Baseball America

2021 PROSPECT HANDBOOK

BASEBALL AMERICA INC. DURHAM, N.C.

Baseball America

2021 PROSPECT HANDBOOK

Editors
J.J. COOPER, MATT EDDY,
KYLE GLASER, CHRIS HILBURN-TRENKLE
AND JOSH NORRIS

Assistant Editors
BEN BADLER, TEDDY CAHILL,
MARK CHIARELLI, CARLOS COLLAZO
AND JOE HEALY

Database and Application Development
BRENT LEWIS

Contributing Writers
MIKE DIGIOVANNA, ANDRE FERNANDEZ,
LACY LUSK, JON MEOLI,
BILL MITCHELL, NICK PIECORO,
ALEX SPEIER, EMILY WALDON,
TIM WILLIAMS AND JEFF WILSON

Design & Production
JAMES ALWORTH AND LEAH TYNER

Cover Photo
JULIO RODRIGUEZ
BY JAMIE SCHWABEROW/GETTY IMAGES

FOR ADDITIONAL COPIES
VISIT OUR WEBSITE AT **BASEBALLAMERICA.COM** OR CALL **1-800-845-2726** TO ORDER.

US $34.95, PLUS SHIPPING AND HANDLING PER ORDER. EXPEDITED SHIPPING AVAILABLE.

DISTRIBUTED BY SIMON & SCHUSTER

ISBN: 978-1-7355482-1-0

STATISTICS PROVIDED BY MAJOR LEAGUE BASEBALL ADVANCED MEDIA AND COMPILED BY BASEBALL AMERICA.

Baseball America

ESTABLISHED 1981 • P.O. Box 12877, Durham, NC 27709 • Phone (919) 682-9635

INTRODUCTION

DECEMBER 18, 2020

The Baseball America Prospect Handbook debuted in 2001, at the dawn of the new century. Twenty years later, Albert Pujols, Miguel Cabrera, Adam Wainwright and a few others are the last remaining active players from that first edition.

Before long, we'll see the first Hall of Famer inducted from the Prospect Handbook era. Our bet is on Ichiro Suzuki, the Mariners' No. 2 prospect in 2001.

We hope and expect there will be Hall of Famers of the 2040s and 2050s in the pages that follow. But this is not just another edition of the Prospect Handbook. In many ways, this has been the most challenging version to compile and complete since the original book in 2001.

In 2001, the challenge was expanding the team Top 10 Prospects lists—something BA had been doing since 1983—to full Top 30 Prospects rankings. The additional challenge was speeding up the production timeline in order to print a book in December and have it delivered to readers in a timely manner.

In 2020, the challenge was quite different. For the first time since the birth of the minor leagues in the 1870s, there was no minor league season. As that reality became apparent around the middle of the year, we worried about how we could produce a Prospect Handbook that matched the caliber of past editions. We didn't want to present readers with a rehash of last year's content.

As we produced the book, we were encouraged to realize that even in a year without minor league games, there was plenty of new information to gather and disseminate. Between major league callups and graduations, alternate training site scrimmages and, most importantly, instructional league games, many of the prospects in this book got a chance to develop—and our rankings and reports reflect their progress.

We also wanted to be careful not to overreact to this new information. A step forward or a step back at instructional league is not the same as a breakout season in the Florida State League. We have endeavored not to overlook the significant amount of scouting insight and performance data on a player's résumé when adding what we learned about them in 2020. For players who contracted Covid-19, weighing how their performance was affected was tricky.

With teams shuffling players on and off of major league rosters more regularly, we have expanded beyond the Top 30 Prospects to include summary capsules on at least 10 more prospects of note in each organization. With a five-round draft and no minor league games, the Draft Analysis pages have been removed this year. We hope you understand these tweaks and find them useful.

We look forward to a more normal baseball season and Prospect Handbook in 2022, but we are proud of this book you hold in your hands, and we hope it provides a bit of normalcy in this unusual time.

J.J. COOPER AND MATT EDDY
EXECUTIVE EDITORS, BASEBALL AMERICA

ABOUT THE 2021 EDITION:

■ To bring you more detailed scouting reports and more relevant information, we reduced the statistical display for prospects ranked outside of an organization's top 10. Each player's most recent professional performance data is shown, whether in the major leagues in 2020 or minor leagues in 2019.

■ We have embedded "Top Rookie" and "Breakout" prospect tags in each chapter to curate and highlight relevant information for readers. As many as three rookies and breakouts appear in each chapter.

■ Each chapter contains a "More Prospects To Know" section immediately following the Top 30 Prospects to provide summary reports on at least 10 more prospects of note.

■ The atypical nature of the 60-game MLB season created a scenario where a greater number of prospects than usual spent most of the season in the major leagues but did not exhaust their eligibility for the Prospect Handbook. For our purposes, these players are still considered prospects even if they are ineligible for 2021 Rookie of the Year awards. Notable examples of this phenomenon include the Angels' Jo Adell, the Mets' Andres Gimenez and the Rangers' Leody Taveras.

EDITOR'S NOTE: The transactions deadline for this book was Dec. 10, 2020. You can find players who changed organizations by using the index in the back.

>> For the purposes of this book, a prospect is any player who is signed with a major league organization and who has not exceeded 130 at-bats, 50 innings or 30 relief appearances or in the major leagues, regardless of major league service time.

L = Low. M = Medium. H = High. V = Very High. X= Extreme.

TABLE OF CONTENTS

L = Low. M = Medium. H = High. V = Very High. X= Extreme.

CHICAGO WHITE SOX

STARTS ON PAGE 98

No. Player, Pos.	Grade/Risk
1. Andrew Vaughn, 1B	60/H
2. Michael Kopech, RHP	60/H
3. Nick Madrigal, 2B	55/M
4. Garrett Crochet, LHP	55/H
5. Jared Kelley, RHP	55/X
6. Matthew Thompson, RHP	50/X
7. Jonathan Stiever, RHP	45/H
8. Andrew Dalquist, RHP	50/X
9. Luis Gonzalez, OF	45/H
10. Gavin Sheets, OF	45/H
11. Codi Heuer, RHP	40/M
12. Blake Rutherford, OF	45/H
13. Jimmy Lambert, RHP	45/H
14. Bryan Ramos, 3B	50/X
15. Matt Foster, RHP	40/M
16. Micker Adolfo, OF	45/H
17. Jake Burger, 3B	45/X
18. Kade McClure, RHP	40/H
19. Bryce Bush, OF	45/X
20. James Beard, OF	45/X
21. Cabrera Weaver, OF	45/X
22. Damon Gladney, 3B	45/X
23. Bailey Horn, LHP	40/H
24. Benyamin Bailey, OF	45/X
25. Yolbert Sanchez, SS	45/X
26. Jose Rodriguez, SS	45/X
27. Zack Collins, C	40/H
28. Tyler Johnson, RHP	40/H
29. Caleb Freeman, RHP	40/H
30. Chase Krogman, OF	40/H

CINCINNATI REDS

STARTS ON PAGE 114

No. Player, Pos.	Grade/Risk
1. Jose Garcia, SS	55/H
2. Austin Hendrick, OF	60/X
3. Jonathan India, 2B/3B	55/H
4. Tyler Stephenson, C	50/M
5. Hunter Greene, RHP	60/X
6. Tejay Antone, RHP	45/L
7. Nick Lodolo, LHP	55/H
8. Rece Hinds, 3B	55/X
9. Tony Santillan, RHP	50/H
10. Mike Siani, OF	50/V
11. Christian Roa, RHP	50/V
12. Ivan Johnson, 2B	50/V
13. Lyon Richardson, RHP	45/H
14. Vladimir Gutierrez, RHP	45/H
15. Noah Davis, RHP	50/X
16. Tyler Callihan, 2B	50/X
17. Bryce Bonnin, RHP	45/H
18. Michel Triana, 1B	50/X
19. Jackson Miller, C	50/X
20. Jose De Leon, RHP	45/H
21. Allen Cerda, OF	50/X
22. T.J. Friedl, OF	40/M
23. Jared Solomon, RHP	45/X
24. Luis Mey, RHP	45/X
25. Riley O'Brien, RHP	40/H
26. Yan Contreras, SS	45/X
27. Brandon Bailey, RHP	40/H
28. Graham Ashcraft, RHP	45/X
29. Joel Kuhnel, RHP	40/H
30. Joe Boyle, RHP	45/X

CLEVELAND INDIANS

STARTS ON PAGE 130

No. Player, Pos.	Grade/Risk
1. Triston McKenzie, RHP	60/H
2. Nolan Jones, 3B	60/H
3. Tyler Freeman, SS	55/H
4. Bo Naylor, C	55/V
5. George Valera, OF	55/V
6. Gabriel Arias, SS	55/V
7. Brayan Rocchio, SS	55/V
8. Daniel Espino, RHP	55/X
9. Ethan Hankins, RHP	55/X
10. Aaron Bracho, 2B	55/X
11. Gabriel Rodriguez, SS	55/X
12. Carson Tucker, SS	50/H
13. Logan S. Allen, LHP	45/M
14. Emmanuel Clase, RHP	50/H
15. Tanner Burns, RHP	50/H
16. Joey Cantillo, LHP	50/H
17. Carlos Vargas, RHP	50/H
18. Owen Miller, SS	45/M
19. Scott Moss, LHP	45/M
20. Logan T. Allen, LHP	50/H
21. Bobby Bradley, 1B	45/M
22. Sam Hentges, LHP	50/V
23. Ernie Clement, SS	45/H
24. Lenny Torres, RHP	50/X
25. Yordys Valdes, SS	50/X
26. Angel Martinez, SS	50/X
27. Yu Chang, 3B/SS	40/M
28. Daniel Johnson, OF	40/M
29. Jose Pastrano, SS	50/X
30. Eli Morgan, RHP	45/H

COLORADO ROCKIES

STARTS ON PAGE 146

No. Player, Pos.	Grade/Risk
1. Brendan Rodgers, SS	55/M
2. Zac Veen, OF	60/X
3. Ryan Rolison, LHP	50/H
4. Michael Toglia, 1B	50/H
5. Aaron Schunk, 3B	50/H
6. Chris McMahon, RHP	50/H
7. Colton Welker, 3B/1B	50/H
8. Brenton Doyle, OF	50/H
9. Ryan Vilade, OF/3B	50/H
10. Helcris Olivarez, LHP	50/X
11. Ryan Castellani, RHP	40/M
12. Grant Lavigne, 1B	45/H
13. Drew Romo, C	50/X
14. Jameson Hannah, OF	45/H
15. Adael Amador, SS	50/X
16. Ben Bowden, LHP	40/M
17. Karl Kauffman, RHP	45/H
18. Sam Weatherly, LHP	45/H
19. Eddy Diaz, SS	50/X
20. Ryan Feltner, RHP	45/H
21. Tommy Doyle, RHP	45/H
22. Gavin Hollowell, RHP	45/H
23. Julio Carreras, 3B/SS	45/X
24. Ezequiel Tovar, SS	45/X
25. Yanquiel Fernandez, OF	45/X
26. Yoan Aybar, LHP	40/H
27. Will Ethridge, RHP	40/H
28. Yonathan Daza, OF	40/H
29. Bladimir Restituyo, 2B/OF	45/X
30. Niko Decolati, OF	40/V

DETROIT TIGERS

STARTS ON PAGE 162

No. Player, Pos.	Grade/Risk
1. Spencer Torkelson, 1B	70/H
2. Tarik Skubal, LHP	60/M
3. Casey Mize, RHP	60/H
4. Matt Manning, RHP	60/H
5. Riley Greene, OF	60/H
6. Isaac Paredes, 3B	50/M
7. Dillon Dingler, C	50/H
8. Daz Cameron, OF	45/M
9. Daniel Cabrera, OF	50/H
10. Gage Workman, 3B	50/H
11. Alex Faedo, RHP	50/V
12. Joey Wentz, LHP	50/V
13. Parker Meadows, OF	50/V
14. Roberto Campos, OF	50/X
15. Bryant Packard, OF	45/H
16. Trei Cruz, SS	45/H
17. Akil Baddoo, OF	45/H
18. Kody Clemens, 2B	45/H
19. Beau Burrows, RHP	45/H
20. Jake Rogers, C	40/M
21. Derek Hill, OF	40/M
22. Colt Keith, 3B	45/X
23. Adinso Reyes, SS	45/X
24. Sergio Alcantara, SS	40/H
25. Cooper Johnson, C	40/H
26. Eliezer Alfonzo, C	40/H
27. Franklin Perez, RHP	45/X
28. Alex Lange, RHP	40/H
29. Jose De La Cruz, OF	45/X
30. Zack Short, SS	40/H

TABLE OF CONTENTS

L = Low. M = Medium. H = High. V = Very High. X= Extreme.

MILWAUKEE BREWERS

STARTS ON PAGE 258

No. Player, Pos.	Grade/Risk
1. Brice Turang, SS	55/H
2. Garrett Mitchell, OF	60/X
3. Hedbert Perez, OF	60/X
4. Antoine Kelly, LHP	55/V
5. Ethan Small, LHP	50/H
6. Freddy Zamora, SS	55/X
7. Mario Feliciano, C	50/H
8. Aaron Ashby, LHP	50/H
9. Zavier Warren, C	50/V
10. Jeferson Quero, C	50/X
11. Eduardo Garcia, SS	50/X
12. Carlos Rodriguez, OF	50/X
13. Drew Rasmussen, RHP	45/H
14. Justin Topa, RHP	40/M
15. Jesus Parra, 3B/2B	50/X
16. David Hamilton, SS/2B	45/V
17. Nick Kahle, C	45/V
18. Hayden Cantrelle, SS	45/V
19. Luis Medina, OF	45/X
20. Alec Bettinger, RHP	40/H
21. Dylan File, RHP	40/H
22. Abner Uribe, RHP	45/X
23. Jheremy Vargas, SS	45/X
24. Joey Wiemer, OF	45/X
25. Corey Ray, OF	40/H
26. Angel Perdomo, LHP	40/H
27. Clayton Andrews, LHP/OF	40/H
28. Tristen Lutz, OF	40/H
29. Phil Bickford, RHP	40/H
30. Micah Bello, OF	40/V

MINNESOTA TWINS

STARTS ON PAGE 274

No. Player, Pos.	Grade/Risk
1. Alex Kirilloff, OF/1B	65/H
2. Royce Lewis, SS/3B	60/H
3. Trevor Larnach, OF	60/H
4. Ryan Jeffers, C	55/M
5. Jhoan Duran, RHP	55/H
6. Jordan Balazovic, RHP	55/H
7. Aaron Sabato, 1B	50/H
8. Matt Canterino, RHP	50/H
9. Blayne Enlow, RHP	50/H
10. Gilberto Celestino, OF	50/H
11. Cole Sands, RHP	50/H
12. Brent Rooker, OF	45/M
13. Misael Urbina, OF	55/X
14. Jorge Alcala, RHP	50/H
15. Keoni Cavaco, 3B	55/X
16. Lamonte Wade, OF	40/L
17. Alerick Soularie, OF	50/H
18. Matt Wallner, OF	50/H
19. Josh Winder, RHP	50/H
20. Cody Stashak, RHP	40/L
21. Edwar Colina, RHP	45/H
22. Chris Vallimont, RHP	45/H
23. Emmanuel Rodriguez, OF	50/X
24. Dakota Chalmers, RHP	50/X
25. Travis Blankenhorn, 3B	40/M
26. Ben Rortvedt, C	40/H
27. Wander Javier, SS	45/X
28. Yunior Severino, 2B	45/X
29. Jovani Moran, LHP	40/H
30. Marco Raya, RHP	45/X

NEW YORK METS

STARTS ON PAGE 290

No. Player, Pos.	Grade/Risk
1. Francisco Alvarez, C	60/V
2. Ronny Mauricio, SS	60/V
3. Andres Gimenez, SS/2B	50/M
4. Matt Allan, RHP	60/X
5. Pete Crow-Armstrong, OF	55/V
6. Brett Baty, 3B	55/V
7. Mark Vientos, 3B	50/H
8. J.T. Ginn, RHP	55/X
9. David Peterson, LHP	45/M
10. Josh Wolf, RHP	50/X
11. Isaiah Greene, OF	50/X
12. Junior Santos, RHP	50/X
13. Alex Ramirez, OF	50/X
14. Robert Dominguez, RHP	50/X
15. Jose Butto, RHP	45/H
16. Shervyen Newton, SS/2B	45/H
17. Jaylen Palmer, 3B/OF	45/H
18. Thomas Szapucki, LHP	45/H
19. Freddy Valdez, OF	50/X
20. Endy Rodriguez, C/OF	50/X
21. Sam McWilliams, RHP	40/H
22. Oscar de la Cruz, RHP	40/H
23. Jordany Ventura, RHP	45/X
24. Ryley Gilliam, RHP	40/H
25. Marcel Renteria, RHP	40/H
26. Michel Otañez, RHP	40/H
27. Joander Suarez, RHP	40/V
28. Jake Mangum, OF	40/V
29. Josh Cornielly, RHP	40/V
30. Tylor Megill, RHP	40/V

NEW YORK YANKEES

STARTS ON PAGE 306

No. Player, Pos.	Grade/Risk
1. Jasson Dominguez, OF	65/X
2. Deivi Garcia, RHP	55/M
3. Clarke Schmidt, RHP	55/M
4. Luis Gil, RHP	55/V
5. Austin Wells, C	50/H
6. Oswald Peraza, SS	50/H
7. Alexander Vizcaino, RHP	50/H
8. Miguel Yajure, RHP	45/M
9. Yoendrys Gomez, RHP	50/H
10. Luis Medina, RHP	55/X
11. Roansy Contreras, RHP	50/H
12. Estevan Florial, OF	50/H
13. Ezequiel Duran, 2B	50/H
14. Kevin Alcantara, OF	50/X
15. Alexander Vargas, SS	50/X
16. Canaan Smith, OF	45/H
17. Anthony Volpe, SS	50/X
18. T.J. Sikkema, LHP	45/H
19. Beck Way, RHP	45/H
20. Albert Abreu, RHP	45/H
21. Matt Sauer, RHP	50/X
22. Everson Pereira, OF	50/X
23. Antonio Cabello, OF	50/X
24. Raimfer Salinas, OF	50/X
25. Antonio Gomez, C	50/X
26. Josh Smith, 2B	45/H
27. Anthony Seigler, C	50/X
28. Michael King, RHP	40/M
29. Nick Nelson, RHP	40/M
30. Brooks Kriske, RHP	40/M

OAKLAND ATHLETICS

STARTS ON PAGE 322

No. Player, Pos.	Grade/Risk
1. Tyler Soderstrom, C	60/X
2. AJ Puk, LHP	60/X
3. Daulton Jefferies, RHP	55/H
4. Robert Puason, SS	55/X
5. Logan Davidson, SS	50/H
6. Nick Allen, SS	50/H
7. Luis Barrera, OF	45/M
8. Jonah Heim, C	45/M
9. Greg Deichmann, OF	45/H
10. James Kaprielian, RHP	50/X
11. Sheldon Neuse, 3B/2B	40/M
12. Brayan Buelvas, OF	50/X
13. Austin Beck, OF	45/H
14. Jeff Criswell, RHP	45/H
15. Junior Perez, OF	50/X
16. Jordan Weems, RHP	40/M
17. Austin Allen, C	40/M
18. Jordan Diaz, 3B	50/X
19. Grant Holmes, RHP	45/H
20. Tyler Baum, RHP	45/H
21. Kyle McCann, C	45/H
22. Gus Varland, RHP	50/X
23. Michael Guldberg, OF	40/H
24. Jeremy Eierman, SS	40/H
25. Skye Bolt, OF	40/H
26. Colin Peluse, RHP	40/H
27. Drew Millas, C	40/H
28. Miguel Romero, RHP	40/H
29. Lazaro Armenteros, OF	45/X
30. Seth Brown, 1B/OF	40/H

L = Low. M = Medium. H = High. V = Very High. X= Extreme.

TABLE OF CONTENTS

SEATTLE MARINERS

STARTS ON PAGE 418

No. Player, Pos.	Grade/Risk
1. Julio Rodriguez, OF	70/H
2. Jarred Kelenic, OF	65/H
3. Logan Gilbert, RHP	60/H
4. Emerson Hancock, RHP	60/H
5. Noelvi Marte, SS	60/V
6. Taylor Trammell, OF	55/H
7. George Kirby, RHP	55/H
8. Cal Raleigh, C	50/H
9. Juan Then, RHP	50/H
10. Andres Muñoz, RHP	55/X
11. Brandon Williamson, LHP	50/H
12. Levi Stoudt, RHP	50/H
13. Adam Macko, LHP	50/H
14. Isaiah Campbell, RHP	50/H
15. Wyatt Mills, RHP	45/M
16. Zach DeLoach, OF	50/H
17. Connor Phillips, RHP	50/H
18. Austin Shenton, 3B	50/H
19. Milkar Perez, 3B	50/X
20. Joey Gerber, RHP	40/M
21. Anthony Misiewiecz, LHP	40/M
22. Yohan Ramirez, RHP	40/M
23. Jake Fraley, OF	40/M
24. Alberto Rodriguez, OF	45/V
25. Kaden Polcovich, 2B/OF	45/V
26. Jose Corniell, RHP	45/X
27. Sam Carlson, RHP	45/X
28. Carter Bins, C	40/H
29. Jonatan Clase, OF	45/X
30. Sam Haggerty, 2B/OF	40/H

TAMPA BAY RAYS

STARTS ON PAGE 434

No. Player, Pos.	Grade/Risk
1. Wander Franco, SS	75/H
2. Randy Arozarena, OF	60/M
3. Vidal Brujan, 2B	55/H
4. Shane McClanahan, LHP	55/H
5. Shane Baz, RHP	60/X
6. Brendan McKay, LHP	60/X
7. Xavier Edwards, 2B/SS	55/H
8. Nick Bitsko, RHP	55/X
9. J.J. Goss, RHP	55/X
10. Joe Ryan, RHP	50/H
11. Ronaldo Hernandez, C	50/H
12. Greg Jones, SS	50/H
13. Taylor Walls, SS	45/M
14. Josh Lowe, OF	50/H
15. Brent Honeywell, RHP	55/X
16. Seth Johnson, RHP	50/H
17. Alika Williams, SS	50/H
18. Kevin Padlo, 3B	45/M
19. Taj Bradley, RHP	50/V
20. Moises Gomez, OF	50/V
21. Nick Schnell, OF	50/V
22. Josh Fleming, LHP	40/M
23. Ryan Thompson, RHP	40/M
24. Pedro Martinez, SS	50/X
25. Heriberto Hernandez, OF/1B	50/X
26. John Doxakis, LHP	45/H
27. Ian Seymour, LHP	45/H
28. Osleivis Basabe, SS	50/X
29. Caleb Sampen, RHP	45/H
30. Drew Strotman, RHP	45/H

TEXAS RANGERS

STARTS ON PAGE 450

No. Player, Pos.	Grade/Risk
1. Josh Jung, 3B	60/H
2. Sam Huff, C	55/H
3. Leody Taveras, OF	50/M
4. Dane Dunning, RHP	50/M
5. Cole Winn, RHP	55/X
6. Justin Foscue, 2B	50/H
7. Maximo Acosta, SS	50/X
8. Luisangel Acuña, SS	50/X
9. Hans Crouse, RHP	50/X
10. Anderson Tejeda, SS	45/H
11. Bayron Lora, OF	50/X
12. Sherten Apostel, 3B	45/H
13. Ronny Henriquez, RHP	45/H
14. Davis Wendzel, 3B/2B	45/H
15. Steele Walker, OF	45/H
16. Evan Carter, OF	50/X
17. David Garcia, C	50/X
18. Ricky Vanasco, RHP	50/X
19. Owen White, RHP	50/X
20. Kyle Cody, RHP	45/H
21. DeMarcus Evans, RHP	40/M
22. Joe Palumbo, LHP	45/V
23. Chris Seise, SS	45/V
24. A.J. Alexy, RHP	40/H
25. Avery Weems, RHP	40/H
26. Bubba Thompson, OF	40/H
27. Keithron Moss, 2B	45/X
28. Yerry Rodriguez, RHP	40/H
29. Alex Speas, RHP	45/X
30. Tyler Phillips, RHP	40/H

TORONTO BLUE JAYS

STARTS ON PAGE 466

No. Player, Pos.	Grade/Risk
1. Nate Pearson, RHP	70/H
2. Austin Martin, SS	65/H
3. Jordan Groshans, SS	60/H
4. S. Woods Richardson, RHP	60/H
5. Alejandro Kirk, C	55/M
6. Orelvis Martinez, SS	60/V
7. Alek Manoah, RHP	55/H
8. Gabriel Moreno, C	55/H
9. Adam Kloffenstein, RHP	55/V
10. Miguel Hiraldo, SS	55/V
11. C.J. Van Eyk, RHP	50/H
12. Otto Lopez, SS/2B	50/H
13. Estiven Machado, SS	50/X
14. Eric Pardinho, RHP	50/X
15. Thomas Hatch, RHP	40/M
16. Leonardo Jimenez, SS	50/X
17. Victor Mesia, C	50/X
18. Rikelbin de Castro, SS	50/X
19. Patrick Murphy, RHP	45/H
20. Anthony Kay, LHP	40/M
21. Santiago Espinal, SS/2B	40/M
22. Will Robertson, OF	45/V
23. Nick Frasso, RHP	45/V
24. Trent Palmer, RHP	45/V
25. Dasan Brown, OF	45/X
26. Joey Murray, RHP	40/H
27. Tanner Morris, SS	40/H
28. Yosver Zulueta, RHP	45/X
29. Sem Robberse, RHP	45/X
30. Phil Clarke, C	40/H

WASHINGTON NATIONALS

STARTS ON PAGE 482

No. Player, Pos.	Grade/Risk
1. Cade Cavalli, RHP	55/H
2. Jackson Rutledge, RHP	55/H
3. Cole Henry, RHP	50/H
4. Yasel Antuna, SS	55/X
5. Andry Lara, RHP	50/X
6. Jeremy De La Rosa, OF	50/X
7. Tim Cate, LHP	45/H
8. Eddy Yean, RHP	50/X
9. Mason Denaburg, RHP	50/X
10. Wil Crowe, RHP	45/H
11. Matt Cronin, LHP	45/H
12. Drew Mendoza, 1B	45/H
13. Jackson Cluff, SS	45/H
14. Sammy Infante, SS	50/X
15. Seth Romero, LHP	45/H
16. Israel Pineda, C	45/V
17. Tres Barrera, C	40/H
18. Daniel Marte, OF	45/X
19. Ben Braymer, LHP	40/H
20. Holden Powell, RHP	40/H
21. Steven Fuentes, RHP	40/H
22. Roismar Quintana, OF	45/X
23. Tyler Dyson, RHP	40/H
24. Jake Irvin, RHP	45/X
25. Joan Adon, RHP	45/X
26. Jakson Reetz, C	40/H
27. Sterling Sharp, RHP	40/H
28. Andry Arias, OF	45/X
29. Jackson Tetreault, RHP	40/V
30. Nick Banks, OF	40/V

BA GRADES

For the 10th year, Baseball America has assigned Grades and Risk Factors for each of the 900 prospects in the Prospect Handbook. For the BA Grade, we used a 20-to-80 scale, similar to the scale scouts use, to keep it familiar. However, most major league clubs put an overall numerical grade on players, called the Overall Future Potential or OFP. Often the OFP is merely an average of the player's tools.

The BA Grade is not an OFP. It's a measure of a prospect's value, and it attempts to gauge the player's realistic ceiling. We've continued to adjust our grades to try to be more realistic, and less optimistic, and keep refining the grade vetting process. The majority of the players in this book rest in the 50 High/45 Medium range, because the vast majority of worthwhile prospects in the minors are players who either have a chance to be everyday regulars but are far from that possibility, or players who are closer to the majors but who are likely to be role players and useful contributors. Few future franchise players or perennial all-stars graduate from the minors in any given year. The goal of the Grade/Risk system is to allow readers to take a quick look at how strong their team's farm system is, and how much immediate help the big league club can expect from its prospects. Have a minor leaguer who was traded from one organization to another after the book went to press? Use the player's Grade/Risk and see where he would rank in his new system.

BA GRADE
50 **Risk: High**

It also helps with our organization talent rankings, but those will not simply flow, in formulaic fashion, from the Grade/Risk results because we incorporate a lot of factors into our talent rankings, including the differences in risk between pitchers and hitters. Hitters have a lower injury risk and are safer bets.

BA Grade Scale

GRADE	HITTER ROLE	PITCHER ROLE	EXAMPLES
75-80	Franchise Player	No. 1 starter	Mike Trout, Mookie Betts, Max Scherzer
65-70	Perennial All-Star	No. 2 starter	George Springer, Paul Goldschmidt, Aaron Nola
60	Occasional All-Star	No. 3 starter, Game's best reliever	Michael Conforto, Marcell Ozuna, Liam Hendriks
55	First-Division Regular	No. 3/No. 4 starter, Elite closer	Nick Castellanos, Marco Gonzales, Brad Hand
50	Solid-Average Regular	No. 4 starter, Elite setup reliever	Cesar Hernandez, Mike Fiers, Shane Greene
45	Second-Division Regular/Platoon	No. 5 starter, Lower-leverage reliever	Freddy Galvis, Tommy Milone, Pedro Baez
40	Reserve	Fill-in starter, Mopup reliever	Greg Allen, Tom Eshelman, Luis Cessa

RISK FACTORS

LOW: Likely to reach realistic ceiling; certain big league career, barring injury.

MEDIUM: Some work left to refine their tools, but a polished player.

HIGH: Most top draft picks in their first seasons, players with plenty of projection left, players with a significant flaw left to correct or players whose injury history is worrisome.

VERY HIGH: Recent draft picks with a limited track record of success or injury issues.

EXTREME: Teenagers in Rookie ball, players with significant injury histories or players whose struggle with a key skill (especially control for pitchers or strikeouts for hitters).

BA GRADES

Explaining The 20-80 Scouting Scale

None of the authors of this book is a scout, but we speak extensively to scouts to report on the prospects and scouting reports enclosed in the Prospect Handbook. So we use their lingo, and the 20-80 scouting scale is part of that. Many of these grades are measurable data, such as fastball velocity and speed (usually timed from home to first or in workouts over 60 yards). A fastball grade doesn't stem solely from its velocity—command and life are crucial elements as well—but throwing 100 mph will earn a player an 80 grade. Secondary pitches are graded in a similar fashion. The more swings-and-misses a pitch induces from hitters and the sharper the bite of the movement, the better the grade.

Velocity steadily has increased over the past decade. Not long ago, an 88-91 mph fastball was considered major league average, but current data shows that is now below-average. Big league starting pitchers now sit 92-93 mph on average. You can reduce the scale by 1 mph for lefthanders as they on average throw with slightly reduced velocity. Fastballs earn their grades based on the average range of the pitch over the course of a typical outing, not touching or bumping the peak velocity on occasion.

A move to the bullpen complicates in another direction. Pitchers airing it out for one inning should throw harder than someone trying to last six or seven innings, so add 1-2 mph for relievers. Yes, nowadays an 80 fastball for a reliever needs to sit 98-99 mph with movement and command.

Hitting ability is as much a skill as it is a tool, but the physical elements—hand-eye coordination, swing mechanics, bat speed—are key factors in the hit tool grade. Raw power generally is measured by how far a player can hit the ball, but game power is graded by how many home runs the hitter projects to hit in the majors, preferably an average over the course of a career. We have tweaked our power grades based on the recent rise in home run rates.

Arm strength can be evaluated by observing the velocity and carry of throws, measured in workouts with radar guns or measured in games for catchers with pop times—the time it takes from the pop of the ball in the catcher's mitt to the pop of the ball in the fielder's glove at second base. Defense takes different factors into account by position but starts with proper footwork and technique, incorporates physical attributes such as hands, short-area quickness and fluid actions, then adds subtle skills such as instincts and anticipation as a last layer.

Not every team uses the wording below. Some use a 2-to-8 scale without half-grades, and others use above-average and plus synonymously. But for the Handbook, consider this BA's 20-80 scale.

20: As bad as it gets for a big leaguer. Think Billy Hamilton's power or Jeff Mathis' hitting ability.

30: Poor, but not unplayable, such as Brandon Belt's speed.

40: Below-average, such as Rafael Devers' defense or Sonny Gray's control.

45: Fringe-average. Dylan Bundy's fastball and Kurt Suzuki's arm qualify.

50: Major league average. Eddie Rosario's speed.

55: Above-average. Nick Castellanos' power.

60: Plus. Marcus Semien's speed or Stephen Strasburg's control.

70: Plus-Plus. Among the best tools in the game, such as Corey Seager's arm, Patrick Corbin's slider or Francisco Lindor's defense.

80: Top of the scale. Some scouts consider only one player's tool in all of the major leagues to be 80. Think of Aaron Judge's power, Byron Buxton's speed or Aroldis Chapman's fastball.

20-80 Measurables

HIT

Grade	Batting Avg
80	.315+
70	295-.315
60	280-.295
55	265-.280
50	250-.265
45	235-.250
40	220-.235
30	200-.220
20	.200 or less

POWER

Grade	Home Runs
80	40+
70	34-39
60	28-33
55	23-27
50	19-22
45	14-18
40	10-13
30	5-9
20	0-4

SPEED

Home-First (In Secs.)

Grade	RHH—LHH
80	4.00—3.90
70	4.10—4.00
65	4.15—4.05
60	4.20—4.10
55	4.25—4.15
50	4.30—4.20
45	4.35—4.25
40	4.40—4.30
30	4.50—4.40
20	4.60—4.50

FASTBALL

Velocity (Starters)

Grade	Velocity
80	97+ mph
70	96
60	95
55	94
50	92-93
45	91
40	89-90
30	87-88
20	86 or less

ARM STRENGTH

Catcher: Pop Times To Second Base (In Seconds)

Grade	Time
80	< 1.90
70	1.90-1.94
60	1.95-1.99
50	2.00-2.04
40	2.05-2.09
30	2.10-2.14
20	> 2.15

MINOR LEAGUE DEPTH CHART

AN OVERVIEW

The depth chart for each organization provides a big-picture look at minor league talent. This shows you at a glance what kind of talent resides in a system.

Players are usually listed on the depth charts where we think they'll ultimately end up—not necessarily the position they currently play. To help you better understand why players are slotted at particular positions, we show you here what scouts look for in the ideal candidate at each spot, with individual tools ranked in descending order.

LF
Power
Hitting
Fielding
Arm Strength
Speed

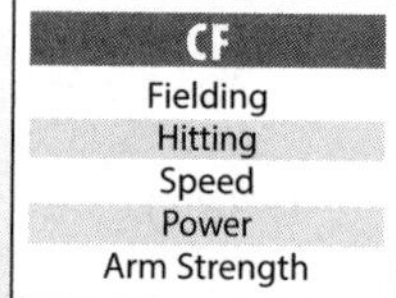

CF
Fielding
Hitting
Speed
Power
Arm Strength

RF
Power
Hitting
Arm Strength
Fielding
Speed

3B
Power
Hitting
Fielding
Arm Strength
Speed

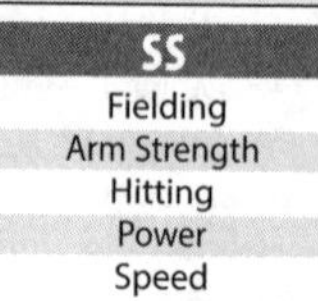

SS
Fielding
Arm Strength
Hitting
Power
Speed

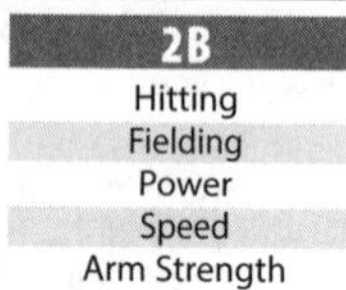

2B
Hitting
Fielding
Power
Speed
Arm Strength

1B
Power
Hitting
Fielding
Arm Strength
Speed

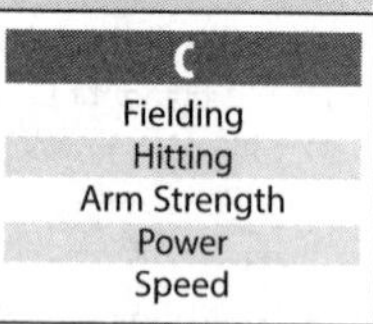

C
Fielding
Hitting
Arm Strength
Power
Speed

STARTING PITCHERS

No. 1 starter
- Two plus pitches
- Average third pitch
- Plus-plus command
- Plus makeup

No. 2 starter
- Two plus pitches
- Average third pitch
- Average command
- Average makeup

No. 3 starter
- One plus pitch
- Two average pitches
- Average command
- Average makeup

No. 4-5 starters
- Command of two major league pitches
- Average velocity
- Consistent breaking ball
- Decent changeup

CLOSER
- One dominant pitch
- Second plus pitch
- Plus command
- Plus-plus makeup

SETUP MAN
- Plus fastball
- Second above-average pitch
- Average command

POSITION RANKINGS

To provide yet another layer of context, we rank prospects at all eight field positions plus righthanded and lefthanded starting pitchers. The rankings go at least 10 deep at each position, with more space afforded to glamour positions, e.g. shortstop and righthanded starter, as well as stocked positions.

We grade players' tools on the 20-80 scouting scale, where 50 is average. The tools listed for position players are ability to hit for average (HIT), hit for power (POW), speed (SPD), fielding ability (FLD) and arm (ARM). The tools listed for pitchers are fastball (FB), curveball (CB), slider (SL), changeup (CHG), other (OTH) and control (CTL). The "other" category can be a splitter, cutter or screwball.

Included as the final categories are BA Grades and Risk levels on a scale ranging from low to extreme.

CATCHER

No	Player	Org	HIT	POW	SPD	FLD	ARM	BA Grade	Risk
1.	Adley Rutschman	Orioles	70	70	40	60	70	70	High
2.	Luis Campusano	Padres	55	55	30	50	55	60	High
3.	Joey Bart	Giants	45	60	40	50	60	60	High
4.	Francisco Alvarez	Mets	50	60	30	50	60	60	Very High
5.	Ryan Jeffers	Twins	55	50	20	60	45	55	Medium
6.	Keibert Ruiz	Dodgers	60	45	30	55	50	55	Medium
7.	Daulton Varsho	D-backs	55	50	55	50	45	55	Medium
8.	Alejandro Kirk	Blue Jays	70	50	20	45	50	55	Medium
9.	Tyler Soderstrom	Athletics	60	60	40	40	55	60	Extreme
10.	Sam Huff	Rangers	40	70	40	45	60	55	High

FIRST BASE

No	Player	Org	HIT	POW	SPD	FLD	ARM	BA Grade	Risk
1.	Spencer Torkelson	Tigers	60	80	45	55	50	70	High
2.	Andrew Vaughn	White Sox	60	60	30	50	50	60	High
3.	Triston Casas	Red Sox	55	65	40	55	50	60	High
4.	Ryan Mountcastle	Orioles	60	60	50	40	30	55	Medium
5.	Bobby Dalbec	Red Sox	40	70	45	50	70	50	Medium
6.	Lewin Diaz	Marlins	50	60	40	60	50	50	High
7.	Michael Toglia	Rockies	50	60	45	60	50	50	High
8.	Aaron Sabato	Twins	50	70	30	40	40	50	High
9.	Pavin Smith	D-backs	55	45	45	55	55	45	Medium
10.	Mason Martin	Pirates	45	60	30	50	45	45	High

SECOND BASE

No	Player	Org	HIT	POW	SPD	FLD	ARM	BA Grade	Risk
1.	Nick Madrigal	White Sox	60	30	60	50	50	55	Medium
2.	Jeter Downs	Red Sox	55	55	50	50	50	55	Medium
3.	Nick Gonzales	Pirates	70	45	55	50	50	55	High
4.	Vidal Brujan	Rays	60	40	80	55	50	55	High
5.	Michael Busch	Dodgers	60	60	45	40	45	55	High
6.	Xavier Edwards	Rays	60	30	60	55	45	55	High
7.	Jonathan India	Reds	55	55	45	50	55	55	High
8.	Aaron Bracho	Indians	55	50	55	50	45	55	Extreme
9.	Chase Strumpf	Cubs	55	50	45	50	45	50	High
10.	Justin Foscue	Rangers	55	55	40	45	50	50	High

THIRD BASE

No	Player	Org	HIT	POW	SPD	FLD	ARM	BA Grade	Risk
1.	Ke'Bryan Hayes	Pirates	60	50	55	70	60	60	Medium
2.	Nolan Jones	Indians	60	60	50	50	60	60	High
3.	Nolan Gorman	Cardinals	45	70	40	45	60	60	High
4.	Josh Jung	Rangers	60	60	40	50	55	60	High
5.	Isaac Paredes	Tigers	55	50	40	45	55	50	Medium
6.	Kody Hoese	Dodgers	60	50	40	55	45	55	High
7.	Brett Baty	Mets	40	60	40	45	60	55	Very High
8.	Jordan Walker	Cardinals	45	60	45	45	55	55	Extreme
9.	Aaron Schunk	Rockies	55	50	45	50	60	50	High
10.	Rece Hinds	Reds	40	70	50	45	70	55	Extreme

POSITION RANKINGS

SHORTSTOP

No	Player	Org	HIT	POW	SPD	FLD	ARM	BA Grade	Risk
1.	Wander Franco	Rays	80	60	50	50	55	75	High
2.	CJ Abrams	Padres	70	50	80	60	50	70	Very High
3.	Marco Luciano	Giants	60	70	40	50	60	70	Very High
4.	Austin Martin	Blue Jays	70	55	55	50	50	65	High
5.	Bobby Witt Jr.	Royals	60	60	60	60	60	70	Very High
6.	Royce Lewis	Twins	45	55	70	55	55	60	High
7.	Brendan Rodgers	Rockies	55	55	50	55	60	55	Medium
8.	Jordan Groshans	Blue Jays	60	60	50	50	60	60	High
9.	Oneil Cruz	Pirates	50	70	60	50	60	60	High
10.	Noelvi Marte	Mariners	60	55	50	50	60	60	Very High
11.	Ronny Mauricio	Mets	50	50	40	60	60	60	Very High
12.	Andres Gimenez	Mets	50	40	70	60	50	50	Medium
13.	Geraldo Perdomo	D-backs	55	40	55	60	55	55	High
14.	Tyler Freeman	Indians	60	40	50	50	55	55	High
15.	Jose Garcia	Reds	50	50	50	60	60	55	High
16.	Jazz Chisholm	Marlins	40	60	55	55	55	55	High
17.	Brice Turang	Brewers	60	40	60	50	50	55	High
18.	Orelvis Martinez	Blue Jays	60	60	45	40	60	60	Very High
19.	Gabriel Arias	Indians	45	55	40	70	70	55	Very High
20.	Liover Peguero	Pirates	60	50	55	50	50	55	Very High

CENTER FIELD

No	Player	Org	HIT	POW	SPD	FLD	ARM	BA Grade	Risk
1.	Cristian Pache	Braves	45	55	70	80	70	65	Medium
2.	Jarred Kelenic	Mariners	70	60	55	50	60	65	High
3.	Jasson Dominguez	Yankees	60	70	70	60	60	65	Extreme
4.	Brandon Marsh	Angels	55	50	60	60	70	60	High
5.	Corbin Carroll	D-backs	60	50	70	60	45	60	High
6.	Robert Hassell	Padres	60	50	55	55	55	60	Extreme
7.	Garrett Mitchell	Brewers	55	55	80	60	60	60	Extreme
8.	Brennen Davis	Cubs	50	60	60	50	60	55	High
9.	Alek Thomas	D-backs	60	45	60	60	45	55	High
10.	Taylor Trammell	Mariners	55	45	55	50	40	55	High
11.	Leody Taveras	Rangers	50	40	70	60	60	50	Medium
12.	Jarren Duran	Red Sox	55	45	70	50	45	55	High
13.	Pete Crow-Armstrong	Mets	50	40	60	70	55	55	Very High
14.	Jordyn Adams	Angels	50	40	80	60	50	55	Very High
15.	Luis Matos	Giants	55	55	55	55	55	60	Extreme

CORNER OUTFIELD

No	Player	Org	HIT	POW	SPD	FLD	ARM	BA Grade	Risk
1.	Julio Rodriguez	Mariners	60	70	45	55	70	70	High
2.	Jo Adell	Angels	50	70	70	50	60	65	High
3.	Dylan Carlson	Cardinals	55	55	55	55	45	60	Medium
4.	Randy Arozarena	Rays	55	60	70	50	55	60	Medium
5.	Alex Kirilloff	Twins	70	60	40	50	50	65	High
6.	Riley Greene	Tigers	60	55	50	55	50	60	High
7.	Drew Waters	Braves	55	55	60	60	55	60	High
8.	JJ Bleday	Marlins	60	60	50	55	60	60	High
9.	Trevor Larnach	Twins	50	60	40	45	50	60	High
10.	Heston Kjerstad	Orioles	50	70	40	50	60	60	High
11.	Heliot Ramos	Giants	50	55	50	55	55	55	High
12.	Kristian Robinson	D-backs	45	70	60	55	50	60	Extreme
13.	Zac Veen	Rockies	55	60	50	50	55	60	Extreme
14.	Austin Hendrick	Reds	50	60	45	40	60	60	Extreme
15.	George Valera	Indians	60	55	50	50	50	55	Very High

RIGHTHANDER

No	Pitcher	Team	FB	CB	SL	CHG	OTH	CTL	BA Grade	Risk
1.	Sixto Sanchez	Marlins	80	55	55	70		60	70	High
2.	Nate Pearson	Blue Jays	80	50	70	55		55	70	High
3.	Ian Anderson	Braves	55	50		60		60	60	Medium
4.	Casey Mize	Tigers	60	50	60		70*	55	60	High
5.	Triston McKenzie	Indians	60	60	55	55		60	60	High
6.	Luis Patiño	Padres	70	45	60	55		50	60	High
7.	Michael Kopech	White Sox	80	50	60	50		50	60	High
8.	Spencer Howard	Phillies	65	55	60	55		55	60	High
9.	Grayson Rodriguez	Orioles	70	50	60	55		60	60	High
10.	Matt Manning	Tigers	60	60		55		55	60	High
11.	Max Meyer	Marlins	70		70	55		55	60	High
12.	Logan Gilbert	Mariners	60	60	55	60		55	60	High
13.	Emerson Hancock	Mariners	60	50	55	60		60	60	High
14.	S. Woods Richardson	Blue Jays	60	50	55	60		60	60	High
15.	Deivi Garcia	Yankees	55	60	50	60		55	55	Medium
16.	Clarke Schmidt	Yankees	60	60		45		50	55	Medium
17.	Quinn Priester	Pirates	60	60	40	50		55	60	Extreme
18.	Edward Cabrera	Marlins	70	60		50		50	55	High
19.	Mick Abel	Phillies	60	45	60	50		55	60	Extreme
20.	Matt Allan	Mets	70	60		60		50	60	Extreme
21.	Shane Baz	Rays	70	40	70	45		40	60	Extreme
22.	Josiah Gray	Dodgers	60		55	45		55	55	High
23.	Jackson Kowar	Royals	60	50		70		55	55	High
24.	Forrest Whitley	Astros	60	55	55	60	55†	40	60	Extreme
25.	Hunter Greene	Reds	70		60	45	55†	55	60	Extreme
26.	Dane Dunning	Rangers	55	50	60	55		55	50	Medium
27.	Jhoan Duran	Twins	70	50			70*	50	55	High
28.	Chris Rodriguez	Angels	70	55	60	60		55	60	Extreme
29.	Bryan Mata	Red Sox	70	40	60	50		45	55	High
30.	Jordan Balazovic	Twins	60	55		50		55	55	High
31.	Bryse Wilson	Braves	55	40	50	55		55	50	Medium
32.	Alek Manoah	Blue Jays	60		55	50		50	55	High
33.	Cade Cavalli	Nationals	70	55	60	55		50	55	High
34.	Jackson Rutledge	Nationals	70	50	60	50		50	55	High
35.	Adbert Alzolay	Cubs	60	50	60	55		45	50	Medium
36.	Bobby Miller	Dodgers	70	50	60	55		50	55	High
37.	Daulton Jefferies	Athletics	55		50	60		70	55	High
38.	Ryan Pepiot	Dodgers	60	45	50	70		45	55	High
39.	Adam Kloffenstein	Blue Jays	55	50	55	50		50	55	Very High
40.	Luis Gil	Yankees	70	50	50	45		45	55	Very High

* Splitter. † Cutter.

LEFTHANDER

No	Pitcher	Team	FB	CB	SL	CHG	OTH	CTL	BA Grade	Risk
1.	MacKenzie Gore	Padres	60	55	60	60		60	70	High
2.	Tarik Skubal	Tigers	60	55	60	50		55	60	Medium
3.	Daniel Lynch	Royals	70	50	60	55		55	60	High
4.	Asa Lacy	Royals	70	55	60	60		55	60	High
5.	Matthew Liberatore	Cardinals	60	60	50	55		55	60	High
6.	D.L. Hall	Orioles	70	55	50	60		45	60	High
7.	Brailyn Marquez	Cubs	80	45	60	50		45	60	High
8.	Garrett Crochet	White Sox	80	60		40		50	55	High
9.	Adrian Morejon	Padres	60	60		60		45	55	High
10.	Shane McClanahan	Rays	70	60	60	50		45	55	High
11.	A.J. Puk	Athletics	80	45	70	50		45	60	Extreme
12.	Brendan McKay	Rays	60	50	*55	50		60	60	Extreme
13.	Reid Detmers	Angels	50	60	50	45		55	55	High
14.	Ryan Weathers	Padres	60		55	50		60	55	High
15.	Trevor Rogers	Marlins	55	50 CUT	55	55		50	50	Medium

TALENT RANKINGS

Organization	2020	2019	2018	2017	2016
1. Tampa Bay Rays	1	2	5	11	13

A dozen major league organizations have never topped our talent rankings. This is the fifth time the Rays lead the way, thanks to an incredible bounty of talented middle infield prospects led by No. 1 prospect Wander Franco plus Vidal Brujan, Xavier Edwards, Greg Jones, Taylor Walls and Alika Williams.

Organization	2020	2019	2018	2017	2016
2. Seattle Mariners	5	17	30	21	28

Baseball's worst farm system three years ago, the Mariners now are stacked at the top, led by outfielders Julio Rodriguez and Jarred Kelenic. A mix of big-ticket international signings (Noelvi Marte) and first-round pitchers (Logan Gilbert, Emerson Hancock and George Kirby) create one of the most formidable Top 10s in the game.

Organization	2020	2019	2018	2017	2016
3. San Diego Padres	2	1	3	9	25

MacKenzie Gore, Luis Patiño, Adrian Morejon and Ryan Weathers make up one of the best pitching prospect quartets in baseball. C.J. Abrams, Luis Campusano and Robert Hassell headline a well-rounded position player group, but few aside from Campusano have played above Class A. The system is less deep after myriad trades.

Organization	2020	2019	2018	2017	2016
4. Toronto Blue Jays	6	3	8	20	24

Righthander Nate Pearson leads the way, but the Blue Jays' bats stand out most. The addition of Austin Martin to go with Jordan Groshans and Orelvis Martinez gives them a strong infield crop, and Alejandro Kirk and Gabriel Moreno are standouts behind the plate. A mix of promising breakout candidates is ready behind them.

Organization	2020	2019	2018	2017	2016
5. Detroit Tigers	11	14	20	25	26

Adding Spencer Torkelson and Riley Greene in the last two drafts has enhanced the position player depth in the organization. The ascent of the Tigers' system is based heavily on their elite talent at the top, which also includes starting pitchers Tarik Skubal, Casey Mize and Matt Manning.

Organization	2020	2019	2018	2017	2016
6. Atlanta Braves	4	4	1	1	3

Outfielder Cristian Pache and righthander Ian Anderson give the Braves two of the game's best position and pitching prospects at the top of a strong list. There's a precipitous drop-off not long after them, however, as the lower levels of the system have thinned due to the team's penalties for violating international signing rules.

Organization	2020	2019	2018	2017	2016
7. Baltimore Orioles	12	22	17	27	27

Catcher Adley Rutschman is the crown jewel of an improved farm system, but the bulk of the potential impact talent remains in the lower levels, with more supplementary players higher up. The Orioles are still feeling the impact of ownership's disregard for signing Latin American prospects until just recently.

Organization	2020	2019	2018	2017	2016
8. Minnesota Twins	7	8	12	22	10

The Twins have a nice balance of talent at different positions, with a pair of corner bats (Alex Kiriloff and Trevor Larnach) and catcher Ryan Jeffers ready to be contributors in 2021. Righthander Jhoan Duran and Jordan Balazovic head a deep group of righthanders. Talented shortstop Royce Lewis is the X-factor.

Organization	2020	2019	2018	2017	2016
9. Los Angeles Dodgers	3	10	9	2	1

Even after graduating Gavin Lux, Dustin May, Brusdar Graterol and Tony Gonsolin in 2020, the Dodgers still have a deep, well-rounded group of pitchers and position players spread across all levels of the minors. The system's strength is more depth than top-level talent, but Keibert Ruiz and Josiah Gray are ready for the big leagues.

Organization	2020	2019	2018	2017	2016
10. Miami Marlins	9	25	24	29	29

Marlins fans can dream of a rotation fronted by Sixto Sanchez, Max Meyer, Edward Cabrera and Trevor Rogers. The system doesn't have the same caliber of hitting prospects as many teams above them on this list, though outfielder J.J. Bleday could enter that group with a big 2021 season.

Organization	2020	2019	2018	2017	2016
11. Cleveland Indians	19	15	21	18	17

Cleveland's pitching development has been exceptional in recent years, but the farm system now slants toward position players. Nolan Jones, Tyler Freeman, Bo Naylor and George Valera give the club a solid nucleus of position players, while last year's trade of Mike Clevinger added depth.

Organization	2020	2019	2018	2017	2016
12. St. Louis Cardinals	14	11	13	12	14

St. Louis can rue the ones that got away—Zac Gallen, Randy Arozarena, Luke Voit and Marco Gonzales— but its system still has a nice mix of premium prospects, led by outfielder Dylan Carlson, as well as intriguing recent additions like Jordan Walker, Masyn Winn and Edwin Nuñez.

Organization	2020	2019	2018	2017	2016
13. Kansas City Royals	18	27	29	26	21

Kansas City's heavy investment in college pitchers started to pay off in 2020 with debuts from Brady Singer and Kris Bubic. It should reap further dividends with Daniel Lynch, Asa Lacy and Jackson Kowar not far behind. The biggest boost will be when shortstop Bobby Witt Jr. arrives in Kansas City.

Organization	2020	2019	2018	2017	2016
14. San Francisco Giants	13	28	25	24	19

Marco Luciano is a potential superstar, and Joey Bart and Heliot Ramos should be big league regulars. Beyond that trio, the Giants have done an excellent job filling their system with interesting players at the lower levels, though they are thin on starting pitching prospects.

Organization	2020	2019	2018	2017	2016
15. Pittsburgh Pirates	24	18	16	7	11

Ke'Bryan Hayes reached the majors and immediately became one of the Pirates' best players. Behind him, the benefits of selecting at the top of the draft are piling up. Righthander Quinn Priester is a potential breakout star, Nick Gonzales can really hit—and Pittsburgh drafts No. 1 overall in 2021.

Organization	2020	2019	2018	2017	2016
16. New York Yankees	17	20	2	3	16

After the top three of Jasson Dominguez, Deivi Garcia and Clarke Schmidt, the Yankees' system is packed with low-level prospects with lots of upside and lots of volatility. After the canceled 2020 minor league season, 2021 will be crucial in determining the system's outlook.

17. Arizona Diamondbacks	10	21	26	28	22

The D-backs have a strong top five of position players who mostly have advanced offensive approaches and play in the middle of the diamond, though they're all in the lower levels aside from Daulton Varsho. They have spent the last two drafts adding athletic power pitchers behind them.

18. Cincinnati Reds	29	7	10	13	12

The Reds system could crack the top 10 a year from now if high-ceiling prospects like Austin Hendrick and Rece Hinds click. But the team's swing-for-the-fences approach carries plenty of risk, as well. Getting a breakout season from Hunter Greene, back from Tommy John surgery, would be a boost.

19. New York Mets	25	19	27	15	15

The Mets' last two drafts supply six of their top prospects—Matt Allan, Pete Crow-Armstrong, Brett Baty, J.T. Ginn, Josh Wolf and Isaiah Greene—while Francisco Alvarez and Ronny Mauricio signed internationally. The organization wonders what could have been had it kept 2018 draft picks Jarred Kelenic and Simeon Woods Richardson.

20. Chicago White Sox	8	6	4	5	23

This is exactly what the farm system should look like near the end of a big league rebuild. A host of talented young players are blossoming in the majors, while a few more will follow close behind from the upper levels of the farm system. But the depth of talent thins thereafter.

21. Boston Red Sox	22	30	23	14	4

After developing Mookie Betts, Xander Bogaerts and Rafael Devers, Boston's farm system emptied during its push for a World Series title in 2018. The system is slowly restocking now, with a mixture of bat-first prospects like Triston Casas and Bobby Dalbec and athletic outfielders like Jarren Duran and Gilberto Jimenez.

22. Chicago Cubs	21	29	28	16	20

The Cubs graduated position players like Kris Bryant, Javier Baez, Kyle Schwarber, Willson Contreras and Ian Happ—and traded away Gleyber Torres and Eloy Jimenez—to build a perennial playoff contender. They are now beginning to backfill their system with the likes of Brailyn Marquez, Brennen Davis, Miguel Amaya and Ed Howard.

23. Los Angeles Angels	16	13	14	30	30

The Angels' win-now approach hasn't paid off in recent years, and it means the farm system has never fully restocked. A bounceback from Jo Adell is crucial for the franchise, and the system thins out quickly after tooled-up prospects Brandon Marsh, Chris Rodriguez and Jordyn Adams behind him.

24. Texas Rangers	20	24	22	23	7

No team has been crushed by pitching injuries more in recent years than the Rangers. It's hard to find one of the team's pitching prospects who hasn't missed time. Leody Taveras, Sam Huff and Anderson Tejeda are nearly ready on the position player side, but Texas needs some of its pitchers to arrive as well.

25. Colorado Rockies	28	23	19	10	6

For a team with two winning seasons in the last decade, you'd like to see a stronger farm system. Colorado hasn't seen many returns from having six top-10 picks in the past nine drafts, but No. 1 prospect Brendan Rodgers is ready to step into a regular role and Zac Veen provides some hope for the 2020s.

26. Houston Astros	27	5	11	4	2

No longer consistently picking at the top of the draft has caused the Astros' system to slide. The strength of their minor league pipeline is a stable of bat-missing pitchers with high-velocity, high-spin fastballs—many of whom were low-dollar international signings and later-round draft picks—but the organization lacks impact hitters.

27. Philadelphia Phillies	26	12	7	6	8

With the graduation of third baseman Alec Bohm, the Phillies have one of the thinnest systems in baseball. The organization added quality arms in the 2020 draft such as Mick Abel and Carson Ragsdale to pair with Spencer Howard, but Dave Dombrowski will need to add quality hitters through the draft and the international market.

28. Milwaukee Brewers	30	26	6	8	9

The Brewers have a promising trio of position prospects in the middle of the diamond with Brice Turang, Garrett Mitchell and Hedbert Perez. They have some quality lefthanders too, but the system has a glaring gap in the upper levels, where the Brewers are particularly thin on hitters.

29. Oakland Athletics	15	9	18	17	18

The early returns on 2020 first-round pick Tyler Soderstrom are promising, but A.J. Puk's injury woes continue to pile up. The A's have some complementary players who could help in 2021, they lack impact talent, players who comfortably project as regulars and also depth.

30. Washington Nationals	23	16	15	19	5

The Nationals have a trio of college pitchers from their last two drafts at the top of their system, but none of Cade Cavalli, Jackson Rutledge or Cole Henry is a Top 100 Prospect. After that trio, the talent level in the system falls off sharply. In fairness, 22-year-old Juan Soto is still younger than a lot of the best prospects in this book.

Arizona Diamondbacks

BY NICK PIECORO

An interesting thing has happened with the Diamondbacks' farm system over the past two years: It has gone from being largely devoid of power pitchers to being overloaded with them, to the point an argument could be made pitching is the future of the organization.

That might be a stretch with the D-backs' top five prospects all currently position players. But with the pitchers who come next, it's not hard to envision a future rotation filled with power stuff.

That development is especially critical given what happened in 2020. The D-backs finished last in the National League West because their starting pitching collapsed, finishing with a 5.04 ERA in the pandemic-shortened season. The team finished 25-35 and saw longtime standouts Archie Bradley and Robbie Ray traded away as the team became unexpected sellers at the trade deadline.

Much of the newfound pitching inventory has arrived in the previous two drafts. The D-backs took a series of gambles on athletes in the 2019 draft, betting on their ability to develop in a professional atmosphere. Their selections at the top of the 2020 draft were a little safer—and some of the early returns have been tantalizing.

"Our pitching the last two years has taken big leaps overall," farm director Josh Barfield said. "I think it's a combination of our amateur scouting doing a great job of identifying talented pitchers . . . (and) I think we do a really good job of developing pitchers and identifying their strengths and helping them address their weaknesses."

The pitchers all have one thing in common: athleticism. Blake Walston is a former high school quarterback. Tommy Henry is a standout golfer who can kick 50-yard field goals. Drey Jameson, Ryne Nelson and Conor Grammes were all position players as well as pitchers in college. All have taken tangible developmental strides since signing.

In 2020, the D-backs used four of their five draft picks to further lock in on pitchers. With their top two selections, they landed a pair of relatively polished college arms in Duke's Bryce Jarvis and Miami's Slade Cecconi. Both project as future starters.

Few of these pitchers will make it. Even fewer will make it as starters. But many of them have ceilings that can change the trajectory of a franchise. If even one of them develops into a frontline starter, the D-backs would be pleased.

"All of a sudden, we have a whole group of really interesting arms," Barfield said. "The more interesting arms you can collect, the better chance you have of those guys popping."

CHRISTIAN PETERSEN/GETTY IMAGES

Daulton Varsho is the rare D-backs position prospect who has upper-level experience.

PROJECTED 2024 LINEUP

Position	Player	Age
Catcher	Daulton Varsho	27
First Base	Pavin Smith	28
Second Base	Ketel Marte	30
Third Base	Eduardo Escobar	35
Shortstop	Geraldo Perdomo	24
Left Field	Corbin Carroll	23
Center Field	Alek Thomas	24
Right Field	Kristian Robinson	23
Designated Hitter	Christian Walker	33
No. 1 Starter	Zac Gallen	28
No. 2 Starter	Madison Bumgarner	34
No. 3 Starter	Luke Weaver	30
No. 4 Starter	Slade Cecconi	25
No. 5 Starter	Caleb Smith	32
Closer	Stefan Crichton	32

The pitchers complement a position player group that is rich on outfielders but light in infielders, particularly following last year's trade of shortstop Liover Peguero to the Pirates in a deal for Starling Marte.

Most of the position players, with the exception of catcher/outfielder Daulton Varsho, have yet to play above Class A and remain far from sure things. At the same time, most are relatively advanced for their age and have mature approaches at the plate, making them somewhat less risky.

As the position players matriculate, there will be little doubt the system's strength is pitching. After the bottom fell out in 2020, the D-backs hope it will lead them back to playoff contention. ■

1 CORBIN CARROLL, OF

Born: Aug. 21, 2000. **B-T:** L-L. **HT:** 5-10. **WT:** 165.
Drafted: HS—Seattle, 2019 (1st round).
Signed by: Dan Ramsay.

TRACK RECORD: Carroll was viewed as an advanced high school hitter when the Diamondbacks selected him with the 16th overall pick in 2019 and signed him for $3,745,500 to forgo a UCLA commitment. He lived up to that billing during his pro debut, hitting .299/.409/.481 as he advanced to short-season Hillsboro and showed an encouraging blend of power (18 extra-base hits in 42 games), speed (18 stolen bases in 19 tries) and plate discipline (29 walks and 41 strikeouts). Carroll continued to impress with his play at the alternate training site in 2020, when he excelled against far more advanced pitchers. He looked so mature in his all-around game that some wondered, albeit prematurely, if he might be the rare fast-to-the-majors high school player.

SCOUTING REPORT: Carroll is undersized physically at a listed 5-foot-10. That gives him something in common not only with other prospects in Arizona's system but also Mookie Betts, Andrew Benintendi and Jackie Bradley Jr., all of whom were drafted by the Red Sox under Amiel Sawdaye, who now oversees amateur scouting for the D-backs. Carroll is strong, wiry and tremendously athletic. He has a fluid lefthanded swing he uses to spray hard line drives to all fields. His approach is mature beyond his years with an innate understanding of the strike zone, an ability to recognize spin and a knack for swinging at pitches on which he can do damage. Carroll is quick to make adjustments and showed during his time at the alternate training site that pitchers couldn't get him out the same way twice. He has plus-plus speed and gets out of the box quickly, which allows him to beat out his share of infield hits. Carroll's raw power is impressive and he can drive balls with authority in games, but evaluators caution he might be more of a 10-15 home run type whose speed will help inflate his slugging percentages early in his career before he grows into more power as he matures. He projects as a plus defender in center field and can shift to both corners without issue. His fringe-average arm strength is the only part of his game that leaves something to be desired. Carroll's excellent makeup and determined work ethic create optimism he will make the most of his abilities and reach his full potential.

THE FUTURE: Carroll has played 42 career games and still has much to prove—including that he can maintain his level of play across a full season—but he has fewer areas of his game that need refining than most 20-year-olds. Many D-backs officials see Carroll as the player in their system most likely to become a star, with comparisons ranging from Benintendi to Adam Eaton to Johnny Damon. ■

BILL MITCHELL

BA GRADE
60 Risk: High

SCOUTING GRADES
Hit: 60. **Power:** 50. **Run:** 70.
Field: 60. **Arm:** 45.

Projected future grades on 20-80 scouting scale.

BEST TOOLS

Best Hitter for Average	Corbin Carroll
Best Power Hitter	Kristian Robinson
Best Strike-Zone Discipline	Pavin Smith
Fastest Baserunner	Corbin Carroll
Best Athlete	Drey Jameson
Best Fastball	Conor Grammes
Best Curveball	Luis Frias
Best Slider	Levi Kelly
Best Changeup	J.B. Bukauskas
Best Control	Tyler Holton
Best Defensive Catcher	Jose Herrera
Best Defensive Infielder	Geraldo Perdomo
Best Infield Arm	Blaze Alexander
Best Defensive Outfielder	Alek Thomas
Best Outfield Arm	Alvin Guzman

Year	Age	Club (League)	Class	AVG	G	AB	R	H	2B	3B	HR	RBI	BB	SO	SB	OBP	SLG
2019	18	Hillsboro (NWL)	SS	.326	11	43	13	14	3	4	0	6	5	12	2	.408	.581
	18	Diamondbacks (AZL)	R	.288	31	111	23	32	6	3	2	14	24	29	16	.409	.450
Minor League Totals				.299	42	154	36	46	9	7	2	20	29	41	18	.409	.487

2 DAULTON VARSHO, C/OF

ALEX TRAUTWIG/MLB PHOTOS VIA GETTY IMAGES

Born: July 2, 1996. **B-T:** L-R. **Ht:** 5-10. **Wt:** 205. **Drafted:** Wisconsin-Milwaukee, 2017 (2nd round supplemental). **Signed by:** Rick Short.

TRACK RECORD: Varsho, the son of former major leaguer Gary Varsho, performed well at summer camp in July before earning a big league callup a week into the season. Things didn't go well initially, but the competitiveness of Varsho's at-bats improved as the season progressed. He posted an .822 OPS over his final 74 plate appearances, looking more like the productive hitter he was in the minors.

SCOUTING REPORT: Like many hitters in their first big league exposure, Varsho got caught in between during many of his early at-bats and was either too aggressive or too passive. He got more comfortable as the season progressed and began showing the decisive, compact swing that has long yielded predictions of an above-average hitter with average power. Varsho is a natural catcher, but his above-average speed and surprising athleticism convinced the D-backs to try him out in center field. He played both spots in his big league debut and was passable at each. His below-average arm strength was more noticeable in the outfield than behind the plate.

THE FUTURE: Varsho doesn't have much left to prove in the minors, but he also doesn't have a clear role on the 2021 big league roster. He will try to win a spot in spring training and carry over his strong finish from 2020.

SCOUTING GRADES: **Hitting:** 55 **Power:** 50 **Running:** 55 **Fielding:** 50 **Arm:** 45

Year	Age	Club (League)	Class	AVG	G	AB	R	H	2B	3B	HR	RBI	BB	SO	SB	OBP	SLG
2017	20	Hillsboro (NWL)	SS	.311	50	193	36	60	16	3	7	39	17	30	7	.368	.534
2018	21	Visalia (CAL)	HiA	.286	80	304	44	87	11	3	11	44	30	71	19	.363	.451
	21	Diamondbacks (AZL)	R	.500	3	12	4	6	2	1	1	1	0	1	0	.500	1.083
2019	22	Jackson (SL)	AA	.301	108	396	85	119	25	4	18	58	42	63	21	.378	.520
2020	23	Arizona (NL)	MAJ	.188	37	101	16	19	5	2	3	9	12	33	3	.287	.366
Major League Totals				.188	37	101	16	19	5	2	3	9	12	33	3	.287	.366
Minor League Totals				.301	241	905	169	272	54	11	37	142	89	165	47	.372	.507

3 GERALDO PERDOMO, SS

ALEX TRAUTWIG/MLB PHOTOS VIA GETTY IMAGES

Born: Oct. 22, 1999. **B-T:** B-R. **Ht:** 6-3. **Wt:** 184. **Signed:** Dominican Republic, 2016. **Signed by:** Junior Noboa/Elvis Cruz.

TRACK RECORD: After signing for just $70,000 in 2016, Perdomo quickly looked like a bargain with his elite plate discipline and ability to play shortstop. After an impressive U.S. debut in 2018, Perdomo advanced to high Class A in 2019 and took a star turn as a 19-year-old in the Arizona Fall League. The D-backs brought him to their alternate training site in 2020.

SCOUTING REPORT: Perdomo primarily stands out on defense but has plenty of offensive tools as well. The switch-hitter controls the strike zone, has good bat speed from both sides of the plate and has posted solid results against both lefties and righties. Mostly a singles and doubles hitter, Perdomo said he added 17 pounds of good weight to his athletic frame after the 2019 season and could still add more. Perdomo is a graceful defender who would be a slightly above-average major league shortstop right now and could be a plus defender in the future. He has soft, reliable hands and an above-average arm, while his above-average speed gives him plenty of range. Nearly fluent in English, Perdomo is viewed as a team leader.

THE FUTURE: Perdomo is set to open 2021 at Double-A. The D-backs have Nick Ahmed signed through 2023, so Perdomo has time to develop his offensive game.

SCOUTING GRADES: **Hitting:** 55 **Power:** 40 **Running:** 55 **Fielding:** 60 **Arm:** 55

Year	Age	Club (League)	Class	AVG	G	AB	R	H	2B	3B	HR	RBI	BB	SO	SB	OBP	SLG
2017	17	D-backs1 (DSL)	R	.238	63	214	42	51	3	2	1	11	60	37	16	.410	.285
2018	18	Hillsboro (NWL)	SS	.301	30	103	20	31	3	2	3	14	18	23	9	.421	.456
	18	Missoula (PIO)	R	.455	6	22	3	10	0	1	0	2	7	4	1	.586	.545
	18	Diamondbacks (AZL)	R	.314	21	86	20	27	4	2	1	8	14	17	14	.416	.442
2019	19	Kane County (MWL)	LoA	.268	90	314	48	84	16	3	2	36	56	56	20	.394	.357
	19	Visalia (CAL)	HiA	.301	26	93	15	28	5	0	1	11	14	11	6	.407	.387
Minor League Totals				.278	236	832	148	231	31	10	8	82	169	148	66	.411	.368

4 KRISTIAN ROBINSON, OF

CRAIG MITCHELLDYER/HILLSBORO HOPS

BA GRADE

60 **Risk: Extreme**

Born: Dec. 11, 2000. **B-T:** R-R. **HT:** 6-3. **WT:** 215. **Signed:** Bahamas, 2017. **Signed by:** Cesar Geronimo/Craig Shipley.

TRACK RECORD: Robinson signed for $2.5 million in 2017 and quickly impressed the organization with his maturity, mindset and athleticism. He put together a strong season in the short-season Northwest League before a promotion to the low Class A Midwest League at age 18 in 2019, and he showed up to spring training in 2020 with a slimmed-down physique after experimenting with a paleo diet in the offseason. Robinson joined the alternate training site in August and finished the year in instructional league.

SCOUTING REPORT: Robinson's natural athleticism, gargantuan raw power and plus speed give him the building blocks for massive upside. He does things few players can, including hitting a home run into the Chase Field pool area in three consecutive at-bats during alternate site play. But while his power and speed are undeniable, concerns about how often he swings and misses are starting to raise questions about his ability to reach his ceiling. He projects as a fringe-average hitter who strikes out often, though he's still young and has relatively little experience against quality pitchers coming from the Bahamas. Observers believe he could still make huge strides in all facets of development, including on defense, where he is a potential above-average defender on an outfield corner.

THE FUTURE: Robinson was hurt by a lack of reps in 2020. He'll look to make up for lost time in 2021.

SCOUTING GRADES: **Hitting:** 45 **Power:** 70 **Running:** 60 **Fielding:** 55 **Arm:** 50

Year	Age	Club (League)	Class	AVG	G	AB	R	H	2B	3B	HR	RBI	BB	SO	SB	OBP	SLG
2018	17	Missoula (PIO)	R	.300	17	60	13	18	1	0	3	10	11	21	5	.419	.467
	17	Diamondbacks (AZL)	R	.272	40	162	35	44	11	0	4	31	16	46	7	.341	.414
2019	18	Hillsboro (NWL)	SS	.319	44	163	29	52	10	1	9	35	23	47	14	.407	.558
	18	Kane County (MWL)	LoA	.217	25	92	14	20	3	1	5	16	8	30	3	.294	.435
Minor League Totals				.281	126	477	91	134	25	2	21	92	58	144	29	.366	.474

5 ALEK THOMAS, OF

TAYLOR JACKSON/ARIZONA DIAMONDBACKS

BA GRADE

55 **Risk: High**

Born: April 28, 2000. **B-T:** L-L. **HT:** 5-11. **WT:** 175. **Drafted:** HS—Chicago, 2018 (2nd round). **Signed by:** Nate Birtwell.

TRACK RECORD: Thomas' father Allen is a former minor league outfielder who has spent the past 17 years as the strength and conditioning coach for the White Sox. The junior Thomas was drafted by the D-backs in the second round in 2018 and hit his way up to high Class A in his first full season. He spent the 2020 season at the alternate training site and held his own against upper-level pitchers.

SCOUTING REPORT: Thomas packs a punch despite his undersized, 5-foot-11 frame. He has a lot going on in his swing with busy hands, a pronounced leg kick and an aggressive weight transfer, but he manages to get on time. Thomas can generate loud contact that yields extra bases, and he uses his plus speed to take the extra 90 feet. He has a chance to grow into double-digit home run power, but most of his impact will be felt in the form of doubles and triples. He has an aggressive approach but has taken steps to being more selective. In an organization filled with talented defensive outfielders, Thomas is regarded as the best of the group and a potential plus defender in center field, though his arm is a tick below-average.

THE FUTURE: Thomas is expected to push his way to Double-A to start 2021. His game calls to mind Adam Eaton, Brett Gardner and other smaller, impactful outfielders.

SCOUTING GRADES: **Hitting:** 60 **Power:** 45 **Running:** 60 **Fielding:** 60 **Arm:** 45

Year	Age	Club (League)	Class	AVG	G	AB	R	H	2B	3B	HR	RBI	BB	SO	SB	OBP	SLG
2018	18	Missoula (PIO)	R	.341	28	123	26	42	11	1	2	17	11	19	4	.396	.496
	18	Diamondbacks (AZL)	R	.325	28	123	24	40	3	5	0	10	13	18	8	.394	.431
2019	19	Kane County (MWL)	LoA	.312	91	353	63	110	21	7	8	48	43	72	11	.393	.479
	19	Visalia (CAL)	HiA	.255	23	94	13	24	2	0	2	7	9	33	4	.327	.340
Minor League Totals				.312	170	693	126	216	37	13	12	82	76	142	27	.385	.455

6 SLADE CECCONI, RHP

Born: June 24, 1999. **B-T:** R-R. **HT:** 6-4. **WT:** 224. **Drafted:** Miami, 2020 (1st round supplemental). **Signed by:** Eric Cruz.

TRACK RECORD: Cecconi was an intriguing draft prospect as a high school senior, but an injury kept him off the field and steered him to Miami. He posted solid results with the Hurricanes and his stuff, presence and strike-throwing ability enticed the D-backs to draft him 33rd overall as an eligible sophomore. Cecconi quickly validated the selection with dominant showings at the alternate training site and instructional league, drawing reviews as the organization's best pitching prospect.

SCOUTING REPORT: Working with a prototype 6-foot-4 pitcher's frame, Cecconi has a methodical, under-control delivery from which he unleashes monster stuff. His fastball sits at 95 mph and touches 98 with impressive life. He backs up his heater with a wipeout slider that is another plus pitch. His curveball is a bit loopy but still gives hitters trouble, serving as a good change of speed. His changeup is a fringy offering that is a clear fourth pitch. Cecconi throws strikes and earns praise for his command, but he does have a history of leaving the ball over the plate too much or falling off as his starts wear on.

THE FUTURE: Cecconi looked like a polished starter who could marry explosive stuff with overpowering results in his first look over the summer in 2020. But he still has to show he can pitch deep into games and maintain his best stuff over a long season.

SCOUTING GRADES: **Fastball:** 60 **Slider:** 60 **Curveball:** 55 **Changeup:** 45 **Control:** 55

Year	Age	Club (League)	Class	W	L	ERA	G	GS	IP	H	HR	BB	SO	BB/9	SO/9	WHIP	AVG
2020	21	Did not play—No minor league season															

7 BRYCE JARVIS, RHP

Born: Dec. 26, 1997. **B-T:** L-R. **HT:** 6-2. **WT:** 195. **Drafted:** Duke, 2020 (1st round). **Signed by:** George Swain.

TRACK RECORD: Jarvis, the son of longtime major league pitcher Kevin Jarvis, had long been a well-regarded prospect, but his stock jumped in 2020 after he worked at Driveline and Cressey Sports Performance to add velocity and sharpen his secondary pitches. He threw a 15-strikeout perfect game against Cornell in February and became the highest-drafted player in Duke history when the D-backs took him 18th overall.

SCOUTING REPORT: The D-backs viewed Jarvis as a polished and potentially fast-moving college pitcher after he sat 93-96 mph with plus command of his fastball and a changeup and slider that were both above-average in the spring. Jarvis exceeded expectations in the brief 2020 college season, but he crashed back to earth by struggling at the alternate training site and instructional league. He showed subpar fastball command and little deception while serving up many home runs. Jarvis' strong four starts in the abbreviated 2020 college season were vastly better than the rest of his career, so there were some questions whether it was sustainable. On the positive side, he earned high marks for his competitiveness and cerebral approach. His changeup also showed plus at its best, and he began showcasing a new curveball.

THE FUTURE: There early indications suggest Jarvis might not be quite as close to the majors as originally believed. He will try to rediscover his best form with a full season in 2021.

SCOUTING GRADES: **Fastball:** 55 **Slider:** 55 **Curveball:** 45 **Changeup:** 55 **Control:** 55

Year	Age	Club (League)	Class	W	L	ERA	G	GS	IP	H	HR	BB	SO	BB/9	SO/9	WHIP	AVG
2020	22	Did not play—No minor league season															

8 BLAKE WALSTON, LHP

Born: June 28, 2001. **B-T:** L-L. **HT:** 6-5. **WT:** 195. **Drafted:** HS—Wilmington, N.C., 2019 (1st round). **Signed by:** George Swain.

TAYLOR JACKSON/ARIZONA DIAMONDBACKS

BA GRADE
55 Risk: Extreme

TRACK RECORD: The D-backs grabbed the projectable, athletic Walston with the second of their two first-round picks in 2019, and they were pleased with the initial returns. Walston added significant weight and strength and spent the 2020 season at the alternate training site, where he faced advanced competition and performed relatively well.

SCOUTING REPORT: Walston has a lot of promise but is still a young pitcher learning to maintain his best stuff. His fastball velocity can reach the mid 90s but is inconsistent, and he's still making mechanical adjustments to get better separation between his average curveball and plus slider. His changeup remains a work in progress. Walston's intensity level fluctuated at the alternate site, leading to speculation that the lack of true competition—of games that counted—was a detriment to his focus. Others wondered if he needed adversity to get the most of his ability. Walston also saw his command and velocity suffer when he got into the middle innings of games. He earned praise for his work and preparation off the field.

THE FUTURE: Walston missed out on the development that comes from grinding out a full season. He should get the chance to do that in 2021 and will aim to show his best stuff on a more consistent basis.

SCOUTING GRADES: **Fastball:** 55 **Slider:** 60 **Curveball:** 50 **Changeup:** 45 **Control:** 50

Year	Age	Club (League)	Class	W	L	ERA	G	GS	IP	H	HR	BB	SO	BB/9	SO/9	WHIP	AVG
2019	18	Hillsboro (NWL)	SS	0	0	3.00	3	3	6	6	0	2	6	3.0	9.0	1.33	.240
	18	Diamondbacks (AZL)	R	0	0	1.80	3	2	5	2	0	0	11	0.0	19.8	0.40	.118
Minor League Totals				0	0	2.45	6	5	11	8	0	2	17	1.6	13.9	0.91	.200

9 PAVIN SMITH, 1B/OF

TOP ROOKIE

Born: Feb. 6, 1995. **B-T:** L-L. **HT:** 6-2. **WT:** 210. **Drafted:** Virginia, 2017 (1st round). **Signed by:** Rick Matsko.

ALEX TRAUTWIG/MLB PHOTOS VIA GETTY IMAGES

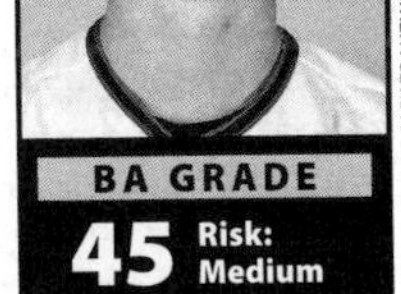

TRACK RECORD: Smith was one of the best pure hitters in the 2017 draft and went seventh overall to the D-backs. He struggled at the start of his professional career, but turned things around midway through the 2019 season at Double-A Jackson. He pushed his way to the majors late in 2020 and hit .270/.341/.405 in 44 plate appearances, showing flashes of the kind of big leaguer he could become.

SCOUTING REPORT: In many ways, Smith is the same player he was coming out of college. He has excellent strike-zone awareness, good bat-to-ball skills and sneaky solid athleticism. The D-backs believe he also has made strides in other areas. He made adjustments to allow him to better stay back and hit the bottom of the ball at the alternate training site, translating to more power. He also has "transformed himself physically," in the words of D-backs general manager Mike Hazen, adding speed and quickness. The club now feels comfortable with him in left and right field in addition to first base, where he is above-average. Smith has an above-average arm and is a fringe-average runner.

THE FUTURE: Smith turned in competitive at-bats during his September cameo. His ability to play the outfield increases his likelihood of impacting the 2021 roster.

SCOUTING GRADES: **Hitting:** 55 **Power:** 45 **Running:** 45 **Fielding:** 55 **Arm:** 55

Year	Age	Club (League)	Class	AVG	G	AB	R	H	2B	3B	HR	RBI	BB	SO	SB	OBP	SLG
2017	21	Hillsboro (NWL)	SS	.318	51	195	34	62	15	2	0	27	27	24	2	.401	.415
2018	22	Visalia (CAL)	HiA	.255	120	439	63	112	25	1	11	54	57	65	3	.343	.392
2019	23	Jackson (SL)	AA	.291	123	440	62	128	29	6	12	67	59	61	2	.370	.466
2020	24	Arizona (NL)	MAJ	.270	12	37	7	10	0	1	1	4	5	8	1	.341	.405
Major League Totals				.270	12	37	7	10	0	1	1	4	5	8	1	.341	.405
Minor League Totals				.281	294	1074	159	302	69	9	23	148	143	150	7	.364	.426

10 CORBIN MARTIN, RHP

TOP ROOKIE

ALEX TRAUTWIG/MLB PHOTOS VIA GETTY IMAGES

BA GRADE
55 Risk: Extreme

Born: Dec. 28, 1995. **B-T:** R-R. **HT:** 6-2. **WT:** 225. **Drafted:** Texas A&M, 2017 (2nd round). **Signed by:** Noel Gonzales-Luna (Astros).

TRACK RECORD: Martin jumped on the fast track after being drafted by the Astros in the second round in 2017 and reached the majors in 2019. That rise was interrupted by an elbow injury that required Tommy John surgery in July 2019—less than a month before the D-backs acquired him in the Zack Greinke deal. Just as Martin was approaching a return in 2020, he suffered a strained left oblique that effectively ended his season.

SCOUTING REPORT: Martin returned to the mound in the fall, appearing in intrasquad games and instructional league, and looked mostly like his normal self. His velocity was a tick down, ranging from 92-95 mph, but he also was not throwing at full intensity. Before surgery, Martin had a solid four-pitch mix, with his fastball complemented by a slider, curveball and changeup that all graded average to above. He's since tinkered with a new grip on his curveball and received good feedback on it, helping solidify it as a potentially above-average pitch. He's previously shown above-average control when healthy.

THE FUTURE: Martin will enter spring training as one of the club's rotation depth options and will try to climb his way into the front five at some point during the year. He has previously shown No. 3 or 4 starter potential but has to stay healthy and show his stuff comes all the way back.

SCOUTING GRADES: **Fastball:** 55 **Slider:** 50 **Curveball:** 55 **Changeup:** 50 **Control:** 55

Year	Age	Club (League)	Class	W	L	ERA	G	GS	IP	H	HR	BB	SO	BB/9	SO/9	WHIP	AVG
2018	22	Corpus Christi (TL)	AA	7	2	2.97	21	18	103	84	7	28	96	2.4	8.4	1.09	.205
	22	Fayetteville (CAR)	HiA	2	0	0.00	4	3	19	4	0	7	26	3.3	12.3	0.58	.057
2019	23	Houston (AL)	MAJ	1	1	5.59	5	5	19	23	8	12	19	5.6	8.8	1.81	.250
	23	Round Rock (PCL)	AAA	2	1	3.13	9	8	37	33	2	18	45	4.3	10.8	1.37	.188
2020	24	Did not play—Injured															
Major League Totals				1	1	5.59	5	5	19	23	8	12	19	5.6	8.8	1.81	.288
Minor League Totals				11	4	2.58	44	33	192	141	10	62	210	2.9	9.8	1.06	.203

11 CONOR GRAMMES, RHP

BREAKOUT

BA GRADE
50 Risk: Very High

Born: July 13, 1997. **B-T:** R-R. **HT:** 6-2. **WT:** 205. **Drafted:** Xavier, 2019 (5th round). **Signed by:** Jeremy Kehrt.

TRACK RECORD: Grammes was a two-way player who spent more time as a position player than a pitcher at Xavier. Intrigued by his quick arm and athleticism, the D-backs drafted Grammes as a pitcher in the fifth round in 2019 despite his limited experience on the mound. The early returns, albeit not in a normal minor league setting, were encouraging in 2020.

SCOUTING REPORT: Grammes has some of the best pure stuff in the D-backs' organization. His fastball routinely sat 97-100 mph during instructional league and he backed it up with a hard, 87-88 mph slider and mid-80s power curveball that both drew above-average grades. Grammes also has a firm, upper-80s changeup, but it lags behind his two breaking balls. Grammes walked more than six batters per nine innings in college. His control has made strides, but his command remains a work in progress. With the cancellation of the 2020 minor league season, he has not had the opportunity to show he can go deep into games or maintain his stuff over a full season.

THE FUTURE: Grammes is most likely a future hard-throwing reliever. Given how much he has improved since being drafted and his relative lack of pitching experience, starting isn't out of the question if he keeps making strides.

Year	Age	Club (League)	Class	W	L	ERA	G	GS	IP	H	HR	BB	SO	BB/9	SO/9	WHIP	AVG
2019	21	Hillsboro (NWL)	SS	0	1	4.11	9	6	15	11	0	8	20	4.7	11.7	1.24	.169
Minor League Totals				0	1	4.11	9	6	15	11	0	8	20	4.7	11.7	1.24	.200

12 LEVI KELLY, RHP

BA GRADE
50 Risk: Very High

Born: May 14, 1999. **B-T:** R-R. **HT:** 6-4. **WT:** 205. **Drafted:** HS—Bradenton, Fla., 2018 (8th round). **Signed by:** Luke Wrenn.

TRACK RECORD: The D-backs took a flier on the projectable Kelly in the eighth round in 2018. He rewarded them with a dominant season in the low Class A Midwest League in his first full season and continued to impress in 2020. Kelly opened eyes at summer camp and continued to pitch well at the alternate training site before tiring at the end of the year.

SCOUTING REPORT: Kelly's fastball sits 94-96 mph and touches 98, but his best weapon is a wipeout slider that was nearly unhittable for much of the summer at the alternate site. He also throws a splitter that serves as a change of pace offering and added a curveball, giving him the potential for a well-rounded starter's arsenal. Kelly's fastball command comes and goes, and some observers would like to see him dial back the intensity in his high-effort delivery, which leads to fringy control. He is highly competitive and has a great work ethic.

THE FUTURE: Kelly needs to tighten up his command and third pitch to remain in the rotation. The D-backs know if starting doesn't work out, he would fit nicely in the back of a bullpen.

Year	Age	Club (League)	Class	W	L	ERA	G	GS	IP	H	HR	BB	SO	BB/9	SO/9	WHIP	AVG
2019	20	Kane County (MWL)	LoA	5	1	2.15	22	22	100	72	4	39	126	3.5	11.3	1.11	.176
Minor League Totals				5	1	2.03	26	26	106	75	4	41	132	3.5	11.2	1.09	.196

13 A.J. VUKOVICH, 3B/OF

BREAKOUT
BA GRADE
50 Risk: Extreme

Born: July 20, 2001. **B-T:** R-R. **HT:** 6-5. **WT:** 210. **Drafted:** HS—East Troy, Wis., 2020 (4th round). **Signed by:** Nate Birtwell.

TRACK RECORD: Vukovich was a two-sport star in high school who was a finalist for Wisconsin's Mr. Basketball. The D-backs drafted him in the fourth round in 2020 and signed him for $1.25 million, the equivalent of second-round money, to forgo a Louisville commitment. Vukovich made a loud first impression at instructional league in the fall, impressing the organization with consistent hard contact and a mature routine and work ethic.

SCOUTING REPORT: Vukovich is lean and lanky and has more athleticism than might be apparent at first glance. Despite his big frame and long levers, his swing is relatively short and direct with few moving parts. With his stance slightly closed, he wears out the right-center field gap. He shows a good approach, a feel for finding the barrel and plus power potential. Defense hasn't been a focus for Vuckovich, but he made strides in his fundamentals at third base during the fall. He still has a long way to go and might end up shifting to an outfield corner. He is a below-average runner.

THE FUTURE: Vukovich should hit enough for an outfield corner. Some observers believe he could develop into a Nick Castellanos type.

Year	Age	Club (League)	Class	AVG	G	AB	R	H	2B	3B	HR	RBI	BB	SO	SB	OBP	SLG
2020	18	Did not play—No minor league season															

14 SETH BEER, 1B/DH

BA GRADE
45 Risk: Medium

Born: Sept. 18, 1996. **B-T:** L-R. **HT:** 6-3. **WT:** 225. **Drafted:** Clemson, 2018 (1st round). **Signed by:** Gavin Dickey (Astros).

TRACK RECORD: Beer put up gaudy numbers at Clemson to become the first freshman to win the Dick Howser Trophy in 2016. The Astros drafted him 28th overall in 2018 and sent him to the D-backs in the Zack Greinke trade a year later. After hitting .289/.389/.516 and reaching Double-A in his first full season, Beer spent 2020 at the D-backs' alternate site and was arguably their best hitter there.

SCOUTING REPORT: Beer isn't just a bat-first player—he appears to be bat only. He has a mature approach, a smooth, strong swing and above-average raw power. He's hit for average and power at every level and projects to continue to do so. Despite the work he has put in to improve defensively, he hasn't made much progress. His footwork at first base is not good, nor are his hands. He is worse in the outfield based on near bottom-of-the-scale speed. Even if he could be a poor-yet-passable defender, it likely would not be good enough for the D-backs, who put a premium on defense.

THE FUTURE: If the universal DH is here to stay, that gives Beer a possible path with the D-backs. Even then, they value flexibility, which Beer does not provide. He can hit, but his future likely lies in a different organization.

Year	Age	Club (League)	Class	AVG	G	AB	R	H	2B	3B	HR	RBI	BB	SO	SB	OBP	SLG
2019	22	Jackson (SL)	AA	.205	24	88	8	18	7	0	1	17	8	25	0	.297	.318
	22	Corpus Christi (TL)	AA	.299	63	234	40	70	9	0	16	52	24	58	0	.407	.543
	22	Fayetteville (CAR)	HiA	.328	35	128	24	42	8	0	9	34	14	30	0	.414	.602
Minor League Totals				.294	189	710	111	209	38	0	38	145	71	162	1	.388	.508

15 TOMMY HENRY, LHP

BA GRADE
45 Risk: High

Born: July 29, 1997. **B-T:** L-L. **HT:** 6-3. **WT:** 205. **Drafted:** Michigan, 2019 (2nd round supplemental). **Signed by:** Jeremy Kehrt.

TRACK RECORD: Henry had a dominant run in the College World Series in 2019, shortly after the D-backs made him the highest-drafted Michigan pitcher in 25 years. The club liked his pitch mix and his athleticism, hoping it would translate into further development. Though the 2020 minor league season was cut short by the pandemic, Henry's early returns were encouraging at the alternate training site.

SCOUTING REPORT: Henry's fluctuations in velocity were a concern leading up to the draft, but his fastball ticked up—and stayed there—during his time at the alternate site, sitting at 93 mph and topping out at 95. He credited the uptick to a better incorporation of his lower half along with long-tossing and work with weighted balls. Henry's above-average slider is generally viewed as his primary secondary offering, but his average changeup made strides to the point that Henry has called it his favorite pitch. He also picked up a curveball this year that has promise. Henry's best asset is his plus control.

THE FUTURE: Henry's ceiling would be higher if he could find a dominant, go-to secondary pitch. Until then, he projects as a back-end starter.

Year	Age	Club (League)	Class	W	L	ERA	G	GS	IP	H	HR	BB	SO	BB/9	SO/9	WHIP	AVG
2019	21	Hillsboro (NWL)	SS	0	0	6.00	3	3	3	4	0	0	4	0.0	12.0	1.33	.267
Minor League Totals				0	0	6.00	3	3	3	4	0	0	4	0.0	12.0	1.33	.286

16 RYNE NELSON, RHP

BA GRADE
45 Risk: High

Born: Feb. 1, 1998. **B-T:** R-R. **HT:** 6-4. **WT:** 190. **Drafted:** Oregon, 2019 (2nd round). **Signed by:** Dan Ramsay.

TRACK RECORD: Nelson shifted his focus to pitching at Oregon in 2019 after spending his first two years as a two-way player. He struggled with command and control and was dropped from the Ducks' rotation to the bullpen, but his power stuff convinced the D-backs to draft him in the second round. He showed up at instructional league in 2020 looking like a different pitcher, giving the D-backs hope he could develop into a starter.

SCOUTING REPORT: Nelson has a lighting-fast arm that generates fastballs that sit 94-95 mph, touch 98 and have excellent life through the zone. He has two additional weapons in his curveball and slider. His curveball is the better pitch when he throws it hard in the 83 mph range, while his slider generates good sweep despite Nelson's high arm slot. He made big strides with his changeup, but it remains his fourth-best offering. Nelson's control has always been the question mark. The progress he made to average was a bright spot in 2020 for the D-backs, who no longer have to squint to see a future starter.

THE FUTURE: Nelson will need to continue progressing to stick in the rotation. High Class A is likely his next test.

Year	Age	Club (League)	Class	W	L	ERA	G	GS	IP	H	HR	BB	SO	BB/9	SO/9	WHIP	AVG
2019	21	Hillsboro (NWL)	SS	0	1	2.89	10	7	19	15	1	10	26	4.8	12.5	1.34	.195
Minor League Totals				0	1	2.89	10	7	18	15	1	10	26	4.8	12.5	1.34	.227

17 LUIS FRIAS, RHP

BA GRADE
45 Risk: High

Born: May 23, 1998. **B-T:** R-R. **HT:** 6-3. **WT:** 235. **Signed:** Dominican Republic, 2015. **Signed by:** Jose Ortiz/Junior Noboa.

TRACK RECORD: Frias is a big-bodied power pitcher the D-backs signed for $50,000 in 2015. He reached the low Class A Midwest League in 2019 and spent 2020 at the alternate training site, where he was occasionally hit hard by more advanced hitters.

SCOUTING REPORT: Frias has the building blocks to be a starting pitcher. His fastball sits in the mid-to-upper 90s and his spike curveball serves as his out pitch. He added a splitter in 2019 and began throwing a slider in 2020, something he hopes to use as a called-strike pitch. As with other power arms in the system, his command remains a work in progress. There was some sense among the organization that his occasional struggles at the alternate site, much of which stemmed from pitches that caught too much of the plate, could help drive home the importance of improved command.

THE FUTURE: Frias' profile remains relatively unchanged from previous years. If he can make strides with the consistency of his command and his secondary stuff, he could become an innings-eating mid-rotation starter. Otherwise, he fits best in relief.

Year	Age	Club (League)	Class	W	L	ERA	G	GS	SV	IP	H	HR	BB	SO	K/9	WHIP	AVG
2019	21	Hillsboro (NWL)	SS	3	3	1.99	10	10	0	50	36	0	17	72	13.0	1.07	.205
	21	Kane County (MWL)	LoA	3	1	4.39	6	6	0	27	22	1	12	29	9.8	1.28	.225
Minor League Totals				10	11	3.10	43	40	0	182	141	2	83	206	10.2	1.23	.212

18 DREY JAMESON, RHP

BA GRADE 45 Risk: High

Born: Aug. 17, 1997. **B-T:** R-R. **HT:** 6-0. **WT:** 165. **Drafted:** Ball State, 2019 (1st round supplemental). **Signed by:** Jeremy Kehrt.

TRACK RECORD: Jameson is undersized and the product of humble roots. He was raised by a single mom who worked two jobs, an upbringing that helped shape his competitive nature. He was initially a two-way player at Ball State but ultimately developed into the program's ace and best pitching prospect since Bryan Bullington was the No. 1 overall pick in the 2002 draft. The D-backs took Jameson with the 34th overall pick in 2019 and signed him for $1.4 million.

SCOUTING REPORT: Despite his small frame, Jameson generates some of the best velocity in the organization. He pumps fastballs that sit in the mid 90s as a starter and 98-100 mph in relief with his super-quick arm speed. But Jameson does so with significant effort, taking away his ability to command it. His fastball also gets hit more than would be expected, raising questions about a potential lack of deception. Jameson has a full repertoire, including a slider, curveball and changeup that all have average potential, though his breaking pitches are inconsistent and sometimes blend together.

THE FUTURE: Jameson may need to tone down his delivery in order to gain consistency with his location and the shape of his secondary stuff. In the eyes of many, he is looking more and more like a future late-inning reliever.

Year	Age	Club (League)	Class	W	L	ERA	G	GS	IP	H	HR	BB	SO	BB/9	SO/9	WHIP	AVG
2019	21	Hillsboro (NWL)	SS	0	0	6.17	8	8	12	14	1	9	12	6.9	9.3	1.97	.241
Minor League Totals			.	0	0	6.17	8	8	11	14	1	9	12	6.9	9.3	1.97	.292

19 JAKE McCARTHY, OF

BREAKOUT

BA GRADE 45 Risk: High

Born: July 30, 1997. **B-T:** L-L. **HT:** 6-3. **WT:** 215. **Drafted:** Virginia, 2018 (1st round supplemental). **Signed by:** Rick Matsko.

TRACK RECORD: McCarthy received a $1.65 million bonus as the 39th overall pick in 2018, following his older brother Joe on a path from Virginia to the professional ranks. He immediately went about working to rebuild his swing, an effort that was sidetracked by injuries that limited him to just 53 games with high Class A Visalia in 2019.

SCOUTING REPORT: McCarthy showed up to instructional league in 2020 looking completely different. He put on some 20 pounds of good weight, and just as noticeable were the changes to his swing. Once rigid and upper-body driven, it is now more athletic while incorporating a leg kick. McCarthy was perhaps the D-backs' most productive hitter during the fall, a performance that teased flashes of an above-average hitter with 20-plus home run power and re-established his prospect value. McCarthy remains an excellent defender whose speed plays well in center field. He saw time at first base during instructs, a move designed to increase his versatility.

THE FUTURE: McCarthy's transformation brings to mind the swing changes made by former D-backs outfielder Mitch Haniger. He'll now try to show he can carry that success into 2021 and sustain it.

Year	Age	Club (League)	Class	AVG	G	AB	R	H	2B	3B	HR	RBI	BB	SO	SB	OBP	SLG
2019	21	Visalia (CAL)	HiA	.277	53	195	29	54	13	3	2	30	17	52	18	.341	.405
Minor League Totals				.283	111	414	63	117	30	7	5	52	40	93	39	.360	.425

20 WILDERD PATIÑO, OF

BA GRADE 50 Risk: Extreme

Born: July 18, 2001. **B-T:** R-R. **HT:** 6-1. **WT:** 175. **Signed:** Venezuela, 2017. **Signed by:** Cesar Geronimo/Kristians Pereira.

TRACK RECORD: Patiño needed surgery on the growth plate in his right elbow in the spring of 2017, prompting the Rangers to back out of a $1.3 million agreement. The D-backs swooped in and signed him for $985,000, then had Patiño undergo revision surgery. He returned the following summer and broke out in 2019, when he hit .349/.403/.472 in the Rookie-level Arizona League and earned a late promotion.

SCOUTING REPORT: Patiño has the raw materials to be an impact major leaguer. His strong, physical frame can produce above-average power to all fields and he has plus speed and athleticism in the outfield. His game remains raw, however. He has made adjustments at the plate, including the way he grips the bat, but could stand to make more. He primarily needs to tone down his aggressiveness, which works against him and will get further exploited against advanced pitchers. Patiño is not as sharp a defender as others in the system and may be forced to a corner. His fringe-average arm may limit him to left field.
THE FUTURE: Patiño was among those most hurt by the lack of a minor league season, given how much development is still needed. He should open 2021 at low Class A.

Year	Age	Club (League)	Class	AVG	G	AB	R	H	2B	3B	HR	RBI	BB	SO	SB	OBP	SLG
2019	17	Missoula (PIO)	R	.229	10	35	6	8	1	2	0	4	2	14	1	.300	.371
	17	Diamondbacks (AZL)	R	.349	30	106	18	37	4	3	1	21	11	32	13	.403	.472
Minor League Totals				.294	74	252	38	74	11	5	1	34	29	70	20	.384	.389

21 BLAZE ALEXANDER, SS/2B

BA GRADE 45 **Risk:** High

Born: June 11, 1999. **B-T:** R-R. **HT:** 6-0. **WT:** 175. **Drafted:** HS—Bradenton, Fla., 2018 (11th round). **Signed by:** Luke Wrenn.

TRACK RECORD: The younger brother of Braves minor league C.J. Alexander, Blaze signed with the D-backs for an over-slot $500,000 bonus as an 11th-rounder in 2018. He had a loud debut followed by a so-so first full professional season at low Class A Kane County. His only 2020 action came during instructional league, which was cut short by a rib injury.
SCOUTING REPORT: Alexander has the athletic frame and actions of a big leaguer. His calling card has always been his rifle arm, which has long graded near the top of the 20-to-80 scouting scale. Alexander began to show burgeoning power production during spring training but tends to be overly streaky and needs to better maintain his approach and swing from at-bat to at-bat. Optimistic projections peg him as a potential fringe-average hitter with average power, but he'll need time to get there. Alexander can play shortstop but might fit best as a multi-positional infielder.
THE FUTURE: Alexander will be looking to pick up lost developmental at-bats in 2021. Many see him as a future super-utility type like the Athletics' Chad Pinder.

Year	Age	Club (League)	Class	AVG	G	AB	R	H	2B	3B	HR	RBI	BB	SO	SB	OBP	SLG
2019	20	Kane County (MWL)	LoA	.262	97	343	56	90	12	4	7	47	42	89	14	.355	.382
Minor League Totals				.288	152	553	108	159	31	9	12	89	73	141	24	.378	.441

22 DOMINIC FLETCHER, OF

BA GRADE 45 **Risk:** High

Born: Sept. 2, 1997. **B-T:** L-L. **HT:** 5-9. **WT:** 185. **Drafted:** Arkansas, 2019 (2nd round supplemental). **Signed by:** Nate Birtwell.

TRACK RECORD: The younger brother of Angels infielder David Fletcher, Dominic became the highest-drafted player from Arkansas in four years when the D-backs took him 75th overall pick in 2019. He performed well in the low Class A Midwest League out of the draft and earned good reviews for his play at the alternate training site in 2020.
SCOUTING REPORT: Like his older brother, Fletcher is a fundamentally sound player. He is at his best when he uses his line-drive swing to spray balls to all fields. He can occasionally get pull-happy. Fletcher has solid raw power, which he occasionally taps into during games. He has fringe-average speed but is nevertheless a good defender in center field on account of his good jumps and routes. D-backs people rave about his style of play and believe his ceiling might be higher than some believe, just as happened with his brother.
THE FUTURE: Fletcher doesn't get the attention of other outfielders in the system, but it wouldn't be a shock if he outperforms many others with bigger raw tools. He draws optimistic comparisons with Kole Calhoun, with many others seeing at least a reserve outfielder in the major leagues.

Year	Age	Club (League)	Class	AVG	G	AB	R	H	2B	3B	HR	RBI	BB	SO	SB	OBP	SLG
2019	21	Kane County (MWL)	LoA	.318	55	214	33	68	14	1	5	28	22	50	1	.389	.463
Minor League Totals				.318	55	214	33	68	14	1	5	28	22	50	1	.389	.463

23 TRISTIN ENGLISH, 3B

BA GRADE 45 **Risk:** High

Born: May 14, 1997. **B-T:** R-R. **HT:** 6-3. **WT:** 210. **Drafted:** Georgia Tech, 2019 (3rd round). **Signed by:** Hudson Belinsky.

TRACK RECORD: English was a two-way player at Georgia Tech and had Tommy John surgery following his freshman year. A strong showing in the Cape Cod League in his return followed by a successful redshirt sophomore season raised English's stock as a position player, prompting the D-backs to select him in the third round in 2019. He put together a solid debut and was impressive during spring training in 2020 before the coronavirus pandemic shut camps down.

SCOUTING REPORT: English has a relatively compact swing geared toward center and right field that generates plus raw power. It can appear a bit stiff at times, but he has a natural feel for finding the barrel. He remains an aggressive hitter who is continuing to work on refining the zone. English's hands work well at third base and he has a monster arm. He is tall with a thick, strong build, but there are concerns his added strength was a detriment to his athleticism.

THE FUTURE: English's bat has won over believers so far. He still has to show he can produce against more advanced pitchers and will try to do so in 2021.

Year	Age	Club (League)	Class	AVG	G	AB	R	H	2B	3B	HR	RBI	BB	SO	SB	OBP	SLG
2019	22	Hillsboro (NWL)	SS	.290	50	193	32	56	12	2	7	30	13	24	1	.356	.482
Minor League Totals				.290	50	193	32	56	12	2	7	30	13	24	1	.356	.482

24 HUMBERTO MEJIA, RHP

BA GRADE 45 Risk: High

Born: March 3, 1997. **B-T:** R-R. **HT:** 6-3. **WT:** 235. **Signed:** Panama, 2013. **Signed by:** Luis Cordoba/Albert Gonzalez (Marlins).

TRACK RECORD: Signed by the Marlins for $50,000 in 2013, Mejia moved slowly through their system in part due to shoulder issues. He stayed healthy in 2019, pitched well enough at the Class A levels to earn a spot on the 40-man roster and found himself in the majors in 2020 after the Marlins' Covid-19 outbreak decimated their pitching staff. The D-backs acquired him at the trade deadline as one of three players for Starling Marte.

SCOUTING REPORT: Mejia has a frame that looks capable of handling a starter's workload and a slightly crossfire delivery that creates deception. At his best, he can pair his low-to-mid-90s fastball with two above-average breaking balls and a changeup, all thrown with solid command. But Mejia's stuff looked pedestrian after the trade, with his curveball and slider blending together and neither looking like put-away pitches. The D-backs are intrigued by his distinct pitch shapes and above-average command history and hope he can succeed using his repertoire to attack a game plan.

THE FUTURE: Despite Mejia's time in the majors, the D-backs don't see him as major league ready. He'll open 2021 in the upper minors and has the potential to emerge as a back-end starter.

Year	Age	Club (League)	Class	W	L	ERA	G	GS	IP	H	HR	BB	SO	BB/9	SO/9	WHIP	AVG
2020	23	Miami (NL)	MAJ	0	2	5.40	3	3	10	13	3	6	11	5.4	9.9	1.90	.310
Major League Totals				0	2	5.40	3	3	10	13	3	6	11	5.4	9.9	1.90	.310
Minor League Totals				13	16	2.40	59	43	277	218	17	62	268	2.0	8.7	1.01	.214

25 J.B. BUKAUSKAS, RHP

BA GRADE 50 Risk: Extreme

Born: Oct. 11, 1996. **B-T:** R-R. **HT:** 6-0. **WT:** 210. **Drafted:** North Carolina, 2017 (1st round). **Signed by:** Tim Bittner (Astros).

TRACK RECORD: Bukauskas was an All-American and a Golden Spikes Award finalist at North Carolina, but he has struggled to either stay healthy or put everything together since being selected 15th overall by the Astros in 2017. The D-backs acquired him as part of the Zack Greinke deal in July 2019 and brought him to the alternate training site in 2020.

SCOUTING REPORT: When it clicks, Bukauskas can be overpowering. His mid-to-upper-90s fastball is explosive, his slider is a wipeout pitch that has late, sharp action and his power 89-91 mph changeup might be the best in the system. But Bukauskas has continued to struggle with both his below-average control and his command, looking at times as if he were trying to make perfect pitches rather than attacking the zone. He also falls in love with his slider and doesn't throw his changeup enough. After battling injuries in previous years, he managed to stay mostly healthy in 2020.

THE FUTURE: Arrows are pointing more and more toward a future relief role for Bukauskas. His high-octane stuff gives him a late-inning ceiling if he can figure out his control.

Year	Age	Club (League)	Class	W	L	ERA	G	GS	IP	H	HR	BB	SO	BB/9	SO/9	WHIP	AVG
2019	22	Jackson (SL)	AA	0	1	7.71	2	2	7	10	0	5	11	6.4	14.1	2.14	.286
	22	Corpus Christi (TL)	AA	2	4	5.25	20	14	86	81	8	54	98	5.7	10.3	1.58	.213
Minor League Totals				6	7	4.06	39	33	161	140	9	88	189	4.9	10.5	1.41	.235

26 JEFERSON ESPINAL, OF

BA GRADE 50 **Risk:** Extreme

Born: June 7, 2002. **B-T:** L-L. **HT:** 6-0. **WT:** 185. **Signed:** Dominican Republic, 2018. **Signed by:** Cesar Geronimo/Omar Rogers.

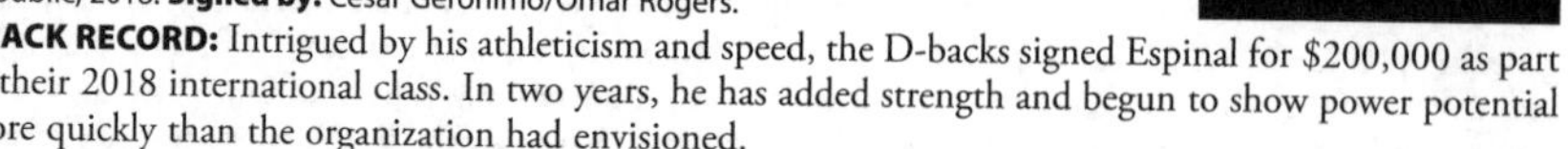

TRACK RECORD: Intrigued by his athleticism and speed, the D-backs signed Espinal for $200,000 as part of their 2018 international class. In two years, he has added strength and begun to show power potential more quickly than the organization had envisioned.

SCOUTING REPORT: Espinal has near top-of-the-scale speed, good bat-to-ball ability and the makings of a good approach. He routinely hit balls hard at instructional league, often going the other way or staying up the middle. He has put on about 20 pounds since signing, drawing comparisons to fellow prospect Wilderd Patiño's powerful frame. He has a chance to stick in center field, though his reads and routes could use work. He draws praise for his makeup and work ethic. The one knock on his game is his below-average arm strength.

THE FUTURE: Espinal has a long way to go, but his early performance gives the D-backs another outfielder to dream on. He has a chance to open the 2021 season at low Class A.

Year	Age	Club (League)	Class	AVG	G	AB	R	H	2B	3B	HR	RBI	BB	SO	SB	OBP	SLG
2019	17	D-backs1 (DSL)	R	.358	47	187	36	67	9	2	2	14	15	45	22	.412	.460
	17	Diamondbacks (AZL)	R	.286	9	35	6	10	1	0	0	7	8	11	4	.419	.314
Minor League Totals				.347	56	222	42	77	10	2	2	21	23	56	26	.413	.437

27 LIAM NORRIS, LHP

BA GRADE 45 **Risk:** Extreme

Born: Aug. 13, 2001. **B-T:** L-L. **HT:** 6-4. **WT:** 215. **Drafted:** HS—Cary, N.C., 2020 (3rd round). **Signed by:** George Swain.

TRACK RECORD: Well-known on the showcase circuit for years, Norris entered his senior season at Green Hope High in Cary, N.C., having shown poor command and control in the recent past. He looked much improved in the spring before the coronavirus pandemic shut everything down, and the D-backs got multiple early looks at him to feel confident the progression was not a mirage. They selected him in the third round and gave him an above-slot $800,000 bonus to forgo a North Carolina commitment.

SCOUTING REPORT: Norris has a big body he is still growing into and a clean arm action. He impressed during instructional league with both his strike-throwing and ability to repeat his delivery, though he wasn't as consistent as he needs to be. His fastball ranged from 92-96 mph, and some believe he still has the physical projection to get stronger and add more velocity. His 79-82 mph curveball has good break and depth and is a potentially average pitch, slightly ahead of his fringy slider and changeup.

THE FUTURE: Norris will need to stay on top of his conditioning and show he can maintain his stuff and command over a full season. If he can, he has the weapons to stick in the rotation.

Year	Age	Club (League)	Class	W	L	ERA	G	GS	IP	H	HR	BB	SO	BB/9	SO/9	WHIP	AVG
2020	18	Did not play--No minor league season															

28 JUSTIN MARTINEZ, RHP

BA GRADE 50 **Risk:** Extreme

Born: July 30, 2001. **B-T:** R-R. **HT:** 6-3. **WT:** 195. **Signed:** Dominican Republic, 2018. **Signed by:** Cesar Geronimo/Jose Ortiz.

TRACK RECORD: When the D-backs signed Martinez for $50,000 in 2018, he had been pitching for just six months, had below-average control and lacked the feel to spin a breaking ball. He improved rapidly and now, nearly three years later, has begun to win over believers when it comes to his potential to be a major league starter.

SCOUTING REPORT: Martinez has plenty of size, strength and athleticism. His fastball sits in the mid 90s, scratches 99 mph and is unique in that it sometimes cuts and sinks. He has picked up a slider that can be sharp and sweepy but remains inconsistent. He also throws a splitter that provides good separation, but he needs to throw more strikes with it. His mechanics are raw and he tends to rush down the mound, but there's not much effort in his arm action and delivery.

THE FUTURE: The strides Martinez has made given his short time on the mound lends credence to those who think he can continue trending upward. He has a ways to go, but his upside is tantalizing.

Year	Age	Club (League)	Class	W	L	ERA	G	GS	IP	H	HR	BB	SO	BB/9	SO/9	WHIP	AVG
2019	17	Missoula (PIO)	R	0	0	0.00	3	0	4	1	0	4	7	9.0	15.8	1.25	.050
	17	Diamondbacks (AZL)	R	0	1	3.24	6	2	17	12	0	11	23	5.9	12.4	1.38	.158
	17	D-backs2 (DSL)	R	1	2	3.06	9	8	35	29	0	22	48	5.6	12.2	1.44	.181
Minor League Totals				1	8	4.95	33	22	100	93	3	75	108	6.8	9.7	1.68	.240

29 STUART FAIRCHILD, OF

BA GRADE 40 Risk: High

Born: March 17, 1996. **B-T:** R-R. **HT:** 6-0. **WT:** 190. **Drafted:** Wake Forest, 2017 (2nd round). **Signed by:** Perry Smith (Reds).

TRACK RECORD: Fairchild's well-rounded skill set prompted the Reds to take him with the 38th overall pick in 2017. Though his power was slow to emerge, he gained a reputation for being a heady, instinctual player capable of outperforming his tools. He began the 2020 season at the Reds' alternate training site and was traded to Arizona with Josh VanMeter at the trade deadline for Archie Bradley.

SCOUTING REPORT: Fairchild is a sum-is-better-than-the-parts type of player. He has good strike-zone awareness and a mature approach that makes him a headache for opposing pitchers. He has worked to simplify his swing, starting his hands farther from his body to become more direct. Fairchild makes a fair amount of contact and his gap-to-gap power is good for a steady volume of doubles, as well as the occasional home run. He's a good defender at all three outfield positions and has an average arm.

THE FUTURE: Some evaluators see Fairchild as the righthanded half of a platoon, but most see a likely fourth outfielder. He will start 2021 at either Double-A or Triple-A and is likely to surface in the majors at some point.

Year	Age	Club (League)	Class	AVG	G	AB	R	H	2B	3B	HR	RBI	BB	SO	SB	OBP	SLG
2019	23	Daytona (FSL)	HiA	.258	67	248	32	64	17	2	8	37	25	60	3	.335	.440
	23	Chattanooga (SL)	AA	.275	42	153	25	42	12	1	4	17	19	23	3	.380	.444
Minor League Totals				.272	295	1060	158	288	60	13	24	134	111	246	41	.356	.421

30 BRANDON PFAADT, RHP

BA GRADE 40 Risk: High

Born: Oct. 15, 1998. **B-T:** R-R. **HT:** 6-4. **WT:** 230. **Drafted:** Bellarmine (Ky.), 2020 (5th round). **Signed by:** Jeremy Kehrt.

TRACK RECORD: Pfaadt became just the ninth player to be drafted out of Division II Bellarmine in Louisville and the highest since Todd Wellemeyer was a fourth-rounder in 2000. Pfaadt is one of four family members to play baseball there; grandfather Bob and older brother Brady preceded him, while his younger brother Brett will be a sophomore this year.

SCOUTING REPORT: Pfaadt uses an old-school delivery, bringing his hands up over his head, then drives down the mound with a strong, prototypical starter's frame. His fastball sat 94-95 mph in instructional league with a power changeup in the upper 80s and a pair of breaking pitches that blend together and/or pop out of his hand. He throws strikes, but his command could stand to improve. Pfaadt's velocity tended to dip in the middle innings in college, so he will have to prove he can maintain stuff deep into games.

THE FUTURE: Pfaadt is working to incorporate his lower half more in his delivery and needs to make his curveball and slider two distinct pitches, but he has a lot of starter attributes. He will likely open 2021 at one of the organization's Class A affiliates.

Year	Age	Club (League)	Class	W	L	ERA	G	GS	IP	H	HR	BB	SO	BB/9	SO/9	WHIP	AVG
2020	21	Did not play—No minor league season															

MORE PROSPECTS TO KNOW

31 ALVIN GUZMAN, OF

Athletic and toolsy, Guzman has a very high ceiling, but at age 19 he's still young and raw, making him about as close to a prospect lottery ticket as they come.

32 TAYLOR WIDENER, RHP

Widener got himself into better shape and regained much of the pure stuff that had backed up on him in 2019. After showing he could get major league hitters out in 2020, he figures to be in the mix for a bullpen job in spring training.

33 ANDY YOUNG, 2B/OF

Young bounced between the big leagues and the alternate site in 2020, largely putting together good at-bats when he was in the majors. His defensive home remains in question but he looks at least like a capable, professional hitter.

34 JON DUPLANTIER, RHP

More arm troubles—this time his elbow—wiped out Duplantier's 2020 season and raised questions about his future role. More arrows are pointing toward the bullpen giving his issues staying healthy as a starter.

35 DIOMEDE SIERRA, LHP

SLEEPER

Sierra is lefthanded, throws 95 mph and has a potential wipeout slider. His control needs to improve, but there's enough there to dream.

36 JOSH GREEN, RHP

Green previously had the best two-seam fastball in the organization and was one of the best pitchers in the minors at inducing ground balls. But the pitch lost significant sink in 2020, perhaps due to his focus on other pitches. Rediscovering his bread and butter will be paramount.

37 MATT TABOR, RHP

Tabor is a strike-thrower with a low-90s fastball, average secondary stuff and excellent pitching acumen. He's a potential back-end starter who could benefit from good game-planning.

38 RILEY SMITH, RHP

Smith reached the majors in 2020 and was terrific out of the bullpen for the D-backs. He pounded the zone and saw his stuff tick up a bit in relief. He figures to be in the mix for a bullpen job in the spring.

39 WYATT MATHISEN, 3B

Mathisen made wholesale swing changes in recent years, tapping into power that hadn't been there before. He has become a big league depth option waiting for an opportunity.

40 TYLER HOLTON, LHP

Holton has good control and an excellent changeup, but he sits around 88 mph and has little margin for error.

TOP PROSPECTS OF THE DECADE

Year	Player, Pos	2020 Org
2011	Jarrod Parker, RHP	Did not play
2012	Trevor Bauer, RHP	Reds
2013	Tyler Skaggs, LHP	Deceased
2014	Archie Bradley, RHP	Reds
2015	Archie Bradley, RHP	Reds
2016	Dansby Swanson, SS	Braves
2017	Anthony Banda, LHP	Rays
2018	Jon Duplantier, RHP	D-backs
2019	Jazz Chisholm, SS	Marlins
2020	Daulton Varsho, C/OF	D-backs

TOP DRAFT PICKS OF THE DECADE

Year	Player, Pos	2020 Org
2011	Trevor Bauer, RHP	Reds
2012	Stryker Trahan, C	Did not play
2013	Braden Shipley, RHP	Royals
2014	Touki Toussaint, RHP	Braves
2015	Dansby Swanson, SS	Braves
2016	Anfernee Grier, OF (1st round supp)	D-backs
2017	Pavin Smith, 1B	D-backs
2018	*Matt McLain, SS	UCLA
2019	Corbin Carroll, OF	D-backs
2020	Bryce Jarvis, RHP	D-backs

* Did not sign

DEPTH CHART

ARIZONA DIAMONDBACKS

TOP 2021 ROOKIES	RANK
Daulton Varsho, C/OF	2
Pavin Smith, 1B/OF	9
Corbin Martin, RHP	10
BREAKOUT PROSPECTS	**RANK**
Conor Grammes, RHP	11
A.J. Vukovich, 3B/OF	13
Jake McCarthy, OF	19

SOURCE OF TOP 30 TALENT

Homegrown	25	Acquired	5
College	12	Trade	5
Junior college	0	Rule 5 draft	0
High school	7	Independent league	0
Nondrafted free agent	0	Free agent/waivers	0
International	6		

LF
A.J. Vukovich (13)
Jorge Barrosa
Junior Franco
Angel Ortiz

CF
Corbin Carroll(1)
Alek Thomas (5)
Jake McCarthy (19)
Wilderd Patiño (20)
Dominic Fletcher (23)
Alvin Guzman

RF
Kristian Robinson (4)
Jeferson Espinal (26)
Stuart Fairchild (29)

3B
Tristin English (22)
Wyatt Mathisen
Deyvison De Los Santos
Ronny Polanco

SS
Geraldo Perdomo (3)
Lewin de la Cruz
Juan Corniel

2B
Blaze Alexander (21)
Andy Young
Buddy Kennedy
Glenallen Hill Jr.

1B
Pavin Smith (9)
Seth Beer (14)

C
Daulton Varsho (2)
Jose Herrera
Dominic Miroglio

LHP

LHSP
Blake Walston (8)
Tommy Henry (15)
Liam Norris (27)
Tyler Holton

LHRP
Diomede Sierra
Andrew Saalfrank
Julio Frias

RHP

RHSP
Slade Cecconi (6)
Bryce Jarvis (7)
Corbin Martin (10)
Conor Grammes (11)
Ryne Nelson (16)
Luis Frias (17)
Humberto Mejia (24)
Justin Martinez (28)
Matt Tabor

RHRP
Levi Kelly (12)
Drey Jameson (18)
J.B. Bukauskas (25)
Brandon Pfaadt (30)
Taylor Widener
Jon Duplantier
Josh Green
Riley Smith
Zach Pop
Jhosmer Alvarez
Matt Peacock
Cristian Pacheco
Chester Pimentel

Atlanta Braves

BY CARLOS COLLAZO

After winning back-to-back National League East titles in 2018 and 2019, the Braves made it a three-peat in 2020. Atlanta finished with a 35-25 record, good for second in the National League to only the eventual World Series-champion Dodgers.

While Atlanta fans have gotten used to regular season success again, the Braves also won their first playoff series since 2001. The team beat the Reds 2-0 in the NL Wild Card Series and topped the Marlins 3-0 in the NL Division Series. The Braves jumped out to a 3-1 series lead against the Dodgers in the NL Championship Series before falling in seven games.

The Braves were led by franchise cornerstone Freddie Freeman, who hit .341/.462/.640 with 13 home runs and led MLB in runs (51) and doubles (23). Freeman was Baseball America's Major League Player of the Year and collected his first NL MVP award after previously finishing in the top 10 in voting four times.

Once again, Braves general manager Alex Anthopoulos showed a shrewd ability to add talent on the free agent market. Marcell Ozuna, the club's primary DH, led the league in home runs (18), RBIs (56) and total bases (145) after signing a one-year deal. Behind Freeman and Ozuna, the Braves finished second in the majors in runs scored.

Atlanta's starting rotation was middle of the pack, even after losing righthander Mike Soroka for the year when he tore his Achilles' tendon in just his third start. With Soroka sidelined, the Braves turned to two other young pitchers to steady the rotation.

Lefthander Max Fried went 7-0, 2.25 over 11 starts and finished fifth in NL Cy Young Award voting. Righander Ian Anderson made his major league debut and went 3-2, 1.95 over six starts while striking out 11.4 batters per nine innings. He added three consecutive scoreless starts in the postseason before starting Game 7 of the NLCS. Between Soroka and Anderson, the Braves have shown an uncanny ability to usher prep arms quickly to the major league rotation, a trend that bodes well with a collection of young pitchers still in their system.

While the Braves will need to replace Ozuna after he left in free agency and start thinking about Freeman's next contract—his current deal expires after the 2021 season—the franchise remains in excellent shape with a core that includes Ronald Acuña Jr., Ozzie Albies, Dansby Swanson and Austin Riley.

While the farm system is trending downward, there are still reinforcements ready to contribute in the majors as soon as 2021, led by outfielders Cristian Pache and Drew Waters. Pache debuted in 2020 and was part of Atlanta's postseason roster.

The lower levels of the system aren't as deep and the team will need to see steps forward from high-risk, high-upside players to ensure internal reinforcements are still coming beyond 2021.

Atlanta's restrictions on signing international players, part of their punishment for violating international signing rules under former general manager John Coppollela, will expire after the 2020-21 signing period. The lifting of those restrictions will be critical to restocking the lower levels of the farm system. ■

RICH VON BIBERSTEIN/ICON SPORTSWIRE VIA GETTY IMAGES

Max Fried stepped into the role of staff ace—and thrived—following Mike Soroka's injury.

PROJECTED 2024 LINEUP

Position	Player	Age
Catcher	Shea Langeliers	26
First Base	Freddie Freeman	34
Second Base	Ozzie Albies	27
Third Base	Austin Riley	27
Shortstop	Dansby Swanson	30
Left Field	Drew Waters	25
Center Field	Cristian Pache	25
Right Field	Ronald Acuña Jr.	26
Designated Hitter	William Contreras	26
No. 1 Starter	Mike Soroka	26
No. 2 Starter	Max Fried	30
No. 3 Starter	Ian Anderson	26
No. 4 Starter	Kyle Wright	28
No. 5 Starter	Bryse Wilson	26
Closer	Touki Toussaint	28

1 CRISTIAN PACHE, OF

Born: Nov. 19, 1998. **B-T:** R-R. **HT:** 6-2. **WT:** 215.
Signed: Dominican Republic, 2015.
Signed by: Matias Laureano.

TRACK RECORD: Signed by the Braves for $1.4 million when he was 16, Pache progressively tapped into more power as he climbed the minor league ladder and, after spending the 2019 season at Double-A and Triple-A, made his big league debut in 2020. Pache had a reserve role during parts of the regular season and saw just four at-bats. He was included on the Braves' postseason roster and stepped into a starting role in the National League Championship Series after Adam Duvall suffered an oblique injury. Shortly thereafter, Pache became the seventh major leaguer to hit his first home run in the playoffs, while showcasing the outstanding defense in center field that has been hyped for years.

SCOUTING REPORT: Pache's postseason offered the Braves a glimpse of what's to come. After adding around 30 pounds over the last three years, Pache is solidly built with enough raw power to keep pitchers honest. His strengths still lie on the defensive side of the ball. Pache has the plus-plus speed to cover enough ground in even the most expansive outfields, and his instincts and arm strength elevate him to the level of potentially one of the best center fielders in baseball. He reads the ball off the bat well, takes efficient routes and has the athleticism and natural timing to make highlight-reel diving catches and jumps at the wall. His plus-plus arm makes runners think twice about taking an extra base. It would be a surprise if he never won a Gold Glove. Pache has upside as a hitter, too. The Braves were happy enough with his growth in 2020 to put him on the big league roster. He has enough bat speed to handle the velocity of the modern game, and he pairs it with solid pitch selection and strike-zone recognition. What could limit him as a hitter is an extreme pull tendency at the plate. He hit between 50% and 59% of his batted balls to his pull side from 2017 to 2019 in the minors. For context, the major league average pull rate in 2020 was 41%. And while Pache does have plus raw power, all of his in-game home runs have gone to the far pull side in left field. Figuring out how to use the opposite field will be necessary for Pache to become an average hitter, and a missed 2020 minor league season might have hampered that development.

THE FUTURE: After more than holding his own for the Braves in short stints in 2020, Pache should become an outfield regular in 2021. He will immediately be one of the game's most exciting young defensive players with the potential to deliver above-average offensive production and pair that with multiple Gold Gloves. ■

BEST TOOLS

Best Hitter for Average	Drew Waters
Best Power Hitter	Bryce Ball
Best Strike-Zone Discipline	Braden Shewmake
Fastest Baserunner	Cristian Pache
Best Athlete	Cristian Pache
Best Fastball	Kyle Muller
Best Curveball	Kyle Muller
Best Slider	Huascar Ynoa
Best Changeup	Ian Anderson
Best Control	Nolan Kingham
Best Defensive Catcher	Shea Langeliers
Best Defensive Infielder	Braden Shewmake
Best Infield Arm	Beau Philip
Best Defensive Outfielder	Cristian Pache
Best Outfield Arm	Cristian Pache

Year	Age	Club (League)	Class	AVG	G	AB	R	H	2B	3B	HR	RBI	BB	SO	SB	OBP	SLG
2018	19	Mississippi (SL)	AA	.260	29	104	10	27	3	1	1	7	5	28	0	.294	.337
	19	Florida (FSL)	HiA	.285	93	369	46	105	20	5	8	40	15	69	7	.311	.431
2019	20	Mississippi (SL)	AA	.278	104	392	50	109	28	8	11	53	34	104	8	.340	.474
	20	Gwinnett (IL)	AAA	.274	26	95	13	26	8	1	1	8	9	18	0	.337	.411
2020	21	Atlanta (NL)	MAJ	.250	2	4	0	1	0	0	0	0	0	2	0	.250	.250
Major League Totals				.250	2	4	0	1	0	0	0	0	0	2	0	.250	.250
Minor League Totals				.283	428	1649	207	467	76	30	21	171	115	347	58	.331	.404

2 IAN ANDERSON, RHP

TOP ROOKIE

SCOTT AUDETTE/MLB PHOTOS VIA GETTY IMAGES

BA GRADE

60 Risk: Medium

Born: May 2, 1998. **B-T:** R-R. **HT:** 6-3. **WT:** 170. **Drafted:** HS—Clifton Park, N.Y., 2016 (1st round). **Signed by:** Greg Morhardt.

TRACK RECORD: Anderson quickly ascended the minors after being drafted third overall in 2016 and made a tremendous impact in his big league debut. Called up after injuries eviscerated the Braves' rotation, Anderson was one of the game's best pitchers in September and October. He allowed two earned runs in 18.2 postseason innings, opening with three consecutive scoreless outings and starting Game 7 of the NLCS

SCOUTING REPORT: Anderson does a tremendous job limiting hard contact and generating whiffs with his three-pitch mix. His fastball sits around 94 mph and gives hitters a unique look with low spin rates and more drop than a typical fastball. That pairs wonderfully with an 86-88 mph changeup that generated a 40% whiff rate in his debut. It has less movement than typical changeups, but plays well because he sells it like a fastball out of his overhand arm slot. Anderson's confidence and ability to throw it for strikes makes his changeup a plus offering. His curveball is his third pitch, but it is enough of a different look to keep hitters off balance. While no single pitch is a true wipeout, his ability to tunnel them and command the ball makes his arsenal deadly, especially with his ability to consistently change hitters' eye levels.

THE FUTURE: Anderson has solidified his place as the Braves' No. 3 starter. The development of his breaking ball will determine if he becomes more.

SCOUTING GRADES: **Fastball:** 55 **Curveball:** 50 **Changeup:** 60 **Control:** 60

Year	Age	Club (League)	Class	W	L	ERA	G	GS	IP	H	HR	BB	SO	BB/9	SO/9	WHIP	AVG
2018	20	Mississippi (SL)	AA	2	1	2.33	4	4	19	14	0	9	24	4.2	11.2	1.19	.175
	20	Florida (FSL)	HiA	2	6	2.52	20	20	100	73	2	40	118	3.6	10.6	1.13	.176
2019	21	Mississippi (SL)	AA	7	5	2.68	21	21	111	82	8	47	147	3.8	11.9	1.16	.177
	21	Gwinnett (IL)	AAA	1	2	6.57	5	5	25	23	5	18	25	6.6	9.1	1.66	.204
2020	22	Atlanta (NL)	MAJ	3	2	1.95	6	6	32	21	1	14	41	3.9	11.4	1.08	.172
Major League Totals				3	2	1.95	6	6	32	21	1	14	41	3.9	11.4	1.08	.172
Minor League Totals				17	21	2.91	80	80	377	294	16	169	451	4.0	10.8	1.23	.214

3 DREW WATERS, OF

TOP ROOKIE

SCOTT AUDETTE/MLB PHOTOS VIA GETTY IMAGES

BA GRADE

60 Risk: High

Born: Dec. 30, 1998. **B-T:** B-R. **HT:** 6-2. **WT:** 185. **Drafted:** HS—Woodstock, Ga., 2017 (2nd round). **Signed by:** Dustin Evans.

TRACK RECORD: A local Georgia product drafted in the second round in 2016, Waters steadily climbed the minor league ladder and won the Double-A Southern League's batting title and MVP award in 2019. The switch-hitter finished the year in Triple-A, played for Team USA's Olympic qualifying team in the fall and spent 2020 at the alternate training site, where he focused on his righthanded swing and improving his approach.

SCOUTING REPORT: Waters is a long, lean athlete with a loose, handsy swing that gives him above-average hitting potential. He is extremely aggressive in his pitch selection and has worked to become a more patient, selective hitter, particularly after his strikeout rate ballooned against upper-level arms. Waters has above-average power potential from both sides, but how much he accesses in games will depend on his pitch selection. His defense is underrated given his proximity to Cristian Pache in the system. He is capable of playing center field as a plus runner with above-average arm strength.

THE FUTURE: The canceled minor league season hurt Waters' ability to develop his offense against high-level arms. If his 2020 work translates in games, he should become a regular in Atlanta's outfield.

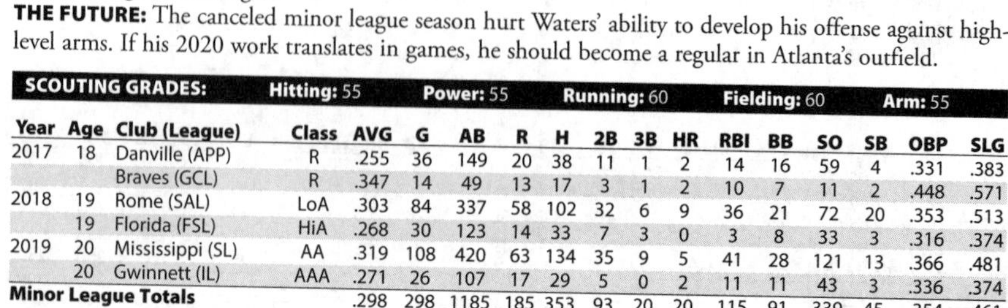

SCOUTING GRADES: **Hitting:** 55 **Power:** 55 **Running:** 60 **Fielding:** 60 **Arm:** 55

Year	Age	Club (League)	Class	AVG	G	AB	R	H	2B	3B	HR	RBI	BB	SO	SB	OBP	SLG
2017	18	Danville (APP)	R	.255	36	149	20	38	11	1	2	14	16	59	4	.331	.383
		Braves (GCL)	R	.347	14	49	13	17	3	1	2	10	7	11	2	.448	.571
2018	19	Rome (SAL)	LoA	.303	84	337	58	102	32	6	9	36	21	72	20	.353	.513
	19	Florida (FSL)	HiA	.268	30	123	14	33	7	3	0	3	8	33	3	.316	.374
2019	20	Mississippi (SL)	AA	.319	108	420	63	134	35	9	5	41	28	121	13	.366	.481
	20	Gwinnett (IL)	AAA	.271	26	107	17	29	5	0	2	11	11	43	3	.336	.374
Minor League Totals				.298	298	1185	185	353	93	20	20	115	91	339	45	.354	.461

4 SHEA LANGELIERS, C

SCOTT AUDETTE/MLB PHOTOS VIA GETTY IMAGES

BA GRADE
55 Risk: High

Born: Nov. 18, 1997. **B-T:** R-R. **HT:** 6-0. **WT:** 205. **Drafted:** Baylor, 2019 (1st round). **Signed by:** Darin Vaughan.

TRACK RECORD: The No. 2 catcher in the 2019 draft behind Adley Rutschman, Langeliers was drafted ninth overall by the Braves and signed for an under-slot $3.9 million. Considered the best defensive backstop in the class, he immediately went to low Class A Rome for his pro debut and was a standout performer at the Braves' alternate training site in 2020.

SCOUTING REPORT: Langeliers lives up to his reputation as a high-level defender by pairing a standout, 70-grade arm with impressive hands in receiving and a desire to consistently improve. He threw out 41% of basestealers in his pro debut and shows all the traits of at least a plus defender behind the plate. Langeliers has solid offensive tools as well. He impressed Braves officials with his ability to drive the ball with authority to right field at the alternate site, especially after he mostly pulled the ball in his debut. His bat projects more average than above and he still needs more reps against upper-level pitchers. Langeliers puts together quality at-bats and has enough strength to project average power.

THE FUTURE: Langeliers' defense behind the plate will carry him up the ladder. He has a chance to become a first-division regular as long as his bat continues to develop.

SCOUTING GRADES: **Hitting:** 50 **Power:** 50 **Running:** 40 **Fielding:** 60 **Arm:** 70

Year	Age	Club (League)	Class	AVG	G	AB	R	H	2B	3B	HR	RBI	BB	SO	SB	OBP	SLG
2019	21	Rome (SAL)	LoA	.255	54	216	27	55	13	0	2	34	17	55	0	.310	.343
Minor League Totals				.255	54	216	27	55	13	0	2	34	17	55	0	.310	.343

5 BRYSE WILSON, RHP

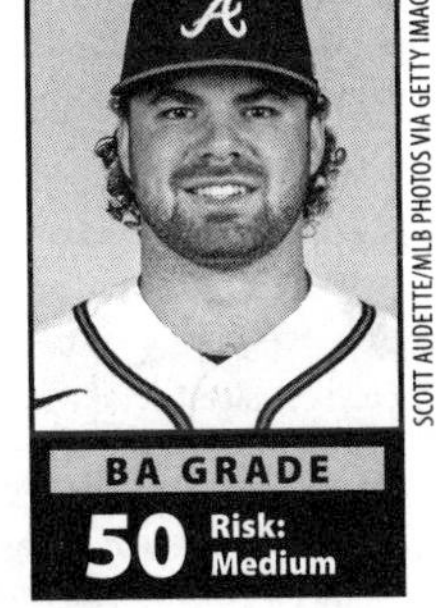

SCOTT AUDETTE/MLB PHOTOS VIA GETTY IMAGES

BA GRADE
50 Risk: Medium

Born: Dec. 20, 1997. **B-T:** R-R. **HT:** 6-2. **WT:** 225. **Drafted:** HS—Hillsborough, N.C., 2016 (4th round). **Signed by:** Billy Best.

TRACK RECORD: Wilson has pitched in the majors in minor roles during each of the last three seasons but still has just 42.2 big league innings. He was called on to start Game 4 of the NL Championship Series against Clayton Kershaw, and he responded by outpitching the future Hall of Famer over six innings, allowing only one run and one hit.

SCOUTING REPORT: A durable righthander, Wilson has impressive fastball command and knows how to establish the strike zone early. He throws four-seam and two-seam fastballs that each average 93-95 mph. He gets ahead of hitters with first-pitch strikes using both. Wilson's best secondary pitch has always been his changeup, which sits around 85-86 mph with solid drop. Some evaluators believe it could be a plus offering. Wilson's best breaking ball is a hard slider that could be classified as a cutter due to its lack of horizontal movement and firm velocity in the 87-89 mph range. He occasionally throws a curveball in the upper 70s, but the pitch has below-average spin and is a distant fifth offering.

THE FUTURE: Wilson profiles as a back-of-the-rotation workhorse type who will throw strikes and compete. He'll be just 23 in 2021 and still has plenty of time to continue adjusting and improving.

SCOUTING GRADES: **Fastball:** 55 **Slider:** 50 **Curveball:** 40 **Changeup:** 55 **Control:** 55

Year	Age	Club (League)	Class	W	L	ERA	G	GS	IP	H	HR	BB	SO	BB/9	SO/9	WHIP	AVG
2017	19	Rome (SAL)	LoA	10	7	2.50	26	26	137	105	8	37	139	2.4	9.1	1.04	.192
2018	20	Atlanta (NL)	MAJ	1	0	6.43	3	1	7	8	0	6	6	7.7	7.7	2.00	.242
	20	Mississippi (SL)	AA	3	5	3.97	15	15	77	77	3	26	89	3.0	10.4	1.34	.230
	20	Gwinnett (IL)	AAA	3	0	5.32	5	3	22	20	6	3	28	1.2	11.5	1.05	.230
	20	Florida (FSL)	HiA	2	0	0.34	5	5	27	16	0	7	26	2.4	8.8	0.86	.154
2019	21	Atlanta (NL)	MAJ	1	1	7.20	6	4	20	26	5	10	16	4.5	7.2	1.80	.280
	21	Gwinnett (IL)	AAA	10	7	3.42	21	21	121	120	12	26	118	1.9	8.8	1.21	.238
2020	22	Atlanta (NL)	MAJ	1	0	4.02	6	2	16	18	2	9	15	5.2	8.6	1.72	.286
Major League Totals				3	1	5.91	15	7	42	52	7	25	37	5.3	7.8	1.80	.306
Minor League Totals				29	20	2.94	81	76	410	354	29	107	429	2.4	9.4	1.12	.230

6 WILLIAM CONTRERAS, C

SCOTT AUDETTE/MLB PHOTOS VIA GETTY IMAGES

BA GRADE
55 **Risk: High**

Born: Dec. 24, 1997. **B-T:** R-R. **HT:** 6-0. **WT:** 180. **Signed:** Venezuela, 2015. **Signed by:** Rolando Petit.

TRACK RECORD: The younger brother of two-time all-star catcher Willson Contreras, William impressed in the South Atlantic League as a 20-year-old in 2018 before advancing to Double-A Mississippi in 2019. His improved defensive focus allowed the Braves to feel comfortable calling him up for his major league debut in July after both Travis d'Arnaud and Tyler Flowers showed coronavirus symptoms.

SCOUTING REPORT: Contreras is a solid athlete for a catcher, has a strong throwing arm and shows plus raw power at the plate. He previously struggled with consistency and focus as a defender, but he made massive strides in 2020 spring training and throughout the year. He worked hard to improve his defense with catching coordinator J.D. Closser to the point where some now believe he could become a plus defender. He moves well behind the plate and has improved as both a receiver and blocker. At the plate, Contreras has the raw power to homer to all fields, but most of his in-game power has gone to his pull side. He has a tendency to chase at times, but generally puts together quality at-bats with a good two-strike approach.

THE FUTURE: Contreras may be ready for an expanded major league role in 2021. He has a chance to become an everyday catcher as long as his defensive improvements hold.

SCOUTING GRADES: **Hitting:** 50 **Power:** 50 **Running:** 40 **Fielding:** 55 **Arm:** 60

Year	Age	Club (League)	Class	AVG	G	AB	R	H	2B	3B	HR	RBI	BB	SO	SB	OBP	SLG
2017	19	Danville (APP)	R	.290	45	169	29	49	10	1	4	25	24	30	1	.379	.432
2018	20	Rome (SAL)	LoA	.293	82	307	54	90	17	1	11	39	29	73	1	.360	.463
	20	Florida (FSL)	HiA	.253	23	83	3	21	7	0	0	10	6	16	0	.300	.337
2019	21	Mississippi (SL)	AA	.246	60	191	24	47	9	0	3	17	15	40	0	.306	.340
	21	Florida (FSL)	HiA	.263	50	190	26	50	11	0	3	22	14	44	0	.324	.368
2020	22	Atlanta (NL)	MAJ	.400	4	10	0	4	1	0	0	1	0	4	0	.400	.500
Major League Totals				.400	4	10	0	4	1	0	0	1	0	4	0	.400	.500
Minor League Totals				.279	339	1184	165	330	68	6	22	153	110	239	4	.345	.402

7 KYLE MULLER, LHP

SCOTT AUDETTE/MLB PHOTOS VIA GETTY IMAGES

BA GRADE
50 **Risk: High**

Born: Oct. 7, 1997. **B-T:** R-L. **HT:** 6-7. **WT:** 250. **Drafted:** HS—Dallas, 2016 (2nd round). **Signed by:** Nate Dion.

TRACK RECORD: Muller has come a long way since the Braves drafted him out of high school in 2016. After sitting in the upper 80s in his first full season, Muller filled out his large, 6-foot-7 frame and now has the best fastball in Atlanta's system. After topping out at 98 mph in 2019, Muller sat 95-97 mph and touched 100 at the Braves' alternate training site in 2020.

SCOUTING REPORT: Muller's calling card is his fastball. Its plus-plus velocity plays up even further with high spin rates that generate plenty of whiffs at the top of the zone. The pitch plays especially well with Muller's extension toward home plate out of his huge frame. Muller has worked hard to refine his secondaries, focusing on improving his curveball and changeup, while also adding a slider to the mix. He has flashed above-average potential with all three but needs to improve his consistency with all of them. Muller will also need to sharpen his fastball control after averaging 5.5 walks per nine innings at Double-A in 2019.

THE FUTURE: The Braves see Muller as a starter and believe he has the athleticism and work ethic to make the necessary gains in control and secondary pitch quality to succeed in that role. If he stalls, his stuff will play in the bullpen.

SCOUTING GRADES: **Fastball:** 70 **Slider:** 50 **Curveball:** 55 **Changeup:** 50 **Control:** 45

Year	Age	Club (League)	Class	W	L	ERA	G	GS	IP	H	HR	BB	SO	BB/9	SO/9	WHIP	AVG
2017	19	Danville (APP)	R	1	1	4.15	11	11	48	43	5	18	49	3.4	9.3	1.28	.208
2018	20	Mississippi (SL)	AA	4	1	3.10	5	5	29	22	3	6	27	1.9	8.4	0.97	.190
	20	Rome (SAL)	LoA	3	0	2.40	6	6	30	24	3	8	23	2.4	6.9	1.07	.202
	20	Florida (FSL)	HiA	4	2	3.24	14	14	81	80	2	32	79	3.6	8.8	1.39	.237
2019	21	Mississippi (SL)	AA	7	6	3.14	22	22	112	81	5	68	120	5.5	9.7	1.33	.173
Minor League Totals				20	10	3.03	68	67	326	264	18	144	336	4.0	9.3	1.25	.223

8 BRADEN SHEWMAKE, SS

SCOTT AUDETTE/MLB PHOTOS VIA GETTY IMAGES

BA GRADE
50 Risk: High

Born: Nov. 19, 1997. **B-T:** L-R. **HT:** 6-4. **WT:** 190. **Drafted:** Texas A&M, 2019 (1st round). **Signed by:** Darin Vaughan.

TRACK RECORD: Shewmake was one of college baseball's best hitters during his three years at Texas A&M and the Braves drafted him in the first round at No. 21 overall in 2019. He continued proving his hitting prowess by batting .318 at low Class A Rome and earning a promotion to Double-A in his pro debut. He spent the 2020 season at the Braves' alternate training site.

SCOUTING REPORT: Shewmake is an athletic, 6-foot-4 shortstop who possesses defensive versatility, a high baseball IQ and a natural feel for hitting. He has a solid, contact-oriented swing with above-average bat speed. He gets the most out of his natural abilities with a solid approach at the plate. His power isn't exceptional, but he has already added about 10 pounds since college and evaluators believe he could grow into 15-20 home runs if he continues to add more strength. The Braves will continue to run Shewmake out at shortstop, where he has solid instincts that make his reliable but unspectacular glove and arm play up. He's a better runner than expected from a player his height, getting to plus times underway.

THE FUTURE: Shewmake needs more time to acclimate to upper-level pitching, but he's already moving quickly. He projects as a super utility type for most scouts who can play all over the infield and potentially the outfield, if necessary.

SCOUTING GRADES: **Hitting:** 55 **Power:** 50 **Running:** 60 **Fielding:** 50 **Arm:** 50

Year	Age	Club (League)	Class	AVG	G	AB	R	H	2B	3B	HR	RBI	BB	SO	SB	OBP	SLG
2019	21	Mississippi (SL)	AA	.217	14	46	7	10	0	0	0	1	4	11	2	.288	.217
	21	Rome (SAL)	LoA	.318	51	201	37	64	18	2	3	39	21	29	11	.389	.473
Minor League Totals				.300	65	247	44	74	18	2	3	40	25	40	13	.371	.425

9 JARED SHUSTER, LHP

BA GRADE
50 Risk: High

Born: Aug. 3, 1998. **B-T:** L-L. **HT:** 6-3. **WT:** 210. **Drafted:** Wake Forest, 2020 (1st round). **Signed by:** Billy Best.

TRACK RECORD: Shuster took a giant leap last spring at Wake Forest, going from a middling lefty who sat 88-92 mph to touching 97 while also showing radically improved control. The Braves bought into his improvement and drafted him in the first round, No. 25th overall and signed him for just under $2.2 million, continuing their recent trend of selecting college players with their first picks.

SCOUTING REPORT: A 6-foot-3 lefthander, Shuster stands out for his impressive pitchability. He walked just nine batters in 58.1 innings between Wake Forest and the Cape Cod League, and Braves officials were impressed with his ability to locate both of his secondary offerings. Shuster's improved fastball now sits 92-95 mph and can reach higher as needed. His best pitch is his changeup. It's a true plus offering with impressive tumble that he throws with confidence. Shuster's slider is fringier and can get slurvy at times but has a chance to be average with continued development. He has improved his control enough to be an above-average strike-thrower, though he will need to prove it in pro ball.

THE FUTURE: Shuster's fastball and changeup give him a solid foundation. He has to show he can hold his improved velocity over a full season and sharpen his slider, which will be his main goals in 2021.

SCOUTING GRADES: **Fastball:** 50 **Slider:** 50 **Changeup:** 60 **Control:** 55

Year	Age	Club (League)	Class	W	L	ERA	G	GS	IP	H	HR	BB	SO	BB/9	SO/9	WHIP	AVG
2020	21	Did not play—No minor league season															

10 TUCKER DAVIDSON, LHP

BA GRADE
50 Risk: High

SCOTT AUDETTE/MLB PHOTOS VIA GETTY IMAGES

Born: March 25, 1996. **B-T:** L-L. **HT:** 6-2. **WT:** 215. **Drafted:** Midland (Texas) JC, 2016 (19th round). **Signed by:** Nate Dion.

TRACK RECORD: An unheralded 19th-round pick, Davidson steadily climbed the minors one level at a time until a breakthrough 2019, when he logged a 2.15 ERA in 25 starts between Double-A and Triple-A. He began 2020 at the alternate training site and earned his first big league callup on Sept. 26, when he pitched 1.2 innings of relief against the Red Sox.

SCOUTING REPORT: Davidson became more efficient in his delivery in 2020, implementing his lower half more effectively to help him hold his velocity. His fastball sits around 92 mph and has been up to 97, and his development should help him maintain an above-average fastball. Formerly a fastball/curveball pitcher, Davidson added a slider and it now looks like his best breaking ball, with above-average potential in the mid-to-upper 80s. His curveball has above-average vertical depth and can be average if he can land it consistently. Davidson throws a changeup, but it's his fourth offering. He walked four batters in his big league debut, and his walk rate has been a tick below-average in his minor league career.

THE FUTURE: Questions about Davidson's durability and control lead scouts to believe he profiles as a reliever in the majors. The Braves haven't given up on him as a starter.

SCOUTING GRADES: **Fastball:** 55 **Slider:** 55 **Curveball:** 50 **Changeup:** 45 **Control:** 50

Year	Age	Club (League)	Class	W	L	ERA	G	GS	IP	H	HR	BB	SO	BB/9	SO/9	WHIP	AVG
2017	21	Rome (SAL)	LoA	5	4	2.60	31	12	104	96	4	30	101	2.6	8.8	1.22	.227
2018	22	Florida (FSL)	HiA	7	10	4.18	24	24	118	120	5	58	99	4.4	7.5	1.50	.233
2019	23	Mississippi (SL)	AA	7	6	2.03	21	21	111	88	5	45	122	3.7	9.9	1.20	.196
	23	Gwinnett (IL)	AAA	1	1	2.84	4	4	19	20	0	9	12	4.3	5.7	1.53	.244
2020	24	Atlanta (NL)	MAJ	0	1	10.80	1	1	2	3	1	4	2	21.6	10.8	4.20	.333
Major League Totals				0	1	10.80	1	1	1	3	1	4	2	21.6	10.8	4.20	.333
Minor League Totals				20	24	2.86	91	62	381	356	15	146	366	3.5	8.6	1.32	.252

11 MICHAEL HARRIS, OF

Born: March 7, 2001. **B-T:** B-L. **HT:** 6-0. **WT:** 195. **Drafted:** HS—Stockbridge, Ga., 2019 (3rd round)**. Signed by:** Kirk Fredriksson.

TRACK RECORD: An athletic, two-way player out of Stockbridge High just south of Atlanta, Harris preferred hitting and the Braves liked his upside enough to draft him in the third round as a position player. After showing exciting tools in 2019, Harris spent 2020 at the alternate training site working to improve his offensive approach.

SCOUTING REPORT: Harris faced some of the team's top pitching prospects at the alternate site and impressed with the quality of his at-bats. He has above-average power potential and a chance to be an above-average hitter as well, though he has holes in his swing he will need to close against upper-level pitching. A solid athlete who is an above-average runner underway, Harris has spent most of his time in center and right field. He ultimately projects to be a right fielder with plenty of arm strength for the position.

THE FUTURE: Harris is one of the organization's most exciting lower-level prospects. He is slated to begin 2021 at one of the Class A levels.

Year	Age	Club (League)	Class	AVG	G	AB	R	H	2B	3B	HR	RBI	BB	SO	SB	OBP	SLG
2019	18	Rome (SAL)	LoA	.183	22	82	11	15	2	1	0	11	9	22	3	.269	.232
	18	Braves (GCL)	R	.349	31	109	15	38	6	3	2	16	9	20	5	.403	.514
Minor League Totals				.277	53	191	26	53	8	4	2	27	18	42	8	.344	.393

12 HUASCAR YNOA, RHP

BA GRADE
45 Risk: Medium

Born: May 28, 1998. **B-T:** R-R. **HT:** 6-2. **WT:** 220. **Signed:** Dominican Republic, 2014. **Signed by:** Fred Guerrero (Twins).

TRACK RECORD: The Braves acquired Ynoa in a 2017 trade with the Twins that sent lefthander Jaime Garcia and catcher Anthony Recker to Minnesota. Ynoa progressed through the minors quickly after joining the Braves and appeared in the majors each of the last two seasons as both a starter and a reliever. He made nine appearances during the 2020 season with shaky results, but came up big with four shutout innings of relief against the Dodgers in Game 5 of the NLCS.

SCOUTING REPORT: Ynoa has a three-pitch mix topped by a fastball that sits in the 95-96 mph range. His fastball has a low spin rate that limits his ability to get whiffs up in the zone, but it does allow him to get grounders at an above-average rate. Ynoa backs it up with a slider that averages 86 mph and a changeup in the same velocity band. All three of his pitches are at least average offerings. His slider is his best as a plus pitch with downward bite. Ynoa's biggest challenge will be to improve his below-average command and control. He frequently misses the strike zone and will need to execute his pitches more consistently.
THE FUTURE: Ynoa's pitch mix is that of a back-of-the-rotation starter, but his control makes it more likely he ends up a reliever. Either way, he'll play a role for the Braves in 2021.

Year	Age	Club (League)	Class	W	L	ERA	G	GS	IP	H	HR	BB	SO	BB/9	SO/9	WHIP	AVG
2020	22	Atlanta (NL)	MAJ	0	0	5.82	9	5	22	23	2	13	17	5.4	7.1	1.66	.277
Major League Totals				0	0	7.30	11	5	24	29	3	14	20	5.1	7.3	1.74	.296
Minor League Totals				17	34	4.32	88	79	372	348	28	170	389	4.1	9.4	1.39	.243

13 JASSEEL DE LA CRUZ, RHP

BA GRADE
50 Risk: High

Born: June 26, 1997. **B-T:** R-R. **HT:** 6-1. **WT:** 195. **Signed:** Dominican Republic, 2015. **Signed by:** Matias Laureano.
TRACK RECORD: A late-bloomer who signed for a $55,000 bonus out of the Dominican Republic, De la Cruz hit his stride in pro ball and showed he could succeed as a starter against upper-level competition at Double-A Mississippi in 2019. The Braves brought him to the alternate training site in 2020 and called him up to the majors in September, although he didn't appear in a game before being sent back down.
SCOUTING REPORT: De la Cruz has two loud offerings, including a plus-plus fastball that sat 97 mph and touched 100 mph at the alternate site. He pairs it with a hard, vertical slider that earns above-average to plus grades. De la Cruz will need to improve his fastball command to fully optimize the two-pitch tandem. He throws strikes but doesn't have the command to pinpoint the ball, largely due to his long arm action in the back of his delivery. He has made strides in the control department, giving some hope he could remain a starter. He's made progress with his changeup to give him a usable third offering.
THE FUTURE: De la Cruz has had success as a starter, but most scouts think he'd be best suited as a reliever. He'll open 2021 in Triple-A.

Year	Age	Club (League)	Class	W	L	ERA	G	GS	IP	H	HR	BB	SO	BB/9	SO/9	WHIP	AVG
2019	22	Rome (SAL)	LoA	0	1	2.50	4	4	18	19	1	5	22	2.5	11.0	1.33	.253
	22	Florida (FSL)	HiA	3	1	1.93	4	4	28	12	0	7	26	2.3	8.4	0.68	.117
	22	Mississippi (SL)	AA	4	7	3.83	17	16	87	71	7	37	73	3.8	7.6	1.24	.193
Minor League Totals				16	17	3.63	76	50	292	238	17	124	260	3.8	8.0	1.24	.223

14 PATRICK WEIGEL, RHP

BA GRADE
45 Risk: Medium

Born: July 8, 1994. **B-T:** R-R. **HT:** 6-6. **WT:** 240. **Drafted:** Houston, 2015 (7th round). **Signed by:** Darin Vaughan.
TRACK RECORD: The Braves' 2016 minor league pitcher of the year, Weigel had Tommy John surgery the following year and missed most of 2018 as well. He returned in 2019 with a solid season at Triple-A Gwinnett and saw his stuff return to its pre-injury form. The Braves brought Weigel to the alternate training site in 2020 and called him up for his major league debut on Sept. 4, although Weigel struggled with two hits, two runs and three walks allowed in two-third of an inning against the Nationals.
SCOUTING REPORT: Weigel's fastball typically sits around 95 mph and has touched 97-98. The pitch is solid-average in longer stints with good carry and running life and can be a plus offering in shorter outings. Weigel worked to reshape his slider into a sweepier pitch with more horizontal break at the alternate site. If the changes hold, the Braves believe Weigel's slider will get more swings and misses and have one of the best sliders in the system. Weigel also throws an average changeup to give him the needed third pitch to start, but his control is fringy.
THE FUTURE: Weigel fits best as a swingman or multi-inning reliever with his stuff playing up in shorter outings. He should be ready to help the Braves pitching staff in 2021.

Year	Age	Club (League)	Class	W	L	ERA	G	GS	IP	H	HR	BB	SO	BB/9	SO/9	WHIP	AVG
2020	25	Atlanta (NL)	MAJ	0	0	27.00	1	0	1	2	0	3	0	40.5	0.0	7.50	.667
Major League Totals				0	0	27.00	1	0	0	2	0	3	0	40.5	0.0	7.50	.667
Minor League Totals				23	13	3.15	86	74	362	280	27	150	346	3.7	8.6	1.19	.215

15 DAYSBEL HERNANDEZ, RHP

Born: Sept. 15, 1996. **B-T:** R-R. **HT:** 5-10. **WT:** 220. **Signed:** Cuba, 2017. **Signed by:** Rolando Petit.

TRACK RECORD: Hernandez spent two seasons pitching for Pinar Del Rio in Cuba's major league, Serie Nacional, and signed with the Braves for $190,000 in 2017. He spent 2019 as the closer at high Class A Florida and got back on the field in 2020 during instructional league.

SCOUTING REPORT: Hernandez has some of the most electric stuff in the Braves system. He pitches with a powerful fastball/slider combination out of the bullpen, with his heater consistently in the 96-99 mph range and his slider a plus weapon. Hernandez had the highest swinging strike rate in the Florida State League among pitchers who threw at least 50 innings and the fifth-highest in all of high Class A. What holds Hernandez back is his control, which was below-average in the FSL and downright troubling when he walked 10 batters in 11.1 innings in the Arizona Fall League. The Braves were impressed with how polished he looked at instructional league, so the hope is he has taken a step forward. He has the demeanor, mentality and stuff to pitch in high-leverage situations.

THE FUTURE: Hernandez is one of the Braves' better relief prospects. He has late-game potential.

Year	Age	Club (League)	Class	W	L	ERA	G	GS	IP	H	HR	BB	SO	BB/9	K/9	WHIP	AVG
2019	22	Florida (FSL)	HiA	5	2	1.71	35	0	53	34	2	23	70	3.9	12.0	1.08	.184
Minor League Totals				7	4	2.88	56	0	90	62	4	46	106	4.6	10.5	1.19	.193

16 BRYCE ELDER, RHP

BA GRADE
45 Risk: High

Born: May 19, 1999. **B-T:** R-R. **HT:** 6-2. **WT:** 220. **Drafted:** Texas, 2020 (5th round). **Signed by:** Darin Vaughan.

TRACK RECORD: Elder spent his freshman year as a reliever at Texas before moving into the rotation as a sophomore. He quickly became one of the Longhorns' top starters and was off to a dominant start in 2020 before the season shut down. The Braves drafted him in the fifth round and signed him for an above-slot $847,500 bonus.

SCOUTING REPORT: Elder has a solid three-pitch mix and throws lots of strikes. He throws his sinking fastball in the 88-93 mph range and his above-average slider is his out pitch. He also mixes in a solid changeup. While other pitchers have more stuff, Elder is a safer bet to remain a starter. He has an advanced feel for pitching and the Braves love his ability to manipulate the baseball. They think he can successfully add a four-seam fastball and curveball to his arsenal to develop a vertical pitch profile in addition to his current horizontal sinker/slider profile. Elder avoids damage by inducing lots of groundouts and is a smart pitcher who knows what to throw in what situations.

THE FUTURE: Elder has a chance to be back-of-the-rotation starter. His pro debut awaits in 2021.

Year	Age	Club (League)	Class	W	L	ERA	G	GS	IP	H	HR	BB	SO	BB/9	SO/9	WHIP	AVG
2020	21	Did not play—No minor league season															

17 ALEX JACKSON, C

BA GRADE
40 Risk: Medium

Born: Dec. 25, 1995. **B-T:** R-R. **HT:** 6-2. **WT:** 215. **Drafted:** HS—San Diego, 2014 (1st round). **Signed by:** Gary Patchett (Mariners).

TRACK RECORD: Jackson's won BA's High School Player of the Year Award and was the sixth overall pick in 2014, but he flopped in the Mariners' system and was traded to the Braves after the 2016 season for Max Povse and Rob Whalen. The Braves moved Jackson from the outfield to catcher, his original position, and he began to regain his footing. He made his major league debut in 2019 and returned to Atlanta in 2020, albeit for just five games.

SCOUTING REPORT: Jackson's loudest tool is his raw power. He hits titanic home runs in batting practice and earns the occasional 80 grade, but he doesn't get to it in games. Jackson is a prolific free swinger who strikes out frequently and is a bottom-of-the-scale hitter. He rarely makes contact, but hits the ball hard when he does. Jackson has improved dramatically as a defender over the last few years and now has a chance to be solid-average behind the plate. His framing metrics are good and his plus arm strength allowed him to throw out 50% of basestealers at Triple-A Gwinnett in 2019.

THE FUTURE: Jackson's improved defense and raw power give him a chance to be a backup catcher. He won't be more unless his hitting ability improves dramatically.

Year	Age	Club (League)	Class	AVG	G	AB	R	H	2B	3B	HR	RBI	BB	SO	SB	OBP	SLG
2020	24	Atlanta (NL)	MAJ	.286	5	7	0	2	1	0	0	0	0	4	0	.286	.429
Major League Totals				.100	9	20	0	2	1	0	0	0	1	9	0	.182	.150
Minor League Totals				.233	471	1692	245	395	96	7	76	280	145	567	6	.317	.433

18 BRYCE BALL, 1B

BA GRADE
45 Risk: High

Born: July 8, 1998. **B-T:** L-R. **HT:** 6-6. **WT:** 240. **Drafted:** Dallas Baptist, 2019 (24th round). **Signed by:** Ray Corbett.

TRACK RECORD: The Braves may have found a late-round gem in Ball. The 24th-round pick hit .329/.395/.628 in his pro debut across the Rookie-level Appalachian and low Class A South Atlantic leagues in 2019. The Braves brought Ball to the alternate training site in 2020, where he asserted himself as one of the top power hitters in the system.

SCOUTING REPORT: With a hulking, 6-foot-6, 240-pound frame, Ball has plus-plus raw power and pairs it with solid plate discipline and a clean lefthanded swing. He needs to prove he can hit upper-level pitching and keep his strikeout rate in check, but in a system light on true power hitters, Ball tops the list in terms of home run potential. Ball worked to improve his defense at first base at the alternate site. He played the position sparingly in college and remains raw around the bag.

THE FUTURE: Ball's upside is all in his bat. He'll try to show his debut wasn't a mirage in 2021.

Year	Age	Club (League)	Class	AVG	G	AB	R	H	2B	3B	HR	RBI	BB	SO	SB	OBP	SLG
2019	20	Danville (APP)	R	.324	41	145	37	47	12	0	13	38	22	30	0	.410	.676
	20	Rome (SAL)	LoA	.337	21	86	14	29	6	0	4	14	4	20	0	.367	.547
Minor League Totals				.329	62	231	51	76	18	0	17	52	26	50	0	.395	.628

19 FREDDY TARNOK, RHP

Born: Nov. 24, 1998. **B-T:** R-R. **HT:** 6-3. **WT:** 185. **Drafted:** HS—Riverview, Fla., 2017 (3rd round). **Signed by:** Justin Clark.

TRACK RECORD: Tarnok was a two-way player in high school the Braves drafted as a pitcher. For someone new to pitching full-time, he held his own in his full-season debut at low Class A Rome but hit a wall with a 4.87 ERA in 19 starts at high Class A Florida in 2019. Tarnok spent 2020 working out remotely at a facility in Florida. He did not participate in instructional league after he dropped a weight on his foot and broke a toe.

SCOUTING REPORT: Tarnok spent the summer working to get a better feel for his delivery. His fastball previously peaked at 95 mph but ran up to 99 mph in bullpen sessions during his remote workouts. His changeup is one of the best in the Braves system and he throws it with confidence to both lefties and righties. Tarnok is still working to settle on a breaking ball. He has toyed with both a curveball and a slider and Braves officials prefer his slider at the moment. Tarnok has steadily improved his control each year, but it's still fringe-average.

THE FUTURE: Tarnok has progressed but needs to show it will hold. He'll see Double-A in 2021.

Year	Age	Club (League)	Class	W	L	ERA	G	GS	IP	H	HR	BB	SO	BB/9	SO/9	WHIP	AVG
2019	20	Braves (GCL)	R	0	1	3.38	3	3	8	3	1	1	9	1.1	10.1	0.50	.100
	20	Florida (FSL)	HiA	3	7	4.87	19	19	98	105	6	36	82	3.3	7.5	1.44	.244
Minor League Totals				8	16	4.29	57	41	197	189	12	81	184	3.7	8.4	1.37	.249

20 VICTOR VODNIK, RHP

BA GRADE
45 Risk: High

Born: Oct. 9, 1999. **B-T:** R-R. **HT:** 6-0. **WT:** 200. **Drafted:** HS—Rialto, Calif., 2018 (4th round). **Signed by:** Kevin Martin.

TRACK RECORD: Vodnik was the first player drafted out of Rialto (Calif.) High since Ricky Nolasco in 2001. He was plenty raw, but the Braves signed him for an above-slot $200,000 because of his natural arm strength. After a rough pro debut, Vodnik posted a 2.93 ERA in 23 appearances for low Class A Rome in 2019, working mostly in long relief. The Braves brought him to the alternate training site late in 2020 and included him in instructional league.

SCOUTING REPORT: Vodnik is undersized but strong. He fires an above-average fastball that sits at 94 mph and touches 98. His breaking ball is slurvy, looking more like a slider some days and like a curveball on others. He shows natural ability to spin the ball, but developing a more consistent shape will be key moving forward. Vodnik made progress with a changeup that previously lacked consistency at the alternate site. He'll need a reliable third pitch if he wants to start. His control was a question mark when he was drafted, but he's kept his walks reasonable so far in his pro career.

THE FUTURE: Vodnik likely ends up a hard-throwing reliever. Some believe he might be able to start.

Year	Age	Club (League)	Class	W	L	ERA	G	GS	IP	H	HR	BB	SO	BB/9	SO/9	WHIP	AVG
2019	19	Rome (SAL)	LoA	1	3	2.94	23	3	67	55	1	24	69	3.2	9.2	1.17	.201
Minor League Totals				2	4	3.38	27	3	72	63	2	25	78	3.1	9.8	1.22	.234

21 WILLIAM WOODS, RHP

BREAKOUT
BA GRADE
45 Risk: High

Born: Dec. 29, 1998. **B-T:** R-R. **HT:** 6-3. **WT:** 200. **Drafted:** Dyersburg (Tenn.) JC, 2018 (23rd round). **Signed by:** JD French.

TRACK RECORD: Woods was a low-profile prospect out of Dyersburg (Tenn.) JC in 2018, signing for just $125,000 as a 23rd-round pick. After struggling in his debut in the Rookie-level Gulf Coast League, Woods' velocity ticked up in 2019 and again in 2020, when he impressed Braves officials at the alternate training site.

SCOUTING REPORT: In a year when it was hard for any prospect to enhance his stock, Woods was one of the biggest risers in Atlanta's system. By filling out a frame that's now 6-foot-3, 200 pounds, Woods' fastball has climbed into the mid-to-high 90s. The pitch has solid carry and plays well alongside a hard slider that has a chance to be above-average. His third pitch is a changeup that is still developing but shows promise Woods will need to improve his control. He's walked 4.9 batters per nine innings over his minor league career and is a below-average strike-thrower overall.

THE FUTURE: The Braves have split Woods between starting and relieving. With his velocity gains, he's a potential breakout candidate for 2021.

Year	Age	Club (League)	Class	W	L	ERA	G	GS	IP	H	HR	BB	SO	BB/9	SO/9	WHIP	AVG
2019	20	Rome (SAL)	LoA	1	5	3.35	20	7	51	38	4	29	58	5.1	10.2	1.31	.174
Minor League Totals				1	6	4.14	30	11	71	60	4	39	78	4.9	9.8	1.38	.225

22 VAUGHN GRISSOM, SS

Born: Jan. 5, 2001. **B-T:** R-R. **HT:** 6-3. **WT:** 180. **Drafted:** HS—Oviedo, Fla., 2019 (11th round). **Signed by:** Jon Bunnell.

TRACK RECORD: Grissom showed an intriguing set of tools in high school and was seen by scouts frequently as a teammate of eventual Tigers first-round pick Riley Greene. The Braves liked his upside enough to draft him in the 11th round and gave him an above-slot $347,500 bonus. Grissom impressed in a solid pro debut in the Rookie-level Arizona League, and the Braves brought him to the alternate training site in 2020.

SCOUTING REPORT: Grissom has an advanced offensive game with solid bat-to-ball skills and a good feel for the strike zone. He makes plenty of contact and could develop solid-average or better power as he continues to add strength to his 6-foot-3 frame and learns to elevate the ball. Scouts noted his swing sometimes flattened out in high school and he hit the ball on the ground nearly half the time in his pro debut. Currently a shortstop, Grissom will play both third and second base in 2021 to try and develop some defensive versatility. He has solid hands and arm strength, but his range is stretched at shortstop.

THE FUTURE: The Braves hope Grissom turns into a contact hitter with some power who can play around the infield. He'll make his full-season debut in 2021.

Year	Age	Club (League)	Class	AVG	G	AB	R	H	2B	3B	HR	RBI	BB	SO	SB	OBP	SLG
2019	18	Braves (GCL)	R	.288	44	160	22	46	7	1	3	23	16	27	3	.361	.400
Minor League Totals				.288	44	160	22	46	7	1	3	23	16	27	3	.361	.400

23 JESSE FRANKLIN, OF

BA GRADE
45 Risk: High

Born: Dec. 1, 1998. **B-T:** L-L. **HT:** 6-1. **WT:** 215. **Drafted:** Michigan, 2020 (3rd round). **Signed by:** Jeremy Gordon.

TRACK RECORD: Franklin was the headliner of Michigan's 2017 recruiting class. He led the team in homers, slugging and RBIs as a freshman and carried the team to the College World Series finals as a sophomore. Franklin didn't play in 2020 due to a broken collarbone, but the Braves still drafted him in the third round and signed him for $497,500.

SCOUTING REPORT: Franklin has a solid all-around game and outstanding baseball instincts. He takes a professional approach at the plate and competes in the box, and Braves officials were happy with how he performed at the alternate training site after signing. He has solid power potential and hit double-digit home runs at Michigan in both of his full seasons. Franklin can play all three outfield positions. He's a slightly above-average runner with an excellent first step and takes good routes to the ball. A fringe-average arm might make him best suited for left field.

THE FUTURE: Franklin projects a solid contributor in the outfield. His pro debut awaits in 2021.

Year	Age	Club (League)	Class	AVG	G	AB	R	H	2B	3B	HR	RBI	BB	SO	SB	OBP	SLG
2020	21	Did not play—No minor league season															

24 KASEY KALICH, RHP

Born: April 25, 1998. **B-T:** R-R. **HT:** 6-3. **WT:** 220. **Drafted:** Texas A&M, 2019 (4th round). **Signed by:** Darin Vaughan.

TRACK RECORD: Kalich transferred to Texas A&M from Blinn (Texas) JC and struck out 13.5 batters per nine in the Aggies' bullpen in 2019. The Braves liked his stuff in relief and drafted him in the fourth round. Kalich posted a 1.31 ERA with 22 strikeouts in 20.2 innings at low Class A Rome in an impressive pro debut.

SCOUTING REPORT: Kalich overwhelms hitters with a powerful two-pitch combination. His fastball sits in the mid-90s and reaches 98 mph. His slider is firm enough that some evaluators label it a cutter. Both pitches have above-average potential. Kalich has worked on a curveball and changeup, but he doesn't rely much on either of those pitches. He dominated despite below-average control in his pro debut and will need to improve against higher-level hitters.

THE FUTURE: Kalich has the stuff to pitch in late relief. He'll get there if his control improves.

Year	Age	Club (League)	Class	W	L	ERA	G	GS	IP	H	HR	BB	SO	BB/9	SO/9	WHIP	AVG
2019	21	Rome (SAL)	LoA	1	1	1.31	13	0	21	9	0	10	22	4.4	9.6	0.92	.102
	21	Braves (GCL)	R	0	0	0.00	1	0	1	1	0	1	2	9.0	18.0	2.00	.200
Minor League Totals				1	1	1.25	14	0	21	10	0	11	24	4.6	10.0	0.97	.143

25 TREY HARRIS, OF

BA GRADE 45 Risk: High

Born: Jan. 15, 1996. **B-T:** R-R. **HT:** 5-8. **WT:** 215. **Drafted:** Missouri, 2018 (32nd round). **Signed by:** JD French.

TRACK RECORD: After struggling his first three seasons at Missouri, Harris hit .316/.413/.516 in a breakout senior season in 2018. The Braves drafted him in the 32nd round and gave him a $10,000 bonus. Harris has continued to hit in pro ball. He owns a .317/.395/.480 career slash line in two seasons between the Class A levels and Double-A.

SCOUTING REPORT: Harris has a fringe-average hit tool and solid power potential. He is an aggressive hitter who doesn't walk much, but he has a great feel to square up fastballs. Most of his power goes to his pull side, though he has the strength to use the opposite field as well. Harris will need to monitor his weight and could slow down to an average or fringy runner. His average arm plays better in left field than right. Braves officials believe he's a better defender than he gets credit for.

THE FUTURE: Harris is set to start back at Double-A in 2021. It will be a good test to see if he can handle upper-level pitching.

Year	Age	Club (League)	Class	AVG	G	AB	R	H	2B	3B	HR	RBI	BB	SO	SB	OBP	SLG
2019	23	Mississippi (SL)	AA	.281	41	146	15	41	7	3	2	12	4	33	1	.318	.411
	23	Rome (SAL)	LoA	.366	56	202	38	74	14	4	8	44	20	32	4	.437	.594
	23	Florida (FSL)	HiA	.303	34	122	20	37	5	0	4	17	12	26	3	.388	.443
Minor League Totals				.317	184	659	107	209	44	9	15	102	64	117	15	.395	.480

26 GREYSON JENISTA, OF/1B

BA GRADE 45 Risk: High

Born: Dec. 7, 1996. **B-T:** L-R. **HT:** 6-4. **WT:** 210. **Drafted:** Wichita State, 2018 (2nd round). **Signed by:** Nate Dion.

TRACK RECORD: Jenista hit .318/.430/.487 at Wichita State and was the MVP of the Cape Cod League prior to his junior year, leading the Braves to draft him 49th overall. Jenista faced doubts in college whether his big raw power would translate in games, and those concerns have become realized as a pro. He reached Double-A in his first full season but posted a .349 slugging percentage.

SCOUTING REPORT: Jensita has worked with minor league hitting coach Mike Bard to improve his swing mechanics and find consistency at the plate. He previously tinkered constantly with his swing, so finding a setup he's comfortable and confident with heading into the 2021 season will be critical. Jenista does have plus raw power to his pull-side and the opposite field, but he needs to find a way to access it more consistently. Defensively, Jenista is adequate in a corner outfield spot and has also spent time at first base. He's a solid runner now but could slow down with his large frame.

THE FUTURE: Jenista will head back to Double-A in 2021. Finding a swing that can access his power is his main goal.

Year	Age	Club (League)	Class	AVG	G	AB	R	H	2B	3B	HR	RBI	BB	SO	SB	OBP	SLG
2019	22	Mississippi (SL)	AA	.243	74	222	18	54	4	1	5	26	27	75	2	.324	.338
	22	Florida (FSL)	HiA	.223	56	202	24	45	14	1	4	29	27	70	1	.312	.361
Minor League Totals				.244	191	647	75	158	27	6	13	89	77	186	7	.322	.365

27 LOGAN BROWN, C

Born: Sept. 14, 1996. **B-T:** L-R. **HT:** 6-0. **WT:** 195. **Drafted:** Southern Indiana, 2018 (35th round). **Signed by:** Kevin Barry.

TRACK RECORD: Brown's father, Kevin, had a seven-year career as a backup catcher. Logan signed with the Braves as a 35th-round pick out of Division II Southern Indiana and has begun following in his father's footsteps. He spent his first full season at the Class A levels and hit just one home run, but his defense stood out and the Braves brought him to the alternate training site in 2020.

SCOUTING REPORT: Brown's defense is his calling card. He's a strong receiver who pitchers love throwing to and who does everything teams want to see defensively. He has solid, reliable hands and can frame pitches, block and call a solid game. He has easy plus arm strength and threw out 40 percent of basestealers in his pro debut. Brown leaves much to be desired offensively. He's a ground ball hitter with some contact skills, but offers very little impact and does not control the strike zone.

THE FUTURE: Brown's defense is good enough to give him a shot at being a backup catcher. His offense will need to improve for him to get even there.

Year	Age	Club (League)	Class	AVG	G	AB	R	H	2B	3B	HR	RBI	BB	SO	SB	OBP	SLG
2019	22	Rome (SAL)	LoA	.301	51	193	25	58	11	1	1	26	11	39	0	.351	.383
	22	Florida (FSL)	HiA	.240	48	175	12	42	7	0	0	20	6	44	0	.269	.280
Minor League Totals				.272	136	482	50	131	23	1	4	62	28	99	0	.321	.349

28 BEAU PHILIP, SS

Born: Oct. 23, 1998. **B-T:** R-R. **HT:** 6-0. **WT:** 190. **Drafted:** Oregon State, 2019 (2nd round). **Signed by:** Cody Martin.

TRACK RECORD: After two seasons at San Joaquin Delta (Calif.) JC, Philip transferred to Oregon State and hit .312 while playing a solid shortstop. The Braves drafted him 60th overall in 2019 and signed him an under-slot $697,500 bonus. Philip hit .193 in an underwhelming pro debut and got back on the field in instructional league in 2020.

SCOUTING REPORT: Philip is a defense-first shortstop with utility tools but a light bat. He pairs reliable hands with good footwork and has solid range to both sides defensively. He particularly excels on plays up the middle. He has plus arm strength and reached 95 mph on the mound as a pitcher in junior college. Philip showed less contact ability in his pro debut than he did in college but has always struggled against breaking stuff. He has well below-average raw power and doesn't project to add more to a small frame.

THE FUTURE: Philip will be exposed to second and third base in 2021 to prepare for a potential utility role. He'll aim for a bounceback year at the plate at the Class A levels.

Year	Age	Club (League)	Class	AVG	G	AB	R	H	2B	3B	HR	RBI	BB	SO	SB	OBP	SLG
2019	20	Danville (APP)	R	.193	55	207	27	40	6	0	4	20	26	51	5	.297	.280
Minor League Totals				.193	55	207	27	40	6	0	4	20	26	51	5	.297	.280

29 STEPHEN PAOLINI, OF

BA GRADE
45 Risk: Extreme

Born: Nov. 23, 2000. **B-T:** L-L. **HT:** 6-2. **WT:** 195. **Drafted:** HS—Trumbull, Conn., 2019 (5th round). **Signed by:** Ted Lekas.

TRACK RECORD: A relatively unknown prospect in high school, the Braves were one of the only teams on Paolini but liked his raw tools. They took him in the fifth round in 2019 and gave him a $597,500 bonus to forgo an Elon commitment. Paolini hit just .192 in the Rookie-level Gulf Coast League in his pro debut and went to instructional league in 2020.

SCOUTING REPORT: Paolini has just 35 professional games under his belt in pro ball and is still something of an unknown, but he has a strong collection of tools. He has plus speed and a projectable, 6-foot-2 frame that could allow him to grow into average power. He'll need plenty of time and patience to get to that power. His swing has some moving parts, including a big leg kick, that create timing issues. He does have solid bat speed and is a patient hitter. Paolini has the speed to handle center field, but the Braves have exposed him in all three outfield positions

THE FUTURE: Paolini has the tools to dream on an everyday player, but he needs plenty of at-bats to develop his offensive game. He'll make his full season debut in 2020.

Year	Age	Club (League)	Class	AVG	G	AB	R	H	2B	3B	HR	RBI	BB	SO	SB	OBP	SLG
2019	18	Braves (GCL)	R	.192	35	120	15	23	6	0	0	8	22	37	2	.315	.242
Minor League Totals				.192	35	120	15	23	6	0	0	8	22	37	2	.315	.242

30 SPENCER STRIDER, RHP

BA GRADE **45** Risk: Extreme

Born: Oct. 28, 1998. **B-T:** R-R. **HT:** 6-0. **WT:** 195. **Drafted:** Clemson, 2020 (4th round). **Signed by:** Billy Best.

TRACK RECORD: Strider was a high-profile recruit in high school and led Clemson in strikeouts as a freshman, whiffing 70 batters in just 51 innings. He missed his sophomore season after having Tommy John surgery, but he returned to the mound as a junior and struck out 19 batters in 12 innings before the season shut down. The Braves drafted him in the fourth round and signed him for a $449,300 signing bonus.

SCOUTING REPORT: Strider is undersized at just 6-feet tall, but he has a big, four-seam fastball that gets into the mid-90s. He also has the feel to spin a breaking ball, but the Braves aren't yet sure if he should focus on developing a hard slider or a curveball. Strider also throws a changeup, but it is well behind his fastball and breaking ball. Strider was at the team's alternate training site, where he tried to adjust to the professional strike zone. It's unlikely Strider ever has average command, but he is athletic enough to repeat his delivery and throw strikes. The Braves love his makeup.

THE FUTURE: Strider carries plenty of risk given the Tommy John surgery already on his resume. He projects best as a reliever.

Year	Age	Club (League)	Class	W	L	ERA	G	GS	IP	H	HR	BB	SO	BB/9	SO/9	WHIP	AVG
2020	21	Did not play—No minor league season															

MORE PROSPECTS TO KNOW

31 JUSTIN DEAN, OF

Dean was voted the best defensive outfielder in the South Atlantic League in 2019 and has 70-grade speed. He's shown on-base skills and is selective at the plate, but his hit tool needs improvement.

32 RICKY DEVITO, RHP

SLEEPER

DeVito was the Big East Conference pitcher of the year in 2018 but got hit around during his junior year in 2019. His fastball has improved in pro ball, his breaking ball is solid and some scouts put plus grades on his changeup.

33 JEREMY WALKER, RHP

Walker transitioned to the bullpen in 2019 and made his big league debut as a ground-ball oriented reliever. He would have seen innings with Atlanta again in 2020 if not for a right shoulder impingement.

34 CJ ALEXANDER, 3B

Alexander came crashing down to earth in 2019 after a loud and impressive pro debut. An elbow injury limited him in 2019, but now that he's healthy he has a chance to bounce back in 2021.

35 JARED JOHNSON, RHP

A pop-up prospect in the 2019 draft class, Johnson had little interest from Division I schools. That changed when he started throwing 97 mph with shocking ease. Johnson is plenty raw and remains a project, but he showed improvement with his delivery and added velocity to his slider during instructs.

36 NOLAN KINGHAM, RHP

Kingham has the best control in Atlanta's system, but his stuff is below-average across the board. He's never struck out more than 7.3 batters per nine innings going back to his college days at Texas, so he needs to add more velocity or improve his breaking ball.

37 JOSH GRAHAM, RHP

Graham is already 27 years old but has one of the better changeups in the system. Changeup-reliant relievers are rare, but Graham did take a step forward in Double-A Mississippi in 2019.

38 TYLER OWENS, RHP

Owens is undersized but he has a fastball that's been into the upper 90s and a solid slider. He was mostly used in a starting role in his pro debut, but profiles better as a reliever given his size.

39 TREY RILEY, RHP

Riley has loud pure stuff but has never shown an ability to harness it. He signed for $450,000 out of Logan (Ill.) JC thanks to a fastball that he ran up to 97 mph and an above-average slider, but after two pro seasons he sports a 7.71 ERA and has walked 7.4 batters per nine innings.

40 MAHKI BACKSTROM, 1B

Backstrom has loud power potential with a large, 6-foot-5, 220-pound frame and impressive bat speed. He had a solid debut in the Rookie-level Gulf Coast League, where he hit .300/.402/.457, and spent 2020 working on his defense.

TOP PROSPECTS OF THE DECADE

Year	Player, Pos.	2020 Org
2011	Julio Teheran, RHP	Angels
2012	Julio Teheran, RHP	Angels
2013	Julio Teheran, RHP	Angels
2014	Lucas Sims, RHP	Reds
2015	Jose Peraza, 2B	Red Sox
2016	Sean Newcomb, LHP	Braves
2017	Dansby Swanson, SS	Braves
2018	Ronald Acuña Jr., OF	Braves
2019	Austin Riley, 3B	Braves
2020	Cristian Pache, OF	Braves

TOP DRAFT PICKS OF THE DECADE

Year	Player, Pos.	2020 Org
2011	Sean Gilmartin, LHP	Rays
2012	Lucas Sims, RHP	Reds
2013	Jason Hursh, RHP	Did not play
2014	Braxton Davidson, OF	Braves
2015	Kolby Allard, LHP	Rangers
2016	Ian Anderson, RHP	Braves
2017	Kyle Wright, RHP	Braves
2018	*Carter Stewart, RHP	SoftBank (Japan)
2019	Shea Langeliers, C	Braves
2020	Jared Shuster, LHP	Braves

*Did not sign.

DEPTH CHART

ATLANTA BRAVES

TOP 2021 ROOKIES	RANK
Cristian Pache, OF	1
Ian Anderson, RHP	2
Drew Waters, OF	3
BREAKOUT PROSPECTS	**RANK**
William Woods, RHP	21
Vaughn Grissom, 3B	22

SOURCE OF TOP 30 TALENT

Homegrown	28	Acquired	2
College	13	Trade	2
Junior college	2	Rule 5 draft	0
High school	9	Independent league	0
Nondrafted free agent	0	Free agent/waivers	0
International	4		

LF
Jesse Franklin (23)
Trey Harris (25)
Greyson Jenista (26)

CF
Cristian Pache (1)
Drew Waters (3)
Stephen Paolini (29)
Justin Dean

RF
Michael Harris (11)
Tyler Neslony
Brandon Parker

3B
Vaughn Grissom (22)
CJ Alexander

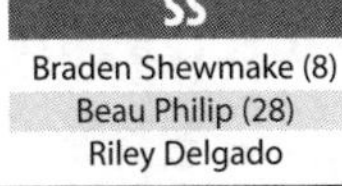

SS
Braden Shewmake (8)
Beau Philip (28)
Riley Delgado

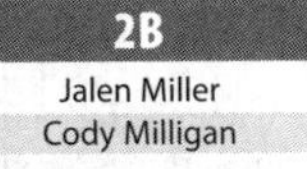

2B
Jalen Miller
Cody Milligan

1B
Bryce Ball (18)
Mahki Backstrom

C
Shea Langeliers (4)
William Contreras (6)
Alex Jackson (17)
Logan Brown (27)

LHP

LHSP	LHRP
Kyle Muller (7)	Phil Pfeifer
Jared Shuster (9)	Thomas Burrows
Tucker Davidson (10)	Corbin Clouse
Hayden Deal	Tanner Lawsen
Gabriel Noguera	Jake Higginbotham
Mitch Stallings	Miguel Jerez

RHP

RHSP	RHRP
Ian Anderson (2)	Huascar Ynoa (12)
Bryse Wilson (5)	Jasseel De La Cruz (13)
Bryce Elder (16)	Patrick Weigel (14)
William Woods (21)	Daysbel Hernández (15)
Ricky Devito	Victor Vodnik (19)
Nolan Kingham	Freddy Tarnok (20)
	Kasey Kalich (24)
	Spencer Strider (30)
	Jeremy Walker
	Jared Johnson
	Josh Graham
	Tyler Owens
	Trey Riley
	Luis Mora
	A.J. Puckett

Baltimore Orioles

BY JON MEOLI

For an organization almost solely focused on the future and creating a contending team through scouting and player development, a pandemic-caused shutdown in the second year of the Orioles' rebuild under executive vice president and general manager Mike Elias was particularly unwelcome in Baltimore.

Even in those conditions, though, the Orioles were still able to acquire young players to contribute to Elias' vision of an elite talent pipeline to Camden Yards.

Another year with a high draft position led the Orioles to an impressive six-player haul in the shortened draft. Trades of pitchers Richard Bleier, Mychal Givens, Miguel Castro, and Tommy Milone allowed them to add both teenage Latin American talent and high-minors depth to the mix. They continued with the trade of Jose Iglesias after the season.

Most crucially, the Orioles' development staff worked at the team's alternate training site, in Bowie, Md., with young top prospects like catcher Adley Rutschman and pitchers Grayson Rodriguez and DL Hall. Those at-bats and innings should help continue their rises to the majors. Others, like teenage shortstop Gunnar Henderson and righthander Kyle Bradish opened eyes in the organization with their efforts at the alternate site.

Young big leaguers like Cedric Mullins and DJ Stewart found their swings and their confidence at the alternate site and helped the major league team after scuffling early. Rookie starters Dean Kremer and Keegan Akin, plus slugging outfielder Ryan Mountcastle, all used the alternate site as a finishing school before impressive major league debuts in the summer.

These young players contributed to an overall improvement under manager Brandon Hyde, with the Orioles in contention for the expanded playoffs through the final week of the season despite finishing 25-35. Thanks to those young starters and a revamped bullpen featuring once and current prospects like lefthander Tanner Scott and righthanders Hunter Harvey and Dillon Tate, the Orioles' pitching staff improved by more than a full run in 2020 with an increased strikeout rate and fewer walks and home runs allowed.

When the rebuilding project officially turns a corner and leads to a contending team in Baltimore is still unclear. Many of the Orioles top prospects have no upper minors experience, and those who are coming to the majors project to be more complementary pieces than stars on a winning team. The organization's prospect strength is in the influx of talent that will be in the low minors in 2021.

Elias and domestic scouting operations supervisor Brad Ciolek have targeted proven college bats early in the last two drafts, and filled it out with pitching that fits the program and preferences of director of pitching Chris Holt. The Orioles have rejoined the Latin American scouting world, with millions of dollars invested in international talent since the middle of 2018 and 15 players coming stateside for instructional league as a result.

Under farm director Matt Blood, these players will be brought along using a modern hitting philosophy from a new group of coaches. Both the pitching and hitting side emphasize building on players' strengths with strong early returns. Still, a year without a minor league season makes it difficult to know just how effective those methods will be to producing impact major leaguers, and when they'll arrive. ■

G FIUME/GETTY IMAGES

The emergence of young starting pitchers, like Dean Kremer, improves the Orioles' outlook.

PROJECTED 2024 LINEUP

Position	Player	Age
Catcher	Adley Rutschman	25
First Base	Trey Mancini	32
Second Base	Adam Hall	25
Third Base	Jordan Westburg	25
Shortstop	Gunnar Henderson	23
Left Field	Anthony Santander	29
Center Field	Austin Hays	28
Right Field	Heston Kjerstad	25
Designated Hitter	Ryan Mountcastle	27
No. 1 Starter	Grayson Rodriguez	24
No. 2 Starter	DL Hall	25
No. 3 Starter	John Means	31
No. 4 Starter	Dean Kremer	28
No. 5 Starter	Keegan Akin	29
Closer	Mike Baumann	28

1 ADLEY RUTSCHMAN, C

Born: Feb. 6, 1998. **B-T:** B-R. **HT:** 6-2. **WT:** 216.
Drafted: Oregon State, 2019 (1st round).
Signed by: Brandon Verley.

JOE ROBBINS/GETTY IMAGES

BA GRADE
70 **Risk: High**

SCOUTING GRADES
Hit: 70. **Power:** 70. **Run:** 40. **Field:** 60. **Arm:** 70.

Projected future grades on 20-80 scouting scale.

TRACK RECORD: Rutschman was a generational talent in college at Oregon State, leading the Beavers to the College World Series title as a sophomore in 2018 and winning the Golden Spikes Award as the nation's best player as a junior in 2019. His performance at the 2018 College World Series was historic. As Rutschman helped propel the Beavers to their third national championship he set a CWS record with 17 hits to go with 13 RBIs and a .649 on-base percentage. He entered his draft year in 2019 as one of the most exciting, highly anticipated draft prospects ever. The Orioles made Rutschman the No. 1 overall pick in the 2019 draft and signed him to a then-record $8.1 million bonus. Rutschman climbed from the Rookie-level Gulf Coast League through the short-season New York-Penn League to help low Class A Delmarva on its playoff run in 2019, crushing two home runs and adding eight RBIs in just 12 games. Rutschman gained valuable experience in major league spring training before spending the summer dominating the team's alternate site at Bowie, Md.

SCOUTING REPORT: The switch-hitting Rutschman rebuilt his swing in college to gear for more power and consistency. He continues to find ways to refine and make his swing more efficient as he learns the professional game. He went through an adjustment period at the Bowie camp after the coronavirus shutdown period halted most of his work, but he quickly revealed the all-fields power and consistent hard contact that give him potential to be a plus-plus hitter with plus-plus power at his peak. He ended the summer as the best performer at the camp. His offensive production is aided by advanced plate discipline. Rutschman is clear in which pitches he's able to drive and which he should lay off. He'll likely see increased benefit from that when pitchers are around the strike zone more and umpires improve at the higher levels of the minors. Rutschman's above-average pop times and advanced receiving skills behind the plate give him the physical tools to be a plus major league catcher. His work at the Bowie camp helped him gain experience calling pitches to an advanced pitcher's plan and gave him invaluable insight into how pitchers and fellow catchers with major league experience see the game. All those tools are enhanced by a reputation as a fantastic teammate and tireless worker who elevates both himself and everyone around him with his approach to the game.

THE FUTURE: Rutschman is the game's best catching prospect and one of the most exciting minor leaguers in all of baseball. The Orioles envision a generational offensive producer at his peak, standout defense behind the plate and multiple all-star nods. Rutschman's path to Baltimore may have been slowed by the lack of a 2020 minor league season, but if he starts in Double-A next spring, he could push for a major league debut at the end of 2021, or else be up early in 2022. ■

BEST TOOLS

Best Hitter for Average	Adley Rutschman
Best Power Hitter	Adley Rutschman
Best Strike-Zone Discipline	Adley Rutschman
Fastest Baserunner	Adam Hall
Best Athlete	Jordan Westburg
Best Fastball	DL Hall
Best Curveball	DL Hall
Best Slider	Mike Baumann
Best Changeup	Grayson Rodriguez
Best Control	Alex Wells
Best Defensive Catcher	Adley Rutschman
Best Defensive Infielder	Jordan Westburg
Best Infield Arm	Coby Mayo
Best Defensive Outfielder	Ryan McKenna
Best Outfield Arm	Yusniel Diaz

Year	Age	Club (League)	Class	AVG	G	AB	R	H	2B	3B	HR	RBI	BB	SO	SB	OBP	SLG
2019	21	Orioles (GCL)	R	.143	5	14	3	2	0	0	1	3	2	2	1	.250	.357
	21	Aberdeen (NYP)	SS	.325	20	77	11	25	7	1	1	15	12	16	0	.413	.481
	21	Delmarva (SAL)	LoA	.154	12	39	5	6	1	0	2	8	6	9	0	.261	.333
Minor League Totals				.254	37	130	19	33	8	1	4	26	20	27	1	.351	.423

2 GRAYSON RODRIGUEZ, RHP

DAN KUBUS

Born: Nov. 16, 1999. **B-T:** L-R. **HT:** 6-5. **WT:** 220. **Drafted:** HS—Nacogdoches, Texas, 2018 (1st round). **Signed by:** Thom Dreier.

TRACK RECORD: Rodriguez blossomed late as a high school senior and was drafted 11th overall by the Orioles in 2018, signing for $4.3 million. He overpowered the low Class A South Atlantic League in his full-season debut in 2019 and shared the Orioles' minor league pitcher of the year award. The Orioles brought him to their alternate training site at Bowie, Md., for the 2020 season.

SCOUTING REPORT: Two months at the Orioles' secondary camp allowed Rodriguez a chance to further hone the consistency of his clean, sturdy delivery. His four-seam fastball sat 95-98 mph with plus-plus potential all summer, and for the second straight year got harder as the season went on. Rodriguez quickly learned a changeup in 2019 and it remains an above-average pitch at 82-85 mph. His curveball has good shape but lacks power in the mid 70s, leaving his low-80s slider as the more effective of his breaking balls. The experience at the alternate site helped Rodriguez start to understand pitching to a plan against older hitters whom he can't simply overpower.

THE FUTURE: Rodriguez is the foremost piece of the Orioles' pitching-driven rebuilding plan. He has a chance to be at least a mid-rotation starter and has countless top-of-the-rotation traits. He should reach Double-A at some time in 2021.

SCOUTING GRADES: **Fastball:** 70 **Slider:** 60 **Curveball:** 50 **Changeup:** 55 **Control:** 60

Year	Age	Club (League)	Class	W	L	ERA	G	GS	IP	H	HR	BB	SO	BB/9	SO/9	WHIP	AVG
2018	18	Orioles (GCL)	R	0	2	1.40	9	8	19	17	0	7	20	3.3	9.3	1.24	.213
2019	19	Delmarva (SAL)	LoA	10	4	2.68	20	20	94	57	4	36	129	3.4	12.4	0.99	.151
Minor League Totals				10	6	2.46	29	28	113	74	4	43	149	3.4	11.8	1.03	.183

3 DL HALL, LHP

DAN KUBUS

Born: Sept. 19, 1998**. B-T:** L-L. **HT:** 6-0. **WT:** 180. **Drafted:** HS—Valdosta, Ga., 2017 (1st round)**. Signed by:** Arthur McConnehead.

TRACK RECORD: Hall surprisingly fell to the Orioles at No. 21 overall in the 2017 draft, and the club felt lucky to get him there and signed him for $3 million. The 2019 Futures Game participant returned fully healthy in 2020 after an oblique injury ended his season early last year and spent the summer at the team's alternate training site in Bowie, Md.

SCOUTING REPORT: Hall was challenged as a 20-year-old at the alternate site but made strides with his plan of attack and showed more trust in his electric four-pitch mix. Though he doesn't consistently command it, his fastball sat 95-98 mph over the summer. Hall's slider and curveball previously blended together, but they now have distinct shapes with the slider at 82-84 mph and the curveball remaining in the 76-79 mph range but with more depth. His best secondary pitch is a swing-and-miss changeup at 82-85 mph. Hall has struggled with walks throughout his career. Maintaining a repeatable delivery that allows him to consistently locate his fastball will be his next challenge.

THE FUTURE: Hall was slated to start 2020 at Double-A and should open there in 2021. He has a chance to develop into a mid-rotation starter with the stuff to be more, but that hinges on his ability to iron out his fastball command.

SCOUTING GRADES: **Fastball:** 70 **Slider:** 50 **Curveball:** 55 **Changeup:** 60 **Control:** 45

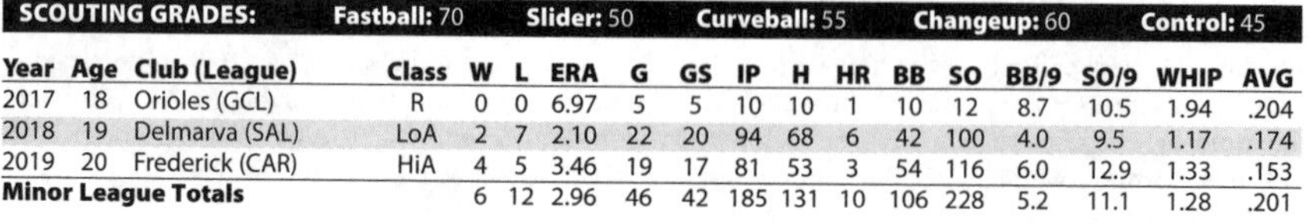

Year	Age	Club (League)	Class	W	L	ERA	G	GS	IP	H	HR	BB	SO	BB/9	SO/9	WHIP	AVG
2017	18	Orioles (GCL)	R	0	0	6.97	5	5	10	10	1	10	12	8.7	10.5	1.94	.204
2018	19	Delmarva (SAL)	LoA	2	7	2.10	22	20	94	68	6	42	100	4.0	9.5	1.17	.174
2019	20	Frederick (CAR)	HiA	4	5	3.46	19	17	81	53	3	54	116	6.0	12.9	1.33	.153
Minor League Totals				6	12	2.96	46	42	185	131	10	106	228	5.2	11.1	1.28	.201

4 HESTON KJERSTAD, OF

Born: Feb. 12, 1999. **B-T:** L-R. **HT:** 6-3. **WT:** 205. **Drafted:** Arkansas, 2020 (1st round). **Signed by:** Ken Guthrie.

BA GRADE
60 Risk: High

TRACK RECORD: The Orioles surprised the industry when they made Kjerstad the No. 2 overall pick in the 2020 draft, but their scouts and analysts loved the Arkansas star's offensive profile. He signed for $5.2 million, which was more than $2.5 million under slot. A three-year starter for the Razorbacks and stalwart for USA Baseball's Collegiate National Team, Kjerstad has grown into prolific power and likely would have been a Golden Spikes Award contender in 2020.

SCOUTING REPORT: Kjerstad's promise is built on an impactful lefthanded bat with plus-plus raw power. He has a fair bit of movement in his swing and will swing and miss, but his much-improved plate coverage leads the Orioles to believe he can be an above-average hitter with all-fields power. He turns around hard line drives on pitches anywhere in the strike zone and cut down his strikeout and chase rates in his shortened junior year. Kjerstad is a below-average runner but can stand in a corner outfield spot. His above-average arm fits in right field.

THE FUTURE: Kjerstad was drafted as a middle-of-the-order complement to Adley Rutschman as future cornerstones of the Orioles' lineup. His power alone could put him on an all-star team in the right year. He is set to begin his pro career at the Class A levels and could move quickly.

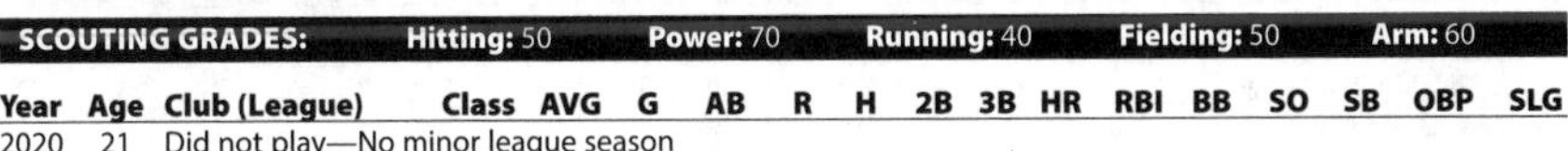

SCOUTING GRADES: **Hitting:** 50 **Power:** 70 **Running:** 40 **Fielding:** 50 **Arm:** 60

Year	Age	Club (League)	Class	AVG	G	AB	R	H	2B	3B	HR	RBI	BB	SO	SB	OBP	SLG
2020	21	Did not play—No minor league season															

5 RYAN MOUNTCASTLE, OF

Born: Feb. 18, 1997. **B-T:** R-R. **HT:** 6-3. **WT:** 195. **Drafted:** HS—Oviedo, Fla., 2015 (1st round). **Signed by:** Kelvin Colon.

TOP ROOKIE

MIKE CARLSON/MLB PHOTOS VIA GETTY IMAGES

BA GRADE
55 Risk: Medium

TRACK RECORD: A tour around the diamond that began at shortstop and included stops at third base and first base eventually delivered Mountcastle to where he belonged: the heart of the Orioles' major league lineup. Now a left fielder, Mountcastle took the team's mandate to improve his plate discipline and defense and, in August, earned what was a productive callup to Baltimore.

SCOUTING REPORT: Mountcastle's work to add strength to what began as a lanky frame and produce more loft with his swing has created an offensive profile built for the modern game. He delivers all-fields power and a swing geared for hard contact in all parts of the zone. Mountcastle's elite hands and good bat speed allow him to cover the whole plate and then some, though the team is trying to harness that and have him focus on where he can do the most damage. In left field, Mountcastle's deceptive athleticism will allow him, with experience, to make the necessary plays at a position where his well below-average arm won't be punished.

THE FUTURE: Mountcastle's potential at the plate was always enough to make him a first-division regular, especially as a left fielder or first baseman. There's little stopping him from being at least that for the 2021 Orioles.

SCOUTING GRADES: **Hitting:** 60 **Power:** 60 **Running:** 50 **Fielding:** 40 **Arm:** 30

Year	Age	Club (League)	Class	AVG	G	AB	R	H	2B	3B	HR	RBI	BB	SO	SB	OBP	SLG
2017	20	Bowie (EL)	AA	.222	39	153	18	34	13	0	3	15	3	35	0	.239	.366
	20	Frederick (CAR)	HiA	.314	88	360	63	113	35	1	15	47	14	61	8	.343	.542
2018	21	Bowie (EL)	AA	.297	102	394	63	117	19	4	13	59	26	79	2	.341	.464
2019	22	Norfolk (IL)	AAA	.312	127	520	81	162	35	1	25	83	24	130	2	.344	.527
2020	23	Baltimore (AL)	MAJ	.333	35	126	12	42	5	0	5	23	11	30	0	.386	.492
Major League Totals				.333	35	126	12	42	5	0	5	23	11	30	0	.386	.492
Minor League Totals				.295	524	2078	301	612	137	10	70	274	101	446	27	.328	.471

6 GUNNAR HENDERSON, SS

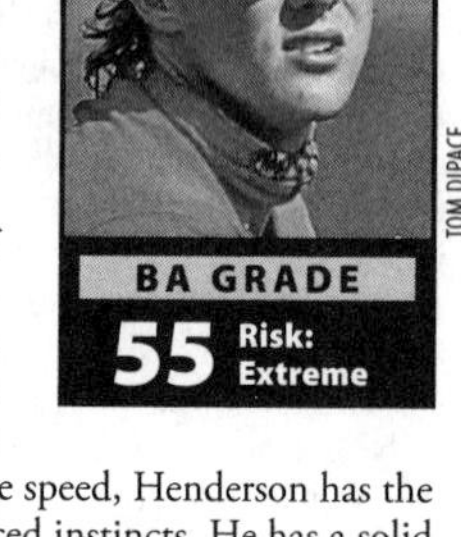
TOM DIPACE

BA GRADE
55 Risk: Extreme

Born: June 29, 2001. **B-T:** L-R. **HT:** 6-3. **WT:** 195. **Drafted:** HS—Selma, Ala., 2019 (2nd round). **Signed by:** David Jennings.

TRACK RECORD: The Orioles selected Henderson with the first pick of the second round in 2019 and signed him away from an Auburn commitment with an above-slot $2.3 million bonus. He got used to pro ball in the Rookie-level Gulf Coast League in 2019, and the Orioles added him to their alternate training site in the second week of August. As the youngest player there, Henderson struggled early before making strides against older competition.

SCOUTING REPORT: The Orioles quickly identified Henderson's lower half was lagging behind his top half at the alternate site, and the resulting adjustments allowed him to cover the plate better and have quality at-bats against advanced pitchers. Henderson's bat control gives him the potential to be an above-average hitter, and his adjustments may allow him to tap into his plus raw power during games more consistently. Despite a bigger frame and average speed, Henderson has the athleticism to stick at shortstop with at least an above-average arm and advanced instincts. He has a solid fallback option at third base, where his bat would play just fine.

THE FUTURE: Henderson's camp time made the Orioles more bullish about his upside as an everyday shortstop who can hit for power. He will still likely start at low Class A in 2021.

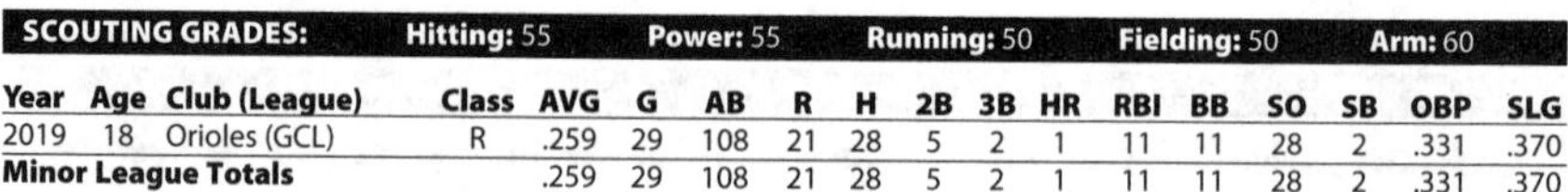

SCOUTING GRADES: **Hitting:** 55 **Power:** 55 **Running:** 50 **Fielding:** 50 **Arm:** 60

Year	Age	Club (League)	Class	AVG	G	AB	R	H	2B	3B	HR	RBI	BB	SO	SB	OBP	SLG
2019	18	Orioles (GCL)	R	.259	29	108	21	28	5	2	1	11	11	28	2	.331	.370
Minor League Totals				.259	29	108	21	28	5	2	1	11	11	28	2	.331	.370

7 YUSNIEL DIAZ, OF

MIKE CARLSON/MLB PHOTOS VIA GETTY IMAGES

BA GRADE
50 Risk: High

Born: Oct. 7, 1996. **B-T:** R-R. **HT:** 6-1. **WT:** 195. **Signed:** Cuba, 2015. **Signed by:** Ismael Cruz/Miguel Tosar/Roman Barinas (Dodgers).

TRACK RECORD: Diaz signed with the Dodgers for $15.5 million out of Cuba and came to the Orioles in the July 2018 trade that sent Manny Machado to Los Angeles. He has been stuck at Double-A Bowie since and returned there to spend the summer at the alternate training site in 2020. Diaz stayed healthy and performed well at the alternate site, but couldn't crack a crowded major league outfield group.

SCOUTING REPORT: The Orioles challenged Diaz both at the plate and in the outfield this summer to try to foster some growth. While Diaz has a good understanding of the strike zone, he can either stay under control and be an above-average hitter with average power, or sell out for plus power and sacrifice average. A combination of both seems unlikely at this point, though he hit plenty of home runs in the secondary camp. Diaz is best suited defensively as an average corner outfielder with a plus arm, though he can play center field as needed.

THE FUTURE: Diaz shows flashes of a special player when the lights come on, and the expectation is he can be a productive big leaguer once he gets there. He will have to perform at Triple-A in 2021 to get that chance.

SCOUTING GRADES: **Hitting:** 50 **Power:** 55 **Running:** 45 **Fielding:** 50 **Arm:** 60

Year	Age	Club (League)	Class	AVG	G	AB	R	H	2B	3B	HR	RBI	BB	SO	SB	OBP	SLG
2017	20	Tulsa (TL)	AA	.333	31	108	15	36	8	0	3	13	10	29	2	.390	.491
	20	R. Cucamonga (CAL)	HiA	.278	83	331	42	92	15	3	8	39	35	73	7	.343	.414
2018	21	Tulsa (TL)	AA	.314	59	220	36	69	10	4	6	30	41	39	8	.428	.477
	21	Bowie (EL)	AA	.239	38	134	23	32	5	1	5	15	18	28	4	.329	.403
2019	22	Bowie (EL)	AA	.262	76	286	45	75	19	4	11	53	32	67	0	.335	.472
	22	Aberdeen (NYP)	SS	.333	3	9	0	3	3	0	0	0	1	1	0	.455	.667
	22	Frederick (CAR)	HiA	.273	6	22	0	6	0	0	0	2	3	7	0	.360	.273
Minor League Totals				.278	381	1440	210	401	68	19	42	209	169	318	28	.355	.440

8 MIKE BAUMANN, RHP

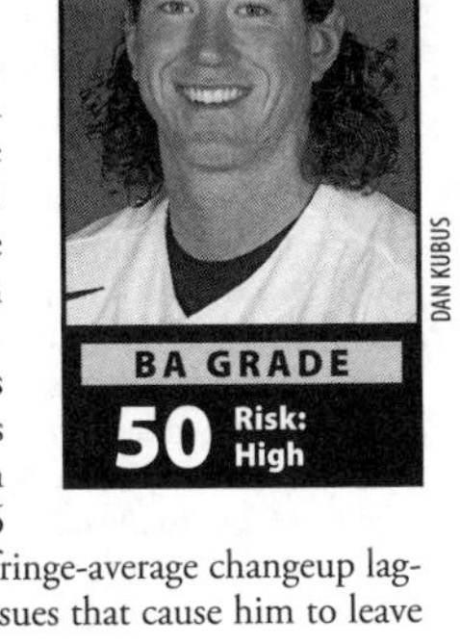
DAN KUBUS

BA GRADE
50 Risk: High

Born: Sept. 10, 1995. **B-T:** R-R. **HT:** 6-4. **WT:** 225. **Drafted:** Jacksonville, 2017 (3rd round). **Signed by:** Arthur McConnehead.

TRACK RECORD: A third-round pick who signed for $500,000 in 2017, Baumann quickly overpowered hitters at the lower levels and rose to Double-A Bowie in 2019. He threw a nine-inning no-hitter there and earned a share of the Orioles minor league pitcher of the year award after striking out 142 hitters in 124 innings. He was one of the most buzzworthy pitchers at the alternate training site in 2020, but a flexor mass strain in his elbow shut him down in August.

SCOUTING REPORT: Baumann pitches off a high-spin four-seam fastball that's routinely 93-96 mph and touches 99, yet yields mostly ground balls. His plus slider at 89-90 mph bites like a cutter and breaks bats like one, too, giving him another power offering. During the 2020 shutdown, he worked on a 12-to-6 curveball with good depth and spin that's his clear third pitch now, with his fringe-average changeup lagging behind. Baumann learned the adjustment required to correct delivery issues that cause him to leave pitches up in the zone at times.

THE FUTURE: Baumann's short-term health is a concern, but the pitcher he was before showed a mid-rotation ceiling. Added to the 40-man roster in November, he will likely start 2021 at Triple-A if healthy.

SCOUTING GRADES: **Fastball:** 60 **Slider:** 60 **Curveball:** 50 **Changeup:** 45 **Control:** 50

Year	Age	Club (League)	Class	W	L	ERA	G	GS	IP	H	HR	BB	SO	BB/9	SO/9	WHIP	AVG
2017	21	Aberdeen (NYP)	SS	4	2	1.31	10	9	41	25	2	19	41	4.1	8.9	1.06	.149
	21	Orioles (GCL)	R	0	0	0.00	1	1	1	2	0	0	2	0.0	18.0	2.00	.400
2018	22	Frederick (CAR)	HiA	8	5	3.88	17	17	93	82	9	40	59	3.9	5.7	1.32	.210
	22	Delmarva (SAL)	LoA	5	0	1.42	7	7	38	23	0	13	47	3.1	11.1	0.95	.160
2019	23	Bowie (EL)	AA	6	2	2.31	13	11	70	45	2	21	65	2.7	8.4	0.94	.168
	23	Frederick (CAR)	HiA	1	4	3.83	11	11	54	40	2	24	77	4.0	12.8	1.19	.179
Minor League Totals				24	13	2.82	59	56	297	217	15	117	291	3.6	8.8	1.12	.204

9 DEAN KREMER, RHP

TOP ROOKIE

MIKE CARLSON/MLB PHOTOS VIA GETTY IMAGES

BA GRADE
45 Risk: Medium

Born: Jan. 7, 1996. **B-T:** R-R. **HT:** 6-3. **WT:** 180. **Drafted:** Nevada-Las Vegas, 2016 (14th round). **Signed by:** Brian Compton (Dodgers).

TRACK RECORD: A 14th-round pick of the Dodgers out of Nevada-Las Vegas in 2016, Kremer came to the Orioles in the July 2018 trade for Manny Machado while on his way to leading the minor leagues with 176 strikeouts that year. In September 2020, he became the first prospect from the trade to reach the majors and delivered three strong starts for the Orioles before struggling in his final outing.

SCOUTING REPORT: Kremer's 2018 breakout came as he switched to a more vertical attack. He primarily works with a four-seam fastball in the low-to-mid 90s with significant ride and a swing-and-miss curveball in the mid 70s. Kremer primarily relies on those two pitches, but during the quarantine period he brought his cutter along to the point it became a weapon against hitters on both sides of the plate in the big leagues. His changeup remains the fourth pitch in his arsenal and is seen as a long-term growth area. Kremer lacks overpowering stuff, but his pitch mix and above-average control gets him plenty of swings and misses.

THE FUTURE: Kremer's strikeout proclivity makes him a good bet to be part of the long-term rotation. His September callup showed he's ready and should be in Baltimore's 2021 Opening Day rotation.

SCOUTING GRADES: **Fastball:** 55 **Cutter:** 50 **Curveball:** 60 **Changeup:** 40 **Control:** 55

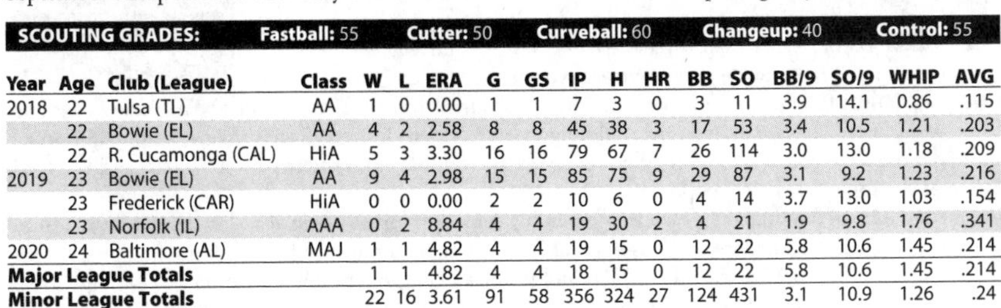

Year	Age	Club (League)	Class	W	L	ERA	G	GS	IP	H	HR	BB	SO	BB/9	SO/9	WHIP	AVG
2018	22	Tulsa (TL)	AA	1	0	0.00	1	1	7	3	0	3	11	3.9	14.1	0.86	.115
	22	Bowie (EL)	AA	4	2	2.58	8	8	45	38	3	17	53	3.4	10.5	1.21	.203
	22	R. Cucamonga (CAL)	HiA	5	3	3.30	16	16	79	67	7	26	114	3.0	13.0	1.18	.209
2019	23	Bowie (EL)	AA	9	4	2.98	15	15	85	75	9	29	87	3.1	9.2	1.23	.216
	23	Frederick (CAR)	HiA	0	0	0.00	2	2	10	6	0	4	14	3.7	13.0	1.03	.154
	23	Norfolk (IL)	AAA	0	2	8.84	4	4	19	30	2	4	21	1.9	9.8	1.76	.341
2020	24	Baltimore (AL)	MAJ	1	1	4.82	4	4	19	15	0	12	22	5.8	10.6	1.45	.214
Major League Totals				1	1	4.82	4	4	18	15	0	12	22	5.8	10.6	1.45	.214
Minor League Totals				22	16	3.61	91	58	356	324	27	124	431	3.1	10.9	1.26	.24

10 KEEGAN AKIN, LHP

MIKE CARLSON/MLB PHOTOS VIA GETTY IMAGES

BA GRADE
45 Risk: Medium

Born: April 1, 1995. **B-T:** L-L. **HT:** 6-0. **WT:** 225. **Drafted:** Western Michigan, 2016 (2nd round). **Signed by:** Dan Durst.

TRACK RECORD: From the moment he entered the organization in a pitching-heavy 2016 draft class, Akin's climb to the big league has been as low key as his personality. He arrived in Baltimore in Aug. 2020 and went on to strike out 12.3 batters per nine innings, mostly as a starter, as the Orioles went young in their rotation at the end of the 60-game season.

SCOUTING REPORT: Just as it did at every level in the minors, Akin's "invisi-ball" fastball was effective in missing bats and getting weak contact in the big leagues. Delivered at mostly 92-95 mph, the pitch has elite vertical movement, jumps on hitters due to Akin's deceptive delivery, and benefits from the lefty's ability to throw it inside to both lefties and righties. Akin spent all of 2019 at Triple-A Norfolk working on his slider and changeup, both of which were in the low 80s, but during the shutdown he worked on a slower curveball that was often his primary breaking ball in the majors.

THE FUTURE: Akin's ceiling as a back-end starter didn't change in his major league cameo. He will at least occupy the back of the Orioles' rotation until the younger wave of starting pitchers are ready to challenge him. He could still provide value as a swingman but will remain in the rotation in 2021.

SCOUTING GRADES: **Fastball:** 55 **Slider:** 45 **Curveball:** 55 **Changeup:** 50 **Control:** 50

Year	Age	Club (League)	Class	W	L	ERA	G	GS	IP	H	HR	BB	SO	BB/9	SO/9	WHIP	AVG
2017	22	Frederick (CAR)	HiA	7	8	4.14	21	21	100	89	12	46	111	4.1	10.0	1.35	.210
2018	23	Bowie (EL)	AA	14	7	3.27	25	25	138	114	16	58	142	3.8	9.3	1.25	.199
2019	24	Norfolk (IL)	AAA	6	7	4.73	25	24	112	109	10	61	131	4.9	10.5	1.51	.228
2020	25	Baltimore (AL)	MAJ	1	2	4.56	8	6	26	27	3	10	35	3.5	12.3	1.44	.262
Major League Totals				1	2	4.56	8	6	25	27	3	10	35	3.5	12.3	1.44	.262
Minor League Totals				27	23	3.78	80	79	376	327	38	172	413	4.1	9.9	1.33	.233

11 JORDAN WESTBURG, SS

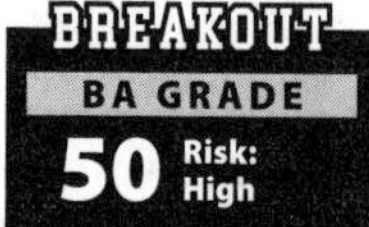
BREAKOUT
BA GRADE
50 Risk: High

Born: Feb. 18, 1999. **B-T:** R-R HT: 6-3. **WT:** 203. **Drafted:** Mississippi State, 2020 (1st round supplemental). **Signed by:** David Jennings.

TRACK RECORD: A breakout summer in the Cape Cod League carried into an improved spring for Westburg at Mississippi State before the college season shut down. The Orioles drafted him 30th overall and signed him for $2.37 million. Westburg made his organizational debut in instructional league and impressed as one of the top performers in camp.

SCOUTING REPORT: Of all the developments Westburg made over his college career, the Orioles were glad to see one continue into the camp: his refined batting eye. Swing-and-miss issues have plagued Westburg at times, but he cut down on his chasing and swung at good pitches in the fall. That development allowed him to better tap into his plus power to all fields and be at least an average hitter. Westburg's athleticism and defense were never a concern. He's a tremendous athlete and plus runner with the instincts and actions to stay at shortstop and the arm to move to third base if needed.

THE FUTURE: Everything Westburg does defensively would make him a useful major leaguer. His continued progress with the bat will what elevates him to a solid everyday player.

Year	Age	Club (League)	Class	AVG	G	AB	R	H	2B	3B	HR	RBI	BB	SO	SB	OBP	SLG
2020	21	Did not play—No minor league season															

12 KYLE BRADISH, RHP

BA GRADE
50 Risk: High

Born: Sept. 12, 1996. **B-T:** R-R. **HT:** 6-4. **WT:** 190. **Drafted:** New Mexico State, 2018 (4th round). **Signed by:** Chad Hermansen (Angels).

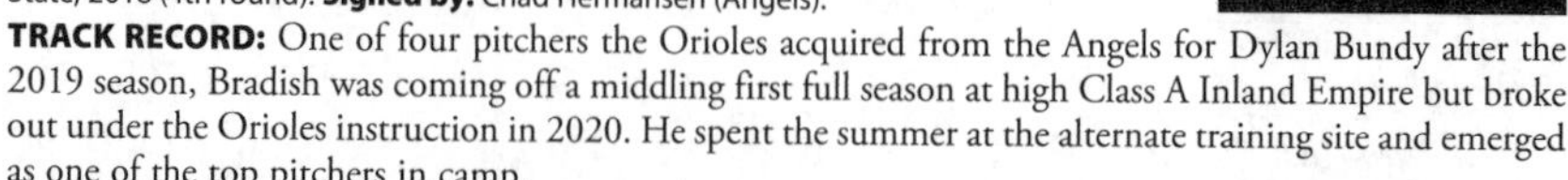

TRACK RECORD: One of four pitchers the Orioles acquired from the Angels for Dylan Bundy after the 2019 season, Bradish was coming off a middling first full season at high Class A Inland Empire but broke out under the Orioles instruction in 2020. He spent the summer at the alternate training site and emerged as one of the top pitchers in camp.

SCOUTING REPORT: While there's some effort in his delivery, Bradish's high arm slot allows him to utilize a unique, vertical-attacking arsenal. His work at home after the shutdown helped him refine his delivery and sit consistently 92-94 mph and reach 96 on his unusual cutting, riding fastball. His 87-88 mph average changeup can be firm but benefits from him maintaining his arm speed and selling it well. Bradish also uses two distinct breaking balls with an above-average slider in the mid-80s and plunging curveball in the low 80s. He keeps hitters off balance by using all four pitches in advantageous spots, but he needs to cut down on his walks that have been a problem since college.

THE FUTURE: Bradish will need to have long-term success to make the Bundy trade seem worthwhile. There's a chance he can slot into the No. 4 spot in a big league rotation quickly.

Year	Age	Club (League)	Class	W	L	ERA	G	GS	IP	H	HR	BB	SO	BB/9	SO/9	WHIP	AVG
2019	22	Inland Empire (CAL)	HiA	6	7	4.28	24	18	101	90	9	53	120	4.7	10.7	1.42	.203
Minor League Totals				6	7	4.28	24	18	101	90	9	53	120	4.7	10.7	1.42	.235

13 HUNTER HARVEY, RHP

BA GRADE
50 Risk: High

Born: Dec. 9, 1994. **B-T:** R-R. **HT:** 6-3 WT: 210. **Drafted:** HS—Catawba, N.C., 2013 (1st round). **Signed by:** Chris Gale.

TRACK RECORD: Harvey was the Orioles' top prospect after signing for a $1.95 million bonus in 2013 and dominating low Class A Delmarva in his first full season. Elbow injuries that led to Tommy John surgery along with subsequent shoulder issues meant the only healthy season was 2019, when he made his major league debut in the Orioles' bullpen. He missed most of the 2020 season with forearm soreness.

SCOUTING REPORT: Through his health issues, Harvey has maintained an electric fastball that sits in the upper 90s and reaches 99 mph, though it can be flat at times. While he's always had at least an above-average breaking ball, Harvey added a splitter in 2019 that flashed above-average but wasn't as consistent in 2020. That can be his primary out pitch should he throw it with proper arm speed instead of trying to slow down and get better shape on it. Harvey throws strikes with average control, but he's never shown the ability to stay on the mound for long.

THE FUTURE: Harvey's health remains difficult to rely on. Still, with any luck he can be a top-level setup man in the majors.

Year	Age	Club (League)	Class	W	L	ERA	G	GS	IP	H	HR	BB	SO	BB/9	SO/9	WHIP	AVG
2020	25	Baltimore (AL)	MAJ	0	2	4.15	10	0	9	8	2	2	6	2.1	6.2	1.15	.242
Major League Totals				1	2	3.00	17	0	15	11	3	6	17	3.6	10.2	1.13	.200
Minor League Totals				11	16	3.67	73	58	252	222	24	86	300	3.1	10.7	1.22	.236

14 BRUCE ZIMMERMANN, LHP

Born: Feb. 9, 1995. **B-T:** L-L. **HT:** 6-2. **WT:** 215. **Drafted:** Mount Olive (N.C.), 2017 (5th round). **Signed by:** Billy Best (Braves).

TRACK RECORD: Zimmermann transferred from Towson University, which is located in Baltimore County, and was drafted by the Braves out of Division II Mount Olive, but it didn't take long for him to come home as part of the Orioles' return in the Kevin Gausman trade in 2018. Zimmermann was masterful in the Double-A Eastern League in 2019 before making his major league debut in 2020.

SCOUTING REPORT: A specialized strength program and mechanical work at Driveline Baseball had Zimmermann throwing harder this summer, with his fastball still sitting 90-93 mph with some hop and reaching 95 mph on occasion. He uses a solid-average changeup against righthanded hitters and can throw a mid-80s slider to both sides, although it is more of a fringy offering. He also features a slower, fringy curveball. While not overpowering, Zimmermann has a plan on the mound and average control. He needs to locate everything, especially his fastball, to be effective.

THE FUTURE: Zimmermann won't be guaranteed a rotation spot in 2021, but he has the mettle to hang on to one if given the chance. Long-term, he's likely an up-and-down starter or swingman.

Year	Age	Club (League)	Class	W	L	ERA	G	GS	IP	H	HR	BB	SO	BB/9	SO/9	WHIP	AVG
2020	25	Baltimore (AL)	MAJ	0	0	7.71	2	1	7	6	2	2	7	2.6	9.0	1.14	.222
Major League Totals				0	0	7.71	2	1	7	6	2	2	7	2.6	9.0	1.14	.222
Minor League Totals				18	14	3.20	61	60	298	277	22	105	303	3.2	9.2	1.28	.245

15 ADAM HALL, SS/2B

BA GRADE **50** Risk: Very High

Born: May 22, 1999. **B-T:** R-R. **HT:** 6-0. **WT:** 170. **Drafted:** HS—London, Ont., 2017 (2nd round). **Signed by:** Chris Reitsma.

TRACK RECORD: The Orioles have spent the last five years using early draft picks on infielders, including taking Hall with the 60th overall pick in 2017 and signing him for $1.3 million. Hall was a South Atlantic League all-star with low Class A Delmarva in his full season debut in 2019 and returned to the field in 2020 for instructional league.

SCOUTING REPORT: A year away from game action is particularly impactful for young hitters, and the coronavirus pandemic and corresponding shutdown meant Hall didn't get much chance to grow. A gap hitter who hits line drives and turns them into extra-base hits with his plus speed, Hall remains a future average hitter whose power may top out at 15 home runs. He could be an average shortstop with cleaner actions, with second base a fallback. Like many youngsters, he is a player with considerable talent but needs repetitions to grow and develop.

THE FUTURE: What could have been a breakout season for Hall turned into a lost one. His speed, versatility and makeup keep him on track for a major league future either as an everyday infielder or utilityman.

Year	Age	Club (League)	Class	AVG	G	AB	R	H	2B	3B	HR	RBI	BB	SO	SB	OBP	SLG
2019	20	Delmarva (SAL)	LoA	.298	122	463	78	138	22	4	5	45	45	117	33	.385	.395
Minor League Totals				.301	186	694	117	209	32	8	6	71	62	177	56	.382	.396

16 KEVIN SMITH, LHP

BA GRADE **45** Risk: High

Born: May 13, 1997. **B-T:** L-L. **HT:** 6-5. **WT:** 200. **Drafted:** Georgia, 2018 (7th round). **Signed by:** Tommy Jackson (Mets).

TRACK RECORD: Smith made it to Double-A Binghamton by the end of his first full season in 2019 and was the Mets' minor league pitcher of the year. The Orioles acquired him at the 2020 trade deadline as the top player in the return for reliever Miguel Castro.

SCOUTING REPORT: Smith joins a well-stocked group of lefthanders without premium velocity in the Orioles' system, but he distinguishes himself by how he creates deception with a lower arm slot from his tall frame. He has both a two-seam and four-seam fastball around 90 mph that helps him attack lefties. His slider can be a plus pitch and he has an average but effective changeup. He throws everything with average control. The combination of Smith's deception and pitchability helped him strike out 10 batters per nine innings in his pro debut despite a lack of big velocity.

THE FUTURE: Smith profiles as a No. 5 starter with the pitches to be an effective reliever if needed. There should be plenty of opportunity in the Orioles' rotation soon.

Year	Age	Club (League)	Class	W	L	ERA	G	GS	IP	H	HR	BB	SO	BB/9	SO/9	WHIP	AVG
2019	22	Binghamton (EL)	AA	3	2	3.45	6	6	31	25	1	15	28	4.3	8.0	1.28	.238
	22	St. Lucie (FSL)	HiA	5	5	3.05	17	17	86	83	5	24	102	2.5	10.7	1.25	.223
Minor League Totals				12	8	2.75	35	26	140	120	7	45	158	2.9	10.1	1.17	.237

17 ZAC LOWTHER, LHP

BA GRADE **45** Risk: High

Born: April 30, 1996. **B-T:** L-L. **HT:** 6-2. **WT:** 235. **Drafted:** Xavier, 2017 (2nd round supplemental). **Signed by:** Adrian Dorsey.

TRACK RECORD: Lowther won the Orioles minor league pitcher of the year award in 2018 and was an Eastern League all-star at Double-A Bowie in 2019. He didn't get to pitch much in 2020. He suffered an oblique injury during the coronavirus shutdown that made him a late addition to the alternate training site and finished the year in instructional league, where he visibly wasn't at his best.

SCOUTING REPORT: For all his good results, Lowther has never done it with dominating stuff. He gets tremendous extension in his delivery that allows his 88-91 mph fastball to jump on hitters and make it difficult to square up. Lowther generally has good command but can lose it for spells, and needs it to be perfect considering neither his changeup nor his high-spin curveball project to be more than average pitches. He worked during the shutdown to add a slider in the 80-81 mph range to give him two defined breaking balls.

THE FUTURE: Lowther has a ceiling as a No. 5 or depth starter, but that ceiling isn't far off. He'll start 2021 at Triple-A and has a chance to make his major league debut during the year.

Year	Age	Club (League)	Class	W	L	ERA	G	GS	IP	H	HR	BB	SO	BB/9	SO/9	WHIP	AVG
2019	23	Bowie (EL)	AA	13	7	2.55	26	26	148	102	8	63	154	3.8	9.4	1.11	.172
Minor League Totals				23	13	2.26	61	59	326	223	17	109	380	3.0	10.5	1.02	.194

18 ALEXANDER WELLS, LHP

BA GRADE 45 **Risk:** High

Born: Feb. 27, 1997. **B-T:** L-L. **HT:** 6-1. **WT:** 190. **Signed:** Australia, 2015. **Signed by:** Brett Ward/Mike Snyder.

TRACK RECORD: A $300,000 international signee, Wells has been an all-star at every level in the minors in his four professional seasons. He went back to his native Australia after spring training shut down due to the coronavirus pandemic and did not return for safety reasons this summer, instead opting to work out and pitch in his home country.

SCOUTING REPORT: Wells' four-seam fastball lives around 88-91 mph, and his plus command allows him to hit his spots inside to both lefthanded and righthanded batters. His changeup has plus potential to give him a swing-and-miss offering. His average curveball was his only breaking ball until he recently began throwing a harder slider to have an offering nearer his fastball in velocity. That pitch progressed well in his remote work. Even if the jump in velocity many have waited for never comes, Wells' command and pitchability mean his success is no fluke.

THE FUTURE: Wells is a soft-tossing lefty with a No. 5 starter profile. He'll begin 2021 in Triple-A and has a chance to make his major league debut during the year.

Year	Age	Club (League)	Class	W	L	ERA	G	GS	IP	H	HR	BB	SO	BB/9	SO/9	WHIP	AVG
2019	22	Bowie (EL)	AA	8	6	2.95	24	24	137	123	10	24	105	1.6	6.9	1.07	.231
Minor League Totals				30	24	2.82	86	86	475	431	46	76	369	1.4	7.0	1.07	.239

19 HUDSON HASKIN, OF

BA GRADE 45 **Risk:** High

Born: Dec. 31, 1998. **B-T:** R-R. **HT:** 6-2. **WT:** 200. **Drafted:** Tulane, 2020 (2nd round). **Signed by:** David Jennings.

TRACK RECORD: Haskin comes from the same Connecticut high school, Avon Old Farms, that produced a five-tool outfielder in Astros star George Springer. Haskin hit from day one at Tulane and was drafted 39th overall by the Orioles in 2020 as a draft-eligible sophomore, signing for $1.91 million.

SCOUTING REPORT: Haskin has a chance to be the total package more than any other outfielder in the Orioles' system. He's at least a plus runner and has the tools to be an above-average center fielder with an above-average arm. Haskins' swing can get a little long and isn't for everyone. He has unique mechanics geared more for line drives than loft, but the Orioles like the work he's done on it and his moldable nature. An average hitter with 15-20 home runs is possible with further development. Haskin's work ethic and discipline are an asset.

THE FUTURE: Haskin's progress with his swing and approach will determine how high he climbs. All the tools are there for him to be a well-rounded, everyday regular.

Year	Age	Club (League)	Class	AVG	G	AB	R	H	2B	3B	HR	RBI	BB	SO	SB	OBP	SLG
2020	21	Did not play—No minor league season															

20 LUIS GONZALEZ, OF

BREAKOUT

BA GRADE 50 **Risk:** Extreme

Born: Nov. 2, 2002. **B-T:** L-L. **HT:** 6-4. **WT:** 185. **Signed:** Dominican Republic, 2019. **Signed by:** Rafael Belen.

TRACK RECORD: The Orioles brought more than a dozen players from their 2018 and 2019 international signing classes to Florida for instructional league, the first fruits of their return to the Latin American market after years of dormancy. One of the crown jewels of those efforts is Gonzalez, who signed for $475,000 in 2019, the Orioles' largest bonus awarded that year.

SCOUTING REPORT: Gonzalez brought what could grow into plus power to the U.S., wowing the Orioles' staff with tape-measure home runs. Some work will be required with his swing to quicken his trigger, but there's belief he could grow into an average hitter as he develops an approach. His performance against live pitching has been uneven, though, with long arms that get him tied up and timing issues he will need to improve to cut down on his whiffs. Gonzalez has a tall, lean frame that's very projectable, with slightly below-average speed that will probably slow down as he fills out and limit him to a corner outfield spot.

THE FUTURE: Gonzalez still hasn't played an organized game without any Dominican Summer League action in 2020, but could come stateside for a professional debut next summer. The Orioles' see great potential for an everyday slugging corner outfielder, though that ceiling is years away.

Year	Age	Club (League)	Class	AVG	G	AB	R	H	2B	3B	HR	RBI	BB	SO	SB	OBP	SLG
2020	17	Did not play—No minor league season															

21 TERRIN VAVRA, SS/2B

BA GRADE
45 Risk: High

Born: May 12, 1997. **B-T:** L-R. **HT:** 6-1. **WT:** 185. **Drafted:** Minnesota, 2018 (3rd round). **Signed by:** Brett Baldwin (Rockies).

TRACK RECORD: Vavra comes from a baseball family. His father Joe was the Tigers' hitting coach in 2020 and his brothers Tanner and Trey both played professionally. Terrin is carving out quite a path for himself. He was an All-American at Minnesota, was drafted by the Rockies in the third round and won the MVP of the low Class A South Atlantic League in his first full season in 2019. The Orioles acquired him at the 2020 trade deadline as part of the Mychal Givens trade.

SCOUTING REPORT: Vavra is a difficult out for pitchers and walked as many times as he struck out (62) in 2019. He boasts an advanced approach and a smooth, line-drive swing from the left side that allows him to square the ball up and drive it. While Vavra has average speed, he's an above-average baserunner with good jumps and instincts. He has good actions on the infield, but his fringe-average arm limits him to second base. The Orioles tried him in left field and center field in the fall.

THE FUTURE: Vavra has all the makings of a trustworthy big leaguer who can give his team consistent at-bats and handle multiple positions. He likely fits as a platoon player or second-division regular.

Year	Age	Club (League)	Class	AVG	G	AB	R	H	2B	3B	HR	RBI	BB	SO	SB	OBP	SLG
2019	22	Asheville (SAL)	LoA	.318	102	374	79	119	32	1	10	52	62	62	18	.409	.489
Minor League Totals				.313	146	543	101	170	40	5	14	78	88	102	27	.405	.483

22 RYAN MCKENNA, OF

BA GRADE
45 Risk: High

Born: Feb. 14, 1997. **B-T:** R-R. **HT:** 5-11. **WT:** 185. **Drafted:** HS—Dover, N.H., 2015 (4th round). **Signed by:** Kirk Fredriksson.

TRACK RECORD: McKenna was always a long-lead prospect as a New England high schooler, but even in that context he has never had a sustained period of high-level production outside of a half-season at high Class A Frederick in 2018. McKenna spent 2020 at the alternate training site, where he focused on improving all aspects of his offensive game.

SCOUTING REPORT: McKenna worked to improve his approach at the alternate site, benefiting from the organization's new hitting coaches and philosophy. Hitting the ball harder was a point of emphasis, too. McKenna is at his best when he takes an all-fields approach that allows him to spray line drives instead of changing his swing for power. He will likely top out as an average hitter with below-average power, and needs work to reach even those thresholds. McKenna is a plus runner with good instincts on the bases and has long shown the ability to play an above-average center field with an above-average arm.

THE FUTURE: McKenna's speed and defense will keep getting him chances. He's going to have to improve at the plate to win even a bench role in the majors leagues.

Year	Age	Club (League)	Class	AVG	G	AB	R	H	2B	3B	HR	RBI	BB	SO	SB	OBP	SLG
2019	22	Bowie (EL)	AA	.232	135	488	78	113	26	6	9	54	59	121	25	.321	.365
Minor League Totals				.264	460	1680	269	443	95	14	28	178	196	415	72	.350	.387

23 DREW ROM, LHP

BA GRADE
45 Risk: High

Born: Dec. 15, 1999. **B-T:** L-L. **HT:** 6-2. **WT:** 170. **Drafted:** HS—Fort Thomas, Ky., 2018 (4th round). **Signed by:** Adrian Dorsey.

TRACK RECORD: Rom had a strong commitment to Michigan as Kentucky's Mr. Baseball in 2018, but he signed with the Orioles instead for an above-slot $650,000 bonus. After an all-star debut at low Class A Delmarva in 2019, Rom pitched against former big leaguers in a local developmental league during the summer coronavirus shutdown and finished the year in instructional league.

SCOUTING REPORT: Rom is one of many soft-tossing Orioles lefties whose fastball sits around 90 mph. His athletic frame and delivery give hope his velocity will tick up, but it's currently no more than a fringe-average pitch. Rom' pitch mix was able to keep low-level hitters off balance for elite strikeout rates for a teenager in 2019. He features a curveball, slider and changeup that all have average potential. He is a fringe-average strike-thrower who boasts more control than command at present. The hope is that as Rom matures physically, he could gain more power with his easy delivery and a true out pitch will emerge.

THE FUTURE: Rom will be part of a crowded low-minors rotation mix in the Orioles system in 2021. He'll need to add power to reach his ceiling as a back-end starter.

Year	Age	Club (League)	Class	W	L	ERA	G	GS	IP	H	HR	BB	SO	BB/9	SO/9	WHIP	AVG
2019	19	Delmarva (SAL)	LoA	6	3	2.93	21	15	95	83	5	33	122	3.1	11.5	1.22	.217
Minor League Totals				6	5	2.64	31	24	126	103	6	39	150	2.8	10.7	1.13	.218

24 KYLE STOWERS, OF

BREAKOUT
BA GRADE
45 Risk: High

Born: Jan. 2, 1998. **B-T:** L-L. **HT:** 6-3. **WT:** 200. **Drafted:** Stanford, 2019 (2nd round supplemental). **Signed by:** Scott Walter.

TRACK RECORD: A glut of prospect outfielders didn't stop the Orioles from loading up on more early in the 2019 draft, led by Stowers in the supplemental second round. He signed for a $884,200 bonus and was a New York-Penn League all-star with short-season Aberdeen in his professional debut, but didn't get any organized action in 2020 until instructional league.

SCOUTING REPORT: Stowers boasted some of the highest average exit velocities among college hitters in 2019. He will show plus power with a nice swing when he gets the barrel to the ball, but he swings and misses too much to be more than an .240-.250 hitter, at best. He has the athleticism and reads to cover in center field in a pinch, but he's likely better suited for right field long term.

THE FUTURE: Stowers has the pieces to be an everyday right fielder if he can make enough contact to consistently tap into his power. There are significant questions whether he will be able to do so.

Year	Age	Club (League)	Class	AVG	G	AB	R	H	2B	3B	HR	RBI	BB	SO	SB	OBP	SLG
2019	21	Aberdeen (NYP)	SS	.216	55	204	19	44	13	1	6	23	20	53	5	.289	.377
Minor League Totals				.216	55	204	19	44	13	1	6	23	20	53	5	.289	.377

25 GARRETT STALLINGS, RHP

BA GRADE
45 Risk: High

Born: Aug. 8, 1997. **B-T:** R-R. **HT:** 6-1. **WT:** 210. **Drafted:** Tennessee, 2019 (5th round). **Signed by:** Joel Murrie (Angels).

TRACK RECORD: Stallings served as the Friday night starter at Tennessee and was drafted in the fifth round by the Angels in 2019. He did not pitch after signing, but he briefly pitched at the Angels' alternate training site in 2020 before finishing in instructional league. The Orioles, encouraged by what they saw at instructs, acquired Stallings and righthander Jean Pinto in exchange for Jose Iglesias after the season.

SCOUTING REPORT: Stallings is a polished righthander who mixes his pitches, limits his walks and lasts deep into his starts. His fastball sits 90-92 mph and his short, sharp mid-80s slider is his best secondary offering. Stallings mixes in an average low-80s changeup he commands well and a big, upper-70s curveball he is trying to throw for more strikes early in the count. He has a smooth, up-tempo delivery that is easy to repeat and allows him to command and sequence his four-pitch repertoire effectively.

THE FUTURE: Stallings has a chance to move fast because of his command, advanced feel for pitching and business-like approach. His lack of a plus pitch limits his ceiling to a back-of-the-rotation starter.

Year	Age	Club (League)	Class	W	L	ERA	G	GS	IP	H	HR	BB	SO	BB/9	SO/9	WHIP	AVG
2019	21	Did not play—Injured															

26 ANTHONY SERVIDEO, SS

Born: March 11, 1999. **B-T:** L-R HT: 5-10. **WT:** 175. **Drafted:** Mississippi, 2020 (3rd round). **Signed by:** David Jennings.

TRACK RECORD: Servideo joins the Orioles with club roots already in place. His grandfather Curt Blefary played four seasons in Baltimore and was a World Series champion with the 1966 Orioles. Serviedo had a difficult summer in the Cape Cod League in 2019, but he returned to Ole Miss in the spring and showed the ability to play shortstop while making significant offensive improvements. The Orioles drafted him in the third round and signed him for an above-slot $950,000 bonus.

SCOUTING REPORT: Servideo only began playing shortstop in 2020, but the Orioles love the ability and mindset he brings in playing all over the field for the good of the team. His athleticism serves him well in both his prospects for staying at shortstop, in terms of his reactions and range, and on the bases, where he runs well. His defense, at this point, is his calling card even if he ends up playing somewhere other than short. Servideo's defense and speed are his main assets. He's a below-average hitter with little power potential, but he may hit just enough in a utility role.

THE FUTURE: Servideo will need to further build on his breakout junior season to be more than a fringe major leaguer. He will make his pro debut in 2021.

Year	Age	Club (League)	Class	AVG	G	AB	R	H	2B	3B	HR	RBI	BB	SO	SB	OBP	SLG
2020	21	Did not play—No minor league season															

27 COBY MAYO, 3B

BA GRADE
45 Risk: Extreme

Born: Dec. 10, 2001. **B-T:** R-R. **HT:** 6-5. **WT:** 215. **Drafted:** HS—Parkland, Fla, 2020 (4th round). **Signed by:** Brandon Verley.

TRACK RECORD: A Florida commit from the same high school as Cubs star Anthony Rizzo, Mayo showed prodigious power both on the showcase circuit and against good prep competition in games. The Orioles drafted him in the fourth round and signed him for $1.75 million, more than $1 million over slot. Mayo got his first taste of professional baseball in instructional league.

SCOUTING REPORT: Mayo boasts plus-plus raw power but needs to adjust his swing to get to it. His main goal is to get his swing shortened and smooth enough to hit for average and make enough contact to tap into that power in games. Mayo had scout interest as a pitcher in high school and boasts a plus arm at third base. He has a big frame and is a fringe-average runner, but the hope is he can stay agile and fit enough to be an average defensive third baseman in time.

THE FUTURE: Mayo is a long way from his ceiling as a power-hitting third baseman. He'll make his pro debut in 2021.

Year	Age	Club (League)	Class	AVG	G	AB	R	H	2B	3B	HR	RBI	BB	SO	SB	OBP	SLG
2020	18	Did not play—No minor league season															

28 TYLER NEVIN, 1B/3B

BA GRADE
40 Risk: High

Born: May 29, 1997. **B-T:** R-R. **HT:** 6-4. **WT:** 225. **Drafted:** HS—Poway, Calif., 2015 (1st round supplemental). **Signed by:** Jon Lukens (Rockies).

TRACK RECORD: The son of former all-star third baseman Phil Nevin, Tyler signed with the Rockies for $2 million as the 38th overall pick in the 2015 draft. He battled a series of injuries after signing, including to his hamstring, wrist and groin, but still hit his way to Double-A as a 21-year-old. The Orioles acquired Nevin as part of the haul for Mychal Givens at the 2020 trade deadline.

SCOUTING REPORT: Nevin is a prototypical corner infielder after beginning his career at third base and now settling in at first base. He has plus raw power, but with a smooth swing geared for line drives, he hasn't been able to tap into it in games. Nevin hits the ball hard, especially to the right-center gap like his dad, and is working to start driving it over the wall. He has an advanced approach that leads to high walk totals and advantageous counts. Nevin doesn't offer much defensively at either corner and has a fringy arm, so it will be on his bat to get him to the majors.

THE FUTURE: Nevin's positional profile creates a high offensive bar. He'll need to translate his hard contact into power production to be more than a bench player.

Year	Age	Club (League)	Class	AVG	G	AB	R	H	2B	3B	HR	RBI	BB	SO	SB	OBP	SLG
2019	22	Hartford (EL)	AA	.251	130	466	60	117	26	2	13	61	65	90	6	.345	.399
Minor League Totals				.286	366	1362	198	390	88	7	36	193	155	274	23	.362	.441

29 DARELL HERNAIZ, SS

BA GRADE
45 Risk: Extreme

Born: Aug. 3, 2001. **B-T:** R-R. **HT:** 6-1. **WT:** 170. **Drafted:** HS—El Paso, Texas, 2019 (5th round). **Signed by:** John Gillette.

TRACK RECORD: Hernaiz stood out as a toolsy infielder who was still 17 years old at the time of the 2019 draft. The Orioles drafted him in the fifth round and signed him for a below-slot $400,000 to forgo a Texas Tech commitment. Hernaiz posted a .371 on-base percentage in the Rookie-level Gulf Coast League after signing and impressed opposing scouts during 2020 instructional league.

SCOUTING REPORT: Hernaiz's youth shows at times, but there's plenty for the Orioles to mold. He has natural contact skills and projects for average power with the loft in his swing. Further refinement of his mechanics and approach could boost his offensive output. Hernaiz is a tremendous athlete who can stay up the middle on the infield dirt. He has the actions and instincts to stick at shortstop and average arm that will play at third base if he outgrows the position.

THE FUTURE: From a developmental standpoint, the Orioles thought young high school hitters would be the ones most affected by the loss of the 2020 minor league season. The hope is the year away doesn't knock Hernaiz too far off his long-term projection as a solid utilityman.

Year	Age	Club (League)	Class	AVG	G	AB	R	H	2B	3B	HR	RBI	BB	SO	SB	OBP	SLG
2019	17	Orioles (GCL)	R	.263	29	99	19	26	2	1	2	8	17	26	5	.371	.364
Minor League Totals				.263	29	99	19	26	2	1	2	8	17	26	5	.371	.364

30 CARTER BAUMLER, RHP

BA GRADE
45 **Risk: Extreme**

Born: Jan. 31, 2002. **B-T:** R-R HT: 6-2. **WT:** 195. **Drafted:** HS—West Des Moines, Iowa, 2020 (5th round). **Signed by:** Scott Thomas.

TRACK RECORD: Not many teams got to see Baumler in 2020 as a cold-weather pitcher in Iowa, but the Orioles were sent Edgertronic video to keep up with his work in the spring. They drafted him in the fifth round and signed him away from a strong Texas Christian commitment for $1.5 million as the only pitcher in their six-player draft class. Baumler impressed at instructional league, but he left an outing with an elbow injury and subsequently had Tommy John surgery.

SCOUTING REPORT: Baumler's injury came as a surprise because he has a sound, simple delivery and a clean arm path. Before surgery, his fastball sat 88-92 mph with room for more velocity as he filled out and gained strength. He showed advanced feel for a potentially average changeup and could spin a slider that flashed average potential. The hope was Baumler would get into player development, fill out and all his stuff would tick up. Now, he'll likely be out until 2022.

THE FUTURE: The Orioles liked what they saw from Baumler at instructs but will have to wait at least a year for him to get back on the mound. If his stuff returns, there's a feeling he could be a mid-rotation starter at his peak.

Year	Age	Club (League)	Class	W	L	ERA	G	GS	IP	H	HR	BB	SO	BB/9	SO/9	WHIP	AVG
2020	18	Did not play—No minor league season															

MORE PROSPECTS TO KNOW

31 RYLAN BANNON, 3B/2B

Part of the Manny Machado trade return, Bannon has a powerful swing and good plate discipline but is still working to find a defensive home.

32 BRENAN HANIFEE, RHP

SLEEPER

A sinkerballer who got away from his bread and butter in 2019, Hanifee used the shutdown to get back on track and improve his delivery to make his breaking ball and changeup more consistent.

33 CODY SEDLOCK, RHP

Sedlock was the Orioles' top pick in 2016, but injuries have knocked him off track. He regained his four-seam fastball in 2019 and has the quality of secondary pitches to have a starter's mix going forward.

34 DILLON TATE, RHP

The fourth overall pick in 2015 is on his third organization, but has found a home in the Orioles' bullpen as a potential setup man. He can maintain a mid-90s sinker and has a usable slider and changeup.

35 LUIS ORTIZ, LHP

Ortiz was another featured international signing in 2019 and signed for a $400,000 bonus. His fastball is already up to 95 mph and has room to tick up as he grows into his lean frame.

36 BLAINE KNIGHT, RHP

Knight was a starter at Arkansas and signed for an above-slot $1.1 million as the Orioles' third-round pick in 2018, but by the end of 2019 had lost his delivery. The Orioles believe he can turn it around.

37 ISAAC BELLONY, OF

One of the final international signings the Orioles made in the Dan Duquette era, Bellony signed for $220,000 in 2018 and shows switch-hitting prowess, good speed and strong arm.

38 OFELKY PERALTA, RHP

With an upper-90s fastball, Peralta has long tantalized the Orioles but was brought along too quickly earlier in his career. A reset back to low Class A Delmarva in 2019 helped, and the Orioles hope they can continue to develop his pitches and keep him in the strike zone.

39 ISAAC MATTSON, RHP

Mattson was one of four pitchers the Orioles acquired from the Angels for Dylan Bundy in 2019. He has a high-spin, low-90s fastball and good command and poise on the mound.

40 LEONEL SANCHEZ, SS

Signed for $400,000 in the Orioles' 2019 international class, Sanchez is a glove-first shortstop with good actions at the position. His bat will need to come a long way as he progresses..•

TOP PROSPECTS OF THE DECADE

Year	Player, Pos	2020 Org
2011	Manny Machado, SS	Padres
2012	Dylan Bundy, RHP	Angels
2013	Dylan Bundy, RHP	Angels
2014	Dylan Bundy, RHP	Angels
2015	Dylan Bundy, RHP	Angels
2016	Dylan Bundy, RHP	Angels
2017	Chance Sisco, C	Orioles
2018	Austin Hays, OF	Orioles
2019	Yusniel Diaz, OF	Orioles
2020	Adley Rutschman, C	Orioles

TOP DRAFT PICKS OF THE DECADE

Year	Player, Pos	2020 Org
2011	Dylan Bundy, RHP	Angels
2012	Kevin Gausman, RHP	Giants
2013	Hunter Harvey, RHP	Orioles
2014	Brian Gonzalez, LHP (3rd round)	Orioles
2015	D.J. Stewart, OF	Orioles
2016	Cody Sedlock, RHP	Orioles
2017	D.L. Hall, LHP	Orioles
2018	Grayson Rodriguez, RHP	Orioles
2019	Adley Rutschman, C	Orioles
2020	Heston Kjerstad, OF	Orioles

DEPTH CHART

BALTIMORE ORIOLES

TOP 2021 ROOKIES	RANK
Ryan Mountcastle, 1B	5
Dean Kremer, RHP	9
BREAKOUT PROSPECTS	**RANK**
Jordan Westburg, SS	11
Luis Gonzalez, OF	20
Kyle Stowers, OF	24

SOURCE OF TOP 30 TALENT

Homegrown	22	Acquired	8
College	9	Trade	8
Junior college	0	Rule 5 draft	0
High school	11	Independent league	0
Nondrafted free agent	0	Free agent/waivers	0
International	2		

LF
Ryan Mountcastle (5)
Ryan McKenna (22)
Stiven Acevedo

CF
Hudson Haskin (19)
Zach Watson
Isaac Bellony

RF
Heston Kjerstad (4)
Yusniel Diaz (7)
Luis Gonzalez (20)
Kyle Stowers (24)
Johnny Rizer

3B
Coby Mayo (27)
Rylan Bannon
JC Encarnacion
Toby Welk

SS
Gunnar Henderson (6)
Jordan Westburg (11)
Anthony Servideo (26)
Darell Hernaiz (29)
Leonel Sanchez
Mason McCoy

2B
Adam Hall (15)
Terrin Vavra (21)

1B
Tyler Nevin (28)
Andrew Daschbach

C
Adley Rutschman (1)
Brett Cumberland

LHP

LHSP
DL Hall (3)
Keegan Akin (10)
Bruce Zimmermann (14)
Kevin Smith (16)
Zac Lowther (17)
Alexander Wells (18)
Drew Rom (23)
Luis Ortiz
Josh Rogers

LHRP
Zack Muckenhirn

RHP

RHSP
Grayson Rodriguez (2)
Mike Baumann (8)
Dean Kremer (9)
Kyle Bradish (12)
Garrett Stallings (25)
Carter Baumler (30)
Brenan Hanifee
Cody Sedlock
Blaine Knight
Ofelky Peralta
Dan Hammer
Connor Gillispie
Kyle Brnovic

RHRP
Hunter Harvey (13)
Dillon Tate
Isaac Mattson

Boston Red Sox

BY ALEX SPEIER

On Feb. 10, 2020, Red Sox chief baseball officer Chaim Bloom—less than four months into his job—was tasked with explaining the inexplicable. Why had the Red Sox traded franchise icon Mookie Betts, along with David Price, to the Dodgers?

"Our mission, our charge as a department, is to compete consistently, year in and year out, and to put ourselves in a position to win as many championships as we can," Bloom said. "And that's behind everything we do. And we can only accomplish that goal with a talent base at all levels of the organization that is deep, broad and sustainable."

From 2014 to 2019, Betts had represented the face of a "deep, broad, and sustainable" homegrown core that powered the Red Sox to a championship in 2018. Yet the elite talent that had flowed steadily through the farm system to the big league roster from 2014 to 2017 encountered drought conditions.

The Red Sox believed Betts wanted to test free agency and further believed that their farm system needed a massive influx of young talent to avoid a multi-year valley.

Betts became the vehicle for the acceleration of that replenishing. Bloom traded the superstar—along with Price, a secondary piece whose inclusion was motivated chiefly by salary relief—for outfielder Alex Verdugo, who is under team control through at least 2024; and shortstop Jeter Downs and catcher Connor Wong, a pair of up-the-middle prospects who finished 2019 in Double-A.

The trade of Betts and Price, in conjunction with the season-long absence of Chris Sale to Tommy John surgery and Eduardo Rodriguez to myocarditis following a Covid-19 infection, and a woeful lack of rotation depth, sent the Red Sox spiraling to a 24-36 record and a last-place finish in the American League East. While the major league results proved awful, the team took steps toward improving its long-term talent base.

With the Red Sox out of contention as soon as the season started, the team moved aggressively as sellers, trading relievers Brandon Workman and Heath Hembree, first baseman Mitch Moreland and outfielder Kevin Pillar for prospects including starter Connor Seabold, third baseman Hudson Potts, outfielder Jeisson Rosario and reliever Jacob Wallace. Late in the season, Boston received encouraging debuts from power-hitting corner infielder Bobby Dalbec and starter Tanner Houck.

At the alternate training site, those trade acquisitions joined Downs and Wong, top prospect Triston Casas, pitchers Bryan Mata and Jay Groome, outfielder Jarren Duran, and 2020 first-rounder Nick Yorke in making favorable impressions. A Red Sox farm system that had seemed thin at the upper levels now appears closer to providing quality big league depth and future impact.

Those additions and arrivals, combined with an excellent Red Sox debut from Verdugo and the fact that the Red Sox will have the fourth pick in the 2021 draft—their highest selection since 1967—suggest that the team is closer to re-establishing a young talent base capable of sustaining competitiveness. When that competitive window re-opens in the big leagues remains to be seen. ■

BILLIE WEISS/BOSTON RED SOX/GETTY IMAGES

Incoming chief baseball officer Chaim Bloom was tasked with trading icon Mookie Betts.

PROJECTED 2024 LINEUP

Position	Player	Age
Catcher	Christian Vazquez	33
First Base	Triston Casas	24
Second Base	Jeter Downs	25
Third Base	Rafael Devers	27
Shortstop	Xander Bogaerts	31
Left Field	Andrew Benintendi	29
Center Field	Jarren Duran	27
Right Field	Alex Verdugo	28
Designated Hitter	Bobby Dalbec	29
No. 1 Starter	Chris Sale	35
No. 2 Starter	Eduardo Rodriguez	31
No. 3 Starter	Bryan Mata	25
No. 4 Starter	Jay Groome	25
No. 5 Starter	Tanner Houck	28
Closer	Darwinzon Hernandez	27

1 TRISTON CASAS, 1B

Born: Jan. 15, 2000. **B-T:** L-R. **HT:** 6-5. **WT:** 245.
Drafted: HS—Plantation, Fla., 2018 (1st round).
Signed by: Willie Romay.

TRACK RECORD: Casas combined elite power in high school with a surprisingly mature approach that became evident against advanced competition in showcase events and playing for USA Baseball's 18U National Team. The Red Sox drafted Casas 26th overall in 2018 and signed him for just over $2.5 million. After most of his 2018 pro debut was wiped out following a strained thumb ligament, his 2019 minor league season with low Class A Greenville didn't disappoint. He joined Xander Bogaerts as the only Red Sox teenagers in more than half a century to hit 20 or more homers in one year and ranked as the top infield prospect in the South Atlantic League. He ranked among the SAL leaders in homers (19), RBIs (78) and slugging (.472). Casas was set to open 2020 in high Class A before the coronavirus pandemic wiped out the minor league season, and he joined the team's alternate training site in late August. He arrived in tremendous shape and ready to hit against more experienced pitchers and held his own against pitchers with Triple-A and major league experience.

SCOUTING REPORT: Casas already has the size and strength to launch moonshots from left-center to right field. He has some swing-and-miss to his game, like most big power hitters, but he has shown the self-awareness and aptitude to cover holes. That trait was evident at the alternate site, where he showed an improved ability to turn on and backspin velocity on the inner half, while continuing to drive pitches away to the opposite field. That all-fields approach is evidence of a player committed to being more than an all-or-nothing hitter. Casas, who considers Joey Votto a model, spreads out his stance and chokes up with two strikes in order to control his strikeout rate. His strike-zone awareness ranks among the best in the system. While Casas was drafted as a third baseman, his future is at first base, where he has a chance to be at least an above-average defender with a long wingspan and solid arm strength. Casas is uncommonly mature, showing both an interest in feedback while also having the self-understanding to filter what works for him. He has worked out with big leaguers in South Florida for years, something that helped him remain unfazed against older competition.

THE FUTURE: Casas made a compelling case to open 2021 at Double-A with his performance at the alternate site. Some in the organization believe he is sufficiently advanced to fast-track to the majors by the end of the season. Even if Casas travels a more conservative time frame, Red Sox officials believe he will become a middle-of-the-lineup staple for years to come. In an era where first basemen are rarely considered top prospects, Casas has an offensive ceiling that allows him to fit the bill. ■

BEST TOOLS

Best Hitter for Average	Triston Casas
Best Power Hitter	Bobby Dalbec
Best Strike-Zone Discipline	Triston Casas
Fastest Baserunner	Jarren Duran
Best Athlete	Gilberto Jimenez
Best Fastball	Bryan Mata
Best Curveball	Jay Groome
Best Slider	Tanner Houck
Best Changeup	Connor Seabold
Best Control	Thad Ward
Best Defensive Catcher	Kole Cottam
Best Defensive Infielder	Matthew Lugo
Best Infield Arm	Bobby Dalbec
Best Defensive Outfielder	Jeisson Rosario
Best Outfield Arm	Gilberto Jimenez

Year	Age	Club (League)	Class	AVG	G	AB	R	H	2B	3B	HR	RBI	BB	SO	SB	OBP	SLG
2018	18	Red Sox (GCL)	R	.000	2	4	0	0	0	0	0	0	1	2	0	.200	.000
2019	19	Greenville (SAL)	LoA	.254	118	422	64	107	25	5	19	78	58	116	3	.349	.472
	19	Salem (CAR)	HiA	.429	2	7	2	3	1	0	1	3	0	2	0	.429	1.000
Minor League Totals				.254	122	433	66	110	26	5	20	81	59	120	3	.349	.476

2 JETER DOWNS, 2B/SS

BRACE HEMMELGARN/MLB PHOTOS VIA GETTY IMAGES

BA GRADE
55 Risk: Medium

Born: July 27, 1998. **B-T:** R-R. **HT:** 5-11. **WT:** 180. **Drafted:** HS—Miami Gardens, Fla., 2017 (1st round supplemental). **Signed by:** Hector Otero (Reds).

TRACK RECORD: Unlike the eponymous Yankees superstar for whom he's named, Downs already has become accustomed to changing teams. The Reds traded Downs to the Dodgers before the 2019 season, and when the Red Sox pivoted away from Brusdar Graterol in the Mookie Betts blockbuster, Los Angeles shipped him to Boston prior to spring training in 2020. Downs made his Red Sox debut at the alternate training site and was one of the team's top performers in Pawtucket.

SCOUTING REPORT: Downs has an efficient swing with impressive whip, driving the ball from gap to gap for doubles and homers. His bat speed buys time for good pitch recognition, allowing him both to manage the strike zone and identify pitches to drive. Downs has crushed lefthanders while doing enough against righties to suggest a potential regular. While he has mainly spent time at shortstop, his solid but unspectacular range suggests a future at second base. Downs features average speed that plays up with his excellent baseball IQ and strong feel for the game.

THE FUTURE: Downs could open 2021 in Triple-A with a solid spring and will be part of Boston's depth equation. With offense down at second base across the majors in recent years, Downs projects as an above-average regular at the position with a chance to be an all-star.

SCOUTING GRADES: **Hitting:** 55 **Power:** 55 **Running:** 50 **Fielding:** 50 **Arm:** 50

Year	Age	Club (League)	Class	AVG	G	AB	R	H	2B	3B	HR	RBI	BB	SO	SB	OBP	SLG
2017	18	Billings (PIO)	R	.267	50	172	31	46	3	3	6	29	27	32	8	.370	.424
2018	19	Dayton (MWL)	LoA	.257	120	455	63	117	23	2	13	47	52	103	37	.351	.402
2019	20	Tulsa (TL)	AA	.333	12	48	14	16	2	0	5	11	6	10	1	.429	.688
	20	R. Cucamonga (CAL)	HiA	.269	107	412	78	111	33	4	19	75	54	97	23	.354	.507
Minor League Totals				.267	289	1087	186	290	61	9	43	162	139	242	69	.359	.458

3 BOBBY DALBEC, 1B/3B

BRACE HEMMELGARN/MLB PHOTOS VIA GETTY IMAGES

Born: June 29, 1995. **B-T:** R-R. **HT:** 6-4. **WT:** 225. **Drafted:** Arizona, 2016 (4th round). **Signed by:** Vaughn Williams.

TRACK RECORD: Dalbec's elite power made him a first-round candidate in the 2016 draft, but his struggles as a junior caused him to slip to the fourth round. The Red Sox signed the two-way standout for $650,000. He made that slide look misguided in pro ball with a combined 59 home runs in 2018 and 2019, sixth-most in the minors. He continued that power display with eight home runs in 19 games in his 2020 big league debut.

SCOUTING REPORT: Dalbec has massive all-fields power with enough strength and leverage to allow even some mis-hits to leave the yard to right field. He also has sizable holes for big league pitchers to exploit, both on elevated fastballs as well as breaking balls and offspeed pitches below the zone. The cerebral Dalbec posted a 42% strikeout rate in the big leagues but has shown the ability to adjust and lower his strikeout rate throughout his pro career. While Dalbec spent most of his time at first base in Boston, he continues to be somewhat stiff there and remains a work in progress. He is more natural at third base, where he is a solid defender and his arm plays as double-plus—but he's blocked by Rafael Devers.

THE FUTURE: Dalbec's first exposure to the majors validated the impression he can become a valuable power hitter and corner infielder. He'll open 2021 back in Boston.

SCOUTING GRADES: **Hitting:** 40 **Power:** 70 **Running:** 45 **Fielding:** 50 **Arm:** 70

Year	Age	Club (League)	Class	AVG	G	AB	R	H	2B	3B	HR	RBI	BB	SO	SB	OBP	SLG
2018	23	Salem (CAR)	HiA	.256	100	344	59	88	27	2	26	85	60	130	3	.372	.573
	23	Portland (EL)	AA	.261	29	111	14	29	8	1	6	24	6	46	0	.323	.514
2019	24	Pawtucket (IL)	AAA	.257	30	113	12	29	4	0	7	16	5	29	0	.301	.478
	24	Portland (EL)	AA	.234	105	359	57	84	15	2	20	57	68	110	6	.371	.454
2020	25	Boston (AL)	MAJ	.263	23	80	13	21	3	0	8	16	10	39	0	.359	.600
Major League Totals				.263	23	80	13	21	3	0	8	16	10	39	0	.359	.600
Minor League Totals				.261	383	1370	218	358	83	7	79	256	189	480	16	.362	.505

4 BRYAN MATA, RHP

TOP ROOKIE

BRACE HEMMELGARN/MLB PHOTOS VIA GETTY IMAGES

BA GRADE

55 Risk: High

Born: May 3, 1999. **B-T:** R-R. **HT:** 6-3. **WT:** 225. **Signed:** Venezuela, 2016.
Signed by: Alex Requena/Eddie Romero.

TRACK RECORD: Signed for just $25,000 during the 2015-16 international signing period, Mata quickly emerged as one of the organization's top pitching prospects. After reaching Double-A in 2019, he made his way to the alternate training site in 2020 and solidified his standing as the pitcher with the best pure stuff in Boston's system.

SCOUTING REPORT: Mata has a diverse arsenal of pitches anchored by a mid-to-high-90s two-seam fastball and a nasty slider that tunnels well off his two-seamer. His two-seamer and slider have the shape and power of plus offerings or better, eliciting bad contact and swings and misses. His four-seamer, changeup and curveball are inconsistent but create options to attack righties and lefties in different parts of the zone. Below-average control remains the focus of Mata's development, but he has improved, dropping his walk rate from 7.3 per nine innings in 2018 to 3.6 per nine in 2019. To continue that progress, Mata adjusted his delivery at the alternate site in hopes that fewer moving parts will result in a more consistent attack on the strike zone.

THE FUTURE: Mata's combination of big stuff but below-average control suggests a No. 3 or 4 starter. He has a chance to put himself on the radar as a major league depth option in 2021.

SCOUTING GRADES: **Fastball:** 70 **Slider:** 60 **Curveball:** 40 **Changeup:** 50 **Control:** 45

Year	Age	Club (League)	Class	W	L	ERA	G	GS	IP	H	HR	BB	SO	BB/9	SO/9	WHIP	AVG
2017	18	Greenville (SAL)	LoA	5	6	3.74	17	17	77	75	3	26	74	3.0	8.6	1.31	.230
2018	19	Salem (CAR)	HiA	6	3	3.50	17	17	72	58	1	58	61	7.3	7.6	1.61	.177
2019	20	Salem (CAR)	HiA	3	1	1.75	10	10	51	38	1	18	52	3.2	9.1	1.09	.176
	20	Portland (EL)	AA	4	6	5.03	11	11	54	54	6	24	59	4.0	9.9	1.45	.231
Minor League Totals				22	20	3.40	69	69	315	279	13	145	307	4.1	8.8	1.35	.242

5 JARREN DURAN, OF

BRACE HEMMELGARN/MLB PHOTOS VIA GETTY IMAGES

BA GRADE

55 Risk: High

Born: Sept. 5, 1996. **B-T:** L-R. **HT:** 6-2. **WT:** 200. **Drafted:** Long Beach State, 2018 (7th round). **Signed by:** Justin Horowitz.

TRACK RECORD: In college, Duran was a second baseman whose speed and offensive performance pointed to bottom-of-the-order or utility skills. Area scout Justin Horowitz believed Duran had more potential based on his bat life and strength and that he could unlock greater defensive impact in the outfield. In his first full season in 2019, Duran raced to Double-A Portland, then made offseason swing adjustments that led to eight home runs at the alternate training site in 2020.

SCOUTING REPORT: Duran's swing was originally calibrated to take advantage of his plus-plus speed with a flat bat path that resulted in grounders and liners to all fields. Duran has since lowered his hands in his stance, an alteration that allowed him to keep a clear path to turn on inside pitches. With more aggressive swings may come an uptick in strikeouts, but Duran's speed and ability to spray liners on two-strike counts should help sustain solid batting averages. Duran relies more on speed than route efficiency to track balls in the outfield but has shown enough improvement to convince the Red Sox that he has a future in center. His arm is below-average.

THE FUTURE: Duran's speed gives him an avenue to the majors. If his swing adjustments hold, he could become a dynamic power-speed threat.

SCOUTING GRADES: **Hitting:** 55 **Power:** 45 **Running:** 70 **Fielding:** 50 **Arm:** 45

Year	Age	Club (League)	Class	AVG	G	AB	R	H	2B	3B	HR	RBI	BB	SO	SB	OBP	SLG
2018	21	Greenville (SAL)	LoA	.367	30	128	24	47	9	1	1	15	5	22	12	.396	.477
	21	Lowell (NYP)	SS	.348	37	155	28	54	5	10	2	20	11	26	12	.393	.548
2019	22	Salem (CAR)	HiA	.387	50	199	49	77	13	3	4	19	23	44	18	.456	.543
	22	Portland (EL)	AA	.250	82	320	41	80	11	5	1	19	23	84	28	.309	.325
Minor League Totals				.322	199	802	142	258	38	19	8	73	62	176	70	.376	.446

6 JAY GROOME, LHP

Born: Aug. 23, 1998. **B-T:** L-L. **HT:** 6-6. **WT:** 250. **Drafted:** HS—Barnegat, N.J., 2016 (1st round). **Signed by:** Ray Fagnant.

BA GRADE
55 Risk: Very High

TRACK RECORD: One of the top high school talents in the 2016 draft, Groome has pitched just 66 minor league innings because of injuries, including having Tommy John surgery that wiped out his 2018 season and most of 2019. The Red Sox sent him to their alternate training site in 2020 to get innings, and he held his own against more advanced hitters while offering a reminder of why he'd been so highly-regarded as an amateur.

SCOUTING REPORT: Groome has the raw materials of a lefthanded starter, including a powerful build, a controlled, repeatable delivery and giant hands that allow him to manipulate the ball. He typically works at 92-94 mph with his four-seam fastball, and the deception in his delivery resulted in lots of whiffs on fastballs at the alternate site. The plus-plus curveball he featured pre-Tommy John has not come back, but still flashes above-average to plus. Groome emphasized his changeup while rehabbing, and the pitch projects as average. He's also started experimenting with a slider, and could feature either that or a cutter as a fourth pitch.

THE FUTURE: Groome possesses mid-rotation potential but still has a lot to prove, including whether he can stay healthy over a full season. He'll likely open 2021 in high Class A.

SCOUTING GRADES: **Fastball:** 55 **Slider:** 50 **Curveball:** 55 **Changeup:** 50 **Control:** 55

Year	Age	Club (League)	Class	W	L	ERA	G	GS	IP	H	HR	BB	SO	BB/9	SO/9	WHIP	AVG
2017	18	Greenville (SAL)	LoA	3	7	6.70	11	11	44	44	6	25	58	5.1	11.8	1.56	.221
	18	Lowell (NYP)	SS	0	2	1.64	3	3	11	5	0	5	14	4.1	11.5	0.91	.114
2018	19	Did not play—Injured															
2019	20	Red Sox (GCL)	R	0	0	0.00	2	2	2	2	0	0	3	0.0	13.5	1.00	.250
	20	Lowell (NYP)	SS	0	0	4.50	1	1	2	3	0	1	3	4.5	13.5	2.00	.273
Minor League Totals				3	9	5.18	20	20	66	57	6	35	88	4.8	12.0	1.39	.227

7 GILBERTO JIMENEZ, OF

Born: July 8, 2000. **B-T:** B-R. **HT:** 5-11. **WT:** 220. **Signed:** Dominican Republic, 2017. **Signed by:** Eddie Romero/Manny Nanita.

BA GRADE
55 Risk: Very High

TRACK RECORD: Jimenez signed for just $10,000 out of the Dominican Republic but quickly surpassed many players who signed for more. He began switch-hitting after signing with the Red Sox and was a standout in the college-heavy short-season New York-Penn League as an 18-year-old. The 2020 season, unfortunately, represented a lost year of development after he wasn't invited to the alternate site camp.

SCOUTING REPORT: Jimenez represents one of the most intriguing talents in the Red Sox organization: a player with the athleticism, strength, hand-eye coordination and elite speed to perform well even while learning. He is still developing his swing path after a choppy approach to the ball resulted in a 64% percent groundball rate in 2019. Nonetheless, his sub-four seconds times to first base allow him to turn many of those grounders into hits, particularly from the left side. Jimenez is still learning to hit lefthanded but batted .374 against righties in 2019, and all three of his homers came while hitting lefthanded. His plus-plus speed and arm strength suggest impact potential both on the bases and in center or right field.

THE FUTURE: The 2021 season should offer Jimenez his first exposure to full-season ball. There's a lot of development left, but he has a ceiling rivaled by few in the system.

SCOUTING GRADES: **Hitting:** 55 **Power:** 45 **Running:** 70 **Fielding:** 60 **Arm:** 70

Year	Age	Club (League)	Class	AVG	G	AB	R	H	2B	3B	HR	RBI	BB	SO	SB	OBP	SLG
2018	17	Red Sox1 (DSL)	R	.319	67	257	42	82	10	8	0	22	19	40	20	.384	.420
2019	18	Lowell (NYP)	SS	.359	59	234	35	84	11	3	3	19	13	38	14	.393	.470
Minor League Totals				.338	126	491	77	166	21	11	3	41	32	78	30	.388	.444

8 TANNER HOUCK, RHP

TOP ROOKIE

BRACE HEMMELGARN/MLB PHOTOS VIA GETTY IMAGES

BA GRADE
50 Risk: Medium

Born: June 29, 1996. **B-T:** R-R. **HT:** 6-5. **WT:** 220. **Drafted:** Missouri, 2017 (1st round). **Signed by:** Todd Gold.

TRACK RECORD: When the Red Sox drafted Houck, they believed he had the athleticism and aptitude to add to his sinker/slider and emerge as a starter. In 2020, Houck made good on that belief as he refined his delivery and pitch mix over two months at the alternate training site and made a dazzling big league debut with one earned run over 17 innings while dominating three playoff teams.

SCOUTING REPORT: Houck quieted his crossfire delivery at the alternate site to establish better direction to home plate. He also raised his low three-quarters arm slot a tick, establishing a better release point for his 90-93 mph sinker, 92-94 four-seamer and low-80s slider. After struggling for much of his career to handle lefthanded hitters, Houck shelved his changeup in favor of a splitter, which he rarely used in the big leagues but shows potential as a viable third pitch. He demonstrated excellent poise in the majors and adapted well to whatever was working, alternately emphasizing his two- and four-seam fastballs while displaying a wipeout slider against which hitters were 0-for-15 with 10 strikeouts.

THE FUTURE: Houck put himself in position to open 2021 in the big league rotation with his debut performance. The development of his splitter will likely determine his career path.

SCOUTING GRADES: **Fastball:** 55 **Slider:** 60 **Splitter:** 45 **Control:** 45

Year	Age	Club (League)	Class	W	L	ERA	G	GS	IP	H	HR	BB	SO	BB/9	SO/9	WHIP	AVG
2017	21	Lowell (NYP)	SS	0	3	3.63	10	10	22	21	0	8	25	3.2	10.1	1.30	.214
2018	22	Salem (CAR)	HiA	7	11	4.24	23	23	119	110	11	60	111	4.5	8.4	1.43	.212
2019	23	Pawtucket (IL)	AAA	0	0	3.24	16	2	25	19	3	14	27	5.0	9.7	1.32	.153
	23	Portland (EL)	AA	8	6	4.25	17	15	83	86	4	32	80	3.5	8.7	1.43	.238
2020	24	Boston (AL)	MAJ	3	0	0.53	3	3	17	6	1	9	21	4.8	11.1	0.88	.113
Major League Totals				3	0	0.53	3	3	17	6	1	9	21	4.8	11.1	0.88	.113
Minor League Totals				15	20	4.08	66	50	249	236	18	114	243	4.1	8.8	1.41	.249

9 NICK YORKE, 2B

LIPO CHING/THE MERCURY NEWS VIA GETTY IMAGES

BA GRADE
50 Risk: Extreme

Born: April 2, 2002. **B-T:** R-R. **HT:** 6-0. **WT:** 200. **Drafted:** HS—San Jose, Calif., 2020 (1st round). **Signed by:** Josh Labandeira.

TRACK RECORD: The Red Sox stunned the industry when they drafted Yorke with the 17th overall pick in 2020, but the team had years of familiarity that informed its willingness to buck consensus. Area scout Josh Labandeira believed Yorke's ability to drive the ball to center and right-center field at an early age harbored similarities to what he'd seen in the minors playing against David Wright. The Red Sox signed Yorke for a below-slot $2.7 million bonus and invited him to the alternate training site, where he reached base in seven of 10 plate appearances.

SCOUTING REPORT: There is an ease about Yorke in the batter's box, where his quickly accelerating bat allows him an extra beat to recognize pitches and make smart swing decisions. He barrels balls to the entire field, creating the potential for high batting averages and on-base percentages with high extra-base hits totals. Yorke gained 15 pounds his senior season to add more power to his game, but he always projects to hit for average over power. While Yorke will move off his high school position of shortstop, the Red Sox believe he can stay in the middle of the diamond at second base.

THE FUTURE: Yorke should open 2021 in low Class A. The Red Sox believe his advanced bat and uncommon maturity could allow him to jump on the fast track.

SCOUTING GRADES: **Hitting:** 60 **Power:** 45 **Running:** 40 **Fielding:** 50 **Arm:** 50

Year	Age	Club (League)	Class	AVG	G	AB	R	H	2B	3B	HR	RBI	BB	SO	SB	OBP	SLG
2020	18	Did not play—No minor league season															

10 THAD WARD, RHP

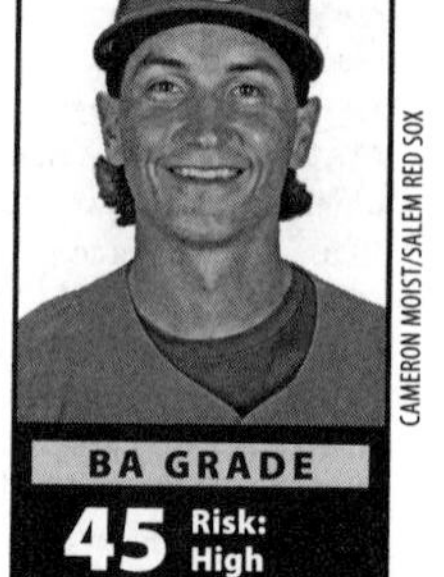
CAMERON MOIST/SALEM RED SOX

BA GRADE
45 **Risk: High**

born: Jan. 16, 1997. **B-T:** R-R. **HT:** 6-3. **WT:** 192. **Drafted:** Central Florida, 2018 (5th round). **Signed by:** Stephen Hargett.

TRACK RECORD: Ward was largely overlooked as a swingman who worked chiefly out of the bullpen at Central Florida. The Red Sox thought he had the ability to emerge as at least a reliever and might be able to start, so they took a flier on him in the fifth round in 2018. Ward rewarded that decision with a standout 2019 season in which both his ERA (2.14) and strikeout rate (11.2 per nine innings) were among the best in the minors by any pitcher who threw at least 100 innings. He spent the canceled 2020 season working out on his own and developing a changeup.

SCOUTING REPORT: Thanks to strength gains in pro ball, Ward's sinker ticked up from a low-90s offering to a 93-96 mph pitch in 2019. Both that pitch and a cutter he developed in 2019 allow him to miss barrels and generate weak contact early in counts. Ward's mid-80s slider is his putaway pitch. While those three pitches are his primary options, Ward is willing to employ additional pitches—including a four-seamer and changeup—to further unbalance opponents and to give him game-planning options. He has an easy delivery but struggles with walks at times.

THE FUTURE: Ward likely will open 2021 in Double-A. He has back-of-the-rotation potential.

SCOUTING GRADES: **Fastball:** 50 **Slider:** 60 **Cutter:** 50 **Changeup:** 45 **Control:** 45

Year	Age	Club (League)	Class	W	L	ERA	G	GS	IP	H	HR	BB	SO	BB/9	SO/9	WHIP	AVG
2018	21	Lowell (NYP)	SS	0	3	3.77	11	11	31	33	2	12	27	3.5	7.8	1.45	.246
2019	22	Salem (CAR)	HiA	3	3	2.33	12	12	54	38	4	32	70	5.3	11.7	1.30	.167
	22	Greenville (SAL)	LoA	5	2	1.99	13	13	72	51	2	25	87	3.1	10.8	1.05	.171
Minor League Totals				8	8	2.46	36	36	157	122	8	69	184	4.0	10.5	1.21	.214

11 CONNOR SEABOLD, RHP

BA GRADE
45 **Risk: High**

Born: Jan. 24, 1996. **B-T:** R-R. **HT:** 6-2. **WT:** 190. **Drafted:** Cal State Fullerton, 2017 (3rd round). **Signed by:** Demerius Pittman (Phillies).

TRACK RECORD: Seabold came to the Red Sox from the Phillies as a pitcher with a solid three-pitch mix. After Seabold finished 2018 in Double-A, an oblique injury at the start of 2019 limited him to 56.1 innings and prevented him from advancing. Nonetheless, he looked like a potential big league starter at Reading and then in the Arizona Fall League, where he recorded a 1.06 ERA with 22 strikeouts and three walks in 17 innings. That led Boston to target him in an August 2020 trade as part of the return for relievers Brandon Workman and Heath Hembree.

SCOUTING REPORT: Seabold's three-pitch mix includes a 90-93 mph fastball that sometimes ticks up slightly higher, an excellent changeup with sink and fade and a below-average slider that plays up because of command and deception. Toward the end of his month at the alternate training site, Seabold started to incorporate a fringy curveball. Though Seabold's stuff lacks a wow factor, his feel for pitching, sequencing, strike-throwing and competitiveness gives him a strong chance to emerge as a back-end starter.

THE FUTURE: Seabold will likely open 2021 in Triple-A. He has a chance to serve as a big league depth starter during the year.

Year	Age	Club (League)	Class	W	L	ERA	G	GS	IP	H	HR	BB	SO	BB/9	SO/9	WHIP	AVG
2019	23	Phillies East (GCL)	R	0	1	11.57	1	1	2	6	0	0	2	0.0	7.7	2.57	.375
	23	Reading (EL)	AA	3	1	2.25	7	7	40	35	2	10	36	2.3	8.1	1.13	.222
	23	Clearwater (FSL)	HiA	1	0	1.00	2	1	9	4	1	1	10	1.0	10.0	0.56	.125
	23	Phillies West (GCL)	R	0	0	0.00	2	2	5	1	0	0	10	0.0	18.0	0.20	.063
Minor League Totals				11	10	3.52	40	34	196	163	19	46	203	2.1	9.3	1.06	.222

12 NOAH SONG, RHP

BA GRADE
50 **Risk: Extreme**

Born: May 28, 1997. **B-T:** R-R. **HT:** 6-4. **WT:** 200. **Drafted:** Navy, 2019 (4th round). **Signed by:** Reed Gragnani.

TRACK RECORD: Song came to the Red Sox with a first-round college pedigree and arsenal but uncertainty given his service obligation as a Naval Academy graduate. The Red Sox hoped that Song might be able to fulfill his service obligation while also pitching in pro ball, a notion that seemed to gain steam when he was allowed to pitch for Team USA at the 2019 Premier12 tournament. His request to pursue a dual track languished for more than a year after he graduated, and he reported to flight school last summer.

SCOUTING REPORT: Song arrived in Annapolis with a mid-80s fastball, but gained considerable strength that translated into easy mid-90s velocity with a putaway slider from a repeatable delivery as a senior. He seldom used his curveball or changeup in college, but both pitches impressed in short-season Lowell and the Premier12 in 2019.

THE FUTURE: Song can petition for a military service waiver in May 2021—two years after he graduated—but no one knows when, or if, such a request might be granted. If he's given permission to return to baseball, it's hard to forecast what kind of pitcher he'll be after at least a year and a half away from competition.

Year	Age	Club (League)	Class	W	L	ERA	G	GS	IP	H	HR	BB	SO	BB/9	SO/9	WHIP	AVG
2019	22	Lowell (NYP)	SS	0	0	1.06	7	7	17	10	0	5	19	2.6	10.1	0.88	.154
Minor League Totals				0	0	1.06	7	7	17	10	0	5	19	2.7	10.1	0.88	.167

13 CHRIS MURPHY, LHP

BA GRADE **45** Risk: High

Born: June 5, 1998. **B-T:** L-L. **HT:** 6-1. **WT:** 175. **Drafted:** San Diego, 2019 (6th round). **Signed by:** J.J. Altobelli.

TRACK RECORD: In college, Murphy displayed a swing-and-miss fastball as the anchor of a mix that as a junior produced 12.2 strikeouts per nine innings, which ranked 23rd in Division I, but control issues pushed him to the sixth round. The walks, however, were partly a product of an effort to force chases out of the zone in two-strike counts. In Murphy's pro debut in short-season Lowell in 2019, he excelled with a more aggressive approach and he continued to impress at instructional league in 2020.

SCOUTING REPORT: Despite some effort in his delivery, Murphy still has harnessed his mechanics in pro ball in a fashion that has allowed him to work in the zone with a four-pitch mix. His fastball—which averaged 93 mph and topped at 95 in instructional league—has deception and life at the top of the zone, and his changeup is a plus pitch that plays off of it. Murphy complements those two pitches with both a below-average slider and curveball that have been sufficient to keep both lefties and righties honest. In pro ball, he's proven capable of applying data to identify where his stuff is most effective.

THE FUTURE: So long as he throws enough strikes, Murphy's four-pitch mix gives him a chance to move relatively quickly through the system as a potential No. 5 starter.

Year	Age	Club (League)	Class	W	L	ERA	G	GS	IP	H	HR	BB	SO	BB/9	SO/9	WHIP	AVG
2019	21	Lowell (NYP)	SS	0	1	1.08	10	10	33	23	1	7	34	1.9	9.2	0.90	.162
Minor League Totals				0	1	1.08	10	10	33	23	1	7	34	1.9	9.2	0.90	.197

14 MATTHEW LUGO, SS

BREAKOUT

BA GRADE **45** Risk: High

Born: May 9, 2001. **B-T:** R-R. **HT:** 6-1. **WT:** 185. **Drafted:** HS—Manati, P.R., 2019 (2nd round). **Signed by:** Edgar Perez.

TRACK RECORD: The nephew of Carlos Beltran, Lugo emerged as an early-round draftee in 2019 thanks to potential plus power along with the athleticism to stay on the middle infield. Drafted in the second round, he got off to a sizzling start in his pro debut in 2019 before fading down the stretch. Minor wrist soreness prevented him from playing games at instructional league in 2020.

SCOUTING REPORT: Scout Edgar Perez saw a number of traits in Lugo that led the Red Sox to sign him for $1.1 million. Among those traits were athleticism, projectability, strength to create above-average power potential, maturity and baseball acumen to create confidence in his ability to advance through the minors. Lugo is described as strikingly mature in his routines and work, including strength work that led one evaluator to describe him as, pound for pound, the strongest prospect in the system. While many expected him to move to second base in pro ball, he has made significant strides at shortstop and many with the Red Sox now believe he can stick at the position.

THE FUTURE: Lugo should start 2021 in full-season ball, with the potential to emerge eventually as a bat-first middle infielder.

Year	Age	Club (League)	Class	AVG	G	AB	R	H	2B	3B	HR	RBI	BB	SO	SB	OBP	SLG
2019	18	Red Sox (GCL)	R	.257	39	136	19	35	5	1	1	12	15	36	3	.342	.331
	18	Lowell (NYP)	SS	.250	2	8	0	2	0	0	0	1	0	2	0	.250	.250
Minor League Total				.257	41	144	19	37	5	1	1	13	15	38	3	.337	.326

15 CONNOR WONG, C

Born: May 9, 1996. **B-T:** R-R. **HT:** 6-1. **WT:** 181. **Drafted:** Houston, 2017 (3rd round). **Signed by:** Clint Bowers (Dodgers).

TRACK RECORD: Wong started college as a shortstop but broadened his resume as a sophomore, when he spent time behind the plate for Houston and moved around the infield and outfield. His versatility, power, and athleticism—he had 12 homers and 26 steals as a junior—led the Dodgers to draft him in the third round in 2017. His defensive versatility and power potential made him attractive to the Red Sox, who acquired him as the third player in the deal that sent Mookie Betts and David Price to the Dodgers.

SCOUTING REPORT: Wong is deceivingly wiry, a physically unimposing presence who nonetheless has the athleticism and strength to make an impact in a number of areas. He typically sells out on his swing, resulting in a pull-heavy approach that emphasizes launch but renders him vulnerable to offspeed pitches and has yielded a strikeout rate of nearly 31%. Still, his hard contact has translated to both power and high batting averages on balls in play over three minor league seasons. Wong is still developing his technical skills behind the plate, but he's considered a solid receiver with the intelligence and body control to handle the position and the athleticism to play other infield spots.

THE FUTURE: Wong's swing-and-miss issues likely cap his ceiling as a reserve, but his versatility could make him more valuable than the typical backup catcher. He'll likely open 2021 in Triple-A as a depth option.

Year	Age	Club (League)	Class	AVG	G	AB	R	H	2B	3B	HR	RBI	BB	SO	SB	OBP	SLG
2019	23	Tulsa (TL)	AA	.349	40	149	17	52	9	1	9	31	11	50	2	.393	.604
	23	R. Cucamonga (CAL)	HiA	.245	71	274	39	67	15	6	15	51	21	93	9	.306	.507
Minor League Totals				.275	241	904	139	249	50	9	48	160	77	308	18	.342	.510

16 BLAZE JORDAN, 3B/1B

BA GRADE
50 Risk: Extreme

Born: Dec. 19, 2002. **B-T:** R-R. **HT:** 6-2. **WT:** 220. **Drafted:** HS—Southaven, Miss., 2020 (3rd round). **Signed by:** Danny Watkins.

TRACK RECORD: Jordan's power as an amateur bordered on legendary after videos of him blasting 500-foot homers started circulating when he was 13. Yet questions about his all-around game and the consensus view of his likely future at first base left him on the board until the third round of the 2020 draft, when the Red Sox signed him away from a Mississippi State commitment with a $1.75 million bonus.

SCOUTING REPORT: Jordan generates his tremendous power with size and a well-synced kinetic chain that seems to transfer every drop of his frame into contact. One evaluator noted some similarities with Matt Holliday. He's a show-stopper in batting practice and has shown in games that his power can play against both velocity and breaking pitches. As might be expected of a high school draftee, his approach is immature and he's prone to chase pitches. Jordan is somewhat stiff at third base, and the general expectation is that he'll end up at first base. The Red Sox felt that he responded well to coaching at third during instructional league.

THE FUTURE: Jordan will be 18 for the entire 2021 season because he reclassified to become draft eligible a year earlier than his peers. He has always looked comfortable against older competition, creating the likelihood that he'll open at a full-season affiliate. Whether he defies doubts and sticks at third or moves to first, he has a chance to emerge as a middle-of-the-order bat if his pitch and strike-zone recognition develop.

Year	Age	Club (League)	Class	AVG	G	AB	R	H	2B	3B	HR	RBI	BB	SO	SB	OBP	SLG
2020	17	Did not play—No minor league season															

17 GARRETT WHITLOCK, RHP

Born: June 11, 1996. **B-T:** R-R. **HT:** 6-5. **WT:** 190. **Drafted:** Alabama-Birmingham, 2017 (18th round). **Signed by:** Mike Wagner (Yankees).

TRACK RECORD: Whitlock's draft-eligible sophomore season at Alabama-Birmingham in 2017 was thrown off by food poisoning and a back strain. His strong turn in the Cape Cod League in 2016 was enough to convince the Yankees to sign him as an 18th-rounder for nearly $250,000, a total that counted against the Yankees' bonus pool He had Tommy John surgery in the middle of the 2019 season but was recovered by December 2020, when the Red Sox selected him in the major league Rule 5 draft.

SCOUTING REPORT: Whitlock's main weapons are a low-to-mid-90s fastball and a hard-darting slider. His lower arm slot gives his fastball excellent sinking life and has made him a reliable groundball pitcher. Whitlock also throws a changeup in the low-to-mid 80s, but the pitch lags behind his fastball and slider. The 2019 season was Whitlock's first long look at Double-A, but his injury limited him to 70.1 innings.

THE FUTURE: Boston's pitching was not good in 2020 and was exacerbated by losses of Chris Sale to Tommy John surgery and Eduardo Rodriguez to Covid-19. Whitlock has a chance to stick in either the rotation or bullpen, giving him a chance to stick on the major league roster as a Rule 5 pick.

Year	Age	Club (League)	Class	W	L	ERA	G	GS	IP	H	HR	BB	SO	BB/9	SO/9	WHIP	AVG
2019	23	Trenton (EL)	AA	3	3	3.07	14	14	70	73	4	18	57	2.3	7.3	1.29	.246
Minor League Totals				12	8	2.41	42	38	205	180	8	59	201	2.6	8.8	1.16	.236

18 BRAINER BONACI, SS

BA GRADE 50 **Risk:** Extreme

Born: July 9, 2002. **B-T:** B-R. **HT:** 5-10. **WT:** 175. **Signed:** Venezuela, 2018. **Signed by:** Manny Padron/Junior Vizcaino/Eddie Romero.

TRACK RECORD: Bonaci's balanced skill set impressed the Red Sox when they signed him for $290,000 as a 16-year-old, and his early performance as a professional has added to the sense of his potential. He hit .279/.356/.397 in the Dominican Summer League in 2019, and he continued to hold his own against older competition at instructional league in 2020.

SCOUTING REPORT: The switch-hitting Bonaci has gotten stronger by adding about 35 pounds since signing, strength that generates steady, hard contact with some power. That power is amplified by his advanced approach, strike-zone management from both sides of the plate and good bat-to-ball skills. He shows the hands, range, and above-average arm to stick at shortstop, with speed to have further impact on the bases.

THE FUTURE: Bonaci is advanced for his age, with a chance to move quickly through the lower levels. His well-rounded game gives him an unusually solid floor for a player who's never played full-season ball, with a chance to emerge as an average to above-average everyday shortstop.

Year	Age	Club (League)	Class	AVG	G	AB	R	H	2B	3B	HR	RBI	BB	SO	SB	OBP	SLG
2019	16	Red Sox1 (DSL)	R	.279	61	229	34	64	14	2	3	37	23	40	18	.356	.397
Minor League Totals				.279	61	229	34	64	14	2	3	37	23	40	18	.356	.397

19 BRAYAN BELLO, RHP

BA GRADE 45 **Risk:** High

Born: May 17, 1999. **B-T:** R-R. **HT:** 6-1. **WT:** 170. **Signed:** Dominican Republic, 2016. **Signed by:** Manny Nanita/Todd Claus/Rollie Pino.

TRACK RECORD: Bello built on a dominant pro debut in the Dominican Summer League in 2018 with a strong spring in 2019, convincing the Red Sox to push him to low Class A Greenville in his age-20 season. He struggled through the first three months of 2019 before a breakthrough fueled by both a greater willingness to attack the strike zone and improved command over his last 10 starts.

SCOUTING REPORT: Bello's fastball sat at 94-95 mph and topped at 98 at instructional league in 2020, but a long arm path creates problems with deception and command. His continually improving velocity gives his fastball a chance to reach above-average if his command improves. His changeup is average with the potential to be better than that, while his mid-80s slider—a pitch he honed at instructs—could go from average to plus. He's prone to being tentative, but he's a good athlete with a quick arm and pitches that suggest enough starter potential to make him a popular ask in trade proposals.

THE FUTURE: Bello should start in high Class A. He has the absolute ceiling of a No. 4 starter.

Year	Age	Club (League)	Class	W	L	ERA	G	GS	IP	H	HR	BB	SO	BB/9	SO/9	WHIP	AVG
2019	20	Greenville (SAL)	LoA	5	10	5.43	25	25	118	135	9	38	119	2.9	9.1	1.47	.257
Minor League Totals				12	12	4.04	39	38	185	174	9	48	193	2.3	9.4	1.20	.244

20 JEISSON ROSARIO, OF

BA GRADE 45 **Risk:** High

Born: Oct. 22, 1999. **B-T:** L-L. **HT:** 6-1. **WT:** 191. **Signed:** Dominican Republic, 2016. **Signed by:** Felix Feliz/Ysrael Rojas/Alvin Duran (Padres).

TRACK RECORD: One of the top prospects in the 2016-17 international signing class, Rosario signed for $1.85 million with the Padres based on his athleticism, speed and a projectable frame. The Padres' 40-man crunch led them to deal Rosario to the Red Sox in 2020 as part of a two-prospect package for Mitch Moreland.

SCOUTING REPORT: Rosario is an electrifying athlete who can do standing backflips and throw with both hands, but his in-game contributions have been modest. His patience has created an extraordinary walk rate of nearly 15% for his career and a .376 on-base percentage but also results in late swing decisions that lead to grounders and weak, opposite-field contact. Evaluators are routinely frustrated by the infrequency with which he swings. He glides in center field with efficient routes and a solid arm, but his speed has ticked down from plus when he signed and now projects as average or slightly above. His above-average arm would fit in a corner spot, too.

THE FUTURE: Rosario's most likely future is as a backup outfielder, but his youth still gives him time to reach a regular's ceiling. The Red Sox added him to their 40-man roster in November.

Year	Age	Club (League)	Class	AVG	G	AB	R	H	2B	3B	HR	RBI	BB	SO	SB	OBP	SLG
2019	19	Lake Elsinore (CAL)	HiA	.242	120	430	67	104	14	4	3	35	87	114	11	.372	.314
Minor League Totals				.264	289	1053	177	278	41	9	7	93	186	258	37	.376	.340

21 JONATHAN ARAUZ, 2B/SS

BA GRADE **40** Risk: Medium

Born: Aug. 3, 1998. **B-T:** B-R. **HT:** 6-0. **WT:** 195. **Signed:** Panama, 2014.
Signed by: Norman Anciani (Phillies).

TRACK RECORD: Arauz signed with the Phillies in 2014 and was traded to the Astros after the 2015 season as a low-level throw-in in the deal that sent Ken Giles to Houston. He was suspended for a drug of abuse in his second season with the Astros, then was selected by Boston in the 2019 Rule 5 draft. He made his big league debut on July 24 and got into 25 games with the Red Sox.

SCOUTING REPORT: In 2020, Arauz lived up to his reputation as a light-hitting infielder who can play on both sides of the keystone. His average exit velocity was 85.3 mph, which would have ranked among the lowest figures in the game if he had garnered more at-bats. He saw action at shortstop, second base, third base and DH over the course of the season. Arauz is not particularly fleet of foot, and his sprint speed of 25.9 feet per second ranked in the 28th percentile of qualified big leaguers.

THE FUTURE: Arauz's role in 2020 was roughly the same as what he'll play in 2021 barring an injury to a Red Sox regular infielder. The key difference is that with his Rule 5 restrictions lifted he may be optioned to the minor leagues.

Year	Age	Club (League)	Class	AVG	G	AB	R	H	2B	3B	HR	RBI	BB	SO	SB	OBP	SLG
2020	21	Boston (AL)	MAJ	.250	25	72	8	18	2	0	1	9	8	21	0	.325	.319
Major League Totals				.250	25	72	8	18	2	0	1	9	8	21	0	.325	.319
Minor League Totals				.243	406	1484	195	360	73	17	24	153	150	283	18	.317	.363

22 ALDO RAMIREZ, RHP

BA GRADE **50** Risk: Extreme

Born: May 6, 2001. **B-T:** R-R. **HT:** 6-0. **WT:** 180. **Signed:** Mexico, 2018.
Signed by: Sotero Torres/Eddie Romero/Todd Claus.

TRACK RECORD: Ramirez was advanced enough to pitch in the Mexican League as a 16-year-old in 2018 before the Red Sox purchased him from Aguascalientes for $550,000. His maturity and understanding of his three-pitch mix allowed him to dominate in his 2018 pro debut in the Dominican Summer League. He held his own as an 18-year-old in the New York-Penn League in 2019, when he struck out 9.2 per nine innings in the college-heavy league.

SCOUTING REPORT: Ramirez typically worked in the low 90s with his fastball in Lowell but arrived at instructional league in 2020 having added strength. His fastball took a corresponding velocity bump and now sits at 93 mph and tops out at 96. His fastball doesn't have a lot of deception, though he does spot it well, and his feel for his curveball and changeup help them play above their grades.

THE FUTURE: Ramirez currently has the stuff of a swingman or back-of-the-rotation starter, but his feel for pitching and command give him a chance to exceed that projection. Those traits also give him a chance to be given aggressive assignments relative to his age.

Year	Age	Club (League)	Class	W	L	ERA	G	GS	IP	H	HR	BB	SO	BB/9	SO/9	WHIP	AVG
2019	18	Lowell (NYP)	SS	2	3	3.94	14	13	62	59	5	16	63	2.3	9.2	1.22	.210
Minor League Totals				3	5	3.16	24	18	91	76	7	25	83	2.5	8.2	1.11	.221

23 CHIH-JUNG LIU, RHP

BA GRADE **50** Risk: Extreme

Born: April 7, 1999. **B-T:** B-R. **HT:** 6-0. **WT:** 180. **Signed:** Taiwan, 2019.
Signed by: Louie Lin/Brett Ward/Chris Becerra/Eddie Romero.

TRACK RECORD: Liu was a two-way player in high school, went to college as a shortstop, then dominated when committing full-time to the mound in 2019, when he was the Asian Baseball Championship's MVP. The Red Sox signed Liu for $750,000 after seeing him throw high-90s fastballs with a slider, curve and splitter in multi-inning relief stints in 2019.

SCOUTING REPORT: Liu lacked access to full training facilities during the coronavirus shutdown, so his fastball was down to averaging 91 mph and topping out at 94 in instructional league. His fastball still

had impressive riding life at the front of an array of five pitches—which now includes a changeup—that showed potential to grade anywhere from fringe-average to above-average. It's still too early in Liu's development for the Red Sox to pinpoint which of his five pitches work best when grouped with one another.
THE FUTURE: Liu's future has more variance than most, but his athletic delivery, varied repertoire and past success could help find a spot in a rotation.

Year	Age	Club (League)	Class	W	L	ERA	G	GS	IP	H	HR	BB	SO	BB/9	SO/9	WHIP	AVG
2020	21	Did not play—No minor league season															

24 HUDSON POTTS, 3B

BA GRADE **45** Risk: High

Born: Oct. 28, 1998. **B-T:** R-R. **HT:** 6-3. **WT:** 205. **Drafted:** HS—Southlake, Texas, 2016 (1st round). **Signed by:** Matt Schaffner (Padres).
TRACK RECORD: Potts was a surprise first-round selection and under-slot signing by the Padres in 2016, but his early professional performance, including 39 homers in his first two full seasons, seemed to validate the selection. He went backward as a 20-year-old in Double-A in 2019, but his plus power remained and he was young for the level. The Red Sox acquired him in the 2020 deadline trade that sent Mitch Moreland to San Diego.
SCOUTING REPORT: Though Potts has plus to double-plus raw power, he has increasingly struggled to get to it in games thanks to concerning swing-and-miss issues on pitches both in and out of the zone. Though he's shown the ability to drill balls to the opposite field, he's also had issues rushing to his front side and becoming more pull-oriented, with rising groundball rates over two years in Double-A. He has shown adequate tools at third base but has started incorporating other positions, and should see time at second base and first base in addition to third base in 2021.
THE FUTURE: Despite Potts' steps back, he still has time to reach his ceiling. The Red Sox added him to their 40-man roster in November.

Year	Age	Club (League)	Class	AVG	G	AB	R	H	2B	3B	HR	RBI	BB	SO	SB	OBP	SLG
2019	20	Padres 1 (AZL)	R	.667	4	12	3	8	1	0	1	6	0	3	0	.692	1.000
	20	Amarillo (TL)	AA	.227	107	409	56	93	23	1	16	59	32	128	3	.290	.406
Minor League Totals				.256	423	1639	239	419	94	9	57	224	120	463	17	.315	.428

25 JACOB WALLACE, RHP

BA GRADE **40** Risk: High

Born: Aug. 13, 1998. **B-T:** R-R. **HT:** 6-1. **WT:** 190. **Drafted:** Connecticut, 2019 (3rd round). **Signed by:** Mike Garlatti (Rockies).
TRACK RECORD: Wallace's selection by the Rockies in 2019 continued a trend—Colorado had also selected Connecticut relievers in 2012 and 2018. With the Rockies trading Wallace to the Red Sox at midseason for outfielder Kevin Pillar, Wallace will now try to join another UConn product, Matt Barnes, in Boston's bullpen.
SCOUTING REPORT: Wallace is a pure reliever prospect, but his pitch mix should allow him to move through the system rather quickly. His fastball sits in the mid 90s and can touch a few ticks higher. He pairs it with a snappy mid-80s slider with a spin rate of 2,800 revolutions per minute that hitters in the short-season Northwest League struggled to identify and put in play. Wallace was working on a changeup in 2019 as well. NWL hitters swung and missed at Wallace's pitches nearly 17% of the time, ranking him 12th among league pitchers with at least 20 innings. Wallace is twitchy and athletic and has the uptempo, aggressive delivery befitting of a late-inning stopper.
THE FUTURE: Wallace's power arsenal should allow him to start 2021 at least at high Class A and get him to Double-A rather quickly.

Year	Age	Club (League)	Class	W	L	ERA	G	GS	IP	H	HR	BB	SO	BB/9	SO/9	WHIP	AVG
2019	20	Boise (NWL)	SS	0	0	1.29	22	0	21	9	1	9	29	3.9	12.4	0.86	.113
Minor League Totals				0	0	1.29	22	0	21	9	1	9	29	3.9	12.4	0.86	.129

26 CEDDANNE RAFAELA, SS/2B

BA GRADE **40** Risk: High

Born: Sept. 18, 2000. **B-T:** R-R. **HT:** 5-8. **WT:** 145. **Signed:** Curacao, 2017. **Signed by:** Dennis Neuman/Rollie Pino/Todd Claus.
TRACK RECORD: Though Rafaela didn't look much bigger when he signed for $10,000 as a 16-year-old than he did when playing for Curacao in the Little League World Series as an 11-year-old, he's shown not only plus running speed but also surprisingly loud contact in the lower minors. His track record includes a .244/.319/.409 batting line with six home runs and nine stolen bases in the Rookie-level Gulf Coast

League and short-season Lowell in 2019.

SCOUTING REPORT: Rafaela is hard to miss. His high-energy style of play is evident in every aspect of the game and he turns heads with his unexpected bat speed and ability to put a charge in pitches in the zone, particularly against lefthanders. However, his bat-to-ball skills can work against him given that he's a free-swinger who is prone to weak contact against pitches outside the zone. Still, he has a chance to offer relatively solid impact as a versatile up-the-middle player, at least at second base and shortstop with the possibility of future work in center field.

THE FUTURE: Rafaela's ability to hone his aggressiveness will dictate his future. His most likely role is as a versatile reserve.

Year	Age	Club (League)	Class	AVG	G	AB	R	H	2B	3B	HR	RBI	BB	SO	SB	OBP	SLG
2019	18	Red Sox (GCL)	R	.248	41	153	30	38	1	4	6	17	14	28	9	.329	.425
	18	Lowell (NYP)	SS	.182	3	11	0	2	0	0	0	1	0	3	0	.167	.182
Minor League Totals				.259	98	367	61	95	10	6	9	46	28	70	28	.323	.392

27 ANDREW POLITI, RHP

BA GRADE 40 Risk: High

Born: June 4, 1996. **B-T:** R-R. **HT:** 6-0. **WT:** 195. **Drafted:** Seton Hall, 2018 (15th round). **Signed by:** Ray Fagnant.

TRACK RECORD: The Red Sox took Politi as an unheralded 15th-round selection in 2018 after a redshirt junior year in which he had a 5.44 ERA but struck out 12.6 batters per nine innings, mostly out of the bullpen.

SCOUTING REPORT: Politi entered pro ball with a mid-90s four-seam fastball that features elite spin and movement, as well as a mid-80s curveball that gave him the basis of a north-south attack. The addition of an 89-93 mph cutter in 2019 set the stage for a dominant performance at high Class A Salem over his final 50 innings of 2019, a run in which he posted a 1.42 ERA and struck out 63 batters. He moved from the bullpen to the rotation during that stretch, making five starts. Politi is also working on a changeup. The effort in his delivery leads to skepticism about his ability to start, but based on what he showed in late 2019 and then in 2020 at instructional league, the Red Sox will give him a chance in the rotation.

THE FUTURE: Politi has the solid floor of a big league reliever with a chance that his cutter and changeup could open additional doors as an opener, bulk reliever or even starter.

Year	Age	Club (League)	Class	W	L	ERA	G	GS	IP	H	HR	BB	SO	BB/9	SO/9	WHIP	AVG
2019	23	Salem (CAR)	HiA	5	2	3.55	33	5	79	56	4	37	96	4.2	11.0	1.18	.165
	23	Wilmington (CAR)	HiA	0	0	0.00	1	1	4	2	0	0	6	0.0	13.5	0.50	.154
Minor League Totals				6	3	3.76	54	5	107	86	6	47	139	3.9	11.6	1.24	.217

28 EDUARD BAZARDO, RHP

BA GRADE 40 Risk: High

Born: Sept. 1, 1995. **B-T:** R-R. **HT:** 6-0. **WT:** 165. **Signed:** Venezuela, 2014. **Signed by:** Alex Requena/Eddie Romero.

TRACK RECORD: Bazardo signed for $8,000 as an undersized 18-year-old in Venezuela. Though he always featured a potentially plus breaking ball with huge spin rates, and he has been a consistently excellent late-innings performer as a pro, he was left unprotected and went undrafted in the 2019 Rule 5 draft. During the shutdown, Bazardo stayed at the Red Sox's Dominican academy, where he added 10 pounds and emerged at instructional league with a fastball that ticked up from the low 90s to hold at 94-97 mph.

SCOUTING REPORT: Bazardo always featured excellent arm speed, the ability to spin the ball and a willingness to attack the strike zone. He started his pro career as a fastball/curveball pitcher who struggled against lefthanded hitters, but the addition of a slider helped him even his splits. He profiled as a depth reliever before his velocity bump allowed his fastball to tick up a grade or two. He's also started developing a splitter.

THE FUTURE: Bazardo probably profiles as a mid-innings reliever, but his four-pitch mix and command give him a chance as a swingman or an opener. His addition to the 40-man roster reflects the possibility he could reach the big leagues in 2021.

Year	Age	Club (League)	Class	W	L	ERA	G	GS	IP	H	HR	BB	SO	BB/9	SO/9	WHIP	AVG
2019	23	Salem (CAR)	HiA	5	2	3.55	33	5	79	56	4	37	96	4.2	11.0	1.18	.165
	23	Wilmington (CAR)	HiA	0	0	0.00	1	1	4	2	0	0	6	0.0	13.5	0.50	.154
Minor League Totals				6	3	3.76	54	5	107	86	6	47	139	3.9	11.6	1.24	.217

29 NICK DECKER, OF

Born: Oct. 2, 1999. **B-T:** L-L. **HT:** 6-0. **WT:** 200. **Drafted:** HS—Tabernacle, N.J., 2018 (2nd round). **Signed by:** Ray Fagnant.

TRACK RECORD: The Red Sox were drawn to Decker's bat speed, power potential, athleticism and passion for the game in the 2018 draft. He convinced them to sign him for slightly above slot at $1.25 million in the second round, though a fractured wrist largely kept Decker off the field in 2018.

SCOUTING REPORT: Decker possesses wiry strength and showed the all-fields raw power of an outfield corner at short-season Lowell in 2019, when he posted a .247/.328/.471 line with an impressive .224 isolated slugging percentage. Strikeouts are a concern because he not only chases pitches but also misses some hittable offerings in the strike zone, which is more likely the product of inconsistent timing in the weight transfer in his crouch than hand-eye coordination issues. Decker's balance improved in cage work at instructional league, but those efforts didn't show up in games. His durability is a question.

THE FUTURE: Decker has the power, range and arm to have potential to emerge as an everyday right fielder, though the greater likelihood is that he'll become a more valuable part of an outfield platoon.

Year	Age	Club (League)	Class	AVG	G	AB	R	H	2B	3B	HR	RBI	BB	SO	SB	OBP	SLG
2019	19	Lowell (NYP)	SS	.247	53	170	23	42	10	5	6	25	21	59	4	.328	.471
Minor League Totals				.247	55	174	24	43	11	5	6	25	22	60	4	.330	.471

30 JEREMY WU-YELLAND, LHP

Born: June 24, 1999. **B-T:** L-L. **HT:** 6-2. **WT:** 210. **Drafted:** Hawaii, 2020 (4th round). **Signed by:** J.J. Altobelli.

TRACK RECORD: While Wu-Yelland pitched just 13 innings as a junior before the shutdown, his fastball/slider combination from a low three-quarters arm slot left opposing hitters feeling uncomfortable, particularly in four shutout innings against Vanderbilt. The Red Sox signed him to a below-slot bonus of $200,000 as a fourth-round pick in 2020.

SCOUTING REPORT: Wu-Yelland is one of the most explosive, powerful pitchers in Boston's system, with the stuff to match. Though he usually worked at 94 mph at Hawaii, he regularly sat at 95-96 and topped out at 97 with his two-seamer and four-seamer in instructional league. Both his fastball and slider possess plus life from a low arm slot—which is reminiscent of Francisco Liriano—which made opposing hitters uncomfortable. He also has shown the ability to shape a changeup against righthanded hitters. His control is wildly inconsistent—he walked 5.6 batters per nine innings in college—and he had a number of innings end early in instructs to manage his workload.

THE FUTURE: Wu-Yelland will get a chance to start, and if his control and changeup develop, he could surprise by staying on a rotation track. Most likely, though, he has a future as a reliever.

Year	Age	Club (League)	Class	W	L	ERA	G	GS	IP	H	HR	BB	SO	BB/9	SO/9	WHIP	AVG
2020	21	Did not play—No minor league season															

MORE PROSPECTS TO KNOW

31 CAMERON CANNON, 2B

Cannon was an excellent college performer for three years at Arizona before struggling while trying to force power in his 2019 pro debut, but the Red Sox believe their 2019 top pick got back to a more balanced and productive approach at instructional league in 2020.

32 RYAN ZEFERJAHN, RHP

The Kansas-bred righthander has developed from a thrower into a pitcher and moved from a two-seamer to a four-seamer. He pairs it with a power slider. He's likely a reliever.

33 BRENDAN CELLUCCI, LHP

The former Tulane closer has a pair of plus pitches in his upper-90s fastball and slider. He could jump on a fast track if he improves his control. He'll likely open 2021 at a Class A level.

34 BRANDON HOWLETT, 3B

The 21st-round pick in 2018 had a tremendous first pro summer but then struggled at low Class A as a 19-year-old in 2019. But he's shown enough of an approach and strength to believe in his upside.

35 WILKELMAN GONZALEZ, RHP

The 18-year-old, signed out of Venezuela in 2018, has improved steadily in pro ball. He now pitches at 92 mph and touches 95, with a chance for a plus breaking ball and feel for a changeup.

36 BRADLEY BLALOCK, RHP

SLEEPER

Blalock pitched at 87-91 mph as an amateur but boosted his fastball by two grades at age 19 during the shutdown. He sat in the low 90s and frequently touched 95 mph with an easy delivery at instructional league. He also has feel for both a curveball and slider.

37 NATHANAEL CRUZ, RHP

The tall, slender 17-year-old already works in the low 90s with an advanced changeup for his relative inexperience. His slider still has a ways to go, but he has starter projection and has made significant strides in his year-plus since signing.

38 DURBIN FELTMAN, RHP

Drafted as a potential fast-track power reliever in 2018, Feltman instead struggled badly in Double-A in 2019. His four-seam fastball velocity (97 mph) and the ability to command it at the top of the zone to set up a sharp mid-80s slider returned in instructs, giving him the look of a big league reliever.

39 TYLER ESPLIN, OF

Esplin seemed to be turning a developmental corner as a 19-year-old in low Class A Greenville in 2019. His frequent hard contact is currently sabotaged by high groundball rates, but he's making progress both getting the ball in the air and using the whole field. A player with size and strength has shown enough improvement to give hope that an offensive breakthrough could be coming.

40 SHANE DROHAN, LHP

The Florida State lefthander has an intriguing three-pitch mix but badly needs to improve his control and command before he can turn potential into results.

TOP PROSPECTS OF THE DECADE

Year	Player, Pos	2020 Org
2011	Jose Iglesias, SS	Orioles
2012	Will Middlebrooks, 3B	Did not play
2013	Xander Bogaerts, SS	Red Sox
2014	Xander Bogaerts, SS/3B	Red Sox
2015	Blake Swihart, C	Rangers
2016	Yoan Moncada, 3B	White Sox
2017	Andrew Benintendi, OF	Red Sox
2018	Jay Groome, LHP	Red Sox
2019	Bobby Dalbec, 3B	Red Sox
2020	Triston Casas, 1B	Red Sox

TOP DRAFT PICKS OF THE DECADE

Year	Player, Pos	2020 Org
2011	Matt Barnes, RHP	Red Sox
2012	Deven Marrero, SS	Did not play
2013	Trey Ball, LHP	Did not play
2014	Michael Chavis, SS	Red Sox
2015	Andrew Benintendi, OF	Red Sox
2016	Jay Groome, LHP	Red Sox
2017	Tanner Houck, RHP	Red Sox
2018	Triston Casas, 3B	Red Sox
2019	Cameron Cannon, SS (2nd round)	Red Sox
2020	Nick Yorke, 2B	Red Sox

DEPTH CHART

BOSTON RED SOX

TOP 2021 ROOKIES	RANK
Bobby Dalbec, 1B	3
Bryan Mata, RHP	4
Tanner Houck, RHP	8
BREAKOUT PROSPECTS	**RANK**
Matthew Lugo, SS	14

SOURCE OF TOP 30 TALENT

Homegrown	22	Acquired	8
College	7	Trade	6
Junior college	0	Rule 5 draft	2
High school	7	Independent league	0
Nondrafted free agent	0	Free agent/waivers	0
International	8		

LF
Tyler Esplin
Bryan Gonzalez

CF
Jarren Duran (5)
Gilberto Jimenez (7)
Jeisson Rosario (20)
Eduardo Lopez

RF
Nick Decker (29)
Juan Chacon
Darel Belen

3B
Hudson Potts (24)
Brandon Howlett

SS
Matthew Lugo (14)
Brainer Bonaci (18)
C.J. Chatham

2B
Jeter Downs (2)
Nick Yorke (9)
Jonathan Arauz (21)
Ceddanne Rafaela (26)
Cameron Cannon

1B
Triston Casas (1)
Bobby Dalbec (3)
Blaze Jordan (16)

C
Connor Wong (15)
Deivy Grullon

LHP

LHSP
Jay Groome (6)
Chris Murphy (13)
Shane Drohan

LHRP
Jeremy Wu-Yelland (30)
Brendan Cellucci

RHP

RHSP
Bryan Mata (4)
Thad Ward (10)
Connor Seabold (11)
Noah Song (12)
Garrett Whitlock (17)
Brayan Bello (19)
Aldo Ramirez (22)
Chih-Jung Liu (23)
Wilkelman Gonzalez
Bradley Blalock
Nathanael Cruz
Brian Van Belle

RHRP
Tanner Houck (8)
Jacob Wallace (25)
Andrew Politi (27)
Eduard Bazardo (28)
Ryan Zeferjahn
Durbin Feltman
Dylan Spacke

Chicago Cubs

BY KYLE GLASER

Nothing lasts forever.

After the Cubs' most consistent run of success in over a century, the organization enters 2021 in flux.

Theo Epstein, the architect of the rebuild that brought the Cubs their first World Series championship in 108 years, resigned as president of baseball operations after the 2020 season. More than 100 employees in business and baseball operations were laid off due to revenue losses from the coronavirus pandemic, including many top scouts. Jon Lester departed in free agency, and Kyle Schwarber and Albert Almora were not tendered contracts, leaving just six players remaining from the 2016 champions.

More change is coming. Anthony Rizzo, Kris Bryant and Javier Baez are all set to be free agents after the 2021 season. Re-signing all of them would be prohibitively expensive and, realistically, isn't likely to happen. The Cubs have some tough decisions looming, with the hope their improving farm system can help soften the blow of the departures.

There are reasons to be optimistic. Jed Hoyer, Epstein's longtime top lieutenant, ascended to president of baseball operations and was every bit a part of the Cubs successful rebuild. The Cubs won the National League Central in 2020 under first-year manager David Ross, a step in the right direction after they were a wild card in 2018 and missed the playoffs altogether in 2019. Outfielder Ian Happ, catcher Willson Contreras and infielder David Bote give the Cubs young position players to build with in addition to whichever of their marquee talents they re-sign. Righthanders Yu Darvish and Kyle Hendricks remain under contract and effective at the front of the rotation.

But in order to backfill the looming talent departures and extend the franchise's run of success, the Cubs farm system is going to have to deliver. The first test comes this season, with Lester, Jose Quintana and Tyler Chatwood all gone and leaving holes in the rotation. Top pitching prospect Brailyn Marquez made his big league debut in 2020 and righthander Adbert Alzolay took a step forward in his second stint in the majors, providing hope the Cubs already have the necessary reinforcements in-house.

The Cubs overhauled their scouting and player development staffs after the 2019 season. The new groups did not get a chance to show what they could do because of the canceled 2020 minor league season, but steps forward at the alternate training site from Marquez, Alzolay, outfielder Brennen Davis, catcher Miguel Amaya and third baseman Christopher Morel were promising.

After a multitude of prospect-for-veteran trades between 2015 and 2019, most notably the ones that sacrificed Gleyber Torres and Eloy Jimenez, the Cubs largely held on to their top prospects at the 2020 trade deadline, knowing they are going to need them sooner rather than later. Combined with the progress of many high-profile international signings and positive early returns on their 2018 to 2020 draft classes, the Cubs' farm system is in better shape than it has been in years.

Seeing how that system progresses will be critical this season—both to keep the Cubs' competitive window open, and to stabilize the organization's long-term outlook. ■

NUCCIO DINUZZO/GETTY IMAGES

Theo Epstein turned over baseball operations to Jed Hoyer as the Cubs enter a new era.

PROJECTED 2024 LINEUP

Position	Player	Age
Catcher	Miguel Amaya	25
First Base	Anthony Rizzo	34
Second Base	Nico Hoerner	27
Third Base	David Bote	31
Shortstop	Ed Howard	22
Left Field	Cole Roederer	24
Center Field	Ian Happ	29
Right Field	Brennen Davis	24
Designated Hitter	Victor Caratini	30
No. 1 Starter	Kyle Hendricks	34
No. 2 Starter	Brailyn Marquez	25
No. 3 Starter	Adbert Alzolay	29
No. 4 Starter	Kohl Franklin	24
No. 5 Starter	Alec Mills	32
Closer	Ryan Jensen	26

1 BRAILYN MARQUEZ, LHP

Born: Jan. 30, 1999. **B-T:** L-L. **HT:** 6-4. **WT:** 185.
Signed: Dominican Republic, 2015.
Signed by: Mario Encarnacion/Jose Serra/Alex Suarez/Louie Eljaua.

JONATHAN DANIEL/GETTY IMAGES

BA GRADE
60 **Risk: High**

SCOUTING GRADES
Fastball: 80. **Curveball:** 45. **Slider:** 60. **Changeup:** 50. **Control:** 45.

Projected future grades on 20-80 scouting scale.

TRACK RECORD: The Cubs signed Marquez out of the Dominican Republic for $600,000 in 2015, the largest signing bonus given to any lefthanded pitcher in that year's international class. Marquez progressively filled out his projectable frame and began touching 98 mph as a starter in the short-season Northwest League in 2018, then in 2019 began sitting in the upper 90s and touched 102 mph as he conquered both Class A levels. The Cubs sent him to their alternate training site in 2020, where he held his own facing more experienced hitters. He received his first callup on the final day of the regular season, but struggled in his lone appearance.

SCOUTING REPORT: Marquez generates some of the easiest velocity of any pitching prospect. His fastball sits 97-98 mph and frequently touches triple digits with startlingly little effort. He holds his velocity through his starts and has steadily become more durable every season. Marquez can dominate with his fastball alone and often does, but he is still working to improve his fastball command. He has long limbs and a thick midsection, so the Cubs have had to work with him to remain athletic in his delivery and get his upper and lower body synced up. Marquez throws his fastball for strikes when he's on time in his delivery, but when he isn't, it sails to his arm side or gets pulled into the righthanded batter's box. Marquez previously threw a mid-80s slider as his breaking ball, but he began working on pitch design at the alternate site and separated out a slider and curveball. His slider now sits in the upper 80s with added power and tunnels well off of his fastball. His mid-80s, slurvy curveball is a change-of-pace option he can land for strikes. Marquez rounds out his arsenal with a hard 89-91 mph changeup that gets more swings and misses every year. He sells his changeup with his arm speed and has improved his command to make it a more consistent weapon. Marquez goes right after hitters and isn't afraid to challenge them, though he still has spurts of wildness. He is continuing to work on landing his secondary pitches in the strike zone and maintaining consistent fastball command. He has a good feel for making adjustments on the mound and self-correcting any delivery flaws, which has helped his control gradually improve each year.

THE FUTURE: Marquez features explosive, top-of-the-rotation stuff from the left side.Whether he continues to improve his control will determine if he reaches his ceiling or ends up in the bullpen, where he would have closer potential. ■

BEST TOOLS

Best Hitter for Average	Chase Strumpf
Best Power Hitter	Brennen Davis
Best Strike-Zone Discipline	Miguel Amaya
Fastest Baserunner	Zach Davis
Best Athlete	Brennen Davis
Best Fastball	Brailyn Marquez
Best Curveball	Riley Thompson
Best Slider	Cory Abbott
Best Changeup	Kohl Franklin
Best Control	Keegan Thompson
Best Defensive Catcher	PJ Higgins
Best Defensive Infielder	Ed Howard
Best Infield Arm	Christopher Morel
Best Defensive Outfielder	Cole Roederer
Best Outfield Arm	Eddy Martinez

Year	Age	Club (League)	Class	W	L	ERA	G	GS	IP	H	HR	BB	SO	BB/9	SO/9	WHIP	AVG
2018	19	Eugene (NWL)	SS	1	4	3.21	10	10	48	46	5	14	52	2.6	9.8	1.26	.234
	19	South Bend (MWL)	LoA	0	0	2.57	2	2	7	7	0	2	7	2.6	9.0	1.29	.226
2019	20	Myrtle Beach (CAR)	HiA	4	1	1.71	5	5	26	21	1	7	26	2.4	8.9	1.06	.198
	20	South Bend (MWL)	LoA	5	4	3.61	17	17	77	64	4	43	102	5.0	11.9	1.38	.193
2020	21	Chicago (NL)	MAJ	0	0	67.50	1	0	1	2	0	3	1	40.5	13.5	7.50	.500
Major League Totals				0	0	67.50	1	0	0	2	0	3	1	40.5	13.5	7.50	.500
Minor League Totals				16	12	3.19	57	55	257	232	14	101	287	3.5	10.1	1.30	.240

2 BRENNEN DAVIS, OF

Born: Nov. 2, 1999. **B-T:** R-R. **HT:** 6-4. **WT:** 175. **Drafted:** HS—Chandler, Ariz., 2018 (2nd round). **Signed by:** Steve McFarland.

TRACK RECORD: Davis starred in both baseball and basketball in high school and signed with the Cubs for $1.1 million after they drafted him 62nd overall in 2018. He had a standout first full season at low Class A South Bend, but was limited to 50 games after he was hit by a pitch and fractured his right index finger. He returned healthy in 2020 and spent the year holding his own against older pitchers at the Cubs' alternate training site.

SCOUTING REPORT: Davis is a long, lean athlete dripping with physical projection. His long levers and growing strength give him plus raw power to his pull side and allow him to drive the ball hard up the middle and the opposite way. Davis crushes breaking balls, but he has had to work hard to get on time against plus velocity and is still progressing. He's a fast learner who makes quick adjustments and controls the strike zone. Davis is a plus runner underway in the outfield and has a plus arm, but he projects to slow down as he fills out. He may begin his career in center field before eventually moving to right.

THE FUTURE: Davis has all the tools to become an everyday outfielder for the Cubs. He should see the upper minors during the 2021 season.

SCOUTING GRADES: **Hitting:** 50 **Power:** 60 **Running:** 60 **Fielding:** 50 **Arm:** 60

Year	Age	Club (League)	Class	AVG	G	AB	R	H	2B	3B	HR	RBI	BB	SO	SB	OBP	SLG
2018	18	Cubs 2 (AZL)	R	.298	18	57	9	17	2	0	0	3	10	12	6	.431	.333
2019	19	South Bend (MWL)	LoA	.305	50	177	33	54	9	3	8	30	18	38	4	.381	.525
Minor League Totals				.303	68	234	42	71	11	3	8	33	28	50	10	.394	.479

3 MIGUEL AMAYA, C

ADAM GLANZMAN/MLB PHOTOS VIA GETTY IMAGES

Born: March 9, 1999. **B-T:** R-R. **HT:** 6-2. **WT:** 230. **Signed:** Panama, 2015. **Signed by:** Marino Encarnacion/Jose Serra/Alex Suarez/Louie Eljaua.

TRACK RECORD: Amaya starred for Panama in international tournaments as an amateur and signed with the Cubs for $1 million in 2015. He quickly stood out and represented the Cubs in both the 2018 and 2019 Futures Games, then impressed manager David Ross with his physicality and work ethic during major league spring training in 2020. Amaya spent the summer at the Cubs' alternate training site gaining experience working with older pitchers.

SCOUTING REPORT: Amaya is a big, physical backstop who looks the part of a major league catcher. He matured greatly at the alternate site camp and improved his focus, motivation and investment on defense, helping his receiving and pitch framing improve to average. He has a quick exchange and a plus arm that shuts down running games. Amaya is a patient hitter who controls the strike zone and swings at the right pitches. He has the strength to hit 20 or more home runs, but he frequently hits the ball on the ground and is still learning to elevate.

THE FUTURE: Cubs officials were pleased with Amaya's improved work ethic behind the plate at the alternate site camp. That development has him in line to be the Cubs' catcher of the future.

SCOUTING GRADES: **Hitting:** 50 **Power:** 55 **Running:** 30 **Fielding:** 50 **Arm:** 60

Year	Age	Club (League)	Class	AVG	G	AB	R	H	2B	3B	HR	RBI	BB	SO	SB	OBP	SLG
2017	18	Eugene (NWL)	SS	.228	58	228	21	52	14	1	3	26	11	49	1	.266	.338
2018	19	South Bend (MWL)	LoA	.256	116	414	54	106	21	2	12	52	50	91	1	.349	.403
2019	20	Myrtle Beach (CAR)	HiA	.235	99	341	50	80	24	0	11	57	54	69	2	.351	.402
Minor League Totals				.243	331	1191	154	289	71	3	27	157	136	236	13	.334	.375

4 ED HOWARD, SS

Born: Jan. 29, 2002. **B-T:** R-R. **HT:** 6-2. **WT:** 185. **Drafted:** HS—Chicago, 2020 (1st round). **Signed by:** John Pedrotty.

BILL MITCHELL

BA GRADE
55 Risk: Extreme

TRACK RECORD: Howard led Chicago's Jackie Robinson West to the Little League World Series championship game in 2014 and emerged as the top prep shortstop in the 2020 draft class after a standout career at Mount Carmel High, 15 miles south of Wrigley Field. Howard didn't get to play his senior year before the coronavirus pandemic canceled his high school season, but the Cubs had seen enough of the hometown product to draft him 16th overall and sign him for $3.745 million to forgo an Oklahoma commitment.

SCOUTING REPORT: Howard is a gifted defensive shortstop who is mature beyond his years. He makes both flashy plays and routine ones with his reliable hands and a plus, accurate arm. He has a solid internal clock and moves fluidly across the diamond, showing impressive body control for his age and also elite athleticism. Howard makes contact in the strike zone against fastballs and recognizes spin, but he needs to refine his approach and add strength to impact the ball. Optimistic evaluators project .260 with 15-18 home runs as Howard's modest offensive ceiling. His elite work ethic gives him a chance to surpass those expectations.

THE FUTURE: Howard's defense gives him a strong foundation. How his offense develops will determine if he becomes the Cubs' shortstop of the future.

SCOUTING GRADES: **Hitting:** 50 **Power:** 45 **Running:** 55 **Fielding:** 60 **Arm:** 60

Year	Age	Club (League)	Class	AVG	G	AB	R	H	2B	3B	HR	RBI	BB	SO	SB	OBP	SLG
2020	18	Did not play—No minor league season															

5 ADBERT ALZOLAY, RHP

Born: May 1, 1995. **B-T:** R-R. **HT:** 6-1. **WT:** 208. **Signed:** Dominican Republic, 2012. **Signed by:** Julio Figueroa/Hector Ortega.

TOP ROOKIE

ADAM GLANZMAN/MLB PHOTOS VIA GETTY IMAGES

BA GRADE
50 Risk: Medium

TRACK RECORD: Alzolay signed with the Cubs for just $10,000 when he was 17. He soared to Double-A in a breakout 2017 season, but injuries to his lat and biceps limited him the next two years. He still made his major league debut in 2019 and returned to the majors in 2020, where he posted a 2.96 ERA in six appearances, working mostly as a spot starter and long reliever.

SCOUTING REPORT: Alzolay added a two-seam fastball and slider to his repertoire in 2020, giving him five distinct pitches. His fastballs both range from 93-97 mph, with his riding four-seamer more effective than his fading two-seamer, and his mid-80s slider has become a dominant swing-and-miss pitch. He has both a vertical, late-breaking version of his slider and a sharp, horizontal one when he moves to more of a cutter grip. His changeup is an above-average pitch that runs away from lefties and his snapping, low-80s curveball is a solid offering that gets a lot of called strikes. Alzolay pounds the strike zone when he has a good pace, but his control and deception suffer when he rushes through his delivery.

THE FUTURE: Alzolay's expanded pitch mix has solidified his future as part of the Cubs' rotation. He should take his place there in 2021.

SCOUTING GRADES: **Fastball:** 60 **Slider:** 60 **Curveball:** 50 **Changeup:** 55 **Control:** 45

Year	Age	Club (League)	Class	W	L	ERA	G	GS	IP	H	HR	BB	SO	BB/9	SO/9	WHIP	AVG
2017	22	Myrtle Beach (CAR)	HiA	7	1	2.98	15	15	82	65	8	22	78	2.4	8.6	1.07	.198
	22	Tennessee (SL)	AA	0	3	3.03	7	7	33	27	0	12	30	3.3	8.3	1.19	.200
2018	23	Iowa (PCL)	AAA	2	4	4.76	8	8	40	43	4	13	27	2.9	6.1	1.41	.251
2019	24	Chicago (NL)	MAJ	1	1	7.30	4	2	12	13	4	9	13	6.6	9.5	1.78	.217
	24	Iowa (PCL)	AAA	2	4	4.41	15	15	65	53	10	31	91	4.3	12.5	1.29	.188
	24	Myrtle Beach (CAR)	HiA	0	1	11.25	1	1	4	7	1	2	3	4.5	6.8	2.25	.350
2020	25	Chicago (NL)	MAJ	1	1	2.95	6	4	21	12	1	13	29	5.5	12.2	1.17	.169
Major League Totals				2	2	4.54	10	6	33	25	5	22	42	5.9	11.2	1.40	.207
Minor League Totals				33	27	3.63	105	84	491	425	41	145	448	2.7	8.2	1.16	.232

6 KOHL FRANKLIN, RHP

Born: Sept. 9, 1999. **B-T:** R-R. **HT:** 6-4. **WT:** 190. **Drafted:** HS—Broken Arrow, Okla., 2018 (6th round). **Signed by:** Ty Nichols.

BA GRADE

50 Risk: High

TRACK RECORD: Franklin is the nephew of 12-year major league pitcher Ryan Franklin and came from the same Oklahoma high school that produced Brad Penny and Archie Bradley. The Cubs liked his size and pedigree and drafted him in the sixth round in 2018 despite the fact he missed most of his senior year with a broken foot. Franklin signed for an above-slot $540,000 bonus and saw his stuff jump as he climbed to low Class A South Bend the following summer.

SCOUTING REPORT: Franklin checks all the boxes for a young pitcher with a projectable 6-foot-4 frame, an athletic delivery and three pitches he can throw for strikes. He pounds the strike zone with a 92-95 mph fastball and shows advanced feel for an 80-84 changeup. His biggest development has been his curveball, now a big breaker at 75-77 mph with increased depth that gets batters swinging and missing over the top. Franklin's frame and athleticism provide optimism he will add velocity and develop above-average control in time. He's thrown just 50.2 professional innings and needs to show he can maintain his stuff and command over an expanded workload.

THE FUTURE: The Cubs believe Franklin has the upside of a mid-rotation starter. He's on track for full-season ball in 2021.

SCOUTING GRADES: **Fastball:** 60 **Curveball:** 60 **Changeup:** 50 **Control:** 55

Year	Age	Club (League)	Class	W	L	ERA	G	GS	IP	H	HR	BB	SO	BB/9	K/9	WHIP	AVG
2018	18	Cubs 2 (AZL)	R	0	1	6.23	5	3	9	5	0	6	8	6.2	8.3	1.27	.161
2019	19	Eugene (NWL)	SS	1	3	2.31	10	10	39	31	2	14	49	3.2	11.3	1.15	.214
	19	South Bend (MWL)	LoA	0	0	3.00	1	1	3	0	0	5	3	15.0	9.0	1.67	.000
Minor League Totals				1	4	3.02	16	14	50	36	2	25	60	4.4	10.7	1.20	.194

7 RYAN JENSEN, RHP

Born: Nov. 23, 1997. **B-T:** R-R. **HT:** 6-0. **WT:** 180. **Drafted:** Fresno State, 2019 (1st round). **Signed by:** Gabe Zappin.

TRACK RECORD: Jensen began as a reliever at Fresno State before transitioning to the rotation as a sophomore. He blossomed as a junior, winning Mountain West Conference pitcher of the year honors, and the Cubs drafted him 27th overall and signed him for $2 million. Jensen pitched a 2.25 ERA in his pro debut at short-season Eugene, but also struggled with his control with 14 walks and 19 strikeouts in 12 innings.

SCOUTING REPORT: Jensen is a tremendous athlete with loads of raw arm strength. His fastball is a plus-plus offering that ticked up to 95-100 mph based on data the Cubs received during the shutdown, and it plays up further with plus armside life. Jensen's mid-80s slider continues to get sharper the more he throws it and projects to be an above-average pitch. Jensen rarely threw a changeup in college and is still in the early stages of developing one. He is relatively new to starting, so his control and feel to pitch are still developing. Some Cubs officials believe Jensen is athletic enough to become an average strike-thrower, but others are less bullish.

THE FUTURE: Jensen's changeup and control will be key to watch in his first full season in 2021. If they stall, his fastball and slider combination will play in high-leverage relief.

SCOUTING GRADES: **Fastball:** 70 **Slider:** 55 **Changeup:** 40 **Control:** 45

Year	Age	Club (League)	Class	W	L	ERA	G	GS	IP	H	HR	BB	SO	BB/9	SO/9	WHIP	AVG
2019	21	Eugene (NWL)	SS	0	0	2.25	6	6	12	7	0	14	19	10.5	14.3	1.75	.123
Minor League Totals				0	0	2.25	6	6	12	7	0	14	19	10.5	14.3	1.75	.171

8 CHRISTOPHER MOREL, 3B

ANDREW WOOLLEY/FOUR SEAM IMAGES

BA GRADE
50 Risk: High

Born: June 24, 1999. **B-T:** R-R. **HT:** 6-0. **WT:** 140. **Signed:** Dominican Republic, 2015. **Signed by:** Jose Estevez/Gian Guzman/Jose Serra.

TRACK RECORD: The Cubs signed Morel for $800,000 as part of their stellar 2015 international signing class that included Brailyn Marquez, Miguel Amaya and current Tigers third baseman Isaac Paredes. Morel struggled initially after signing but broke out at low Class A South Bend in 2019 before sustaining a season-ending knee injury. The Cubs brought him to their alternate training site in 2020, where he impressed facing older pitchers.

SCOUTING REPORT: Morel has some of the loudest tools in the Cubs' system. He has massive, plus raw power, is a plus runner and has a cannon for a right arm. Morel's issue is he often plays too fast. He's an aggressive, free swinger who chases fastballs up and breaking balls down and away and rushes plays in the infield, resulting in too many throwing errors. He reeled in his approach to stay up the middle at the alternate site and improved greatly over the course of camp, giving the Cubs hope he will hit enough to get to his power. He's an average defender at third base who can also stand in at shortstop and second base. The Cubs plan to experiment with him in center field to expand his versatility.

THE FUTURE: Morel made great strides at the alternate site in 2020. He'll see if they hold in 2021.

SCOUTING GRADES: **Hitting:** 45 **Power:** 60 **Running:** 60 **Fielding:** 50 **Arm:** 70

Year	Age	Club (League)	Class	AVG	G	AB	R	H	2B	3B	HR	RBI	BB	SO	SB	OBP	SLG
2017	18	Cubs (DSL)	R	.220	61	223	44	49	6	2	7	40	35	37	23	.332	.359
2018	19	Eugene (NWL)	SS	.165	25	91	7	15	2	0	1	8	0	29	0	.172	.220
	19	Cubs 1 (AZL)	R	.257	29	113	20	29	6	0	2	12	11	28	1	.331	.363
2019	20	South Bend (MWL)	LoA	.284	73	257	36	73	15	7	6	31	11	60	9	.320	.467
Minor League Totals				.243	188	684	107	166	29	9	16	91	57	154	33	.308	.382

9 CHASE STRUMPF, 2B

BA GRADE
50 Risk: High

Born: March 8, 1998. **B-T:** R-R. **HT:** 6-1. **WT:** 191. **Drafted:** UCLA, 2019 (2nd round). **Signed by:** Tom Myers.

TRACK RECORD: Strumpf preceded Royce Lewis, the No. 1 overall pick in the 2017 draft, as the shortstop at national power JSerra High in Southern California. Strumpf went on to a decorated three-year career at UCLA, capped by winning Most Outstanding Player of the Los Angeles Regional his junior year. The Cubs drafted him in the second round, No. 64 overall, and signed him for just over $1.05 million. He reached low Class A for six games in his pro debut.

SCOUTING REPORT: Strumpf is a consistent, mature hitter with a patient approach and knack for putting the barrel on the ball. He works counts, takes his walks and lines the ball hard to the gaps when he gets a pitch to hit. Strumpf is mostly a contact hitter, but he has sneaky power the Cubs believe will translate into more home runs as he takes a more aggressive approach. Strumpf makes all the routine plays at second base and has shown better arm strength in pro ball than he did in college, allowing him to play the left side of the infield as needed. Strumpf has dealt with foot, back and wrist injuries in the last three years, so health is a concern.

THE FUTURE: Strumpf has a chance to develop into a steady, everyday second baseman who hits for average and possibly power. He'll move to full-season ball in 2021.

SCOUTING GRADES: **Hitting:** 55 **Power:** 50 **Running:** 45 **Fielding:** 50 **Arm:** 45

Year	Age	Club (League)	Class	AVG	G	AB	R	H	2B	3B	HR	RBI	BB	SO	SB	OBP	SLG
2019	21	Cubs 2 (AZL)	R	.182	7	22	5	4	3	0	0	1	7	7	0	.406	.318
	21	Eugene (NWL)	SS	.292	26	89	17	26	8	0	2	14	15	28	2	.405	.449
	21	South Bend (MWL)	LoA	.125	6	24	3	3	1	0	1	2	1	7	0	.214	.292
Minor League Totals				.244	39	135	25	33	12	0	3	17	23	42	2	.374	.400

10 RILEY THOMPSON, RHP

BA GRADE
50 **Risk: High**

Born: July 9, 1996. **B-T:** L-R. **HT:** 6-3. **WT:** 205. **Drafted:** Louisville, 2018 (11th round). **Signed by:** Jacob Williams.

TRACK RECORD: Thompson had Tommy John surgery his freshman year at Louisville and struggled to throw strikes when he returned, leaving him with a career 5.82 ERA despite solid stuff. The Cubs drafted him in the 11th round and gave him an above-slot $200,000 bonus because they believed they could fix his control. Thompson rewarded that faith in his first full season at low Class A South Bend, going 8-6, 3.06 in 21 starts and, most importantly, walking fewer than three batters per nine innings.

SCOUTING REPORT: Thompson has a prototypical starter's build and three pitches he can throw for strikes. He attacks the zone with a high-spin fastball that ranges from 90-96 mph and complements it with a high-spin, mid-80s curveball that shows flashes of being a putaway pitch. Thompson found a changeup grip that worked for him in his first instructional league, settling on a "Vulcan" grip, and the result was a sinking change that gets swings and misses in the strike zone. Thompson's command and control have improved the further he's moved away from Tommy John surgery, in part because he's throwing with more conviction and confidence.

THE FUTURE: Both the Cubs and opposing evaluators believe Thompson is a solid future starter. He should see the upper minors at some point in 2021

SCOUTING GRADES:	Fastball: 55	Curveball: 60	Changeup: 50	Control: 50

Year	Age	Club (League)	Class	W	L	ERA	G	GS	IP	H	HR	BB	SO	BB/9	K/9	WHIP	AVG
2018	21	Eugene (NWL)	SS	0	2	2.84	9	8	25	24	1	9	25	3.2	8.9	1.30	.253
2019	22	South Bend (MWL)	LoA	8	6	3.06	21	21	94	85	9	31	87	3.0	8.3	1.23	.239
Minor League Totals				8	8	3.02	30	29	119	109	10	40	112	3.0	8.5	1.25	.242

11 CORY ABBOTT, RHP

BA GRADE
45 **Risk: Medium**

Born: Sept. 20, 1995. **B-T:** R-R. **HT:** 6-2. **WT:** 220. **Drafted:** Loyola Marymount, 2017 (2nd round). **Signed by:** Tom Myers.

TRACK RECORD: Abbott didn't attract much attention in college until he learned a new slider grip from watching videos of Noah Syndergaard. Armed with his new slider, Abbott became an All-American his junior year and threw the first perfect game in Loyola Marymount history. The Cubs drafted him 67th overall and signed him for just over $900,000. Abbott continued his ascent in pro ball and led the Double-A Southern League in strikeouts in 2019. He spent 2020 at the Cubs' alternate training site.

SCOUTING REPORT: Abbott's success starts with his slider. It's a short, firm offering at 86-88 mph he commands to both sides of the plate. Lefties struggle with the break and righties don't pick it up out of his slightly crossfire delivery, allowing Abbott to get both swings and misses and called strikes with it. He also has a hard, 12-to-6 curveball that gets batters swinging over the top. Abbott's fastball sits 90-92 mph and tops out at 94, but it plays well up in the zone with an elevated spin rate. His changeup is a nonfactor. Abbott is competitive, durable and adjusts quickly. He commands all his pitches and moves the ball around the strike zone.

THE FUTURE: Abbott is in line for his major league debut in 2021. He projects as a solid, durable starter or swingman.

Year	Age	Club (League)	Class	W	L	ERA	G	GS	IP	H	HR	BB	SO	BB/9	SO/9	WHIP	AVG
2019	23	Tennessee (SL)	AA	8	8	3.01	26	26	147	112	15	52	166	3.2	10.2	1.12	.187
Minor League Totals				16	14	2.84	53	53	275	220	24	94	315	3.1	10.3	1.14	.218

12 BURL CARRAWAY, LHP

Born: May 27, 1999. **B-T:** L-L. **HT:** 6-0. **WT:** 173. **Drafted:** Dallas Baptist, 2020 (2nd round). **Signed by:** Todd George.

TRACK RECORD: Carraway cemented himself as the top reliever in the 2020 draft class when he made five appearances for USA Baseball's Collegiate National Team and didn't allow a run. He followed with a dominant showing as Dallas Baptist's closer as a junior before the season shut down. The Cubs drafted him in the second round, No. 51 overall, and signed him for $1.05 million.

SCOUTING REPORT: Carraway brings high-octane stuff from the left side. His fastball sits 96-98 mph and explodes out of his hand, getting on batters even quicker than they expect. He complements his fastball

with a sharp, knee-buckling curveball in the mid 70s with 1-to-7 shape that is another plus pitch at its best. Carraway is a pure reliever with a slight frame and a high-effort delivery, which leads to inconsistent control. His wildness sometimes helps him by making batters uncomfortable in the box, but other times he sprays his fastball around and struggles to land his breaking ball.
THE FUTURE: Carraway has the stuff to move quickly to the Cubs bullpen. He has a chance to pitch in high-leverage relief if he can throw strikes more consistently.

Year	Age	Club (League)	Class	W	L	ERA	G	GS	IP	H	HR	BB	SO	BB/9	SO/9	WHIP	AVG
2020	21	Did not play—No minor league season															

13 COLE ROEDERER, OF

Born: Sept. 24, 1999. **B-T:** L-L. **HT:** 6-0. **WT:** 175. **Drafted:** HS—Newhall, Calif., 2018 (2nd round supplemental). **Signed by:** Tom Myers.

TRACK RECORD: Roederer was the latest standout to come out of Hart High in suburban Los Angeles, following James Shields, Tyler Glasnow and Trevor Bauer. He suffered a separated right shoulder just before the draft, but the Cubs still selected him 77th overall and gave him an above-slot $1.2 million signing bonus to forgo a UCLA commitment. Roederer had a strong pro debut in the Rookie-level Arizona League, but he began selling out for power and struggled in his first full season at low Class A South Bend.
SCOUTING REPORT: Roederer shows plenty of promising tools. He has a quick, direct swing from the left side that produces hard contact, is an above-average runner and defender in center field and has developed a physical, athletic frame. Roederer's issue is his approach. He gets too pull happy and tries to hit the ball as far as he can rather than focusing on contact. As a result, pitchers dominate him with changeups he's too far out in front of. Roederer hits elevated fastballs. but has yet to show he can stay back and adjust to offspeed pitches.
THE FUTURE: Roederer has the tools to be an everyday center fielder. Whether he adjusts his approach will determine if he gets there.

Year	Age	Club (League)	Class	AVG	G	AB	R	H	2B	3B	HR	RBI	BB	SO	SB	OBP	SLG
2019	19	South Bend (MWL)	LoA	.224	108	384	45	86	19	4	9	60	52	112	16	.319	.365
Minor League Totals				.238	144	526	75	125	23	8	14	84	70	149	29	.328	.392

14 LUIS VERDUGO, SS/3B

Born: Oct. 12, 2000. **B-T:** R-R. **HT:** 6-0. **WT:** 172. **Signed:** Mexico, 2017. **Signed by:** Sergio Hernandez/Louie Eljaua.

TRACK RECORD: The Cubs paid $1.2 million to the Mexico City Red Devils for the rights to sign Verdugo in 2017, continuing the club's scouting push into Mexico. Verdugo struggled in his first year after signing, but he rebounded with a strong year in the Rookie-level Arizona League in 2019 and was targeted by other clubs at the 2020 trade deadline.
SCOUTING REPORT: Verdugo's main draw is his bat. He is a mature hitter with a selective approach and solid bat speed. He has a lot of moving parts in his swing and gets streaky when he falls in and out of sync, but at his best he controls the zone, rarely strikes out and drives the ball hard to all fields. Verdugo signed as a shortstop but projects to move to third base as he fills out. He has solid actions in the field and throws well from varied angles on the run, although he occasionally plays too fast and makes errors as a result.
THE FUTURE: Verdugo has a chance to hit for average and power as an everyday third baseman. He's many years from that ceiling and will aim to make his full-season debut in 2021.

Year	Age	Club (League)	Class	AVG	G	AB	R	H	2B	3B	HR	RBI	BB	SO	SB	OBP	SLG
2019	18	Cubs 2 (AZL)	R	.305	53	197	40	60	9	2	5	38	19	39	8	.367	.447
Minor League Totals				.252	100	373	68	94	13	3	9	58	36	84	13	.318	.375

15 CHRIS CLARKE, RHP

Born: May 13. **B-T:** R-R. **HT:** 6-7. **WT:** 212. **Drafted:** Southern California, 2019 (4th round). **Signed by:** Tom Myers.

TRACK RECORD: Clarke had Tommy John surgery in high school and struggled his first two years at Southern California, but he clicked working with Bethesda pitching coach Bill Sizemore in the Cal Ripken Collegiate League after his sophomore season. Clarke followed with a breakthrough junior year as the Trojans' closer and was drafted by the Cubs in the fourth round, signing for $426,600.
SCOUTING REPORT: Clarke's success came as a closer, but the Cubs believe he can start. He's a big, 6-foot-7 righthander who throws a lot of strikes with a sinking 92-95 mph fastball and a big-breaking curveball

in the low 80s that he commands to make it a plus or better pitch. His sinking heater and downer curveball induce a steady stream of ground balls and prevent hard contact in the air. Clarke complements his two primary pitches with a darting slider in the mid 80s and a changeup with solid depth. He is a good athlete for his size and has a smooth, repeatable delivery that allows him to fill up the strike zone.
THE FUTURE: Clarke will jump to full-season ball in 2021. He will continue developing as a starter and has a fallback as a late-inning reliever.

Year	Age	Club (League)	Class	W	L	ERA	G	GS	IP	H	HR	BB	SO	BB/9	SO/9	WHIP	AVG
2019	21	Eugene (NWL)	SS	0	1	1.96	9	8	23	20	2	4	26	1.6	10.2	1.04	.217
Minor League Totals				0	1	1.96	9	8	23	20	2	4	26	1.6	10.2	1.04	.230

16 MICHAEL MCAVENE, RHP

BREAKOUT
BA GRADE
45 Risk: High

Born: Aug. 24, 1997. **B-T:** R-R. **HT:** 6-3. **WT:** 210. **Drafted:** Louisville, 2019 (3rd round). **Signed by:** Jacob Williams.
TRACK RECORD: McAvene had Tommy John surgery his freshman year at Louisville but rebounded to become the Cardinals' lockdown closer by the time he was a junior. The Cubs drafted him in the third round and signed him for $500,000, then sent him out as a starter at short-season Eugene in his pro debut.
SCOUTING REPORT: McAvene has a high-powered arsenal fronted by a 93-96 mph fastball that touches 98-99 in short stints. He has a high-effort delivery with a pronounced head whack, but he's strong enough to repeat his mechanics and pound the strike zone. His fastball gets lots of swings and misses in the strike zone, and he complements it with a hard, sharp slider with unique depth that has a chance to be a wipeout offering. He has rarely used a changeup in his career and needs to develop one.
THE FUTURE: McAvene's history, pitch mix and effortful delivery point to a relief future, but the Cubs see the athleticism and control to give him a chance to start. He's set to make his full-season debut in 2021.

Year	Age	Club (League)	Class	W	L	ERA	G	GS	IP	H	HR	BB	SO	BB/9	SO/9	WHIP	AVG
2019	21	Eugene (NWL)	SS	0	0	1.42	6	6	13	5	0	4	20	2.8	14.2	0.71	.102
Minor League Totals				0	0	1.42	6	6	12	5	0	4	20	2.8	14.2	0.71	.119

17 KEVIN MADE, SS

BA GRADE
50 Risk: Extreme

Born: Sept. 10, 2002. **B-T:** R-R. **HT:** 6-1. **WT:** 160. **Signed:** Dominican Republic, 2019. **Signed by:** Louis Eljaua/Jose Serra/Gian Guzman.
TRACK RECORD: Made trained in the same program as fellow Cubs 2019 international signee Ronnier Quintero and signed for $1.5 million out of the Dominican Republic. He hit well in games as an amateur and was set to make his pro debut in 2020 before the coronavirus pandemic canceled the minor league season.
SCOUTING REPORT: Made is a wiry, high-waisted athlete with a lot of present ability and plenty of room to get stronger. His quick hands and strong wrists give him surprising thump for his lean frame, and he makes a lot of contact with good hand-eye coordination and a mature, selective approach. As he adds weight and strength, he has the potential to hit for both average and power. Made should stick at shortstop even as he gets bigger. He has good instincts and actions at the position, ranges well in all directions and has a plus, accurate arm that could become plus-plus as he gets stronger.

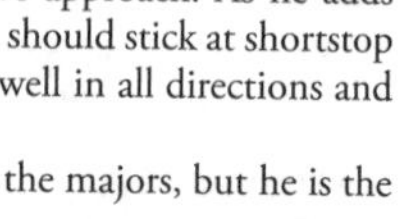

THE FUTURE: Made is set to make his professional debut in 2021. He's far from the majors, but he is the Cubs' best pure shortstop prospect outside of Ed Howard.

Year	Age	Club (League)	Class	AVG	G	AB	R	H	2B	3B	HR	RBI	BB	SO	SB	OBP	SLG
2019	16	Did not play—Signed 2020 contract															

18 JUSTIN STEELE, LHP

BA GRADE
40 Risk: Medium

Born: July 11, 1995. **B-T:** L-L. **HT:** 6-2. **WT:** 205. **Drafted:** HS—Lucedale, Miss., 2014 (5th round). **Signed by:** J.P. Davis.
TRACK RECORD: Steele became the highest-drafted Mississippi high school pitcher in 15 years when the Cubs selected him in the fifth round in 2014 and signed him for $1 million. He had Tommy John surgery in 2017, missed most of 2018 recovering and was limited by an oblique injury in 2019, but he rebounded to earn his first big league callup in 2020. He didn't get to pitch before returning to the alternate site camp, and then suffered a hamstring injury.
SCOUTING REPORT: The Cubs prepared Steele for a bullpen role at the alternate site and saw his stuff tick up in shorter stints. His fastball jumped to 94-96 mph with riding life, and he integrated a sharp, mid-

80s slider into his arsenal that was rarely used before. He still has his downer, 76-80 mph curveball that was his best pitch as a starter and a usable changeup with late fade. Steele struggled to keep a consistent rhythm in his delivery as a starter and suffered control problems, but he throws enough strikes in relief.
THE FUTURE: The Cubs haven't given up on Steele as a starter but like what he offers in the bullpen. His major league debut should come in 2021.

Year	Age	Club (League)	Class	W	L	ERA	G	GS	IP	H	HR	BB	SO	BB/9	SO/9	WHIP	AVG
2019	23	Tennessee (SL)	AA	0	6	5.59	11	11	39	45	3	20	42	4.7	9.8	1.68	.308
Minor League Totals				16	23	3.62	80	75	320	320	14	131	316	3.7	8.9	1.41	.263

19 ALFONSO RIVAS, 1B

BA GRADE
45 Risk: High

Born: Sept. 3, 1996. **B-T:** L-L. **HT:** 6-0. **WT:** 188. **Drafted:** Arizona, 2018 (4th round). **Signed by:** Scott Cousins (Athletics).
TRACK RECORD: Rivas was regarded as one of the college baseball's best pure hitters at Arizona and was drafted by the A's in the fourth round in 2018. He raced to Triple-A in his first full season and followed with a strong showing in the Arizona Fall League, leading the Cubs to acquire him for Tony Kemp.
SCOUTING REPORT: Rivas is a bit of a throwback as a sweet-swinging first baseman with modest power. He is extremely disciplined at the plate and rarely chases outside the strike zone. He's a tough at-bat who grinds pitchers down, draws his walks and hits the ball where it's pitched, using the whole field. Rivas mostly lines singles and doubles into the outfield. Evaluators question whether he will surpass 15 home runs, but believe he may hit enough doubles for a decent slugging percentage. Rivas is a top-notch defensive first baseman who briefly pitched in college and has above-average arm strength.
THE FUTURE: Rivas' professional approach and hitting ability have him close to the majors. Whether he accesses more power will determine if he becomes an everyday player.

Year	Age	Club (League)	Class	AVG	G	AB	R	H	2B	3B	HR	RBI	BB	SO	SB	OBP	SLG
2018	21	Vermont (NYP)	SS	.285	61	214	33	61	16	1	1	28	36	44	7	.397	.383
2019	22	Las Vegas (PCL)	AAA	.406	8	32	2	13	2	1	1	5	2	7	0	.441	.625
	22	Stockton (CAL)	HiA	.283	114	431	60	122	24	3	8	55	66	113	2	.383	.408
Minor League Totals				.290	183	677	95	196	42	5	10	88	104	164	9	.390	.411

20 JORDAN NWOGU, OF

BA GRADE
45 Risk: High

Born: March 10, 1999. **B-T:** R-R. **HT:** 6-3. **WT:** 235. **Drafted:** Michigan, 2020 (3rd round). **Signed by:** John Pedrotty.
TRACK RECORD: Nwogu attended Michigan on academic scholarship to study computer engineering and was a recruited walk-on to the baseball team. He was nearly cut in fall ball but rebounded to become a three-year starting outfielder. He led the Wolverines in on-base percentage and slugging percentage as a sophomore to lead them to the College World Series finals and was off to a scorching start in 2020 before the season shut down. The Cubs drafted him in the third round and signed him for $678,600.
SCOUTING REPORT: Nwogu received Division I football scholarship offers in high school and is still built like a linebacker at 6-foot-3, 235 pounds. That strength and size yields plus-plus raw power to go with plus speed on the bases. Scouts aren't sure Nwogu's funky, top-hand heavy swing will work against pro pitching. He does have a good bat path and controls the strike zone, providing optimism he'll make enough contact to access his power. Nwogu played left field before moving to center at Michigan, but projects to move back to left with his uneven routes and below-average arm.
THE FUTURE: Nwogu's future depends on his swing development. He has a chance to become a power-hitting corner outfielder.

Year	Age	Club (League)	Class	AVG	G	AB	R	H	2B	3B	HR	RBI	BB	SO	SB	OBP	SLG
2020	21	Did not play—No minor league season															

21 YOHENDRICK PINANGO, OF

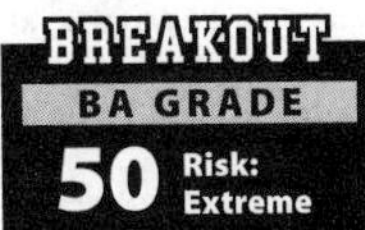

Born: May 7, 2002. **B-T:** L-L. **HT:** 5-11. **WT:** 170. **Signed:** Venezuela, 2018. **Signed by:** Julio Figeuroa/Hector Ortega/Louie Eljaua.
TRACK RECORD: Pinango hit well in games as an amateur in Venezuela and was one of the Cubs' top signings in their 2018 international class. He burnished his reputation as a top hitter in his pro debut in the Rookie-level Dominican Summer League, leading the league with 86 hits and finishing fourth with a .358 batting average.
SCOUTING REPORT: Pinango has unique bat-to-ball skills for his age. He is a patient hitter who rarely

chases and has an advanced feel for picking out pitches he can drive. Pinango has a quick, impactful swing and drives the ball hard to all fields on a line. He has doubles power now and may grow into home run power as he matures physically. Pinango enhances his offensive game with his speed and went 27-for-34 on stolen bases in the DSL. He plays center field now and has a chance to stick there, although he may move to a corner depending on how his body develops.

THE FUTURE: The Cubs already consider Pinango one of the best pure hitters in their system. He should make his stateside debut in 2021.

Year	Age	Club (League)	Class	AVG	G	AB	R	H	2B	3B	HR	RBI	BB	SO	SB	OBP	SLG
2019	17	Cubs1 (DSL)	R	.358	62	240	43	86	20	0	0	36	27	20	27	.427	.442
Minor League Totals				.358	62	240	43	86	20	0	0	36	27	20	27	.427	.442

22 TYSON MILLER, RHP

BA GRADE
40 Risk: Medium

Born: July 29, 1995. **B-T:** R-R. **HT:** 6-4. **WT:** 225. **Drafted:** California Baptist, 2016 (4th round). **Signed by:** Alex Lontayo.

TRACK RECORD: Miller was drafted by the Cubs in the fourth round out of Division II California Baptist following a dominant showing in the Cape Cod League the previous summer. He progressively made his way up the minors and took a step forward at the Cubs' alternate training site in 2020, leading to his major league debut in August.

SCOUTING REPORT: Miller is a big, sturdy righthander who generates lots of natural movement on his pitches. His 90-95 mph fastball features natural cutting action and late ride at the top of the strike zone, and he backs it up with a true cutter in the upper 80s that also plays at the top of the zone. Miller mostly relies on those two pitches. He has a low-to-mid-80s slider that cuts late and a changeup, but both are fringy-to-below average offerings. Miller struggled with his control in the majors but was efficient in the minors with above-average control. He stays off of barrels and generates soft contact more than swings and misses.

THE FUTURE: The Cubs used Miller as a spot starter/long reliever in his debut. He'll try to force his way into a larger role in 2021.

Year	Age	Club (League)	Class	W	L	ERA	G	GS	IP	H	HR	BB	SO	BB/9	SO/9	WHIP	AVG
2020	24	Chicago (NL)	MAJ	0	0	5.40	2	1	5	2	1	3	0	5.4	0.0	1.00	.125
Major League Totals				0	0	5.40	2	1	5	2	1	3	0	5.4	0.0	1.00	.125
Minor League Totals				24	25	4.05	85	74	413	386	45	123	365	2.7	8.0	1.23	.245

23 KEEGAN THOMPSON, RHP

BA GRADE
45 Risk: High

Born: March 13, 1995. **B-T:** R-R. **HT:** 6-1. **WT:** 210. **Drafted:** HS—Auburn, 2017 (3rd round). **Signed by:** Alex McClure.

TRACK RECORD: Thompson was Auburn's ace since he stepped foot on campus as a freshman, but missed his junior year after having Tommy John surgery and his stuff wasn't as crisp when he returned. The Cubs still drafted him in the third round in 2017 and signed him for $511,900. Thompson moved quickly to Double-A in his first full season, but he made only one start in 2019 before going on the injured list with elbow inflammation and received a platelet-rich plasma injection. He returned to pitch well in the Arizona Fall League and spent 2020 at the alternate training site.

SCOUTING REPORT: Thompson is the proverbial "bulldog" on the mound who stays on the attack, fills up the strike zone and doesn't give in. His stuff is modest with a 90-93 mph fastball, above-average 85-87 mph slider, average 79-81 mph curveball and average 83-85 mph changeup, but expertly sequences his pitches to keep hitters off balance. He moves the ball around the strike zone with plus control and avoids self-induced mistakes like walks, hit batters and wild pitches.

THE FUTURE: The Cubs added Thompson to the 40-man roster after the 2020 season. If healthy, he has a chance to make his major league debut in 2021.

Year	Age	Club (League)	Class	W	L	ERA	G	GS	IP	H	HR	BB	SO	BB/9	SO/9	WHIP	AVG
2019	24	Cubs 1 (AZL)	R	0	2	7.20	2	2	5	4	1	0	5	0.0	9.0	0.80	.190
	24	Tennessee (SL)	AA	0	0	0.00	1	1	5	0	0	1	8	1.8	14.4	0.20	.000
Minor League Totals				10	10	3.46	35	29	158	134	11	39	151	2.2	8.6	1.09	.227

24 RONNIER QUINTERO, C

Born: Nov. 13, 2002. **B-T:** L-R. **HT:** 6-0. **WT:** 175. **Signed:** Venezuela, 2019. **Signed by:** Jose Serra/Gian Guzman/Louie Eljaua.

TRACK RECORD: Quintero stood out from the time he was 15 in Venezuela and emerged as the top catching prospect in the 2019 international class. He trained in the Dominican Republic and signed with the Cubs for $2.9 million, a franchise-record bonus for an international amateur.

SCOUTING REPORT: Quintero is a big, lefthanded power hitter. He has a quick, impactful swing and lifts the ball to produce hard contact from right field to left-center. He keeps his swing short for a power hitter and stays inside the ball to drive it the other way when needed. Quintero projects to hit for both power and average, but his future defensive home is less certain. The Cubs believe he can remain a catcher. Others are less sure because of questions about his receiving. His plus arm will play at any position.

THE FUTURE: Quintero will make his professional debut in 2021. He has a chance to be a catcher who hits in the middle of a lineup, but is many years away.

Year	Age	Club (League)	Class	AVG	G	AB	R	H	2B	3B	HR	RBI	BB	SO	SB	OBP	SLG
2019	16	Did not play—Signed 2020 contract															

25 JACK PATTERSON, LHP

Born: Aug. 3, 1995. **B-T:** L-L. **HT:** 6-0. **WT:** 210. **Drafted:** Bryant, 2018 (32nd round). **Signed by:** Matt Sherman.

TRACK RECORD: Patterson took a line drive to the head in college that caused severe concussion symptoms for nearly two years, but he recovered to win Northeast Conference pitcher of the year as a senior in 2018. The Cubs drafted him in the 32nd round. Patterson posted a 1.69 ERA as he jumped three levels to Double-A in his first full season, and the Cubs brought him to their alternate training site in 2020.

SCOUTING REPORT: Patterson's fastball previously sat 88-91 mph but rose to 91-94 mph after the Cubs made an adjustment to his lower half. That velocity bump has helped him be more aggressive, and he still has advanced pitchability from when he threw softer. Patterson complements his fastball with a downer, low-80s curveball that helps him generate ground balls. He is capable of missing bats, but he primarily induces weak contact on the ground. His changeup is developing but flashes average. Patterson struggled with walks in college, but he's shown an easy, efficient delivery and improved strike-throwing in pro ball.

THE FUTURE: Patterson fits in the Cubs' plans as a future swingman or lefthanded reliever. He has a chance to make his major league debut in 2021.

Year	Age	Club (League)	Class	W	L	ERA	G	GS	IP	H	HR	BB	SO	BB/9	SO/9	WHIP	AVG
2019	23	Myrtle Beach (CAR)	HiA	2	0	0.00	5	5	24	8	0	8	24	3.0	9.1	0.68	.090
	23	South Bend (MWL)	LoA	5	1	2.34	16	1	42	29	0	18	47	3.8	10.0	1.11	.172
	23	Tennessee (SL)	AA	1	0	2.63	3	3	14	11	1	6	9	4.0	5.9	1.24	.204
Minor League Totals				10	2	2.04	35	15	114	83	4	42	113	3.3	8.9	1.09	.203

26 MANUEL RODRIGUEZ, RHP

BA GRADE
40 Risk: High

Born: Aug. 6, 1996. **B-T:** R-R. **HT:** 5-11. **WT:** 205. **Signed:** Mexico, 2016. **Signed by:** Sergio Hernandez/Louie Eljaua.

TRACK RECORD: Rodriguez won the Mexican League's rookie of the year award in 2015 as Yucatan's closer. The Cubs signed him for $400,000 the following year, their largest bonus during the 2016-17 international period. Rodriguez averaged 12.4 K/9 at high Class A Myrtle Beach and was added to the Cubs' 40-man roster before the 2020 season. He turned heads in spring training, but suffered a forearm strain just before camps shut down.

SCOUTING REPORT: Rodriguez has a power arsenal befitting a late-game reliever. His four-seam fastball checks in at 95-98 mph with ride and cut and his heavy two-seamer sits 94-97 mph, giving him two power offerings he overpowers batters with. He complements his fastballs with a power, downer curveball in the mid 80s that generates a lot of swing-and-misses, as well as a softer, sweepier breaking ball to disrupt batters' timing. Rodriguez struggled to throw strikes when he was younger, but a more consistent delivery has helped him pound the strike zone and cut his walks significantly.

THE FUTURE: Rodriguez emerged fully healthy after rehabbing at the Cubs complex in Arizona. He has the stuff to join the Cubs bullpen in the near future.

Year	Age	Club (League)	Class	W	L	ERA	G	GS	IP	H	HR	BB	SO	BB/9	SO/9	WHIP	AVG
2019	22	Myrtle Beach (CAR)	HiA	1	3	3.45	35	0	47	43	1	17	65	3.3	12.4	1.28	.218
Minor League Totals				10	9	4.24	155	0	184	176	8	101	229	4.9	11.2	1.50	.249

27 D.J. HERZ, LHP

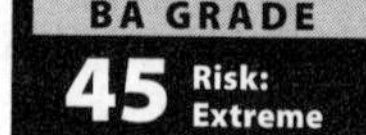

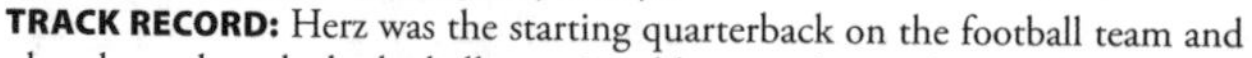

BA GRADE 45 **Risk: Extreme**

Born: Jan. 4, 2001. **B-T:** L-R. **HT:** 6-2. **WT:** 175. **Drafted:** HS—Fayetteville, N.C., 2019 (8th round). **Signed by:** Billy Swoope.

TRACK RECORD: Herz was the starting quarterback on the football team and played guard on the basketball team in addition to being the ace lefthander at Terry Sanford (N.C.) High. Crosschecker Tim Adkins highlighted Herz early in the draft scouting process, and the Cubs selected him in the eighth round and signed him for an above-slot $500,000 to forgo a North Carolina commitment.

SCOUTING REPORT: Herz sat 88-91 mph in high school, but he made a delivery adjustment in spring training and saw his velocity and spin rates jump. He formerly pitched with a crossfire delivery, but once he altered his stride direction more toward the plate, he began sitting 92-95 mph. His curveball also gained 4 mph, up to 81 mph, and added an additional 400 rpm's of spin. Herz shows advanced feel for a changeup to give him the three-pitch mix to start. He still has to show he can maintain his stride direction in games, which will help him improve his fringy control. He is an excellent athlete who draws rave reviews for his work ethic.

THE FUTURE: The Cubs believe Herz would have broken out with a full season in 2020. He'll get the chance in 2021.

Year	Age	Club (League)	Class	W	L	ERA	G	GS	IP	H	HR	BB	SO	BB/9	SO/9	WHIP	AVG
2019	18	Cubs 2 (AZL)	R	0	1	2.61	6	6	10	10	0	8	8	7.0	7.0	1.74	.200
Minor League Totals				0	1	2.61	6	6	10	10	0	8	8	7.0	7.0	1.74	.238

28 NELSON VELAZQUEZ, OF

BA GRADE 40 **Risk: High**

Born: Dec. 26, 1998. **B-T:** R-R. **HT:** 6-0. **WT:** 190. **Drafted:** HS—Carolina, P.R, 2017 (5th round). **Signed by:** Edwards Guzman.

TRACK RECORD: Velazquez initially attended high school in Florida before moving back to Puerto Rico and becoming one of the island's top draft prospects. The Cubs drafted him in the fifth round in 2017 and signed him for $400,000. Velazquez struggled to translate his tools into production his first two seasons, but he appeared to break through at low Class A South Bend in 2019 despite missing two months with an oblique strain.

SCOUTING REPORT: Velazquez has plenty of tools to dream on. His compact, muscular build produces solid bat speed and plus raw power. He can drive balls the opposite way as well as his pull-side, and he is a good athlete with above-average speed and a plus arm in right field. Velazquez is an aggressive hitter who takes big swings and struggles to make adjustments at times, preventing him from accessing his power in games. He shows some natural feel for the barrel but still has to improve his overall approach and consistency at the plate.

THE FUTURE: Velazquez has the range, arm and raw power to profile in right field. He'll try to build on his contact gains in 2021.

Year	Age	Club (League)	Class	AVG	G	AB	R	H	2B	3B	HR	RBI	BB	SO	SB	OBP	SLG
2019	20	South Bend (MWL)	LoA	.286	72	262	33	75	16	4	4	34	21	77	5	.338	.424
	20	Cubs 2 (AZL)	R	.316	6	19	4	6	1	0	2	5	2	5	0	.381	.684
Minor League Totals				.253	213	767	104	194	41	8	25	96	68	245	25	.319	.425

29 RICHARD GALLARDO, RHP

BA GRADE 45 **Risk:** Extreme

Born: Sept. 6, 2001. **B-T:** R-R. **HT:** 6-1. **WT:** 187. **Signed:** Venezuela, 2018. **Signed by:** Hector Ortega/Louie Eljaua/Manuel Pestana/Carlos Figueroa.

TRACK RECORD: Gallardo starred for Venezuela at the 15U World Cup in 2016 and stuck out six of the seven batters he faced during MLB's international showcase the following year. Considered by some clubs to be the best pitching prospect in the 2018 international class, Gallardo signed with the Cubs and reached short-season Eugene in his first professional season.

SCOUTING REPORT: Gallardo's stuff was more pedestrian than expected in his pro debut, but he shows impressive command and feel for pitching for his age. Gallardo's fastball averages 91 mph and tops out at 94. His body doesn't offer much projection, but he could still add a tick of velocity as he gets stronger. Gallardo locates his curveball to both sides of the plate and has a chance to make it an above-average pitch as he adds power to it. He shows good feel for a nascent changeup. None of Gallardo's pitches jump out, but he throws strikes and keeps the ball down.

THE FUTURE: Gallardo's youth, feel and command of three pitches provide hope he can grow into a back-end starter. He's set for his full-season debut in 2021.

Year	Age	Club (League)	Class	W	L	ERA	G	GS	IP	H	HR	BB	SO	BB/9	SO/9	WHIP	AVG
2019	17	Cubs 1 (AZL)	R	0	2	4.15	11	9	30	32	1	12	23	3.6	6.8	1.45	.239
	17	Eugene (NWL)	SS	0	0	2.25	2	1	4	2	0	2	2	4.5	4.5	1.00	.125
Minor League Totals				0	2	3.93	13	10	34	34	1	14	25	3.7	6.6	1.40	.256

30 BRENDON LITTLE, LHP

BA GRADE 40 **Risk:** High

Born: Aug. 11, 1996. **B-T:** L-L. **HT:** 6-1. **WT:** 195. **Drafted:** State JC of Florida, 2017 (1st round). **Signed by:** John Koronka.

TRACK RECORD: Little began his college career at North Carolina before transferring to State JC of Florida as a sophomore. He dominated the JC circuit and was drafted by the Cubs in the first round, No. 27 overall, and signed for $2.2 million. Little's velocity declined as he battled a lat strain in 2019, but he returned healthy and throwing harder than ever in 2020.

SCOUTING REPORT: Little regained his college velocity and then some in 2020, sitting 94-95 mph and touching 97-98 mph in short bursts during spring training. He mainly focused on developing his slider and was beginning to form it as a mid-80s, sharp breaker. He also has a hammer curveball in the low-80s that flashes above-average and a changeup that is progressing. Little has long had power stuff but struggled to control it, with issues repeating his delivery the main culprit. He also gets tentative at times instead of attacking hitters.

THE FUTURE: Little's velocity jump has the Cubs encouraged for 2021. He still needs to show he can maintain it over a full season and throw consistent strikes.

Year	Age	Club (League)	Class	W	L	ERA	G	GS	IP	H	HR	BB	SO	BB/9	SO/9	WHIP	AVG
2019	22	Cubs 1 (AZL)	R	0	0	3.68	2	2	7	4	2	4	9	4.9	11.0	1.09	.138
	22	Myrtle Beach (CAR)	HiA	2	1	5.95	4	4	20	21	2	9	23	4.1	10.5	1.53	.233
	22	South Bend (MWL)	LoA	0	1	1.91	6	6	28	18	0	13	25	4.1	7.9	1.09	.158
Minor League Totals				7	15	5.05	40	39	173	170	14	78	159	4.1	8.3	1.43	.253

MORE PROSPECTS TO KNOW

31 RAFAEL MOREL, SS

Christopher Morel's younger brother has intriguing contact skills and has started to grow into power.

32. ANDY WEBER, SS

SLEEPER

The lefthanded-hitting shortstop has a long track record of hitting and can ably play both middle infield positions.

33. KOEN MORENO, RHP

The 2020 fifth-round pick is a super-athletic righthander who shows feel for three pitches and has room to grow into more velocity.

34. EDMOND AMERICAAN, OF

The wiry, athletic outfielder shows hints of power but still needs refinement as a hitter.

35. TREVOR MEGILL, RHP

Megill is a massive righthander with a mid-90s fastball and downer curveball. He should be ready to help the Cubs' bullpen in 2021.

36. FABIAN PERTUZ, 3B/SS

The young Colombian has an impressive swing, but still has to prove himself outside of complex leagues.

37. ETHAN HEARN, C

The physical catcher has big lefthanded power and can stay behind the plate, but he needs to show he can make enough contact.

38. YONATHAN PERLAZA, 2B/OF

A favorite of opposing scouts, Perlaza is a versatile defender and a smart, patient hitter with growing power

39. LUKE LITTLE, LHP

The flame-throwing lefty is a lottery ticket with elite velocity but well below-average present control.

40. P.J. HIGGINS, C

Higgins is an older catcher who is an excellent defender and leader. He has a chance to reach the majors late and have an Erik Kratz-type career.

TOP PROSPECTS OF THE DECADE

Year	Player, Pos.	2020 Org
2011	Chris Archer, RHP	Pirates
2012	Brett Jackson, OF	Did not play
2013	Javier Baez, SS	Cubs
2014	Javier Baez, SS	Cubs
2015	Kris Bryant, 3B	Cubs
2016	Gleyber Torres, SS	Yankees
2017	Eloy Jimenez, OF	White Sox
2018	Aramis Ademan, SS	Cubs
2019	Nico Hoerner, SS	Cubs
2020	Brailyn Marquez, LHP	Cubs

TOP DRAFT PICKS OF THE DECADE

Year	Player, Pos.	2020 Org
2011	Javier Baez, SS	Cubs
2012	Albert Almora, OF	Cubs
2013	Kris Bryant, 3B	Cubs
2014	Kyle Schwarber, C	Cubs
2015	Ian Happ, OF	Cubs
2016	Thomas Hatch, RHP (3rd round)	Blue Jays
2017	Brendon Little, LHP	Cubs
2018	Nico Hoerner, SS	Cubs
2019	Ryan Jensen, RHP	Cubs
2020	Ed Howard, SS	Cubs

DEPTH CHART

CHICAGO CUBS

TOP 2021 ROOKIES	RANK
Adbert Alzolay, RHP	5
BREAKOUT PROSPECTS	**RANK**
Michael McAvene, RHP	16
Yohendrick Pinango, OF	21
D.J. Herz, LHP	27

SOURCE OF TOP 30 TALENT

Homegrown	29	Acquired	1
College	13	Trade	1
Junior college	0	Rule 5 draft	0
High school	6	Independent league	0
Nondrafted free agent	0	Free agent/waivers	0
International	10		

LF
Jordan Nwogu (20)
Yohendrick Pinango (21)
Yonathan Perlaza

CF
Brennen Davis (2)
Cole Roederer (13)

RF
Nelson Velazquez (28)
Edmond Americaan

3B
Christopher Morel (8)
Luis Verdugo (14)
Fabian Pertuz

SS
Ed Howard (4)
Kevin Made (17)
Rafael Morel
Andy Weber

2B
Chase Strumpf (9)
Trent Giambrone
Juan Mora

1B
Alfonso Rivas (19)
Jared Young
Matt Mervis

C
Miguel Amaya (3)
Ronnier Quintero (24)
Ethan Hearn
P.J. Higgins
Brayan Altuve

LHP

LHSP	LHRP
Brailyn Marquez (1)	Burl Carraway (12)
Jack Patterson (25)	Justin Steele (18)
D.J. Herz (27)	Luke Little
Brendon Little (30)	Wyatt Short

RHP

RHSP	RHRP
Adbert Alzolay (5)	Ryan Jensen (7)
Kohl Franklin (6)	Michael McAvene (16)
Riley Thompson (10)	Manuel Rodriguez (26)
Cory Abbott (11)	Trevor Megill
Chris Clarke (15)	James Norwood
Tyson Miller (22)	Michael Rucker
Keegan Thompson (23)	Dakota Mekkes
Richard Gallardo (29)	Ben Leeper
Koen Moreno	Hunter Bigge
Yovanny Cruz	
Duncan Robinson	
Javier Assad	

Chicago White Sox

BY JOSH NORRIS

They're almost there.

After years of rebuilding through smart trades and high draft picks, the White Sox made it back to the playoffs in 2020, albeit under the shroud of a tournament expanded to 16 teams and a season shortened to 60 games because of the novel coronavirus pandemic.

Still, the White Sox pushed the American League Central-winning Twins all season and finished only one game back, while qualifying for the postseason for the first time since 2008.

In the offseason, sensing the precipice was near, Chicago added catcher Yasmani Grandal and lefty Dallas Keuchel via free agency, signed top prospect Luis Robert to a big league deal and had righty Michael Kopech ready to go, fresh from Tommy John surgery.

Then came the pandemic, which caused Kopech to opt out of the season. It also meant a season playing games only against opponents from the Central division teams and in ballparks which had to pipe in crowd noise because the pandemic meant fans were shut out.

Even so, the White Sox still benefited greatly from contributions from young stars like righthander Lucas Giolito, who threw a no-hitter, and shortstop Tim Anderson, who nearly repeated as the AL batting champion.

The team also got boosts from rookies like Robert, who started fast but scuffled in September as the league adjusted to him; second baseman Nick Madrigal, starter Dane Dunning and relievers Codi Heuer and Matt Foster.

Another gift came late in the season, when 2020 first-rounder Garrett Crochet made his big league debut and immediately became a premier fireballer. His fastball averaged 100 mph, and his slider gave him one of the nastiest one-two punches. When he debuted, Crochet became the first player since Mike Leake in 2010 to go straight from the draft to the big leagues without playing a minor league game.

In the postseason, the White Sox fell to the Athletics and were struck by bad luck when Crochet and budding star Eloy Jimenez each had to leave with injuries during the team's season-ending Game 3 loss in the Wild Card Series.

Though the year finished with a bit of a whimper, the White Sox clearly made progress toward returning to prominence.

After the season, the White Sox wasted no time making changes. They let go of manager Rick Renteria and replaced him with Tony La Russa, who last managed in 2011 and who immediately came under fire for a DUI arrest earlier in the year.

In December, the White Sox beefed up their roster even further by sending Dunning and prospect lefty Avery Weems to the Rangers for 33-year-old righthander Lance Lynn, who finished sixth in AL Cy Young Award voting in 2020. The acquisition only strengthened an enviable rotation topped by Giolito and Keuchel.

The talented roster, combined with the returns of Kopech, the encores of Madrigal (who had shoulder surgery after the season), Robert and Crochet, and potential impact bat Andrew Vaughn waiting in the wings, should help the White Sox make it even deeper in the playoffs in 2021. ■

NICK WOSIKA/ICON SPORTSWIRE VIA GETTY IMAGES

Preseason No. 1 prospect Luis Robert flashed five-tool ability in a strong rookie season.

PROJECTED 2024 LINEUP

Position	Player	Age
Catcher	Yasmani Grandal	35
First Base	Andrew Vaughn	27
Second Base	Nick Madrigal	27
Third Base	Yoan Moncada	29
Shortstop	Tim Anderson	31
Left Field	Eloy Jimenez	27
Center Field	Luis Robert	26
Right Field	Luis Gonzalez	28
Designated Hitter	Jose Abreu	37
No. 1 Starter	Lucas Giolito	29
No. 2 Starter	Michael Kopech	28
No. 3 Starter	Dylan Cease	28
No. 4 Starter	Garrett Crochet	25
No. 5 Starter	Reynaldo Lopez	30
Closer	Matt Foster	29

1 ANDREW VAUGHN, 1B

BORN: April 3, 1998. **B-T:** R-R. **HT:** 6-0. **WT:** 214.
Drafted: California, 2019 (1st round).
Signed by: Adam Virchis.

RON VESELY/GETTY IMAGES

BA GRADE	SCOUTING GRADES
60 Risk: High	**Hit:** 60. **Power:** 60. **Run:** 30. **Field:** 50. **Arm:** 50.

Projected future grades on 20-80 scouting scale.

TRACK RECORD: By the time he left California, Vaughn had established himself as one of the nation's most decorated college baseball players. He was a part of USA Baseball's Collegiate National Team following both his freshman and sophomore years, when he teamed with future White Sox prospects Nick Madrigal and Steele Walker (since traded). He won the Golden Spikes Award as the nation's top college player his sophomore year, then followed by hitting .374/.539/.704 as a junior for the Golden Bears. The White Sox used the third overall pick on Vaughn in 2019 and signed him for $7,221,200. He spent most of his professional debut at low Class A Kannapolis and high Class A Winston-Salem, where evaluators were impressed by the amount of hard contact he made despite numbers that might not jump off the page. He spent the 2020 season at Chicago's alternate training site in Schaumburg, Ill.

SCOUTING REPORT: When Vaughn joined the White Sox, the team wanted to install a concrete, day-to-day routine that would help him manage the grind of professional baseball. He settled on one that featured a front-flip drill designed to keep his legs underneath him during his swing, and evaluators inside the organization say it has helped him become a better hitter. Vaughn does an excellent job keeping his upper and lower halves synced throughout the course of his swing. He gets the barrel to the zone quickly and keeps it there a long while. Vaughn also shows an excellent approach befitting a top-five pick. He knows when he can do the most damage and works each at-bat to get himself into those situations. The combination of his swing and approach allows him to make consistent loud contact and drive balls from line to line. He projects to hit for a high average and for plus power, with his physical frame and natural strength yielding high-velocity rockets off the bat that carry out to left and left-center field. Vaughn has shown a minor weakness against changeups from righthanders, but that may be a sample size issue that will work itself out once he gets regular at-bats in game settings. Defensively, Vaughn continues to hone in his footwork around the first base bag. He played some third base at the alternate site, but he's a well below-average runner with limited range and remains a first baseman long-term. He projects to be an average defender in time with an average arm.

THE FUTURE: Vaughn is ready for his first taste of the upper levels and could get a shot at the majors late in 2021. No matter when he arrives, he has the look of a classic masher ready to take the reins from 2020 American League MVP Jose Abreu in the middle of a talented White Sox lineup. ■

BEST TOOLS

Best Hitter for Average	Nick Madrigal
Best Power Hitter	Andrew Vaughn
Best Strike-Zone Discipline	Andrew Vaughn
Fastest Baserunner	James Beard
Best Athlete	Matthew Thompson
Best Fastball	Garrett Crochet
Best Curveball	Jonathan Stiever
Best Slider	Garrett Crochet
Best Changeup	Jared Kelley
Best Control	Bernardo Flores Jr
Best Defensive Catcher	Seby Zavala
Best Defensive Infielder	Nick Madrigal
Best Infield Arm	Zach Remillard
Best Defensive Outfielder	Duke Ellis
Best Outfield Arm	Micker Adolfo

Year	Age	Club (League)	Class	AVG	G	AB	R	H	2B	3B	HR	RBI	BB	SO	SB	OBP	SLG
2019	21	White Sox (AZL)	R	.600	3	15	3	9	2	0	1	4	0	3	0	.625	.933
	21	Kannapolis (SAL)	LoA	.253	23	83	14	21	7	0	2	11	14	18	0	.388	.410
	21	Winston-Salem (CAR)	HiA	.252	29	107	16	27	8	0	3	21	16	17	0	.349	.411
Minor League Totals				.278	55	205	33	57	17	0	6	36	30	38	0	.384	.449

2 MICHAEL KOPECH, RHP

TOP ROOKIE

BA GRADE

60 Risk: High

DAVE DUROCHIK/MLB PHOTOS VIA GETTY IMAGES

Born: April 30, 1996. **B-T:** R-R. **HT:** 6-3. **WT:** 205. **Drafted:** HS—Mount Pleasant, Texas, 2014 (1st round). **Signed by:** Tim Collinsworth (Red Sox).

TRACK RECORD: The White Sox acquired Kopech from the Red Sox in 2016 as part of the package for lefty Chris Sale. He made his major league debut for the White Sox in 2018 and flashed immense potential in four starts, but a torn elbow ligament led to Tommy John surgery that cost him all of 2019. He opted out of the 2020 season due to the coronavirus pandemic.

SCOUTING REPORT: Kopech is the classic power pitcher armed with a fastball that sits in the mid-to-upper 90s and peaks at 102 mph. He backs up his heater with a wicked slider that projects as a plus pitch. Kopech started throwing a two-seam fastball as a way to improve his changeup in the minors and earned his first callup after the pitch improved to average. His next step is to improve his curveball so it doesn't blend with his slider, which would give him a full four-pitch arsenal. Kopech's electric arm speed and high-octane arsenal have made it difficult for him to consistently throw strikes at times, but he has the athleticism and delivery to project for average control as he continues to harness his raw power.

THE FUTURE: Kopech looked electric before spring training was shut down. The White Sox expect him to compete for a spot at the top of the rotation alongside Lucas Giolito in 2021.

SCOUTING GRADES: **Fastball:** 80 **Slider:** 60 **Curveball:** 50 **Changeup:** 50 **Control:** 50

Year	Age	Club (League)	Class	W	L	ERA	G	GS	IP	H	HR	BB	SO	BB/9	K/9	WHIP	AVG
2017	21	Birmingham (SL)	AA	8	7	2.87	22	22	119	77	6	60	155	4.5	11.7	1.15	.184
	21	Charlotte (IL)	AAA	1	1	3.00	3	3	15	15	0	5	17	3.0	10.2	1.33	.263
2018	22	Charlotte (IL)	AAA	7	7	3.70	24	24	126	101	9	60	170	4.3	12.1	1.27	.219
	22	Chicago (AL)	MAJ	1	1	5.02	4	4	14	20	4	2	15	1.3	9.4	1.53	.328
2019	23	Did not play—Injured															
2020	24	Did not play—Opted out of season															
Major League Totals				1	1	5.02	4	4	14	20	4	2	15	1.3	9.4	1.53	.328
Minor League Totals				24	22	3.05	85	84	395	286	18	194	514	4.4	11.7	1.21	.203

3 NICK MADRIGAL, 2B

DAVE DUROCHIK/MLB PHOTOS VIA GETTY IMAGES

Born: March 5, 1997. **B-T:** R-R. **HT:** 5-7. **WT:** 165. **Drafted:** Oregon State, 2018 (1st round). **Signed by:** Mike Gange.

TRACK RECORD: Madrigal was an unconventional top draft prospect because of his 5-foot-7 stature, but he was a prolific hitter at Oregon State and was drafted fourth overall by the White Sox in 2018. Madrigal burnished his reputation as an elite contact hitter with just 21 strikeouts in 705 minor league plate appearances. He made his major league debut on July 3, but he missed three weeks with a separated shoulder that required offseason surgery.

SCOUTING REPORT: Madrigal is an aggressive hitter who makes tons of contact, rarely walks and doesn't show much home run power. His swing is short, quick and geared for line drives. He lines the ball to all fields and is almost wholly a singles and doubles hitter. Madrigal has nearly bottom-of-the-scale power, but he plays to his strengths and doesn't try to do too much. Madrigal is a plus runner who stole 35 bases in his final minor league season in 2019. He is a steady, sound defender with quick feet and soft hands, though his arm strength is average at best.

THE FUTURE: The White Sox are optimistic Madrigal's surgery will not affect his future. He projects as a top-of-the order menace who sprays balls around the diamond and wreaks havoc on the bases.

SCOUTING GRADES: **Hitting:** 60 **Power:** 30 **Running:** 60 **Fielding:** 50 **Arm:** 50

Year	Age	Club (League)	Class	AVG	G	AB	R	H	2B	3B	HR	RBI	BB	SO	SB	OBP	SLG
2018	21	Kannapolis (SAL)	LoA	.341	12	44	9	15	3	0	0	6	1	0	2	.347	.409
	21	Winston-Salem (CAR)	HiA	.306	26	98	14	30	4	0	0	9	5	5	6	.355	.347
	21	White Sox (AZL)	R	.154	5	13	2	2	0	0	0	1	1	0	0	.353	.154
2019	22	Birmingham (SL)	AA	.341	42	164	30	56	11	2	1	16	14	5	14	.400	.451
	22	Charlotte (IL)	AAA	.331	29	118	26	39	6	1	1	12	13	5	4	.398	.424
	22	Winston-Salem (CAR)	HiA	.272	49	191	20	52	10	2	2	27	17	6	17	.346	.377
2020	23	Chicago (AL)	MAJ	.340	29	103	8	35	3	0	0	11	4	7	2	.376	.369
Major League Totals				.340	29	103	8	35	3	0	0	11	4	7	2	.376	.369
Minor League Totals				.309	163	628	101	194	34	5	4	71	51	21	43	.371	.398

4 GARRETT CROCHET, LHP

TOP ROOKIE

BA GRADE 55 Risk: High

CALEB JONES/TENNESSEE ATHLETICS

Born: June 21, 1999. **B-T:** L-L. **HT:** 6-6. **WT:** 218. **Drafted:** Tennessee, 2020 (1st round). **Signed by:** Phil Gulley.

TRACK RECORD: Crochet bounced between the rotation and bullpen his first two seasons at Tennessee and made only one start before the 2020 season shut down. The White Sox had history with him and drafted him 11th overall. Crochet then raced to the majors roughly three months after being drafted and overpowered hitters with a fastball that averaged 100 mph in relief. He made six scoreless relief appearances, including the postseason, but left his final outing with forearm tightness.

SCOUTING REPORT: Crochet brings elite velocity from the left side at 96-99 mph as a starter and 100-102 as a reliever. The White Sox taught him to work through the ball rather than around it at the alternate training site, which helped give his fastball a little extra riding life and finish and make it a true 80-grade pitch. Crochet threw his fastball nearly 85% of the time in his debut, but he also has a power slider in the mid 80s. The White Sox tweaked his grip to give it a more consistent break and help it play as a plus pitch. Crochet's low-90s changeup is extremely firm and a below-average pitch he'll need to improve in order to start. He improved his delivery at the alternate site to better work down the mound and has a chance at average control.

THE FUTURE: Crochet should be healthy in time for spring training. There's still debate over whether he'll end up a starter or reliever, but there's no question he'll be a weapon in any role.

SCOUTING GRADES: **Fastball:** 80 **Curveball:** 60 **Changeup:** 40 **Control:** 50

Year	Age	Club (League)	Class	W	L	ERA	G	GS	IP	H	HR	BB	SO	BB/9	SO/9	WHIP	AVG
2020	21	Chicago (AL)	MAJ	0	0	0.00	5	0	6	3	0	0	8	0.0	12.0	0.50	.143
Major League Totals				0	0	0.00	5	0	6	3	0	0	8	0.0	12.0	0.50	.143

5 JARED KELLEY, RHP

BA GRADE 55 Risk: Extreme

BILL MITCHELL

Born: Oct. 3, 2001. **B-T:** R-R. **HT:** 6-3. **WT:** 230. **Drafted:** HS—Refugio, Texas, 2020 (2nd round). **Signed by:** Tyler Wilt.

TRACK RECORD: Kelley surprisingly fell out of the first round in the 2020 draft after ranking as one of the top prep pitchers in the class. The White Sox quickly selected him in the second round, No. 47 overall, and signed him away from a Texas commitment for $3 million, nearly double slot value. Kelley reported to the team's alternate training site after signing and finished the year at instructional league, where he was one of the top pitchers in Arizona.

SCOUTING REPORT: Kelley stands out for his strong, classic pitcher's frame and the ease with which he pumps 95-97 mph fastballs. The White Sox worked with him on staying behind his fastball to help it maintain its axis and riding life through the zone. That makes it a potential plus-plus pitch. Kelley's low-80s changeup is another potential plus offering that plays well off his fastball and keeps hitters off-balance. His slider is a work in progress, with the White Sox emphasizing throwing it with intent in order to maintain mid-80s velocity. Kelley has a sturdy, durable build that should help him log innings and throw strikes, but he doesn't have much room to get bigger.

THE FUTURE: Kelley is set to make his pro debut in 2021. If all goes well, he has a chance to become a mid-to-front-of-the-rotation starter.

SCOUTING GRADES: **Fastball:** 70 **Slider:** 50 **Changeup:** 60 **Control:** 55

Year	Age	Club (League)	Class	W	L	ERA	G	GS	IP	H	HR	BB	SO	BB/9	K/9	WHIP	AVG
2020	18	Did not play—No minor league season															

6 MATTHEW THOMPSON, RHP

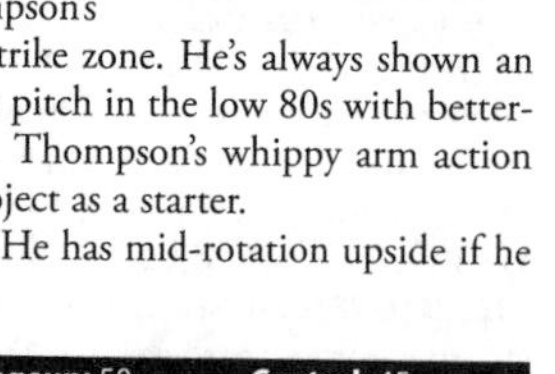

BILL MITCHELL

BA GRADE
50 **Risk: Extreme**

Born: Aug. 11, 2000. **B-T:** R-R. **HT:** 6-3. **WT:** 195. **Drafted:** HS—Cypress, Texas, 2019 (2nd round). **Signed by:** Chris Walker.

TRACK RECORD: Thompson gained recognition in high school as a live-armed pitcher who could pump low-to-mid-90s fastballs with relative ease. The White Sox drafted him in the second round in 2019 and signed him for an above-slot $2.1 million. Thompson made his pro debut with two outings in the Rookie-level Arizona League and spent the 2020 season at the team's alternate training site before finishing the year at instructional league.

SCOUTING REPORT: Thompson returned in 2020 in better physical shape and is now regarded as the best athlete in Chicago's farm system. The organization worked to keep his body in sync throughout his delivery and tried to eliminate a bit of a leg kick in his delivery. Those alterations helped him stay through his pitches better, and the result was a crisper arsenal. Thompson's fastball now sits 92-95 mph and touches 97 with carry through the strike zone. He's always shown an advanced feel to spin the ball, and now his curveball is a bona fide plus pitch in the low 80s with better-defined break. His changeup is a clear third pitch but flashes average. Thompson's whippy arm action limits his control to fringe-average, but he throws enough strikes to project as a starter.

THE FUTURE: Thompson is set to move to the Class A levels in 2020. He has mid-rotation upside if he continues developing at his current rate.

SCOUTING GRADES: **Fastball:** 60 **Curveball:** 60 **Changeup:** 50 **Control:** 45

Year	Age	Club (League)	Class	W	L	ERA	G	GS	IP	H	HR	BB	SO	BB/9	K/9	WHIP	AVG
2019	18	White Sox (AZL)	R	0	0	0.00	2	2	2	2	0	0	2	0.0	9.0	1.00	.250
Minor League Totals				0	0	0.00	2	2	2	2	0	0	2	0.0	9.0	1.00	.250

7 JONATHAN STIEVER, RHP

DAVE DUROCHIK/MLB PHOTOS VIA GETTY IMAGES

BA GRADE
45 **Risk: High**

Born: May 12, 1997. **B-T:** R-R. **HT:** 6-2. **WT:** 205. **Drafted:** Indiana, 2018 (5th round). **Signed by:** Justin Weschsler.

TRACK RECORD: Stiever spent two years at the front of Indiana's rotation and was drafted by the White Sox in the fifth round in 2018. He broke out with 154 strikeouts in 145 innings in his first full season in 2019 as he conquered both Class A levels. The White Sox brought him to their alternate training site in 2020 and he made his major league debut Sept. 13 with a start against the Tigers.

SCOUTING REPORT: Stiever has an average fastball that sits 92-93 mph and touches 95, but what separates him is his breaking pitches. His curveball is a true downer at 73-77 mph with nearly five feet of drop and has a chance to be plus, while his 83-86 mph slider has sharper vertical bite and should be at least above-average. He did not command either pitch particularly well in the majors, but both have a chance to be out pitches if he can land them in the strike zone consistently. Stiever's mid-80s changeup is a work in progress but has a chance to be average. The White Sox have worked with Stiever to stay through his delivery and work downhill. The improvements give him a chance to throw enough strikes to be competitive, even with fringe-average control.

THE FUTURE: Stiever will open 2021 back in the minors. He has back-of-the-rotation potential if he can harness command of his secondaries.

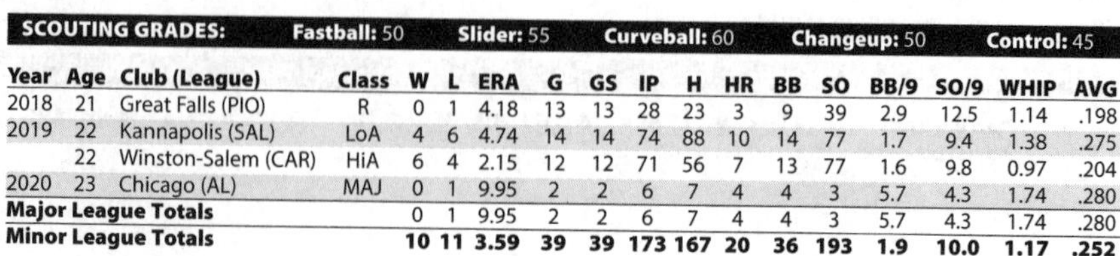

SCOUTING GRADES: **Fastball:** 50 **Slider:** 55 **Curveball:** 60 **Changeup:** 50 **Control:** 45

Year	Age	Club (League)	Class	W	L	ERA	G	GS	IP	H	HR	BB	SO	BB/9	SO/9	WHIP	AVG
2018	21	Great Falls (PIO)	R	0	1	4.18	13	13	28	23	3	9	39	2.9	12.5	1.14	.198
2019	22	Kannapolis (SAL)	LoA	4	6	4.74	14	14	74	88	10	14	77	1.7	9.4	1.38	.275
	22	Winston-Salem (CAR)	HiA	6	4	2.15	12	12	71	56	7	13	77	1.6	9.8	0.97	.204
2020	23	Chicago (AL)	MAJ	0	1	9.95	2	2	6	7	4	4	3	5.7	4.3	1.74	.280
Major League Totals				0	1	9.95	2	2	6	7	4	4	3	5.7	4.3	1.74	.280
Minor League Totals				**10**	**11**	**3.59**	**39**	**39**	**173**	**167**	**20**	**36**	**193**	**1.9**	**10.0**	**1.17**	**.252**

8 ANDREW DALQUIST, RHP

Born: Nov. 13, 2000. **B-T:** R-R. **HT:** 6-1. **WT:** 175. **Drafted:** HS—Redondo Beach, Calif., 2019 (3rd round). **Signed by:** Mike Baker.

BILL MITCHELL

BA GRADE
50 Risk: Extreme

TRACK RECORD: Dalquist went from relative anonymity to a top draft prospect with a big senior year at Redondo (Calif.) Union High. The White Sox drafted him in the third round in 2019 and signed him for an above-slot $2 million. Dalquist made his pro debut with three scoreless appearances in the Rookie-level Arizona League and spent 2020 at the alternate training site before finishing at instructional league.

SCOUTING REPORT: Dalquist moved to Arizona to be closer to the White Sox's minor league complex and made significant strength gains. His fastball ticked up from the low 90s to sitting 94-95 mph with late tailing action. His slider is an above-average pitch with solid break when he throws it in the low-to-mid 80s, but it shows more cutter-type break when he overthrows it. Dalquist removed some of the slurviness from his mid-70s curveball and now shows a crisp, deep, 11-to-5 break on the pitch. Dalquist's changeup shows fine separation from his fastball, but he needs to do a better job finishing the pitch to get it to play to its average potential. Dalquist throws everything for strikes with an easy, athletic delivery and generates some deception, as well.

THE FUTURE: Dalquist needs to show he can hold his improvements over a full season. If he can, he has mid-rotation potential.

SCOUTING GRADES: **Fastball:** 60 **Slider:** 55 **Curveball:** 50 **Changeup:** 50 **Control:** 50

Year	Age	Club (League)	Class	W	L	ERA	G	GS	IP	H	HR	BB	SO	BB/9	SO/9	WHIP	AVG
2019	18	White Sox (AZL)	R	0	0	0.00	3	3	3	2	0	2	2	6.0	6.0	1.33	.154
Minor League Totals				0	0	0.00	3	3	3	2	0	2	2	6.0	6.0	1.33	.182

9 LUIS GONZALEZ, OF

Born: Sept. 10, 1995. **B-T:** L-L. **HT:** 6-1. **WT:** 190. **Drafted:** New Mexico, 2017 (3rd round). **Signed by:** John Kazanas.

DAVE DUROCHIK/MLB PHOTOS VIA GETTY IMAGES

BA GRADE
45 Risk: High

TRACK RECORD: Gonzalez pitched and hit at New Mexico but was universally regarded as a better prospect as a position player. The White Sox drafted him in the third round in 2017 as an outfielder and signed him for $517,000. Gonzalez struggled at Double-A in 2019, but he redeemed himself with a strong showing at the alternate training site in 2020 and made his major league debut Aug. 18.

SCOUTING REPORT: Gonzalez has long had gifted hands, solid bat speed and a patient, mature approach at the plate. The White Sox tweaked his lower half after the 2019 season, including reinstalling a toe tap he had previously discarded, and the result was a more rhythmic swing. With his improvements and an emphasis on letting the ball travel deep and using the whole field, Gonzalez shows the potential to be an average hitter. He has more line-drive gap power than home run power, but he has the bat speed to impact the ball and drive it over the fence on occasion. Gonzalez is a well-rounded athlete capable of playing all three outfield spots. He is best in a corner, where his plus arm strength is an asset.

THE FUTURE: Gonzalez will head back to the minors to start 2021. How his swing improvements hold will determine if he reaches his everyday ceiling.

SCOUTING GRADES: **Hitting:** 50 **Power:** 45 **Running:** 50 **Fielding:** 55 **Arm:** 60

Year	Age	Club (League)	Class	AVG	G	AB	R	H	2B	3B	HR	RBI	BB	SO	SB	OBP	SLG
2017	21	Kannapolis (SAL)	LoA	.245	63	233	26	57	13	4	2	12	38	50	2	.356	.361
	21	Great Falls (PIO)	R	.118	4	17	3	2	1	0	0	3	4	3	0	.286	.176
2018	22	Kannapolis (SAL)	LoA	.300	55	230	35	69	16	2	8	26	21	57	7	.358	.491
	22	Winston-Salem (CAR)	HiA	.313	62	252	50	79	24	3	6	45	27	46	3	.376	.504
2019	23	Birmingham (SL)	AA	.247	126	473	63	117	18	4	9	59	47	89	17	.316	.359
2020	24	Chicago (AL)	MAJ	.000	3	1	1	0	0	0	0	0	0	1	0	.500	.000
Major League Totals				.000	3	1	1	0	0	0	0	0	0	1	0	.500	.000
Minor League Totals				.269	310	1205	177	324	72	13	25	145	137	245	29	.344	.412

10 GAVIN SHEETS, 1B/OF

DAVE DUROCHIK/MLB PHOTOS VIA GETTY IMAGES

Born: April 23, 1996. **B-T:** L-L. **HT:** 6-4. **WT:** 245. **Drafted:** Wake Forest, 2017 (2nd round). **Signed by:** Abe Fernandez.

TRACK RECORD: Sheets zoomed up draft boards after a power surge during his junior year, hitting 21 home runs in 240 at-bats for Wake Forest. The White Sox drafted him 49th overall and signed him for $2 million. Sheets' power didn't show up initially as a pro, leading some to believe it might have been a mirage, but he broke out in 2019 with 16 homers at Double-A Birmingham and seemed prime for even further gains in 2020.

SCOUTING REPORT: Sheets used the coronavirus shutdown to get in better shape, and the White Sox saw enough athleticism to try him in left field at instructional league. Outside scouts who saw him at the position believe it is a legitimate option. In the box, Sheets continued working to utilize his lower half more in his swing, and the results are some of the best exit velocities in the organization and a newfound ability to pull offspeed pitches with authority. He does better on pitches in the upper half of the zone, and working to do damage on pitches in all parts of the zone will be his next step.

THE FUTURE: With left field now an option, Sheets has a clearer path to the big leagues because he was behind top prospect Andrew Vaughn on the first base depth chart. He'll open 2021 at Triple-A.

SCOUTING GRADES: **Hitting:** 45 **Power:** 55 **Running:** 45 **Fielding:** 50 **Arm:** 50

Year	Age	Club (League)	Class	AVG	G	AB	R	H	2B	3B	HR	RBI	BB	SO	SB	OBP	SLG
2017	21	Kannapolis (SAL)	LoA	.266	52	192	16	51	10	0	3	25	20	34	0	.346	.365
	21	White Sox (AZL)	R	.500	4	12	3	6	2	0	1	3	3	0	0	.625	.917
2018	22	Winston-Salem (CAR)	HiA	.293	119	437	58	128	28	2	6	61	52	81	1	.368	.407
2019	23	Birmingham (SL)	AA	.267	126	464	56	124	18	1	16	83	54	99	3	.345	.414
Minor League Totals				.280	301	1105	133	309	58	3	26	172	129	214	4	.358	.408

11 CODI HEUER, RHP

BA GRADE 40 Risk: Medium

Born: July 3, 1996. **B-T:** R-R. **HT:** 6-5. **WT:** 195. **Drafted:** Wichita State, 2018 (6th round). **Signed by:** Robbie Cummings.

TRACK RECORD: After a successful career as a starter at Wichita State, Heuer moved to the bullpen in his first full season as a pro and immediately found success. Combined between high Class A and Double-A, Heuer whiffed 8.6 per nine innings. He made his big league debut on July 24 and was a part of Chicago's prospect-laden bullpen the rest of the way.

SCOUTING REPORT: Heuer operates primarily with two pitches: An upper-90s sinker and a devastating high-80s slider which induced a 67% whiff rate in 23.2 big league innings. The growth of the slider was huge in fueling Heuer's rise to Chicago. High-speed cameras showed flaws in the way he was delivering the pitch, and the resulting tweaks to his release point and hand positioning allowed him to get on top of the ball more often for consistent, sharp break. Heuer also gets deception because of the way he hides the ball in the back of his delivery.

THE FUTURE: Heuer's role in 2020 is likely where he'll settle going forth—a power-armed reliever who pitches late innings and can rack up plenty of strikeouts. He should begin 2021 back in Chicago.

Year	Age	Club (League)	Class	W	L	ERA	G	GS	IP	H	HR	BB	SO	BB/9	SO/9	WHIP	AVG
2020	23	Chicago (AL)	MAJ	3	0	1.52	21	0	24	12	1	9	25	3.4	9.5	0.89	.145
Major League Totals				3	0	1.52	21	0	23	12	1	9	25	3.4	9.5	0.89	.145
Minor League Totals				6	5	3.24	56	14	105	108	4	29	100	2.5	8.5	1.30	.263

12 BLAKE RUTHERFORD, OF

BA GRADE 45 Risk: High

Born: May 2, 1997. **B-T:** L-R. **HT:** 6-2. **WT:** 210. **Drafted:** HS—Canoga Park, Calif., 2016 (1st round). **Signed by:** Bobby Dejardin (Yankees).

TRACK RECORD: After one season in the Yankees' system, Rutherford was dealt to the White Sox for third baseman Todd Frazier and relievers David Robertson and Tommy Kahnle. Since joining his new organization, Rutherford has continued to try to add strength and produce enough power to profile in a corner outfielder. He spent the summer at the team's alternate training site, but could not attend official instructional league because he is part of the 40-man roster.

SCOUTING REPORT: Though the coronavirus pandemic canceled the minor league season, Rutherford was afforded development time at the ATS. There he continued to work on learning how to pull the ball with authority. He worked with Brewers star Christian Yelich over the offseason and brought those lessons to camp, where he worked on getting the barrel on plane quickly and meeting the ball in the strike zone. The result was double-digit home runs against some of the White Sox's higher level pitching. Defensively, his fringe-average speed and below-average throwing arm likely limits him to left field, where he could play to help get Eloy Jimenez to DH.

THE FUTURE: The 2020 season would have been eye-opening for Rutherford, who would have played at the team's hitter-friendly Triple-A park in Charlotte. If his power didn't play there, it would have raised serious red flags. He'll try that path again in 2021.

Year	Age	Club (League)	Class	AVG	G	AB	R	H	2B	3B	HR	RBI	BB	SO	SB	OBP	SLG
2019	22	Birmingham (SL)	AA	.265	118	438	50	116	17	3	7	49	37	118	9	.319	.365
Minor League Totals				.280	367	1395	185	390	75	18	19	174	122	314	34	.337	.400

13 JIMMY LAMBERT, RHP

BA GRADE
45 Risk: High

Born: Nov. 18. 1994. **B-T:** R-R. **HT:** 6-2. **WT:** 190. **Drafted:** Fresno State, 2016 (5th round). **Signed by:** Adam Virchis.

TRACK RECORD: Lambert, whose younger brother Peter pitches for the Rockies, got scouts' attention with an excellent five-game stretch at Double-A Birmingham in 2018. He tore his ulnar collateral ligament shortly thereafter and had Tommy John. Under normal circumstances, Lambert would have missed a good chunk of the season finishing his rehab before returning to the minors. With no minor league season, he instead got a chance to make his big league debut.

SCOUTING REPORT: At his best, Lambert pitches with a four-seam fastball that averaged around 93 mph and touched 96 during his two-game stint in the big leagues. He backs it up with a trio of pitches that each could reach above-average. He went to his low-80s changeup and downer, mid-70s curveball in near-equal measure in the majors, and the White Sox particularly like the action his high arm slot creates on his changeup. His fourth pitch is a short, sharp mid-80s slider, which he threw twice in the big leagues (for consecutive swinging strikes against the Twins' Miguel Sano).

THE FUTURE: Lambert's season ended when he strained his right forearm and had to be placed on the injured list. He should be ready to go for spring training, however, and could find himself back in the big leagues at some point.

Year	Age	Club (League)	Class	W	L	ERA	G	GS	IP	H	HR	BB	SO	BB/9	SO/9	WHIP	AVG
2020	25	Chicago (AL)	MAJ	0	0	0.00	2	0	2	2	0	0	2	0.0	9.0	1.00	.250
Major League Totals				0	0	0.00	2	0	2	2	0	0	2	0.0	9.0	1.00	.250
Minor League Totals				24	24	4.07	70	68	342	346	32	107	325	2.8	8.5	1.32	.265

14 BRYAN RAMOS, 3B

BREAKOUT
BA GRADE
50 Risk: Extreme

Born: March 12, 2002. **B-T:** R-R. **HT:** 6-2. **WT:** 190. **Signed:** Cuba, 2018. **Signed by:** Ruddy Moreta/Doug Laumann/Marco Paddy.

TRACK RECORD: After impressing as an amateur in Cuba, Ramos earned a $300,000 bonus and was skipped over the Dominican Summer League in favor of a pro debut in the Rookie-level Arizona League. There, he hit for average and power and performed well as one of just three players in the league who were born in 2002.

SCOUTING REPORT: After missing out on much-needed development in 2020 thanks to the novel coronavirus pandemic, Ramos was intriguing at instructional league. He's a strong player with big bat speed who can impress in batting practice but still needs to work on timing and consistent direction to the ball in his swing. He's a fairly free swinger, especially early in the count, which could hamper his ability to hit. He's a below-average runner, but the White Sox see enough athleticism to possibly try him at second base in addition to his traditional spot at third.

THE FUTURE: No matter when the season begins, Ramos will play all year at 19. He's likely to stay back in the AZL before moving to low Class A. He will take patience, but has one of the system's higher upsides.

Year	Age	Club (League)	Class	AVG	G	AB	R	H	2B	3B	HR	RBI	BB	SO	SB	OBP	SLG
2019	17	White Sox (AZL)	R	.277	51	188	36	52	10	2	4	26	19	44	3	.353	.415
Minor League Totals				.277	51	188	36	52	10	2	4	26	19	44	3	.353	.415

15 MATT FOSTER, RHP

Born: Jan. 27, 1995. **B-T:** R-R. **HT:** 6-0. **WT:** 210. **Drafted:** Alabama, 2016 (20th round). **Signed by:** Warren Hughes.

TRACK RECORD: Foster was drafted out of high school by the D-backs but chose to head to Gulf Coast State JC for two seasons before transferring to Alabama for his junior year. He moved to the bullpen at Alabama and has stayed there as a pro outside of two appearances as an opener in 2020. Foster made his big league debut on Aug. 1

SCOUTING REPORT: Foster moved slowly through the White Sox system and was on the cusp of the big leagues before the coronavirus pandemic shelved the minor league season before it began. The righthander operates primarily with three pitches—a four-seam fastball that averaged 94 mph and was lauded for its riding life up in the zone, a changeup with roughly 10 mph of separation from his fastball and a slider thrown a tick faster than his changeup. Foster got whiff rates of better than 34% on both of his secondary pitches. His changeup made exceptional progress at instructional league in 2017 thanks to tutelage with pitching coach J.R. Perdew. Foster commands his arsenal well and has weapons for both righties and lefties.

THE FUTURE: Like fellow Top 30 Prospect and 2020 rookie Codi Heuer, Foster has earned a permanent spot in the White Sox bullpen.

Year	Age	Club (League)	Class	W	L	ERA	G	GS	IP	H	HR	BB	SO	BB/9	SO/9	WHIP	AVG
2020	25	Chicago (AL)	MAJ	6	1	2.20	23	2	29	16	2	9	31	2.8	9.7	0.87	.162
Major League Totals				6	1	2.20	23	2	28	16	2	9	31	2.8	9.7	0.87	.162
Minor League Totals				6	8	2.52	132	0	182	135	14	53	218	2.6	10.8	1.03	.207

16 MICKER ADOLFO, OF

BA GRADE
45 Risk: High

Born: Sept. 11, 1996. **B-T:** R-R. **HT:** 6-4. **WT:** 255. **Signed:** Dominican Republic, 2013. **Signed by:** Marco Paddy.

TRACK RECORD: Adolfo signed with the White Sox with the idea that he'd grow into his body and develop big-time power. Four years later, he proved them right by hitting 16 home runs at low Class A Kannapolis. His development has been slowed, however, first by Tommy John surgery in 2019 and then the coronavirus pandemic in 2020.

SCOUTING REPORT: Adolfo easily possesses the most juice in the system. He's a hulking man who takes a huge cut and can quickly lose mistakes to the deepest parts of any park. The question is: Can he cut down enough on his strikeouts to access that power often enough to make himself a big league regular? The White Sox coaching staff worked with Adolfo at the alternate training site to maintain his posture and find a more consistent, less steep bat path that he can trust will help him do the same damage as his old swing. Defensively, his 80-grade arm would be a weapon in right field, where he can potentially be an average defender with fringe-average speed.

THE FUTURE: Adolfo will begin 2021 at one of the team's upper-level affiliates in the hopes of returning to the form that saw him star at high Class A in 2018. There's a lot of rust to kick off, but the reward might be worth the wait.

Year	Age	Club (League)	Class	AVG	G	AB	R	H	2B	3B	HR	RBI	BB	SO	SB	OBP	SLG
2019	22	Birmingham (SL)	AA	.205	23	78	5	16	7	0	0	9	14	36	0	.337	.295
	22	White Sox (AZL)	R	.260	13	50	8	13	5	0	2	3	7	21	0	.362	.480
Minor League Totals				.249	364	1368	194	341	86	7	40	184	121	504	7	.323	.410

17 JAKE BURGER, 3B

Born: April 10, 1996. **B-T:** R-R. **HT:** 6-2. **WT:** 210. **Drafted:** Missouri State, 2017 (1st round). **Signed by:** Clay Overcash.

TRACK RECORD: The White Sox were extremely high on Burger's combination of skills and makeup when they drafted him, and the latter has come into play over the last couple of years as he's dealt with a twice-ruptured left Achilles tendon and a bruised heel that cost him all of the 2018 and 2019 seasons. In 2020, Burger played for a bit in a semi-pro league in the midwest before heading to Chicago's alternate training site and instructional league.

SCOUTING REPORT: It has been a long road back for Burger, who worked at instructs on adjusting his posture to the point where he could better control his barrel on pitches up in the zone. Scouts at instructs also saw a small hitch in his swing that caused him to hit off his front foot at times. Despite that, they liked his bat speed, all-fields power and projected him to hit 20-plus homers if he reaches his peak. Defensively, the injuries have taken their toll, but not as much as would be expected. He is OK moving laterally, has some trouble coming in on balls, and shows above-average arm strength.

THE FUTURE: Despite the two injuries, the White Sox still believed enough in Burger's future to add him to the 40-man roster over the winter. Given the time he's lost, Burger will likely need to start at least at high Class A.

Year	Age	Club (League)	Class	AVG	G	AB	R	H	2B	3B	HR	RBI	BB	SO	SB	OBP	SLG
2019	23	Did not play—Injured															
Minor League Totals				.263	51	194	25	51	10	2	5	29	14	30	0	.336	.412

18 KADE MCCLURE, RHP

BA GRADE 40 Risk: High

Born: Feb. 12, 1996. **B-T:** R-R. **HT:** 6-7. **WT:** 230. **Drafted:** Louisville, 2017 (6th round). **Signed by:** Phil Gulley.

TRACK RECORD: The son of a former NFL quarterback and a college volleyball player, McClure was excellent for three seasons at Louisville before the White Sox took him in 2017. He missed most of the 2018 season with a knee injury, then dominated at the lower levels in 2019 and impressed again at instructional league in 2020.

SCOUTING REPORT: McClure worked with White Sox biomechanist Ben Hansen to increase the power in his delivery, and the result was a fastball that ticked up to the low 90s with flecks of 95. His go-to offspeed pitch is a potentially average, sweepy slider, and he rounds out his repertoire with a potentially average curveball and a fringy changeup. None of his stuff jumps off the page, but the sum of the parts could allow him to eat innings in the back of a rotation.

THE FUTURE: McClure will be 25 once the season starts, so he'll need to move quickly through the upper levels in order to show the White Sox what he's got.

Year	Age	Club (League)	Class	W	L	ERA	G	GS	IP	H	HR	BB	SO	BB/9	SO/9	WHIP	AVG
2019	23	Kannapolis (SAL)	LoA	2	3	3.09	10	10	55	56	3	12	50	2.0	8.1	1.23	.238
	23	Winston-Salem (CAR)	HiA	2	3	3.39	12	12	66	64	8	17	49	2.3	6.6	1.22	.233
Minor League Totals				8	7	3.05	40	30	174	166	14	46	160	2.4	8.3	1.22	.247

19 BRYCE BUSH, OF

BA GRADE 45 Risk: Extreme

Born: Dec. 14, 1999. **B-T:** R-R. **HT:** 6-0. **WT:** 200. **Drafted:** HS—Warren, Mich, 2018 (33rd round). **Signed by:** Justin Wechsler.

TRACK RECORD: Originally committed to Mississippi State, Bush was swayed to sign with Chicago thanks to a bonus of $290,000 which ranked as the second-highest in 2018's 33rd round and the sixth-highest in the White Sox's class. He's struggled with swing-and-miss issues as a pro, but shows enough flashes of talent that there's still plenty of hope.

SCOUTING REPORT: The White Sox always knew Bush was going to be a bit of a project, but they were willing to wait. His raw gifts include a pair of extremely strong hands that he uses to power his bat through the zone and generate exceptional raw power. Now, the swing and strike zone discipline must be refined. He struggled especially against sliders in 2019 at low Class A, and scouts who saw him at instructional league noticed a strong tendency to step in the bucket. In 2019, Bush moved from third base to the outfield, where his athleticism and plus throwing arm could be put to better use.

THE FUTURE: Bush sorely needed 2020, but at least got a chance to get some at-bats at instructional league. Once 2021 begins, he's likely to move to high Class A to continue working to turn his tools into skills.

Year	Age	Club (League)	Class	AVG	G	AB	R	H	2B	3B	HR	RBI	BB	SO	SB	OBP	SLG
2019	19	Kannapolis (SAL)	LoA	.201	67	254	29	51	12	5	5	33	27	92	4	.285	.346
	19	White Sox (AZL)	R	.000	4	9	0	0	0	0	0	0	0	2	0	.000	.000
Minor League Totals				.234	109	402	53	94	21	6	8	51	45	119	8	.318	.376

20 JAMES BEARD, OF

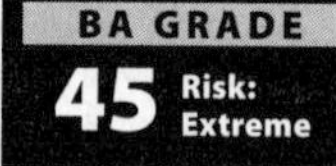

Born: Sept. 24, 2000. **B-T:** R-R. **HT:** 5-10. **WT:** 170. **Drafted:** HS—Brookhaven, Miss., 2019 (4th round). **Signed by:** Warren Hughes.

TRACK RECORD: Beard is a speed merchant of the highest order. He's the fastest player in the White Sox's system by a longshot, and he was the fastest player in his draft class overall. He also showed a modicum of power as an amateur, and the White Sox saw enough potential to take the time to let those tools grow into skills.

SCOUTING REPORT: Because of the novel coronavirus pandemic and a minor leg injury from the instructional league, Beard didn't get much time to develop in 2020. At his best, Beard is an 80-grade runner with strong hands the White Sox believe will help him tap into double-digit home run power. He needs plenty of refinement as a hitter, though, and team officials saw some progress with his swing, but he'll need plenty more as he gets older. He also has to do a better job controlling the strike zone. His speed also serves him well in center field, where he projects to stick.

THE FUTURE: Once the 2021 season begins, Beard could stick back in the Rookie-level Arizona League before moving to low Class A.

Year	Age	Club (League)	Class	AVG	G	AB	R	H	2B	3B	HR	RBI	BB	SO	SB	OBP	SLG
2019	18	White Sox (AZL)	R	.213	31	127	19	27	4	1	2	12	8	54	9	.270	.307
Minor League Totals				.213	31	127	19	27	4	1	2	12	8	54	9	.270	.307

21 CABRERA WEAVER, OF

BA GRADE
45 Risk: Extreme

Born: Dec. 1, 1999. **B-T:** R-R. **HT:** 6-3. **WT:** 180. **Drafted:** HS—Snellville, Ga., 2018 (7th round). **Signed by:** Kevin Burrell.

TRACK RECORD: Out of high school, the White Sox liked Weaver's blend of athleticism and relatively polished tools. The $226,200 bonus he received was the highest for his draft round. He held his own at Rookie-level Great Falls in 2019 and then impressed scouts with moderate improvements at instructional league.

SCOUTING REPORT: At instructional league, Weaver appeared to fill out his body a little bit more and showed the corresponding strength gains. Scouts noted that he's shortened his swing a bit, which gives them a little more confidence in his ability to hit, though there's still a ways to go in that area. The White Sox have tried to get him to use his legs a bit more in his swing. He's a plus runner with a below-average arm who should stick in center field.

THE FUTURE: Weaver is exactly the kind of player who was hurt the most by a lack of a minor league season. He'll likely head to low Class A in 2021, when he'll work to build on the gains he's made.

Year	Age	Club (League)	Class	AVG	G	AB	R	H	2B	3B	HR	RBI	BB	SO	SB	OBP	SLG
2019	19	Great Falls (PIO)	R	.254	62	236	30	60	13	5	2	18	18	85	10	.317	.377
Minor League Totals				.252	112	385	56	97	18	8	3	29	36	137	18	.337	.364

22 DAMON GLADNEY, 3B

BA GRADE
45 Risk: Extreme

Born: July 14, 2001. **B-T:** R-R. **HT:** 6-3. **WT:** 195. **Drafted:** HS—Dyer, Ind., 2019 (16th round). **Signed by:** J.J. Lally.

TRACK RECORD: Gladney impressed the White Sox during a private workout at their big league park before the draft, when he showed enough power to convince them he was worth a flier. He was also a part of their Amateur City Elite program, where he showed strong makeup that heartened the White Sox. He socked eight home runs in the Rookie-level Arizona League, which was second on his team behind Jose Rodriguez.

SCOUTING REPORT: Gladney started his instructional league with a bang, hitting three home runs in three games and posting exit velocities up to 114 mph. The White Sox want him to focus on using his legs more in his swing and sharpening his pitch-recognition skills, which were a clear area of improvement after 82 strikeouts in 201 AZL at-bats in 2019. Scouts questioned his footwork and throwing arm at third base, and wondered if first base might be his long-term home.

THE FUTURE: Gladney could move to low Class A to start 2021, but he might also benefit from more seasoning at the lowest levels. He has intriguing power, but there's a lot of work to be done.

Year	Age	Club (League)	Class	AVG	G	AB	R	H	2B	3B	HR	RBI	BB	SO	SB	OBP	SLG
2019	17	White Sox (AZL)	R	.264	50	201	27	53	5	2	8	25	10	82	1	.309	.428
Minor League Totals				.264	50	201	27	53	5	2	8	25	10	82	1	.309	.428

23 BAILEY HORN, LHP

BA GRADE 40 **Risk: High**

Born: Jan. 15, 1998. **B-T:** L-L. **HT:** 6-2. **WT:** 212. **Drafted:** Auburn, 2020 (5th round). **Signed by:** Warren Hughes.

TRACK RECORD: Horn had Tommy John surgery during his sophomore season at McLennan (Texas) JC, but still got to Auburn in 2019 and helped pitch the Tigers to the College World Series. He'd started well in 2020 before the novel coronavirus pandemic ended the season.

SCOUTING REPORT: Horn works with a three-pitch mix, fronted by a 90-94 mph fastball with tailing action. He backs it up with a potentially plus curveball and a slider that lags behind just a bit. He's also thrown an inconsistent changeup. The White Sox are particularly intrigued by Horn's athleticism, his aggressive mentality on the mound and the carry he gets on his fastball. They plan to continue developing him as a starter but will need to see his command and control improve if he is to remain in that role.

THE FUTURE: Because of his college pedigree, Horn should start his pro career at high Class A with a chance to move to Double-A by season's end.

Year	Age	Club (League)	Class	W	L	ERA	G	GS	IP	H	HR	BB	SO	BB/9	SO/9	WHIP	AVG
2020	22	Did not play—No minor league season															

24 BENYAMIN BAILEY, OF

BA GRADE 45 **Risk: Extreme**

Born: Sept. 18, 2001. **B-T:** R-R. **HT:** 6-4. **WT:** 215. **Signed:** Panama, 2019. **Signed by:** Ricardo Ortiz.

TRACK RECORD: Signed for just $35,000 in April 2019, Bailey was considered somewhat of a sleeper prospect among that year's international class. He produced in the Dominican Summer League and then impressed during Dominican instructional league as well.

SCOUTING REPORT: In Bailey, the White Sox see a player with a blend of potentially above-average power and speed. Evaluators saw a rusty player at the team's instructional league, where he showed big-time power during batting practice but struggled with pitch recognition during games and tended to step in the bucket on swings. Scouts there also saw a player who'd slowed down quite a bit and will have to play in a corner outfield spot.

THE FUTURE: After a long layoff, Bailey will look to get back into the swing of things in 2021, when he's likely to spend most of the year in the Rookie-level Arizona League but could reach low Class A.

Year	Age	Club (League)	Class	AVG	G	AB	R	H	2B	3B	HR	RBI	BB	SO	SB	OBP	SLG
2019	17	White Sox (DSL)	R	.324	55	185	41	60	12	3	2	19	52	40	10	.477	.454
Minor League Totals				.324	55	185	41	60	12	3	2	19	52	40	10	.477	.454

25 YOLBERT SANCHEZ, SS

BA GRADE 45 **Risk: Extreme**

Born: March 3, 1997. **B-T:** R-R. **HT:** 5-11. **WT:** 176. **Signed:** Cuba, 2019. **Signed by:** Marco Paddy.

TRACK RECORD: Sanchez earned the top international bonus handed out by the White Sox in 2019. He was teammates with Luis Robert as an amateur in Cuba on the country's U18 national team. He started his career in the Dominican Summer League, where he was among the league's older players.

SCOUTING REPORT: Sanchez reported to instructional league in Arizona and looked particularly rusty. Internal and external evaluators saw a player who'd gotten thicker during the shutdown, lacked an approach at the plate and showed a willingness to chase. Scouts also saw a player who will not be able to stick at shortstop because of below-average speed and fringy arm strength. The White Sox are optimistic he'll be able to regain some of what they saw when they signed him once he gets more consistent reps.

THE FUTURE: Because Sanchez will be 23 once the season starts, the clock is ticking. He has little experience as a pro and will likely need to start at low Class A to give the White Sox the best chance to see what he can do.

Year	Age	Club (League)	Class	AVG	G	AB	R	H	2B	3B	HR	RBI	BB	SO	SB	OBP	SLG
2019	22	White Sox (DSL)	R	.297	29	111	19	33	8	1	2	12	15	12	3	.386	.441
Minor League Totals				.297	29	111	19	33	8	1	2	12	15	12	3	.386	.441

26 JOSE RODRIGUEZ, SS

Born: May 13, 2001. **B-T:** R-R. **HT:** 5-11. **WT:** 175. **Signed:** Dominican Republic, 2018. **Signed by:** Ruddy Moreta.

TRACK RECORD: Two seasons after signing, Rodriguez has been productive at both of the system's lowest levels. He tied for fourth in the Rookie-level Arizona League in home runs in 2019, with nine, and was one of just 13 players in the league with a slugging percentage better than .500.

SCOUTING REPORT: Rodriguez's reports from instructional league were uneven. He plays with aggression that can border on recklessness, but also can play above-average defense when everything goes right. At the plate, he badly needs to reel in his approach. Scouts in Arizona saw an overly free swinger with a loopy swing who stepped in the bucket and had a particular weakness against sliders. When everything clicks in his swing, though, there's surprising power and ability to use the whole field, though the White Sox would like him to work more on going the opposite way. He's a below-average runner.

THE FUTURE: Rodriguez has a lot of work to do to refine his game, and he'll resume that quest in low Class A. If everything clicks, he could fill a middle-infield utility role with a bit of pop.

Year	Age	Club (League)	Class	AVG	G	AB	R	H	2B	3B	HR	RBI	BB	SO	SB	OBP	SLG
2019	18	White Sox (AZL)	R	.293	44	188	28	55	7	3	9	31	9	45	7	.328	.505
Minor League Totals				.292	104	415	59	121	20	6	11	54	18	74	23	.323	.448

27 ZACK COLLINS, C

Born: Feb. 6, 1995. **B-T:** L-R. **HT:** 6-3. **WT:** 220. **Drafted:** Miami, 2016 (1st round). **Signed by:** Jose Ortega.

TRACK RECORD: Collins as an amateur was lauded for his combination of plate discipline and power, both of which have shown up throughout his minor league career. He's got by far the best knowledge of the strike zone in the system, despite a large amount of strikeouts.

SCOUTING REPORT: Collins' extreme plate discipline plays like a double-edged sword. One thė one hand, he sees a ton of pitches and works walks. On the other, getting deep into counts leads to strikeouts. He has a hand hitch in his swing that, when everything is right, can be counteracted with quick hands through the zone. He has plenty of raw power but needs to make more contact to get to it more often. He's a subpar defender who has a strong throwing arm but slow-twitch mechanics that make it difficult for him to catch runners trying to steal. He could also stand to sharpen his receiving skills.

THE FUTURE: Collins was the third catcher in 2020, behind Yasmani Grandal and James McCann, but could move up with McCann gone. He has the ceiling of backup with more impact offensively.

Year	Age	Club (League)	Class	AVG	G	AB	R	H	2B	3B	HR	RBI	BB	SO	SB	OBP	SLG
2020	25	Chicago (AL)	MAJ	.063	9	16	1	1	1	0	0	0	2	5	0	.167	.125
Major League Totals				.167	36	102	11	17	4	1	3	12	16	44	0	.286	.314
Minor League Totals				.244	362	1218	209	297	70	5	59	213	283	431	5	.385	.455

28 TYLER JOHNSON, RHP

Born: Aug. 21, 1995. **B-T:** R-R. **HT:** 6-3. **WT:** 210. **Drafted:** South Carolina, 2017 (5th round). **Signed by:** Kevin Burrell.

TRACK RECORD: Johnson dealt with biceps and triceps inflammation and a stress reaction in college, but the White Sox were still high enough on his potential to take him in the fifth round. He dominated at the system's lower levels in 2018, but then was limited to just 31.1 innings in 2019 by a strained right lat muscle suffered in the spring.

SCOUTING REPORT: Johnson's allure comes from a mid-90s fastball and a slider that flashes plus but needs more consistency. The pitch had a lot of variance in 2019, and at times almost looked like an over-hand curveball when he'd try to flip it in for an early-count strike. At the alternate training site, Johnson worked to get the slider to above-average or plus more often. He also has feel for an average changeup. Johnson also worked on learning the finer points of pitching instead of simply relying on pure velocity.

THE FUTURE: Johnson will likely start the season at Triple-A Charlotte and has a chance to reach the big leagues at some point in 2021. He was protected on the 40-man roster over the winter.

Year	Age	Club (League)	Class	W	L	ERA	G	GS	IP	H	HR	BB	SO	BB/9	SO/9	WHIP	AVG
2019	23	Birmingham (SL)	AA	2	0	3.44	12	0	18	10	3	6	23	2.9	11.3	0.87	.141
	23	Winston-Salem (CAR)	HiA	0	1	1.80	7	0	10	6	1	4	15	3.6	13.5	1.00	.146
	23	White Sox (AZL)	R	0	0	0.00	3	0	3	5	0	0	5	0.0	15.0	1.67	.385
Minor League Totals				12	2	2.27	85	0	115	82	6	45	169	3.5	13.2	1.10	.197

29 CALEB FREEMAN, RHP

Born: Feb. 23, 1998. **B-T:** R-R. **HT:** 6-1. **WT:** 195. **Drafted:** Texas Tech, 2019 (15th round). **Signed by:** Ryan Dorsey.

TRACK RECORD: Freeman had a rough junior year at Texas Tech. After starting the season as the closer, his velocity and command of the strike zone dipped and he got shelled in 14.2 innings. Nonetheless, the White Sox trusted the stuff rather than the results and have been rewarded.

SCOUTING REPORT: Freeman is a classic case of country hardball. He brings a mid-90s, lively fastball that touched 96 in instructs and reached 98 in college and complements it with a pair of breaking balls. Evaluators were higher on his 78-82 mph curveball than his slider, which comes in a tick harder. The White Sox also like Freeman's makeup, which is aggressive on the mound but mature and willing to learn off the field. Establishing a consistent routine has helped him harness his stuff.

THE FUTURE: Freeman's future is squarely in the bullpen, but if he carries his success from instructs into 2021 he could move quickly. He's likely to start 2021 at one of Chicago's Class A affiliates.

Year	Age	Club (League)	Class	W	L	ERA	G	GS	IP	H	HR	BB	SO	BB/9	SO/9	WHIP	AVG
2019	21	Kannapolis (SAL)	LoA	0	0	4.15	2	0	4	3	1	2	5	4.2	10.4	1.15	.167
	21	Great Falls (PIO)	R	1	1	0.00	5	0	7	3	0	1	12	1.4	16.2	0.60	.103
	21	White Sox (AZL)	R	3	1	2.63	10	0	14	9	1	6	21	4.0	13.8	1.10	.155
Minor League Totals				4	2	2.19	17	0	24	15	2	9	38	3.3	13.9	0.97	.170

30 CHASE KROGMAN, OF

BA GRADE
40 Risk: High

Born: Feb. 27, 2001. **B-T:** L-L. **HT:** 5-11. **WT:** 180. **Drafted:** HS—Liberty, Mo., 2019 (34th round). **Signed by:** Robbie Cummings.

TRACK RECORD: Considering where they drafted him, the White Sox bet relatively big on Krogman in 2019 when they signed him to a $190,000 bonus which ranked as the highest of that round and the sixth-highest of their entire class. The money bought him out of a commitment to Missouri State. He made a quick, seven-game cameo at Rookie-level Great Falls.

SCOUTING REPORT: Scouts who saw Krogman at instructs were mildly intrigued by his bat speed and potential for lefthanded power because of his strength and knowledge of the strike zone. The White Sox see a player who loves the game and can play a corner outfield position, which would likely be right field because of his strong throwing arm that produced 90 mph fastballs off the mound as an amateur.

THE FUTURE: Krogman will be 21 when the season begins, which could lead the White Sox to start him at low Class A.

Year	Age	Club (League)	Class	AVG	G	AB	R	H	2B	3B	HR	RBI	BB	SO	SB	OBP	SLG
2019	18	White Sox (AZL)	R	.190	7	21	2	4	0	0	0	1	1	6	0	.227	.190
Minor League Totals				.190	7	21	2	4	0	0	0	1	1	6	0	.227	.190

MORE PROSPECTS TO KNOW

31 LENYN SOSA, SS

SLEEPER

Sosa is a young infielder who showed intriguing pop in 2019, with 35 doubles, albeit with a lot of swing-and-miss.

32 ALEXANDER COMAS, OF

The high-upside Dominican has struggled at the lowest levels but there's still raw power to bet on as he matures.

33 LUIS MIESES, OF

Evaluators still see some power potential in Mieses, who will be 21 for most of 2021, especially if he can add more loft to his swing.

34 DUKE ELLIS, OF

The 2019 20th-rounder hasn't played an official pro game but already earned the nod as the organization's best defensive outfielder.

35 YOELVIN SILVEN, LHP

In a system without much in the way of pitching from Latin America, Silven stands out as an intriguing, far-away project. He touched 96 at instructs.

36 VICTOR TORRES, C

A Puerto Rican backstop whom the White Sox selected in the 11th round in 2019 has a ceiling as a backup catcher but missed an entire year of development.

37 JEFFERSON MENDOZA, C

The Venezuelan catcher showed better in 2019 while repeating the Dominican Summer League but needs to polish his game on both sides of the ball.

38 LENCY DELGADO, SS

The 2018 fourth-rounder was interesting at Rookie-level Great Falls in 2019 but doesn't stand out among a crowded pack of similarly skilled middle infielders.

39 SEBY ZAVALA, C

The system's best defensive catcher was stuck behind Yasmani Grandal, James McCann and Zack Collins on the road to Chicago but could be a backup somewhere else.

40 YERMIN MERCEDES, C

Mercedes is a big boy with a big swing and a whole lot of fun to his game. He got one big league at-bat in 2020. Mercedes will be 28 in 2021.

TOP PROSPECTS OF THE DECADE

Year	Player, Pos	2020 Org
2011	Chris Sale, LHP	Red Sox
2012	Addison Reed, RHP	Did not play
2013	Courtney Hawkins, OF	Independent League
2014	Jose Abreu, 1B	White Sox
2015	Carlos Rodon, LHP	White Sox
2016	Tim Anderson, SS	White Sox
2017	Yoan Moncada, 2B/3B	White Sox
2018	Eloy Jimenez, OF	White Sox
2019	Eloy Jimenez, OF	White Sox
2020	Luis Robert, OF	White Sox

TOP DRAFT PICKS OF THE DECADE

Year	Player, Pos	2020 Org
2011	Keenyn Walker, OF (1st round supp)	Did not play
2012	Courtney Hawkins, OF	Independent League
2013	Tim Anderson, SS	White Sox
2014	Carlos Rodon, LHP	White Sox
2015	Carson Fulmer, RHP	Pirates
2016	Zack Collins, C	White Sox
2017	Jake Burger, 3B	White Sox
2018	Nick Madrigal, SS	White Sox
2019	Andrew Vaughn, 1B	White Sox
2020	Garrett Crochet, LHP	White Sox

DEPTH CHART

CHICAGO WHITE SOX

TOP 2021 ROOKIES	RANK
Michael Kopech, RHP	2
Nick Madrigal, 2B	3
Garrett Crochet, LHP	4
BREAKOUT PROSPECTS	**RANK**
Bryan Ramos, 3B	14
Jake Burger, 3B	17

SOURCE OF TOP 30 TALENT

Homegrown	28	Acquired	2
College	15	Trade	2
Junior college	0	Rule 5 draft	0
High school	8	Independent league	0
Nondrafted free agent	0	Free agent/waivers	0
International	5		

LF
Blake Rutherford (12)
Anderson Comas

CF
James Beard (20)
Cabrera Weaver (21)
Luis Mieses
Duke Ellis

RF
Luis Gonzalez (9)
Micker Adolfo (16)
Bryce Bush (19)
Benyamin Bailey (24)
Chase Krogman (30)

3B
Bryan Ramos (14)
Jake Burger (17)
Damon Gladney (22)
Zach Remillard
Ti'Quan Forbes

SS
Yolbert Sanchez (25)
Jose Rodriguez (26)
Lenyn Sosa
Luis Curbelo
Lency Delgado

2B
Nick Madrigal (3)

1B
Andrew Vaughn (1)
Gavin Sheets (10)

C
Zack Collins (27)
Victor Torres
Jefferson Mendoza
Yermin Mercedes
Seby Zavala

LHP

LHSP	LHRP
Garrett Crochet (4)	Bailey Horn (23)
Konnor Pilkington	Anderson Severino
Bernardo Flores Jr.	Ronaldo Guzman
Taylor Varnell	Yoelvin Silven

RHP

RHSP	RHRP
Michael Kopech (2)	Codi Heuer (11)
Jared Kelley (5)	Matt Foster (15)
Matthew Thompson (6)	Tyler Johnson (28)
Jonathan Stiever (7)	Caleb Freeman (29)
Andrew Dalquist (8)	Alex McRae
Jimmy Lambert (13)	Emilio Vargas
Kade McClure (18)	McKinley Moore
Jason Bilous	Will Kincanon
Cooper Bradford	Alec Hansen
Chase Solesky	Zack Burdi
Davis Martin	

Cincinnati Reds

BY JJ COOPER

It seemed reasonable to think that Reds president of baseball operations Dick Williams' job was secure when the Reds made the expanded 2020 postseason, even if the team failed to score a run in two games against the Braves and made a quick exit.

A week later, Williams surprised everyone when he announced he was stepping down to pursue other interests and spend more time with his family. Soon afterward, the Reds announced that general manager Nick Krall would be the team's decision-maker. His title remained the same, but now he reports directly to owner Bob Castellini.

Krall inherited a difficult situation.

The Reds boasted one of the best rotations in baseball in 2020 thanks to a dominating season from Cy Young Award winner Trevor Bauer as well as excellent seasons from Sonny Gray and Luis Castillo and the solid contributions of homegrown starters Tyler Mahle and Tejay Antone.

But Bauer became a free agent when the season ended. Closer Raisel Iglesias was traded to the Angels to cut payroll. Righthander Archie Bradley, a useful 2020 trade pickup as a setup man, was non-tendered.

The Reds' lineup was not nearly as effective as the pitching staff. Cincinnati finished 13th in the National League in runs scored, but the lineup largely returns for 2021 while the rotation and bullpen will have to be reworked.

First baseman Joey Votto has reached the point in his contract where his salary—$25 million per year for at least the next three years—far outweighs his production.

It's hard to find a team in the NL Central on the rise. The Cubs, Brewers and Cardinals all discussed cutting payroll heading into 2021, but the Reds were the team making the biggest cuts.

It's not clear whether Cincinnati is looking to win in the short term or retool for the long term. The current roster seems to indicate that the Reds are trying to win now, but the farm system is a couple of years away from making a big impact. After a late surge pushed Cincinnati to 31-29 in a shortened 2020 season, it's not clear whether the Reds have enough firepower to contend for a playoff spot over a longer season, especially if the playoffs return to their pre-2020 format.

Cincinnati has a few minor leaguers who could make significant impacts in 2021, but third baseman Jonathan India and catcher Tyler Stephenson don't have clear paths to everyday at-bats and shortstop Jose Garcia may need further time in the minors.

MICHAEL HICKEY/GETTY IMAGES

Cy Young Award winner Trevor Bauer helped the Reds reach October for the first since 2013.

PROJECTED 2024 LINEUP

Position	Player	Age
Catcher	Tucker Barnhart	33
First Base	Tyler Stephenson	27
Second Base	Jonathan India	27
Third Base	Eugenio Suarez	32
Shortstop	Jose Garcia	26
Left Field	Austin Hendrick	22
Center Field	Nick Senzel	29
Right Field	Rece Hinds	23
Designated Hitter	Jesse Winker	30
No. 1 Starter	Luis Castillo	31
No. 2 Starter	Hunter Greene	24
No. 3 Starter	Nick Lodolo	26
No. 4 Starter	Tyler Mahle	29
No. 5 Starter	Tejay Antone	30
Closer	Tony Santillan	26

But the Reds' farm system's chances to make a big impact are likely a few years away. Picking Rece Hinds and Austin Hendrick in back-to-back drafts gave the team a pair of potential middle-of-the-order thumpers, but both will need significant development. Getting Hunter Greene back on the mound could provide another boost, but the 2017 first-round pick needs to show that his fastball's results can match its impressive radar gun readings.

Getting back to the playoffs for the first time since 2013 was impressive. Now, a team that finished fourth or fifth in the NL Central in each of the previous six seasons has to prove it wasn't an anomaly. ■

1 JOSE GARCIA, SS

Born: April 5, 1998. **B-T:** R-R. **HT:** 6-2. **WT:** 175.
Signed: Cuba, 2017.
Signed by: Chris Buckley/Tony Arias/Miguel Machado/Jim Stoeckel/Bob Engle/Hector Otero.

TRACK RECORD: The Reds have a long history of signing Cuban prospects and have gotten strong payoffs for their proclivity, most notably Aroldis Chapman and Raisel Iglesias. Garcia became the latest Cuban to join the Reds when he signed for $5 million as part of their strong 2016-17 international signing class that also included shortstop Alfredo Rodriguez and righthander Vladimir Gutierrez. Garcia was slowed by a shoulder injury in 2018 but broke out to lead the high Class A Florida State League with 46 extra-base hits in 2019. He hit four home runs in 13 games in spring training with the Reds in 2020, which helped convince the club to fast track him to the majors once baseball resumed after the coronavirus shutdown. The Reds called Garcia up in late August despite the fact he had never played above high Class A and immediately made him their everyday shortstop. He struggled with the aggressive jump and hit .194/.206/.194 before eventually turning the starting job back over to Freddy Galvis, but the Reds still used Garcia as a defensive replacement and pinch-runner and included him on their playoff roster.

SCOUTING REPORT: Jumping to the majors proved to be too much, too soon for Garcia, but he's not a finished product as a hitter. He has good hand-eye coordination, solid bat control in the strike zone and more power than most middle infielders. As bad as his debut was, Garcia has the potential to be an average hitter with average or even a tick above-average power one day. His swing is simple, and his size and strength give him the ability to yank home runs and drive doubles in the gaps. Garcia's approach got pull-heavy in the majors and he had difficulty laying off of breaking balls down and away, giving pitchers an easy plan of attack. Garcia hit .300 against lefties and .167 against righthanders, largely because of his struggles against sliders that broke away from him. Many of Garcia's hitting issues can be chalked up to inexperience, and he has the potential to eventually hit .255-.260 with 15 home runs if he can build off his rough MLB debut. The Reds knew his aggressiveness at the plate was a potential issue, but they brought him up anyway because they love his glove. Garcia has the tools to be a plus defender at shortstop with a quick first step, excellent body control, soft hands, plus range and a plus arm.

THE FUTURE: Garcia is the Reds' shortstop of the future, but that future might not begin until late 2021 or 2022. He needs more time in the minors to face quality breaking balls in a less pressurized environment. His solid glove will give his bat plenty of chances to catch up. ■

JOE ROBBINS/GETTY IMAGES

BA GRADE
55 **Risk: High**

SCOUTING GRADES
Hit: 50. **Power:** 50. **Run:** 50. **Field:** 60. **Arm:** 60

Projected future grades on 20-80 scouting scale.

BEST TOOLS

Best Hitter for Average	Tyler Stephenson
Best Power Hitter	Rece Hinds
Best Strike-Zone Discipline	TJ Friedl
Fastest Baserunner	Jacob Hurtubise
Best Athlete	Michael Siani
Best Fastball	Joe Boyle
Best Curveball	Graham Ashcraft
Best Slider	Jared Solomon
Best Changeup	Jose De Leon
Best Control	Nick Lodolo
Best Defensive Catcher	Mark Kolozsvary
Best Defensive Infielder	Jose Garcia
Best Infield Arm	Rece Hinds
Best Defensive Outfielder	Michael Siani
Best Outfield Arm	Austin Hendrick

Year	Age	Club (League)	Class	AVG	G	AB	R	H	2B	3B	HR	RBI	BB	SO	SB	OBP	SLG
2018	20	Dayton (MWL)	LoA	.245	125	482	61	118	22	4	6	53	19	112	13	.290	.344
2019	21	Daytona (FSL)	HiA	.280	104	404	58	113	37	1	8	55	25	83	15	.343	.436
2020	22	Cincinnati (NL)	MAJ	.194	24	67	4	13	0	0	0	2	1	26	1	.206	.194
Major League Totals				.194	24	67	4	13	0	0	0	2	1	26	1	.206	.194
Minor League Totals				.261	229	886	119	231	59	5	14	108	44	195	28	.315	.386

2 AUSTIN HENDRICK, OF

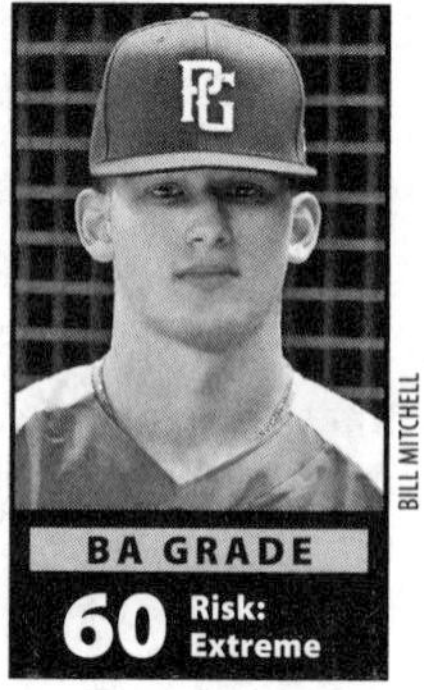

BILL MITCHELL

Born: June 15, 2001. **B-T:** L-L. **HT:** 6-0. **WT:** 195. **Drafted:** HS—Imperial, Pa., 2020 (1st round). **Signed by:** Jeff Brookens.

TRACK RECORD: Just four years after the Twins drafted Alex Kirilloff with the 15th pick in the first round as a lefthanded-hitting corner outfielder coming out of the Pittsburgh area, the Reds made Austin Hendrick the 12th pick in the 2020 draft as a lefthanded-hitting corner outfielder coming out of the Pittsburgh area. Hendrick had a loud summer leading into his senior year and showed off some of the best power in the 2020 draft class. He cleared Wrigley Field's right field scoreboard during the Under Armour All-America Game home run derby and continued to mash throughout the showcase circuit. The coronavirus pandemic canceled Hendrick's high school season before it started, but the Reds still drafted him 12th overall and signed him for $4 million to pass up a Mississippi State commitment.

SCOUTING REPORT: Hendrick is a middle-of-the-order slugger in the making. His plus-plus raw power allows him to hit the ball out to all fields, and his exceptional bat speed allows him to turn around any fastball. Hendrick has a bat wrap that adds some length to his swing and leads to swings and misses, but he's still a potential above-average hitter and shows enough selectivity to draw walks and post solid on-base percentages. Hendrick has plenty of work to do defensively. His fringe-average speed and plus arm fit in right field, but his routes and reads are well below average.

THE FUTURE: Hendrick fits the profile of an everyday outfielder whose bat carries him to the majors. He'll make his pro debut in 2021.

SCOUTING GRADES: **Hitting:** 50 **Power:** 60 **Running:** 45 **Fielding:** 40 **Arm:** 60

Year	Age	Club (League)	Class	AVG	G	AB	R	H	2B	3B	HR	RBI	BB	SO	SB	OBP	SLG
2020	18	Did not play—No minor league season															

3 JONATHAN INDIA, 2B/3B

ALEX TRAUTWIG/MLB PHOTOS VIA GETTY IMAGES

Born: Dec. 15, 1996. **B-T:** R-R. **HT:** 6-0. **WT:** 200. **Drafted:** Florida, 2018 (1st round). **Signed by:** Sean Buckley.

TRACK RECORD: A top draft prospect coming out of high school, India had two solid but unspectacular seasons at Florida, but they didn't seem to offer many hints of what turned into a dominant junior season. He hit .350/.497/.717 with 21 home runs to vault up draft boards, and the Reds drafted him fifth overall and signed him for just under $5.3 million. India was again more solid than spectacular in his first taste of pro ball, but he still reached Double-A at the end of his first full season. He spent 2020 at the Reds' alternate training site in Mason, Ohio.

SCOUTING REPORT: If there was a star of the Reds' alternate site workouts it was India. Much like his third year at Florida, India seemed to take a step forward in his third year of pro ball. He did a better job of driving balls to the opposite field, and in turn his power to left and center field seemed to pick up. India has long had mature at-bats and controlled the strike zone, and the developments increased the confidence he'll fulfill his potential as an above-average hitter with average or better power. India has moved around the infield but is most comfortable at third base, where he has average range. He flashes above-average arm strength, but at times his throws lack zip and are inaccurate, leading many to surmise his best long-term position will be second base.

THE FUTURE: India projects as more of a solid regular than star, but Great American Ball Park could help his power numbers spike. He could make his big league debut in 2021.

SCOUTING GRADES: **Hitting:** 55 **Power:** 55 **Running:** 45 **Fielding:** 50 **Arm:** 55

Year	Age	Club (League)	Class	AVG	G	AB	R	H	2B	3B	HR	RBI	BB	SO	SB	OBP	SLG
2018	21	Greeneville (APP)	R	.261	14	46	11	12	2	1	3	12	15	12	1	.452	.543
	21	Billings (PIO)	R	.250	3	8	1	2	0	0	0	0	0	4	0	.400	.250
	21	Dayton (MWL)	LoA	.229	27	96	17	22	7	0	3	11	13	28	5	.339	.396
2019	22	Daytona (FSL)	HiA	.256	87	317	50	81	15	5	8	30	37	84	7	.346	.410
	22	Chattanooga (SL)	AA	.270	34	111	24	30	3	0	3	14	22	26	4	.414	.378
Minor League Totals				.254	165	578	103	147	27	6	17	67	87	154	17	.369	.410

4 TYLER STEPHENSON, C

TOP ROOKIE

ALEX TRAUTWIG/MLB PHOTOS VIA GETTY IMAGES

BA GRADE

50 Risk: Medium

Born: Aug. 16, 1996. **B-T:** R-R. **HT:** 6-4. **WT:** 225. **Drafted:** HS—Kennesaw, Ga., 2015 (1st round). **Signed by:** John Poloni.

TRACK RECORD: Drafted 11th overall in 2015, Stephenson made his major league debut in 2020 and homered in his first at-bat. After a breather at the alternate training site, he returned to Cincinnati a month later and hit a walk-off home run in his fifth game. It was an impressive start and fitting reward after an injury-filled minor league career. Stephenson had missed time with a concussion, wrist injury and thumb injury.

SCOUTING REPORT: Stephenson fits the model of the bat-first catcher. His swing is quite compact for someone with long arms, and he has toned down the bat waggle and leg kick he had early in his pro career. The changes may sap his power to a minor extent, but they have helped him make more consistent contact. Stephenson recognizes spin well for a young hitter and altogether shows the attributes of an above-average hitter with average power. Stephenson's pitch framing and blocking behind the plate have improved to average, but his game-calling needs work. His long arm action on his throws takes away from his plus arm strength.

THE FUTURE: Stephenson's bat is major league-ready, but his defense may not be. If the National League has the DH again in 2021, it would help Stephenson get regular at-bats in the majors while continuing to polish his catching. It's going to be hard to push Tucker Barnhart and his excellent defense aside in the short term, but Stephenson should be the Reds catcher of the future if he keeps refining his defense.

SCOUTING GRADES: **Hitting:** 55 **Power:** 50 **Running:** 30 **Fielding:** 45 **Arm:** 60

Year	Age	Club (League)	Class	AVG	G	AB	R	H	2B	3B	HR	RBI	BB	SO	SB	OBP	SLG
2017	20	Dayton (MWL)	LoA	.278	80	295	39	82	22	0	6	50	44	58	2	.374	.414
2018	21	Daytona (FSL)	HiA	.250	109	388	60	97	20	1	11	59	45	98	1	.338	.392
2019	22	Chattanooga (SL)	AA	.285	89	312	47	89	19	1	6	44	37	60	0	.372	.410
2020	23	Cincinnati (NL)	MAJ	.294	8	17	4	5	0	0	2	6	2	9	0	.400	.647
Major League Totals				.294	8	17	4	5	0	0	2	6	2	9	0	.400	.647
Minor League Totals				.263	376	1348	195	355	81	3	28	187	162	310	3	.350	.390

5 HUNTER GREENE, RHP

BA GRADE

60 Risk: Extreme

Born: Aug. 6, 1999. **B-T:** R-R. **HT:** 6-4. **WT:** 215. **Drafted:** HS—Sherman Oaks, Calif., 2017 (1st round). **Signed by:** Rick Ingalls.

TRACK RECORD: A two-way star at Notre Dame High in Sherman Oaks, Calif., Greene was a legitimate first round talent as a shortstop with a cannon of an arm and plus power potential. But the Reds and most teams thought Greene's 100 mph fastball needed to become his pro focus. The Reds drafted him second overall in 2017 and signed him for $7.23 million. He struggled early in his pro career and was shut down in July 2018 with an elbow ligament sprain. Greene attempted to rehab the injury, but eventually had Tommy John surgery that sidelined him for all of 2019. He returned in 2020 and spent the year at the Reds' alternate training site.

SCOUTING REPORT: Greene showed his velocity was back to its pre-injury levels at the alternate site. He sat 96-97 mph and touched 102, though his stuff played well below its velocity. His four-seamer lacks vertical movement to help miss bats and his sinker is relatively straight. Greene added a promising but inconsistent 90-93 mph cutter at the alternate site. His 80-85 mph slider is a bigger, sweepier pitch that flashes plus. Greene's fringe-average changeup needs refinement to give him a pitch for lefties, who have hit .321/.411/.571 against him. Greene's easy delivery gives him a chance for above-average control, though he's pitched below that so far in pro ball.

THE FUTURE: Greene's delivery and effortless velocity fit as a starter, but his repertoire needs work. He'll return to game action for the first time in two years in 2021.

SCOUTING GRADES: **Fastball:** 70 **Slider:** 60 **Cutter:** 55 **Changeup:** 45 **Control:** 55

Year	Age	Club (League)	Class	W	L	ERA	G	GS	IP	H	HR	BB	SO	BB/9	K/9	WHIP	AVG
2017	17	Billings (PIO)	R	0	1	12.46	3	3	4	8	0	1	6	2.1	12.5	2.08	.400
2018	18	Dayton (MWL)	LoA	3	7	4.48	18	18	68	66	6	23	89	3.0	11.7	1.30	.251
2019	19	Did not play—Injured															
Minor League Totals				3	8	4.95	21	21	72	74	6	24	95	3.0	11.8	1.35	.261

6 TEJAY ANTONE, RHP

TOP ROOKIE

ALEX TRAUTWIG/MLB PHOTOS VIA GETTY IMAGES

BA GRADE
45 Risk: Low

Born: Dec. 5, 1993. **B-T:** R-R. **HT:** 6-4. **WT:** 205. **Drafted:** Weatherford (Texas) JC, 2014 (5th round). **Signed by:** Byron Ewing.

TRACK RECORD: A high school teammate of Noah Syndergaard, Antone mixed 88-91 mph sinkers and cutters when the Reds drafted him out of Weatherford (Texas) JC. His development was slowed by Tommy John surgery in 2017. His steady velocity improvement took a jump in 2020, when he proved a wonderful surprise for the Reds.

SCOUTING REPORT: Antone made small mechanical tweaks in 2020, including an ability to load into his back leg, to help him go from throwing 91-95 mph two-seamers in 2019 to 94-98 in 2020 while also improving his command. Everything played better because of his improved velocity. His fastball is relatively straight, but the improved velocity helped him generate swings and misses when he elevated. His mid-80s slider is now a true plus pitch that he throws as much as his fastball. It has tight, late tilt and is effective diving away from righties and in on lefties' hands. His above-average curveball doesn't look much different than his slider, but it's slower (78-82 mph) with a bigger, more vertical break and elite spin rates. Antone's average 86-90 mph changeup has some late drop. Antone's biggest issue is that he doesn't throw anything that runs away from lefties, who had a .711 OPS against him compared to righthanded hitters' .446 OPS. He'll have to fix that to earn a spot in the rotation long term.

THE FUTURE: Before 2020, Antone looked ticketed to be an up-and-down starter. Now he's at least a setup man, and if he can better handle lefties, he could be a starter.

SCOUTING GRADES: **Fastball:** 55 **Slider:** 60 **Curveball:** 55 **Changeup:** 50 **Control:** 50

Year	Age	Club (League)	Class	W	L	ERA	G	GS	IP	H	HR	BB	SO	BB/9	SO/9	WHIP	AVG
2017	23	Did not play—Injured															
2018	24	Daytona (FSL)	HiA	6	3	4.03	17	17	96	95	6	29	82	2.7	7.7	1.29	.232
2019	25	Louisville (IL)	AAA	4	8	4.65	14	13	72	93	7	31	70	3.9	8.8	1.73	.304
	25	Chattanooga (SL)	AA	7	4	3.38	13	13	75	63	4	22	63	2.7	7.6	1.14	.221
2020	26	Cincinnati (NL)	MAJ	0	3	2.80	13	4	35	20	4	16	45	4.1	11.5	1.02	.165
Major League Totals				0	3	2.80	13	4	35	20	4	16	45	4.1	11.5	1.02	.165
Minor League Totals				39	35	3.74	111	109	611	679	39	164	460	2.4	6.8	1.38	.283

7 NICK LODOLO, LHP

ALEX TRAUTWIG/MLB PHOTOS VIA GETTY IMAGES

BA GRADE
55 Risk: High

Born: Feb. 5, 1998. **B-T:** L-L. **HT:** 6-6. **WT:** 202. **Drafted:** Texas Christian, 2019 (1st round). **Signed by:** Paul Scott.

TRACK RECORD: A supplemental first-round pick of the Pirates (41st overall) in 2016, Lodolo opted to head to Texas Christian instead of signing. That proved to be a wise choice. After a dominant junior year at TCU, he was nearly universally viewed as the best pitcher available in one of the worst drafts ever for pitching. The Reds made him the only pitcher taken in the top 10.

SCOUTING REPORT: Lodolo is a 6-foot-6 lefty with plus control of his three-pitch arsenal, but his stuff simply wasn't good enough to beat advanced hitters at the alternate training site. Lodolo's fastball sat 90-94 mph, a tick or two slower than his debut, and his armside command was not particularly sharp. The unique challenges of the 2020 season may be a reason for those issues, but he'll need to improve them moving forward. Lodolo's plus curveball with good depth and late snap is his best weapon and projects as a plus pitch. He has worked on throwing his changeup against both righties and lefties, but it is still in the early stages of development and has a long way to go to get to average.

THE FUTURE: Lodolo's ceiling has always been more of a mid-rotation starter than an ace. He needs to improve his velocity, fastball command and changeup to get there.

SCOUTING GRADES: **Fastball:** 55 **Curveball:** 60 **Changeup:** 50 **Control:** 60

Year	Age	Club (League)	Class	W	L	ERA	G	GS	IP	H	HR	BB	SO	BB/9	SO/9	WHIP	AVG
2019	21	Dayton (MWL)	LoA	0	0	2.57	2	2	7	6	0	0	9	0.0	11.6	0.86	.214
	21	Billings (PIO)	R	0	1	2.38	6	6	11	12	1	0	21	0.0	16.7	1.06	.261
Minor League Totals				0	1	2.45	8	8	18	18	1	0	30	0.0	14.7	0.98	.247

8 RECE HINDS, 3B

Born: Sept 5, 2000. **B-T:** R-R. **HT:** 6-4. **WT:** 215. **Drafted:** HS—Bradenton, Fla., 2019 (2nd round). **Signed by:** Sean Buckley.

TRACY PROFFITT/FOUR SEAM IMAGES

BA GRADE
55 **Risk: Extreme**

TRACK RECORD: Hinds had some of the best power in the 2019 draft but struggled to get to it because he swung and missed so often. The Reds drafted him in the second round, No. 49 overall, and signed him for $1,797,500. Hinds played only three games in 2019 due to a quad injury, but he reported to the alternate training site in 2020 and steadily improved. He built on a successful summer with an excellent instructional league that included five home runs, including a monster home run that cleared the batter's eye at the Reds' complex in Goodyear, Ariz.

SCOUTING REPORT: Hinds has an extremely high ceiling thanks to massive power potential. He has top-of-the-scale 80-grade raw power. Hinds' development as a hitter was the most encouraging development of 2020. He showed improved ability to lay off breaking balls and make consistent contact, though it needs to remain a developmental focus. He has plenty of bat speed and his hands work well enough to give his swing some malleability. He has massive, plus-plus raw power when he connects and posted exit velocities as high as 117 mph in instructs. Hinds' plus-plus arm is an asset at third base, but his footwork has to improve and his range is fringy. Many evaluators believe he eventually will be an above-average right fielder, where his average speed will fit.

THE FUTURE: Hinds still has a lot of work to do (and a resume of eight career plate appearances), but his power potential and athleticism give him a high ceiling. He has impressed with his drive and intelligence.

SCOUTING GRADES: **Hitting:** 40 **Power:** 70 **Running:** 50 **Fielding:** 40 **Arm:** 70

Year	Age	Club (League)	Class	AVG	G	AB	R	H	2B	3B	HR	RBI	BB	SO	SB	OBP	SLG
2019	18	Greeneville (APP)	R	.000	3	8	1	0	0	0	0	1	2	3	0	.200	.000
Minor League Totals				.000	3	8	1	0	0	0	0	1	2	3	0	.200	.000

9 TONY SANTILLAN, RHP

Born: April 15, 1997. **B-T:** R-R. **HT:** 6-3. **WT:** 240. **Drafted:** HS—Arlington, Texas, 2015 (2nd round). **Signed by:** Byron Ewing.

ALEX TRAUTWIG/MLB PHOTOS VIA GETTY IMAGES

BA GRADE
50 **Risk: High**

TRACK RECORD: After a slow but steady progression through the Reds' farm system, Santillan battled through a shoulder injury in 2019 at Double-A Chattanooga and saw his stuff and control take a step back. He looked more like his old self in 2020 at the alternate training site and put himself back on the radar as an option for the Reds in 2021 and beyond.

SCOUTING REPORT: Santillan is a bit of a slow starter every season but generally rounds himself into form. At his best, Santillan's fastball works effectively in the low 90s and touches 98 mph with late, vertical life to get swings and misses. Santillan's 84-88 mph slider has solid bite and projects as a plus pitch to give him an effective secondary, but he lacks a third option. His 87-90 mph changeup is well below-average because it lacks deception and flattens out too often. Santillan has some effort in his delivery, leading to stretches of below-average control.

THE FUTURE: Santillan was added to the 40-man roster before the 2020 season, so he still has multiple options remaining. Santillan's most likely future is as a two-pitch power reliever whose fastball and slider play up in shorter stints. The Reds will give him a chance to see if he can improve his changeup and control at Triple-A and remain a potential starter.

SCOUTING GRADES: **Fastball:** 60 **Slider:** 60 **Changeup:** 40 **Control:** 45

Year	Age	Club (League)	Class	W	L	ERA	G	GS	IP	H	HR	BB	SO	BB/9	SO/9	WHIP	AVG
2017	20	Dayton (MWL)	LoA	9	8	3.38	25	24	128	104	9	56	128	3.9	9.0	1.25	.195
2018	21	Daytona (FSL)	HiA	6	4	2.70	15	15	87	81	5	22	73	2.3	7.6	1.19	.224
	21	Pensacola (SL)	AA	4	3	3.61	11	11	62	65	8	16	61	2.3	8.8	1.30	.243
2019	22	Chattanooga (SL)	AA	2	8	4.84	21	21	102	110	8	54	92	4.7	8.1	1.60	.237
Minor League Totals				24	28	3.94	95	93	468	434	38	199	457	3.8	8.8	1.35	.246

10 MICHAEL SIANI, OF

BA GRADE
50 Risk: Very High

Born: July 16, 1999. **B-T:** L-L. **HT:** 6-1. **WT:** 188. **Drafted:** HS—Philadelphia, 2018 (4th round). **Signed by:** Jeff Brookens.

TRACK RECORD: Lefthanded-hitting outfielders run in the Siani family. Michael received an over-slot $2 million bonus as a fourth-round pick in 2018; his younger brother Sammy was a supplemental first-round pick of the Pirates in 2019; and youngest brother Jake is a member of the 2021 high school class. Mike struggled some in his 2019 full-season debut in the low Class A Midwest League, but the Reds still brought him to their alternate training site at the end of the 2020 season.

SCOUTING REPORT: Siani faces questions about his bat, but there's little doubt about his defense. He is a plus runner with excellent range in center field and has Gold Glove potential. He gets excellent jumps, runs precise routes and has a plus arm that yielded 18 assists in his first pro season. As a hitter, Siani has a direct swing path but tends to over-swing. He has a little bit of gap power that will likely improve as he matures and gets stronger, but he's better suited to be a table-setter who uses the entire field and takes advantage of his plus speed on the bases.

THE FUTURE: Siani is years away from being ready for the majors as a hitter. His defense will buy him time to make the necessary approach and strength improvements.

SCOUTING GRADES: Hitting: 50 | Power: 40 | Running: 60 | Fielding: 70 | Arm: 60

Year	Age	Club (League)	Class	AVG	G	AB	R	H	2B	3B	HR	RBI	BB	SO	SB	OBP	SLG
2018	18	Greeneville (APP)	R	.288	46	184	24	53	6	3	2	13	16	35	6	.351	.386
2019	19	Dayton (MWL)	LoA	.253	121	466	75	118	10	6	6	39	46	109	45	.333	.339
Minor League Totals				.263	167	650	99	171	16	9	8	52	62	144	51	.338	.352

11 CHRISTIAN ROA, RHP

BA GRADE
50 Risk: Very High

Born: April 2, 1999. **B-T:** R-R. **HT:** 6-4. **WT:** 220. **Drafted:** Texas A&M, 2020 (2nd round). **Signed by:** Mike Partida.

TRACK RECORD: After two years as a reliever and fill-in starter for Texas A&M, Roa moved into the Aggies' weekend rotation and had an uneven four starts before the coronavirus pandemic ended the college season, but the Reds and other teams were enthused by what they saw. Roa had sports hernia surgery that kept him from pitching at the alternate training site or instructional league.

SCOUTING REPORT: Roa has four pitches that project as average or above-average, and his spin rates and movement profiles are promising. He has a clean arm action and a durable frame and above-average control. Roa will succeed in pro ball if he can throw strikes and mix his pitches to keep hitters from sitting on his average, 92-94 mph fastball. Roa can throw his above-average slider for strikes or bury it, and his above-average changeup's deception gets awkward swings and misse. His average curveball is useful as a change of pace option early in counts.

THE FUTURE: Roa's varied assortment of usable pitches, frame and delivery should lead him to be a fourth or fifth starter. If he can sharpen the slider or changeup a little further he could end up being even better.

Year	Age	Club (League)	Class	W	L	ERA	G	GS	IP	H	HR	BB	SO	BB/9	SO/9	WHIP	AVG
2020	21	Did not play—No minor league season															

12 IVAN JOHNSON, 2B

Born: Oct. 11, 1998. **B-T:** B-R. **HT:** 6-0. **WT:** 190. **Drafted:** Chipola (Fla.) JC, 2019 (4th round). **Signed by:** John Poloni.

TRACK RECORD: After playing infrequently as a freshman at Georgia, Johnson transferred to Chipola (Fla.) JC and had a loud sophomore season. He hit .389/.500/.606 and became the year's highest drafted junior college position player. After a productive debut, Johnson was one of the most consistent and impressive hitters at the Reds' instructional league in 2020.

SCOUTING REPORT: Johnson is one of the Reds' better pure hitters. Solid swings from both sides of the plate give him a shot to be a plus hitter, and his competitiveness and intelligence at the plate stand out even more. He uses the whole field and he has fringe-average power that should continue to improve. For now, Johnson is a surprisingly competent shortstop. His fringy range is offset by steady reliability, quick hands and an accurate arm. He has fringe-average speed, but his mature body should slow him down a touch. He's a safe bet to stay in the infield and could end up as an above-average second baseman.

THE FUTURE: Johnson's blend of usable tools and skills give him a solid path to a big league role. The pandemic means the Reds have a backlog of middle infielders ready for Class A, which could lead to Johnson going straight to high Class A.

Year	Age	Club (League)	Class	AVG	G	AB	R	H	2B	3B	HR	RBI	BB	SO	SB	OBP	SLG
2019	20	Greeneville (APP)	R	.255	46	188	27	48	10	1	6	22	18	46	11	.327	.415
Minor League Totals				.255	46	188	27	48	10	1	6	22	18	46	11	.327	.415

13 LYON RICHARDSON, RHP

BA GRADE 45 **Risk: High**

Born: Jan. 18, 2000. **B-T:** B-R. **HT:** 6-2. **WT:** 192. **Drafted:** HS—Jensen Beach, Fla., 2018 (2nd round). **Signed by:** Stephen Hunt.

TRACK RECORD: Richardson seemed on his way to being a two-way contributor at Florida, but he pitched his way into the second round out of high school by bringing his fastball into the upper 90s. Richardson struggled in his pro debut but bounced back with a reliable and durable season at low Class A Dayton in 2019. The Reds brought him to the alternate training site in 2020.

SCOUTING REPORT: Richardson is a better athlete than most pitchers, but so far he has struggled to match the dominance he flashed as an amatuer. At the alternate site, his strike-throwing simply wasn't consistent enough to outwit more advanced hitters. Stuff-wise, he started to show the mid-90s velocity he'd flashed in high school more consistently, albeit in shorter stints. He generally sat 90-93 when he was taking the ball every fifth day in Dayton. In high school, Richardson's curveball showed power and depth. Now, it's a softer, potentially average pitch thrown in the mid 70s. His below-average changeup needs refinement. Despite a stiff delivery, Richardson could have average control but below-average command.

THE FUTURE: As a pro, Richardson's stuff has been more average than plus. He should head to high Class A in 2021.

Year	Age	Club (League)	Class	W	L	ERA	G	GS	IP	H	HR	BB	SO	BB/9	SO/9	WHIP	AVG
2019	19	Dayton (MWL)	LoA	3	9	4.15	26	26	113	126	10	33	106	2.6	8.5	1.41	.254
Minor League Totals				3	14	4.76	37	37	141	163	13	49	130	3.1	8.3	1.50	.284

14 VLADIMIR GUTIERREZ, RHP

BA GRADE 45 **Risk: High**

Born: Sept. 18, 1995. **B-T:** R-R. **HT:** 6-1. **WT:** 190. **Signed:** Cuba, 2016. **Signed by:** Tony Arias/Chris Buckley.

TRACK RECORD: Gutierrez was expected to be a fast-mover when the Reds signed him for $4.7 million in Sept. 2016. Four seasons later, Gutierrez has yet to make his MLB debut. He struggled to pitch with the more lively Triple-A ball in 2019. He was suspended for 80 games after testing positive for the performance-enhancing drug stanozolol. Gutierrez did get approval from MLB to report to instructional league and pitched as a starter for Licey in the Dominican League.

SCOUTING REPORT: Gutierrez's velocity took a jump in spring training before his suspension. He showed that same 94-96 mph velocity at the end of instructional league. His changeup and curve have both flashed above-average, but too often he's focused on strike-throwing and the quality of his stuff suffers. He can vary the break of his curve, making it a sweepier strike or a harder pitch he buries in advantageous counts. Gutierrez has average control.

THE FUTURE: Gutierrez has 20 games remaining to serve on his suspension, so his 2021 season will be delayed. The Reds added him to the 40-man roster despite his PED suspension. He's more likely to end up as a reliever, but he could fill a back-end role if the opportunity arises.

Year	Age	Club (League)	Class	W	L	ERA	G	GS	IP	H	HR	BB	SO	BB/9	SO/9	WHIP	AVG
2019	23	Louisville (IL)	AAA	6	11	6.04	27	27	137	144	26	48	117	3.2	7.7	1.40	.236
Minor League Totals				22	29	4.98	73	73	387	391	54	105	356	2.4	8.3	1.28	.259

15 NOAH DAVIS, RHP

BA GRADE 50 **Risk: Extreme**

Born: April 22, 1997. **B-T:** R-R. **HT:** 6-2. **WT:** 195. **Drafted:** UC Santa Barbara, 2018 (11th round). **Signed by:** Rick Ingalls.

TRACK RECORD: As a freshman, Davis served as UC Santa Barbara's No. 2 starter behind ace Shane Bieber as the Gauchos made their first College World Series. Davis pitched through a significant toe injury as a freshman, but an elbow injury derailed his junior season after just three appearances. He had Tommy John surgery in March 2018. The Reds drafted him knowing he wouldn't pitch until a year after he was drafted.

SCOUTING REPORT: Davis impressed in the Rookie-level Pioneer League in his return to the mound in 2019. He battled some shoulder soreness at instructs, but got back on the mound and showed a potentially plus fastball and slider. Davis' top-end velocity bumped up to 96 at instructs, but he sat 91-94 as a starter in 2019. His fastball has solid carry. He also throws a curveball that isn't as impressive as his slider. Davis' changeup needs to improve if he's going to remain a starter. Davis' control has wavered in his limited pro action, but he could eventually get to average control.

THE FUTURE: Davis is ready to jump to high Class A in 2021. Between injuries and the pandemic, he's not gotten to pitch much, but his patience may pay off before long. He has potential to be a No. 4 starter.

Year	Age	Club (League)	Class	W	L	ERA	G	GS	IP	H	HR	BB	SO	BB/9	SO/9	WHIP	AVG
2019	22	Billings (PIO)	R	1	1	2.10	8	8	34	27	4	13	30	3.4	7.9	1.17	.175
	22	Reds (AZL)	R	0	2	7.88	5	5	8	13	4	0	5	0.0	5.6	1.63	.448
Minor League Totals				1	3	3.19	13	13	42	40	8	13	35	2.8	7.4	1.25	.248

16 TYLER CALLIHAN, 2B

Born: June 22, 2000. **B-T:** L-R. **HT:** 6-0. **WT:** 205. **Drafted:** HS—Jacksonville, Fla., 2019 (3rd round). **Signed by:** Sean Buckley.

TRACK RECORD: Callihan was one of the most advanced hitters in the 2019 high school class. He impressed scouts with his ability to square up quality pitchers and velocity. In his pro debut in 2019, he largely lived up to those expectations, showing a solid swing, although he was somewhat allergic to taking a walk. He struggled at the Reds' instructional league in 2020.

SCOUTING REPORT: Callihan's bat has long been ahead of his glove. A high school shortstop, there are questions about whether Callihan has the quickness to handle second or third base long-term. His hands work fine, but he seemed a step slow at instructional league. His arm is above-average and could fit in an outfield corner. He played some catcher in high school, which could be another option. Callihan has a shot to be an above-average hitter with above-average power, though he needs to pair his solid hand-eye coordination with improved plate discipline. Like many young lefthanded hitters, he needs plenty of at-bats against lefties, but his swing and fast hands should continue to work.

THE FUTURE: The Reds hope that Callihan will bounce back after a rough instructional league. Finding a defensive home remains a priority, but his bat should give him chances to find a fit.

Year	Age	Club (League)	Class	AVG	G	AB	R	H	2B	3B	HR	RBI	BB	SO	SB	OBP	SLG
2019	19	Greeneville (APP)	R	.250	52	204	27	51	10	5	5	26	9	46	9	.286	.422
	19	Billings (PIO)	R	.400	5	20	3	8	0	1	1	7	1	4	2	.429	.650
Minor League Totals				.263	57	224	30	59	10	6	6	33	10	50	11	.298	.442

17 BRYCE BONNIN, RHP

Born: Oct. 11, 1998. **B-T:** R-R. **HT:** 6-2. **WT:** 190. **Drafted:** Texas Tech, 2020 (3rd round). **Signed by:** Paul Scott.

TRACK RECORD: After a year in Arkansas' bullpen, Bonnin transferred to Texas Tech, where he moved into the rotation and missed both bats and the strike zone. Bonnin made four uneven starts in 2020, which led to a 7.36 ERA in his pandemic-shortened draft year.

SCOUTING REPORT: Bonnin has the stuff to get outs in the majors. His 93-97 mph plus fastball will touch 99, and his plus 85-87 mph slider is even more of a weapon. His crossfire delivery leads to his slider cutting across the plate with plenty of lateral bite. Bonnin has a hard high-80s, well below-average changeup which needs to improve if he is to remain a starter. Though his delivery adds deception, it has also led to below-average command and control. His lengthy arm action involves a plunge and a wrap in the back, which makes it difficult for his arm to be on time.

THE FUTURE: Most likely, Bonnin ends up as a power reliever who can attack hitters with a plus fastball and a plus slider. For now, the Reds will likely let him start as he tries to throw strikes more consistently.

Year	Age	Club (League)	Class	W	L	ERA	G	GS	IP	H	HR	BB	SO	BB/9	SO/9	WHIP	AVG
2020	21	Did not play—No minor league season															

18 MICHEL TRIANA, 1B

BA GRADE
50 Risk: Extreme

Born: Nov. 23, 1999. **B-T:** L-R. **HT:** 6-3. **WT:** 230. **Signed:** Cuba, 2019. **Signed by:** Reds international scouting department.

TRACK RECORD: Triana has had a long wait to play in an official game. He was one of the best players on Cuba's 18U national team in 2017, but he headed to the Dominican Republic in 2018 to showcase for U.S. teams. The Reds signed him for $1.3 million and then sent him to the unofficial tricky league. He was supposed to make his U.S. debut in 2020 but thanks to the coronavirus pandemic he couldn't get a visa for instructional league.

SCOUTING REPORT: Triana worked out for teams as a third baseman, but the Reds took one look at his big, mature frame and immediately slid him to first base, where his skill set will profile. He has plus raw power, but his line-drive swing doesn't always lift the ball over the fence. He showed some issues with breaking balls in the Tricky League, but that can somewhat be chalked up to rust. He could end up as an asset defensively at first thanks to good feet and soft hands.
THE FUTURE: The Reds and Triana have had a long wait to see what he can do in actual games. He has the tools to be a MLB regular at first base if everything develops, but it's hard to feel confident until he gets tested by minor league pitchers.

Year	Age	Club (League)	Class	AVG	G	AB	R	H	2B	3B	HR	RBI	BB	SO	SB	OBP	SLG
2019	20	Did not play—Signed 2020 contract															

19 JACKSON MILLER, C

BA GRADE
50 Risk: Extreme

Born: Jan. 3, 2002. **B-T:** L-R. **HT:** 6-0. **WT:** 195. **Drafted:** HS—New Port Richey, Fla., 2020 (2nd round supplemental). **Signed by:** Sean Buckley.
TRACK RECORD: Teams have gotten understandably nervous about taking prep catchers high in the draft. The Reds, though, have been better than most at scouting prep catchers, picking Devin Mesoraco, Tucker Barnhart, Tyler Stephenson and Joey Votto in the 21st century. A former shortstop, Miller impressed scouts as a well-rounded, athletic backstop.
SCOUTING REPORT: Miller does everything pretty well. Like most catchers, he's a below-average runner who likely will slow further. Other than that, everything projects as fringe-average or better. His lefty swing is simple, repeatable and has the potential to make him an average hitter who produces line-drive doubles to the gap and power that could get to fringe-average. His arm is average, but his soft hands and quiet receiving give him the tools to be an above-average receiver.
THE FUTURE: Miller was viewed as a breakout candidate if there had been a 2020 high school season. Instead, his 2020 season was limited to a few games before the shutdown and some work in instructional league. High school catchers take a while to develop, but Miller has the tools to be a big league regular.

Year	Age	Club (League)	Class	AVG	G	AB	R	H	2B	3B	HR	RBI	BB	SO	SB	OBP	SLG
2020	18	Did not play—No minor league season															

20 JOSE DE LEON, RHP

BA GRADE
45 Risk: High

Born: Aug. 7, 1992. **B-T:** R-R. **HT:** 6-2. **WT:** 215. **Drafted:** Southern, 2013 (24th round). **Signed by:** Matt Paul (Dodgers).
TRACK RECORD: A two-time Top 100 prospect, De Leon made his major league debut with the Dodgers in 2016. He's still prospect-eligible because injuries have ravaged his career, beginning with shoulder inflammation and ending with Tommy John surgery in 2018 that affected his stuff well into 2019. De Leon was acquired by the Reds for cash after the 2019 season and he had a pair of stints in the bullpen.
SCOUTING REPORT: At the end of 2020, De Leon showed glimpses of the form that once made him a top prospect. He regained 3-4 mph on his fastball, turning a 91-92 mph below-average offering back into at least an average pitch. De Leon's fastball doesn't have to be great, but if it's 94-96, it sets up a plus 85-87 mph changeup. De Leon has always thrown the changeup with excellent deception, but his improved arm speed helps him sell it better and it has excellent fading action. His slider improved as well. He doesn't command it as well as his fastball and changeup, but it has plenty of lateral sweep away from righties.
THE FUTURE: Durability will remain a concern considering De Leon's injury history, but a year after the Reds helped Lucas Sims return to prominence, De Leon could be the next reclamation project to click.

Year	Age	Club (League)	Class	W	L	ERA	G	GS	IP	H	HR	BB	SO	BB/9	SO/9	WHIP	AVG
2020	27	Cincinnati (NL)	MAJ	0	0	18.00	5	0	6	6	1	11	10	16.5	15.0	2.83	.250
Major League Totals				4	0	8.49	13	4	29	32	7	24	34	7.3	10.3	1.89	.271
Minor League Totals				27	16	3.35	96	87	425	347	37	145	564	3.1	11.9	1.16	.220

21 ALLAN CERDA, OF

BREAKOUT
BA GRADE
50 Risk: Extreme

Born: Nov. 24, 1999. **B-T:** R-R. **HT:** 6-3. **WT:** 170. **Signed:** Dominican Republic, 2017. **Signed by:** Felix Romero.

TRACK RECORD: After spending big in 2016, the Reds were in the international penalty box, restricted to spending $300,000 or less on signings in 2017. The Reds signed only one player for even $100,000 that year (Leonardo Seminati), but they found Cerda as a low-cost signee who's paid off. Cerda posted the second-best on-base percentage (.402) on the 2018 DSL Reds and was just as impressive in the Rookie-level Appalachian League in 2019. He was invited to instructional league in 2020.

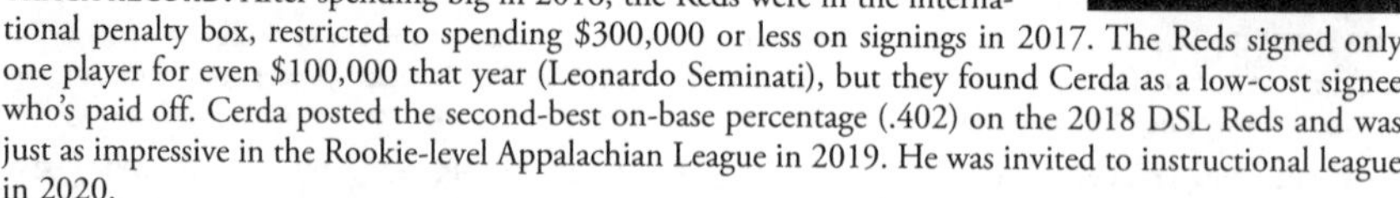

SCOUTING REPORT: Cerda has plenty of tools at his disposal. He has a chance to stick in center field while hitting for power and impressed in the Appalachian League with his feel for the game. He's an above-average runner who flashes an above-average glove in center and has a plus arm that could also fit in right field. Cerda swings and misses too much, but he has survival skills because he also shows a picky batting eye, drawing walks when pitchers try to stay away from his above-average power.

THE FUTURE: Cerda is ready for full-season ball. He has an athletic build, and has a chance to retain his speed to pair with solid power potential.

Year	Age	Club (League)	Class	AVG	G	AB	R	H	2B	3B	HR	RBI	BB	SO	SB	OBP	SLG
2019	19	Greeneville (APP)	R	.220	39	132	22	29	6	0	9	27	20	56	2	.360	.470
Minor League Totals				.249	90	305	57	76	17	0	15	61	45	101	5	.384	.452

22 T.J. FRIEDL, OF

BA GRADE
40 Risk: Medium

Born: Aug. 4, 1995. **B-T:** L-L. **HT:** 5-10. **WT:** 180. **Signed:** Nevada, 2016 (NDFA). **Signed by:** Rich Bordi/Sam Grossman.

TRACK RECORD: Thanks to draft rule changes, Friedl holds a record that may go unbroken for years. Friedl went overlooked as a draft-eligible sophomore, but after an impressive summer with USA Baseball, he set off a bidding war and signed with the Reds for $735,000. Now, nondrafted free agents are limited to signing for $20,000, or 2.7 percent of Freidl's bonus.

SCOUTING REPORT: After an injury-plagued 2019 season when he was slowed by a shoulder injury and then shut down because of an ankle injury, Friedl spent the summer at the Reds' alternate training site. There, he once again showed he's a pesky hitter who loves to work counts but doesn't really put much fear in a pitcher's heart. Freidl's well below-average power makes him more of a bottom-of-the-order bat, but he gets on base and should be an average hitter with a contact-oriented approach. He's a plus runner who can play above-average defense in center or left field. His arm is below-average.

THE FUTURE: Friedl has been unpicked in back-to-back Rule 5 drafts. He's a fourth or fifth outfielder whose value is limited by his lack of impact, but he's ready for Triple-A and could help the Reds if injuries hit.

Year	Age	Club (League)	Class	AVG	G	AB	R	H	2B	3B	HR	RBI	BB	SO	SB	OBP	SLG
2019	23	Chattanooga (SL)	AA	.235	65	226	38	53	11	4	5	28	29	50	13	.347	.385
Minor League Totals				.277	339	1265	211	351	68	21	20	134	147	260	66	.369	.412

23 JARED SOLOMON, RHP

BA GRADE
45 Risk: Extreme

Born: June 10, 1997. **B-T:** R-R. **HT:** 6-2. **WT:** 192. **Drafted:** Lackawanna (Pa.) JC, 2017 (11th round). **Signed by:** Lee Seras.

TRACK RECORD: When the Reds drafted Solomon, they were taking a chance on a pitcher with a lot of work ahead. Solomon's performance in junior college wasn't spectacular, but Reds scout Lee Seras believed there was more to come. Three years later, Solomon was throwing 4-5 mph harder at instructional league with a much sharper slider. He tore his right ulnar collateral near the end of instructs and needed Tommy John surgery.

SCOUTING REPORT: Other than Rece Hinds, no Reds player impressed more at instructs than Solomon. He's added strength and uses his legs better in his delivery. Solomon sat 93-97 mph and touched 99, up from the 92-94 he threw in college. His improved arm speed also paid off in a better and harder slider that sat 87-89 mph with significant tilt. Working with two plus pitches, Solomon had the look of a potentially dominating reliever. He also has a seldom-thrown, below-average changeup. Solomon has been a starter for the Reds so far, but he's more likely to end up as a two-pitch power reliever.

THE FUTURE: The Reds were impressed enough by Solomon's improved stuff that they added him to the 40-man roster despite the injury and his lack of experience above Class A. He will miss all of 2021 while he recovers.

Year	Age	Club (League)	Class	W	L	ERA	G	GS	IP	H	HR	BB	SO	BB/9	SO/9	WHIP	AVG
2019	22	Daytona (FSL)	HiA	2	8	4.30	15	15	73	74	5	34	65	4.2	8.0	1.47	.213
	22	Dayton (MWL)	LoA	1	3	3.43	11	11	42	42	0	27	46	5.8	9.9	1.64	.218
Minor League Totals				9	16	3.82	52	47	226	219	12	109	221	4.3	8.8	1.45	.252

24 LUIS MEY, RHP

BREAKOUT

BA GRADE

45 Risk: Extreme

Born: June 24, 2001. **B-T:** R-R. **HT:** 6-2. **WT:** 180. **Signed:** Dominican Republic, 2017. **Signed by:** Felix Romero.

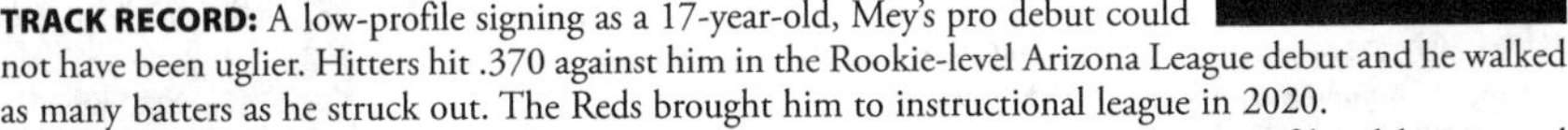

TRACK RECORD: A low-profile signing as a 17-year-old, Mey's pro debut could not have been uglier. Hitters hit .370 against him in the Rookie-level Arizona League debut and he walked as many batters as he struck out. The Reds brought him to instructional league in 2020.

SCOUTING REPORT: Mey has the building blocks to be a future MLB starter, even if his debut seemed inauspicious. Mey's fastball sat 93-96 mph at instructional league and can touch 99. His delivery is very smooth and repeatable and he uses a loose arm to generate easy velocity. In addition to his plus fastball, Mey's 80-84 mph slider is potentially average, although he gets on the side of it too often now, which negates some of its depth. Mey doesn't have a third consistent pitch. Mey's control is currently well below-average, but his delivery and athleticism should allow him to significantly improve as he matures and gets stronger.

THE FUTURE: Mey has the athleticism, repeatable delivery and fluid arm action of a potential starter, even if he's still half-decade away from Cincinnati. The 2021 season will be big for him to show he's made strides toward reaching his significant potential.

Year	Age	Club (League)	Class	W	L	ERA	G	GS	IP	H	HR	BB	SO	BB/9	SO/9	WHIP	AVG
2019	18	Reds (AZL)	R	0	5	8.39	13	12	40	64	4	28	28	6.4	6.4	2.32	.302
Minor League Totals				0	5	8.39	13	12	39	64	4	28	28	6.4	6.4	2.32	.370

25 RILEY O'BRIEN, RHP

BA GRADE

40 Risk: High

Born: Feb. 6, 1995. **B-T:** R-R. **HT:** 6-4. **WT:** 170. **Drafted:** College of Idaho, 2017 (8th round). **Signed by:** Paul Kirsch (Rays).

TRACK RECORD: An astute pick as a $7,500 seventh-rounder out of the College of Idaho, an NAIA school, O'Brien has a long track record of success in the minors, although his 2019 season ended early because of a sore elbow. The Reds picked him up from the Rays in a trade for lefthander Cody Reed after Reed was designated for assignment.

SCOUTING REPORT: O'Brien's 91-95 mph fastball is above-average and flashes plus. He can elevate for swings and misses and tops out at 97. His slider flashes plus as well, but it's erratic. O'Brien's control has been fringe-average, but his command is below-average. His changeup has never really developed.

THE FUTURE: O'Brien's time as a starter may be running out. The Reds added him to their 40-man roster in the offseason, but the cancelled 2020 minor league season means he'll enter 2021 as a 25-year-old who has yet to pitch in Triple-A. O'Brien's future is likely as an up-and-down reliever who hopes to blossom into a middle-innings option.

Year	Age	Club (League)	Class	W	L	ERA	G	GS	IP	H	HR	BB	SO	BB/9	SO/9	WHIP	AVG
2019	24	Montgomery (SL)	AA	5	6	3.93	14	11	69	56	4	29	72	3.8	9.4	1.24	.189
	24	Charlotte, FL (FSL)	HiA	2	0	1.59	6	6	34	20	2	15	35	4.0	9.3	1.03	.152
Minor League Totals				16	10	2.83	56	40	232	163	11	103	250	4.0	9.7	1.15	.199

26 YAN CONTRERAS, SS

BA GRADE

45 Risk: Extreme

Born: Jan. 30, 2001. **B-T:** R-R. **HT:** 6-2. **WT:** 185. **Drafted:** HS—Aguadilla, P.R, 2019 (12th round). **Signed by:** Hector Otero.

TRACK RECORD: The actual on-field track record of Contreras as a hitter is pretty limited. Scouts were somewhat concerned about his bat when he was in high school, and he did not hit in 20 games in the Rookie-level Arizona League in 2019 before he was sidelined by a wrist injury. He impressed at the plate at the Excellence Tournament in the leadup to the draft and he showed improved power and exit velocities at instructional league in 2020.

SCOUTING REPORT: Contreras' defense at shortstop is his calling card for now. He's an athletic shortstop with plus hands and a plus arm who should be at least an above-average defender. He's also an above-average runner. Now, the question is whether his bat will develop to let him be an everyday regular at short. He's a well-below-average hitter with well-below-average power for now, but there is promise. He needs to keep getting stronger, but his frame gives him the chance to add weight and strength. He has solid bat-to-ball skills, although he needs to improve his pitch recognition.

THE FUTURE: If everything clicks, Contreras will be a steal of a 12th-round pick, but his bat has a long way to go. He should be ready for low Class A in 2021.

Year	Age	Club (League)	Class	AVG	G	AB	R	H	2B	3B	HR	RBI	BB	SO	SB	OBP	SLG
2019	18	Reds (AZL)	R	.145	20	69	8	10	1	2	0	2	14	25	4	.298	.217
Minor League Totals				.145	20	69	8	10	1	2	0	2	14	25	4	.298	.217

27 BRANDON BAILEY, RHP

BA GRADE
40 Risk: High

Born: Oct. 19, 1994. **B-T:** R-R. **HT:** 5-10. **WT:** 194. **Drafted:** Gonzaga, 2016 (6th round). **Signed by:** Jim Coffman (Athletics).

TRACK RECORD: When Bailey made the Astros' Opening Day roster in 2020—at the same time and on the same team as his Gonzaga teammate Taylor Jones—he became the fourth member of the Chickasaw nation to reach the majors. Bailey was a Rule 5 pick of the Orioles in 2019, but was sent back to the Astros during 2020 spring training. After spending most of the season at the Astros' alternate training site, the Reds acquired Bailey for cash considerations when the Astros were looking to clear 40-man roster space.

SCOUTING REPORT: Bailey's listed 5-foot-10 height might be a little generous, but he's long succeeded thanks to getting extremely high spin rates on his above-average, 92-94 mph fastball, which means it plays better than its velocity readings. His changeup is a second above-average pitch and has solid fade and excellent deception. He also throws a 1-to-7 curve and a cutterish slider that are both fringe-average. Bailey has average command and fringe-average control. He has to work the edges and is not afraid to miss high or low when behind in counts.

THE FUTURE: Bailey has long been a spin-rate monster. After making his MLB debut in 2020 he needs to show in 2021 that he can stick around. He fits as a useful lower-leverage reliever who can go multiple innings.

Year	Age	Club (League)	Class	W	L	ERA	G	GS	IP	H	HR	BB	SO	BB/9	SO/9	WHIP	AVG
2020	25	Houston (AL)	MAJ	0	0	2.45	5	0	7	6	1	3	4	3.7	4.9	1.23	.231
Major League Totals				0	0	2.45	5	0	7	6	1	3	4	3.7	4.9	1.23	.231
Minor League Totals				16	16	3.07	83	58	349	263	32	134	405	3.5	10.4	1.14	.208

28 GRAHAM ASHCRAFT, RHP

BA GRADE
45 Risk: Extreme

Born: Feb. 11, 1998. **B-T:** L-R. **HT:** 6-2. **WT:** 220. **Drafted:** Alabama-Birmingham, 2019 (6th round). **Signed by:** Jonathan Reynolds.

TRACK RECORD: Ashcraft was one of the top high school players in Alabama in 2016. He led the state with 16 home runs as a junior, but then impressed even more on the mound as a senior as he touched 99 mph. He made five starts for Mississippi State as a freshman, then missed the next year and a half due to hip injuries. He flashed more potential at Alabama-Birmingham in 2019 and pitched reasonably effectively in the Rookie-level Appalachian League after signing.

SCOUTING REPORT: Ashcraft has the potential for two plus pitches. He may not touch 99 mph anymore but he will bump it up to 97, and his plus curveball is better than his fastball. The shutdown did Ashcraft no favors. More than anything, he needs regular innings to develop. He has thrown less than 140 innings combined since high school. Ashcraft's command and control remain below-average, but they have made strides in pro ball—he walked six batters per nine during his abbreviated college career.

THE FUTURE: Ashcraft's stuff is as good as almost any Reds pitching prospect's arsenal, but his injuries and the pandemic have left him behind on the development curve. A full, healthy 2021 in full season ball would be a big step.

Year	Age	Club (League)	Class	W	L	ERA	G	GS	IP	H	HR	BB	SO	BB/9	SO/9	WHIP	AVG
2019	21	Greeneville (APP)	R	2	4	4.53	13	13	54	51	2	21	60	3.5	10.1	1.34	.231
Minor League Totals				2	4	4.53	13	13	53	51	2	21	60	3.5	10.1	1.34	.243

29 JOEL KUHNEL, RHP

BA GRADE **40** Risk: High

Born: Feb. 19, 1995. **B-T:** R-R. **HT:** 6-4. **WT:** 280. **Drafted:** Texas-Arlington, 2016 (11th round). **Signed by:** Byron Ewing.

TRACK RECORD: A starter at Texas-Arlington, Kuhnel has been a closer at every step up the ladder in the minors. In the majors, he's had a much less pressure-packed role. The Reds ourighted him off the 40-man roster after the season and he went unclaimed by the other 29 teams.

SCOUTING REPORT: Kuhnel's velocity was down a tick in 2020. He still sat around 95 mph and touched 97, but that was down from the 97-98 he regularly touched in his brief MLB stint in 2019. He has touched 100 in the minors. It may not seem like much, but Kuhnel relies on his velocity because the movement profiles of his pitches are relatively pedestrian. Righthanded hitters don't have to worry about anything running in or significantly away from them, as Kuhnel's average four-seam and two-seam fastballs both are relatively straight and his average slider has more depth than tilt. Kuhnel demonstrated above-average control in the lower minors, where his plus velocity gave hitters fits, but his command is less refined.

THE FUTURE: Kuhne's big arm gives him a shot to be a low-leverage reliever. He likely will get another shot in Cincinnati in 2021, but his lack of an out pitch will likely keep him from a significant role.

Year	Age	Club (League)	Class	W	L	ERA	G	GS	IP	H	HR	BB	SO	BB/9	SO/9	WHIP	AVG
2020	25	Cincinnati (NL)	MAJ	1	0	6.00	3	0	3	4	2	0	3	0.0	9.0	1.33	.308
Major League Totals				2	0	4.97	14	0	12	12	3	5	12	3.6	8.5	1.34	.240
Minor League Totals				8	12	3.28	151	0	192	199	15	38	174	1.8	8.2	1.23	.264

30 JOE BOYLE, RHP

Born: Aug. 14, 1999. **B-T:** R-R. **HT:** 6-7. **WT:** 240. **Drafted:** Notre Dame, 2020 (5th round). **Signed by:** Tyler Gibbons.

TRACK RECORD: Boyle made just 32 appearances in three seasons with the Fighting Irish, largely because he walked 48 batters in 36 innings. Few pitchers with his resume get drafted, but fewer still throw as hard. In the 2019 Cape Cod League, he struck out 39 batters and posted a 2.14 ERA in 21 effective innings in front of packs of scouts.

SCOUTING REPORT: Boyle is one of the hardest throwers in pro ball. He sits in the upper 90s, touched 102 mph in the Northwoods League in the summer after his freshman year and 101 mph when pitching on the Cape. Boyle's fastball doesn't have an elite movement profile, but he throws hard enough that if he's throwing strikes he's hard to square up. He scrapped his curve and switched to a plus-plus slider. He has a fringy changeup as well. If he can locate the fastball, his slider can finish off hitters, but he needs to greatly improve his control.

THE FUTURE: The Reds will send Boyle out every fifth day with the hope that steady work will help him find the strike zone. Like many recent Reds draftees, he's high risk, but there are few pitchers with two 70s on their scouting report.

Year	Age	Club (League)	Class	W	L	ERA	G	GS	IP	H	HR	BB	SO	BB/9	SO/9	WHIP	AVG
2020	20	Did not play—No minor league season															

MORE PROSPECTS TO KNOW

31 JACOB HEATHERLY, LHP

Control issues and shoulder soreness have kept Heatherly, the Reds' third round pick in 2017, from harnessing his mid-90s fastball and potentially plus curveball.

32 BRAYLIN MINIER, SS

Minier was the Reds' biggest signing from Latin America in 2019. A lefty hitter with a whippy bat, he may end up at second or third, but his hands and feet give him infield skills to go with a solid bat.

33 ALFREDO RODRIGUEZ, SS

Rodriguez's glove is MLB-caliber, but he's yet to show he can hit enough to earn a lineup spot. He's been Rule 5-eligible and unpicked in back-to-back years.

34 RYAN HENDRIX, RHP

Hendrix has a hard, downer curve that almost looks like a splitter. That and a mid-90s fastball should make him a useful reliever if he throws the breaking ball more and improves his control.

35 MAC WAINWRIGHT, OF

While Wainwright played more football than baseball in high school, he turned down scholarship offers as a wide receiver to go pro. The Reds are counting on Wainwright's strength to help him become a power-hitting, athletic outfielder.

36 DEBBY SANTANA, 3B

A $70,000 signing from the Reds' 2016 international signing class, Santana has a chance to be an above-average hitter with above-average raw power. His eventual defensive home is less clear.

37 CASE WILLIAMS, RHP

Williams was drafted by the Rockies but never got to throw a pitch for them, as Colorado traded him in the deal that sent Robert Stephenson to Colorado. Williams has an 89-93 mph fastball and a potentially useful mid-70s curve that needs more consistency.

38 GUS STEIGER, SS

Steiger was one of the top-ranked nondrafted free agents to sign in 2020. He showed he could play shortstop at instructional league and profiles as a productive utility infielder.

39 ALEXANDER JOHNSON, RHP

SLEEPER

A 36th-round find from Buffalo, N.Y., Johnson sits 89-91 mph now, but the 6-foot-6 righty has a quick arm, a projectable frame and every now and then will pop the mitt at 94-95.

40 JAKE STEVENSON, RHP

A 10th-round, low-cost senior sign in 2019, Stevenson has an above-average 94-96 mph fastball and a potentially above-average slider. His control needs to improve.

41 JACOB HURTUBISE, OF

Hurtubise was an undrafted free agent because of the shortened 2020 draft. The Army graduate is a plus-plus runner with a plus arm. That and a contact-heavy approach at the plate could make him a useful extra outfielder.

TOP PROSPECTS OF THE DECADE

Year	Player, Pos	2020 Org
2011	Aroldis Chapman, LHP	Yankees
2012	Devin Mesoraco, C	Did not play
2013	Billy Hamilton, OF	Cubs
2014	Robert Stephenson, RHP	Reds
2015	Robert Stephenson, RHP	Reds
2016	Robert Stephenson, RHP	Reds
2017	Nick Senzel, 3B/2B	Reds
2018	Nick Senzel, 3B/2B	Reds
2019	Nick Senzel, 3B/2B	Reds
2020	Hunter Greene, RHP	Reds

TOP DRAFT PICKS OF THE DECADE

Year	Player, Pos	2020 Org
2011	Robert Stephenson, RHP	Reds
2012	Nick Travieso, RHP	Did not play
2013	Phillip Ervin, OF	Reds
2014	Nick Howard, RHP	Royals
2015	Tyler Stephenson, C	Reds
2016	Nick Senzel, 3B	Reds
2017	Hunter Greene, RHP	Reds
2018	Jonathan India, 3B	Reds
2019	Nick Lodolo, LHP	Reds
2020	Austin Hendrick, OF	Reds

DEPTH CHART

CINCINNATI REDS

TOP 2021 ROOKIES	RANK
Jonathan India, 2B/3B	3
Tyler Stephenson, C	4
Tejay Antone, RHP	6
BREAKOUT PROSPECTS	**RANK**
Ivan Johnson, 2B	12
Allan Cerda, OF	21
Luis Mey, RHP	24

SOURCE OF TOP 30 TALENT

Homegrown	27	Acquired	3
College	8	Trade	3
Junior college	3	Rule 5 draft	0
High school	10	Independent league	0
Nondrafted free agent	1	Free agent/waivers	0
International	5		

LF

Austin Hendrick (2)
Leonardo Seminati

CF

Michael Siani (10)
Allan Cerda (21)
T.J. Friedl (22)
Mac Wainwright
Jacob Hurtubise

RF

Rece Hinds (8)

3B

Alejo Lopez

SS

Jose Garcia (1)
Yan Contreras (26)
Braylin Minier
Alfredo Rodriguez
Gus Steiger

2B

Jonathan India (3)
Ivan Johnson (12)
Tyler Callihan (16)

1B

Michel Triana (18)
Debby Santana

C

Tyler Stephenson (4)
Jackson Miller (19)
Eric Yang
Daniel Vellojin

LHP

LHSP	LHRP
Nick Lodolo (7)	Evan Kravetz
Jacob Heatherly	

RHP

RHSP	RHRP
Hunter Greene (5)	Vladimir Gutierrez (14)
Tejay Antone (6)	Bryce Bonnin (17)
Tony Santillan (9)	Jared Solomon (23)
Christian Roa (11)	Riley O'Brien (25)
Lyon Richardson (13)	Brandon Bailey (27)
Noah Davis (15)	Graham Ashcraft (28)
Jose De Leon (20)	Joel Kuhnel (29)
Luis Mey (24)	Joe Boyle (30)
Case Williams	Ryan Hendrix
Alexander Johnson	Jake Stevenson
Matt Pidich	Carson Spiers
	Braxton Roxby

Cleveland Indians

BY TEDDY CAHILL

The sky turns dark and overcast in Cleveland every year as winter descends. Layers and layers of gray clouds shroud the city for months, dimming the lights at Progressive Field.

The clouds rolled in off Lake Erie on the heels of another playoff disappointment for the Indians, who were swept at home by the Yankees in the Wild Card Series. The loss extended the club's World Series drought to 72 years, the longest in the sport.

To add to the frustration, the winter brought further belt tightening and renewed speculation about the future of Francisco Lindor. The team's electric shortstop has not signed a long-term contract and has only one more season before he reaches free agency. The team has already seen core players Trevor Bauer, Michael Brantley, Mike Clevinger, Jason Kipnis and Corey Kluber all depart over the last two years as the club aims to keep its payroll in check.

The Indians have fallen behind the Twins in the American League Central standings in each of the last two years. Now, they must also contend with the White Sox, who are ramping up under new manager Tony La Russa. Viewed in that light, it is easy to see a dark winter ahead for the Indians.

But the gray clouds above the corner of Carnegie and Ontario contain multitudes. Shane Bieber has taken over as the team's unquestioned ace and won the AL Cy Young Award after going 8-1, 1.63. Jose Ramirez finished second in AL MVP voting after hitting .292/.386/.607 with 17 home runs. Both are under team control for at least the next three seasons.

Cleveland's pitching pipeline continues to flow. James Karinchak and Triston McKenzie are the latest homegrown pitchers to come up and impress in the major leagues.

The club's farm system is the deepest it has been in years and its most exciting prospects continue to work toward Cleveland. McKenzie will still be a rookie in 2021, and Nolan Jones and Tyler Freeman will soon make an impact, too. Daniel Espino, Ethan Hankins, Bo Naylor, Brayan Rocchio and George Valera are further away, but they also could form the core of a top-five farm system a year from now.

The Indians were also able to retain both team president Chris Antonetti and general manager Mike Chernoff, despite both being rumored in job searches to lead baseball operations for the Mets and Phillies. The team's front office has had impressive continuity, and since Antonetti and Chernoff were promoted to their current roles in October 2015, only the Dodgers and Astros have won more games than the Indians.

Now, that group must navigate the difficult transition from one core, and its window of contention, to another. With Bieber and Ramirez leading the way, the Indians have their cornerstones. Finding the right pieces to fit around them will be the key in the short term to managing that changeover. Cleveland's front office has a strong track record in trades and professional scouting, giving optimism they will be up to the task.

Winter in Cleveland is cold and bleak, and this year is no different. But it is a city of relentless hope. The sun will clear the clouds in spring, and the Indians will again be playoff contenders. ■

JASON MILLER/GETTY IMAGES

Indians ace Shane Bieber won the Cy Young Award and anchors a young, talented core.

PROJECTED 2024 LINEUP

Catcher	Bo Naylor	24
First Base	Josh Naylor	27
Second Base	Tyler Freeman	25
Third Base	Jose Ramirez	30
Shortstop	Gabriel Arias	24
Left Field	Nolan Jones	26
Center Field	Oscar Mercado	29
Right Field	George Valera	23
Designated Hitter	Franmil Reyes	28
No. 1 Starter	Shane Bieber	29
No. 2 Starter	Triston McKenzie	26
No. 3 Starter	Zach Plesac	29
No. 4 Starter	Daniel Espino	23
No. 5 Starter	Aaron Civale	29
Closer	James Karinchak	28

1 TRISTON MCKENZIE, RHP

Born: Aug. 2, 1997. **B-T:** R-R. **HT:** 6-5. **WT:** 165.
Drafted: HS—Palm Beach, Fla., 2015 (1st round supp).
Signed by: Juan Alvarez.

MARK CUNNINGHAM/MLB PHOTOS VIA GETTY IMAGES

TRACK RECORD: The last few years have been up-and-down for McKenzie, but he finished 2020 on a decidedly upward trajectory. He made his major league debut three weeks after his 23rd birthday, excelled down the stretch and earned a spot on the Indians' playoff roster. It was quite the turnaround after McKenzie missed all of 2019 with an upper back injury. Scouts have questioned McKenzie's durability since the Indians drafted him 42nd overall in 2015 due to his rail-thin 6-foot-5, 165-pound frame, but he's excelled when healthy. He won the high Class A Carolina League's pitcher of the year award in 2017 and ranked second in the minors with 186 strikeouts. He reached Double-A the following year as a 20-year-old and put together a strong summer despite being one of the youngest players in the Eastern League. That performance carried into the big leagues in 2020, despite a 24-month gap between competitive games. McKenzie struck out 10 batters in six innings in his debut, the second-most in a debut in franchise history, and posted a 3.24 ERA with 42 strikeouts and just nine walks in 33.1 innings down the stretch to help the Indians secure a playoff spot. McKenzie made one postseason appearance, allowing two runs on one hit and two walks and striking out two in 1.2 innings of the Indians' Game 2 loss to the Yankees in the AL Wild Card Series.

SCOUTING REPORT: Even with his skinny frame, McKenzie's fastball averages 93 mph and has reached 97. He holds that velocity well and while it dips in the middle of his starts, he shows the ability to reach back for more and finish strong. McKenzie's fastball plays up and gets swings and misses thanks to tremendous extension out of his delivery and a high spin rate. McKenzie also has a good feel for spinning his curveball and gets good depth on the offering, making it an out pitch that draws consensus plus grades from evaluators. His slider and changeup both improved over the last year to help round out his arsenal. His slider was especially impressive and showed it can be an above-average, swing-and-miss offering. McKenzie commands the ball well and earns praise for his makeup and understanding of his craft. He may never fill out his lean frame, so learning how to manage a starter's workload remains a point of emphasis and will be critical for him to reach mid-to-front of the rotation ceiling.

THE FUTURE: McKenzie's big league debut was everything the Indians could have hoped for, especially given the unique nature of his long gap between games given the delayed start to the 2020 season. He has a chance to be Cleveland's next great homegrown starter and should open the 2021 season in the big league rotation. ■

BEST TOOLS

Best Hitter for Average	Tyler Freeman
Best Power Hitter	Bobby Bradley
Best Strike-Zone Discipline	Ernie Clement
Fastest Baserunner	Quentin Holmes
Best Athlete	Will Benson
Best Fastball	Daniel Espino
Best Curveball	Triston McKenzie
Best Slider	Kyle Nelson
Best Changeup	Logan T. Allen
Best Control	Eli Morgan
Best Defensive Catcher	Bo Naylor
Best Defensive Infielder	Brayan Rocchio
Best Infield Arm	Gabriel Arias
Best Defensive Outfielder	Steven Kwan
Best Outfield Arm	Johnathan Rodriguez

Year	Age	Club (League)	Class	W	L	ERA	G	GS	IP	H	HR	BB	SO	BB/9	SO/9	WHIP	AVG
2017	19	Lynchburg (CAR)	HiA	12	6	3.46	25	25	143	105	14	45	186	2.8	11.7	1.05	.185
2018	20	Akron (EL)	AA	7	4	2.68	16	16	91	63	8	28	87	2.8	8.6	1.00	.174
2019	21	Did not play—Injured															
2020	22	Cleveland (AL)	MAJ	2	1	3.24	8	6	33	21	6	9	42	2.4	11.3	0.90	.179
Major League Totals				2	1	3.24	8	6	33	21	6	9	42	2.4	11.3	0.90	.179
Minor League Totals				26	16	2.68	60	59	329	230	26	98	394	2.7	10.8	1.00	.194

2 NOLAN JONES, 3B

Born: May 7, 1998. **B-T:** L-R. **HT:** 6-2. **WT:** 185. **Drafted:** HS—Bensalem, Pa., 2016 (2nd round). **Signed by:** Mike Kanen.

MIKE JANES/FOUR SEAM IMAGES

BA GRADE
60 Risk: High

TRACK RECORD: The Indians viewed Jones as one of the best prep hitters in the 2016 draft and were surprised he was still available at No. 55, when they made him their second selection. He lived up to that reputation in pro ball, showing off his offensive ability at every stop and earning a selection to the 2019 Futures Game in Cleveland. Jones finished the season in Double-A and spent 2020 at the alternate training site before finishing at the instructional league.

SCOUTING REPORT: Jones has an easy lefthanded swing and uses the whole field. He is a patient hitter and led all Indians minor leaguers in walks in both 2018 and 2019, though his patience also means he gets into deep counts and strikes out. He has plus raw power and has started to turn that into in-game production. Jones profiles at third base but has long faced questions whether he will stay at the position. He has plus arm strength and has worked hard to improve his glove work, infield actions and agility, especially ranging to his right. The Indians like their position players to be versatile and have started working Jones into the outfield and first base.

THE FUTURE: Jones still needs seasoning before he reaches Cleveland. He's closing in on the majors, and his offensive ability will get him into the lineup sooner rather than later.

SCOUTING GRADES: **Hitting:** 60 **Power:** 60 **Running:** 50 **Fielding:** 50 **Arm:** 60

Year	Age	Club (League)	Class	AVG	G	AB	R	H	2B	3B	HR	RBI	BB	SO	SB	OBP	SLG
2017	19	Mahoning Valley (NYP)	SS	.317	62	218	41	69	18	3	4	33	43	60	1	.430	.482
2018	20	Lake County (MWL)	LoA	.279	90	323	46	90	12	0	16	49	63	97	2	.393	.464
	20	Lynchburg (CAR)	HiA	.298	30	104	23	31	9	0	3	17	26	34	0	.438	.471
2019	21	Akron (EL)	AA	.253	49	178	33	45	10	2	8	22	31	63	2	.370	.466
	21	Lynchburg (CAR)	HiA	.286	77	252	48	72	12	1	7	41	65	85	5	.435	.425
Minor League Totals				.283	340	1184	201	335	66	8	38	171	251	388	13	.409	.448

3 TYLER FREEMAN, SS

Born: May 21, 1999. **B-T:** R-R. **HT:** 6-0. **WT:** 170. **Drafted:** HS—Rancho Cucamonga, Calif., 2017 (2nd round supplemental). **Signed by:** Mike Bradford.

BA GRADE
55 Risk: High

TRACK RECORD: Freeman has been a top hitter at nearly every stop since the Indians drafted him in the supplemental second round in 2017. He led the short-season New York-Penn League in batting (.352) and slugging (.511) in 2018 and climbed to high Class A Lynchburg in 2019, where he hit .319/.354/.397 as a 20-year-old at two stops. The Indians brought him to their alternate training site in Eastlake, Ohio in 2020 with most of their other top prospects.

SCOUTING REPORT: Freeman stands out for his excellent hitting ability and natural feel for the barrel. He has a very aggressive approach and rarely walks, but when he swings, he makes contact. Freeman got stronger during the shutdown and started showing more power over the summer. His bat speed and ability to consistently square balls up give him double-digit home run power despite his modest size. Freeman was drafted as a shortstop and has improved his hands, infield actions and instincts. He's still an average runner with average arm strength, which limits his range and may push him to second base.

THE FUTURE: Regardless of where he ends up defensively, Freeman's bat will stand out. He's likely to get his first taste of Double-A in 2021.

SCOUTING GRADES: **Hitting:** 60 **Power:** 40 **Running:** 50 **Fielding:** 50 **Arm:** 55

Year	Age	Club (League)	Class	AVG	G	AB	R	H	2B	3B	HR	RBI	BB	SO	SB	OBP	SLG
2017	18	Indians 1 (AZL)	R	.297	36	128	19	38	9	0	2	14	7	12	5	.364	.414
2018	19	Mah. Valley (NYP)	SS	.352	72	270	49	95	29	4	2	38	8	22	14	.405	.511
2019	20	Lake County (MWL)	LoA	.292	61	236	51	69	16	3	3	24	18	28	11	.382	.424
	20	Lynchburg (CAR)	HiA	.319	62	257	38	82	16	2	0	20	8	25	8	.354	.397
Minor League Totals				.319	231	891	157	284	70	9	7	96	41	87	38	.379	.441

4 BO NAYLOR, C

Born: Feb. 21, 2000. **B-T:** L-R. **HT:** 6-0. **WT:** 195. **Drafted:** HS—Mississauga, Ont., 2018 (1st round). **Signed by:** Mike Kanen.

BA GRADE 55 Risk: Very High

TRACK RECORD: Naylor compiled a long track record of success as an amateur, especially facing premier competition with the Canadian junior national team. That helped ease his transition to pro ball after the Indians drafted him 29th overall in 2018. Naylor held his own in the low Class A Midwest League in 2019 and spent 2020 at the alternate training site. Midway through the season, the Indians acquired his older brother Josh from the Padres in the trade that sent Mike Clevinger to San Diego.

SCOUTING REPORT: Naylor had perhaps the best offensive performance of any prospect at the alternate site. He has an advanced hit tool thanks to his smooth swing, pitch recognition and approach. His solid-average power hasn't always played in games, but he makes consistent hard contact and has the ability to drive the ball. Naylor is an above-average runner and his athleticism plays well behind the plate. He earns high grades for pitch framing and he threw out 37% of basestealers in 2019. Naylor still has work to do to refine his defense, but he's shown enough to quell talk of a potential move to third base, where he played a lot as an amateur.

THE FUTURE: Naylor will be just 21 in 2021 and remains ahead of the curve. He may see Double-A during the season.

SCOUTING GRADES: **Hitting:** 55 **Power:** 50 **Running:** 50 **Fielding:** 55 **Arm:** 60

Year	Age	Club (League)	Class	AVG	G	AB	R	H	2B	3B	HR	RBI	BB	SO	SB	OBP	SLG
2018	18	Indians 2 (AZL)	R	.274	33	117	17	32	3	3	2	17	21	28	5	.381	.402
2019	19	Lake County (MWL)	LoA	.243	107	399	60	97	18	10	11	65	43	104	7	.313	.421
Minor League Totals				.250	140	516	77	129	21	13	13	82	64	132	12	.329	.417

5 GEORGE VALERA, OF

Born: Nov. 13, 2000. **B-T:** L-L. **HT:** 5-10. **WT:** 160. **Signed:** Dominican Republic, 2017. **Signed by:** Jhonathan Leyba/Domingo Toribio.

PAXTON REMBIS

BA GRADE 55 Risk: Very High

TRACK RECORD: The Indians made a splash internationally in 2017 and signed Valera, the fifth-ranked player in the class, for $1.3 million. He was born in New York and lived there until his family moved to the Dominican Republic when he was 13. After a broken hamate bone limited him to six games in 2018, Valera spent most of 2019 with short-season Mahoning Valley—where he was the youngest position player in the league—before a late-season promotion to low Class A Lake County. The Indians brought him to their alternate training site in 2020.

SCOUTING REPORT: Valera has a loose, compact swing and keeps his bat in the zone for a long time. His feel for the barrel, bat-to-ball skills, pitch recognition and plate discipline all help him make consistent, hard contact and give him the kind of hitting ability the Indians covet. He has above-average raw power and gets to it in games, hitting eight home runs in 46 games as an 18-year-old in the New York-Penn League. Valera profiles as a corner outfielder with average speed and arm strength.

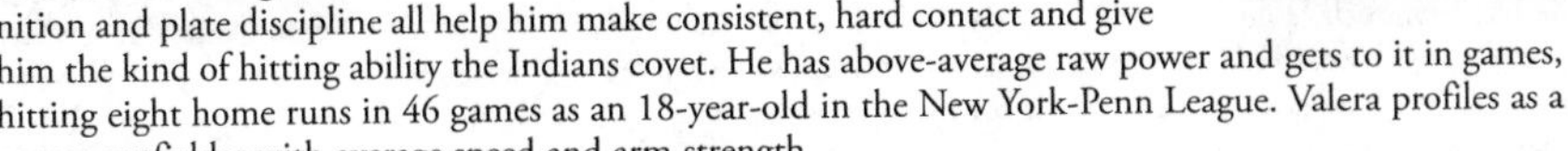

THE FUTURE: Valera has proved advanced enough to handle challenging assignments. He has moved slower than anticipated between his injury and the canceled 2020 minor league season, but that could change in a hurry once 2021 begins.

SCOUTING GRADES: **Hitting:** 60 **Power:** 55 **Running:** 50 **Fielding:** 50 **Arm:** 50

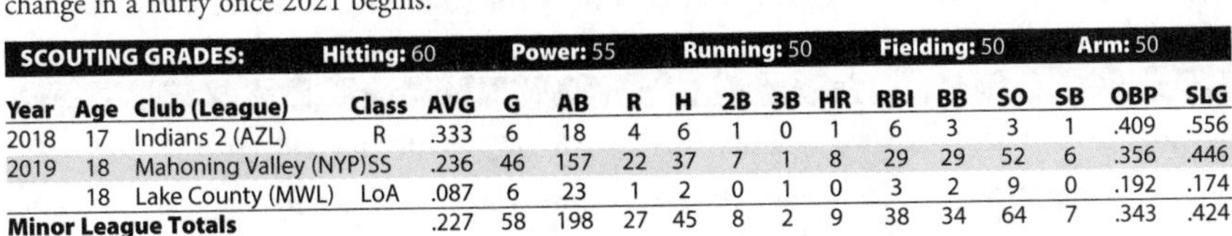

Year	Age	Club (League)	Class	AVG	G	AB	R	H	2B	3B	HR	RBI	BB	SO	SB	OBP	SLG
2018	17	Indians 2 (AZL)	R	.333	6	18	4	6	1	0	1	6	3	3	1	.409	.556
2019	18	Mahoning Valley (NYP)	SS	.236	46	157	22	37	7	1	8	29	29	52	6	.356	.446
	18	Lake County (MWL)	LoA	.087	6	23	1	2	0	1	0	3	2	9	0	.192	.174
Minor League Totals				.227	58	198	27	45	8	2	9	38	34	64	7	.343	.424

6 GABRIEL ARIAS, SS

Born: Feb. 27, 2000. **B-T:** R-R. **HT:** 6-1. **WT:** 201. **Signed:** Venezuela, 2016.
Signed by: Luis Prieto/Yfrain Linares/Trevor Schumm (Padres).

BA GRADE
55 Risk: Very High

TRACK RECORD: Arias was one of the top prospects in the 2016 international class and signed with the Padres for $1.9 million. He stood out defensively from the start of his career and broke out offensively in the second half of 2019 at high Class A Lake Elsinore, finishing fourth in the California League in batting (.302). The Indians acquired him at the 2020 trade deadline in the deal that sent Mike Clevinger to San Diego.

SCOUTING REPORT: Arias is a good athlete with a lot of raw ability. The righthanded hitter has a smooth swing, and his wiry strength and bat speed give him above-average raw power. His plate discipline is not as advanced. He improved his strikeout rate in 2019, but still whiffed in 25% of his plate appearances and his walk rate halved at the same time. Improving his pitch recognition and approach at the plate will be critical to maintain his offensive progress. Arias has few questions defensively. He has advanced infield actions, clean hands and plus-plus arm strength. Despite his below-average speed, he has plenty of range for the position and makes all the plays necessary.

THE FUTURE: Arias will likely head to Double-A in 2021. He'll need to prove his offensive breakout is sustainable outside of the Cal League.

SCOUTING GRADES: **Hitting:** 50 **Power:** 55 **Running:** 40 **Fielding:** 70 **Arm:** 70

Year	Age	Club (League)	Class	AVG	G	AB	R	H	2B	3B	HR	RBI	BB	SO	SB	OBP	SLG
2017	17	Fort Wayne (MWL)	LoA	.242	16	62	8	15	1	0	0	4	2	16	1	.266	.258
	17	Padres (AZL)	R	.275	37	153	18	42	6	3	0	13	10	51	4	.329	.353
2018	18	Fort Wayne (MWL)	LoA	.240	124	455	54	109	27	3	6	55	41	149	3	.302	.352
2019	19	Lake Elsinore (CAL)	HiA	.302	120	477	62	144	21	4	17	75	25	128	8	.339	.470
Minor League Totals				.270	297	1147	142	310	55	10	23	147	78	344	16	.319	.396

7 BRAYAN ROCCHIO, SS

Born: Jan. 13, 2001. **B-T:** R-R. **HT:** 5-10. **WT:** 150. **Signed:** Venezuela, 2017.
Signed by: Jhonathan Leyba.

PAXTON REMBIS

BA GRADE
55 Risk: Very High

TRACK RECORD: Aaron Bracho and George Valera were the headliners of the Indians' 2017 international class, but Rocchio has proven a top signing as well. Signed for $125,000, Rocchio quickly moved to short-season Mahoning Valley in 2019 and held his own as the league's third-youngest player. He returned to Venezuela during the early days of the coronavirus pandemic in 2020 and was unable to return to the U.S. due to travel restrictions, but he continued playing in a makeshift league throughout the year.

SCOUTING REPORT: Rocchio doesn't stand out physically but is nicknamed "The Professor" for his high baseball IQ and game awareness. A switch-hitter, he has a smooth, consistent swing from both sides of the plate and excellent pitch recognition. He's an aggressive hitter and consistently barrels the ball.
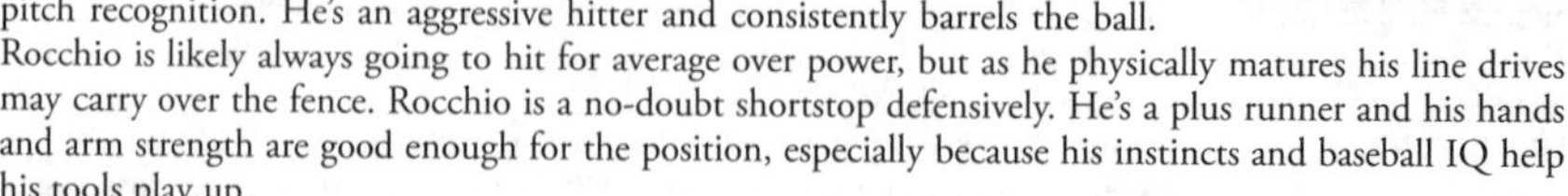
Rocchio is likely always going to hit for average over power, but as he physically matures his line drives may carry over the fence. Rocchio is a no-doubt shortstop defensively. He's a plus runner and his hands and arm strength are good enough for the position, especially because his instincts and baseball IQ help his tools play up.

THE FUTURE: Rocchio played his way to an accelerated track and even a lost 2020 season shouldn't slow him much. Once he returns to the U.S., he'll jump right back into the mix.

SCOUTING GRADES: **Hitting:** 55 **Power:** 30 **Running:** 60 **Fielding:** 55 **Arm:** 50

Year	Age	Club (League)	Class	AVG	G	AB	R	H	2B	3B	HR	RBI	BB	SO	SB	OBP	SLG
2018	17	Indians (DSL)	R	.323	25	99	19	32	2	3	1	12	5	14	8	.391	.434
	17	Indians 2 (AZL)	R	.343	35	143	21	49	10	1	1	17	10	17	14	.389	.448
2019	18	Mahoning Valley (NYP)	SS	.250	69	268	33	67	12	3	5	27	20	40	14	.310	.373
Minor League Totals				.290	129	510	73	148	24	7	7	56	35	71	36	.348	.406

8 DANIEL ESPINO, RHP

Born: Jan. 5, 2001. **B-T:** R-R. **HT:** 6-1. **WT:** 205. **Drafted:** HS—Statesboro, Ga., 2019 (1st round). **Signed by:** Ethan Purser.

BILL MITCHELL

BA GRADE
55 Risk: Extreme

TRACK RECORD: Espino was born in Panama before moving with his family to the U.S. when he was 15. He enrolled at Georgia Premier Academy and adopted a professional mindset that was readily apparent to the Indians after they selected him 24th overall in the 2019 draft. He became the first high school player the Indians promoted to short-season Mahoning Valley in his pro debut since Francisco Lindor in 2011, and he spent 2020 at the alternate training site.

SCOUTING REPORT: Espino is shorter than what most teams look for in a righthander, but his excellent athleticism, explosiveness and flexibility helps him access his lower half in a way most pitchers cannot. The result is a plus-plus fastball that sits at 96 mph and reaches 99. Espino throws both a curveball and slider, with the slider earning better grades as a potential plus pitch. He also throws a firm changeup that needs refining but has a chance to give him a fourth at least average offering. Espino has a long arm action but typically pitches with average control. He'll need to refine his command as he faces more advanced hitters who are less susceptible to chasing his offspeed stuff.

THE FUTURE: Espino will be just 20 when the 2021 season begins. The Indians will likely take a cautious tack with him, but he may force their hand.

SCOUTING GRADES: **Fastball:** 70 **Slider:** 60 **Curveball:** 50 **Changeup:** 50 **Control:** 50

Year	Age	Club (League)	Class	W	L	ERA	G	GS	IP	H	HR	BB	SO	BB/9	SO/9	WHIP	AVG
2019	18	Mahoning Valley (NYP)	SS	0	2	6.30	3	3	10	9	1	5	18	4.5	16.2	1.40	.200
	18	Indians 1 (AZL)	R	0	1	1.98	6	6	14	7	1	5	16	3.3	10.5	0.88	.132
Minor League Totals				0	3	3.80	9	9	23	16	2	10	34	3.8	12.9	1.10	.186

9 ETHAN HANKINS, RHP

Born: May 23, 2000. **B-T:** R-R. **HT:** 6-6. **WT:** 200. **Drafted:** HS—Gainesville, Ga., 2018 (1st round). **Signed by:** C.T. Bradford.

PAXTON REMBIS

BA GRADE
55 Risk: Extreme

TRACK RECORD: Hankins was considered arguably the top high school player in the 2018 draft class before a shoulder injury cost him most of his senior season. The Indians were thrilled to be able to draft him with the final pick of the first round. After cautiously introducing him to pro ball, the Indians let him loose in 2019. He posted a 2.55 ERA in 60 innings between short-season Mahoning Valley and low Class A Lake County. He pitched at the alternate training site in 2020.

SCOUTING REPORT: Hankins has a long, lean, 6-foot-6 frame and uncommon athleticism for a pitcher his size. His fastball typically sits in the mid 90s and can run up to 97 mph with plus life. Hankins has the makings of quality secondary pitches, but they'll need to become more consistent offerings. His slider and changeup both have the ability to be above-average offerings and he also throws a bigger curveball, though it lags behind his other pitches. Hankins controls his arsenal well, but it will be important for him to maintain his delivery as he grows into his large frame.

THE FUTURE: Hankins' impressive first season was a reminder of his enormous upside. He and Daniel Espino make for an impressive 1-2 punch the Indians hope will stick together all the way to the majors.

SCOUTING GRADES: **Fastball:** 60 **Slider:** 55 **Changeup:** 50 **Control:** 50

Year	Age	Club (League)	Class	W	L	ERA	G	GS	IP	H	HR	BB	SO	BB/9	SO/9	WHIP	AVG
2018	18	Indians 2 (AZL)	R	0	0	6.00	2	2	3	4	0	0	6	0.0	18.0	1.33	.286
2019	19	Lake County (MWL)	LoA	0	3	4.64	5	5	21	20	3	12	28	5.1	11.8	1.50	.213
	19	Mahoning Valley (NYP)	SS	0	0	1.40	9	8	39	23	1	18	43	4.2	10.0	1.06	.149
Minor League Totals				0	3	2.71	16	15	63	47	4	30	77	4.3	11.0	1.22	.212

10 AARON BRACHO, 2B

Born: April 24, 2001. **B-T:** B-R. **HT:** 5-11. **WT:** 175. **Signed:** Venezuela, 2017. **Signed by:** Hernan Albornoz/Rafael Cariel.

BILL MITCHELL

BA GRADE
55 Risk: Extreme

TRACK RECORD: The Indians went big on the 2017 international market and Bracho was a part of that, signing for $1.5 million out of Venezuela as a top 20 player in the class. He missed the 2018 season due to an arm injury, but made his pro debut in 2019 and hit .281/.402/.570 as he ascended to short-season Mahoning Valley. Like the rest of the Indians' top prospects, Bracho spent 2020 at the alternate training site.

SCOUTING REPORT: A switch-hitter, Bracho has a smooth, compact swing from both sides of the plate and produces good bat speed. He has an advanced approach and posted nearly as many walks (28) as strikeouts (29) in his pro debut. Listed at 5-foot-11, Bracho has more pop than his frame suggests and could end up hitting for at least average power. He hit eight home runs and slugged .570 in 38 games in his debut—big numbers for an teen middle infielder. Bracho was signed as a shortstop but has already moved to second base. His hands and range are good enough to keep him there, but he projects to be more of an offensive second baseman.

THE FUTURE: It's been apparent why Bracho had as much hype as he did as an amateur. Now that he's healthy, he should be ready for his first taste of full-season ball in 2021.

SCOUTING GRADES: Hitting: 55 Power: 50 Running: 55 Fielding: 50 Arm: 45

Year	Age	Club (League)	Class	AVG	G	AB	R	H	2B	3B	HR	RBI	BB	SO	SB	OBP	SLG
2018	17	Did not play--Injured															
2019	18	Mahoning Valley (NYP)	SS	.222	8	27	5	6	1	0	2	4	5	8	0	.344	.481
	18	Indians 2 (AZL)	R	.296	30	108	25	32	10	2	6	29	23	21	4	.416	.593
Minor League Totals				.281	38	135	30	38	11	2	8	33	28	29	4	.402	.570

11 GABRIEL RODRIGUEZ, SS

BA GRADE
55 Risk: Extreme

Born: Feb. 22, 2002. **B-T:** R-R. **HT:** 6-2. **WT:** 174. **Signed:** Venezuela, 2018. **Signed by:** Hernan Albornoz.

TRACK RECORD: The Indians' 2018 international signing class wasn't as big as the 2017 group that produced three of the club's Top 10 prospects, but Rodriguez gives it a true headliner. The Venezuelan was the eighth-ranked player overall in the 2018 class and had an impressive professional debut in 2019, earning a midseason promotion to the Rookie-level Arizona League. He stayed in Arizona in 2020, playing at instructional league.

SCOUTING REPORT: Rodriguez stands out for his consistency and all-around tools. He has a short, simple swing and an advanced approach at the plate. As he physically matures, he figures to develop at least average power and he has already shown the ability to drive balls to all fields. He's still learning to get to that power potential, and part of that adjustment is learning how to take his power-packed batting practice swing into games. Rodriguez has a bigger frame and may eventually outgrow shortstop. His strong arm and instincts will allow him to stay in the infield, likely at third base, if he does need to move.

THE FUTURE: Rodriguez is advanced enough to follow an aggressive developmental track, much like the premium players in the 2017 class. He'll be 19 when the 2021 season opens and should soon be ready for low Class A.

Year	Age	Club (League)	Class	AVG	G	AB	R	H	2B	3B	HR	RBI	BB	SO	SB	OBP	SLG
2019	17	Indians (DSL)	R	.238	38	143	25	34	7	4	3	29	15	27	3	.335	.406
	17	Indians 1 (AZL)	R	.215	18	65	7	14	3	0	0	10	4	22	1	.288	.262
Minor League Totals				.231	56	208	32	48	10	4	3	39	19	49	4	.321	.361

12 CARSON TUCKER, SS

Born: Jan. 24, 2002. **B-T:** R-R. **HT:** 6-2. **WT:** 180. **Drafted:** HS—Phoenix, 2020 (1st round). **Signed by:** Ryan Perry.

TRACK RECORD: Tucker was a solid player on the showcase circuit in the summer of 2019, but he took a step forward during the offseason when he grew two inches and put on 10-15 pounds of muscle. Limited to just a few high school games due to the coronavirus pandemic, he showed enough to convince the Indians to draft him 23rd overall, bettering his older brother Cole Tucker, who went 24th overall in 2014 to the Pirates.

SCOUTING REPORT: Tucker has solid all-around tools and stands out most for his feel for hitting and infield actions. He has a short, consistent swing and makes a lot of contact—a combination that should make him at least an average hitter. His swing is more geared to hitting line drives, but he can flash above-average power and his offseason strength gains should help him get to it. He's at least a plus runner. Tucker has worked hard at his defense and has a good natural feel for the position. His actions, above-average arm and speed give him the tools to be an above-average defender.

THE FUTURE: Tucker fits in with the growing stable of young shortstops in the organization and will make his professional debut in 2021.

Year	Age	Club (League)	Class	AVG	G	AB	R	H	2B	3B	HR	RBI	BB	SO	SB	OBP	SLG
2020	18	Did not play—No minor league season															

13 LOGAN ALLEN, LHP

Born: May 23, 1997. **B-T:** R-L. **HT:** 6-3. **WT:** 200. **Drafted:** HS—Bradenton, Fla, 2015. (8th round). **Signed by:** Stephen Hargett (Red Sox).

TRACK RECORD: Allen has been well traveled since the Red Sox drafted him in 2015 and signed him to an over-slot deal. He was traded that fall to the Padres as a part of the package for Craig Kimbrel and then reached San Diego in June 2019. A month later, he was traded to Cleveland as a part of the three-team deal that sent Trevor Bauer to the Reds. He spent most of 2020 at the alternate training site, but did get a couple stints in Cleveland out of the bullpen.

SCOUTING REPORT: Allen has a strong frame and a solid four-pitch mix. His fastball velocity ticked up a bit in 2020, averaging 94 mph and regularly reaching 96. His above-average changeup and average slider are his main secondary offerings, and he also will occasionally mix in a fringe-average curveball. He can throw his full arsenal for strikes, but he still needs to refine his command to get the most out of his stuff.

THE FUTURE: Allen's ability to pitch both in the bullpen and rotation is valuable, though he's still looking to establish himself in a role. He'll again be in the mix for a spot on the Indians' staff in 2021.

Year	Age	Club (League)	Class	W	L	ERA	G	GS	IP	H	HR	BB	SO	BB/9	SO/9	WHIP	AVG
2020	23	Cleveland (AL)	MAJ	0	0	3.38	3	0	11	12	1	7	7	5.9	5.9	1.78	.293
Major League Totals				2	3	5.40	12	4	38	48	5	20	24	4.7	5.6	1.77	.320
Minor League Totals				29	24	3.31	94	88	440	386	30	154	459	3.2	9.4	1.23	.235

14 EMMANUEL CLASE, RHP

TOP ROOKIE
BA GRADE
50 Risk: High

Born: March 18, 1998. **B-T:** R-R. **HT:** 6-2. **WT:** 205. **Signed:** Dominican Republic, 2015. **Signed by:** Chris Kemp/Emengildo Diaz (Padres).

TRACK RECORD: Since signing with the Padres in 2015, Clase has been traded twice. He went to the Rangers in 2018 for Brett Nicholas, then to Cleveland in 2019 for Corey Kluber. In May 2020, Clase was suspended for 80 games after testing positive for PEDs. When MLB reduced the 2020 season to 60 games, it also reduced Clase's suspension to the full 2020 season.

SCOUTING REPORT: Clase has an electric fastball that regularly reaches the upper 90s and has touched 101 mph. His slider took a step forward in 2019, becoming a more consistent pitch as he improved his arm speed when throwing it and started locating it better. The pitch is now at least an average offering and plays well with his fastball, which has excellent natural cutting action.

THE FUTURE: Clase's suspension and the season's interruption obscured the fact that in late February he suffered a strained teres major muscle in his shoulder, which was projected to shut him down for a few months. He spent much of 2020 rehabbing in Arizona and will enter the 2021 season healthy and ready to pitch high-leverage innings.

Year	Age	Club (League)	Class	W	L	ERA	G	GS	IP	H	HR	BB	SO	BB/9	SO/9	WHIP	AVG
2019	21	Texas (AL)	MAJ	2	3	2.31	21	1	23	20	2	6	21	2.3	8.1	1.11	.225
	21	Frisco (TL)	AA	1	2	3.35	33	1	38	34	1	8	39	1.9	9.3	1.12	.210
	21	Down East (CAR)	HiA	2	0	0.00	6	0	7	4	0	1	11	1.3	14.1	0.71	.160
Major League Totals				2	3	2.31	21	1	23	20	2	6	21	2.3	8.1	1.11	.230
Minor League Totals				10	9	3.06	92	19	191	178	7	70	195	3.3	9.2	1.30	.242

15 TANNER BURNS, RHP

BA GRADE **50** Risk: High

Born: Dec. 28, 1998. **B-T:** R-R. **HT:** 6-0. **WT:** 215. **Drafted:** Auburn, 2020 (1st round supplemental). **Signed by:** C.T. Bradford.

TRACK RECORD: Burns was the top-ranked player from the 2017 high school class to make it to college. He stepped into the rotation at Auburn and starred throughout his college career, learning alongside Casey Mize and under Tim Hudson. The Indians drafted him with the 36th overall pick in 2020, the highest they have drafted a college pitcher since Drew Pomeranz fifth overall in 2010.

SCOUTING REPORT: Burns has solid all-around stuff and a good understanding of pitching. His fastball sits 93-94 mph and reaches 97. It's a plus pitch that plays up thanks to his ability to consistently locate it. He throws both a curveball and a slider and has worked to make them two distinct pitches. Both flash above-average potential, with his curve typically showing better. He also throws a changeup with good sinking action, though he didn't need it much in college. Burns earns praise for his dedication, makeup and desire to learn.

THE FUTURE: There is a lot to like between Burns' stuff, aptitude and the Indians' track record of success developing college pitchers. He could move quickly in 2021.

Year	Age	Club (League)	Class	W	L	ERA	G	GS	IP	H	HR	BB	SO	BB/9	SO/9	WHIP	AVG
2020	21	Did not play—No minor league season															

16 JOEY CANTILLO, LHP

BA GRADE **50** Risk: High

Born: Dec. 18, 1999. **B-T:** L-L. **HT:** 6-4. **WT:** 200. **Drafted:** HS—Kailua, Hawaii, 2017 (16th round). **Signed by:** Justin Baughman (Padres).

TRACK RECORD: Cantillo drew limited draft interest after sitting in the mid 80s in high school, but the Padres were intrigued when he touched 91 mph in a pre-draft workout. They selected him in the 16th round and went well over slot to sign him away from his Kentucky commitment. Cantillo broke out in 2019 and led the Padres organization in strikeouts (144). He was traded to Cleveland at the 2020 trade deadline as a part of the return for Mike Clevinger.

SCOUTING REPORT: Cantillo has a projectable frame and has already seen his velocity tick up as he's physically matured, with more still potentially to come. He throws his fastball in the upper 80s and the high-spin rate he gets on the pitch helps it play better than its velocity. His changeup is a plus pitch and has the ability to miss bats. His curveball lags behind his other two offerings, but with added power could become an average pitch. He throws a lot of strikes and has a good understanding of how to attack hitters.

THE FUTURE: Cantillo offers solid upside as a three-pitch starter if he grows into more velocity and refines his curveball. He may be ready for Double-A in 2021.

Year	Age	Club (League)	Class	W	L	ERA	G	GS	IP	H	HR	BB	SO	BB/9	SO/9	WHIP	AVG
2019	19	Lake Elsinore (CAL)	HiA	1	1	4.61	3	3	14	12	2	7	16	4.6	10.5	1.39	.190
	19	Fort Wayne (MWL)	LoA	9	3	1.93	19	19	98	58	3	27	128	2.5	11.8	0.87	.164
Minor League Totals				13	7	2.51	41	32	168	112	5	55	221	2.9	11.8	0.99	.187

17 CARLOS VARGAS, RHP

BREAKOUT

BA GRADE **50** Risk: High

Born: Oct. 13, 1999. **B-T:** R-R. **HT:** 6-3. **WT:** 180. **Signed:** Dominican Republic, 2016. **Signed by:** Rafael Espinal.

TRACK RECORD: Vargas was the Indians' top signing in the 2016 international class, signing for $275,000. Though he wasn't a high-profile prospect at the time, the Indians landed a premium arm. Even though he has yet to advance past short-season, the Indians were impressed enough with his progress to add him to the 40-man roster in November.

SCOUTING REPORT: When he signed as a 17-year-old in 2016, Vargas had an ultra-projectable frame and was already throwing 93 mph. His velocity has ticked up as expected and his fastball now reaches 100 mph and sits in the upper 90s. His slider sits around 90 mph and is a plus pitch at its best. His changeup can be an average pitch and gives him a viable third offering. He improved his strike-throwing in 2019, cutting his walk rate considerably. He still needs to refine his command and learn how to get the most out of his electric stuff.

THE FUTURE: Vargas has considerable upside and has given plenty of reason for optimism at the outset of his career. He'll get his first taste of A ball in 2021.

Year	Age	Club (League)	Class	W	L	ERA	G	GS	IP	H	HR	BB	SO	BB/9	SO/9	WHIP	AVG
2019	19	Mahoning Valley (NYP)	SS	6	4	4.52	15	15	78	73	4	24	71	2.8	8.2	1.25	.225
Minor League Totals				7	6	4.34	25	24	112	106	6	48	112	3.9	9.0	1.38	.252

18 OWEN MILLER, SS

BA GRADE
45 Risk: Medium

Born: Nov. 15, 1996. **B-T:** R-R. **HT:** 6-0. **WT:** 190. **Drafted:** Illinois State, 2018 (3rd round). **Signed by:** Troy Hoerner (Padres).

TRACK RECORD: Miller was a standout from the beginning at Illinois State, starting every game in his career and hitting .345 over three seasons. After an impressive professional debut, he spent 2019 in Double-A and led the Texas League with 147 hits. He was traded to the Indians in August as a part of the package for Mike Clevinger and spent the rest of the season at the alternate training site before finishing the year at instructional league.

SCOUTING REPORT: Miller's standout tools are his hittability and defensive versatility. He has a balanced swing, consistently squares balls up and uses the whole field to hit. His swing is geared toward making contact, but he can drive the ball, especially to the pull side, and has fringe-average power. Miller is a consistent, reliable defender whose tools play up thanks to his feel for the game. He's mostly played shortstop, but he has experience all around the infield. His fringe-average arm and average range may ultimately push him to second base.

THE FUTURE: Miller's tools don't measure up to some of the other infielders in the system, but he's a better player than the sum of his parts. His feel for hitting and defensive versatility are a valuable combination.

Year	Age	Club (League)	Class	AVG	G	AB	R	H	2B	3B	HR	RBI	BB	SO	SB	OBP	SLG
2019	22	Amarillo (TL)	AA	.290	130	507	76	147	28	2	13	68	46	86	5	.355	.430
Minor League Totals				.307	205	805	116	247	47	5	17	101	65	127	9	.367	.441

19 SCOTT MOSS, LHP

BA GRADE
45 Risk: Medium

Born: Oct. 6, 1994. **B-T:** L-L. **HT:** 6-6. **WT:** 225. **Drafted:** Florida, 2016 (4th round). **Signed by:** Greg Zunino (Reds).

TRACK RECORD: Tommy John surgery sidelined Moss for his first two seasons at Florida but he broke out with a dominant start in the 2016 Southeastern Conference tournament, and the Reds drafted him in the fourth round. He's shown solid stuff in pro ball, and was included in the trade that sent Trevor Bauer to the Reds. He got to Triple-A after the trade and spent 2020 at the alternate training site.

SCOUTING REPORT: Moss has a big, strong frame and since getting into pro ball has proved to be dependable, throwing more than 130 innings from 2017-19. His fastball sits in the low 90s, gets up to 94 mph, and is capable of producing swings and misses. He combines it with a slider that can be plus and a changeup that makes for a quality third option. Moss pitched with average control early in his career but saw his walk rate balloon in 2019. The Indians have worked with him to get back to throwing more strikes since he joined the organization, but it's unlikely he'll ever have better than average command.

THE FUTURE: Moss did not make his major league debut in 2020, but, given the circumstances of the season, only so much can be taken from that. He'll likely return to Triple-A and figures to be in the mix for a spot in the big leagues in 2021.

Year	Age	Club (League)	Class	W	L	ERA	G	GS	IP	H	HR	BB	SO	BB/9	SO/9	WHIP	AVG
2019	24	Akron (EL)	AA	2	0	0.00	2	2	10	3	0	5	13	4.5	11.7	0.80	.079
	24	Columbus (IL)	AAA	2	1	1.93	4	4	19	12	1	8	23	3.9	11.1	1.07	.158
	24	Chattanooga (SL)	AA	6	5	3.44	20	20	102	84	7	57	123	5.0	10.9	1.38	.193
Minor League Totals				41	17	3.28	87	87	436	383	34	173	456	3.6	9.4	1.27	.234

20 LOGAN T. ALLEN, LHP

BA GRADE
50 Risk: High

Born: Sept. 5, 1998. **B-T:** R-L. **HT:** 6-0. **WT:** 180. **Drafted:** Florida International, 2020 (2nd round). **Signed by:** Jhonathan Leyba.

TRACK RECORD: Allen was the 2017 Florida Gatorade Player of the Year, then impressed at Florida International and for USA Baseball's Collegiate National Team. The Indians drafted him in the second round in 2020, completing the pair of lefthanded Logan Allens from Florida after trading for Logan S. Allen a year prior.

SCOUTING REPORT: Allen stands out for his feel and competitiveness on the mound, with the knocks on him long being his size and lack of a big arm. His fastball velocity ticked up during the brief 2020 college season, averaging 90 mph and touching 95, up from averaging 89 and touching 93. The pitch plays up thanks to some deception in his delivery and his ability to locate it. His best pitch is his changeup, which is a plus offering and a weapon he can use against both lefthanders and righthanders. He started exclusively throwing a slider in the fall of 2019 and it has the potential to be average. His control was among the best in the draft class and he's a good athlete. A two-way player at FIU, there is some hope that his stuff could improve now that he's solely focused on pitching.

THE FUTURE: After nothing but success as an amateur, Allen will have to prove himself in pro ball. He'll begin that journey in 2021 and is advanced enough to handle an assignment to high Class A.

Year	Age	Club (League)	Class	W	L	ERA	G	GS	IP	H	HR	BB	SO	BB/9	SO/9	WHIP	AVG
2020	21	Did not play—No minor league season															

21 BOBBY BRADLEY, 1B

Born: May 29, 1996. **B-T:** L-R. **HT:** 6-1. **WT:** 225. **Drafted:** HS—Gulfport, Miss., 2014 (3rd round). **Signed by:** Mike Bradford.

TRACK RECORD: Bradley has been one of the most productive players in the system since being drafted in 2014, and in 2019 he made his major league debut. He hit at every level along the way to Cleveland, including hitting a career-high 33 home runs in 107 games at Triple-A in 2019. He did not appear in a game for the Indians in 2020 and spent the summer at the alternate training site.

SCOUTING REPORT: Bradley's raw power is the best in the system, and he has shown he is adept at getting to it in games. He has a strong, physical frame and creates excellent bat speed that allows him to drive the ball out to all fields. That power comes with a lot of swing and miss, and in Triple-A he struck out in a third of his plate appearances. Bradley is a well below-average runner with an average arm, limiting him to first base.

THE FUTURE: To get a true feel for what he can become, Bradley needs an extended run in the big leagues. The Indians have several more experienced options for first base and DH and breaking through that group won't be easy. Bradley is still just 24 but it feels like 2021 will be a crucial season for him.

Year	Age	Club (League)	Class	AVG	G	AB	R	H	2B	3B	HR	RBI	BB	SO	SB	OBP	SLG
2019	23	Cleveland (AL)	MAJ	.178	15	45	4	8	5	0	1	4	4	20	0	.245	.356
	23	Columbus (IL)	AAA	.264	107	402	65	106	23	0	33	74	46	153	0	.344	.567
Major League Totals				.178	15	45	4	8	5	0	1	4	4	20	0	.245	.356
Minor League Totals				.254	647	2401	374	609	125	17	147	490	305	779	13	.342	.504

22 SAM HENTGES, LHP

BA GRADE
50 Risk: Very High

Born: July 18, 1996. **B-T:** L-L. **HT:** 6-8. **WT:** 245. **Drafted:** HS—Arden Hills, Minn., 2014 (4th round). **Signed by:** Les Pajari.

TRACK RECORD: Hentges didn't pitch much until he was a junior in high school and was one of the youngest players in the 2014 draft class. He had Tommy John surgery in 2016, but had a breakout 2018 in high Class A. That breakout slowed in Double-A Akron in 2019, though he improved as the season went on and was added to the 40-man roster. He pitched well at the alternate training site in 2020.

SCOUTING REPORT: Hentges has a big, physical frame that he has grown into since signing and he has the powerful fastball to match. His fastball averages about 93 mph and he can run it into the upper 90s. He overpowered hitters with it early in his career and now is learning to rely more on his secondary stuff. His three offspeed offerings have potential—his curveball flashes plus, his changeup has promise and his cutter gives him another option. Like many big, young pitchers, Hentges needs to improve his control and take better advantage of his height to pitch down in the zone. His arm action can be long, hurting his ability to repeat his delivery.

THE FUTURE: Hentges is a 6-foot-8 lefthander with a big arm who is still just 24. He needs to refine some of the finer parts of his game, but the potential is still easy to see.

Year	Age	Club (League)	Class	W	L	ERA	G	GS	IP	H	HR	BB	SO	BB/9	SO/9	WHIP	AVG
2019	22	Akron (EL)	AA	2	13	5.11	26	26	129	148	11	64	126	4.5	8.8	1.65	.252
Minor League Totals				14	32	4.34	95	85	406	420	30	193	433	4.3	9.6	1.51	.268

23 ERNIE CLEMENT, SS

BA GRADE
45 Risk: High

Born: March 22, 1996. **B-T:** R-R. **HT:** 6-0. **WT:** 170. **Drafted:** Virginia, 2017 (4th round). **Signed by:** Bob Mayer.

TRACK RECORD: Clement's success at Virginia translated well to the professional ranks and he raced to Double-A Akron in 2018, his first full professional season. A right abductor strain slowed him in 2019, but he still played well enough to finish the season with Triple-A. He spent 2020 at the alternate training site and then instructional league.

SCOUTING REPORT: Clement embodies the saying, "Good things happen when you put the ball in play." He has an aggressive approach and an uncanny knack for putting the bat on the ball. He has minimal power and instead sprays the ball all over the field and takes advantage of his plus speed to get on base. Clement has above-average instincts defensively and good hands. The biggest concern about his ability to stay at shortstop is his arm strength, which is fringy for the position. His versatility allows him to play anywhere on the infield and he also has experience as a center fielder.

THE FUTURE: The Indians have toolsier shortstops than Clement, but he's proven to be capable of playing the position. He's fast approaching the major leagues and could debut in 2021 in a variety of roles.

Year	Age	Club (League)	Class	AVG	G	AB	R	H	2B	3B	HR	RBI	BB	SO	SB	OBP	SLG
2019	23	Akron (EL)	AA	.261	98	394	46	103	15	3	1	24	26	33	16	.314	.322
	23	Columbus (IL)	AAA	.545	3	11	3	6	1	0	0	4	2	1	1	.615	.636
Minor League Totals				.279	248	999	153	279	51	6	3	74	75	81	41	.336	.351

24 LENNY TORRES, RHP

BREAKOUT
BA GRADE
50 Risk: Extreme

Born: Oct. 15, 2000. **B-T:** R-R. **HT:** 6-1. **WT:** 190. **Drafted:** HS—Beacon, N.Y., 2018 (1st round supplemental). **Signed by:** Mike Kanen.

TRACK RECORD: Torres didn't pitch much growing up but quickly showed big upside on the mound after starting to focus on it late in his high school career. He made a smooth transition to pro ball and in 2018 excelled in the Rookie-level Arizona League. His progress was slowed in 2019, however, when he had Tommy John surgery in May and missed the whole season. He spent 2020 at the Indians' complex in Arizona and was back to full health in time for instructional league.

SCOUTING REPORT: Torres doesn't have a big frame at a listed 6-foot-1, but he has a quick arm and can run his fastball up to 97 mph. The pitch typically sits 94 and he pairs it with a slider that has plus potential. He is working to implement a changeup, which at its best has hard downer action. His control is also an area of focus, though he surprised with his strike-throwing ability during his professional debut.

THE FUTURE: Before the draft, Torres faced lots of questions about whether he could be a starter in pro ball because of his size and lack of a third pitch. His injury raised those concerns again, but the Indians are optimistic he'll be able to take the necessary steps in his development. He'll be ready for Class A in 2021.

Year	Age	Club (League)	Class	W	L	ERA	G	GS	IP	H	HR	BB	SO	BB/9	SO/9	WHIP	AVG
2019	18	Did not play—Injured															
Minor League Totals				0	0	1.76	6	5	15	14	0	4	22	2.4	12.9	1.17	.24

25 YORDYS VALDES, SS

BA GRADE
50 Risk: Extreme

Born: Aug. 16, 2001. **B-T:** B-R. **HT:** 6-0. **WT:** 170. **Drafted:** HS—Hollywood, Fla., 2019 (2nd round). **Signed by:** Jhonathan Leyba.

TRACK RECORD: Valdes was born in Cuba, where his father played in the Serie Nacional, and moved with his family to Florida when he was 12. Though he was young for the 2019 draft class, he was one of the best prep defenders in the nation. He played at instructional league in 2020.

SCOUTING REPORT: Valdes had a glove-over-bat profile as an amateur and that has continued to be the case since entering the Indians' system. The natural righthanded hitter began switch-hitting when he got to America and almost all of his high school plate appearances came from the left side. He's made strides as a lefthanded hitter but he's still clearly better from the right side. He has a wiry frame and should be able to add more impact offensively as he physically matures. Valdes shines defensively. He has a plus arm, can make all the throws from shortstop and gets rid of the ball quickly. He's an average runner, but that plays up on the bases and in the field thanks to his quickness and instincts.

THE FUTURE: The Indians have a bevy of exciting shortstops, especially in the lower levels of the system, and Valdes fits right in with the group.

Year	Age	Club (League)	Class	AVG	G	AB	R	H	2B	3B	HR	RBI	BB	SO	SB	OBP	SLG
2019	17	Indians 1 (AZL)	R	.179	43	162	17	29	3	1	2	11	16	53	15	.251	.247
Minor League Totals				.179	43	162	17	29	3	1	2	11	16	53	15	.251	.247

26 ANGEL MARTINEZ, SS

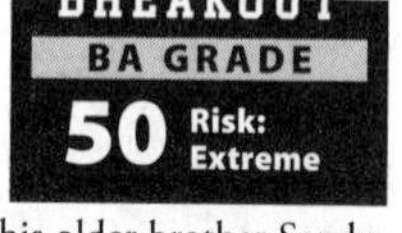

Born: Jan. 27, 2002. **B-T:** B-R. **HT:** 6-0. **WT:** 165. **Signed:** Dominican Republic, 2018. **Signed by:** Jhonathan Leyba.

TRACK RECORD: Martinez is the son of former big league catcher Sandy Martinez, who now is the Nationals' Dominican Summer League manager, and his older brother Sandy Martinez Jr. is a prospect in the D-backs system. As a result, Angel grew up around the diamond and has an advanced understanding of the game. He made his professional debut in 2019 in the DSL and impressed as a 17-year-old. He came to the Indians' complex in Arizona for instructional league in 2020.

SCOUTING REPORT: Martinez isn't the most toolsy of the Indians' lower-level infielders, but his baseball IQ and maturity make all his tools play up. The switch-hitter has a simple swing from both sides and can drive the ball to all fields. He has advanced plate discipline and walked as much as he struck out in the DSL—a rarity—and has good physicality that plays as doubles power. Martinez is an average runner, but still covers a lot of ground thanks to his instincts and makes sound decisions defensively. That, as well as his plus arm, gives him a chance to stay at shortstop.

THE FUTURE: Martinez could make a jump in 2021 as he makes his U.S. debut.

Year	Age	Club (League)	Class	AVG	G	AB	R	H	2B	3B	HR	RBI	BB	SO	SB	OBP	SLG
2019	17	Indians (DSL)	R	.306	56	222	37	68	10	7	1	27	29	29	11	.402	.428
Minor League Totals				.306	56	222	37	68	10	7	1	27	29	29	11	.402	.428

27 YU CHANG, 3B/SS

BA GRADE
40 Risk: Medium

Born: Aug. 18, 1995. **B-T:** R-R. **HT:** 6-1. **WT:** 175. **Signed:** Taiwan, 2013. **Signed by:** Jason Lynn.

TRACK RECORD: Chang was a prominent prep player in Taiwan and was one of the top amateur free agents to sign out of Asia in 2013. His prospect profile rose as his power developed in the minor leagues, especially upon reaching the upper levels. He made his major league debut in June 2019 and has seen action in each of the last two years.

SCOUTING REPORT: Chang has solid all-around offensive tools and while his 24 home runs in 2017 now look more aberrational, he still has continued to produce. He is a patient hitter, but his willingness to work deep in counts leads to an elevated strikeout rate. Though Chang may not pass the eye test at shortstop, he can make all the plays at the position and is an average defender with average or better speed and arm strength. He's capable of playing anywhere on the infield—which he did in Cleveland in 2020—and has seen the majority of his big-league action at third base.

THE FUTURE: Chang is 25 and the Indians have waves of dynamic infielders closing in on the big leagues. If he is to seize an everyday role, 2021 is a critical season for him.

Year	Age	Club (League)	Class	AVG	G	AB	R	H	2B	3B	HR	RBI	BB	SO	SB	OBP	SLG
2020	24	Cleveland (AL)	MAJ	.182	10	11	1	2	0	0	0	1	2	4	0	.308	.182
Major League Totals				.179	38	84	9	15	2	1	1	7	13	26	0	.289	.262
Minor League Totals				.251	577	2119	342	532	122	24	74	314	212	586	41	.326	.436

28 DANIEL JOHNSON, OF

BA GRADE
40 Risk: Medium

Born: July 11, 1995. **B-T:** L-L. **HT:** 5-10. **WT:** 185. **Drafted:** New Mexico State, 2016 (5th round). **Signed by:** Mitch Sokol (Nationals).

TRACK RECORD: Originally drafted by the Nationals in 2016, the Indians acquired Johnson as a part of the package for Yan Gomes in November 2018. He had a strong introduction to his new organization the following year, leading the system in doubles (34) and ranking third in hits (140). In 2020, he made his major league debut, appearing in five games.

SCOUTING REPORT: Johnson has quick hands at the plate and does a good job of barreling balls, especially against righthanded pitching. His strength and bat speed give him above-average raw power, which he's done a good job of getting to in games. It does come with a fair amount of swing and miss, however, and he's struck out in 22% of his plate appearances in the upper levels. Johnson has plus speed and arm strength and can play all three outfield positions. He probably fits best in right field, which is where he has the most experience.

THE FUTURE: The Indians started the offseason by non-tendering Delino DeShields and Tyler Naquin, leaving their outfield picture open. Johnson will go to spring training competing for a job and should return to Cleveland sometime in 2021.

Year	Age	Club (League)	Class	AVG	G	AB	R	H	2B	3B	HR	RBI	BB	SO	SB	OBP	SLG
2020	24	Cleveland (AL)	MAJ	.083	5	12	0	1	0	0	0	0	1	5	0	.154	.083
Major League Totals				.083	5	12	0	1	0	0	0	0	1	5	0	.154	.083
Minor League Totals				.284	411	1601	235	454	91	22	49	198	117	352	69	.344	.460

29 JOSE PASTRANO, SS

BA GRADE
50 **Risk: Extreme**

Born: Sept. 12, 2002. **B-T:** B-R. **HT:** 5-11. **WT:** 145. **Signed:** Venezuela, 2019. **Signed by:** Gustavo Benzan.

TRACK RECORD: The Indians continued to be aggressive on the international market in 2019 and Pastrano, a Venezuelan native, was the club's biggest signing. His older brother, also named Jose Pastrano, plays in the Athletics' organization, but the younger Pastrano is viewed as the superior prospect.

SCOUTING REPORT: Pastrano stands out for his athleticism and understanding of the game. A switch-hitter, he has a short, direct swing and a good feel for the strike zone. He uses the whole field to hit and has enough physical projection to see his doubles power increase in time, but he's likely to be hit over power in the long run. Pastrano might have been the best defensive shortstop in the international class. He's a plus runner with quick hands, good infield actions and above-average arm strength.

THE FUTURE: Pastrano finished the 2020 season at instructional league. The 18-year-old is a part of the burgeoning group of talented middle infielders at the lower levels of the organization and will make his professional debut in 2021.

Year	Age	Club (League)	Class	AVG	G	AB	R	H	2B	3B	HR	RBI	BB	SO	SB	OBP	SLG
2019	16	Did not play—Signed 2020 contract															

30 ELI MORGAN, RHP

BA GRADE
45 **Risk: High**

Born: May 13, 1996. **B-T:** R-R. **HT:** 5-10. **WT:** 190. **Drafted:** Gonzaga, 2017 (8th round). **Signed by:** Conor Glassey.

TRACK RECORD: Morgan has built an impressive track record of success over the last five years, dating to his time at Gonzaga. He's produced at every level, reaching Triple-A in 2019, and has averaged 10.2 strikeouts and 2.3 walks per nine innings in the minor leagues. While his shorter stature and below-average velocity have meant he's kept a lower profile despite that production, the Indians added him to their 40-man roster in November after he spent the summer at the alternate training site.

SCOUTING REPORT: Morgan has never thrown hard and while his fastball can reach 93-94 mph, it typically sits 89-90. The pitch plays up thanks to some deception in his delivery and his ability to locate it. His best pitch is his changeup, which has excellent fading action. It's a plus offering that he can throw in any situation and locate well. His breaking ball has improved, giving him a viable third pitch. Morgan understands what he needs to do to get outs and works hard to refine his pitches.

THE FUTURE: As a short righthander whose best pitch is his changeup, Morgan has an unusual profile. But he's been successful everywhere he's pitched. He'll likely get a chance in 2021 to show what he can do in Cleveland.

Year	Age	Club (League)	Class	W	L	ERA	G	GS	IP	H	HR	BB	SO	BB/9	SO/9	WHIP	AVG
2019	23	Akron (EL)	AA	6	4	3.79	19	18	102	100	12	33	104	2.9	9.2	1.30	.231
	23	Columbus (IL)	AAA	0	1	5.40	1	1	5	5	0	2	2	3.6	3.6	1.40	.227
	23	Lynchburg (CAR)	HiA	3	1	1.87	6	6	34	19	3	5	40	1.3	10.7	0.71	.156
Minor League Totals				21	15	3.08	66	57	319	272	28	83	360	2.3	10.2	1.11	.229

MORE PROSPECTS TO KNOW

31 JOSE TENA, SS

Tena is another impressive prospect from the Indians' 2017 international class. He's an advanced hitter and a plus athlete with a chance to stick at shortstop.

32 PETEY HALPIN, OF

The Indians' 2020 third-rounder, Halpin is a good athlete with the chance to be an above-average hitter. He's gotten stronger in the last year and if that added strength equates to more power, he could make a jump in pro ball.

33 TREVOR STEPHAN, RHP

A 2020 Rule 5 pick from the Yankees, Stephan bounced between high Class A and Double-A as a starter in 2018 and 2019 but has struggled with control in Double-A and likely fits in the bullpen. He attacks hitters with a good fastball/slider combination and his funky delivery helps his stuff play up.

34 WILL BENSON, OF

Benson was the Indians' first-round pick in 2016 and has long stood out for his combination of power, size and athleticism. He hasn't been able to put it all together to reach his considerable ceiling, however, and has especially struggled with making enough consistent contact.

35 NICK SANDLIN, RHP

Sandlin looked to be ticketed to join the Indians' bullpen after reaching Triple-A in June 2019, but suffered a forearm strain the next month. He was healthy in 2020 and now again looks like he'll bring his funky low arm slot and fastball-slider combination to Cleveland.

36 JUNIOR SANQUINTIN, SS

SLEEPER

Sanquintin was the Indians' second-biggest signing in the 2018 international class, behind only Gabriel Rodriguez. He's a switch-hitter who produces premium bat speed and above-average raw power.

37 JEAN CARLOS MEJIA, RHP

Mejia broke out in 2018 and was added to the 40-man roster that fall. He hasn't had a chance to build on that success, as he was limited by a hip injury in 2019 and then lost the 2020 season. He has a big frame, a big arm and a good feel for spin—a profile that gives him a chance as a starter or reliever.

38 JOSE FERMIN, 2B

Fermin has solid all-around tools and has a good feel at the plate. He's walked more than he's struck out in each of the last two seasons and has the versatility to play anywhere on the infield.

39 LUIS DURANGO JR, OF

Durango was one of the top players in Panama in 2019 and was the Indians' second-biggest signing in the international class, behind only Jose Pastrano. He has an advanced hitting approach and well above-average speed. He has a chance to fit a traditional top-of-the-order, center field profile.

40 KYLE NELSON, LHP

Drafted in the 15th round in 2017, Nelson worked his way through the minor leagues thanks to a wipeout slider. He made his major league debut in 2020 and figures to again be in the mix in the Indians' bullpen in 2020. He profiles best as a matchup reliever but could grow into a bigger role in time.

TOP PROSPECTS OF THE DECADE

Year	Player, Pos	2020 Org
2011	Lonnie Chisenhall, 3B	Did not play
2012	Francisco Lindor, SS	Indians
2013	Francisco Lindor, SS	Indians
2014	Francisco Lindor, SS	Indians
2015	Francisco Lindor, SS	Indians
2016	Bradley Zimmer, OF	Indians
2017	Francisco Mejia, C	Padres
2018	Francisco Mejia, C	Padres
2019	Triston McKenzie, RHP	Indians
2020	Nolan Jones, 3B	Indians

TOP DRAFT PICKS OF THE DECADE

Year	Player, Pos	2020 Org
2011	Francisco Lindor, SS	Indians
2012	Tyler Naquin, OF	Indians
2013	Clint Frazier, OF	Yankees
2014	Bradley Zimmer, OF	Indians
2015	Brady Aiken, LHP	Indians
2016	Will Benson, OF	Indians
2017	Quentin Holmes, OF (2nd round)	Indians
2018	Bo Naylor, C	Indians
2019	Daniel Espino, RHP	Indians
2020	Carson Tucker, SS	Indians

DEPTH CHART

CLEVELAND INDIANS

TOP 2021 ROOKIES	RANK
Triston McKenzie, RHP	1
Emmanuel Clase, RHP	14
BREAKOUT PROSPECTS	**RANK**
Carlos Vargas, RHP	17
Lenny Torres, RHP	24
Angel Martinez, SS	26

SOURCE OF TOP 30 TALENT

Homegrown	23	Acquired	7
College	4	Trade	7
Junior college	0	Rule 5 draft	0
High school	11	Independent league	0
Nondrafted free agent	0	Free agent/waivers	0
International	8		

LF
George Valera (5)
Oscar Gonzalez

CF
Petey Halpin
Luis Durango Jr.
Steven Kwan

RF
Daniel Johnson (28)
Will Benson
Johnathan Rodriguez

3B
Nolan Jones (2)
Yu Chang (27)
Junior Sanquintin
Christian Cairo
Jhonkensy Noel

SS
Tyler Freeman (3)
Gabriel Arias (6)
Brayan Rocchio (7)
Gabriel Rodriguez (11)
Carson Tucker (12)
Owen Miller (18)
Ernie Clement (23)
Yordys Valdes (25)
Angel Martinez (26)
Jose Pastrano (29)

2B
Aaron Bracho (10)
Jose Tena
Jose Fermin
Richie Palacios

1B
Bobby Bradley (21)
Joe Naranjo

C
Bo Naylor (4)
Bryan Lavastida
Yainer Diaz

LHP

LHSP
Logan Allen (13)
Joey Cantillo (16)
Scott Moss (19)
Logan T. Allen (20)
Sam Hentges (22)
Adam Scott
Raymond Burgos

LHRP
Kyle Nelson
Tim Herrin
Anthony Gose

RHP

RHSP
Triston McKenzie (1)
Daniel Espino (8)
Ethan Hankins (9)
Tanner Burns (15)
Carlos Vargas (17)
Lenny Torres (24)
Eli Morgan (30)
Jean Carlos Mejia
Cody Morris
Hunter Gaddis
Mason Hickman

RHRP
Emanuel Clase (14)
Trevor Stephan
Nick Sandlin
Jordan Humphreys
Robert Broom
Nick Mikolajchak

Colorado Rockies

BY JOE HEALY

The Rockies were flying high at the end of the 2018 season. They were coming off of back-to-back postseason appearances, boasted a talented team full of mostly homegrown players, and with much of that talent young and under team control, it appeared a lengthy window of contention had just flown wide open.

Two years later, the Rockies' core is still largely intact, but that promise has not been fulfilled. They dropped to fourth place in the National League West in 2019 and finished fourth again during the pandemic-shortened 2020 season, unable to take advantage of an expanded playoff field to return to the postseason.

Now, the organization faces questions about the future of its big-name stars. Third baseman Nolan Arenado has generated speculation about his willingness to remain in Denver despite signing a lengthy extension in early 2019. Shortstop Trevor Story is a free agent after the 2021 season. Righthander Jon Gray, a workhorse in the rotation for the last five seasons, will also be a free agent after 2021.

The Rockies' player development challenge is finding the next crop of cornerstone pieces, and those players haven't shown themselves yet.

Some of that is because the Rockies simply graduated so much high-end talent in the years leading up to their 2017 and 2018 postseason appearances that it naturally left the system depleted. That's simply the circle of life when building a team around homegrown players.

But it's also because the next group of players have hit their fair share of snags, chief among them shortstop Brendan Rodgers, the third overall pick in the 2015 draft. The top prospect in the system for the last four years, Rodgers has had his season scuttled by injuries two years in a row. Others, like righthander Peter Lambert, have also suffered injuries, and still others, like Sam Hilliard, endured tough sophomore campaigns after promising big league debuts.

Even further back in prospect history, players like Ryan McMahon, Garrett Hampson, Raimel Tapia and David Dahl have had their moments but struggled to stay consistently productive and/or healthy. The Rockies even non-tendered Dahl in the offseason and he quickly signed with the Rangers.

The good news is the Rockies have reached a critical mass of position player prospects at the upper levels of the minors, and some of them are likely to reach the majors in short order. That could be a panacea for a lineup that has struggled to get consistent production outside of Arenado or Story the last two seasons.

For the Rockies to compete again, they will need some of their prospects to have a big impact right away. Or, if the organization hits the reset button and trades some of the established stars on the roster, many of those same players will be pressed into major roles immediately.

Either way, the 2021 season is a pivotal time for the Rockies' top prospects, and how they perform will determine the Rockies long-term outlook. ■

JUSTIN EDMONDS/GETTY IMAGES

As free agency looms for shortstop Trevor Story, the Rockies' window of success could be closing.

PROJECTED 2024 LINEUP

Position	Player	Age
Catcher	Drew Romo	22
First Base	Michael Toglia	25
Second Base	Brendan Rodgers	27
Third Base	Nolan Arenado	33
Shortstop	Trevor Story	31
Left Field	Brenton Doyle	26
Center Field	Garrett Hampson	29
Right Field	Zac Veen	21
Designated Hitter	Aaron Schunk	26
No. 1 Starter	German Marquez	29
No. 2 Starter	Jon Gray	32
No. 3 Starter	Kyle Freeland	31
No. 4 Starter	Ryan Rolison	26
No. 5 Starter	Chris McMahon	25
Closer	Yency Almonte	30

1 BRENDAN RODGERS, SS/2B

Born: Aug. 9, 1996. **B-T:** R-R. **HT:** 6-0. **WT:** 204.
Drafted: HS—Lake Mary, Fla., 2015 (1st round).
Signed by: John Cedarburg.

TRACK RECORD: Rodgers was the top prospect in the 2015 draft thanks to his precocious hitting ability, promising power potential and ability to stick up the middle defensively. The Rockies drafted him third overall, behind Southeastern Conference shortstops Dansby Swanson and Alex Bregman, and signed him for a franchise-record $5.5 million. While Swanson and Bregman have found success in the big leagues, Rodgers' career has stalled due to injuries. Shoulder surgery limited his big league time in 2019 to just 25 games and resulted in him being handled with extreme caution in 2020. A tweaked hamstring suffered at the alternate training site delayed his return to Colorado, where he once again struggled offensively. Through 32 big league games he has hit .196/.235/.227 with four walks and 33 strikeouts

SCOUTING REPORT: While Rodgers' standing as a prospect has suffered, both because of injuries and decaying enthusiasm about his tools, he still has the ceiling of an impact player. He's still 24 years old, and there is little doubt he can be an above-average hitter if he stays healthy. Rodgers' quick wrists, bat speed and ability to make consistent hard contact earn high marks, and he projects to have above-average power. Historically, the knock on Rodgers has been his lack of walks and a strikeout rate that has ballooned in his small big league sample. At present, he can hit any fastball but struggles with big league-caliber breaking balls. While his pitch recognition and patience will continue to be question marks until he proves otherwise, they have been an area of focus over the last two years and he has shown progress. A natural shortstop, Rodgers is still a work in progress defensively at second base. He has more than enough arm strength and athleticism for the position and has spent time working on the finer points of the keystone, including his angles to the ball, moving better to his left and working to soften his hands. There is confidence he can be an above-average defender at second base if he winds up there.

THE FUTURE: Rodgers will get another chance in 2021 to entrench himself with fellow homegrown stars Nolan Arenado and Trevor Story, who play third base and shortstop in Colorado. Rodgers might still be the franchise's shortstop of the future, but with Story there for at least another year, his best path to playing time will be at second base. If Rodgers gets the playing time he needs and makes a leap in 2021, an infield featuring Rodgers, Story and Arenado could be one of the most dynamic in baseball. ■

BEST TOOLS

Best Hitter for Average	Brendan Rodgers
Best Power Hitter	Michael Toglia
Best Strike-Zone Discipline	Grant Lavigne
Fastest Baserunner	Bladimir Restituyo
Best Athlete	Brenton Doyle
Best Fastball	Riley Pint
Best Curveball	Ryan Rolison
Best Slider	Tommy Doyle
Best Changeup	Ryan Rolison
Best Control	Antonio Santos
Best Defensive Catcher	Drew Romo
Best Defensive Infielder	Ezequiel Tovar
Best Infield Arm	Julio Carreras
Best Defensive Outfielder	Yonathan Daza
Best Outfield Arm	Yonathan Daza

Year	Age	Club (League)	Class	AVG	G	AB	R	H	2B	3B	HR	RBI	BB	SO	SB	OBP	SLG
2017	20	Lancaster (CAL)	HiA	.383	51	222	44	85	21	3	12	46	6	35	2	.403	.667
	20	Hartford (EL)	AA	.260	38	150	20	39	5	0	6	17	8	36	0	.323	.413
2018	21	Albuquerque (PCL)	AAA	.232	19	69	5	16	4	0	0	5	1	16	0	.264	.290
	21	Hartford (EL)	AA	.275	95	357	49	98	23	2	17	62	30	76	12	.342	.493
2019	22	Colorado (NL)	MAJ	.224	25	76	8	17	2	0	0	7	4	27	0	.272	.250
	22	Albuquerque (PCL)	AAA	.350	37	143	34	50	10	1	9	21	14	27	0	.413	.622
2020	23	Colorado (NL)	MAJ	.095	7	21	1	2	1	0	0	2	0	6	0	.095	.143
Major League Totals				.196	32	97	9	19	3	0	0	9	4	33	0	.235	.227
Minor League Totals				.296	387	1526	247	452	102	8	66	245	109	325	24	.352	.503

2 ZAC VEEN, OF

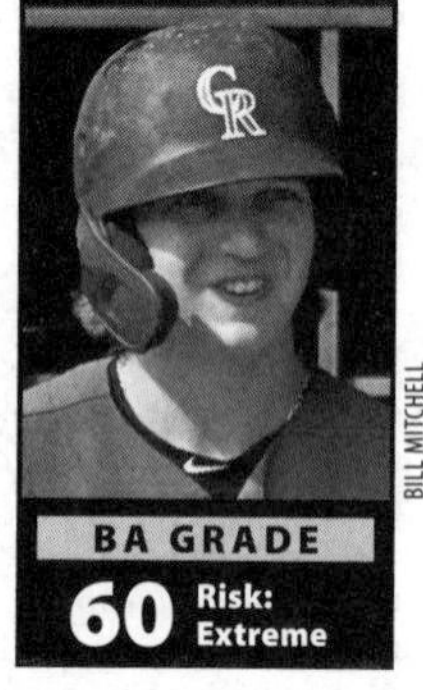

BILL MITCHELL

Born: Dec. 12, 2001. **B-T:** L-R. **HT:** 6-5. **WT:** 200. **Drafted:** HS—Port Orange, Fla., 2020 (1st round). **Signed by:** John Cedarburg.

TRACK RECORD: Veen used a big junior season at Spruce Creek High outside of Orlando to rocket up draft boards. A late push in 2020 took him from a back-of-the-first-round prospect to the ninth overall pick, where the Rockies drafted him and signed him for $5 million to forgo a Florida commitment. Veen participated in instructional league and held his own against high-velocity arms.

SCOUTING REPORT: Veen is a fantastic athlete with an exceptional batting eye and a natural feel to hit. He possesses leverage in his swing and plus power to the pull side, and there is confidence power to all fields will come. Veen is 6-foot-5, 200 pounds, but the Rockies think the lefthanded hitter can add another 15-20 pounds to an already-sturdy frame. Opinions on Veen's long-term hitting potential vary, but most see at least an average hitter with the potential for 30 home runs. Veen has the athleticism and average speed to play center field now, but as he grows he may be a better fit in right field, where his above-average arm would fit nicely.

THE FUTURE: Few doubt Veen's offensive ceiling as a middle of the order slugger. The Rockies are eager to get him into the system and begin his development in earnest, most likely at low Class A in 2021.

SCOUTING GRADES: **Hitting:** 55 **Power:** 60 **Running:** 50 **Fielding:** 50 **Arm:** 55

Year	Age	Club (League)	Class	AVG	G	AB	R	H	2B	3B	HR	RBI	BB	SO	SB	OBP	SLG
2020	18	Did not play—No minor league season															

3 RYAN ROLISON, LHP

BA GRADE
50 Risk: High

ROBERT BINDER/MLB PHOTOS VIA GETTY IMAGES

Born: July 11, 1997. **B-T:** B-L. **HT:** 6-2. **WT:** 213. **Drafted:** Mississippi, 2018 (1st round). **Signed by:** Zack Zulli.

TRACK RECORD: Rolison was a key piece of Mississippi's No. 1-ranked recruiting class in 2016, and he lived up his potential in Oxford, striking out 184 batters in 159 career innings on the way to being drafted in the first round, 22nd overall, as an eligible sophomore in 2018. In 2019, Rolison did as well as could be expected in hitter-friendly Lancaster. Rolison spent time at both the Rockies' alternate training site and at instructional league in 2020.

SCOUTING REPORT: Rolison gets hitters out with his intellect, feel to pitch and ability to make quick adjustments. He primarily sets hitters up with his low-90s fastball and finishes them with a plus curveball he can manipulate the spin and shape of. The Rockies are excited about the continued development of a changeup that shows average potential. Rolison is sometimes listed as having a slider, but it's actually a modified version of his curveball, which is also in the upper 70s. Rolison has shown plus control in the minors with 2.7 walks per nine innings, but the Rockies would like to see him improve his command to his arm side.

THE FUTURE: The lack of eye-popping stuff limits Rolison's ceiling, but his command and pitchability give him a chance to be a rotation mainstay. He'll see Double-A in 2021.

SCOUTING GRADES: **Fastball:** 50 **Curveball:** 60 **Changeup:** 50 **Control:** 60

Year	Age	Club (League)	Class	W	L	ERA	G	GS	IP	H	HR	BB	SO	BB/9	SO/9	WHIP	AVG
2018	20	Grand Junction (PIO)	R	0	1	1.86	9	9	29	15	2	8	34	2.5	10.6	0.79	.138
2019	21	Lancaster (CAL)	HiA	6	7	4.87	22	22	116	129	22	38	118	2.9	9.1	1.44	.253
	21	Asheville (SAL)	LoA	2	1	0.61	3	3	15	8	0	2	14	1.2	8.6	0.68	.151
Minor League Totals				8	9	3.94	34	34	160	152	24	48	166	2.7	9.3	1.25	.247

4 MICHAEL TOGLIA, 1B

Born: Aug. 16, 1998. **B-T:** B-L. **HT:** 6-5. **WT:** 226. **Drafted:** UCLA, 2019 (1st round). **Signed by:** Matt Hattabaugh.

COURTESY OF BOISE HAWKS

BA GRADE
50 **Risk: High**

TRACK RECORD: The Rockies drafted Toglia in the 37th round out of high school and picked him again in the first round, No. 23 overall, after an accomplished career at UCLA. Toglia went to the short-season Northwest League in his pro debut, showing the power and defense that made him a coveted prospect, and spent 2020 at the alternate training site.

SCOUTING REPORT: Despite his hulking 6-foot-5, 226-pound frame, the switch-hitting Toglia is more of a contact hitter than a slugger. He takes a patient approach and drives the ball hard on a line from the left side of the plate. He's much less dangerous righthanded, but he's worked hard on his load and trigger to get into a better hitting position from that side. Toglia is streaky and flashes plus power from the left side when he's hot. The Rockies believe adjustments to his timing can make him an average hitter with plus power in time. Toglia is a plus defender at first base with smooth actions, sound footwork and good instincts around the bag. The Rockies are working him in the outfield to enhance his versatility.

THE FUTURE: Toglia is advanced but still has to prove himself over a full minor league season. The Rockies envision him becoming a middle of the order slugger.

SCOUTING GRADES: **Hitting:** 50 **Power:** 60 **Running:** 45 **Fielding:** 60 **Arm:** 50

Year	Age	Club (League)	Class	AVG	G	AB	R	H	2B	3B	HR	RBI	BB	SO	SB	OBP	SLG
2019	20	Boise (NWL)	SS	.248	41	145	25	36	7	0	9	26	28	45	1	.369	.483
Minor League Totals				.248	41	145	25	36	7	0	9	26	28	45	1	.369	.483

5 AARON SCHUNK, 3B

Born: July 24, 1997. **B-T:** R-R. **HT:** 6-2. **WT:** 205. **Drafted:** Georgia, 2019 (2nd round). **Signed by:** Sean Gamble.

COURTESY OF BOISE HAWKS

BA GRADE
50 **Risk: High**

TRACK RECORD: A third baseman and closer at Georgia, Schunk dropped pitching after being drafted in the second round in 2019. He began his pro career with a bang by hitting .306/.370/.503 with short-season Boise and ranking as the Northwest League's No. 4 prospect despite dealing with knee inflammation that limited him at the end of the season. He spent 2020 at the alternate training site before finishing in instructional league.

SCOUTING REPORT: Schunk doesn't have the loudest tools in the system, but observers see him as the type of player who will get the most from his skills. He has the arm and athleticism to be an average third baseman and also took to second base when the Rockies played him there at the alternate site. Offensively, Schunk controls the strike zone, stays inside the ball and drives it from gap to gap. His approach and bat speed give him a chance to hit for average with enough power to get frequent at-bats. Schunk made recent positive changes physically as well, slimming down over the course of the year while maintaining his strength during the coronavirus shutdown.

THE FUTURE: Schunk's maturity and work ethic could help him move quickly. His bat will be what pushes him forward, but his newfound versatility on the infield can only help.

SCOUTING GRADES: **Hitting:** 55 **Power:** 50 **Running:** 45 **Fielding:** 50 **Arm:** 60

Year	Age	Club (League)	Class	AVG	G	AB	R	H	2B	3B	HR	RBI	BB	SO	SB	OBP	SLG
2019	21	Boise (NWL)	SS	.306	46	173	31	53	12	2	6	23	14	25	4	.370	.503
Minor League Totals				.306	46	173	31	53	12	2	6	23	14	25	4	.370	.503

6 CHRIS MCMAHON, RHP

JC RIDLEY/MIAMI HURRICANES

Born: Feb. 4, 1999. **B-T:** R-R. **HT:** 6-2. **WT:** 217. **Drafted:** Miami, 2020 (2nd round). **Signed by:** Rafael Reyes.

TRACK RECORD: Offseason meniscus surgery forced McMahon to miss the start of his freshman year at Miami in 2018, and a minor back injury slowed him for a short period of time as a sophomore. But when he was on the mound, McMahon was excellent for the Hurricanes. He put up a 2.55 ERA with 123 strikeouts in 112.1 career innings, leading the Rockies to draft him 46th overall in 2020 and sign him for $1,637,400.

SCOUTING REPORT: McMahon's best offering is a fastball that sits 95-96 mph and was located well when he participated in instructional league. He complements his fastball with a solid-average slider and changeup that has a chance to be a plus offering down the line. The consistency of those secondary offerings will be key for McMahon. He throws strikes with average control, and the Rockies like the mound presence and moxie that he brings to his craft. McMahon's athleticism, three-pitch repertoire and arm strength should keep him alive as a starter.

THE FUTURE: McMahon has yet to officially debut and he'll have to prove himself in 2021. The Rockies are already pleased with what they've seen so far and think they have a potential mid-rotation starter.

SCOUTING GRADES: **Fastball:** 60 **Slider:** 55 **Changeup:** 55 **Control:** 50

Year	Age	Club (League)	Class	W	L	ERA	G	GS	IP	H	HR	BB	SO	BB/9	SO/9	WHIP	AVG
2020	21	Did not play—No minor league season															

7 COLTON WELKER, 3B/1B

ROBERT BINDER/MLB PHOTOS VIA GETTY IMAGES

Born: Oct. 9, 1997. **B-T:** R-R. **HT:** 6-1. **WT:** 235. **Drafted:** HS—Parkland, Fla., 2016 (4th round). **Signed by:** Rafael Reyes.

TRACK RECORD: Welker's pro career got off to a flying start, highlighted by winning the California League batting title with a .333 average in 2018. He started strong at Double-A in 2019, hitting .308 with power through 56 games, before fading badly down the stretch and suffering a shoulder injury that cut his season short. The Rockies brought Welker to the alternate training site in 2020 and added him to the 40-man roster after the season.

SCOUTING REPORT: Welker rose to Double-A at a young age thanks to above-average hitting ability and solid plate discipline, and those traits will be his ticket to the majors. His downturn late in 2019 came when he got outside of himself, tried to do too much and his swing got out of sync. Average power could come naturally if he doesn't try to force it. Welker has a big body and his feet slow down when he carries too much weight, which hurts him at third base. His hands and above-average arm work at the hot corner, but his size and resulting lack of mobility might force him to first base, a position he played with greater regularity at Double-A in 2019.

THE FUTURE: Welker can flat-out hit when he stays within himself. His defensive value is likely to be limited, so he'll have to hit his way to the big leagues.

SCOUTING GRADES: **Hitting:** 55 **Power:** 45 **Running:** 40 **Fielding:** 45 **Arm:** 55

Year	Age	Club (League)	Class	AVG	G	AB	R	H	2B	3B	HR	RBI	BB	SO	SB	OBP	SLG
2017	19	Asheville (SAL)	LoA	.350	67	254	32	89	18	1	6	33	18	42	5	.401	.500
2018	20	Lancaster (CAL)	HiA	.333	114	454	74	151	32	0	13	82	42	103	5	.383	.489
2019	21	Hartford (EL)	AA	.252	98	353	37	89	23	1	10	53	32	68	2	.313	.408
Minor League Totals				.313	330	1271	181	398	88	4	34	204	105	241	18	.364	.469

8 BRENTON DOYLE, OF

ZACHARY LUCY FOUR SEAM IMAGES

BA GRADE
50 **Risk: High**

Born: May 14, 1998. **B-T:** R-R. **HT:** 6-3. **WT:** 200. **Drafted:** Shepherd (W.Va.), 2019 (4th round). **Signed by:** Ed Santa.

TRACK RECORD: Doyle originally committed to Virginia Military Institute before landing at Division II Shepherd (W.Va.) instead. He looked like a Division I player at the level and was drafted in the fourth round in 2019 by the Rockies. Doyle led the Rookie-level Pioneer League in batting average (.383) and on-base percentage (.477) during a smashing pro debut. He returned to the field in 2020 during instructional league.

SCOUTING REPORT: Doyle has a lot of tools that jump out. His plus speed and strong arm give him the defensive versatility to settle in at any of the three outfield positions. He has plus power at the plate, giving him the potential to be a dynamic power-speed threat. Doyle does swing and miss at times and will have to answer questions about his contact skills against upper-level pitching, but so far he has kept his strikeout numbers manageable. A tweak Doyle made in 2019—he stood up taller in his stance—granted him more leverage for power and helped him see the ball longer to avoid chasing out of the zone as frequently.

THE FUTURE: Doyle continues to perform as the pitching he faces gets better. He has the tools to emerge as an everyday outfielder if he can keep that up.

SCOUTING GRADES: **Hitting:** 50 **Power:** 60 **Running:** 60 **Fielding:** 50 **Arm:** 65

Year	Age	Club (League)	Class	AVG	G	AB	R	H	2B	3B	HR	RBI	BB	SO	SB	OBP	SLG
2019	21	Grand Junction (PIO)	R	.383	51	180	42	69	11	3	8	33	31	47	17	.477	.611
Minor League Totals				.383	51	180	42	69	11	3	8	33	31	47	17	.477	.611

9 RYAN VILADE, OF

ROBERT BINDER/MLB PHOTOS VIA GETTY IMAGES

BA GRADE
50 **Risk: High**

Born: Feb. 18, 1999. **B-T:** R-R. **HT:** 6-2. **WT:** 226. **Drafted:** HS—Stillwater, Okla., 2017 (2nd round). **Signed by:** Jesse Retzlaf.

TRACK RECORD: Drafted in the second round in 2017, Vilade was the Rockies' top pick that year because they lost their first-rounder for signing free agent Ian Desmond. Vilade was drafted for his bat, and he hasn't disappointed, batting .291/.368/.428 while rising to high Class A, albeit all while playing at hitter-friendly locales.

SCOUTING REPORT: Vilade is traditionally a slow starter but tends to round into form as the season progresses. He has a flat, impactful swing that makes a lot of contact, and he's added strength that has pushed his weight up from 200 to 226 pounds. That stands to help his power, though his swing path is more geared for line drives and makes him more of a doubles hitter than a home run threat. He's always been able to go the other way effectively and has learned when to turn on the inside pitch while still staying up the middle on balls out over the plate. Vilade's defense is a different story. Despite his average speed, his slow reactions and limited range made him a liability at both shortstop and third base. The Rockies moved him to the outfield to give him another defensive option.

THE FUTURE: Vilade has the tools to hit himself to the big leagues. His defensive progress in the outfield will be key to watch in 2021.

SCOUTING GRADES: **Hitting:** 55 **Power:** 45 **Running:** 50 **Fielding:** 40 **Arm:** 50

Year	Age	Club (League)	Class	AVG	G	AB	R	H	2B	3B	HR	RBI	BB	SO	SB	OBP	SLG
2017	18	Grand Junction (PIO)	R	.308	33	117	23	36	3	2	5	21	27	31	5	.438	.496
2018	19	Asheville (SAL)	LoA	.274	124	457	77	125	20	4	5	44	49	96	17	.353	.368
2019	20	Lancaster (CAL)	HiA	.303	128	509	92	154	27	10	12	71	56	95	24	.367	.466
Minor League Totals				.291	285	1083	192	315	50	16	22	136	132	222	46	.369	.428

10 HELCRIS OLIVAREZ

Born: Aug. 8, 2000. **B-T:** L-L. **HT:** 6-3. **WT:** 200. **Signed:** Dominican Republic, 2016. **Signed by:** Rolando Fernandez/Arnaldo Gomez/Orlando Medina/Frank Roa.

BILL MITCHELL

BA GRADE
50 **Risk: Extreme**

TRACK RECORD: Olivarez was relatively anonymous after signing with the Rockies for $77,000 and spent parts of three seasons in the Dominican Summer League. He broke out in 2019 and averaged 11.8 strikeouts per nine innings at Rookie-level Grand Junction in his U.S. debut, albeit with a heavy dose of walks. Olivarez went to the alternate training site in 2020, turned heads in instructional league and was added to the 40-man roster after the season.

SCOUTING REPORT: Olivarez may be just 20 years old, but at 6-foot-3, 200 pounds, he is built like a grown man. His fastball sits 94-96 mph, touches 97 and is one of the best in the Rockies' system. His curveball is an above-average offering and is his go-to putaway pitch. His changeup flashes plus but is inconsistent. Olivarez is fully bilingual and exudes confidence on the mound. The only questions are his durability and control. He has yet to throw more than 60.2 innings in a season and is an inconsistent strike-thrower who will be stretched to reach average control.

THE FUTURE: Olivarez's arm is special and he has the makeup to get the most from his abilities. He has the makings of a hard-throwing lefthanded starter if he can improve his control.

SCOUTING GRADES: **Fastball:** 60 **Curveball:** 55 **Changeup:** 50 **Control:** 50

Year	Age	Club (League)	Class	W	L	ERA	G	GS	IP	H	HR	BB	SO	BB/9	SO/9	WHIP	AVG
2017	16	Rockies (DSL)	R	0	1	3.55	18	1	33	24	0	17	35	4.6	9.5	1.24	.170
2018	17	Rockies (DSL)	R	4	1	2.78	9	9	36	25	1	22	36	5.6	9.1	1.32	.170
	17	Colorado (DSL)	R	2	0	1.42	4	4	19	11	0	4	24	1.9	11.4	0.79	.151
2019	18	Rockies (DSL)	R	1	0	0.64	3	3	14	7	0	7	21	4.5	13.5	1.00	.127
	18	Grand Junction (PIO)	R	3	4	4.82	11	11	47	47	9	24	61	4.6	11.8	1.52	.222
Minor League Totals				10	6	3.22	45	28	148	114	10	74	177	4.5	10.7	1.27	.212

11 RYAN CASTELLANI, RHP

BA GRADE
40 **Risk: Medium**

Born: April 1, 1996. **B-T:** R-R. **HT:** 6-1. **WT:** 218. **Drafted:** HS—Phoenix, 2014 (2nd round). **Signed by:** Chris Forbes.

TRACK RECORD: Castellani's mechanics broke down in 2018 and he logged an 8.31 ERA at Triple-A in 2019 before having season-ending surgery to remove bone chips in his elbow. His run of misfortune continued when he tested positive for Covid-19 before the 2020 season, but he rebounded to have a strong summer camp and earned his first major league callup. Castellani made 10 appearances (nine starts) and posted a 5.82 ERA.

SCOUTING REPORT: Castellani comes at hitters with a three-quarter arm slot that generates unique movement on his pitches. His fastball sits 92-93 mph and touches 96 mph with a lot of horizontal movement. His short, mid-80s slider is his best pitch and generated a 50 percent whiff rate in his debut. Castellani's mid-80s changeup was his fourth pitch in the past, but it proved effective against lefties and he increasingly went to it in the majors. He also added an upper-70s curveball that was largely ineffective against big league hitters. Consistency and throwing strikes are the challenges for Castellani moving forward. He walked more batters than he struck out in his debut and has had below-average walk rates since Double-A.

THE FUTURE: Castellani has a shot to be a back-end starter if his control improves. Mostly likely, he fits in the bullpen.

Year	Age	Club (League)	Class	W	L	ERA	G	GS	IP	H	HR	BB	SO	BB/9	SO/9	WHIP	AVG
2020	24	Colorado (NL)	MAJ	1	4	5.82	10	9	43	37	12	26	25	5.4	5.2	1.45	.236
Major League Totals				1	4	5.82	10	9	43	37	12	26	25	5.4	5.2	1.45	.236
Minor League Totals				28	43	4.80	126	126	653	677	60	235	531	3.2	7.3	1.40	.267

12 GRANT LAVIGNE, 1B

BA GRADE **45** Risk: High

Born: Aug. 27, 1999. **B-T:** L-R. **HT:** 6-4. **WT:** 220. **Drafted:** HS—Bedford, N.H., 2018 (1st round supplemental). **Signed by:** Mike Garlatti.

TRACK RECORD: A prep product out of New Hampshire, where the high school season is short and the quality of play is inconsistent, Lavigne is one of the most inexperienced domestic prospects in the Rockies system. He made a big first impression in 2018 with Rookie-level Grand Junction, but struggled at low Class A Asheville in his first full season in 2019.

SCOUTING REPORT: Lavigne possesses a beautiful lefthanded swing. It makes surprisingly little impact given his large, 6-foot-4 frame, but he has a chance to increasingly hit for power as he fills out. Lavigne has excellent strike zone discipline, giving him an intriguing combination of patience and power potential. The Rockies believe he'll be an impact hitter as he gains confidence and experience. Lavigne needs work defensively at first base. He's a good athlete for his size and has a strong work ethic, but his hands and footwork need a lot of improvement for him to become average.

THE FUTURE: The Rockies were pleased with the quality of the at-bats Lavigne took in instructional league. Given his inexperience, he needs a full season of at-bats in 2021 as much as anyone.

Year	Age	Club (League)	Class	AVG	G	AB	R	H	2B	3B	HR	RBI	BB	SO	SB	OBP	SLG
2019	19	Asheville (SAL)	LoA	.236	126	440	52	104	19	0	7	64	68	129	8	.347	.327
Minor League Totals				.272	185	646	97	176	32	2	13	102	113	169	20	.390	.389

13 DREW ROMO, C

BA GRADE **50** Risk: Extreme

Born: Aug. 29, 2001. **B-T:** B-R. **HT:** 6-1. **WT:** 205. **Drafted:** HS—The Woodlands, Texas, 2020 (1st round supplemental). **Signed by:** Jeff Edwards.

TRACK RECORD: Romo's reputation as an elite defensive catcher stretches back to his days as a high school freshman. Questions about his bat became amplified during his abbreviated senior year, but the Rockies still drafted him 35th overall and signed him for $2,095,800 to forgo a Louisiana State commitment.

SCOUTING REPORT: Romo is everything a team could want behind the plate. He's mature and shows advanced defensive ability with soft hands, excellent receiving and blocking skills and a plus, accurate arm. He loves to catch and doesn't want to take a day off. The switch-hitter has long faced offensive questions and took a step backward during his brief senior season with a slow, uphill swing that concerned many evaluators. But Romo impressed in a small sample at instructional league, showing a compact stroke with average raw power from both sides of the plate and a good grasp of the strike zone. The average major league catcher hit .229/.310/.385 in 2020 and Romo has a chance to attain that, especially with help from hitter-friendly Coors Field.

THE FUTURE: The track record of defense-first high school catchers is terrible, but the Rockies think Romo can buck the trend. His advanced defensive skills will buy time for his offense to develop.

Year	Age	Club (League)	Class	AVG	G	AB	R	H	2B	3B	HR	RBI	BB	SO	SB	OBP	SLG
2020	18	Did not play—No minor league season															

14 JAMESON HANNAH, OF

BA GRADE **45** Risk: High

Born: Aug. 10, 1997. **B-T:** L-L. **HT:** 5-9. **WT:** 185. **Drafted:** Dallas Baptist, 2018 (2nd round). **Signed by:** Chris Reilly (Athletics).

TRACK RECORD: Hannah has already been on the move a lot in his young career. Drafted by the Athletics 50th overall out of Dallas Baptist in 2018, he was traded to the Reds for Tanner Roark at the 2019 trade deadline. The Reds then shipped him to the Rockies with Robert Stephenson after the 2020 season in exchange for Jeff Hoffman and minor league righthander Case Williams.

SCOUTING REPORT: Hannah is an impressive athlete who does a lot of things well if nothing great. He has a good approach at the plate, doesn't give away at-bats and makes frequent contact with a line-drive stroke. Home run power isn't in the cards, but he has the strength to wear out the gaps and rack up extra-base hits using his plus speed. Hannah is a solid defender at all three outfield positions, although his fringy arm strength precludes him from playing right field on a regular basis.

THE FUTURE: Hannah's likely future is a reserve outfielder who puts together competitive at-bats and moves around to all three positions. If he can find a way to impact the ball more consistently, a future as a regular isn't out of reach.

Year	Age	Club (League)	Class	AVG	G	AB	R	H	2B	3B	HR	RBI	BB	SO	SB	OBP	SLG
2019	21	Daytona (FSL)	HiA	.224	18	67	6	15	3	1	0	6	9	16	2	.325	.299
	21	Stockton (CAL)	HiA	.283	92	375	48	106	25	3	2	31	29	88	6	.341	.381
Minor League Totals				.275	133	528	68	145	32	5	3	47	47	128	14	.340	.371

15 ADAEL AMADOR, SS

Born: April 11, 2003. **B-T:** R-R. **HT:** 5-11. **WT:** 180. **Signed:** Dominican Republic, 2019 Signed by: Rolando Fernandez/Martin Cabrera.

TRACK RECORD: Amador signed with the Rockies for $1.5 million in 2019, but the club is still waiting for its first look at him. What would have been his debut season was scuttled by the coronavirus pandemic, and a broken hamate bone in October held him out of competition in instructional league.

SCOUTING REPORT: Amador is more advanced than many international signees at his age and experience level. The switch-hitter has a clean swing from both sides of the plate, good plate discipline and he has a unique ability for his age to manage a swing to do damage and another swing to fend off strikeouts. He's grown a couple of inches since signing and has added strength and power, though average power remains his likely ceiling. Defensively, Amador shows the kind of good footwork and plus arm strength that could help him stick at shortstop, but where he ends up remains to be seen depending on how his body develops.

THE FUTURE: The Rockies are eager to get Amador on the field. He has the makings of a potential everyday player but is a long ways away.

Year	Age	Club (League)	Class	AVG	G	AB	R	H	2B	3B	HR	RBI	BB	SO	SB	OBP	SLG
2019	17	Did not play—Signed 2020 contract															

16 BEN BOWDEN, LHP

Born: Oct. 21, 1994. **B-T:** L-L. **HT:** 6-4. **WT:** 249. **Drafted:** Vanderbilt, 2016 (2nd round). **Signed by:** Scott Corman.

TRACK RECORD: After a successful college career at Vanderbilt, including winning a national title in 2014, Bowden pitched his way to the doorstep of the big leagues leading up to 2020. The shortened season, plus minor back and shoulder injuries, kept him from debuting, but he spent the year at the alternate training site and was a member of the Rockies' taxi squad for their last road trip.

SCOUTING REPORT: Bowden mainly relies on the two-pitch mix of his fastball and changeup. His fastball sits 92-94 mph and can reach as high as 97 mph. He pairs his heater with a plus changeup in the low 80s that he uses effectively against both righties and lefties. Bowden has a slider he can mix in, but it is decidedly his third pitch. Bowden is still working to be consistent with his fastball command and is sharpening his feel for how to best mix his pitches. He has consistently dominated lefthanded batters but has been hit-or-miss against righties.

THE FUTURE: Bowden appears ready to compete for a spot in the Rockies' bullpen in 2021. He should settle into a middle relief role.

Year	Age	Club (League)	Class	W	L	ERA	G	GS	IP	H	HR	BB	SO	BB/9	SO/9	WHIP	AVG
2019	24	Albuquerque (PCL)	AAA	1	3	5.88	22	0	26	29	4	17	37	5.9	12.8	1.77	.242
	24	Hartford (EL)	AA	0	0	1.05	26	0	26	8	1	7	42	2.5	14.7	0.58	.088
Minor League Totals				8	6	3.60	123	0	127	112	14	59	186	4.2	13.2	1.34	.232

17 KARL KAUFFMANN, RHP

Born: Aug. 15, 1997. **B-T:** R-R. **HT:** 6-2. **WT:** 200. **Drafted:** Michigan, 2019 (2nd round supplemental). **Signed by:** Ed Santa.

TRACK RECORD: Kauffmann enjoyed a successful career at Michigan and helped the Wolverines finish as runner-up at the 2019 College World Series. The Rockies drafted Kauffmann in the supplemental second round and elected to rest him after a long college season, so he has yet to pitch an official game after the coronavirus pandemic canceled the 2020 minor league season.

SCOUTING REPORT: Kauffmann has solid stuff and a reputation for being a dogged competitor. His sinking fastball that sits in the low 90s is his best offering, and he also has an above-average changeup that he varies well and an average slider. Full seasons of pro baseball are a different animal, but there is little doubt about Kauffmann's durability as a starting pitcher. He throws plenty of strikes with average control.

THE FUTURE: Kauffmann's durability, strike-throwing ability and competitiveness give him a good shot to be a solid back-of-the-rotation starter. He'll aim to make his pro debut in 2021.

Year	Age	Club (League)	Class	W	L	ERA	G	GS	IP	H	HR	BB	SO	BB/9	SO/9	WHIP	AVG
2019	21	Did not play															

18 SAM WEATHERLY, LHP

Born: May 28, 1999. **B-T:** L-L. **HT:** 6-4. **WT:** 205. **Drafted:** Clemson, 2020 (3rd round). **Signed by:** Jordan Czarniecki.

TRACK RECORD: Weatherly pitched exclusively out of the bullpen his first two seasons at Clemson and piled up strikeouts and walks in just about equal measure. He found his stride as a starter in 2020 before the season shut down, leading the Rockies to draft him in the third round and sign him for $755,300.

SCOUTING REPORT: Stuff is not a question with Weatherly. He throws his fastball 92-96 mph from the left side with a plus slider. He also has a changeup in his repertoire, but it's a clear third pitch. The question with Weatherly is consistency of those pitches, and to put more of a fine point on it, whether he can command them well enough to continue as a starter. Weatherly is an intellectual pitcher who understands the craft, but his control is well below-average and will need lots of work.

THE FUTURE: The Rockies are committed to having Weatherly debut as a starter. His electric stuff should make him an effective short reliever if he fails to stick in the rotation.

Year	Age	Club (League)	Class	W	L	ERA	G	GS	IP	H	HR	BB	SO	BB/9	SO/9	WHIP	AVG
2020	21	Did not play—No minor league season															

19 EDDY DIAZ, SS

Born: Feb. 14, 2000. **B-T:** R-R. **HT:** 6-0. **WT:** 175. **Signed:** Cuba, 2017. **Signed by:** Rolando Fernandez/Orlando Medina.

TRACK RECORD: Diaz signed with the Rockies for $750,000 in 2017 as the club's first-ever Cuban signee. After two solid seasons in the Dominican Summer League, he went to Rookie-level Grand Junction in 2019 and continued to hit until a knee injury cost him the final month of the season.

SCOUTING REPORT: A proven fastball hitter, Diaz has work to do against good breaking balls. The one unsightly stat at Grand Junction compared to his previous seasons in the DSL was the jump in his strikeout rate, although it still wasn't alarming. Diaz is a contact hitter and doesn't have a home run in his career yet, but the Rockies believe he has some gap power that will fit with his middle infield profile. His plus speed makes him a weapon on the bases. The Rockies plan to play Diaz all around the infield. He has the athleticism to stay up the middle, even if that ends up meaning second base.

THE FUTURE: Diaz is a developing table-setter who can also provide defensive versatility. He's a better in-game player than he is a practice or showcase player, and that bodes well for his ability to compete as he moves up.

Year	Age	Club (League)	Class	AVG	G	AB	R	H	2B	3B	HR	RBI	BB	SO	SB	OBP	SLG
2019	19	Grand Junction (PIO)	R	.331	39	166	32	55	12	3	0	10	8	33	20	.366	.440
Minor League Totals				.317	126	479	111	152	32	12	0	44	58	71	104	.397	.434

20 RYAN FELTNER, RHP

BREAKOUT
BA GRADE
45 Risk: High

Born: Sep. 2, 1996. **B-T:** R-R. **HT:** 6-4. **WT:** 190. **Drafted:** Ohio State, 2018 (4th round). **Signed by:** Ed Santa.

TRACK RECORD: Feltner had an up-and-down career at Ohio State that featured more stuff than polish, but the Rockies took a chance and drafted him in the fourth round in 2018. He showed well after signing but struggled to a 5.07 ERA in his first full season at low Class A Asheville. Feltner returned to the mound in 2020 in instructional league and dominated, putting wind in his sails heading into 2021.

SCOUTING REPORT: Feltner has power stuff with a fastball that ranges from 94-97 mph and averaged 95 mph during instructs. His above-average changeup is his best secondary offering and he made strides with the slider to make it a potentially average pitch. The Rockies lauded the way Feltner used the pandemic-induced layoff to get better in a remote setting. They were particularly pleased with how well he pounded the strike zone in the fall after below-average control had been a concern in the past.

THE FUTURE: Feltner has the durability and three-pitch mix to be a starting pitcher. It all comes down to how well he can maintain his control improvements over the course of a full season.

Year	Age	Club (League)	Class	W	L	ERA	G	GS	IP	H	HR	BB	SO	BB/9	SO/9	WHIP	AVG
2019	22	Asheville (SAL)	LoA	9	9	5.07	25	25	119	137	12	46	116	3.5	8.8	1.54	.265
Minor League Totals				9	9	4.21	34	34	149	153	13	50	155	3.0	9.3	1.36	.267

21 TOMMY DOYLE, RHP

BA GRADE 45 Risk: High

Born: May 1, 1996. **B-T:** R-R. **HT:** 6-6. **WT:** 244. **Drafted:** Virginia, 2017 (2nd round supplemental). **Signed by:** Jordan Czarniecki.

TRACK RECORD: Doyle found his stride as a closer at Virginia and continued to shine in that role as a professional, saving a combined 37 games in his first two seasons at the Class A levels. Doyle pitched well at the alternate training site in 2020 and was fast-tracked to the majors, but he struggled with the jump and allowed six hits and six runs in 2.1 innings over three appearances.

SCOUTING REPORT: Doyle boasts an excellent one-two punch in a 95-97 mph fastball and a wipeout slider that is the best in the Rockies system. He also has a changeup, but it's a below-average pitch and is very much a work in progress. The development of that third pitch, whether a changeup or something else, could be the key to Doyle becoming a truly dominant reliever. He keeps his high-octane stuff in the strike zone with average control.

THE FUTURE: The Rockies compare Doyle to Scott Oberg in terms of stuff and the fact neither had the smoothest introduction to the major leagues. He is likely to start 2021 back in the minors but should be back in the majors at some point.

Year	Age	Club (League)	Class	W	L	ERA	G	GS	IP	H	HR	BB	SO	BB/9	SO/9	WHIP	AVG
2020	24	Colorado (NL)	MAJ	0	0	23.14	3	0	2	6	0	4	2	15.4	7.7	4.29	.462
Major League Totals				0	0	23.14	3	0	2	6	0	4	2	15.4	7.7	4.29	.462
Minor League Totals				12	12	3.12	110	0	115	105	8	35	132	2.7	10.3	1.21	.236

22 GAVIN HOLLOWELL, RHP

BREAKOUT

BA GRADE 45 Risk: High

Born: Nov. 4, 1997. **B-T:** R-R. **HT:** 6-7. **WT:** 215. **Drafted:** St. John's, 2019 (6th round). **Signed by:** Mike Garlatti.

TRACK RECORD: Hollowell spent three years anchoring St. John's bullpen and was selected in the sixth round in 2019 after a somewhat disappointing junior season. He bounced back once he arrived in pro ball and dominated the Rookie-level Pioneer League as Grand Junction's closer, notching seven saves in eight tries and with 30 strikeouts and five walks in 18.2 innings.

SCOUTING REPORT: Hollowell has the classic fastball/slider combination common in the best bullpen arms in the game. His fastball sits at 95 mph and can reach the high 90s and his slider is a plus offering in its own right. The Rockies worked with Hollowell on standing tall in his delivery, which has allowed him to get more out of his 6-foot-7 frame and throw downhill. Hollowell was a bit old for the Pioneer League in 2019, but the Rockies feel that his dominance was real.

THE FUTURE: Hollowell's two plus pitches and mentality to pitch at the end of games give him a chance to emerge as a high-leverage reliever. He'll move to full-season ball in 2021.

Year	Age	Club (League)	Class	W	L	ERA	G	GS	IP	H	HR	BB	SO	BB/9	SO/9	WHIP	AVG
2019	21	Grand Junction (PIO)	R	3	0	2.89	17	0	19	14	2	5	30	2.4	14.5	1.02	.182
Minor League Totals				3	0	2.89	17	0	18	14	2	5	30	2.4	14.5	1.02	.200

23 JULIO CARRERAS, 3B/SS

BA GRADE 45 Risk: Extreme

Born: Jan. 12, 2000. **B-T:** R-R. **HT:** 6-2. **WT:** 190. **Signed:** Dominican Republic, 2018. **Signed by:** Rolando Fernandez/Frank Roa.

TRACK RECORD: Carreras signed for just $15,000 in the Rockies' 2018 international signing class, but he quickly proved a bargain. He hit well in his pro debut in the Dominican Summer League and followed up with another strong showing stateside in 2019, batting .294/.369/.466 at Rookie-level Grand Junction.

SCOUTING REPORT: With a projectable body and leverage in his swing, Carreras projects for 20-home run power and could grow into more as he continues to fill out and get stronger. He has some length in his swing that leads to concerns about whiffs against better competition, but so far it hasn't been a problem. Carreras is a great athlete with good actions and plus arm strength in the infield. He's primarily a third baseman and projects to stay there, but he has the defensive skills to play second base or even shortstop in a pinch. The Rockies are working on letting his natural athleticism show in the field rather than him trying to force quicker actions.

THE FUTURE: Carreras is set to begin the 2021 season at low Class A. How his bat plays in his first taste of full-season ball will be telling.

Year	Age	Club (League)	Class	AVG	G	AB	R	H	2B	3B	HR	RBI	BB	SO	SB	OBP	SLG
2019	19	Grand Junction (PIO)	R	.294	67	262	51	77	14	8	5	38	25	63	14	.369	.466
Minor League Totals				.292	135	490	109	143	25	15	11	69	56	109	30	.383	.471

24 EZEQUIEL TOVAR, SS

BA GRADE 45 **Risk:** Extreme

Born: Aug. 1, 2001. **B-T:** R-R. **HT:** 6-0. **WT:** 162. **Signed:** Venezuela, 2017. **Signed by:** Rolando Fernandez/Orlando Medina.

TRACK RECORD: The top signing in the Rockies' 2018 international signing class, Tovar increased his strength upon turning pro and has excelled despite continually being among the youngest players in each league. In fact, the Rockies had to initially send him to short-season Boise in 2019 rather than Rookie-level Grand Junction in 2019 due to Colorado-specific labor laws that made him unable to play in the state as a 17-year-old. He returned to the field in 2020 for instructional league.

SCOUTING REPORT: Tovar is the best defensive infielder in the Rockies system. The club believes he could not only be a major league shortstop right now, but that he will contend for Gold Gloves down the road. He has great actions, plus speed and range and plus arm strength that make him a good fit at shortstop. Originally a switch hitter, Tovar now hits exclusively from the right side, which the club thinks will help give him a chance to be an average hitter. He has put on 10-15 pounds since last year, but it remains to be seen if that will translate into additional power.

THE FUTURE: Tovar is a good enough defender to be a difference-maker. How high he climbs will depend on how his bat comes along.

Year	Age	Club (League)	Class	AVG	G	AB	R	H	2B	3B	HR	RBI	BB	SO	SB	OBP	SLG
2019	17	Boise (NWL)	SS	.249	55	217	22	54	4	2	2	13	16	52	13	.304	.313
	17	Grand Junction (PIO)	R	.264	18	72	12	19	2	2	0	3	10	17	4	.357	.347
Minor League Totals				.255	108	419	63	107	10	8	2	28	48	102	33	.335	.332

25 YANQUIEL FERNANDEZ, OF

BA GRADE 45 **Risk:** Extreme

Born: Jan. 1, 2003. **B-T:** L-L. **HT:** 6-2. **WT:** 200. **Signed:** Cuba, 2019. **Signed by:** Rolando Fernandez/Marc Russo/Raul Gomez.

TRACK RECORD: Fernandez signed with the Rockies for $295,000 in 2019, making him a key piece of the international signing class that also included Adael Amador. He was considered to be one of the best lefthanded power bats available in the class but did not get a chance to make his pro debut in 2020 due to the coronavirus pandemic.

SCOUTING REPORT: Fernandez cuts an imposing figure in the batter's box even at just 17 years old. He has plus power and is to project as a middle-of-the-order bat if everything goes well. The Rockies only expect him to get stronger and potentially tick up another power grade. While he's certainly a power hitter first, he uses his hands well, controls the strike zone and has a chance to be an average hitter. Fernandez has a strong arm in the outfield but a lack of foot speed may limit him to a corner and a below-average defender.

THE FUTURE: Fernandez is a long way from the big leagues, but his big power could lead him to make a splash in his debut in 2021.

Year	Age	Club (League)	Class	AVG	G	AB	R	H	2B	3B	HR	RBI	BB	SO	SB	OBP	SLG
2019	16	Did not play—Signed 2020 contract															

26 YOAN AYBAR, LHP

BA GRADE 40 **Risk:** High

Born: July 3, 1997. **B-T:** L-L. **HT:** 6-2. **WT:** 210. **Signed:** Dominican Republic, 2013. **Signed by:** Jonathan Cruz/Eddie Romero (Red Sox).

TRACK RECORD: Aybar spent four seasons in the Red Sox system as an outfielder but didn't show enough plate discipline or the ability to translate raw power into in-game power. He converted to pitching and has moved steadily, ending the 2019 season at high Class A. The Rockies acquired him after the 2020 season in a trade for infielder Christian Koss and immediately placed him on their 40-man roster.

SCOUTING REPORT: Aybar has electric pure stuff that could allow him to have a role in a big league bullpen. His fastball sits in the mid 90s and has reached 99 mph. He also employs a slider/cutter hybrid he's comfortable using as a putaway offering. It's the finer points, such as incorporating more deception into his delivery, moving the ball around and improving command that still need work, but that's understandable given how raw he is as a pitcher. His control is below-average and needs work.

THE FUTURE: Aybar is in a position to debut in Denver at some point, but in order to get there he will need to cut down on his walks.

Year	Age	Club (League)	Class	W	L	ERA	G	GS	IP	H	HR	BB	SO	BB/9	SO/9	WHIP	AVG
2019	21	Salem (CAR)	HiA	0	0	1.80	4	0	5	2	0	1	3	1.8	5.4	0.60	.111
	21	Greenville (SAL)	LoA	1	3	4.88	40	0	52	34	1	40	67	7.0	11.7	1.43	.145
Minor League Totals				3	4	4.45	61	0	85	61	1	55	97	5.8	10.3	1.36	.196

27 WILL ETHRIDGE, RHP

BA GRADE 40 Risk: High

Born: Dec. 20, 1997. **B-T:** R-R. **HT:** 6-5. **WT:** 240. **Drafted:** Mississippi, 2019 (5th round). **Signed by:** Zach Zulli.

TRACK RECORD: After serving as a reliever for Mississippi for two years, Ethridge jumped into the rotation for the 2019 season and excelled, pushing him up draft boards. The Rockies drafted him in the fifth round and sent him to short-season Boise, where he posted a 3.82 ERA in nine starts.

SCOUTING REPORT: At 6-foot-5 and 240 pounds, Ethridge looks the part of a traditional rotation workhorse, and the Rockies are looking for him to become one. He doesn't have standout stuff and that limits his ceiling, but has a solid, well-rounded pitch mix that includes a fastball that sits in the low-90s, and an average slider and changeup that can both generate swings and misses. The Rockies see particular upside in further refining his slider. Etheridge locates everything well with average control, understands how to mix his pitches and is always in attack mode on the mound.

THE FUTURE: Moving to full-season ball in 2021 will be a good chance for Ethridge to prove his durability as a starter. He projects as a potential back-of-the-rotation or depth arm.

Year	Age	Club (League)	Class	W	L	ERA	G	GS	IP	H	HR	BB	SO	BB/9	SO/9	WHIP	AVG
2019	21	Boise (NWL)	SS	0	2	3.82	9	9	31	29	1	6	21	1.8	6.2	1.14	.230
Minor League Totals				0	2	3.82	9	9	30	29	1	6	21	1.8	6.2	1.14	.250

28 YONATHAN DAZA, OF

BA GRADE 40 Risk: High

Born: Feb. 28, 1994. **B-T:** R-R. **HT:** 6-2. **WT:** 207. **Signed:** Venezuela, 2010. **Signed by:** Rolando Fernandez/Carlos Gonzalez/Orlando Medina.

TRACK RECORD: Daza put together an impressive track record as a hitter in the minor leagues with a career .318 average, but that didn't translate to success in his first taste of the big leagues in 2019. His reputation as a plus defender, however, is still intact.

SCOUTING REPORT: Daza is the best defensive outfielder prospect in the Rockies farm system. His plus speed makes him a fit for center field and his borderline plus-plus arm is the best among any outfielder in the organization. Offensively, a flat swing that produces line drives and grounders means he doesn't project to add much power, but the Rockies see that as a feature rather than a bug. Daza focuses on being a hitter with a high contact rate and on-base skills.

THE FUTURE: The Rockies see Daza as a fully-formed player. He's a great fit as an extra outfielder and will remain in that role barring a late-career surprise.

Year	Age	Club (League)	Class	AVG	G	AB	R	H	2B	3B	HR	RBI	BB	SO	SB	OBP	SLG
2019	25	Colorado (NL)	MAJ	.206	44	97	7	20	1	1	0	3	7	21	1	.257	.237
	25	Albuquerque (PCL)	AAA	.364	89	387	67	141	30	4	11	48	25	52	12	.404	.548
Major League Totals				.206	44	97	7	20	1	1	0	3	7	21	1	.257	.237
Minor League Totals				.318	683	2624	401	834	170	28	30	365	133	378	96	.359	.438

29 BLADIMIR RESTITUYO, 2B/OF

BA GRADE 45 Risk: Extreme

Born: July 2, 2001. **B-T:** R-R. **HT:** 5-10. **WT:** 151. **Signed:** Dominican Republic, 2017. **Signed by:** Rolando Fernandez/Frank Roa.

TRACK RECORD: Restituyo signed with the Rockies for $200,000 on his 16th birthday in 2017. After two seasons in the Dominican Summer League, he debuted stateside in 2019 and held his own as an 18-year-old in the college-heavy Northwest League.

SCOUTING REPORT: Restituyo's standout tool is his plus speed, which will give him a chance to develop into a center fielder over time as he learns the finer points of the position. He has quick hands and good hand-eye coordination, which bodes well for his projection as an average hitter. A projectable body also suggests he could add more power, which is presently below-average. The one glaring weakness in Restituyo's offensive skill set is that he rarely walks. He'll have to figure out that part of his game to truly reach his potential. Given his youth, he has time to do just that.

THE FUTURE: Restituyo has the makings of a table-setter type in the lineup, but he'll need to walk more to fill that role. His speed and defensive versatility give him some potential as a utilityman.

Year	Age	Club (League)	Class	AVG	G	AB	R	H	2B	3B	HR	RBI	BB	SO	SB	OBP	SLG
2019	17	Boise (NWL)	SS	.259	55	228	28	59	13	0	4	25	2	56	16	.266	.368
	17	Grand Junction (PIO)	R	.310	20	84	13	26	4	2	2	14	2	13	6	.326	.476
Minor League Totals				.284	135	549	84	156	28	9	10	72	13	120	38	.307	.423

30 NIKO DECOLATI, OF

BA GRADE 40 **Risk:** Very High

Born: Aug. 12, 1997. **B-T:** R-R. **HT:** 6-1. **WT:** 215. **Drafted:** Loyola Marymount, 2018 (6th round). **Signed by:** Matt Hattabaugh.

TRACK RECORD: Decolati pressed in his draft season at Loyola Marymount and fell to the sixth round as a result, but his loud tools showed in an impressive 2018 debut at Rookie-level Grand Junction. He missed the start of the 2019 season with a broken right wrist and never got going once he took the field for low Class A Asheville, batting .264/.334/.399 while his strikeout rate increased and his walk rate decreased.

SCOUTING REPORT: After playing third base and shortstop in college, Decolati moved to the outfield in pro ball and took to it well. He has enough arm for right field and has surprised some with how well he's played center field, where his plus speed is an asset. Offensively he has a tendency to chase pitches out of the zone, but when he gets pitches he can drive, he shows impressive raw power. The Rockies like the chances that he puts it all together because of his drive and will to improve.

THE FUTURE: Decolati is a plus all-around athlete, albeit one with some rough edges right now. He'll be tested at high Class A in 2021.

Year	Age	Club (League)	Class	AVG	G	AB	R	H	2B	3B	HR	RBI	BB	SO	SB	OBP	SLG
2019	21	Asheville (SAL)	LoA	.265	77	291	42	77	13	4	6	38	13	80	15	.334	.399
Minor League Totals				.294	146	554	97	163	28	7	17	94	47	136	32	.373	.462

MORE PROSPECTS TO KNOW

31 JIMMY HERRON, OF

Herron uses a compact swing to hit line drives, and while he won't leave the yard too often, he has the speed to get extra bases by running out doubles and triples.

32 RILEY PINT, RHP

Control issues have knocked Pint from his perch among the Rockies' top prospects, but his electric raw stuff gives him a chance to rise in a bullpen role. Pint was the fourth overall pick in the 2016 draft.

33 ANTONIO SANTOS, RHP

Santos got hit around in his big league debut in 2020, but he has excellent control and can fill in as either a spot starter or depth bullpen option.

34 REAGAN TODD, LHP

SLEEPER

Todd is 25 years old, but he dominated at two stops in the system in 2019 and impressed in instructional league. His fastball sits 95-96 mph and he has a quality breaking ball to match.

35 EVER MOYA, LHP

Moya showed well in his stateside debut in 2019 after a conversion to the bullpen full time. The physical 6-foot-5, 220-pound lefthander works with a fastball in the mid 90s.

36 DANIEL MONTAÑO, OF

A $2 million signee out of Venezuela in 2015, Montaño has the speed for center field and the arm for right field, but has yet to show he can hit.

37 P.J. POULIN, LHP

Poulin has excelled in late relief with a 2.63 ERA and 20 saves in 82 career professional innings. He works from a low slot with a low-90s fastball and a slider.

38 LUCAS GILBREATH, LHP

Gilbreath's outlook has changed after a move to the bullpen. His velocity jumped from the low 90s to the high 90s, leading the Rockies to add him to their 40-man roster.

39 WILLIE MACIVER, C

MacIver is a good athlete behind the plate with a good arm, but he's lacking as a hitter. The lack of catching depth in the Rockies' system will give him a chance to rise.

40 BRET BOSWELL, 2B

Boswell has steadily climbed through the system and reached Double-A Hartford in 2019. He possesses good power for a middle infielder and has more than enough range and arm to be a solid second baseman.

TOP PROSPECTS OF THE DECADE

Year	Player, Pos	2020 Org
2011	Tyler Matzek, LHP	Braves
2012	Drew Pomeranz, LHP	Padres
2013	Nolan Arenado, 3B	Rockies
2014	Jon Gray, RHP	Rockies
2015	David Dahl, OF	Rockies
2016	Jon Gray, RHP	Rockies
2017	Brendan Rodgers, SS	Rockies
2018	Brendan Rodgers, SS	Rockies
2019	Brendan Rodgers, SS/2B	Rockies
2020	Brendan Rodgers, SS/2B	Rockies

TOP DRAFT PICKS OF THE DECADE

Year	Player, Pos	2020 Org
2011	Tyler Anderson, LHP	Giants
2012	David Dahl, OF	Rockies
2013	Jon Gray, RHP	Rockies
2014	Kyle Freeland, LHP	Rockies
2015	Brendan Rodgers, SS	Rockies
2016	Riley Pint, RHP	Rockies
2017	Ryan Vilade, 3B (2nd round)	Rockies
2018	Ryan Rolison, LHP	Rockies
2019	Michael Toglia, 1B	Rockies
2020	Zac Veen, OF	Rockies

DEPTH CHART

COLORADO ROCKIES

TOP 2021 ROOKIES	RANK
Brendan Rodgers, SS	1
BREAKOUT PROSPECTS	**RANK**
Ryan Feltner, RHP	20
Gavin Hollowell, RHP	22

SOURCE OF TOP 30 TALENT

Homegrown	28	Acquired	2
College	13	Trade	2
Junior college	0	Rule 5 draft	0
High school	7	Independent league	0
Nondrafted free agent	0	Free agent/waivers	0
International	8		

LF
Ryan Vilade (9)
Yanquiel Fernandez (25)
Casey Golden

CF
Brenton Doyle (8)
Jameson Hannah (14)
Yonathan Daza (28)

RF
Zac Veen (2)
Niko Decolati (30)
Jimmy Herron
Mylz Jones

3B
Aaron Schunk (5)
Colton Welker (7)
Julio Carreras (23)

SS
Adael Amador (15)
Eddy Diaz (19)
Ezequiel Tovar (24)
Jack Blomgren
Alan Trejo

2B
Brendan Rodgers (1)
Bladimir Restituyo (29)
Bret Boswell

1B
Michael Toglia (4)
Grant Lavigne (12)

C
Drew Romo (13)
Willie MacIver
Dom Nunez
Max George

LHP

LHSP	LHRP
Ryan Rolison (3)	Ben Bowden (16)
Helcris Olivarez (10)	Yoan Aybar (26)
Sam Weatherly (18)	Reagan Todd
	Ever Moya
	PJ Poulin
	Lucas Gilbreath

RHP

RHSP	RHRP
Chris McMahon (7)	Tommy Doyle (21)
Ryan Castellani (11)	Gavin Hollowell (22)
Karl Kauffman (17)	Riley Pint
Ryan Feltner (20)	Jordan Sheffield
Will Ethridge (27)	Justin Lawrence
Antonio Santos	
Juan Mejia	
Shelby Lackey	
Garrett Schilling	
Will Gaddis	

Detroit Tigers

BY EMILY WALDON

On the heels of a dismal 114-loss season in 2019, the Tigers' front office looked slightly different leading into 2020. The revisions came through the organization's desire to move a focus on analytics, sports science and player development to the forefront.

Among the changes, former quality control coach Joe Vavra received a promotion to hitting coach, opening the quality control position for Josh Paul, who spent the previous three seasons as the Angels' bench coach. In player development, the Tigers hired Kenny Graham as their new farm director, replacing Dave Owen, who transitioned to minor league field coordinator. Graham had spent the previous four seasons as the Brewers' hitting coordinator.

The Tigers' hope in adding Graham was to place a greater focus on the development of their hitting prospects. In addition to revising the existing positions, the Tigers created two new roles in player development.

Dr. Georgia Giblin was no stranger to working with the Tigers via a prior performance science partnership between Detroit and the University of Michigan. Her knowledge of the organization and the direction the Tigers are hoping to go led to her selection as director of performance science.

Dan Hubbs, who spent 12 seasons as the pitching coach at California and served as the head coach at Southern California from 2013 to 2019 was selected to leverage data as a tool for cultivating higher-level performance throughout the organization. The Tigers hired him as director of pitching development and strategies.

With these key additions to the staff in place, the Tigers' were ready to go. But then the coronavirus pandemic happened.

The 2020 minor league season was canceled and an entire crop of prospects lost most, if not all, of their chances at development.

With a condensed 60-game season in the majors, the Tigers were forced to expedite the debuts of multiple minor leaguers in order to bolster their roster for the unorthodox season. The results were ugly. The team finished 23-35 and lost 19 of their final 25 games.

Casey Mize, Tarik Skubal, Isaac Paredes, and Daz Cameron were among many who would have normally had more time in the minors before their major league debuts. None fared particularly well, showing how much the lost chance at more development in the minors negatively affected their preparedness for the majors.

In the condensed five-round draft in 2020, the Tigers, for the second time in the last three years, had the No. 1 overall pick. The draft provided an opportunity for Detroit to buttress its pitching-heavy system with a dose of high-upside hitters. Focused on strengthening that position depth, the Tigers selected Arizona State slugger Spencer Torkelson at No. 1 overall followed by five additional position players.

With a more balanced system, an overhauled front office and some of their top prospects getting their first taste of the majors, the Tigers are moving closer to a return to relevancy.

When manager Ron Gardenhire retired in the final weeks of the season, the Tigers moved quickly to hire former Astros manager A.J. Hinch as his replacement. Hinch was suspended all of 2020 as punishment for his role in Houston's sign-stealing scandal, but the Tigers will now entrust him to lead the team out of the rebuild and into contention, just as he did the Astros. ■

MARK CUNNINGHAM/MLB PHOTOS VIA GETTY IMAGES

Rookie shortstop Willi Castro provided an unexpected spark to an improving lineup core.

PROJECTED 2024 LINEUP

Position	Player	Age
Catcher	Dillon Dingler	25
First Base	Spencer Torkelson	24
Second Base	Niko Goodrum	32
Third Base	Isaac Paredes	25
Shortstop	Willi Castro	27
Left Field	Daz Cameron	27
Center Field	Victor Reyes	29
Right Field	Riley Greene	23
Designated Hitter	Jeimer Candelario	30
No. 1 Starter	Tarik Skubal	27
No. 2 Starter	Casey Mize	27
No. 3 Starter	Matt Manning	26
No. 4 Starter	Spencer Turnbull	31
No. 5 Starter	Alex Faedo	28
Closer	Gregory Soto	29

1 SPENCER TORKELSON, RHP

Born: Aug. 26, 1999. **B-T:** R-R. **HT:** 6-1. **WT:** 220.
Drafted: Arizona State, 2020 (1st round).
Signed by: Joey Lothrop.

MARK CUNNINGHAM/MLB PHOTOS VIA GETTY IMAGES

TRACK RECORD: Torkelson was a jack-of-all trades at Casa Grande High in Petaluma, Calif., playing football and basketball in addition to baseball and spending time as both a pitcher and position player on the diamond. He ranked No. 436 on Baseball America's draft rankings, but went undrafted out of high school, a decision teams quickly came to regret. As a freshman at Arizona State, Torkelson led the nation with 25 home runs and smashed Barry Bonds' school freshman home run record. He followed up by batting .351/.446/.707 with 23 home runs as a sophomore and entered his junior season on the verge of breaking the Sun Devils' career home run record and entering the national top 10. Torkelson drew 31 walks in 17 games in 2020 as opponents gave him the Bonds treatment and simply pitched around him, but he still managed to hit six home runs in limited action before the season was shut down because of the coronavirus pandemic. The Tigers decided he was their pick early in the process and wasted no time selecting him No. 1 overall, signing him for a draft record $8.146 million bonus. The only surprise was that they announced Torkelson as a third baseman, despite the fact he spent nearly his entire career playing first base in college.

SCOUTING REPORT: Torkelson's power is enormous, but he's far from an all-or-nothing slugger. A strong, physical righthanded hitter, Torkelson has plus bat speed and manages the strike zone with ease. His advanced barrel control and hand-eye coordination are complemented by exceptional timing. He hits all types of pitches, draws walks and makes balls disappear with his 80-grade power. In short, he projects to be a game-changing offensive force in the middle of a lineup. Torkelson has occasionally struggled against low breaking balls, but scouts don't cite it as common enough to be labeled as a red flag. Even with that minor concern, evaluators project Torkelson to hit .280 with 40-plus homers on the high end and .260 with 30-plus home runs on the low end. Torkelson is a good athlete for his size, but despite being drafted as a third baseman, his long-term position is likely first base. He is an above-average defender there with an average arm, solid athleticism and footwork and fringe-average speed. Some evaluators believe he could play left field if necessary, though it would take time for him to learn the position. No matter what position he plays, Torkelson's boundless offensive gifts will help him fit the profile.

BA GRADE	SCOUTING GRADES
70 Risk: High	**Hit:** 60. **Power:** 80. **Run:** 45. **Field:** 55. **Arm:** 50.

Projected future grades on 20-80 scouting scale.

BEST TOOLS

Best Hitter for Average	Spencer Torkelson
Best Power Hitter	Spencer Torkelson
Best Strike-Zone Discipline	Spencer Torkelson
Fastest Baserunner	Parker Meadows
Best Athlete	Parker Meadows
Best Fastball	Jason Foley
Best Curveball	Keider Montero
Best Slider	Alex Faedo
Best Changeup	Casey Mize
Best Control	Paul Richan
Best Defensive Catcher	Jake Rogers
Best Defensive Infielder	Cole Peterson
Best Infield Arm	Sergio Alcantara
Best Defensive Outfielder	Derek Hill
Best Outfield Arm	Riley Greene

THE FUTURE: Torkelson joined the Tigers' alternate training site group after signing and continued play during instructional league in Lakeland, Fla. Once regular season play resumes, expect the Tigers to challenge Torkelson with an aggressive path to the big leagues. He draws frequent comparisons with Paul Konerko as a potential all-star and face of the franchise. If Torkelson follows the aggressive development path of college stars such as Mark Teixeira, Kris Bryant or Anthony Rendon, he could be ready for a full-time job in 2022. ■

Year	Age	Club (League)	Class	AVG	G	AB	R	H	2B	3B	HR	RBI	BB	SO	SB	OBP	SLG
2020	20	Did not play—No minor league season															

2 TARIK SKUBAL, LHP

TOP ROOKIE

TONY FIRRIOLO/MLB PHOTOS VIA GETTY IMAGES

BA GRADE
60 Risk: Medium

Born: Nov. 20, 1996. **B-T:** L-L. **HT:** 6-3. **WT:** 215. **Drafted:** Seattle, 2018 (9th round). **Signed by:** Dave Dangler.

TRACK RECORD: Skubal missed the 2017 season at Seattle University recovering from Tommy John surgery but pitched well enough in his return for the Tigers to draft him in the ninth round in 2018. He vaulted into top prospect conversations following a jaw-dropping stint with Double-A Erie that concluded with a 2.13 ERA and 17.4 strikeouts per nine innings. He made his major league debut on Aug. 18 and made eight appearances.

SCOUTING REPORT: Skubal's biggest selling point is his 94-98 mph fastball with late life. It's an overpowering pitch he can locate to both sides of the plate, though his command was scattered in his debut. Skubal's secondaries are still developing. He flashes a plus slider and an above-average curveball, and he should be able to land them in the strike zone more often as he develops confidence in them. His changeup boasts plus movement and is effective when mixed properly, but it still lacks consistency compared to the rest of his arsenal. Skubal uses his 6-foot-3 frame to create a natural downhill attack against hitters and stays in and around the strike zone.

THE FUTURE: Skubal's debut showed that his command and secondaries still need work. His arsenal still gives him the ceiling of at least a mid-rotation starter.

SCOUTING GRADES: **Fastball:** 60 **Slider:** 60 **Curveball:** 55 **Changeup:** 50 **Control:** 55

Year	Age	Club (League)	Class	W	L	ERA	G	GS	IP	H	HR	BB	SO	BB/9	SO/9	WHIP	AVG
2018	21	Connecticut (NYP)	SS	0	0	0.75	4	0	12	8	0	2	17	1.5	12.8	0.83	.186
	21	West Michigan (MWL)	LoA	2	0	0.00	3	0	7	5	0	1	11	1.2	13.5	0.82	.192
	21	Tigers West (GCL)	R	1	0	0.00	2	1	3	2	0	1	5	3.0	15.0	1.00	.154
2019	22	Erie (EL)	AA	2	3	2.13	9	9	42	25	2	18	82	3.8	17.4	1.02	.147
	22	Lakeland (FSL)	HiA	4	5	2.58	15	15	80	62	5	19	97	2.1	10.9	1.01	.194
2020	23	Detroit (AL)	MAJ	1	4	5.63	8	7	32	28	9	11	37	3.1	10.4	1.22	.235
Major League Totals				1	4	5.63	8	7	32	28	9	11	37	3.1	10.4	1.22	.235
Minor League Totals				9	8	2.11	33	25	145	102	7	41	212	2.5	13.2	0.99	.195

3 CASEY MIZE, RHP

TONY FIRRIOLO/MLB PHOTOS VIA GETTY IMAGES

Born: May 1, 1997. **B-T:** R-R. **HT:** 6-3. **WT:** 220. **Drafted:** Auburn, 2018 (1st round). **Signed by:** Justin Henry.

TRACK RECORD: Mize established himself as the nation's best pitcher at Auburn and was the easy choice for the Tigers to take with the No. 1 overall pick in 2018. He raced to Double-A in his first full season, twirling a no-hitter in his Erie debut, but he went on the injured list with shoulder soreness late in the season and showed noticeably diminished stuff when he returned. Mize began the 2020 season at the alternate training site and made his major league debut on Aug. 19 but struggled to an 0-3, 6.99 mark in seven starts.

SCOUTING REPORT: Mize looks the part of a frontline starter with three power pitches out of a physical, 6-foot-3 frame. His fastball sits 93-96 mph and gets swings and misses in the strike zone when his command is on. His best pitch is his diving splitter in the mid 80s with late drop away from hitters on both sides of the plate. His third potential plus pitch is an upper-80s breaking ball he shapes between a cutter and a true slider. He also throws a low-80s curveball that lags behind his other offerings. Mize struggled with his fastball command and general control in his debut, which sapped the effectiveness of his splitter. He's been seen a plus strike-thrower throughout his career.

THE FUTURE: Mize's debut wasn't pretty, and he will have to improve his command to bounce back in 2021. His track record and arsenal give Tigers officials confidence he's still a potential frontline starter.

SCOUTING GRADES: **Fastball:** 60 **Splitter:** 70 **Slider:** 60 **Curveball:** 50 **Control:** 55

Year	Age	Club (League)	Class	W	L	ERA	G	GS	IP	H	HR	BB	SO	BB/9	SO/9	WHIP	AVG
2018	21	Lakeland (FSL)	HiA	0	1	4.63	4	4	12	13	2	2	10	1.5	7.7	1.29	.271
	21	Tigers West (GCL)	R	0	0	0.00	1	1	2	0	0	1	4	4.5	18.0	0.50	.000
2019	22	Erie (EL)	AA	6	3	3.20	15	15	79	69	5	18	76	2.1	8.7	1.11	.214
	22	Lakeland (FSL)	HiA	2	0	0.88	6	6	31	11	0	5	30	1.5	8.8	0.52	.103
2020	23	Detroit (AL)	MAJ	0	3	6.99	7	7	28	29	7	13	26	4.1	8.3	1.48	.252
Major League Totals				0	3	6.99	7	7	28	29	7	13	26	4.1	8.3	1.48	.252
Minor League Totals				8	4	2.71	26	26	123	93	7	26	120	1.9	8.8	0.97	.209

4 MATT MANNING, RHP

TONY FIRRIOLO/MLB PHOTOS VIA GETTY IMAGES

Born: Jan. 28, 1998. **B-T:** R-R. **HT:** 6-6. **WT:** 195. **Drafted:** HS—Sacramento, 2016 (1st round). **Signed by:** Scott Cerny.

TRACK RECORD: The son of former NBA power forward Rich Manning, Matt was committed to St. Mary's to play both basketball and baseball but instead signed with the Tigers as the ninth overall pick in 2016. After overcoming some developmental growing pains during his first full season, Manning ascended three levels the following year and won Eastern League pitcher of the year in 2019 at Double-A Erie. He began 2020 at the alternate training site but was shut down in late August with a right forearm strain. He was back throwing and working out at instructional league.

SCOUTING REPORT: Manning possesses a natural, athletic fluidity to his 6-foot-6 frame and generates excellent extension on his pitches. His fastball sits 92-95 mph and touches 98. His plus curveball features sharp, downward action that plays well off his heater. Manning's changeup flashes above-average with sinking action, but it still needs further improvement. Manning has worked incessantly to refine his delivery and repeat his arm slot. His tempo, athleticism and penchant for attacking the strike zone give him potential above-average control.

THE FUTURE: Manning still has to polish his changeup and overall delivery. Once he does, he'll be closer to fulfilling his frontline starter potential.

SCOUTING GRADES: **Fastball:** 60 **Curveball:** 60 **Changeup:** 55 **Control:** 55

Year	Age	Club (League)	Class	W	L	ERA	G	GS	IP	H	HR	BB	SO	BB/9	SO/9	WHIP	AVG
2017	19	Connecticut (NYP)	SS	2	2	1.89	9	9	33	27	0	14	36	3.8	9.7	1.23	.194
	19	West Michigan (MWL)	LoA	2	0	5.60	5	5	18	14	0	11	26	5.6	13.2	1.42	.177
2018	20	Erie (EL)	AA	0	1	4.22	2	2	11	11	0	4	13	3.4	11.0	1.41	.239
	20	Lakeland (FSL)	HiA	4	4	2.98	9	9	51	32	4	19	65	3.3	11.4	0.99	.156
	20	West Michigan (MWL)	LoA	3	3	3.40	11	11	56	47	3	28	76	4.5	12.3	1.35	.198
2019	21	Erie (EL)	AA	11	5	2.56	24	24	134	93	7	38	148	2.6	10.0	0.98	.176
Minor League Totals				22	17	3.04	70	70	331	251	16	121	410	3.3	11.1	1.12	.207

5 RILEY GREENE, OF

MARK CUNNINGHAM/MLB PHOTOS VIA GETTY IMAGES

BA GRADE
60 Risk: High

Born: Sept. 28, 2000. **B-T:** L-L. **HT:** 6-3. **WT:** 200. **Drafted:** HS—Oviedo, Fla., 2019 (1st round). **Signed by:** R.J. Burgess.

TRACK RECORD: A few teams considered Greene the best high school player in the 2019 draft class, ahead of the more touted Bobby Witt Jr., and the Tigers locked onto him early before taking him with the fifth overall pick. Greene made good on those predictions by shooting up to low Class A in his draft year, a rare rise for a high school prospect. He continued with an impressive cameo during big league spring training before camps were shut down by the coronavirus pandemic and spent the summer at the Tigers' alternate training site.

SCOUTING REPORT: Greene is a supremely talented hitter with a unique mix of skill and maturity. He does immense damage with a fluid, powerful stroke from the left side, but he also manages the strike zone with impressive patience and possesses sound control of the barrel. He's a consensus plus hitter and, with his frame still developing, scouts believe Greene should develop 20-plus home run power as he matures physically. While there was some discussion of Greene remaining in center field, his average speed makes him a better fit in right field, where his average arm strength will play.

THE FUTURE: Greene has the offensive potential to join Spencer Torkelson as a cornerstone of the Tigers' lineup for years to come. In 2021, he'll get a second chance at a first full season.

SCOUTING GRADES: **Hitting:** 60 **Power:** 55 **Running:** 50 **Fielding:** 55 **Arm:** 50

Year	Age	Club (League)	Class	AVG	G	AB	R	H	2B	3B	HR	RBI	BB	SO	SB	OBP	SLG
2019	18	Connecticut (NYP)	SS	.295	24	88	12	26	3	1	1	7	11	25	1	.380	.386
	18	West Michigan (MWL)	LoA	.219	24	96	13	21	2	2	2	13	6	26	4	.278	.344
	18	Tigers West (GCL)	R	.351	9	37	9	13	3	0	2	8	5	12	0	.442	.595
Minor League Totals				.271	57	221	34	60	8	3	5	28	22	63	5	.347	.403

6 ISAAC PAREDES, 3B

TONY FIRRIOLO/MLB PHOTOS VIA GETTY IMAGES

BA GRADE **50** Risk: Medium

Born: Feb. 18, 1999. **B-T:** R-R. **HT:** 5-11. **WT:** 213. **Signed:** Mexico, 2015. **Signed by:** Sergio Hernandez/Louie Eljaua (Cubs).

TRACK RECORD: The Tigers acquired Paredes with Jeimer Candelario in the 2017 trade that sent Alex Avila and Justin Wilson to the Cubs. Paredes quickly established himself as one of the top up-and-coming hitters in the Tigers' system and, after a strong showing at Double-A Erie in 2019, made his major league debut for the Tigers in 2020. He appeared in 34 games down the stretch and hit .220 with one home run.

SCOUTING REPORT: Paredes doesn't have the most athletic figure, but he can hit. He has long displayed an understanding of how to handle opposing pitchers beyond his years and boasts elite strike-zone discipline. His approach and advanced barrel control yield above-average contact ability, and his mix of strength, approach and feel for the barrel give him a chance to hit for average power. Paredes came up as a shortstop but is purely a third baseman now with his portly, fully developed frame. He has the arm strength for the hot corner and projects to hit enough to profile at the position.

THE FUTURE: Paredes is in line to be the Tigers' Opening Day third baseman in 2021. He has enough offensive skill to be a first-division player, but he's going to have to watch his fitness.

SCOUTING GRADES: **Hitting:** 55 **Power:** 50 **Running:** 40 **Fielding:** 45 **Arm:** 55

Year	Age	Club (League)	Class	AVG	G	AB	R	H	2B	3B	HR	RBI	BB	SO	SB	OBP	SLG
2017	18	South Bend (MWL)	LoA	.264	92	337	49	89	25	0	7	49	29	54	2	.343	.401
	18	West Michigan (MWL)	LoA	.217	32	115	16	25	3	0	4	21	13	13	0	.323	.348
2018	19	Erie (EL)	AA	.321	39	131	20	42	9	0	3	22	19	22	1	.406	.458
	19	Lakeland (FSL)	HiA	.259	84	301	50	78	19	2	12	48	32	54	1	.338	.455
2019	20	Erie (EL)	AA	.282	127	478	63	135	23	1	13	66	57	61	5	.368	.416
2020	21	Detroit (AL)	MAJ	.220	34	100	7	22	4	0	1	6	8	24	0	.278	.290
Major League Totals				.220	34	100	7	22	4	0	1	6	8	24	0	.278	.290
Minor League Totals				.274	424	1541	221	422	93	6	40	232	163	226	13	.355	.420

7 DILLON DINGLER, C

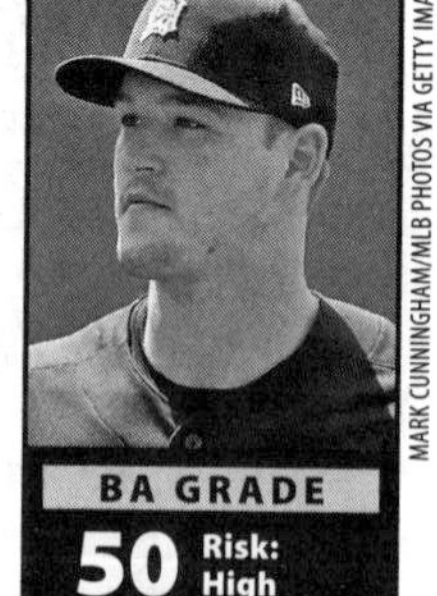

MARK CUNNINGHAM/MLB PHOTOS VIA GETTY IMAGES

BA GRADE **50** Risk: High

Born: Sept. 17, 1998. **B-T:** R-R. **HT:** 6-3. **WT:** 210. **Drafted:** Ohio State, 2020 (2nd round). **Signed by:** Austin Cousino.

TRACK RECORD: Dingler split his time between catcher and center field his freshman year at Ohio State before moving back behind the plate full-time as a sophomore. He impressed with his athleticism and natural catch-and-throw skills and became a top draft prospect as a junior in 2020 once he started hitting. Dingler tied for the Big Ten Conference lead with five home runs in 13 games before the season shut down due to the coronavirus pandemic. The Tigers drafted him in the second round, No. 32 overall, and signed him for $1,952,300.

SCOUTING REPORT: Dingler has a strong, durable frame to handle the grind of catching and is more athletic than most catchers his size. He's a natural leader who was a Buckeyes team captain and his receiving and framing are continuously improving. Dingler threw out 50% of runners in college with his nearly plus-plus arm strength and shuts down running games. Dingler is less prolific offensively, but he controls the strike zone and knows how to work a count. His power surge occurred after he recovered from a broken hamate bone, but scouts mostly regard him as an ambush hitter.

THE FUTURE: Dingler needs to continue to refine his receiving and develop as a hitter but is the favorite to become the Tigers' catcher of the future.

SCOUTING GRADES: **Hitting:** 50 **Power:** 50 **Running:** 55 **Fielding:** 55 **Arm:** 65

Year	Age	Club (League)	Class	AVG	G	AB	R	H	2B	3B	HR	RBI	BB	SO	SB	OBP	SLG
2020	21	Did not play—No minor league season															

8 DAZ CAMERON, OF

Born: Jan. 15, 1997. **B-T:** R-R. **HT:** 6-2. **WT:** 185. **Drafted:** HS—McDonough, Ga., 2015 (1st round supplemental). **Signed by:** Gavin Dickey (Astros).

TONY FIRRIOLO/MLB PHOTOS VIA GETTY IMAGES

BA GRADE
45 **Risk: Medium**

TRACK RECORD: The son of former all-star center fielder Mike Cameron, Daz was one of three prospects the Tigers acquired from the Astros in the Justin Verlander trade. Cameron has struggled to hit aside from a brief stint at Double-A Erie in 2018, but he still spent all of 2019 at Triple-A and made his major league debut in 2020, where he hit .193 in 17 games.

SCOUTING REPORT: It's easy to catch a glimpse of Cameron's defensive bloodlines watching him play the outfield. His pure speed and arm strength are average, but he has an advanced feel for the game that helps everything play up. He's a capable defender in center field and can play both corners without issue. Cameron is not a natural hitter and struggles to make consistent contact. He knows the strike zone, but he swings through hittable pitches in the zone and struggles with pitch recognition at times. Cameron's offensive value is dependent on him tapping into his natural power and making impact on contact, because he doesn't make contact very often.

THE FUTURE: Cameron's defensive ability will keep him on the major league roster while he tries to figure out his offensive game. His father was a late bloomer offensively, so the hope is Daz will be, too.

SCOUTING GRADES: **Hitting:** 40 **Power:** 45 **Running:** 55 **Fielding:** 55 **Arm:** 55

Year	Age	Club (League)	Class	AVG	G	AB	R	H	2B	3B	HR	RBI	BB	SO	SB	OBP	SLG
2017	20	Quad Cities (MWL)	LoA	.271	119	442	78	120	29	8	13	72	45	107	32	.350	.462
	20	West Michigan (MWL)	LoA	.250	3	8	1	2	0	0	0	1	3	4	0	.455	.250
2018	21	Erie (EL)	AA	.285	53	200	32	57	12	5	5	35	25	53	12	.367	.470
	21	Toledo (IL)	AAA	.211	15	57	8	12	4	1	0	6	2	15	2	.246	.316
	21	Lakeland (FSL)	HiA	.259	58	216	35	56	9	3	3	20	25	69	10	.346	.370
2019	22	Toledo (IL)	AAA	.214	120	448	68	96	22	6	13	43	62	152	17	.330	.377
2020	23	Detroit (AL)	MAJ	.193	17	57	4	11	2	1	0	3	2	19	1	.220	.263
Major League Totals				.193	17	57	4	11	2	1	0	3	2	19	1	.220	.263
Minor League Totals				.247	460	1706	275	421	85	29	37	215	201	509	109	.338	.396

9 DANIEL CABRERA, OF

Born: Sept. 5, 1998. **B-T:** L-L. **HT:** 6-1. **WT:** 196. **Drafted:** Louisiana State, 2020 (2nd round supplemental). **Signed by:** Mike Smith.

STEVE FRANZ/LSU ATHLETICS

BA GRADE
50 **Risk: High**

TRACK RECORD: Cabrera was a top draft prospect in high school but fell to the 26th round due to his strong commitment to Louisiana State. He hit .305 with 22 home runs and 116 RBIs in a decorated three-year career at LSU and was drafted by the Tigers with the 62nd overall pick in 2020. Cabrera signed for $1.21 million and made his organizational debut during instructional league.

SCOUTING REPORT: Cabrera's calling card is his bat. He possesses a fluid, simple stroke from the left side, complemented by good hand-eye coordination and bat speed. He shoots line drives to all fields and is an extremely consistent hitter who avoids prolonged slumps. Cabrera's power is more of a question mark. Some believe he'll be able to tap into his above-average raw power with his natural ability to find the barrel, while others question whether he will be able to get to it against better pitching. Originally a left fielder, Cabrera transitioned to right field and has the above-average arm strength and athleticism to stick there. He is an average runner.

THE FUTURE: Cabrera has a chance to move quickly as an advanced college hitter. He'll go as far as his bat takes him and has a chance to develop into a solid, everyday outfielder if his power comes.

SCOUTING GRADES: **Hitting:** 55 **Power:** 45 **Running:** 50 **Fielding:** 50 **Arm:** 55

Year	Age	Club (League)	Class	AVG	G	AB	R	H	2B	3B	HR	RBI	BB	SO	SB	OBP	SLG
2020	21	Did not play—No minor league season															

10 GAGE WORKMAN, 3B

MIKE JANES/FOUR SEAM IMAGES

Born: Oct. 24, 1999. **B-T:** B-R. **HT:** 6-4. **WT:** 195. **Drafted:** Arizona State, 2020 (4th round). **Signed by:** Joey Lothrop.

TRACK RECORD: The son of Padres 1996 third-round pick Widd Workman, Gage followed in his father's footsteps by heading to Arizona State, where Widd played in the '90s. Workman grabbed attention as a sophomore, hitting .330/.413/.528 over 57 games, and continued to excel during the abbreviated 2020 season. The Tigers selected Workman in the fourth round and signed him for $1 million, keeping him in the same organization as his college teammate Spencer Torkelson.

SCOUTING REPORT: Workman is an athletic, powerful switch-hitter with impressive raw power. He shows more feel for hitting from the left side of the plate but is able to get to his power from both sides. Workman strikes out more than is ideal, even for a power hitter, and needs to learn how to work counts to his advantage. His average speed and range, clean hands and above-average arm fit at third base. Workman moves better than most for his size and has enough athleticism to handle shortstop in a pinch.

THE FUTURE: Workman's power potential and defensive ability give him a chance to be an everyday third baseman. He'll need to work on cutting down on strikeouts in his pro debut in 2021.

SCOUTING GRADES: **Hitting:** 50 **Power:** 55 **Speed:** 55 **Fielding:** 50 **Arm:** 55

Year	Age	Club (League)	Class	AVG	G	AB	R	H	2B	3B	HR	RBI	BB	SO	SB	OBP	SLG
2020	20	Did not play—No minor league season															

11 ALEX FAEDO, RHP

Born: Nov. 12, 1995. **B-T:** R-R. **HT:** 6-5. **WT:** 225. **Drafted:** Florida, 2017 (1st round). **Signed by:** RJ Burgess.

TRACK RECORD: Faedo went 28-6 in three years at Florida and was named Most Outstanding Player of the 2017 College World Series after leading the Gators to the national title. The Tigers drafted him 18th overall and signed him for $3.5 million. Faedo suffered a mysterious drop in velocity in his first full season, but he rebounded in 2019 to finish third in the Double-A Eastern League with 134 strikeouts. He expected to compete for a spot in the majors in 2020, but he tested positive for Covid-19 in July and was shut down with a forearm strain in late August after a brief stint at the alternate training site. He subsequently had Tommy John surgery in December.

SCOUTING REPORT: When healthy, Faedo's fastball sits 91-93 mph and touches 95. His main weapon is his slider. It's an above-average pitch and he can manipulate its length depending if he's trying to land it for a strike or get a batter to chase. Faedo's changeup is a fringe-average offering he needs to throw more regularly to become an average pitch. He is an intense competitor who goes right after hitters, throws strikes and draws rave reviews for his makeup.

THE FUTURE: Faedo's competitive edge and three-pitch mix are enough for scouts to project a back-of-the-rotation starter. He will resume his quest to reach the major leagues in 2022.

Year	Age	Club (League)	Class	W	L	ERA	G	GS	IP	H	HR	BB	SO	BB/9	SO/9	WHIP	AVG
2018	22	Erie (EL)	AA	3	6	4.95	12	12	60	54	15	22	59	3.3	8.9	1.27	.213
	22	Lakeland (FSL)	HiA	2	4	3.10	12	12	61	49	3	13	51	1.9	7.5	1.02	.199
2019	23	Erie (EL)	AA	6	7	3.90	22	22	115	104	17	25	134	2.0	10.5	1.12	.220
Minor League Totals				11	17	3.96	46	46	236	207	35	60	244	2.3	9.3	1.13	.232

12 JOEY WENTZ, LHP

BA GRADE
50 Risk: Very High

Born: Oct. 6, 1997. **B-T:** L-L. **HT:** 6-5. **WT:** 220. **Drafted:** HS—Prairie Village, Kan., 2016 (1st round supplemental). **Signed by:** Nate Dion (Braves).

TRACK RECORD: Wentz was selected 40th overall by the Braves in 2016 and won South Atlantic League pitcher of the year in his first full season. He missed much of the 2018 season with an oblique injury and was traded to the Tigers in 2019 as part of the deal for Shane Greene. Instead of making his Tigers debut in 2020 as planned, Wentz had Tommy John surgery in March.

SCOUTING REPORT: Wentz leads his three-pitch mix with a fastball that sits comfortably at 91-93 mph with late life. While his fastball doesn't have the same velocity as the other top arms, its action through the zone is enough to generate plenty of swings and misses. Wentz complements his heater with a mid-to-high-70s curveball with late break, making it difficult for opposing hitters to identify early. Wentz's mid-

80s changeup is his strongest secondary offering and projects as an above-average pitch. Wentz projects to make a living off of his deception rather than overwhelming velocity.
THE FUTURE: Wentz still has more rehab time ahead of him. His pitch mix and durable frame allow him to project as a back-end starter.

Year	Age	Club (League)	Class	W	L	ERA	G	GS	IP	H	HR	BB	SO	BB/9	K/9	WHIP	AVG
2019	21	Mississippi (SL)	AA	5	8	4.72	20	20	103	90	13	45	100	3.9	8.7	1.31	.239
	21	Erie (EL)	AA	2	0	2.10	5	5	26	20	3	4	37	1.4	13.0	0.94	.213
Minor League Totals				19	19	3.22	79	79	371	292	23	144	395	3.5	9.6	1.17	.219

13 PARKER MEADOWS, OF

BA GRADE
50 Risk: Very High

Born: Nov. 2, 1999. **B-T:** L-R. **HT:** 6-5. **WT:** 205. **Drafted:** HS—Loganville, Ga., 2018 (2nd round). **Signed by:** Bryson Barber.
TRACK RECORD: The younger brother of Rays outfielder Austin Meadows, Parker was drafted in the second round by the Tigers in 2018 and signed for an above-slot $2.5 million to forgo a Clemson commitment. After slashing .290/.377/.473 in his pro debut, Meadows struggled in 2019 at low Class A West Michigan as one of the Midwest League's youngest players. The Tigers brought him to their alternate training site late in the 2020 season.
SCOUTING REPORT: Meadows moves exceptionally well for his 6-foot-5 frame and is athletic enough to navigate his long arms and legs on both sides of the ball. He has the strength and leverage to access plus raw power, but he struggles to time up pitches because of a lengthy bat path. Whether he can make enough contact will depend on him shortening his swing. Defensively, Meadows profiles near the top of the organization in speed and athleticism and takes good reads and solid routes in center field, though scouts are split on whether he'll stick there as he continues to fill out a large frame.
THE FUTURE: Meadows has plenty of athleticism and physicality to dream on, but will need time. He'll see high Class A in 2021.

Year	Age	Club (League)	Class	AVG	G	AB	R	H	2B	3B	HR	RBI	BB	SO	SB	OBP	SLG
2019	19	West Michigan (MWL)	LoA	.221	126	443	52	98	15	2	7	40	47	113	14	.296	.312
Minor League Totals				.233	154	536	72	125	18	3	11	50	57	144	17	.310	.340

14 ROBERTO CAMPOS, OF

BA GRADE
50 Risk: Extreme

Born: June 14, 2003. **B-T:** R-R. **HT:** 6-3. **WT:** 200. **Signed:** Cuba, 2019. **Signed by:** Aldo Perez/Oliver Arias.
TRACK RECORD: Campos grabbed enough attention during the 2019 international signing period to land a $2.85 million from the Tigers, the largest bonus for any Cuban player in the class. His expected pro debut in 2020 was delayed by the coronavirus pandemic, and he did not participate in instructional league either.
SCOUTING REPORT: A solid 6-foot-3, 200 pounds already at 17 years old, Campos has plus-plus raw power and shows the instinct to hit to all fields. He controls the strike zone well for his age and has an advanced approach. With Campos' body still developing, the Tigers are optimistic he will be an impact hitter. His defensive projections are more uncertain. He is still learning to play the outfield and shows the average speed and plus arm strength that will fit in right field, but he is still raw and needs reps.
THE FUTURE: Campos' hitting ability gives him a solid foundation. He has many years of development ahead, but the Tigers hope he can develop into an everyday right fielder.

Year	Age	Club (League)	Class	AVG	G	AB	R	H	2B	3B	HR	RBI	BB	SO	SB	OBP	SLG
2019	16	Did not play—Signed 2020 contract															

15 BRYANT PACKARD, OF

BA GRADE 45 Risk: High

Born: Oct. 6, 1997. **B-T:** L-R. **HT:** 6-3. **WT:** 200. **Drafted:** East Carolina, 2019 (5th round). **Signed by:** Taylor Black.

TRACK RECORD: Packard won American Athletic Conference player of the year as a sophomore at East Carolina. He was hampered by back discomfort and a wrist injury as a junior, but the Tigers still drafted him in the fifth round and signed him for $386,600. Packard immediately hit upon signing and climbed three levels up to high Class A Lakeland in his pro debut. His only 2020 action came in instructional league due to the coronavirus pandemic.

SCOUTING REPORT: Packard shows good hitter's instincts and possesses a natural ability to drive the ball. He controls the strike zone and has fluid barrel control, allowing him to pick out hittable pitches and square them up consistently. Packard isn't much of a runner, but his plus raw power allows him to rack up extra-base hits. Defensively, Packard is simply adequate in a corner with well below-average speed and a well below-average arm. Scouts wonder if he'll have to move to first base.

THE FUTURE: Packard is going to have to mash in order to make up for his defensive shortcomings, but he may have the bat to do it. He should see the upper minors at some point in 2021.

Year	Age	Club (League)	Class	AVG	G	AB	R	H	2B	3B	HR	RBI	BB	SO	SB	OBP	SLG
2019	21	Lakeland (FSL)	HiA	.118	5	17	2	2	0	0	0	2	2	5	0	.250	.118
	21	Connecticut (NYP)	SS	.351	11	37	5	13	2	0	0	2	6	9	1	.432	.405
	21	West Michigan (MWL)	LoA	.309	23	81	14	25	6	0	3	12	13	24	1	.404	.494
Minor League Totals				.296	39	135	21	40	8	0	3	16	21	38	2	.392	.422

16 TREI CRUZ, SS

BA GRADE 45 Risk: High

Born: July 5, 1998. **B-T:** B-R. **HT:** 6-2. **WT:** 200. **Drafted:** Rice, 2020 (3rd round). **Signed by:** Bryce Mosier.

TRACK RECORD: Cruz is the son of former outfielder Jose Cruz Jr. and the grandson of longtime outfielder Jose Cruz. Trei was drafted by the Astros in 2017 and the Nationals in 2019 but opted not to sign either time. After making significant improvements on both sides of the ball his junior year at Rice, Cruz was drafted by the Tigers in the third round and signed for $900,000. After signing, Cruz played in the independent Constellation Energy League before heading to instructional league.

SCOUTING REPORT: The switch-hitting Cruz has a solid track record of hitting, particularly from the left side, and plus raw power. His extremely aggressive approach has precluded him from getting to that power so far, but the Tigers hope further development will allow him to tap into it in games. Cruz has played second base, third base and shortstop. His soft hands and plus arm should permit him to stay in the dirt, but his below-average speed makes shortstop a stretch.

THE FUTURE: Cruz has work to do to access his power and solidify a defensive position. His hitting ability gives him a solid foundation to work from as he begins his pro career in 2021.

Year	Age	Club (League)	Class	AVG	G	AB	R	H	2B	3B	HR	RBI	BB	SO	SB	OBP	SLG
2020	21	Did not play—No minor league season															

17 AKIL BADDOO, OF

BA GRADE 45 Risk: High

Born: Aug. 16, 1998. **B-T:** L-L. **HT:** 6-1. **WT:** 210. **Drafted:** HS—Conyers, Ga., 2016 (2nd round supplemental). **Signed by:** Jack Powell (Twins).

TRACK RECORD: The Twins drafted Baddoo 74th overall in 2016 and signed him for $750,000, intrigued by his present strength and bat-to-ball skills. While Baddoo has been limited by injuries, including a Tommy John surgery in 2019, he has shown an exciting blend of power and speed when healthy. The Tigers took a shot on his upside potential by selecting him with the third pick in the major league phase of the 2020 Rule 5 draft.

SCOUTING REPORT: The Twins believed Baddoo had a chance for average hitting ability and average power, though the elevated strikeout rates he had shown in Class A put that hitting ability projection out at risk. His swing got a bit too steep, which limited the time his barrel was in the zone. Baddoo struck out nearly 30% of the time in a 29-game stint in the high Class A Florida State League in 2019 after posting a 24% strikeout rate in the low Class A Midwest League in 2018 over 113 games. Baddoo is a plus athlete and runner who can handle all three outfield positions. Some scouts think he's solidly above-average in center field, while others believe he's better in the corners. A below-average arm makes left field a distinct possibility.

THE FUTURE: Baddoo's power, speed and outfield versatility make him a candidate to become a fourth outfielder. He'll have to improve his bat-to-ball skills and cut down the whiffs to project as a regular.

Year	Age	Club (League)	Class	AVG	G	AB	R	H	2B	3B	HR	RBI	BB	SO	SB	OBP	SLG
2019	20	Fort Myers (FSL)	HiA	.214	29	117	15	25	3	3	4	9	12	39	6	.290	.393
Minor League Totals				.249	233	862	170	215	44	21	21	93	140	231	47	.357	.422

18 KODY CLEMENS, 2B

BA GRADE **45** Risk: High

Born: May 15, 1996. **B-T:** L-R. **HT:** 6-1. **WT:** 170. **Drafted:** Texas, 2018 (3rd round). **Signed by:** Matt Lea.

TRACK RECORD: Clemens has a pedigree few can match. He is the son of seven-time Cy Young Award winner Roger Clemens and won Big 12 Conference player of the year at Texas in 2018, leading the Tigers to draft him in the third round. Clemens struggled to hit in his first full season but still made his way to Double-A by the end of the year. He spent 2020 in the independent Constellation Energy League and again struggled to hit, batting .233/.291/.456.

SCOUTING REPORT: Clemens has an average, well-rounded toolset, but his aggressive approach overshadows it and leads to diminished production. He has worked to trim his swings and misses, and he does have developing double-digit home run power, but it will be up to him to make adjustments to make more contact moving forward. Clemens is a competitive, instinctual ballplayer with solid situational awareness on the bases and in the field. He steals bases efficiently despite just fringe-average speed and is a solid second baseman who plays with an extra dose of grit.

THE FUTURE: Clemens will need to make more contact against advanced pitching in order to reach the majors. That will be his main goal in 2021.

Year	Age	Club (League)	Class	AVG	G	AB	R	H	2B	3B	HR	RBI	BB	SO	SB	OBP	SLG
2019	23	Erie (EL)	AA	.170	13	47	5	8	2	0	1	4	6	18	0	.278	.277
	23	Dunedin (FSL)	HiA	.333	2	6	2	2	2	0	0	0	2	2	0	.500	.667
	23	Lakeland (FSL)	HiA	.238	115	411	43	98	24	7	11	59	45	101	11	.314	.411
Minor League Totals				.248	180	649	72	161	38	9	17	83	74	158	15	.327	.413

19 BEAU BURROWS, RHP

BA GRADE **45** Risk: High

Born: Sept. 18, 1996. **B-T:** R-R. **HT:** 6-2. **WT:** 210. **Drafted:** HS—Weatherford, Texas, 2015 (1st round). **Signed by:** Chris Wimmer.

TRACK RECORD: The Tigers drafted the touted Burrows 22nd overall in the 2015 draft and pushed him aggressively, highlighted by an assignment to Double-A as a 20-year-old. Burrows struggled with injuries and inconsistency once he got to the upper levels and posted a 5.51 ERA at Triple-A in 2019, but the Tigers still brought him up to the majors in 2020. He made five relief appearances and allowed four runs in 6.2 innings.

SCOUTING REPORT: Burrows' fastball sits comfortably at 92-95 mph and touches a few ticks higher. His curveball was much more successful prior to Triple-A, but under the right guidance it could still land as a fringe-average offering. There have been improvements to Burrows' changeup but it still lacks consistency. Burrows hasn't leaned on his slider much in recent years. Instead, he's tried to learn a cutter, but it has a ways to go as well. While the consistency of his four-pitch mix fluctuates, Burrows has enough confidence in his pitches to mix them fairly evenly.

THE FUTURE: Without a true out pitch, it's hard to project Burrows as much more than a low-leverage reliever. Simply improving any of his offspeeds would raise his ceiling slightly.

Year	Age	Club (League)	Class	W	L	ERA	G	GS	IP	H	HR	BB	SO	BB/9	SO/9	WHIP	AVG
2020	23	Detroit (AL)	MAJ	0	0	5.40	5	0	7	8	3	1	3	1.4	4.1	1.35	.286
Major League Totals				0	0	5.40	5	0	6	8	3	1	3	1.4	4.1	1.35	.286
Minor League Totals				30	26	3.61	100	98	468	426	34	177	433	3.4	8.3	1.29	.245

20 JAKE ROGERS, C

BA GRADE **40** Risk: Medium

Born: April 18, 1995. **B-T:** R-R. **HT:** 6-1. **WT:** 192. **Drafted:** Tulane, 2016 (3rd round). **Signed by:** Justin Cryer (Astros).

TRACK RECORD: Viewed as the top defensive catcher in the 2016 draft class, Rogers was drafted by the Astros in the third round and traded to the Tigers a year later with Daz Cameron and Franklin Perez for Justin Verlander. Rogers rose through Double-A and Triple-A up to the majors for his debut in 2019, but he spent all of 2020 at the alternate training site and did not receive a callup.

SCOUTING REPORT: Rogers shines behind the plate defensively. He has cat-like quickness and footwork and plus arm strength. He has improved his ability to properly block and frame. He draws praise for his attitude and work ethic, and pitchers like throwing to him. Rogers' offense is a different story. An uphill

swing leads to inconsistent contact and struggles against offspeed pitches, in particular. Rogers does have some raw power, but he doesn't project to make enough contact to get to it.
THE FUTURE: Rogers needs a swing change in order to be in the lineup every day, even with his defensive abilities. His most likely outcome is a backup catcher.

Year	Age	Club (League)	Class	AVG	G	AB	R	H	2B	3B	HR	RBI	BB	SO	SB	OBP	SLG
2019	24	Detroit (AL)	MAJ	.125	35	112	11	14	3	0	4	8	13	51	0	.222	.259
	24	Erie (EL)	AA	.302	28	86	17	26	3	1	5	21	19	26	0	.429	.535
	24	Toledo (IL)	AAA	.223	48	166	29	37	10	1	9	31	18	53	0	.321	.458
Major League Totals				.125	35	112	11	14	3	0	4	8	13	51	0	.222	.259
Minor League Totals				.242	333	1185	181	287	63	9	52	194	153	336	22	.338	.442

21 DEREK HILL, OF

Born: Dec. 30, 1995. **B-T:** R-R. **HT:** 6-2. **WT:** 190. **Drafted:** HS—Elk Grove, Calif., 2014 (1st round). **Signed by:** Scott Cerny.

TRACK RECORD: The 23rd overall pick in 2014, Hill was sidetracked by injuries almost as soon as his career began. He missed time with lower back pain when he signed, was limited by a recurring quad injury in 2015 and had Tommy John surgery late in the 2016 season. Hill played 100 games in a season for the first time in 2018 and steadily made his way up the minors, culminating in his big league debut in 2020.
SCOUTING REPORT: Even after all his injuries, Hill remains an explosive athlete. He dazzles defensively in center field with his plus-plus speed and outstanding defensive skills. Few doubt he would be one of the top defensive center fielders in the major leagues with regular playing time. Hill has discovered some power as he's gotten stronger, but he's a below-average hitter who swings and misses too frequently to be in the lineup everyday. He struck out in half of his plate appearances in his big league debut and doesn't have the approach or swing conducive to big league success.
THE FUTURE: Hill's defense is exceptional, but without significant improvements as a hitter, he's no more than a bench option.

Year	Age	Club (League)	Class	AVG	G	AB	R	H	2B	3B	HR	RBI	BB	SO	SB	OBP	SLG
2020	24	Detroit (AL)	MAJ	.091	15	11	3	1	0	0	0	0	1	6	0	.167	.091
Major League Totals				.091	15	11	3	1	0	0	0	0	1	6	0	.167	.091
Minor League Totals				.243	477	1804	284	439	64	29	23	169	164	513	156	.313	.349

22 COLT KEITH, 3B

BREAKOUT
BA GRADE
45 Risk: Extreme

Born: Aug. 14, 2001. **B-T:** L-R. **HT:** 6-2. **WT:** 220. **Drafted:** HS—Biloxi, Miss., 2020 (5th round). **Signed by:** Mike Smith.

TRACK RECORD: Keith was Mississippi's high school player of the year as a junior in 2019 and stood out as one of the best hitters on the high school showcase circuit the following summer. The Tigers drafted him in the fifth round in 2020 and signed him for $500,000 to forgo an Arizona State commitment. Keith played shortstop and pitched in high school, but the Tigers drafted him as a third baseman and sent him out to the hot corner in instructional league.
SCOUTING REPORT: Keith has an impressive array of tools that include plus raw power, plus arm strength and plus speed. He mostly got by on his natural athleticism in high school and didn't face the strongest competition on a daily basis in Mississippi, but he shows the ability to pull the ball for home runs and drive the ball hard on a line to the opposite field. Keith's natural loft and bat speed should lead to power as his body continues to develop and he adjusts to more advanced pitchers. Keith has advanced glove work and the arm for third base. He could also slide to right field if needed.
THE FUTURE: Keith will face a steep adjustment against professional pitchers. If he shows he can handle it, he has the athleticism and tools to be a breakout prospect in the system.

Year	Age	Club (League)	Class	AVG	G	AB	R	H	2B	3B	HR	RBI	BB	SO	SB	OBP	SLG
2020	18	Did not play—No minor league season															

23 ADINSO REYES, SS

BA GRADE
45 Risk: Extreme

Born: Oct. 22, 2001. **B-T:** R-R. **HT:** 6-1. **WT:** 195. **Signed:** Dominican Republic, 2018. **Signed by:** Aldo Perez.

TRACK RECORD: Signed by the Tigers for $1.45 million, Reyes hit .331/.379/.508 in a loud pro debut in the Dominican Summer League in 2019. His expected U.S. debut in 2020 was derailed by the coronavirus pandemic, but he got on the field in instructional league.
SCOUTING REPORT: Reyes has impressive natural strength and fluid swing. He drives the ball to all fields

and projects to grow into plus power as he gets older. Reyes' impact potential is exciting, but he is still working to improve his pitch recognition and streamline a lengthy swing. He has worked to improve his pitch recognition while streamlining a lengthy swing. He is still getting a feel for his developing frame. Reyes is a shortstop now and moves well in the field, but he will likely move to third base as he gets bigger. He has enough arm strength to stay on the left side of the infield.
THE FUTURE: Reyes is intriguing but largely unproven. He'll make his U.S. debut in the Rookie-level Gulf Coast League in 2021.

Year	Age	Club (League)	Class	AVG	G	AB	R	H	2B	3B	HR	RBI	BB	SO	SB	OBP	SLG
2019	17	Tigers1 (DSL)	R	.331	62	242	44	80	20	1	7	48	14	51	3	.379	.508
Minor League Totals				.331	62	242	44	80	20	1	7	48	14	51	3	.379	.508

24 SERGIO ALCANTARA, SS

BA GRADE 40 **Risk: High**

Born: July 10, 1996. **B-T:** B-R. **HT:** 5-9. **WT:** 151. **Drafted:** Dominican Republic, 2012. **Signed by:** Junior Noboa (D-backs).
TRACK RECORD: Originally signed by the D-backs in 2012, Alcantara arrived in Detroit as one of three players acquired for J.D. Martinez in 2017. The slick-fielding, light-hitting shortstop spent back-to-back seasons at Double-A Erie in 2018 and 2019 before jumping to Detroit for his big league debut in 2020.
SCOUTING REPORT: One of the most fluid infield defenders in Detroit's system, Alcantara mixes clean hands, easy footwork, quick-twitch reflexes and near-elite arm strength to handle the shortstop with ease. At the plate, Alcantara does a decent job of working counts but will need to produce louder contact if he hopes to project as an average hitter. Alcantara's size works against the notion of any more projectable power. He hit just .143/.217/.381 in his first taste of the majors.
THE FUTURE: Alcantara is strictly a defensive replacement in the middle infield. He is ready to fill that role now and should return to the majors in 2021.

Year	Age	Club (League)	Class	AVG	G	AB	R	H	2B	3B	HR	RBI	BB	SO	SB	OBP	SLG
2020	23	Detroit (AL)	MAJ	.143	10	21	2	3	0	1	1	1	2	4	0	.217	.381
Major League Totals				.143	10	21	2	3	0	1	1	1	2	4	0	.217	.381
Minor League Totals				.256	631	2266	317	580	86	14	9	187	289	447	57	.340	.318

25 COOPER JOHNSON, C

BA GRADE 40 **Risk: High**

Born: April 25, 1998. **B-T:** R-R. **HT:** 6-0. **WT:** 215. **Drafted:** Mississippi, 2019 (6th round). **Signed by:** Mike Smith.
TRACK RECORD: Johnson never hit much in college at Mississippi, but his defense behind the plate was so outstanding, the Tigers still drafted him in the sixth round in 2019. He began his career at short-season Connecticut and held his own before he was promoted to low Class A West Michigan, where he was overwhelmed by more advanced pitchers. After the coronavirus pandemic canceled the 2020 minor league season, Johnson got back on the field at instructional league.
SCOUTING REPORT: Johnson is everything teams want behind the plate from a defensive standpoint. He's an excellent receiver and blocker, he runs a pitching staff expertly and his plus-plus arm shuts down running games. Johnson's ability to hit at the higher levels is questionable, at best. He is fair at managing the strike zone and he has some barrel control, but he struggles to read offspeed pitches and has a long swing that leads to lots of strikeouts. He doesn't impact the ball and thus has little projectable power.
THE FUTURE: Johnson's defense gives him an outside chance of reaching the majors as a backup, but his bat will have to make significant improvements for him to even reach that. He'll head back to the Class A level in 2021.

Year	Age	Club (League)	Class	AVG	G	AB	R	H	2B	3B	HR	RBI	BB	SO	SB	OBP	SLG
2019	21	Connecticut (NYP)	SS	.234	14	47	5	11	3	0	0	6	8	15	0	.357	.298
	21	West Michigan (MWL)	LoA	.179	27	84	13	15	4	0	2	11	15	28	2	.320	.298
Minor League Totals				.198	41	131	18	26	7	0	2	17	23	43	2	.333	.298

26 ELIEZER ALFONZO, C

BA GRADE **40** Risk: High

Born: Sept. 23, 1999. **B-T:** B-R. **HT:** 5-10. **WT:** 155. **Signed:** Venezuela, 2016. **Signed by:** Alejandro Rodriguez/Raul Leiva.

TRACK RECORD: Alfonzo signed with the Tigers out of Venezuela in 2016 and has slowly made his way up the minor league ladder. After spending two seasons in Rookie ball, Alfonzo jumped to short-season Connecticut in 2019 and hit .318/.342/.374 with seven doubles and 24 RBIs. The Tigers brought him to instructional league in 2020.

SCOUTING REPORT: Alfonzo has a nice blend of skills, even if he lacks a plus tool. He has a short, compact swing geared for plenty of contact but not a lot of power. He has strong knowledge of the strike zone and doesn't strike out very often. Alfonzo moves well behind the plate and threw out 51% of basestealers with his above-average arm. He is also praised for his leadership qualities and work ethic.

THE FUTURE: Alfonzo's blend of decent offensive and defensive skills give him a chance to be a backup catcher. He'll move to full-season ball in 2021.

Year	Age	Club (League)	Class	AVG	G	AB	R	H	2B	3B	HR	RBI	BB	SO	SB	OBP	SLG
2019	19	Connecticut (NYP)	SS	.318	48	179	16	57	7	0	1	24	8	17	2	.342	.374
Minor League Totals				.316	155	509	69	161	22	2	2	71	63	52	13	.392	.379

27 FRANKLIN PEREZ, RHP

BA GRADE **45** Risk: Extreme

Born: Dec. 6, 1997. **B-T:** R-R. **HT:** 6-3. **WT:** 197. **Signed:** Venezuela, 2014. **Signed by:** Oz Ocampo/Oscar Alvarado (Astros).

TRACK RECORD: Perez was one of three players the Tigers received from the Astros in 2017 for Justin Verlander. The others—outfielder Daz Cameron and catcher Jake Rogers—have reached the big leagues. Perez, meanwhile, has thrown just 27 innings since the trade because of various injuries and has yet to pitch above high Class A. The Tigers brought him to the alternate training site in 2020 and continued to get him innings in instructional league.

SCOUTING REPORT: Perez's pure stuff has never been in question, but he cannot stay healthy enough to show it to anyone. He's dealt with a lat strain and repeated shoulder injuries. At his best, Perez works with a mid-90s fastball, a mid-80s changeup and a downer curveball. He introduced a slider in 2017, as well, before being traded to Detroit. All his pitches with the exception of his slider have flashed plus, and he throws strikes with above-average control. Now he just needs to get on the mound and stay healthy.

THE FUTURE: Despite his injury history, Perez landed on the Tigers' 40-man roster after the 2019 season. If his health keeps him from starting, he has enough stuff to stick in a late-inning bullpen role.

Year	Age	Club (League)	Class	W	L	ERA	G	GS	IP	H	HR	BB	SO	BB/9	SO/9	WHIP	AVG
2019	21	Lakeland (FSL)	HiA	0	0	2.35	2	2	8	7	1	5	6	5.9	7.0	1.57	.212
Minor League Totals				10	12	3.56	59	45	230	212	11	73	234	2.9	9.2	1.24	.243

28 ALEX LANGE, RHP

BA GRADE **40** Risk: High

Born: Oct. 2, 1995. **B-T:** R-R. **HT:** 6-3. **WT:** 197. **Drafted:** Louisiana State, 2017 (1st round). **Signed by:** Kevin Ellis (Cubs).

TRACK RECORD: Drafted 30th overall by the Cubs in 2017, Lange was sent to the Tigers at the 2019 trade deadline as part of the return for Nick Castellanos. He made his Tigers organizational debut at Double-A Erie and pitched to a 3.45 ERA in nine starts, albeit with a concerning number of walks. He followed with a strong stint as a reliever in the Arizona Fall League and was brought to the alternate training site in 2020.

SCOUTING REPORT: Lange is a starter for now, but his max-effort delivery and below-average control have him ticketed for relief in the long term. His 90-93 mph fastball is a fringe-average pitch that lacks life, and his curveball is an average pitch. His curveball shows hard bite and can miss bats but doesn't quite project as better than average. Lange also has a slider, but it's not consistent enough to be much more than fringe-average.

THE FUTURE: Lange's fastball could tick up in relief, where his control would be less of an issue. That's his likely role in the majors and he should be in line to make his debut in 2021.

Year	Age	Club (League)	Class	W	L	ERA	G	GS	IP	H	HR	BB	SO	BB/9	SO/9	WHIP	AVG
2019	23	Erie (EL)	AA	2	1	3.45	9	0	16	13	0	8	15	4.6	8.6	1.34	.213
	23	Myrtle Beach (CAR)	HiA	1	9	7.36	11	11	48	58	4	26	51	4.9	9.6	1.76	.254
	23	Tennessee (SL)	AA	2	3	3.92	7	7	39	36	4	19	28	4.4	6.5	1.41	.214
Minor League Totals				11	22	4.54	54	45	232	220	14	94	208	3.7	8.1	1.35	.251

29 JOSE DE LA CRUZ, OF

Born: July 3, 2002. **B-T:** R-R. **HT:** 6-1. **WT:** 195. **Signed:** Dominican Republic, 2018. **Signed by:** Aldo Perez/Carlos Santana.

TRACK RECORD: The Tigers signed de la Cruz for $1.8 million, the largest bonus in their 2018 international class, then watched as he put together a stellar pro debut in the Dominican Summer League the following year. De la Cruz's 11 home runs placed him in a three-way tie for the DSL lead, and the Tigers brought him to the U.S. for instructional league in 2020.

SCOUTING REPORT: De la Cruz is an aggressive player in all facets of the game. He has plus bat speed, swings often and makes hard contact when he connects, though he also swings and misses quite a bit. He struck out 30% of the time in the DSL and will have to manage that moving forward. De la Cruz's plus speed and plus arm allow him to profile at any of the three outfield positions. He plays center field for now but may shift to right field as he gets bigger and stronger.

THE FUTURE: De la Cruz's future is tied to how much he can reduce his swings and misses. He'll start 2021 in the Rookie-level Gulf Coast League.

Year	Age	Club (League)	Class	AVG	G	AB	R	H	2B	3B	HR	RBI	BB	SO	SB	OBP	SLG
2019	17	Tigers2 (DSL)	R	.307	56	225	55	69	13	5	11	39	18	75	16	.375	.556
Minor League Totals				.307	56	225	55	69	13	5	11	39	18	75	16	.375	.556

30 ZACK SHORT, SS

Born: May 29, 1995. **B-T:** R-R. **HT:** 5-10. **WT:** 180. **Drafted:** Sacred Heart, 2016 (17th round). **Signed by:** Matt Sherman (Cubs).

TRACK RECORD: A product of a talented Sacred Heart team, Short was selected by the Cubs in the 17th round in 2016 and signed for $80,000. The same year, Short's college teammate Jason Foley signed with the Tigers as a nondrafted free agent. Short quickly developed a reputation as a defensive wizard and rose to Triple-A in 2019, though his season was interrupted by a broken hand. The Tigers acquired him for Cameron Maybin at the 2020 trade deadline.

SCOUTING REPORT: Short's skill set is led by his defensive abilities. He's a twitchy athlete who can handle shortstop easily, with light footwork and impressive rage. At the plate, Short's undersized frame works against him and leaves little room for any power projection. He is capable of an occasional home run thanks to a quick stroke through the zone, but his swing is more geared for line drives to all fields.

THE FUTURE: Short is on the Tigers' 40-man roster and should make his major league debut in 2021. He should provide valuable infield depth.

Year	Age	Club (League)	Class	AVG	G	AB	R	H	2B	3B	HR	RBI	BB	SO	SB	OBP	SLG
2019	24	Cubs 1 (AZL)	R	.375	6	16	5	6	2	0	0	3	8	4	0	.600	.500
	24	Iowa (PCL)	AAA	.211	41	133	22	28	9	0	6	17	21	50	2	.338	.414
	24	Tennessee (SL)	AA	.250	16	64	7	16	3	2	0	5	9	18	0	.338	.359
Minor League Totals				.241	371	1288	220	310	79	11	37	162	261	345	43	.377	.405

MORE PROSPECTS TO KNOW

31 NICK QUINTANA, 3B

The 2019 second-round pick went directly to low Class A in his pro debut but struggled and was demoted to short-season Connecticut. His plus bat speed produces above-average raw power, but an elevated strikeout rate holds him back.

32 PAUL RICHAN, RHP

With plus control and a repeatable delivery, Richan has a strong chance of landing as a dependable back-end starter or long reliever. He and Alex Lange formed the trade return from the Cubs for Nick Castellanos.

33 JACOB ROBSON, OF

Despite his size, Robson's aggressive defense, speed and knack for consistent contact have him positioned as an outfield option off the bench.

34 ZACK HESS, RHP

SLEEPER

The natural downhill plane from Hess' 6-foot-6 frame makes him a valued potential bullpen piece and a sleeper candidate for 2021.

35 WENCEEL PEREZ, SS

Perez has enough athletic ability to be a utility option under the right development staff, but he needs to improve his maturity on the field.

36 BROCK DEATHERAGE, OF

Deatherage has struggled at the plate, but his near-elite speed helps him maintain his status as one of the top defenders in the Tigers' system.

37 KYLE FUNKHOUSER, RHP

Although Funkhouser's control will likely push him to the bullpen, his pitch mix remains effective enough in short spurts to work in a relief role.

38 WILKEL HERNANDEZ, RHP

Following Tommy John surgery in Oct. 2020, Hernandez is expected to return to in-game activity in 2022. Some scouts still see a solid future.

39 WLADIMIR PINTO, RHP

Pinto's high-octane fastball should carry him until he can streamline his offspeed mix. He projects as a potential multi-inning reliever.

40 GERSON MORENO, RHP

Moreno is still rounding into form from Tommy John surgery but could provide bullpen depth once he returns to full strength.

TOP PROSPECTS OF THE DECADE

Year	Player, Pos	2020 Org
2011	Jacob Turner, RHP	Did not play
2012	Jacob Turner, RHP	Did not play
2013	Nick Castellanos ,3B/OF	Reds
2014	Nick Castellanos, 3B/OF	Reds
2015	Steven Moya, OF	Orix (Japan)
2016	Michael Fulmer, RHP	Tigers
2017	Matt Manning, RHP	Tigers
2018	Franklin Perez, RHP	Tigers
2019	Casey Mize, RHP	Tigers
2020	Casey Mize, RHP	Tigers

TOP DRAFT PICKS OF THE DECADE

Year	Player, Pos	2020 Org
2011	James McCann, C (2nd round)	White Sox
2012	Jake Thompson, RHP (2nd round)	Angels
2013	Jonathon Crawford, RHP	Independent League
2014	Derek Hill, OF	Tigers
2015	Beau Burrows, RHP	Tigers
2016	Matt Manning, RHP	Tigers
2017	Alex Faedo, RHP	Tigers
2018	Casey Mize, RHP	Tigers
2019	Riley Greene, OF	Tigers
2020	Spencer Torkelson, 3B	Tigers

DEPTH CHART

DETROIT TIGERS

TOP 2021 ROOKIES	RANK
Tarik Skubal, LHP	2
Casey Mize, RHP	3
BREAKOUT PROSPECTS	**RANK**
Colt Keith, 3B	22

SOURCE OF TOP 30 TALENT

Homegrown	21	Acquired	9
College	10	Trade	8
Junior college	0	Rule 5 draft	1
High school	6	Independent league	0
Nondrafted free agent	0	Free agent/waivers	0
International	5		

LF
Bryant Packard (15)
Troy Stokes Jr.
Danny Woodrow

CF
Daz Cameron (8)
Parker Meadows (13)
Akil Baddoo (17)
Derek Hill (21)
Jose De La Cruz (29)
Jacob Robson
Brock Deatherage

RF
Riley Greene (5)
Daniel Cabrera (9)
Roberto Campos (14)
Kingston Liniak
Ulrich Bojarski

3B
Isaac Paredes (6)
Gage Workman (10)
Colt Keith (22)
Nick Quintana

SS
Trei Cruz (16)
Adinso Reyes (23)
Sergio Alcantara (24)
Zack Short (30)
Wenceel Perez
Jose King

2B
Kody Clemens (18)
Andre Lipcius

1B
Spencer Torkelson (1)

C
Dillon Dingler (7)
Jake Rogers (20)
Cooper Johnson (25)
Eliezer Alfonzo (26)

LHP

LHSP	LHRP
Tarik Skubal (2)	Jack O'Loughlin
Joey Wentz (12)	Adam Wolf

RHP

RHSP	RHRP
Casey Mize (3)	Alex Lange (28)
Matt Manning (4)	Paul Richan
Alex Faedo (11)	Zack Hess
Beau Burrows (19)	Kyle Funkhouser
Franklin Perez (27)	Wladimir Pinto
Wilkel Hernandez	Gerson Moreno
Elvin Rodriguez	Jason Foley
	John Schreiber
	Bryan Garcia
	Nolan Blackwood
	Hugh Smith
	Yunior Perez

Houston Astros

BY BEN BADLER

In January 2020, the commissioner's office penalized the Astros for their sign-stealing violations, prompting owner Jim Crane to fire general manager Jeff Luhnow and manager A.J. Hinch.

The Astros, dealing with the fallout from the scandal, slumped to a 29-31 record in the pandemic-shortened season but rallied to reach Game 7 of the American League Championship Series under new manager Dusty Baker and new general manager James Click.

The Astros are still positioned to contend in 2021, but their farm system has declined. Some of that is a natural byproduct of consistently winning and picking later in the draft. Penalties from their sign-stealing violations, namely the loss of first-and second-round picks in 2020 and 2021, won't help.

What would make a huge impact for the Astros is a leap forward from righthander Forrest Whitley, who remains the team's top prospect. Once the top pitching prospect in baseball, Whitley is growing further removed from that title, with concerns mounting about whether he will reach his frontline starter projections. After suffering through a miserable 2019, he mostly stayed on the sidelines during 2020 with elbow pain.

Meanwhile, the Astros' ability to identify and develop overlooked pitching prospects from Latin America has been beneficial. In an international arena focused on players signing at 16, former international scouting boss Oz Ocampo (who is now with the Pirates) and Roman Ocumarez have an outstanding track record of signing "older" players at low cost who become quality big leaguers and some of the organization's best prospects.

Dominican lefthander Framber Valdez, signed for $10,000 when he was 21, developed into a mid-rotation starter in 2020. Dominican righthander Cristian Javier, another $10,000 signing just before his 18th birthday, finished third in AL Rookie of the Year voting. Righthander Jose Urquidy, signed out of Mexico at 19, looks like he should stick in the rotation.

The Astros have more on the way, including No. 2 prospect Luis Garcia as well as Bryan Abreu, Enoli Paredes and Nivaldo Rodriguez.

The entire Astros farm system is heavy on pitching, even more so after they used their top 2020 draft pick on prep righthander Alex Santos. Their domestic scouting staff has shown a knack for finding pitchers in the later rounds of the draft, with righthanders Shawn Dubin, Brandon Bielak and Brett Conine all potential major league starters selected in the 11th round or later. The Astros' pitching development program has done a good job of helping pitchers throw harder and maximize their strengths.

BOB LEVEY/GETTY IMAGES

Dominican lefthander Framber Valdez emerged as one of the Astros' top starting pitchers.

PROJECTED 2024 LINEUP

Position	Player	Age
Catcher	Korey Lee	25
First Base	Abraham Toro	27
Second Base	Jose Altuve	34
Third Base	Alex Bregman	30
Shortstop	Carlos Correa	29
Left Field	Kyle Tucker	27
Center Field	Colin Barber	23
Right Field	Chas McCormick	29
Designated Hitter	Yordan Alvarez	27
No. 1 Starter	Lance McCullers Jr.	30
No. 2 Starter	Framber Valdez	30
No. 3 Starter	Cristian Javier	27
No. 4 Starter	Forrest Whitley	26
No. 5 Starter	Jose Urquidy	29
Closer	Luis Garcia	27

The Astros have several young pitchers who could make contributions in 2021, but the options to find offensive help are slimmer. With their returning lineup, that's not an overwhelming concern. The Astros have enough pieces to continue contending, but they're going to need help from their farm system.

Soon Click will face the difficult challenge of keeping the Astros' playoff streak alive while simultaneously building the system back up for the organization's long-term future. ■

1 FORREST WHITLEY, RHP

Born: Sept. 15, 1997. **B-T:** R-R. **HT:** 6-7. **WT:** 238.
Drafted: HS—San Antonio, 2016 (1st round).
Signed by: Noel Gonzales-Luna.

TRACK RECORD: It's hard to know what to make of Whitley at this point. Drafted 17th overall out of high school in 2016, he ranks as the Astros' No. 1 prospect for the fourth straight season. Whitley ranked as the No. 10 prospect in baseball entering the 2018 season, coming off a year in which he reached Double-A as a 19-year-old. In 2018, Whitley missed the start of the season with a 50-game suspension due to a positive test for a performance-enhancing drug. He then threw just 26 innings in the regular season because he missed time with oblique and lat muscle injuries before returning for an impressive Arizona Fall League. His 2019 was ugly, with a double-digit ERA in Triple-A and command and shoulder issues, though he did throw well again in the AFL. Whitley opened 2020 at spring training, where his velocity was a little bit down. Once he got ramped up at the Astros' alternate training site, he was regularly into the mid 90s with the rest of his arsenal intact. He was dominating in his last outing before he left with elbow pain and was shut down the rest of the year.

SCOUTING REPORT: Heading into 2021, it has now been three full seasons since Whitley pitched like a future ace back in 2017. He has flashed upside in the interim, but the red flags are whipping harder than ever. At his best, Whitley has pitched at 92-97 mph and hit 99. He mixes in a low-90s cutter, a hard slider with power and depth, a curveball with good rotation and a changeup that's plus at times with good sink and fade. It's a deep arsenal, but Whitley's command, delivery issues and health problems have added significantly more risk to his profile the last few years. Whitley showed remarkable body control for a young 6-foot-7 pitcher earlier in his career, but a variety of mechanical alterations over the years has thrown him out of whack, though optimistic scouts think he could follow other tall pitchers and sync it up later in his career. Since Whitley only pitched at the alternate site and didn't go to instructional league, where opposing scouts could have seen him, he's even more challenging for other teams to evaluate.

TOP ROOKIE

BOB LEVEY/GETTY IMAGES

BA GRADE

60 Risk: Extreme

SCOUTING GRADES

Fastball: 60. **CHG:** 60. **CB:** 55. **SL:** 55. **CT:** 55. **Control:** 40.

Projected future grades on 20-80 scouting scale.

BEST TOOLS

Best Hitter for Average	Chas McCormick
Best Power Hitter	Zach Daniels
Best Strike-Zone Discipline	Grae Kessinger
Fastest Baserunner	Zach Daniels
Best Athlete	Zach Daniels
Best Fastball	Hunter Brown
Best Curveball	Bryan Abreu
Best Slider	Bryan Abreu
Best Changeup	Luis Garcia
Best Control	Brett Conine
Best Defensive Catcher	Korey Lee
Best Defensive Infielder	Jeremy Peña
Best Infield Arm	Freudis Nova
Best Defensive Outfielder	Jake Meyers
Best Outfield Arm	Richi Gonzalez

THE FUTURE: There's still a chance Whitley develops into an anchor in Houston's rotation, but it hasn't been trending in that direction. He is still just 23 and has the most well-rounded arsenal in the Astros' farm system. With the way he finished 2020, Whitley likely starts 2021 in Triple-A and could make his major league debut in 2021. ■

Year	Age	Club (League)	Class	W	L	ERA	G	GS	IP	H	HR	BB	SO	BB/9	SO/9	WHIP	AVG
2017	19	Corpus Christi (TL)	AA	0	0	1.84	4	2	15	8	1	4	26	2.5	16.0	0.82	.143
	19	Quad Cities (MWL)	LoA	2	3	2.91	12	10	46	42	2	21	67	4.1	13.0	1.36	.215
	19	Fayetteville (CAR)	HiA	3	1	3.16	7	6	31	28	2	9	50	2.6	14.4	1.18	.217
2018	20	Corpus Christi (TL)	AA	0	2	3.76	8	8	26	15	2	11	34	3.8	11.6	0.99	.139
2019	21	Round Rock (PCL)	AAA	0	3	12.21	8	5	24	35	9	15	29	5.5	10.7	2.05	.294
	21	Corpus Christi (TL)	AA	2	2	5.56	6	6	23	18	2	19	36	7.5	14.3	1.63	.175
	21	Astros (GCL)	R	0	2	8.31	2	2	4	2	0	9	10	18.7	20.8	2.54	.080
	21	Fayetteville (CAR)	HiA	1	0	2.16	2	2	8	4	0	1	11	1.1	11.9	0.60	.129
Minor League Totals				9	15	4.71	57	47	197	171	18	95	289	4.3	13.2	1.35	.232

2 LUIS GARCIA, RHP

TOP ROOKIE

BA GRADE

50 Risk: Medium

Born: Dec. 13, 1996. **B-T:** R-R. **HT:** 6-1. **WT:** 244. **Signed:** Venezuela, 2017. **Signed by:** Oz Ocampo/Tom Shafer/Roman Ocumarez/David Brito.

TRACK RECORD: The Astros signed Garcia out of Venezuela in 2017 for $20,000 when he was a 20-year-old touching the low 90s. He started to touch the mid 90s later that summer. After reaching high Class A Fayetteville in 2019, Garcia made his major league debut in Sept. 2020, then threw two scoreless innings as the opener in Houston's 4-3 victory in Game 5 of the American League Championship Series.

SCOUTING REPORT: Garcia pitches off a fastball that ranges from 92-97 mph. His best pitch is his plus changeup with late sink and fade that flashes as a 70 on the 20-80 scale. Garcia sells it to look like a fastball out of his hand, but its 11 mph of separation consistently gets both lefties and righties waving out front. His low-80s slider is an average pitch that he used effectively last year, with sharp, late break at times. His 76-78 mph curveball is a fringe-average pitch that blends too much into his slider. Garcia also introduced a hard 86-88 mph cutter with mixed results. He has a track record of missing bats, though his command is still below-average.

THE FUTURE: Garcia has the swing-and-miss stuff to develop into a mid-rotation starter if his location improves. He's a potential closer if he stays in the bullpen.

SCOUTING GRADES: **Fastball:** 55 **Slider:** 50 **Curveball:** 45 **Cutter:** 40 **Changeup:** 70 **Control:** 45

Year	Age	Club (League)	Class	W	L	ERA	G	GS	IP	H	HR	BB	SO	BB/9	SO/9	WHIP	AVG
2017	20	Astros (DSL)	R	1	1	1.64	6	1	11	13	1	4	18	3.3	14.7	1.55	.277
2018	21	Quad Cities (MWL)	LoA	7	2	2.48	19	10	69	58	4	33	70	4.3	9.1	1.32	.200
	21	Tri-City (NYP)	SS	0	0	0.00	5	3	16	7	0	8	28	4.4	15.4	0.92	.106
2019	22	Quad Cities (MWL)	LoA	4	0	2.93	9	6	43	23	4	16	60	3.3	12.6	0.91	.138
	22	Fayetteville (CAR)	HiA	6	4	3.02	15	12	66	43	5	34	108	4.7	14.8	1.17	.157
2020	23	Houston (AL)	MAJ	0	1	2.92	5	1	12	7	1	5	9	3.6	6.6	0.97	.167
Major League Totals				0	1	2.92	5	1	12	7	1	5	9	3.7	6.6	0.97	.167
Minor League Totals				18	7	2.50	54	32	205	144	14	95	284	4.2	12.5	1.17	.196

3 JEREMY PEÑA, SS

MARY DECICCO/MLB PHOTOS VIA GETTY IMAGES

BA GRADE

50 Risk: High

Born: Sept. 22, 1997. **B-T:** R-R. **HT:** 6-0. **WT:** 202. **Drafted:** Maine, 2018 (3rd round). **Signed by:** Bobby St. Pierre.

TRACK RECORD: The son of former big leaguer Geronimo Peña, Jeremy stood out for his defense at Maine before signing with the Astros for $535,000 as a third-round pick in 2018. He had an excellent full-season debut through two levels of Class A, then followed it up in 2020 with a strong showing playing winter ball in the Dominican Republic.

SCOUTING REPORT: Peña is a plus defender at shortstop, where he has smooth actions, good instincts and range to go with a plus arm. He signed with a lean, lively frame and has since added around 20 pounds while retaining his athleticism and slightly above-average speed. Scouts were more skeptical of Peña's bat as an amateur, but his swing has evolved from a handsy version in college into one that better incorporates his whole body. He now better leverages his explosiveness and creates a more adjustable swing path to go with his solid bat-to-ball skills and a sound grasp for the strike zone. The added strength has helped Peña's ability to drive the ball, but he still has below-average power, though he has a chance for more because of his contact frequency.

THE FUTURE: Some scouts view Peña as a reserve infielder, but his defense and contact skills give him a chance to develop into an everyday shortstop.

SCOUTING GRADES: **Hitting:** 50 **Power:** 40 **Running:** 55 **Fielding:** 60 **Arm:** 60

Year	Age	Club (League)	Class	AVG	G	AB	R	H	2B	3B	HR	RBI	BB	SO	SB	OBP	SLG
2018	20	Tri-City (NYP)	SS	.250	36	136	22	34	5	0	1	10	18	19	3	.340	.309
2019	21	Quad Cities (MWL)	LoA	.293	66	242	44	71	8	4	5	41	35	57	17	.389	.421
	21	Fayetteville (CAR)	HiA	.317	43	167	28	53	13	3	2	13	12	33	3	.378	.467
Minor League Totals				.290	145	545	94	158	26	7	8	64	65	109	23	.374	.407

4 ALEX SANTOS, RHP

BILL MITCHELL

BA GRADE
55 **Risk: Extreme**

Born: Feb. 10, 2002. **B-T:** R-R. **HT:** 6-3. **WT:** 215. **Drafted:** HS—Bronx, N.Y., 2020 (2nd round supp). **Signed by:** Bobby St. Pierre.

TRACK RECORD: Major League Baseball made the Astros surrender their first- and second-round picks in 2020 as penalties for their illegal sign-stealing. With their first pick at No. 72 overall, Houston drafted Santos, who didn't get to pitch during the 2020 high school season in New York due to the pandemic. Instead, Santos regularly threw bullpens at the Citius Baseball facility his father co-owns and sent his Rapsodo data. After signing for $1.25 million, Santos went to instructional league in Florida.

SCOUTING REPORT: Santos pitches off a low-to-mid-90s fastball with a high spin rate that should help him get swings and misses when he pitches up in the zone. He shows feel for two secondary pitches. The most advanced one is his curveball, which is a potential plus pitch which can miss bats with its tight rotation. His changeup—a pitch Santos didn't really need in high school—made strides in 2020 and gives him a chance for a third average or better pitch. Santos has a strong, athletic build and the strike-throwing ability to project as a starter.

THE FUTURE: High school pitchers are risky—especially given the lack of looks at Santos during his draft year—but he has one of the best combinations of upside and starter traits in the Astros' system.

SCOUTING GRADES: **Fastball:** 55 **Curveball:** 60 **Changeup:** 50 **Control:** 55

Year	Age	Club (League)	Class	W	L	ERA	G	GS	IP	H	HR	BB	SO	BB/9	SO/9	WHIP	AVG
2020	18	Did not play—No minor league season															

5 BRYAN ABREU, RHP

MARY DECICCO/MLB PHOTOS VIA GETTY IMAGES

BA GRADE
50 **Risk: High**

Born: April 22, 1997. **B-T:** R-R. **HT:** 6-1. **WT:** 204. **Signed:** Dominican Republic, 2013. **Signed by:** Oz Ocampo/Marc Russo/Rafael Belen.

TRACK RECORD: Abreu was a $40,000 signing at 16 out of the Dominican Republic in 2013 who spent two years in the Dominican Summer League and didn't reach full-season ball until his fifth minor league season. Since then his stock has climbed, and he made his big league debut as a reliever in a 2019 September callup. Abreu struggled in four relief appearances for Houston at the start of 2020 before the Astros sent him down to their alternate training site in Corpus Christi, Texas.

SCOUTING REPORT: Abreu pitches at 92-95 mph and has the ability to dial it up to 97. His money-maker is his breaking stuff. He has an innate feel to spin a pair of swing-and-miss pitches in his mid-80s slider and low-80s curveball. His slider, which he threw more than any other pitch in 2020, earns plus to plus-plus grades, with hard, late break and two-plane depth. That same tight spin shows up with his curveball, a plus pitch that's similar to his slider but with more top-to-bottom shape. He rarely uses his well below-average changeup. Below-average control has hampered Abreu, whose upper and lower halves get disconnected.

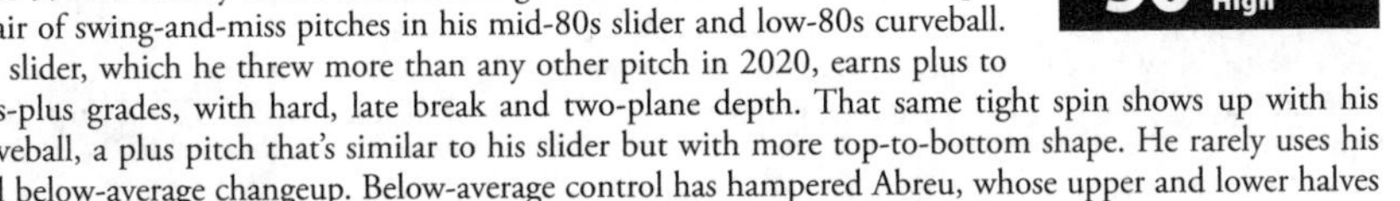

THE FUTURE: If Abreu can straighten out his control problems, he has the stuff to pitch in the middle of a rotation.

SCOUTING GRADES: **Fastball:** 55 **Slider:** 70 **Curveball:** 60 **Changeup:** 30 **Control:** 40

Year	Age	Club (League)	Class	W	L	ERA	G	GS	IP	H	HR	BB	SO	BB/9	SO/9	WHIP	AVG
2017	20	Greeneville (APP)	R	1	3	7.98	8	6	29	29	4	21	40	6.4	12.3	1.70	.215
2018	21	Quad Cities (MWL)	LoA	4	1	1.64	10	5	38	22	2	17	68	4.0	16.0	1.02	.144
	21	Tri-City (NYP)	SS	2	0	1.13	4	2	16	11	2	6	22	3.4	12.4	1.06	.177
2019	22	Houston (AL)	MAJ	0	0	1.04	7	0	9	4	0	3	13	3.1	13.5	0.81	.125
	22	Corpus Christi (TL)	AA	6	2	5.05	20	13	77	60	6	48	101	5.6	11.9	1.41	.178
	22	Fayetteville (CAR)	HiA	1	0	3.68	3	3	15	9	2	6	25	3.7	15.3	1.02	.153
2020	23	Houston (AL)	MAJ	0	0	2.70	4	0	3	1	0	7	3	18.9	8.1	2.40	.091
Major League Totals				0	0	1.50	11	0	12	5	0	10	16	7.5	12.0	1.25	.125
Minor League Totals				18	15	4.48	88	43	287	223	18	174	368	5.5	11.5	1.38	.215

6 TYLER IVEY, RHP

BA GRADE
50 Risk: High

Born: May 12, 1996. **B-T:** R-R. **HT:** 6-4. **WT:** 195. **Drafted:** Grayson (Texas) JC, 2017 (3rd round). **Signed by:** Jim Stevenson.

TRACK RECORD: Ivey transferred from Texas Tech to Grayson (Texas) JC for his sophomore year in 2017, when he signed with the Astros for $450,000 as a third-rounder. Ivey has missed a lot of bats and thrown a lot of strikes, but he had trouble staying on the field in 2019 due to a sprained elbow ligament.

SCOUTING REPORT: What immediately jumps out about Ivey is his unorthodox delivery. It's a funky, herky-jerky motion with a head whack that he's toned down a bit, but the Astros have mostly left him alone because he's able to repeat it and throw strikes consistently. Ivey's mechanics add deception to a high-spin fastball that sits in the low 90s with the ability to reach 95 mph. It's effective up in the zone and pairs nicely with his plus curveball which has good rotation and top-to-bottom shape to miss bats and has led to high strikeout rates up through Double-A. Ivey can have success with his fastball/curve combo, but he has deepened his repertoire to include a hard, cutter-like slider and occasional changeup.

THE FUTURE: There's some durability risk with Ivey, but he has the stuff and control to develop into a mid-rotation starter. If he ends up in the bullpen, he could become a multi-inning relief threat with high-leverage potential.

SCOUTING GRADES: **Fastball:** 50 **Slider:** 50 **Curveball:** 60 **Changeup:** 40 **Control:** 55

Year	Age	Club (League)	Class	W	L	ERA	G	GS	IP	H	HR	BB	SO	BB/9	SO/9	WHIP	AVG
2017	21	Tri-City (NYP)	SS	0	3	5.94	11	7	36	41	2	12	41	3.0	10.2	1.46	.252
	21	Astros (GCL)	R	0	0	0.00	1	1	2	1	0	2	3	9.0	13.5	1.50	.125
2018	22	Quad Cities (MWL)	LoA	1	3	3.46	9	6	42	36	2	8	53	1.7	11.4	1.06	.211
	22	Fayetteville (CAR)	HiA	3	3	2.69	15	12	70	50	3	21	82	2.7	10.5	1.01	.176
2019	23	Corpus Christi (TL)	AA	4	0	1.57	11	8	46	28	5	16	61	3.1	11.9	0.96	.152
	23	Astros (GCL)	R	0	0	0.00	2	2	3	0	0	3	5	9.0	15.0	1.00	.000
	23	Fayetteville (CAR)	HiA	0	0	0.00	1	1	3	0	0	1	2	3.0	6.0	0.33	.000
Minor League Totals				8	9	3.07	50	37	202	156	12	63	247	2.8	11.0	1.08	.207

7 KOREY LEE, C

BA GRADE
50 Risk: Very High

Born: July 25, 1998. **B-T:** R-R. **HT:** 6-2. **WT:** 210. **Drafted:** California, 2019 (1st round). **Signed by:** Tom Costic.

TRACK RECORD: The Astros pulled a surprise with their first-round pick, at No. 32 overall, in 2019 when they drafted Lee, whom other clubs thought would be available in later rounds. The Astros had more conviction in his bat and signed him for $1.75 million. He had a solid debut that summer in the short-season New York-Penn League, then in 2020 came over to Houston's alternate training site later in the summer before going to Florida for instructional league.

SCOUTING REPORT: Lee didn't do much to distinguish himself offensively during his first two years at California, but he elevated his stock by hitting .337/.416/.619 during his draft year. He has slightly above-average raw power, though it hasn't shown as much in pro games because he was pulling a lot of balls on the ground. He worked since then to condense his stride and to drive the ball in the air more consistently, with promising returns at instructs. Lee moved around the field as a sophomore before working regularly behind the plate as a junior, and he has quickly made himself into a quality receiver. He's a good athlete for a catcher and has a plus arm.

THE FUTURE: Lee has the upside to be an everyday catcher if everything clicks. He should start 2021 at one of Houston's Class A affiliates.

SCOUTING GRADES: **Hitting:** 45 **Power:** 55 **Running:** 40 **Fielding:** 50 **Arm:** 60

Year	Age	Club (League)	Class	AVG	G	AB	R	H	2B	3B	HR	RBI	BB	SO	SB	OBP	SLG
2019	20	Tri-City (NYP)	SS	.268	64	224	31	60	6	4	3	28	28	49	8	.359	.371
Minor League Totals				.268	64	224	31	60	6	4	3	28	28	49	8	.359	.371

8 HUNTER BROWN, RHP

Born: Aug. 29, 1998. **B-T:** R-R. **HT:** 6-2. **WT:** 203. **Drafted:** Wayne State, 2019 (5th round). **Signed by:** Scott Oberhelman.

TRACK RECORD: Brown went to Division II Wayne State in Detroit, where he did little to distinguish himself until his junior year in 2019. That's when he posted a 2.43 ERA with 114 strikeouts in 85.1 innings and showed more power to his stuff, prompting the Astros to draft him in the fifth round and sign him for $325,000. Brown made his pro debut that summer in the short-season New York-Penn league, then in 2020 was a standout at instructional league.

SCOUTING REPORT: Brown began his time at Wayne State scraping the low 90s, but he now has a power fastball that gets to the mid-to-upper 90s in short bursts and ranges from 92-100 mph as a starter. He gets good angle on his fastball, which has late riding life to help him miss bats. He throws all of his pitches with power, including a hard curveball that's a plus offering, and a slider and changeup that both have average or better potential. Brown has starter stuff, but he is wild and will need to improve his well below-average control.

THE FUTURE: It will take a lot of improvement for Brown to get to even fringe-average control, but if he can throw enough strikes he has a chance to develop into a mid-rotation starter. Otherwise, scouts see him as a potential candidate for multi-inning relief.

SCOUTING GRADES: **Fastball:** 70 **Slider:** 50 **Curveball:** 60 **Changeup:** 50 **Control:** 40

Year	Age	Club (League)	Class	W	L	ERA	G	GS	IP	H	HR	BB	SO	BB/9	SO/9	WHIP	AVG
2019	20	Tri-City (NYP)	SS	2	2	4.56	12	6	24	13	0	18	33	6.8	12.5	1.31	.116
Minor League Totals				2	2	4.56	12	6	23	13	0	18	33	6.9	12.6	1.31	.157

9 COLIN BARBER, OF

MIKE JANES/FOUR SEAM IMAGES

Born: Dec. 4, 2000. **B-T:** L-L. **HT:** 6-0. **WT:** 194. **Drafted:** HS—Chico, Calif., 2019 (4th round). **Signed by:** Tim Costic.

TRACK RECORD: Barber signed an above-slot deal of $1 million with the Astros as a fourth-round pick in 2019. With the 2020 minor league season canceled, Barber's summer started in Joliet, Ill., where he was one of the youngest hitters in the independent City of Champions Cup league. Later on, the Astros added Barber to their alternate training site, where he was the youngest player in camp, then in the fall went to instructional league.

SCOUTING REPORT: Barber is a focused, diligent worker with a fast bat and above-average raw power. He takes a fairly simple, direct cut that produces hard contact from the left side, albeit with some swing-and-miss. He has had a tendency to roll over with his top hand, leading to too many grounders to his pull side. He has worked to stay through the ball better, which should help his power show up more in games. He has a patient approach, sometimes to the point where scouts would like to see him be more aggressive on pitches he can drive. Barber is an above-average runner with a chance to stick in center field with an average arm that could play in right field.

THE FUTURE: Barber's potential stands out in a farm system which is light on young position players. He will likely start 2021 with an assignment to one of Houston's Class A affiliates.

SCOUTING GRADES: **Hitting:** 45 **Power:** 55 **Running:** 55 **Fielding:** 50 **Arm:** 50

Year	Age	Club (League)	Class	AVG	G	AB	R	H	2B	3B	HR	RBI	BB	SO	SB	OBP	SLG
2019	18	Astros (GCL)	R	.263	28	99	19	26	5	1	2	6	19	29	2	.387	.394
Minor League Totals				.263	28	99	19	26	5	1	2	6	19	29	2	.387	.394

10 GRAE KESSINGER, SS/3B

BA GRADE
50 Risk: Very High

Born: Aug. 25, 1997. **B-T:** R-R. **HT:** 6-2. **WT:** 204. **Drafted:** Mississippi, 2019 (2nd round). **Signed by:** Travis Coleman.

TRACK RECORD: Kessinger's father Kevin played in the minors for the Cubs, and his uncle Keith played in the majors. His grandfather Don has the most accomplished baseball career in the family as a six-time all-star shortstop for the Cubs before becoming Mississippi's coach. Grae signed with the Astros for $750,000 as a second-rounder in 2019. With the 2020 season canceled, Kessinger focused on his conditioning before heading to instructional league.

SCOUTING REPORT: Kessinger is a fundamentally sound player who gets the most out of tools which grade mostly as 40s and 50s. It starts with good bat control, pitch recognition and a disciplined offensive approach, enabling him to make frequent contact with all pitch types and draw walks. He has below-average raw power, but he hits the ball hard and his feel for the barrel could allow him to produce sneaky pop later, especially if he's able to get his hips and legs into his swing more. An average runner and thrower, Kessinger doesn't have the typical first-step burst and range scouts prefer at shortstop. He reads the ball well off the bat and is a reliable defender on balls he gets to, so second or third base could work.

THE FUTURE: Some scouts see Kessinger as a future utilityman with risk he could hit a wall against upper-level pitchers.

SCOUTING GRADES: Hitting: 50 | Power: 40 | Running: 50 | Fielding: 45 | Arm: 50

Year	Age	Club (League)	Class	AVG	G	AB	R	H	2B	3B	HR	RBI	BB	SO	SB	OBP	SLG
2019	21	Quad Cities (MWL)	LoA	.224	50	170	25	38	6	0	2	17	26	32	8	.333	.294
	21	Tri-City (NYP)	SS	.268	12	41	5	11	4	0	0	3	3	4	1	.333	.366
Minor League Totals				.232	62	211	30	49	10	0	2	20	29	36	9	.333	.308

11 ENOLI PAREDES, RHP

BA GRADE
45 Risk: Medium

Born: Sept. 28, 1995. **B-T:** R-R. **HT:** 5-11. **WT:** 171. **Signed:** Dominican Republic, 2015. **Signed by:** Oz Ocampo/Roman Ocumarez.

TRACK RECORD: Few players in the Dominican Republic get signed when they're 20, but the Astros took a chance on Paredes for a $10,000 bonus in 2015. He progressively gained velocity, ascended the minors and rose to Houston's bullpen in 2020. Paredes earned the trust of manager Dusty Baker and began pitching high-leverage innings by the end of the season, ultimately finishing with a 3.05 ERA in 22 appearances.

SCOUTING REPORT: Paredes has outstanding arm speed on a fastball that sits 94-97 mph and touches 99 mph. He is primarily a two-pitch reliever, zipping his fastball past hitters and complementing it with a plus slider he can add and subtract from, ranging from the low 80s all the way to 89 mph. He has an innate feel to impart tight spin on his slider, giving him a putaway pitch with good tilt across the zone. Paredes throws an occasional curveball and rarely uses his below-average changeup. He has a high-energy delivery that gets out of control at times, making it difficult to corral his stuff.

THE FUTURE: Paredes should play an important role in Houston's bullpen in 2021. Improving his below-average control could make him a potential closer.

Year	Age	Club (League)	Class	W	L	ERA	G	GS	IP	H	HR	BB	SO	BB/9	SO/9	WHIP	AVG
2020	24	Houston (AL)	MAJ	3	3	3.05	22	0	21	18	1	11	20	4.8	8.7	1.40	.237
Major League Totals				3	3	3.05	22	0	20	18	1	11	20	4.8	8.7	1.40	.237
Minor League Totals				13	14	2.41	66	26	235	130	8	103	297	3.9	11.4	0.99	.160

12 CHAS MCCORMICK, OF

BA GRADE
45 Risk: Medium

Born: April 19, 1995. **B-T:** R-R. **HT:** 6-0. **WT:** 208. **Drafted:** Millersville (Pa.), 2017, (21st round). **Signed by:** Zach Clark.

TRACK RECORD: McCormick entered pro ball with little fanfare as a 21st-round senior sign for $1,000 out of Division II Millersville (Pa.). He quietly performed well up through Triple-A in 2019, made hard contact at the alternate training site in 2020 and even earned a spot on the Astros' postseason roster, though he didn't play. He played winter ball in the Dominican Republic after the season.

SCOUTING REPORT: McCormick has excellent strike-zone judgment and had more walks than strike-outs in his last full season in 2019. That disciplined approach helps him frequently get on base. When McCormick does swing, he has solid bat-to-ball skills, average raw power and a knack for getting the ball

airborne. More pull-oriented earlier in his career, McCormick is best when he stays through the middle of the field and uses the right-center gap. McCormick has played all three outfield spots with most of his time in the corners. He's a tick above-average runner who could handle center field, but he is a plus defender in a corner with good instincts and reactions off the bat.
THE FUTURE: There isn't much projection left with McCormick, whom some scouts see as a reserve outfielder. There's a chance he can be an everyday player who chips in with his on-base skills and glove.

Year	Age	Club (League)	Class	AVG	G	AB	R	H	2B	3B	HR	RBI	BB	SO	SB	OBP	SLG
2019	24	Round Rock (PCL)	AAA	.262	57	191	39	50	3	3	10	44	28	34	7	.347	.466
	24	Corpus Christi (TL)	AA	.277	53	177	26	49	3	3	4	22	39	28	9	.426	.395
Minor League Totals				.276	281	968	152	267	38	11	20	143	125	148	41	.360	.400

13 SHAWN DUBIN, RHP

BREAKOUT
BA GRADE
45 Risk: High

Born: Sept. 6, 1995. **B-T:** R-R. **HT:** 6-1. **WT:** 171. **Drafted:** Georgetown (Ky.), 2018 (13th round). **Signed by:** Travis Coleman.
TRACK RECORD: When Buffalo shut down its baseball program, Dubin transferred to NAIA Georgetown (Ky.) for his senior year. After signing with the Astros for $1,000 in 2018, he added velocity in 2019 and led the high Class A Carolina League with 132 strikeouts in just 98.2 innings. The Astros brought him to their alternate training site in 2020.
SCOUTING REPORT: Dubin came into pro ball with a fast arm. With added weight, he now pitches at 92-96 mph and can hit 99 with late riding life when he pitches up in the zone. Dubin's slider is his key pitch. It's a plus offering with tight rotation and good tilt when it's on, but it can be inconsistent and has a shorter, cutter-like break at times. His solid-average curveball and fringe-average changeup round out his repertoire. Dubin has some effort in his delivery and struggled to throw strikes in college. He has fringe-average control and has kept his walks reasonable, if still a tick high.
THE FUTURE: Dubin has a chance to start. Along with his mechanics, the way his fastball and slider would play up in short stints leads some scouts to think he's better suited for a bullpen role.

Year	Age	Club (League)	Class	W	L	ERA	G	GS	IP	H	HR	BB	SO	BB/9	SO/9	WHIP	AVG
2019	23	Quad Cities (MWL)	LoA	1	0	0.75	3	1	12	7	0	4	19	3.0	14.3	0.92	.149
	23	Fayetteville (CAR)	HiA	6	5	3.92	22	18	99	71	3	42	132	3.8	12.0	1.15	.169
Minor League Totals				9	6	3.79	39	24	140	101	7	57	182	3.7	11.7	1.13	.198

14 BRETT CONINE, RHP

BA GRADE
45 Risk: High

Born: Oct. 16, 1996. **B-T:** R-R. **HT:** 6-3. **WT:** 210. **Drafted:** Cal State Fullerton, 2018 (11th round). **Signed by:** Ryan Leake.
TRACK RECORD: Conine has a chance to make an unusual transformation from college closer to major league starter. After saving 25 games over three years at Cal State Fullerton, Conine spent his first full season with the Astros as a starter and went 8-4, 2.20 as he climbed to Double-A. The Astros brought him to their alternate training site in 2020 and he continued to progress before wrapping up in instructional league.
SCOUTING REPORT: Conine doesn't fit the profile of a typical former closer. He relies on mixing four pitches and throwing strikes rather than overpowering anyone. Conine's fastball ranges from 90-95 mph. He backs it up with a solid-average curveball that's his go-to pitch for a strikeout and an average changeup he has the confidence to throw against lefties and righties. Conine sprinkles in a fringe-average slider, though it's more of an early-count offering that doesn't miss as many bats as his curve. His control could be plus and he's adept at moving the ball around the zone.
THE FUTURE: Conine will open 2021 in the upper levels and could make his major league debut during the season. He has the potential to stick around as a back-end starter.

Year	Age	Club (League)	Class	W	L	ERA	G	GS	IP	H	HR	BB	SO	BB/9	SO/9	WHIP	AVG
2019	22	Corpus Christi (TL)	AA	1	0	2.00	4	2	18	20	1	6	14	3.0	7.0	1.44	.253
	22	Quad Cities (MWL)	LoA	3	2	1.91	6	5	33	19	3	6	40	1.6	10.9	0.76	.154
	22	Fayetteville (CAR)	HiA	4	2	2.42	15	8	63	52	3	17	80	2.4	11.4	1.09	.202
Minor League Totals				9	5	2.16	36	18	146	114	7	40	171	2.5	10.5	1.05	.212

15 JAIRO SOLIS, RHP

Born: Dec. 22, 1999. **B-T:** R-R. **HT:** 6-2. **WT:** 209. **Signed:** Venezuela, 2016. **Signed by:** Oz Ocampo/Tom Shafer/Roman Ocumarez/Enrique Brito.

TRACK RECORD: Solis signed with the Astros for $450,000 after touching 91 mph as a 16-year-old. He quickly advanced to the low Class A Midwest League at 18, but he suffered an elbow injury and missed the end of the 2018 season and all of 2019 after having Tommy John surgery. Solis returned to pitch at instructional league in 2020 and showed enough that the Astros added him to the 40-man roster.

SCOUTING REPORT: Solis rose quickly as one of the Astros' most promising pitchers, especially given his starter traits relative to some of the organization's hard-throwing but erratic arms. At his best, Solis pitched with good angle on a lively fastball sitting at 91-95 mph and reaching 98. He was back to working in the low-to-mid 90s at instructs in 2020. Solis flashes an above-average changeup with late tumble and he has shown a feel for both a curveball and slider, though they can get slurvy. He's an athletic pitcher who has shown solid control at times, though it escapes him at other times.

THE FUTURE: The arrows pointed in the right direction once Solis got back on the mound in 2020. He could reach Double-A by the end of 2021.

Year	Age	Club (League)	Class	W	L	ERA	G	GS	IP	H	HR	BB	SO	BB/9	SO/9	WHIP	AVG
2018	18	Quad Cities (MWL)	LoA	2	5	3.55	13	11	51	49	1	32	51	5.7	9.1	1.60	.218
Minor League Totals				5	7	3.05	28	21	112	100	4	53	120	4.3	9.6	1.37	.240

16 TYLER BROWN, RHP

BA GRADE
45 Risk: Very High

Born: Oct. 2, 1998. **B-T:** R-R. **HT:** 6-4. **WT:** 242. **Drafted:** Vanderbilt, 2020 (3rd round). **Signed by:** Landon Townsley.

TRACK RECORD: Brown probably could have started at another school, but he pitched in relief for a Vanderbilt team that won the 2019 College World Series with one of the best rotations in the country. After the 2020 coronavirus pandemic cut his junior year short, Brown signed with the Astros for $577,000 as a third-round pick.

SCOUTING REPORT: Brown has a deeper repertoire than most relievers, operating off a fastball that sits 91-94 mph and can reach 96. He throws frequent strikes with his fastball and complements it with an above-average slider, an average changeup and a slightly below-average curve. It's a starter's pitch mix, but Brown had Tommy John surgery in high school and some scouts think his delivery is better suited to relief.

THE FUTURE: Brown will likely begin his career as a tandem starter at one of the Class A levels in 2021. His pitch mix gives him a chance to start and he has a fallback as a potential high-leverage reliever if he ends up in the bullpen.

Year	Age	Club (League)	Class	W	L	ERA	G	GS	IP	H	HR	BB	SO	BB/9	SO/9	WHIP	AVG
2020	21	Did not play—No minor league season															

17 ZACH DANIELS, OF

BREAKOUT
BA GRADE
50 Risk: Extreme

Born: Jan. 23, 1999. **B-T:** R-R. **HT:** 6-1. **WT:** 210. **Drafted:** Tennessee, 2020 (4th round). **Signed by:** Landon Townsley.

TRACK RECORD: Daniels showed exciting tools but piled up strikeouts his first two seasons at Tennessee, hitting .161/.339/.344 as a freshman, then .200/.262/.417 as a sophomore and his struggles continued that summer in the Cape Cod League. He began 2020 like he was on the verge of a breakthrough, batting .357/.478/.750 through 17 games until the coronavirus pandemic shut the season down before Southeastern Conference play. The Astros bought into his improvement and drafted him in the fourth round, signing him for $400,000 before he went to instructional league.

SCOUTING REPORT: Daniels has the loudest combination of tools and athleticism in the Astros' system. He's a power sprinter with plus-plus speed, running the 60-yard dash under 6.4 seconds. He's an explosive, quick-twitch athlete with the strength and bat speed to drive the ball with plus raw power in batting practice, but whether it will click in games is a question mark. His swing isn't long, but there is extra noise in his trigger and his swing path doesn't keep his barrel in the zone for long, leading to lots of swings and misses. Daniels has the speed to play center field and an average arm, but he moved around all three outfield spots at Tennessee and spent most of his junior year at DH.

THE FUTURE: Daniels' glimmer of offensive performance gives hope he may be starting to turn the corner, with athleticism that should help him make adjustments. He's likely to open 2021 in low Class A.

Year	Age	Club (League)	Class	AVG	G	AB	R	H	2B	3B	HR	RBI	BB	SO	SB	OBP	SLG
2020	21	Did not play—No minor league season															

18 FREUDIS NOVA, SS

BA GRADE
50 Risk: Extreme

Born: Jan. 12, 2000. **B-T:** R-R. **HT:** 6-1. **WT:** 190. **Signed:** Dominican Republic, 2016. **Signed by:** Oz Ocampo/Roman Ocumarez/Jose Lima.

TRACK RECORD: Nova was one of the top players in the 2016 international class and signed with the Astros for $1.2 million. He reached low Class A Quad Cities in 2019, where his athleticism and raw tools stood out more than his performance. At instructional league in 2020, Nova left scouts disappointed between his declining athleticism and performance, but the Astros still added him to their 40-man roster after the season.

SCOUTING REPORT: Nova didn't show the same quick-twitch to his actions that he had shown in the past, a concern for a player whose value has been tied more to his tools than his pure hitting ability. Nova does have solid-average raw power to pull a fastball over the fence when a pitcher makes a mistake, but he struggles with pitch recognition and his free-swinging approach gets him in trouble. Nova has a strong arm for the left side of the diamond, but he has slowed down as he's filled out, leading to more concerns that he's a third baseman rather than a shortstop, with hands that need improvement to stick in the dirt.

THE FUTURE: Youth is still on Nova's side to rebound as he enters his age-20 season and returns to the structure of a normal year. The 2021 season will be critical for his prospect status.

Year	Age	Club (League)	Class	AVG	G	AB	R	H	2B	3B	HR	RBI	BB	SO	SB	OBP	SLG
2019	19	Quad Cities (MWL)	LoA	.259	75	282	35	73	20	1	3	29	15	68	10	.301	.369
Minor League Totals				.268	163	594	86	159	29	2	13	73	36	122	27	.320	.389

19 JORDAN BREWER, OF

BA GRADE
45 Risk: Very High

Born: Aug. 1, 1997. **B-T:** R-L. **HT:** 6-1. **WT:** 195. **Drafted:** Michigan, 2019 (3rd round). **Signed by:** Scott Oberhelman.

TRACK RECORD: After starring in football and baseball in high school, Brewer went to Lincoln Trail (Ill.) JC for two seasons before transferring to Michigan. Swing adjustments helped him take off and become the 2019 Big Ten player of the year as he led the Wolverines to the College World Series finals. The Astros took him in the third round and signed him for $500,000. Brewer scuffled in his pro debut and missed time with a toe injury, then had left knee surgery in April 2020 that kept him off the field the entire year.

SCOUTING REPORT: Brewer has the backward profile of a lefthanded thrower who bats righthanded. While he hit well at Michigan, his tools stand out more than his pure hitting ability. He's a potential power/speed threat in center field, with his power and wheels both grading out plus. Brewer has worked to better incorporate his lower half into his swing, but it's not the most adjustable stroke, which leaves him with holes. Brewer has the speed for center field but mostly played on the corners at Michigan.

THE FUTURE: Brewer's athleticism and history of making swing changes bode well, but his bat will be tested by better pitching. He should be ready for the start of spring training in 2021.

Year	Age	Club (League)	Class	AVG	G	AB	R	H	2B	3B	HR	RBI	BB	SO	SB	OBP	SLG
2019	21	Tri-City (NYP)	SS	.130	16	54	5	7	0	0	1	3	2	6	2	.161	.185
Minor League Totals				.130	16	54	5	7	0	0	1	3	2	6	2	.161	.185

20 SHAY WHITCOMB, SS

BREAKOUT
BA GRADE
45 Risk: Very High

Born: Sept. 28, 1998. **B-T:** R-R. **HT:** 6-3. **WT:** 200. **Drafted:** UC San Diego, 2020 (5th round). **Signed by:** Ryan Leake.

TRACK RECORD: Whitcomb played at Division II at UC San Diego and elevated his stock with a strong summer after his sophomore year in the Cape Cod League, where he hit .303/.371/.606 with eight home runs in 34 games. He was the 160th and final pick of the five-round draft in 2020, signing for $56,000 before reporting to instructional league.

SCOUTING REPORT: Whitcomb's Cape performance increased scouts' confidence in his ability to hit better pitching. He has the ability to turn around good velocity and drive the ball for above-average raw power. There could be more power to unlock as he works to hit from a sturdier base on his back side and get into a better hitting position, an adjustment he seemed to be working through during instructs. What Whitcomb does at the plate drives his value. He's an average runner who doesn't have the footwork or range for shortstop, with his arm probably pushing him to second base, though he could see time at third.

THE FUTURE: Whitcomb fits the mold of players with hitterish tendencies the Astros have targeted in recent years. He should start 2021 at one of the team's Class A affiliates.

Year	Age	Club (League)	Class	AVG	G	AB	R	H	2B	3B	HR	RBI	BB	SO	SB	OBP	SLG
2020	21	Did not play—No minor league season															

21 DAURI LORENZO, SS

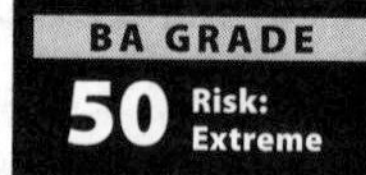

Born: Oct. 29, 2002. **B-T:** B-R. **HT:** 6-0. **WT:** 195. **Signed:** Dominican Republic, 2019. **Signed by:** Roman Ocumarez/Francisco Ulloa/Leocadio Guevara.

TRACK RECORD: Lorenzo landed a $1.8 million bonus as Houston's top international signing in 2019. His pro debut was delayed by the coronavirus pandemic, but he held his own in instructional league. He faced a stable of hard-throwing pitchers with full-season experience and got work at Dominican instructs.

SCOUTING REPORT: Lorenzo shows a knack for slowing the game down and managing his at-bats with a mature approach for his age, even against much more advanced pitchers than he was accustomed to facing. He's an offensive-minded shortstop whose strengths should be putting the ball in play and getting on base. A switch-hitter with a better swing and more rhythm from the right side, Lorenzo has good bat-to-ball skills, keeps the barrel through the hitting zone a long time and uses his hands well in his swing, with the ability to adjust even when he drifts open early. He's mostly a line-drive hitter with doubles power, and while he got stronger in 2020, he doesn't project to be a big power threat. Lorenzo has solid-average speed and arm strength, but he doesn't have the quick-burst athleticism or instincts of other shortstops, so he most likely ends up at second base.

THE FUTURE: Lorenzo will still be the same age as a high school senior next season. He should open in the Rookie-level Gulf Coast League.

Year	Age	Club (League)	Class	AVG	G	AB	R	H	2B	3B	HR	RBI	BB	SO	SB	OBP	SLG
2020	17	Did not play—No minor league season															

22 BRANDON BIELAK, RHP

BA GRADE
40 Risk: Medium

Born: April 2, 1996. **B-T:** L-R. **HT:** 6-2. **WT:** 208. **Drafted:** Notre Dame, 2017 (11th round). **Signed by:** Nick Venuto.

TRACK RECORD: Bielak is one of several pitchers the Astros drafted after the 10th round who have emerged as legitimate prospects. He quickly climbed the minors and made his big league debut as a starter in 2020, but he got blown up as his command vanished and moved to the bullpen down the stretch.

SCOUTING REPORT: Bielak's fastball ranges from 91-96 mph. He mixes in four other pitches, the best of which is an 85-88 mph changeup that flashes above-average with sink and fade. Bielak has a deeper, more horizontal break than most other pitchers on his 88-91 mph cutter. It's an average pitch, as is his curveball, and he throws a fringe-average slider as well. Bielak was a solid strike-thrower throughout his minor league career, but he lost feel for the zone in the majors, which led to hitters teeing off on his fastball.

THE FUTURE: Bielak has enough stuff to pitch in the back of a rotation, but will need to locate better to stick in that role. He could get another crack in 2021.

Year	Age	Club (League)	Class	W	L	ERA	G	GS	IP	H	HR	BB	SO	BB/9	SO/9	WHIP	AVG
2020	24	Houston (AL)	MAJ	3	3	6.75	12	6	32	39	9	17	26	4.8	7.3	1.75	.305
Major League Totals				3	3	6.75	12	6	32	39	9	17	26	4.8	7.3	1.75	.305
Minor League Totals				20	13	2.94	58	41	272	215	19	94	292	3.1	9.7	1.13	.217

23 JUAN SANTANDER, C

BA GRADE
45 Risk: Extreme

Born: Dec. 9, 2002. **B-T:** R-R. **HT:** 6-3. **WT:** 215. **Signed:** Venezuela, 2019. **Signed by:** Roman Ocumarez/Jose Palacios/Enrique Brito.

TRACK RECORD: Santander was one of the best catchers in the 2019 international class and signed with the Astros for $700,000. He has yet to make his official pro debut due to the coronavirus pandemic, but he was able to participate in the Tricky League (an unofficial league for July 2 signings) and Dominican instructional league in 2019 as well as Dominican instructs again in 2020.

SCOUTING REPORT: Santander stands out for his physicality and offensive upside for a catcher. He hits from a solid base, keeps his weight back, and while there's some length to his swing, he has quick hands to catch up to good velocity. He has a slight uppercut to hit the ball in the air and has a chance to grow into average power, especially if he can incorporate his whole body into his swing rather than relying on his hands. Santander has a large build for a catcher that he will need to maintain. He has done that so far, resulting in quicker footwork on throws with solid-average arm strength. He's a leader among his teammates and has the intangibles teams love in a catcher.

THE FUTURE: Santander has a lot to like, but he's still a teenager several years away. He will make his pro debut in 2021.

Year	Age	Club (League)	Class	AVG	G	AB	R	H	2B	3B	HR	RBI	BB	SO	SB	OBP	SLG
2020	17	Did not play—No minor league season															

24 JOJANSE TORRES, RHP

BA GRADE
40 Risk: Medium

Born: Aug. 4, 1995. **B-T:** R-R. **HT:** 6-1. **WT:** 185. **Signed:** Dominican Republic, 2018. **Signed by:** Roman Ocumarez.

TRACK RECORD: The Astros haven't shied away from signing pitchers in their late teens or early 20s in a Latin American scouting world focused on 16-year-old signings. Even for the Astros, Torres was older for a Dominican signing when they inked him for $150,000 at 22. Torres made the signing look prescient with a strong full-season debut at the Class A levels in 2019. He was with the major league team for exhibition games in July, but elbow issues prevented him from pitching during the regular season.

SCOUTING REPORT: Torres ran his fastball up to 98 mph that first year in the DSL in 2018, then in 2019 was regularly touching 100 mph. Torres has a huge fastball that stands out in a system deep with power arms. His heater sits 95-100 mph and he throws it with an aggressive, grip-it-and-rip-it approach. He shows feel for a changeup that has good velocity separation off his fastball. It has the best chance among his offspeed stuff to develop into a solid-average or better pitch. Torres also throws a slider and curveball that are both inconsistent. He has overpowered lower-level competition, but his control needs to get better against more discerning hitters.

THE FUTURE: Torres has just 135 innings with the Astros, so there's some hope his control and secondary feel can improve. The most likely outcome is a reliever, with Double-A probably his next stop.

Year	Age	Club (League)	Class	W	L	ERA	G	GS	IP	H	HR	BB	SO	BB/9	SO/9	WHIP	AVG
2019	23	Quad Cities (MWL)	LoA	3	0	0.56	7	1	16	9	1	8	26	4.5	14.6	1.06	.138
	23	Fayetteville (CAR)	HiA	9	0	1.94	17	9	79	50	2	38	81	4.3	9.3	1.12	.153
Minor League Totals				13	2	1.86	37	18	135	95	4	54	155	3.6	10.3	1.10	.193

25 BLAKE TAYLOR, LHP

BA GRADE
40 Risk: Medium

Born: Aug. 17, 1995. **B-T:** L-L. **HT:** 6-3. **WT:** 220. **Drafted:** HS—Dana Point, Calif., 2013 (2nd round). **Signed by:** Brian Tracy (Pirates).

TRACK RECORD: The Pirates drafted Taylor when he was 17 with the 51st overall pick in 2013 and traded him to the Mets one year later as part of the deal for Ike Davis. He largely scuffled in the low minors until he moved to the bullpen and vaulted up to Triple-A in 2019. The Astros acquired him after the season in the deal for Jake Marisnick. Taylor made his major league debut in 2020 and earned the trust of manager Dusty Baker to pitch crucial innings as the season progressed, appearing in eight of the Astros' 13 playoff games.

SCOUTING REPORT: Taylor sticks out as a lefty in a system full of righthanded power arms. He comes at hitters with a 92-95 mph fastball that tops out at 97 with late cut that induces a lot of weak contact. His mid-80s slider is a solid-average pitch at its best when he keeps it at the bottom of the zone, though sometimes it flattens out and stays up, allowing hitters to do damage. He's primarily a two-pitch reliever with a below-average changeup he rarely throws. Taylor's control is below-average, but he was able to get out of sticky situations last year by drawing soft contact.

THE FUTURE: Taylor should return to a middle relief role in Houston in 2021. Better command will be key for him to stick.

Year	Age	Club (League)	Class	W	L	ERA	G	GS	IP	H	HR	BB	SO	BB/9	SO/9	WHIP	AVG
2020	24	Houston (AL)	MAJ	2	1	2.18	22	0	21	13	2	12	17	5.2	7.4	1.21	.173
Major League Totals				2	1	2.18	22	0	20	13	2	12	17	5.2	7.4	1.21	.173
Minor League Totals				10	23	4.08	106	52	321	279	14	177	292	5.0	8.2	1.42	.234

26 ELVIS GARCIA, RHP

Born: Sept. 24, 2002. **B-T:** R-R. **HT:** 5-11. **WT:** 186. **Signed:** Venezuela, 2019. **Signed by:** Roman Ocumarez/Jose Palacios.

TRACK RECORD: With all of the electric arms the Astros scouts have signed and developed out of Latin America in recent years, it would be wise to watch for who might be in their next wave. It could be Garcia, who signed for $180,000 on July 2, 2019, at 16 and quickly trended up after signing. His pro debut was delayed by the coronavirus pandemic, but he participated in Dominican instructional league at the end of 2020.

SCOUTING REPORT: Garcia signed with a fastball that touched 91 mph. After reporting to the Astros' academy, he increased his peak velocity to 94 mph with late riding life to miss bats up in the zone. Garcia isn't very big, but he's athletic with fast arm speed. He still lacks strength, so there's projection for him to continue throwing harder as he physically matures. What helps separate Garcia from his peers are his feel for pitching and starter traits, with easy arm action and a smooth delivery. His curveball has good depth

and shape and shows signs of being a future plus pitch. He hasn't focused much on his changeup but has flashed a feel for that pitch as well.
THE FUTURE: Garcia is a long way away, but the arrows are pointing in the right direction. He will make his pro debut in 2021.

Year	Age	Club (League)	Class	W	L	ERA	G	GS	IP	H	HR	BB	SO	BB/9	SO/9	WHIP	AVG
2020	17	Did not play—No minor league season															

27 RICHI GONZALEZ, OF

BA GRADE 45 Risk: Extreme

Born: Dec. 29, 2002. **B-T:** R-R. **HT:** 6-3. **WT:** 185. **Signed:** Dominican Republic, 2019. **Signed by:** Roman Ocumarez.

TRACK RECORD: Gonzalez signed for $310,000 on July 2, 2019, with tools that had started trending up leading into the signing date and continued after he got to the Astros' Dominican academy. He impressed in both the Tricky League (an unofficial league for July 2 signings) and Dominican instructional league in 2019, but his expected pro debut in 2020 was wiped out by the coronavirus pandemic aside from time at the end of the year at Dominican instructs.

SCOUTING REPORT: Scouts saw a lot of Gonzalez in the Dominican Republic early in the evaluation process, but later on he looked like a different player. Gonzalez has grown taller while retaining a lean, athletic frame. He has impressive raw tools, including plus speed and a plus arm from center field that could grow to plus-plus as he fills out, to the point where pitching could be a backup plan. That's not on the radar, though, as Gonzalez has performed well so far in unofficial games and live batting practice sessions. He has a habit of barring his arm in his swing, which adds some length, but he can drive balls out of the park to the middle of the field with solid-average raw power and a chance to grow into more.

THE FUTURE: Gonzalez has yet to be tested in official games, but he teases the potential to be a power/speed threat who could rise up this list next year. His pro debut in 2021 will be telling.

Year	Age	Club (League)	Class	AVG	G	AB	R	H	2B	3B	HR	RBI	BB	SO	SB	OBP	SLG
2020	17	Did not play—No minor league season															

28 BLAIR HENLEY, RHP

BA GRADE 40 Risk: High

Born: May 14, 1997. **B-T:** R-R. **HT:** 6-3. **WT:** 190. **Drafted:** Texas, 2019 (7th round). **Signed by:** Kris Gross.

TRACK RECORD: An unsigned 22nd-round pick of the Yankees out of high school, Henley spent three years in the starting rotation at Texas as a solid but unsensational performer. The Astros drafted him in the seventh round and signed him for $150,000. Henley dominated with a 1.60 ERA over 11 appearances in the New York-Penn League after signing, although most of it came in relief.

SCOUTING REPORT: The Astros are trying to squeeze velocity gains out of Henley the way they have with other pitchers in recent years. His fastball is already up a little bit and sits in the low 90s with the ability to touch 94 mph. Henley is moving away from a two-seamer he relied on in college to throw more four-seamers up in the zone to try to miss more bats. His separator is a plus slider with extremely tight spin (over 3,000 revolutions per minute) and sharp bite to dive underneath barrels. His changeup is a below-average pitch. Henley showed uneven control in college, but was significantly better throwing strikes in his pro debut.

THE FUTURE: Henley isn't overpowering, but his slider is a legitimate weapon that could carry him to the majors. He should start 2021 at one of the Class A levels.

Year	Age	Club (League)	Class	W	L	ERA	G	GS	IP	H	HR	BB	SO	BB/9	SO/9	WHIP	AVG
2019	22	Tri-City (NYP)	SS	1	1	1.60	11	2	34	29	1	8	46	2.1	12.3	1.10	.210
	22	Astros (GCL)	R	0	0	0.00	1	1	3	1	0	1	4	3.0	12.0	0.67	.091
Minor League Totals				1	1	1.47	12	3	36	30	1	9	50	2.2	12.3	1.06	.219

29 PETER SOLOMON, RHP

BA GRADE
40 Risk: High

Born: Aug. 16, 1996. **B-T:** R-R. **HT:** 6-4. **WT:** 201. **Drafted:** Notre Dame, 2017 (4th round). **Signed by:** Nick Venuto.

TRACK RECORD: Solomon turned in a dominant performance in the Cape Cod League after his sophomore year, but he stumbled as a junior at Notre Dame was demoted to the bullpen. The Astros still took him in the fourth round in 2017 and developed him as a starter. Solomon flourished in pro ball, but he made just two starts at high Class A Fayetteville in 2019 before having season-ending Tommy John surgery. The Astros added him to their 40-man roster after the 2020 season despite the missed time.

SCOUTING REPORT: Solomon finished his rehab and showed the same stuff he had before the operation. He has a four-pitch arsenal topped by a fastball that sits in the low-to-mid 90s with late riding life to hop over bats. He has a pair of breaking balls in a downer curveball that flashes above-average and a fringe-average slider, and he also has a below-average changeup that has taken a back seat to other development priorities. Solomon struggled with walks in college but was better in pro ball prior to surgery.

THE FUTURE: Solomon is set to return to official games in 2021. He has a chance to develop into a back-of-the-rotation starter, though his eventual ticket to the big leagues might come through a bullpen role.

Year	Age	Club (League)	Class	W	L	ERA	G	GS	IP	H	HR	BB	SO	BB/9	SO/9	WHIP	AVG
2019	22	Fayetteville (CAR)	HiA	0	0	2.35	2	2	8	7	1	4	14	4.7	16.4	1.43	.212
Minor League Totals				9	1	2.30	27	16	109	85	3	36	128	3.0	10.5	1.11	.213

30 AUSTIN HANSEN, RHP

Born: Aug. 25, 1996. **B-T:** R-R. **HT:** 6-0. **WT:** 195. **Drafted:** Oklahoma, 2018 (8th round). **Signed by:** Jim Stevenson.

TRACK RECORD: A closer at Oklahoma his junior year, Hansen is one of several college relievers the Astros have drafted and developed in their tandem-starter system. Hansen had success in that role in 2019 as he climbed to high Class A Fayetteville and got continued work at instructional league in 2020.

SCOUTING REPORT: Hansen pitches with a fastball in the low-to-mid 90s and can reach back for 98 mph. He has an above-average slider that is his putaway pitch, and the combination of his fastball and slider helped him strike out 33% of the batters he faced in 2019. Hansen primarily relies on those two pitches, but his feel for spin shows up on a curveball with good depth. He also throws an occasional below-average changeup. Hansen's delivery has a lot of effort, which gives him some deception but also impedes his command and control, leading to too many walks.

THE FUTURE: Hansen will continue to develop as a starter, but his stuff, delivery and control all suggest a likely return to the bullpen. He'll open at Double-A in 2021.

Year	Age	Club (League)	Class	W	L	ERA	G	GS	IP	H	HR	BB	SO	BB/9	SO/9	WHIP	AVG
2019	22	Quad Cities (MWL)	LoA	4	1	0.86	9	7	42	20	1	19	52	4.1	11.2	0.94	.121
	22	Fayetteville (CAR)	HiA	3	2	3.10	14	7	52	32	4	32	76	5.5	13.1	1.22	.144
Minor League Totals				9	6	2.02	37	16	124	66	7	63	173	4.6	12.5	1.03	.152

MORE PROSPECTS TO KNOW

31 ANDRE SCRUBB, RHP

The Astros needed lots of bullpen reinforcements in 2020 and called on Scrubb, who walked 20 in 23.2 innings but still had a 1.90 ERA, mixing a 91-96 mph fastball with a hard curveball.

32 CIONEL PEREZ, LHP

Perez has pitched in parts of three major league seasons and attacks hitters with a mid-90s fastball and a solid slider, but control remains an obstacle.

33 TAYLOR JONES, 1B

At 6-foot-7, Jones spent time on the mound at Gonzaga before becoming a full-time hitter. He made his brief major league debut in 2020 and has hit at every level up through Triple-A.

34 JAIRO LOPEZ, RHP

Lopez didn't look sharp at instructional league in 2020, but at his best the 20-year-old Venezuelan sits in the low 90s with feel to spin a pair of breaking balls.

35 NIVALDO RODRIGUEZ, RHP

Rodriguez hadn't pitched above high Class A prior to 2020, when he got the surprise callup to Houston's bullpen. He doesn't have a plus pitch and needs more minor league development time, but he could eventually solidify himself as a middle relief option with a 91-95 fastball and a hard breaking ball.

36 HUMBERTO CASTELLANOS, RHP

A pure relief prospect the Astros signed out of Mexico, Castellanos was one of many rookies to get innings out of Houston's bullpen in 2020. His fastball is light and sits around 90 mph, but he has a diverse pitch mix with his curveball, slider and changeup that he will throw in any count.

37 JIMMY ENDERSBY, RHP

SLEEPER

Endersby signed out of Division II Concordia-Irvine as an undrafted free agent after the five-round 2020 draft. He shows an innate feel for spin on both his 90-95 mph four-seam fastball and breaking stuff.

38 LUIS SANTANA, 2B/3B

Acquired from the Mets in the 2019 trade for J.D. Davis, Santana has a small, compact 5-foot-8 frame and is limited defensively, but he has a lot of hitter-ish tendencies and knack for putting the ball in play.

39 YOHANDER MARTINEZ, SS/3B/2B

Martinez hit .313/.439/.383 in 66 games in the Dominican Summer League as a 17-year-old in 2019, showing good strike-zone judgment, solid bat-to-ball skills from a compact, line-drive swing.

40 JAKE MEYERS, OF

Meyers spent 2020 at the alternate training site and showed good defensive instincts in center field. He struggled offensively in his brief time in Double-A in 2019 and will need to show more at the plate to break in as a reserve outfielder•

TOP PROSPECTS OF THE DECADE

Year	Player, Pos	2020 Org
2011	Jordan Lyles, RHP	Rangers
2012	Jon Singleton, 1B/OF	Did not play
2013	Carlos Correa, SS	Astros
2014	Carlos Coyrrea, SS	Astros
2015	Carlos Correa, SS	Astros
2016	A.J. Reed, 1B	Did not play
2017	Francis Martes, RHP	Astros
2018	Forrest Whitley, RHP	Astros
2019	Forrest Whitley, RHP	Astros
2020	Forrest Whitley, RHP	Astros

TOP DRAFT PICKS OF THE DECADE

Year	Player, Pos	2020 Org
2011	George Springer, OF	Astros
2012	Carlos Correa, SS	Astros
2013	Mark Appel, RHP	Did not play
2014	*Brady Aiken, LHP	Indians
2015	Alex Bregman, SS	Astros
2016	Forrest Whitley, RHP	Astros
2017	J.B. Bukauskas, RHP	D-backs
2018	Seth Beer, OF	D-backs
2019	Korey Lee, C	Astros
2020	Alex Santos, RHP (2nd round supp)	Astros

* Did not sign

DEPTH CHART

HOUSTON ASTROS

TOP 2021 ROOKIES	RANK
Forrest Whitley, RHP	1
Luis Garcia, RHP	2
BREAKOUT PROSPECTS	**RANK**
Shawn Dubin, RHP	13
Zach Daniels, OF	17
Shay Whitcomb, SS	20

SOURCE OF TOP 30 TALENT

Homegrown	29	Acquired	1
College	15	Trade	1
High School	3	Rule 5 draft	0
Junior College	1	Independent leagues	0
Nondrafted free agent	0	Free agents/waivers	0
International	10		

LF

J.J. Matijevic
Bryan de la Cruz

CF

Colin Barber (9)
Zach Daniels (17)
Jordan Brewer (19)
Richi Gonzalez (27)
Jake Meyers

RF

Chas McCormick (12)

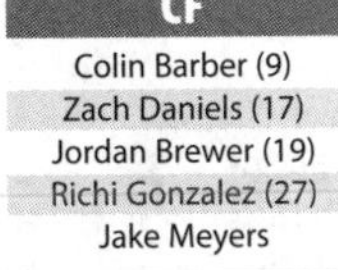

3B

Grae Kessinger (10)
Cristian Gonzalez

SS

Jeremy Peña (3)
Freudis Nova (18)
Dauri Lorenzo (21)

2B

Shay Whitcomb (20)
Luis Santana
Yohander Martinez

1B

Taylor Jones

C

Korey Lee (7)
Juan Santander (23)
Garrett Stubbs
C.J. Stubbs
Nathan Perry

LHP

LHSP	LHRP
Ryan Hartman	Blake Taylor (25)
Parker Mushinski	Cionel Perez

RHP

RHSP	RHRP
Forrest Whitley (1)	Enoli Paredes (11)
Luis Garcia (2)	Tyler Brown (16)
Alex Santos (4)	Brandon Bielak (22)
Bryan Abreu (5)	Jojanse Torres (24)
Tyler Ivey (6)	Austin Hansen (30)
Hunter Brown (8)	Andre Scrubb
Shawn Dubin (13)	Nivaldo Rodriguez
Brett Conine (14)	Humberto Castellanos
Jairo Solis (15)	Zack Matthews
Elvis Garcia (26)	
Blair Henley (28)	
Peter Solomon (29)	
Jairo Lopez	
Jimmy Endersby	

Kansas City Royals

BY BILL MITCHELL

The Royals have taken a big leap forward in terms of building up their farm system the last three years.

Now they're hoping to start taking a step forward in the major leagues.

The Royals went 26-34 in the pandemic-shortened 2020 season. New manager Mike Matheny oversaw the club's fourth straight losing season, but there were some positive developments. Rookie pitchers Brady Singer and Kris Bubic made their debuts and held their own in the rotation, while Josh Staumont proved to be a dominant relief option out of the bullpen.

The Royals hope that was just the start of the wave that will get them back to playoff contention.

KC™

The organization has placed a heavy emphasis on drafting and developing pitchers during its rebuild. Nearly two-thirds of their Top 30 Prospects are pitchers, including four of their top five prospects.

The latest addition was Texas A&M lefthander Asa Lacy, whom they took fourth overall in 2020. They went back to the pitching well to add intriguing high school righthander Ben Hernandez in the second round.

While pitching is the dominant demographic at the top of their farm system, the Royals aren't necessarily short on position players. Shortstop Bobby Witt Jr. had an outstanding summer playing older competition at the alternate training site, and outfielders Kyle Isbel and Khalil Lee both took steps forward.

Seventeen-year-old Dominican outfielder Erick Peña had to wait until the fall to get on the field but made up for the time by participating first in the Royals' postseason program at Kauffman Stadium before heading to instructional league. Shortstop Nick Loftin, drafted out of Baylor in the supplemental first round in 2020, showed himself to be a solid all-around ballplayer who should play above his tools.

The Royals face challenges, however. They have recently put more of an emphasis on drafting raw, untested athletes who need more time at the lower levels. The cancellation of the 2020 minor league season due to the coronavirus pandemic figures to hit them as hard as any organization in baseball given how many of their position player prospects are in need of development.

But not all was lost on the field in 2020. In addition to the emergence of Singer, Bubic and Staumont, team leader Salvador Perez returned after missing all of 2019 after having Tommy John surgery injury and hit .333/.353/.633 with a team-leading 11 home runs despite playing in just 37 games. Whit Merrifield put together another standout season and the Royals added more prospects to their collection through a series of trades, including sending Trevor Rosenthal to the Padres at the trade deadline.

As the new prospects prepare to take over, some of the old ones are bowing out.

Veteran outfielder Alex Gordon, the No. 2 overall pick of the 2005 draft, announced his retirement after the season, ending a 14-year career spent entirely with the Royals. He earned one more Gold Glove award in 2020, the eighth of his career. ■

ED ZURGA/GETTY IMAGES

Rookie Brady Singer proved ready for his big league debut, and more arms are on the way.

PROJECTED 2024 LINEUP

Position	Player	Age
Catcher	Salvador Perez	34
First Base	Hunter Dozier	32
Second Base	Adalberto Mondesi	28
Third Base	Nick Loftin	25
Shortstop	Bobby Witt Jr.	24
Left Field	Franchy Cordero	29
Center Field	Kyle Isbel	26
Right Field	Whit Merrifield	35
Designated Hitter	Jorge Soler	32
No. 1 Starter	Daniel Lynch	27
No. 2 Starter	Asa Lacy	25
No. 3 Starter	Brady Singer	27
No. 4 Starter	Brad Keller	28
No. 5 Starter	Jackson Kowar	27
Closer	Josh Staumont	30

1 BOBBY WITT JR., SS

Born: June 14, 2000. **B-T:** R-R. **HT:** 6-1. **WT:** 185.
Drafted: HS—Colleyville, Texas, 2019 (1st round).
Signed by: Chad Lee

TRACK RECORD: The son of 16-year major league pitcher Bobby Witt, Bobby Jr. has been around the game his entire life. He blossomed into a regular at premier national showcases while at Colleyville (Texas) Heritage High and shined on the national stage when he won the high school home run derby in Washington D.C. prior to the 2018 All-Star Game. He won Baseball America's High School Player of the Year award in 2019 and was drafted second overall by the Royals. He signed for a franchise-record $7.789 million. Witt made his pro debut in the Rookie-level Arizona League and was slated to head to full-season ball in 2020 before the coronavirus pandemic canceled the minor league season. Witt also gave a little bit of a preview of his future during spring training, when he went 2-for-5 with a double, an RBI, a stolen base and a pair of walks during his big league cameos. He spent the early days of the pandemic working out with major and minor league players near his Texas home, joined the Royals for summer camp in July, spent the remainder of the season at their alternate training site and finished up at instructional league camp at Kauffman Stadium.

SCOUTING REPORT: Witt projects as a premier starting shortstop with five impact tools. He struggled a bit in his pro debut and raised concerns about how much he swung and missed, but that's now a distant memory after he began getting more aggressive in his approach. He showed signs of turning the corner at 2019 instructional league and took a big jump in 2020 while facing more advanced pitchers. Witt comes to his hit tool through plus bat speed and a short, compact, low-maintenance swing. The swing-and-miss concerns disappeared with his improved approach, and he vastly improved hitting with two strikes. He now projects to be at least an above-average hitter, and possibly plus. Witt's plus power has never been in question, and there is now increased confidence he will make enough contact to get to it regularly. Already a plus runner with solid instincts on the bases, Witt worked regularly with Royals coaches to become even better instinctually. There is no doubt about him defensively. He projects to be a solid shortstop with elite hands, a good first step and good body control, rounding out the package with a plus, accurate arm. Witt also saw time at third base during the summer and handled the position well.

SCOTT WINTERS/ICON SPORTSWIRE VIA GETTY IMAGES

BA GRADE
70 **Risk:** **Very High**

SCOUTING GRADES
Hit: 60. **Power:** 60. **Run:** 60. **Field:** 60. **Arm:** 60.

Projected future grades on 20-80 scouting scale.

BEST TOOLS

Best Hitter for Average	Kyle Isbel
Best Power Hitter	Seuly Matias
Best Strike-Zone Discipline	Nick Loftin
Fastest Baserunner	Nick Heath
Best Athlete	Bobby Witt Jr.
Best Fastball	Daniel Lynch
Best Curveball	Alec Marsh
Best Slider	Asa Lacy
Best Changeup	Jackson Kowar
Best Control	Jonathan Bowlan
Best Defensive Catcher	MJ Melendez
Best Defensive Infielder	Nick Pratto
Best Infield Arm	Kelvin Gutierrez
Best Defensive Outfielder	Khalil Lee
Best Outfield Arm	Seuly Matias

THE FUTURE: Witt still has to show he can maintain his improved approach and contact skills over a full season, but there is now increased confidence that he will reach his ceiling as an all-star shortstop in the mold of Troy Tulowitzki. Even with the missed season, he made enough progress that a Double-A assignment seems likely at some point in 2021 before the big move to Kansas City in 2022. Then, he could be on the road to becoming the offensive centerpiece of a pitching-rich team. ■

Year	Age	Club (League)	Class	AVG	G	AB	R	H	2B	3B	HR	RBI	BB	SO	SB	OBP	SLG
2019	19	Royals (AZL)	R	.262	37	164	30	43	2	5	1	27	13	35	9	.317	.354
Minor League Totals				.262	37	164	30	43	2	5	1	27	13	35	9	.317	.354

2 DANIEL LYNCH, LHP

TOP ROOKIE

JENNIFER STEWART/MLB PHOTOS VIA GETTY IMAGES

BA GRADE

60 Risk: High

Born: Nov. 17, 1996. **B-T:** L-L. **HT:** 6-6. **WT:** 190. **Drafted:** Virginia, 2018 (1st round). **Signed by:** Jim Farr.

TRACK RECORD: One of three college pitchers drafted by the Royals in the first round in 2018, Lynch missed time with arm discomfort in his first full season but starred in the Arizona Fall League to finish 2019. He earned an invitation to major league spring training in 2020, continued working with the big leaguers during summer camp and spent the season at the alternate training site.

SCOUTING REPORT: Lynch's velocity jumped between college and pro ball and he continues to maintain those extra miles per hour. His fastball explodes on hitters at 94-97 mph and touches 99 with life and sinking action out of his long, lanky frame. Lynch's best secondary pitch is a hard, mid-80s slider with late bite and depth at the bottom of the zone, and he's worked to gain the confidence in his changeup to throw it to both lefties and righties. He rounds out his arsenal with an average curveball he can locate for strikes. At the alternate site, Lynch improved his mechanics to better repeat his delivery. His three-quarters arm slot features a clean motion, granting him above-average control of his potent stuff.

THE FUTURE: Lynch should team with Asa Lacy to give the Royals a pair of lefties at the top of their rotation before long. His major league debut is on the horizon in 2021.

SCOUTING GRADES: **Fastball:** 70 **Slider:** 60 **Curveball:** 50 **Changeup:** 55 **Control:** 55

Year	Age	Club (League)	Class	W	L	ERA	G	GS	IP	H	HR	BB	SO	BB/9	SO/9	WHIP	AVG
2018	21	Burlington (APP)	R	0	0	1.59	3	3	11	9	0	2	14	1.6	11.1	0.97	.191
	21	Lexington (SAL)	LoA	5	1	1.58	9	9	40	35	1	6	47	1.4	10.6	1.03	.229
2019	22	Royals (AZL)	R	0	0	1.00	3	3	9	6	0	3	12	3.0	12.0	1.00	.182
	22	Wilmington (CAR)	HiA	5	2	3.10	15	15	78	76	4	23	77	2.6	8.8	1.26	.232
	22	Burlington (APP)	R	1	0	4.00	2	2	9	13	1	3	7	3.0	7.0	1.78	.333
Minor League Totals				11	3	2.50	32	32	147	139	6	37	157	2.3	9.6	1.19	.251

3 ASA LACY, LHP

CRAIG BISACRE/TEXAS A&M ATHLETICS

Born: June 2, 1999. **B-T:** L-L. **HT:** 6-4. **WT:** 215. **Drafted:** Texas A&M, 2020 (1st round). **Signed by:** Josh Hallgren.

TRACK RECORD: Lacy cemented his status as the top pitcher in the 2020 draft with a 0.75 ERA and 46 strikeouts in 24 innings for Texas A&M before the season shut down. The Royals, ecstatic he was still available, drafted him fourth overall and signed him for $6.67 million. Lacy reported to the alternate training site but missed a couple of weeks due to an eye issue. He returned to participate in the instructional league program at Kauffman Stadium.

SCOUTING REPORT: Lacy earned frequent plaudits as the best college lefthander scouts had seen in years. A big, physical southpaw at 6-foot-4, 215 pounds, he comfortably works 92-96 mph and touches 98 with solid ride on his fastball. Lacy's slider is his strikeout pitch. It's an 87-90 mph wipeout offering that neither righthanded nor lefthanded batters can touch. His changeup flashes plus potential and his curveball was even better than expected in camp, flashing plus as well. All of Lacy's stuff plays up with the deception he generates from a fluid, downhill delivery. His command is more average than plus, but he throws strikes and his stuff overpowers hitters even without precise command.

THE FUTURE: Lacy has front-of-the-rotation potential and could move quickly to the majors. He should see Double-A at some point in 2021.

SCOUTING GRADES: **Fastball:** 70 **Slider:** 60 **Curveball:** 55 **Changeup:** 60 **Control:** 55

Year	Age	Club (League)	Class	W	L	ERA	G	GS	IP	H	HR	BB	SO	BB/9	K/9	WHIP	AVG
2020	20	Did not play—No minor league season															

4 JACKSON KOWAR, RHP

TOP ROOKIE

JENNIFER STEWART/MLB PHOTOS VIA GETTY IMAGES

BA GRADE

55 Risk: High

Born: Oct. 4, 1996. **B-T:** R-R. **HT:** 6-5. **WT:** 180. **Drafted:** Florida, 2018 (1st round). **Signed by:** Jim Buckley.

TRACK RECORD: Kowar teamed with Brady Singer to lead Florida to the 2017 College World Series title as the Gators' top two starters. The Royals drafted both of them in the first round in 2018, Singer with the 18th pick and Kowar with the 33rd. Kansas City kept them together as they ascended to Double-A. Singer jumped to the majors in 2020, but Kowar stayed back at the alternate training site for the duration of the summer.

SCOUTING REPORT: Kowar's changeup is the gem of his arsenal. It's a nasty, plus-plus offering at 83-85 mph that confounds hitters with its trapdoor action. It generates swings and misses from both lefthanded and righthanded hitters, and he's comfortable throwing it in any count. Kowar pairs his changeup with a two-seam fastball that checks in at 93-96 mph with armside sink. He has a tendency to overthrow his fastball, so he worked at the alternate site to keep his delivery more under control and improve his fastball command. Kowar's mid-70s curveball is a work in progress, but it's a potentially average pitch he is learning to locate on both sides of the plate. He throws plenty of strikes with at least average control.

THE FUTURE: Kowar's major league debut should come in 2021. He projects to join Singer in the middle of the Royals' rotation for years to come.

SCOUTING GRADES: **Fastball:** 60 **Curveball:** 50 **Changeup:** 70 **Control:** 55

Year	Age	Club (League)	Class	W	L	ERA	G	GS	IP	H	HR	BB	SO	BB/9	SO/9	WHIP	AVG
2018	21	Lexington (SAL)	LoA	0	1	3.42	9	9	26	19	2	12	22	4.1	7.5	1.18	.178
2019	22	Wilmington (CAR)	HiA	5	3	3.53	13	13	74	68	4	22	66	2.7	8.0	1.22	.218
	22	NW Arkansas (TL)	AA	2	7	3.51	13	13	74	73	8	21	78	2.5	9.4	1.26	.235
Minor League Totals				7	11	3.50	35	35	174	160	14	55	166	2.8	8.6	1.23	.243

5 KRIS BUBIC, LHP

JENNIFER STEWART/MLB PHOTOS VIA GETTY IMAGES

BA GRADE

50 Risk: Medium

Born: Aug. 19, 1997. **B-T:** L-L. **HT:** 6-3. **WT:** 220. **Drafted:** Stanford, 2018 (1st round supplemental). **Signed by:** Josh Hallgren.

TRACK RECORD: One of five college pitchers taken by the Royals on the first day of the 2018 draft, Bubic led the minors with 185 strikeouts in 2019 and jumped straight from high Class A to the majors in 2020. He made a favorable impression on manager Mike Matheny in spring training with his approach and demeanor and held his own after his callup, logging a 4.32 ERA with a strikeout rate of 8.8 per nine innings over 10 starts despite the massive jump in level.

SCOUTING REPORT: Bubic is a polished lefthander who relies on his ability to mix and locate three pitches. His fastball sits 90-92 mph and can touch 94. The pitch itself is unremarkable, but it pairs well with an above-average changeup in the low 80s he's able to keep down in the zone. Bubic's curveball is his third pitch, but it was his most effective offering in the majors as an average pitch with 1-to-7 shape and solid bite. Bubic has a strong, durable body and generates some deception by hiding the ball in his delivery. He has the potential for above-average control but did not show it in the majors.

THE FUTURE: Bubic has a chance to settle in as a solid, back-end starter as long as he sharpens his command and control. He's in the mix for a rotation spot in 2021.

SCOUTING GRADES: **Fastball:** 50 **Curveball:** 55 **Changeup:** 50 **Control:** 55

Year	Age	Club (League)	Class	W	L	ERA	G	GS	IP	H	HR	BB	SO	BB/9	SO/9	WHIP	AVG
2018	20	Idaho Falls (PIO)	R	2	3	4.03	10	10	38	38	2	19	53	4.5	12.6	1.50	.253
2019	21	Lexington (SAL)	LoA	4	1	2.08	9	9	48	27	3	15	75	2.8	14.2	0.88	.164
	21	Wilmington (CAR)	HiA	7	4	2.30	17	17	102	76	3	27	110	2.4	9.7	1.01	.215
2020	22	Kansas City (MLB)		1	6	4.32	10	10	50	52	8	22	49	4.0	8.8	1.48	.263
Minor League Totals				13	8	2.59	36	36	187	141	8	61	238	2.9	11.4	1.08	.211
Major League Totals				1	6	4.32	10	10	50	52	8	22	49	4.0	8.8	1.48	.263

6 KYLE ISBEL, OF

JENNIFER STEWART/MLB PHOTOS VIA GETTY IMAGES

BA GRADE
50 **Risk: High**

Born: March 3, 1997. **B-T:** L-R. **HT:** 5-11. **WT:** 183. **Drafted:** Nevada-Las Vegas, 2018 (3rd round). **Signed by:** Kenny Munoz.

TRACK RECORD: Isbel delivered a sensational pro debut after the Royals drafted him in the third round in 2018. He hit .326 with seven home runs and 26 stolen bases in 64 games, spending the majority of his time with low Class A Lexington. But Isbel's progress was stalled in 2019 by injuries to his hamstring and hamate bone. He finished the year on a high note with a strong showing in the Arizona Fall League and spent 2020 at the Royals' alternate training site.

SCOUTING REPORT: When healthy, Isbel shows a solid set of tools across the board to go with fast-twitch athleticism. He consistently puts together good at-bats with a swing naturally geared to hit line drives. Isbel showed emerging power at the alternate site during the summer that gave the Royals hope he could approach 15-20 home runs to go with high batting averages. A second baseman in college, Isbel is still relatively new to the outfield and improved his routes and jumps working with Royals coach Mitch Maier. With plus speed, a quick first step and more experience in the outfield, Isbel projects to be a plus defender with an average arm. He's a gamer who plays above his tools.

THE FUTURE: Isbel is penciled in as the Royals' center fielder of the future. He should see the upper minors in 2021.

SCOUTING GRADES: **Hitting:** 50 **Power:** 40 **Running:** 60 **Fielding:** 60 **Arm:** 50

Year	Age	Club (League)	Class	AVG	G	AB	R	H	2B	3B	HR	RBI	BB	SO	SB	OBP	SLG
2018	21	Idaho Falls (PIO)	R	.381	25	105	27	40	10	1	4	18	14	17	12	.454	.610
	21	Lexington (SAL)	LoA	.289	39	159	30	46	12	1	3	14	12	43	12	.345	.434
2019	22	Royals (AZL)	R	.360	7	25	9	9	2	0	2	7	2	5	3	.407	.680
	22	Wilmington (CAR)	HiA	.216	52	194	26	42	7	3	5	23	15	44	8	.282	.361
Minor League Totals				.284	123	483	92	137	31	5	14	62	43	109	35	.347	.455

7 ERICK PEÑA, OF

BILL MITCHELL

BA GRADE
55 **Risk: Extreme**

Born: Feb. 20, 2003. **B-T:** L-R. **HT:** 6-3. **WT:** 180. **Signed:** Dominican Republic, 2019. **Signed by:** Edis Perez.

TRACK RECORD: Peña was one of the top players in the 2019 international class and signed with the Royals for $3,897,500 on July 2. He was scheduled to make his professional debut in 2020, but the coronavirus pandemic limited him to working out at his home in the Dominican Republic. He joined the Royals for instructional camps in Kansas City and Surprise, Ariz.

SCOUTING REPORT: Peña is a big, physical hitter with excellent balance, strong hands and a level swing. He shows advanced bat-to-ball skills for his age and has a chance to develop plus power as he fills out his 6-foot-3, 180-pound frame. Peña's offensive ceiling is high, but it's all projection—he will be 18 years old in 2021, has yet to play a professional game and struggled with swings and misses at instructs. Peña's lower half has thickened up since he signed, cementing his future as a corner outfielder. He showed improvement defensively this summer with a good feel for reading fly balls and an average arm. Peña has a strong work ethic, is mature for his age and is already fluent in English.

THE FUTURE: Peña doesn't turn 18 until spring training and still has a lot of growth ahead. He has a chance to be the Royals' right fielder of the future, but it will take time.

SCOUTING GRADES: **Hitting:** 50 **Power:** 55 **Running:** 50 **Fielding:** 55 **Arm:** 50

Year	Age	Club (League)	Class	AVG	G	AB	R	H	2B	3B	HR	RBI	BB	SO	SB	OBP	SLG
2020	17	Did not play—No minor league season															

8 NICK LOFTIN, SS

ERIC GUEL

BA GRADE
50 Risk: High

Born: Sept. 25, 1998. **B-T:** R-R. **HT:** 6-1. **WT:** 185. **Drafted:** Baylor, 2020 (1st round supplemental). **Signed by:** Josh Hallgren

TRACK RECORD: Loftin took over as Baylor's shortstop midway through his freshman year and posted an OPS above .800 in each of his three seasons for the Bears. He showed increased power in 2020 to raise his draft stock before the season shut down, and the Royals drafted him 32nd overall and signed him for $3 million. Loftin spent the summer working out at home in Corpus Christi, Texas, before joining the Royals' advanced instructional league program in Kansas City.

SCOUTING REPORT: Loftin possesses mostly average tools that play up because of his high baseball IQ. He has prototypical leadoff skills as a hitter with a clean, simple swing geared for contact. He has some emerging pull-side power, but doubles and triples are more his game than home runs. Loftin is a solid, instinctual defender who can play both middle-infield positions. He has enough arm strength for shortstop and the athleticism to move around the field. Loftin has just average speed, but his instincts help put him in position to make every play.

THE FUTURE: Loftin is the type of player whose final product will be greater than the sum of his individual tools. The Royals dream of him developing into another Whit Merrifield, who starred at South Carolina but wasn't viewed as an impact big leaguer while a prospect.

SCOUTING GRADES: **Hitting:** 55 **Power:** 40 **Running:** 50 **Fielding:** 55 **Arm:** 40

Year	Age	Club (League)	Class	AVG	G	AB	R	H	2B	3B	HR	RBI	BB	SO	SB	OBP	SLG
2020	21	Did not play—No minor league season															

9 KHALIL LEE, OF

JENNIFER STEWART/MLB PHOTOS VIA GETTY IMAGES

BA GRADE
45 Risk: Medium

Born: June 26, 1998. **B-T:** L-L. **HT:** 5-10. **WT:** 192. **Drafted:** HS—Oakton, Va., 2016 (3rd round). **Signed by:** Jim Farr.

TRACK RECORD: The Royals have pushed Lee aggressively since they drafted him in the third round in 2016, including sending him to Double-A as a 20-year-old. Lee was set to spend the 2020 season at Triple-A, but he instead spent the summer at the alternate training site and finished up with the instructional program at Kauffman Stadium.

SCOUTING REPORT: Lee is an impressive athlete whose biggest need is to reduce his strikeout rate. He struck out 154 times in 129 games in 2019 and has a 34% strikeout rate in his career. He made strides at the alternate training site by hunting specific pitches and staying out of two-strike counts. Lee hasn't been able to get to his above-average raw power because of his swing-and-miss issues, but he has enough thump to reach double-digit home runs. Lee worked with Royals outfield coach Mitch Maier to improve his instincts and jumps in the outfield and take better advantage of his above-average speed. Even if he can't stay in center field, his plus arm will be enough for an outfield corner. Lee is an aggressive and instinctive baserunner who stole 53 bases in 65 attempts in his last full season.

THE FUTURE: Lee has a chance to become part of the Royals' outfield, but only if his contact improvements hold. He'll be tested at Triple-A.

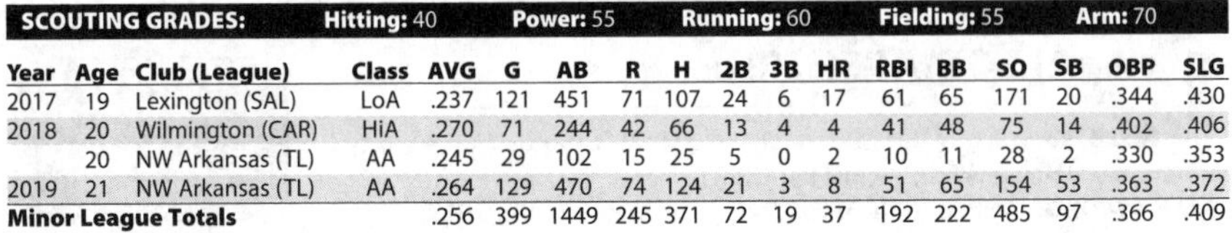

SCOUTING GRADES: **Hitting:** 40 **Power:** 55 **Running:** 60 **Fielding:** 55 **Arm:** 70

Year	Age	Club (League)	Class	AVG	G	AB	R	H	2B	3B	HR	RBI	BB	SO	SB	OBP	SLG
2017	19	Lexington (SAL)	LoA	.237	121	451	71	107	24	6	17	61	65	171	20	.344	.430
2018	20	Wilmington (CAR)	HiA	.270	71	244	42	66	13	4	4	41	48	75	14	.402	.406
	20	NW Arkansas (TL)	AA	.245	29	102	15	25	5	0	2	10	11	28	2	.330	.353
2019	21	NW Arkansas (TL)	AA	.264	129	470	74	124	21	3	8	51	65	154	53	.363	.372
Minor League Totals				.256	399	1449	245	371	72	19	37	192	222	485	97	.366	.409

10 JONATHAN BOWLAN, RHP

BA GRADE
50 Risk: High

Born: Dec. 1, 1996. **B-T:** R-R. **HT:** 6-6. **WT:** 248. **Drafted:** Memphis, 2018 (2nd round). **Signed by:** Travis Ezi.

TRACK RECORD: The Royals drafted the massive, husky Bowlan in the second round in 2018 and signed him for $697,500. They implored him to get in better shape and he responded, slimming down and adding strength each year since being drafted. Bowlan's career highlight came when he threw a no-hitter at high Class A Wilmington in 2019. He was a late addition to the Royals' alternate training site in 2020 before taking part in their instructional league program in Kansas City.

SCOUTING REPORT: Bowlan is an intimidating presence at 6-foot-6, 248 pounds and throws a heavy, 93-96 mph fastball that jumps on hitters with the extension he generates out of his delivery. Both of Bowlan's secondary pitches flash above-average potential. His darting, low-80s slider has late bite and he shows feel for a changeup he will throw to both righthanded and lefthanded hitters. Despite his big body, Bowlan repeats his delivery with a clean arm action and pounds the strike zone. He has above-average life and deception on all of his pitches and goes right after hitters.

THE FUTURE: Bowlan projects as a workhorse toward the back of a rotation. With the Royals flush with rotation prospects, he could also thrive in a multi-inning relief role.

SCOUTING GRADES: **Fastball:** 55 **Slider:** 55 **Changeup:** 50 **Control:** 60

Year	Age	Club (League)	Class	W	L	ERA	G	GS	IP	H	HR	BB	SO	BB/9	SO/9	WHIP	AVG
2018	21	Idaho Falls (PIO)	R	1	4	6.94	9	9	35	51	6	9	23	2.3	5.9	1.71	.309
2019	22	Wilmington (CAR)	HiA	5	3	2.95	13	12	76	66	5	13	76	1.5	9.0	1.03	.244
	22	Lexington (SAL)	LoA	6	2	3.36	13	11	70	55	4	10	74	1.3	9.6	0.93	.198
Minor League Totals				12	9	3.88	35	32	181	172	15	32	173	1.6	8.6	1.13	.250

11 AUSTIN COX, LHP

BA GRADE
50 Risk: High

Born: March 28, 1997. **B-T:** L-L. **HT:** 6-4. **WT:** 185. **Drafted:** Mercer, 2018 (5th round). **Signed by:** Jim Buckley.

TRACK RECORD: Cox was coming off a strong 2019 season split between the two Class A levels just over a year after being drafted from Mercer in the fifth round. He spent the summer at the alternate training site, adjusting to facing more advanced hitters and working on his secondary pitches.

SCOUTING REPORT: The strength of Cox's repertoire is a plus fastball that he gets to both sides of the plate in the 90-94 mph range. He delivers his pitches with good arm speed and a low-effort, repeatable delivery. Complementing the fastball is a plus curveball in the high 70s with downer movement and good depth. His slider is a newer pitch, offering a different shape from the curveball, and he worked all summer on the changeup, trying to get feel for it and gain comfort with the pitch. The pitches play up because of how well Cox commands them, and he's learning to be more competitive in the zone.

THE FUTURE: With two plus pitches and outstanding command, Cox would certainly not be out of place as a power arm near the back of the bullpen if he never develops a solid third pitch. He'll likely head to Double-A for the start of the 2021 season.

Year	Age	Club (League)	Class	W	L	ERA	G	GS	IP	H	HR	BB	SO	BB/9	SO/9	WHIP	AVG
2019	22	Wilmington (CAR)	HiA	3	3	2.77	11	10	55	53	6	16	52	2.6	8.5	1.25	.202
	22	Lexington (SAL)	LoA	5	3	2.75	13	13	75	59	5	22	77	2.6	9.2	1.08	.177
Minor League Totals				9	7	2.96	33	32	164	141	12	53	180	2.9	9.9	1.18	.229

12 ALEC MARSH, RHP

Born: May 14, 1998. **B-T:** R-R. **HT:** 6-2. **WT:** 220. **Drafted:** Arizona State, 2019 (2nd round supplemental). **Signed by:** Kenny Munoz.

TRACK RECORD: Drafted in the second supplemental round in 2019 from Arizona State, Marsh began his career with a promising pro debut at Rookie-level Idaho Falls where he showed use of four pitches and significantly lowered his walk rates from his college career. After pitching a few games in a pop-up league in Texas, Marsh reported to the Royals alternate training site late in the summer.

SCOUTING REPORT: The biggest change for Marsh during the summer of 2020 was an increase in his fastball velocity. Previously sitting 90-94 mph with both a two-seamer and a four-seamer, he added several ticks and is now touching 99 mph. The extra velo changes his profile, especially with the new high-powered fastball being complemented by his cerebral approach to pitching and solid secondary pitches. His best secondary is an 11-to-5 power curveball that has good shape and depth, which he pairs with a short, tight slider resembling a cutter. He previously needed more separation between the breaking balls but they now look like different pitches, with the curveball averaging 80 mph and the slider 86 mph. He has feel for a solid-average or better changeup that he throws with good arm speed and natural sink. Marsh delivers his pitches from the same arm slot with a clean, repeatable delivery.

THE FUTURE: If he maintains the velocity increase, Marsh profiles as a solid, reliable mid-rotation starter. He'll make his full-season debut in 2021.

Year	Age	Club (League)	Class	W	L	ERA	G	GS	IP	H	HR	BB	SO	BB/9	SO/9	WHIP	AVG
2019	21	Idaho Falls (PIO)	R	0	1	4.05	13	13	33	30	5	4	38	1.1	10.3	1.02	.213
Minor League Totals				0	1	4.05	13	13	33	30	5	4	38	1.1	10.3	1.02	.238

13 NICK PRATTO, 1B

Born: Oct. 6, 1998. **B-T:** L-L. **HT:** 6-1. **WT:** 195. **Drafted:** HS—Huntington Beach, Calif., 2017 (1st round). **Signed by:** Rich Amaral.

TRACK RECORD: Pratto had a long amateur track record, notching the winning hit in the 2011 Little League World Series and starring for USA Baseball's junior national teams throughout high school. The Royals drafted him 14th overall in 2017 and signed him for $3.45 million. Pratto was supposed to be a polished hitter who could move fast, but he's instead struggled to make contact and hit .191/.278/.310 at high Class A Wilmington in 2019. He spent 2020 at the Royals' alternate training site.

SCOUTING REPORT: Pratto's swing was non-functional in games, so he refined his body and hand movement at the alternate site to find a more efficient bat path and get his bat in the zone sooner. He had also been overly passive at the plate, but the Royals saw progress that resulted in an uptick in his walk rate and hard-hit rate and a drop in his strikeout rate at the alternate site. Pratto has always been a standout defender at first base with good hands and footwork. He's a below-average runner but has sneaky instincts that allow his speed to play up on the bases.

THE FUTURE: Pratto still has to prove he can hit in live games. If he doesn't, he was a standout pitcher in high school and could move to the mound.

Year	Age	Club (League)	Class	AVG	G	AB	R	H	2B	3B	HR	RBI	BB	SO	SB	OBP	SLG
2019	20	Wilmington (CAR)	HiA	.191	124	419	48	80	21	1	9	46	49	164	17	.278	.310
Minor League Totals				.240	303	1102	152	265	69	6	27	142	118	372	49	.316	.387

14 BEN HERNANDEZ, RHP

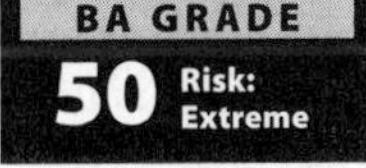

Born: July 1, 2001. **B-T:** R-R. **HT:** 6-2. **WT:** 205. **Drafted:** HS—Chicago, 2020 (2nd round). **Signed by:** Scott Melvin.

TRACK RECORD: Hernandez didn't get a high school season in 2020 because of the coronavirus pandemic, but that didn't affect his draft stock. The Royals drafted the Chicago-area product in the second round and gave him a $1.45 million bonus to forgo an Illinois-Chicago commitment. An advanced pitcher well ahead of his years, Hernandez finally was able to don a Royals uniform for the fall instructional league program in Arizona.

SCOUTING REPORT: Hernandez resembles fellow Royals farmhand Jackson Kowar because of his potent fastball-changeup combination. Some observers say Hernandez has the best changeup they've ever seen from a high school pitcher, and he showed in live batting practice sessions in the fall he can get swings and misses with it. His fastball is another plus pitch with easy velocity and was up to 96 mph at instructional league. A mid-70s curveball is his third pitch and is a tight, sharp offering with good depth, but he needs to throw it with more power and arm speed. Hernandez has good feel for pitching and a nice, easy delivery.

THE FUTURE: He should be able to move more quickly than the normal high school product. An assignment to low Class A to start his pro career is not out of the question.

Year	Age	Club (League)	Class	W	L	ERA	G	GS	IP	H	HR	BB	SO	BB/9	SO/9	WHIP	AVG
2020	18	Did not play—No minor league season															

15 CARLOS HERNANDEZ, RHP

BA GRADE **45** Risk: High

Born: March 11, 1997. **B-T:** R-R. **HT:** 6-4. **WT:** 250. **Signed:** Venezuela, 2016. **Signed by:** Richard Castro/Joelvis Gonzalez.

TRACK RECORD: Signed for $15,000 as a 19-year-old, Hernandez was already an older international signee and fell behind in his development due to a rib injury in 2019 that prevented him from advancing beyond low Class A. That inexperience didn't stop the Royals from jumping the native Venezuelan straight to the big leagues for five games in 2020, when he posted a 4.91 ERA in 13.2 innings.

SCOUTING REPORT: It's all about the fastball for Hernandez. His four-seamer averaged 96 mph and touched triple digits during his time in Kansas City. Hernandez has an easy delivery and the ball comes out of his hand with natural angle, helping it play up despite a lack of significant movement. Hernandez's primary offspeed pitch is a mid-80s hard curveball with 12-to-6 movement that flashes plus. He also throws a hard, split-changeup at 85-90 mph and a below-average slider. Hernandez's control is fringe-average, but he throws enough strikes for a bullpen role.

THE FUTURE: Hernandez needs more seasoning in the minors and will likely head to Double-A in 2021. He'll continue to develop as a starter, but he is most likely to end up in a bullpen role when he reaches the major leagues.

Year	Age	Club (League)	Class	W	L	ERA	G	GS	IP	H	HR	BB	SO	BB/9	SO/9	WHIP	AVG
2020	23	Kansas City (AL)	MAJ	0	1	4.91	5	3	15	19	4	6	13	3.7	8.0	1.70	.317
Major League Totals				0	1	4.91	5	3	14	19	4	6	13	3.7	8.0	1.70	.317
Minor League Totals				10	14	4.56	42	41	199	194	20	74	212	3.3	9.6	1.34	.253

16 MJ MELENDEZ, C

BA GRADE **45** Risk: High

Born: Nov. 28, 1998. **B-T:** L-R. **HT:** 6-1. **WT:** 185. **Drafted:** HS—Miami, 2017 (2nd round). **Signed by:** Alex Mesa.

TRACK RECORD: Drafted in the second round in 2017 and paid a well over-slot bonus of just over $2 million, Melendez had a disastrous 2019, hitting .163/.260/.311 at high Class A Wilmington. He spent the summer at the Royals' alternate training site followed by the instructional league program held at Kauffman Stadium in order to get as many at-bats as possible.

SCOUTING REPORT: Melendez has worked on applying mechanical changes to his swing. He cut down on his leg kick, quieted the noise in his swing and worked hard to reduce the amount of pitches he chases out of the zone. Melendez also continued refining his alignment in the batter's box and understanding what pitches he could drive. Even if everything clicks, Melendez projects as no more than a below-average hitter, but his physicality may give him enough power to hit enough for a catcher. Melendez's best tool defensively is a cannon of an arm with a quick release. He's athletic behind the plate and receives and blocks well.

THE FUTURE: Melendez profiles as a low-average, moderate-power type of hitter with catching skills that will play in the majors. A Double-A assignment awaits in 2021.

Year	Age	Club (League)	Class	AVG	G	AB	R	H	2B	3B	HR	RBI	BB	SO	SB	OBP	SLG
2019	20	Wilmington (CAR)	HiA	.163	110	363	34	59	23	2	9	54	44	165	7	.260	.311
Minor League Totals				.219	268	950	111	208	57	14	32	157	113	368	15	.308	.409

17 NOAH MURDOCK, RHP

BREAKOUT BA GRADE **45** Risk: High

Born: Aug. 20, 1998. **B-T:** R-R. **HT:** 6-8. **WT:** 190. **Drafted:** Virginia, 2019 (7th round). **Signed by:** Jim Farr.

TRACK RECORD: Murdock had Tommy John surgery his sophomore year at Virginia and wasn't at peak form when he came back, posting a 6.30 ERA his redshirt sophomore season. The Royals saw his 6-foot-8 frame and mid-90s fastball and decided he was worthy of a flier in the seventh round. Murdock had a solid pro debut at Rookie-level Burlington and worked out remotely during the 2020 coronavirus shutdown, keeping in close contact with the Royals coaches. He got back on the field at the Royals' fall instructional program in Kansas City.

SCOUTING REPORT: Murdock's velocity continues to increase the further he moves away from surgery. His fastball has ticked up to sit 96-97 mph and touch 99 mph with deception from his long arms and high arm slot. His main secondary is a 79-82 mph slider, which some observers call a slurve, that now profiles as a future above-average pitch. It has more depth than normal because of his arm slot and release. His 82-85 mph changeup is a future solid-average pitch, and everything he throws has sink and angle from his towering release point. Murdock has worked on repeating his delivery and commanding his secondary pitches and has a chance for average control.

THE FUTURE: Murdock will keep starting until he shows he can't. He'll get his first chance at full-season ball in 2021.

Year	Age	Club (League)	Class	W	L	ERA	G	GS	IP	H	HR	BB	SO	BB/9	SO/9	WHIP	AVG
2019	20	Burlington (APP)	R	3	1	2.17	11	6	37	35	2	11	43	2.7	10.4	1.23	.223
Minor League Totals				3	1	2.17	11	6	37	35	2	11	43	2.7	10.4	1.23	.246

18 RONALD BOLAÑOS, RHP

BA GRADE 45 Risk: High

Born: Aug. 23, 1996. **B-T:** R-R. **HT:** 6-3. **WT:** 220. **Signed:** Cuba, 2016. **Signed by:** Chris Kemp/Trevor Schumm (Padres).

TRACK RECORD: Bolaños originally signed with the Padres in 2016 for $2.25 million after a decorated amateur career in his native Cuba. The Royals acquired him as part of the trade for reliever Tim Hill prior to the start of the 2020 season. Bolaños spent most of the year at the alternate training site and made two abbreviated starts in Kansas City.

SCOUTING REPORT: Bolaños is a big-bodied righthander with four pitches, highlighted by a fastball that sits 93-95 mph and can get into the upper 90s. He gives hitters different looks by adding cut, sink or rise to his heater. Bolaños' best offspeed pitch is a tight-spinning curveball. He's working on throwing it harder as it's often too soft of a pitch. He gets plenty of spin on his mid-80s slider and infrequently adds a high-80s changeup with cut action. Bolaños needs to smooth out his delivery to get better control of his diverse repertoire.

THE FUTURE: Bolaños could thrive in a middle relief role but will continue to get chances to make it as a starter. He stands a good chance at opening the 2021 season in the Royals bullpen.

Year	Age	Club (League)	Class	W	L	ERA	G	GS	IP	H	HR	BB	SO	BB/9	SO/9	WHIP	AVG
2020	23	Kansas City (AL)	MAJ	0	2	12.27	2	2	4	8	2	3	2	7.4	4.9	3.00	.471
Major League Totals				0	4	6.94	7	5	23	25	5	15	21	5.8	8.1	1.71	.275
Minor League Totals				24	18	4.38	66	57	324	311	27	137	311	3.8	8.6	1.38	.254

19 EDWARD OLIVARES, OF

BA GRADE 40 Risk: Medium

Born: March 6, 1996 **B-T:** R-R. **HT:** 6-2. **WT:** 186. **Signed:** Venezuela, 2014. **Signed by:** Ismael Cruz/Luis Marquez/Jose Contreras (Blue Jays).

TRACK RECORD: Originally signed by Toronto in 2014 for only $1,000, Olivares has now been traded twice in his career. The Blue Jays traded him to the Padres for Yangervis Solarte after the 2017 season and the Royals acquired him from San Diego for closer Trevor Rosenthal at the 2020 trade deadline. Olivares had a standout year at Double-A Amarillo in 2019, but wasn't quite ready for the majors and hit .240/.267/.375 in 101 plate appearances for the Padres and Royals.

SCOUTING REPORT: Olivares uses a compact swing at the plate and flashes above-average power, but struggles with pitch selection. He's generally improved each year and has the athleticism to make adjustments, but he hasn't shown enough consistently for evaluators to consider him more than a fringe-average hitter. Olivares' above-average speed allows him to cover plenty of ground in the outfield with his long strides, but he needs to improve his routes. He shows an above-average arm and is an above-average runner with good instincts on the bases.

THE FUTURE: Olivares should be at least a fourth outfielder, but he's been more tools and athleticism than production so far. He's in line for more playing time with the Royals in 2021.

Year	Age	Club (League)	Class	AVG	G	AB	R	H	2B	3B	HR	RBI	BB	SO	SB	OBP	SLG
2020	24	San Diego (NL)	MAJ	.176	13	34	4	6	1	0	1	3	2	14	0	.222	.294
	24	Kansas City (AL)	MAJ	.274	18	62	5	17	1	1	2	7	2	11	0	.292	.419
Major League Totals				.240	31	96	9	23	2	1	3	10	4	25	0	.267	.375
Minor League Totals				.274	469	1824	317	500	93	27	52	249	138	361	103	.342	.440

20 TYLER ZUBER, RHP

BA GRADE 40 Risk: Medium

Born: June 6, 1995. **B-T:** R-R. **HT:** 5-11. **WT:** 175. **Drafted:** Arkansas State, 2017 (6th round). **Signed by:** Matt Price.

TRACK RECORD: Righthanded relievers under 6 feet tall tend to fly under the radar. Zuber put together a strong 2019 between high Class A and Double-A and jumped to the Royals' bullpen in 2020. He made 23 appearances and posted a 4.09 ERA, although he struggled badly with walks.

SCOUTING REPORT: Zuber dominates with a mid-90s fastball with late hop through the zone that he delivers with a lightning fast arm. His above-average slider is his go-to secondary offering in the mid 80s, and he also has a curveball in the low 80s he'll mix in to slow down hitters. He commands both breaking balls better than he does his fastball. Zuber's changeup came along nicely in 2020 and was an effective pitch against lefties, projecting average overall. Zuber's stuff plays in the strike zone, but he walked 20 batters in 22 innings in his debut and will have to show better control.

THE FUTURE: Zuber has a good chance to break camp in 2021 with a role in the Royals' bullpen. If he can get his control right, he should settle in as a long reliever.

Year	Age	Club (League)	Class	W	L	ERA	G	GS	IP	H	HR	BB	SO	BB/9	SO/9	WHIP	AVG
2020	25	Kansas City (AL)	MAJ	1	2	4.09	23	0	22	15	4	20	30	8.2	12.3	1.59	.197
Major League Totals				1	2	4.09	23	0	22	15	4	20	30	8.2	12.3	1.59	.197
Minor League Totals				8	10	2.96	105	0	133	116	7	39	177	2.6	11.9	1.16	.236

21 JON HEASLEY, RHP

BA GRADE **45** Risk: High

Born: Jan. 27, 1997. **B-T:** R-R. **HT:** 6-3. **WT:** 215. **Drafted:** Oklahoma State, 2018 (13th round). **Signed by:** Chad Lee.

TRACK RECORD: Heasley didn't quite live up to expectations at Oklahoma State and fell to the 13th round of the 2018 draft. He found his stride in his full-season debut and went 8-5, 3.12 at low Class A Lexington, albeit against mostly younger competition. The Royals added Heasley to the alternate training site in September and kept him in Kansas City for their fall instructional league program at Kauffman Stadium.

SCOUTING REPORT: Heasley is a competitor on the mound with four average or better pitches. He started throwing from a higher slot at Lexington. The move helped his velocity and his fastball now touches 97 mph with a high spin rate. Heasley's best secondary is a potential plus curveball that plays well off the fastball with 12-to-6 movement and heavy break. A changeup that is tough on hitters from both sides gives Heasley a third quality pitch. He rounds out the arsenal with a slider that he uses infrequently but has late, short break. He ties everything together with average control.

THE FUTURE: Heasley's stuff looked great in his pro debut, but he'll be more tested by age-appropriate competition. That should come in 2021.

Year	Age	Club (League)	Class	W	L	ERA	G	GS	IP	H	HR	BB	SO	BB/9	SO/9	WHIP	AVG
2019	22	Lexington (SAL)	LoA	8	5	3.12	25	20	113	93	11	34	120	2.7	9.6	1.13	.199
Minor League Totals				9	8	3.75	37	31	163	148	15	50	155	2.8	8.5	1.21	.236

22 LUCIUS FOX, SS

BA GRADE **45** Risk: High

Born: July 2, 1997. **B-T:** B-R. **HT:** 6-1. **WT:** 190. **Signed:** Bahamas, 2015. **Signed by:** Jose Alou/Joe Salermo (Giants).

TRACK RECORD: After starting his high school career in Florida, Fox returned to his native Bahamas and re-classified as an international prospect. That move paid off when the Giants gave him a $6 million signing bonus, the largest in the 2015 international class. San Francisco traded Fox to the Rays one year later in the deal for Matt Moore, and the Rays flipped him to the Royals at the 2020 trade deadline for Brett Phillips. Fox joined the Royals' alternate training site after the trade and also saw time at instructional league.

SCOUTING REPORT: Fox's best attributes are traits that can't be taught, with plus-plus speed and an obvious energy and passion for the game. He has the tools and athleticism to be a big league regular, but his bat has not developed. He struggles with consistency in his routine and needs to get better in his pitch selection. He lacks the strength to impact the baseball but shows good barrel control and walks at a high rate. Fox is an above-average defender at shortstop with good hands and is capable of handling other infield positions. He uses his speed well on the bases, with 123 stolen bases in four minor league seasons.

THE FUTURE: Fox could be a regular shortstop with more production at the plate. If not, his speed and defense may be enough to earn him a role as a utility player.

Year	Age	Club (League)	Class	AVG	G	AB	R	H	2B	3B	HR	RBI	BB	SO	SB	OBP	SLG
2019	21	Durham (IL)	AAA	.143	15	42	6	6	0	1	0	1	6	15	2	.250	.190
	21	Montgomery (SL)	AA	.230	104	365	60	84	16	8	3	33	53	89	37	.340	.342
Minor League Totals				.244	417	1564	244	382	58	18	11	128	191	392	123	.337	.325

23 ZACH HAAKE, RHP

BA GRADE 45 Risk: High

Born: Oct. 8, 1996. **B-T:** R-R. **HT:** 6-5. **WT:** 186. **Drafted:** Kentucky, 2018 (6th round). **Signed by:** Mike Farrell.

TRACK RECORD: Haake has had an up-and-down career that included an 8.47 ERA at Kentucky his junior season. The Royals still drafted him in the sixth round based on his loud stuff and were rewarded when he posted a 2.85 ERA in 18 starts for low Class A Lexington. Haake missed nearly two months with shoulder soreness, however, and his only 2020 action came during the Royals' fall instructional program.

SCOUTING REPORT: Haake's strength is a 93-97 mph fastball with good life that is capable of beating hitters up in the zone. His best secondary pitch is a potential plus changeup that looks like a slider because it cuts so much before dropping quickly. He also throws a slider with 11-to-5 break, which flashes plus and has good late movement. Haake is athletic but doesn't always repeat his delivery and has fringe-average control. He has a history of struggling to get through an order a second time.

THE FUTURE: Haake has the repertoire to remain in the rotation with more consistency and a cleaner delivery. He has the stuff to thrive in a bullpen role if those developments don't come.

Year	Age	Club (League)	Class	W	L	ERA	G	GS	IP	H	HR	BB	SO	BB/9	SO/9	WHIP	AVG
2019	22	Idaho Falls (PIO)	R	0	0	0.00	1	1	4	2	0	3	4	6.2	8.3	1.15	.118
	22	Lexington (SAL)	LoA	4	6	2.85	18	18	76	60	2	36	90	4.3	10.7	1.27	.190
Minor League Totals				4	6	2.55	26	25	95	71	3	43	108	4.1	10.2	1.20	.210

24 SEULY MATIAS, OF

BA GRADE 45 Risk: Very High

Born: Sept. 4, 1998. **B-T:** R-R. **HT:** 6-3. **WT:** 204. **Signed:** Dominican Republic, 2015. **Signed by:** Fausto Morel.

TRACK RECORD: Matias made a splash with 31 home runs at low Class A Lexington in 2018, but that came with an alarming 35% strikeout rate. He got exposed by better pitching and hit .148 with four home runs in 57 games at high Class A Wilmington in 2019 before a broken hand ended his season. Matias returned healthy in 2020 and spent the summer at the alternate training site before heading to instructional league.

SCOUTING REPORT: Matias has explosive, plus-plus raw power, but he needs to undergo massive swing changes in order to hit higher-level pitching. He has started the process by lowering his hands and becoming more relaxed with his setup, creating a cleaner path to the baseball. That result was more of a line-drive approach, with his power playing well with that swing path. Even with the change, Matias has a long way to go. The next step is creating a better connection between his lower half and his hands. Defensively, Matias possesses prototypical right field skills, especially with a plus-plus arm.

THE FUTURE: Matias' tools are tantalizing, but it's not going to be a quick process to improve his swing. A return to high Class A to start the 2021 season may be best.

Year	Age	Club (League)	Class	AVG	G	AB	R	H	2B	3B	HR	RBI	BB	SO	SB	OBP	SLG
2019	20	Wilmington (CAR)	HiA	.148	57	189	23	28	10	4	4	22	25	98	2	.259	.307
Minor League Totals				.218	261	945	146	206	48	10	50	152	89	387	12	.299	.449

25 SCOTT BLEWETT, RHP

BA GRADE 40 Risk: High

Born: April 10, 1996. **B-T:** R-R. **HT:** 6-6. **WT:** 245. **Drafted:** HS—Baldwinsville, N.Y., 2014 (2nd round). **Signed by:** Bobby Gandolfo.

TRACK RECORD: It's been a slow climb for the New York high school product since he was drafted in the second round in 2014, but Blewett made it to the majors for two appearances in 2020. He spent most of the summer at the alternate training site before getting called up briefly at the end of September.

SCOUTING REPORT: Blewett has a tall, bulky frame that has added 30 pounds since being drafted. He delivers his 92-96 mph four-seam fastball with sink out of a high, three-quarter slot, and added a two-seamer in 2020. He also added a mid-80s slider with 12-to-6 break he uses to get swings-and-misses as an above-average pitch. Blewett still has an average curveball, but it's taken a back seat to his slider. He occasionally mixes in a firm changeup in the upper 80s. with good action. His ability to repeat his delivery has improved in the past year, providing hope he can get to average control.

THE FUTURE: Without a plus pitch and uncertain control, Blewett projects more as a spot starter or long reliever than a rotation mainstay. He should get another chance to pitch in the majors in 2021.

Year	Age	Club (League)	Class	W	L	ERA	G	GS	IP	H	HR	BB	SO	BB/9	SO/9	WHIP	AVG
2020	24	Kansas City (AL)	MAJ	0	0	6.00	2	0	3	6	0	1	4	3.0	12.0	2.33	.400
Major League Totals				0	0	6.00	2	0	3	6	0	1	4	3.0	12.0	2.33	.400
Minor League Totals				33	45	5.00	127	123	646	706	73	245	529	3.4	7.4	1.47	.279

26 ANGEL ZERPA, LHP

BA GRADE **40** Risk: High

Born: Sept. 27, 1999. **B-T:** L-L. **HT:** 6-0. **WT:** 211. **Signed:** Venezuela, 2016. **Signed by:** Richard Castro/Joelvis Gonzalez/Orlando Estevez.

TRACK RECORD: The Royals surprisingly added Zerpa to the 40-man roster after the 2020 season. The 21-year-old Venezuelan lefty has yet to pitch above the Rookie-levels, but he's pitched well so far with a 2.95 ERA in 38 career appearances, including 31 starts.

SCOUTING REPORT: Zerpa pitches from a lower slot with a short-armed delivery. He's a consistent strike thrower with a feel for the strike zone, particularly with his 89-94 mph fastball with plenty of sink. Zerpa commands his secondary pitches, notably a high-70s slider with sweep and a mid-80s changeup with good drop. He'll need to continue to rely on his pitchability since there's not much projection left in his body, but he gives batters a different look.

THE FUTURE: Zerpa will head to spring training with the big league team before returning to the minor leagues. The hope is he becomes a lefthanded reliever.

Year	Age	Club (League)	Class	W	L	ERA	G	GS	IP	H	HR	BB	SO	BB/9	SO/9	WHIP	AVG
2019	19	Idaho Falls (PIO)	R	0	0	4.15	1	1	4	5	0	1	4	2.1	8.3	1.38	.250
	19	Burlington (APP)	R	6	3	3.33	12	11	51	41	6	13	51	2.3	8.9	1.05	.202
Minor League Totals				12	13	2.95	38	31	168	145	11	37	128	2.0	6.9	1.08	.234

27 YEFRI DEL ROSARIO, RHP

BA GRADE **45** Risk: Extreme

Born: Sept. 23, 1999. **B-T:** R-R. **HT:** 6-2. **WT:** 180. **Signed:** Dominican Republic, 2016. **Signed by:** Jonathan Cruz (Braves).

TRACK RECORD: Del Rosario originally signed with the Braves in 2016 for $1 million but was later declared a free agent as part of Atlanta's punishment for violating international signing rules. The Royals signed him for $665,000 and he quickly shot up to low Class A Lexington in his first season in the organization. Del Rosario's progress was stunted when he missed all of 2019 with a nerve issue, but he returned in 2020 to participate in the Royals' fall instructional league camp at Kauffman Stadium.

SCOUTING REPORT: Del Rosario is throwing as well as ever, with a 92-95 mph fastball with late life to both sides of the plate. He throws with a sneaky arm action and his pitches jump on hitters. He's still fine-tuning his 80-mph curveball, which flashes plus with good shape, and his changeup has good action but he needs to better follow through on it. Del Rosario is still growing and continues to add strength. His control is fringy but has a chance to improve as he matures physically and moves further away from injury.

THE FUTURE: Del Rosario hasn't pitched in an official game in two years, but he's a tantalizing righthander with lots of potential. He should see high Class A in 2021.

Year	Age	Club (League)	Class	W	L	ERA	G	GS	IP	H	HR	BB	SO	BB/9	SO/9	WHIP	AVG
2018	18	Lexington (SAL)	LoA	6	5	3.19	15	15	79	69	10	29	72	3.3	8.2	1.24	.205
Minor League Totals				7	6	3.33	28	23	116	107	11	43	108	3.3	8.4	1.29	.238

28 SAMUEL VALERIO, RHP

BA GRADE **45** Risk: Extreme

Born: Oct. 8, 2001. **B-T:** R-R. **HT:** 6-4. **WT:** 220. **Drafted:** Dominican Republic, 2018. **Signed by:** Edis Perez

TRACK RECORD: It didn't take long for a buzz to start circulating at instructional league about the hefty young Dominican regularly hitting triple-digits in outings for the Royals. Valerio's fastball sat in the high 80s when he signed in 2018 for $242,500, but it wasn't long until that velocity started creeping up.

SCOUTING REPORT: It's all about the fastball for Valerio. The ball flies out of his hand with plenty of hop to it, getting heavy sink and downhill plane. He sits 96-99 mph with the heater and has touched 102. He has a nice, easy delivery but needs to repeat it better to locate his pitches. Valerio's secondary pitches are behind his fastball. His 79-81 mph curveball has downer movement and could be a plus pitch with more consistency. He doesn't often use the hard, 88-89 mph changeup. Valerio is still growing into his body but there's already strength in the lower half. He has a chance to reach fringe-average control if he can be more consistent in his delivery.

THE FUTURE: There's a lot to dream on with Valerio, but he's very far away. His plus-plus fastball gives him a carrying asset.

Year	Age	Club (League)	Class	W	L	ERA	G	GS	IP	H	HR	BB	SO	BB/9	SO/9	WHIP	AVG
2019	17	Royals1 (DSL)	R	3	1	4.62	11	4	25	23	1	13	31	4.6	11.0	1.42	.198
Minor League Totals				3	1	4.62	11	4	25	23	1	13	31	4.6	11.0	1.42	.240

29 DARRYL COLLINS, OF

BA GRADE
45 Risk: Extreme

Born: Sept.16, 2001. **B-T:** L-R. **HT:** 6-2. **WT:** 195. **Signed:** Netherlands, 2018. **Signed by:** Nick Leto.

TRACK RECORD: Collins is the rare baseball prospect from The Netherlands, but his athleticism and ability to hit that have attracted more interest than his nationality. He began his pro career in the Rookie-level Arizona League and hit .320/.401/.436 as a 17-year-old. He left early to represent his nation at the Under 18 World Cup in Korea and was named to the All-World team. Collins got back on the field in 2020 at instructional league.

SCOUTING REPORT: Collins has added strength since his debut season without affecting his athleticism. He's more of a hit over power type, with plus bat speed and a good approach at the plate. Since he's likely to be limited to left field, Collins will need to develop more power. He's a plus runner underway but projects as more of an average runner or a tick above as he continues to grow. A below-average arm will keep him out of right field. He is mature for his age and a hard worker.

THE FUTURE: Collins still has a long way to go. A corner outfielder with power questions and an unorthodox profile, he may still have the hitting potential to make it work.

Year	Age	Club (League)	Class	AVG	G	AB	R	H	2B	3B	HR	RBI	BB	SO	SB	OBP	SLG
2019	17	Royals (AZL)	R	.320	48	181	24	58	7	7	0	25	22	30	1	.401	.436
Minor League Totals				.320	48	181	24	58	7	7	0	25	22	30	1	.401	.436

30 BREWER HICKLEN, OF

BA GRADE
40 Risk: High

Born: Feb. 9, 1996. **B-T:** R-R. **HT:** 6-2. **WT:** 208. **Drafted:** Alabama-Birmingham, 2017 (7th round). **Signed by:** Nick Hamilton.

TRACK RECORD: Hicklen was a two-sport star who played wide receiver at Alabama-Birmingham until the school dropped its football program in 2017. With his focus solely on baseball, he had a breakout season that spring and was drafted in the seventh round by the Royals. Hicklen advanced to high Class A Wilmington in 2019 and showed an impressive combination of power and speed with 34 extra-base hits and 39 stolen bases, albeit with 140 strikeouts. He returned to the field in 2020 at instructional league.

SCOUTING REPORT: A strong, physical talent with plus-plus speed, Hicklen is capable of playing all three outfield positions. He has a chance to be at least an average defender, but he struggles with routine plays at times. His above-average arm will be enough for right field. Hicklen is working to get the parts of his swing to work together as he continues to improve the timing and rhythm of his toe tap. His struggles with good velocity and pitches with horizontal movement will limit his offensive upside, but he should be able to get to at least average power. Hicklen plays with an aggressive football mentality and demonstrates elite makeup and leadership skills.

THE FUTURE: Hicklen has the physical skills to be a reserve outfielder, with the added bonus of exceptional leadership that will help a clubhouse.

Year	Age	Club (League)	Class	AVG	G	AB	R	H	2B	3B	HR	RBI	BB	SO	SB	OBP	SLG
2019	23	Wilmington (CAR)	HiA	.263	125	419	70	110	13	7	14	51	55	140	39	.363	.427
Minor League Totals				.283	268	952	178	269	46	15	36	142	101	310	90	.368	.476

MORE PROSPECTS TO KNOW

31 WILMIN CANDELARIO, SS

Candelario is still raw but hit well in the DSL in his pro debut in 2019 and has the quick, fluid actions and arm to play at shortstop.

32 RICHARD LOVELADY, LHP

Lovelady has some funk as a lefty reliever, but the new three-batter minimum rule means he has to develop his changeup in order to handle righthanders.

33 JUAN CARLOS NEGRET, OF

The Cuban native had a strong instructional league as he continued to mature physically. He makes solid contact at the plate and his average or better arm will keep him in right field.

34 TYLER GENTRY, OF

The Royals' third-round pick in 2020, Gentry showed plus raw power at Alabama but struggled with breaking balls at instructs.

35 SEBASTIAN RIVERO, C

SLEEPER

Rivero made some s swing adjustments and got bigger and stronger, making him a potential breakout candidate in 2021. He's an excellent defensive catcher with great leadership skills behind the plate.

36 KELVIN GUTIERREZ, 3B

Acquired from the Nationals in 2018, Gutierrez remains a strong defender at third base but has not yet developed the power needed for a corner infielder.

37 WILL KLEIN, RHP

Kansas City's fifth-round pick in 2020 from Eastern Illinois, Klein has a big fastball up to 98 mph as part of a four-pitch mix. It's more of a reliever delivery, his role until his final year in college, and after starting his pro career in the rotation he'll likely settle into the bullpen long-term.

38 DANIEL TILLO, LHP

Tillo was shut down late in summer camp with UCL damage and had Tommy John surgery in late July. He will be out of action until the 2022 season.

39 GRANT GAMBRELL, RHP

Gambrell has a big, strong body and intriguing four-pitch mix. His fastball sits 90-95 mph with good tilt and he flashes a wipeout slider.

40 CHRISTIAN CHAMBERLAIN, LHP

The Royals' 2020 fourth round pick from Oregon State, Chamberlain is undersized but goes right at hitters with his lively 92-94 mph fastball.

TOP PROSPECTS OF THE DECADE

Year	Player, Pos	2020 Org
2011	Eric Hosmer, 1B	Padres
2012	Mike Montgomery, LHP	Royals
2013	Kyle Zimmer, RHP	Royals
2014	Kyle Zimmer, RHP	Royals
2015	Adalberto Mondesi, SS	Royals
2016	Adalberto Mondesi, SS	Royals
2017	Josh Staumont, RHP	Royals
2018	Nick Pratto, 1B	Royals
2019	Brady Singer, RHP	Royals
2020	Bobby Witt Jr., SS	Royals

TOP DRAFT PICKS OF THE DECADE

Year	Player, Pos	2020 Org
2011	Bubba Starling, OF	Royals
2012	Kyle Zimmer, RHP	Royals
2013	Hunter Dozier, SS	Royals
2014	Brandon Finnegan, LHP	Reds
2015	Ashe Russell, RHP	Royals
2016	A.J. Puckett, RHP (2nd round)	White Sox
2017	Nick Pratto, 1B	Royals
2018	Brady Singer, RHP	Royals
2019	Bobby Witt Jr., SS	Royals
2020	Asa Lacy, LHP	Royals

DEPTH CHART

KANSAS CITY ROYALS

TOP 2021 ROOKIES	RANK
Daniel Lynch, LHP	2
Jackson Kowar, RHP	4
BREAKOUT PROSPECTS	**RANK**
Alec Marsh, RHP	12
Noah Murdock, RHP	17

SOURCE OF TOP 30 TALENT

Homegrown	26	Acquired	4
College	14	Trade	3
Junior college	0	Rule 5 draft	0
High school	6	Independent league	0
Nondrafted free agent	0	Free agent/waivers	1
International	6		

LF
Edward Olivares (19)
Darryl Collins (29)

CF
Kyle Isbel (6)
Erick Peña (7)
Khalil Lee (9)
Nick Heath
Brady McConnell

RF
Seuly Matias (24)
Brewer Hicklen (30)
Juan Carlos Negret
Tyler Gentry

3B
Kelvin Gutierrez
Emmanuel Rivera

SS
Bobby Witt Jr. (1)
Nick Loftin (8)
Lucius Fox (22)
Wilmin Candelario
Maikel Garcia

2B
Michael Massey
Clay Dungan
Erick Mejia

1B
Nick Pratto (13)
Vinnie Pasquantino

C
MJ Melendez (16)
Sebastian Rivero
Omar Henandez

LHP

LHSP	LHRP
Daniel Lynch (2)	Richard Lovelady
Asa Lacy (3)	Christian Chamberlain
Kris Bubic (5)	
Austin Cox (11)	
Angel Zerpa (26)	
Daniel Tillo	

RHP

RHSP	RHRP
Jackson Kowar (4)	Tyler Zuber (20)
Jonathan Bowlan (10)	Brandon Marklund
Alec Marsh (12)	Will Klein
Ben Hernandez (14)	John McMillon
Carlos Hernandez (15)	Carlos Sanabria
Noah Murdock (17)	
Ronald Bolaños (18)	
Jon Heasley (21)	
Zach Haake (23)	
Scott Blewett (25)	
Yefri Del Rosario (27)	
Samuel Valerio (28)	
Grant Gambrell	

Los Angeles Angels

BY MIKE DIGIOVANNA

After a fifth straight losing season and sixth without a playoff berth, even with the expanded postseason in 2020, the Angels had an offseason of upheaval.

General manager Billy Eppler was fired after a disappointing 26-34 season. Team president John Carpino joined manager Joe Maddon on a postseason video call that sounded more like a reckoning than a postmortem, with Carpino acknowledging "something is not right in our organization."

The Angels, who have not won a playoff game since 2009 despite employing the best player in baseball—Mike Trout—for the past nine years, are actively trying to fix that. The first step was hiring Perry Minasian to be their new general manager after a successful stint as a Braves assistant GM.

The issues Carpino referred to, and what Minasian inherits, are a major league team that lacks both starpower and depth on the pitching staff, is too old in some spots on the field and too young in others and a farm system that has produced major leaguers but few stars in recent years.

The Angels have drafted, signed and developed plenty of solid big leaguers, such as Griffin Canning, Tyler Skaggs, Kole Calhoun, David Fletcher and C.J. Cron over the past decade or so.

But they've produced only one star position player in Trout and one potential ace in Garrett Richards, both picked in 2009.

The Angels thought five-tool outfielder Jo Adell, their most highly touted homegrown prospect since Trout, would snap that streak, but Adell's lackluster major league debut exposed holes in his swing and defense. At 21, with a strong work ethic and immense physical skills, Adell could still become a star, but it's clear he's not ready for an Angels team trying to make the playoffs now.

The Angels will need to hit on more top draft picks and international signings to supplement their big league roster with young, high-end talent that will help push them into playoff contention.

There are reasons for optimism. Top pitching prospect Chris Rodriguez appears fully recovered from the back injuries that sidelined him for most of 2018 and 2019, and top 2020 draft pick Reid Detmers could crack the rotation soon.

A willingness to pursue more high-risk, high-reward prospects has yielded intriguing pitchers such as Jack Kochanowicz, Hector Yan, Erik Rivera and William Holmes.

Top outfield prospects Brandon Marsh and Jordyn Adams feature dynamic tools, and the system is deep in athletic middle infielders such as Jeremiah Jackson, Kyren Paris and Arol Vera.

JAYNE KAMIN-ONCEA/GETTY IMAGES

Rookie Jared Walsh mashed nine home runs in 32 games after adjusting his hitting setup.

PROJECTED 2024 LINEUP

Position	Player	Age
Catcher	Max Stassi	33
First Base	Jared Walsh	30
Second Base	David Fletcher	30
Third Base	Anthony Rendon	34
Shortstop	Jeremiah Jackson	24
Left Field	Jo Adell	25
Center Field	Mike Trout	32
Right Field	Brandon Marsh	26
Designated Hitter	Shohei Ohtani	29
No. 1 Starter	Shohei Ohtani	29
No. 2 Starter	Griffin Canning	28
No. 3 Starter	Chris Rodriguez	25
No. 4 Starter	Reid Detmers	24
No. 5 Starter	Jack Kochanowicz	23
Closer	Oliver Ortega	27

The emergence of the less-heralded Fletcher, who hit .319 and shined defensively in 2020, and Jared Walsh, who hit .293 with nine homers in 32 games, could fill holes at shortstop and first base in 2021, freeing up more money for pitching.

Owner Arte Moreno gave assurances that a payroll that has hovered in the $170 million range for five years will not go down, meaning the Angels should compete for a premier free-agent pitcher or two.

The addition of a front-end starter and a key reliever and big contributions from the farm system would go a long way toward the Angels—and Trout—ending their lengthy playoff drought. ■

1 JO ADELL, OF

Born: April 8, 1999. **B-T:** R-R. **HT:** 6-3. **WT:** 215.
Drafted: HS—Louisville, 2017 (1st round).
Signed by: John Burden.

TRACK RECORD: The 10th overall pick in 2017, Adell made his major league debut in 2020 and flashed some of the tools that made him the organization's most touted draft pick since Mike Trout. In his peak moment, he crushed a 437-foot homer to left field that left his bat at 110 mph and also hit a 107 mph laser off the top of the right field wall in a 16-3 Angels victory against the Mariners. But that performance was more the exception than the rule during an uneven rookie season marked by a high strikeout rate, lengthy power droughts and several defensive gaffes. Adell had just 27 games of Triple-A experience when he was called up in early August to replace slumping veteran Justin Upton. His lack of upper-level experience showed. He looked overmatched at the plate, hitting .161/.212/.266 with a 42% strikeout rate, and was uncomfortable and unsure of himself in right field. He committed a rare four-base error in which a fly ball popped out of his glove and over the wall on Aug. 9 and had another ball pop out of his glove over the fence on the final day of the season.

SCOUTING REPORT: Despite Adell's ugly debut, evaluators still view him as a potential impact player. He is a broad-shouldered, muscular and dynamic athlete who boasts plus-plus raw power, excellent bat speed and quick hands that allow him to drive the ball to all fields and get to high pitches. He has plus speed, which translates into more first-to-third sprints than stolen bases, a plus arm and a work ethic and willingness to learn that draw rave reviews from coaches. Major league pitchers exposed holes in a swing that was too long at times and an approach that made him too vulnerable to secondary pitches. A month into the season, Adell tried to alter his swing path to get the ball in the air more and quieted his stance to remove some movement from his pre-swing setup. His pitch recognition and plate discipline improved with experience, even if the results didn't come. He was more mechanical and less fluid in right field during his first month in the big leagues, but his jumps and reads off the bat improved as he grew more comfortable and confident over the final month.

THE FUTURE: Lofty expectations for Adell were tempered by his shaky rookie season, but like Aaron Judge and other future stars who had rough debuts, he has the talent, maturity and intelligence to make the necessary adjustments. With more experience, he still projects to develop into an all-star-caliber player. ■

JOHN MCCOY/GETTY IMAGES

BA GRADE
65 **Risk: High**

SCOUTING GRADES
Hit: 50. **Power:** 70. **Run:** 70. **Field:** 50. **Arm:** 60.

Projected future grades on 20-80 scouting scale.

BEST TOOLS

Best Hitter for Average	Brandon Marsh
Best Power Hitter	Jo Adell
Best Strike-Zone Discipline	Brandon Marsh
Fastest Baserunner	Jordyn Adams
Best Athlete	Jordyn Adams
Best Fastball	Chris Rodriguez
Best Curveball	Reid Detmers
Best Slider	Chris Rodriguez
Best Changeup	William Holmes
Best Control	Reid Detmers
Best Defensive Catcher	Jack Kruger
Best Defensive Infielder	Livan Soto
Best Infield Arm	Kevin Maitan
Best Defensive Outfielder	Brandon Marsh
Best Outfield Arm	Brandon Marsh

Year	Age	Club (League)	Class	AVG	G	AB	R	H	2B	3B	HR	RBI	BB	SO	SB	OBP	SLG
2017	18	Angels (AZL)	R	.288	31	118	18	34	6	6	4	21	10	32	5	.351	.542
	18	Orem (PIO)	R	.376	18	85	25	32	5	2	1	9	4	17	3	.411	.518
2018	19	Inland Empire (CAL)	HiA	.290	57	238	46	69	19	3	12	42	15	63	9	.345	.546
	19	Rocket City (SL)	AA	.238	17	63	14	15	6	0	2	6	6	22	2	.324	.429
	19	Burlington (MWL)	LoA	.326	25	95	23	31	7	1	6	29	11	26	4	.398	.611
2019	20	Inland Empire (CAL)	HiA	.280	6	25	4	7	1	0	2	5	1	10	0	.333	.560
	20	Rocket City (SL)	AA	.308	43	159	28	49	15	0	8	23	19	41	6	.390	.553
	20	Salt Lake (PCL)	AAA	.264	27	121	22	32	11	0	0	8	10	43	1	.321	.355
2020	21	Los Angeles (AL)	MAJ	.161	38	124	9	20	4	0	3	7	7	55	0	.212	.266
Major League Totals				.161	38	124	9	20	4	0	3	7	7	55	0	.212	.266
Minor League Totals				.298	224	904	180	269	70	12	35	143	76	254	30	.361	.518

2 BRANDON MARSH, OF

TOP ROOKIE

ROBERT BINDER/MLB PHOTOS VIA GETTY IMAGES

BA GRADE
60 Risk: High

Born: Dec. 18, 1997. **B-T:** L-R. **HT:** 6-4. **WT:** 215. **Drafted:** HS—Buford, Ga., 2016 (2nd round). **Signed by:** Todd Hogan.

TRACK RECORD: Marsh has been a standout on the field since the Angels drafted him in the second round in 2016, but he's also been frequently sidelined by injuries. That continued in 2020 when he suffered an elbow strain in spring training and missed part of summer camp for undisclosed reasons. He returned to spend August and September at the alternate training site and built on the offensive adjustments he made in 2019 with Double-A Mobile.

SCOUTING REPORT: Marsh is a high-level athlete who blends big tools with impressive instincts. He is a plus runner who displays excellent routes and reads in center field, has a plus-plus, accurate arm and has an athletic swing that drives the ball hard to the gaps. His game-planning and understanding of how opponents are pitching him continues to grow, and his improved pull-side power in the second half of 2019 has fueled optimism he can approach 20 home runs at his peak. The Angels introduced Marsh to first base at the alternate site. He initially balked at the idea, but grew to enjoy the position and attacked it with the same vigor he displays in the outfield.

THE FUTURE: With his bat continuing to develop, Marsh should join Mike Trout and Jo Adell to give the Angels a star-studded outfield in the near future. He is set to begin 2021 at Triple-A.

SCOUTING GRADES: **Hitting:** 55 **Power:** 50 **Running:** 60 **Fielding:** 60 **Arm:** 70

Year	Age	Club (League)	Class	AVG	G	AB	R	H	2B	3B	HR	RBI	BB	SO	SB	OBP	SLG
2017	19	Orem (PIO)	R	.350	39	177	47	62	13	5	4	44	9	35	10	.396	.548
2018	20	Inland Empire (CAL)	HiA	.256	93	371	59	95	15	6	7	46	52	118	10	.348	.385
	20	Burlington (MWL)	LoA	.295	34	132	26	39	12	1	3	24	21	40	4	.390	.470
2019	21	Angels (AZL)	R	.048	5	21	1	1	0	0	0	2	0	8	1	.048	.048
	21	Rocket City (SL)	AA	.300	96	360	48	108	21	2	7	43	47	92	18	.383	.428
Minor League Totals				.288	267	1060	181	305	61	14	21	159	129	292	43	.368	.431

3 CHRIS RODRIGUEZ, RHP

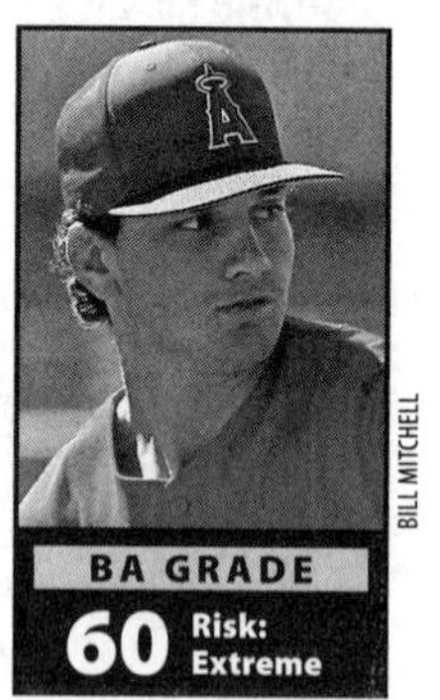

BILL MITCHELL

BA GRADE
60 Risk: Extreme

Born: July 20, 1998. **B-T:** R-R. **HT:** 6-2. **WT:** 185. **Drafted:** HS—Miami, 2016 (4th round). **Signed by:** Ralph Reyes.

TRACK RECORD: Rodriguez has flashed wicked stuff since the Angels drafted him in the fourth round in 2016, but he's pitched just 77.2 innings in four seasons. He missed the 2018 season with a stress reaction in his lower back and made just three starts in 2019 before having season-ending back surgery to repair a stress fracture. Rodriguez returned in 2020 and earned high praise from big leaguers during summer camp. He threw about 65-70 innings between the alternate training site and instructional league.

SCOUTING REPORT: Rodriguez has a tantalizing four-pitch mix on par with any pitching prospect. His fastball comfortably sits 94-95 mph and touches 98 with hard sink and tailing life. All three of his secondary pitches flash plus, and he commands them better than his fastball. His slider is a wipeout offering at 87-91 mph, his big overhand curveball in the mid 80s gets batters swinging over the top, and his upper-80s changeup with screwball-like action might be his best pitch. Rodriguez matured physically and gained a better feel for his delivery over the past year, helping him grow into potentially above-average control. He spent the summer learning how to manipulate his pitches to create different movement.

THE FUTURE: Rodriguez has the ingredients of a front-of-the-rotation starter, but he has to show he can stay healthy. He should get his first taste of the upper minors in 2021.

SCOUTING GRADES: **Fastball:** 70 **Slider:** 60 **Curveball:** 55 **Changeup:** 60 **Control:** 55

Year	Age	Club (League)	Class	W	L	ERA	G	GS	IP	H	HR	BB	SO	BB/9	SO/9	WHIP	AVG
2017	18	Burlington (MWL)	LoA	1	2	5.84	6	6	25	32	1	7	24	2.6	8.8	1.58	.288
	18	Orem (PIO)	R	4	1	6.40	8	8	32	35	1	7	32	1.9	8.9	1.30	.240
2018	19	Did not play—Injured															
2019	20	Inland Empire (CAL)	HiA	0	0	0.00	3	3	9	6	0	4	13	3.9	12.5	1.07	.167
Minor League Totals				5	3	4.75	24	22	77	79	2	21	86	2.4	10.0	1.29	.262

4 REID DETMERS, LHP

MLB PHOTOS VIA GETTY IMAGES

BA GRADE

55 Risk: High

Born: July 8, 1999. **B-T:** L-L. **HT:** 6-2. **WT:** 210. **Drafted:** Louisville, 2020 (1st round). **Signed by:** John Burden.

TRACK RECORD: Detmers set Louisville's single-season record with 167 strikeouts as a sophomore in 2019 and allowed only one earned run in three starts for USA Baseball's Collegiate National team the following summer. He dominated with a 1.23 ERA and 48 strikeouts in 22 innings before the 2020 season shut down and solidified himself as one of the top pitchers in the draft class. The Angels drafted him 10th overall and signed him for $4.67 million. Detmers reported to the alternate training site after signing and threw just over 50 innings between there and instructional league.

SCOUTING REPORT: Detmers is the archetype of a polished college lefthander. His fastball averages 92 mph but generates swings and misses at the top of the strike zone with its high spin rate and late, riding action. His best pitch is a big-breaking curveball in the mid 70s he can drop in the zone for strikes or bury in the dirt for chases. Detmers also has an upper-80s slider that locks up lefthanded hitters, and he's getting a better feel for a low-80s changeup he didn't throw much in college. Detmers moves the ball around the strike zone with above-average control. He mixes and matches his pitches and keeps hitters guessing.

THE FUTURE: Detmers should move quickly up the Angels' system. He projects as a solid No. 3 or 4 starter.

SCOUTING GRADES: **Fastball:** 50 **Slider:** 50 **Curveball:** 60 **Changeup:** 45 **Control:** 55

Year	Age	Club (League)	Class	W	L	ERA	G	GS	IP	H	HR	BB	SO	BB/9	SO/9	WHIP	AVG
2020	20	Did not play—No minor league season															

5 JORDYN ADAMS, OF

BA GRADE

55 Risk: Very High

Born: Oct. 18, 1999. **B-T:** R-R. **HT:** 6-2. **WT:** 195. **Drafted:** HS—Cary, N.C., 2018 (1st round). **Signed by:** Chris McAlpin.

TRACK RECORD: Adams was committed to play both football and baseball at North Carolina but opted to sign with the Angels after they made him the 17th overall pick in 2018. He rose to high Class A in his first full season and spent 2020 at the alternate training site, where he accumulated roughly 200 at-bats and impressed coaches and teammates with his jaw-dropping speed and athleticism.

SCOUTING REPORT: Adams was set to play wide receiver in college and brings that elite athleticism to the diamond. He is an 80-grade runner with excellent bat speed and wiry strength, but he's still learning to translate those tools into production. He has a mature feel for the strike zone and rarely chases offspeed pitches, but he often hits weak ground balls and is still learning how to make his best swings in games. He showed growth with five home runs at the alternate site. After committing 13 errors in 2019, including when he outran balls in the gaps, Adams has refined his jumps and is running cleaner routes in center field. He has improved his arm strength to average and shows flashes of being a plus defensive center fielder, including when he made three home run-robbing catches at the alternate site.

THE FUTURE: Adams has huge upside, but a lot depends on his swing development. He could see Double-A in 2021.

SCOUTING GRADES: **Hitting:** 50 **Power:** 40 **Running:** 80 **Fielding:** 60 **Arm:** 50

Year	Age	Club (League)	Class	AVG	G	AB	R	H	2B	3B	HR	RBI	BB	SO	SB	OBP	SLG
2018	18	Angels (AZL)	R	.243	20	70	8	17	2	2	0	5	10	23	5	.354	.329
	18	Orem (PIO)	R	.314	9	35	5	11	4	1	0	8	4	7	0	.375	.486
2019	19	Inland Empire (CAL)	HiA	.229	9	35	7	8	1	1	1	1	5	14	0	.325	.400
	19	Angels (AZL)	R	.538	3	13	4	7	1	0	0	4	1	3	4	.571	.615
	19	Burlington (MWL)	LoA	.250	97	372	52	93	15	2	7	31	50	94	12	.346	.358
Minor League Totals				.259	138	525	76	136	23	6	8	49	70	141	21	.353	.371

6 JEREMIAH JACKSON, SS/2B

Born: March 26, 2000. **B-T:** R-R. **HT:** 6-0. **WT:** 180. **Drafted:** HS—Mobile, Ala., 2018 (2nd round). **Signed by:** J.T. Zink.

ZACHARY LUCY/FOUR SEAM IMAGES

BA GRADE
50 **Risk: Extreme**

TRACK RECORD: Jackson signed for $1.194 million as a 2018 second-round pick and made a quick impression by hitting a Pioneer League-record 23 homers at Rookie-level Orem in 2019. That power, however, came with a concerning 33% strikeout rate. Jackson joined the Angels' alternate training site in early August and finished the year in instructional league, where he was limited by an oblique injury.

SCOUTING REPORT: Jackson is a slim-bodied middle infielder with eye-popping power for his size. He generates plus bat speed with an old-school flick of the wrist and has the pop to approach 30 homers as he matures physically. Jackson's power is tantalizing, but he still swings and misses too much to get to it consistently. He looked overmatched against more advanced pitching in his first two weeks at the alternate site, but his at-bats grew more competitive and he made more consistent contact in the final month. Jackson is athletic enough to play shortstop and second base, and he mixed in a little third base last summer. He has above-average arm strength but needs to improve his accuracy.

THE FUTURE: It's easy to dream of Jackson becoming a power-hitting middle infielder, but he has to make more contact. That will be his primary goal in his full-season debut.

SCOUTING GRADES:	Hitting: 40	Power: 60	Running: 55	Fielding: 45	Arm: 55

Year	Age	Club (League)	Class	AVG	G	AB	R	H	2B	3B	HR	RBI	BB	SO	SB	OBP	SLG
2018	18	Angels (AZL)	R	.317	21	82	13	26	4	2	5	14	7	25	6	.374	.598
	18	Orem (PIO)	R	.198	22	91	13	18	6	3	2	9	8	34	4	.260	.396
2019	19	Orem (PIO)	R	.266	65	256	47	68	14	2	23	60	24	96	5	.333	.605
Minor League Totals				.261	108	429	73	112	24	7	30	83	39	155	15	.326	.559

7 JACK KOCHANOWICZ, RHP

Born: Dec. 22, 2000. **B-T:** L-R. **HT:** 6-6. **WT:** 220. **Drafted:** HS—Philadelphia, 2019 (3rd round). **Signed by:** Kennard Jones.

BILL MITCHELL

BA GRADE
50 **Risk: Extreme**

TRACK RECORD: The Angels made Kochanowicz a high-round prep pitcher draftee, a rare step for them. Taken in the third round in 2019 and signed for an over-slot $1.25 million, he spent the final weeks of 2020 at the alternate training site before heading to instructional league. He stood out in Arizona as he improved his fastball command, made progress with his changeup and gained a better mechanical feel for how his large frame works on the mound.

SCOUTING REPORT: Kochanowicz checks in at 6-foot-6, 220 pounds, but his delivery is athletic and relatively fluid. His lively fastball ranged from 90-95 mph when he signed and now sits 93-94 and touches 97 with ride up in the zone. The Angels love his work ethic and believe he will gain even more velocity as he continues to mature and add strength. Kochanowicz's high-spin, big-breaking curveball with late horizontal movement gives him a second potential plus pitch. His changeup is still developing but shows average potential. Kochanowicz is a natural strike-thrower for his age and should have no trouble maintaining at least average control with his clean delivery.

THE FUTURE: Kochanowicz shows the ingredients of a mid-rotation starter and maybe more, but he's still a young kid yet to pitch in a professional game. He will make his official pro debut in 2021.

SCOUTING GRADES:	Fastball: 60	Curveball: 60	Changeup: 50	Control: 50

Year	Age	Club (League)	Class	W	L	ERA	G	GS	IP	H	HR	BB	SO	BB/9	SO/9	WHIP	AVG
2019	18	Did not play															

8 JAHMAI JONES, 2B/OF

ROBERT BINDER/MLB PHOTOS VIA GETTY IMAGES

BA GRADE
45 Risk: High

Born: Aug. 4, 1997. **B-T:** R-R. **HT:** 6-0. **WT:** 204. **Drafted:** HS—Norcross, Ga., 2015 (2nd round). **Signed by:** Todd Hogan.

TRACK RECORD: The son of former NFL linebacker Andre Jones, Jahmai cycled through multiple swing changes in the minors and clicked in the second half of 2019 when he hit .292 with a .370-on base percentage from July on at Double-A Mobile. He followed up with a strong showing in the Arizona Fall League and earned his first big league callup in August 2020.

SCOUTING REPORT: Jones has a promising foundation with solid athleticism, advanced plate discipline, an excellent work ethic and natural leadership skills. He's at his best when he takes a level, direct swing and struggled when he tried to implement a launch-angle swing at the Angels' request. With his swing back in order, Jones hit seven homers at the alternate site and did a better job of hitting with two strikes and driving the ball the other way. He makes enough contact to project as an average hitter and has enough thump to approach double-digit home runs. Originally an outfielder, Jones struggled with a transition to second base but has grown to look more natural at the position. His range to both sides, the smoothness of his double-play turns and arm have all improved to average.

THE FUTURE: Jones projects as a solid utility player if he can maintain his best swing. He is set to open 2021 at Triple-A Salt Lake and will be in position to return to the majors during the year.

SCOUTING GRADES: Hitting: 50 Power: 40 Running: 60 Fielding: 50 Arm: 45

Year	Age	Club (League)	Class	AVG	G	AB	R	H	2B	3B	HR	RBI	BB	SO	SB	OBP	SLG
2017	19	Inland Empire (CAL)	HiA	.302	41	172	32	52	11	3	5	17	13	43	9	.368	.488
	19	Burlington (MWL)	LoA	.272	86	346	54	94	18	4	9	30	32	63	18	.338	.425
2018	20	Inland Empire (CAL)	HiA	.235	75	298	47	70	10	5	8	35	43	63	13	.338	.383
	20	Rocket City (SL)	AA	.245	48	184	33	45	10	4	2	20	24	51	11	.335	.375
2019	21	Rocket City (SL)	AA	.234	130	482	66	113	22	3	5	50	50	109	9	.308	.324
2020	22	Los Angeles (AL)	MAJ	.429	3	7	2	3	0	0	0	1	0	2	0	.429	.429
Major League Totals				.429	3	7	2	3	0	0	0	1	0	2	0	.429	.429
Minor League Totals				.258	484	1900	317	491	90	24	35	202	205	404	96	.338	.386

9 HECTOR YAN, LHP

ROBERT BINDER/MLB PHOTOS VIA GETTY IMAGES

BA GRADE
45 Risk: High

Born: April 26, 1999. **B-T:** L-L. **HT:** 5-11. **WT:** 209. **Signed:** Dominican Republic, 2015. **Signed by:** Domingo Garcia/Alfredo Ulloa.

TRACK RECORD: Yan spent three years in Rookie ball after signing for $80,000 but broke out in 2019, when he finished second in the Midwest League with 148 strikeouts and limited opponents to a .190 average. He got valuable experience facing big leaguers at summer camp in 2020 and spent the year at the alternate training site, throwing just under 40 innings, before finishing the year in the Dominican League.

SCOUTING REPORT: Yan has a funky, low three-quarters arm slot and cross-body delivery that generates a ton of deception but also below-average control. His fastball averaged 94 mph and touched 98 during his breakout 2019, but he struggled to regain that velocity after the long layoff in 2020 and sat in the 92-93 mph range throughout the summer. Yan's low-80s curveball has excellent depth and his mid-80s changeup with late fade flashes average. Yan also throws a low-80s splitter that has been an out pitch for him at times, but it's thrown with such a low spin rate—usually under 1,000 rpms—that it appears to knuckle at times, making it difficult to command.

THE FUTURE: The Angels will keep Yan in the rotation as long as they can to see if he improves his control. If not, his mix of stuff and funk will play in relief.

SCOUTING GRADES: Fastball: 55 Splitter: 45 Curveball: 50 Changeup: 45 Control: 40

Year	Age	Club (League)	Class	W	L	ERA	G	GS	IP	H	HR	BB	SO	BB/9	SO/9	WHIP	AVG
2017	18	Angels (AZL)	R	0	1	4.96	10	5	16	10	0	11	21	6.1	11.6	1.29	.139
2018	19	Orem (PIO)	R	0	4	4.55	10	10	30	29	3	20	29	6.1	8.8	1.65	.218
2019	20	Burlington (MWL)	LoA	4	5	3.39	26	20	109	74	5	52	148	4.3	12.2	1.16	.153
Minor League Totals				6	10	3.30	53	42	185	136	8	98	231	4.8	11.2	1.26	.207

10 KYREN PARIS, SS

Born: Nov. 11, 2001. **B-T:** R-R. **HT:** 6-0. **WT:** 180. **Drafted:** HS—Oakley, Calif., 2019 (2nd round). **Signed by:** Brian Tripp.

TRACK RECORD: Paris signed for an above-slot $1.4 million as a second-round pick in 2019 but was limited to three games after signing by a broken hamate bone. He spent the final month of 2020 at the alternate training site, where he was one of the youngest players in camp. Paris looked overmatched the first two weeks, but his at-bats grew more competitive over time.

SCOUTING REPORT: Paris has a sound righthanded swing and a line-drive approach that allows him to drive the ball with authority to the opposite field. He has quick hands and good timing and possesses a natural feel to hit. Paris is known for his contact skills more than his power, but he opened eyes when he drove a home run off lefthander Patrick Sandoval over the 395-foot center field wall at the alternate site. Paris played second and third base at the alternate site, but with his above-average speed and arm, he should be able to stick at shortstop.

THE FUTURE: Paris has a chance to grow into an everyday infielder. He'll start 2021 at the Rookie level.

SCOUTING GRADES: **Hitting:** 50 **Power:** 45 **Running:** 55 **Fielding:** 55 **Arm:** 55

Year	Age	Club (League)	Class	AVG	G	AB	R	H	2B	3B	HR	RBI	BB	SO	SB	OBP	SLG
2019	17	Angels (AZL)	R	.300	3	10	4	3	1	0	0	2	3	4	0	.462	.400
Minor League Totals				.300	3	10	4	3	1	0	0	2	3	4	0	.462	.400

11 OLIVER ORTEGA, RHP

Born: Oct. 2, 1996. **B-T.:** R-R. **HT:** 6-0. **WT:** 200. **Signed:** Dominican Republic, 2014. **Signed by:** Domingo Garcia/Alfredo Ulloa.

TRACK RECORD: Ortega, who signed for just $10,000 in 2014, missed all of 2017 with a stress reaction in his back and was not considered much of a prospect until the 2019 season. A velocity bump helped him rack up 135 strikeouts in 111 innings between high Class A Inland Empire and Double-A Mobile. His only 2020 action came playing winter ball in the Dominican Republic.

SCOUTING REPORT: Ortega complements a fastball that averages 95 mph and touches 98 mph with a funky 12-to-6 knuckle curveball that averages 83 mph and sometimes spins like a lefthanded breaking ball. Both are plus pitches that draw plenty of swings and misses. Ortega mostly throws those two pitches, but he does have an upper-80s mph changeup he'll occasionally throw. His control is inconsistent.

THE FUTURE: If Ortega can improve his strike-throwing, he could develop into a back-of-the-rotation starter. Most likely, he ends up a reliever whose fastball and knuckle-curve play up in shorter bursts.

Year	Age	Club (League)	Class	W	L	ERA	G	GS	IP	H	HR	BB	SO	BB/9	SO/9	WHIP	AVG
2019	22	Inland Empire (CAL)	HiA	4	5	3.34	21	16	94	67	8	49	121	4.7	11.5	1.23	.162
	22	Rocket City (SL)	AA	0	3	8.64	5	5	17	23	0	8	14	4.3	7.6	1.86	.284
Minor League Totals				11	19	3.83	72	46	265	212	15	126	285	4.3	9.7	1.27	.218

12 JOSE ALBERTO RIVERA, RHP

BA GRADE
45 Risk: Very High

Born: Feb. 14, 1997. **B-T:** R-R. **HT:** 6-3. **WT:** 200. **Signed:** Dominican Republic, 2016. **Signed by:** Oz Ocampo/Roman Ocumarez/Leocadio Guevara (Astros).

TRACK RECORD: The Astros signed Rivera for $10,000 in 2016 and he didn't make his full-season debut until he was 22 in 2019. By then, his fastball exploded to over 100 mph. When the Astros didn't protect Rivera on their 40-man roster after the 2020 season, the Angels selected him in the Rule 5 draft.

SCOUTING REPORT: Rivera has electric arm speed and produces a fastball that ranges from 97-102 mph with lively tailing action. He throws a split-changeup in the mid 80s that has progressed to flash above-average and has a hard slider in the mid-80s as well, but it's inconsistent and he struggles to locate it. Rivero has an aggressive, high-energy delivery he will need to corral in order to improve his fringe-average control.

THE FUTURE: The Astros developed Rivera as starter, but his stuff, delivery and control all point to a future as a power reliever. He'll get the chance to fill that role for the Angels in 2021.

Year	Age	Club (League)	Class	W	L	ERA	G	GS	IP	H	HR	BB	SO	BB/9	SO/9	WHIP	AVG
2019	22	Quad Cities (MWL)	LoA	5	5	3.81	18	11	76	61	2	36	95	4.3	11.3	1.28	.191
Minor League Totals				9	12	3.63	44	21	161	120	11	74	185	4.1	10.3	1.20	.205

13 D'SHAWN KNOWLES, OF

Born: Jan. 16, 2001. **B-T:** B-R. **HT:** 5-11. **WT:** 180. **Signed:** Bahamas, 2017. **Signed by:** Carlos Gomez.

TRACK RECORD: Knowles, who signed out of the Bahamas for $850,000, struggled in a repeat season at Rookie-level Orem in 2019 and was not brought to the alternate training site in 2020. But he spent six weeks at instructional league in Arizona, where he earned rave reviews for his strong defense at all three outfield spots, improved baserunning and plate discipline and his ability to make more consistent contact from both sides of the plate.

SCOUTING REPORT: Knowles is a gap-to-gap contact hitter with plus speed. He has a clean, compact, quiet swing from both sides and average raw power potential, with more pop coming from the left side. He has a chance to hit for more power as he gets bigger and his bat-to-ball skills improve. Knowles was introduced to second base at instructional league in 2019 and will continue to explore the position moving forward. His arm is strong enough to play three outfield spots, and it should play up in the infield.

THE FUTURE: Knowles projects as a high on-base percentage, speedy utility man more than a regular. He will likely start 2021 at low Class A.

Year	Age	Club (League)	Class	AVG	G	AB	R	H	2B	3B	HR	RBI	BB	SO	SB	OBP	SLG
2019	18	Orem (PIO)	R	.241	64	253	38	61	11	4	6	28	26	76	5	.310	.387
Minor League Totals				.274	122	475	84	130	24	7	11	57	54	141	14	.348	.423

14 AROL VERA, SS

BA GRADE
45 Risk: Extreme

Born: Sept. 12, 2002. **B-T:** B-R. **HT:** 6-3. **WT:** 215. **Signed:** Venezuela, 2019. **Signed by:** Marion Urdaneta/Andres Garcia/Joel Chicarelli.

TRACK RECORD: Vera signed for $2 million as a 16-year-old as part of the Angels' renewed commitment to Latin America. He was confined to an Arizona apartment complex during the coronavirus shutdown in 2020 and put on a little too much weight by the time he reported to instructional league in the fall. Even with the added weight, he showed a tool set that remains intriguing.

SCOUTING REPORT: The switch-hitting Vera has an advanced understanding of the strike zone and good bat-to-ball skills from both sides. He works counts and rarely swings at pitches outside the strike zone. He's more of a line-drive hitter but should hit for more power as he matures physically and gains strength. Vera is athletic in the field with quick hands, a strong arm and an ability to throw from all angles at shortstop. He's an average runner now but will likely slow down as he fills out.

THE FUTURE: Vera is too gifted of an infielder to move off of shortstop for now. If he continues to add weight, he might project more as a third baseman.

Year	Age	Club (League)	Class	AVG	G	AB	R	H	2B	3B	HR	RBI	BB	SO	SB	OBP	SLG
2019	16	Did not play															

15 ERIK RIVERA, LHP/OF

BREAKOUT
BA GRADE
45 Risk: Extreme

Born: April 2, 2001. **B-T:** L-L. **HT:** 6-2. **WT:** 200. **Drafted:** HS—Gurabo, P.R., 2019 (4th round). **Signed by:** Omar Rodriguez.

TRACK RECORD: Rivera impressed enough at the Puerto Rico Baseball Academy to be selected in the fourth round in 2019 and was announced by the Angels as a two-way player. He continued to take at-bats as a designated hitter in instructional league in 2020, but he appears to have more upside as a pitcher.

SCOUTING REPORT: Rivera has a smooth, athletic delivery and induces plenty of swings and misses with a fastball that averages 92 mph and touches 95 mph. His 77 mph curveball resembles a slider, with a little more sweep than depth, and an emphasis in the fall was adding velocity to, and improving the command of, his breaking pitch. Rivera has shown improvement on an 83 mph changeup that has some fade. At the plate, Rivera has plenty of raw power but has struggled to make consistent contact.

THE FUTURE: Rivera should reach low Class A in 2021. He may continue to get at-bats, but his future is firmly as a pitcher. He projects as a mid-to-back-of-the-rotation starter or possibly a swingman.

Year	Age	Club (League)	Class	AVG	G	AB	R	H	2B	3B	HR	RBI	BB	SO	SB	OBP	SLG
2019	18	Angels (AZL)	R	.208	21	72	8	15	4	0	0	9	9	31	0	.313	.264
Minor League Totals				.208	21	72	8	15	4	0	0	9	9	31	0	.313	.264

16 JOSE BONILLA, SS/3B

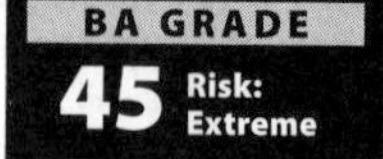

Born: April 2, 2002. **B-T:** R-R. **HT:** 6-1. **WT:** 190. **Signed:** Dominican Republic, 2019. **Signed by:** Domingo Garcia.

TRACK RECORD: Bonilla signed for $600,000 in 2019 and showed good pull-side power with occasional opposite-field pop during a 20-game stint in the Dominican Summer League. He stayed in shape by playing sandlot ball in the Dominican Republic during the coronavirus shutdown and was a full participant in instructional league in the fall.

SCOUTING REPORT: Bonilla has a clean bat path that allows him to barrel baseballs consistently and produce high-end exit velocities, and he has a natural launch angle that helps him hit the ball into the air. As he grows and adds muscle, he has a chance to hit for average power. The stout-framed Bonilla is not as athletic as many of the organization's top middle-infield prospects, but he's a smooth, polished defender with a plus-plus arm that allows him to make throws from deep in the hole. The Angels love Bonilla's work ethic and baseball IQ.

THE FUTURE: Though he handles shortstop well, Bonilla's body type might necessitate a move to third base. He will likely start 2021 in the Rookie-level Arizona League.

Year	Age	Club (League)	Class	AVG	G	AB	R	H	2B	3B	HR	RBI	BB	SO	SB	OBP	SLG
2019	17	Angels (DSL)	R	.284	20	74	13	21	5	2	0	6	14	19	0	.402	.405
Minor League Totals				.284	20	74	13	21	5	2	0	6	14	19	0	.402	.405

17 ALEXANDER RAMIREZ, OF

BA GRADE
45 Risk: Extreme

Born: Aug. 29, 2002. **B-T:** R-R. **HT:** 6-3. **WT:** 210. **Signed:** Dominican Republic, 2018. **Signed by:** Frank Tejeda.

TRACK RECORD: The Angels signed Ramirez for $1 million based on the belief he had the power potential to grow into a middle-of-the-order slugger. He showed that pop as a 17-year-old with 17 extra-base hits, including four homers, over 39 games in the Dominican Summer League in his pro debut. Ramirez was quarantined in an Arizona apartment last summer during the coronavirus shutdown and slowed by a sore shoulder during fall instructional league.

SCOUTING REPORT: Ramirez is big, strong and muscular with an athletic frame, and he can hit the ball a long way. But there is some swing-and-miss in his game—he struck out in one-third of his plate appearances in 2019—and his bat-to-ball skills, timing and ability to hit breaking balls all need work. Ramirez is an average runner who is still learning to manage his long strides. Though he has solid defensive instincts in the outfield and an above-average throwing arm, Ramirez is still growing into his body and has occasional coordination issues.

THE FUTURE: Ramirez projects as a power-hitting corner outfielder, but the Angels will continue to challenge him by playing him in center field as much as they can. He will likely open 2021 in the Rookie-level Arizona League.

Year	Age	Club (League)	Class	AVG	G	AB	R	H	2B	3B	HR	RBI	BB	SO	SB	OBP	SLG
2019	16	Angels (DSL)	R	.234	39	154	37	36	8	5	4	19	16	59	6	.328	.429
Minor League Totals				.234	39	154	37	36	8	5	4	19	16	59	6	.328	.429

18 DENNY BRADY, RHP

Born: Jan. 18, 1997. **B-T:** R-R. **HT:** 6-1. **WT:** 200. **Drafted:** Mercer County (N.J.) JC, 2017 (7th round). **Signed by:** Ryan Leahy.

TRACK RECORD: Brady showed excellent command and an attack-the-zone mentality in his first three professional seasons, striking out 157 and walking 44 in 144 2/3 innings as he climbed to high Class A. He had a brief stint at the alternate training site in 2020 before finishing in instructional league, where he placed an emphasis on getting ahead in counts and putting away hitters quicker.

SCOUTING REPORT: Brady gets well above average ride on a fastball that averages 93 mph, and he throws two different 82-mph breaking balls. One resembles a slider and one is more of a curveball depending on how he manipulates the ball, with his curveball drawing above-average grades. His improving mid-80s changeup has some fading action but doesn't have much depth. Brady has average control and is starting to understand how his stuff works: the more he stays in attack mode, the better his results usually are.

THE FUTURE: Brady has a chance to land as a back-of-the-rotation starter, but he is more likely to reach the big leagues as a middle reliever. He will likely start 2021 at Double-A.

Year	Age	Club (League)	Class	W	L	ERA	G	GS	IP	H	HR	BB	SO	BB/9	SO/9	WHIP	AVG
2019	22	Inland Empire (CAL)	HiA	3	9	3.64	17	10	77	78	4	25	86	2.9	10.1	1.34	.234
Minor League Totals				4	15	4.11	43	23	144	152	7	44	157	2.7	9.8	1.35	.269

19 ADRIAN PLACENCIA, SS/2B

Born: June 2, 2003. **B-T:** B-R. **HT:** 5-11. **WT:** 170. **Signed:** Dominican Republic, 2019. **Signed by:** Jochy Cabrera.

TRACK RECORD: The switch-hitting Placencia signed with the Angels for $1.1 million as one of the youngest players in the 2019-20 international signing class. He did not play for an affiliate after signing, so the Angels got their first extended look at him during instructional league last fall.

SCOUTING REPORT: Still only 17, Placencia doesn't have the size right now to generate much impact at the plate. He does have a sound swing, uses his hands well, puts together quality at-bats and makes decently hard contact when he finds the barrel. Despite his size, the natural lift in his swing gives him a chance to develop average or better raw power as he matures physically and gains strength. Defensively, Placencia has smooth actions, soft hands and an average arm with a quick exchange at shortstop. He is a below-average runner.

THE FUTURE: Placencia is not quite as advanced as fellow 2019 international signee Arol Vera in terms of baseball IQ and maturity, but he's extremely athletic with explosive movements. He will likely start 2021 in the Dominican Summer League.

Year	Age	Club (League)	Class	AVG	G	AB	R	H	2B	3B	HR	RBI	BB	SO	SB	OBP	SLG
2019	16	Did not play—Signed 2020 contract															

20 PACKY NAUGHTON, LHP

Born: April 16, 1996. **B-T:** R-L. **HT:** 6-2. **WT:** 195. **Drafted:** Virginia Tech, 2017 (9th round). **Signed by:** Jeff Brookens (Reds).

TRACK RECORD: Naughton was named the Reds minor league player of the year in 2019 after going 11-12, 3.32 between high Class A Daytona and Double-A Chattanooga. The Angels acquired him for Brian Goodwin at the 2020 trade deadline. Naughton was durable enough to throw more than 150 innings in both 2018 and 2019 and spent 2020 at the alternate training sites of the Reds and Angels.

SCOUTING REPORT: Naughton is a crafty lefthander who works from a slightly funky, low-three-quarters arm slot that adds deception to his three-pitch mix. He throws his fastball in the low-90s with average command, but his best weapon is a changeup he throws with excellent deception, depth and some armside run. Naughton can spin a breaking ball with some shape, but his curveball isn't nearly as effective as his changeup and fastball. He is able to repeat his delivery and has above-average control.

THE FUTURE: Naughton will likely start 2021 at Triple-A. His lack of high-octane stuff relegates him to the back of the rotation, but with his advanced feel for pitching, durability and control, he should provide starting pitching depth.

Year	Age	Club (League)	Class	W	L	ERA	G	GS	IP	H	HR	BB	SO	BB/9	SO/9	WHIP	AVG
2019	23	Daytona (FSL)	HiA	5	2	2.63	9	9	51	49	2	9	50	1.6	8.8	1.13	.234
	23	Chattanooga (SL)	AA	6	10	3.66	19	19	106	109	8	26	81	2.2	6.9	1.28	.244
Minor League Totals				19	25	3.59	70	68	371	384	27	89	331	2.2	8.0	1.27	.267

21 SADRAC FRANCO, RHP

Born: June 4, 2000. **B-T:** R-R. **HT:** 6-0. **WT:**190. **Signed:** Panama, 2017. **Signed by:** Carlos Ramirez/Lebi Ochoa.

TRACK RECORD: Franco signed for $50,000 in 2017 and excited the Angels with his raw arm strength, but the injury bug has bitten him. He spent the first two and a half months of 2019 in extended spring training rehabilitating a forearm injury, which led to a major elbow injury after he made eight starts at Rookie-league Orem. Franco had Tommy John surgery following the season and did not pitch at all in 2020.

SCOUTING REPORT: Franco added 25-30 pounds in his first two professional seasons. He vaulted up the organization's depth chart because of his command of a fastball that averages 94 mph and touches 98 mph with riding action at the top of the zone, a considerable boost from his previous peak velocity of 94 mph.Franco has struggled with the command of his secondary pitches. He has a mid-80s changeup with significant fade and depth and an upper-70s curveball that lags behind his changeup.

THE FUTURE: Franco should be ready to go in spring training. He could develop into a starter if he gains better control of his offspeed pitches. If not, his fastball should play up even more in shorter relief stints.

Year	Age	Club (League)	Class	W	L	ERA	G	GS	IP	H	HR	BB	SO	BB/9	SO/9	WHIP	AVG
2019	19	Orem (PIO)	R	0	2	5.04	8	8	25	28	5	13	25	4.7	9.0	1.64	.233
Minor League Totals				3	7	5.21	29	12	76	80	6	37	75	4.4	8.9	1.54	.265

22 WILLIAM HOLMES, RHP/OF

BREAKOUT
BA GRADE
45 Risk: Extreme

Born: Dec. 22, 2000. **B-T:** R-R. **HT:** 6-3. **WT:** 220. **Drafted:** HS—Detroit, 2018 (5th round). **Signed by:** Drew Dominguez.

TRACK RECORD: Holmes, formerly known as William English, signed as a two-way player for an over-slot $700,000 bonus in 2018. He hit .320 with a .920 OPS in 43 Rookie-level at-bats in his pro debut, but he appears to have more upside as a pitcher.

SCOUTING REPORT: Holmes is a physical specimen with a broad-shouldered, muscular, athletic frame and huge hands. His fastball sits at 93 mph and touches 97 mph with occasional cutting action. His 81-82-mph changeup spins like a lefthanded slider at times because of the way he naturally pronates his forearm and has a chance to be a plus pitch. Holmes needs to get more depth and better command of his 76-79 mph curveball. Holmes has raw power at the plate, but his promise as a pitcher is too great for him to focus on hitting.

THE FUTURE: Holmes could develop into a starter if can add a little velocity and master his curveball as a third pitch. His fastball-changeup combination might also play in the back of the bullpen.

Year	Age	Club (League)	Class	W	L	ERA	G	GS	IP	H	HR	BB	SO	BB/9	SO/9	WHIP	AVG
2019	18	Angels (AZL)	R	0	2	5.71	7	6	17	15	2	16	25	8.3	13.0	1.79	.183
	18	Orem (PIO)	R	0	0	3.86	2	2	7	4	2	4	13	5.1	16.7	1.14	.148
Minor League Totals				0	2	5.18	9	8	24	19	4	20	38	7.4	14.1	1.60	.224

23 LIVAN SOTO, SS/2B

BA GRADE
40 Risk: High

Born: June 22, 2000. **B-T:** L-R. **HT:** 5-11. **WT:** 180. **Signed:** Venezuela, 2017. **Signed by:** Rolando Petit (Braves).

TRACK RECORD: Soto is one of 12 former Braves prospects who were declared free agents by MLB in 2017 as punishment for Atlanta's violation of international signing rules. He signed with the Angels and gained 15 pounds, but the added strength did not result in more power. Soto hit only one home run and seven doubles in 273 Rookie-level and low Class A at-bats in 2019. His only 2020 action came at instructional league.

SCOUTING REPORT: Soto is one of the best defenders in the Angels system with good instincts and fast-twitch actions, a good first step, quick hands and a strong arm. Though his best position is shortstop, he's also grown into a plus defender at second base. Soto has solid bat-to-ball skills and an advanced approach at the plate—he has almost as many walks (84) as strikeouts (94) in three minor league seasons—but he lacks pop and is a slightly below-average runner.

THE FUTURE: Soto is still only 20 and has time to develop, but unless he hits for more power, he projects more as a utility player. He will begin 2021 at one of the Class A levels.

Year	Age	Club (League)	Class	AVG	G	AB	R	H	2B	3B	HR	RBI	BB	SO	SB	OBP	SLG
2019	19	Angels (AZL)	R	.214	7	28	4	6	2	0	0	1	1	4	0	.241	.286
	19	Burlington (MWL)	LoA	.220	64	245	24	54	5	0	1	20	32	40	6	.311	.253
Minor League Totals				.241	162	618	83	149	22	0	1	46	84	94	22	.335	.282

24 ORLANDO MARTINEZ, OF

BA GRADE
40 Risk: High

Born: Feb. 17, 1998. **B-T:** L-L. **HT:** 5-11. **WT:** 195. **Signed:** Cuba, 2017. **Signed by:** Frankie Thon Jr.

TRACK RECORD: Martinez played in Cuba's 18U national league in 2016 and led the circuit in batting average while finishing second in slugging percentage behind only Luis Robert. Martinez signed with the Angels for $250,000 the following year and showed promising power at high Class A Inland Empire in 2019, hitting 12 homers, 21 doubles and four triples in 88 games.

SCOUTING REPORT: Martinez has a smooth lefthanded swing, good contact skills and a hit-over-power profile overall. When he gets a pitch he's looking for he can do damage, especially to the pull-side gap. His power tends to show up in flashes and he does have double-digit home run potential. Marinez is only an average runner but gets great jumps off the bat and runs efficient routes, which allows him to get to balls in the gaps and play all three outfield positions. He has an average, accurate arm.

THE FUTURE: Martinez projects as a versatile extra outfielder in the major leagues. He will move to Double-A in 2021.

Year	Age	Club (League)	Class	AVG	G	AB	R	H	2B	3B	HR	RBI	BB	SO	SB	OBP	SLG
2019	21	Inland Empire (CAL)	HiA	.263	88	380	55	100	21	4	12	49	36	79	5	.325	.434
Minor League Totals				.280	153	646	93	181	38	5	17	84	57	144	14	.337	.433

25 DAVID CALABRESE, OF

BA GRADE
45 **Risk: Extreme**

Born: Sept. 26, 2002. **B-T:** L-R. **HT:** 5-10. **WT:** 165. **Drafted:** HS—Thornhill, Ont., 2020 (3rd round). **Signed by:** Chris Cruz.

TRACK RECORD: The speedy Calabrese impressed scouts at the Future Stars Series in 2019 at Fenway Park, where he ran a 6.47-second 60-yard dash, hit several doubles and made a few highlight-reel plays in center field. The Ontario native wasn't able to showcase his ability with Team Canada in 2020 due to the coronavirus pandemic, but the Angels still drafted him in the third round and signed him for $744,200 to turn down a scholarship to Arkansas.

SCOUTING REPORT: Calabrese has a simple, efficient swing from the left side. He doesn't offer much in the way of power with his short, thin frame, but he has a good rhythm at the plate and the elite speed to be a base-stealing threat. Once he gains a more consistent bat path, he should develop into a solid gap-to-gap hitter. Calabrese shows good instincts on both sides of the ball and has the potential to be a plus defender with his plus-plus closing speed and ability to cover a lot of ground in center field.

THE FUTURE: Calabrese has the athleticism and speed to stick in center field. It remains to be seen how much strength he develops in order to impact the ball.

Year	Age	Club (League)	Class	AVG	G	AB	R	H	2B	3B	HR	RBI	BB	SO	SB	OBP	SLG
2020	17	Did not play—No minor league season															

26 ZACH LINGINFELTER, RHP

BREAKOUT
BA GRADE
40 **Risk: High**

Born: April 10, 1997. **B-T:** L-R. **HT:** 6-5. **WT:** 240. **Drafted:** Tennessee, 2019 (9th round). **Signed by:** Joel Murrie.

TRACK RECORD: Linginfelter logged a 5.64 ERA at Tennessee in 2019, but he also struck out more than a batter per inning and showed flashes of excellence. The Angels drafted him in the ninth round and signed him for $150,800. He did not pitch for an affiliate after signing, but was a full participant in the 2020 instructional league.

SCOUTING REPORT: The big-bodied Linginfelter has plenty of stuff. His four-seam fastball sits 94-95 mph and touches 98 mph, and he's experimenting with a two-seam fastball that has a little bit of run. His short, late-breaking curveball in the mid-80s looks promising, though his upper 80s slider and a firm changeup, which has some split-finger action, are works in progress. Repetition and consistency are key for Linginfelter moving forward. He has a great arm, but his delivery too often falls apart as he closes himself off and loses feel for the strike zone.

THE FUTURE: Linginfelter will remain in the rotation for now. His fastball-slider mix and his bulldog mentality on the mound may make him better suited for the bullpen.

Year	Age	Club (League)	Class	W	L	ERA	G	GS	IP	H	HR	BB	SO	BB/9	SO/9	WHIP	AVG
2020	23	Did not play—No minor league season															

27 AARON HERNANDEZ, RHP

BA GRADE
40 **Risk: High**

Born: Dec. 2, 1996. **B-T:** R-R. **HT:** 6-1. **WT:** 170. **Drafted:** Texas A&M-Corpus Christi, 2018 (3rd round). **Signed by:** Rudy Vasquez.

TRACK RECORD: Hernandez took a winding road in college that included being declared academically ineligible for a year. He struggled in his first pro season at high Class A Inland Empire, where he walked 5.7 batters per nine innings and was dropped from the rotation at one point, but he rebounded with a strong showing as a starter in the Arizona Fall League. His only 2020 action came during instructional league.

SCOUTING REPORT: Hernandez's four-seam fastball averages 92-93 mph with average run. He flashed 96 mph in college, but he hasn't approached that as a pro and he's struggled to hold his velocity for more than three or four innings. Both of his breaking balls, a low-80s slider and upper-70s curveball, have a chance to be swing-and-miss pitches with better command. A tumbling mid-80s changeup might be his best pitch. Hernandez has a fairly clean delivery, but he sometimes loads differently with some pitches and has a tendency to yank his slider.

THE FUTURE: Hernandez's stuff may eventually play up in shorter bursts out of the bullpen. He is set to open 2021 in Double-A.

Year	Age	Club (League)	Class	W	L	ERA	G	GS	IP	H	HR	BB	SO	BB/9	SO/9	WHIP	AVG
2019	22	Inland Empire (CAL)	HiA	1	4	4.46	20	15	73	75	6	46	81	5.7	10.0	1.67	.223
Minor League Totals				1	4	4.46	20	15	72	75	6	46	81	5.7	10.0	1.67	.269

28 ROBINSON PINA, RHP

Born: Nov. 26, 1998. **B-T:** R-R. **HT:** 6-4. **WT:** 215. **Signed:** Dominican Republic, 2017. **Signed by:** Francisco Tejeda.

TRACK RECORD: Pina was not considered an elite prospect when he signed for $50,000 in 2017, but he shot up when he scrapped his changeup in favor of a split-fingered fastball after the 2018 season. The big-bodied, broad-shouldered righthander took off with the new pitch and struck out 146 in 108 innings at low Class A Burlington in 2019. His only 2020 action came in the instructional league.

SCOUTING REPORT: Pina's fastball sits 93 mph and touches 95 mph with average run. His 84-mph splitter sometimes looks like a straight changeup with a little more depth. Pina also throws an 84-mph curveball with a short break that resembles a slider, but the breaking ball has a tendency to back up on him at times. Pina needs to keep the curveball on the outer half of the plate, and out of the nitro zone, of righthanded hitters.

THE FUTURE: Pina will continue pitching in the rotation. His bulldog mentality and mastery of his fastball-splitter mix might eventually be a better fit in the bullpen.

Year	Age	Club (League)	Class	W	L	ERA	G	GS	IP	H	HR	BB	SO	BB/9	SO/9	WHIP	AVG
2019	20	Burlington (MWL)	LoA	5	8	3.83	26	21	108	85	5	61	146	5.1	12.2	1.35	.171
Minor League Totals				10	12	3.72	60	33	203	157	6	104	254	4.6	11.2	1.28	.210

29 WERNER BLAKELY, SS/2B

BA GRADE
45 Risk: Extreme

Born: Feb. 21, 2002. **B-T:** L-R. **HT:** 6-3 **WT:** 185. **Drafted:** HS—Detroit, 2020 (4th round). **Signed by:** Drew Dominguez.

TRACK RECORD: Blakely lost his senior high school season to the coronavirus pandemic, but he was a beast as a junior at Detroit's Edison Academy, batting .469 (45 for 96) with five homers, 11 doubles, seven triples, 38 RBIs, 44 runs and 26 stolen bases in 26 attempts. The Angels drafted him in the fifth round and bought him out of an Auburn commitment for $900,000. He got his first pro action in the instructional league in the fall.

SCOUTING REPORT: Blakely has the long, lean and wiry athletic frame of his idol, Derek Jeter. He had some of the best pure shortstop actions in the 2020 draft class, but there is a rawness to his game that raises some concern. He moves fluidly around the field and has a potentially plus arm, but a highlight-reel play will sometimes be followed by a bobble of a routine grounder. Blakely has a tendency to get long in his swing, but his above-average hand-eye coordination makes up for some deficiencies in the batter's box. There is upside for power as Blakely packs more muscle onto his athletic frame, and he has the speed to develop into a base-stealing threat.

THE FUTURE: A prototypical high-risk, high-reward prospect, Blakely will likely go from extended spring training to the Rookie-level Arizona League in 2021.

Year	Age	Club (League)	Class	AVG	G	AB	R	H	2B	3B	HR	RBI	BB	SO	SB	OBP	SLG
2020	18	Did not play—No minor league season															

30 ADAM SEMINARIS, LHP

BA GRADE
40 **Risk: High**

Born: Oct. 19, 1998. **B-T:** R-L. **HT:** 6-0 **WT:** 185. **Drafted:** HS—Long Beach State, 2020 (5th round). **Signed by:** Ben Diggins.

TRACK RECORD: Seminaris was off to one of the hottest starts in the nation with 1.23 ERA, 36 strikeouts and three walks in 22 innings for Long Beach State before the coronavirus pandemic shut down the college season. The Angels drafted him in the fifth round and signed him for an under-slot $140,000. He reported to the alternate training site after signing and finished the year in the instructional league.

SCOUTING REPORT: Seminaris won't wow scouts with stuff, but he is polished and has an advanced feel for pitching. He creates some deception with his high-three-quarters arm slot and crossfire delivery. The Angels expect Seminaris' sinking two-seam fastball, which sits between 88-90 mph, to get up to 92 mph. He gets decent horizontal movement on a 76-mph slurvy curveball and some fading action on an 83-mph changeup. He also has a low 80s-slider. How quickly Seminaris moves through the system will depend on his command and his ability to change speeds and sequence pitches in a way that keeps hitters off-balance.

THE FUTURE: Seminaris has the potential to be a back-of-the-rotation starter. His pitchability could help him move quickly.

Year	Age	Club (League)	Class	W	L	ERA	G	GS	IP	H	HR	BB	SO	BB/9	SO/9	WHIP	AVG
2020	21	Did not play—No minor league season															

MORE PROSPECTS TO KNOW

31. AUSTIN WARREN, RHP

The 25-year-old reliever has a 94-mph fastball and sharp 87-mph slider, which helped him strike out 77 in 57.2 innings at high Class A Inland Empire and Double-A Mobile in 2019.

32. KEVIN MAITAN, 3B

The strong-armed, power-hitting 21-year-old has improved defensively, but he needs to improve his plate discipline and trim down from the 247 pounds he weighed in the fall.

33. STIWARD AQUINO, RHP

At 6-foot-6 and 215 pounds, the 21-year-old from the Dominican Republic touched 96 mph with his fastball in 2019 after missing 2018 due to Tommy John surgery.

34. CONNOR HIGGINS, LHP

SLEEPER

The 6-foot-5, 240 pound lefty from Arizona State has used his mid-to-upper 90s cut fastball to strike out 98 in 78.2 innings in his first two pro seasons. He could move quickly through the system if he can command his considerable stuff.

35. JOSE REYES, OF

The 20-year-old from the Dominican Republic has a smooth lefthanded swing with gap-to-gap power and can play three outfield spots.

36. GREG VELIZ, RHP

A 15th-round pick out of Miami in 2019, the righthander with a sharp slider struck out 36 and walked nine in 29.1 innings in his pro debut.

37. DYLAN KING, RHP

Injured when he was drafted out of Belmont University in 2018, King used a balanced four-pitch mix to strike out 48 batters in 38.1 innings in his pro debut.

38. TRENT DEVEAUX, OF

The 20-year-old from the Bahamas has plus speed, is an above-average defender with a strong arm and is beginning to flash some power, but he has to mature mentally.

39. JACK KRUGER, C

Kruger is a solid hitter with good receiving skills but a subpar throwing arm, making him the best backstop in a system that is extremely thin in catching prospects.

40. IBANDEL ISABEL, 1B

The minor league free agent signee has mesmerizing raw power but also a 35% career strikeout rate.

TOP PROSPECTS OF THE DECADE

Year	Player, Pos.	2020 Org
2011	Mike Trout, OF	Angels
2012	Mike Trout, OF	Angels
2013	Kaleb Cowart, 3B	Yankees
2014	Taylor Lindsey, 2B	Did not play
2015	Andrew Heaney, LHP	Angels
2016	Taylor Ward, C	Angels
2017	Jahmai Jones, OF	Angels
2018	Shohei Ohtani, RHP/DH	Angels
2019	Jo Adell, OF	Angels
2020	Jo Adell, OF	Angels

TOP DRAFT PICKS OF THE DECADE

Year	Player, Pos.	2020 Org
2011	C.J. Cron, 1B	Tigers
2012	R.J. Alvarez, RHP (3rd round)	Red Sox
2013	Hunter Green, LHP (2nd round)	Did not play
2014	Sean Newcomb, LHP	Braves
2015	Taylor Ward, C	Angels
2016	Matt Thaiss, C	Angels
2017	Jo Adell, OF	Angels
2018	Jordyn Adams, OF	Angels
2019	Will Wilson, SS	Giants
2020	Reid Detmers, LHP	Angels

DEPTH CHART

LOS ANGELES ANGELS

TOP 2021 ROOKIES	RANK
Brandon Marsh, OF	2
BREAKOUT PROSPECTS	**RANK**
Erik Rivera, LHP/DH	15
William Holmes, RHP/DH	22
Zach Linginfelter, RHP	26

SOURCE OF TOP 30 TALENT

Homegrown	28	Acquired	2
College	4	Trades	1
Junior college	1	Rule 5 draft	1
High school	12	Independent leagues	0
International	11	Free agents/waivers	0
Nondrafted free agents	0		

LF
D'Shawn Knowles (13)
Alexander Ramirez (17)
Brennon Lund

CF
Brandon Marsh (2)
Jordyn Adams (5)
David Calabrese (25)

RF
Jo Adell (1)
Orlando Martinez (24)
Jose Reyes
Torii Hunter Jr.,
Izzy Wilson

3B
Jose Bonilla (16)
Kevin Maitan
Jose Rojas
Junior Aviles

SS
Jeremiah Jackson (6)
Kyren Paris (10)
Arol Vera (14)
Werner Blakely (29).
Ray-Patrick Didder

2B
Jahmai Jones (8)
Adrian Placencia (19)
Livan Soto (23)

1B
Ibandel Isabel
David MacKinnon

C
Jack Kruger
Michael Cruz
Franklin Torres
Harrison Wenson

LHP

LHSP	LHRP
Reid Detmers (4)	Connor Higgins
Hector Yan (9)	Ryan Smith
Erik Rivera (15)	Jack Dashwood
Packy Naughton (20),	Jose Salvador

RHP

RHSP	RHRP
Chris Rodriguez (3)	Oliver Ortega (11)
Jack Kochanowicz (7)	Jose Alberto Rivera (12)
Denny Brady (18)	Sadrac Franco (21)
William Holmes (22)	Zach Linginfelter (26),
Dylan King	Aaron Hernandez, (27)
	Robinson Pina (28)
	Austin Warren
	Greg Veliz
	Stiward Aquino

Los Angeles Dodgers

BY KYLE GLASER

The Dodgers have long been lauded as baseball's "model" organization. They draft and develop better than anyone, they turn retreads into stars and they win games at a rate on par with the best teams in major league history. The only thing missing was a World Series trophy.

That's no longer a problem.

Bolstered by the offseason acquisition of Mookie Betts, the Dodgers stormed to a 43-17 record during the pandemic-shortened 2020 season and won the World Series in six games against the Rays, their first World Series title since 1988.

The Dodgers' vast financial resources gave them an undeniable advantage, but their World Series championship team embodied everything the organization does right.

Half of the 28 players on their World Series roster were homegrown. That included World Series MVP Corey Seager, the pitchers who won (Victor Gonzalez) and saved (Julio Urias) the decisive Game 6 and every pitcher who started a game for them in the postseason (Urias, Clayton Kershaw, Walker Buehler, Dustin May and Tony Gonsolin). Many other key players—Justin Turner, Chris Taylor, Max Muncy, Enrique Hernandez, Austin Barnes—weren't homegrown but were acquired at minimal cost. For all intents and purposes, Dodgers championship was built from within, with the acquisition of Betts the final piece.

The task now is to keep it going. The Dodgers have a dynamic young core led by Seager, Buehler and Cody Bellinger and no long-term financial commitments outside of Betts. Turner became a free agent after the 2020 season and Kershaw and Kenley Jansen are scheduled to be free agents after 2021. The potential departures of clubhouse leaders and franchise icons can never be discounted, but the Dodgers have the players in the organization to keep their dominance going.

Even with all the prospects they've graduated and others they've traded, the Dodgers still have a deep well of homegrown talent. Catcher Keibert Ruiz made his major league debut in 2020 and righthander Josiah Gray is in position to debut in 2021. Big performances at the alternate training site and in instructional league from 2019 first-round picks Kody Hoese and Michael Busch and 2020 first-rounder Bobby Miller provide encouragement for the following wave, and a talented young group of international signees headlined by catcher Diego Cartaya looms in the lower levels.

The Dodgers don't need all of them to make it. With the homegrown standouts they have in the major leagues, they only need their prospects to supplement the core, rather than be the core.

Seager is set to be a free agent after the 2021 season, but Bellinger, Buehler, Will Smith and the rest of their young standouts are all under team control through at least 2023. There may come a day when the Dodgers have to make some tough financial decisions, but with the resources at their disposal, they will be able to keep whoever they desire.

The Dodgers front office, player development and scouting infrastructures that got them here all remain in place. The players who made them a perennial power are almost all back for 2021.

The stage is set for the Dodgers to continue their dominance, and solidify their place as baseball's "model" franchise. ■

KELLY GAVIN/MLB PHOTOS VIA GETTY IMAGES

The Dodgers relied exclusively on homegrown pitchers like Julio Urias to make playoff starts.

PROJECTED 2024 LINEUP

Position	Player	Age
Catcher	Will Smith	29
First Base	Max Muncy	33
Second Base	Gavin Lux	26
Third Base	Kody Hoese	26
Shortstop	Corey Seager	30
Left Field	Andy Pages	22
Center Field	Cody Bellinger	28
Right Field	Mookie Betts	31
Designated Hitter	Michael Busch	26
No. 1 Starter	Walker Buehler	29
No. 2 Starter	Dustin May	26
No. 3 Starter	Julio Urias	27
No. 4 Starter	Tony Gonsolin	30
No. 5 Starter	Josiah Gray	25
Closer	Brusdar Graterol	25

1 KEIBERT RUIZ, C

Born: July 20, 1998. **B-T:** B-R. **HT:** 6-0. **WT:** 225.
Signed: Venezuela 2014.
Signed by: Francisco Cartaya/Pedro Avila.

TRACK RECORD: Ruiz trained at the academy run by former all-star shortstop Carlos Guillen in Venezuela as an amateur and signed with the Dodgers for $140,000 when he turned 16. He was known for his defense when he signed, but his offense quickly became his calling card. Ruiz hit .300 or better at each of his first four stops and zoomed up the minors to play a full season at Double-A at age 19 in 2018, when he ranked as the Texas League's No. 3 prospect. He hit his first speed bump in 2019 when an organizational catching logjam forced him back to Double-A, and he struggled to stay motivated. He looked re-energized after a promotion to Triple-A, but he suffered a season-ending injury when a foul tip fractured his right pinkie finger. Ruiz rode out the early days of the coronavirus pandemic in 2020 at the Dodgers' complex in Arizona, where he improved his physique and worked extensively with Dodgers hitting coach Brant Brown. Ruiz contracted Covid-19 and arrived late to summer camp, but he recovered to make his major league debut on Aug. 16 and homered in his first at-bat.

SCOUTING REPORT: The switch-hitting Ruiz has a preternatural ability to put the bat on the ball. He has elite hand-eye coordination, can manipulate the barrel to cover all parts of the strike zone and rarely swings and misses. Those traits have long given Ruiz the potential to be a plus hitter, but his quality of contact was often lacking. The Dodgers made adjustments in 2020 to get him more upright in his stance and keep his hands closer to his body, and the result was a more direct path that helped him stay inside the ball and produce consistently harder contact. Ruiz is much stronger batting lefthanded and shows average power from that side. His righthanded swing is visually similar but lacks strength and largely produces weak contact. Ruiz is an aggressive hitter who is still learning to pick out pitches he can drive rather than swinging at the first pitch near the strike zone. Once he improves his pitch selection, he has a chance to hit .280 or higher with double-digit home runs. Ruiz is a potentially above-average receiver who has good timing on his blocks and received positive reviews from the big leaguers who threw to him at the alternate training site. His game-planning and game-calling still have room to grow. Ruiz's arm strength is fringy to average, which was an issue in the majors when opponents went 3-for-3 against him on stolen bases.

THE FUTURE: With Will Smith entrenched at catcher, the best Ruiz can hope for is a timeshare with the Dodgers. His offensive abilities and improving defensive skills would make him the catcher of the future for many other teams. ■

SEAN M. HAFFEY/GETTY IMAGES

BA GRADE
55 **Risk: Medium**

SCOUTING GRADES
Hit: 60. **Power:** 45. **Run:** 30. **Field:** 55. **Arm:** 50.

Projected future grades on 20-80 scouting scale.

BEST TOOLS

Best Hitter for Average	Michael Busch
Best Power Hitter	Edwin Rios
Best Strike-Zone Discipline	Jacob Amaya
Fastest Baserunner	Jeren Kendall
Best Athlete	Jeren Kendall
Best Fastball	Josiah Gray
Best Curveball	Jimmy Lewis
Best Slider	Mitch White
Best Changeup	Ryan Pepiot
Best Control	Landon Knack
Best Defensive Catcher	Diego Cartaya
Best Defensive Infielder	Jacob Amaya
Best Infield Arm	Leonel Valera
Best Defensive Outfielder	Jeren Kendall
Best Outfield Arm	Andy Pages

Year	Age	Club (League)	Class	AVG	G	AB	R	H	2B	3B	HR	RBI	BB	SO	SB	OBP	SLG
2018	19	Tulsa (TL)	AA	.268	101	377	44	101	14	0	12	47	26	33	0	.328	.401
2019	20	Oklahoma City (PCL)	AAA	.316	9	38	6	12	0	0	2	9	2	1	0	.350	.474
	20	Tulsa (TL)	AA	.254	76	276	33	70	9	0	4	25	28	21	0	.329	.330
2020	21	Los Angeles (NL)	MAJ	.250	2	8	1	2	0	0	1	1	0	3	0	.250	.625
Major League Totals				.250	2	8	1	2	0	0	1	1	0	3	0	.250	.625
Minor League Totals				.299	387	1439	188	430	76	6	29	199	104	150	4	.351	.420

2 JOSIAH GRAY, RHP

ADAM GLANZMAN/MLB PHOTOS VIA GETTY IMAGES

BA GRADE
55 **Risk: High**

Born: Dec. 21, 1997. **B-T:** R-R. **HT:** 6-1. **WT:** 190. **Drafted:** Le Moyne (N.Y), 2018 (2nd round supplemental). **Signed by:** Lee Seras (Reds).

TRACK RECORD: Gray began his career at Division II Le Moyne as a shortstop but converted to the mound and became one of the top pitchers in the 2018 draft. The Reds selected him 72nd overall and traded him to the Dodgers in the deal for Yasiel Puig and Matt Kemp. Gray jumped three levels to Double-A in 2019, his first season with the Dodgers, and was named the organization's minor league pitcher of the year. He spent 2020 at the alternate training site.

SCOUTING REPORT: Gray is a power pitcher with a strong, athletic physique. He overpowers hitters with a plus fastball that sits 93-96 mph with running life and touches 97-98 in short bursts. Other pitchers throw harder, but Gray's fastball gets more swings and misses with his life and ability to hold his velocity and command deep into games. Gray focused on his secondary pitches at the alternate site and increased the depth and horizontal movement of his mid-80s slider to cement it as an above-average, swing-and-miss pitch. His changeup added tail and drop but remains a fringe-average pitch that's often too firm in the upper-80s. Gray pounds the strike zone with above-average control. He is highly intelligent and an elite competitor who thrives when the lights are brightest.

THE FUTURE: Gray has the stuff and intangibles of a mid-rotation starter. If his changeup improves, he could be more.

SCOUTING GRADES: **Fastball:** 60 **Slider:** 55 **Changeup:** 45 **Control:** 55

Year	Age	Club (League)	Class	W	L	ERA	G	GS	SV	IP	H	HR	BB	SO	K/9	WHIP	AVG
2019	21	Great Lakes (MWL)	LoA	1	0	1.93	5	5	0	23	13	0	7	26	10.0	0.86	.165
	21	R. Cucamonga (CAL)	HiA	7	0	2.14	12	12	0	67	52	3	13	80	10.7	0.97	.209
	21	Tulsa (TL)	AA	3	2	2.75	9	8	0	39	33	0	11	41	9.4	1.12	.228
Minor League Totals				13	4	2.37	38	37	0	182	127	4	48	206	10.2	0.96	.192

3 MICHAEL BUSCH, 2B

BA GRADE
55 **Risk: High**

Born: Nov. 9, 1997. **B-T:** L-R. **HT:** 6-0. **WT:** 207. **Drafted:** North Carolina, 2019 (1st round). **Signed by:** Jonah Rosenthal.

TRACK RECORD: Busch was regarded as one of college baseball's top hitters at North Carolina and was drafted 31st overall by the Dodgers in 2019. He was limited to 10 games in his pro debut after he was hit by a pitch that broke his right hand, but he showed what he could do in 2020. Busch spent the summer at the alternate training site and drew raves as the best hitter in instructional league in Arizona.

SCOUTING REPORT: Busch is all about his bat. He is an exceptionally patient hitter who doesn't chase, fights off close pitches and waits for something he can drive. When he gets it, he unloads on balls with a compact, lefthanded swing with plus bat speed and extension. Busch's swing and approach make him a plus hitter, and he's begun to show plus power with the ability to drive the ball over the fence to both gaps. Busch played first base and left field in college, but the Dodgers are trying to make him a second baseman. He's gotten leaner and more athletic to improve his range, and he dropped his arm slot to give him more zip on his throws, but he's still a likely below-average defender.

THE FUTURE: Busch is following the Max Muncy path as a masher who is playable at second base in short stints. He is poised to move quickly in 2021.

SCOUTING GRADES: **Hitting:** 60 **Power:** 60 **Running:** 45 **Fielding:** 40 **Arm:** 45

Year	Age	Club (League)	Class	AVG	G	AB	R	H	2B	3B	HR	RBI	BB	SO	SB	OBP	SLG
2019	21	Great Lakes (MWL)	LoA	.182	5	11	4	2	0	0	0	2	6	3	0	.474	.182
	21	Dodgers Lasorda (AZL)	R	.077	5	13	1	1	0	0	0	0	1	2	0	.250	.077
Minor League Totals				.125	10	24	5	3	0	0	0	2	7	5	0	.371	.125

4 KODY HOESE, 3B

BA GRADE
55 Risk: High

Born: July 13, 1997. **B-T:** R-R. **HT:** 6-4. **WT:** 200. **Drafted:** Tulane, 2019 (1st round). **Signed by:** Benny Latino.

TRACK RECORD: Hoese went from a 35th-round pick in 2018 to a first-round pick in 2019 after he finished fourth in the nation with 23 home runs at Tulane. He posted an .863 OPS in his pro debut and was the Dodgers' top hitter at the alternate training site in 2020, but he was more pedestrian in instructional league as he battled fatigue and drew mixed reviews from opposing evaluators.

SCOUTING REPORT: Hoese is a well-rounded hitter with a balanced approach and compact swing. He is an adept fastball hitter who frequently finds the barrel and drives the ball to all fields, though he's better against high fastballs than low ones because he gets out of his legs at times. He covers all pitch types and locations when he stays rooted in his lower half. His long levers, wiry strength and knack for the barrel give him 20-plus home run potential. Hoese has calm, reliable hands at third base and reads hops well, but he's not a smooth mover and his arm strength fluctuates widely from below-average to above-average. He worked with Dodgers pitching coordinator Rob Hill at the alternate site to improve his velocity and be more consistent with his arm slot.

THE FUTURE: Hoese looks like a future standout at his best but needs to be more consistent with his swing and throwing stroke. He'll see the upper minors in 2021.

SCOUTING GRADES: Hitting: 55 Power: 50 Running: 40 Fielding: 55 Arm: 45

Year	Age	Club (League)	Class	AVG	G	AB	R	H	2B	3B	HR	RBI	BB	SO	SB	OBP	SLG
2019	21	Great Lakes (MWL)	LoA	.264	22	91	15	24	3	1	2	16	8	14	0	.330	.385
	21	Dodgers Mota (AZL)	R	.357	19	56	14	20	5	1	3	13	10	11	1	.456	.643
Minor League Totals				.299	41	147	29	44	8	2	5	29	18	25	1	.380	.483

5 BOBBY MILLER, RHP

MLB PHOTOS VIA GETTY IMAGES

BA GRADE
55 Risk: High

Born: April 5, 1999. **B-T:** R-R. **HT:** 6-5. **WT:** 220. **Drafted:** Louisville, 2020 (1st round). **Signed by:** Marty Lamb.

TRACK RECORD: Miller bounced between the bullpen and rotation his first two seasons at Louisville and became a full-time starter as a junior. His stuff and control both ticked up through four starts before the coronavirus pandemic shut down the season, and the Dodgers drafted him 29th overall and signed him for $2,197,500. Miller continued improving his stuff and control at the alternate training site and was a revelation in instructional league.

SCOUTING REPORT: Miller is an intimidating presence at 6-foot-5, 220 pounds and has the stuff to match. He has both a four-seam and two-seam fastball that average 95 mph and touch 98 moving in opposite directions, and his mid-80s slider is another plus pitch with three-quarters tilt and late, darting action. Miller got more comfortable with his diving, mid-80s changeup throughout the summer and began throwing it with conviction to hitters on both sides of the plate. His downer curveball in the upper 70s is another pitch he can land for strikes. Miller's stuff is sizzling, but he's still learning how to sequence and get his pitches to play off each other. He throws plenty of strikes but will leave pitches over the plate.

THE FUTURE: Miller has the look and stuff of a power starter. He'll make his pro debut in 2021.

SCOUTING GRADES: Fastball: 70 Slider: 60 Curveball: 50 Changeup: 55 Control: 50

Year	Age	Club (League)	Class	W	L	ERA	G	GS	IP	H	HR	BB	SO	BB/9	SO/9	WHIP	AVG
2020	21	Did not play—No minor league season															

6 DIEGO CARTAYA, C

Born: Sept. 7, 2001. **B-T:** R-R. **HT:** 6-2. **WT:** 199. **Signed:** Venezuela, 2018. **Signed by:** Luis Marquez/Roman Barinas/Cliff Nuiter/Jean Castro.

BA GRADE
60 Risk: Extreme

BILL MITCHELL

TRACK RECORD: Cartaya was Venezuela's top player in the 2018 international signing class and signed with the Dodgers for $2.5 million on July 2. He quickly jumped from the Dominican Summer League to the Rookie-level Arizona League in his pro debut and starred in the AZL as a 17-year-old. One of the youngest players added to a 60-man player pool in 2020, he spent the summer at the alternate training site.

SCOUTING REPORT: Cartaya is highly advanced for his age on both sides of the ball. He shows soft hands in receiving, sets a good target, expertly frames low pitches and has impressive flexibility for his size. Cartaya has plus raw arm strength and has improved at syncing his footwork to get his best throws off more consistently. He still needs refinement but has a chance to be a plus defender with a plus arm. Cartaya has an advanced approach at the plate and projects to hit for average with his short, quick swing and sound bat path. His natural strength and long levers give him power potential, but his swing is primarily geared to shoot the ball the other way.

THE FUTURE: Cartaya has the potential to be a standout, but he's still a teenager who is many years away. He'll make his full-season debut in 2021.

SCOUTING GRADES: **Hitting:** 55 **Power:** 50 **Running:** 30 **Fielding:** 60 **Arm:** 60

Year	Age	Club (League)	Class	AVG	G	AB	R	H	2B	3B	HR	RBI	BB	SO	SB	OBP	SLG
2019	17	Dodgers Bautista (DSL)	R	.240	13	50	11	12	2	2	1	9	5	11	0	.316	.420
	17	Dodgers Mota (AZL)	R	.296	36	135	25	40	10	0	3	13	11	31	1	.353	.437
Minor League Totals				.281	49	185	36	52	12	2	4	22	16	42	1	.343	.432

7 EDWIN RIOS, 3B

Born: April 21, 1994. **B-T:** L-R. **HT:** 6-3. **WT:** 220. **Drafted:** Florida International, 2015 (6th round). **Signed by:** Adrian Casanova.

ADAM GLANZMAN/MLB PHOTOS VIA GETTY IMAGES

TRACK RECORD: Rios finished second in the nation in home runs his junior year at Florida International and was drafted in the sixth round by the Dodgers. He continued to mash throughout the minors, made his major league debut in 2019 and established himself as a key part of the Dodgers in 2020. He hit eight home runs in just 76 at-bats, added two more homers in the National League Championship Series, and finished with a .946 OPS.

SCOUTING REPORT: Rios is a big, physical lefthanded hitter capable of destroying baseballs. His fast hands, long levers and excellent natural timing generate plus-plus power to center and right field. Rios' swing gets long and he is prone to striking out, but he's competitive enough against both righthanded and lefthanded pitchers to project to hit .230 to .240 with slugging percentages in the .500s. Rios used his elite work ethic to transform from a well below-average third baseman into a playable one. He remains better defensively at first base but can bounce between the two infield corners.

THE FUTURE: Rios' defensive improvements and the expected permanent addition of the designated hitter in the NL give him a path to everyday playing time. He's ready to take on a larger role in 2021.

SCOUTING GRADES: **Hitting:** 45 **Power:** 70 **Running:** 40 **Fielding:** 45 **Arm:** 55

Year	Age	Club (League)	Class	AVG	G	AB	R	H	2B	3B	HR	RBI	BB	SO	SB	OBP	SLG
2017	23	Oklahoma City (PCL)	AAA	.296	51	169	23	50	13	0	9	29	18	42	0	.368	.533
	23	Tulsa (TL)	AA	.317	77	306	47	97	21	0	15	62	17	69	1	.358	.533
2018	24	Oklahoma City (PCL)	AAA	.304	88	309	45	94	25	0	10	55	23	110	0	.355	.482
2019	25	Los Angeles (NL)	MAJ	.277	28	47	10	13	2	1	4	8	9	21	0	.393	.617
	25	Oklahoma City (PCL)	AAA	.270	104	393	72	106	23	2	31	91	37	153	2	.340	.575
2020	26	Los Angeles (NL)	MAJ	.250	32	76	13	19	6	0	8	17	4	18	0	.301	.645
Major League Totals				.260	60	123	23	32	8	1	12	25	13	39	0	.338	.634
Minor League Totals				.295	450	1670	264	492	115	4	95	326	126	514	6	.348	.539

8 RYAN PEPIOT, RHP

Born: Aug. 21, 1997. **B-T:** R-R. **HT:** 6-3. **WT:** 215. **Drafted:** Butler, 2019 (3rd round). **Signed by:** Stephen Head.

MIKE JANES/FOUR SEAM IMAGES

BA GRADE
55 Risk: High

TRACK RECORD: Pepiot led the Big East Conference in strikeouts in 2019 but also had the second-most hit batters and third-most walks. The Dodgers bet on his stuff and made him the highest-drafted player in Butler history when they selected him in the third round, No. 102 overall. Pepiot opened eyes in 2020 when he struck out Cody Bellinger, Matt Beaty and Gavin Lux in a dominant two-inning summer camp appearance at Dodger Stadium. He carried that success over to the alternate site and was the Dodgers' best pitcher in camp.

SCOUTING REPORT: Pepiot is a big-bodied righthander with premium stuff. His fastball has ticked up to sit 93-95 mph with riding life, and his changeup is a devastating, plus-plus pitch in the mid 80s with hard movement down and in to righthanded batters. Pepiot focused on the consistency of his slider and began getting reliable tilt down and away to make it an average pitch, and his mid-70s curveball is another usable offering. Pepiot cleaned up his arm action and began locating his fastball to his glove side, giving him average control for the first time. He occasionally sprays his fastball up and in but generally self-corrects.

THE FUTURE: Pepiot has to show he can maintain his control gains over a full season. If he can, he has a chance to be a righthanded power starter.

SCOUTING GRADES: **Fastball:** 60 **Slider:** 50 **Curveball:** 45 **Changeup:** 70 **Control:** 45

Year	Age	Club (League)	Class	W	L	ERA	G	GS	IP	H	HR	BB	SO	BB/9	SO/9	WHIP	AVG
2019	21	Great Lakes (MWL)	LoA	0	0	2.45	9	9	18	13	0	9	21	4.4	10.3	1.20	.171
	21	Dodgers Mota (AZL)	R	0	0	0.00	4	1	5	2	0	4	10	7.2	18.0	1.20	.091
Minor League Totals				0	0	1.93	13	10	23	15	0	13	31	5.0	12.0	1.20	.181

9 MIGUEL VARGAS, 3B

Born: Nov. 17, 1999. **B-T:** R-R. **HT:** 6-3. **WT:** 205. **Signed:** Cuba, 2017. **Signed by:** Roman Barinas/Mike Tosar.

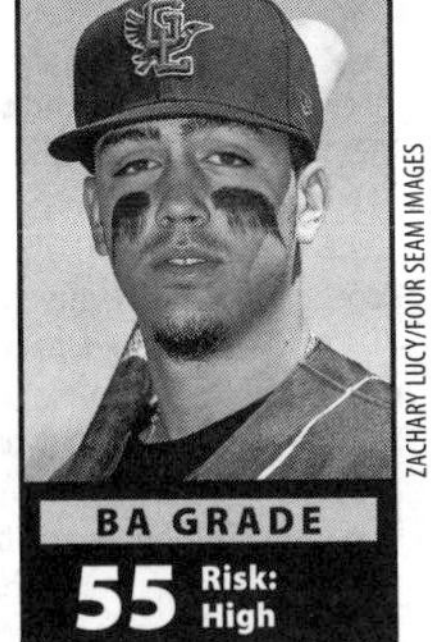

ZACHARY LUCY/FOUR SEAM IMAGES

BA GRADE
55 Risk: High

TRACK RECORD: Vargas is the son of international baseball legend Lazaro Vargas, who played 22 seasons in Cuba and led the country to Olympic gold medals in 1992 and '96. He left the island with his father in 2015 and signed with the Dodgers for $300,000 in 2017. Vargas quickly emerged as one of the top hitters in the Dodgers' system, batting .330 in his pro debut despite not playing for two years. He advanced to high Class A as a 19-year-old in 2019 and stood out in instructional league in 2020.

SCOUTING REPORT: Vargas is a uniquely advanced hitter for his age. He has quick hands, elite hand-eye coordination and drives the ball the other way with authority. Vargas wears out the right-center field gap and racks up doubles, but he's still learning to pull the ball in the air and has yet to show he can turn on velocity inside. The Dodgers see the physical ability to make the adjustment and believe it's a matter of intent. Vargas is a slow mover without a lot of twitch in the field. He's a below-average third baseman and played some second base during instructs, but he is likely a first baseman long term. He has average arm strength.

THE FUTURE: Vargas' hitting ability is that of an everyday player. He'll try to find his best position in 2021.

SCOUTING GRADES: **Hitting:** 60 **Power:** 50 **Running:** 45 **Fielding:** 40 **Arm:** 50

Year	Age	Club (League)	Class	AVG	G	AB	R	H	2B	3B	HR	RBI	BB	SO	SB	OBP	SLG
2017	17	Did not play															
2018	18	Dodgers (AZL)	R	.419	8	31	6	13	3	1	0	2	5	3	1	.514	.581
	18	Ogden (PIO)	R	.394	22	94	25	37	11	1	2	22	8	13	6	.447	.596
	18	Great Lakes (MWL)	LoA	.213	23	75	4	16	1	1	0	6	10	20	0	.307	.253
2019	19	Great Lakes (MWL)	LoA	.325	70	280	53	91	20	2	5	45	35	43	9	.399	.464
	19	R. Cucamonga (CAL)	HiA	.284	54	211	23	60	18	1	2	32	20	40	4	.353	.408
Minor League Totals				.314	177	691	111	217	53	6	9	107	78	119	20	.387	.447

10 ANDY PAGES, OF

Born: Dec. 8, 2000. **B-T:** R-R. **HT:** 6-1. **WT:** 180. **Signed:** Cuba, 2018. **Signed by:** Luis Marquez/Roman Barinas/Manelik Pimentel

STEPHEN SMITH/FOUR SEAM IMAGES

BA GRADE

55 Risk: Very High

TRACK RECORD: Pages was one of the top hitters in Cuba's junior leagues growing up and signed with the Dodgers for $300,000 when he was 17. He struggled in his first pro season but blossomed in year two when he finished second in the Rookie-level Pioneer League in home runs (19) and total bases (153). He stood out for his tools in instructional league in 2020.

SCOUTING REPORT: Pages combines impressive physical ability with a high-level understanding of hitting. He recognizes pitches, has excellent hand-eye coordination and possesses plus power that produces some of the top exit velocities in the Dodgers' system. He drives the ball hard to center and right field and makes loud contact that stays with observers for weeks after. Pages can be overly aggressive and will swing and miss against higher-quality pitches, but he makes adjustments and should improve with experience. He is an intuitive baserunner whose excellent reads and jumps make up for fringe-average speed. Pages has learned to tone down his flair in right field and become a reliable, above-average defender with a plus-plus, albeit sometimes inaccurate, arm.

THE FUTURE: Pages has the makings of an everyday right fielder if he can make enough contact. He is set to make his full-season debut in 2021.

SCOUTING GRADES: **Hitting:** 45 **Power:** 60 **Running:** 45 **Fielding:** 55 **Arm:** 70

Year	Age	Club (League)	Class	AVG	G	AB	R	H	2B	3B	HR	RBI	BB	SO	SB	OBP	SLG
2018	17	Dodgers Shoemaker (DSL)	R	.236	42	140	34	33	8	0	9	33	23	31	9	.393	.486
	17	Dodgers Mota (AZL)	R	.192	10	26	5	5	1	0	1	3	6	4	1	.382	.346
2019	18	Ogden (PIO)	R	.298	63	235	57	70	22	2	19	55	26	79	7	.398	.651
Minor League Totals				.269	115	401	96	108	31	2	29	91	55	114	17	.395	.574

11 ZACH MCKINSTRY, 2B/SS

Born: April 29, 1995. **B-T:** L-R. **HT:** 6-0. **WT:** 180. **Drafted:** Central Michigan, 2016 (33rd round). **Signed by:** Trey Magnuson.

TRACK RECORD: McKinstry hit .325 as a draft-eligible sophomore at Central Michigan and was expected to return to school, but the Dodgers snagged him in the 33rd round and signed him for $100,000. He continued to hit for average in the minors and, like so many other Dodgers prospects, made swing changes to add power and hit 19 home runs between Double-A and Triple-A in 2019. McKinstry spent most of 2020 at the alternate training site and received his first major league callup on Sept. 16, becoming the ninth player from the Dodgers 2016 draft class to reach the majors.

SCOUTING REPORT: McKinstry is a player who does everything well. He's a natural hitter who works counts, uses the whole field and hangs in well against same-side pitching. He's primarily a contact hitter, but his swing changes and added strength have enabled him to drive the ball to his pull-side for home runs. McKinstry is an above-average runner and versatile defender. His best position is second base and he's also average at shortstop and third base with the ability to play left and center field, as well. He has a plus, accurate arm with a quick release.

THE FUTURE: McKinstry is ticketed to replace Kiké Hernandez as the Dodgers do-everything utilityman in 2021. His versatility and contact skills should make him a valuable contributor.

Year	Age	Club (League)	Class	AVG	G	AB	R	H	2B	3B	HR	RBI	BB	SO	SB	OBP	SLG
2020	25	Los Angeles (NL)	MAJ	.286	4	7	1	2	1	0	0	0	0	3	0	.286	.429
Major League Totals				.286	4	7	1	2	1	0	0	0	0	3	0	.286	.429
Minor League Totals				.270	356	1226	182	331	61	14	30	149	147	288	23	.357	.416

12 JACOB AMAYA, SS

BA GRADE

50 Risk: High

Born: Sept. 3, 1998. **B-T:** R-R. **HT:** 6-0. **WT:** 180. **Drafted:** HS—West Covina, Calif., 2017 (11th round). **Signed by:** Bobby Darwin.

TRACK RECORD: Amaya grew up a Dodgers fan in suburban Los Angeles and his grandfather, Frank, was a Dodgers minor leaguer from 1955-58. The Dodgers drafted him in the 11th round in 2017 and signed him for an above-slot $247,500 to forgo a Cal State Fullerton commitment. Amaya immediately established himself as the best defensive infielder in the Dodgers system and progressively grew offensively, culminating in a .381 on-base percentage for low Class A Great Lakes in 2019. The Dodgers brought him to their alternate training site for the final month of the 2020 season.

SCOUTING REPORT: Amaya is a gifted defensive shortstop for his age. He positions himself in the right places with uncanny instincts, has impressive range in every direction, maintains proper footwork and has an above-average, accurate arm. He's improved his consistency with maturity and projects to be at least a plus defender. Amaya has a solid offensive foundation as a patient hitter who recognizes pitches and rarely chases, but his swing is still developing. He worked on his lower half and balance throughout the shutdown and saw an uptick in his quality of contact at the alternate site.
THE FUTURE: Amaya's offensive development will determine if he reaches his everyday ceiling. His defense will buy him time.

Year	Age	Club (League)	Class	AVG	G	AB	R	H	2B	3B	HR	RBI	BB	SO	SB	OBP	SLG
2019	20	Great Lakes (MWL)	LoA	.262	103	386	68	101	25	4	6	58	74	83	4	.381	.394
	20	R. Cucamonga (CAL)	HiA	.250	21	80	14	20	3	2	1	13	7	15	1	.307	.375
Minor League Totals				.273	217	809	153	221	42	10	13	114	147	170	23	.386	.398

13 LUIS RODRIGUEZ, OF

BA GRADE
55 Risk: Extreme

Born: Sept. 16, 2002. **B-T:** R-R. **HT:** 6-2. **WT:** 175. **Signed:** Venezuela, 2019.
Signed by: Roman Barinas/Laiky Uribe/Leon Canelon.

TRACK RECORD: Rodriguez ranked as Venezuela's top prospect in the 2019 international class and signed with the Dodgers for $2,667,500 on July 2. He was set to make his professional debut in 2020, but instead spent the year working out in the Dominican Republic after the coronavirus pandemic canceled the minor league season. He briefly participated in Dominican instructional league in the fall.
SCOUTING REPORT: Rodriguez was a lanky, contact-oriented center fielder when he signed, but his game has changed as he's started to fill out. He's added weight and strength and started focusing on hitting balls as far as he can with his newfound strength. While his power potential has ticked up to plus, he's lost his all-fields approach and become a pull-only hitter who is too aggressive at the plate. Rodriguez plays an adequate center field, but his average speed and growing body portend a possible move to a corner. He has the above-average strength for right field.
THE FUTURE: The Dodgers hope Rodriguez can rediscover his old swing and approach with a return to normalcy in 2021. He'll be 18 all of next season and still has a lot of development left.

Year	Age	Club (League)	Class	AVG	G	AB	R	H	2B	3B	HR	RBI	BB	SO	SB	OBP	SLG
2019	16	Did not play—signed 2020 contract															

14 DJ PETERS, OF

BA GRADE
45 Risk: Medium

Born: Dec. 12, 1995. **B-T:** R-R. **HT:** 6-6. **WT:** 225. **Drafted:** Western Nevada JC, 2016 (4th round). **Signed by:** Tom Kunis.

TRACK RECORD: Peters set Western Nevada JC's single-season home run record in 2016 and was drafted in the fourth round by the Dodgers. He continued to mash in pro ball, winning MVP of the high Class A California League in 2017 and leading the Double-A Texas League in home runs in 2018. Peters' production fell as he advanced to Triple-A in 2019, but the Dodgers still added him to their 40-man roster and carried him on their 2020 postseason taxi squad.
SCOUTING REPORT: Muscular and massive at 6-foot-6, 225 pounds, Peters generates jaw-dropping power with his natural strength and the leverage produced by his long arms. He demolishes anything out over the plate and separates balls and strikes with a sharp eye. Peters has good strike-zone discipline, but his long arms and uphill swing path create holes in his swing. He has a career 31% strikeout rate because he swings and misses so often in the strike zone, especially against inside fastballs. Peters is an impressive athlete for his size with average speed and long strides that allow him to play all three outfield positions. He has plus arm strength but iffy accuracy.
THE FUTURE: Peters' power and outfield versatility give him a chance to carve out a major league role. His debut should come in 2021.

Year	Age	Club (League)	Class	AVG	G	AB	R	H	2B	3B	HR	RBI	BB	SO	SB	OBP	SLG
2019	23	Oklahoma City (PCL)	AAA	.260	57	208	40	54	10	1	12	39	33	75	1	.388	.490
	23	Tulsa (TL)	AA	.241	68	249	31	60	10	1	11	42	28	93	1	.331	.422
Minor League Totals				.269	455	1714	304	461	96	13	92	271	205	615	11	.363	.501

15 VICTOR GONZALEZ, LHP

BA GRADE **40** Risk: Low

Born: Nov. 16, 1995. **B-T:** L-L. **HT:** 6-0. **WT:** 180. **Signed:** Mexico, 2012. **Signed by:** Mike Brito.

TRACK RECORD: A group of Dodgers scouts went to Mexico City in 2012 to evaluate Yasiel Puig and also scouted the local talent. They signed six players off that trip, including Puig, Julio Urias and Gonzalez. Gonzalez failed to advance past low Class A his first four seasons and missed most of 2017 and 2018 after having Tommy John surgery. He returned a new pitcher after surgery and vaulted to the majors in 2020, where he posted a 1.33 ERA in 15 relief appearances and won the decisive Game 6 of the World Series.

SCOUTING REPORT: Gonzalez came up as a starter and has more pitchability and control than a typical reliever. His fastball averages 95 mph and touches 98 mph with late sink and run to his armside. He turned his mid-80s slider from a fringe-average pitch to a dominant, plus-plus offering with late drop that draws lots of chase swings. He also has an average changeup. Gonzalez's fastball and slider dominate both lefthanded and righthanded hitters, and he locates in and out of the zone with plus control.

THE FUTURE: Gonzalez emerged as one of the Dodgers top relievers in 2020. He'll solidify that in 2021.

Year	Age	Club (League)	Class	W	L	ERA	G	GS	IP	H	HR	BB	SO	BB/9	SO/9	WHIP	AVG
2020	24	Los Angeles (NL)	MAJ	3	0	1.33	15	1	20	13	0	2	23	0.9	10.2	0.74	.176
Major League Totals				3	0	1.33	15	1	20	13	0	2	23	0.9	10.2	0.74	.176
Minor League Totals				17	27	4.34	112	76	377	407	31	138	364	3.3	8.7	1.45	.275

16 MITCH WHITE, RHP

BA GRADE **45** Risk: Medium

Born: Dec. 28, 1994. **B-T:** R-R. **HT:** 6-3. **WT:** 210. **Drafted:** Santa Clara, 2016 (2nd round). **Signed by:** Tom Kunis.

TRACK RECORD: White had Tommy John surgery in high school and battled an assortment of injuries after the Dodgers drafted him in the second round in 2016, including a broken toe, general soreness and recurring blisters. White finally stayed healthy in 2020 and pitched consistently well at the alternate training site, resulting in his first major league callup on Aug. 28.

SCOUTING REPORT: White has plenty of stuff but has long been hampered by injuries and inconsistency. His fastball sits 93-94 mph with natural cut. Both his vertical, low-80s curveball and horizontal mid-80s slider are plus pitches at their best. White has long struggled with fastball command and secondary execution, in part due to mechanical issues caused by his injuries. He was consistent at the alternate site and in two scoreless relief appearances in the majors, providing optimism that he's turned a corner.

THE FUTURE: It all comes down to health and consistency for White. The Dodgers saw enough progress to believe he still has a chance to start, but his injury history and pitch mix point to a relief future.

Year	Age	Club (League)	Class	W	L	ERA	G	GS	IP	H	HR	BB	SO	BB/9	SO/9	WHIP	AVG
2020	25	Los Angeles (NL)	MAJ	1	0	0.00	2	0	3	1	0	1	2	3.0	6.0	0.67	.100
Major League Totals				1	0	0.00	2	0	3	1	0	1	2	3.0	6.0	0.67	.100
Minor League Totals				14	15	3.97	75	67	294	257	30	102	311	3.1	9.5	1.22	.231

17 ALEX DE JESUS, SS

BREAKOUT
BA GRADE **55** Risk: Extreme

Born: March 22, 2002. **B-T:** R-R. **HT:** 6-2. **WT:** 170. **Signed:** Dominican Republic, 2018. **Signed by:** Luis Marquez/Laiky Uribe/Manelik Pimentel.

TRACK RECORD: De Jesus signed with the Dodgers for $500,000 during the 2018 international signing period. He needed only 13 games in the Dominican Summer League to earn a promotion to the Rookie-level Arizona League, where he impressed as a 17-year-old. De Jesus spent the 2020 shutdown at home and participated in Dominican instructional league in the fall.

SCOUTING REPORT: De Jesus is rapidly growing into more power to go with an impressive feel for hitting. He has a simple swing that produces natural loft and drives balls hard in the air from gap-to-gap. He swings and misses a bit much, but his youth, bat speed and projectable power give him a chance to be an above-average hitter with above-average power. De Jesus has a quick first step, reliable hands and easy actions at shortstop, but he's a fringe-average runner with below-average range and projects to move to third base. He should be an average third baseman with a plus arm. De Jesus is already bilingual and shows leadership attributes. He does get overly frustrated by failure at times.

THE FUTURE: De Jesus has the foundations of a power-hitting third baseman. He'll see Class A in 2021.

Year	Age	Club (League)	Class	AVG	G	AB	R	H	2B	3B	HR	RBI	BB	SO	SB	OBP	SLG
2019	17	Dodgers Shoemaker (DSL)	R	.296	13	54	8	16	5	0	1	9	8	14	0	.381	.444
	17	Dodgers Mota (AZL)	R	.276	44	163	13	45	8	1	2	25	12	58	5	.326	.374
Minor League Totals				.281	57	217	21	61	13	1	3	34	20	72	5	.340	.392

18 DENNIS SANTANA, RHP

Born: April 12, 1996. **B-T:** R-R. **HT:** 6-2. **WT:** 190. **Signed:** Dominican Republic, 2012. **Signed by:** Bob Engle/Patrick Guerrero/Elvio Jimenez.

TRACK RECORD: Santana signed with the Dodgers as a shortstop in 2012 but converted to pitching one year later. He vaulted up the minors as a starter and reached the majors as a reliever. After brief stints with the Dodgers in 2018 and 2019, Santana made 15 relief appearances in 2020. He struck out more than a batter per inning and his 5.29 ERA was inflated by one bad outing.

SCOUTING REPORT: Santana has loud stuff with a ton of natural movement. His fastball sits 93-94 mph and touches 97 mph with huge sink and run. The pitch moves so much Santana struggles to command it, however, especially to his glove-side. Santana throws his mid-80s slider with big, late drop more often than his fastball. It's a swing and miss offering, but he's also prone to leaving it over the heart of the plate. Santana throws his above-average, 86-89 mph changeup with fade to lefties and gets a lot of chase swings.

THE FUTURE: Santana will be part of the Dodgers bullpen in 2021. He'll have to harness his command to be trusted in high leverage spots.

Year	Age	Club (League)	Class	W	L	ERA	G	GS	IP	H	HR	BB	SO	BB/9	SO/9	WHIP	AVG
2020	24	Los Angeles (NL)	MAJ	1	2	5.29	12	0	17	15	4	7	18	3.7	9.5	1.29	.234
Major League Totals				2	2	6.66	16	0	25	27	5	12	28	4.2	9.8	1.52	.270
Minor League Totals				23	34	4.28	119	74	454	417	33	223	513	4.4	10.2	1.41	.241

19 OMAR ESTEVEZ, 2B

BA GRADE **45** Risk: Medium

Born: Feb. 25, 1998. **B-T:** R-R. **HT:** 5-10. **WT:** 185. **Signed:** Cuba, 2015. **Signed by:** Roman Barinas/Mike Tosar.

TRACK RECORD: The Dodgers invested heavily in Cuban talent during the 2015-16 international period, including signing Estevez for $6 million. Estevez struggled initially, but broke out in 2018 and hit .291/.352/.431 at Double-A in 2019. The Dodgers brought him to their alternate training site in 2020.

SCOUTING REPORT: Estevez reinvented himself as a hitter by doing weighted ball drills. Previously an all-pull hitter, he now makes frequent contact up the middle and drives the ball gap-to-gap for doubles. He was one of the Dodgers' most consistent hitters at the alternate site and shows the contact skills and barrel awareness to project to run into 10-15 home runs. Estevez is more limited on the defensive side of the ball. He is a below-average runner without much range and is stretched playing shortstop. He has decent footwork and enough lateral agility to survive at second base, where his fringe-average arm will play.

THE FUTURE: Estevez will rise as far as his bat takes him. He'll see Triple-A in 2021.

Year	Age	Club (League)	Class	AVG	G	AB	R	H	2B	3B	HR	RBI	BB	SO	SB	OBP	SLG
2019	21	Dodgers Mota (AZL)	R	.300	7	20	7	6	2	0	0	3	2	8	0	.364	.400
	21	Tulsa (TL)	AA	.291	83	299	34	87	24	0	6	36	31	70	0	.352	.431
Minor League Totals				.268	460	1762	230	473	125	7	34	231	137	434	8	.322	.405

20 CLAYTON BEETER, RHP

BA GRADE **50** Risk: High

Born: Oct. 9, 1998. **B-T:** R-R. **HT:** 6-1. **WT:** 205. **Drafted:** Texas Tech, 2020 (2nd round supplemental). **Signed by:** Clint Bowers.

TRACK RECORD: Beeter had Tommy John surgery in high school and redshirted his freshman year at Texas Tech. He took over as the Red Raiders closer when he returned in 2019 and moved into the rotation as their No. 1 starter during the abbreviated 2020 season. The Dodgers drafted Beeter in the supplemental second round, No. 66 overall, and signed him for $1,196,500. He spent the summer at the alternate training site.

SCOUTING REPORT: Beeter boasts two power offerings with a mid-90s fastball that reaches 97 mph and a top-to-bottom, hammer curveball that draws consensus plus grades. His fastball features elite rise and his curveball has sharp downward movement, giving him the north-south profile teams covet. Beeter's changeup and control lag well behind. His changeup is a below-average pitch and his control was firmly below-average at the alternate site. He struggles to repeat his delivery and fails to consistently execute or command his pitches. Even at his best, Beeter flashes only average control.

THE FUTURE: Beeter faced questions in college whether he projected as starter or reliever, and the Dodgers acknowledge he's likely a reliever after what they saw at the alternate site. He'll start for now as he begins his pro career.

Year	Age	Club (League)	Class	W	L	ERA	G	GS	IP	H	HR	BB	SO	BB/9	SO/9	WHIP	AVG
2020	21	Did not play—No minor league season															

21 DEVIN MANN, 2B/3B

BA GRADE 45 Risk: High

Born: Feb. 11, 1997. **B-T:** R-R. **HT:** 6-3. **WT:** 180. **Drafted:** Louisville, 2018 (5th round). **Signed by:** Marty Lamb.

TRACK RECORD: Mann hit .288/.408/.458 over three seasons at Louisville and the Dodgers saw untapped power potential, leading them to draft him in the fifth round. Mann got stronger, made a few swing adjustments and broke out as one of the top power hitters in the high Class A California League in his first full season. He spent 2020 at the alternate training site and continued making power gains.

SCOUTING REPORT: Mann looks like a major leaguer with long levers, wiry strength and an easy swing that produces loud contact. His short, simple swing packs a punch and produces hard contact in the air to left and center field. Mann is a patient hitter who works counts, spoils pitches and isn't fazed by falling behind. He will swing and miss, particularly on the outer half, but keeps his strikeouts reasonable. Finding a position will be Mann's biggest challenge. He is a stiff, slow defender at second base and only marginally better at third. His funky arm action may limit him to first base or left field.

THE FUTURE: Mann's bat will play if he can find a defensive home. He should see Double-A in 2021.

Year	Age	Club (League)	Class	AVG	G	AB	R	H	2B	3B	HR	RBI	BB	SO	SB	OBP	SLG
2019	22	Dodgers Mota (AZL)	R	.000	1	1	0	0	0	0	0	0	1	0	0	.500	.000
	22	R. Cucamonga (CAL)	HiA	.278	98	367	63	102	19	2	19	63	45	93	5	.358	.496
Minor League Totals				.269	168	610	91	164	34	3	21	94	82	147	12	.359	.438

22 KENDALL WILLIAMS, RHP

BREAKOUT

BA GRADE 50 Risk: Extreme

Born: Aug. 24, 2000. **B-T:** R-R. **HT:** 6-6. **WT:** 205. **Drafted:** HS—Bradenton, Fla., 2019 (2nd round). **Signed by:** Brandon Bishoff (Blue Jays).

TRACK RECORD: Williams was IMG Academy's No. 2 starter behind Brennan Malone and boosted his stock with a strong showing at the 2019 National High School Invitational. The Blue Jays drafted him in the second round and signed him for $1,547,500. The Dodgers liked Williams in the draft and acquired him for Ross Stripling at the 2020 trade deadline.

SCOUTING REPORT: Williams is a classic, projectable righthander with a 6-foot-6 frame, a polished delivery and room to grow into more velocity. His fastball presently sits in the low 90s and frequently touches 93-94 mph. His best secondary is a potentially plus changeup that tunnels well off his fastball before dropping off with power fade. Williams is still working to find a breaking ball. He began working on a hard slider in the mid-80s during instructional league with short tilt. Williams has a natural feel to manipulate the baseball and throw strikes from different angles. He should have at least average control.

THE FUTURE: Williams has the ingredients to become a solid starter. His full-season debut awaits in 2021.

Year	Age	Club (League)	Class	W	L	ERA	G	GS	IP	H	HR	BB	SO	BB/9	SO/9	WHIP	AVG
2019	18	Blue Jays (GCL)	R	0	0	1.13	6	5	16	6	0	7	19	3.9	10.7	0.81	.095
Minor League Totals				0	0	1.13	6	5	16	6	0	7	19	3.9	10.7	0.81	.111

23 EDWIN UCETA, RHP

BA GRADE 45 Risk: High

Born: Jan. 9, 1998. **B-T:** R-R. **HT:** 6-0. **WT:** 155. **Signed:** Dominican Republic, 2016. **Signed by:** Luis Marquez/Matt Doppelt.

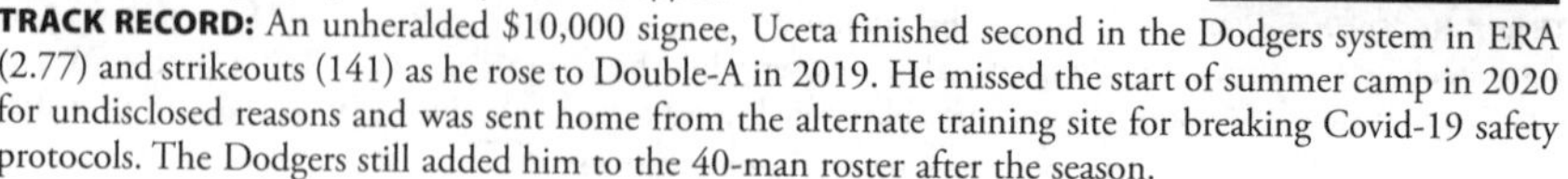

TRACK RECORD: An unheralded $10,000 signee, Uceta finished second in the Dodgers system in ERA (2.77) and strikeouts (141) as he rose to Double-A in 2019. He missed the start of summer camp in 2020 for undisclosed reasons and was sent home from the alternate training site for breaking Covid-19 safety protocols. The Dodgers still added him to the 40-man roster after the season.

SCOUTING REPORT: Uceta is a slight-bodied righthander with impressive feel to pitch. His fastball sits 90-92 mph and touches 94, but it plays up extension and late ride from his lower release height. Uceta's changeup is his out pitch. He sells it with his arm speed and it looks like his fastball out of his hand before dropping off the table with late run and fade in the mid-80s. Uceta expertly plays his fastball and changeup off each other and keeps batters guessing. His upper-70s, slurvy breaking ball remains a work in progress but gets some swings and misses from righthanded batters. Uceta ties everything together with average control.

THE FUTURE: Uceta still has room to fill out and add velocity. He can be a back-end starter if he does.

Year	Age	Club (League)	Class	W	L	ERA	G	GS	IP	H	HR	BB	SO	BB/9	K/9	WHIP	AVG
2019	21	R. Cucamonga (CAL)	HiA	4	0	2.15	10	10	50	47	6	16	65	2.9	11.6	1.25	.241
	21	Tulsa (TL)	AA	7	2	3.21	16	14	73	62	5	33	76	4.1	9.4	1.30	.238
Minor League Totals				20	12	3.73	76	66	331	300	36	105	362	2.9	9.8	1.22	.240

24 MICHAEL GROVE, RHP

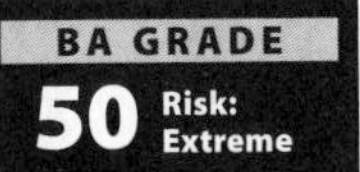

Born: Dec. 18, 1996. **B-T:** R-R. **HT:** 6-3. **WT:** 200. **Drafted:** West Virginia, 2018 (2nd round). **Signed by:** Jonah Rosenthal.

TRACK RECORD: Grove missed most of 2017 and all of 2018 at West Virginia after having Tommy John surgery, but the Dodgers still drafted him in the second round based on the stuff he showed pre-surgery. Grove returned to the mound in 2019 at high Class A Rancho Cucamonga and struggled to a 6.10 ERA with diminished stuff and limited durability. His stuff ticked up in his second year back and he impressed at the alternate training site.

SCOUTING REPORT: Grove is a good athlete with a fast arm and is starting to rediscover his pre-surgery form. After sitting 89-93 mph over two-inning stints in 2019, Grove began holding 92-95 mph over four-inning stints at the alternate site in 2020. He also began to regain the feel for his upper-70s, downer curveball. Grove focused on developing his 80-84 mph, vertical slider and nascent mid-80s changeup at the alternate site. His slider showed flashes of above-average potential and his changeup started tunneling well off his fastball. Grove throws strikes, but his effortful delivery and injury history raise questions about his durability.

THE FUTURE: Grove has to show he can maintain his stuff over a full season. He'll try to do that in 2021.

Year	Age	Club (League)	Class	W	L	ERA	G	GS	IP	H	HR	BB	SO	BB/9	SO/9	WHIP	AVG
2019	22	R. Cucamonga (CAL)	HiA	0	5	6.10	21	21	52	61	7	19	73	3.3	12.7	1.55	.264
Minor League Totals				0	5	6.10	21	21	51	61	7	19	73	3.3	12.7	1.55	.293

25 JIMMY LEWIS, RHP

BREAKOUT
BA GRADE
50 Risk: Extreme

Born: Nov. 2, 2000. **B-T:** R-R. **HT:** 6-6. **WT:** 200. **Drafted:** HS—Austin, Texas, 2019 (2nd round supplemental). **Signed by:** Clint Bowers.

TRACK RECORD: Lewis teamed with Brett Baty to make Lake Travis High in Austin a top destination for scouts in 2019. The Mets drafted Baty 12th overall and the Dodgers took Lewis with the 77th pick. Shoulder inflammation limited Lewis after he signed, but he rehabbed in 2020 and returned to the pitch in instructional league, where he impressed rival evaluators.

SCOUTING REPORT: Lewis is a tall, projectable righthander with a polished delivery and clean arm action that portends a future starter. His fastball sits 90-93 and touches 95 mph with sink and tail at the bottom of the zone. His 78-80 mph, top-to-bottom curveball is inconsistent but flashes plus, and his changeup has quickly progressed to show above-average potential. Lewis stands for his ability to command the ball to both sides of the plate. He repeats his delivery and has an advanced feel to pitch for his age. His father, Jim, was a pitcher drafted in the second round by the Astros in 1991 and reached Triple-A .

THE FUTURE: Lewis still has room to fill out and add velocity. If he does, he has mid-rotation potential, provided his shoulder holds up.

Year	Age	Club (League)	Class	W	L	ERA	G	GS	IP	H	HR	BB	SO	BB/9	SO/9	WHIP	AVG
2019	18	Did not play—Injured															

26 LUKE RALEY, OF

BA GRADE
40 Risk: Medium

Born: Sept. 19, 1994. **B-T:** L-R. **HT:** 6-4. **WT:** 235. **Drafted:** Lake Erie (Ohio), 2016 (7th round). **Signed by:** Marty Lamb.

TRACK RECORD: Raley hit .424/.528/.727 for Division II Lake Erie in 2016 and was drafted by the Dodgers in the seventh round. They traded him to the Twins as part of the package for Brian Dozier in 2018 but re-acquired him with Brusdal Graterol in exchange for Kenta Maeda before the 2020 season. Raley spent the summer at the alternate training site and was one of the top hitters.

SCOUTING REPORT: Raley is incredibly strong with bulging biceps and plus-plus raw power. He frequently hit home runs on top of the parking garage beyond right field at Southern California's Dedeaux Field. His swing is oriented to his pull-side and he needs to improve his plate discipline, but he's productive against both righties and lefties and has the bat speed to be an average hitter. Raley is an average runner and plays hard defensively in left field. He's occasionally too aggressive and collides with other fielders or the wall. He has above-average arm strength despite a funky throwing stroke.

THE FUTURE: Raley's power and sneaky athleticism have long made him a potential sleeper. He's on the 40-man roster and is in position for his major league debut in 2021.

Year	Age	Club (League)	Class	AVG	G	AB	R	H	2B	3B	HR	RBI	BB	SO	SB	OBP	SLG
2019	24	Twins (GCL)	R	.368	5	19	1	7	0	0	1	2	0	2	0	.350	.526
	24	Rochester (IL)	AAA	.302	33	126	28	38	6	0	7	21	7	42	4	.362	.516
Minor League Totals				.288	347	1347	245	388	60	25	46	178	104	355	21	.361	.472

27 GERARDO CARRILLO, RHP

Born: Sept. 3, 1998. **B-T:** R-R. **HT:** 6-1. **WT:** 180. **Signed:** Mexico, 2016. **Signed by:** Mike Brito/Roman Barinas/Juvenal Soto.

TRACK RECORD: Carrillo was a slight righthander with a quick arm when the Dodgers purchased his rights from the Mexican League's Tijuana franchise in 2016. He grew three inches and added 25 pounds after signing and saw a huge uptick in velocity, but also struggled to harness his newfound power. Carrillo spent 2020 at the alternate training site and instructional league. He showed enough progress that the Dodgers added him to their 40-man roster after the season.

SCOUTING REPORT: Carrillo's stuff is undeniable. His sinker sits 94-97 mph with nearly 16 inches of run and his short, 89-91 mph slider is a swing-and-miss pitch that moves in the opposite direction. He generates his power stuff with remarkable ease and holds his velocity deep into his outings. He also flashes an average changeup with late drop and mixes in a below-average, slurvy curveball. Carrillo's issue is his well below-average control. He often throws strikes one inning and can't find the plate the next. He's still learning to control the tempo of his delivery and be on time with his arm.

THE FUTURE: Carrillo likely won't throw enough strikes to start. His stuff will work as a power reliever.

Year	Age	Club (League)	Class	W	L	ERA	G	GS	IP	H	HR	BB	SO	BB/9	SO/9	WHIP	AVG
2019	20	R. Cucamonga (CAL)	HiA	5	9	5.44	23	21	86	87	3	51	86	5.3	9.0	1.60	.215
Minor League Totals				14	12	3.57	50	41	194	172	7	82	168	3.8	7.8	1.31	.235

28 ANDRE JACKSON, RHP

Born: May 1, 1996. **B-T:** R-R. **HT:** 6-3. **WT:** 210. **Drafted:** Utah, 2017 (12th round). **Signed by:** Brian Compton.

TRACK RECORD: Jackson primarily played left field at Utah and pitched briefly as a reliever. He missed the 2017 season after having Tommy John surgery, but the Dodgers liked his arm strength and drafted him as a pitcher in the 12th round. Jackson got healthy, began starting and tied for second in the organization in strikeouts as he advanced to high Class A Rancho Cucamonga in 2019. The Dodgers brought him to the alternate training site in 2020 and added him to their 40-man roster after the season.

SCOUTING REPORT: Jackson is a good athlete with lots of natural arm strength. His fastball sits 95-96 mph and gets swings and misses in the strike zone, and his above-average changeup is one of the best in the organization. He shows natural feel to spin the ball and flashes an average curveball and hard cutter with short tilt. Jackson is still raw and more of a thrower than pitcher. He revamped his delivery and arm action at the alternate site to improve his below-average control, and he lacks the feel for sequencing or command that comes with experience.

THE FUTURE: Jackson is a potential late-bloomer as a converted position player. Double-A awaits in 2021.

Year	Age	Club (League)	Class	W	L	ERA	G	GS	IP	H	HR	BB	SO	BB/9	SO/9	WHIP	AVG
2019	23	Great Lakes (MWL)	LoA	4	1	2.23	10	10	48	29	1	19	50	3.5	9.3	0.99	.153
	23	R. Cucamonga (CAL)	HiA	3	1	3.66	15	15	66	61	5	38	91	5.2	12.3	1.49	.207
Minor League Totals				10	7	3.45	43	42	182	156	9	102	217	5.0	10.7	1.41	.232

29 ROBINSON ORTIZ, LHP

BA GRADE
45 Risk: High

Born: Jan. 4, 2000. **B-T:** L-L. **HT:** 6-0. **WT:** 180. **Signed:** Dominican Republic, 2017. **Signed by:** Luis Marquez/Roman Barinas/Laiky Uribe.

TRACK RECORD: Ortiz fell under the radar as an amateur and signed with the Dodgers for $60,000 a year after he became eligible. He quickly conquered the Rookie levels and had a strong finish at low Class A Great Lakes in 2019. Ortiz returned home to the Dominican Republic during the coronavirus shutdown and participated in Dominican instructional league after the season.

SCOUTING REPORT: Ortiz has a smooth, easy delivery from the left side. His fastball sits 91-93 mph and touches 94-95 with armside life. He has room to fill out and get stronger and throw harder, which the Dodgers expect he will. Ortiz has an advanced feel for an 82-86 mph changeup that draws swings and misses and weak contact from righthanders. His 79-83 mph slider stays off the barrel against lefties. Ortiz mixes his pitches effectively and shows average control with his simple, repeatable delivery.

THE FUTURE: Ortiz has a chance to be a back-of-the-rotation starter if he grows into more velocity. He'll move to high Class A in 2021.

Year	Age	Club (League)	Class	W	L	ERA	G	GS	IP	H	HR	BB	SO	BB/9	SO/9	WHIP	AVG
2019	19	Great Lakes (MWL)	LoA	4	5	4.59	19	18	86	73	10	40	74	4.2	7.7	1.31	.200
Minor League Totals				8	9	4.15	41	38	156	133	12	57	151	3.3	8.7	1.22	.232

30 ZACH REKS, OF

BA GRADE 40 **Risk:** Medium

Born: Nov. 12, 1993. **B-T:** L-R. **HT:** 6-2. **WT:** 190. **Drafted:** Kentucky, 2017 (10th round). **Signed by:** Marty Lamb.

TRACK RECORD: Reks struggled as an Air Force freshman and transferred to Kentucky, where he failed to make the team as a walk-on. He spent the next two years as a student-only until Wildcats assistant coach Rick Eckstein saw him athletically dismount a scooter and asked him to try out again. Reks made the team, became a starting outfielder and was drafted by the Dodgers in the 10th round in 2017 as a senior sign. He quickly made his way up the minors and hit .291/.385/.536 with 28 home runs between Double-A and Triple-A in 2019. The Dodgers brought him to their alternate training site in 2020 and added him to the 40-man roster after the season.

SCOUTING REPORT: Reks' game is simple: he can hit. He gets on plane quickly and has a quick, adjustable swing from the left side that allows him to cover the entire plate. He has an efficient swing path and frequently finds the barrel to generate home run power to all fields. Reks is at least an average hitter with average power, but he's a liability defensively. He's well below-average in left field and struggles both coming in and going back on balls. His arm strength is fringe-average, but he's accurate and has a quick release.

THE FUTURE: Reks will benefit if the National League permanently adopts the designated hitter. He's in position for his major league debut in 2021.

Year	Age	Club (League)	Class	AVG	G	AB	R	H	2B	3B	HR	RBI	BB	SO	SB	OBP	SLG
2019	25	Oklahoma City (PCL)	AAA	.284	89	331	57	94	19	1	19	71	48	104	2	.382	.520
	25	Tulsa (TL)	AA	.310	32	113	29	35	2	1	9	22	15	27	1	.394	.584
Minor League Totals				.300	256	908	155	272	41	4	35	145	114	241	12	.383	.469

MORE PROSPECTS TO KNOW

31 LEONEL VALERA, SS

SLEEPER

Long an athletic defender with a cannon for an arm, Valera has added strength and begun to impact the ball more when he connects.

32 LANDON KNACK, RHP

The senior sign from East Tennessee State is a polished righthander with exceptional control. Most promising, his stuff has begun ticking up.

33 YEINER FERNANDEZ, C

A participant in the 2015 Little League World Series with Venezuela, Fernandez has grown into a versatile athlete with a potential impact bat.

34 JERMING ROSARIO, RHP

The projectable righthander is sitting 92-95 mph with a sharp slider and still has room to get stronger and throw harder.

35 NICK ROBERTSON, RHP

Robertson has emerged as a potential late-relief candidate with a 95-98 mph that features deception and ride and blows hitters away.

36 CODY THOMAS, OF

The former Oklahoma quarterback has loud lefthanded power and is starting to find more consistency at the plate.

37 HYUN-IL CHOI, RHP

The young Korean righthander shows plus command of a polished three-pitch mix and is starting to grow into more velocity.

38 JAKE VOGEL, OF

A touted prep product drafted in the third round in 2020, Vogel has plus-plus speed and sneaky power, but his swing needs a lot of work.

39 CARSON TAYLOR, C

The 2020 fourth-round pick holds a lot of offensive promise as a switch-hitting catcher with elite plate discipline and a good lefthanded swing.

40 JAMES OUTMAN, OF

The freakishly athletic outfielder has rapidly improving baseball skills and offers intriguing potential on both sides of the ball.

TOP PROSPECTS OF THE DECADE

Year	Player, Pos	2020 Org
2011	Dee Strange-Gordon, SS	Mariners
2012	Zach Lee, RHP	Athletics
2013	Hyun-Jin Ryu, LHP	Blue Jays
2014	Joc Pederson, OF	Dodgers
2015	Corey Seager, SS	Dodgers
2016	Corey Seager, SS	Dodgers
2017	Cody Bellinger, 1B	Dodgers
2018	Walker Buehler, RHP	Dodgers
2019	Keibert Ruiz, C	Dodgers
2020	Gavin Lux, SS/2B	Dodgers

TOP DRAFT PICKS OF THE DECADE

Year	Player, Pos	2020 Org
2011	Chris Reed, LHP	Did not play
2012	Corey Seager, 3B	Dodgers
2013	Chris Anderson, RHP	Did not play
2014	Grant Holmes, RHP	Athletics
2015	Walker Buehler, RHP	Dodgers
2016	Gavin Lux, SS	Dodgers
2017	Jeren Kendall, OF	Dodgers
2018	*J.T. Ginn, RHP	Mets
2019	Kody Hoese, 3B	Dodgers
2020	Bobby Miller, RHP	Dodgers

* Did not sign

DEPTH CHART

LOS ANGELES DODGERS

TOP 2021 ROOKIES	RANK
Zach McKinstry, 2B/SS	11
BREAKOUT PROSPECTS	**RANK**
Alex De Jesus, SS	17
Kendall Williams, RHP	22
Jimmy Lewis, RHP	25

SOURCE OF TOP 30 TALENT

Homegrown	28	Acquired	2
College	13	Trade	2
Junior college	1	Rule 5 draft	0
High school	2	Independent league	0
Nondrafted free agent	0	Free agent/waivers	0
International	12		

LF
Luke Raley (26)
Zach Reks (30)
Drew Avans

CF
Luis Rodriguez (13)
Jake Vogel
James Outman

RF
Andy Pages (10)
DJ Peters (14)
Cody Thomas
Donovan Casey

3B
Kody Hoese (4)
Miguel Vargas (9)
Devin Mann (21)
Cristian Santana
Brandon Lewis

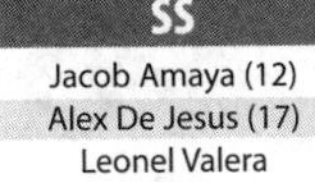

SS
Jacob Amaya (12)
Alex De Jesus (17)
Leonel Valera

2B
Michael Busch (3)
Zach McKinstry (11)
Omar Estevez (19)

1B
Edwin Rios (7)
Dillon Paulson

C
Keibert Ruiz (1)
Diego Cartaya (6)
Yeiner Fernandez
Carson Taylor

LHP

LHSP	LHRP
Robinson Ortiz (29)	Victor Gonzalez (15)
John Rooney	Logan Salow

RHP

RHSP	RHRP
Josiah Gray (2)	Dennis Santana (18)
Bobby Miller (5)	Gerardo Carrillo (27)
Ryan Pepiot (8)	Andre Jackson (28)
Mitch White (16)	Nick Robertson
Clayton Beeter (20)	Josh Sborz
Kendall Williams (22)	Carlos Duran
Edwin Uceta (23)	Marshal Kasowski
Michael Grove (24)	Melvin Jimenez
Jimmy Lewis (25)	Jose Martinez
Landon Knack	
Jerming Rosario	
Hyun-il Choi	
Jeronimo Castro	

Miami Marlins

BY ANDRE FERNANDEZ

Despite a Covid-19 outbreak that decimated their roster at the start of the pandemic-shortened 2020 season, the Marlins made their first playoff appearance since 2003 and advanced to the National League Division Series after a two-game sweep of the Cubs in the NL Wild Card Series. They finished 31-29, for their first winning record since 2009

The Marlins' success didn't occur during a typical 162-game schedule and benefitted from an expanded 16-team postseason field. Still, ending the NL's longest active postseason drought was a positive step for a franchise that has undergone a major rebuild since 2017, when new ownership led by Derek Jeter and venture capitalist Bruce Sherman bought the team from Jeffrey Loria.

Perhaps most encouraging is the Marlins ended their playoff drought while seeing eight of their top 15 prospects make their major league debuts in 2020. Among the most notable was righthander Sixto Sanchez, who made nine starts including a victorious playoff debut against the Cubs at Wrigley Field. Lefthander Trevor Rogers, a 2017 first-round pick, also impressed and maintained a spot in the rotation for most of the regular season.

The rebuild began with the Marlins trading 2017 NL MVP Giancarlo Stanton and Christian Yelich, as well as all-stars Marcell Ozuna, J.T. Realmuto and Dee Gordon over the first two years of the Jeter/Sherman leadership. The return from several of those trades, plus others, which came under the watch of former president of baseball operations Michael Hill, yielded top starters Sanchez and Sandy Alcantara as well as shortstops Jazz Chisholm—at least indirectly—and Jose Devers, outfielder Jesus Sanchez and first baseman Lewin Diaz, among many other prospects.

In early November, the Marlins made a historic move when they hired Kim Ng to replace Hill as their new general manager. Ng became the first female general manager for a North American major sports franchise as well as the first East Asian-American to assume that role in Major League Baseball. Now, it will be Ng's responsibility to see the rebuild through to ensure that Miami's 2020 playoff appearance was the start of a sustained run of success rather than a fluke.

She will have a good foundation from which to work. Before the pandemic, the Marlins committed more resources to scouting, which led to the organization acquiring a strong crop of pitching talent in the 2020 draft, led by Minnesota righthander Max Meyer with the third overall pick.

Outfielder JJ Bleday, their 2019 first-round pick, gives the Marlins a top young position player atop their system.

The Marlins spent a combined $6.25 million to sign Cuban outfielders Victor Victor Mesa and Victor Mesa Jr. in 2018, but have also made solid under-the-radar international signings such as shortstop Jose Salas, righthanders Breidy Encarnacion and Eury Perez as well as shortstops Dalvy Rosario, Ian Lewis and Junior Sanchez.

It all has created optimism heading into 2021. With a competitive big league team and a wealth of farm talent, the Marlins believe they have the foundation to become a World Series championship contender in the next three to four years. ■

MARCELO MARAGNI/MLB PHOTOS VIA GETTY IMAGES

The Marlins hired Kim Ng as the first female GM of a North American major league franchise.

PROJECTED 2024 LINEUP

Position	Player	Age
Catcher	Jorge Alfaro	31
First Base	Lewin Diaz	27
Second Base	Isan Diaz	28
Third Base	Brian Anderson	31
Shortstop	Jazz Chisholm	26
Left Field	Jesus Sanchez	26
Center Field	Lewis Brinson	30
Right Field	JJ Bleday	26
Designated Hitter	Garrett Cooper	34
No. 1 Starter	Sixto Sanchez	25
No. 2 Starter	Sandy Alcantara	28
No. 3 Starter	Max Meyer	25
No. 4 Starter	Pablo Lopez	28
No. 5 Starter	Trevor Rogers	26
Closer	Edward Cabrera	26

1 SIXTO SANCHEZ, RHP

Born: July 29, 1998. **B-T:** R-R. **HT:** 6-0. **WT:** 234.
Signed: Dominican Republic, 2015.
Signed by: Carlos Salas (Phillies).

MARK BROWN/GETTY IMAGES

BA GRADE	SCOUTING GRADES
70 Risk: High	Fastball: 80. Changeup: 70. Slider: 55. Curveball: 55. Control: 60.

Projected future grades on 20-80 scouting scale.

TRACK RECORD: Signed originally by the Phillies for $35,000 in July 2015, Sanchez was part of the return the Marlins received when they traded away J.T. Realmuto after the 2018 season. After Sanchez pitched just 46.2 innings at high Class A in his final season with the Phillies due to right elbow inflammation, the Marlins eased him into his first season in their organization. He pitched a combined 114 innings at high Class A and Double-A, where he went 8-4, 2.53 with 97 strikeouts and 19 walks. In 2020, Sanchez made his big league debut in late August and quickly became a fixture in the Marlins' rotation after going 3-2 with a 3.46 ERA over 39 innings with 33 strikeouts and 11 walks in seven regular-season starts. Sanchez impressed enough to earn a steady spot in the playoff rotation along with Sandy Alcantara and Pablo Lopez.

SCOUTING REPORT: Sanchez's headlining pitch is a double-plus fastball with solid life that averaged nearly 99 mph—the third-highest velocity in the majors in 2020. He touched triple-digits eight times, peaking at 101 mph. Sanchez also throws a two-seamer in the upper 90s with powerful sink. He made great strides with his changeup, his most frequently thrown offspeed pitch. The double-plus offering has solid dive and proved equally tough against lefties and righties, who hit .152 and .145 against the pitch, respectively. His power slider has plus potential, as does a curveball with solid break he used as an additional out pitch. Sanchez is an advanced strike-thrower with a smooth, clean delivery who pitches with a quick yet composed pace. Injury concerns about his elbow have quieted, and he exhibited some of the same plus or better control he did in the minors during his first major league season. Consistency will be key for Sanchez, who struck out 8.2 and walked 1.4 per nine innings during his first five starts and a 3-to-1 strikeout-to-walk ratio overall. Those numbers somewhat masked a tough finish to the season during which he allowed nine earned runs in seven innings, with six walks and four strikeouts.

THE FUTURE: Sanchez was already slotted among the Marlins' top three starters during the 2020 playoffs and should remain a frontline starter if he continues to progress in spring training. Sanchez has the highest upside of any pitcher in the organization, perhaps even perennial all-star potential, with continued development of his fastball command and control of his secondary pitches. He could emerge as the team's No. 1 starter at some point in the next two seasons, when he'll form a young, imposing group with Alcantara, Lopez and possibly Rogers. ■

BEST TOOLS

Best Hitter for Average	Jose Devers
Best Power Hitter	Lewin Diaz
Best Strike-Zone Discipline	JJ Bleday
Fastest Baserunner	Monte Harrison
Best Athlete	Monte Harrison
Best Fastball	Sixto Sanchez
Best Curveball	Braxton Garrett
Best Slider	Max Meyer
Best Changeup	Sixto Sanchez
Best Control	Sixto Sanchez
Best Defensive Catcher	Will Banfield
Best Defensive Infielder	Nasim Nuñez
Best Infield Arm	Jazz Chisholm
Best Defensive Outfielder	Monte Harrison
Best Outfield Arm	Jerar Encarnacion

Year	Age	Club (League)	Class	W	L	ERA	G	GS	IP	H	HR	BB	SO	BB/9	SO/9	WHIP	AVG
2017	18	Lakewood (SAL)	LoA	5	3	2.41	13	13	67	46	1	9	64	1.2	8.6	0.82	.180
	18	Clearwater (FSL)	HiA	0	4	4.55	5	5	28	27	1	9	20	2.9	6.5	1.30	.227
2018	19	Clearwater (FSL)	HiA	4	3	2.51	8	8	47	39	1	11	45	2.1	8.7	1.07	.207
2019	20	Jupiter (FSL)	HiA	0	2	4.91	2	2	11	14	1	2	6	1.6	4.9	1.45	.304
	20	Jacksonville (SL)	AA	8	4	2.53	18	18	103	87	5	19	97	1.7	8.5	1.03	.212
2020	21	Miami (NL)	MAJ	3	2	3.46	7	7	39	36	3	11	33	2.5	7.6	1.21	.250
Major League Totals				3	2	3.46	7	7	39	36	3	11	33	2.5	7.6	1.21	.250
Minor League Totals				23	18	2.58	68	59	335	278	9	64	294	1.7	7.9	1.02	.223

2 JJ BLEDAY, OF

Born: Nov. 10, 1997. **B-T:** L-L. **HT:** 6-2. **WT:** 197. **Drafted:** Vanderbilt, 2019 (1st round). **Signed by:** Christian Castorri.

TRACK RECORD: The Marlins drafted Bleday fourth overall in 2019 and signed him for a franchise-record $6.67 million after he led Vanderbilt to a national championship his junior season and led the nation with 27 home runs. Following his pro debut at high Class A Jupiter in 2019, Bleday was slated to play in Double-A in 2020. Instead, he faced the organization's top-level pitchers at the alternate training site.

SCOUTING REPORT: Bleday uses a fluid swing and solid bat speed to project as a middle-of-the-order hitter with plus power from the left side. He also shows above-average defense and arm strength. Bleday made positive strides when it came to his outfield reads and jumps, according to scouts, while playing both corner spots, as well as center field. Bleday has the fundamentally sound mechanics and speed to handle center but still projects as a corner outfielder, most likely in right field. He also shows above-average strike-zone discipline that complements his above-average defensive skills and average-to-above speed on the bases.

THE FUTURE: Bleday was in the Marlins' 60-player pool and could start the 2021 season at Double-A. He has a chance to fast-track to Miami and secure a starting corner outfield spot before the end of the season.

SCOUTING GRADES: **Hitting:** 60 **Power:** 60 **Running:** 50 **Fielding:** 55 **Arm:** 60

Year	Age	Club (League)	Class	AVG	G	AB	R	H	2B	3B	HR	RBI	BB	SO	SB	OBP	SLG
2019	21	Jupiter (FSL)	HiA	.257	38	140	13	36	8	0	3	19	11	29	0	.311	.379
Minor League Totals				.257	38	140	13	36	8	0	3	19	11	29	0	.311	.379

3 MAX MEYER, RHP

BA GRADE
60 Risk: High

Born: March 12, 1999. **B-T:** L-R. **HT:** 6-0. **WT:** 196. **Drafted:** Minnesota, 2020 (1st round). **Signed by:** Shaeffer Hall.

TRACK RECORD: The Marlins surprised many when they chose Meyer with the third overall pick and made him the first pitcher selected in the 2020 draft. Meyer, a two-time member of USA Baseball's Collegiate National team, signed for $6.7 million—a franchise record even at $520,000 under slot value. After opening his collegiate career as a closer and recording a school-record 16 saves as a freshman, Meyer moved into Minnesota's rotation and posted 10.2 strikeouts per nine innings as a sophomore before dominating in an abbreviated junior campaign.

SCOUTING REPORT: A natural strike-thrower with elite athleticism and explosiveness, Meyer is armed with a double-plus slider and fastball. He throws both with above-average control and a nearly effortless delivery. He throws his slider in the 92-93 mph range with excellent movement and depth. Meyer's four-seamer touched 100 mph in college and averages 95-98 with solid sink. He complements those pitches with a mid-80s changeup with above-average potential.

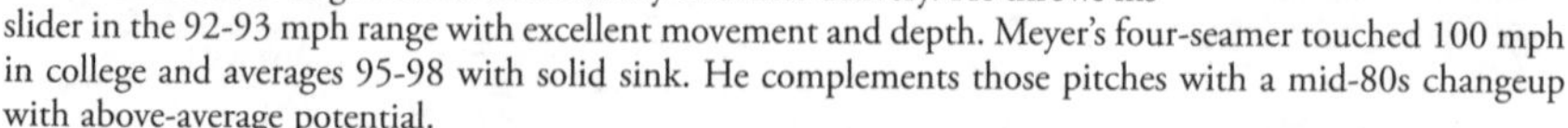

THE FUTURE: Meyer has a chance to rise quickly after showing he could hold his own against older hitters at the alternate training site. His future as a starter or reliever depends on the development of his changeup as a reliable third pitch.

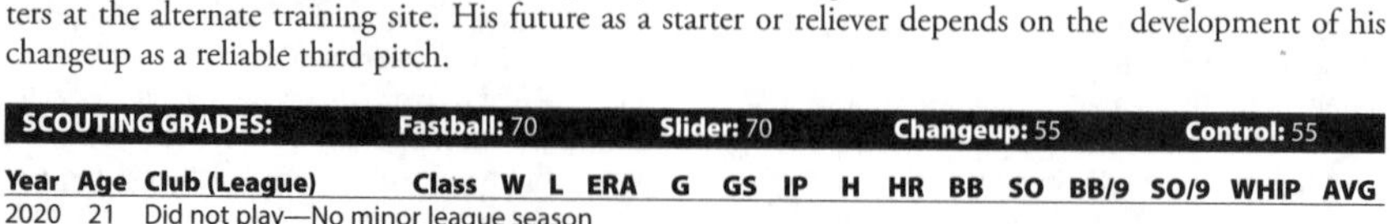

SCOUTING GRADES: **Fastball:** 70 **Slider:** 70 **Changeup:** 55 **Control:** 55

Year	Age	Club (League)	Class	W	L	ERA	G	GS	IP	H	HR	BB	SO	BB/9	SO/9	WHIP	AVG
2020	21	Did not play—No minor league season															

4 JAZZ CHISHOLM, SS

JARED BLAIS/MLB PHOTOS VIA GETTY IMAGES

BA GRADE
55 **Risk: High**

Born: Feb. 1, 1998. **B-T:** L-R. **HT:** 5-11. **WT:** 184. **Signed:** Bahamas, 2015. **Signed by:** Craig Shipley (D-backs).

TRACK RECORD: Chisholm signed with the D-backs for $200,000 in July 2015 and hit 54 home runs combined at low Class A, high Class A and Double-A. The Marlins acquired him at the 2019 trade deadline for right-hander Zac Gallen. After the deal, Chisholm hit .284 with an .877 OPS at Double-A Jacksonville and lowered his strikeout rate by more than 8%. He began the 2020 season at the alternate training site and made his major league debut on Sept. 1.

SCOUTING REPORT: Chisholm has impressive raw tools on both sides of the ball. His smooth, uppercut swing generates solid bat speed and plus power, but his extremely aggressive approach leads to lots of swings and misses. He had a 31% strikeout rate and .107 batting average against fastballs in his debut and may always be a below-average hitter. Chisholm is a twitchy, rangy athlete who displayed above-average defense, speed and arm strength at both shortstop and second base in the majors. His mix of speed and power gives him a chance to be a 20-20 player if he can make enough contact.

THE FUTURE: Chisholm has shown the ability to refine his approach and lower his strikeout rate in the past. He should earn a place on the Marlins' 2021 roster and is on track to be Miami's everyday shortstop as early by 2022.

SCOUTING GRADES: **Hitting:** 40 **Power:** 60 **Running:** 55 **Fielding:** 55 **Arm:** 55

Year	Age	Club (League)	Class	AVG	G	AB	R	H	2B	3B	HR	RBI	BB	SO	SB	OBP	SLG
2017	19	Kane County (MWL)	LoA	.248	29	109	14	27	5	2	1	12	10	39	3	.325	.358
2018	20	Kane County (MWL)	LoA	.244	76	307	52	75	17	4	15	43	30	97	8	.311	.472
	20	Visalia (CAL)	HiA	.329	36	149	27	49	6	2	10	27	9	52	9	.369	.597
2019	21	Jackson (SL)	AA	.204	89	314	51	64	6	5	18	44	41	123	13	.305	.427
	21	Jacksonville (SL)	AA	.284	23	81	6	23	4	2	3	10	11	24	3	.383	.494
2020	22	Miami (NL)	MAJ	.161	21	56	8	9	1	1	2	6	5	19	2	.242	.321
Major League Totals				.161	21	56	8	9	1	1	2	6	5	19	2	.242	.321
Minor League Totals				.255	315	1209	192	308	50	16	56	173	120	408	49	.327	.462

5 EDWARD CABRERA, RHP

TOP ROOKIE

JARED BLAIS/MLB PHOTOS VIA GETTY IMAGES

BA GRADE
55 **Risk: High**

Born: April 13, 1998. **B-T:** R-R. **HT:** 6-4. **WT:** 215. **Signed:** Dominican Republic, 2015. **Signed by:** Albert Gonzalez/Sandy Nin/Domingo Ortega.

TRACK RECORD: The Marlins signed Cabrera for $100,000 in 2015. He progressed steadily and broke out in 2019, when he went 9-4, 2.23 with 116 strikeouts and 31 walks in 96.2 innings while climbing to Double-A. Cabrera was a candidate to make his major league debut in 2020 but dealt with arm and back injuries that halted a potential callup.

SCOUTING REPORT: Cabrera's main weapon is a double-plus, upper-90s fastball with solid sink that can touch 100 mph. That power pitch helped him induce a near 50% groundball rate at Double-A and prevents batters from making hard contact in the air. Cabrera's main secondary is a plus curveball with added depth that has become a solid swing-and-miss pitch. The key to proving himself as a long-term starter will be the development of his change-up, which has showed improved separation from his fastball. Cabrera walked more than three batters per nine innings in Double-A in 2019 and must improve his control, but he has shown an improved, repeatable delivery.

THE FUTURE: Cabrera has a high ceiling that could make him anywhere from a No. 2 to No. 4 starter in the Marlins' rotation, depending on how he commands his secondary pitches. He should start 2021 at Triple-A with a chance for a quick callup.

SCOUTING GRADES: **Fastball:** 70 **Curveball:** 60 **Changeup:** 50 **Control:** 50

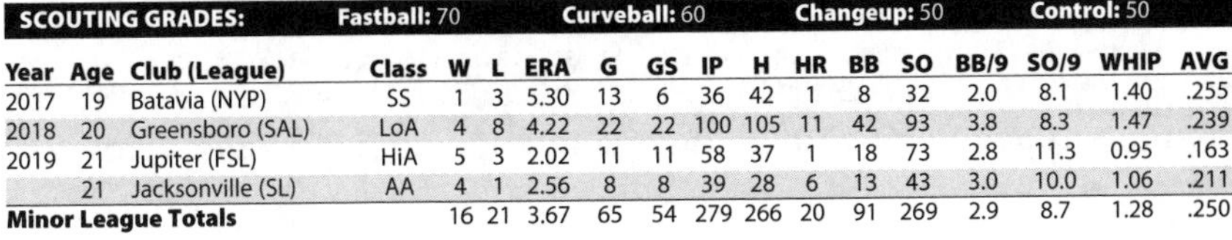

Year	Age	Club (League)	Class	W	L	ERA	G	GS	IP	H	HR	BB	SO	BB/9	SO/9	WHIP	AVG
2017	19	Batavia (NYP)	SS	1	3	5.30	13	6	36	42	1	8	32	2.0	8.1	1.40	.255
2018	20	Greensboro (SAL)	LoA	4	8	4.22	22	22	100	105	11	42	93	3.8	8.3	1.47	.239
2019	21	Jupiter (FSL)	HiA	5	3	2.02	11	11	58	37	1	18	73	2.8	11.3	0.95	.163
	21	Jacksonville (SL)	AA	4	1	2.56	8	8	39	28	6	13	43	3.0	10.0	1.06	.211
Minor League Totals				16	21	3.67	65	54	279	266	20	91	269	2.9	8.7	1.28	.250

6 TREVOR ROGERS, LHP

JARED BLAIS/MLB PHOTOS VIA GETTY IMAGES

BA GRADE
50 Risk: Medium

Born: Nov. 13, 1997. **B-T:** L-L. **HT:** 6-6. **WT:** 217. **Drafted:** HS—Carlsbad, N.M., 2017 (1st round). **Signed by:** Scott Stanley.

TRACK RECORD: The Marlins drafted Rogers 13th overall in 2017 and signed him for an under-slot $3.4 million. He struggled in his debut season at low Class A Greensboro, but broke out in 2019 with a 2.90 ERA and 150 strikeouts in 136 innings at high Class A Jupiter and Double-A Jacksonville. The Marlins called up Rogers for his major league debut on Aug. 25 ahead of other top pitching prospects in the system, and he maintained his rotation spot the rest of the year.

SCOUTING REPORT: Rogers uses a smooth, repeatable delivery to command his solid repertoire of above-average pitches. His fastball averaged 93-94 mph and topped out at 97 with an excellent spin rate of 2,426 rpms in the majors. Rogers tweaked the grip on his slider and exhibited noticeable improvement that prompted his early promotion. Rogers also added a cutter to his arsenal last offseason. One of the biggest keys to his success is a changeup with 5.3 inches more vertical break than average. His varied arsenal, combined with above-average control, helped him record three times as many strikeouts as walks in his big league debut.

THE FUTURE: Rogers handled himself well in the majors. He is in position to earn a spot at the back of the rotation coming out of spring training or perhaps after a brief Triple-A stint.

SCOUTING GRADES: **Fastball:** 55 **Slider:** 55 **Cutter:** 50 **Changeup:** 55 **Control:** 50

Year	Age	Club (League)	Class	W	L	ERA	G	GS	IP	H	HR	BB	SO	BB/9	SO/9	WHIP	AVG
2018	20	Greensboro (SAL)	LoA	2	7	5.82	17	17	73	86	4	27	85	3.3	10.5	1.56	.263
2019	21	Jupiter (FSL)	HiA	5	8	2.53	18	18	110	97	7	24	122	2.0	10.0	1.10	.203
	21	Jacksonville (SL)	AA	1	2	4.50	5	5	26	25	3	9	28	3.1	9.7	1.31	.225
2020	22	Miami (NL)	MAJ	1	2	6.11	7	7	28	32	5	13	39	4.2	12.5	1.61	.283
Major League Totals				1	2	6.11	7	7	28	32	5	13	39	4.2	12.5	1.61	.283
Minor League Totals				8	17	3.92	40	40	209	208	14	60	235	2.6	10.1	1.28	.256

7 LEWIN DIAZ, 1B

JARED BLAIS/MLB PHOTOS VIA GETTY IMAGES

BA GRADE
50 Risk: High

Born: Nov. 19, 1996. **B-T:** L-L. **HT:** 6-4. **WT:** 217. **Signed:** Dominican Republic, 2013. **Signed by:** Fred Guerrero (Twins).

TRACK RECORD: Diaz signed with the Twins for $1.4 million in 2013 but failed to advance past high Class A for five years due to injuries and inconsistency. He appeared to finally break through in 2019 and was acquired by the Marlins for closer Sergio Romo and pitching prospect Chris Vallimont. Diaz's production slipped after the trade, but he still made the Marlins' 60-man player pool in 2020 and received his first big league callup in August.

SCOUTING REPORT: Diaz is a lefthanded power hitter who can drive the ball to all fields. Even when he's not hitting home runs, he has a knack for racking up extra-base hits. He totaled 27 homers, 33 doubles and two triples in 2019, taking many of them to left or left-center field. Diaz doesn't walk much but doesn't strike out at a high rate, either. The Marlins have long felt Diaz's defense at first base was well above-average and major league-ready. Diaz gave them a glimpse at the position while showing off his strong arm and solid mechanics around the bag in his 14-game debut.

THE FUTURE: Diaz's plus defense at first base and potential middle-of-the-order power make him the Marlins' first baseman of the future. He will have a chance to secure the everyday job as early as 2021.

SCOUTING GRADES: **Hitting:** 50 **Power:** 60 **Running:** 40 **Fielding:** 60 **Arm:** 50

Year	Age	Club (League)	Class	AVG	G	AB	R	H	2B	3B	HR	RBI	BB	SO	SB	OBP	SLG
2017	20	Cedar Rapids (MWL)	LoA	.292	121	462	47	135	32	1	12	68	25	79	2	.329	.444
2018	21	Fort Myers (FSL)	HiA	.224	79	294	21	66	11	3	6	35	10	56	1	.255	.344
2019	22	Fort Myers (FSL)	HiA	.290	57	214	34	62	11	1	13	36	14	40	0	.333	.533
	22	Jacksonville (SL)	AA	.200	31	115	16	23	6	0	8	14	11	28	0	.279	.461
	22	Pensacola (SL)	AA	.302	33	126	12	38	16	1	6	26	8	23	0	.341	.587
2020	23	Miami (NL)	MAJ	.154	14	39	2	6	2	0	0	3	2	12	0	.195	.205
Major League Totals				.154	14	39	2	6	2	0	0	3	2	12	0	.195	.205
Minor League Totals				.268	458	1692	192	453	113	9	63	263	123	327	5	.322	.457

8 JESUS SANCHEZ, OF

JARED BLAIS/MLB PHOTOS VIA GETTY IMAGES

BA GRADE
50 **Risk: High**

Born: Oct. 7, 1997. **B-T:** L-R. **HT:** 6-3. **WT:** 222. **Signed:** Dominican Republic, 2014. **Signed by:** Danny Santana (Rays).

TRACK RECORD: Sanchez signed with the Rays for $400,000 in 2014 and rose all the way to Triple-A in 2019. The Marlins acquired him along with reliever Ryne Stanek for righthanders Nick Anderson and Trevor Richards at the 2019 trade deadline. Sanchez hit respectably the rest of the year at Triple-A New Orleans and made the Marlins' 60-man player pool in 2020. The Marlins called him up from the alternate training site to make his major league debut in August.

SCOUTING REPORT: Sanchez generates plenty of bat speed and uses plus raw power to drive the ball to all fields, but he needs more polish as a hitter to go with his outstanding hand-eye coordination. The 6-foot-3 lefthanded hitter has a very pull-heavy approach and struggles with premium velocity, especially on the inner half of the plate. Sanchez's shortcomings were evident during his brief major league stint, when he went 1-for-25 with 11 strikeouts and lost focus and discipline in his approach. Sanchez is a solid defender whose average speed and above-average arm project on an outfield corner.

THE FUTURE: After an ugly major league debut, Sanchez could use more time at Triple-A before returning to the majors. He projects to join JJ Bleday as one of the Marlins' starting corner outfielders of the future.

SCOUTING GRADES: **Hitting:** 45 **Power:** 55 **Running:** 50 **Fielding:** 55 **Arm:** 55

Year	Age	Club (League)	Class	AVG	G	AB	R	H	2B	3B	HR	RBI	BB	SO	SB	OBP	SLG
2017	19	Bowling Green (MWL)	LoA	.305	117	475	81	145	29	4	15	82	32	91	7	.348	.478
2018	20	Montgomery (SL)	AA	.214	27	98	14	21	8	0	1	11	11	21	1	.300	.327
	20	Charlotte, FL (FSL)	HiA	.301	90	359	56	108	24	2	10	64	15	71	6	.331	.462
2019	21	Durham (IL)	AAA	.206	18	63	6	13	2	1	1	5	6	20	0	.282	.317
	21	Montgomery (SL)	AA	.275	78	287	32	79	11	1	8	49	24	65	5	.332	.404
	21	New Orleans (PCL)	AAA	.246	17	65	11	16	1	0	4	9	9	15	0	.338	.446
2020	22	Miami (NL)	MAJ	.040	10	25	1	1	1	0	0	2	4	11	0	.172	.080
Major League Totals				.040	10	25	1	1	1	0	0	2	4	11	0	172	.080
Minor League Totals				.296	464	1799	269	532	98	23	50	304	126	358	29	.342	.459

9 BRAXTON GARRETT, LHP

JARED BLAIS/MLB PHOTOS VIA GETTY IMAGES

BA GRADE
50 **Risk: High**

Born: Aug. 5, 1997. **B-T:** L-L. **HT:** 6-2. **WT:** 202. **Drafted:** HS—Florence, Ala., 2016 (1st round). **Signed by:** Mark Willoughby.

TRACK RECORD: The Marlins drafted Garrett with the No. 7 overall pick in 2016 and went above slot to sign him for $4.1 million. His first season was cut short after he had Tommy John surgery, but he returned to the mound in 2019 and held up over 107 innings while climbing to Double-A. The Marlins added him to their 60-man player pool in 2020 and called him in September up for his first two major league starts.

SCOUTING REPORT: Garrett's arsenal is fronted by low-80s curveball with great depth that is considered the best in the Marlins' system. It's a swing-and-miss pitch that had immediate success in the majors and is a consensus plus offering. Garrett's fastball previously averaged 92-95 mph but dipped to the 88-90 range in the majors, which led to the pitch getting crushed. He also throws an average changeup that is effective against righthanders. Garrett exhibits above-average control and command of all three pitches but had to nibble in the majors with his decreased velocity.

THE FUTURE: Garrett's velocity dip was concerning, but he had barely pitched in Double-A and needs more time in the minors. He is a candidate to land a spot on the back end of the rotation in the coming years.

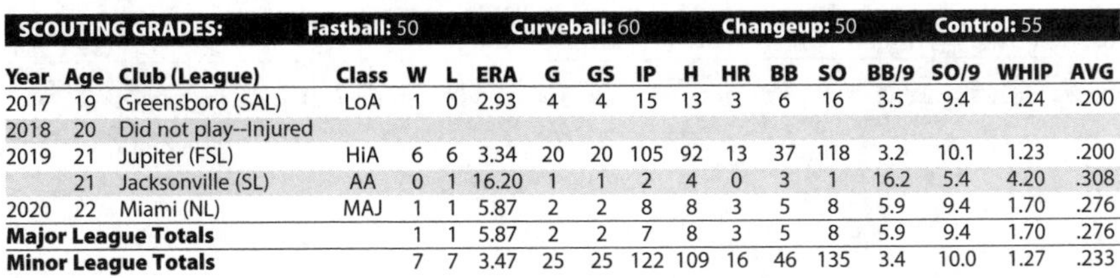

SCOUTING GRADES: **Fastball:** 50 **Curveball:** 60 **Changeup:** 50 **Control:** 55

Year	Age	Club (League)	Class	W	L	ERA	G	GS	IP	H	HR	BB	SO	BB/9	SO/9	WHIP	AVG
2017	19	Greensboro (SAL)	LoA	1	0	2.93	4	4	15	13	3	6	16	3.5	9.4	1.24	.200
2018	20	Did not play--Injured															
2019	21	Jupiter (FSL)	HiA	6	6	3.34	20	20	105	92	13	37	118	3.2	10.1	1.23	.200
	21	Jacksonville (SL)	AA	0	1	16.20	1	1	2	4	0	3	1	16.2	5.4	4.20	.308
2020	22	Miami (NL)	MAJ	1	1	5.87	2	2	8	8	3	5	8	5.9	9.4	1.70	.276
Major League Totals				1	1	5.87	2	2	7	8	3	5	8	5.9	9.4	1.70	.276
Minor League Totals				7	7	3.47	25	25	122	109	16	46	135	3.4	10.0	1.27	.233

10 JOSE DEVERS, SS

JARED BLAIS/MLB PHOTOS VIA GETTY IMAGES

BA GRADE
50 Risk: High

Born: Dec. 7, 1999. **B-T:** L-R. **HT:** 6-0. **WT:** 175. **Signed:** Dominican Republic, 2016. **Signed by:** Juan Rosario (Yankees).

TRACK RECORD: Devers originally signed with the Yankees for $250,000 and was traded to the Marlins with righthander Jorge Guzman and second baseman Starlin Castro in the deal that sent Giancarlo Stanton to New York. Devers' rise through the system has been hindered by shoulder, forearm and groin injuries, but he performed well in the Arizona Fall League in 2019 after hitting a combined .322/.391/.390 in 177 at-bats during his rise to high Class A.

SCOUTING REPORT: Devers needs to add weight and strength to his wiry frame, but he projects as a plus hitter who consistently makes solid contact with a low 15% strikeout rate in 2019. He barreled the ball consistently facing older pitchers at the alternate training site, a development that solidified his standing as the best pure hitter in the Marlins' system. Devers' power will likely always remain well below-average, but his bat-to-ball skills give him a chance to become a top-of-the lineup option in the major leagues. He's a plus runner who enhances his offensive game as an efficient basestealer. Devers is a plus defender at shortstop with range and instincts that make up for his average arm strength.

THE FUTURE: Devers has struggled to stay healthy and must show that he can. He is poised for a jump to Double-A to open 2021.

SCOUTING GRADES: **Hitting:** 55 **Power:** 30 **Running:** 60 **Fielding:** 60 **Arm:** 50

Year	Age	Club (League)	Class	AVG	G	AB	R	H	2B	3B	HR	RBI	BB	SO	SB	OBP	SLG
2017	17	Yankees1 (DSL)	R	.239	11	46	4	11	2	1	0	7	0	16	1	.255	.326
	17	Yankees1 (GCL)	R	.246	42	138	17	34	7	2	1	9	18	21	15	.359	.348
2018	18	Greensboro (SAL)	LoA	.273	85	337	46	92	12	4	0	24	15	49	13	.313	.332
	18	Jupiter (FSL)	HiA	.250	2	8	1	2	0	0	0	2	1	0	0	.333	.250
2019	19	Marlins (GCL)	R	.275	11	40	7	11	3	1	0	2	4	4	3	.370	.400
	19	Jupiter (FSL)	HiA	.325	33	126	13	41	3	1	0	3	8	20	5	.384	.365
	19	Clinton (MWL)	LoA	.455	3	11	5	5	2	0	0	2	2	2	0	.538	.636
Minor League Totals				.278	187	706	93	196	29	9	1	49	48	112	37	.339	.348

11 MONTE HARRISON, OF

Born: Aug. 10, 1995. **B-T:** R-R. **HT:** 6-3. **WT:** 225. **Drafted:** HS—Lee's Summit, Mo., 2014 (2nd round). **Signed by:** Drew Anderson (Brewers).

TRACK RECORD: The Marlins acquired Harrison as part of the trade that sent Christian Yelich to the Brewers before the 2018 season. Harrison had a rough debut in the Marlins' system with 215 strikeouts at Double-A Jacksonville, but he rebounded with a solid showing at Triple-A the following year. The Marlins called Harrison up for his major league debut in 2020, when he had a chance to earn playing time in center field but instead hit .170 with 26 strikeouts in 51 plate appearances.

SCOUTING REPORT: Harrison is a physical, explosive athlete with plus-plus raw power and speed, plus arm strength and the ability to play all three outfield positions. The issue is he struggles to make contact. He's made multiple adjustments to level out his swing throughout his career but still strikes out prodigiously. He is prone to chasing outside the strike zone and, even when doesn't chase, swings and misses way too frequently against all types of pitches in the strike zone. With his current approach and swing, Harrison projects as a well below-average hitter, at best, who will struggle to turn his raw power into production.

THE FUTURE: Harrison's high strikeout rate dampens his tantalizing tools. Whether he can stick on a major league roster in any capacity hinges on him figuring things out at the plate and making more contact.

Year	Age	Club (League)	Class	AVG	G	AB	R	H	2B	3B	HR	RBI	BB	SO	SB	OBP	SLG
2020	24	Miami (NL)	MAJ	.170	32	47	8	8	1	0	1	3	4	26	6	.235	.255
Major League Totals				.170	32	47	8	8	1	0	1	3	4	26	6	.235	.255
Minor League Totals				.245	520	1921	314	471	84	15	61	221	195	677	138	.333	.400

12 DAX FULTON, LHP

Born: Oct. 16, 2001. **B-T:** L-L. **HT:** 6-6. **WT:** 230. **Drafted:** HS—Mustang, Okla., 2020 (2nd round). **Signed by:** James Vilade.

TRACK RECORD: Fulton was considered one of the top high school lefthanders in the 2020 draft class, but he hurt his elbow trying out for USA Baseball's 18U national team and had Tommy John surgery that wiped out his senior year. The Marlins still drafted him 40th overall and signed him for $2.4 million to pass up an Oklahoma commitment. Fulton began throwing bullpens in the fall and returned to the mound in instructional league.

SCOUTING REPORT: With a tall and athletic frame, Fulton is a consistent strike-thrower with his three-pitch mix. His fastball sits 89-93 mph and should tick up as he continues to rehab. The gem of his arsenal is a plus, high-spin curveball he can throw with power and depth. Fulton doesn't use his mid-80s changeup often, but he shows some feel for the offering and it projects as an average pitch. His delivery and arm action looked solid during his rehab work in the fall, providing optimism he'll stay healthy.

THE FUTURE: Fulton has the highest upside of any lefthander in the Marlins' system. He'll make his pro debut in 2021 and try to build innings.

Year	Age	Club (League)	Class	W	L	ERA	G	GS	IP	H	HR	BB	SO	BB/9	SO/9	WHIP	AVG
2020	18	Did not play—No minor league season															

13 KAMERON MISNER, OF

Born: Jan. 8, 1998. **B-T:** L-L. **HT:** 6-4. **WT:** 219. **Drafted:** Missouri, 2019 (1st round supplemental). **Signed by:** Joe Dunigan.

TRACK RECORD: Misner hit .301 with 21 home runs and 50 stolen bases during his three years at Missouri, but struggled his final season due to strikeout issues. The Marlins still drafted him 35th overall in 2019 and signed him for $2.115 million. Misner made a solid pro debut, hitting .270 with two home runs and 11 steals in 163 combined at-bats in the Rookie-level Gulf Coast League and at low Class A Clinton.

SCOUTING REPORT: Misner struggled with falling behind in counts early in his career, but his combination of plus power and above average speed, fielding and arm strength give him well-rounded potential. Misner generates plenty of bat speed using a balanced swing from the left side that produced increased power last fall in Jupiter. His speed makes him a possible 30-30 player with the defensive tools to play all three outfield positions.

THE FUTURE: The original plan in 2020 was for Misner to start at high Class A Jupiter. His continued progress could mean a quick rise through the system with an eye toward a 2022 debut.

Year	Age	Club (League)	Class	AVG	G	AB	R	H	2B	3B	HR	RBI	BB	SO	SB	OBP	SLG
2019	21	Marlins (GCL)	R	.241	8	29	2	7	2	0	0	4	9	7	3	.421	.310
	21	Clinton (MWL)	LoA	.276	34	134	25	37	7	0	2	20	21	35	8	.380	.373
Minor League Totals				.270	42	163	27	44	9	0	2	24	30	42	11	.388	.362

14 CONNOR SCOTT, OF

BA GRADE
45 Risk: High

Born: Oct. 8, 1999. **B-T:** L-L. **HT:** 6-3. **WT:** 187. **Drafted:** HS—Tampa, Fla. 2018 (1st round). **Signed by:** Donavan O'Dowd.

TRACK RECORD: Scott was the Marlins' first draft pick of the Derek Jeter/Bruce Sherman era and signed as the 13th overall pick for $4.03 million out of Plant High in Tampa, the alma mater of Pete Alonso and Kyle Tucker in recent years. Scott was pushed quickly, ascending to high Class A Jupiter at age 19.

SCOUTING REPORT: Scott has plenty of tools but is still learning how to get them to play in games. He struggled early with plate discipline and lifting the ball but has since shown improvement in both areas, allowing him to start tapping into his 15-20 home run potential. He has continued to refine his approach and make strides toward impacting the ball more consistently in order to be an average hitter. Scott's plus speed makes him a base-stealing threat and his above average defensive skills project well at all three outfield positions. His plus arm strength projects well in right field, but his overall tools would make him an average to above average center fielder.

THE FUTURE: Scott remains should see the upper levels in 2021. He'll aim to continue his offensive strides in hopes of becoming an everyday outfielder.

Year	Age	Club (League)	Class	AVG	G	AB	R	H	2B	3B	HR	RBI	BB	SO	SB	OBP	SLG
2019	19	Jupiter (FSL)	HiA	.235	27	98	12	23	4	1	1	5	11	26	2	.306	.327
	19	Clinton (MWL)	LoA	.251	95	378	56	95	24	4	4	36	31	91	21	.311	.368
Minor League Totals				.240	172	655	87	157	31	9	6	54	66	173	32	.310	.342

15 NICK NEIDERT, RHP

Born: Nov. 20, 1996. **B-T:** R-R. **HT:** 6-1. **WT:** 202. **Drafted:** HS—Suwanee, Ga., 2015 (2nd round). **Signed by:** Dustin Evans (Mariners).

TRACK RECORD: A second-round pick of the Mariners in 2015, the Marlins acquired Neidert as part of the trade that sent Dee Gordon to Seattle in 2017. Neidert made it to Triple-A New Orleans in 2019 before having surgery to repair his meniscus. He returned with an impressive five-start performance at the Arizona Fall League and made his Marlins debut in 2020, compiling a 5.40 ERA in four games.

SCOUTING REPORT: Neidert shows command of his 90-92 mph fastball and relies on that command to succeed. He can locate the pitch to both sides of the plate with late movement and often uses it as a complement—rather than as his primary offering—to his plus changeup and average slider. His curveball is still a work in progress. Neidert's solid, repeatable delivery creates good deception with his three-pitch mix to keep hitters off-balance.

THE FUTURE: Neidert's ceiling is a back-end starter or long reliever, but he's ready now and will be a part of the Marlins' pitching staff in 2021.

Year	Age	Club (League)	Class	W	L	ERA	G	GS	IP	H	HR	BB	SO	BB/9	SO/9	WHIP	AVG
2020	23	Miami (NL)	MAJ	0	0	5.40	4	0	8	10	1	2	4	2.2	4.3	1.44	.313
Major League Totals				0	0	5.40	4	0	8	10	1	2	4	2.2	4.3	1.44	.313
Minor League Totals				33	23	3.20	94	94	460	427	41	102	414	2.0	8.1	1.15	.247

16 PEYTON BURDICK, OF

Born: Feb. 26, 1997. **B-T:** R-R. **HT:** 6-0. **WT:** 205. **Drafted:** Wright State, 2019 (3rd round). **Signed by:** Nate Adcock.

TRACK RECORD: The Marlins appear to have found a hidden gem in Burdick, whom they signed below-slot for $397,500 after choosing him with the 82nd overall pick in 2019. Burdick earned Horizon League Player of the Year honors that season after returning from Tommy John surgery and proceeded to slash .308/.407/.542 with 11 home runs and 64 RBIs combined at short-season Batavia and low Class A Clinton.

SCOUTING REPORT: One of the quickest risers in the Marlins' system, Burdick has put himself in the thick of the club's next wave of potential outfielders. His strength is his combination of above-average power to all fields and average to above-average hit tool. Following his impressive season at Clinton, he continued to impact the ball consistently during his work at the alternate training site to solidify himself as a potential impact hitter. Burdick has an above-average arm along average speed. He should be an average defender in either corner outfield spot.

THE FUTURE: Burdick might end up the best of the Marlins' outfield prospects. If he continues to add power and maintain consistency in his swing and approach, he should be an everyday player.

Year	Age	Club (League)	Class	AVG	G	AB	R	H	2B	3B	HR	RBI	BB	SO	SB	OBP	SLG
2019	22	Clinton (MWL)	LoA	.307	63	238	57	73	20	3	10	59	32	67	6	.408	.542
	22	Batavia (NYP)	SS	.318	6	22	3	7	0	1	1	5	2	5	1	.400	.545
Minor League Totals				.308	69	260	60	80	20	4	11	64	34	72	7	.407	.542

17 KYLE NICOLAS, RHP

BREAKOUT
BA GRADE
45 Risk: High

Born: Feb. 22, 1999. **B-T:** R-R. **HT:** 6-4. **WT:** 223. **Drafted:** Ball State, 2020 (2nd round supplemental). **Signed by:** Joe Dunigan.

TRACK RECORD: The nephew of former NFL quarterback Todd Blackledge, Nicolas averaged 14.5 strikeouts per nine innings in four starts during his final season at Ball State before the coronavirus pandemic shut down the college season. The Marlins drafted him with the 61st overall pick and signed him for $1,129,700. Nicolas made his Marlins debut in instructional league.

SCOUTING REPORT: Nicolas was one of the hardest throwers in the 2020 draft, with a plus-plus fastball that sits 96 mph and frequently touches 100 mph. Nicolas has a deceptive, above-average slider that can sometimes touch 90 mph, but there are concerns that he'll be nothing more than a high-leverage reliever unless he can continue to develop his curveball or changeup. Both are fringy to below average offerings, at best. He has the average control to remain a starter if he can find that third offering.

THE FUTURE: Scouts are split whether Nicolas projects as a starter or reliever. His pro debut in 2021 will be telling.

Year	Age	Club (League)	Class	W	L	ERA	G	GS	IP	H	HR	BB	SO	BB/9	SO/9	WHIP	AVG
2020	21	Did not play—No minor league season															

18 JERAR ENCARNACION, OF

BA GRADE
45 Risk: High

Born: Oct. 22, 1997. **B-T:** R-R. **HT:** 6-5. **WT:** 239. **Signed:** Dominican Republic, 2015. **Signed by:** Albert Gonzalez/Sandy Nin.

TRACK RECORD: A former basketball player in the Dominican Republic, Encarnacion got a late start in baseball and signed with the Marlins at age 18 in for $78,000. He had a breakout 2019 in with 16 home runs and 71 RBIs at low Class A Clinton and high Class A Jupiter. He hit three more home runs at the Arizona Fall League, including a grand slam in the championship game.

SCOUTING REPORT: Encarnacion's high strikeout rate was alarming entering 2019, but he was able to lower it from 31% the previous two seasons to 25.3%. His closed stance from the right side generates plenty of power to all fields and his plate discipline on offspeed pitches and breaking balls showed improvement. He likely won't be more than a fringe-average hitter, but his above-average power should make him an offensive contributor. Encarnacion has average speed and is an average defender in right field. His plus arm helped him notch 20 outfield assists in 2019.

THE FUTURE: How Encarnacion refines his approach and plate discipline will dictate how far he climbs. He should see Double-A in 2021.

Year	Age	Club (League)	Class	AVG	G	AB	R	H	2B	3B	HR	RBI	BB	SO	SB	OBP	SLG
2019	21	Jupiter (FSL)	HiA	.253	67	253	27	64	10	1	6	28	17	71	3	.298	.372
	21	Clinton (MWL)	LoA	.298	68	255	34	76	16	0	10	43	23	69	3	.363	.478
Minor League Totals				.261	250	954	125	249	49	7	26	130	60	282	10	.309	.409

19 GRIFFIN CONINE, OF

BA GRADE
45 Risk: High

Born: July 11, 1997. **B-T:** L-R. **HT:** 6-1. **WT:** 213. **Drafted:** Duke, 2018 (2nd round). **Signed by:** Jason Beverlin (Blue Jays).

TRACK RECORD: The son of "Mr. Marlin" Jeff Conine joined his father's former team when the Blue Jays traded him to the Marlins for Jonathan Villar at the 2020 trade deadline. Conine was suspended for 50 games after testing positive for the stimulant ritalinic acid the previous year, but still led the low Class A Midwest League with 22 home runs despite playing just 80 games.

SCOUTING REPORT: Conine has used his quick bat and plus raw power to display plus power to all fields at every stop. The amount he swings and misses is alarming, however, with a 36% strikeout rate against low Class A competition. Conine primarily struggles when pitchers attack him up in the zone. He did show improvement during instructional league in 2020, but he still projects as a fringe-average hitter, at best. Conine is a below-average runner but covers enough ground to be an average defender in right field.

THE FUTURE: Conine will be challenged by better pitching in 2021. How he handles it will determine if he can hit enough to be an everyday major leaguer.

Year	Age	Club (League)	Class	AVG	G	AB	R	H	2B	3B	HR	RBI	BB	SO	SB	OBP	SLG
2019	21	Lansing (MWL)	LoA	.283	80	304	59	86	19	2	22	64	38	125	2	.371	.576
Minor League Totals				.266	137	518	84	138	34	4	29	97	58	190	7	.348	.515

20 NASIM NUNEZ, SS

BA GRADE
50 Risk: Extreme

Born: Aug. 18, 2000. **B-T:** B-R. **HT:** 5-9. **WT:** 158. **Drafted:** HS—Suwanee, Ga. 2019 (2nd round). **Signed by:** Christian Castorri.

TRACK RECORD: One of the top defensive shortstops in the 2019 draft, Nunez was taken 46th overall by the Marlins and signed for $2.2 million. The Marlins brought him to their alternate training site in 2020 and he continued to see game action at instructional league in the fall.

SCOUTING REPORT: Nunez's defensive skills and instincts at shortstop are advanced. His plus speed gives him plenty of range and his plus arm makes him a lock to stay at the position. He has a tendency to make highlight-worthy plays. Nunez makes contact at the plate but his power is well below-average and limits his ability to impact the ball. He struggled primarily against righthanders during his first pro action. Nunez shows a patient approach and uses his speed to steal bases when he gets on, but he has a long way to go to be an average hitter. The Marlins expect him to develop more offensive consistency and impact the ball solidly to all fields as he matures.

THE FUTURE: Already considered one of the top defensive shortstops in the organization, Nunez's offensive development will determine whether he becomes an everyday shortstop.

Year	Age	Club (League)	Class	AVG	G	AB	R	H	2B	3B	HR	RBI	BB	SO	SB	OBP	SLG
2019	18	Marlins (GCL)	R	.211	48	175	37	37	5	1	0	12	34	43	28	.340	.251
	18	Batavia (NYP)	SS	.000	3	10	1	0	0	0	0	0	1	5	0	.091	.000
Minor League Totals				.200	51	185	38	37	5	1	0	12	35	48	28	.327	.238

21 JOSE SALAS, SS

BREAKOUT
BA GRADE
50 Risk: Extreme

Born: April 26, 2003. **B-T:** B-R. **HT:** 6-2. **WT:** 191. **Signed:** Venezuela, 2019. **Signed by:** Fernando Seguignol.

TRACK RECORD: Salas grew up in Orlando, Fla., but moved to Venezuela before high school and signed with the Marlins for $2.8 million during the 2019 international signing period. His father, uncle and grandfather all played pro ball in Venezuela. The Marlins planned for Salas to begin his career in the Rookie-level Gulf Coast League, but he was limited to instructional league in 2020 after the coronavirus pandemic wiped out the minor league season.

SCOUTING REPORT: A fast-twitch athlete with plus speed and an above-average arm, Salas has raw defensive tools that will play well at shortstop. He has a projectable frame that gives him a chance to add strength and power at the plate, although scouts feel he needs to develop more consistency and fluidity in his swing as he matures. Salas has a chance to hit for average and possesses average power, but he's a long way from fulfilling those projections.

THE FUTURE: Salas will make his pro debut in 2021. His offensive development will determine whether he becomes an everyday shortstop.

Year	Age	Club (League)	Class	AVG	G	AB	R	H	2B	3B	HR	RBI	BB	SO	SB	OBP	SLG
2019	16	Did not play—Signed 2020 contract															

22 JORGE GUZMAN, RHP

BA GRADE
45 Risk: High

Born: Jan. 28, 1996. **B-T:** R-R. **HT:** 6-2. **WT:** 246. **Signed:** Dominican Republic, 2014. **Signed by:** Oz Ocampo/Ramon Ocumarez/Francis Mojica (Astros).

TRACK RECORD: Guzman signed with the Astros for $22,500 in 2014. He has been traded twice, first to the Yankees in the Brian McCann deal and later to the Marlins in the Giancarlo Stanton deal. Guzman made a brief yet forgettable major league debut in 2020 when he gave up a pair of home runs and walked a batter in one inning of relief.

SCOUTING REPORT: Guzman has a solid delivery that produces a lot of velocity and a downhill plane, but has struggled with timing issues and thus below-average control. His double-plus fastball is consistently in the 96-98 mph range and tops 100 mph. Guzman learned to locate it better up in the zone at Double-A Jacksonville and developed his slider, which breaks hard and down to the plate. His changeup is an average pitch. Guzman struggled with command and control of all three pitches in his short major league stint and must find a way to achieve consistency.

THE FUTURE: Guzman has a chance to be a hard-throwing reliever but will need to improve his control. He should return to the Marlins at some point in 2021.

Year	Age	Club (League)	Class	W	L	ERA	G	GS	IP	H	HR	BB	SO	BB/9	SO/9	WHIP	AVG
2020	24	Miami (NL)	MAJ	0	0	18.00	1	0	1	2	2	1	0	9.0	0.0	3.00	.400
Major League Totals				0	0	18.00	1	0	1	2	2	1	0	9.0	0.0	3.00	.400
Minor League Totals				18	31	3.70	89	78	396	323	27	200	399	4.5	9.1	1.32	.223

23 ZACH MCCAMBLEY, RHP

BA GRADE
45 Risk: High

Born: May 4, 1999. **B-T:** L-R. **HT:** 6-2. **WT:** 220. **Drafted:** Coastal Carolina, 2020 (3rd round). **Signed by:** Blake Newsome.

TRACK RECORD: Undrafted out of high school because of a knee injury, McCambley pitched both as a starter and reliever at Coastal Carolina. He impressed with a 1.74 ERA in the Cape Cod League the summer before his junior year and carried it through the abbreviated 2020 college season. The Marlins drafted him in the third round and signed him for $775,000.

SCOUTING REPORT: McCambley has a deceptive delivery and fast-paced tempo on the mound. His fastball sits 92-94 mph and can touch 96 mph, and his ability to improve his command will determine whether it becomes a plus offering. He throws a plus curveball with a high spin rate and bite in the upper-70s. The lack of a third pitch has many scouts believing McCambley will be a high-leverage reliever instead of a starter in the majors. His fringe-average control further points to a relief future.

THE FUTURE: McCambley will remain a starter for now. How much he develops a third pitch and improves his control will determine if he stays there.

Year	Age	Club (League)	Class	W	L	ERA	G	GS	IP	H	HR	BB	SO	BB/9	SO/9	WHIP	AVG
2020	21	Did not play—No minor league season															

24 EVAN FITTERER, RHP

Born: June 26, 2000. **B-T:** R-R. **HT:** 6-3. **WT:** 192. **Drafted:** HS—Aliso Viejo, Calif., 2019 (5th round). **Signed by:** Eric Brock.

TRACK RECORD: The Marlins swayed Fitterer from his UCLA commitment with an above-slot $1.5 million signing bonus as a fifth-round pick in 2019. He made his pro debut in the Rookie-level Gulf Coast League and impressed with a 2.38 ERA. The Marlins brought him to their alternate training site in 2020.

SCOUTING REPORT: Fitterer has four pitches that all project as average or better offerings. His fastball sits 91-94 mph with solid sink and cut that induces ground balls consistently. He complements it with an upper-70s curveball that could become a plus pitch in time, as well as a sharp slider that has solid separation from his curveball and an average changeup with good sink. He ties it all together with average control and a polished delivery.

THE FUTURE: Fitterer projects as a possible mid-to-back-of-the-rotation starter. He still has a long way to go and will make his full-season debut in 2021.

Year	Age	Club (League)	Class	W	L	ERA	G	GS	IP	H	HR	BB	SO	BB/9	SO/9	WHIP	AVG
2019	19	Marlins (GCL)	R	0	1	2.38	9	8	23	20	1	12	19	4.8	7.5	1.41	.190
Minor League Totals				0	1	2.38	9	8	22	20	1	12	19	4.8	7.5	1.41	.233

25 JORDAN HOLLOWAY, RHP

Born: June 13, 1996. **B-T:** R-R. **HT:** 6-6. **WT:** 230. **Drafted:** HS—Arvada, Colo., 2014 (20th round). **Signed by:** Scott Stanley.

TRACK RECORD: Holloway signed for $400,000 in 2014 but didn't advance past low Class A for his first five years due largely to injuries, including Tommy John surgery in 2017. He returned and vaulted all the way to the majors in 2020, but his stint was cut short after one appearance when he contracted Covid-19 early in the season.

SCOUTING REPORT: The Marlins remain high on Holloway despite his struggles with consistent fastball command. He possesses a plus fastball that sits 96-97 mph and can exceed 100 mph. He has worked to limit excess movement and simplify his delivery in order to improve his control. He has a plus curveball he also struggles to land in the zone and a changeup that is a usable but fringy offering.

THE FUTURE: Holloway is likely bound to be a reliever. He'll need to improve his consistency and control to stick in a major league bullpen.

Year	Age	Club (League)	Class	W	L	ERA	G	GS	IP	H	HR	BB	SO	BB/9	SO/9	WHIP	AVG
2020	24	Miami (NL)	MAJ	0	0	0.00	1	0	0	2	0	1	0	27.0	0.0	9.00	.667
Major League Totals				0	0	0.00	1	0	0	2	0	1	0	27.0	0.0	9.00	.667
Minor League Totals				13	30	4.64	76	72	304	280	24	166	245	4.9	7.3	1.47	.242

26 DANIEL CASTANO, LHP

BA GRADE
40 Risk: Medium

Born: Sept. 17, 1994. **B-T:** L-L. **HT:** 6-3. **WT:** 231. **Drafted:** Baylor, 2016 (19th round). **Signed by:** Ralph Garr Jr. (Cardinals).

TRACK RECORD: The Cardinals drafted Castano in the 19th round in 2016 and signed him for $130,000. They traded him to the Marlins in the deal for Marcell Ozuna. While many thought of Castano as a throw-in player in the trade, he became one of the surprises of the 2020 season. He made his major league debut in August and made six starts and one relief appearance, finishing with a 3.03 ERA in 29.2 innings.

SCOUTING REPORT: Castano will never light up the radar gun with his fastball, but he attacks the zone and throws all four of his pitches with good movement and average to above-average control. His fastball is fringe-average, sitting 89-90 mph and touching 93 mph. Castano mixes in a changeup, cutter and a slider, the latter of which has above-average potential. Castano is hardly dominating on the mound, but he knows how to set hitters up and stays out of the middle of the plate.

TRACK RECORD: As a lefthander with at least average control, Castano could earn a sustained role either as a low-leverage reliever or fill-in starter in the coming years.

Year	Age	Club (League)	Class	W	L	ERA	G	GS	IP	H	HR	BB	SO	BB/9	SO/9	WHIP	AVG
2020	25	Miami (NL)	MAJ	1	2	3.03	7	6	30	30	3	11	12	3.3	3.6	1.38	.263
Major League Totals				1	2	3.03	7	6	29	30	3	11	12	3.3	3.6	1.38	.263
Minor League Totals				27	24	3.76	80	59	393	418	26	76	335	1.7	7.7	1.26	.270

27 WILL BANFIELD, C

BA GRADE
45 Risk: Very High

Born: Nov. 18, 1999. **B-T:** R-R. **HT:** 6-1. **WT:** 207. **Drafted:** HS—Snellville, Ga., 2018 (2nd round). **Signed by:** Christian Castorri.

TRACK RECORD: Considered the top high school defensive catcher in the 2018 draft, Banfield was drafted 69th overall by the Marlins and signed for an above-slot for $1.8 million. He hit just .199/.252/.310 at low Class A Clinton in his first full season, but he showed enough defensive tools for the Marlins to bring him to their alternate training site in 2020.

SCOUTING REPORT: Banfield is a defense-only catcher who will have to ride his glove to the majors. He has above-average receiving and blocking skills and a plus arm that helped him throw out 46% of attempted basestealers during his first full season in the minors. Banfield showed an improved offensive approach at the alternate training site and flashes above-average power when he finds the barrel, but his swing is grooved and he often gets into bad counts.

THE FUTURE: Banfield has drawn comparisons to Austin Hedges as a gifted defender who won't hit enough to play every day. How his offense progresses will determine if he becomes a major leaguer at all.

Year	Age	Club (League)	Class	AVG	G	AB	R	H	2B	3B	HR	RBI	BB	SO	SB	OBP	SLG
2019	19	Clinton (MWL)	LoA	.199	101	397	44	79	13	2	9	55	25	121	0	.252	.310
Minor League Totals				.209	140	527	56	110	21	3	12	73	36	164	0	.266	.328

28 VICTOR MESA JR., OF

Born: Sept. 8, 2001. **B-T:** L-L. **HT:** 6-0. **WT:** 187. **Signed:** Cuba, 2018. **Signed by:** Fernando Seguignol.

TRACK RECORD: Mesa Jr. signed with the Marlins for $1 million in 2018 at the same time as his more famous brother, Victor Victor Mesa. He's outperformed his brother so far in pro ball, batting .284/.366/.398 in his pro debut in the Rookie-level Gulf Coast League and showing advanced skills for his age.

SCOUTING REPORT: With a smooth swing from the left side and a solid approach to the middle of the field, Mesa Jr. has displayed an above-average hit tool with sneaky power that could increase in time. He has shown an ability to make consistent contact and can still add bulk and strength to his swing, which generates good bat speed despite a tendency to open his front side much too early. Mesa Jr. has shown good instincts at all three outfield spots and has above-average arm strength. His average speed has been enough to track balls down in center field for now, but he projects to move to right field as he matures.

THE FUTURE: Mesa Jr.'s well-rounded game gives him a solid foundation. He'll make his full-season debut in 2021.

Year	Age	Club (League)	Class	AVG	G	AB	R	H	2B	3B	HR	RBI	BB	SO	SB	OBP	SLG
2019	17	Marlins (GCL)	R	.284	47	176	39	50	9	4	1	24	24	29	7	.366	.398
Minor League Totals				.284	47	176	39	50	9	4	1	24	24	29	7	.366	.398

29 JAKE EDER, LHP

Born: Oct. 9, 1998. **B-T:** L-L. **HT:** 6-4. **WT:** 215. **Drafted:** Vanderbilt, 2020 (4th round). **Signed by:** JT Zink.

TRACK RECORD: Eder was one of Vanderbilt's top relievers during its run to the College World Series championship in 2019. He moved to the rotation in 2020 and showed the ability to miss bats in his four starts before the coronavirus pandemic shut down the season, but also a proclivity for walks. The Marlins drafted Eder in the fourth round, signed him for $700,000 and sent him to the alternate training site.

SCOUTING REPORT: Eder has the size and smooth delivery of a starter, but his stuff and control lack consistency. His velocity fluctuates between 89-92 mph and 90-94 mph, which affects his results depending on what he has that day. Eder's curveball is potentially a plus pitch with good break, and his changeup could become at least an average offering in time. Eder has flashed average control in spurts, but pitches more with fringe-average control over the long haul.

THE FUTURE: The Marlins will have Eder work as a starter initially. Whether he stays there will be determined by his ability to be more consistent with his stuff and control.

Year	Age	Club (League)	Class	W	L	ERA	G	GS	IP	H	HR	BB	SO	BB/9	SO/9	WHIP	AVG
2020	21	Did not play—No minor league season															

30 VICTOR VICTOR MESA, OF

BA GRADE
40 **Risk: High**

Born: July 20, 1996. **B-T:** R-R. **HT:** 5-11. **WT:** 185. **Signed:** Cuba, 2018.
Signed by: Fernando Seguignol.

TRACK RECORD: Mesa played six seasons of Cuban baseball before defecting along with his younger brother, Victor Jr., and signing with the Marlins for $5.25 million in 2018. Mesa reached Double-A in his first full season, but put together an underwhelming .235/.274/.263 slash line while showing a concerning lack of tools. He spent 2020 at the Marlins' alternate training site.

SCOUTING REPORT: Mesa struggles to hit the ball with any kind of impact. He often opens up too early and commits his lower half, which robs him of the leverage to generate lift. He has well below-average power and hits the ball on the ground more than 60% of the time. Mesa doesn't swing and miss too often, but he doesn't hit the ball hard enough to be more than a below-average hitter. Mesa flashes plus speed and arm strength in the outfield, but never seems to put it all quite together. He is a base-stealing threat and tracks balls effectively at all three outfield spots.

THE FUTURE: Mesa still hasn't shown he's capable of hitting at higher levels. Cuban signees often face an adjustment period, and the Marlins hope his struggles were merely a product of that trend.

Year	Age	Club (League)	Class	AVG	G	AB	R	H	2B	3B	HR	RBI	BB	SO	SB	OBP	SLG
2019	22	Jupiter (FSL)	HiA	.252	89	357	37	90	5	3	0	26	19	48	15	.295	.283
	22	Jacksonville (SL)	AA	.178	27	107	8	19	2	0	0	3	3	16	3	.200	.196
Minor League Totals				.235	116	464	45	109	7	3	0	29	22	64	18	.274	.263

MORE PROSPECTS TO KNOW

31 BREIDY ENCARNACION, RHP

The 6-foot-3, 185-pound righthander possesses an above-average fastball, a potentially plus curveball and average to above-average changeup. His stuff and smooth delivery could make him a quick riser.

32 OSIRIS JOHNSON, SS

Johnson missed all of 2019 after surgery to repair a stress fracture in his right leg. The 20-year-old cousin of Jimmy Rollins has above-average defensive skills and enough power to project as a productive middle infielder.

33 CHRIS MOKMA, RHP

Mokma is a projectable righthaner with a ceiling as a middle-of-the-rotation starter. He has a solid, repeatable delivery and a low-90s fastball that should add more velocity as he grows into his athletic frame.

34 BRIAN MILLER, OF

Miller hit for a high average at every level until he reached Double-A Jacksonville in late 2018. He profiles as a contact hitter with low swing-and-miss rates and plus speed who can contribute as a bench player.

35 DIOWILL BURGOS, OF

Acquired from the Cardinals for Austin Dean, Burgos has shown flashes of power potential and profiles in right field with his above-average arm strength, but he'll have to cut down on his strikeouts.

36 EURY PEREZ, RHP

SLEEPER

A tall, lanky righthander signed out of the Dominican Republic for $200,000 in 2019, Perez creates easy power with a smooth delivery for a 17-year-old. He possesses a fastball that sits 93-96 mph and should increase in velocity substantially as he fills out.

37 ALEX VESIA, LHP

Vesia jumped from Double-A Jacksonville to the majors in 2020 and struggled. He still projects as a solid lefthanded reliever with his 91-93 mph fastball and promising slider.

38 WILL STEWART, LHP

Stewart's velocity dipped noticeably in 2019, leading to a 5.43 ERA at high Class A Jupiter. He still showed flashes of an average slider that misses bats, giving him a chance to rise if his velocity returns.

39 LUIS PALACIOS, LHP

The Venezuelan lefthander went 13-0, 1.49 over three seasons at the Rookie levels. He will make the jump to full-season ball in 2020.

40 DALVY ROSARIO, SS/3B

Rosario draws positive reviews for his athleticism and power potential. He's still learning to turn those raw tools into production.

TOP PROSPECTS OF THE DECADE

Year	Player, Pos	2020 Org
2011	Matt Dominguez, 3B	Did not play
2012	Christian Yelich, OF	Brewers
2013	Jose Fernandez, RHP	Deceased
2014	Andrew Heaney, LHP	Angels
2015	Tyler Kolek, RHP	Marlins
2016	Tyler Kolek, RHP	Marlins
2017	Braxton Garrett, LHP	Marlins
2018	Sandy Alcantara, RHP	Marlins
2019	Victor Victor Mesa, OF	Marlins
2020	Sixto Sanchez, RHP	Marlins

TOP DRAFT PICKS OF THE DECADE

Year	Player, Pos	2020 Org
2011	Jose Fernandez, RHP	Deceased
2012	Andrew Heaney, LHP	Angels
2013	Colin Moran, 3B	Pirates
2014	Tyler Kolek, RHP	Marlins
2015	Josh Naylor, 1B	Indians
2016	Braxton Garrett, LHP	Marlins
2017	Trevor Rogers, LHP	Marlins
2018	Connor Scott, OF	Marlins
2019	JJ Bleday, OF	Marlins
2020	Max Meyer, RHP	Marlins

DEPTH CHART

MIAMI MARLINS

TOP 2021 ROOKIES	RANK
JJ Bleday, OF	2
Edward Cabrera, RHP	5
BREAKOUT PROSPECTS	**RANK**
Peyton Burdick, OF	16
Jose Salas, SS	21
Kyle Nicolas, RHP	17

SOURCE OF TOP 30 TALENT

Homegrown	20	Acquired	10
College	7	Trade	10
Junior College	0	Rule 5 Draft	0
High School	8	Independent League	0
Nondrafted Free Agent	0	Free Agent/Waivers	0
International	5		

LF

Jesus Sanchez (8)
Peyton Burdick (16)
Victor Victor Mesa (30)
Brian Miller
J.D. Orr

CF

Monte Harrison (11)
Kameron Misner (13)
Connor Scott (14)

RF

JJ Bleday (2)
Jerar Encarnacion (18)
Griffin Conine (19)
Victor Mesa Jr. (28)
Diowill Burgos

3B

Jose Salas (21)
Joe Dunand
Nic Ready

SS

Jazz Chisholm (4)
Jose Devers (10)
Nasim Nunez (20)
Osiris Johnson
Dalvy Rosario
Ian Lewis
Junior Sanchez

2B

Christopher Torres
Riley Mahan
Bryson Brigman

1B

Lewin Diaz (7)
Evan Edwards
Lazaro Alonso
Sean Reynolds

C

Will Banfield (27)
Nick Fortes

LHP

LHSP

Trevor Rogers (6)
Braxton Garrett (9)
Dax Fulton (12)
Daniel Castano (26)
Will Stewart
Luis Palacios

LHRP

Jake Eder (29)
Alex Vesia
Dylan Lee
Sean Guenther
Andrew Nardi

RHP

RHSP

Sixto Sanchez (1)
Max Meyer (3)
Edward Cabrera (5)
Nick Neidert (15)
Kyle Nicolas (17)
Zach McCambley (23)
Evan Fitterer (24)
Paul Campbell
Breidy Encarnacion
Chris Mokma
Eury Perez

RHRP

Jorge Guzman (22)
Jordan Holloway (25)
Tommy Eveld

Milwaukee Brewers

BY BEN BADLER

The Brewers didn't spend a day above .500 in 2020, but the expanded playoffs allowed them to sneak into the postseason.

They exited quickly with a 2-0 sweep at the hands of the Dodgers, but it marked the third straight playoff appearance for the Brewers under president of baseball operations David Stearns and Matt Arnold, who after the season was promoted to general manager.

After the first years of consecutive playoff appearances for the organization since 1981 and '82, where do the Brewers go from here?

Milwaukee entered 2020 with the worst farm system in baseball. That's no longer the case, but the minor league pipeline is still thin on upper-level players who will be ready to contribute in 2021, aside from relievers like Drew Rasmussen and Justin Topa, who made their debuts last season.

The standouts of the system are a trio of position players in the middle of the diamond, starting with shortstop Brice Turang. He's the organization's top prospect, an advanced pure hitter for his age with good strike-zone judgement.

Center fielder Garrett Mitchell has more questions about his hitting ability, but he possesses one of the better tool sets in the minors coming out of UCLA as the Brewers' first-round pick in 2020.

The third potential impact position player in the system is center fielder Hedbert Perez, a 17-year-old Venezuelan with an exciting combination of tools and skills, though he has yet to play an official game in pro ball.

Turang, Perez and the Brewers' other lefthanded hitters got a stiff test against the team's lefty-heavy pitching group at the alternate training site, including Antoine Kelly, Ethan Small, Aaron Ashby and reliever Angel Perdomo. Kelly was the star of the group, improving his stock to the point where he could be a future Top 100 Prospects candidate.

The Brewers have an intriguing group of international prospects at the lower levels from their recent Venezuelan-heavy signing classes, including catcher Jeferson Quero and shortstop Eduardo Garcia. But there is a hole in the upper level of the system, particularly for hitting prospects who project to be average or better regulars, which sticks out relative to other organizations.

That's an especially challenging problem for the Brewers if they want to return to the playoffs in 2021. The club ranked 26th in the majors in runs scored in 2020.

While they lost Yasmani Grandal, Eric Thames and Mike Moustakas coming into the 2020 season, declines in offensive production from Christian Yelich, Ryan Braun and Keston Hiura added to the pain. It's reasonable to believe that Yelich and Hiura can rebound, but that lack of upper-level hitting prospects means the Brewers will need to find other ways to bolster their 2021 lineup.

The Brewers' minor league pipeline is in a better position than it was, but it remains a bottom-third system, with their major league club in a middle tier after a string of playoff appearances.

It will take shrewd moves for the Brewers to make it four in a row—or a reset to bolster their young talent in 2021 and try to contend again in 2022. ■

DYLAN BUELL/GETTY IMAGES

The Brewers will need a rebound from second baseman Keston Hiura if they want to contend.

PROJECTED 2024 LINEUP

Position	Player	Age
Catcher	Jacob Nottingham	29
First Base	Keston Hiura	27
Second Base	Brice Turang	24
Third Base	Luis Urias	27
Shortstop	Orlando Arcia	29
Left Field	Christian Yelich	32
Center Field	Garrett Mitchell	25
Right Field	Hedbert Perez	21
Designated Hitter	Daniel Vogelbach	31
No. 1 Starter	Brandon Woodruff	31
No. 2 Starter	Corbin Burnes	29
No. 3 Starter	Antoine Kelly	24
No. 4 Starter	Adrian Houser	31
No. 5 Starter	Ethan Small	27
Closer	Devin Williams	29

1 BRICE TURANG, SS

Born: Nov. 21, 1999. **B-T:** L-R. **HT:** 6-0. **WT:** 175.
Drafted: HS—Corona, Calif., 2018 (1st round).
Signed by: Wynn Pelzer.

BILL MITCHELL

BA GRADE
55 **Risk: High**

SCOUTING GRADES
Hit: 60. **Power:** 40. **Run:** 60. **Field:** 50. **Arm:** 50.

Projected future grades on 20-80 scouting scale.

TRACK RECORD: Turang became well known in scouting circles early in his high school years after playing for USA Baseball's 15U National Team in 2014. The son of former Mariners outfielder Brian Turang, he put himself in the conversation among the top prep hitters in the country after winning a gold medal with Team USA and making the all-tournament team at the U-18 World Cup in 2017. Turang didn't quite meet the expectations scouts had for him as a high school senior and slid down the first round to the Brewers, who drafted him 21st overall and signed him for $3.411 million. In his first full season in 2019, Turang hit well in the low Class A Midwest League, though he struggled after a promotion to high Class A Carolina as a 19-year-old. With the 2020 season wiped out due to the coronavirus pandemic, Turang reported to the team's alternate training site in Appleton, Wis., where he was the Brewers' best hitter and started to drive the ball with more impact.

SCOUTING REPORT: Turang consistently puts together quality at-bats with his sharp eye for the strike zone and sweet lefthanded swing. He's a patient hitter who doesn't chase much off the plate. He has a calm, balanced swing with good bat-to-ball skills and stays through the ball, leading to an all-fields, line-drive approach. The knock on Turang coming into 2020 was his well below-average power, which got exposed once the Brewers promoted him to the Carolina League. Turang did a better job of driving the ball with more authority in Appleton. The Brewers kept an internal "barrel" board of hitters with exit velocities of 95 mph or better at the alternate site, and Turang was consistently among the leaders throughout the summer. Turang didn't change his swing, but he added strength and adjusted his approach in favorable counts to drive the ball for more damage. He still doesn't project as a big power threat, but evaluators now think 15-20 home runs in his prime is feasible. Turang is a plus runner who has good instincts on the basepaths. He has a solid chance to stay at shortstop, where his hands and feet work well. He's adept at charging in on the ball and ranging toward second base, and he has worked to improve his throws from the hole with his average arm strength.

THE FUTURE: If Turang can continue to show the uptick in his hard-hit rate, he has the components to be an on-base threat who can hit toward the top of a lineup. After what he showed at the alternate training site, he should be ready to jump to Double-A in 2021. ■

BEST TOOLS

Best Hitter for Average	Brice Turang
Best Power Hitter	Mario Feliciano
Best Strike-Zone Discipline	Brice Turang
Fastest Baserunner	Garrett Mitchell
Best Athlete	Garrett Mitchell
Best Fastball	Drew Rasmussen
Best Curveball	Aaron Ashby
Best Slider	Antoine Kelly
Best Changeup	Ethan Small
Best Control	Dylan File
Best Defensive Catcher	Payton Henry
Best Defensive Infielder	Freddy Zamora
Best Infield Arm	Eduardo Garcia
Best Defensive Outfielder	Garrett Mitchell
Best Outfield Arm	Joey Wiemer

Year	Age	Club (League)	Class	AVG	G	AB	R	H	2B	3B	HR	RBI	BB	SO	SB	OBP	SLG
2018	18	Brewers (AZL)	R	.319	13	47	11	15	2	0	0	7	9	6	8	.421	.362
	18	Helena (PIO)	R	.268	29	112	26	30	4	1	1	11	22	28	6	.385	.348
2019	19	Wisconsin (MWL)	LoA	.287	82	303	57	87	13	4	2	31	49	54	21	.384	.376
	19	Carolina (CAR)	HiA	.200	47	170	25	34	6	2	1	6	34	47	9	.338	.276
Minor League Totals				.263	171	632	119	166	25	7	4	55	114	135	44	.374	.343

2 GARRETT MITCHELL, OF

Born: Sept. 4, 1998. **B-T:** L-R. **HT:** 6-3. **WT:** 215. **Drafted:** UCLA, 2020 (1st round). **Signed by:** Daniel Cho/Corey Rodriguez.

DON LIEBIG/ASUCL

BA GRADE
60 **Risk: Extreme**

TRACK RECORD: Mitchell hit .349/.418/.566 as a sophomore at UCLA in 2019 and led the nation with 12 triples. He was off to a strong start in 2020 and had arguably the best pure tools in the draft class, but concerns about his Type 1 diabetes were among the reasons he fell on draft day. He fell to the Brewers at No. 20 overall and signed for $3,242,900. Mitchell made his organizational debut in instructional league, though a strained quad limited his time.

SCOUTING REPORT: A physical, explosive athlete, Mitchell is an 80 runner on the 20-80 scouting scale. He covers huge swaths of ground in center field, where he projects as a plus defender with a plus arm. Mitchell's offensive approach was built around his speed at UCLA. There's some choppiness to his swing, which is geared to hit low line drives and use his wheels to stretch out extra-base hits. Mitchell shows plus raw power in batting practice, but his approach limits his ability to apply it in games. Mitchell has worked on getting his lower half more engaged in his swing to try to do more damage, but it remains to be seen how much power he will be able to unlock.

THE FUTURE: Mitchell can be a polarizing player, but if he can translate his power into games, he has all-star upside. He'll make his pro debut in 2021.

SCOUTING GRADES: **Hitting:** 55 **Power:** 55 **Running:** 80 **Fielding:** 60 **Arm:** 60

Year	Age	Club (League)	Class	AVG	G	AB	R	H	2B	3B	HR	RBI	BB	SO	SB	OBP	SLG
2020	21	Did not play—No minor league season															

3 HEDBERT PEREZ, OF

Born: April 4, 2003. **B-T:** L-L. **HT:** 5-11. **WT:** 180. **Signed:** Venezuela, 2019. **Signed by:** Reinaldo Hidalgo.

BA GRADE
60 **Risk: Extreme**

TRACK RECORD: Perez is the son of former major league outfielder Robert Perez and trained with his father before signing with the Brewers for $700,000 in 2019. His impressive blend of athleticism, tools and advanced baseball skills gave the Brewers confidence to push him to the alternate training site in 2020 as a 17-year-old, making him the youngest player on any 60-man player pool. He held his own there and was one of the Brewers' top performers at instructional league in the fall.

SCOUTING REPORT: Perez could soon be the top prospect in the organization. He has a fast, easy and efficient swing from the left side with strong bat-to-ball skills and a firm grasp of the strike zone. He has at least above-average raw power and could develop more with continued physical growth. Perez has added considerable muscle the past couple of years and is a plus runner with quick acceleration in center field. He reads balls well off the bat and takes efficient routes for a 17-year-old. His strong arm is another plus tool. He's also a fluent English speaker whose maturity and charismatic personality endear him to teammates and coaches.

THE FUTURE: Perez has a chance to be an impact player at a premium position. He's still a teenager who has yet to make his pro debut, but he could be a fast riser through the system.

SCOUTING GRADES: **Hitting:** 60 **Power:** 55 **Running:** 60 **Fielding:** 55 **Arm:** 60

Year	Age	Club (League)	Class	AVG	G	AB	R	H	2B	3B	HR	RBI	BB	SO	SB	OBP	SLG
2020	17	Did not play—No minor league season															

4 ANTOINE KELLY, LHP

BA GRADE
55 Risk: Very High

Born: Dec. 5, 1999. **B-T:** L-L. **HT:** 6-6. **WT:** 205. **Drafted:** Wabash Valley (Ill.) JC, 2019 (2nd round). **Signed by:** Harvey Kuenn Jr.

TRACK RECORD: Kelly led all junior college pitchers with 19.1 strikeouts per nine innings for Wabash Valley (Ill.) JC in 2019 and was drafted by the Brewers in the second round. He signed for $1,025,100 and continued to rack up whiffs with 45 strikeouts in 31.2 innings in his pro debut, which was concentrated in the Rookie-level Arizona League. Despite only one career start above the Rookie level, Kelly was the most electric pitcher at the team's alternate training site in Appleton, Wis., in 2020.

SCOUTING REPORT: Kelly has a big 6-foot-6 frame and continues gaining velocity each year. A low-90s pitcher in high school, Kelly sat 93-97 mph leading up to the draft and started touching 98 over 60-pitch outings in Appleton. Kelly previously relied almost wholly on his fastball, but his secondary stuff ticked up in 2020. His slider is a plus pitch that misses bats, and when his changeup is on it flashes at least average. Kelly throws strikes with all three pitches, though he needs to tighten his fastball command. He's slow to the plate from the stretch and needs to do a better job holding runners.

THE FUTURE: Kelly took a jump in 2020 and has the attributes to develop into a mid-rotation or better starter. He looks poised for a breakout 2021 campaign.

SCOUTING GRADES: **Fastball:** 60 **Slider:** 60 **Changeup:** 50 **Control:** 50

Year	Age	Club (League)	Class	W	L	ERA	G	GS	IP	H	HR	BB	SO	BB/9	K/9	WHIP	AVG
2019	19	Brewers (AZL)	R	0	0	1.26	9	9	29	21	0	5	41	1.6	12.9	0.91	.208
2019	19	Wisconsin (MWL)	LoA	0	1	18.00	1	1	3	5	2	4	4	12.0	12.0	3.00	.417
Minor League Totals				0	1	2.84	10	10	32	26	2	9	45	2.6	12.8	1.11	.230

5 ETHAN SMALL, LHP

ADAM GLANZMAN/MLB PHOTOS VIA GETTY IMAGES

BA GRADE
50 Risk: High

Born: Feb. 14, 1997. **B-T:** L-L. **HT:** 6-3. **WT:** 215. **Drafted:** Mississippi State, 2019 (1st round). **Signed by:** Scott Nichols.

TRACK RECORD: Small had Tommy John surgery at Mississippi State but bounced back to lead the Southeastern Conference in strikeouts and rank second in ERA as a redshirt junior in 2019. The performance vaulted him into the first round, where the Brewers drafted him 28th overall and signed him for $1.8 million. Small breezed through five starts at low Class A Wisconsin and spent 2020 at the Brewers' alternate training site in Appleton, Wis.

SCOUTING REPORT: Small relies on his polish, deception and pitchability. His fastball sits at 89-93 mph and touches 94. It plays up with riding life and is aided by his ability to throw it for strikes to all quadrants of the strike zone. Small hides the ball and messes with hitters' timing by varying his leg lift and tempo in his delivery. His slightly above-average changeup is his best offspeed weapon and plays well off his fastball to generate empty swings or weak contact. Small throws a curveball and added a slider to his mix in 2020, but sharpening his breaking stuff is a focal point. Neither one is average, though his feel for pitching is so good he probably won't be tested until he gets to Double-A.

THE FUTURE: Small's polish is evident and he should move quickly in 2021. He projects as a starter who fits toward the back of a rotation.

SCOUTING GRADES: **Fastball:** 50 **Slider:** 45 **Curveball:** 45 **Changeup:** 55 **Control:** 60

Year	Age	Club (League)	Class	W	L	ERA	G	GS	IP	H	HR	BB	SO	BB/9	K/9	WHIP	AVG
2019	22	Brewers Gold (AZL)	R	0	0	0.00	2	2	3	0	0	0	5	0.0	15.0	0.00	.000
	22	Wisconsin (MWL)	LoA	0	2	1.00	5	5	18	11	0	4	31	2.0	15.5	0.83	.172
Minor League Totals				0	2	0.86	7	7	21	11	0	4	36	1.7	15.4	0.71	.151

6 FREDDY ZAMORA, SS

Born: Nov. 1, 1998. **B-T:** R-R. **HT:** 6-1. **WT:** 190. **Drafted:** Miami, 2020 (2nd round). **Signed by:** Lazaro Llanes.

BA GRADE

55 Risk: Extreme

TRACK RECORD: Zamora entered the 2020 season at Miami considered one of college baseball's top shortstops, but during a preseason practice he suffered a torn anterior cruciate ligament that erased his junior year. Still, the Brewers drafted Zamora in the second round, No. 53 overall, and signed him for $1.15 million. Zamora was still rehabbing throughout the fall and did not play in instructional league.

SCOUTING REPORT: Zamora has the tools to be a plus defender at shortstop, where he has soft hands, solid range and a slightly above-average arm. He was error-prone as a sophomore, so he needs to improve his reliability at the position. An above-average runner, Zamora shows his best tools on the defensive side, but he's a steady hitter with fringe-average raw power who controls the strike zone well. He walked more often than he struck out in each of his two seasons at Miami. He has strong baserunning instincts.

THE FUTURE: Zamora's lost season makes it hard to get a read on his current ability and future projection. When healthy, he showed the makings of a potential steady, everyday player who can stick at shortstop. He is on track to be ready by spring training and should make his pro debut in 2021.

SCOUTING GRADES: **Hitting:** 50 **Power:** 45 **Running:** 55 **Fielding:** 60 **Arm:** 55

Year	Age	Club (League)	Class	AVG	G	AB	R	H	2B	3B	HR	RBI	BB	SO	SB	OBP	SLG
2020	21	Did not play—No minor league season															

7 MARIO FELICIANO, C

Born: Nov. 20, 1998. **B-T:** R-R. **HT:** 6-1. **WT:** 195. **Drafted:** HS—Florida, P.R., 2016 (2nd round supplemental). **Signed by:** Charlie Sullivan.

ADAM GLANZMAN/MLB PHOTOS VIA GETTY IMAGES

BA GRADE

50 Risk: High

TRACK RECORD: The Brewers have pushed Feliciano aggressively since drafting him in the supplemental second round in 2016, but he responded by winning the high Class A Carolina League MVP award as a 20-year-old in 2019, one year after he played just 46 games and had offseason shoulder surgery. Feliciano spent 2020 at the alternate training site in Appleton, Wis., where he was the Brewers' most consistent offensive performer.

SCOUTING REPORT: Feliciano made more frequent contact when he first entered the organization, but has traded contact for power the last two seasons. He has plus raw power and a sound swing, but he chases too many pitches outside the strike zone and needs to become a more disciplined hitter. Feliciano is an offensive-oriented player but should end up good enough defensively to stick behind the plate. He's agile and a good athlete for a catcher with a slightly above-average arm. He threw out 28% of basestealers in 2019, and his throwing showed continued signs of improvement in 2020.

THE FUTURE: Feliciano has a chance to develop into a power-hitting, everyday catcher, but only if he can rein in his aggressive approach and keep his strikeouts manageable. After a cameo at the level in 2019, he'll return to Double-A in 2021.

SCOUTING GRADES: **Hitting:** 40 **Power:** 60 **Running:** 40 **Fielding:** 45 **Arm:** 55

Year	Age	Club (League)	Class	AVG	G	AB	R	H	2B	3B	HR	RBI	BB	SO	SB	OBP	SLG
2017	18	Wisconsin (MWL)	LoA	.251	104	402	47	101	16	2	4	36	34	72	10	.320	.331
2018	19	Brewers (AZL)	R	.286	4	14	0	4	1	0	0	2	2	3	0	.375	.357
	19	Carolina (CAR)	HiA	.205	42	146	20	30	7	1	3	12	13	59	2	.282	.329
2019	20	Carolina (CAR)	HiA	.273	116	440	62	120	25	4	19	81	29	139	2	.324	.477
	20	Biloxi (SL)	AA	.167	3	12	2	2	0	1	0	0	0	4	0	.286	.333
Minor League Totals				.255	298	1131	147	288	54	11	26	147	85	296	16	.315	.391

8 AARON ASHBY, LHP

EVAN MOESTA

BA GRADE
50 **Risk: High**

Born: May 24, 1998. **B-T:** R-L. **HT:** 6-2. **WT:** 181. **Drafted:** Crowder (Mo.) JC, 2018 (4th round). **Signed by:** Drew Anderson.

TRACK RECORD: Ashby, the nephew of former all-star righthander Andy Ashby, arrived at Crowder (Mo.) JC throwing in the mid 80s but was touching 94 mph by the end of his sophomore season. The Brewers drafted him in the fourth round in 2018 and signed him for $520,000. Ashby made an immediate impression and won the organization's minor league pitcher of the year award while climbing to high Class A in 2019. He was a late arrival to the alternate training site in 2020 and struggled, but he was the team's best pitcher during instructional league in the fall.

SCOUTING REPORT: Ashby stood out for both his performance and his enhanced stuff during instructional league, though with the caveat he was largely facing younger, less experienced competition. Ashby's fastball jumped from 90-95 mph to 93-97 in 2020 and overwhelmed hitters from the left side. His solid-average curveball is his most effective secondary pitch, while his fringe-average changeup has flashed a tick better. He also mixes in an occasional slider. Ashby's control can come and go, but he did a better job throwing strikes at instructs.

THE FUTURE: Ashby has a chance to develop into a back-of-the-rotation starter. A high-leverage relief role is possible, too.

SCOUTING GRADES: **Fastball:** 55 **Slider:** 45 **Curveball:** 55 **Changeup:** 45 **Control:** 45

Year	Age	Club (League)	Class	W	L	ERA	G	GS	IP	H	HR	BB	SO	BB/9	K/9	WHIP	AVG
2018	20	Helena (PIO)	R	1	2	6.20	6	3	20	18	3	8	19	3.5	8.4	1.28	.234
	20	Wisconsin (MWL)	LoA	1	1	2.17	7	7	37	40	1	9	47	2.2	11.3	1.31	.274
2019	21	Wisconsin (MWL)	LoA	3	4	3.54	11	10	61	47	4	28	80	4.1	11.8	1.23	.216
	21	Carolina (CAR)	HiA	2	6	3.46	13	13	65	54	1	32	55	4.4	7.6	1.32	.229
Minor League Totals				7	13	3.53	37	33	183	159	9	77	201	3.8	9.9	1.28	.235

9 ZAVIER WARREN, C

BILL MITCHELL

BA GRADE
50 **Risk: Very High**

Born: Jan. 8, 1999. **B-T:** B-R. **HT:** 6-0. **WT:** 190. **Drafted:** Central Michigan, 2020 (3rd round). **Signed by:** Pete Vuckovich Jr.

TRACK RECORD: Warren played catcher in high school and spent time behind the plate at Central Michigan, but he was primarily a shortstop for the Chippewas. The Brewers drafted him as a catcher in the third round in 2020 and signed him for $600,000. After signing, Warren worked on his catching in the independent United Shore League, then went to instructional league and hit well.

SCOUTING REPORT: A switch-hitter, Warren has a good track record of getting on base. He led the Mid-American Conference with a .502 on-base percentage in 2019 and hit .315/.396/.443 that summer in the Cape Cod League. He's a patient hitter with a loose, rhythmic swing and good hand-eye coordination. Warren has a hit-over-power profile, though he makes hard contact from both sides and could be a threat for 15-20 home runs. Warren has the attributes to stay behind the plate with his baseball acumen, agility, hands and average arm strength. He has fallback options with the defensive skills that could fit at third base or perhaps second base. He's an average runner, though he may slow down if he continues to catch.

THE FUTURE: It's not a lock that Warren can stay behind the plate. If he can, his value receives a boost as a switch-hitting catcher with strong on-base skills.

SCOUTING GRADES: **Hitting:** 55 **Power:** 50 **Running:** 50 **Fielding:** 50 **Arm:** 45

Year	Age	Club (League)	Class	AVG	G	AB	R	H	2B	3B	HR	RBI	BB	SO	SB	OBP	SLG
2020	21	Did not play—No minor league season															

10 JEFERSON QUERO, C

Born: Oct. 8, 2002. **B-T:** R-R. **HT:** 5-10. **WT:** 165. **Signed:** Venezuela, 2019. **Signed by:** Reinaldo Hidalgo.

BA GRADE
50 Risk: Extreme

TRACK RECORD: Quero played for Venezuela in the 2015 Little League World Series and emerged as one of the top players in the 2019 international class. He signed with the Brewers for $200,000 and immediately delivered a strong showing in the Tricky League—an unofficial league for July 2 signees—and Dominican instructional league. He reported stateside for instructional league in 2020 and impressed on both sides of the ball.

SCOUTING REPORT: Quero has the tools to develop into a plus defensive catcher. He's quick and athletic behind the plate with advanced blocking and receiving skills for his age. His plus arm helps him record pop times as low as 1.9 seconds on throws to second base. He also draws praise for his intelligence and vocal, high-energy leadership on the field. Quero has hit well so far in unofficial games, even against more advanced competition. He has a sound approach for his age with a knack for making hard contact and driving the ball well to the opposite field. He has solid-average raw power and good bat-to-ball skills.

THE FUTURE: Quero has yet to make his official pro debut, but he has been an arrow-up player since signing. He's one of the Brewers' top breakout candidates heading into 2021.

SCOUTING GRADES: **Hitting:** 50 **Power:** 55 **Running:** 40 **Fielding:** 60 **Arm:** 60

Year	Age	Club (League)	Class	AVG	G	AB	R	H	2B	3B	HR	RBI	BB	SO	SB	OBP	SLG
2020	18	Did not play—No minor league season															

11 EDUARDO GARCIA, SS

BREAKOUT
BA GRADE
50 Risk: Extreme

Born: July 10, 2002. **B-T:** R-R. **HT:** 6-2. **WT:** 188. **Signed:** Venezuela, 2018. **Signed by:** Reinaldo Hidalgo.

TRACK RECORD: Garcia was young for the 2018 international signing class, finalizing a $1.1 million deal with the Brewers when he turned 16. He has played just 10 official games in two years after a broken ankle cut his 2019 season short and the coronavirus pandemic erased the 2020 minor league season. The Brewers pushed Garcia aggressively to their alternate training site in Appleton, where he was understandably overmatched given his age and the level of competition. He looked more comfortable during instructional league against age-appropriate opponents.

SCOUTING REPORT: Garcia has shown promising flashes, but he's difficult to evaluate given his limited playing time. Signed with a skinny 6-foot-2 frame, he has added 25 pounds to a still lean, well-proportioned build. Garcia primarily stands out for his defensive ability at shortstop with soft hands and good defensive actions. He's a tick below-average runner but shows good body control to go with a plus arm. Garcia has added more leverage to his swing, but scouts are mixed on his offensive potential. He hit well during his brief time in the DSL and shows flashes of being an average hitter with 15-home run power, but there's more uncertainty with his bat than his glove.

THE FUTURE: Garcia will make his stateside debut in 2021. How he performs at the plate will be crucial to watch.

Year	Age	Club (League)	Class	AVG	G	AB	R	H	2B	3B	HR	RBI	BB	SO	SB	OBP	SLG
2019	16	Brewers (DSL)	R	.313	10	32	6	10	2	0	1	3	6	9	1	.450	.469
Minor League Totals				.313	10	32	6	10	2	0	1	3	6	9	1	.450	.469

12 CARLOS RODRIGUEZ, OF

BA GRADE
50 Risk: Extreme

Born: Dec. 7, 2000. **B-T:** L-L. **HT:** 5-10. **WT:** 165. **Signed:** Venezuela, 2017. **Signed by:** Jose Rodriguez.

TRACK RECORD: Rodriguez was one of the most advanced pure hitters in the 2017 international class and signed with the Brewers for $1.355 million. He lived up to that reputation by hitting over .320 in each of his first two seasons as a pro. Rodriguez spent time at the alternate training site in 2020, where he wasn't a standout but held his own against significantly older competition and a lefty-heavy pitching group.

SCOUTING REPORT: Rodriguez's bat control is among the best in the Brewers' system. He has a career strikeout rate of just 10% and has a knack for putting the bat to the ball. He doesn't walk much, in part because he makes contact early in counts, and will need to be more selective to enhance his on-base skills. Rodriguez's power is mostly to the gaps. While he added strength in 2020 and started driving the

ball, he's mostly a line-drive hitter with 8-12 home run potential. Where Rodriguez ends up defensively is his biggest question. He's an average runner without the burner speed of a typical center fielder. Some observers like his defensive instincts in center, while others think he looks more comfortable in a corner.
THE FUTURE: There's some tweener outfield risk with Rodriguez, but he has hit at every level so far and that may be enough to carry him.

Year	Age	Club (League)	Class	AVG	G	AB	R	H	2B	3B	HR	RBI	BB	SO	SB	OBP	SLG
2019	18	Brewers Gold (AZL)	R	.318	7	22	5	7	1	0	0	1	0	2	1	.318	.364
	18	Rocky Mountain (PIO)	R	.331	36	151	20	50	3	1	3	12	4	20	4	.350	.424
Minor League Totals				.327	104	410	67	134	17	2	5	46	13	42	19	.356	.415

13 DREW RASMUSSEN, RHP

BA GRADE
45 Risk: High

Born: July 27, 1995. **B-T:** R-R. **HT:** 6-1. **WT:** 225. **Drafted:** Oregon State, 2018 (6th round). **Signed by:** Shawn Whalen.

TRACK RECORD: Rasmussen had Tommy John surgery at Oregon State as a sophomore in 2016. The Rays drafted him 31st overall the following year but didn't sign him due to concerns about his elbow. Rasmussen returned to school and had a second Tommy John surgery that wiped out his 2018 season, but the Brewers still drafted him in the sixth round and signed him for $135,000. Rasmussen returned in 2019 and jumped three levels up to Double-A on the strength of a fastball up to 99 mph. He began the 2020 season at the alternate training site and made his major league debut in August.
SCOUTING REPORT: Rasmussen's best pitch is his fastball, which he pumps at 96-99 mph. The pitch has good life to miss bats when he pitches up in the zone, but his control escapes him at times, leading to too many walks and hard contact. His 85-88 mph slider is a slightly above-average pitch with good bite that could still tick up, though he has trouble landing it in the strike zone. Rasmussen is primarily a fastball/slider pitcher, but he mixes in a fringe-average curveball and an occasional below-average changeup at 89-91 mph.
THE FUTURE: Rasmussen should break camp with the Brewers in 2021. He has the stuff to pitch high-leverage relief innings if he can sharpen his command.

Year	Age	Club (League)	Class	W	L	ERA	G	GS	IP	H	HR	BB	SO	BB/9	SO/9	WHIP	AVG
2020	24	Milwaukee (NL)	MAJ	1	0	5.87	12	0	15	17	3	9	21	5.3	12.3	1.70	.274
Major League Totals				1	0	5.87	12	0	15	17	3	9	21	5.3	12.3	1.70	.274
Minor League Totals				1	3	3.15	27	23	74	57	4	31	96	3.8	11.6	1.18	.216

14 JUSTIN TOPA, RHP

TOP ROOKIE
BA GRADE
40 Risk: Medium

Born: March 7, 1991. **B-T:** R-R. **HT:** 6-4. **WT:** 215. **Drafted:** Long Island-Brooklyn, 2013 (17th round). **Signed by:** Chris Kline (Pirates).

TRACK RECORD: Topa had Tommy John surgery in college in 2011 and, after signing with the Pirates for $70,000 as a 13th-round pick in 2013, had a second Tommy John surgery in 2015. He was released and spent 2017 pitching in the independent Can-Am League before signing a minor league deal with the Rangers in 2018. Topa joined the Brewers on a minor league deal in 2019 and reached Double-A. He generated buzz at the alternate training site and earned his first big league callup in September as a 29-year-old.
SCOUTING REPORT: Topa flourished in his brief time in Milwaukee and didn't look like a fluke. He throws a heavy sinker that sits at 96-99 mph with lively armside run and peaks at 100 mph. His plus slider plays well off his fastball with two-plane depth and deep lateral break. Both pitches are swing-and-miss weapons against both righties and lefties. Topa has demonstrated plus control throughout his career and didn't issue a single walk 7.2 innings with the Brewers.
FUTURE: Already entering his 30s, Topa's window to produce is limited. He has the high-octane stuff to be a key reliever for the Brewers right away in 2021.

Year	Age	Club (League)	Class	W	L	ERA	G	GS	IP	H	HR	BB	SO	BB/9	SO/9	WHIP	AVG
2020	29	Milwaukee (NL)	MAJ	0	1	2.35	6	0	8	7	1	0	12	0.0	14.1	0.91	.233
Major League Totals				0	1	2.35	6	0	7	7	1	0	12	0.0	14.1	0.91	.233
Minor League Totals				13	20	4.84	97	21	215	247	16	57	170	2.4	7.1	1.41	.291

15 JESUS PARRA, 3B/2B

Born: Aug. 30, 2002. **B-T:** R-R. **HT:** 6-3. **WT:** 220. **Signed:** Venezuela, 2018. **Signed by:** Jesus Rodriguez.

TRACK RECORD: Parra signed with the Brewers for $210,000 during the 2018 international signing period as one of the youngest players in the class. He made his pro debut in 2019 in the Dominican Summer League and hit .275/.398/.486 after the all-star break. The Brewers brought Parra to Arizona for instructional league 2020, though he was a late arrival and didn't get many at-bats.

SCOUTING REPORT: Parra is a big, physical infielder with a patient hitting approach for his age, good bat speed and above-average raw power. His power comes with some swing-and-miss, as he struck out 26 percent of the time in the DSL, though he was also just 16 years old nearly the whole season. If he can keep his strikeout rate to a manageable level, his ability to draw walks should help keep his on-base percentage up. A below-average runner, Parra has split time between second base and third base. His range probably fits better at third base. His hands and feet work well for his size and he has a plus arm.

THE FUTURE: Parra will still be 18 in 2021. He will spend most of the year at the Rookie level.

Year	Age	Club (League)	Class	AVG	G	AB	R	H	2B	3B	HR	RBI	BB	SO	SB	OBP	SLG
2019	16	Brewers (DSL)	R	.247	65	227	39	56	15	2	6	37	26	71	9	.361	.410
Minor League Totals				.247	65	227	39	56	15	2	6	37	26	71	9	.361	.410

16 DAVID HAMILTON, SS/2B

BREAKOUT
BA GRADE
45 Risk: Very High

Born: Sept. 29, 1997. **B-T:** L-R. **HT:** 5-10. **WT:** 175. **Drafted:** Texas, 2019 (8th round). **Signed by:** K.J. Hendricks.

TRACK RECORD: Hamilton had a standout sophomore year at Texas and but he ruptured his Achilles tendon and missed his entire junior year. The Brewers still took him in the eighth round and signed him for an above-slot $400,000. Hamilton returned to the field in 2020 and played in the independent Constellation Energy League, where he hit .296/.430/.370 and went 20-for-20 on stolen bases in 27 games. He reported to instructional league and drew attention as a top offensive performer.

SCOUTING REPORT: Hamilton is 22, so he was one of the older players at instructs, but the quality of his at-bats was impressive. He has a sound lefthanded stroke, uses his hands well at the plate and consistently barrels balls while showing a good eye for the strike zone. He doesn't have a ton of home run power, but he's a sound hitter with a good approach. Hamilton is a good athlete and a plus runner. He showed a solid-average arm and played steady defense at both middle-infield positions during instructs.

THE FUTURE: Hamilton is advanced enough that he could jump to high Class A for his pro debut. He has a chance for a breakout season now that he's healthy.

Year	Age	Club (League)	Class	AVG	G	AB	R	H	2B	3B	HR	RBI	BB	SO	SB	OBP	SLG
2020	22	Did not play—No minor league season															

17 NICK KAHLE, C

BA GRADE
45 Risk: Very High

Born: Feb. 28, 1998. **B-T:** R-R. **HT:** 5-10. **WT:** 210. **Drafted:** Washington, 2019 (4th round). **Signed by:** Shawn Whalen.

TRACK RECORD: Kahle had a breakout junior season at Washington in 2019, hitting .339/.506/.532 with more than twice as many walks (59) as strikeouts (28). The Brewers drafted him in the fourth round and he had a solid pro debut in the Rookie-level Pioneer League. With the coronavirus pandemic canceling the 2020 minor league season, Kahle played independent ball in North Dakota for Fargo-Moorhead in the American Association before heading to Arizona for instructional league.

SCOUTING REPORT: Kahle has a short, direct swing and a disciplined offensive approach. He recognizes pitches well and seldom expands the strike zone. Kahle is mostly a doubles threat who might hit 8-12 home runs and will need to be able to do more damage on contact against advanced pitchers. Kahle drew mixed reviews for his defense as an amateur, with scouts praising his blocking and receiving skills but questioning his fringe-average arm. Kahle has made significant progress on his throwing while working with minor league coach Nestor Corredor. He threw out 44% of baserunners in his pro debut and carried that over to instructs in 2020. Kahle also draws positive reviews for his all-around baseball IQ.

THE FUTURE: If Kahle can drive the ball with impact, he has a chance to develop into a high-OBP catcher. He got a taste of high Class A in 2019 and should open back there in 2021.

Year	Age	Club (League)	Class	AVG	G	AB	R	H	2B	3B	HR	RBI	BB	SO	SB	OBP	SLG
2019	21	Carolina (CAR)	HiA	.000	2	5	0	0	0	0	0	0	1	2	0	.167	.000
	21	Rocky Mountain (PIO)	R	.255	40	141	25	36	11	1	6	25	20	36	2	.350	.475
Minor League Totals				.247	42	146	25	36	11	1	6	25	21	38	2	.343	.459

18 HAYDEN CANTRELLE, SS

BA GRADE 45 **Risk: Very High**

Born: Nov. 25, 1998. **B-T:** B-R. **HT:** 5-10. **WT:** 175. **Drafted:** Louisiana-Lafayette, 2020 (5th round). **Signed by:** Craig Smajstrla.

TRACK RECORD: Cantrelle hit well his first two years at Louisiana-Lafayette and batted .315/.427/.438 in the Cape Cod League after his sophomore year. He struggled in his junior season, however, batting .146/.320/.237 before college baseball shut down. The Brewers still drafted him in the fifth round and signed him for $300,000. Cantrelle spent the summer playing in the independent City of Champions Cup league and led his team in on-base percentage before going to Arizona for instructional league.

SCOUTING REPORT: At his best, Cantrelle shows a controlled, compact swing from both sides of the plate and solid feel for the strike zone. His stroke is more contact-oriented from the right side, with more sneaky pop from the left side, though still gives him an on-base over power profile. Cantrelle is a plus runner with the baserunning savvy to be an efficient stolen base threat. He plays with good rhythm and footwork at shortstop and has an average, accurate arm. He's also a potentially above-average defender at second base and his speed makes him an option in center field if needed.

THE FUTURE: Cantrelle doesn't have huge tools, but his high baseball IQ is evident in all phases of the game. He should make his full-season debut in 2021.

Year	Age	Club (League)	Class	AVG	G	AB	R	H	2B	3B	HR	RBI	BB	SO	SB	OBP	SLG
2020	21	Did not play—No minor league season															

19 LUIS MEDINA, OF

BA GRADE 45 **Risk: Extreme**

Born: Feb. 24, 2003. **B-T:** L-L. **HT:** 6-2. **WT:** 199. **Signed:** Venezuela, 2019. **Signed by:** Jose Rodriguez.

TRACK RECORD: The Brewers' 2019 international signing class leaned heavily on Venezuelan players, including outfielder Hedbert Perez and catcher Jeferson Quero. Their biggest bonus went to Medina, who signed for $1.3 million. The Brewers brought him to instructional league in 2020 after the coronavirus shutdown and he struggled to get his timing back against older competition, but the quality of his at-bats improved as he readjusted to live pitching.

SCOUTING REPORT: Medina's best tool is his plus raw power. He has a loose swing, good bat speed and a chance for his power to tick up even more. Medina has a solid idea of the strike zone for his age but can get pull-happy, which gets him to drift out front early and leads to swings and misses. Even when he does pull off the ball, his hands work well enough to still make contact. Medina has played center field, but he projects as a corner outfielder and should develop into an average defender. He's around an average runner with solid defensive instincts and a tick above-average arm that fits in right field.

THE FUTURE: Medina's pro debut awaits in 2021. He's likely to begin in the Rookie-level Arizona League.

Year	Age	Club (League)	Class	AVG	G	AB	R	H	2B	3B	HR	RBI	BB	SO	SB	OBP	SLG
2020	17	Did not play—No minor league season															

20 ALEC BETTINGER, RHP

BA GRADE 40 **Risk: High**

Born: July 13, 1995. **B-T:** R-R. **HT:** 6-2. **WT:** 210. **Drafted:** Virginia, 2017 (10th round). **Signed by:** James Fisher.

TRACK RECORD: Bettinger split between starting and relieving at Virginia before pitching exclusively out of the bullpen as a senior. The Brewers drafted him in the 10th round, signed him for $10,000 and developed him as a starter. Bettinger ranked second in the Double-A Southern League in strikeouts in 2019 and spent 2020 at the alternate training site. The Brewers added him to their 40-man roster after the season.

SCOUTING REPORT: Bettinger doesn't have a plus pitch, but he throws strikes, is durable and has a feel for pitching that has yielded better results than his stuff would suggest. There's some funk and deception in his release, which gives him a little more margin with a fastball that sits 89-93 mph with occasional cutting action and can scrape 94-95 mph. The pitch has good vertical movement, helping him miss bats when he elevates. Bettinger's best secondary pitch is his changeup, which is a solid-average pitch with good sink and fade when it's on. He mixes in a curveball that has been effective against minor leaguers, though it's typically a fringy pitch which might not get major league hitters to bite.

THE FUTURE: Bettinger faces questions about whether his stuff will work against major league hitters. He should open 2021 in Triple-A and is in position to make his debut if he pitches well.

Year	Age	Club (League)	Class	W	L	ERA	G	GS	IP	H	HR	BB	SO	BB/9	SO/9	WHIP	AVG
2019	23	Biloxi (SL)	AA	5	7	3.44	26	26	146	121	13	35	157	2.2	9.7	1.07	.206
Minor League Totals				14	20	4.35	66	58	314	302	30	92	302	2.6	8.7	1.25	.254

21 DYLAN FILE, RHP

BA GRADE
40 Risk: High

Born: June 4, 1996. **B-T:** R-R. **HT:** 6-1. **WT:** 205. **Drafted:** Dixie State, 2017 (21st round). **Signed by:** Jeff Scholzen.

TRACK RECORD: File went to Division II Dixie State, where he won Pacific West Conference freshman of the year in 2015 and co-pitcher of the year in 2017. He has exceeded expectations as a pro, showing a combination of durability and control that has led to success through Double-A. The Brewers brought him to their alternate training site in 2020 and added him to the 40-man roster after the season.

SCOUTING REPORT: File relies on his ability to throw strikes and mix four pitches. His fastball ranges from 88-92 mph and touches 94 in short bursts. He has some deception in his delivery and is able to get elevated swings and misses with his fastball despite below-average velocity. File has plus control, filling the strike zone and hitting his spots. He lacks a true putaway pitch with an average curveball and slider to go with a fringe-average changeup. He gets ahead in counts and sequences hitters effectively.

THE FUTURE: Whether File's stuff will work against advanced hitters remains a question. He'll open 2021 in Triple-A with a chance to make his major league debut during the year.

Year	Age	Club (League)	Class	W	L	ERA	G	GS	IP	H	HR	BB	SO	BB/9	SO/9	WHIP	AVG
2019	23	Carolina (CAR)	HiA	6	4	3.80	12	12	66	71	4	7	63	0.9	8.5	1.18	.260
	23	Biloxi (SL)	AA	9	2	2.79	14	14	81	74	5	15	73	1.7	8.1	1.10	.226
Minor League Totals				24	18	3.65	63	58	330	348	31	63	287	1.7	7.8	1.24	.271

22 ABNER URIBE, RHP

BA GRADE
45 Risk: Extreme

Born: June 20, 2000. **B-T:** R-R. **HT:** 6-2. **WT:** 200. **Signed:** Dominican Republic, 2018. **Signed by:** Elvis Cruz.

TRACK RECORD: Uribe was old enough to sign out of the Dominican Republic in 2017 but wasn't officially registered with Major League Baseball, so the Brewers signed him in 2018 for $85,000. Uribe's fastball topped out in the low 90s when he signed and has since skyrocketed. He began touching the mid 90s in his stateside debut in 2019, then sat 95-98 mph and touched 101 at instructional league in 2020.

SCOUTING REPORT: Uribe has always had fast arm speed, and his velocity spike came as he gained strength and became more consistent with his delivery. He has thrown just 28.1 official innings in three years, mostly as a reliever, so the rest of his development beyond his velocity lags behind. Uribe's fastball command and overall strike-throwing has been erratic and he tends to overthrow. He has shown a feel for a slider that's ahead of his changeup, but because he often falls behind in counts his focus has been on learning how to throw his fastball for strikes.

THE FUTURE: Uribe has a chance to be a power-armed reliever. He'll need to throw strikes to get there.

Year	Age	Club (League)	Class	W	L	ERA	G	GS	IP	H	HR	BB	SO	BB/9	SO/9	WHIP	AVG
2019	19	Rocky Mountain (PIO)	R	2	1	9.00	4	0	7	11	1	7	5	9.0	6.4	2.57	.324
	19	Brewers Blue (AZL)	R	1	1	15.43	3	2	2	4	0	4	2	15.4	7.7	3.43	--
Minor League Totals				5	2	5.72	19	2	28	25	1	21	28	6.7	8.9	1.62	.260

23 JHEREMY VARGAS, SS

BA GRADE
45 Risk: Extreme

Born: May 10, 2003. **B-T:** R-R. **HT:** 5-10. **WT:** 165. **Signed:** Venezuela, 2019. **Signed by:** Jose Rodriguez.

TRACK RECORD: Vargas played for Venezuela in the COPABE 14U Pan American Championship in 2017 and signed with the Brewers for $650,000 two years later. He stood out for his baseball IQ and strong offensive performance as an amateur and has continued to showcase those attributes as a pro, first in the Dominican Republic after signing and during instructional league in 2020.

SCOUTING REPORT: Vargas stands out more in games than in a workout. He doesn't have loud tools or the prettiest swing, but he gets on base, makes frequent contact with good plate discipline and uses the whole field. Vargas is physically behind his peers, so he's mostly a line drive hitter with doubles pop. There's room on his frame to add more strength, but he doesn't project to be a big home run threat. Vargas is an average runner who lacks the quick-twitch actions teams prefer at shortstop, but he has a chance to stick there because of his internal clock, secure hands, solid-average arm and advanced instincts.

THE FUTURE: Vargas will still be 17 on Opening Day 2021. He is set to begin his pro career in the Rookie-level Arizona League.

Year	Age	Club (League)	Class	AVG	G	AB	R	H	2B	3B	HR	RBI	BB	SO	SB	OBP	SLG
2020	17	Did not play—No minor league season															

24 JOEY WIEMER, OF

BA GRADE 45 **Risk:** Extreme

Born: Feb. 11, 1999. **B-T:** R-R. **HT:** 6-5. **WT:** 215. **Drafted:** Cincinnati, 2020 (4th round). **Signed by:** Jeff Bianchi.

TRACK RECORD: The Brewers bet on Wiemer's tools and drafted him in the fourth round in 2020 despite a lack of standout performance in college at Cincinnati. He signed for $150,000 and spent the summer playing for Birmingham Bluefield of the independent United Shore Baseball League. He struggled there before heading to instructional league, where a thumb injury limited his playing time.

SCOUTING REPORT: Wiemer has a fast bat and plus raw power. He isn't a free-swinger, but he hasn't tapped into that power in games and faces questions about his pure hitting ability because of all the moving parts in his unorthodox swing. He loads with a big leg kick, drops his hands from behind his head to just above his waist before raising them back again and unleashing an aggressive hack. All of that creates timing issues and will be tested once he faces better velocity. Wiemer has plus speed underway and good instincts on the basepaths. He runs well enough to play center field, though he projects as a corner outfielder due to his size. He clocked up to 104 mph in outfield throwing drills and has an 80-grade arm.

THE FUTURE: Wiemer will make his pro debut in 2021. If he doesn't hit enough, his arm strength and athleticism make pitching a fallback option.

Year	Age	Club (League)	Class	AVG	G	AB	R	H	2B	3B	HR	RBI	BB	SO	SB	OBP	SLG
2020	21	Did not play—No minor league season															

25 COREY RAY, OF

BA GRADE 40 **Risk:** High

Born: Sept. 22, 1994. **B-T:** L-L. **HT:** 5-11. **WT:** 185. **Drafted:** Louisville, 2016 (1st round). **Signed by:** Jeff Simpson.

TRACK RECORD: The Brewers had high hopes when they drafted Ray fourth overall in 2016. He won MVP of the Double-A Southern League in 2018 but scuffled upon reaching Triple-A in 2019, when a wrist issue limited his playing time. He spent 2020 at the alternate training site.

SCOUTING REPORT: Ray has a promising combination of power and speed, but his swing-and-miss rate has hampered his production. His swing gets long, he has difficulty recognizing offspeed pitches and he chases too many pitches outside the strike zone. Those holes have been exposed against better pitching, with Ray striking out in 32% of his plate appearances at Double-A and Triple-A. Ray is a plus runner who is a dangerous stolen base threat. He is an average defender in center field with an average arm.

THE FUTURE: Ray will open 2021 back at Triple-A. He needs dramatic improvement with his contact rate and strike-zone management to have any kind of major league career.

Year	Age	Club (League)	Class	AVG	G	AB	R	H	2B	3B	HR	RBI	BB	SO	SB	OBP	SLG
2019	24	Brewers Gold (AZL)	R	.533	5	15	5	8	3	0	1	4	1	3	0	.563	.933
	24	San Antonio (PCL)	AAA	.188	53	207	23	39	8	0	7	21	20	89	3	.261	.329
	24	Biloxi (SL)	AA	.250	11	40	5	10	3	0	0	0	6	14	3	.348	.325
Minor League Totals				.235	376	1486	201	349	88	13	47	164	158	496	77	.311	.406

26 ANGEL PERDOMO, LHP

BA GRADE 40 **Risk:** High

Born: May 7, 1994. **B-T:** L-L. **HT:** 6-8. **WT:** 265. **Signed:** Dominican Republic, 2011. **Signed by:** Marino Tejada/Jose Rosario/Ismael Cruz (Blue Jays).

TRACK RECORD: It was a long road to the majors for Perdomo, who signed with the Blue Jays when he was 17. He failed to advance past high Class A in seven seasons and signed with the Brewers as a minor league free agent after 2018. Perdomo saw more success after shifting to the bullpen and spent most of 2020 at the alternate training site. He earned his first major league callup in August.

SCOUTING REPORT: Perdomo has a powerful left arm and a track record of high strikeout rates. He throws slightly across his body, sitting 93-96 mph with the ability to miss bats when he elevates his fastball. He pairs it with a low-80s slider that is inconsistent but flashes plus with long horizontal break across the zone. He also throws an occasional below-average, 88-90 mph changeup. Perdomo frequently fell behind in the count in the majors, which allowed hitters to tee off on his fastball. He is 6-foot-8 and, like a lot of pitchers his size, struggles to sync up his delivery, which leads to below-average control.

THE FUTURE: Perdomo will be 27 in 2021. If he can learn to repeat his delivery and throw more strikes, he could stick around in Milwaukee's bullpen.

Year	Age	Club (League)	Class	W	L	ERA	G	GS	IP	H	HR	BB	SO	BB/9	SO/9	WHIP	AVG
2020	26	Milwaukee (NL)	MAJ	0	0	20.25	3	0	3	3	0	7	5	23.6	16.9	3.75	.273
Major League Totals				0	0	20.25	3	0	2	3	0	7	5	23.6	16.9	3.75	.273
Minor League Totals				25	24	3.39	162	70	504	402	30	260	608	4.6	10.8	1.31	.219

27 CLAYTON ANDREWS, LHP/OF

BA GRADE 40 Risk: High

Born: Jan. 4, 1997. **B-T:** L-L. **HT:** 5-6. **WT:** 165. **Drafted:** Long Beach State, 2018 (17th round). **Signed by:** Dan Houston.

TRACK RECORD: Andrews is a diminutive 5-foot-6, but he has quickly put himself into consideration to make the majors after signing for $75,000 as a 17th-round pick in 2018. A two-way player at Long Beach State, Andrews has primarily been a reliever in pro ball, though he spent time in center field in 2019 when he reached Double-A Biloxi. He pitched particularly well at the alternate training site in 2020.

SCOUTING REPORT: Andrews' fastball sits 89-93 mph with late life up in the zone, and he touched 95 at the alternate site. He pairs his fastball with a plus changeup that gets empty swings and messes with hitters' timing. He also mixes in a sweepy slider that can be an average pitch at times. Andrews is an excellent athlete and has been a solid strike-thrower throughout his career. That athleticism and plus speed shows up in the outfield, where he has strong defensive instincts. The Brewers have let him hit a little and he has shown good bat-to-ball skills with minimal power, albeit in just 63 at-bats.

THE FUTURE: Andrews was in the conversation for a 2020 callup. He projects to be primarily a middle reliever with the versatility to be a defensive replacement, pinch-runner and possible pinch-hitter.

Year	Age	Club (League)	Class	W	L	ERA	G	GS	IP	H	HR	BB	SO	BB/9	SO/9	WHIP	AVG
2019	22	Carolina (CAR)	HiA	2	2	3.86	22	0	28	24	2	10	44	3.2	14.1	1.21	.211
	22	Biloxi (SL)	AA	3	0	2.59	17	0	31	19	3	15	33	4.3	9.5	1.09	.128
Minor League Totals				11	3	2.83	58	0	92	66	8	32	131	3.1	12.8	1.06	.202

28 TRISTEN LUTZ, OF

BA GRADE 40 Risk: High

Born: Aug. 22, 1998. **B-T:** R-R. **HT:** 6-3. **WT:** 210. **Drafted:** HS—Arlington, Texas, 2017 (1st round supplemental). **Signed by:** K.J. Hendricks.

TRACK RECORD: The Brewers drafted Lutz with the 34th overall pick in 2017 and signed him for $2.352 million. He had an excellent start to his pro career, but he's since struggled with strikeouts at both Class A levels. Lutz spent 2020 at the alternate training site in Appleton, Wis.

SCOUTING REPORT: Lutz's best attribute is his above-average power. He's a strong, physical player and a good athlete for his size. Lutz isn't a total free-swinger, but he has had trouble making consistent contact. He has issues making contact in the zone along with some chase tendencies. An average runner, Lutz has spent most of his time in center field but projects to right field, where his slightly above-average arm fits.

THE FUTURE: Lutz has intriguing power, but he will need to make more contact and tighten his plate discipline against more advanced pitching. Double-A is up next.

Year	Age	Club (League)	Class	AVG	G	AB	R	H	2B	3B	HR	RBI	BB	SO	SB	OBP	SLG
2019	20	Carolina (CAR)	HiA	.255	112	420	62	107	24	3	13	54	46	137	3	.335	.419
Minor League Totals				.260	271	1025	160	266	62	10	35	144	108	318	15	.339	.442

29 PHIL BICKFORD, RHP

BA GRADE 40 Risk: High

Born: July 10, 1995. **B-T:** R-R. **HT:** 6-4. **WT:** 200. **Drafted:** JC of Southern Nevada, 2015 (1st round). **Signed by:** Chuck Fick (Giants).

TRACK RECORD: Bickford was drafted 10th overall by the Blue Jays out of high school, didn't sign and was picked in the first round again when the Giants selected him 18th overall in 2015. The Brewers acquired him one year later in the deal for lefthander Will Smith. Bickford flamed out as a starter and moved to the bullpen during the 2018 season. He had several strong outings at the alternate training site in 2020 and got called up for his major league debut on Sept. 1.

SCOUTING REPORT: Bickford overhauled his mechanics and now relies on deception and angle to help his stuff play up. His velocity is below-average, sitting 88-91 mph and scraping 93 mph, down from the mid 90s he sat as an amateur. Bickford has a crossfire delivery where he jumps toward the third base side, creating a difficult angle for righthanded hitters. Along with the movement on his fastball, he gets more uncomfortable swings than would otherwise be expected. Bickford's low-80s slider is a fringy pitch that sweeps across the zone and relies more on his angle than the quality of the pitch. Control was an issue earlier in Bickford's career, but he has made significant strides throwing strikes.

THE FUTURE: Bickford will need more minor league time to begin 2021. He projects as a middle reliever.

Year	Age	Club (League)	Class	W	L	ERA	G	GS	IP	H	HR	BB	SO	BB/9	SO/9	WHIP	AVG
2020	24	Milwaukee (NL)	MAJ	0	0	36.00	1	0	1	4	0	0	2	0.0	18.0	4.00	.571
Major League Totals				0	0	36.00	1	0	1	4	0	0	2	0.0	18.0	4.00	.571
Minor League Totals				11	8	2.98	80	37	226	183	11	87	277	3.5	11.0	1.19	.220

30 MICAH BELLO, OF

Born: July 21, 2000. **B-T:** R-R. **HT:** 5-11. **WT:** 170. **Drafted:** HS—Hilo, Hawaii, 2018 (2nd round supplemental). **Signed by:** Shawn Whalen.

TRACK RECORD: Bello was still 17 when the Brewers drafted him in the supplemental second round and signed him for $550,000, joining lefthander Kodi Medeiros and righthander Jordan Yamamoto as fellow Hawaiian high school picks by the Brewers. He delivered an uneven performance as one of the youngest players in the Rookie-level Pioneer League in 2019, but was one of the more pleasant surprises during instructional league in 2020.

SCOUTING REPORT: Bello hit in the middle of the lineup for the Brewers at instructs, where he showed a solid offensive approach and the ability to hit to all fields. There's still some swing-and-miss to his game and his power is still mostly to the gaps, with occasional home runs to his pull side. Bello has spent time at all three outfield spots. He's a slightly above-average runner who might have enough defensive instincts to play center field, but he might end up fitting better in a corner. He has a plus arm that has helped him record 12 assists in 87 career games in the outfield.

THE FUTURE: Bello has a chance to rise as an extra outfielder. He should start at low Class A in 2021.

Year	Age	Club (League)	Class	AVG	G	AB	R	H	2B	3B	HR	RBI	BB	SO	SB	OBP	SLG
2019	18	Rocky Mountain (PIO)	R	.232	50	177	30	41	9	3	6	20	18	47	5	.308	.418
Minor League Totals				.236	89	331	55	78	13	6	7	35	36	88	15	.315	.375

MORE PROSPECTS TO KNOW

31 ALEXIS RAMIREZ, RHP

Ramirez signed for $10,000 out of the Dominican Republic throwing 88-91 mph, but his velocity has spiked to where he's now sitting 92-95 mph and reaching 97. His control and feel for pitching still need a lot of work.

32 ALEXANDER PEREZ, SS

SLEEPER

Signed out of Venezuela in 2019, Perez has shown good bat control and athleticism and has a good chance to stay at shortstop with a solid-average arm.

33 VICTOR CASTANEDA, RHP

Castaneda missed a lot of bats as a reliever at low Class A Wisconsin in 2019 with a good fastball/splitter combination. He has a chance to be part of Milwaukee's bullpen mix in the coming years.

34 ZACK BROWN, RHP

A rough 2019 season dropped Brown's status, but he has a chance to make his major league debut in 2021, most likely as a reliever.

35 MAX LAZAR, RHP

Lazar posted a 109-to-15 strikeout-to-walk mark in 79 innings for low Class A Wisconsin as a 20-year-old in 2019. He does it with a high-slot fastball that misses bats despite sitting 87-90 mph.

36 THOMAS DILLARD, C/1B/OF

Dillard has shown some offensive promise, but his conversion to catcher has been understandably bumpy.

37 JOSE CABALLERO, SS

Signed out of Venezuela in 2019, Caballero is a true shortstop with outstanding hands and a good internal clock in the field.

38 TYRONE TAYLOR, OF

Taylor doesn't project as an everyday player, but he could hit enough to stick around as a reserve who can play center field with plus speed.

39 PAYTON HENRY, C

Henry is the best defensive catcher in the system, but his free-swinging approach and high strikeout rate limits his offensive upside.

40 EDUARQUI FERNANDEZ, OF

Fernandez has loud tools with big raw power, speed and athleticism, but he will have to address the major strikeout issues he had in Rookie ball.

41 EDINSON MEJIA, RHP

Mejia signed for $10,000 after the 2018 season and only pitched briefly in the Dominican Summer League in 2019, but his velocity grew to reach 96 mph in 2020 as a 19-year-old.

TOP PROSPECTS OF THE DECADE

Year	Player, Pos	2020 Org
2011	Jake Odorizzi, RHP	Twins
2012	Wily Peralta, RHP	Did not play
2013	Wily Peralta, RHP	Did not play
2014	Jimmy Nelson, RHP	Dodgers
2015	Tyrone Taylor, OF	Brewers
2016	Orlando Arcia, SS	Brewers
2017	Lewis Brinson, OF	Marlins
2018	Lewis Brinson, OF	Marlins
2019	Keston Hiura, 2B	Brewers
2020	Brice Turang, SS	Brewers

TOP DRAFT PICKS OF THE DECADE

Year	Player, Pos	2020 Org
2011	Taylor Jungmann, RHP	Independent Lge
2012	Clint Coulter, C	Independent Lge
2013	Devin Williams, RHP (2nd round)	Brewers
2014	Kodi Medeiros, LHP	White Sox
2015	Trent Grisham, OF	Padres
2016	Corey Ray, OF	Brewers
2017	Keston Hiura, 2B	Brewers
2018	Brice Turang, SS	Brewers
2019	Ethan Small, LHP	Brewers
2020	Garrett Mitchell, OF	Brewers

DEPTH CHART

MILWAUKEE BREWERS

TOP 2021 ROOKIES	RANK
Justin Topa, RHP	14
BREAKOUT PROSPECTS	**RANK**
Eduardo Garcia, SS	11
Jesus Parra, 3B/2B	15
David Hamilton, SS/2B	16

SOURCE OF TOP 30 TALENT

Homegrown	27	Acquired	3
College	13	Trade	1
Junior college	2	Rule 5 draft	0
High school	4	Independent league	0
Nondrafted free agent	0	Free agent/waivers	2
International	8		

LF
Pablo Abreu

CF
Garrett Mitchell (2)
Hedbert Perez (3)
Carlos Rodriguez (12)
Corey Ray (25)
Tyrone Taylor
Eduarqui Fernandez

RF
Luis Medina (19)
Joey Wiemer (24)
Tristen Lutz (28)
Micah Bello (30)

3B
Jesus Parra (15)
Alberto Ciprian
Branlyn Jaraba

SS
Brice Turang (1)
Freddy Zamora (6)
Eduardo Garcia (11)
David Hamilton (16)
Hayden Cantrelle (18)
Jheremy Vargas (23)
Alexander Perez
Jose Caballero

2B
Gabe Holt
Drew Smith
Noah Campbell

1B
Thomas Dillard

C
Mario Feliciano (7)
Zavier Warren (9)
Jeferson Quero (10)
Nick Kahle (17)
Payton Henry
Jacob Nottingham

LHP

LHSP	LHRP
Antoine Kelly (4)	Angel Perdomo (26)
Ethan Small (5)	Clayton Andrews (27)
Aaron Ashby (8)	
Nick Bennett	
Brock Begue	

RHP

RHSP	RHRP
Alec Bettinger (20)	Drew Rasmussen (13)
Dylan File (21)	Justin Topa (14)
Abner Uribe (22)	Phil Bickford (29)
Alexis Ramirez	Victor Castaneda
Zack Brown	Bobby Wahl
Max Lazar	Miguel Sanchez
Edinson Mejia	Matt Hardy
Michele Vassalotti	Luke Barker
Reese Olson	
Bowden Francis	
Noah Zavolas	

Minnesota Twins

BY CARLOS COLLAZO

At some point, something has to give.

Despite winning the American League Central for the second straight year and having a run differential of plus-54 that ranked third in the AL, the Twins once again fell short in the playoffs.

Minnesota extended a North American professional sports record of consecutive postseason losses to 18 after dropping back-to-back games to the sub-.500 Astros in the AL Wild Card Series. Only one team in baseball, the Mariners, has not won a postseason game since the most recent Twins postseason victory, which came against the Yankees on Oct. 5, 2004.

Not recording a single postseason win despite making the playoffs in three of the last four years is a tough pill to swallow. And it's worth asking how long Minnesota can keep its competitive window open.

The team went all-in after signing veteran third baseman Josh Donaldson to the largest free agent deal in franchise history, a four-year, $92 million contract. The deal was the second-largest contract the Twins have given a player, second only to Joe Mauer's eight-year, $184 million extension. Donaldson has proven to be a potent, middle-of-the-order bat when healthy, but injuries limited him to just 22 games in 2020.

In fact, the Twins most impactful hitters in 2020 are elders by the standards of today's game, with Donaldson playing his age-34 season and DH Nelson Cruz leading the team with a 169 OPS+ at the ripe age of 39. With Cruz headed for free agency, there was a chance the Twins would have to replace their most important hitter.

The Twins have internal options waiting in the wings of a deep and talented system. How well players like outfielders Alex Kirilloff and Trevor Larnach and shortstop Royce Lewis adapt to the major leagues could decide how long Minnesota is able to remain a perennial contender atop the AL Central.

If that trio follows in the footsteps of catcher Ryan Jeffers, the Twins' future is in good hands. Jeffers, a 2018 second-round pick out of UNC Wilmington, serves as the biggest success story of Minnesota's current player development group.

Seen as a bit of a reach when he was drafted, Jeffers is so far the only second-rounder from the 2018 draft to make the majors. He did so while being one of the best pitch-framers in baseball in 2020—something most amateur scouts didn't see coming—while managing a 118 OPS+ in 26 games during the pandemic-shortened season.

The Twins have plenty of corner outfield prospects ready to make an impact, led by Kirilloff. That depth is a major reason the club felt comfortable not tendering a contract to Eddie Rosario, one of the Twins' top hitters that last four seasons.

BRACE HEMMELGARN/MINNESOTA TWINS/GETTY IMAGES

Josh Donaldson signed the largest free agent deal in Twins history to anchor a potent lineup.

PROJECTED 2024 LINEUP

Position	Player	Age
Catcher	Ryan Jeffers	27
First Base	Alex Kirilloff	26
Second Base	Luis Arraez	27
Third Base	Royce Lewis	25
Shortstop	Jorge Polanco	30
Left Field	Trevor Larnach	27
Center Field	Byron Buxton	30
Right Field	Max Kepler	31
Designated Hitter	Miguel Sano	31
No. 1 Starter	Jose Berrios	30
No. 2 Starter	Michael Piñeda	35
No. 3 Starter	Kenta Maeda	36
No. 4 Starter	Jhoan Duran	26
No. 5 Starter	Randy Dobnak	29
Closer	Jorge Alcala	28

The team has plenty of righthanded pitchers in their system, with Jhoan Duran and Jordan Balazovic leading a group of starters. Minnesota also has numerous internal options to fill potential holes in the bullpen, including Jorge Alcala and Cody Stashak.

Whether that is enough for the Twins to win a playoff game remains to be seen. But at the very least, they should remain in the playoff picture. ■

1 ALEX KIRILLOFF, OF/1B

Born: Nov. 9, 1997. **B-T:** L-L. **HT:** 6-2. **WT:** 215.
Drafted: HS—Pittsburgh, 2016 (1st round).
Signed by: Jay Weitzel.

TRACK RECORD: The 15th overall selection in the 2016 draft, Kirilloff was considered one of the best pure hitters in the class as the son of a hitting coach. Four years later, he is one of the top pure hitting prospects in baseball. Wrist injuries and Tommy John surgery slowed Kirilloff's development, but he still reached Double-A as a 21-year-old in 2019 and made his major league debut in 2020 when the Twins called him up for their American League Wild Card Series. He became the third player in MLB history to make his major league debut in the postseason and also collected his first hit. That should come as no surprise. Kirilloff was rated the best hitter for average in the Twins' system in 2019, 2020 and again in 2021. In four minor league seasons, he is a career .317 hitter. More encouraging was how he finished his time in the Double-A Southern League in 2019. Plagued by a wrist injury all season, Kirilloff got healthy for the playoffs and homered in four straight games against Biloxi in a first-round series.
SCOUTING REPORT: Kirilloff's bat is his most advanced and exceptional tool. While some players might have better pure bat speed, Kirilloff combines a balanced lefthanded swing, strong hands, quick wrists and the ability to make adjustments mechanically and mentally at an elite level. Where some players have to hit to their strengths, Kirilloff has the rare ability to succeed as a hitter in a variety of ways—using the opposite field, turning on the inner half with authority, handling both velocity and breaking stuff and also understanding the strike zone. Those traits, and the fact that he plays with such a low pulse, give him a chance to become a plus-plus hitter. Kirilloff's game is more about contact than power, but that's a testament to his hitting prowess rather than his lack of pop. Kirilloff's exit velocities in Double-A were above-average for the league—around 91 mph—and if he is able to increase his launch angle—which was below-average in 2019—he could have plus power. His power was sapped due to wrist injuries in 2019, but at full health he has all the tools to be a middle-of-the-order masher. He has shown the ability to homer to his pull side and the opposite field. Kirilloff is a below-average runner, but he is smart on the bases and moves around well enough to handle an outfield corner. In the past he's shown plus arm strength, but most see his arm as average.

TOP ROOKIE

BRACE HEMMELGARN/MINNESOTA TWINS/GETTY IMAGES

BA GRADE
65 Risk: High

SCOUTING GRADES
Hit: 70. **Power:** 60. **Run:** 40. **Field:** 50. **Arm:** 50.

Projected future grades on 20-80 scouting scale.

BEST TOOLS

Best Hitter for Average	Alex Kirilloff
Best Power Hitter	Aaron Sabato
Best Strike-Zone Discipline	LaMonte Wade
Fastest Baserunner	Royce Lewis
Best Athlete	Royce Lewis
Best Fastball	Jhoan Duran
Best Curveball	Dakota Chalmers
Best Slider	Edwar Colina
Best Changeup	Cole Sands
Best Control	Jordan Balazovic
Best Defensive Catcher	Ryan Jeffers
Best Defensive Infielder	Royce Lewis
Best Infield Arm	Keoni Cavaco
Best Defensive Outfielder	Gilberto Celestino
Best Outfield Arm	Gilberto Celestino

Kirilloff is a perfectly adequate defender in left or right field, but some scouts think he has above-average defensive potential at first base, which might be his best fit if he continues to get bigger and stronger with age.
THE FUTURE: The Twins have plenty of confidence in Kirilloff's bat, and he is advanced enough to become a regular fixture in their lineup in 2021. Where he plays defensively will depend more on what Minnesota has around him than Kirilloff himself, but his bat is more than enough to profile in left field, right field or at first base. He has a long career in the Twins lineup ahead.■

Year	Age	Club (League)	Class	AVG	G	AB	R	H	2B	3B	HR	RBI	BB	SO	SB	OBP	SLG
2017	19	Did not play—Injured															
2018	20	Cedar Rapids (MWL)	LoA	.333	65	252	36	84	20	5	13	56	24	47	1	.391	.607
	20	Fort Myers (FSL)	HiA	.362	65	260	39	94	24	2	7	45	14	39	3	.393	.550
2019	21	Pensacola (SL)	AA	.283	94	375	47	106	18	2	9	43	29	76	7	.343	.413
Minor League Totals				.317	279	1103	155	350	71	10	36	177	78	194	11	.365	.498

2 ROYCE LEWIS, SS

TOP ROOKIE

BILLIE WEISS/MLB PHOTOS VIA GETTY IMAGES

BA GRADE

60 Risk: High

Born: June 5, 1999. **B-T:** R-R. **HT:** 6-2. **WT:** 200. **Drafted:** HS—San Juan Capistrano, Calif., 2017 (1st round). **Signed by:** John Leavitt.

TRACK RECORD: The Twins made Lewis the first overall pick in the 2017 draft after a decorated career at national prep power JSerra High in southern California. He looked the part of a No. 1 pick with a strong first two seasons, but he hit .236/.290/.371 at high Class A and Double-A in 2019 while struggling with his consistency. Lewis rebounded to win MVP of the Arizona Fall League after the season, and the Twins brought him to their alternate training site in 2020.

SCOUTING REPORT: The most athletic and naturally gifted player in the Twins' system, Lewis has impressive raw tools but is still learning how to translate them into in-game skills. He has plenty of bat speed, but there's lots of movement in his swing and he can get pull-happy, which creates issues in his lower half and bat path through the zone. He has plate coverage issues on the outer half, particularly against sliders. Lewis does have plus raw power, but questions about his swing and pitch selection prevent him from tapping into it. Lewis has focused on his defensive work at shortstop, particularly with his throwing. He's shown progress and has the elite range and quickness to become an above-average defender at the position with continued reps and refinement. He has also looked sharp in stints at third base and played second base and center field, as well.

THE FUTURE: Lewis needs more repetitions against upper-level pitchers to actualize his talent. His athleticism and potential defensive versatility could help the Twins in 2021 if they need him.

SCOUTING GRADES: **Hitting:** 45 **Power:** 55 **Running:** 70 **Fielding:** 55 **Arm:** 55

Year	Age	Club (League)	Class	AVG	G	AB	R	H	2B	3B	HR	RBI	BB	SO	SB	OBP	SLG
2017	18	Twins (GCL)	R	.271	36	133	38	36	6	2	3	17	19	17	15	.390	.414
	18	Cedar Rapids (MWL)	LoA	.296	18	71	16	21	2	1	1	10	6	16	3	.363	.394
2018	19	Cedar Rapids (MWL)	LoA	.315	75	295	50	93	23	0	9	53	24	49	22	.368	.485
	19	Fort Myers (FSL)	HiA	.255	46	188	33	48	6	3	5	21	19	35	6	.327	.399
2019	20	Fort Myers (FSL)	HiA	.238	94	383	55	91	17	3	10	35	27	90	16	.289	.376
	20	Pensacola (SL)	AA	.231	33	134	18	31	9	1	2	14	11	33	6	.291	.358
Minor League Totals				.266	302	1204	210	320	63	10	30	150	106	240	68	.331	.409

3 TREVOR LARNACH, OF

BILLIE WEISS/MLB PHOTOS VIA GETTY IMAGES

BA GRADE

60 Risk: High

Born: Feb. 26, 1997. **B-T:** L-R. **HT:** 6-4. **WT:** 223. **Drafted:** Oregon State, 2018 (1st round). **Signed by:** Kyle Blackwell.

TRACK RECORD: Larnach was always a solid collegiate hitter at Oregon State, but a power explosion in 2018 pushed him up draft boards and made him the 20th overall pick for the Twins. That newly discovered in-game pop translated to pro ball and Larnach raced to Double-A in his first full season in 2019.

SCOUTING REPORT: Larnach has easy plus power to all fields, but his recent focus has been turning on pitches to his pull side. Only three of his 13 homers in 2019 went to his pull side and, because of that, some teams think attacking Larnach in on the hands is the way to get him out. The left-center alley has always been Larnach's natural attack zone, and he can get crossed off in his lower half and be too opposite-field oriented. The Twins focused on making center field his natural direction and believe he has the intelligence and work ethic to make the adjustment. Larnach possesses terrific body control and the length and direction of his bat path gives him a larger margin for error than most. He has average arm strength and should be serviceable but unspectacular in a corner outfield spot.

THE FUTURE: Larnach should bring power and get on base at a solid clip in the majors. He may be ready for his first callup in 2021.

SCOUTING GRADES: **Hitting:** 50 **Power:** 60 **Running:** 40 **Fielding:** 45 **Arm:** 50

Year	Age	Club (League)	Class	AVG	G	AB	R	H	2B	3B	HR	RBI	BB	SO	SB	OBP	SLG
2018	21	Elizabethton (APP)	R	.311	18	61	10	19	5	0	2	16	10	11	2	.413	.492
	21	Cedar Rapids (MWL)	LoA	.297	24	91	17	27	8	1	3	10	11	17	1	.373	.505
2019	22	Fort Myers (FSL)	HiA	.316	84	320	33	101	26	1	6	44	35	74	4	.382	.459
	22	Pensacola (SL)	AA	.295	43	156	26	46	4	0	7	22	22	50	0	.387	.455
Minor League Totals				.307	169	628	86	193	43	2	18	92	78	152	7	.385	.468

4 RYAN JEFFERS, C

TOP ROOKIE

BILLIE WEISS/MLB PHOTOS VIA GETTY IMAGES

BA GRADE
55 Risk: Medium

Born: June 3, 1997. **B-T:** R-R. **HT:** 6-4. **WT:** 235. **Drafted:** UNC Wilmington, 2018 (2nd round). **Signed by:** Matt Williams.

TRACK RECORD: The Twins' selection of Jeffers in the second round of the 2018 draft was seen as a bit of a reach at the time, but it looked like Minnesota was on to something after a strong pro debut. Jeffers solidified that hunch when he rushed all the way to the majors in 2020 and performed on both sides of the ball.

SCOUTING REPORT: Jeffers is big for a catcher at 6-foot-4, 235 pounds but has taken to Minnesota's new-school approach to catching with aplomb. Setting up in one-knee stances, Jeffers has shown outstanding ability to receive, frame and block in the majors. He does a tremendous job stealing low strikes and can improve by getting better at the top half of the zone. Jeffers doesn't control the running game well—14 of 16 basestealers against him were successful in the majors—but he excels in the areas the Twins have made a priority. Offensively, Jeffers has a simple setup with a low-maintenance swing and a chance to be an above-average hitter with average or a tick better power. He occasionally leaks out, but when he holds his back hip and lets the ball travel, he does damage.

THE FUTURE: Jeffers is a success story for the current Twins' player acquisition and development group. He has all the tools to be an everyday catcher.

SCOUTING GRADES: **Hitting:** 55 **Power:** 50 **Running:** 20 **Fielding:** 60 **Arm:** 45

Year	Age	Club (League)	Class	AVG	G	AB	R	H	2B	3B	HR	RBI	BB	SO	SB	OBP	SLG
2018	21	Cedar Rapids (MWL)	LoA	.288	36	139	19	40	10	0	4	17	14	30	0	.361	.446
	21	Elizabethton (APP)	R	.422	28	102	29	43	7	0	3	16	20	16	0	.543	.578
2019	22	Fort Myers (FSL)	HiA	.256	79	281	35	72	11	0	10	40	28	64	0	.330	.402
	22	Pensacola (SL)	AA	.287	24	87	13	25	5	0	4	9	9	19	0	.374	.483
2020	23	Minnesota (AL)	MAJ	.273	26	55	5	15	0	0	3	7	5	19	0	.355	.436
Major League Totals				.273	26	55	5	15	0	0	3	7	5	19	0	.355	.436
Minor League Totals				.296	167	609	96	180	33	0	21	82	71	129	0	.383	.453

5 JHOAN DURAN, RHP

BILLIE WEISS/MLB PHOTOS VIA GETTY IMAGES

BA GRADE
55 Risk: High

Born: Jan. 8, 1998. **B-T:** R-R. **HT:** 6-5. **WT:** 230. **Signed:** Dominican Republic, 2014. **Signed by:** Jose Ortiz/Junior Noboa (D-backs).

TRACK RECORD: The D-backs signed Duran for $65,000 in 2014 and traded him to the Twins in 2018 in the deal that sent Eduardo Escobar to Arizona. Duran showed signs of breaking out before the trade and solidified that trend with the Twins, reaching Double-A in his first season in the organization.

SCOUTING REPORT: Duran is a physically huge pitcher with two plus-plus offerings. The first is a fastball that sits 96-98 mph and frequently reaches triple-digits. The second is his signature "splinker" which combines low-90s sinker velocity and the downward depth of a splitter. Both pitches generate lots of swing and misses, with the splinker in particular piling up whiffs in the zone on a regular basis. Duran focused on improving his high-spin curveball in 2020 at the alternate training site, particularly his ability to land it and improving its spin efficiency. He's also worked on refining a changeup to give him a softer offering. Duran has a big-bodied, arm-strength oriented operation which can get sloppy at times. Whether he can make the adjustments and get his control to average will determine if he remains a starter.

THE FUTURE: The Twins are developing Duran as a starter and believe he has mid-rotation upside. If his command or third pitch development stalls, his stuff will play in relief

SCOUTING GRADES: **Fastball:** 70 **Curveball:** 50 **Splitter:** 70 **Control:** 50

Year	Age	Club (League)	Class	W	L	ERA	G	GS	IP	H	HR	BB	SO	BB/9	SO/9	WHIP	AVG
2017	19	Hillsboro (NWL)	SS	6	3	4.24	11	11	51	44	5	17	36	3.0	6.4	1.20	.203
	19	Diamondbacks (AZL)	R	0	2	7.15	3	3	11	19	0	4	13	3.2	10.3	2.03	.322
2018	20	Kane County (MWL)	LoA	5	4	4.73	15	15	65	69	6	28	71	3.9	9.9	1.50	.238
	20	Cedar Rapids (MWL)	LoA	2	1	2.00	6	6	36	19	2	10	44	2.5	11.0	0.81	.141
2019	21	Fort Myers (FSL)	HiA	2	9	3.23	16	15	78	63	5	31	95	3.6	11.0	1.21	.188
	21	Pensacola (SL)	AA	3	3	4.86	7	7	37	34	2	9	41	2.2	10.0	1.16	.222
Minor League Totals				23	26	3.94	77	76	374	348	23	131	366	3.2	8.8	1.28	.246

6 JORDAN BALAZOVIC, RHP

BA GRADE
55 **Risk: High**

Born: Sept. 17, 1998. **B-T:** R-R. **HT:** 6-5. **WT:** 215. **Drafted:** HS—Mississauga, Ont., 2016 (5th round). **Signed by:** Walt Burrows.

TRACK RECORD: Balazovic was the top Canadian prospect in the 2016 draft class. The Twins took a shot on his lean, projectable frame and developing fastball and signed him for $515,000 in the fifth round. Balazovic broke out with a 2.69 ERA at the Class A levels in 2019 and made the Futures Game. He was a late addition to the alternate training site in 2020.

SCOUTING REPORT: Balazovic's standout fastball command sets up the rest of his arsenal. His heater ranges from 89-96 mph and sits around 93, with above-average carry and deception that helps it play up. His secondaries are solid but not overwhelming. Balazovic throws a curveball in the 78-82 mph range that is potentially an above-average pitch, and his average changeup gives him a third offering to keep hitters off-balance. Balazovic has walked just 2.7 batters per nine innings throughout his minor league career, though he has yet to face upper-level hitters.

THE FUTURE: With a strong, 6-foot-5, 215-pound frame and a long history of good strikeout and walk rates, Balazovic has the foundation to be a part of the Twins' starting rotation in the coming years. His upside will depend on how much he can get out of his secondaries.

SCOUTING GRADES:	Fastball: 55	Curveball: 55	Changeup: 50	Control: 55

Year	Age	Club (League)	Class	W	L	ERA	G	GS	IP	H	HR	BB	SO	BB/9	SO/9	WHIP	AVG
2017	18	Twins (GCL)	R	1	3	4.91	10	3	40	47	5	20	29	4.5	6.5	1.66	.257
2018	19	Cedar Rapids (MWL)	LoA	7	3	3.94	12	11	62	54	5	18	78	2.6	11.4	1.17	.213
2019	20	Cedar Rapids (MWL)	LoA	2	1	2.18	4	4	21	15	1	4	33	1.7	14.4	0.92	.181
	20	Fort Myers (FSL)	HiA	6	4	2.84	15	14	73	52	3	21	96	2.6	11.8	1.00	.163
Minor League Totals				18	12	3.32	49	38	227	194	14	68	252	2.7	10.0	1.15	.226

7 AARON SABATO, 1B

REBECCA LAWSON

BA GRADE
50 **Risk: High**

Born: June 4, 1999. **B-T:** R-R. **HT:** 6-2. **WT:** 230. **Drafted:** North Carolina, 2020 (1st round). **Signed by:** Ty Dawson.

TRACK RECORD: Sabato went undrafted out of high school but made an immediate impact at North Carolina, smashing a freshman program-record 18 homers in 2019. Sabato had some of the best raw power in the 2020 class as a draft-eligible sophomore, prompting the Twins to draft him with the 27th overall pick and sign him for $2.75 million.

SCOUTING REPORT: Sabato's signature trait is his massive power potential. He has near top-of-the-scale raw power and can leave any ballpark from foul pole to foul pole on account of his brute natural strength and massive wrists and forearms. Sabato has a compact operation and a clean rotation in his swing. He doesn't need to cheat to catch up to velocity and isn't overly susceptible to breaking balls, helping him project as an average hitter. He showed good strike zone-recognition in college and should continue to post high on-base percentages. Sabato is strictly limited to first base defensively. He's a below-average defender with a below-average arm and well below-average speed. He's a big, slow mover and may end up becoming a full-time designated hitter.

THE FUTURE: Sabato has the most power potential of any player in the Twins' system. There is a lot of pressure on his bat, but he shows the traits of an impact slugger who can make it work.

SCOUTING GRADES:	Hitting: 50	Power: 70	Running: 30	Fielding: 40	Arm: 40

Year	Age	Club (League)	Class	AVG	G	AB	R	H	2B	3B	HR	RBI	BB	SO	SB	OBP	SLG
2020	21	Did not play—No minor league season															

8 MATT CANTERINO, RHP

Born: Dec. 14, 1997. **B-T:** R-R. **HT:** 6-2. **WT:** 222. **Drafted:** Rice, 2019 (2nd round). **Signed by:** Greg Runser.

TRACK RECORD: Canterino was one of the most consistent and effective starting pitchers in the 2019 draft despite an unorthodox delivery. The Twins drafted him 54th overall out of Rice and signed him for $1.1 million. Canterino reached low Class A in an impressive pro debut and was a late addition to the Twins' alternate training site in 2020.

SCOUTING REPORT: Canterino throws a standard four-pitch mix that includes a fastball, slider, curveball and changeup. His fastball averages 93 mph and plays up with additional life and cutting action as a result of a tweak in his thumb placement. Canterino's 83-85 mph slider is his best secondary. The pitch is above-average, while his slower, upper-70s curveball has more top-to-bottom action and projects as an average pitch. Canterino added 8-10 inches of depth to his changeup at the alternate site after changing his grip and becoming more comfortable with the pitch. His delivery has plenty of moving parts and could be high-maintenance long-term, but he has a track record of throwing strikes with above-average control and staying in sync.

THE FUTURE: Canterino doesn't have loud stuff, but the way he mixes his offerings with solid control helps him project as a potential back-end starter. He should see Double-A in 2021.

BA GRADE
50 Risk: High

SCOUTING GRADES: **Fastball:** 55 **Slider:** 55 **Curveball:** 50 **Changeup:** 50 **Control:** 55

Year	Age	Club (League)	Class	W	L	ERA	G	GS	IP	H	HR	BB	SO	K/9	WHIP	AVG
2019	21	Twins (GCL)	R	0	0	1.80	2	2	5	2	0	1	6	10.8	0.60	.118
	21	Cedar Rapids (MWL)	LoA	1	1	1.35	5	5	20	6	0	7	25	11.3	0.65	.091
Minor League Totals				1	1	1.44	7	7	25	8	0	8	31	11.2	0.64	.096

9 BLAYNE ENLOW, RHP

Born: March 21, 1999. **B-T:** R-R. **HT:** 6-3. **WT:** 210. **Drafted:** HS—St. Amant, La., 2017 (3rd round). **Signed by:** Greg Runser.

TRACK RECORD: Enlow was a projectable, high-upside pitcher out of high school with great feel to spin a breaking ball. The Twins liked him enough to draft him in the third round in 2017 and sign him for an above-slot $2 million to buy him out of a Louisiana State commitment. After reaching high Class A Fort Myers in 2019, Enlow was not included at the Twins alternate training site in 2020 but was brought to instructional league after the season.

SCOUTING REPORT: Enlow has filled out his 6-foot-3 frame and added strength to improve his fastball velocity each year. After getting into the 92-96 mph range at the Class A levels in 2019, Enlow consistently sat 94-97 mph in instructional league in 2020. While his fastball lacks standout movement, he has shown ability to command it. Enlow has two distinct breaking balls that are both average. His slider is firm and resembles a cutter at times in the low 90s, while his curveball is a slurvier offering with occasional depth. Enlow's changeup has progressed to show fading life and sink that complements his fastball nicely. He previously didn't focus much on his changeup, but it progressed significantly this summer and now projects as his best secondary offering. He throws enough strikes with average control.

THE FUTURE: Enlow has progressed in important areas including velocity, physicality and changeup feel. His ceiling is somewhat capped at the back of the rotation unless he can get more from one of his breaking pitches.

BA GRADE
50 Risk: High

SCOUTING GRADES: **Fastball:** 55 **Slider:** 50 **Curveball:** 50 **Changeup:** 55 **Control:** 50

Year	Age	Club (League)	Class	W	L	ERA	G	GS	IP	H	HR	BB	SO	BB/9	SO/9	WHIP	AVG
2017	18	Twins (GCL)	R	3	0	1.33	6	1	20	10	1	4	19	1.8	8.4	0.69	.130
2018	19	Cedar Rapids (MWL)	LoA	3	5	3.26	20	17	94	94	4	35	71	3.4	6.8	1.37	.230
2019	20	Cedar Rapids (MWL)	LoA	4	3	4.57	8	8	41	42	4	15	44	3.3	9.6	1.38	.227
	20	Fort Myers (FSL)	HiA	4	4	3.38	13	12	69	61	4	23	51	3.0	6.6	1.21	.210
Minor League Totals				14	12	3.36	47	38	225	207	13	77	185	3.1	7.4	1.26	.242

10 GILBERTO CELESTINO, OF

BILLIE WEISS/MLB PHOTOS VIA GETTY IMAGES

BA GRADE
50 **Risk: High**

Born: Feb. 13, 1999. **B-T:** R-L. **HT:** 6-0. **WT:** 195. **Signed:** Dominican Republic, 2015. **Signed by:** Oz Ocampo/Roman Ocumarez (Astros).

TRACK RECORD: Celestino was one of the top prospects in the 2015 international class and signed with the Astros for $2.5 million. The Twins acquired him in the 2018 deal that sent righthander Ryan Pressly to Houston. Celestino impressed in his new organization and starred at low Class A Cedar Rapids in 2019. The Twins brought him to their alternate training site in 2020.

SCOUTING REPORT: Celestino isn't the toolsiest player, but he does many things at a high level. He's a plus defender in center field despite being an average runner because of his exceptional reads and route-running. His plus arm also allows him to play right field. Celestino is more hit-over-power, but he has slowly added strength and may develop sneaky power as he continues to grow. He has some moving parts to his setup, including a high leg kick, but he knows his body and his swing well. Celestino has good strike-zone awareness and has improved his ability to hit to all fields. He spent 2020 working to control his stride and load more consistently in order to not be susceptible to elevated fastballs and breaking balls.

THE FUTURE: Celestino has a chance to be an everyday center fielder with an above-average bat. His ability to play all three outfield spots gives him a fallback as reserve outfielder.

SCOUTING GRADES: **Hitting:** 50 **Power:** 40 **Running:** 50 **Fielding:** 60 **Arm:** 60

Year	Age	Club (League)	Class	AVG	G	AB	R	H	2B	3B	HR	RBI	BB	SO	SB	OBP	SLG
2017	18	Greeneville (APP)	R	.268	59	235	38	63	10	2	4	24	22	59	10	.331	.379
2018	19	Corpus Christi (TL)	AA	.000	3	8	0	0	0	0	0	0	0	5	0	.000	.000
	19	Elizabethton (APP)	R	.266	27	109	13	29	4	1	1	13	6	16	8	.308	.349
	19	Tri-City (NYP)	SS	.323	34	127	18	41	8	0	4	21	10	25	14	.387	.480
2019	20	Cedar Rapids (MWL)	LoA	.276	117	450	52	124	24	3	10	51	48	81	14	.350	.409
	20	Fort Myers (FSL)	HiA	.300	8	30	6	9	4	0	0	3	2	4	0	.333	.433
Minor League Totals				.274	304	1150	156	315	62	10	21	131	121	229	61	.346	.400

11 COLE SANDS, RHP

BA GRADE
50 **Risk: High**

Born: July 17, 1997. **B-T:** R-R. **HT:** 6-3. **WT:** 215. **Drafted:** Florida State, 2018 (5th round). **Signed by:** Brett Dowdy.

TRACK RECORD: Sands was drafted by the Twins in the fifth round in 2018 after posting career bests in his strikeout and walk rates at Florida State. He didn't pitch in pro ball that season after dealing with biceps tendonitis, but he had a strong pro debut in 2019 when he posted a 2.68 ERA across three levels and reached Double-A Pensacola.

SCOUTING REPORT: Sands has a strong three-pitch mix including a fastball, curveball and changeup. After sitting around 93 mph in 2019, Sands saw his velo climb and averaged 95 mph in 2020. He delivers the ball from a low three-quarters arm slot that gets on hitters fast. Sands was previously most comfortable with a changeup that flashed plus, but he's made progress with a big, sweeping breaking ball. The pitch averages 2,800 revolutions per minute and could turn into a weapon if he can spot it down and in the zone more frequently. Sands walked a tick too many batters in college, but his control has been above-average in pro ball.

THE FUTURE: With improved fastball velocity and a better curveball, Sands has a path to being more than just a back-end starter. He'll spend 2021 in the upper levels and could make his major league debut.

Year	Age	Club (League)	Class	W	L	ERA	G	GS	IP	H	HR	BB	SO	BB/9	SO/9	WHIP	AVG
2019	21	Cedar Rapids (MWL)	LoA	2	1	3.05	8	8	41	41	0	11	49	2.4	10.7	1.26	.236
	21	Fort Myers (FSL)	HiA	5	2	2.25	9	9	52	36	4	7	53	1.2	9.2	0.83	.213
	21	Pensacola (SL)	AA	0	0	4.50	1	1	4	4	0	1	6	2.3	13.5	1.25	.235
Minor League Totals				7	3	2.68	18	18	97	81	4	19	108	1.8	10.0	1.03	.228

12 BRENT ROOKER, OF/1B

BA GRADE
45 **Risk: Medium**

Born: Nov. 1, 1994. **B-T:** R-R. **HT:** 6-3. **WT:** 225. **Drafted:** Mississippi State, 2017 (1st round supplemental). **Signed by:** Derrick Dunbar.

TRACK RECORD: The Twins drafted Rooker with the 35th overall pick in 2017 after he won Southeastern Conference Player of the Year at Mississippi State. After homering at a steady clip in the minors for three seasons, Rooker made his big league debut in 2020 and continued to show impressive power.

SCOUTING REPORT: Rooker has massive raw power and the ability to hit 25-30 home runs per season. That plus power comes with plenty of strikeouts, however, and his whiff rate eclipsed 34% in 2019 at Triple-A Rochester. The Twins believe Rooker controls the strike zone better than he gets credit for. He does see a decent amount of pitches and has the potential to walk at a solid clip that could offset a low batting average. Rooker's contributions will primarily be on the offensive side of the ball. He's a below-average defender in left field and at first base.
THE FUTURE: Rooker's power should allow him to be a contributor in 2021. He may be a hitter who cycles through first base, DH and the bench as opposed to an everyday player.

Year	Age	Club (League)	Class	AVG	G	AB	R	H	2B	3B	HR	RBI	BB	SO	SB	OBP	SLG
2020	25	Minnesota (AL)	MAJ	.316	7	19	4	6	2	0	1	5	0	5	0	.381	.579
Major League Totals				.316	7	19	4	6	2	0	1	5	0	5	0	.381	.579
Minor League Totals				.267	259	965	157	258	59	4	54	178	119	313	10	.357	.505

13 MISAEL URBINA, OF

BA GRADE 55 Risk: Extreme

Born: April 26, 2002. **B-T:** R-R. **HT:** 6-0. **WT:** 175. **Signed:** Venezuela, 2018. **Signed by:** Fred Guerrero.

TRACK RECORD: Urbina was one of the top Venezuelan prospects in the 2018 international class and signed with the Twins for $2.75 million. He lived up to his billing with a strong 2019 season in the Dominican Summer League, showing solid bat-to-ball skills and batting .279/.382/.443.
SCOUTING REPORT: Urbina has exciting potential, but he is still a fairly raw teenager and needs as many game reps as possible. He has a chance to be an above-average or better hitter thanks to his natural feel for the barrel, but the Twins want him to get less rotational in his swing. The goal is to sync his lower and upper halves to spread the ball around the field better. Urbina doesn't project as a huge power threat, but the canceled 2020 minor league season allowed him to focus on strength gains, and he is in better shape than he was a year ago. Urbina has upside defensively as a plus runner who could stick in center field, but he needs to focus on the details of outfield defense to shore up some rough edges. Urbina has an upbeat personality and an advanced, instinctual baseball mind for his age
THE FUTURE: Urbina possesses some of the most exciting potential in the lower levels of Minnesota's system. He is set to make his stateside debut in 2021.

Year	Age	Club (League)	Class	AVG	G	AB	R	H	2B	3B	HR	RBI	BB	SO	SB	OBP	SLG
2019	17	Twins (DSL)	R	.279	50	183	34	51	14	5	2	26	23	14	19	.382	.443
Minor League Totals				.279	50	183	34	51	14	5	2	26	23	14	19	.382	.443

14 JORGE ALCALA, RHP

BA GRADE 50 Risk: High

Born: July 28, 1995. **B-T:** R-R. **HT:** 6-3. **WT:** 205. **Signed:** Dominican Republic, 2014. **Signed by:** Oz Ocampo/Roman Ocumarez/Leocadio Guevara (Astros).

TRACK RECORD: The Astros signed Alacala as an 18-year-old in 2014 and helped him gain nearly 10 mph on his fastball before flipping him to the Twins in a trade for Ryan Pressly in 2018. After struggling as a starter, Alcala transitioned to the bullpen in late 2019 and he posted a 2.64 ERA over 24 innings in the majors in 2020.
SCOUTING REPORT: Alcala threw four pitches as a starter but now primarily works with two pitches. His plus-plus fastball averages 97 mph and touches 100 mph, while his firm, upper-80s slider generates frequent swings and misses and is a plus pitch. Alcala occasionally throws a firm changeup that has less drop and more armside running action than average changeups, but he only uses it around 10% of the time. Alcala has plenty of athleticism on the mound, but his body control and overall strike-throwing are questionable and erratic.
THE FUTURE: Alcala has the pure stuff to be a closer. He'll need to refine his control to be consistently trusted in high-leverage situations.

Year	Age	Club (League)	Class	W	L	ERA	G	GS	IP	H	HR	BB	SO	BB/9	SO/9	WHIP	AVG
2020	24	Minnesota (AL)	MAJ	2	1	2.63	16	0	24	21	3	8	27	3.0	10.1	1.21	.244
Major League Totals				2	1	2.45	18	0	25	22	3	9	28	3.2	9.8	1.21	.239
Minor League Totals				21	27	3.80	104	62	407	346	30	170	405	3.8	9.0	1.27	.231

15 KEONI CAVACO, SS/3B

Born: June 2, 2001. **B-T:** R-R. **HT:** 6-2. **WT:** 195. **Drafted:** HS—Chula Vista, Calif., 2019 (1st round). **Signed by:** John Leavitt.

TRACK RECORD: Cavaco was far from a household name in the leadup to the 2019 draft but rocketed up draft boards after showing big raw tools his senior year at San Diego-area power Eastlake High. The Twins drafted him 13th overall and signed him for $4.05 million. Cavaco made his pro debut in the Rookie-level Gulf Coast League and struggled mightily, batting .172 with one home run and 35 strikeouts in 92 plate appearances. His only 2020 action came at instructional league.

SCOUTING REPORT: Cavaco has a lot of work to do. He has significant swing-and-miss concerns, particularly against velocity, and the Twins have made a wholesale effort to improve his swing path and approach. Cavaco struggles to land square and keep his hips in line, a basic tenet of hitting that is concerning he hasn't mastered yet. Cavaco has plus bat speed and plus raw power, but he needs massive refinement to get to the point where they are usable in games. Cavaco was drafted as a shortstop and played there in his pro debut, but he projects to move off the position and be an above-average third baseman with a plus arm.

THE FUTURE: The canceled 2020 minor league season hurts, but being able to focus on foundational elements in a low-pressure environment could prove beneficial for Cavaco. He may see low Class A in 2021.

Year	Age	Club (League)	Class	AVG	G	AB	R	H	2B	3B	HR	RBI	BB	SO	SB	OBP	SLG
2019	18	Twins (GCL)	R	.172	25	87	9	15	4	0	1	6	4	35	1	.217	.253
Minor League Totals				.172	25	87	9	15	4	0	1	6	4	35	1	.217	.253

16 LAMONTE WADE, OF/1B

BA GRADE
40 Risk: Low

Born: Jan. 1, 1994. **B-T:** L-L. **HT:** 6-1. **WT:** 205. **Drafted:** Maryland, 2015 (9th round). **Signed by:** John Wilson.

TRACK RECORD: The Twins drafted Wade in the ninth round in 2015 because of his fluid lefthanded swing and chance to stick in center field. He progressively climbed the minors and made his major league debut in 2019. He returned to Minnesota in 2020 and appeared in 16 games while playing all three outfield spots and first base.

SCOUTING REPORT: Wade has arguably the best eye of any player in the Twins system. His patient approach and ability to control the strike zone have yielded a strong walk rate in his brief major league time, helping make up for a lack of impact in his swing. The Twins have tried to open Wade's stance up so he has more room to turn on inside pitches. A solid-average runner, Wade is serviceable at all three outfield positions but is better in the corners. His best defensive position is first base.

THE FUTURE: Wade's on-base skills and defensive versatility give him a chance to stick in a reserve role. He's ready to fill that role now and should be back in the majors in 2021.

Year	Age	Club (League)	Class	AVG	G	AB	R	H	2B	3B	HR	RBI	BB	SO	SB	OBP	SLG
2020	26	Minnesota (AL)	MAJ	.231	16	39	3	9	3	0	0	1	4	9	1	.318	.308
Major League Totals				.211	42	95	13	20	5	1	2	6	15	18	1	.336	.347
Minor League Totals				.276	480	1710	265	472	70	17	40	238	303	281	44	.389	.407

17 ALERICK SOULARIE, 2B/OF

Born: July 5, 1999. **B-T:** R-R. **HT:** 6-0. **WT:** 175. **Drafted:** Tennessee, 2020 (2nd round). **Signed by:** Jack Powell.

TRACK RECORD: The Cardinals drafted Soularie out of San Jacinto (Texas) JC in the 29th round in 2018, but he instead opted to transfer to Tennessee. He upped his draft stock by becoming one of the Volunteers' most reliable hitters in two seasons in Knoxville and finished with a career .336/.448/.586 slash line. The Twins drafted him 59th overall in 2020 and signed him for $900,000.

SCOUTING REPORT: A bit of a throwback player, Soularie has an old-school setup at the plate with a hunched and closed-off stance. His hands do most of the work in his swing and he has demonstrated the bat-to-ball skills to be an average hitter. The Twins want to help him try and access his average raw power, which he didn't do much in college. Primarily a left fielder at Tennessee, Soularie spent most of his time at second base in instructional league after being drafted. He is a solid runner and has the tools to be an adequate infielder, although it's still a work in progress.

THE FUTURE: Soularie is a well-rounded player who can do a little bit of everything. How his power and infield defense develop will determine if he reaches his everyday potential.

Year	Age	Club (League)	Class	AVG	G	AB	R	H	2B	3B	HR	RBI	BB	SO	SB	OBP	SLG
2020	20	Did not play—No minor league season															

18 MATT WALLNER, OF

Born: Dec. 12, 1997. **B-T:** L-R. **HT:** 6-5. **WT:** 220. **Drafted:** Southern Mississippi, 2019 (1st round supplemental). **Signed by:** Derrick Dunbar.

TRACK RECORD: One of the most decorated players in Southern Mississippi history, Wallner set the program's career record with 58 home runs and was drafted 39th overall by the Twins in 2019. He climbed to low Class A in his pro debut, but his feast or famine approach was exposed against pro pitching.

SCOUTING REPORT: Wallner has prototypical right field tools with a large physical frame, plus-plus raw power from the left side and massive arm strength, but that comes with significant swing-and-miss concerns. Wallner struck out 27 percent of the time in his pro debut despite playing largely younger competition. He projects as a below-average hitter who will be almost entirely dependent on his home run production to be an offensive contributor. A fringy runner and athlete, Wallner won't track down many tough balls in the gaps in right field, but he does have a cannon for an arm.

THE FUTURE: Wallner will need to show an improved hit tool to project as a regular. He'll see high Class A in 2021.

Year	Age	Club (League)	Class	AVG	G	AB	R	H	2B	3B	HR	RBI	BB	SO	SB	OBP	SLG
2019	21	Cedar Rapids (MWL)	LoA	.205	12	44	7	9	3	1	2	6	5	14	0	.340	.455
	21	Elizabethton (APP)	R	.269	53	208	35	56	18	1	6	28	19	66	1	.361	.452
Minor League Totals				.258	65	252	42	65	21	2	8	34	24	80	1	.357	.452

19 JOSH WINDER, RHP

BREAKOUT
BA GRADE
50 Risk: High

Born: Oct. 11, 1996. **B-T:** R-R. **HT:** 6-5. **WT:** 210. **Drafted:** Virginia Military Institute, 2018 (7th round). **Signed by:** Matt Williams.

TRACK RECORD: After a strong sophomore season at Virginia Military Institute, Winder slipped during his junior year when his stuff backed up and he got hit around more. The Twins still liked him enough to draft him in the seventh round. Winder rewarded the organization by leading the low Class A Midwest League with a 2.65 ERA in 2019. He followed up by standing out as one of the most improved prospects in the system during 2020 instructional league.

SCOUTING REPORT: An intense worker, Winder took advantage of the time allotted by the coronavirus shutdown to improve. He arrived at instructional league with improved physicality and a better pitch mix across the board. After previously sitting in the low-90s with his fastball, Winder sat 96-97 mph in camp and also improved his slider to above-average. Combined with his average changeup and curveball, he now has the stuff to profile as a major league starter. Winder has a long track record of above-average control. He has a good feel for sequencing and mixing his stuff.

THE FUTURE: Winder's improvements were highly encouraging. He'll try to carry them over into 2021.

Year	Age	Club (League)	Class	W	L	ERA	G	GS	IP	H	HR	BB	SO	BB/9	SO/9	WHIP	AVG
2019	22	Cedar Rapids (MWL)	LoA	7	2	2.65	21	21	126	93	10	30	118	2.1	8.5	0.98	.188
Minor League Totals				10	3	2.90	30	30	164	130	11	36	160	2.0	8.8	1.01	.216

20 CODY STASHAK, RHP

BA GRADE
40 Risk: Low

Born: March 9, 1994. **B-T:** R-R. **HT:** 6-4. **WT:** 185. **Signed:** St. John's, 2015 (13th round). **Signed by:** John Wilson

TRACK RECORD: Stashak was drafted in the 13th round by the Twins in 2015 and signed for $100,000. He spent his first three seasons as a starter before converting to the bullpen in 2018 and shot up the system as a reliever. Stashak made his major league debut in 2019 and returned to the majors in 2020, settling in as a reliable reliever with an unorthodox pitch mix.

SCOUTING REPORT: In an era where relievers are expected to throw in the mid-90s, Stashak has found success sitting 91-92 mph. His slider also has below-average velocity in the 81-83 mph range. Yet, both pitches miss bats. His fastball has elite vertical movement and good carry up in the strike zone, while his slider has solid depth and above-average horizontal movement. He also has a changeup he will occasionally throw. Stashak has standout control of his stuff and makes the most of the movement he has. His walk rate is the second-lowest lowest of any reliever who has thrown at least 30 innings since in 2019.

THE FUTURE: Stashak has proven his ability to keep his team in games despite below-average velocity. He will remain a part of the Twins bullpen plans in 2021.

Year	Age	Club (League)	Class	W	L	ERA	G	GS	IP	H	HR	BB	SO	BB/9	SO/9	WHIP	AVG
2020	26	Minnesota (AL)	MAJ	1	0	3.00	11	0	15	11	2	3	17	1.8	10.2	0.93	.204
Major League Totals				1	1	3.15	29	1	40	40	5	4	42	0.9	9.5	1.10	.258
Minor League Totals				28	15	3.15	123	50	374	317	25	88	381	2.1	9.2	1.08	.229

21 EDWAR COLINA, RHP

BA GRADE **45** Risk: High

Born: May 3, 1997. **B-T:** R-R. **HT:** 5-11. **WT:** 240. **Signed:** Venezuela, 2015. **Signed by:** Jose Leon.

TRACK RECORD: Colina was an older international signee out of Venezuela who received just an $8,000 signing bonus. After starting for four years and working his way up to Triple-A, Colina moved to relief in 2020 and made his major league debut on Sept. 25 against the Reds.

SCOUTING REPORT: Colina has a short but large frame and throws two pitches out of a simple delivery and short arm action. He attacks east-west with a hard, running sinker in the 95-99 mph range and a mid-80s slider with lots of horizontal movement. His slider moves hard and late and he has a better feel to command it than his sinker. Colina has below-average command overall and is susceptible to lefthanded hitters, which got exposed when he gave up three hits, four runs and two walks in his debut.

THE FUTURE: Colina will need to improve his fastball command to be effective in a middle relief role. That will be his primary goal in 2021.

Year	Age	Club (League)	Class	W	L	ERA	G	GS	IP	H	HR	BB	SO	BB/9	SO/9	WHIP	AVG
2020	23	Minnesota (AL)	MAJ	0	0	81.00	1	0	0	4	1	2	0	54.0	0.0	18.00	.800
Major League Totals				0	0	81.00	1	0	0	4	1	2	0	54.0	0.0	18.00	.800
Minor League Totals				19	15	2.80	66	58	324	257	16	140	316	3.9	8.8	1.22	.216

22 CHRIS VALLIMONT, RHP

BA GRADE **45** Risk: High

Born: March 18, 1997. **B-T:** R-R. **HT:** 6-5. **WT:** 220. **Drafted:** Mercyhurst, 2018 (5th round). **Signed by:** Alex Smith (Marlins).

TRACK RECORD: Vallimont posted a 2.54 ERA over three years at Division II Mercyhurst (Pa.) and struck out 147 batters in 80.1 innings as a junior. The Marlins drafted him in the fifth round in 2018 and signed him for $300,000. The Twins acquired Vallimont with Sergio Romo from Miami in a 2019 trade for Lewin Diaz. He showed well at high Class A Fort Myers in his first stint in the organization and was brought to instructional league in 2020.

SCOUTING REPORT: Vallimont has a solid build for a starting pitcher and an intriguing pitch mix. He throws his fastball in the 90-92 mph range with elite carry and can reach back for 95-96 mph. He shows good feel to spin both a slider and curveball that flash average, while his changeup has flashed average but has never been consistent. Vallimont has an advanced feel for pitching and will throw any of his four pitches at any time. He throws everything for strikes with average control.

THE FUTURE: Vallimont has back-of-the-rotation potential with his varied arsenal and advanced feel for pitching. He'll try to show his stuff plays against upper-level hitters in 2021.

Year	Age	Club (League)	Class	W	L	ERA	G	GS	IP	H	HR	BB	SO	BB/9	SO/9	WHIP	AVG
2019	22	Jupiter (FSL)	HiA	2	3	3.50	6	6	36	31	3	11	42	2.8	10.5	1.17	.211
	22	Clinton (MWL)	LoA	4	4	2.99	13	13	69	48	4	26	80	3.4	10.4	1.07	.177
	22	Fort Myers (FSL)	HiA	2	2	3.63	4	4	22	15	0	4	28	1.6	11.3	0.85	.152
Minor League Totals				8	11	3.79	35	34	156	117	10	64	170	3.7	9.8	1.16	.206

23 EMMANUEL RODRIGUEZ, OF

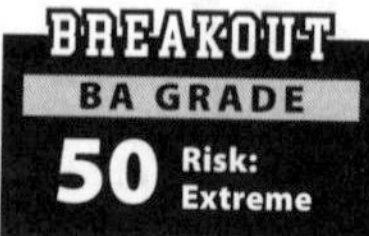

Born: Feb. 28, 2003. **B-T:** L-L. **HT:** 5-11. **WT:** 200. **Signed:** Dominican Republic, 2019 Signed by: Manuel Luciano.

TRACK RECORD: Rodriguez was the Twins' top target in the 2019 international class and signed for $2.5 million. His expected pro debut in 2020 was delayed by the coronavirus pandemic and canceled minor league season.

SCOUTING REPORT: Rodriguez stands out for his low-maintenance swing, direct bat path and plus raw power. He has improved his ability to use the entire field in recent years and the Twins believe he has a chance to become a plus hitter. A hand injury has limited Rodriguez, but he spent time doing throwing drills and long-toss work after struggling with his throwing accuracy and arm stroke during the spring. He has plus arm strength when he's right and is currently a solid-average runner in center field. He projects to slow down as he fills out and may move to right field.

THE FUTURE: Rodriguez is set to make his pro debut in 2021. He has plenty of tools to dream on but is a long ways away.

Year	Age	Club (League)	Class	AVG	G	AB	R	H	2B	3B	HR	RBI	BB	SO	SB	OBP	SLG
2019	16	Did not play—Signed 2020 contract															

24 DAKOTA CHALMERS, RHP

BA GRADE
50 Risk: Extreme

Born: Oct. 8, 1996. **B-T:** R-R. **HT:** 6-3. **WT:** 175. **Drafted:** HS—Cumming, Ga., 2015 (3rd round). **Signed by:** Jemel Spearman (Athletics).

TRACK RECORD: Chalmers signed an over-slot $1.2 million deal with the Athletics as a third-round pick in 2015, but he struggled to throw strikes for three seasons before having Tommy John surgery in 2018. The Twins acquired him for Fernando Rodney that year while he was rehabbing. Chalmers returned to the mound with high Class A Fort Myers at the end of 2019 and spent 2020 at the alternate training site.

SCOUTING REPORT: Chalmers' stuff is undeniable. His fastball is a high-spin 93-96 mph pitch that has touched 100 mph in the past. He complements it with a high-spin curveball that reaches 2,800 revolutions per minute with impressive depth in the low 80s. Both pitches are plus and he also has a fringy changeup. Control is the ultimate question with Chalmers. He has walked 6.6 batters per nine innings in his minor league career and frequently misses the strike zone with all of his pitches.

THE FUTURE: The Twins have confidence Chalmers can improve his control enough to start. His pure stuff profiles nicely in the bullpen as a fallback.

Year	Age	Club (League)	Class	W	L	ERA	G	GS	IP	H	HR	BB	SO	BB/9	SO/9	WHIP	AVG
2019	22	Twins (GCL)	R	1	0	4.05	4	4	13	8	0	8	19	5.4	12.8	1.20	.148
	22	Fort Myers (FSL)	HiA	1	1	3.38	5	5	21	12	0	15	29	6.3	12.2	1.27	.093
Minor League Totals				9	8	3.98	47	39	156	108	9	114	185	6.6	10.7	1.42	.193

25 TRAVIS BLANKENHORN, 2B/OF

Born: Aug. 3, 1996. **B-T:** L-R. **HT:** 6-2. **WT:** 235. **Drafted:** HS—Pottsville, Pa., 2015 (3rd round). **Signed by:** Jay Weitzel.

TRACK RECORD: A standout three-sport athlete in high school, Blankenhorn signed with the Twins for $800,000 as a third-round pick in 2015. After reaching Double-A in a solid 2019 season, Blankenhorn made his major league debut in 2020 and went 1-for-3 with a double in his lone game.

SCOUTING REPORT: Blankenhorn doesn't have any plus tools, but he does a lot of things well. He's a functional hitter who could be fringe-average with average power. He puts together solid at-bats but has never walked much, which limits his ability to get on base. Defensively, Blankenhorn can handle a number of positions adequately including first base, second base, third base and the outfield corners. He has average speed but is an efficient basestealer.

THE FUTURE: Blankenhorn's ceiling is limited, but he does enough things well to contribute in a reserve or utility role. He should start 2021 in Triple-A.

Year	Age	Club (League)	Class	AVG	G	AB	R	H	2B	3B	HR	RBI	BB	SO	SB	OBP	SLG
2020	23	Minnesota (AL)	MAJ	.333	1	3	0	1	1	0	0	0	0	0	0	.500	.667
Major League Totals				.333	1	3	0	1	1	0	0	0	0	0	0	.500	.667
Minor League Totals				.257	462	1742	237	448	87	24	56	244	142	455	38	.325	.431

26 BEN RORTVEDT, C

BA GRADE
40 Risk: High

Born: Sept. 19, 1994. **B-T:** L-R. **HT:** 5-10. **WT:** 205. **Drafted:** HS—Verona, Wis., 2016 (2nd round). **Signed by:** Mark Wilson.

TRACK RECORD: Rortvedt was part of a strong Wisconsin high school class in 2016 that included Gavin Lux. He was drafted 56th overall by the Twins and signed for $900,000. Rortvedt progressed to Double-A Pensacola in 2019 before finishing the year on the injured list with a knee injury. He got back on the field for instructional league in 2020 and was added to the 40-man roster after the season.

SCOUTING REPORT: Rortvedt has standout defensive skills behind the plate. He is an excellent receiver and blocker and draws high praise for his ability to work with pitchers. He has adapted to Minnesota's one-knee catching philosophy with aplomb and has plus arm strength, allowing him to frequently throw runners out from one knee. Rortvedt's offense is a different story. He has a choppy, top-hand heavy swing and slow bat speed, resulting mostly in ground balls and infield flies. He generally hits the ball the other way, so learning to elevate more frequently to his pull side has been an emphasis.

THE FUTURE: Rortvedt's catch-and-throw ability offers him a path to the majors as a backup. Barring a sudden, significant change, he does not project to hit enough to be more.

Year	Age	Club (League)	Class	AVG	G	AB	R	H	2B	3B	HR	RBI	BB	SO	SB	OBP	SLG
2019	21	Fort Myers (FSL)	HiA	.238	24	80	13	19	8	1	2	10	12	16	0	.340	.438
	21	Pensacola (SL)	AA	.239	55	197	19	47	8	0	5	19	23	51	0	.332	.355
Minor League Totals				.240	291	1001	104	240	51	4	16	112	98	201	2	.315	.347

27 WANDER JAVIER, SS

Born: Dec. 29, 1998. **B-T:** R-R. **HT:** 6-1. **WT:** 175. **Signed:** Dominican Republic, 2015. **Signed by:** Fred Guerrero.

TRACK RECORD: A $4 million signee out of the Dominican Republic, Javier was one of the top prospects in the 2015 international class and looked the part in 2016 and 2017. Injuries have dampened his outlook the past few years, along with a tough 2019 season at low Class A Cedar Rapids.

SCOUTING REPORT: By nature a player with a slow heartbeat, Javier has been asked by the Twins to turn up his intensity level and become a more aggressive swinger. He's passive by default, which has allowed him to walk at a solid clip, but also puts him in poor positions to do damage when he decides to swing. Javier had a tendency to lunge on his front side, so he has worked to stay in his back hip. Javier was previously one of the organization's best defensive players with a reliable glove and strong arm at shortstop, but leg injuries have hurt his quick-twitch actions and range.

THE FUTURE: Javier has a lot of work to do to get back on track. He'll be just 22 the entire 2021 season.

Year	Age	Club (League)	Class	AVG	G	AB	R	H	2B	3B	HR	RBI	BB	SO	SB	OBP	SLG
2019	20	Cedar Rapids (MWL)	LoA	.177	80	300	43	53	9	1	11	37	35	116	2	.278	.323
Minor League Totals				.224	130	483	84	108	25	2	17	65	58	170	6	.319	.389

28 YUNIOR SEVERINO, 2B

BA GRADE
45 Risk: Extreme

Born: Oct. 3, 1999. **B-T:** B-R. **HT:** 6-1. **WT:** 190. **Signed:** Dominican Republic, 2016. **Signed by:** Jonathan Cruz (Braves).

TRACK RECORD: Severino originally signed with the Braves in 2016 but was declared a free agent as part of Atlanta's punishment for international signing violations. He then signed with the Twins for $2.5 million. Severino held his own offensively his first few seasons but hit a bump in 2019 at low Class A Cedar Rapids, when his strikeout rate ballooned and a thumb injury cost him several months.

SCOUTING REPORT: Severino fits the mold of an offensive-oriented second baseman who brings power from both sides of the plate. Most of his power comes from the left side, but Severino actually prefers hitting from the right side. The Twins will have him continue as a switch-hitter for now. He'll need to control the strike zone better moving forward to profile as a regular. Severino isn't a great defender with below-average speed and range, but he has a chance to be adequate at second base if he continues to improve his footwork. He has more than enough arm.

THE FUTURE: Severino's strength and power potential give him a chance to rise. He'll open 2021 at one of the Class A levels.

Year	Age	Club (League)	Class	AVG	G	AB	R	H	2B	3B	HR	RBI	BB	SO	SB	OBP	SLG
2019	19	Twins (GCL)	R	.227	6	22	2	5	1	1	1	2	0	6	0	.227	.500
	19	Cedar Rapids (MWL)	LoA	.244	22	78	7	19	7	0	0	8	7	27	0	.302	.333
Minor League Totals				.261	135	524	74	137	35	4	12	67	48	152	0	.325	.412

29 JOVANI MORAN, LHP

Born: April 24, 1997. **B-T:** L-L. **HT:** 6-1. **WT:** 167. **Drafted:** HS—Florida, P.R., 2015 (7th round). **Signed by:** Freddie Thon.

TRACK RECORD: Moran was one of the top pitching prospects out of Puerto Rico in 2015 and signed with the Twins for $275,000 as their seventh-round pick. He worked as a starter in his pro debut but moved quickly to the bullpen and progressed to Double-A Pensacola in 2019. The Twins brought Moran to instructional league in 2020 after the canceled minor league season.

SCOUTING REPORT: Moran racks up strikeouts with his two-pitch combination, but instead of the slider he threw as an amateur, he now relies on a diving changeup to miss bats. His 18.4% swinging-strike ranked fourth in the Southern League in 2019 among pitchers with at least 30 innings. That's because of his changeup, which some scouts have labeled a plus-plus offering. Moran has shown reverse platoon splits throughout his career because his changeup is so effective versus righthanded hitters. His fastball is more of a solid-average pitch, so time will tell how his changeup will fare when advanced hitters don't need to gear up for heat. Moran also has below-average control he needs to improve.

THE FUTURE: Moran's changeup gives him a real weapon in relief. He should open in Triple-A in 2021.

Year	Age	Club (League)	Class	W	L	ERA	G	GS	IP	H	HR	BB	SO	BB/9	SO/9	WHIP	AVG
2019	22	Twins (GCL)	R	0	0	0.00	3	0	3	2	0	2	5	5.4	13.5	1.20	.143
	22	Pensacola (SL)	AA	2	2	4.98	20	0	34	27	3	23	50	6.0	13.1	1.46	.178
Minor League Totals				14	8	2.73	77	7	158	102	6	75	224	4.3	12.8	1.12	.185

30 MARCO RAYA, RHP

Born: Aug. 7, 2002. **B-T:** R-R. **HT:** 6-0. **WT:** 165. **Drafted:** HS—Laredo, Texas, 2020 (4th round). **Signed by:** Trevor Brown.

TRACK RECORD: One of the youngest players in the 2020 draft class, Raya's draft stock was trending up before the coronavirus pandemic shut down the high school season. The Twins liked what they saw enough in a small sample to draft him in the fourth round and sign him for $410,000 to forgo a Texas Tech commitment. Raya made his organizational debut in instructional league after the season.

SCOUTING REPORT: Raya is undersized but shows a solid four-pitch mix and an advanced ability to spin two breaking balls. His fastball sits 92-93 mph and will touch 95-96 mph, but it's presently flat and will need to add some sort of movement in the future. Raya shows a natural feel to spin the ball. His average curveball is ahead of his fringe-average slider at the moment, but both have room to grow. Raya's changeup also projects fringe-average. Raya's idol is Marcus Stroman as a 6-foot righthander, and scouts think his delivery mirrors Stroman's.

THE FUTURE: Raya has back-of-the-rotation potential if he continues to fill out and add strength. He'll make his pro debut in the Rookie-level Gulf Coast League in 2021.

Year	Age	Club (League)	Class	W	L	ERA	G	GS	IP	H	HR	BB	SO	BB/9	SO/9	WHIP	AVG
2020	17	Did not play—No minor league season															

MORE PROSPECTS TO KNOW

31 YENNIER CANO, RHP

A 26-year-old who the Twins signed out of Cuba for $750,000, Cano throws a sinker in the 93-95 mph range and compliments it with a firm split-change and developing slider. He could be a ground-ball-heavy, low-leverage reliever if he can improve his control.

32 LUIS RIJO, RHP

Rijo is a control and command righthander with unremarkable stuff but a good feel for pitching. His low-90s fastball and upper-70s curveball are average, but some evaluators think his changeup could become above-average.

33 NICK GORDON, SS/2B

Gordon is a fine defender at second base or shortstop, but his light bat and well below-average power means a backup or utility role is his likely outcome.

34 WILL HOLLAND, SS

Holland has tools but needs to develop more confidence and a better rhythm and approach at the plate. He could stick at shortstop with the athleticism, range and arm strength necessary for the position.

35 JOSE MIRANDA, 1B/3B

Miranda is a hit collector with the ability to put the bat on the ball at an extremely high rate, but he's a free swinger who needs to optimize his approach to tap into more power.

36 KALAI ROSARIO, OF

A fifth-round draft pick in 2020, Rosario is a solid athlete with enormous raw power but will have to control how much he swings and misses.

37 SETH GRAY, 3B

Gray is a plus defender at the hot corner, but he'll need to iron out some fixable throwing issues. He needs to pull the ball with more authority to access his power potential.

38 CALEB HAMILTON, C/3B

Hamilton is serviceable behind the plate and an instinctive game-caller. He can also play third, second, first and left field.

39 SPENCER STEER, 3B/2B/SS

SLEEPER

Steer is solid in many ways but electric in none. He's a reliable defender within his range at second, shortstop and third base and could be a productive utility player.

40 CHARLES MACK, C

After struggling at third base his first two years, the Twins are going to try Mack behind the plate. His best attributes are his natural strength and power potential.

TOP PROSPECTS OF THE DECADE

Year	Player, Pos.	2020 Org
2011	Kyle Gibson, RHP	Rangers
2012	Miguel Sano, 3B/SS	Twins
2013	Miguel Sano, 3B	Twins
2014	Byron Buxton, OF	Twins
2015	Byron Buxton, OF	Twins
2016	Byron Buxton, OF	Twins
2017	Nick Gordon, SS	Twins
2018	Royce Lewis, SS	Twins
2019	Royce Lewis, SS	Twins
2020	Royce Lewis, SS/3B	Twins

TOP DRAFT PICKS OF THE DECADE

Year	Player, Pos.	2020 Org
2011	Levi Michael, SS	Twins
2012	Byron Buxton, OF	Twins
2013	Kohl Stewart, RHP	Orioles
2014	Nick Gordon, SS	Twins
2015	Tyler Jay, LHP	Reds
2016	Alex Kirilloff, OF	Twins
2017	Royce Lewis, SS	Twins
2018	Trevor Larnach, OF	Twins
2019	Keoni Cavaco, SS	Twins
2020	Aaron Sabato, 1B	Twins

DEPTH CHART

MINNESOTA TWINS

TOP 2021 ROOKIES	RANK
Alex Kirilloff, OF	1
Royce Lewis, SS	2
Ryan Jeffers, C	4
BREAKOUT PROSPECTS	**RANK**
Josh Winder, RHP	19
Emmanuel Rodriguez, OF	23

SOURCE OF TOP 30 TALENT

Homegrown	24	Acquired	6
College	11	Trade	5
High School	9	Rule 5 draft	0
Junior College	0	Independent leagues	0
Nondrafted free agent	0	Free agents/waivers	1
International	4		

LF
Alex Kirilloff (1)
Lamonte Wade (16)
Kalai Rosario

CF
Gilberto Celestino (10)
Misael Urbina (13)
Aaron Whitefield
Jimmy Kerrigan
Willie Joe Garry Jr.

RF
Trevor Larnach (3)
Matt Wallner (18)
Emmanuel Rodriguez (23)
Gabriel Maciel

3B
Keoni Cavaco (15)
Seth Gray
Spencer Steer
Andrew Bechtold

SS
Royce Lewis (2)
Wander Javier (27)
Will Holland

2B
Alerick Soularie (17)
Travis Blankenhorn (25)
Yunior Severino (28)
Nick Gordon

1B
Aaron Sabato (7)
Brent Rooker (12)
Jose Miranda

C
Ryan Jeffers (4)
Ben Rortvedt (26)
Caleb Hamilton
Charles Mack

LHP

LHSP	LHRP
Charlie Barnes	Jovani Moran (29)
Bryan Sammons	Brandon Waddell

RHP

RHSP	RHRP
Jhoan Duran (5)	Jorge Alcala (14)
Jordan Balazovic (6)	Cody Stashak (20)
Matt Canterino (8)	Edwar Colina (21)
Blayne Enlow (9)	Dakota Chalmers (24)
Cole Sands (11)	Yennier Cano
Josh Winder (19)	
Chris Vallimont (22)	
Marco Raya (30)	
Luis Rijo	
Bailey Ober	
Landon Leach	

New York Mets

BY MATT EDDY

The Mets made history last fall—just not in the way they envisioned.

On the field, a team with playoff aspirations stumbled to the third-worst record in the National League, undone by pitching injuries, ineffectiveness and lack of inventory.

Off the field, the Mets sold for a U.S. sports franchise-record $2.475 billion on Oct. 30, when billionaire hedge fund manager Steve Cohen was approved by Major League Baseball owners.

Outgoing Mets owner Fred Wilpon had held at least a minority stake since 1980. In that time he presided over most of the franchise's greatest hits, including a World Series title in 1986 and NL pennants in 2000 and 2015.

Cohen is a lifelong Mets fan whose first act as owner was to reinstall Sandy Alderson, architect of the 2015 pennant-winners, as team president. Alderson supplants general manager Brodie Van Wagenen, whose high-profile trades in two years at the helm not only failed to push the Mets into October but depleted the organization's minor league depth.

Van Wagenen's first trade in Dec. 2018 sacrificed outfielder Jarred Kelenic, now a top 10 overall prospect in the game, to the Mariners for Edwin Diaz and Robinson Cano, plus $100 million of the salary Cano is owed through 2023.

Diaz and Cano have not lived up to their reputations, but even more harmful was that the money owed to Cano affected the Mets' ability to re-sign free agent Zack Wheeler after the 2019 season.

Van Wagenen's other major misfire occurred at the 2019 trade deadline, when he parted with prospect righthander Simeon Woods Richardson for Marcus Stroman as the Mets chased a playoff spot. New York fell short of the postseason and Stroman missed the entire 2020 season, first because of a torn calf muscle and then because he opted out due to the coronavirus pandemic.

The Mets traded pitching prospects Justin Dunn and Anthony Kay in those two trades, and while neither has a high ceiling, simply having them around would have provided depth. The 2020 Mets finished last in the NL with an 86 ERA+ and never seemed to have enough arms for a rotation missing Stroman, Wheeler and Noah Syndergaard, who had Tommy John surgery in March.

It's not all doom and gloom in Queens. The 2020 Mets led the majors with a 122 OPS+. The club's lineup is full of hitters in their primes, including Michael Conforto, Pete Alonso, Jeff McNeil, Dominic Smith and Brandon Nimmo.

Ace Jacob deGrom might be the best pitcher in baseball and is under contract for as many as four more seasons. Stroman and Syndergaard will be back on the Citi Field mound in 2021.

STEVEN RYAN/GETTY IMAGES

Dominic Smith's breakout season embellished the Mets' lineup core of players in their primes.

PROJECTED 2024 LINEUP

Position	Player	Age
Catcher	Francisco Alvarez	22
First Base	Dominic Smith	29
Second Base	Andres Gimenez	25
Third Base	Brett Baty	24
Shortstop	Ronny Mauricio	23
Left Field	Brandon Nimmo	31
Center Field	Pete Crow-Armstrong	22
Right Field	Michael Conforto	31
Designated Hitter	Pete Alonso	29
No. 1 Starter	Jacob deGrom	36
No. 2 Starter	Noah Syndergaard	31
No. 3 Starter	Marcus Stroman	32
No. 4 Starter	Matt Allan	23
No. 5 Starter	J.T. Ginn	25
Closer	Edwin Diaz	30

Still, fortifying the club's rotation, whether in free agency or trades, remains a priority because help is not on the way—at least not any time soon.

For as well as the Mets have attacked the amateur talent sources in recent years, especially domestic and international teenagers, they have a talent gap at the upper levels of the minors.

It won't be enough for the Mets to throw money at free agents. A successful organization needs to do many things well—draft, develop, evaluate, analyze, acquire—and Cohen seems to grasp that.

"You build champions," he said at his introductory press conference," you don't buy them." ■

1 FRANCISCO ALVAREZ, C

Born: Nov. 19, 2001. **B-T:** R-R. **HT:** 5-11. **WT:** 220.
Signed: Venezuela, 2018.
Signed by: Andres Nunez/Ismael Perez.

TRACK RECORD: The Mets made Alvarez the headliner of their 2018 international class by signing the Venezuelan catcher for a franchise-record $2.7 million. He dazzled in his 2019 pro debut by quickly hitting his way out of the Rookie-level Gulf Coast League to the Rookie-level Appalachian League as a 17-year-old. That is the same age and level progression traveled by Vladimir Guerrero Jr. in 2016 and Wander Franco in 2018. Alvarez hit .312 in his pro debut with seven home runs, 21 walks and 37 strikeouts in 42 games. He didn't get a chance to build on his breakout in 2020 because of the coronavirus pandemic and canceled minor league season. Stranded in spring training in mid-March when Venezuela shut its borders, he headed from Port St. Lucie, Fla., to the Mets' alternate training site in Brooklyn in July. He wowed teammates and staff as the most impressive hitter in camp.

SCOUTING REPORT: Alvarez developed exceptionally strong hands and forearms from working for his father's construction company as a youth. He has incredible raw strength, double-plus raw power and he drives the ball to the opposite field exceptionally well. He is a confident two-strike hitter who can spoil pitches and put offspeed and breaking pitches in play with authority. He has the type of bat-to-ball skill, reflexes and flyball profile to deliver first-division offensive production at the catcher position. Alvarez's defensive game requires maintenance, but he will stick at the position. He is a confident, poised defender with solid-average receiving ability and a plus arm. He allowed 15 passed balls in 27 games behind the plate in 2019, calling into question his blocking ability. But some of that is attributable to the one-knee catching technique he is learning. It helps him present low pitches to the umpire to gain strikes for his pitcher but costs him lateral mobility on balls in the dirt and momentum on throws to second base. Alvarez tends to overthrow on stolen base attempts and needs to focus on making clean transfers and accurate throws to the bag. He has the type of outgoing, take-charge attitude to build rapport with pitchers. The next step is building conviction in his pitch calling. Alvarez has a thick build and mature body type even at age 19, but he is flexible enough for the position and determined to be a big league catcher.

THE FUTURE: Alvarez lost at-bats to the pandemic but gained valuable experience with veteran pitchers at the alternate site and at instructional league, where he called his own game. He was slated to head to the Australian Baseball League in the offseason, but when Venezuela opened its borders in the fall, the 19-year-old asked to return home to see family. The young catcher was also feeling worn down after what equated to his first full season. Alvarez is the rare catching prospect who has middle-of-the-order offensive upside, though it will take at least two more full seasons in the minors for his glove to catch up. The wait will be worth it. ■

MIKE JANES/FOUR SEAM IMAGES

BA GRADE
60 **Risk: V. High**

SCOUTING GRADES
Hit: 50. **Power:** 60. **Run:** 30. **Field:** 50. **Arm:** 60.

Projected future grades on 20-80 scouting scale.

BEST TOOLS

Best Hitter for Average	Francisco Alvarez
Best Power Hitter	Brett Baty
Best Strike-Zone Discipline	Brett Baty
Fastest Baserunner	Pete Crow-Armstrong
Best Athlete	Ronny Mauricio
Best Fastball	Matt Allan
Best Curveball	Matt Allan
Best Slider	Marcel Renteria
Best Changeup	Jose Butto
Best Control	Garrison Bryant
Best Defensive Catcher	Nick Meyer
Best Defensive Infielder	Andres Gimenez
Best Infield Arm	Mark Vientos
Best Defensive Outfielder	Pete Crow-Armstrong
Best Outfield Arm	Stanley Consuegra

Year	Age	Club (League)	Class	AVG	G	AB	R	H	2B	3B	HR	RBI	BB	SO	SB	OBP	SLG
2019	17	Mets (GCL)	R	.462	7	26	8	12	4	0	2	10	4	4	0	.548	.846
	17	Kingsport (APP)	R	.282	35	131	24	37	6	0	5	16	17	33	1	.377	.443
Minor League Totals				.312	42	157	32	49	10	0	7	26	21	37	1	.407	.510

2 RONNY MAURICIO, SS

TOM PRIDDY/FOUR SEAM IMAGES

BA GRADE
60 **Risk: Very High**

Born: April 4, 2001. **B-T:** B-R. **HT:** 6-3. **WT:** 166. **Signed:** Dominican Republic, 2017. **Signed by:** Marciano Alvarez/Gerardo Cabrera.

TRACK RECORD: Mauricio is a product of the stellar 2017 international signing class that includes Wander Franco, Julio Rodriguez and Kristian Robinson. While Mauricio hasn't produced like that trio, many scouts believe it's only a matter of time before he does. He was on target to play in the high Class A Florida State League in 2020 before the minor league season was canceled by the coronavirus pandemic. He didn't get to the Mets' alternate training site until mid August because of family issues, then reported to instructional league in October.

SCOUTING REPORT: Mauricio is a switch-hitting shortstop with a lean, high-waisted frame and the type of looseness and bat speed that portend a high upside. He has hit .270 as a pro without notable power, speed or discipline, but his production should improve as his 6-foot-3 frame matures and he improves his pitch selection. Mauricio had one of the highest groundball rates in the South Atlantic League in 2019, so continued strength gains and an improved attack angle are his main development objectives. His timing and efficient bat path suggest future above-average hitting ability with a chance for average power or better. Mauricio is a flashy but efficient defender who has the quick first step and soft hands of a plus shortstop. He makes accurate throws from all angles with a plus arm.

THE FUTURE: If his physical development unfolds the way scouts think it will, Mauricio has a chance to be a first-division shortstop. The lost 2020 season and abbreviated alternate training site appearance deprived Mauricio of valuable repetitions.

SCOUTING GRADES: **Hitting:** 50 **Power:** 50 **Running:** 40 **Fielding:** 60 **Arm:** 60

Year	Age	(League)	Class	AVG	G	AB	R	H	2B	3B	HR	RBI	BB	SO	SB	OBP	SLG
2018	17	Mets (GCL)	R	.279	49	197	26	55	13	3	3	31	10	31	1	.307	.421
	17	Kingsport (APP)	R	.233	8	30	6	7	3	0	0	4	3	9	1	.286	.333
2019	18	Columbia (SAL)	LoA	.268	116	470	62	126	20	5	4	37	23	99	6	.307	.357
Minor League Totals				.270	173	697	94	188	36	8	7	72	36	139	8	.306	.374

3 ANDRES GIMENEZ, SS/2B

MARY DECICCO/MLB PHOTOS VIA GETTY IMAGES

BA GRADE
50 **Risk: Medium**

Born: Sept. 4, 1998. **B-T:** L-R. **HT:** 5-11. **WT:** 161. **Signed:** Venezuela, 2015. **Signed by:** Robert Espejo/Hector Rincones.

TRACK RECORD: The prize of the Mets' 2015 international signing class, Gimenez worked his way to Double-A as a 19-year-old in 2018. He didn't blossom until after the 2019 season, when he hit .371 to win the Arizona Fall League batting title. Expanded 28-man rosters afforded Gimenez the chance to make the Mets' Opening Day roster in 2020. He showed himself to be more than capable as a 21-year-old rookie, while showing growth potential.

SCOUTING REPORT: Gimenez appeared unfazed by the big league spotlight. His strike-zone judgment was sound and he hit his first two home runs to the opposite field. Even if he never develops more than average hitting ability or power, Gimenez has the type of barrel control and speed that makes him difficult to pitch to and defend. He stole eight bases in nine tries to put his double-plus wheels to good use. Gimenez has the soft hands, reflexes and plus arm of a true shortstop and the versatility to handle second base or third base. He made only one error as a rookie and ranked 10th among infielders with five outs above average, according to MLB Statcast.

THE FUTURE: Gimenez wrested playing time from Amed Rosario late in the season. His defensive ability, feel for the game and on-base skills give him a chance to be the club's regular shortstop in 2021.

SCOUTING GRADES: **Hitting:** 50 **Power:** 40 **Running:** 70 **Fielding:** 60 **Arm:** 50

Year	Age	Club (League)	Class	AVG	G	AB	R	H	2B	3B	HR	RBI	BB	SO	SB	OBP	SLG
2017	18	Columbia (SAL)	LoA	.265	92	347	50	92	9	4	4	31	28	61	14	.346	.349
2018	19	Binghamton (EL)	AA	.277	37	137	19	38	9	1	0	16	9	22	10	.344	.358
	19	St. Lucie (FSL)	HiA	.282	85	308	43	87	20	4	6	30	22	70	28	.348	.432
2019	20	Binghamton (EL)	AA	.250	117	432	54	108	22	5	9	37	24	102	28	.309	.387
2020	21	New York (NL)	MAJ	.263	49	118	22	31	3	2	3	12	7	28	8	.333	.398
Major League Totals				.263	49	118	22	31	3	2	3	12	7	28	8	.333	.398
Minor League Totals				.278	393	1438	218	400	80	18	22	152	129	277	93	.356	.405

4 MATT ALLAN, RHP

Born: April 17, 2001. **B-T:** R-R. **HT:** 6-3. **WT:** 225. **Drafted:** HS—Sanford, Fla., 2019 (3rd round). **Signed by:** Jon Updike.

TOM DIPACE

BA GRADE

60 **Risk: Extreme**

TRACK RECORD: The top high school pitcher in the 2019 draft class, Allan slipped to the Mets in the third round because of perceived signability concerns. He came to terms for $2.5 million, more than any prep pitcher in class except for the Pirates' Quinn Priester, the 18th overall pick. Allan had his full-season debut placed on hold by the pandemic and canceled minor league season. He pitched at the Mets' alternate training site in Brooklyn and in instructional league.

SCOUTING REPORT: The Mets rave about Allan's combination of stuff, work ethic and understanding of analytics. He looked better than advertised at the alternate site, armed with his primary two pitches but now abetted by feel for a third pitch. Allan pitches at 96 mph with riding life on his double-plus four-seam fastball. He took a bit off his high-70s curveball and locates the plus pitch for called strikes. His curve has power break and high-end spin at 2,800 to 2,900 revolutions per minute. Allan rounded out his arsenal by gaining feel for a mid-80s changeup with fading life to his arm side. He worked hard to master his hand and wrist position at release, and his changeup was fooling even experienced hitters from both sides of the plate at the alternate site.

THE FUTURE: Allan already has a major league body, average control and the desire to be great. He fits the mold of a front-of-the-rotation starter, especially now that he has a reliable changeup. If he stays healthy he has a floor as a big league No. 3 starter.

SCOUTING GRADES: **Fastball:** 70 **Curveball:** 60 **Changeup:** 55 **Control:** 50

Year	Age	Club (League)	Class	W	L	ERA	G	GS	IP	H	HR	BB	SO	BB/9	SO/9	WHIP	AVG
2019	18	Brooklyn (NYP)	SS	0	0	9.00	1	1	2	5	0	1	3	4.5	13.5	3.00	.455
	18	Mets (GCL)	R	1	0	1.08	5	4	8	5	0	4	11	4.3	11.9	1.08	.147
Minor League Totals				1	0	2.61	6	5	10	10	0	5	14	4.4	12.2	1.45	.250

5 PETE CROW-ARMSTRONG, OF

Born: March 25, 2002. **B-T:** L-L. **HT:** 6-1. **WT:** 180. **Drafted:** HS—Los Angeles, 2020 (1st round). **Signed by:** Rusty McNamara.

BILL MITCHELL

BA GRADE

55 **Risk: Very High**

TRACK RECORD: Crow-Armstrong knows the spotlight. Both of his parents are actors. He starred for USA Baseball's national teams from the age of 12. He played for Harvard-Westlake, the Los Angeles-area high school that produced first-round pitchers Lucas Giolito, Max Fried and Jack Flaherty. The Mets drafted Crow-Armstrong 19th overall in 2020 and signed him for the slot value of $3.359 million to forgo a Vanderbilt commitment. Because of the canceled minor league season, his first action for the Mets occurred at instructional league.

SCOUTING REPORT: As a rising senior, Crow-Armstrong ranked as the best high school prospect in his class. He stumbled on the 2019 showcase circuit but regained his form the following spring before the amateur season was scuttled. Crow-Armstrong was the best defensive outfielder in the 2020 prep class and one of its best hitters and fastest runners. His grace and anticipation in center field give him Gold Glove upside, while his above-average arm is a separator at the position. Crow-Armstrong profiles as a top-of-the-order hitter who offers advanced bat-to-ball skills, a direct swing path and the above-average speed to leg out hits. He could mature into power but is expected to be a hit-over-power offensive player.

THE FUTURE: The Mets laud Crow-Armstrong's competitive makeup, which is a trait the organization has prioritized in recent drafts. That makeup, combined with his skills, helps make him the leading candidate to be the Mets' center fielder of the future.

SCOUTING GRADES: **Hitting:** 50 **Power:** 40 **Running:** 60 **Fielding:** 70 **Arm:** 55

Year	Age	Club (League)	Class	AVG	G	AB	R	H	2B	3B	HR	RBI	BB	SO	SB	OBP	SLG
2020	18	Did not play--No minor league season															

6 BRETT BATY, 3B

BA GRADE
55 Risk: Very High

Born: Nov. 13, 1999. **B-T:** L-R. **HT:** 6-3. **WT:** 210. **Drafted:** HS—Austin, Texas, 2019 (1st round). **Signed by:** Harry Shelton.

TRACK RECORD: Some teams regarded Baty as one of the most promising high school hitters in the 2019 draft. Others viewed his age—19 and a half on draft day—as a non-starter in the first round. The Mets drafted him 12th overall and signed him for $3.9 million, nearly $500,000 under slot. Baty drew walks and hit for power in his 2019 pro debut but struck out too frequently. With the 2020 minor league season canceled, the Mets brought him to their alternate training site in late August. He continued to gain reps at instructional league

SCOUTING REPORT: Strike-zone discipline, hard contact and incredible raw power to all fields are Baty's defining traits. He played power forward for his high school basketball team and is a deceptive athlete. For example, he was one of the fastest players at the Mets' instructional league. Baty struggled to catch up with velocity in his pro debut because he was drifting and not hitting against a firm front side. Baty has made progress but needs to continue hitting through the ball and making more contact. His swing path is steep, with his bat going in and out of the zone quickly, so hitting for average will be a challenge. He has a chance to hit .250 with plenty of walks. Baty has impact power potential and is capable of launching no-doubters to the opposite field. Baty is a capable third baseman with a plus arm. He came to camp toned after an offseason of conditioning and is one of the organization's hardest workers.

THE FUTURE: Baty hits the ball as hard as any Mets prospect, so getting his swing more connected will be the key to realizing his potential. He should make his full-season debut in 2021.

SCOUTING GRADES: Hitting: 40 | Power: 60 | Running: 40 | Fielding: 45 | Arm: 60

Year	Age	Club (League)	Class	AVG	G	AB	R	H	2B	3B	HR	RBI	BB	SO	SB	OBP	SLG
2019	19	Brooklyn (NYP)	SS	.200	4	10	2	2	1	0	0	3	6	3	0	.529	.300
	19	Mets (GCL)	R	.350	5	20	5	7	3	0	1	8	5	6	0	.480	.650
	19	Kingsport (APP)	R	.222	42	158	30	35	12	2	6	22	24	56	0	.339	.437
Minor League Totals				.234	51	188	37	44	16	2	7	33	35	65	0	.368	.452

7 MARK VIENTOS, 3B

BA GRADE
50 Risk: High

Born: Dec. 11, 1999. **B-T:** R-R. **HT:** 6-4. **WT:** 185. **Drafted:** HS—Plantation, Fla., 2017 (2nd round). **Signed by:** Cesar Aranguren.

TRACK RECORD: The youngest player selected in the 2017 draft, Vientos is about a month younger than Brett Baty, the Mets' first-round pick two years later. Vientos reached low Class A in 2019 and showed spurts of power as a 19-year-old with 12 homers and 27 doubles in 110 games, doing most of his damage away from pitcher-friendly Columbia.

SCOUTING REPORT: Vientos combines bat speed with a flyball-hitting approach to produce some of the best exit velocities in the system and an elite hard-hit rate. He can square up just about any fastball but has struggled to pick up and connect with spin from righthanders. That ability should come in time, because Vientos does a great job staying within himself and using the middle of the field. Rival scouts ding him for a grooved bat path and stiffer hitting actions, making him a below-average hitter. The Mets believe it's only a matter of time before Vientos' plus power manifests. Drafted as a shortstop, Vientos shifted to third base as a pro because of slow footspeed, sloppy footwork and a maturing body. He has a chance to stay at third as a below-average to fringy defender with an above-average but sometimes erratic arm.

THE FUTURE: Vientos can take the ball out to any part of the park, but in light of his limitations in terms of hitting for average, plate discipline and defense, some scouts view him more as a second-division player.

SCOUTING GRADES: Hitting: 40 | Power: 60 | Running: 30 | Fielding: 40 | Arm: 50

Year	Age	Club (League)	Class	AVG	G	AB	R	H	2B	3B	HR	RBI	BB	SO	SB	OBP	SLG
2017	17	Mets (GCL)	R	.259	47	174	22	45	12	0	4	24	14	42	0	.316	.397
	17	Kingsport (APP)	R	.294	4	17	1	5	2	0	0	2	1	4	0	.333	.412
2018	18	Kingsport (APP)	R	.287	60	223	32	64	12	0	11	52	37	43	1	.389	.489
2019	19	Columbia (SAL)	LoA	.255	111	416	48	106	27	1	12	62	22	110	1	.300	.411
Minor League Totals				.265	222	830	103	220	53	1	27	140	74	199	2	.329	.429

8 J.T. GINN, RHP

Born: May 20, 1999. **B-T:** R-R. **HT:** 6-2. **WT:** 200. **Drafted:** Mississippi State, 2020 (2nd round). **Signed by:** Jet Butler.

TRACK RECORD: The Dodgers failed to come to terms with Ginn as the 30th overall pick in 2018 out of Brandon (Miss.) High. He instead made his way to Mississippi State, where he was recognized as the Southeastern Conference freshman of the year in 2019. Ginn lined up as a probable first-round talent again in 2020 as an eligible sophomore, but he had Tommy John surgery after three innings and missed the rest of the season. The Mets drafted him in the middle of the second round and signed him for $2.9 million, the equivalent of late first-round money.

SCOUTING REPORT: Ginn had his elbow surgery in March 2020, just before the coronavirus pandemic shut down the season. As a freshman he went 8-4, 3.13 with 105 strikeouts in 86 innings while allowing only one home run. At his best, Ginn works with two plus or better pitches on the 20-80 scouting scale. His heavy sinker features outstanding armside life and premium velocity. The pitch operates in the low-to-mid 90s with a peak of 99 mph. Scouts would like to see him add more sink to his fastball to accompany the outstanding running action. Ginn's slider has vicious two-plane life in the mid 80s and is a major swing-and-miss weapon. He had toyed with a changeup prior to his injury and will resume its development as a pro. It has flashed average. He earns high marks for his feel for pitching and competitiveness.

THE FUTURE: The Mets like Ginn's physical 6-foot-2 frame and work ethic, giving them confidence he can make a full recovery. Scouts who like him see a No. 3 starter upside. Ginn's rehab should be complete in time to break camp with a minor league affiliate in 2021.

SCOUTING GRADES: **Fastball:** 60 **Slider:** 70 **Changeup:** 40 **Control:** 50

Year	Age	Club (League)	Class	W	L	ERA	G	GS	IP	H	HR	BB	SO	BB/9	SO/9	WHIP	AVG
2020	21	Did not play—No minor league season															

9 DAVID PETERSON, LHP

MARY DECICCO/MLB PHOTOS VIA GETTY IMAGES

Born: Sept. 3, 1995. **B-T:** L-L. **HT:** 6-6. **WT:** 240. **Drafted:** Oregon, 2017 (1st round). **Signed by:** Jim Reeves.

TRACK RECORD: The Mets drafted Peterson 20th overall in 2017, the year he struck out 20 batters in a game for Oregon. Three years later they had a major league starter after Peterson received his first callup on July 28. He stayed in the rotation all season, missing two weeks with shoulder fatigue in August, and served as the club's de facto No. 2 starter behind Jacob deGrom. Peterson will not be eligible for the Rookie of the Year award in 2021 because he accrued too much major league service in his debut.

SCOUTING REPORT: Peterson's height, extension and unique slider characteristics make him tough to square up when he's working ahead in the count. Opponents hit just .119 and swung and missed 37% of the time against his sweeping, low-80s slider. Peterson previously sat in the high 80s with his fastball, but after dedicating himself to conditioning and nutrition he came to camp in 2020 sitting 92 mph and held that velocity all season. He also shifted his focus from sinking the ball to throwing four-seam fastballs to give him something competitive up in the zone. Peterson has shown increasing confidence in his fringe changeup, which shows good armside life and complements his sinker. He needs to improve his control, particularly his first-pitch strike rate.

THE FUTURE: Peterson profiles as a back-of-the-rotation starter unless he develops plus fastball command or commits to becoming fully slider-forward. He's ready to fill that role now and should be in the Mets' 2021 Opening Day rotation.

SCOUTING GRADES: **Fastball:** 50 **Slider:** 60 **Changeup:** 40 **Control:** 50

Year	Age	Club (League)	Class	W	L	ERA	G	GS	IP	H	HR	BB	SO	BB/9	SO/9	WHIP	AVG
2017	21	Brooklyn (NYP)	SS	0	0	2.45	3	3	4	4	0	1	6	2.5	14.7	1.36	.250
2018	22	St. Lucie (FSL)	HiA	6	6	4.33	13	13	69	74	1	19	58	2.5	7.6	1.35	.246
	22	Columbia (SAL)	LoA	1	4	1.82	9	9	59	46	1	11	57	1.7	8.6	0.96	.198
2019	23	Binghamton (EL)	AA	3	6	4.19	24	24	116	119	9	37	122	2.9	9.5	1.34	.229
2020	24	New York (NL)	MAJ	6	2	3.44	10	9	50	36	5	24	40	4.3	7.2	1.21	.202
Major League Totals				6	2	3.44	10	9	50	36	5	24	40	4.4	7.3	1.21	.202
Minor League Totals				10	16	3.63	49	49	247	243	11	68	243	2.5	8.8	1.26	.255

10 JOSH WOLF, RHP

TOM DIPACE

BA GRADE
50 **Risk: Extreme**

Born: Sept. 1, 2000. **B-T:** R-R. **HT:** 6-3. **WT:** 170. **Drafted:** HS—Houston, 2019 (2nd round). **Signed by:** Harry Shelton.

TRACK RECORD: Wolf blossomed as a high school senior in 2019 by showing a dramatic uptick in velocity and continuing to throw strikes at his newfound speed. The Mets drafted him 53rd overall that year and signed him for $2.15 million, nearly $800,000 over slot. Wolf made his pro debut in the Rookie-level Gulf Coast League in 2019 but had to work remotely until instructional league in 2020 after not being brought to the Mets' alternate training site.

SCOUTING REPORT: Wolf has a chance to develop three average to above pitches with above-average control. Multiple scouts have likened his body type and athleticism to Walker Buehler when he was in high school. Wolf ranges from 91-96 mph with his fastball and throws strikes. He has potential to pitch in the mid 90s as he matures, with untapped physicality in his lean 6-foot-3 frame. Wolf shows an advanced feel for spin. He calls his breaking ball a curveball but its shape and late, abrupt break at 78-81 mph are more indicative of a slider or slurve. Given his ease of operation, Wolf should be able to pick up a usable changeup and continue throwing strikes.

THE FUTURE: Wolf made the most of his training time at home in Texas and sent regular video updates of bullpen sessions to Mets player development. It will take time, but Wolf has mid-rotation upside and could blossom with a season of regular work in the minor leagues.

SCOUTING GRADES: **Fastball:** 50 **Slider:** 60 **Changeup:** 45 **Control:** 50

Year	Age	Club (League)	Class	W	L	ERA	G	GS	IP	H	HR	BB	SO	BB/9	SO/9	WHIP	AVG
2019	18	Mets (GCL)	R	0	1	3.38	5	5	8	9	0	1	12	1.1	13.5	1.25	.273
Minor League Totals				0	1	3.38	5	5	8	9	0	1	12	1.1	13.5	1.25	.281

11 ISAIAH GREENE, OF

BA GRADE
50 **Risk: Extreme**

Born: Aug. 29, 2001. **B-T:** L-L. **HT:** 6-1. **WT:** 180. **Drafted:** HS—Corona, Calif., 2020 (2nd round supplemental). **Signed by:** Glenn Walker.

TRACK RECORD: Greene first popped the summer after his junior year when he hit well versus USA Baseball's 18U National Team in scrimmages as a member of a scout team. He started slowly as a senior at Corona (Calif.) High in 2020 before the season shut down, but he showed enough previously for the Mets to draft him 69th overall—the supplemental second-round pick they received as compensation for losing free agent Zack Wheeler to the Phillies. Greene signed for an underslot $850,000 to pass up a Missouri commitment and made his organizational debut in instructional league.

SCOUTING REPORT: Greene showed the most advanced hitting approach among the Mets' young players at instructional league. He didn't blink at seeing pro velocity for the first time, hitting 13-for-28 (.464) with 11 walks and seven strikeouts. Greene stands out for his smooth lefthanded stroke, athletic build and frame that can support strength gains. His short, simple swing produces line drives and could translate to plus hitting ability. As he fills out, he should develop more power and could get to above-average if he learns to lift the ball. Greene is an average, effortless runner. His instincts in center field require fine-tuning, and unless he catches up to the speed of the game there, he probably settles in left field with a below-average arm.

THE FUTURE: Greene plays with a quiet confidence that can be construed as lack of effort. If everything clicks, he could develop into a hit-over-power left fielder, a la fellow Southern California prep Garret Anderson.

Year	Age	Club (League)	Class	AVG	G	AB	R	H	2B	3B	HR	RBI	BB	SO	SB	OBP	SLG
2020	18	Did not play—No minor league season															

12 JUNIOR SANTOS, RHP

BA GRADE
50 **Risk: Extreme**

Born: Aug. 16, 2001. **B-T:** R-R. **HT:** 6-8. **WT:** 230. **Signed:** Dominican Republic, 2017. **Signed by:** Anderson Taveras/Gerardo Cabrera.

TRACK RECORD: Santos signed for $275,000 about six weeks after turning 16 in 2017. His 6-foot-8 frame helped him stand out instantly in the Dominican Summer League and then again when he jumped to the Rookie-level Appalachian League in 2019, where he struck out 36 in 40.2 innings as a 17-year-old. Santos broke his foot preparing for the 2020 season and spent the year working on strength and conditioning rather than working off a mound.

SCOUTING REPORT: Santos' height helps create extension in his delivery that aids him in terms of perceived velocity, but it hinders him when it comes to syncing his delivery, throwing strikes and holding baserunners. He pitches at 90-94 mph and hits 95, but his body has room to fill out and carry greater velocity. Santos needs to develop a trusted secondary pitch. His slurvy high-70s breaking ball has above-average spin and could become a weapon if he learns to stay on top of the pitch. Learning to repeat his delivery will help Santos realize better fastball command and consistency with his breaking ball.
THE FUTURE: Santos' injury precluded him from being considered for the alternate training site, and he spent the fall working out at Dominican instructional league. His tantalizing combination of height and projectability make him a rotation prospect, but high-leverage relief is a possibility if he doesn't learn to throw more strikes. He could be ready for low Class A.

Year	Age	Club (League)	Class	W	L	ERA	G	GS	IP	H	HR	BB	SO	BB/9	SO/9	WHIP	AVG
2019	17	Kingsport (APP)	R	0	5	5.09	14	14	41	46	4	25	36	5.5	8.0	1.75	.234
Minor League Totals				1	6	3.67	28	24	90	85	5	31	75	3.1	7.4	1.28	.247

13 ALEX RAMIREZ, OF

Born: Jan. 13, 2003. **B-T:** R-R. **HT:** 6-3. **WT:** 170. **Signed:** Dominican Republic, 2019. **Signed by:** Gerardo Cabrera/Fernando Encarnacion.
TRACK RECORD: The Mets signed Ramirez out of the Dominican Republic for $2.05 million as the headliner of the club's 2019 international class. He was deprived the chance to make his pro debut in 2020 after the coronavirus pandemic canceled the minor league season. Ramirez spent the spring and summer back home before participating in the Mets' instructional league in October.
SCOUTING REPORT: Ramirez is tall with an athletic build and absolutely looks the part of five-tool center fielder. While an optimistic scout could grade Ramirez's power, speed, fielding and arm as future plus tools, his ability to hit will determine whether he realizes his overall potential. His swing features a lot of moving parts, which hinders his timing and could take several years of repetitions to iron out. Ramirez flashes plus power in batting practice and projects as a plus runner, but he must prove himself as a hitter first. His instincts in center field are strong and so is his arm.
THE FUTURE: Ramirez was often overmatched by pitchers at instructs—which is understandable given that he was 17 and had zero games of pro experience—but the Mets were encouraged that he never gave away at-bats. A likely scenario in 2021 includes time in extended spring training before embarking on a half-season in Rookie ball.

Year	Age	Club (League)	Class	AVG	G	AB	R	H	2B	3B	HR	RBI	BB	SO	SB	OBP	SLG
2020	17	Did not play—No minor league season															

14 ROBERT DOMINGUEZ, RHP

BA GRADE
50 Risk: Extreme

Born: Nov. 30, 2001. **B-T:** R-R. **HT:** 6-4. **WT:** 200. **Signed:** Venezuela, 2019. **Signed by:** Ismael Perez/Andres Nuñez.
TRACK RECORD: The Mets signed Dominguez in Nov. 2019 a few days before he turned 18. He was passed over in the 2018 international signing period, but his fortunes changed when he relocated from his native Venezuela to the Dominican Republic. Once in the Dominican, he made mechanical adjustments and his velocity spiked to 97 mph. He spent 2020 working out with about a dozen of the Mets' other Venezuelan prospects in Port St. Lucie, Fla., when those players' homeland shut its borders because of the pandemic.
SCOUTING REPORT: Dominguez peaked at 99 mph late at Dominican instructional league in 2019, making him one of the hardest-throwing teenagers in the world. He was unable to build on that and begin his pro career in 2020, both because of the coronavirus pandemic and because of a minor injury. Dominguez threw on the side during instructional league but didn't participate in games. Still, his premium velocity stood out even on the sidelines and even when not at 100%. Dominguez's fastball features riding life up in the zone, and his ability to continue adding strength to his 6-foot-4 frame suggests he could hold high-end velocity. His curveball flashes average and could one day complement his fastball as he develops feel for spin. He does not have much feel for a changeup.
THE FUTURE: Dominguez draws praise for his aptitude and arm strength. His future role has not come into focus, but back-of-the-rotation starter or high-leverage reliever seem the most realistic.

Year	Age	Club (League)	Class	W	L	ERA	G	GS	IP	H	HR	BB	SO	BB/9	SO/9	WHIP	AVG
2020	18	Did not play—No minor league season															

15 JOSE BUTTO, RHP

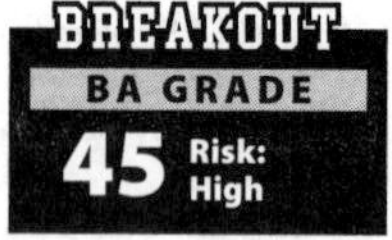

Born: March 19, 1998. **B-T:** R-R. **HT:** 6-1. **WT:** 160. **Signed:** Venezuela, 2017. **Signed by:** Hector Rincones.

TRACK RECORD: Butto signed at age 19 in 2017 and worked his way to low Class A Columbia in 2019. He finished strong to rank among the South Atlantic League top 10 with a 3.62 ERA and 1.17 WHIP. Butto was one of the most impressive pitchers at the Mets' instructional league in 2020, throwing strikes at a high rate, limiting hard contact and striking out a batter per inning.

SCOUTING REPORT: Butto throws the best changeup in the Mets' system. He uses a circle-change grip and sells the low-80s pitch with identical arm speed and tunnel as his fastball. His changeup fades to his arm side and features as much as 13 mph of separation from his fastball. Butto can reach the mid 90s in short outings but parks at 91-94 mph in starts. His fastball has plus spin and plus ride, making the pitch difficult to pick up when located up in the zone. Butto used his time at the alternate training site and instructs to gain confidence in his below-average curveball. The Mets challenged him to up his curve usage from 10% to 20% and spin the pitch straight up and down to complement his riding fastball. He developed enough trust to use it as more than a show-me pitch.

THE FUTURE: While on the short side for a righthanded starter, Butto is solidly built and throws three pitches. He is the Mets' most under-the-radar future starter, probably in a No. 5-type capacity.

Year	Age	Club (League)	Class	W	L	ERA	G	GS	IP	H	HR	BB	SO	BB/9	SO/9	WHIP	AVG
2019	21	Columbia (SAL)	LoA	4	10	3.62	27	25	112	100	8	31	109	2.5	8.8	1.17	.214
Minor League Totals				9	13	3.19	54	44	222	206	17	62	205	2.5	8.3	1.20	.244

16 SHERVYEN NEWTON, SS/2B

Born: April 24, 1999. **B-T:** B-R. **HT:** 6-4. **WT:** 180. **Signed:** Curacao, 2015. **Signed by:** Sendly Reina/Hector Rincones/Harold Herrera/Chris Becerra.

TRACK RECORD: Newton jumped on the prospect map in 2018, his fourth pro season, when he led the Rookie-level Appalachian League with 16 doubles and ranked second with 46 walks. He struggled mightily at low Class A Columbia in 2019, giving away at-bats and generally playing down to the competition as he shared the same infield with shortstop Ronny Mauricio and third baseman Mark Vientos.

SCOUTING REPORT: Tall and rangy when he signed, Newton has continuously added muscle to his frame and stands out among his middle infield peers at 6-foot-4. He shows plus power in batting practice and posts high exit velocities, but pitch recognition and a high swing-and-miss rate limit his impact in games. Those attributes make him a poor bet to hit for average, though he does draw his share of walks. Newton has made the greatest strides on the defensive side, which he showcased at instructional league with his strong fundamentals and leadership. He is a smooth fielder at shortstop with average range and reliable hands. His strong arm makes him a candidate to move around the infield as needed.

THE FUTURE: For a second straight offseason, Newton went unprotected and unselected in the Rule 5 draft. His combination of defensive know-how and power potential make him a possible future reserve infielder, but he is years away from realizing that potential.

Year	Age	Club (League)	Class	AVG	G	AB	R	H	2B	3B	HR	RBI	BB	SO	SB	OBP	SLG
2019	20	Columbia (SAL)	LoA	.209	109	382	35	80	15	2	9	32	37	139	1	.283	.330
Minor League Totals				.246	266	948	154	233	47	14	15	109	155	312	15	.360	.372

17 JAYLEN PALMER, 3B/OF

Born: July 31, 2000. **B-T:** R-R. **HT:** 6-4. **WT:** 195. **Drafted:** HS—Flushing, N.Y., 2018 (22nd round). **Signed by:** John Kosciak.

TRACK RECORD: Palmer grew up in Flushing, N.Y. and played high school ball in the shadow of Citi Field. Drafted in the 22nd round in 2018, he hit .310 in his pro debut in the Rookie-level Gulf Coast League and put himself on the prospect map in 2019, when he ranked among the Rookie-level Appalachian League leaders with 63 hits and 31 walks.

SCOUTING REPORT: Palmer does many things well but lacks an outstanding tool to put him over the top. His biggest area for improvement in 2020 was simply pitch recognition after striking out 39% of the time the year before. To correct that, Palmer made two adjustments. First, he made use of a portable virtual reality machine to help with pitch recognition. Second, he made his swing more effective by working through the ball rather than diving at it. Palmer hits the ball hard consistently and could grow into average power, especially if his recognition gains hold. Drafted as a shortstop, he projects more as an average third baseman. The Mets had him playing outfield at instructional league to increase his versatility. His above-average speed will play there once he becomes more practiced.

THE FUTURE: Palmer has the work ethic and drive to improve, which could be his separating tool. Barring a huge surge in offensive upside, he profiles as a multi-positional player who could play infield and outfield.

Year	Age	Club (League)	Class	AVG	G	AB	R	H	2B	3B	HR	RBI	BB	SO	SB	OBP	SLG
2019	18	Kingsport (APP)	R	.260	62	242	41	63	12	2	7	28	31	108	1	.344	.413
Minor League Totals				.274	87	329	54	90	16	3	8	39	39	135	6	.357	.413

18 THOMAS SZAPUCKI, LHP

BA GRADE
45 **Risk: High**

Born: June 12, 1996. **B-T:** R-L. **HT:** 6-2. **WT:** 181. **Drafted:** HS—Palm Beach Gardens, Fla., 2015 (5th round). **Signed by:** Cesar Aranguren.

TRACK RECORD: Szapucki missed 2018 while recovering from Tommy John surgery but returned in 2019 to throw a career-high 61.2 innings and reach Double-A for one start. Added to the 40-man roster after the 2019 season, he spent 2020 at the Mets' alternate training site.

SCOUTING REPORT: Szapucki pitched with diminished velocity in 2020, clouding his timetable to reach the big leagues unless he recovers that zip on his fastball. He sat at 88 mph at the alternate site after averaging 92 mph the year before and peaking at 95. Szapucki's fastball features plus ride and spin up in the zone, while his curveball shows deep breaking action and high spin in the low 80s. His changeup shows promise and has fringe-average potential as he gains confidence in the pitch. Szapucki is still trying to mentally get through the injury and workload restrictions that have plagued him. The Mets are hopeful his velocity will return after a commitment to strength and conditioning.

THE FUTURE: As a lefthander who can land three pitches for strikes, and whose pitch attributes on his fastball and curveball are promising, Szapucki has a major league future if he recovers his velocity. He is further away than he appeared in 2019 and could require a full minor league season before reaching the majors in 2022.

Year	Age	Club (League)	Class	W	L	ERA	G	GS	IP	H	HR	BB	SO	BB/9	SO/9	WHIP	AVG
2019	23	Binghamton (EL)	AA	0	0	0.00	1	1	4	2	0	1	4	2.3	9.0	0.75	.111
	23	St. Lucie (FSL)	HiA	1	3	3.25	9	9	36	33	1	15	42	3.8	10.5	1.33	.168
	23	Columbia (SAL)	LoA	0	0	2.08	11	8	22	14	1	10	26	4.2	10.8	1.11	.159
Minor League Totals				6	8	2.42	39	33	145	104	4	56	188	3.5	11.7	1.10	.199

19 FREDDY VALDEZ, OF

BA GRADE
50 **Risk: Extreme**

Born: Dec. 6, 2001. **B-T:** R-R. **HT:** 6-3. **WT:** 210. **Signed:** Dominican Republic, 2018. **Signed by:** Fernando Encarnacion/Gerardo Cabrera.

TRACK RECORD: Valdez signed for $1.4 million in 2018 on the strength of his incredible raw power. He hit six home runs in his pro debut as a 17-year-old in 2019, spending most of the season in the Dominican Summer League but appearing in three games in the Rookie-level Gulf Coast League.

SCOUTING REPORT: Valdez records some of the highest average exit velocities in the Mets' system, and lives in the same neighborhood in that regard as Top 10 Prospects Brett Baty and Mark Vientos. During one notable live batting practice session at instructional league, the righthanded-hitting Valdez flexed his plus-plus raw power by driving a pitch about 450 feet down the left-field line. Otherwise, the speed of instructional league play was too fast for Valdez, who was one of the younger players in camp. He doesn't chase out of the zone as much as other hitters his age but struggled to wait on his pitch and do damage. Valdez is a power-over-hit corner outfielder, with below-average hitting ability. His physical, mature body will keep him locked in right field, where he has below-average defensive instincts and a strong arm that is mitigated by a long arm action and slow release.

THE FUTURE: Valdez has strong competitive makeup and is a good teammate. His upward mobility depends on doing damage when he makes contact. His development will take time.

Year	Age	Club (League)	Class	AVG	G	AB	R	H	2B	3B	HR	RBI	BB	SO	SB	OBP	SLG
2019	17	Mets (GCL)	R	.400	3	10	4	4	1	0	1	3	3	3	0	.538	.800
	17	Mets1 (DSL)	R	.268	57	220	36	59	15	3	5	36	28	46	6	.358	.432
Minor League Totals				.274	60	230	40	63	16	3	6	39	31	49	6	.367	.448

20 ENDY RODRIGUEZ, C/OF

BREAKOUT
BA GRADE
50 Risk: Extreme

Born: May 26, 2000. **B-T:** B-R. **HT:** 6-0. **WT:** 170. **Signed:** Dominican Republic, 2018. **Signed by:** Anderson Taveras.

TRACK RECORD: Rodriguez has shown more promise than expected for an international free agent who signed at age 18 and has no fixed position. He has played mostly catcher in the Rookie complex leagues, while showing an intriguing blend of on-base ability and power in two pro seasons. He drew raves at 2020 instructional league for his energetic, vocal leadership.

SCOUTING REPORT: Rodriguez has a slender, athletic build that is atypical for catchers, which explains why he has spent so much time at first base and on the outfield corners. But he worked extensively with catching coach Chad Kreuter at instructs to improve his technique and focus behind the plate. Rodriguez stands out for his flexibility behind the plate and strong hands to present low pitches as strikes. His arm has a chance to be average. Rodriguez is a switch-hitter who has good balance at the plate, a good feel for contact and an innate ability to adjust to secondary pitches. He has shown the type of loft in his swing to hit with power, with the chance to get to average as he matures physically.

THE FUTURE: Rodriguez has a number of promising attributes that could manifest in him becoming a top catching prospect—if he can stick behind the plate. He could get a chance to prove himself at low Class A in the second half of the 2021 season.

Year	Age	Club (League)	Class	AVG	G	AB	R	H	2B	3B	HR	RBI	BB	SO	SB	OBP	SLG
2019	19	Mets (GCL)	R	.293	22	75	14	22	10	1	0	6	10	13	4	.393	.453
	19	Mets1 (DSL)	R	.296	9	27	5	8	4	0	2	8	5	5	0	.457	.667
Minor League Totals				.276	66	217	41	60	20	3	4	37	35	44	6	.389	.452

21 SAM MCWILLIAMS, RHP

TOP ROOKIE
BA GRADE
40 Risk: Medium

Born: Sept. 4, 1995. **B-T:** R-R. **HT:** 6-7. **WT:** 230. **Drafted:** HS—Hendersonville, Tenn., 2014 (8th round). **Signed by:** Nate Dion (Phillies).

TRACK RECORD: The well-traveled McWilliams has been traded twice and selected in the Rule 5 draft in a seven-year pro career. A member of the Rays organization since 2018, he reached Triple-A for a couple months in 2019 and spent 2020 at Tampa Bay's alternate training site. A minor league free agent after the season, McWilliams received multiple major league contract offers. The Mets won out with an offer of $750,000, an unusually high total for a player with no major league experience.

SCOUTING REPORT: McWilliams has worked as a starter for the majority of his career, but the Mets view him as a reliever now that his stuff has ticked up. After previously sitting 93 mph, McWilliams showed up to spring training in 2020 pitching in the mid-to-high 90s and touching 98 mph. He used the time at the Rays' camp to improve his fastball precision and has historically had average or better control despite long limbs on his 6-foot-7 frame. McWilliams' slider has consistently sharp bite, mid-to-high-80s velocity and is his top secondary pitch. He also threw a fringy curveball and changeup as a starter.

THE FUTURE: Few teams have struggled to generate capable bullpen arms like the Mets of recent vintage, giving McWilliams a prime opportunity to establish himself in the bullpen. He has three minor league options remaining but could work his way into middle relief in 2021.

Year	Age	Club (League)	Class	W	L	ERA	G	GS	IP	H	HR	BB	SO	BB/9	SO/9	WHIP	AVG
2019	23	Durham (IL)	AAA	1	6	8.18	11	8	44	72	7	17	43	3.5	8.8	2.02	.327
	23	Montgomery (SL)	AA	6	3	2.05	15	11	88	80	3	30	66	3.1	6.8	1.25	.220
Minor League Totals				30	35	3.85	109	94	535	551	35	156	414	2.6	7.0	1.32	.269

22 OSCAR DE LA CRUZ, RHP

BA GRADE
40 Risk: Medium

Born: March 4, 1995. **B-T:** R-R. **HT:** 6-6. **WT:** 250. **Signed:** Dominican Republic, 2012. **Signed by:** Marcio Encarnacion/Jose Serra (Cubs).

TRACK RECORD: De la Cruz first flashed potential in the short-season Northwest League in 2015, when as 20-year-old he ranked second in the league with 73 strikeouts. He ranked as one of the Cubs' Top 10 prospects three times after his breakout year but never advanced past Double-A before being released in May 2020. The Mets signed him in November as a priority minor league free agent.

SCOUTING REPORT: The Cubs developed de la Cruz as a starter until the second half of the 2019 season, when he moved to the Double-A Tennessee bullpen. His stuff played well in the role—he struck out 49 and walked nine in 37.1 innings with a 1.10 WHIP—and the Mets intend to keep him in a relief role. De la Cruz is a physical freak. His 6-foot-7 stature, long arms and plus extension help his four-seam fastball play up. He sat 92 mph as a starter but as a reliever pitches at 94 and touches 97, delivering the ball from

a lower three-quarters arm slot and from the far third base side of the rubber. De la Cruz's mid-80s straight changeup deceives hitters because it doesn't have the expected fade or bore. A lack of a trusted breaking ball limited him in the rotation but isn't as big an issue in the bullpen.
THE FUTURE: The Mets believe de la Cruz has middle reliever upside in the big leagues, a role he could realize in 2021. He will first have to pitch his way onto the 40-man roster, but his unique extension, arm slot and pitch characteristics could work.

Year	Age	Club (League)	Class	W	L	ERA	G	GS	IP	H	HR	BB	SO	BB/9	SO/9	WHIP	AVG
2019	24	Myrtle Beach (CAR)	HiA	1	0	1.20	3	3	15	14	0	5	17	3.0	10.2	1.27	.219
	24	Tennessee (SL)	AA	4	5	4.09	31	8	81	65	8	29	88	3.2	9.7	1.16	.194
Minor League Totals				31	22	3.45	103	76	428	368	32	130	426	2.7	9.0	1.16	.231

23 JORDANY VENTURA, RHP

TOP ROOKIE
BA GRADE
45 Risk: Very High

Born: July 6, 2000. **B-T:** R-R. **HT:** 6-0. **WT:** 162. **Signed:** Dominican Republic, 2018. **Signed by:** Andres Nuñez.
TRACK RECORD: The Mets signed Ventura when he was 17 in 2018 and sent him straight to the Dominican Summer League, where he made three brief appearances. He began to showcase his ability at three levels in 2019, particularly in the Rookie-level Gulf Coast League, where he struck out 34 and walked eight in 33 innings, blending bat-missing ability and an ability to throw strikes with a varied repertoire.
SCOUTING REPORT: Ventura has an athletic delivery and three promising pitches, but it's really the potential of what he could become that intrigues evaluators. He has an athletic delivery, a quick arm and notable shoulder mobility. He pitches at 91-92 mph and tops at 94 as a teenager, but as he matures and gains strength he could sit a few ticks higher based on his ease of operation. Ventura relies on his fastball, throwing it more than 90% of the time in 2019, but has a nascent feel for his secondaries. His curveball shows occasional late snap, while his changeup is thrown with convincing arm speed. Ventura is a responsive learner and shows aptitude for development. The Mets want him to focus on loading his back side better in his delivery and better incorporating his lower half.
THE FUTURE: Ventura throws enough strikes to project to a rotation role if his pitches come up with growth and experience. He is one of the organization's more intriguing lower-level arms.

Year	Age	Club (League)	Class	W	L	ERA	G	GS	IP	H	HR	BB	SO	BB/9	SO/9	WHIP	AVG
2019	18	Mets (GCL)	R	2	1	4.36	9	7	33	27	2	8	34	2.2	9.3	1.06	.197
	18	Kingsport (APP)	R	0	1	1.13	2	2	8	3	0	6	9	6.8	10.1	1.13	.097
	18	Mets1 (DSL)	R	0	0	3.97	4	4	11	8	1	5	11	4.0	8.7	1.15	.178
Minor League Totals				2	3	3.36	18	14	59	45	3	26	57	4.0	8.7	1.20	.215

24 RYLEY GILLIAM, RHP

BA GRADE
40 Risk: High

Born: Aug. 11, 1996. **B-T:** R-R. **HT:** 5-10. **WT:** 170. **Drafted:** Clemson, 2018 (5th round). **Signed by:** Daniel Coles.
TRACK RECORD: Gilliam led the Atlantic Coast Conference with 11 saves as Clemson's closer in 2018. He has remained a reliever since the Mets drafted him in the fifth round after that year and appeared in 29 games in 2019, including 10 for Triple-A Syracuse. Gilliam has struck out 14 batters per nine innings as a pro but has walked 5 per nine and allowed opponents to hit .250, resulting in a 1.50 WHIP.
SCOUTING REPORT: Gilliam's pitch attributes jump off the page. His performance in pro ball has not. Gilliam sits in the mid 90s with his plus, high-spin fastball. He loves to bury his plus, high-spin curveball for swings and misses. He runs into trouble because his command is poor. He wastes too many pitches and doesn't locate his curve in the zone enough, meaning that experienced hitters just eliminate spin and focus on his fastball. He has worked to develop a mid-80s slider to give him an east-west weapon he can throw for strikes.
THE FUTURE: Gilliam's short stature and twitchy, tightly wound actions consign him to the bullpen. His upside remains high because of the caliber of his fastball and curveball, but he needs to locate both in the zone more often to make progress.

Year	Age	Club (League)	Class	W	L	ERA	G	GS	IP	H	HR	BB	SO	BB/9	SO/9	WHIP	AVG
2019	22	Binghamton (EL)	AA	3	0	4.34	12	0	19	15	1	7	28	3.4	13.5	1.18	.181
	22	St. Lucie (FSL)	HiA	0	0	2.53	7	0	11	8	0	2	16	1.7	13.5	0.94	.190
	22	Syracuse (IL)	AAA	2	0	13.50	10	0	9	19	3	9	12	8.7	11.6	3.00	.345
Minor League Totals				5	1	4.82	46	0	56	53	5	31	87	5.0	14.0	1.50	.250

25 MARCEL RENTERIA, RHP

BA GRADE 40 Risk: High

Born: Sept. 27, 1994. **B-T:** R-R. **HT:** 5-11. **WT:** 185. **Drafted:** New Mexico State, 2017 (6th round). **Signed by:** Kevin Roberson.

TRACK RECORD: Renteria led the Western Athletic Conference with 9.8 strikeouts per nine innings as a New Mexico State redshirt junior in 2017, when the Mets drafted him in the sixth round. He remained in the rotation at low Class A in 2018 before shifting to the bullpen in 2019. While Renteria lost reps because of the canceled 2020 season, he shined at instructional league.

SCOUTING REPORT: Renteria packages a starter's repertoire in a reliever's body. In short bursts he averages 96 mph and throws strikes with conviction. His slider is a legitimate weapon with mid-80s velocity and a high-end spin rate up to 3,000 revolutions per minute. Renteria also throws the rare high-spin changeup with extreme horizontal break. His 5-foot-10 frame and effort level give him more of a bullpen look, but his repertoire and ability to spot pitches in all four quadrants keep him alive as a starter.

THE FUTURE: The Mets nearly added Renteria to the 40-man roster, but he went unselected in the Rule 5 draft. He has a future in middle relief if everything clicks.

Year	Age	Club (League)	Class	W	L	ERA	G	GS	IP	H	HR	BB	SO	BB/9	SO/9	WHIP	AVG
2019	24	Binghamton (EL)	AA	0	0	0.00	1	0	1	1	0	0	2	0.0	18.0	1.00	.250
	24	St. Lucie (FSL)	HiA	1	4	4.62	37	0	62	62	6	26	63	3.8	9.1	1.41	.215
Minor League Totals				7	9	4.76	62	15	151	155	12	56	154	3.3	9.2	1.39	.265

26 MICHEL OTAÑEZ, RHP

BA GRADE 40 Risk: High

Born: July 3, 1997. **B-T:** R-R. **HT:** 6-3. **WT:** 215. **Signed:** Dominican Republic, 2016. **Signed by:** Marciano Alvarez.

TRACK RECORD: Otañez signed out of the Dominican Republic at age 18, missed his age-19 season after having Tommy John surgery and didn't pop on the radar until he was 21 in 2019. Otañez finished that year with short-season Brooklyn and lost a chance to build on that momentum in 2020 when the season was canceled. He did not participate in instructional league because of an unspecified Covid-related issue.

SCOUTING REPORT: Otañez is tall, long-limbed and capable of pumping 97 mph heat with plus vertical ride on his fastball. The Mets love his arm strength—he averages around 95 mph—and work ethic, but he will need to develop his secondary weapons to have a major league future. Otañez increased the power of his curveball from the mid 70s to the low 80s, but his arm swing is stiff and inconsistent, lending more horizontal break than vertical snap to the pitch. Thus, his breaking ball tends to get slurvy. The Mets have pushed Otañez to use his below-average changeup more often, but it makes rare appearances in games.

THE FUTURE: With a more consistent breaking ball, Otañez would profile as a reliever with a north-south attack. His below-average control is also befitting of a bullpen role.

Year	Age	Club (League)	Class	W	L	ERA	G	GS	IP	H	HR	BB	SO	BB/9	SO/9	WHIP	AVG
2019	21	Brooklyn (NYP)	SS	2	1	2.97	7	7	30	26	2	17	26	5.0	7.7	1.42	.200
	21	Kingsport (APP)	R	2	2	3.31	7	7	33	26	1	11	44	3.0	12.1	1.13	.195
Minor League Totals				6	10	4.74	30	26	119	117	5	58	124	4.4	9.3	1.46	.255

27 JOANDER SUAREZ, RHP

BA GRADE 40 Risk: Very High

Born: Feb. 27, 2000. **B-T:** R-R. **HT:** 6-3. **WT:** 181. **Signed:** Venezuela, 2018. **Signed by:** Carlos Perez.

TRACK RECORD: Suarez signed out of Venezuela at age 18 and spent two years in Rookie complex leagues. He tied for fourth in the Rookie-level Gulf Coast League with 47 strikeouts in 2019 and was poised to break camp with a full-season club in 2020 before the minor league season was canceled.

SCOUTING REPORT: Suarez doesn't have a knockout pitch, but batters struggle to square him up. He allowed a .191 opponent average in the GCL in 2019. Suarez pitches at 93 mph with the above-average vertical break the Mets emphasize. His high-80s changeup flashes plus and is his best pitch, more notable for his repeatable arm action. Suarez's straight changeup doesn't feature much sink or movement and is separated by just 4 mph from his fastball. Yet it has played against inexperienced hitters. Suarez has feel for a loopy, below-average curveball that is more of an early-count pitch.

THE FUTURE: Suarez has deception that can't be taught. If the Mets can teach him to develop sink and separation on his changeup, he will become a sleeper for back-of-the-rotation work.

Year	Age	Club (League)	Class	W	L	ERA	G	GS	IP	H	HR	BB	SO	BB/9	SO/9	WHIP	AVG
2019	19	Mets (GCL)	R	1	0	1.79	11	8	40	27	1	16	47	3.6	10.5	1.07	.169
Minor League Totals				1	1	2.66	19	12	61	43	1	21	66	3.1	9.7	1.05	.197

28 JAKE MANGUM, OF

BA GRADE 40 Risk: Very High

Born: March 8, 1996. **B-T:** B-L. **HT:** 6-1. **WT:** 179. **Drafted:** Mississippi State, 2019 (4th round). **Signed by:** Jet Butler.

TRACK RECORD: The son of former NFL defensive back John Mangum, Jake turned down two chances to turn pro so that he could chase history. With a 108-hit senior season at Mississippi State in 2019, he set the Southeastern Conference all-time hits record. The Mets drafted Mangum in the fourth round in 2019 but signed him for just $20,000 as part of a strategy to save bonus pool money for higher draft picks.

SCOUTING REPORT: Mangum looked largely overmatched as a 23-year-old slap hitter in the short-season New York-Penn League in his 2019 pro debut. That drove him to retool his swing by altering his hand position and setup to help boost his exit velocity and improve his attack angle. With two strikes, Mangum reverts to his spread-out stance he used to great effect in college to poke the ball to the opposite field. He could become an average major league hitter, albeit with well below-average power. Mangum is capable at all three outfield spots as a plus runner with an above-average arm. He is most proficient on the corners.

THE FUTURE: Mangum's feel for hitting, discipline, speed and versatility make him a potential fourth outfielder. He'll make his full-season debut in 2021.

Year	Age	Club (League)	Class	AVG	G	AB	R	H	2B	3B	HR	RBI	BB	SO	SB	OBP	SLG
2019	23	Brooklyn (NYP)	SS	.247	53	182	29	45	5	2	0	18	15	26	17	.337	.297
Minor League Totals				.247	53	182	29	45	5	2	0	18	15	26	17	.337	.297

29 JOSH CORNIELLY, RHP

BA GRADE 40 Risk: Very High

Born: Jan. 15, 2001. **B-T:** R-R. **HT:** 6-2. **WT:** 175. **Signed:** Venezuela, 2017. **Signed by:** Carlos Perez.

TRACK RECORD: Cornielly signed as a 17-year-old out of Venezuela in 2018 and debuted that season in the Dominican Summer League. He earned a quick ticket out of the DSL in 2019 after striking out 12 and walking one through 10.1 innings, moving to the Rookie-level Gulf Coast League.

SCOUTING REPORT: Cornielly uses a simple, repeatable delivery and has a tall, well-proportioned starter's body. What he lacks at this stage is a starter's velocity. He pitches at 88 mph and ranges from 87-90 with solid-average control. Cornielly throws an above-average changeup with sharp sink and run. He typically subtracts anywhere from 12-14 mph off his fastball. Cornielly's low-70s curveball is the proverbial work in progress and lacks power and finish. Cornielly is cerebral, detail-oriented and an adherent of pitch metrics—which is crucial for a pitcher like him who has to think one step ahead of the batter.

THE FUTURE: Not many righthanded starters make the majors throwing 88 mph, but the Mets believe Cornielly could have more velocity in the tank. He'll make his full-season debut in 2021.

Year	Age	Club (League)	Class	W	L	ERA	G	GS	IP	H	HR	BB	SO	BB/9	SO/9	WHIP	AVG
2019	18	Mets (GCL)	R	3	2	4.54	10	3	36	43	3	8	40	2.0	10.1	1.43	.272
	18	Mets1 (DSL)	R	1	2	6.10	3	3	10	12	0	1	12	0.9	10.5	1.26	.273
Minor League Totals				8	4	4.28	27	6	73	90	3	17	79	2.1	9.7	1.45	.297

30 TYLOR MEGILL, RHP

BA GRADE 40 Risk: Very High

Born: July 28, 1995. **B-T:** R-R. **HT:** 6-7. **WT:** 230. **Drafted:** Arizona, 2018 (8th round). **Signed by:** Brian Reid.

TRACK RECORD: The Mets snagged Megill as an eighth-round senior sign in 2018 after he spent his junior and senior seasons in the University of Arizona bullpen. He has the weapons, physicality and endurance to start, so the Mets began the process of stretching him out in the rotation in 2019.

SCOUTING REPORT: Megill came to instructional league in 2020 firing bullets. He reached 98 mph with apparent ease and sat in the mid 90s. Megill has a giant 6-foot-7 frame and very high arm slot but throws strikes and flashes average with three secondary pitches. His mid-80s slider has abrupt action but not a lot of depth, while his curveball has short, sharp break in the same velocity band. Megill has added depth to both breaking pitches as he has developed. His changeup plays as average and helps limit damage from lefthanded hitters.

THE FUTURE: Megill has the wide repertoire of average to near-average secondary pitches to keep hitters off-balance. If he can learn to command them, he could be dangerous, most likely as a reliever.

Year	Age	Club (League)	Class	W	L	ERA	G	GS	IP	H	HR	BB	SO	BB/9	SO/9	WHIP	AVG
2019	23	Binghamton (EL)	AA	0	1	5.40	1	1	5	5	0	0	9	0.0	16.2	1.00	.250
	23	St. Lucie (FSL)	HiA	3	4	4.04	7	7	36	36	1	10	42	2.5	10.6	1.29	.235
	23	Columbia (SAL)	LoA	3	2	2.61	14	3	31	23	1	15	41	4.4	11.9	1.23	.178
Minor League Totals				7	9	3.43	32	13	99	82	4	39	128	3.5	11.6	1.21	.220

MORE PROSPECTS TO KNOW

31 CARLOS CORTES, OF

A move from second base to left field puts a lot of pressure on the 5-foot-7 lefthanded hitter's bat, but he may have the bat speed and twitchiness to pull it off.

32 FRANKLYN KILOME, RHP

Tattooed for five homers in 11 innings and a .298 opponent average in his major league debut in 2020, Kilome needs to develop better command of his fastball and trust in a second pitch.

33 JARED ROBINSON, RHP

A 26-year-old reliever signed as a minor league free agent from the Indians' system, Robinson reaches 96 mph with life up in the zone and has a quality slider.

34 COLIN HOLDERMAN, RHP

The 6-foot-7 starter came to instructional league firing fastballs in the mid 90s and touching 97 mph, but he's also 25 with little experience above low Class A.

35 STANLEY CONSUEGRA, OF

The 20-year-old Dominican is tooled up and has one of the system's highest average exit velocities, but he hasn't played since 2018 because of injuries, including a torn anterior cruciate ligament in 2019.

36 ALI SANCHEZ, C

The 24-year-old defensive wizard made his big league debut in 2020, but his bat could be stretched even as a backup catcher.

37 PATRICK MAZEIKA, C/1B

The 27-year-old lefthanded hitter has shown flashes of power and plate discipline but struggles to hit enough for first base or defend enough for catcher.

38 RICHARD BRITO, RHP

SLEEPER

Brito brushed 100 mph before the Mets signed him as a 21-year-old out of Venezuela in 2019. He could not get a visa in 2020 and was sidelined in the Dominican Republic with an injury.

39 WILMER REYES, SS/3B

Reyes was one of the Mets' top hitters at instructional league, hitting .351 with four homers, but he's already 23 and has no experience above short-season ball.

40 JUNIOR TILIEN, SS

Signed at age 17 out of the Dominican Republic in 2019, Tilien is an offensive-oriented shortstop with good bat-to-ball skills, plate discipline and gap power. His speed and arm fit at shortstop if he improves his defensive reliability.

41 ERIC SANTANA, OF

Signed out of the Dominican Republic at age 17 in 2019, Santana is a switch-hitting center fielder with a knack for hitting line drives to all fields. He relies on instincts rather than notable power or speed.

TOP PROSPECTS OF THE DECADE

Year	Player, Pos.	2020 Org
2011	Jenrry Mejia, RHP	Mexican League
2012	Zack Wheeler, RHP	Phillies
2013	Zack Wheeler, RHP	Phillies
2014	Noah Syndergaard, RHP	Mets
2015	Noah Syndergaard, RHP	Mets
2016	Steven Matz, LHP	Mets
2017	Amed Rosario, SS	Mets
2018	Andres Gimenez, SS	Mets
2019	Andres Gimenez, SS	Mets
2020	Ronny Mauricio, SS	Mets

TOP DRAFT PICKS OF THE DECADE

Year	Player, Pos	2020 Org
2011	Brandon Nimmo, OF	Mets
2012	Gavin Cecchini, SS	Independent League
2013	Dominic Smith, 1B	Mets
2014	Michael Conforto, OF	Mets
2015	Desmond Lindsay, OF (2nd round)	Mets
2016	Justin Dunn, RHP	Mariners
2017	David Peterson, LHP	Mets
2018	Jarred Kelenic, OF	Mariners
2019	Brett Baty, 3B	Mets
2020	Pete Crow-Armstrong, OF	Mets

DEPTH CHART

NEW YORK METS

TOP 2021 ROOKIE	RANK
Sam McWilliams, RHP	21
BREAKOUT PROSPECTS	**RANK**
Jose Butto, RHP	15
Endy Rodriguez, C	20
Jordany Ventura, RHP	23

SOURCE OF TOP 30 TALENT

Homegrown	28	Acquired	2
College	6	Trades	0
Junior college	0	Rule 5 draft	0
High school	8	Independent leagues	0
International	14	Free agents/waivers	2
Nondrafted free agents	0		

LF
Isaiah Greene (11)
Carlos Cortes

CF
Pete Crow-Armstrong (5)
Alex Ramirez (13)
Jake Mangum (28)
Eric Santana
Drew Ferguson
Blaine McIntosh

RF
Freddy Valdez (19)
Stanley Consuegra
Scott Ota

3B
Brett Baty (6)
Mark Vientos (7)
Jaylen Palmer (17)
Will Toffey

SS
Ronny Mauricio (2)
Andres Gimenez (3)
Shervyen Newton (16)
Wilmer Reyes
Junior Tilien

2B
Robel Garcia
Wilmer Reyes

1B
Jeremy Vasquez

C
Francisco Alvarez (1)
Endy Rodriguez (20)
Ali Sanchez
Patrick Mazeika

LHP

LHSP	LHRP
David Peterson (9)	Thomas Szapucki (18)

RHP

RHSP	RHRP
Matt Allan (4)	Sam McWilliams (21)
J.T. Ginn (8)	Oscar de la Cruz (22)
Josh Wolf (10)	Ryley Gilliam (24)
Robert Dominguez (14)	Marcel Renteria (25)
Jose Butto (15)	Michel Otañez (26)
Jordany Ventura (23)	Joander Suarez (27)
Tylor Megill (30)	Josh Cornielly (28)
Richard Brito	Franklyn Kilome
Tony Dibrell	Jared Robinson
Jose Acuña	Colin Holderman
	Daison Acosta
	Eric Orze

New York Yankees

BY JOSH NORRIS

The Yankees' highest and lowest points in 2020 both occurred in San Diego.

In the midst of the Winter Meetings, after years of trying through the draft and via trade, the Yankees finally reeled in ace righthander Gerrit Cole. He was their first-round choice in 2008, but instead chose to go to UCLA for three seasons before spending seven seasons with the Pirates and Astros.

Once Cole reached free agency, however, the Yankees pulled out all the stops (and their wallet) and inked him to a nine-year, $324 million contract. In an ideal world, Cole would have been the cherry on top of a roster primed to slice through the American League en route to the World Series.

Then came the novel coronavirus pandemic, which turned the world—and the season—on its side. After months of hemming and hawing, MLB and the Players Association settled on a 60-game interleague but intradivison season, which began with an epic matchup of Cole against Max Scherzer.

Once the year got going, the Yankees ran into the same problems as in previous years. Namely, their biggest sluggers—Aaron Judge and Giancarlo Stanton—missed time with injuries. Combined, the pair played just 51 games in the regular season.

With those two out, catcher Gary Sanchez's continued regression was magnified. His performance became so bad, in fact, that Kyle Higashioka became the starter in the middle of the playoffs.

With the playoff field expanded to 16 in 2020, the Yankees opened the postseason against the Indians, whom they dispatched in two games. That set up a Division Series battle with the Rays, who had quickly become their most-heated rivals.

The series—held in San Diego to reduce travel—carried extra tension after a near-beanball from Yankees closer Aroldis Chapman over the head of Rays utilityman Mike Brosseau sparked a bench-clearing incident in the regular season.

The undertones were clear in Game 5 of the series, when Brosseau turned a protracted at-bat against Chapman into a home run, giving the Rays the lead and the eventual series win.

Like many other teams, the Yankees turned to a plethora of rookies and prospects during the stunted 2020 season. Top pitching prospects Deivi Garcia, Clarke Schmidt and Miguel Yajure each made their debuts, as did outfielder Estevan Florial and relievers Nick Nelson and Brooks Kriske.

Garcia and Schmidt are likely to figure into the Yankees' rotation plans in 2021, especially with Masahiro Tanaka, J.A. Happ and James Paxton all free agents after the season.

MIKE STOBE/GETTY IMAGES

The Yankees courted Gerrit Cole for more than a decade and finally got their man in 2020.

PROJECTED 2024 LINEUP

Position	Player	Age
Catcher	Gary Sanchez	31
First Base	Luke Voit	33
Second Base	Gleyber Torres	27
Third Base	Gio Urshela	32
Shortstop	Oswald Peraza	24
Left Field	Clint Frazier	29
Center Field	Jasson Dominguez	21
Right Field	Aaron Judge	32
Designated Hitter	Giancarlo Stanton	34
No. 1 Starter	Gerrit Cole	32
No. 2 Starter	Luis Severino	30
No. 3 Starter	Deivi Garcia	25
No. 4 Starter	Clarke Schmidt	28
No. 5 Starter	Luis Gil	26
Closer	Jonathan Loaisiga	29

Although the shelved minor league season in 2020 meant young prospects didn't get a chance to add any meaningful development, the Yankees' minor leaguers had it worse than most.

New York did not hold a domestic instructional league, meaning the only players who got to work in-person with coaches after spring training shut down were those at alternate training site during the season or afterward at instructional league in the Dominican Republic.

Though many things were different about 2020, the Yankees' ending remained the same: Another year of reaching the playoffs but failing to end their World Series drought. ■

1 JASSON DOMINGUEZ, OF

Born: Feb. 7, 2003. **B-T:** B-R. **HT:** 5-10. **WT:** 210.
Signed: Dominican Republic, 2019.
Signed by: Juan Rosario/Lorenzo Piron/Edgar Mateo.

TRACK RECORD: Dominguez was one of the Yankees' most celebrated international signings ever and garnered a $5.1 million bonus that tied him with the Athletics' Robert Puason for the highest in the 2019 international class. It was also the highest bonus the Yankees have ever paid to an amateur. The team's only bigger bonuses went to Jose Contreras and Hideki Irabu, who got $6 million and $8 million, respectively, but had professional experience. Dominguez showed early hints of his potential as a 13-year-old when he homered on the first pitch of a tryout and ran a 6.4-second 60-yard dash. His expected U.S. debut in 2020 was as anticipated as any Yankees prospect's over the last decade, but it was delayed a year by the coronavirus pandemic. He did, however, get on the field as part of the Yankees instructional league in the Dominican Republic.

SCOUTING REPORT: Dominguez is as tooled up as any prospect in baseball. All five of his tools show plus potential, with his power and speed garnering double-plus grades that have the Yankees dreaming of a potential 30-30 player. Yankees international scouting director Donny Rowland said Dominguez has "possibly the best combination of tools and performance that I've run across." Dominguez is extremely physical despite not being completely filled out with a body that reminds some of White Sox third baseman Yoan Moncada, and the Yankees note that he tackles two-a-day workouts like a high school football player. Dominguez's bat speed is already as explosive as any player in the organization, with one evaluator comparing it to Clint Frazier, whose bat speed was labeled "legendary" by Yankees general manager Brian Cashman. Beyond his pure bat speed, the switch-hitting Dominguez's bat paths from both sides allow the barrel to get to the strike zone quickly and stay there for a long time. He has already produced exit velocities up to 108 mph from both sides of the plate. Dominguez's offensive potential is tremendous, but he still needs more experience against pitches other than fastballs. He spent part of the shutdown hitting off pitching machines that throw breaking balls in order to help him get used to making better swing decisions. Defensively, Dominguez has experience at shortstop, but the Yankees preferred him in center field because of his 70-grade speed and an advanced feel for route-running in the outfield. His arm ranks as plus not only for its strength but also for the accuracy of his throws.

CLIFF WELCH/ICON SPORTSWIRE VIA GETTY IMAGES

BA GRADE
65 **Risk: Extreme**

SCOUTING GRADES
Hit: 60. **Power:** 70. **Run:** 70. **Field:** 60. **Arm:** 60.

Projected future grades on 20-80 scouting scale.

BEST TOOLS

Best Hitter for Average	Canaan Smith
Best Power Hitter	Jasson Dominguez
Best Strike-Zone Discipline	Canaan Smith
Fastest Baserunner	Jasson Dominguez
Best Athlete	Jasson Dominguez
Best Fastball	Luis Gil
Best Curveball	Clarke Schmidt
Best Slider	Greg Weissert
Best Changeup	Alexander Vizcaino
Best Control	Michael King
Best Defensive Catcher	Antonio Gomez
Best Defensive Infielder	Oswald Peraza
Best Infield Arm	Oswald Peraza
Best Defensive Outfielder	Jasson Dominguez
Best Outfield Arm	Jasson Dominguez

THE FUTURE: After a lost season due to the coronavirus, Dominguez will get a second crack at officially starting his first pro season in 2021. He'll likely start the year in extended spring training before moving to one of the Yankees' Class A levels. Once he debuts, he should move through the system quickly and could become one of baseball's next great Latin American stars. ■

Year	Age	Club (League)	Class	AVG	G	AB	R	H	2B	3B	HR	RBI	BB	SO	SB	OBP	SLG
2019	16	Did not play—Signed 2020 contract															

2 DEIVI GARCIA, RHP

TOP ROOKIE

BA GRADE

55 Risk: Medium

MIKE CARLSON/MLB PHOTOS VIA GETTY IMAGES

Born: May 19, 1999. **B-T:** R-R. **HT:** 5-10. **WT:** 167. **Signed:** Dominican Republic, 2015. **Signed by:** Miguel Benitez.

TRACK RECORD: Garcia opened 2020 at the Yankees' alternate training site and made his big league debut on Aug. 30, capping a storybook rise after he signed for $200,000 as a 16-year-old in 2015. Garcia finished strong enough to earn a spot on the Yankees' postseason roster and started Game 2 of the American League Division Series, albeit for only one inning as an opener.

SCOUTING REPORT: Garcia emerged a changed pitcher in 2020. The Yankees shifted him toward the first base side of the rubber to get more on line toward home plate and toned down the rotational elements of his delivery. The result was substantially improved control. Garcia worked to add more ride to his 91-93 mph fastball that touches 95, helping it play up beyond its pure velocity. The process of adding a slider at the end of 2019 caused Garcia's curveball to lose some of its bite, but once the pitch was re-shaped, it resembled the potential plus offering he had shown in the past. Garcia's changeup was his most frequently used secondary pitch in the majors, with its 11 mph separation leading to a 29% whiff rate.

THE FUTURE: Garcia is in line for a full-time rotation spot in 2021.

SCOUTING GRADES: **Fastball:** 55 **Slider:** 50 **Curveball:** 60 **Changeup:** 60 **Control:** 55

Year	Age	Club (League)	Class	W	L	ERA	G	GS	IP	H	HR	BB	SO	BB/9	SO/9	WHIP	AVG
2018	19	Charleston (SAL)	LoA	2	4	3.76	8	8	41	31	5	10	63	2.2	13.9	1.01	.182
	19	Trenton (EL)	AA	1	0	0.00	1	1	5	0	0	2	7	3.6	12.6	0.40	.000
	19	Tampa (FSL)	HiA	2	0	1.27	6	6	28	19	0	8	35	2.5	11.1	0.95	.174
2019	20	Scranton/W-B (IL)	AAA	1	3	5.40	11	6	40	39	8	20	45	4.5	10.1	1.48	.239
	20	Trenton (EL)	AA	4	4	3.86	11	11	54	43	2	26	87	4.4	14.6	1.29	.183
	20	Tampa (FSL)	HiA	0	2	3.06	4	4	18	14	0	8	33	4.1	16.8	1.25	.192
2020	21	New York (AL)	MAJ	3	2	4.98	6	6	34	35	6	6	33	1.6	8.7	1.19	.254
Major League Totals				3	2	4.98	6	6	34	35	6	6	33	1.6	8.7	1.19	.254
Minor League Totals				17	20	3.37	65	57	293	211	23	125	416	3.8	12.8	1.14	.202

3 CLARKE SCHMIDT, RHP

Born: Feb. 20, 1996. **B-T:** R-R. **HT:** 6-1. **WT:** 200. **Drafted:** South Carolina, 2017 (1st round). **Signed by:** Billy Godwin.

TRACK RECORD: The Yankees drafted Schmidt in 2017 knowing he would need Tommy John surgery. He missed most of 2018 recovering but returned in 2019 and bullied his way to Double-A. The Yankees called Schmidt up for his big league debut in September.

SCOUTING REPORT: Schmidt initially dominated hitters with a powerful two-seam fastball and a filthy power curveball thrown in the mid 80s. The Yankees used the downtime during the coronavirus shutdown to give him a four-seamer, which gave him a pitch that played better against lefthanded hitters as well as an offering that rode up in the zone to pair with his signature curveball. Schmidt throws both fastballs in the 95 mph range, but they really just set up his power curve. It's a tight-spinning weapon that averages 3,085 rpms and dives straight down, garnering a 44% whiff rate in the majors. It's a consensus plus pitch that gets batters to swing over the top. Schmidt rounds out his arsenal with a seldom-used, high-80s changeup that doesn't fool lefties.

THE FUTURE: Schmidt will look to cement a spot in the Yankees' rotation in 2021. He has barely pitched above the Class A levels and may need more time in the minors.

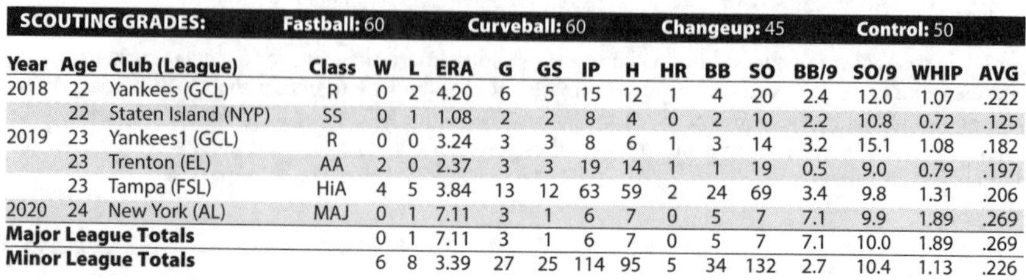

SCOUTING GRADES: **Fastball:** 60 **Curveball:** 60 **Changeup:** 45 **Control:** 50

Year	Age	Club (League)	Class	W	L	ERA	G	GS	IP	H	HR	BB	SO	BB/9	SO/9	WHIP	AVG
2018	22	Yankees (GCL)	R	0	2	4.20	6	5	15	12	1	4	20	2.4	12.0	1.07	.222
	22	Staten Island (NYP)	SS	0	1	1.08	2	2	8	4	0	2	10	2.2	10.8	0.72	.125
2019	23	Yankees1 (GCL)	R	0	0	3.24	3	3	8	6	1	3	14	3.2	15.1	1.08	.182
	23	Trenton (EL)	AA	2	0	2.37	3	3	19	14	1	1	19	0.5	9.0	0.79	.197
	23	Tampa (FSL)	HiA	4	5	3.84	13	12	63	59	2	24	69	3.4	9.8	1.31	.206
2020	24	New York (AL)	MAJ	0	1	7.11	3	1	6	7	0	5	7	7.1	9.9	1.89	.269
Major League Totals				0	1	7.11	3	1	6	7	0	5	7	7.1	10.0	1.89	.269
Minor League Totals				6	8	3.39	27	25	114	95	5	34	132	2.7	10.4	1.13	.226

4 LUIS GIL, RHP

MIKE CARLSON/MLB PHOTOS VIA GETTY IMAGES

BA GRADE
55 **Risk: Very High**

Born: June 3, 1998. **B-T:** R-R. **HT:** 6-2. **WT:** 185. **Signed:** Dominican Republic, 2014. **Signed by:** Luis Lajara (Twins).

TRACK RECORD: Gil signed with the Twins for $90,000 in 2014 and was traded to the Yankees for outfielder Jake Cave before the 2018 season. He took off after the trade and rose to high Class A Tampa in 2019, earning a place on the Yankees' 40-man roster after the season. He spent 2020 at the alternate training site, where he built on previous developmental gains.

SCOUTING REPORT: Gil is a power-armed righthander with an upper-90s fastball. The Yankees worked with him at the alternate site to give the pitch riding life at the top of the zone while weeding out the version that bleeds into two-seam territory, helping it move toward its plus-plus potential. Gil's slider is a new addition to his arsenal, replacing his curveball, and ranges from 82-88 mph while showing average promise with more development. The Yankees like the movement and shape of Gil's low-90s changeup, but would like to see him execute the pitch more consistently. To that end, they asked him to shift the way he holds the changeup in an effort to make it more enticing to batters than it is currently. Gil has long struggled with walks and needs a lot of work to reach even average control.

THE FUTURE: Gil gained valuable experience at the alternate training site. He has a chance to reach Double-A in 2021.

SCOUTING GRADES: **Fastball:** 70 **Slider:** 50 **Changeup:** 50 **Control:** 45

Year	Age	Club (League)	Class	W	L	ERA	G	GS	IP	H	HR	BB	SO	BB/9	SO/9	WHIP	AVG
2017	19	Twins (DSL)	R	0	2	2.59	14	14	42	31	2	20	49	4.3	10.6	1.22	.175
2018	20	Staten Island (NYP)	SS	0	2	5.40	2	2	7	11	1	6	10	8.1	13.5	2.55	.282
	20	Pulaski (APP)	R	2	1	1.37	10	10	39	21	1	25	58	5.7	13.3	1.17	.130
2019	21	Charleston, SC (SAL)	LoA	4	5	2.39	17	17	83	60	1	39	112	4.2	12.1	1.19	.171
	21	Tampa (FSL)	HiA	1	0	4.85	3	3	13	11	0	8	11	5.5	7.6	1.46	.139
Minor League Totals				8	12	2.74	62	46	207	149	7	124	264	5.4	11.5	1.32	.200

5 AUSTIN WELLS, C

MIKE CHRISTY/ARIZONA ATHLETICS

BA GRADE
50 **Risk: High**

Born: July 12, 1999. **B-T:** L-R. **HT:** 6-1. **WT:** 200. **Drafted:** Arizona, 2020 (1st round). **Signed by:** Troy Afenir.

TRACK RECORD: Wells attended Las Vegas high school powerhouse Bishop Gorman, then matriculated to Arizona, where his father played. Wells was a draft-eligible sophomore who produced with the Wildcats following a standout summer in the Cape Cod League. The Yankees, who drafted Wells in the 35th round in 2018, saw fit to pick him again at No. 28 overall and signed him for $2.5 million.

SCOUTING REPORT: The Yankees covet lefthanded power, which Wells has in ample supply. He has a strong frame, a simple swing and outstanding knowledge of the strike zone that helped him register more walks (46) than strikeouts (43) in college. He projects to hit for both average and power and be a potential middle-of-the-order hitter. The Yankees believe Wells can remain at catcher, but they're in the minority. He has trouble blocking pitches and isn't particularly mobile behind the plate, and his long history of elbow troubles leads to fringy arm strength at best. The Yankees see a strong receiver who could benefit from the organization's new one-knee philosophy installed by big league catching coordinator Tanner Swanson.

THE FUTURE: Wells will get pro instruction for the first time in 2021. Even if he can't stick at catcher, his bat should help him move quickly up the system.

SCOUTING GRADES: **Hitting:** 60 **Power:** 55 **Running:** 50 **Fielding:** 40 **Arm:** 45

Year	Age	Club (League)	Class	AVG	G	AB	R	H	2B	3B	HR	RBI	BB	SO	SB	OBP	SLG
2020	20	Did not play—No minor league season															

6 OSWALD PERAZA, SS

Born: June 15, 2000. **B-T:** R-R. **HT:** 5-11. **WT:** 186. **Signed:** Venezuela, 2016. **Signed by:** Roney Calderon/Jose Gavidia.

TRACK RECORD: Signed for $175,000 in the same international class as righthander Roansy Contreras and shortstop Jose Devers, Peraza spent the first few years of his career impressing evaluators with his tools despite middling production at the lower levels. The Yankees did not include him in their 60-man player pool because he had yet to play above low Class A, so he didn't get any formal, in-person instruction in 2020 after the coronavirus shutdown.

SCOUTING REPORT: Peraza's top skill is his ability to put the barrel on the ball. He consistently produces louder exit velocities than his small stature would suggest, including a peak velocity of 110 mph. He overwhelmingly hits singles, but Peraza has worked hard with instructors to put the ball in the air more so his hard contact will go deep into the outfield. Defensively, Peraza is a twitchy athlete with smooth actions at shortstop, excellent range, a quick transfer and strong arm. Those ingredients will keep him at the position as a potential plus defender. He is a plus runner who stole 23 bases in 30 attempts in 2019.

THE FUTURE: Peraza may deal with some rust after a season-long layoff. He is likely to open the year at high Class A once the minor leagues begin. The Yankees added him to the 40-man roster in November.

SCOUTING GRADES:	Hitting: 50	Power: 40	Running: 60	Fielding: 60	Arm: 60

Year	Age	Club (League)	Class	AVG	G	AB	R	H	2B	3B	HR	RBI	BB	SO	SB	OBP	SLG
2017	17	Yankees (DSL)	R	.361	10	36	10	13	3	2	0	10	7	2	1	.467	.556
	17	Yankees2 (GCL)	R	.266	48	184	34	49	10	1	0	24	16	36	12	.363	.332
2018	18	Pulaski (APP)	R	.250	36	140	25	35	3	2	1	11	14	41	8	.333	.321
2019	19	Charleston, SC (SAL)	LoA	.273	46	183	31	50	5	0	2	13	16	28	18	.348	.333
	19	Staten Island (NYP)	SS	.241	19	79	7	19	1	1	2	7	5	9	5	.294	.354
Minor League Totals				.267	159	622	107	166	22	6	5	65	58	116	44	.350	.346

7 ALEXANDER VIZCAINO, RHP

MIKE CARLSON/MLB PHOTOS VIA GETTY IMAGES

Born: May 22, 1997. **B-T:** R-R. **HT:** 6-1. **WT:** 172. **Signed:** Dominican Republic, 2016. **Signed by:** Juan Rosario.

TRACK RECORD: Vizcaino signed for just $14,000 and began his career with three nondescript seasons, but he broke out in 2019 on the strength of a greatly improved changeup to go with his explosive fastball. The Yankees, impressed with his gains, brought him to their alternate training site in 2020 despite the fact he has yet to pitch above high Class A.

SCOUTING REPORT: Vizcaino is an elite athlete who is one of the fastest runners and highest jumpers in the Yankees' system. He pairs that athleticism with a powerful right arm that generates upper-90s fastballs and a plus-plus changeup, which helped him strike out more than a batter per inning in 2019. Vizcaino's slider was a point of focus at the alternate training site. Rather than change the pitch itself, the Yankees tweaked Vizcaino's delivery with a bit of a hip turn to help him stay closed and on-line toward the plate. Those alterations helped him land his slider more consistently and play as an average pitch. Vizcaino throws all his pitches for strikes but still needs to add strength to his frame, which will help improve his durability.

THE FUTURE: After a summer facing more experienced hitters, he may open 2021 at Double-A. He was added to the 40-man roster in November.

SCOUTING GRADES:	Fastball: 60	Slider: 50	Changeup: 70	Control: 55

Year	Age	Club (League)	Class	W	L	ERA	G	GS	IP	H	HR	BB	SO	BB/9	SO/9	WHIP	AVG
2017	20	Pulaski (APP)	R	3	5	5.79	12	11	51	69	9	23	49	4.0	8.6	1.79	.283
2018	21	Charleston, SC (SAL)	LoA	0	1	13.50	1	1	4	8	2	2	2	4.5	4.5	2.50	.364
	21	Pulaski (APP)	R	3	3	4.50	11	11	54	49	7	21	55	3.5	9.2	1.30	.212
2019	22	Charleston, SC (SAL)	LoA	5	5	4.41	16	16	88	80	6	27	101	2.8	10.4	1.22	.202
	22	Tampa (FSL)	HiA	1	1	4.28	5	5	27	33	2	11	27	3.6	8.9	1.61	.280
Minor League Totals				12	20	4.89	56	50	259	279	30	97	261	3.4	9.1	1.45	.276

8 MIGUEL YAJURE, RHP

Born: May 1, 1998. **B-T:** R-R. **HT:** 6-1. **WT:** 175. **Signed:** Venezuela, 2015.
Signed by: Cesar Suarez/Ricardo Finol.

MIKE CARLSON/MLB PHOTOS VIA GETTY IMAGES

BA GRADE
45 **Risk: Medium**

TRACK RECORD: The Yankees signed Yajure out of Venezuela for $30,000 in 2015 on the strength of two innings at a tryout. He missed the 2017 season after having Tommy John surgery, returned in 2018 and broke out in 2019 as he jumped to Double-A. The Yankees added Yajure to their 40-man roster after the 2019 season. He made his big league debut on Aug. 31, 2020.

SCOUTING REPORT: Yajure added velocity through a weighted-ball program and a series of delivery tweaks after the 2019 season that were designed to better incorporate his lower half. The result was a nearly 2 mph jump in his average velocity, up to 92 mph in 2020. Yajure complements his enhanced four-seamer with a cutter, slider, curveball and changeup. His high-80s changeup, which he feels comfortable throwing against both righties and lefties, is his go-to secondary pitch and shows above-average potential. His curveball is a 12-to-6 breaker thrown in the low 80s and forms an ideal tunnel with his four-seamer. His cutter and slider were added to give him more options against righthanders. Yajure struggled with walks in 2020 but had above-average control in the minors.

THE FUTURE: Yajure likely will start 2021 at Triple-A. He should return to the majors during the season.

SCOUTING GRADES: **Fastball:** 55 **Cutter:** 50 **Curveball:** 60 **Changeup:** 55 **Control:** 55

Year	Age	Club (League)	Class	W	L	ERA	G	GS	IP	H	HR	BB	SO	BB/9	SO/9	WHIP	AVG
2017	19	Did not play--Injured															
2018	20	Charleston, SC (SAL)	LoA	4	3	3.90	14	14	65	64	3	15	56	2.1	7.8	1.22	.237
2019	21	Trenton (EL)	AA	1	0	0.82	2	2	11	9	0	2	11	1.6	9.0	1.00	.205
	21	Tampa (FSL)	HiA	8	6	2.26	22	18	128	110	5	28	122	2.0	8.6	1.08	.215
2020	22	New York (AL)	MAJ	0	0	1.29	3	0	7	3	1	5	8	6.4	10.3	1.14	.130
Major League Totals				0	0	1.29	3	0	7	3	1	5	8	6.4	10.3	1.14	.130
Minor League Totals				14	13	2.47	61	54	291	261	10	70	246	2.2	7.6	1.13	.241

9 YOENDRYS GOMEZ, RHP

Born: Oct. 15, 1999. **B-T:** R-R. **HT:** 6-3. **WT:** 175. **Signed:** Venezuela, 2016.
Signed by: Alan Atacho.

BA GRADE
50 **Risk: High**

TRACK RECORD: After his projectable body and fastball earned him a $50,000 signing bonus, Gomez quickly began impressing evaluators. He bypassed the short-season New York-Penn League on the way to low Class A in 2019 and whiffed just less than a batter an inning. Gomez's 2020 season was wiped out by the pandemic, but he spent the time away working remotely with Yankees minor league pitching coach Dustin Glant.

SCOUTING REPORT: Gomez has a lean body and a whippy arm to go with broad shoulders that lead evaluators to believe he could gain more strength, which is exactly what the Yankees want him to do. The gains he made over the offseason helped bump his average fastball velocity to 95 mph in the few innings he got in spring training. He had also been working with the Yankees' pitching development team to add a slider to what had been an arsenal of fastball, curveball and changeup. Evaluators who saw Gomez last year projected his low-80s curveball as a potential plus pitch, while they wanted to see more consistency from his changeup. A polished strike-thrower, Gomez must improve the quality of his strikes.

THE FUTURE: Gomez was not at the alternate training site this year and should return to low Class A in 2021.

SCOUTING GRADES: **Fastball:** 60 **Slider:** 50 **Curveball:** 60 **Changeup:** 50 **Control:** 55

Year	Age	Club (League)	Class	W	L	ERA	G	GS	IP	H	HR	BB	SO	BB/9	SO/9	WHIP	AVG
2017	17	Yankees (DSL)	R	0	3	4.78	10	8	32	36	2	12	32	3.4	9.0	1.50	.250
	17	Yankees2 (GCL)	R	0	0	12.00	1	1	3	5	0	6	1	18.0	3.0	3.67	.278
2018	18	Yankees1 (GCL)	R	3	1	2.33	10	9	39	27	1	15	43	3.5	10.0	1.09	.168
	18	Yankees (DSL)	R	1	0	1.00	2	2	9	2	0	7	7	7.0	7.0	1.00	.061
2019	19	Charleston, SC (SAL)	LoA	0	3	6.08	6	6	27	28	2	9	25	3.0	8.4	1.39	.235
	19	Pulaski (APP)	R	4	2	2.12	6	6	30	26	1	10	28	3.0	8.5	1.21	.210
Minor League Totals				8	9	3.69	35	32	139	124	6	59	136	3.8	8.8	1.32	.243

10 LUIS MEDINA, RHP

Born: May 3, 1999. **B-T:** R-R. **HT:** 6-3. **WT:** 195. **Signed:** Dominican Republic, 2015. **Signed by:** Juan Rosario.

MIKE CARLSON/MLB PHOTOS VIA GETTY IMAGES

BA GRADE
55 Risk: Extreme

TRACK RECORD: Medina already touched 100 mph by the time he was 16 years old and signed with the Yankees for $280,000 out of the Dominican Republic. Medina has continued to throw hard in pro ball, but his control has been non-existent and he has yet to advance past high Class A. The Yankees still added Medina to the 40-man roster after the 2019 season and brought him to the alternate training site in 2020.

SCOUTING REPORT: Medina has the best pure stuff in the Yankees' system. All three of his pitches are potentially plus, including an upper-90s fastball that peaked at 102 mph at the alternate site and a double-plus, hammer curveball. But that stuff is a tease more often than not because of his poor command and control. He has averaged 7.1 walks per nine innings in his career with a heavy dose of wild pitches annually. Medina began showing improvement with decreased fastball usage but still needs more work. Medina controls his changeup best of his three pitches and often uses the potential plus offering to get back in counts.

THE FUTURE: Medina has a long way to go to get to even playable control, but his stuff will buy him time. He may see Double-A in 2021.

SCOUTING GRADES: **Fastball:** 70 **Curveball:** 70 **Changeup:** 60 **Control:** 40

Year	Age	Club (League)	Class	W	L	ERA	G	GS	IP	H	HR	BB	SO	BB/9	SO/9	WHIP	AVG
2017	18	Yankees (DSL)	R	1	1	5.74	4	3	16	17	0	10	17	5.7	9.8	1.72	.233
	18	Pulaski (APP)	R	1	1	5.09	6	6	23	14	1	14	22	5.5	8.6	1.22	.141
2018	19	Pulaski (APP)	R	1	3	6.25	12	12	36	32	3	46	47	11.5	11.8	2.17	.174
2019	20	Charleston, SC (SAL)	LoA	1	8	6.00	20	20	93	86	9	67	115	6.5	11.1	1.65	.201
	20	Tampa (FSL)	HiA	0	0	0.84	2	2	11	7	0	3	12	2.5	10.1	0.94	.163
Minor League Totals				4	13	5.51	47	46	183	158	13	144	217	7.1	10.7	1.65	.232

11 ROANSY CONTRERAS, RHP

Born: Nov. 7, 1999. **B-T:** R-R. **HT:** 6-0. **WT:** 197. **Signed:** Dominican Republic, 2016. **Signed by:** Juan Rosario.

BA GRADE
50 Risk: High

TRACK RECORD: Though the Yankees were in the international penalty box in 2016, they still unearthed several gems in shortstops Jose Devers (since traded to Miami), Oswald Peraza and Contreras, who was a product of the same training program in the D.R. that produced current Yankees Gary Sanchez and Miguel Andujar. Contreras was part of a talented group of pitchers at low Class A in 2019 but was not part of the team's 60-man player pool over the summer.

SCOUTING REPORT: Of the Yankees' group at Charleston, Contreras has the lowest ceiling but the highest floor. He had a small uptick in velocity and averaged 95 mph with his fastball in spring training. The biggest flashpoint in his development, however, will be the development of a consistent breaking ball. In 2019, his breaking ball was more of a slurve. Now, the Yankees' pitching development team wants to see if they can get it to act more like a slider so it will pair better with his fastball. Before the shutdown, Contreras tried tinkering with different grips to achieve that goal. Evaluators outside of the organization were fans of Contreras' changeup, noting that it featured both horizontal and vertical movement and was thrown with enough confidence to be effective against both righties and lefties.

THE FUTURE: After a year of missed development—though he worked remotely with new Yankees pitching coach Dustin Glant during the shutdown—Contreras is likely to begin 2021 at high Class A. He was added to the 40-man roster over the winter.

Year	Age	Club (League)	Class	W	L	ERA	G	GS	IP	H	HR	BB	SO	BB/9	SO/9	WHIP	AVG
2019	19	Charleston, SC (SAL)	LoA	12	5	3.33	24	24	132	105	10	36	113	2.4	7.7	1.07	.187
Minor League Totals				16	11	3.25	50	47	249	209	19	74	207	2.7	7.5	1.14	.225

12 ESTEVAN FLORIAL, OF

Born: Nov. 25, 1997. **B-T:** L-L. **HT:** 6-1. **WT:** 195. **Signed:** Haiti, 2015. **Signed by:** Esteban Castillo.

TRACK RECORD: Off limits in the 2017 trade that brought Sonny Gray to New York, Florial had his career sidetracked by a pair of broken bones in his hands in 2018 and 2019. The injuries limited Florial to just 158 games in two seasons, costing him valuable development time. He made a big league cameo in 2020 and collected his first MLB hit on Aug. 28.

SCOUTING REPORT: Because he is on the 40-man roster, Florial was at the team's alternate training site all summer. There, he faced a mixture of wily, high-level arms he hadn't been exposed to outside of big league spring training. His goal has long been to improve his command of the strike zone, and he made strides in that department at the ATS while also using his potentially plus power to swat 12 home runs and produce an average exit velocity of 91.3 mph. His plus speed and instincts will allow him to profile in center field, and his plus arm gives him an extra defensive weapon.

THE FUTURE: After a summer facing veteran arms, Florial might be ready to move to Triple-A in 2021 for more polish. He still has a ceiling of a regular with impact offensively and defensively.

Year	Age	Club (League)	Class	AVG	G	AB	R	H	2B	3B	HR	RBI	BB	SO	SB	OBP	SLG
2020	22	New York (AL)	MAJ	.333	1	3	0	1	0	0	0	0	0	2	0	.333	.333
Major League Totals				.333	1	3	0	1	0	0	0	0	0	2	0	.333	.333
Minor League Totals				.273	392	1507	261	412	73	24	42	213	182	484	73	.353	.437

13 EZEQUIEL DURAN, 2B

BREAKOUT
BA GRADE
50 Risk: High

Born: May 22, 1999. **B-T:** R-R. **HT:** 5-10. **WT:** 202. **Signed:** Dominican Republic, 2017. **Signed by:** Juan Rosario/Raymon Sanchez/Victor Mata.

TRACK RECORD: Clerical issues meant that Duran had to wait a little later than most to turn professional, but he eventually signed—for just $10,000—and immediately proved worth the investment. The best example of what Duran can do came in July 2019, when he hit .333/.392/.630 with six homers for short-season Staten Island. He ranked No. 7 in the New York-Penn League's Top 20.

SCOUTING REPORT: Evaluators both inside and outside the organization are intrigued by Duran's abilities. Scouts see a player with hit and power tools that range from average to plus, and bat speed and exit velocities that rank among the best of the system's middle infield prospects. He's made strides in pitch recognition and swing decisions, which should unlock more of his potential. On defense he shows above-average speed, average range and a plus arm that could allow him to fill in at shortstop if needed.

THE FUTURE: Duran participated in the Yankees' instructional league in the Dominican Republic in December and will start 2021 at a Class A level. He has the ceiling of an everyday second baseman with offensive impact.

Year	Age	Club (League)	Class	AVG	G	AB	R	H	2B	3B	HR	RBI	BB	SO	SB	OBP	SLG
2019	20	Staten Island (NYP)	SS	.256	66	246	49	63	12	4	13	37	25	77	11	.329	.496
Minor League Totals				.249	134	526	95	131	25	10	20	68	37	157	22	.307	.449

14 KEVIN ALCANTARA, OF

BREAKOUT
BA GRADE
50 Risk: Extreme

Born: July 12, 2002. **B-T:** R-R. **HT:** 6-6. **WT:** 205. **Signed:** Dominican Republic, 2018. **Signed by:** Edgar Mateo/Juan Piron.

TRACK RECORD: The Yankees were aggressive on the 2018 international market, signing five of the top 50 players. Alcantara ranked No. 15 on that list and has arguably the highest ceiling of the group, which also included catcher and fellow Top 30 prospect Antonio Gomez. He performed well in the Rookie-level Gulf Coast League, where he ranked as the circuit's No. 8 prospect.

SCOUTING REPORT: Tall and lithe, Alcantara's body reminds some of Marlins outfielder Lewis Brinson. He's added nearly 20 pounds since signing, and the Yankees believe there's room for even more. His long strides allow him to cover plenty of ground in center field, where his well above-average speed shows up more often than on times from home to first. Alcantara is an aggressive hitter with a big leg kick that can cause him to get out of sync at times. His approach will be tested as he moves through the minors—especially without two levels between the GCL and low Class A—and he'll need to keep his swing in rhythm as much as possible to unlock his true offensive potential.

THE FUTURE: After spending the shutdown in the Dominican Republic, Alcantara finally got back on the field in a semi-official capacity at the Yankees' D.R. instructional league. He should crack low Class A at some point in 2021 and has one of the higher ceilings among the Yankees' group of lower-level prospects.

Year	Age	Club (League)	Class	AVG	G	AB	R	H	2B	3B	HR	RBI	BB	SO	SB	OBP	SLG
2019	16	Yankees1 (GCL)	R	.260	32	123	19	32	5	2	1	13	3	27	3	.289	.358
	16	Yankees (DSL)	R	.237	9	38	7	9	3	1	0	6	5	9	2	.348	.368
Minor League Totals				.255	41	161	26	41	8	3	1	19	8	36	5	.305	.360

15 ALEXANDER VARGAS, SS

BA GRADE 50 Risk: Extreme

Born: Oct. 29, 2001. **B-T:** B-R. **HT:** 5-11. **WT:** 175. **Signed:** Cuba, 2018. **Signed by:** Edgar Mateo/Esteban Castillo/Rudy Gomez.

TRACK RECORD: The Yankees went big on the international market in 2018, including a foray into Cuba to nab Vargas, who had been expected to sign with Cincinnati, for $2.5 million. He started his career in the Rookie-level Gulf Coast League, where his quick-twitch athleticism helped him rank No. 9 among the league's Top 20 prospects.

SCOUTING REPORT: The most exciting part about Vargas' development is the addition of roughly 30 pounds of good weight without sacrificing his ability to play a strong defensive shortstop. Vargas' new body also allowed him to reduce a big leg kick in favor of a much quieter swing, which the Yankees believe will go a long way toward him handling high-velocity fastballs. He's a double-plus runner with soft hands and skilled feet and an arm that has improved to correspond with his gains in the weight room.

THE FUTURE: Vargas was at the Yankees' instructional league in the D.R. and should be able to reach low Class A once the minor leagues get going in 2021. He has the ceiling of a leadoff-type shortstop.

Year	Age	Club (League)	Class	AVG	G	AB	R	H	2B	3B	HR	RBI	BB	SO	SB	OBP	SLG
2019	17	Yankees1 (GCL)	R	.219	40	155	23	34	5	5	1	16	14	22	13	.301	.335
	17	Yankees (DSL)	R	.289	8	38	6	11	5	2	0	2	4	6	2	.364	.526
Minor League Totals				.233	48	193	29	45	10	7	1	18	18	28	15	.313	.373

16 CANAAN SMITH, OF

BREAKOUT

BA GRADE 45 Risk: High

Born: April 30, 1999. **B-T:** L-R. **HT:** 6-0. **WT:** 215. **Drafted:** HS—Rockwall, Texas, 2017 (4th round). **Signed by:** Mike Leuzinger.

TRACK RECORD: Smith showed well in his first taste of pro ball after his draft year, then scuffled in 2018 in the college-heavy New York-Penn League. He rebounded in 2019 at low Class A Charleston, where he became one of just 15 players in the minors with 30 or more doubles, 10 or more home runs and 15 or more stolen bases.

SCOUTING REPORT: Smith hits balls hard. He averaged an 89.4 mph exit velocity in 2019 and has peaked at 110. He shows strong pitch-recognition skills, handles velocity well and posted an excellent swinging-strike rate of just 9.7%. Despite the success, scouts have mild concerns that Smith could be exploited by upper-level pitchers who do better jobs changing speeds and throwing offspeed pitches for strikes. Smith shows average athleticism, a fringy arm and below-average defense in left field. He's an average runner who steals bases on instincts rather than pure speed.

THE FUTURE: Because the Yankees did not hold instructional league, Smith missed a full season of development. He should begin 2021 in high Class A and could hit his way to a role as big league regular.

Year	Age	Club (League)	Class	AVG	G	AB	R	H	2B	3B	HR	RBI	BB	SO	SB	OBP	SLG
2019	20	Charleston, SC (SAL)	LoA	.307	124	449	67	138	32	3	11	74	74	108	16	.405	.465
Minor League Totals				.280	226	788	109	221	50	4	19	118	139	204	21	.389	.426

17 ANTHONY VOLPE, SS

BA GRADE 50 Risk: Extreme

Born: April 28, 2001. **B-T:** R-R. **HT:** 5-11. **WT:** 180. **Drafted:** HS—Morristown, N.J., 2019 (1st round). **Signed by:** Matt Hyde.

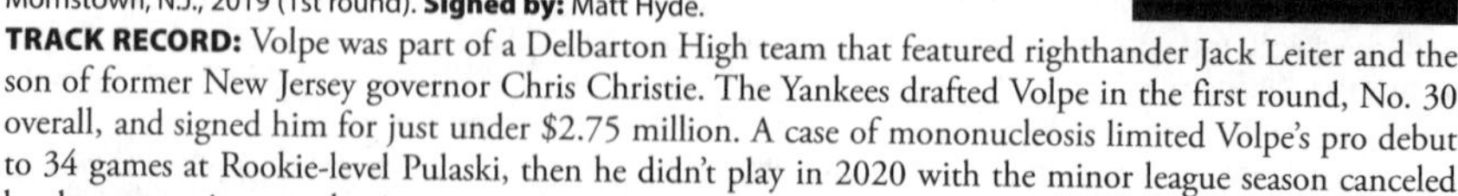

TRACK RECORD: Volpe was part of a Delbarton High team that featured righthander Jack Leiter and the son of former New Jersey governor Chris Christie. The Yankees drafted Volpe in the first round, No. 30 overall, and signed him for just under $2.75 million. A case of mononucleosis limited Volpe's pro debut to 34 games at Rookie-level Pulaski, then he didn't play in 2020 with the minor league season canceled by the coronavirus pandemic.

SCOUTING REPORT: Volpe has an innate ability to square balls up and produce quality contact. His main goal during the shutdown was to add strength to his lean frame, and the Yankees say he's added 15 pounds of muscle since being drafted. Volpe needs to continue to get stronger to impact the ball more, but he has the tools to hit for average. Defensively, Volpe earns high marks for his quickness and instincts at shortstop and shows enough arm strength to stick at the position in the long-term. He's an above-average runner.

THE FUTURE: Volpe will still be 19 on Opening Day and has time on his side to make the needed physical gains. Depending on his camp performance, he'll open in either extended spring training or low Class A.

Year	Age	Club (League)	Class	AVG	G	AB	R	H	2B	3B	HR	RBI	BB	SO	SB	OBP	SLG
2019	18	Pulaski (APP)	R	.215	34	121	19	26	7	2	2	11	23	38	6	.349	.355
Minor League Totals				.215	34	121	19	26	7	2	2	11	23	38	6	.349	.355

18 T.J. SIKKEMA, LHP

BA GRADE
45 Risk: High

Born: July 25, 1998. **B-T:** L-L. **HT:** 6-0. **WT:** 221. **Drafted:** Missouri, 2019 (1st round supplemental). **Signed by:** Steve Lemke.

TRACK RECORD: Sikkema broke onto the scene as a member of Mizzou's bullpen, where he tied Tanner Houck's record for freshman wins. He transitioned into the rotation as a sophomore and then used a combination of stuff and guile to earn a supplemental first-round selection. He spent 2019 in the short-season New York-Penn League, where he struck out 13 against one walk in 11 innings.

SCOUTING REPORT: In a system starved for lefties, Sikkema leads the way at the position. He stands out for the varied ways he uses his arsenal. He brings a four-seam fastball that sits in the low 90s and tops out at 95. He backs it up with a deep, powerful slurve and a potentially average changeup. He also adds deception by changing arm slots from true overhand to low three-quarters. The move reduces the velocity on the fastball but adds running life to Sikkema's armside.

THE FUTURE: The loss of the minor league season and the Yankees' lack of domestic instructional league meant that Sikkema missed a year of in-person development. He should jump to high Class A to begin his career, and has the ceiling of a back-end starter.

Year	Age	Club (League)	Class	W	L	ERA	G	GS	IP	H	HR	BB	SO	BB/9	SO/9	WHIP	AVG
2019	20	Staten Island (NYP)	SS	0	0	0.84	4	4	11	6	0	1	13	0.8	11.0	0.66	.150
Minor League Totals				0	0	0.84	4	4	10	6	0	1	13	0.8	11.0	0.66	.158

19 BECK WAY, RHP

BA GRADE
45 Risk: High

Born: Aug. 6, 1999. **B-T:** R-R. **HT:** 6-4. **WT:** 200. **Drafted:** Northwest Florida State JC, 2020 (4th round). **Signed by:** Chuck Bartlett.

TRACK RECORD: Way started his college career at Division II Belmont Abbey before transferring to Northwest Florida State. He sat out 2019 because of the move, then struck out 58 hitters in 40 innings before the season was shut down by the novel coronavirus pandemic. Though the Yankees took Way in the fourth round, he was actually their second pick after losing their second- and third-round choices to the Astros as compensation for signing Gerrit Cole. He was one of the best junior college prospects on the board.

SCOUTING REPORT: Way brings a three-pitch mix, started with an expertly commanded four-seam fastball that sits in the 92-94 mph range and touches 97. He backs it up with a potentially plus changeup and an inconsistent but intriguing slider. He meshes all three together with above-average control, which should allow him to move relatively quickly.

THE FUTURE: The Yankees' lack of domestic instructional league meant Way won't debut until 2021, when he could begin at a Class A level. He has the ceiling of a back-end starter.

Year	Age	Club (League)	Class	W	L	ERA	G	GS	IP	H	HR	BB	SO	BB/9	SO/9	WHIP	AVG
2020	20	Did not play—No minor league season															

20 ALBERT ABREU, RHP

BA GRADE
45 Risk: High

Born: Sept. 26, 1995. **B-T:** R-R. **HT:** 6-2. **WT:** 190. **Signed:** Dominican Republic, 2013. **Signed by:** Oz Ocampo/Rafael Belen/Francis Mojica (Astros)

TRACK RECORD: Acquired by New York in 2016 for Brian McCann, Abreu has spent his tenure with the Yankees teasing at his potential and frustrating coaches with his inconsistency. While the majority of his work in the minor leagues was as a starter, Abreu's two big league appearances in 2020 were as a reliever, which is likely where his future lies.

SCOUTING REPORT: There is no doubting Abreu's stuff. His fastball has long been in the mid 90s and his curveball, slider and changeup each has its moments as well. Evaluators see two main issues with Abreu: consistency and approach. His short-stride delivery leads to timing issues with his arm stroke, which produces scattershot control and command. He also has problems throwing his offspeed pitches for early-count strikes, opting instead to try to use putaway pitches which hitters aren't inclined to chase. Of the 21 offspeed pitches he threw in the big leagues, just three were swung at and missed.

THE FUTURE: Until he figures out how to use his stuff to the best of its ability, Abreu is likely a reliever. He should be in the mix for a spot in New York's pen again in 2021.

Year	Age	Club (League)	Class	W	L	ERA	G	GS	IP	H	HR	BB	SO	BB/9	SO/9	WHIP	AVG
2020	24	New York (AL)	MAJ	0	1	20.25	2	0	1	4	1	2	2	13.5	13.5	4.50	.500
Major League Totals				0	1	20.25	2	0	1	4	1	2	2	13.5	13.5	4.50	.500
Minor League Totals				19	30	3.77	105	87	439	373	31	211	446	4.3	9.1	1.33	.228

21 MATT SAUER, RHP

BA GRADE
50 Risk: Extreme

Born: Jan. 21, 1999. **B-T:** R-R. **HT:** 6-4. **WT:** 195. **Drafted:** HS—Santa Maria, Calif., 2017 (2nd round). **Signed by:** Bobby Dejardin.

TRACK RECORD: The Yankees spent just shy of $2.5 million on Sauer after a big velocity jump in his senior year of high school. He was impressive in his first full year as a pro, then started well in 2019 before a torn ulnar collateral ligament led to Tommy John surgery. He would have been ready toward the middle of the 2020 season, but the shelved minor league season gave him more time.

SCOUTING REPORT: Before the surgery, Sauer was showing a fastball in the 92-95 mph range. He backed the fastball up with a slider and a changeup that each showed above-average or plus. Scouts outside the org were impressed with the stuff, but wanted to see him utilize it better and get more swings and misses.

THE FUTURE: Because the Yankees didn't hold domestic instructional league, Sauer has not gotten into a game since April 11, 2019. He's likely to head to low Class A, where the season will be of extra emphasis because he'll need to be protected on the 40-man roster after the year.

Year	Age	Club (League)	Class	W	L	ERA	G	GS	IP	H	HR	BB	SO	BB/9	SO/9	WHIP	AVG
2019	20	Charleston, SC (SAL)	LoA	0	1	2.08	2	2	9	6	0	6	8	6.2	8.3	1.38	.154
Minor League Totals				3	9	3.92	21	21	87	79	3	32	65	3.3	6.7	1.27	.237

22 EVERSON PEREIRA, OF

Born: April 10, 2001. **B-T:** R-R. **HT:** 5-10. **WT:** 191. **Signed:** Venezuela, 2017. **Signed by:** Roney Calderon.

TRACK RECORD: The Yankees spent big money on their 2017 international class, including $1.5 million on Pereira, who jumped over the Dominican Summer League in favor of a stateside pro debut at Rookie-level Pulaski. He played there all season as a 17-year-old and ranked No. 7 among the league's Top 20 prospects. His 2019 season, spent in the New York-Penn League, was cut short by a severely sprained ankle.

SCOUTING REPORT: Like many Venezuelans, Pereira was stuck in the U.S. once the novel coronavirus pandemic shut down the sport. Instead, he's been training in Orlando, Fla. Though his numbers weren't impressive in his first two seasons, the Yankees were heartened by Pereira's above-average bat speed and exit velocities. Now, he needs to get more experience against quality breaking balls. He's got above-average speed and instincts, which helps him both in the outfield and on the bases.

THE FUTURE: The 2021 season will be doubly important for Pereira. Because he will be eligible for the Rule 5 Draft, the Yankees will need to decide whether he's worthy of 40-man protection. He has the upside of an everyday center fielder, but there's a long way to go.

Year	Age	Club (League)	Class	AVG	G	AB	R	H	2B	3B	HR	RBI	BB	SO	SB	OBP	SLG
2019	18	Staten Island (NYP)	SS	.171	18	70	9	12	3	0	1	3	4	26	3	.216	.257
Minor League Totals				.236	59	237	30	56	11	2	4	29	19	86	6	.292	.350

23 ANTONIO CABELLO, OF

Born: Nov. 1, 2000. **B-T:** R-R. **HT:** 5-11. **WT:** 216. **Signed:** Venezuela, 2017. **Signed by:** Darwin Bracho.

TRACK RECORD: After Shohei Ohtani chose the Angels, the Yankees pivoted and reallocated their remaining international money on Cabello and Raimfer Salinas. Cabello moved stateside after a quick tune-up in the Dominican Summer League but lost time after suffering a dislocated shoulder at instructional league after the 2018 season. He struggled in the Rookie-level Appalachian League in 2019 but still showed scouts impressive tools.

SCOUTING REPORT: At first, evaluators are confused about how to square Cabello's thicker body with his position in center field. Then they see a player with a combination of speed and athleticism albeit with some stiffness to his swing at times. The Yankees worked with Cabello to get his bat on a path designed to keep the barrel in the zone for a longer time, which would help him do damage on a wider variety of pitches. They also wanted to create a better angle to the ball, which would help more of his mishits go in the air rather than on the ground. He's not a slam dunk in center field, but the Yankees will continue to develop him at the position.

THE FUTURE: Cabello was part of the Yankees' group at instructional league in the Dominican Republic, where he got to kick off at least a little of the rust from the canceled 2020 season. He should open 2021 at low Class A.

Year	Age	Club (League)	Class	AVG	G	AB	R	H	2B	3B	HR	RBI	BB	SO	SB	OBP	SLG
2019	18	Pulaski (APP)	R	.211	56	227	31	48	10	4	3	19	19	77	5	.280	.330
Minor League Totals				.251	102	386	57	97	19	9	8	40	46	117	15	.344	.409

24 RAIMFER SALINAS, OF

BA GRADE
50 Risk: Extreme

Born: Dec. 31, 2000. **B-T:** R-R. **HT:** 5-11. **WT:** 195. **Signed:** Venezuela, 2017. **Signed by:** Darwin Bracho.

TRACK RECORD: When Shohei Ohtani declined the Yankees' offer in 2017, the team turned their attention and remaining slot money to a pair of promising Latin outfielders: Antonio Cabello and Salinas. His 2018 season was limited to 11 games by injuries to his knee and ring finger, which led to him repeating the Rookie-level Gulf Coast League in 2019.

SCOUTING REPORT: In 2019, the Yankees worked with Salinas to find a swing that got to the strike zone quicker and stayed there longer. As with many players at that level, they also worked with him to refine his command of the strike zone and get him to unleash on pitches he could drive. Outside scouts noted a player whose shorter arms give him a better chance to more quickly close holes in the zone, as well as someone who looked calm in the box. He's an explosive runner who has a chance to stick in center field.

THE FUTURE: Though he wasn't at the alternate training site, Salinas did get a taste of in-person instruction at the Yankees' Dominican Republic instructional league in December. He's got a lot of catching up to do, but there's still a ceiling waiting to be achieved.

Year	Age	Club (League)	Class	AVG	G	AB	R	H	2B	3B	HR	RBI	BB	SO	SB	OBP	SLG
2019	18	Yankees2 (GCL)	R	.270	42	159	25	43	10	2	3	15	7	45	11	.329	.415
Minor League Totals				.240	53	196	29	47	11	2	3	17	14	55	15	.326	.362

25 ANTONIO GOMEZ, C

BA GRADE
50 Risk: Extreme

Born: Nov. 13, 2001. **B-T:** R-R. **HT:** 6-2. **WT:** 216. **Signed:** Venezuela, 2018. **Signed by:** Edgar Mateo/Raul Gonzalez.

TRACK RECORD: Gomez ranked as the No. 14 player in the 2018 international class and then got enough at-bats in the Rookie-level Gulf Coast League to rank fifth among its Top 20 prospects despite a bout with biceps soreness.

SCOUTING REPORT: Gomez was lauded as an amateur for his blend of offensive and defensive tools, and both have shown up in his brief pro career. His swing stays in the zone long enough and with sufficient loft to both pull balls with authority and go the other way when necessary. He's a mature, athletic defender who has adapted well to the Yankees' new knee-down catching technique. He regularly produces pop times in the 1.8-1.9-second range, and in 2019 threw out 50% of attempted basestealers.

THE FUTURE: The novel coronavirus pandemic kept Gomez from working in-person with Yankees coaches in 2020, even at the team's instructional league in the Dominican Republic. He might return to the GCL to start 2021, but should find his way to low Class A at some point.

Year	Age	Club (League)	Class	AVG	G	AB	R	H	2B	3B	HR	RBI	BB	SO	SB	OBP	SLG
2019	17	Yankees1 (GCL)	R	.255	14	47	9	12	4	0	1	7	3	7	0	.314	.404
	17	Yankees (DSL)	R	.600	1	5	2	3	1	0	0	1	1	2	0	.667	.800
Minor League Totals				.288	15	52	11	15	5	0	1	8	4	9	0	.351	.442

26 JOSH SMITH, 2B

Born: Aug. 7, 1997. **B-T:** L-R. **HT:** 5-9. **WT:** 175. **Drafted:** Louisiana State, 2019 (2nd round). **Signed by:** Mike Leuzinger.

TRACK RECORD: After an excellent track record of production in the Cape Cod League and Louisiana State, Smith produced as expected in the short-season New York-Penn League after signing in 2019. He ranked as the No. 16 prospect on the circuit.

SCOUTING REPORT: Smith doesn't have a standout tool, but he doesn't have any glaring weaknesses either. The Yankees will continue to develop him at shortstop, but he'll get plenty of exposure at other infield spots as well. He's one of the system's best pure contact-makers and shows excellent plate discipline. Put simply: He swings at the right pitches.

THE FUTURE: Smith's pedigree is strong enough that he could begin at high Class A in 2021.

Year	Age	Club (League)	Class	AVG	G	AB	R	H	2B	3B	HR	RBI	BB	SO	SB	OBP	SLG
2019	21	Staten Island (NYP)	SS	.324	33	111	17	36	6	1	3	15	25	17	6	.450	.477
Minor League Totals				.324	33	111	17	36	6	1	3	15	25	17	6	.450	.477

27 ANTHONY SEIGLER, C

BA GRADE **50** **Risk: Extreme**

Born: June 20, 1999. **B-T:** B-B. **HT:** 6-0. **WT:** 200. **Drafted:** HS—Cartersville, Ga., 2018 (1st round). **Signed by:** Darryl Monroe.

TRACK RECORD: Seigler stood out as an amateur for his ability to switch-hit and switch-pitch. The Yankees liked him at the plate and behind it, but Seigler hasn't gotten any extended chance to show what he can do. A hamstring injury and a concussion limited him to just 24 games in 2018, and a broken left knee cost him all but 30 games at low Class A in 2019.

SCOUTING REPORT: Defensively, Seigler is still strong, and he made gains in the weight room as well. He's taken well to the Yankees' new knee-down approach to catching and flashes a plus throwing arm. Offensively, there is room to grow. Scouts haven't seen much in the way of impact bat speed, and he's produced just seven extra-base hits in 176 minor league at-bats. He knows the strike zone well and doesn't swing and miss often, but his best chance at value is likely going to come on defense.

THE FUTURE: With no minor league season and no domestic instructional league, Seigler missed out on chances to develop after spring training. The glut of prospects behind him means Seigler could move to high Class A in 2021.

Year	Age	Club (League)	Class	AVG	G	AB	R	H	2B	3B	HR	RBI	BB	SO	SB	OBP	SLG
2019	20	Charleston, SC (SAL)	LoA	.175	30	97	10	17	3	0	0	6	20	28	1	.328	.206
Minor League Totals				.216	54	176	21	38	6	0	1	15	34	40	1	.350	.267

28 MICHAEL KING, RHP

BA GRADE **40** **Risk: Medium**

Born: May 25, 1994. **B-T:** R-R. **HT:** 6-3. **WT:** 210. **Drafted:** Boston College, 2016 (20th round). **Signed by:** Steve Payne (Marlins).

TRACK RECORD: King was acquired by New York in the 2017 deal that sent Garrett Cooper and Caleb Smith to Miami. King moved quickly through the Yankees system after the trade but missed most of the 2019 season with a stress fracture and a setback in his rehab. He made his MLB debut later that year, and returned to the big leagues as a swingman in 2020.

SCOUTING REPORT: King is a bit of anomaly in a system built on big righthanders with big velocity. Instead, King gets his outs by mixing and matching an array of pitches in all quadrants of the strike zone. This year, he primarily went with a mix of a low-90s sinker, low-80s curveball and mid-80s changeup. He sprinkled in a four-seamer every now and then as well. Both of his fastballs and his changeup showed above-average vertical break. His rate of 3.71 walks per nine innings was the highest of his career.

THE FUTURE: King is likely to fill the role of spot starter and swingman going forward, and should have a spot in New York's bullpen in 2021.

Year	Age	Club (League)	Class	W	L	ERA	G	GS	IP	H	HR	BB	SO	BB/9	SO/9	WHIP	AVG
2020	25	New York (AL)	MAJ	1	2	7.76	9	4	27	30	5	11	26	3.7	8.8	1.54	.278
Major League Totals				1	2	7.22	10	4	28	32	5	11	27	3.5	8.5	1.50	.274
Minor League Totals				28	19	2.93	77	58	387	343	26	69	322	1.6	7.5	1.06	.238

29 NICK NELSON, RHP

BA GRADE **40** **Risk: Medium**

Born: Dec. 5, 1995. **B-T:** R-R. **HT:** 6-0. **WT:** 216. **Drafted:** Gulf Coast State (Fla.) JC, 2016 (4th round). **Signed by:** Mike Wagner.

TRACK RECORD: Nelson was a two-way player in college, but the Yankees liked him better on the mound. By focusing solely on pitching, the team hoped Nelson would gain a better handle on his excellent natural stuff. Added to the 40-man roster after 2019, Nelson made 11 big league relief appearances in the regular season and was included on the rosters for both rounds of the playoffs.

SCOUTING REPORT: Nelson stayed back in Tampa over the offseason to work on taking his stuff to the next level. The result was a fastball with a tick more velocity and a slider with new, sweepier break than his previous version, which gave him a more effective weapon against righties. Nelson's high-80s changeup is his most advanced pitch, though both it and his slider induced swinging-strike rates of better than 32% in the big leagues. He also throws a high-70s, downer curveball that works best for early-count strikes.

THE FUTURE: Nelson has settled into his likely long-term role: Middle-innings reliever who can rack up strikeouts. He'll be in the mix for the 2021 bullpen.

Year	Age	Club (League)	Class	W	L	ERA	G	GS	IP	H	HR	BB	SO	BB/9	SO/9	WHIP	AVG
2020	24	New York (AL)	MAJ	1	0	4.79	11	0	21	20	4	11	18	4.8	7.8	1.50	.256
Major League Totals				1	0	4.79	11	0	20	20	4	11	18	4.8	7.8	1.50	.256
Minor League Totals				19	24	3.65	76	74	333	286	14	178	387	4.8	10.5	1.39	.233

30 BROOKS KRISKE, RHP

BA GRADE
40 Risk: Medium

Born: Feb. 3, 1994. **B-T:** R-R. **HT:** 6-3. **WT:** 190. **Drafted:** Southern California, 2016 (6th round). **Signed by:** Dave Keith.

TRACK RECORD: A near-exclusive reliever at Southern California, Kriske showed a big uptick in velocity between his junior and senior seasons and earned a $100,000 bonus from New York. He had Tommy John surgery roughly two months after his pro debut, then dominated for two seasons in the minors upon his return. He was added to the 40-man after the 2019 season, then made four big league appearances in 2020.

SCOUTING REPORT: Kriske works primarily with two pitches—a mid-90s fastball that peaked at 97 in the big leagues, as well as a splitter with devastating trap-door action in the high 80s. He also uses a low-80s slider, but threw it just seven times in the big leagues. The Yankees particularly like the riding action Kriske gets on his four-seamer. Now they'd like to see him command his splitter and slider better in order to make them more effective.

THE FUTURE: Kriske should have a shot at returning to the big leagues to open 2021. He has a ceiling as a middle-innings reliever who can strike out plenty of hitters.

Year	Age	Club (League)	Class	W	L	ERA	G	GS	IP	H	HR	BB	SO	BB/9	SO/9	WHIP	AVG
2020	26	New York (AL)	MAJ	0	0	14.73	4	0	4	3	1	7	8	17.2	19.6	2.73	.200
Major League Totals				0	0	14.73	4	0	3	3	1	7	8	17.2	19.6	2.73	.200
Minor League Totals				5	7	1.97	72	0	105	71	3	43	135	3.7	11.5	1.08	.193

MORE PROSPECTS TO KNOW

31 RYDER GREEN, OF

The 2018 third-rounder has intriguing power and made steps in 2019 toward refining his approach. Because he profiles in a corner, the power will need to continue to show up as he develops.

32 MAIKOL ESCOTTO, SS

SLEEPER

Escotto raked in the Dominican Summer League in 2019. He used a compact swing to do damage against hard and soft stuff and showed exit velocities up to 106 mph.

33 TREVOR HAUVER, OF/2B

The Yankees' final pick in the 2020 draft can play in the infield or outfield and showed the ability to hit for average and power at Arizona State. He still needs to cut down some swing and miss.

34 BARRETT LOSEKE, RHP

The Yankees like Loseke's combination of a mid-90s fastball that shows cutting and riding action. He pairs it with a slider he developed over the offseason and unveiled in spring training.

35 HAYDEN WESNESKI, RHP

A reliever prospect, Wesneski brings a sinker, slider and cutter from a lower arm slot and put up a 5-to-1 strikeout-to-walk rate in his first pro experience.

36 KEN WALDICHUK, LHP

The southpaw from Saint Mary's can bring his fastball up to 98 mph and struck out 49 in 29.1 innings in 2019 in the Appalachian League

37 MITCH SPENCE, RHP

The Yankees are intrigued by the way Spence's fastball moves, and compare it to the one thrown by Chad Green. He also flashes a solid slider and struck out 29 against just four walks in his pro debut.

38 ANTHONY GARCIA, OF

Though he's a long way away, Garcia has special power from both sides of the plate and a huge frame that could hold even more strength.

39 BRANDON LOCKRIDGE, OF

Lockridge flew somewhat under the radar, but his mix of speed, defense and moderate power is reminiscent of what Dustin Fowler showed a few years ago.

40 MATT KROOK, LHP

The Yankees took Krook from the Rays in the minor league Rule 5 draft. He has electric velocity and sink from the left side, but he needs to harness his command and control.

TOP PROSPECTS OF THE DECADE

Year	Player, Pos	2020 Org
2011	Jesus Montero, C	Did not play
2012	Jesus Montero, C	Did not play
2013	Mason Williams, OF	Orioles
2014	Gary Sanchez, C	Yankees
2015	Luis Severino, RHP	Yankees
2016	Jorge Mateo, SS	Padres
2017	Gleyber Torres, SS	Yankees
2018	Gleyber Torres, SS	Yankees
2019	Estevan Florial, OF	Yankees
2020	Jasson Dominguez, OF	Yankees

TOP DRAFT PICKS OF THE DECADE

Year	Player, Pos	2020 Org
2011	Dante Bichette Jr., 3B (1st round supp)	Nationals
2012	Ty Hensley, RHP	Independent League
2013	Eric Jagielo, 3B	Did not play
2014	Jacob Lindgren, LHP (2nd round)	White Sox
2015	James Kaprielian, RHP	Athletics
2016	Blake Rutherford, OF	White Sox
2017	Clarke Schmidt, RHP	Yankees
2018	Anthony Seigler, C	Yankees
2019	Anthony Volpe, SS	Yankees
2020	Austin Wells, C	Yankees

DEPTH CHART

NEW YORK YANKEES

TOP 2021 ROOKIES	RANK
Deivi Garcia, RHP	2
Clarke Schmidt, RHP	3
BREAKOUT PROSPECTS	**RANK**
Ezequiel Duran, 2B	13
Kevin Alcantara, OF	14
Canaan Smith, OF	16

SOURCE OF TOP 30 TALENT

Homegrown	27	Acquired	3
College	6	Trade	3
Junior college	1	Rule 5 draft	0
High school	4	Independent league	0
Nondrafted free agent	0	Free agent/waivers	0
International	16		

LF
Canaan Smith (16)
Jake Sanford
Trey Amburgey

CF
Jasson Dominguez (1)
Estevan Florial (12)
Kevin Alcantara (14)
Everson Pereira (22)
Antonio Cabello (23)
Raimfer Salinas (24)
Brandon Lockridge

RF
Ryder Green
Josh Stowers
Anthony Garcia

3B
Oswaldo Cabrera
Enger Castellano
Andres Chapparo

SS
Oswald Peraza (6)
Alexander Vargas (15)
Anthony Volpe (17)
Maikol Escotto
Thairo Estrada
Roberto Chirinos
Marcos Cabrera

2B
Ezequiel Duran (13)
Josh Smith (26)
Trevor Hauver
Diego Castillo

1B
Chris Gittens
Dermis Garcia
Brandon Wagner

C
Austin Wells (5)
Antonio Gomez (25)
Anthony Seigler (27)

LHP

LHSP	LHRP
T.J. Sikkema (18)	Matt Krook
Jake Agnos	Trevor Lane
Ken Waldichuk	James Reeves
Josh Maciejewski	
Alfredo Garcia	

RHP

RHSP	RHRP
Deivi Garcia (2)	Albert Abreu (20)
Clarke Schmidt (3)	Michael King (28)
Luis Gil (4)	Nick Nelson (29)
Alexander Vizcaino (7)	Brooks Kriske (30)
Miguel Yajure (8)	Reggie McClain
Yoendrys Gomez (9)	Hayden Wesneski
Luis Medina (10)	Barret Loseke
Roansy Contreras (11)	Mitch Spence
Beck Way (19)	Tanner Myatt
Matt Sauer (21)	Glenn Otto
	Aaron McGarity
	Nelson Alvarez
	Frank German
	Shawn Semple
	Yoljeldriz Diaz

Oakland Athletics

BY MARK CHIARELLI

For a team on a 97-win pace in 2020, mirroring their total from both 2019 and 2018, there's a surprising amount of apprehension surrounding the A's this winter.

There is, of course, the annual concern of Oakland's payroll flexibility, which is only exacerbated by baseball's perceived economic struggles stemming from a shortened, fanless 2020 season amid the coronavirus pandemic.

The A's reportedly laid off roughly 20% of their employees across business and baseball operations in October, months after issuing widespread furloughs across baseball operations. Owner John Fisher even briefly decided to suspend the $400 per month stipend the organization paid to minor leaguers, although he reversed that decision in early June following significant public backlash. Such budget tightening comes during an offseason when two core players—2019 MVP candidate Marcus Semien and all-star closer Liam Hendriks—hit free agency.

And then there's Billy Beane.

Beane has proven quite adept at navigating Oakland's precarious financial footprint in his more than 20 years atop the organization. But the Wall Street Journal reported in October that Beane's investment venture, RedBall Acquisition Corp., is prepared to merge with Fenway Sports Group, owned by Red Sox owner John Henry.

The merger would allow Beane's group to purchase a minority stake in FSG and take the company public, creating a tricky situation for Beane, who also has a minority ownership stake in the A's. MLB forbids anyone holding an ownership stake in multiple teams.

Beane was reportedly ready to sever his ties to baseball and join FSG, which also owns the Liverpool soccer club in the English Premier League, and pursue soccer interests. The merger, however, had not been approved as of December, casting a shadow over Oakland's offseason.

The A's have a resilient baseball operations staff. In some ways, they're already equipped to negotiate the unusual challenges presented in 2020.

Much of their player development staff remains intact and general manager David Forst, a longtime lieutenant of Beane, remains. They have a long track record of maximizing the abilities of players overlooked by the industry, and they'll need to flex those muscles again. Oakland has one of baseball's weaker systems following the graduations of Jesus Luzardo and Sean Murphy. Yet another injury clouding A.J. Puk's immediate future doesn't help, either.

THEARON W. HENDERSON/GETTY IMAGES

Catcher Sean Murphy joined a young position core in 2020, but is there help on the way?

PROJECTED 2024 LINEUP

Catcher	Sean Murphy	29
First Base	Matt Olson	30
Second Base	Logan Davidson	26
Third Base	Matt Chapman	31
Shortstop	Nick Allen	25
Left Field	Tyler Soderstrom	22
Center Field	Ramon Laureano	29
Right Field	Luis Barrera	28
Designated Hitter	Greg Deichmann	29
No. 1 Starter	Jesus Luzardo	26
No. 2 Starter	Frankie Montas	31
No. 3 Starter	A.J. Puk	29
No. 4 Starter	Sean Manaea	32
No. 5 Starter	Daulton Jefferies	28
Closer	Lou Trivino	32

But the early returns on their top 2020 draft pick, Tyler Soderstrom, suggest they may have nabbed a steal at No. 26 overall. Many in the organization believe Soderstrom is the best high school hitter they've seen in years, reminding some of Eric Chavez or Ben Grieve.

The top of the system also has several players—such as Daulton Jefferies or Luis Barrera—who appear ready to help Oakland in 2021.

Even amid a stressful offseason, those are promising signs for the defending AL West champions, who continue trying to find creative ways to maximize their competitive window while young stars Matt Chapman and Matt Olson remain under team control through 2023.

So while the faces and circumstances may change, Oakland arrives at a place it's been before: Needing to figure out a way to do more with potentially less. ■

1 TYLER SODERSTROM, C

Born: Nov. 24, 2001. **B-T:** L-R. **HT:** 6-2. **WT:** 205.
Drafted: HS—Turlock, Calif., 2020 (1st round).
Signed by: Kevin Mello.

BILL MITCHELL

BA GRADE	SCOUTING GRADES
60 **Risk:** Extreme	**Hit:** 60. **Power:** 60. **Run:** 40. **Field:** 40. **Arm:** 55.

Projected future grades on 20-80 scouting scale.

TRACK RECORD: Soderstrom surged into the top tier of the 2020 draft class after a blistering summer on the showcase circuit. Scouts singled him out as one of the most steady and consistent performers they saw all summer. His rise culminated with the Athletics drafting him No. 26 overall and signing him for $3.3 million to forgo a UCLA commitment. It was the second-largest bonus ever given to a prep catcher, behind only No. 1 overall pick Joe Mauer's $5.1 million from the Twins in 2001. The A's promptly sent the 18-year-old Soderstrom into a win-now environment at the alternate training site and watched their top pick hit nearly .500 with three home runs in his first week. He continued to dominate at instructional league, where he posted a .441 on-base percentage and earned raves as one of the top hitters in Arizona.

SCOUTING REPORT: Soderstrom is regularly compared with Eric Chavez and Ben Grieve in terms of high school hitters to pass through Oakland's system, and the A's believe he has the potential to be better than both. Soderstrom already posts exit velocities as high as 108 mph and has an exceptionally advanced approach that belies his youth. He has the physicality reminiscent of a college pick–when the A's measured him at their alternate site, they found he was an an inch taller and 15 pounds heavier than his listed height and weight at the time of the draft. There's more physical projection to go and it's easy to envision 30-home run potential with loads of walks and a high OBP. Hardly an all-or-nothing slugger, Soderstrom has a polished lefthanded swing and projects to be a plus hitter. Soderstrom is much less polished defensively behind the plate and mostly succeeded on raw ability as a prep. His skills were tested immediately at the alternate site and he struggled at times, especially blocking and receiving. Still, Soderstrom shows above-average arm strength, solid athleticism and a desire to improve. His arm stroke will need to get shorter and his foowork will have to improve if he is going to stick at catcher. His father Steve was drafted sixth overall by the Giants in 1993 and pitched one season in the majors. He instilled the work ethic and drive needed to succeed in his son. The A's labeled Soderstrom a "baseball rat" with a meticulous work ethic and say it's too early to consider a move off catcher. If his bat proves to be too far ahead of his glove, he has enough athleticism that scouts see him as an option at first, third, right or left field.

THE FUTURE: Soderstrom's bat is advanced to the point Oakland believes he could jump straight to high Class A in 2021. He's more likely to begin at low Class A, which would put less stress on his defense. The A's will give Soderstrom every chance to develop as a catcher, but a future move to a corner infield or outfield spot can't be ruled out, especially if it allows Soderstrom to jump on a potential fast track to Oakland. ■

BEST TOOLS

Best Hitter for Average	Sheldon Neuse
Best Power Hitter	Kyle McCann
Best Strike-Zone Discipline	Jonah Heim
Fastest Baserunner	Buddy Reed
Best Athlete	Buddy Reed
Best Fastball	Wandisson Charles
Best Curveball	Miguel Romero
Best Slider	Richard Guasch
Best Changeup	Daulton Jefferies
Best Control	Daulton Jefferies
Best Defensive Catcher	Drew Millas
Best Defensive Infielder	Nick Allen
Best Infield Arm	Jeremy Eierman
Best Defensive Outfielder	Buddy Reed
Best Outfield Arm	Buddy Reed

Year	Age	Club (League)	Class	AVG	G	AB	R	H	2B	3B	HR	RBI	BB	SO	SB	OBP	SLG
2020	18	Did not play—No minor league season															

2 A.J. PUK, LHP

TOP ROOKIE

BA GRADE 60 Risk: Extreme

KELLY GAVIN/MLB PHOTOS VIA GETTY IMAGES

Born: April 25, 1995. **B-T:** L-L. **HT:** 6-7. **WT:** 238. **Drafted:** Florida, 2016 (1st round). **Signed by:** Trevor Schaffer.

TRACK RECORD: For all of Puk's tantalizing ability, he has not been able to stay healthy since the Athletics drafted him sixth overall in 2016. Puk had Tommy John surgery and missed all of the 2018 season, briefly returned in 2019 and made his major league debut, then missed all of 2020 with a pair of left shoulder strains. He was shut down in September and had shoulder surgery after the season.

SCOUTING REPORT: Puk showed his upside when the A's deployed the 6-foot-7 lefty out of their bullpen in 2019 while chasing a playoff spot. His fastball sits 96-100 mph and explodes on hitters with unique angle and impressive extension out of his imposing frame. He pairs it with a vicious upper-80s power slider that dives at the back foot of righthanded hitters, and he's gaining confidence in his burgeoning changeup. Puk also features a low-80s curveball that flashes average. Even with just average control, he generates a ton of whiffs—12.9 strikeouts per nine innings in the minors—and uncomfortable at-bats. Health remains Puk's biggest obstacle. He's thrown just 194.1 innings combined in five professional seasons.

THE FUTURE: The A's hope Puk will be ready for spring training following his surgery. Injuries have clouded his future, but his arm is too good to give up on.

SCOUTING GRADES: **Fastball:** 80 **Slider:** 70 **Curveball:** 45 **Changeup:** 50 **Control:** 45

Year	Age	Club (League)	Class	W	L	ERA	G	GS	IP	H	HR	BB	SO	BB/9	SO/9	WHIP	AVG
2018	23	Did not play—Injured															
2019	24	Oakland (AL)	MAJ	2	0	3.18	10	0	11	10	1	5	13	4.0	10.3	1.32	.213
	24	Midland (TL)	AA	0	0	4.32	6	1	8	9	2	3	13	3.2	14.0	1.44	.257
	24	Las Vegas (PCL)	AAA	4	1	4.91	9	0	11	7	3	3	16	2.5	13.1	0.91	.159
	24	Stockton (CAL)	HiA	0	0	6.00	3	3	6	5	2	4	9	6.0	13.5	1.50	.200
2020	25	Did not play—Injured															
Major League Totals				2	0	3.18	10	0	11	10	1	5	13	4.0	10.3	1.32	.238
Minor League Totals				10	15	3.98	55	38	183	152	10	70	262	3.4	12.9	1.21	.220

3 DAULTON JEFFERIES, RHP

TOP ROOKIE

BA GRADE 55 Risk: High

KELLY GAVIN/MLB PHOTOS VIA GETTY IMAGES

Born: Aug. 2, 1995. **B-T:** L-R. **HT:** 6-2. **WT:** 185. **Drafted:** California, 2016 (1st round supplemental). **Signed by:** Jermaine Clark.

TRACK RECORD: Jefferies battled shoulder woes his final year in college, but the Athletics still drafted him 37th overall from California. He continued to struggle with injuries in pro ball and missed most of 2017 and 2018 after having Tommy John surgery. Jefferies rebounded with a dominant 2019 season that included 93 strikeouts against just nine walks as he rose to Double-A. He turned in an impressive summer at the alternate training site in 2020 and was rewarded with his first big league callup in mid September.

SCOUTING REPORT: An athletic but undersized righty, Jefferies boasts an impressive fastball/changeup combination and peppers the strike zone with plus command. His fastball sits 92-95 mph as a starter and 94-97 in short bursts, and he locates it deftly to both sides of the plate. Jefferies' plus changeup is his jewel and can make hitters look foolish when it bottoms out. His breaking stuff is less refined—his average slider is sometimes mistaken for a cutter—but can play up because of his command.

THE FUTURE: Building innings and maintaining health is the last step of Jefferies' progression. He did that successfully at the alternate site in 2020 and should compete for a rotation spot in 2021.

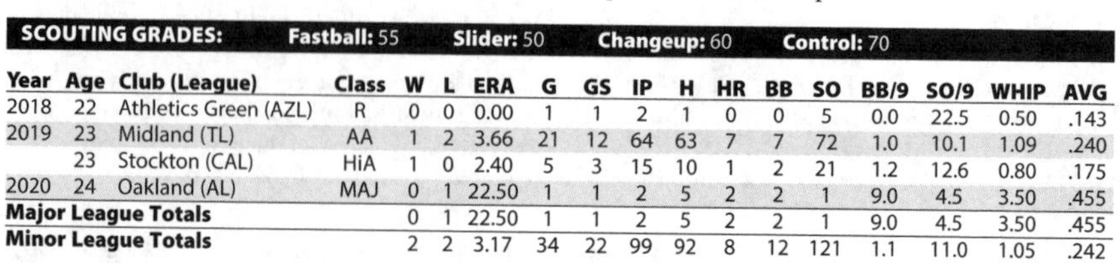

SCOUTING GRADES: **Fastball:** 55 **Slider:** 50 **Changeup:** 60 **Control:** 70

Year	Age	Club (League)	Class	W	L	ERA	G	GS	IP	H	HR	BB	SO	BB/9	SO/9	WHIP	AVG
2018	22	Athletics Green (AZL)	R	0	0	0.00	1	1	2	1	0	0	5	0.0	22.5	0.50	.143
2019	23	Midland (TL)	AA	1	2	3.66	21	12	64	63	7	7	72	1.0	10.1	1.09	.240
	23	Stockton (CAL)	HiA	1	0	2.40	5	3	15	10	1	2	21	1.2	12.6	0.80	.175
2020	24	Oakland (AL)	MAJ	0	1	22.50	1	1	2	5	2	2	1	9.0	4.5	3.50	.455
Major League Totals				0	1	22.50	1	1	2	5	2	2	1	9.0	4.5	3.50	.455
Minor League Totals				2	2	3.17	34	22	99	92	8	12	121	1.1	11.0	1.05	.242

4 ROBERT PUASON, SS

BILL MITCHELL

BA GRADE
55 **Risk: Extreme**

Born: Sept. 11, 2002. **B-T:** B-R. **HT:** 6-3. **WT:** 165. **Signed:** Dominican Republic, 2019. **Signed by:** Amauris Reyes.

TRACK RECORD: The Athletics signed Puason for $5.1 million out of the Dominican Republic in 2019, which tied the Yankees' Jasson Dominguez for the largest bonus that signing period. The coronavirus pandemic thwarted Puason's professional debut, but the A's brought him to their alternate training site in 2020 as one of just three teenagers alongside a mostly older, win-now group.

SCOUTING REPORT: Puason is tooled up in a way that makes him easy to dream on. He's a twitchy athlete with a wiry, projectable body and has shown a knack for barreling the ball from both sides of the plate. His long levers and projectable frame suggest more power is on the way, too. The A's believe Puason can stick at shortstop in the long run, aided by his athletic ability and 70-grade arm, and he's a plus runner now. While his tools are evident, it's also clear Puason is still a ways away. He struggled at times with the speed of the game at both the ATS and during instructional league. Puason has worked to improve his English since coming to the U.S., including taking classes at Arizona State.

THE FUTURE: The alternate site was a helpful, eye-opening experience for the 17-year-old Puason. He'll look to take all he learned into his pro debut in 2021.

SCOUTING GRADES: **Hitting:** 50 **Power:** 50 **Running:** 60 **Fielding:** 60 **Arm:** 70

Year	Age	Club (League)	Class	AVG	G	AB	R	H	2B	3B	HR	RBI	BB	SO	SB	OBP	SLG
2019	16	Did not play—Signed 2020 contract															

5 LOGAN DAVIDSON, SS

KELLY GAVIN/MLB PHOTOS VIA GETTY IMAGES

BA GRADE
50 **Risk: High**

Born: Dec. 26, 1997. **B-T:** B-R. **HT:** 6-3. **WT:** 185. **Drafted:** Clemson, 2019 (1st round). **Signed by:** Neil Avent.

TRACK RECORD: Davidson displayed big tools but struggled to consistently hit at Clemson. The Athletics drafted him 29th overall in 2019 and sent him to short-season Vermont, where he hit .239/.345/.332 in 54 games to further raise questions about his hitting ability. But Davidson arrived at the alternate training site in 2020 with increased physicality and took some of the biggest strides of anyone.

SCOUTING REPORT: The switch-hitting Davidson has impressive tools with above-average raw power, above-average speed, plus arm strength and excellent throwing accuracy. The question has always been his bat. Davidson has been dogged about his ability to hit with wood dating back to an unimpressive Cape Cod League stint, and there is length in his swing that leads to swings and misses. Davidson displays solid pitch recognition, however, and the A's were impressed with his approach at the alternate site, generating hopes he can be a fringe-average hitter and access enough of his power to play every day. A taller shortstop, Davidson worked to clean up his actions and has the athleticism to stick at the position. He also played second base and third base at the alternate site.

THE FUTURE: The A's were encouraged by Davidson's gains in a disjointed 2020, particularly hitting from the left side.

SCOUTING GRADES: **Hitting:** 45 **Power:** 55 **Running:** 55 **Fielding:** 55 **Arm:** 60

Year	Age	Club (League)	Class	AVG	G	AB	R	H	2B	3B	HR	RBI	BB	SO	SB	OBP	SLG
2019	21	Vermont (NYP)	SS	.239	54	205	42	49	7	0	4	12	31	55	5	.345	.332
Minor League Totals				.239	54	205	42	49	7	0	4	12	31	55	5	.345	.332

6 NICK ALLEN, SS

KELLY GAVIN/MLB PHOTOS VIA GETTY IMAGES

BA GRADE
50 Risk: High

Born: Oct. 8, 1998. **B-T:** R-R. **HT:** 5-8. **WT:** 166. **Drafted:** HS—San Diego, 2017 (3rd round). **Signed by:** Anthony Aliotti.

TRACK RECORD: Allen earned a reputation as a defensive wizard as an amateur and signed with the Athletics for $2 million as a third-round pick in 2017, nearly triple the slot amount. He began to progress offensively at high Class A Stockton in 2019 before a high ankle sprain wiped out the second half of his season. Allen returned healthy in 2020 and spent the summer at the alternate training site in San Jose before finishing at instructional league.

SCOUTING REPORT: One of the top defensive shortstops in the minors, Allen is a Gold Glove-caliber defender who was nicknamed "Magic Man" by his coaches in Stockton. He is a twitchy, instinctive defender who glides to the ball, has superb hands, covers a wide range with his plus speed and has a plus, accurate arm to convert every play. The 5-foot-8 infielder fights a glove-only perception and led the Cal League in doubles before his season-ending injury in 2019. Allen has good hand-eye coordination, and the A's have worked with him to avoid chasing power—and fastballs up in the zone—and instead focus on a gap-to-gap approach, using fellow undersized infielder David Fletcher as a blueprint.

THE FUTURE: How Allen progresses as a hitter will determine whether he's a slick-fielding backup or something more.

SCOUTING GRADES: **Hitting:** 50 **Power:** 30 **Running:** 60 **Fielding:** 70 **Arm:** 60

Year	Age	Club (League)	Class	AVG	G	AB	R	H	2B	3B	HR	RBI	BB	SO	SB	OBP	SLG
2017	18	Athletics Green (AZL)	R	.254	35	138	26	35	3	2	1	14	13	28	7	.322	.326
2018	19	Beloit (MWL)	LoA	.239	121	460	51	110	17	6	0	34	34	85	24	.301	.302
2019	20	Stockton (CAL)	HiA	.292	72	288	45	84	22	5	3	25	28	52	13	.363	.434
Minor League Totals				.258	228	886	122	229	42	13	4	73	75	165	44	.324	.349

7 LUIS BARRERA, OF

KELLY GAVIN/MLB PHOTOS VIA GETTY IMAGES

Born: Nov 15, 1995. **B-T:** L-L. **HT:** 6-0. **WT:** 205. **Signed:** Dominican Republic, 2012. **Signed by:** Raymond Abreu.

TRACK RECORD: Signed out of the Dominican Republic in 2012, Barrera is on the doorstep of the majors after a slow climb through the system. A shoulder injury cut his 2019 season short at Double-A Midland, but he returned healthy in 2020 and was one of the Athletics' top standouts at the alternate training site. He hit nearly .450 in camp at San Jose and won the program's batting title on the final day.

SCOUTING REPORT: Barrera is a bit of a throwback as a dynamic slasher with a fervent passion for the game. He is a line drive-oriented hitter, though the A's believe he has 15-home run potential with a slightly altered approach. Barrera is aggressive, sometimes to a fault, but he makes enough contact to make it work. The A's believe he has developed a bit more selectivity. Barrera's plus speed shows up both on the basepaths and in the outfield, where he's an above-average defender with a strong arm who could play all three positions. Consistency was the missing ingredient for Barrera, but A's officials say they saw much more of it at the alternate site.

THE FUTURE: Oakland's starting outfield mix is mostly set entering 2021. Barrera could force his way into at least a part-time role if he carries his momentum into spring training.

SCOUTING GRADES: **Hitting:** 50 **Power:** 45 **Running:** 60 **Fielding:** 55 **Arm:** 60

Year	Age	Club (League)	Class	AVG	G	AB	R	H	2B	3B	HR	RBI	BB	SO	SB	OBP	SLG
2017	21	Stockton (CAL)	HiA	.228	35	114	15	26	2	0	4	16	8	25	3	.276	.351
	21	Beloit (MWL)	LoA	.277	73	278	41	77	13	7	3	22	16	61	13	.320	.406
2018	22	Midland (TL)	AA	.328	36	131	24	43	8	4	0	18	9	18	13	.378	.450
	22	Stockton (CAL)	HiA	.284	88	313	51	89	18	7	3	46	32	63	10	.354	.415
2019	23	Midland (TL)	AA	.321	54	224	35	72	9	11	4	24	12	48	9	.357	.513
Minor League Totals				.280	438	1576	234	441	72	37	21	183	132	321	62	.337	.412

8 JONAH HEIM, C

KELLY GAVIN/MLB PHOTOS VIA GETTY IMAGES

BA GRADE
45 Risk: Medium

Born: June 27, 1995. **B-T:** B-R. **HT:** 6-4. **WT:** 220. **Drafted:** HS—Amherst, NY, 2013 (4th round). **Signed by:** Kirk Fredriksson (Orioles).

TRACK RECORD: Heim took a circuitous path to his major league debut in 2020. Drafted out of high school by the Orioles in 2013, he's been traded twice: first by Baltimore to the Rays in 2016 for Steve Pearce, then a year later by the Rays to Oakland for Joey Wendle. Heim didn't break camp with Oakland in 2020, but the A's installed him as Sean Murphy's backup midway through the season and kept him on their playoff roster.

SCOUTING REPORT: Heim is a strong defender with impressive receiving and blocking chops, especially considering his 6-foot-4 frame. He has a solid-average arm that plays up with his strong accuracy. Long branded a glove-first catcher, Heim's bat has begun to catch up the last two seasons. He controls the strike zone as well as any player in the system and has begun to show moderate all-fields power to go along with his average hitting ability. Oakland challenged Heim prior to last season to play with more energy and assertiveness, and he responded by assuming more of a leadership role.

THE FUTURE: Heim should compete for a backup role again in 2021. Some in the A's organization believe his ceiling is a second-division regular, but it will be tough for him to start in Oakland with Murphy entrenched behind the plate.

SCOUTING GRADES: **Hitting:** 50 **Power:** 45 **Running:** 30 **Fielding:** 60 **Arm:** 55

Year	Age	Club (League)	Class	AVG	G	AB	R	H	2B	3B	HR	RBI	BB	SO	SB	OBP	SLG
2017	22	Bowling Green (MWL)	LoA	.268	77	291	45	78	17	1	9	53	27	57	0	.327	.426
	22	Charlotte, FL (FSL)	HiA	.218	16	55	3	12	3	0	0	8	3	17	1	.262	.273
2018	23	Midland (TL)	AA	.182	39	137	16	25	4	0	1	11	10	22	0	.238	.234
	23	Stockton (CAL)	HiA	.292	80	312	41	91	21	1	7	49	29	60	3	.353	.433
2019	24	Midland (TL)	AA	.282	50	181	20	51	12	0	5	34	24	27	0	.370	.431
	24	Las Vegas (PCL)	AAA	.358	35	106	22	38	9	0	4	19	11	18	0	.412	.557
2020	25	Oakland (AL)	MAJ	.211	13	38	5	8	0	0	0	5	3	3	0	.268	.211
Major League Totals				.211	13	38	5	8	0	0	0	5	3	3	0	.268	.211
Minor League Totals				.250	517	1802	214	451	106	4	36	236	164	326	10	.314	.373

9 GREG DEICHMANN, OF

KELLY GAVIN/MLB PHOTOS VIA GETTY IMAGES

Born: May 31, 1995. **B-T:** L-R. **HT:** 6-2. **WT:** 190. **Drafted:** Louisiana State, 2017 (2nd round). **Signed by:** Kelcey Mucker.

TRACK RECORD: Bizarre injuries have plagued Deichmann since 2017, when he was hit in the face by a pitch as a junior at Louisiana State. He dealt with a combination of hamate, wrist and shoulder injuries in 2018 and 2019, but was healthy for the 2019 Arizona Fall League and hit nine homers in 23 games. That was enough for the Athletics to bring Deichmann to their alternate training site in 2020, and they added him to their 40-man roster after the season.

SCOUTING REPORT: Deichmann's carrying tool is his plus raw power from the left side. He has the bat speed and lower body strength to hit 25-30 home runs in the majors, but it will likely come with a low average and elevated strikeout rate. Scouts have been concerned about Deichmann's grooved swing since college, and he hit just .219 with a 30% strikeout rate at Double-A in 2019. Deichmann simplified his movements and made mechanical adjustments in 2020 to restore some athleticism to his swing in hopes of getting to his plus raw power more frequently. Defensively, Deichmann projects to be an average right fielder with an above-average arm.

THE FUTURE: The A's were encouraged by Deichmann's performance at the alternate site. Now he needs consistent at-bats—and to control the strike zone better—to build on it.

SCOUTING GRADES: **Hitting:** 40 **Power:** 60 **Running:** 50 **Fielding:** 50 **Arm:** 55

Year	Age	Club (League)	Class	AVG	G	AB	R	H	2B	3B	HR	RBI	BB	SO	SB	OBP	SLG
2017	22	Vermont (NYP)	SS	.274	46	164	31	45	10	4	8	30	28	40	4	.385	.530
2018	23	Athletics Green (AZL)	R	.289	11	38	9	11	2	2	1	7	5	8	0	.372	.526
	23	Stockton (CAL)	HiA	.199	47	166	18	33	14	0	6	21	17	63	0	.276	.392
2019	24	Midland (TL)	AA	.219	80	301	42	66	10	2	11	36	34	103	19	.300	.375
Minor League Totals				.232	184	669	100	155	36	8	26	94	84	214	23	.320	.426

10 JAMES KAPRIELIAN, RHP

Born: March 2, 1994. **B-T:** R-R. **HT:** 6-3. **WT:** 225. **Drafted:** UCLA, 2015 (1st round). **Signed by:** Bobby DeJardin (Yankees).

KELLY GAVIN/MLB PHOTOS VIA GETTY IMAGES

BA GRADE **50** Risk: Extreme

TRACK RECORD: That Kaprielian pitched in the majors for the first time in 2020 is a feel-good story in itself. A 2015 first-rounder of the Yankees who was traded to Oakland in the Sonny Gray deal, Kaprielian missed most of the 2016 season with a flexor strain and all of 2017 and 2018 recovering from Tommy John surgery and a subsequent bout with shoulder soreness. He returned in 2019, albeit under a monitored workload, and opened 2020 at the alternate training site. He received his first callup on Aug. 16 and made two appearances out of the Athletics' bullpen.

SCOUTING REPORT: Kaprielian's stuff continues to inch toward a return to form, though it's still not where it was coming out of college. His fastball is back up to 93-95 mph as a starter and averaged 95 in relief. While his secondaries haven't fully returned, he has the most trust in his above-average 85-86 mph slider with tight shape. Kaprielian's curveball and changeup also show average potential, and he throws everything for strikes with above-average control. Kaprielian's delivery remains effortful, leading to long-term health concerns.

THE FUTURE: The A's are eager to see what Kaprielian looks like in 2021 now that his stuff is on the mend. He can reach his back-of-the-rotation potential only if health permits.

SCOUTING GRADES: Fastball: 55 Slider: 55 Curveball: 50 Changeup: 50 Control: 55

Year	Age	Club (League)	Class	W	L	ERA	G	GS	IP	H	HR	BB	SO	BB/9	SO/9	WHIP	AVG
2017	23	Did not play—Injured															
2018	24	Did not play—Injured															
2019	25	Midland (TL)	AA	2	1	1.63	7	5	28	18	2	8	26	2.6	8.5	0.94	.168
	25	Las Vegas (PCL)	AAA	0	0	2.25	1	1	4	6	0	0	6	0.0	13.5	1.50	.333
	25	Stockton (CAL)	HiA	2	2	4.46	11	10	36	35	6	8	43	2.0	10.7	1.18	.230
2020	26	Oakland (AL)	MAJ	0	0	7.36	2	0	4	4	2	2	4	4.9	9.8	1.64	.267
Major League Totals				0	0	7.36	2	0	3	4	2	2	4	4.9	9.8	1.64	.267
Minor League Totals				6	5	2.96	27	22	97	77	9	23	111	2.1	10.3	1.03	.216

11 SHELDON NEUSE, 3B/2B

BA GRADE **40** Risk: Medium

Born: Dec. 10, 1994. **B-T:** R-R. **HT:** 6-0. **WT:** 232. **Drafted:** Oklahoma, 2016 (2nd round). **Signed by:** Ed Gustafson (Nationals).

TRACK RECORD: The A's acquired Neuse from the Nationals at the 2017 trade deadline in the deal that also netted them Jesus Luzardo. Neuse made his big league debut in 2019 and was in the mix to be the A's second baseman in 2020, but he failed to win the job and spent the season at the alternate training site.

SCOUTING REPORT: Neuse is mostly the same player he has been the past two years. He has above-average raw power and impressive barrel control, but there are concerns about his strike-zone control after he posted a 31% strikeout rate in limited big league at-bats and a 32% strikeout rate at Triple-A Nashville in 2018. He chases fastballs up in the zone and has a hard time holding off on them. Neuse is a stocky athlete with surprisingly adequate athleticism defensively, where he's aided by a plus arm. His natural fit is third base, but he has moved around the diamond in an effort to boost his versatility.

THE FUTURE: Concerns about Neuse's consistency at the plate held him back in 2020. Tightening his approach and increasing his defensive versatility will be key as he vies to return to the majors in 2021.

Year	Age	Club (League)	Class	AVG	G	AB	R	H	2B	3B	HR	RBI	BB	SO	SB	OBP	SLG
2019	24	Oakland (AL)	MAJ	.250	25	56	3	14	3	0	0	7	4	19	0	.295	.304
	24	Las Vegas (PCL)	AAA	.317	126	498	99	158	31	2	27	102	56	132	3	.389	.550
Major League Totals				.250	25	56	3	14	3	0	0	7	4	19	0	.295	.304
Minor League Totals				.294	414	1565	233	460	88	11	49	247	141	442	23	.354	.458

12 BRAYAN BUELVAS, OF

Born: June 8, 2002. **B-T:** R-R. **HT:** 5-11. **WT:** 155. **Signed:** Colombia, 2019. **Signed by:** Tito Quintero.

TRACK RECORD: The A's invited three teenagers to their alternate training site: Tyler Soderstrom, their 2020 first-round pick; Robert Puason, their $5.1 million international signing in 2019; and Buelvas. Unlike his contemporaries, Buelvas arrived with considerably less pedigree after signing out of Colombia for just $100,000. But all he's done is impress since then, including posting a

.300/.392/.506 line as a 17-year-old in the Rookie-level Arizona League in 2019.

SCOUTING REPORT: Buelvas does everything well despite lacking an obvious carrying tool. He's an instinctual player with an advanced approach for such a young hitter. Buelvas' 5-foot-11 frame has room for projection, although the A's don't envision much raw power. He has shown a penchant for finding the barrel and taking competitive at-bats against more experienced pitching. Buelvas' arm is average now, with a chance to reach above-average, and his speed gives him a shot to stick in center field. He didn't post gaudy statistics at either the alternate site or instructional league, but the A's love his passion for the game, work ethic and competitiveness.

THE FUTURE: The A's trust Buelvas' makeup enough to keep pitting him against older competition. Starting 2021 at low Class A isn't out of the question.

Year	Age	Club (League)	Class	AVG	G	AB	R	H	2B	3B	HR	RBI	BB	SO	SB	OBP	SLG
2019	17	Athletics Green (AZL)	R	.300	44	160	26	48	10	7	3	27	22	46	12	.392	.506
	17	Athletics (DSL)	R	.244	23	78	4	19	5	1	0	14	8	14	4	.330	.333
Minor League Totals				.282	67	238	30	67	15	8	3	41	30	60	16	.372	.450

13 AUSTIN BECK, OF

BA GRADE 45 Risk: High

Born: Nov. 21, 1998. **B-T:** R-R. **HT:** 6-1. **WT:** 200. **Drafted:** HS—Lexington, N.C., 2017 (1st round). **Signed by:** Neil Avent.

TRACK RECORD: The A's drafted Beck sixth overall in 2017, banking on his athleticism despite a torn ACL that wiped out his senior showcase summer. After a solid if unspectacular first full season in 2018 at low Class A Beloit, a quad injury limited him to 85 uneven games at high Class A Stockton in 2019. Beck was not invited to the alternate training site in 2020 but did accrue at-bats during the fall at instructional league.

SCOUTING REPORT: Beck boasts impressive athleticism across the board, highlighted by his potential plus raw power, plus arm strength and plus speed, the latter of which allows him to play an above-average center field. Beck has lightning-fast hands at the plate, which can sometimes work against him when he struggles to keep his bat in the strike zone long enough to make contact. Beck made adjustments to his swing in search of more launch angle which, combined with subpar pitch recognition, led to a 34% strikeout rate with Stockton in 2019.

THE FUTURE: Beck hasn't lived up to his draft status, but he has consistently been young for his level and didn't have a long track record against top pitching as an amateur. He's in need of consistent at-bats after a lost 2020.

Year	Age	Club (League)	Class	AVG	G	AB	R	H	2B	3B	HR	RBI	BB	SO	SB	OBP	SLG
2019	20	Stockton (CAL)	HiA	.251	85	338	40	85	22	4	8	49	24	126	2	.302	.411
Minor League Totals				.268	249	983	121	263	58	12	12	137	71	294	17	.317	.388

14 JEFF CRISWELL, RHP

BA GRADE 45 Risk: High

Born: March 10, 1999. **B-T:** R-R. **HT:** 6-4. **WT:** 225. **Drafted:** Michigan, 2020 (2nd round). **Signed by:** Rich Sparks.

TRACK RECORD: Criswell's stuff intrigued teams as a high schooler, but most wanted to see him go to school and add strength. He immediately stepped in as a high-leverage reliever at Michigan as a freshman, helped the Wolverines to the College World Series as a sophomore and appeared as their No. 1 starter in the shortened 2020 season. The A's drafted Criswell in the second round in 2020 and signed him for a $1 million bonus. His father, Brian, was drafted by the A's in 1984 and reached Double-A.

SCOUTING REPORT: A physical righty with impressive arm strength, Criswell already has one of the loudest arsenals in the A's system. His fastball sat at 95 mph and touched 98 in instructional league. He throws both a power curveball and a slider that flash plus and pairs them with a changeup that has average potential. Criswell has long faced reliever concerns because of his effortful delivery and spotty control—he walked 4.5 batters per 9 innings in college—but the A's were impressed with his analytical aptitude, experience working with high-speed video and willingness to make changes to his delivery.

THE FUTURE: Criswell will need to hone in on his delivery to stay on a starter track. The A's intend to leave him in the rotation for now.

Year	Age	Club (League)	Class	W	L	ERA	G	GS	IP	H	HR	BB	SO	BB/9	SO/9	WHIP	AVG
2020	21	Did not play—No minor league season															

15 JUNIOR PEREZ, OF

BREAKOUT
BA GRADE
50 Risk: Extreme

Born: July 4, 2001. **B-T:** R-R. **HT:** 6-1. **WT:** 180. **Signed:** Dominican Republic, 2017. **Signed by:** Felix Perez/Trevor Schumm (Padres).

TRACK RECORD: The Padres signed Perez for $300,000 in 2017, banking on power potential once he filled out his 6-foot-1 frame. He showed that power as a 17-year-old in the Rookie-level Arizona League in 2019, batting .268/.349/.512 with 11 homers in 209 at-bats. The A's took notice and acquired Perez as the player to be named later in a trade for Jorge Mateo.

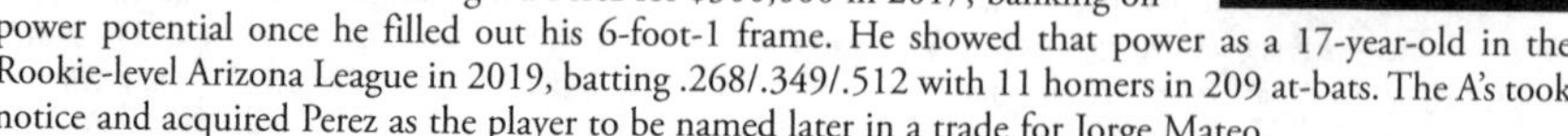

SCOUTING REPORT: Perez's ability to make adjustments in the Arizona League impressed the Padres. He stopped chasing as many pitches and did more damage as the year went on, posting a .283/.345/.572 line over his final 36 games while hitting 10 of his 11 homers. He will swing and miss, but not at a disqualifying level for a player his age. His physicality leaves room to dream on even more power to come. Defensively, Perez has experience at all three positions, but he is likely destined for a corner as he continues to mature and slow down.

THE FUTURE: Perez should reach low Class A at some point in 2021. He'll team with Brayan Buelvas to give the A's a pair of exciting young outfielders in Stockton's lineup.

Year	Age	Club (League)	Class	AVG	G	AB	R	H	2B	3B	HR	RBI	BB	SO	SB	OBP	SLG
2018	16	Padres (DSL)	R	.176	61	204	26	36	6	2	3	26	53	80	12	.354	.270
2019	17	Padres (AZL)	R	.268	51	209	44	56	14	2	11	39	24	59	11	.349	.512
Minor League Totals				.223	112	413	70	92	20	4	14	65	77	139	23	.351	.392

16 JORDAN WEEMS, RHP

BA GRADE
40 Risk: Medium

Born: Nov. 7, 1992. **B-T:** L-R. **HT:** 6-foot-3. **WT:** 175. **Drafted:** HS—Columbus, Ga., 2011 (3rd round). **Signed by:** Tim Hyers (Red Sox).

TRACK RECORD: The Red Sox drafted Weems as a high school catcher in 2011. Five years later, after having posted a .568 OPS through 1,027 at-bats, Boston converted him to pitching. Weems stayed in the Red Sox system through 2019 and reached Triple-A Pawtucket before signing a minor league deal with the A's after the season. He made the A's bullpen out of summer camp and appeared in nine games, posting a 3.21 ERA.

SCOUTING REPORT: Strictly a reliever, Weems employs a fastball-heavy approach and throws it nearly two-thirds of the time. It's an above-average fastball that sits 95-96 mph with more rise than the average MLB fastball thrown at that velocity. He pairs it with an 86 mph changeup that gets swings and misses from lefthanded hitters and an 85-86 mph slider than handles righties. Weems hides the ball well, adding some deception, and you can't miss his Noah Syndergaard-esque long blonde hair. His control is below-average, but he throws enough strikes in the bullpen.

THE FUTURE: Depending on how the A's proceed with free agents Liam Hendriks, Joakim Soria and Yusmeiro Petit, Weems could be in line for high-leverage relief opportunities in 2021. He should be a solid middle reliever at the very least.

Year	Age	Club (League)	Class	W	L	ERA	G	GS	IP	H	HR	BB	SO	BB/9	SO/9	WHIP	AVG
2020	27	Oakland (AL)	MAJ	0	0	3.21	9	0	14	10	1	7	18	4.5	11.6	1.21	.200
Major League Totals				0	0	3.21	9	0	14	10	1	7	18	4.5	11.6	1.21	.200
Minor League Totals				13	8	3.87	127	2	200	175	13	104	208	4.7	9.4	1.40	.241

17 AUSTIN ALLEN, C

BA GRADE
40 Risk: Medium

Born: Jan. 16, 1994. **B-T:** L-R. **HT:** 6-2. **WT:** 220. **Drafted:** Florida Tech, 2015 (4th round). **Signed by:** William Bosque (Padres).

TRACK RECORD: The A's acquired Allen from the Padres after the 2019 season for Jurickson Profar and installed him as their backup catcher. Allen hit at least .280 with 20 homers every year from 2017-19 in the minors, but he struck out 14 times in 32 plate appearances with Oakland and was optioned to the alternate training site in August.

SCOUTING REPORT: A powerful slugging type dating back to his days at Division II Florida Tech, almost all of Allen's value is tied to his bat. He regularly gets to his lefthanded power, mostly to the pull side, and has solid timing and feel to hit. He's long been dogged by concerns over his defense—namely his mobility and game-calling —and projects as a below-average defender at best. His slow transfer and below-average arm lead opponents to run on him at will.

THE FUTURE: The addition of the 26th roster spot helps Allen, who can play first base in a pinch and provides lefthanded thump off the bench. He will again compete for a backup role behind Sean Murphy in 2021.

Year	Age	Club (League)	Class	AVG	G	AB	R	H	2B	3B	HR	RBI	BB	SO	SB	OBP	SLG
2020	26	Oakland (AL)	MAJ	.194	14	31	1	6	1	0	1	3	1	14	0	.219	.323
Major League Totals				.208	48	96	5	20	5	0	1	6	7	35	0	.262	.292
Minor League Totals				.296	472	1800	258	532	121	2	75	300	153	369	1	.354	.490

18 JORDAN DIAZ, 3B

BA GRADE **50** Risk: Extreme

Born: Aug. 13, 2000. **B-T:** R-R. **HT:** 5-10. **WT:** 175. **Signed:** Colombia, 2016. **Signed by:** Jose Quintero.

TRACK RECORD: Oakland signed Diaz for $275,000 during the 2016 international signing period on the strength of his bat. He made his professional debut as a 16-year-old, slowly worked his way through the lower levels and posted a respectable .264/.307/.430 slash line as a teenager in the college-heavy New York-Penn League in 2019.

SCOUTING REPORT: Diaz has always possessed hitter-ish qualities dating back to his days as an amateur in Colombia. He has natural bat-to-ball skills and generates a ton of hard contact. He has a thicker build and is close to maxed out physically, inviting questions about both his power potential and ability to stick at third base, where he shows off an average arm but inconsistent footwork. The A's want to see Diaz improve his focus and approach, hoping he can turn in quality at-bats on a more consistent basis.

THE FUTURE: Diaz internally draws comparisons to Renato Nunez, another A's international signee who flourished into a power-hitting, everyday player with Baltimore. Diaz will still be just 20 years old in 2021 and should begin the year at low Class A.

Year	Age	Club (League)	Class	AVG	G	AB	R	H	2B	3B	HR	RBI	BB	SO	SB	OBP	SLG
2019	18	Vermont (NYP)	SS	.264	70	277	31	73	17	1	9	47	18	46	2	.307	.430
Minor League Totals				.262	168	600	70	157	35	3	10	92	43	94	5	.317	.380

19 GRANT HOLMES, RHP

BA GRADE **45** Risk: High

Born: March 26, 1996. **B-T:** L-R. **HT:** 6-0. **WT:** 224. **Drafted:** HS—Conway, S.C., 2014 (1st round). **Signed by:** Lon Joyce (Dodgers).

TRACK RECORD: Holmes arrived in the A's system following a 2016 trade that sent Rich Hill and Josh Reddick to the Dodgers. He missed almost all of 2018 with a right shoulder injury, but returned to Double-A Midland in 2019 and gained momentum as the season progressed. He spent 2020 at the alternate training site in San Jose.

SCOUTING REPORT: Stuff has never been an issue for Holmes. He attacks hitters with a heavy 92-94 mph fastball that generates plenty of ground balls and a power curveball that draws plus grades and is among the best in Oakland's system. He recently added a cutter and also throws a changeup, which are both at least average, and all of his stuff plays up in shorter outings. But hitters have a surprisingly easy time squaring Holmes up, leading the A's to tinker with his long-armed delivery and sequencing in the hopes of adding more deception. So far it's yielded mixed results. His control is fringe-average.

THE FUTURE: Holmes should start 2021 in the rotation at Triple-A. He could ultimately be better suited for a spot in Oakland's bullpen if he doesn't display better deception and command.

Year	Age	Club (League)	Class	W	L	ERA	G	GS	IP	H	HR	BB	SO	BB/9	SO/9	WHIP	AVG
2019	23	Midland (TL)	AA	6	5	3.31	22	16	82	71	9	27	76	3.0	8.4	1.20	.210
	23	Las Vegas (PCL)	AAA	0	0	1.93	1	1	5	6	1	1	5	1.9	9.6	1.50	.333
Minor League Totals				36	31	3.98	115	100	526	502	45	211	538	3.6	9.2	1.35	.252

20 TYLER BAUM, RHP

Born: Jan. 14, 1998. **B-T:** R-R. **HT:** 6-2. **WT:** 195. **Drafted:** North Carolina, 2019 (2nd round). **Signed by:** Neil Avent.

TRACK RECORD: Baum was a three-year starter at North Carolina before the A's made him a second-round pick in 2019 and signed him to a $900,000 bonus. He posted a 4.70 ERA over 30.2 innings for short-season Vermont after signing and was assigned to the alternate training site in 2020.

SCOUTING REPORT: Baum was lights out his first week of the alternate site, running his fastball up to 96 mph and stymying older A's hitters. But his stuff faded over the duration of camp, leading the A's to wonder if he simply ran out of gas. When he's on, Baum features a 92-94 mph fastball with plenty of movement. His curveball has enough shape and tightness to project as a potential out-pitch, but it sometimes blends with his average slider. He also flashes an average changeup. Baum worked to cut his walk rate in college and carried those improvements over to pro ball, but he still has fringy control and his command remains a concern.

THE FUTURE: Baum is one of many A's pitching prospects toeing the starter vs. reliever line. The A's will look for him to iron out his velocity and command fluctuations in 2021.

Year	Age	Club (League)	Class	W	L	ERA	G	GS	IP	H	HR	BB	SO	BB/9	SO/9	WHIP	AVG
2019	21	Vermont (NYP)	SS	0	3	4.70	11	11	31	29	4	7	34	2.1	10.0	1.17	.246
Minor League Totals				0	3	4.70	11	11	31	29	4	7	34	2.1	10.0	1.17	.246

21 KYLE MCCANN, C

BA GRADE
45 Risk: High

Born: Dec. 2, 1997. **B-T:** L-R. **HT:** 6-2. **WT:** 217. **Drafted:** Georgia Tech, 2019 (4th round). **Signed by:** Jemel Spearman.

TRACK RECORD: The A's drafted McCann (no relation to Brian) out of catching factory Georgia Tech in 2019, where he started behind the plate as a junior after spending his first two seasons at first base in deference to Joey Bart. McCann flashed plenty of power to go along with plenty of strikeouts in his pro debut with short-season Vermont in 2019. He was assigned to Oakland's alternate training site in 2020, where he was aided by the tutelage of veteran catcher Carlos Perez.

SCOUTING REPORT: The A's labeled McCann as one of their biggest risers at the alternate site, a welcome development after he struggled mightily in his pro debut. Massive all-fields power is McCann's calling card, albeit with limited contact. He has a tendency to get pull-happy at times and projects as no more than a below-average hitter. It was strides he made defensively that impressed the A's the most. He showed an increased attention to detail and a willingness to improve his blocking, mobility and receiving. Those developments lead the A's to believe he could still develop into an adequate defensive catcher. He also plays an average first base right now.

THE FUTURE: The 2021 season will be revealing for McCann. He still must prove he's the player the A's saw at the alternate site instead of the one who floundered in his pro debut.

Year	Age	Club (League)	Class	AVG	G	AB	R	H	2B	3B	HR	RBI	BB	SO	SB	OBP	SLG
2019	21	Vermont (NYP)	SS	.192	55	198	23	38	7	1	7	25	25	81	0	.289	.343
	21	Athletics Gold (AZL)	R	.400	5	20	10	8	2	2	2	7	5	6	0	.520	1.000
Minor League Totals				.211	60	218	33	46	9	3	9	32	30	87	0	.312	.404

22 GUS VARLAND, RHP

Born: Nov. 6, 1996. **B-T:** L-R. **HT:** 6-1. **WT:** 205. **Drafted:** Concordia-St. Paul (Minn.), 2018 (14th round). **Signed by:** Derek Lee.

TRACK RECORD: The A's identified Varland as a breakout candidate in 2018 when he carved up hitters (1.04 ERA in 60 innings) across three levels after being drafted in the 14th round out of Division III Concordia-St. Paul. Elbow discomfort led the A's to shut Varland down at high Class A Stockton in July 2019 and he subsequently had Tommy John surgery. He returned to the mound in 2020 during instructional league.

SCOUTING REPORT: Varland's high-spin fastball induces plenty of whiffs or soft contact up in the zone and he commands it well. He threw just eight innings at instructs but his velocity crept up to 94-95 mph, which is a slight bump if he can sustain it. Varland also mixes in a tight-spinning, above-average slider and a below-average changeup that could use refinement. Varland pitches with deception because of some extra arm length in his delivery, although that has also caused additional stress on his elbow. The A's worked with Varland to add more flex to his elbow upon foot strike to alleviate strain. He showed above-average control prior to surgery but has to show it has come back.

THE FUTURE: The A's remain excited about Varland. He should rise to Double-A at some point in 2021 as long as he stays healthy.

Year	Age	Club (League)	Class	W	L	ERA	G	GS	IP	H	HR	BB	SO	BB/9	SO/9	WHIP	AVG
2019	22	Stockton (CAL)	HiA	2	1	2.39	5	4	26	23	3	8	27	2.7	9.2	1.18	.217
Minor League Totals				2	2	1.54	18	15	64	46	4	16	77	2.2	10.8	0.96	.199

23 MICHAEL GULDBERG, OF

BA GRADE **40** Risk: High

Born: Jun. 22, 1999. **B-T:** R-R. **HT:** 6-0. **WT:** 171. **Drafted:** Georgia Tech, 2020 (3rd round). **Signed by:** Jemel Spearman.

TRACK RECORD: The A's drafted Guldberg, a favorite of area scout Jemel Spearman, in the third round of the shortened 2020 draft. Missed developmental time because of a 2018 shoulder injury and the 2020 coronavirus pandemic meant Guldberg had less track record than a typical college hitter, but he did rank second in the Atlantic Coast Conference with a .355 batting average as a sophomore. He was a top performer at instructional league before a minor leg injury shut him down.

SCOUTING REPORT: The A's believe Guldberg can stick in center field despite playing mostly left field in college. He's a quick-twitch, wiry athlete who pairs quality defensive instincts with his plus running ability. He has experience playing second base and the A's may eventually get him occasional reps there, too. Guldberg takes a contact-oriented approach to the plate from the right side and has impressive bat speed. He lacks physicality but the A's say he showed sneaky raw power in batting practice.

THE FUTURE: Guldberg fits the mold of a versatile utilityman. He'll make his pro debut in 2021.

Year	Age	Club (League)	Class	AVG	G	AB	R	H	2B	3B	HR	RBI	BB	SO	SB	OBP	SLG
2020	21	Did not play—No minor league season															

24 JEREMY EIERMAN, SS

BA GRADE **40** Risk: High

Born: Sept. 10, 1996. **B-T:** R-R. **HT:** 6-0. **WT:** 205. **Drafted:** Missouri State, 2018 (2nd round supplemental). **Signed by:** Al Skorupa.

TRACK RECORD: Eierman surged up draft boards as a sophomore at Missouri State, but his power numbers dropped as a junior and led him to fall to the supplemental second round. Eierman's offensive regression has continued in pro ball. He hit just .208/.270/.357 with 177 strikeouts at high Class A Stockton in 2019, the fourth-most strikeouts in all of minor league baseball.

SCOUTING REPORT: It's easy to take notice of Eierman's plus raw power in batting practice, but an inability to make consistent contact has hampered his ability to unlock that power regularly. Eierman has tinkered with his mechanics often over the last three years and Oakland spent time remaking both his approach and his stride. The early returns were encouraging—he walked as much as he struck out in a limited instructional league sample size—but there is still concern over his ability to make consistent contact. Even with a more mature, filled-out frame, Eierman is an above-average defender with a plus arm capable of playing multiple infield positions.

THE FUTURE: A return to high Class A could be in order for Eierman, where the A's hope he continues to display a better hitting approach.

Year	Age	Club (League)	Class	AVG	G	AB	R	H	2B	3B	HR	RBI	BB	SO	SB	OBP	SLG
2019	22	Stockton (CAL)	HiA	.208	131	501	57	104	22	7	13	64	39	177	11	.270	.357
Minor League Totals				.217	193	748	93	162	30	9	21	90	52	247	21	.274	.365

25 SKYE BOLT, OF

BA GRADE **40** Risk: High

Born: Jan. 15, 1994. **B-T:** B-R. **HT:** 6-2. **WT:** 187. **Drafted:** North Carolina, 2015 (4th round). **Signed by:** Neil Avent.

TRACK RECORD: Bolt made his major league debut in 2019, hitting a double in 10 at-bats. He wasn't a September callup initially and only got the nod after an injury to Mark Canha. He spent 2020 at the alternate training site in San Jose.

SCOUTING REPORT: A switch-hitter more effective from the left side, Bolt teases with his athletic skill set but has yet to fully capitalize on it. He has a keen eye at the plate and bettered his strikeout rates as he moved through minor leagues, helping to mitigate his fringe-average hit tool. Defensively, Bolt can comfortably play any outfield position, aided by his above-average speed and arm strength. He has struggled with injuries since the A's drafted him in 2015 out of North Carolina.

THE FUTURE: Bolt faces stiff competition in pursuit of a bench role in Oakland's outfield. His legs and glove give him a shot.

Year	Age	Club (League)	Class	AVG	G	AB	R	H	2B	3B	HR	RBI	BB	SO	SB	OBP	SLG
2019	25	Oakland (AL)	MAJ	.100	5	10	1	1	1	0	0	0	1	3	0	.182	.200
	25	Las Vegas (PCL)	AAA	.269	89	305	57	82	19	3	11	61	37	94	7	.350	.459
Major League Totals				.100	5	10	1	1	1	0	0	0	1	3	0	.182	.200
Minor League Totals				.249	480	1714	262	427	99	21	54	252	214	482	47	.335	.426

26 COLIN PELUSE, RHP

BREAKOUT
BA GRADE
40 Risk: High

Born: Jun 11, 1998. **B-T:** R-R. **HT:** 6-3. **WT:** 240. **Drafted:** Wake Forest, 2019 (9th round). **Signed by:** Neil Avent.

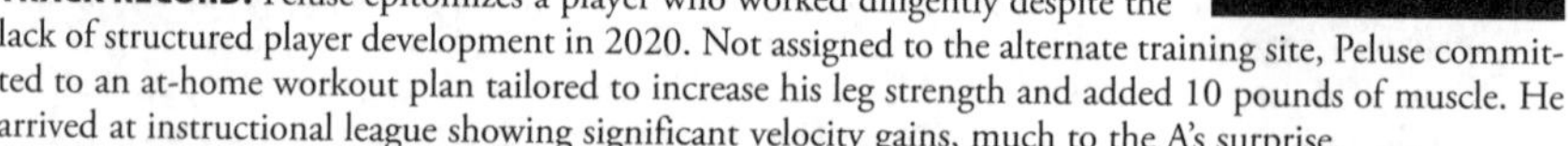

TRACK RECORD: Peluse epitomizes a player who worked diligently despite the lack of structured player development in 2020. Not assigned to the alternate training site, Peluse committed to an at-home workout plan tailored to increase his leg strength and added 10 pounds of muscle. He arrived at instructional league showing significant velocity gains, much to the A's surprise.

SCOUTING REPORT: Peluse's fastball sat 96 mph and touched 98 at instructs, a marked increase from his low-90s readings in college. His slider was already a plus pitch, showing late life and more drop than a typical slider. His changeup is firm, sitting at 88-89 mph, and the A's worked to soften it a bit during instructional league. Peluse already possessed one of the better deliveries among Oakland's starting pitching prospects and showed solid command and control during his time at Wake Forest, walking 3.18 batters per nine innings.

THE FUTURE: The A's hope Peluse sustains his velocity gains. He'll try to show he can in his first taste of full-season ball in 2021.

Year	Age	Club (League)	Class	W	L	ERA	G	GS	IP	H	HR	BB	SO	BB/9	SO/9	WHIP	AVG
2019	21	Vermont (NYP)	SS	2	1	2.25	8	5	24	21	1	6	26	2.3	9.8	1.13	.202
Minor League Totals				2	1	2.25	8	5	24	21	1	6	26	2.3	9.8	1.13	.226

27 DREW MILLAS, C

BA GRADE
40 Risk: High

Born: Jan. 15, 1998. **B-T:** B-R. **HT:** 6-2. **WT:** 205. **Drafted:** Missouri State, 2019 (7th round). **Signed by:** Steve Abney.

TRACK RECORD: Millas was considered one of the top defensive college catchers in the 2019 draft class, but puzzling offensive struggles hindered his stock and dropped him to the seventh round. A subsequent injury to the UCL in his throwing arm combined with a blood clotting issue in his right armpit postponed his professional debut. Millas arrived at instructional league in 2020 fully healthy and immediately impressed the A's.

SCOUTING REPORT: Millas was a three-sport star in high school, also playing quarterback and point guard, and it shows behind the plate. He's an agile defender, a solid receiver and displays prototypical leadership skills, making him a favorite for pitchers to throw to. His arm is above-average even despite the injury. The switch-hitting Millas is a better hitter from the left side, where he projects as an average hitter with solid bat speed, although there were swing-and-miss concerns in college. His power is below-average and limits the offensive impact he projects to make.

THE FUTURE: Millas' glove will help him move through Oakland's system. How far his bat comes along will ultimately determine how far he rises.

Year	Age	Club (League)	Class	AVG	G	AB	R	H	2B	3B	HR	RBI	BB	SO	SB	OBP	SLG
2019	21	Did not play—Injured															

28 MIGUEL ROMERO, RHP

BA GRADE
40 Risk: High

Born: April 23, 1994. **B-T:** B-R. **HT:** 6-0. **WT:** 202. **Signed:** Cuba, 2017. **Signed by:** J.C. de la Cruz.

TRACK RECORD: The A's signed Romero from Cuba in 2017 as a 23-year-old. He has primarily worked out of the bullpen and posted a 3.96 ERA in 45 appearances at Triple-A Las Vegas in 2019. He spent 2020 at the alternate training site in San Jose, where he showcased a new changeup he learned by watching videos on the internet.

SCOUTING REPORT: Romero has long looked the part of a major league reliever. His fastball sits 95 mph with sink and touches 98. He pairs it with an 86-88 mph breaking ball that shows late life. He previously struggled to commit to a third pitch, allowing hitters to sit on his heater if command of his breaking ball went awry, but his new changeup could be the answer to those problems and has the look of a potentially plus pitch. Romero's control is firmly below-average and his walk rate has increased successively at each new level.

THE FUTURE: The A's continue to ask Romero to focus more on the little things like holding runners, but there's no denying the arsenal. He could help the A's bullpen in 2021.

Year	Age	Club (League)	Class	W	L	ERA	G	GS	SV	IP	H	HR	BB	SO	K/9	WHIP	AVG
2019	25	Las Vegas (PCL)	AAA	4	1	3.96	45	1	3	73	65	11	36	81	10.0	1.39	.234
Minor League Totals				9	5	4.13	103	6	17	163	152	22	64	189	10.4	1.32	.24

29 LAZARO ARMENTEROS, OF

BA GRADE
45 Risk: Extreme

Born: May 22, 1999. **B-T:** R-R. **HT:** 6-0. **WT:** 182. **Signed:** Cuba, 2016. **Signed by:** Raul Gomez.

TRACK RECORD: Armenteros landed the largest bonus of any A's international signing in 2016 at $3 million, but he has yet to translate his enticing tools into production as a professional. He struck out 227 times at high Class A Stockton in 2019, the most strikeouts of any player in the minor leagues, and was not invited to either the alternate training site or instructional league in 2020.

SCOUTING REPORT: Armenteros has tantalizing plus raw power and speed. The issue is he rarely gets to that plus raw power. Armenteros' swing doesn't stay in the strike zone very long and he has struggled with pitch recognition, especially on breaking balls. He often swings wildly and is an easy out for pitchers who can land a breaking ball in the zone. Armenteros' speed does play when he gets on base and helps him play an average outfield, although he's limited to left field because of a below-average arm.

THE FUTURE: Armenteros has mostly confounded the A's so far as a professional. He's still just 21 years old and has a combination of tools they don't want to give up on.

Year	Age	Club (League)	Class	AVG	G	AB	R	H	2B	3B	HR	RBI	BB	SO	SB	OBP	SLG
2019	20	Stockton (CAL)	HiA	.222	126	459	65	102	22	5	17	61	73	227	22	.336	.403
Minor League Totals				.250	252	925	138	231	39	11	29	123	128	399	42	.356	.410

30 SETH BROWN, 1B/OF

Born: July 13, 1992. **B-T:** L-L. **HT:** 6-1. **WT:** 223. **Drafted:** Lewis-Clark State (Idaho), 2015 (19th round). **Signed by:** Jim Coffman.

TRACK RECORD: A 19th-round pick out of NAIA Lewis-Clark State, Brown had a Cinderella rise to the majors and hit well in his debut in 2019. He made a brief, seven-game cameo with Oakland in 2020 and spent the rest of the summer at the alternate training site.

SCOUTING REPORT: Brown re-tooled his swing in search of more launch angle prior to 2017 and unlocked considerable power. It has yet to translate to the big leagues in a very small sample size -- zero homers in 88 at-bats—but his plus raw power is as good as any in the A's system. He makes solid contact and has a chance to be an average hitter against righthanders as part of a platoon. Brown has worked hard to improve his outfield defense in the hopes of enhancing his versatility and giving him more avenues to playing time. He's a fine defender at first base.

THE FUTURE: The A's continue to look for more lefthanded bats, and some believe the 28-year-old Brown can still carve out a part-time role as a thumper.

Year	Age	Club (League)	Class	AVG	G	AB	R	H	2B	3B	HR	RBI	BB	SO	SB	OBP	SLG
2020	27	Oakland (AL)	MAJ	.000	7	5	0	0	0	0	0	0	0	2	0	.000	.000
Major League Totals				.275	33	80	11	22	8	2	0	13	7	25	1	.341	.425
Minor League Totals				.274	573	2183	364	598	126	26	92	391	234	592	39	.344	.482

MORE PROSPECTS TO KNOW

31 HOGAN HARRIS, LHP

Harris is a pitchability lefty with a reliable three-pitch mix. Improved command is the key to achieving his ceiling as a back-of-the-rotation starter.

32 WANDISSON CHARLES, RHP

The A's added Charles to their 40-man roster in November. He has the best fastball in the system, flirting with 100 mph, and could help the A's bullpen in the second half of 2021.

33 BUDDY REED, OF

Few prospects match the raw tools the switch-hitting Reed displays, but the 25-year-old has yet to show he can make enough contact to produce offensively.

34 BRIAN HOWARD, RHP

The 6-foot-9 righty creates uncomfortable angle for hitters but has struggled to maintain his stuff in starts. A move to the bullpen would allow his fastball to play up to 95-96 mph more regularly.

35 RICHARD GUASCH, RHP

SLEEPER

The 22-year-old hasn't pitched above low Class A, but his fastball sits at 94 mph, he has the best slider in the system and the A's like his repeatable delivery.

36 JONAH BRIDE, 3B

Bride lacks a carrying tool but has a mature approach at the plate. He's the type of player who stands out over time, not necessarily in a quick glimpse.

37 PARKER DUNSHEE, RHP

Dunshee amassed nearly 100 innings between the alternate training site and instructional league. He needs to further refine his command to make up for nondescript stuff.

38 DANE ACKER, RHP

The A's selected Acker in the fourth round of the 2020 draft and think he has more projection. His fastball currently sits 93 mph and he has a solid-average curveball, but he doesn't throw as many strikes as his repeatable delivery would suggest.

39 STEVIE EMANUELS, RHP

The Washington product wowed scouts prior to college baseball's shutdown and the A's took him in the fifth round of the 2020 draft. His high-spin slider is his best pitch, but there's still a decent amount of projection involved.

40 JALEN GREER, SS

Greer is raw as a 2019 fifth-rounder out of Chicago, but he added muscle to his frame over the last year and has an enticing set of tools, which includes plus running ability and above-average raw power.

TOP PROSPECTS OF THE DECADE

Year	Player, Pos	2020 Org
2011	Grant Green, SS	Did not play
2012	Jarrod Parker, RHP	Did not play
2013	Addison Russell, SS	Kiwoom (Korea)
2014	Addison Russell, SS	Kiwoom (Korea)
2015	Daniel Robertson, SS	Giants
2016	Franklin Barreto, SS	Angels
2017	Franklin Barreto, SS	Angels
2018	A.J. Puk, LHP	Athletics
2019	Jesus Luzardo, LHP	Athletics
2020	Jesus Luzardo, LHP	Athletics

TOP DRAFT PICKS OF THE DECADE

Year	Player, Pos	2020 Org
2011	Sonny Gray, RHP	Reds
2012	Addison Russell, SS	Kiwoom (Korea)
2013	Billy McKinney, OF	Brewers
2014	Matt Chapman, 3B	Athletics
2015	Richie Martin, SS	Orioles
2016	A.J. Puk, LHP	Athletics
2017	Austin Beck, OF	Athletics
2018	Kyler Murray, OF	NFL
2019	Logan Davidson, SS	Athletics
2020	Tyler Soderstrom, C	Athletics

DEPTH CHART

OAKLAND ATHLETICS

TOP 2021 ROOKIES	RANK
A.J. Puk, LHP	2
Daulton Jefferies, RHP	3
BREAKOUT PROSPECTS	**RANK**
Brayan Buelvas, OF	12
Junior Perez, OF	15
Colin Peluse, RHP	26

SOURCE OF TOP 30 TALENT

Homegrown	23	Acquired	7
College	15	Trade	6
Junior college	0	Rule 5 draft	0
High school	2	Independent league	0
Nondrafted free agent	0	Free agent/waivers	1
International	6		

LF
Junior Perez (15)
Lazaro Armenteros (29)
Tyler Ramirez

CF
Luis Barrera (7)
Brayan Buelvas (12)
Austin Beck (13)
Michael Guldberg (23)
Skye Bolt (25)
Buddy Reed

RF
Greg Deichmann (9)

3B
Sheldon Neuse (11)
Jordan Diaz (18)
Jonah Bride
Joshwan Wright

SS
Robert Puason (4)
Logan Davidson (5)
Nick Allen (6)
Jeremy Eierman (24)
Jalen Greer

2B
Marcos Brito
Yerdel Vargas

1B
Seth Brown (30)
Mikey White
Lawrence Butler

C
Tyler Soderstrom (1)
Jonah Heim (8)
Austin Allen (17)
Kyle McCann (21)
Drew Millas (27)

LHP

LHSP
A.J. Puk (2)
Hogan Harris
Dalton Sawyer

LHRP
Zack Erwin

RHP

RHSP
Daulton Jefferies (3)
James Kaprielian (10)
Jeff Criswell (14)
Grant Holmes (19)
Tyler Baum (20)
Gus Varland (22)
Colin Peluse (26)
Richard Guasch
Parker Dunshee
Dane Acker
Stevie Emanuels

RHRP
Jordan Weems (16)
Miguel Romero (28)
Wandisson Charles
Brian Howard
Brady Feigl

Philadelphia Phillies

BY CHRIS HILBURN-TRENKLE

A season that began with expectations the Phillies would return to the playoffs for the first time since 2011 ended with heartbreak.

On the final day of the pandemic-shorted season, the Phillies were shut out by the Rays in a game they needed to win to earn a postseason bid.

Unlike the 2019 season, when Philadelphia was done in by a rotation that produced just one pitcher with an ERA under 4.00, the Phillies' bullpen was the culprit in 2020. Philadelphia relievers pitched to a league-worst 7.06 ERA while pitching the fewest innings (177) of any bullpen in MLB and ended the season as one of the worst units in the history of the game.

That disappointment led to a front office shakeup. General manager Matt Klentak was "reassigned" to another position in the organization, and in December the Phillies hired famed executive Dave Dombrowski as president of baseball operations.

The Phillies haven't had a winning record since 2012, but even still Dombrowski inherits a Phillies team with pieces to work with. The Phillies ranked fourth in the majors in runs scored, sixth in home runs and 10th in starters' ERA. The team got encouraging contributions from Bryce Harper, Didi Gregorius, J.T. Realmuto and Aaron Nola, saw a step forward from Zach Eflin and watched their big offseason signing—Zack Wheeler—pitch up to expectations.

The Phillies also welcomed their top two prospects to the big leagues, and both Alec Bohm and Spencer Howard showed flashes of promise. Bohm quickly took over as the team's everyday third baseman in August and was one of baseball's top rookies, hitting .338/.400/.481. Howard pitched to a 5.81 ERA in seven starts, but showed four above-average pitches and encouraged officials within the organization.

Now, the team enters a transition period. In addition to the front office shakeup, Realmuto, Gregorius, Jake Arrieta and Jay Bruce became free agents after the season. With big bats in the lineup, a strong starting pitching core and a bottom-tier farm system, the Phillies expect to win now and hired Dombrowski to do so.

Still, there have been some promising developments in the minors. In the first year under new scouting director Brian Barber, the Phillies landed top high school pitcher Mick Abel with the 15th overall pick and drafted decorated Arkansas shortstop Casey Martin in the third round.

With the 2020 draft reduced to just five rounds, the Phillies targeted nondrafted free agents who they would have considered in the sixth to 15th rounds. They signed 12 NDFAs, all pitchers.

While the Phillies added some talented young arms to the organization, their system remains relatively light on hitters. Bohm and 2019 first-round shortstop Bryson Stott give them a pair of young hitters to work with, but the organization will look to add more in the years ahead.

In the short term, the most pressing issue for the Phillies is to end their postseason drought amid a difficult economic environment following a season of fanless games due to the coronavirus pandemic. They hired Dombrowski to do just that, and if that means trading away the few prospects they have to enhance present value, he's likely going to do it. ■

MITCHELL LEFF/GETTY IMAGES

Top prospect Alec Bohm adapted quickly to the big leagues, batting .338/.400/.481 as a rookie.

PROJECTED 2024 LINEUP

Position	Player	Age
Catcher	Rafael Marchan	25
First Base	Alec Bohm	27
Second Base	Luis Garcia	23
Third Base	Scott Kingery	30
Shortstop	Bryson Stott	26
Left Field	Adam Haseley	28
Center Field	Simon Muzziotti	25
Right Field	Bryce Harper	31
Designated Hitter	Rhys Hoskins	31
No. 1 Starter	Aaron Nola	31
No. 2 Starter	Zack Wheeler	34
No. 3 Starter	Spencer Howard	27
No. 4 Starter	Mick Abel	22
No. 5 Starter	Zach Eflin	30
Closer	Francisco Morales	24

1 SPENCER HOWARD, RHP

Born: July 28, 1996. **B-T:** R-R. **HT:** 6-3. **WT:** 210.
Drafted: Cal Poly, 2017 (2nd round).
Signed by: Shane Bowers.

BEST TOOLS

Best Hitter for Average	Bryson Stott
Best Power Hitter	Baron Radcliff
Best Strike-Zone Discipline	Bryson Stott
Fastest Baserunner	Corbin Williams
Best Athlete	Corbin Williams
Best Fastball	Spencer Howard
Best Curveball	Zach Warren
Best Slider	Francisco Morales
Best Changeup	Kyle Dohy
Best Control	Ethan Lindow
Best Defensive Catcher	Rafael Marchan
Best Defensive Infielder	Arquimedes Gamboa
Best Infield Arm	Jonathan Guzman
Best Defensive Outfielder	Simon Muzziotti
Best Outfield Arm	Jhailyn Ortiz

TRACK RECORD: Howard got into Cal Poly on academics and planned to play for the school's club team, but he made the varsity team during walk-on tryouts as a freshman. He blossomed physically and went from throwing 84-85 mph at the tryout to sitting 92-93 and touching 96 by the time he was a redshirt sophomore in the Mustangs' rotation. The Phillies drafted him in the second round, No. 45 overall, in 2017 and signed him for $1.15 million. Howard battled through an arm injury his first full season but recovered to throw a no-hitter in the South Atlantic League playoffs. He reached Double-A in 2019 and followed with an impressive stint in the Arizona Fall League. Howard looked like one of the Phillies' best pitchers in summer camp, and it didn't take long for him to make his first big league start. He took the bump on Aug. 9 against the Braves. His season hit a hiccup when he missed time with shoulder stiffness. Despite some rockiness, including a 5.92 ERA overall, Howard flashed four above-average or better pitches and impressed the Phillies' staff.

SCOUTING REPORT: Howard has a strong, sturdy build at 6-foot-2, 205 pounds and tops his arsenal with a nearly plus-plus fastball. The pitch comfortably sits 94 mph, bumps 98 and has touched 100 in the past. Howard showed the ability to throw his fastball to all four quadrants of the zone in 2020, though he mainly threw the pitch up or missed down the middle. His fastball shows above-average movement and above-average spin, and he leans on it heavily, throwing it more than half the time. All three of Howard's secondary pitches show above-average potential, including his changeup. His changeup made rapid improvement, going from below-average in 2017 to flashing plus by 2019. The pitch sits 79-80 mph, plays up with solid deception and features late tumble at its best. Howard's slider is his most-used secondary. The pitch sits 84-85 mph and has some late tilt. It's his primary swing-and-miss pitch and generated a nearly 41% whiff rate in his debut. Howard's curveball flashes plus 12-to-6 shape but needs further refinement. Howard has an easy, repeatable delivery that suggests future above-average control, though he didn't show it in his debut. Howard adjusted well to being ushered to the big leagues early in the season. The Phillies were impressed by his stuff, feel and confidence attacking the zone.

THE FUTURE: Howard profiles as a potential No. 2 or 3 starter with four above-average or better pitches if everything comes together. He should continue to improve and adjust with more starts under his belt. Barring an unforeseen development, he should start the 2021 season back in the Phillies' rotation. ■

Year	Age	Club (League)	Class	W	L	ERA	G	GS	IP	H	HR	BB	SO	BB/9	SO/9	WHIP	AVG
2017	20	Williamsport (NYP)	SS	1	1	4.45	9	9	28	22	0	18	40	5.7	12.7	1.41	.179
2018	21	Lakewood (SAL)	LoA	9	8	3.78	23	23	112	101	6	40	147	3.2	11.8	1.26	.217
2019	22	Phillies East (GCL)	R	0	0	11.57	1	1	2	3	1	1	3	3.9	11.6	1.71	.250
	22	Reading (EL)	AA	1	0	2.35	6	6	31	20	2	9	38	2.6	11.2	0.95	.164
	22	Clearwater (FSL)	HiA	2	1	1.29	7	7	35	19	1	5	48	1.3	12.3	0.69	.152
	22	Phillies West (GCL)	R	0	0	0.00	1	1	3	1	0	1	5	3.0	15.0	0.67	.091
2020	23	Philadelphia (NL)	MAJ	1	2	5.92	6	6	24	30	6	10	23	3.7	8.5	1.64	.300
Major League Totals				1	2	5.92	6	6	24	30	6	10	23	3.7	8.5	1.64	.300
Minor League Totals				13	10	3.28	47	47	211	166	10	74	281	3.2	12.0	1.14	.215

2 MICK ABEL, RHP

Born: Aug. 18, 2001. **B-T:** R-R. **HT:** 6-5. **WT:** 190. **Drafted:** HS—Portland, Ore., 2020 (1st round). **Signed by:** Zach Friedman.

MLB PHOTOS VIA GETTY IMAGES

BA GRADE 60 Risk: Extreme

TRACK RECORD: Abel jumped on scouts' radars when he struck out 2019 No. 5 overall pick Riley Greene as a junior, and he kept their attention leading up to his senior year. He entered 2020 considered arguably the top high school pitcher in the nation, but his season was canceled by the coronavirus pandemic before he could throw a pitch. The Phillies still made him the first prep pitcher selected when they drafted him 16th overall and signed him for $4.08 million to forgo an Oregon State commitment.

SCOUTING REPORT: Abel has an athletic, projectable build at 6-foot-5, 190 pounds and a clean delivery. His four-seam fastball is a plus pitch that sat 90-94 mph in game action and began reaching 97-100 mph during summer workouts at a facility near his home. Abel complements his fastball with a plus 82-86 mph slider as well as an 81-85 mph changeup with tumble and late fade at its best. Abel ties his potent arsenal together with above-average control. He showed how advanced he was by striking out 12 of 15 batters he faced in an informal outing against minor leaguers in Oregon.

THE FUTURE: Abel has a long way to go, but he has the ceiling of a top-of-the-rotation starter. He took part in instructional league and is set to make his pro debut in 2021.

SCOUTING GRADES: **Fastball:** 60 **Slider:** 60 **Curveball:** 45 **Changeup:** 50 **Control:** 55

Year	Age	Club (League)	Class	W	L	ERA	G	GS	IP	H	HR	BB	SO	BB/9	SO/9	WHIP	AVG
2020	18	Did not play—No minor league season															

3 BRYSON STOTT, SS

Born: Oct. 6, 1997. **B-T:** L-R. **HT:** 6-3. **WT:** 200. **Drafted:** Nevada-Las Vegas, 2019 (1st round). **Signed by:** Mike Garcia.

WILLIAMSPORT CROSSCUTTERS

TRACK RECORD: The Phillies took Stott with the 14th overall pick in 2019 after a standout career at UNLV. He continued to perform with an .816 OPS in 44 games in his pro debut in the short-season New York-Penn League. The Phillies brought Stott to their alternate training site in 2020, where he faced more advanced pitchers, worked on his strength and conditioning and concentrated on hitting the ball to all fields.

SCOUTING REPORT: Stott is a solid all-around player who doesn't have many holes in his game. He makes at-bats tough on pitchers and rarely chases out of the strike zone. He struggles some against high velocity, which he worked on at the alternate site. Stott has been too pull-happy at times, but the Phillies were impressed with the progress he showed hitting the ball to all fields. He has solid bat speed and showed an uptick in his power. Stott is an above-average runner who has good actions at shortstop, with above-average range and an above-average arm. He impressed the organization with his daily routine and earned high marks for his makeup.

THE FUTURE: Stott should experience his first taste of the upper minors in 2021. He projects to stick in the middle of the diamond and be a solid contributor on both sides of the ball.

SCOUTING GRADES: **Hitting:** 50 **Power:** 50 **Running:** 55 **Fielding:** 55 **Arm:** 55

Year	Age	Club (League)	Class	AVG	G	AB	R	H	2B	3B	HR	RBI	BB	SO	SB	OBP	SLG
2019	21	Williamsport (NYP)	SS	.274	44	157	27	43	8	2	5	24	22	39	5	.370	.446
	21	Phillies East (GCL)	R	.667	4	9	3	6	1	1	1	3	2	0	0	.727	1.333
Minor League Totals				.295	48	166	30	49	9	3	6	27	24	39	5	.391	.494

4 FRANCISCO MORALES, RHP

Born: Oct. 27, 1999. **B-T:** R-R. **HT:** 6-5. **WT:** 260. **Signed:** Venezuela, 2016.
Signed by: Jesus Mendez.

MICHAEL DILL

BA GRADE
50 Risk: Very High

TRACK RECORD: Morales was one of the top pitchers in the 2016 international class and signed with the Phillies for $720,000. He experienced a breakthrough in 2019 at low Class A Lakewood with a 3.82 ERA and just over 12 strikeouts per nine innings. Morales spent the 2020 season in Orlando working on his changeup and his strength and conditioning. He was listed at 260 pounds at instructional league, up from 185 when he signed.

SCOUTING REPORT: Morales has the best stuff of any pitcher in the organization outside of Spencer Howard and Mick Abel. Morales has a fast, loose arm and generates two power pitches in a 93-97 mph fastball and sharp, 85-89 mph slider that routinely misses bats. Both are plus-plus pitches and play up with deception from his slight crossfire delivery. The development of Morales' changeup will dictate whether he ends up in a rotation or bullpen. His changeup has rarely fooled hitters, and he needs to add deception or movement to the pitch. Morales needs to keep his release point consistent and establish more extension out front, but he competes hard, has a strong presence and shows potentially average control.

THE FUTURE: Morales has a chance to be a mid-rotation starter if he can get his changeup to average. If he doesn't, he has a solid fallback option as a high-leverage reliever.

SCOUTING GRADES: **Fastball:** 70 **Slider:** 70 **Changeup:** 40 **Control:** 50

Year	Age	Club (League)	Class	W	L	ERA	G	GS	IP	H	HR	BB	SO	BB/9	SO/9	WHIP	AVG
2017	17	Phillies East (GCL)	R	3	2	3.05	10	9	41	34	1	20	44	4.4	9.6	1.31	.189
2018	18	Williamsport (NYP)	SS	4	5	5.27	13	13	56	54	6	33	68	5.3	10.9	1.54	.209
2019	19	Lakewood (SAL)	LoA	1	8	3.82	27	15	97	82	8	46	129	4.3	12.0	1.32	.197
Minor League Totals				8	15	4.08	50	37	194	170	15	99	241	4.6	11.2	1.38	.231

5 RAFAEL MARCHAN, C

Born: Feb. 25, 1999. **B-T:** B-R. **HT:** 5-9. **WT:** 196. **Signed:** Venezuela, 2015.
Signed by: Jesus Mendez.

THE PHILLIES/MILES KENNEDY

BA GRADE
45 Risk: High

TRACK RECORD: Marchan played shortstop as an amateur in Venezuela but moved behind the plate before signing with the Phillies for $200,000 in 2015. He caught manager Joe Girardi's eye in big league camp for his defense and intelligence and was added to the Phillies' 60-man player pool. The Phillies called him up on Sept. 14 and he went 4-for-8 and hit his first professional home run.

SCOUTING REPORT: Marchan's calling card is his excellent defense behind the plate. He has above-average blocking skills, a plus arm and maturity beyond his years for handling pitchers. He runs well for a catcher and is a good athlete. Marchan is firmly defense-first, but he has taken steps forward as a hitter. He has solid bat-to-ball skills and bat control that allows him to line the ball to all fields. He showed a knack for hitting breaking balls at the alternate training site and seemed to gain confidence the more he faced advanced pitchers. Marchan's flat swing isn't conducive to home runs, but he showed he could drive the ball with an average exit velocity of 92 mph in his limited big league sample.

THE FUTURE: Marchan handled his own against advanced competition in 2020. He should, at the very least, provide top-flight defense and plus makeup behind the plate.

SCOUTING GRADES: **Hitting:** 45 **Power:** 30 **Running:** 40 **Fielding:** 70 **Arm:** 60

Year	Age	Club (League)	Class	AVG	G	AB	R	H	2B	3B	HR	RBI	BB	SO	SB	OBP	SLG
2017	18	Phillies East (GCL)	R	.238	30	84	10	20	5	0	0	10	4	8	1	.290	.298
2018	19	Williamsport (NYP)	SS	.301	51	196	28	59	8	2	0	12	11	18	9	.343	.362
2019	20	Lakewood (SAL)	LoA	.271	63	236	21	64	16	0	0	20	24	31	1	.347	.339
	20	Clearwater (FSL)	HiA	.231	22	78	6	18	4	0	0	3	6	8	1	.291	.282
2020	21	Philadelphia (NL)	MAJ	.500	3	8	3	4	0	0	1	3	1	2	0	.556	.875
Major League Totals				.500	3	8	3	4	0	0	1	3	1	2	0	.556	.875
Minor League Totals				.285	210	765	88	218	40	3	0	79	61	79	18	.342	.345

6 LUIS GARCIA, SS

Born: Oct. 1, 2000. **B-T:** B-R. **HT:** 5-11. **WT:** 195. **Signed:** Dominican Republic, 2017. **Signed by:** Carlos Salas.

BA GRADE

45 Risk: High

TRACK RECORD: Garcia was one of the top prospects in a deep 2017 international class that included Wander Franco and Julio Rodriguez. He signed with the Phillies for $2.5 million and won the Rookie-level Gulf Coast League batting title in his 2018 pro debut. The Phillies sent Garcia to low Class A Lakewood in 2019, but he hit under .200 for most of the year and struggled to impact the ball.

SCOUTING REPORT: The switch-hitting Garcia shows all the tools to hit. He has short, quick swings from both sides of the plate, catches up to velocity, recognizes pitches and puts together good at-bats. He simply lacked strength, so he spent 2020 working on his body and added 20 pounds to his frame. The increase led to a career-high 107 mph maximum exit velocity during instructional league, and his bat speed also showed significant improvement. In theory, he should now be able to generate more power and make it harder for outfielders to play him shallow. Garcia is a plus defender at shortstop with soft hands, smooth footwork and above-average arm strength. He's an average runner with enough range for the position.

THE FUTURE: If Garcia can be even a fringe-average hitter, his defense will carry him to the majors. He will try to show that his strength gains made a difference in 2021.

SCOUTING GRADES: **Hitting:** 45 **Power:** 40 **Running:** 50 **Fielding:** 60 **Arm:** 55

Year	Age	Club (League)	Class	AVG	G	AB	R	H	2B	3B	HR	RBI	BB	SO	SB	OBP	SLG
2018	17	Phillies West (GCL)	R	.369	43	168	33	62	11	3	1	32	15	21	12	.433	.488
2019	18	Lakewood (SAL)	LoA	.186	127	467	36	87	14	3	4	36	44	132	9	.261	.255
Minor League Totals				.235	170	635	69	149	25	6	5	68	59	153	21	.306	.317

7 YHOSWAR GARCIA, OF

Born: Sept. 13, 2001. **B-T:** R-R. **HT:** 6-1. **WT:** 155. **Signed:** Venezuela, 2020. **Signed by:** Ebert Velasquez.

TRACK RECORD: Garcia initially expected to sign with the Phillies in 2019 but was delayed a year due to an age-discrepancy issue. He had originally represented himself to be a year younger than his actual age. Garcia officially signed in March but became stuck in his home country of Venezuela due to travel restrictions put in place during the coronavirus pandemic. He spent the year at home running and working on his conditioning.

SCOUTING REPORT: Nicknamed "The Drone," Garcia shows outstanding speed and athleticism. He has good contact skills at the plate, where he works as a line-drive hitter from the right side with gap-to-gap power. Garcia is not expected to be a huge home run threat, but he should add more power to his 6-foot-1, 155-pound frame as he matures. That would give him at least average pop. Garcia is a plus runner, giving him the potential to be a threat at the top of the order. He is a standout defender in center field with the speed, instincts and range to stay at the position. He has the potential to develop a plus arm as he gets stronger.

THE FUTURE: Garcia has yet to play a professional game and has a long way to go to reach his ceiling as a top-of-the-order center fielder. His pro debut should come in 2021.

SCOUTING GRADES: **Hitting:** 55 **Power:** 40 **Running:** 60 **Fielding:** 55 **Arm:** 50

Year	Age	Club (League)	Class	AVG	G	AB	R	H	2B	3B	HR	RBI	BB	SO	SB	OBP	SLG
2020	18	Did not play—No minor league season															

8 SIMON MUZZIOTTI, OF

Born: Dec. 27, 1998. **B-T:** L-L. **HT:** 6-1. **WT:** 198. **Signed:** Venezuela, 2016. **Signed by:** Claudio Scerrato.

TRACK RECORD: Muzziotti originally signed with the Red Sox but was declared a free agent by Major League Baseball after Boston was found to have violated international signing rules. The Phillies picked him up for $750,000. Muzziotti hit .287 with 21 doubles and 21 steals in the pitcher-friendly Florida State League in 2019 and impressed the Phillies with his ability to drive the ball in spring training before camps shut down. He got back on the field in Clearwater in October for instructional league.

BA GRADE
45 Risk: High

SCOUTING REPORT: Muzziotti is a lanky contact hitter whose best tool is his bat. He flashes above-average hitting ability from the left side with quick hands, solid bat speed and a natural feel for contact. He has a steep, downhill bat path that generates ground balls and line drives, and he is primarily a gap-to-gap hitter. Phillies coaches are working on adding more loft to his swing to increase his flyball rate. Defensively, Muzziotti is the top center fielder in the system with solid routes, quick reads off the bat and the plus speed to cover plenty of ground. He has an average arm and earns high marks for his makeup and intelligence.

THE FUTURE: Muzziotti has the tools to be a table-setter at the top of the lineup. He'll move as fast as his bat takes him.

SCOUTING GRADES: Hitting: 55 Power: 40 Running: 55 Fielding: 60 Arm: 50

Year	Age	Club (League)	Class	AVG	G	AB	R	H	2B	3B	HR	RBI	BB	SO	SB	OBP	SLG
2017	18	Phillies East (GCL)	R	.269	33	134	20	36	4	6	0	14	7	8	8	.305	.388
	18	Clearwater (FSL)	HiA	.286	2	7	2	2	0	0	0	0	0	2	1	.286	.286
2018	19	Lakewood (SAL)	LoA	.263	68	278	33	73	12	2	1	20	14	40	18	.299	.331
	19	Phillies East (GCL)	R	.091	6	22	2	2	0	0	0	2	2	1	1	.167	.091
2019	20	Clearwater (FSL)	HiA	.287	110	425	52	122	21	3	3	28	32	60	21	.337	.372
Minor League Totals				.268	273	1069	130	287	43	13	4	86	70	127	57	.314	.344

9 JOHAN ROJAS, OF

Born: Aug. 14, 2000. **B-T:** R-R. **HT:** 6-0. **WT:** 175. **Signed:** Dominican Republic, 2018. **Signed by:** Carlos Salas.

TRACK RECORD: The Phillies signed the unheralded Rojas for just $10,000 in the same international period that netted them Luis Garcia. Rojas had an encouraging debut season in the Rookie-level Dominican Summer League in 2018 and held his own as a teenager with short-season Williamsport in 2019. Rojas spent the summer adding muscle to his frame before heading to instructional league.

BA GRADE
50 Risk: Extreme

SCOUTING REPORT: Rojas is an athletic, toolsy outfielder with impressive bat speed, but he will need to work on his pitch selection, especially against fastballs. He has at least an average hit tool, with a short, compact swing with minimal movement. The ball jumps off his bat, as evidenced by exit velocities over 110 mph in 2019. He is working to get more lift on the ball to cut down on his high groundball rate. With his added strength, Rojas projects for average power and has shown the ability to hit the ball to all fields in the minor leagues. The Phillies believe he can play all three outfield spots with above-average defensive ability, an average arm, plus speed and a high-energy approach.

THE FUTURE: Rojas' upside is matched by few prospects in the system. He will need to work on improving his approach and chase rates to reach his ceiling as an everyday big leaguer.

SCOUTING GRADES: Hitting: 50 Power: 50 Running: 60 Fielding: 60 Arm: 50

Year	Age	Club (League)	Class	AVG	G	AB	R	H	2B	3B	HR	RBI	BB	SO	SB	OBP	SLG
2018	17	Phillies Red (DSL)	R	.320	68	259	42	83	12	4	2	31	18	37	19	.376	.421
2019	18	Williamsport (NYP)	SS	.244	42	164	17	40	5	6	2	11	5	29	11	.273	.384
	18	Phillies West (GCL)	R	.311	18	74	13	23	6	5	0	4	9	12	3	.393	.527
Minor League Totals				.294	128	497	72	146	23	15	4	46	32	78	33	.346	.425

10 NICK MATON, SS

TONY FIRRIOLO/MLB PHOTOS VIA GETTY IMAGES

BA GRADE
45 Risk: High

Born: Feb. 18, 1997. **B-T:** L-R. **HT:** 6-2. **WT:** 183. **Drafted:** Lincoln Land (Ill) JC, 2017 (7th round). **Signed by:** Justin Morgenstern.

TRACK RECORD: Maton, whose older brother Phil is an Indians reliever, signed with the Phillies for just over $350,000 as a seventh-round pick in 2017 and sped past many players taken ahead of him. He reached Double-A in 2019, then impressed during spring training in 2020 and spent the summer at the alternate training site facing older pitchers.

SCOUTING REPORT: Maton is a solid athlete with a knack for catching up to velocity. He's an average hitter from the left side who gets on base at a solid clip. The ball jumped off his bat at the alternate site, and the Phillies felt he improved his pitch recognition facing more advanced pitchers. Maton's power is mostly to the gaps, but he's shown enough power to project 10-12 home runs as he adds strength to his frame. Maton is an above-average defender at shortstop who has worked hard to improve his range. He has the above-average arm strength to play the left side of the infield and saw time at both third base and second base at the alternate site. He earns high marks for his makeup, instincts and routine.

THE FUTURE: Maton has the tools and mindset to be a useful, versatile infielder in the major leagues. He will likely return to Double-A in 2021.

SCOUTING GRADES: Hitting: 50 Power: 40 Running: 50 Fielding: 55 Arm: 55

Year	Age	Club (League)	Class	AVG	G	AB	R	H	2B	3B	HR	RBI	BB	SO	SB	OBP	SLG
2017	20	Williamsport (NYP)	SS	.252	58	210	34	53	9	1	2	13	30	47	10	.350	.333
2018	21	Lakewood (SAL)	LoA	.256	114	406	52	104	26	5	8	51	43	103	5	.330	.404
2019	22	Clearwater (FSL)	HiA	.276	93	337	35	93	14	3	5	45	41	71	11	.358	.380
	22	Reading (EL)	AA	.210	21	62	6	13	3	0	2	6	9	14	1	.306	.355
Minor League Totals				.259	286	1015	127	263	52	9	17	115	123	235	27	.342	.378

11 CASEY MARTIN, SS

BA GRADE
50 Risk: Extreme

Born: April 7, 1999. **B-T:** R-R. **HT:** 5-11. **WT:** 175. **Drafted:** Arkansas, 2020 (3rd round). **Signed by:** Tommy Field.

TRACK RECORD: Martin broke onto the scene with 13 home runs and a .974 OPS his freshman year to help Arkansas come within a few outs of winning the College World Series. He regressed each successive season, however, and concerns about his aggressiveness caused him to fall to the third round of the 2020 draft. The Phillies stopped his slide at No. 87 overall and signed him for $1.3 million, nearly double slot value.

SCOUTING REPORT: Martin has excellent tools, including plus raw power, plus speed, plus arm strength and defense that flashes plus, but he struggles to utilize those tools in games. He struck out 165 times in 148 collegiate games and is a below-average hitter with his overly aggressive approach. Martin does damage when he connects, but he needs to cut down on his swings and misses and improve his pitch recognition greatly. He has been pull-happy at times, and the Phillies have encouraged him to use the whole field. Martin has good range at shortstop and a strong arm, but he lacks polish and needs to improve his consistency and reliability. Otherwise, he could end up at third base, second or center field.

THE FUTURE: Martin is one of the toolsiest players in the system. He's somewhat boom or bust, but the right adjustments could help him move quickly.

Year	Age	Club (League)	Class	AVG	G	AB	R	H	2B	3B	HR	RBI	BB	SO	SB	OBP	SLG
2020	21	Did not play—No minor league season															

12 ADONIS MEDINA, RHP

BA GRADE
45 Risk: High

Born: Dec. 18, 1996. **B-T:** R-R. **HT:** 6-1. **WT:** 187. **Signed:** Dominican Republic, 2014. **Signed by:** Carlos Salas.

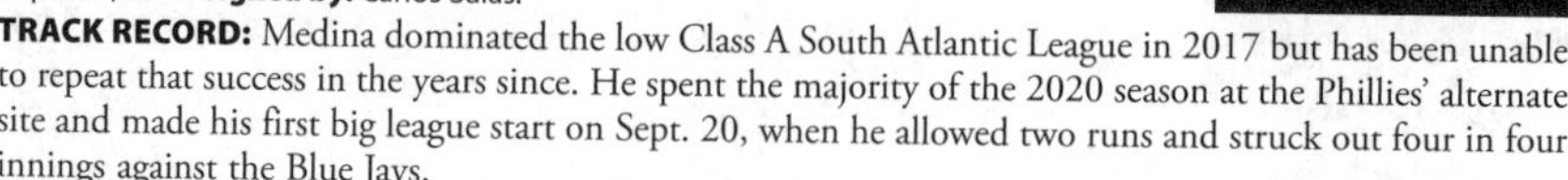

TRACK RECORD: Medina dominated the low Class A South Atlantic League in 2017 but has been unable to repeat that success in the years since. He spent the majority of the 2020 season at the Phillies' alternate site and made his first big league start on Sept. 20, when he allowed two runs and struck out four in four innings against the Blue Jays.

SCOUTING REPORT: Medina features a three-pitch mix out of a clean delivery with good arm action, led by his average fastball that generally sits 92-93 mph and touches 95. He produces solid cutting action on the pitch and commands it well, with the ability to throw it to both sides of the plate. Medina's best offspeed offering is his above-average slider, which has some three-quarter break but often comes out as a slurvy pitch. Medina's changeup shows solid fade and has the potential to become plus, but he struggles to throw it for strikes. The Phillies were pleased by the progress Medina made, especially with his slider. He will need to continue improving his changeup to subdue lefthanded hitters.

THE FUTURE: Medina should start 2021 in the upper minors before returning to the majors later in the season. If he can't bring his changeup along enough to start, his fastball and slider should play up in a bullpen role.

Year	Age	Club (League)	Class	W	L	ERA	G	GS	IP	H	HR	BB	SO	BB/9	SO/9	WHIP	AVG
2020	23	Philadelphia (NL)	MAJ	0	1	4.50	1	1	4	3	0	3	4	6.8	9.0	1.50	.200
Major League Totals				0	1	4.50	1	1	4	3	0	3	4	6.8	9.0	1.50	.200
Minor League Totals				31	28	3.60	100	87	473	420	35	156	429	3.0	8.2	1.22	.236

13 MICKEY MONIAK, OF

BA GRADE **45** Risk: High

Born: May 13, 1998. **B-T:** L-R. **HT:** 6-2. **WT:** 195. **Drafted:** HS—Carlsbad, Calif., 2016 (1st round). **Signed:** Mike Garcia.

TRACK RECORD: The 2016 BA High School Player of the Year and No. 1 overall pick in the draft followed his best season as a professional in 2019—52 extra-base hits as a 21-year-old at Double-A Reading while showing increased strength—by earning a spot at the alternate training site in 2020. He impressed the Phillies with his play and earned his first major league callup at the end of the season, posting three hits in 14 at-bats.

SCOUTING REPORT: A lack of above-average tools across the board leads evaluators to believe Moniak will be a fourth or fifth outfielder. He provides solid defense at all three outfield spots and could stick in center, where his arm is average. The lefthanded hitter does a good job getting the barrel on the ball and has worked on cutting down his free-swinging approach, taking pitches early in the count and increasing his bat speed. Moniak still has some projection left, but his bat and power will likely top out at slightly below average and he's drawn just 94 walks in over 1,500 at-bats. He has average speed.

THE FUTURE: Moniak has a chance to make the team as a reserve in 2021. His approach and hit tool must improve in order for him to earn a starting spot.

Year	Age	Club (League)	Class	AVG	G	AB	R	H	2B	3B	HR	RBI	BB	SO	SB	OBP	SLG
2020	22	Philadelphia (NL)	MAJ	.214	8	14	3	3	0	0	0	0	4	6	0	.389	.214
Major League Totals				.214	8	14	3	3	0	0	0	0	4	6	0	.389	.214
Minor League Totals				.256	402	1540	193	394	89	26	22	194	94	355	42	.302	.390

14 ERIK MILLER, LHP

BREAKOUT

BA GRADE **45** Risk: High

Born: Feb. 13, 1998. **B-T:** L-L. **HT:** 6-5. **WT:** 240. **Drafted:** Stanford, 2019 (4th round). **Signed by:** Joey Davis.

TRACK RECORD: Miller showed enough in his three seasons at Stanford (17-9, 3.68) to merit a fourth-round selection in the 2019 draft. The bulky lefthander pitched across three levels after signing, culminating with a sharp stint at low Class A Lakewood. Miller impressed the Phillies with his repertoire in spring training and was added to the team's instructional league roster in the fall.

SCOUTING REPORT: Miller is an imposing lefthander on the mound. His fastball has increased in velocity and now sits in the mid 90s, topping out at 96 mph. Miller does a good job hiding the ball and it shows running life with carry up in the zone, giving it the potential to be a plus pitch. His slider is another plus offering that sits 80-84 mph and induces swings and misses with three-quarter tilt and big crossbreak. Miller mostly relies on those two pitches, but also has an 84-86 mph changeup with some turnover action. He is working to increase the repeatability of his delivery in order to improve his below-average control.

THE FUTURE: If Miller's changeup keeps improving and he starts to attack the zone consistently, he should profile as a back-end starter. Otherwise, his fastball and slider will play in relief.

Year	Age	Club (League)	Class	W	L	ERA	G	GS	IP	H	HR	BB	SO	BB/9	SO/9	WHIP	AVG
2019	21	Lakewood (SAL)	LoA	1	0	2.08	3	2	13	10	0	6	17	4.2	11.8	1.23	.182
	21	Williamsport (NYP)	SS	0	0	0.90	6	4	20	13	0	7	29	3.2	13.1	1.00	.151
	21	Phillies West (GCL)	R	0	0	3.00	2	1	3	2	0	2	6	6.0	18.0	1.33	.154
Minor League Totals				1	0	1.50	11	7	36	25	0	15	52	3.8	13.0	1.11	.188

15 ENYEL DE LOS SANTOS, RHP

BA GRADE
40 Risk: Medium

Born: Dec. 25, 1995. **B-T:** R-R. **HT:** 6-3. **WT:** 235. **Signed:** Dominican Republic, 2014. **Signed by:** Eddy Toledo/Domingo Toribio (Mariners).

TRACK RECORD: De Los Santos was acquired from the Padres for Freddy Galvis and made 12 appearances for the Phillies between 2018 and 2019. He did not pitch in the majors in 2020, instead joining the alternate training site in late August and working on repeating his delivery, improving his command and locating his breaking ball for strikes.

SCOUTING REPORT: De Los Santos has a big arm with an above-average fastball that ranges from 92-98 mph, but he has struggled to consistently locate the pitch, especially on the outer half to righthanded hitters. His changeup is fringe-average but does a good job of falling away from lefthanded hitters. De Los Santos spent the bulk of his time at the alternate training site working on his breaking ball. His slider sits 80-83 mph but shows 12-to-6 shape at times that makes it resemble a curveball. De Los Santos has struggled to locate the pitch, and the Phillies worked with him to repeat his delivery to improve his consistency. The club believes the breaking ball can be above-average if he can tighten it up and learn to land it.

THE FUTURE: De Los Santos most likely profiles as a reliever. The Phillies need bullpen arms and his fastball should play up in the role.

Year	Age	Club (League)	Class	W	L	ERA	G	GS	IP	H	HR	BB	SO	BB/9	SO/9	WHIP	AVG
2019	23	Philadelphia (NL)	MAJ	0	1	7.36	5	1	11	13	4	5	9	4.1	7.4	1.64	.283
	23	Lehigh Valley (IL)	AAA	5	7	4.40	19	19	94	81	16	35	83	3.4	7.9	1.23	.205
Major League Totals				1	1	5.70	12	3	30	32	6	13	24	3.9	7.2	1.50	.288
Minor League Totals				39	23	3.57	106	100	554	485	56	182	499	3.0	8.1	1.20	.237

16 LOGAN SIMMONS, SS

BREAKOUT
BA GRADE
45 Risk: Very High

Born: April 11, 2000. **B-T:** R-R. **HT:** 6-2. **WT:** 180. **Drafted:** HS—Macon, Ga., 2018 (6th round). **Signed by:** Aaron Jersild.

TRACK RECORD: Simmons made a quick impression after being drafted in the sixth round in 2018, highlighted by hitting 12 home runs with a .520 slugging percentage at short-season Williamsport in 2019. The athletic middle infielder spent the summer of 2020 helping coach East Cobb teams in Atlanta before getting added to the instructional league roster.

SCOUTING REPORT: Simmons has impressive power and added even more after spending the summer working on his conditioning. He's added 30 pounds of muscle from the time he was drafted and came out hitting the ball hard in instructs. Simmons is athletic but still has some rawness in his game, particularly as a hitter. He shows quick bat speed but tends to sell out too much for power with a pull-happy approach. He also needs to work on staying in the strike zone. Simmons has a strong, average to above-average arm, but doesn't have good actions at shortstop and the Phillies still aren't sure where he will end up defensively. He's moved around the infield, but could even end up in left field eventually. He is a fringe-average runner.

THE FUTURE: Simmons was one of the players in the organization most hurt by not having a minor league season. He should make his full-season debut in 2021.

Year	Age	Club (League)	Class	AVG	G	AB	R	H	2B	3B	HR	RBI	BB	SO	SB	OBP	SLG
2019	19	Williamsport (NYP)	SS	.234	51	171	31	40	7	3	12	34	20	54	5	.333	.520
Minor League Totals				.233	83	266	52	62	14	3	15	45	29	84	7	.338	.477

17 LOGAN O'HOPPE, C

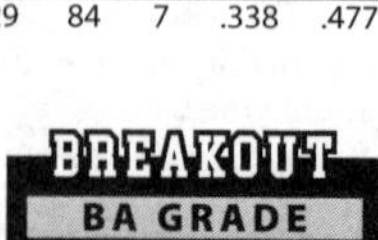

Born: Feb. 9, 2000. **B-T:** R-R. **HT:** 6-2. **WT:** 185. **Drafted:** HS—West Islip, N.Y., 2018 (23rd round). **Signed by:** Alex Agostino.

TRACK RECORD: Immensely popular within the organization, O'Hoppe was picked by the Phillies as a 23rd-rounder in 2018 and wasted no time before posting a .943 OPS in the Rookie-level Gulf Coast League. He struggled in short-season ball in 2019, but slugged .483 as a 19-year-old over the winter in the Australian Baseball League.The Phillies brought him to the alternate training site in 2020.

SCOUTING REPORT: O'Hoppe's program at the alternate site was focused around his contact skills, hitting approach and cutting down his strikeout rate. By the final two months his strikeout rate was down to 10% after sitting north of 27% in 2019. How those adjustments translate into real games will go a long way in projecting his hit tool, which presently is below-average. He has fringe-average bat speed and average power, but he tends to have a pull-happy approach. O'Hoppe draws rave reviews for his work ethic, makeup, leadership and ability to call a game behind the plate. He's an above-average defender with

strong blocking skills who works well with pitchers. He has average arm strength.
THE FUTURE: Few doubt O'Hoppe can catch in the majors, but his bat could take a couple years. He'll make his full-season debut in 2021.

Year	Age	Club (League)	Class	AVG	G	AB	R	H	2B	3B	HR	RBI	BB	SO	SB	OBP	SLG
2019	19	Williamsport (NYP)	SS	.216	45	162	20	35	12	2	5	26	12	49	3	.266	.407
Minor League Totals				.277	79	271	39	75	22	3	7	47	22	77	5	.326	.458

18 CRISTOPHER SANCHEZ, LHP

BA GRADE **40** Risk: High

Born: Dec. 12, 1996. **B-T:** L-L. **HT:** 6-5. **WT:** 165. **Signed:** Dominican Republic, 2013. **Signed by:** Daniel Santana (Rays).

TRACK RECORD: Signed out of the Dominican Republic by the Rays in 2013, Sanchez spent three seasons in the Dominican Summer League and two in the Rookie-level Appalachian League. He broke out and jumped all the way from high Class A to Triple-A Durham in 2019, leading the Phillies to acquire him for Curtis Mead after the season. He made his organizational debut at the alternate training site in 2020.
SCOUTING REPORT: Sanchez is a power pitcher with an electric fastball that sits in the mid 90s and tops out at 98 mph. His low three-quarters crossfire delivery makes it hard for hitters to see the ball, but also hurts Sanchez's fastball command. His mid-80s slider flashes above-average to plus at times and works down and in on righthanded hitters. His changeup sits in the low 80s with little movement and he struggles to command it. Sanchez is extremely raw for his age and spent the summer gaining experience against advanced hitters at the alternate site. His control remains well below average.
THE FUTURE: Sanchez should start 2021 back in Triple-A. He might not be far from assuming a role in the Phillies bullpen.

Year	Age	Club (League)	Class	W	L	ERA	G	GS	IP	H	HR	BB	SO	BB/9	SO/9	WHIP	AVG
2019	22	Durham (IL)	AAA	0	0	20.25	1	0	1	2	0	2	0	13.5	0.0	3.00	.286
	22	Bowling Green (MWL)	LoA	3	1	2.01	11	4	40	28	3	11	37	2.5	8.3	0.97	.155
	22	Charlotte, FL (FSL)	HiA	1	0	1.85	12	6	34	28	0	13	36	3.4	9.5	1.21	.183
Minor League Totals				17	16	4.53	90	40	270	287	14	113	219	3.8	7.3	1.48	.272

19 ANDRICK NAVA, C

BA GRADE **45** Risk: Extreme

Born: Oct. 6, 2001. **B-T:** B-R. **HT:** 5-11. **WT:** 225. **Signed:** Venezuela, 2018. **Signed by:** Rafael Alvarez/Romulo Oliveros.

TRACK RECORD: Nava signed for $400,000 in 2018 and the Phillies were confident enough in him as a hitter that they had him start his pro career in the Gulf Coast League in 2019 as a 17-year-old. The switch-hitter did not disappoint, hitting .314 and showing little swing and miss, and he was added to the Phillies instructional league roster this fall to give him reps behind and at the plate.
SCOUTING REPORT: Generally considered the top hitter among the Phillies stable of catchers, Nava shows an advanced approach at the plate for his age, with advanced bat control, strong hands and the ability to hit from both sides of the plate. Nava makes quality contact, with his bat-to-ball skills and bat speed standing out. Nava doesn't have much power at the moment, with little projection left in his body at 5-foot-11, 225 pounds. He's still raw defensively, but has solid catch and throw skills—he threw out 32% of baserunners in 2019. He's a decent receiver and has shown improvement in blocking balls in the dirt. Nava's arm is fringe-average and he does a good job of handling pitchers for his age. He's a slow runner.
THE FUTURE: Like many other young players, Nava was hurt by not having a minor league season. His hitting ability should allow him to handle his first assignment at full-season ball next summer.

year	Age	Club (League)	Class	AVG	G	AB	R	H	2B	3B	HR	RBI	BB	SO	SB	OBP	SLG
2019	17	Phillies West (GCL)	R	.314	44	156	25	49	6	0	1	20	8	20	1	.349	.372
Minor League Totals				.314	44	156	25	49	6	0	1	20	8	20	1	.349	.372

20 JOJO ROMERO, LHP

BA GRADE **40** Risk: High

Born: Sept. 9, 1996. **B-T:** L-L. **HT:** 5-11. **WT:** 200. **Drafted:** Yavapai (Ariz.) JC, 2016 (4th round). **Signed by:** Brad Holland.

TRACK RECORD: Romero bounced back and forth between Double-A and Triple-A in 2019 and appeared to figure it out at the end of the season, capped by a strong showing in the Arizona Fall League. The Phillies brought him to the alternate site in 2020 and called him up for his big league debut Aug. 21. Romero went on to make 12 relief appearances and allowed 13 hits and nine earned runs in 10.2 innings, albeit with 10 strikeouts against only two walks.

SCOUTING REPORT: After showing signs of decreased velocity on his fastball, Romero sat 95 mph in the major leagues and showed an average heater he was capable of leaning on against big league hitters. He's worked to throw his slider harder, tighter and more effectively in the strike zone and showed a high-spin breaking ball in the mid-80s in his debut, but at times hitters were able to tee off on it. Romero's changeup was previously an above-average pitch, but was used infrequently in 2020. He has average control.
THE FUTURE: The Phillies have a need for bullpen arms. Romero will likely continue to pitch in that role in 2021.

Year	Age	Club (League)	Class	W	L	ERA	G	GS	IP	H	HR	BB	SO	BB/9	SO/9	WHIP	AVG
2020	23	Philadelphia (NL)	MAJ	0	0	7.59	12	0	11	13	1	2	10	1.7	8.4	1.41	.310
Major League Totals				0	0	7.59	12	0	11	13	1	2	10	1.7	8.4	1.41	.310
Minor League Totals				26	20	3.69	75	75	392	371	31	135	351	3.1	8.0	1.29	.250

21 DAMON JONES, LHP

BA GRADE
40 Risk: High

Born: Sept. 30, 1994. **B-T:** L-L. **HT:** 6-5. **WT:** 225. **Drafted:** Washington State, 2017 (18th round). **Signed by:** Hilton Richardson.

TRACK RECORD: The Phillies took a flier on Jones in the 18th round of the 2017 draft despite two underwhelming seasons at Washington State. He improved significantly as a pro after adding velocity at Driveline Baseball and ditching his windup, which in turn helped his command. He spent the summer of 2020 at the Phillies alternate site.
SCOUTING REPORT: Jones has impressive stuff but has trouble throwing strikes. His above-average fastball sits 92-94 mph and tops out at 96 and his best pitch is his high-spin, low-80s slider. He gets excellent horizontal movement on the pitch and it's a true swing-and-miss offering. His changeup doesn't show movement and is thrown too close in velocity to his fastball at 86-88 mph, making it a below-average pitch. Jones has a strong body and a big arm with good extension out of his delivery, but has to improve his control to start. He spent the summer working against advanced hitters in uncomfortable at-bats and needs to improve at attacking the strike zone and consistently landing his pitches in the strike zone.
THE FUTURE: The Phillies believe that Jones can be a back-end starter. His stuff will play in the bullpen if his control doesn't improve.

Year	Age	Club (League)	Class	W	L	ERA	G	GS	IP	H	HR	BB	SO	BB/9	SO/9	WHIP	AVG
2019	24	Lehigh Valley (IL)	AAA	0	1	6.62	8	8	34	27	4	26	33	6.9	8.7	1.56	.185
	24	Reading (EL)	AA	1	0	0.82	4	4	22	9	0	9	31	3.7	12.7	0.82	.093
	24	Clearwater (FSL)	HiA	4	3	1.54	11	11	58	38	3	24	88	3.7	13.6	1.06	.165
Minor League Totals				17	14	3.34	59	45	253	202	14	129	313	4.6	11.1	1.30	.220

22 JAMARI BAYLOR, SS

BA GRADE
45 Risk: Extreme

Born: Aug. 25, 2000. **B-T:** R-R. **HT:** 5-11. **WT:** 190. **Drafted:** HS—Richmond, Va., 2019 (3rd round). **Signed by:** Kellum McKeon.

TRACK RECORD: An athletic prep shortstop, Baylor signed with the Phillies for $675,000 after they drafted him in the third round in 2019. He played in just four games in the Rookie-level Gulf Coast League after signing due to a hamstring injury. He spent 2020 recovering from another hamstring injury before joining instructional league in the fall.
SCOUTING REPORT: Baylor has an exciting blend of tools highlighted by his speed, athleticism, hitting ability and arm strength. He has strong bat-to-ball skills and solid bat speed and spent the fall working to clean up unnecessary hitches in his swing. Baylor impressed evaluators at instructs with his added strength, setting career highs in exit velocity and crossing 105 mph multiple times. Baylor has above-average arm strength, but his actions are slow and there is some concern he might have to move from shortstop to second base, third or the outfield.
THE FUTURE: Baylor should make his full-season debut next summer. His main goals are to continue working on his approach and stay healthy.

Year	Age	Club (League)	Class	AVG	G	AB	R	H	2B	3B	HR	RBI	BB	SO	SB	OBP	SLG
2019	18	Phillies West (GCL)	R	.273	4	11	4	3	2	0	0	0	1	2	0	.333	.455
Minor League Totals				.273	4	11	4	3	2	0	0	0	1	2	0	.333	.455

23 CONNOR BROGDON, RHP

BA GRADE
40 Risk: High

Born: Jan. 29, 1995. **B-T:** R-R. **HT:** 6-6. **WT:** 205. **Drafted:** Lewis-Clark State (Idaho), 2017 (10th round). **Signed by:** Hilton Richardson.

TRACK RECORD: A 2017 10th-rounder from NAIA power Lewis-Clark State, Brogdon is a big, hard-throwing righthander who logged a 2.50 ERA in three minor league seasons and earned a spot at the Phillies alternate training site in 2020. He made his major league debut in August and became one of the few reliable members of the Phillies' MLB-worst bullpen, pitching to a 3.97 ERA in nine appearances with 17 strikeouts, five walks and five hits allowed in 11.1 innings.

SCOUTING REPORT: Brogdon's arsenal is headlined by a plus fastball that averages 95 mph and has a high spin rate between 2,400-2,500 rpm. In the past he's thrown a 79-83 mph slider that doesn't have much power and featured slurvy action, but he ditched the pitch in the majors. His circle changeup averages 84 mph with good deception and plus fading life. Major league hitters struggled against the pitch, producing just two hits in 16 at-bats—both singles—and striking out eight times. Brogdon has average control.

THE FUTURE: Brogdon solidified himself as a valuable weapon out of the bullpen. He will need to cut down on his walk rate and continue staying aggressive in the zone.

Year	Age	Club (League)	Class	W	L	ERA	G	GS	IP	H	HR	BB	SO	BB/9	SO/9	WHIP	AVG
2020	25	Philadelphia (NL)	MAJ	1	0	3.97	9	0	11	5	3	5	17	4.0	13.5	0.88	.128
Major League Totals				1	0	3.97	9	0	11	5	3	5	17	4.0	13.5	0.88	.128
Minor League Totals				14	6	2.50	98	7	180	127	14	58	230	2.9	11.5	1.03	.196

24 RAMON ROSSO, RHP

BA GRADE
40 Risk: High

Born: June 9, 1996. **B-T:** R-R. **HT:** 6-4. **WT:** 240. **Signed:** Dominican Republic, 2017. **Signed by:**

TRACK RECORD: Rosso's breakout 2018 season at the Class A levels was followed by an encouraging performance at Double-A in 2019, though he struggled after a promotion to Triple-A. The Phillies included Rosso on their Opening Day roster and he spent the year bouncing back and forth between the majors and the alternate training site, ultimately going 0-1, 6.52 in seven appearances.

SCOUTING REPORT: Rosso is a burly righthander whose stuff is improving, but his control still needs work. His fastball sits 93-94 mph with above-average spin, touching 97, and has some running action to both sides of the plate. His slurvy slider sits 84-85 mph with an above-average spin rate but needs to be tightened. His changeup is just a show-me pitch. The Phillies have pushed Rosso to stretch out his delivery more and want to see him attack hitters in the strike zone. His control is fringe-average and he walked eight batters in 9.2 innings in his major league debut.

THE FUTURE: Rosso profiles as a middle reliever in the majors. The Phillies hold out some hope he can be a back-end starter if he improves his changeup.

Year	Age	Club (League)	Class	W	L	ERA	G	GS	IP	H	HR	BB	SO	BB/9	SO/9	WHIP	AVG
2020	24	Philadelphia (NL)	MAJ	0	1	6.52	7	1	10	9	1	8	11	7.4	10.2	1.76	.243
Major League Totals				0	1	6.52	7	1	9	9	1	8	11	7.5	10.2	1.76	.243
Minor League Totals				23	10	2.80	62	60	322	259	25	111	360	3.1	10.1	1.15	.221

25 ABRAHAN GUTIERREZ, C

BA GRADE
40 Risk: High

Born: Oct. 31, 1999. **B-T:** R-R. **HT:** 6-2. **WT:** 214. **Signed:** Venezuela, 2017. **Signed by:** Carlos Salas.

TRACK RECORD: Gutierrez signed with the Phillies in 2017 after his contract with the Braves was voided when MLB penalized Atlanta for violating international signing rules. He fared well in the Rookie-level Gulf Coast League in 2018, but struggled to a .246/.314/.318 slash line in his first taste of full-season ball at low Class A Lakewood in 2019. Gutierrez spent 2020 working hard to improve his conditioning and added strength to his frame.

SCOUTING REPORT: Gutierrez is a line-drive hitter despite showing average raw power in batting practice. He does a solid job controlling the strike zone and rarely chases outside of it. While Gutierrez doesn't swing and miss much, he struggles to consistently make hard contact as a result of below-average bat speed and a long swing. The result most often is weak ground balls and popups. Defensively, Gutierrez receives well and offers a low target behind the plate. He handles pitchers well and has average arm strength, ultimately projecting as an average defender.

THE FUTURE: Gutierrez will attempt to turn his physical gains into better production. He projects as a backup catcher if he can quicken his bat speed and make harder contact.

Year	Age	Club (League)	Class	AVG	G	AB	R	H	2B	3B	HR	RBI	BB	SO	SB	OBP	SLG
2019	19	Lakewood (SAL)	LoA	.246	83	289	23	71	9	0	4	27	28	62	3	.314	.318
Minor League Totals				.269	159	580	62	156	28	1	6	69	48	99	5	.328	.352

26 ETHAN LINDOW, LHP

Born: Oct. 15, 1998. **B-T:** R-L. **HT:** 6-3. **WT:** 180. **Drafted:** HS—Locust Grove, Ga., 2017 (5th round). **Signed by:** Aaron Jersild.

TRACK RECORD: Lindow seemed destined for college until he began working out with Tom Glavine, whose son played travel ball with Lindow, before his senior year of high school. Glavine's instruction led to an uptick in Lindow's velocity and the sharpness of his breaking ball, leading the Phillies to draft him in the fifth round. Lindow went 5-4, 2.52 in 26 starts across the Class A levels in his full-season debut in 2019. The Phillies decided not to send him to the alternate training site or instructional league in 2020, opting instead to preserve his arm after he worked on his conditioning over the summer.

SCOUTING REPORT: Lindow has a solid four-pitch mix with plus control from the left side, but he's going to need to add velocity. Lindow's fastball sits just 89-90 mph and touches 93, although it's solid riding life helps it play up to a fringe-average pitch. His 73-77 mph curveball is his best secondary as an above-average offering with three-quarter break and depth. His changeup is also above-average at 82-84 mph with good fade and deception and his 81-83 mph slider is an average pitch that resembles a cutter. Lindow works quickly and hides the ball well in his delivery.

THE FUTURE: Lindow has performed at every stop and has the pitch mix to settle in the back of a rotation. Whether he adds more velocity will determine if he gets there.

Year	Age	Club (League)	Class	W	L	ERA	G	GS	IP	H	HR	BB	SO	BB/9	SO/9	WHIP	AVG
2019	20	Lakewood (SAL)	LoA	5	2	2.66	23	13	95	73	4	20	103	1.9	9.8	0.98	.184
	20	Clearwater (FSL)	HiA	0	2	1.69	3	3	16	17	0	2	16	1.1	9.0	1.19	.258
Minor League Totals				10	8	2.68	47	37	208	174	8	53	216	2.3	9.3	1.09	.224

27 JHAILYN ORTIZ, OF

Born: Nov. 18, 1998. **B-T:** R-R. **HT:** 6-3. **WT:** 264. **Signed:** Dominican Republic, 2015. **Signed by:** Sal Agostinelli.

TRACK RECORD: Signed out of the Dominican Republic for $4 million, Ortiz has shown light-tower power but struggled to make contact at every level. He's hit .227 in 1,167 minor league at-bats, capped by a .200 average at high Class A Clearwater in 2019. His only 2020 action came during instructional league.

SCOUTING REPORT: Ortiz takes huge swings to try and access his 70-grade power, but he does not have good timing and is far too rotational with his swing. He struggles adjusting to offspeed pitches and upper-end velocity and chases far too often. The Phillies have emphasized working on pitch-recognition skills as well as hitting the ball the other way. Even if he can make those improvements, it's hard to imagine him making enough contact to be a major leaguer. Ortiz is a below-average defender in right field and may be destined for first base. He is a below-average runner who will need to watch his conditioning after arriving at instructs weighing 264 pounds.

THE FUTURE: Ortiz does not currently project as a major leaguer in any capacity. His power may buy him time to figure things out.

Year	Age	Club (League)	Class	AVG	G	AB	R	H	2B	3B	HR	RBI	BB	SO	SB	OBP	SLG
2019	20	Clearwater (FSL)	HiA	.200	115	430	57	86	15	3	19	65	36	149	2	.272	.381
Minor League Totals				.227	319	1167	164	265	57	7	48	169	106	397	17	.307	.411

28 JONATHAN GUZMAN, SS

Born: Aug. 17, 1999. **B-T:** R-R. **HT:** 6-0. **WT:** 200. **Signed:** Dominican Republic, 2015. **Signed by:** Carlos Salas.

TRACK RECORD: Signed out of the Dominican Republic in 2015, Guzman slowly rose through the system and made his full-season debut in 2019, hitting .251/.298/.316 with three home runs and 31 stolen bases at low Class A Lakewood. He was included in the Phillies instructional league roster in 2020, where he worked on his plate discipline and overall approach.

SCOUTING REPORT: Regarded as the best defensive shortstop in the system, Guzman is a plus defender with strong range, smooth actions and plus arm strength. His bat is far behind his glove, however. Guzman is a well below-average hitter with bottom-of-the-scale power. He is attempting to increase his bat speed while working on his approach to be more patient and work counts better. Phillies officials feel he's made some improvement in that area and are encouraged by his ability to get the barrel on the ball. Guzman doesn't project to hit for much impact and is likely limited to a backup ceiling in the major leagues. He is a plus runner who can steal a lot of bases.

THE FUTURE: Guzman should head to high Class A in 2021. He needs to improve offensively in order to project as a reserve who can play multiple positions and is a threat on the basepaths.

Year	Age	Club (League)	Class	AVG	G	AB	R	H	2B	3B	HR	RBI	BB	SO	SB	OBP	SLG
2019	19	Lakewood (SAL)	LoA	.251	123	475	55	119	18	2	3	40	32	97	31	.298	.316
Minor League Totals				.252	294	1133	129	285	40	5	7	82	78	213	52	.303	.314

29 CARSON RAGSDALE, RHP

BA GRADE
40 Risk: High

Born: May 25, 1998. **B-T:** R-R. **HT:** 6-8. **WT:** 217. **Drafted:** South Florida, 2020 (4th round). **Signed by:** Bryce Harman.

TRACK RECORD: Ragsdale worked out of the bullpen at South Florida his first two seasons and missed all of 2019 after having Tommy John surgery. He returned in 2020 and blossomed in a starting role, posting a 2.84 ERA with 37 strikeouts in 19 innings. The Phillies drafted Ragsdale in the fourth round and signed him for a below-slot $225,000. He made his organizational debut in instructional league in the fall.

SCOUTING REPORT: Despite a huge 6-foot-8 frame, Ragsdale has solid body control and the Phillies believe he has a chance to start. He gets good extension and has a repeatable, three-quarter delivery, although he does have some length to his arm action. Ragsdale's fastball sat 90-93 mph in college and humped up to 94-96 mph during short stints in instructional league. He pairs his above-average fastball with a curveball that some believe is average, although the Phillies think could be a plus pitch. His changeup is fringy at best and will need to show improvement for him to stay a starter. He has fringe-average control.

THE FUTURE: Ragsdale will make his professional debut in 2021. If his changeup and control don't improve, he has a future as a power reliever.

Year	Age	Club (League)	Class	W	L	ERA	G	GS	IP	H	HR	BB	SO	BB/9	SO/9	WHIP	AVG
2020	22	Did not play—No minor league season															

30 MAURICIO LLOVERA, RHP

BA GRADE
40 Risk: High

Born: April 17, 1996. **B-T:** R-R. **HT:** 5-11. **WT:** 224. **Signed:** Venezuela, 2014. **Signed by:** Carlos Salas.

TRACK RECORD: Llovera first jumped on radars for his power fastball in 2017 and moved full-time into the rotation in 2018 at high Class A Clearwater. He pitched well there, but his fastball velocity decreased in 2019 at Double-A Reading and he missed part of the season with forearm tightness. Llovera spent most of 2020 at the Phillies alternate training site. He received his first major league callup on Sept. 6 and allowed five hits and four runs in his lone inning of work.

SCOUTING REPORT: After brushing 99 mph at his peak, Llovera's drop in velocity in 2019 was alarming and he did not come close to throwing as hard at either the alternate site or the majors. His fastball now averages 93 mph and tops out at 95. His average slider sits 80-83 mph and his changeup sits in the mid 80s with good deception and arm speed. Llovera creates good angle in his delivery and hides the ball well, but he has just fringe-average control.

THE FUTURE: Llovera's fastball velocity will be something to monitor. He profiles as a middle reliever either way.

Year	Age	Club (League)	Class	W	L	ERA	G	GS	IP	H	HR	BB	SO	BB/9	SO/9	WHIP	AVG
2020	24	Philadelphia (NL)	MAJ	0	0	36.00	1	0	1	5	0	1	1	9.0	9.0	6.00	.625
Major League Totals				0	0	36.00	1	0	1	5	0	1	1	9.0	9.0	6.00	.625
Minor League Totals				22	20	3.45	89	64	372	316	24	124	402	3.0	9.7	1.18	.228

MORE PROSPECTS TO KNOW

31 EDUAR SEGOVIA, RHP

SLEEPER

After impressive stints in the Dominican Summer League and Rookie-level Gulf Coast League in 2018 and 2019, respectively, Segovia's fastball was up to 97 mph at instructional league to go along with an average to above-average slider.

32 NOAH SKIRROW, RHP

Skirrow has a fastball that has topped out in the mid-90s but sat 87-92 mph in 2020, part of the reason he went undrafted out of Liberty. He pairs the pitch with a strong breaking ball, giving him two average or better pitches if he can regain his previous velocity.

33 BEN BROWN, RHP

Brown pitched well before having Tommy John surgery in 2019. He returned to the mound during 2020 instructional league and he showed a fastball up to 95 mph with a with a solid breaking ball.

34 MATT VIERLING, OF

Vierling is a toolsy outfielder who can play all three outfield spots and was hitting the ball hard at instructs, with some exit velocities over 110 mph.

35 DOMINIC PIPKIN, RHP

Pipkin has an explosive fastball that tops out at 98 mph to go with a mid-70s curveball that has the potential to be above average. His control and command remain question marks.

36 JONATHAN HUGHES, RHP

The nondrafted free agent signee from Georgia Tech impressed officials at instructional league with a 94-96 mph fastball, a high-spin breaking ball and a potentially average changeup.

37 BLAKE BROWN, RHP

The nondrafted free agent from UNC Asheville impressed at instructional league with a fastball that reaches triple-digits to go along with two fringe-average secondaries.

38 BARON RADCLIFF, OF

The team's 2020 fifth-rounder from Georgia Tech, Radcliff drew rave reviews for his 80-grade power and bat speed at instructional league. He needs to improve at making consistent contact and dealing with offspeed pitches.

39 JAKE MCKENNA, LHP

The prep lefthander from New Jersey has a good frame at 6-foot-6 with some projection remaining, a curveball that has the potential to be above average and a fringe-average fastball up to 91 mph.

40 BILLY SULLIVAN, RHP

Sullivan was excellent as a Delaware freshman but missed all of 2019 and 2020 after having Tommy John surgery. The nondrafted free agent signee returned to the mound in instructional league and showed a fastball that averaged 96 mph and touched 99 mph to go with an effective slider.

TOP PROSPECTS OF THE DECADE

Year	Player, Pos	2020 Org
2011	Domonic Brown, OF	Did not play
2012	Trevor May, RHP	Twins
2013	Jesse Biddle, LHP	Reds
2014	Maikel Franco, 3B	Royals
2015	J.P. Crawford, SS	Mariners
2016	J.P. Crawford, SS	Mariners
2017	J.P. Crawford, SS	Mariners
2018	J.P. Crawford, SS	Mariners
2019	Sixto Sanchez, RHP	Marlins
2020	Spencer Howard, RHP	Phillies

TOP DRAFT PICKS OF THE DECADE

Year	Player, Pos	2020 Org
2011	Larry Greene, OF (1st round supp)	Did not play
2012	Shane Watson, RHP (1st round supp)	Did not play
2013	J.P. Crawford, SS	Mariners
2014	Aaron Nola, RHP	Phillies
2015	Cornelius Randolph, SS	Phillies
2016	Mickey Moniak, OF	Phillies
2017	Adam Haseley, OF	Phillies
2018	Alec Bohm, 3B	Phillies
2019	Bryson Stott, SS	Phillies
2020	Mick Abel, RHP	Phillies

DEPTH CHART

PHILADELPHIA PHILLIES

TOP 2021 ROOKIES	RANK
Spencer Howard, RHP	1
BREAKOUT PROSPECTS	**RANK**
Erik Miller, LHP	14
Logan Simmons, SS	16
Logan O'Hoppe, C	17

SOURCE OF TOP 30 TALENT

Homegrown	28	Acquired	2
College	6	Trades	2
Junior college	3	Rule 5 draft	0
High school	6	Independent leagues	0
Nondrafted free agents	0	Free agents/waivers	0
International	13		

LF
Mickey Moniak (13)

CF
Yhoswar Garcia (7)
Simon Muzziotti (8)
Johan Rojas (9)

RF
Matt Vierling
Baron Radcliff

3B
Logan Simmons (16)

SS
Bryson Stott (3)
Luis Garcia (6)
Nick Maton (10)
Casey Martin (11)
Jamari Baylor (22)
Jonathan Guzman (28)
Arquimedes Gamboa

2B
Wilfredo Flores
Daniel Brito
Nicolas Torres

1B
Jhailyn Ortiz (27)

C
Rafael Marchan (5)
Logan O'Hoppe (17)
Andrick Nava (19)
Abrahan Gutierrez (25)
Rodolfo Duran

LHP

LHSP	LHRP
Erik Miller (14)	Cristopher Sanchez (18)
Ethan Lindow (26)	JoJo Romero (20)
Cole Irvin	Damon Jones (21)
David Parkinson	Zach Warren
Jake McKenna	Kyle Dohy
Kyle Young	

RHP

RHSP	RHRP
Spencer Howard (1)	Connor Brogdon (23)
Mick Abel (2)	Ramon Rosso (24)
Adonis Medina (12)	Carson Ragsdale (29)
Francisco Morales (4)	Mauricio Llovera (30)
Enyel de los Santos (15)	Noah Skirrow
Eduar Segovia	Victor Santos
Ben Brown	Colton Eastman
Blake Brown	Carlos Betancourt
Billy Sullivan	Ian Hamilton
Jonathan Hughes	
Buddy Hayward	

Pittsburgh Pirates

BY TIM WILLIAMS

The Pirates are in transition.

Ben Cherington took over as general manager at the end of 2019 and was tasked with getting the organization back to the point when it had one of the best teams in the majors and one of the best farm systems in the game.

The Pirates finished with the worst record in the major leagues at 19-41 in the pandemic-shortened 2020 season, but Cherington added several talented prospects to the system while updating the organization's use of analytics and technology to assist with player development.

Cherington worked quickly, adding four of the organization's Top 10 Prospects in less than a year. He acquired shortstop Liover Peguero and righthander Brennan Malone in a January 2020 trade with Arizona for Starling Marte. Peguero was fresh off ranking as the No. 1 prospect in the Rookie-level Pioneer League. Malone was Arizona's first-round pick in 2019 out of high school.

Six months later, Pittsburgh added New Mexico State shortstop Nick Gonzales and South Carolina righthander Carmen Mlodzinski in the shortened five-round 2020 draft.

In Pittsburgh, righthander Mitch Keller and third baseman Ke'Bryan Hayes both made impacts to give the Pirates young cornerstones to build on. Keller finished an injury-shortened season on a strong note with 11 hitless innings over his final two starts. Hayes was impressive in limited play, winning National League rookie of the month honors in September after batting .376/.442/.682 with five home runs in 85 at-bats. His OPS ranked fourth best in the majors in September.

The system's pitching depth is stronger than its position depth. Righthander Quinn Priester, the club's first-round pick out of high school in 2019, leads the way on the pitching side after bumping his fastball up to the upper 90s in 2020. He received an invitation to the Pirates' alternate training site in Altoona, Pa., before his 20th birthday. Priester is joined by hard-throwing righthanders Cody Bolton and Tahnaj Thomas in addition to Malone and Mlodzinski.

Oneil Cruz leads the position player pool, which received a boost with the additions of Peguero and Gonzales. That trio could form three-quarters of the Pirates' infield of the future, though Cruz's status is unclear after he was involved in an offseason motor vehicle collision that killed three people in his native Dominican Republic.

The Pirates have a great opportunity to add to the mix. The consolation prize for their miserable 2020 season is the No. 1 overall pick in the 2021 draft, a year where a number of tantalizing pitching prospects are available, including Vanderbilt righthanders Kumar Rocker and Jack Leiter.

The biggest issue for the Pirates under former GM Neal Huntington wasn't that they lacked talent, but that they couldn't maximize that talent in the majors. Cherington has already started overhauling Pittsburgh's player development processes, making several changes including the reassignment of farm director Larry Broadway.

The 2021 season will be a key one to watch for the development changes in the system, and to see which prospects are on track to join Hayes and Keller in 2022 and beyond. ■

MARY DECICCO/MLB PHOTOS VIA GETTY IMAGES

General manager Ben Cherington has added talent and analytical insight to the organization.

PROJECTED 2024 LINEUP

Position	Player	Age
Catcher	Jacob Stallings	34
First Base	Josh Bell	31
Second Base	Nick Gonzales	25
Third Base	Ke'Bryan Hayes	27
Shortstop	Liover Peguero	23
Left Field	Bryan Reynolds	29
Center Field	Cole Tucker	27
Right Field	Oneil Cruz	25
Designated Hitter	Colin Moran	31
No. 1 Starter	Mitch Keller	28
No. 2 Starter	Quinn Priester	23
No. 3 Starter	Joe Musgrove	31
No. 4 Starter	Steven Brault	32
No. 5 Starter	Cody Bolton	26
Closer	Tahnaj Thomas	25

1 KE'BRYAN HAYES, 3B

Born: Jan. 28, 1997. **B-T:** R-R. **HT:** 5-10. **WT:** 205.
Drafted: HS—Tomball, Texas, 2015 (1st round).
Signed by: Tyler Stohr.

TRACK RECORD: The Pirates drafted Hayes with the 32nd overall pick in 2015. He's the son of former major league third baseman Charlie Hayes, who played for the Pirates in 1996 and spent 14 years in the majors. His brother Tyree also pitched professionally. Hayes entered the 2020 season as the Pirates' top position prospect but tested positive for Covid-19 during summer camp, which set his progress back. He returned in late July and made his major league debut in September, exploding onto the scene with numbers that were among the best of the rookie class. He hit .376/.422/.682 with seven doubles, two triples and five home runs in 95 plate appearances. His 1.124 OPS ranked fourth among qualified batters in September, when he won National League rookie of the month, providing hope for Pirates fans looking for a young prospect to emerge as a cornerstone of their rebuild.

SCOUTING REPORT: Hayes' calling card has long been his defense at third base. He has a chance to win multiple Gold Glove awards with smooth hands, quick reactions, good routes to the ball and plus arm strength. He's an asset defensively for the Pirates whether they want a traditionally strong third baseman or if they want to get creative with defensive shifts. Hayes has the range to play shortstop in a pinch and is a great candidate to move around the field in different defensive alignments. Hayes' offense has been improving the last few years and his power took a big leap in 2020. Hayes made adjustments to his swing mechanics by opening up his stance and changing his hand position. His biggest change was mental. He prioritized hard contact, as opposed to just making contact, and worked with his father during the coronavirus quarantine period to get the ball in the air more often. The result was the most power than Hayes has had in his career without sacrificing his average or plate discipline. Hayes' video-game September numbers will come down—his .450 batting average on balls in play is one of the highest in history for a batter with at least 90 PAs—but he is capable of hitting .300 with 15-20 homers a year with a high on-base percentage. Hayes is an above-average runner who adds value on the bases in addition to his bat and glove.

TOP ROOKIE

JUSTIN BERL/GETTY IMAGES

BA GRADE 60 Risk: Medium

SCOUTING GRADES Hit: 60. Power: 50. Run: 55. Field: 70. Arm: 60.

Projected future grades on 20-80 scouting scale.

BEST TOOLS

Best Hitter for Average	Nick Gonzales
Best Power Hitter	Oneil Cruz
Best Strike-Zone Discipline	Ke'Bryan Hayes
Fastest Baserunner	Jasiah Dixon
Best Athlete	Oneil Cruz
Best Fastball	Blake Cederlind
Best Curveball	Quinn Priester
Best Slider	Cody Bolton
Best Changeup	James Marvel
Best Control	Aaron Shortridge
Best Defensive Catcher	Christian Kelly
Best Defensive Infielder	Ke'Bryan Hayes
Best Infield Arm	Oneil Cruz
Best Defensive Outfielder	Jared Oliva
Best Outfield Arm	Travis Swaggerty

THE FUTURE: Hayes has the potential to be an offensive cornerstone the Pirates build their lineup around. He obviously won't hit .376 over a full season as pitchers adjust to him, but a few .300 seasons are not out of the question. Hayes could be a perennial all-star third baseman who hits for average and power and wins Gold Gloves with regularity thanks to his range and plus arm. He's also one of the fastest third basemen in the game, too, according to MLB Statcast. Hayes will be the Pirates' Opening Day third baseman in 2021 and figures to keep that status as long as he remains in Pittsburgh. ■

Year	Age	Club (League)	Class	AVG	G	AB	R	H	2B	3B	HR	RBI	BB	SO	SB	OBP	SLG
2017	20	Bradenton (FSL)	HiA	.278	108	421	66	117	16	7	2	43	41	76	27	.345	.363
2018	21	Altoona (EL)	AA	.293	117	437	64	128	31	7	7	47	57	84	12	.375	.444
2019	22	Indianapolis (IL)	AAA	.265	110	427	64	113	30	2	10	53	43	90	12	.336	.415
	22	West Virginia (NYP)	SS	.111	3	9	1	1	1	0	0	2	2	2	1	.250	.222
2020	23	Pittsburgh (NL)	MAJ	.376	24	85	17	32	7	2	5	11	9	20	1	.442	.682
Major League Totals				.376	24	85	17	32	7	2	5	11	9	20	1	.442	.682
Minor League Totals				.279	461	1731	254	483	96	18	25	202	188	335	66	.354	.399

2 ONEIL CRUZ, SS

MIKE CARLSON/MLB PHOTOS VIA GETTY IMAGES

BA GRADE **60** Risk: High

Born: Oct. 4, 1998. **B-T:** L-R. **HT:** 6-7. **WT:** 210. **Signed:** Dominican Republic, 2015. **Signed by:** Patrick Guerrero/Franklin Taveras/Bob Engle (Dodgers).

TRACK RECORD: Cruz signed with the Dodgers for $950,000 in 2015 and was traded to the Pirates two years later for Tony Watson. He cemented his status as the most athletic and dynamic prospect in the Pirates' system during his ascent to Double-A in 2019 and spent the 2020 season at the alternate training site. He was arrested in his native Dominican Republic in September for allegedly driving under the influence in a car crash that killed three people.

SCOUTING REPORT: Though it might seem odd to see a 6-foot-7 player at shortstop, Cruz can handle the position. He has plus speed and moves around well at short despite his height. Cruz has a plus arm and the Pirates have better infield options, so he may end up in right field in the future. Cruz is a dynamic prospect due to his elite raw power that comes from his long arms and strength in his hands and wrists. He has hit for average in the minors, but because of his lanky body and long levers, there are long-term concerns about whether pitchers will find holes in his strike zone to exploit.

THE FUTURE: Cruz faces up to five years in prison if convicted. If he's able to play, he has the tools to anchor the middle of the Pirates' lineup with power and speed.

SCOUTING GRADES: **Hitting:** 50 **Power:** 70 **Running:** 60 **Fielding:** 50 **Arm:** 60

Year	Age	Club (League)	Class	AVG	G	AB	R	H	2B	3B	HR	RBI	BB	SO	SB	OBP	SLG
2017	18	Great Lakes (MWL)	LoA	.240	89	342	51	82	9	1	8	36	28	110	8	.293	.342
	18	West Virginia (SAL)	LoA	.218	16	55	9	12	2	1	2	8	8	22	0	.317	.400
2018	19	West Virginia (SAL)	LoA	.286	103	402	66	115	25	7	14	59	34	100	11	.343	.488
2019	20	Pirates (GCL)	R	.600	3	10	0	6	1	0	0	1	1	1	1	.636	.700
	20	Bradenton (FSL)	HiA	.301	35	136	21	41	6	1	7	16	8	38	7	.345	.515
	20	Altoona (EL)	AA	.269	35	119	14	32	8	3	1	17	15	35	3	.346	.412
Minor League Totals				.274	336	1251	189	343	69	18	32	160	116	350	41	.335	.435

3 NICK GONZALES, SS/2B

BA GRADE **55** Risk: High

Born: May 27, 1999. **B-T:** R-R. **HT:** 5-10. **WT:** 190. **Drafted:** New Mexico State, 2020 (1st round). **Signed by:** Derrick Van Dusen.

TRACK RECORD: Gonzales became the first draftee of the Ben Cherington era for the Pirates, signing for $5,432,400 as the seventh overall pick in 2020. That capped off an impressive transformation after he joined New Mexico State as a walk-on and went on to lead the nation in hitting as a sophomore by batting .432/.532/.773 in 2019. Gonzales proved he has no mere high-altitude mirage that summer when he hit .351 with seven home runs in the wood-bat Cape Cod League and claimed MVP honors. He hit 12 home runs in 82 plate appearances in his brief junior season before the coronavirus pandemic shut everything down.

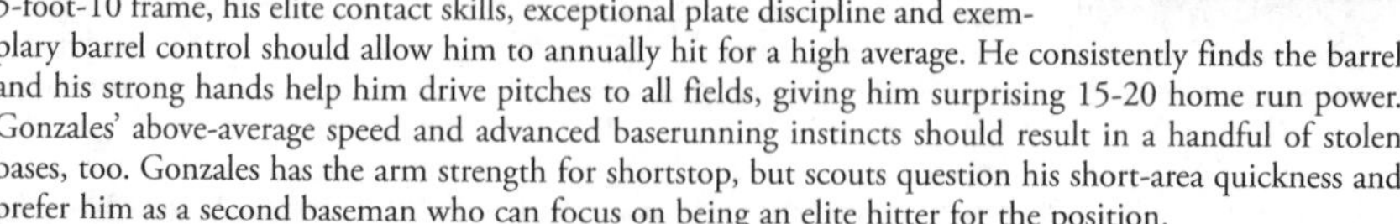

SCOUTING REPORT: Gonzales' carrying tool is his bat. Despite his slight, 5-foot-10 frame, his elite contact skills, exceptional plate discipline and exemplary barrel control should allow him to annually hit for a high average. He consistently finds the barrel and his strong hands help him drive pitches to all fields, giving him surprising 15-20 home run power. Gonzales' above-average speed and advanced baserunning instincts should result in a handful of stolen bases, too. Gonzales has the arm strength for shortstop, but scouts question his short-area quickness and prefer him as a second baseman who can focus on being an elite hitter for the position.

THE FUTURE: Scouts view Gonzales as a future all-star second baseman capable of competing for batting titles. He is advanced enough to jump on the fast track to the majors and arrive in Pittsburgh at some point in 2022.

SCOUTING GRADES: **Hitting:** 70 **Power:** 45 **Running:** 55 **Fielding:** 50 **Arm:** 50

Year	Age	Club (League)	Class	AVG	G	AB	R	H	2B	3B	HR	RBI	BB	SO	SB	OBP	SLG
2020	21	Did not play—No minor league season															

4 QUINN PRIESTER, RHP

Born: Sept. 15, 2000. **B-T:** R-R. **HT:** 6-3. **WT:** 195. **Drafted:** HS—Cary, Ill., 2019 (1st round). **Signed by:** Anthony Wycklendt.

MIKE JANES/FOUR SEAM IMAGES

BA GRADE
60 Risk: Extreme

TRACK RECORD: The Pirates drafted Priester out of high school with the 18th overall pick in 2019. He hadn't even turned 20 when the Pirates sent him to their alternate training site in 2020, but he was impressive enough facing some of the best hitting prospects in the system to show he may be a fast mover despite his youth.

SCOUTING REPORT: Priester's fastball jumped to 96-98 mph in short stints at the alternate site, an encouraging development after he sat in the low 90s and touched 97 mph in his pro debut. He throws both a two-seam fastball with movement and a four-seamer he controls better. Priester complements his fastballs up with a plus low-80s curveball he can land for strikes or get swings and misses with. He improved his changeup by learning to consistently throw it like a fastball. Priester improved his control by staying taller in his delivery and keeping his upper and lower body in sync. He's made strides figuring out how to sequence and tunnel each pitch to improve his entire mix. In addition to his physical talents, Priester is a studious learner who quickly picks up the game's newest trends on pitch mechanics and deception.

THE FUTURE: The Pirates are prepared to move Priester aggressively with his stuff and smarts. He has the potential to eventually join Mitch Keller at the front of the Pirates' rotation.

SCOUTING GRADES: **Fastball:** 60 **Slider:** 40 **Curveball:** 60 **Changeup:** 50 **Control:** 55

Year	Age	Club (League)	Class	W	L	ERA	G	GS	IP	H	HR	BB	SO	BB/9	SO/9	WHIP	AVG
2019	18	Pirates (GCL)	R	1	1	3.03	8	7	33	29	1	10	37	2.8	10.2	1.19	.207
	18	West Virginia (NYP)	SS	0	0	4.50	1	1	4	3	0	4	4	9.0	9.0	1.75	.158
Minor League Totals				1	1	3.19	9	8	36	32	1	14	41	3.4	10.1	1.25	.235

5 LIOVER PEGUERO, SS

Born: Dec. 31, 2000. **B-T:** R-R. **HT:** 6-1. **WT:** 160. **Signed:** Dominican Republic, 2017. **Signed by:** Cesar Geronimo (D-backs).

HOPS

BA GRADE
55 Risk: Very High

TRACK RECORD: The first big move Pirates general manager Ben Cherington made was to trade center fielder Starling Marte to the D-backs for Peguero and righthanded pitching prospect Brennan Malone in January 2020. The previous year, Peguero ranked as the No. 1 prospect in the Rookie-level Pioneer League and finished the campaign at short-season Hillsboro. The Pirates sent him to their alternate training site in 2020 to challenge him against older competition.

SCOUTING REPORT: Peguero is a dynamic athlete with a long track record of hitting the ball hard. He has a strong, wiry build and has a natural feel for finding the barrel. He has worked the last two years to tone down his aggressive approach and be more selective at the plate. If those improvements continue, he has the feel for quality contact to be a plus hitter with average power as he fills out. Peguero improved his defense at shortstop with Arizona prior to the trade and continued his work at the position all year with the Pirates. He has above-average speed and the long strides to handle the outfield if he has to move.

THE FUTURE: Peguero's bat will always be above his glove, but he has a chance to be the Pirates' shortstop of the future as long his defensive strides continue. He is slated to jump to full-season ball in 2021.

SCOUTING GRADES: **Hitting:** 60 **Power:** 50 **Running:** 55 **Fielding:** 50 **Arm:** 50

Year	Age	Club (League)	Class	AVG	G	AB	R	H	2B	3B	HR	RBI	BB	SO	SB	OBP	SLG
2018	17	D-backs1 (DSL)	R	.309	22	81	14	25	3	3	1	16	6	12	4	.356	.457
	17	Diamondbacks (AZL)	R	.197	19	66	8	13	0	0	0	5	5	17	3	.254	.197
2019	18	Hillsboro (NWL)	SS	.262	22	84	13	22	4	2	0	11	8	17	3	.333	.357
	18	Missoula (PIO)	R	.364	38	143	34	52	7	3	5	27	12	34	8	.410	.559
Minor League Totals				.299	101	374	69	112	14	8	6	59	31	80	18	.354	.428

6 CODY BOLTON, RHP

PITTSBURGH PIRATES

BA GRADE
50 Risk: High

Born: June 19, 1998. **B-T:** R-R. **HT:** 6-3. **WT:** 185. **Drafted:** HS—Tracy, Calif., 2017 (6th round). **Signed by:** Mike Sansoe.

TRACK RECORD: The Pirates drafted Bolton in the sixth round in 2017 and signed him for an over-slot $300,000 bonus. He was shut down with forearm soreness after nine starts in 2018 and received a platelet-rich plasma injection, but he came back throwing harder with better control in 2019 and vaulted up to Double-A. He spent 2020 at the alternate training site in Altoona, Pa.

SCOUTING REPORT: Bolton has grown into his projectable frame and now sits 93-96 mph on a consistent basis, while touching 98. He has both a four-seam fastball and a two-seamer he keeps in the bottom part of the zone in the low 90s, forcing hitters to look for two different fastballs in two different parts of the zone. Bolton added a cutter in 2019 and has developed it into a potentially above-average pitch that pairs nicely with his two-seamer. His average changeup gives him a competitive offering against lefthanded hitters and gives him the third pitch needed to start. Bolton pounds the strike zone out of his low three-quarters arm slot and keeps his walks to a minimum.

THE FUTURE: Bolton has the body, stuff and control to profile as a No. 4 or 5 type starter. If his development stalls, he has a fallback as a power reliever with his fastball/cutter combination.

SCOUTING GRADES: **Fastball:** 60 **Slider:** 55 **Changeup:** 50 **Control:** 55

Year	Age	Club (League)	Class	W	L	ERA	G	GS	IP	H	HR	BB	SO	BB/9	SO/9	WHIP	AVG
2017	19	Pirates (GCL)	R	0	2	3.16	9	9	26	23	1	8	22	2.8	7.7	1.21	.213
2018	20	West Virginia (SAL)	LoA	3	3	3.65	9	9	44	43	6	7	45	1.4	9.1	1.13	.240
2019	21	Altoona (EL)	AA	2	3	5.85	9	9	40	37	6	16	33	3.6	7.4	1.33	.222
	21	Bradenton (FSL)	HiA	6	3	1.61	12	12	62	39	1	14	69	2.0	10.1	0.86	.173
Minor League Totals				11	11	3.36	39	39	171	142	14	45	169	2.4	8.9	1.09	.222

7 TAHNAJ THOMAS, RHP

PIRATES

BA GRADE
50 Risk: High

Born: June 16, 1999. **B-T:** R-R. **HT:** 6-4. **WT:** 190. **Signed:** Bahamas, 2016. **Signed by:** Koby Perez (Indians).

TRACK RECORD: Thomas trained as a shortstop in the Bahamas and moved to the mound only after signing with the Indians for $200,000 in 2016. The Pirates acquired Thomas in the November 2018 that trade sent Jordan Luplow and Max Moroff to Cleveland. Thomas' velocity spiked and his control improved after the trade, helping him emerge as one of the top pitchers in the Rookie-level Appalachian League in 2019.

SCOUTING REPORT: Thomas hasn't pitched in a live game since 2019 because of the coronavirus pandemic, but he was sitting 95-99 mph and touching 101 with Bristol at the end of that season. His fastball gets swings and misses with plus life up in the zone, and he has steadily improved his control to become an average strike-thrower. Thomas relies heavily on his fastball, but his slider flashes above-average potential and generates swings and misses at its best. His changeup is a fringe-average offering he uses sparingly.

THE FUTURE: Thomas has the kind of overpowering fastball that dominates hitters, but he needs to refine his secondary pitches. He has a chance to stick as a starter if he can improve his changeup or find another offspeed pitch. If not, he can be a dominant reliever with his fastball/slider combination.

SCOUTING GRADES: **Fastball:** 70 **Slider:** 55 **Changeup:** 45 **Control:** 50

Year	Age	Club (League)	Class	W	L	ERA	G	GS	IP	H	HR	BB	SO	BB/9	SO/9	WHIP	AVG
2017	18	Indians (DSL)	R	0	2	3.38	3	3	5	3	0	8	5	13.5	8.4	2.06	.111
	18	Indians 1 (AZL)	R	0	3	6.00	13	10	33	35	4	25	29	6.8	7.9	1.82	.227
2018	19	Indians 1 (AZL)	R	0	0	4.58	8	6	20	13	2	10	27	4.6	12.4	1.17	.163
2019	20	Bristol (APP)	R	2	3	3.17	12	12	48	40	5	14	59	2.6	11.0	1.12	.200
Minor League Totals				2	8	4.32	36	31	106	91	11	57	120	4.8	10.2	1.39	.230

8 BRENNAN MALONE, RHP

ZACHARY LUCY/FOUR SEAM IMAGES

BA GRADE **55** Risk: Extreme

Born: Sept. 8, 2000. **B-T:** R-R. **HT:** 6-4. **WT:** 205. **Drafted:** HS—Bradenton, Fla., 2019 (1st round). **Signed by:** Matt Mercurio (D-backs).

TRACK RECORD: The D-backs drafted Malone with the 33rd pick in the 2019 draft and signed him for an above-slot $2.2 million to keep him from a North Carolina commitment. The Pirates acquired him with Liover Peguero for Starling Marte in January 2020. Malone reported to the Pirates' alternate training site in Altoona, Pa., after the coronavirus pandemic canceled the minor league season, but he was never cleared for on-field activity.

SCOUTING REPORT: Malone is a physical, projectable pitcher still learning to harness his potent stuff. His fastball sits at 93 mph and touches the upper 90s with heavy sink, and his slider is a potential plus pitch with late, sharp break. He focused on developing his curveball during the shutdown and transformed it from a slurvy pitch to a spike-curveball that shows average potential. His changeup isn't consistent but flashes average potential. Malone has a strong, durable frame and an athletic delivery, but he can be a bit wild and spent the shutdown working to shorten his arm path in an attempt to throw more strikes more consistently.

THE FUTURE: Malone made his Pirates debut in instructional league and should see full-season ball in 2021. He has mid-rotation potential but is a long way from that ceiling.

SCOUTING GRADES: **Fastball:** 60 **Slider:** 60 **Curveball:** 50 **Changeup:** 50 **Control:** 45

Year	Age	Club (League)	Class	W	L	ERA	G	GS	IP	H	HR	BB	SO	BB/9	SO/9	WHIP	AVG
2019	18	Hillsboro (NWL)	SS	0	0	0.00	1	0	1	0	0	0	1	0.0	9.0	0.00	.000
	18	Diamondbacks (AZL)	R	1	2	5.14	6	3	7	4	0	5	7	6.4	9.0	1.29	.133
Minor League Totals				1	2	4.50	7	3	8	4	0	5	8	5.6	9.0	1.13	.148

9 JI-HWAN BAE, SS

GRASSHOPPERS/JAK KERLEY

BA GRADE **50** Risk: High

Born: July 26, 1999. **B-T:** L-R. **HT:** 6-1. **WT:** 170. **Signed:** South Korea, 2018. **Signed by:** Fu-chun Chiang/Tony Harris.

TRACK RECORD: Bae originally signed with the Braves but was declared a free agent after Major League Baseball ruled the Braves violated international signing rules. The Pirates signed him in early 2018 for $1.25 million. Bae was convicted of assaulting his girlfriend in South Korea and served a 30-game suspension during the 2019 season. He returned to low Class A Greensboro in late May and won the South Atlantic League batting title with a .323 average. The Pirates brought him to their alternate training site in 2020.

SCOUTING REPORT: Bae projects as a prototypical top-of-the-order shortstop with a contact bat and plus speed. He makes some of the best contact in the system and uses his speed to beat out infield singles and take extra bases when he drives the ball into the gaps. Bae lacks home run power with his slight build, so his slugging contributions will come from doubles and triples. Bae has the range to be an above-average defender at shortstop, but his lack of arm strength raises questions about his ability to stick at the position. His assault conviction raises obvious concerns about his makeup.

THE FUTURE: Bae has a chance to develop into a table-setter at the top of the order or a No. 8 or 9 hitter who provides value with his speed and defense. He may see Double-A in 2021.

SCOUTING GRADES: **Hitting:** 60 **Power:** 30 **Running:** 70 **Fielding:** 55 **Arm:** 40

Year	Age	Club (League)	Class	AVG	G	AB	R	H	2B	3B	HR	RBI	BB	SO	SB	OBP	SLG
2018	18	Pirates (GCL)	R	.271	35	129	24	35	6	2	0	13	15	16	10	.362	.349
2019	19	Greensboro (SAL)	LoA	.323	86	328	69	106	25	5	0	38	43	77	31	.403	.430
Minor League Totals				.309	121	457	93	141	31	7	0	51	58	93	41	.391	.407

10 CARMEN MLODZINSKI, RHP

ALLEN SHARPE

BA GRADE
50 **Risk: High**

Born: Feb. 19, 1999. **B-T:** R-R. **HT:** 6-2. **WT:** 231. **Drafted:** South Carolina, 2020 (1st round supplemental). **Signed by:** Cam Murphy.

TRACK RECORD: Mlodzinski was one of the 2020 draft's biggest question marks due to a lack of track record. He suffered a broken foot that limited him to three starts in 2019, made six starts in the Cape Cod League the following summer and had just four outings before the coronavirus pandemic shut down the 2020 college season. His stuff was undeniable, though, and the Pirates drafted him 31st overall and signed him for $2.05 million to turn pro as a redshirt sophomore.

SCOUTING REPORT: Mlodzinski throws a heavy sinking fastball that sits 92-94 mph and has reached 98. He throws a slider and a cutter that have flashed plus potential, especially during an impressive performance in the Cape. Both pitches were less sharp in the spring, however, with the slider lacking depth and tilt, and his cutter sitting at a reduced 89-91 mph. Mlodzinski has a fringe-average curveball and a below-average changeup that need to be improved. He throws strikes and generates a lot of ground balls with his fastball, but he's still trying to find a consistent swing-and-miss pitch.

THE FUTURE: Mlodzinski is capable of being a groundball-oriented starter at the back of a rotation. He needs to find a consistent second pitch.

SCOUTING GRADES: **Fastball:** 60 **Slider:** 55 **Cutter:** 55 **Changeup:** 40 **Control:** 55

Year	Age	Club (League)	Class	W	L	ERA	G	GS	IP	H	HR	BB	SO	BB/9	K/9	WHIP	AVG
2020	21	Did not play—No minor league season															

11 TRAVIS SWAGGERTY, OF

BA GRADE
50 **Risk: High**

Born: Aug. 19, 1997. **B-T:** L-L. **HT:** 5-10. **WT:** 183. **Drafted:** South Alabama, 2018 (1st round). **Signed by:** Darren Mazeroski.

TRACK RECORD: The Pirates drafted Swaggerty 10th overall in 2018 and gave him a $4.4 million bonus based on the power-speed combination he showed at South Alabama. Swaggerty's speed has translated to pro ball, but his power has not. Swaggerty hit a combined .257/.339/.381 in his first two seasons, topping out at high Class A. The Pirates brought him to their alternate training site in 2020.

SCOUTING REPORT: Swaggerty has the potential for average or better tools across the board, but he simply doesn't make enough contact. He tends to sell out for power, leading to a lot of swings and misses and a decline in his overall offensive game. Swaggerty worked to clean up his hitting mechanics, but the lost 2020 minor league season didn't give him a chance to show off the results of his work. He draws plenty of walks, which allows his plus speed to play on the bases. Swaggerty's defense is ahead of his offense. He's a plus defender with the range and above-average arm strength to be the Pirates' center fielder of the future.

THE FUTURE: Swaggerty has to start making more contact. If he can, he has the tools to be an everyday outfielder.

Year	Age	Club (League)	Class	AVG	G	AB	R	H	2B	3B	HR	RBI	BB	SO	SB	OBP	SLG
2019	21	Bradenton (FSL)	HiA	.265	121	457	79	121	20	3	9	40	57	116	23	.347	.381
Minor League Totals				.257	173	658	107	169	30	5	14	60	79	174	32	.339	.381

12 JARED JONES, RHP

BA GRADE
55 **Risk: Extreme**

Born: Aug. 6, 2001. **B-T:** L-R. **HT:** 6-1. **WT:** 180. **Drafted:** HS—La Mirada, Calif., 2020 (2nd round). **Signed by:** Brian Tracy.

TRACK RECORD: Jones was a well-known draft prospect after playing for USA Baseball's Junior National Team three times as a two-way player. The Pirates drafted him 44th overall as a pitcher in 2020 and gave him an above-slot $2.2 million bonus to pry him from a Texas commitment. Jones' father Keith played two seasons in the minors. Cousins Randy and Ron Flores both pitched in the majors.

SCOUTING REPORT: Jones is undersized but already owns a lively 96-99 mph fastball thanks to his electric arm speed. He pairs it with a sharp, above-average, mid-80s slider, and he is developing a changeup. The Pirates have worked with Jones on adjusting his effortful delivery to improve both his command and control. He showed power potential and above-average speed as a high school outfielder, but he was a bit of a free-swinger and the Pirates typically stick to developing players on one side of the game.

THE FUTURE: Some evaluators peg Jones as a bullpen candidate because of his size and effortful delivery. The Pirates will give him every chance to develop his changeup and remain on a starter track.

Year	Age	Club (League)	Class	W	L	ERA	G	GS	IP	H	HR	BB	SO	BB/9	SO/9	WHIP	AVG
2020	18	Did not play—No minor league season															

13 JT BRUBAKER, RHP

BA GRADE 45 Risk: Medium

Born: Nov. 17, 1993. **B-T:** R-R. **HT:** 6-3. **WT:** 185. **Drafted:** Akron, 2015 (6th round). **Signed by:** Trevor Haley.

TRACK RECORD: A sixth-round pick out of Akron in 2015, Brubaker slowly climbed the minors and appeared on the cusp of the majors in 2019, but a forearm strain followed by right elbow irritation limited him to six starts. He returned healthy in 2020 and made the Pirates' Opening Day roster, beginning the year in the bullpen before moving into the rotation. In his nine starts, Brubaker recorded a 5.53 ERA with 41 strikeouts and 16 walks in 42.1 innings.

SCOUTING REPORT: Brubaker's fastball sits 93-94 mph with plenty of horizontal movement and generates a lot of ground balls. Both his upper-80s slider and low-80s curveball are swing-and-miss offerings that played against major leaguers. His curveball is a slurvy pitch that grades at least average, while his short slider flashes plus when paired with his hard sinker. Brubaker also flashes an average changeup and at least average control. He has a tall, muscular frame that can handle a starter's workload, though his recent arm injuries are reason for pause.

THE FUTURE: The Pirates will give Brubaker a shot to win a rotation spot out of spring training in 2021. He should settle in as a back-of-the-rotation starter.

Year	Age	Club (League)	Class	W	L	ERA	G	GS	IP	H	HR	BB	SO	BB/9	SO/9	WHIP	AVG
2020	26	Pittsburgh (NL)	MAJ	1	3	4.94	11	9	47	48	6	17	48	3.2	9.1	1.37	.262
Major League Totals				1	3	4.94	11	9	47	48	6	17	48	3.2	9.1	1.37	.262
Minor League Totals				31	28	3.60	101	99	514	514	37	155	433	2.7	7.6	1.30	.262

14 NICK GARCIA, RHP

BA GRADE 50 Risk: Very High

Born: April 20, 1999. **B-T:** L-R. **HT:** 6-4. **WT:** 215. **Drafted:** Chapman (Calif.), 2020 (3rd round). **Signed by:** Brian Tracy.

TRACK RECORD: Garcia was one of the biggest risers on the West Coast in the 2020 draft, with many Southern California area scouts writing him in as the top pitching prospect in the area. Garcia played third base as a freshman at Division III Chapman in Orange, Calif., but converted to pitching as a sophomore and was named Most Outstanding Player of the D-III College World Series. As a junior, Garcia moved into a starting role and saw his draft stock take off, eventually signing for $1.2 million in the third round.

SCOUTING REPORT: While Garcia is new to pitching, he possesses starter traits, with a strong 6-foot-4, 215-pound frame and an easy and smooth delivery that allowed him to pound the strike zone with a three-pitch mix in college. His fastball typically sat in the 92-95 mph range, but he could run it up to 98 at his best. Garcia also mixed in a pair of potentially above-average secondary offerings with an upper-80s slider and a cutter in the same velocity range. Garcia has also thrown a curveball and a changeup, though both pitches were used infrequently and will need further refinement to profile as consistently average offerings.

THE FUTURE: Garcia comes with plenty of risk as a D-III arm who has yet to be tested consistently against high-quality hitters, but given his surprising polish and pitch-mix has plenty of upside as well.

Year	Age	Club (League)	Class	W	L	ERA	G	GS	IP	H	HR	BB	SO	BB/9	SO/9	WHIP	AVG
2020	21	Did not play—No minor league season															

15 JOSE SORIANO, RHP

BA GRADE 50 Risk: Extreme

Born: Oct. 20, 1998. **B-T:** R-R. **HT:** 6-3 **WT:** 210. **Signed:** Dominican Republic, 2016. **Signed by:** Domingo Garcia/Alfredo Ulloa (Angels).

TRACK RECORD: Soriano weighed 170 pounds when he signed with the Angels for $70,000 in 2016. He grew to a muscular 210 pounds by the time of his breakout season at low Class A Burlington in 2019. He entered 2020 looking to build on that momentum but suffered an elbow injury and had season-ending Tommy John surgery just before the start of spring training. The Pirates drafted Soriano with the No. 1 pick in the major league phase of the 2020 Rule 5 draft.

SCOUTING REPORT: Soriano has an ideal pitcher's body at 6-foot-3, 210 pounds. He is athletic with long, loose limbs and a smooth, rhythmic delivery that is easy to repeat. After previously sitting in the low 90s, Soriano's fastball averaged 96 mph and touched 100 in 2019 as he grew into his newfound strength. He has an advanced feel for a high-spin, low-80s curveball with 11-to-5 shape and solid depth. His upper-80s changeup shows swing-and-miss potential but is too firm at times. Soriano has struggled with walks, but he has improved his control as he's grown into his body and sharpened the timing and mechanics of his delivery.

THE FUTURE: Soriano is set to return during the 2021 season. If his stuff and control comes back, he has a chance to develop into a hard-throwing starting pitcher. The rebuilding Pirates should have the roster space and patience to carry Soriano all season to satisfy the Rule 5 requirements.

Year	Age	Club (League)	Class	W	L	ERA	G	GS	IP	H	HR	BB	SO	BB/9	SO/9	WHIP	AVG
2019	20	Angels (AZL)	R	0	1	1.93	3	3	5	5	0	3	8	5.8	15.4	1.71	.217
	20	Burlington (MWL)	LoA	5	6	2.55	17	15	78	53	5	48	84	5.6	9.7	1.30	.164
Minor League Totals				11	20	2.76	61	57	238	176	10	134	218	5.1	8.2	1.30	.210

16 MASON MARTIN, 1B

BREAKOUT
BA GRADE
45 Risk: High

Born: June 2, 1999. **B-T:** L-R. **HT:** 6-1. **WT:** 224. **Drafted:** HS—Kennewick, Wash., 2017 (17th round). **Signed by:** Max Kwan.

TRACK RECORD: The Pirates drafted Martin in the 17th round in 2017 based on his prodigious power potential and signed him for an over-slot $350,000 bonus, equivalent to fifth-round money. Martin delivered on that promise by hitting 35 home runs across the Class A levels in 2019, winning the organization's minor league player of the year award. The Pirates brought him to their alternate training site in 2020.

SCOUTING REPORT: Martin has plus raw power and can drive the ball out to all fields, including towering home runs to his pull side. The downside to Martin's power is it comes with plenty of strikeouts, raising questions about how much he'll get to it against upper-level pitchers. Martin worked with Triple-A hitting coach Jon Nunnally on developing a better eye at the plate at the alternate site. They focused on setting the top of his zone and recognizing breaking pitches earlier, which will hopefully reduce his strikeouts. Defensively, Martin has improved his fringe-average glove to the point where he's not considered a liability at first base, but his value is mostly derived from his power.

THE FUTURE: Martin is expected to open the year at Double-A. If he shows a more discerning eye, he could jump on to the fast track to the majors.

Year	Age	Club (League)	Class	AVG	G	AB	R	H	2B	3B	HR	RBI	BB	SO	SB	OBP	SLG
2019	20	Greensboro (SAL)	LoA	.262	82	301	58	79	19	3	23	83	46	103	8	.361	.575
	20	Bradenton (FSL)	HiA	.239	49	176	32	42	13	1	12	46	22	65	0	.333	.528
Minor League Totals				.248	274	977	185	242	58	5	60	209	160	358	13	.360	.502

17 BRAXTON ASHCRAFT, RHP

BREAKOUT
BA GRADE
45 Risk: High

Born: Oct. 5, 1999. **B-T:** L-R. **HT:** 6-5. **WT:** 204. **Drafted:** HS—Robinson, Texas, 2018 (2nd round). **Signed by:** Phil Huttmann.

TRACK RECORD: The Pirates made Ashcraft their second-round pick in 2018 and signed him for $1.825 million to forgo his commitment to Baylor. He was a two-sport star in high school, also excelling at wide receiver, and had surgery on his non-throwing shoulder after the 2019 season to clean up an old football injury. He returned to the field for instructional league in 2020 and looked noticeably better, with his fastball ticking up 2-3 mph and much more polish all-around.

SCOUTING REPORT: Ashcraft has the classic projectable pitcher's frame with room to continue filling out. His improved fastball now ranges from 93-96 mph and sits 94. The pitch generates a high volume of ground balls with its natural sink. Ashcraft has improved his changeup to a pitch that can at least be an average offering. He also improved his slider to get a sharper break on the pitch and it now flashes above-average. Ashcraft has solid control and the Pirates believe his surgery will help iron out some of the command issues he's had so far.

THE FUTURE: Ashcraft should start at one of the Class A levels in 2021. He projects as a back-of-the-rotation starter but could be more if he continues to fill out and add velocity.

Year	Age	Club (League)	Class	W	L	ERA	G	GS	IP	H	HR	BB	SO	BB/9	SO/9	WHIP	AVG
2019	19	West Virginia (NYP)	SS	1	9	5.77	11	11	53	49	4	22	39	3.7	6.6	1.34	.210
Minor League Totals				1	10	5.48	16	16	70	65	6	27	51	3.4	6.5	1.30	.240

18 MICHAEL BURROWS, RHP

BA GRADE
45 Risk: High

Born: Nov. 8, 1999. **B-T:** R-R. **HT:** 6-1. **WT:** 192. **Drafted:** HS—Waterford, Conn., 2018 (11th round). **Signed by:** Eddie Charles.

TRACK RECORD: The Pirates took Burrows in the 11th round in 2018 and gave him an above-slot $500,000 bonus—fourth-round money—to forgo a commitment to Connecticut. He quickly showed more polish than a typical high school pitcher and spent his first full season as a starter in the college-heavy New York-Penn League. The Pirates brought him to instructional league in 2020 after the coronavirus pandemic canceled the minor league season.

SCOUTING REPORT: Burrows' mid-90s fastball touches as high as 96 mph with good sinking movement. His curveball has some late break, grading as above-average with the chance to be an out pitch in the future. Burrows' solid frame suggests he's capable of compiling innings in the rotation. His fringe-average changeup will need improvement and he walked 4.1 batters per nine innings in 2019, but his control has average upside. He has rapidly shown improvements in his velocity and breaking stuff and has room to make further gains.

THE FUTURE: Burrows has the potential to be a back-of-the-rotation starter or a multi-inning reliever working off his fastball/curveball combination. He is set to begin 2021 at one of the Class A levels.

Year	Age	Club (League)	Class	W	L	ERA	G	GS	IP	H	HR	BB	SO	BB/9	SO/9	WHIP	AVG
2019	19	West Virginia (NYP)	SS	2	3	4.33	11	11	44	44	2	20	43	4.1	8.9	1.47	.228
Minor League Totals				2	3	3.28	15	14	57	50	2	24	52	3.8	8.1	1.28	.235

19 CAL MITCHELL, OF

BA GRADE
45 Risk: High

Born: March 8, 1999. **B-T:** L-L. **HT:** 6-0. **WT:** 216. **Drafted:** HS—San Diego, 2017 (2nd round). **Signed by:** Brian Tracy.

TRACK RECORD: Mitchell has shown tantalizing offensive upside since the Pirates took him in the second round in 2017. He's shown a smooth stroke and an increased ability to hit for power, capped by 15 homers in the pitcher-friendly Florida State League in 2019, but also far too many swings and misses. He spent 2020 at instructional league working to fix that.

SCOUTING REPORT: Known mainly as a contact hitter when he was drafted, Mitchell's profile has changed as he's matured. His driving tool is now the plus raw power in his lefthanded bat. He's shown an ability to hit to all fields and also displays a patient approach at the plate. At the same time, Mitchell chases the power far too often and gets into trouble when he tries to pull the ball. He is going to have to make more contact because he doesn't offer much defensively. Mitchell is slated for left field as a below-average runner and fringe-average defender with an arm that grades as average at best.

THE FUTURE: Mitchell should start 2021 in Double-A. If he can figure things out at the plate, the Pirates don't have many prospects blocking his path to PNC Park.

Year	Age	Club (League)	Class	AVG	G	AB	R	H	2B	3B	HR	RBI	BB	SO	SB	OBP	SLG
2019	20	Bradenton (FSL)	HiA	.251	118	451	54	113	21	2	15	64	32	142	1	.304	.406
Minor League Totals				.262	280	1053	126	276	61	5	27	149	97	286	7	.328	.406

20 JARED OLIVA, OF

BA GRADE
45 Risk: High

Born: Nov. 27, 1995. **B-T:** R-R. **HT:** 6-2. **WT:** 195. **Drafted:** Arizona, 2017 (7th round). **Signed by:** Derrick Van Dusen.

TRACK RECORD: Oliva has exceeded expectations at every stop since he walked on at Arizona and quickly became a starter. The Pirates made him a seventh-round pick in 2017 and he moved quickly through the system. Oliva made his major league debut in 2020, appearing in six games.

SCOUTING REPORT: Oliva is a streaky hitter, but he makes enough contact to hit for average. He mostly deploys a line-drive approach and has just fringe-average power potential. Oliva's greatest strength is his plus-plus speed, which makes him both a basestealing threat and an above-average defender in center field with plenty of range. He has average arm strength and can play the corners as needed.

THE FUTURE: Oliva is ready now to be a reserve outfielder in the majors with his speed and defensive acumen. He'll need to continue making gains with the bat to become more.

Year	Age	Club (League)	Class	AVG	G	AB	R	H	2B	3B	HR	RBI	BB	SO	SB	OBP	SLG
2020	24	Pittsburgh (NL)	MAJ	.188	6	16	0	3	0	0	0	0	0	6	1	.188	.188
Major League Totals				.188	6	16	0	3	0	0	0	0	0	6	1	.188	.188
Minor League Totals				.274	287	1065	175	292	58	17	15	106	99	252	84	.348	.403

21 BLAKE CEDERLIND, RHP

BA GRADE **40** Risk: Medium

Born: Jan. 4, 1996. **B-T:** R-R. **HT:** 6-4. **WT:** 215. **Drafted:** Merced (Calif.) JC, 2016 (5th round). **Signed by:** Mike Sansoe.

TRACK RECORD: Cederlind's fastball sat in the mid 90s as a starter when the Pirates drafted him out of junior college in the fifth round in 2016. His velocity ticked up significantly after a move to the bullpen and sent him soaring up the system. The Pirates called him up for his major league debut in 2020, and he made five appearances in relief.

SCOUTING REPORT: Cederlind made the most of his time in Pittsburgh, flashing a fastball that averaged 98 mph and touched 101. He pairs his explosive heater with a 90 mph cutter that is a plus, swing-and-miss pitch that played well in his major league debut. Cederlind's fringe-average control is still a concern, despite showing marginal improvement after moving to the bullpen. His stuff is so lively that he's able to get swings and misses even when he misses his spot.

THE FUTURE: Cederlind has a late-inning mentality and the stuff to match. He should be back in the Pirates bullpen for at least part of the 2021 season.

Year	Age	Club (League)	Class	W	L	ERA	G	GS	IP	H	HR	BB	SO	BB/9	SO/9	WHIP	AVG
2020	24	Pittsburgh (NL)	MAJ	0	0	4.50	5	0	4	3	0	1	4	2.3	9.0	1.00	.200
Major League Totals				0	0	4.50	5	0	4	3	0	1	4	2.3	9.0	1.00	.200
Minor League Totals				11	10	4.93	108	14	184	178	16	93	178	4.5	8.7	1.47	.254

22 RODOLFO CASTRO, 2B

BA GRADE **45** Risk: High

Born: May 21, 1999. **B-T:** B-R. **HT:** 6-0. **WT:** 210. **Signed:** Dominican Republic, 2015. **Signed by:** Rene Gayo, Juan Mercaso, and Jose Ortiz.

TRACK RECORD: The shortened 2020 season was something of a breakout for Castro, who originally signed for $150,000 out of the Dominican Republic in 2015 and had yet to advance past high Class A. He showed a more mature, refined skill set at the Pirates' alternate training site, impressing the club enough that they added him to their 40-man roster after the season

SCOUTING REPORT: Castro is very toolsy but has been very raw to this point, with swing-and-miss concerns at the plate and defensive inconsistencies in the infield. He improved his defensive work in 2020, and the Pirates believe he can play second base, shortstop and third base in the majors. He's a switch-hitter with above-average or better raw power from each side. He has above-average speed, giving him plenty of range in the field and allowing him to steal bases. The biggest downside to his game has been his strikeout tendencies and general lack of contact skills.

THE FUTURE: Castro is unlikely to hit for average but can contribute with his power and defensive versatility. He will likely open 2021 back in the minors.

Year	Age	Club (League)	Class	AVG	G	AB	R	H	2B	3B	HR	RBI	BB	SO	SB	OBP	SLG
2019	20	Greensboro (SAL)	LoA	.242	61	215	33	52	13	2	14	46	18	68	6	.306	.516
	20	Bradenton (FSL)	HiA	.243	57	202	26	49	13	1	5	27	13	54	1	.288	.391
Minor League Totals				.249	332	1182	160	294	72	14	39	184	100	317	19	.310	.432

23 MAX KRANICK, RHP

BREAKOUT **BA GRADE** **40** Risk: High

Born: July 21, 1997. **B-T:** R-R. **HT:** 6-3. **WT:** 214. **Drafted:** HS—Archbald, Pa., 2016 (11th round). **Signed by:** Dan Radcliff.

TRACK RECORD: Kranick fell to the 11th round in 2016 because of signability concerns stemming from his commitment to Virginia. The Pirates stopped his slide and convinced him to sign for an over-slot $300,000 bonus. Kranick kick-started his development with solid seasons at low Class A in 2018 and high Class A in 2019. The Pirates brought him to the alternate training site in 2020 and added him to the 40-man roster after the season.

SCOUTING REPORT: Kranick dealt with shoulder fatigue and tightness early in his career, so he turned to former major league reliever Vic Black to help with weighted ball drills to increase strength. He also shortened his arm path and gained velocity throughout the process. Kranick's fastball sat 93-94 mph and touched 98 at the Pirates' alternate training site. He ditched his two-seam fastball entirely, instead focusing on his four-seamer and curveball combination. His four-seamer features more movement up in the zone and he worked with former big league closer Joel Hanrahan on tunneling the curveball to look like the fastball out of the hand. Kranick also has an average slider and below-average changeup. He throws strikes with above-average control.

THE FUTURE: Kranick should start in Double-A in 2021. His newfound velocity and arm strength give him a good chance to reach the majors.

Year	Age	Club (League)	Class	W	L	ERA	G	GS	IP	H	HR	BB	SO	BB/9	SO/9	WHIP	AVG
2019	21	Bradenton (FSL)	HiA	6	7	3.79	20	20	109	100	11	30	78	2.5	6.4	1.19	.222
Minor League Totals				12	14	3.34	51	47	245	225	20	58	194	2.1	7.1	1.16	.244

24 ALEXANDER MOJICA, 3B

BA GRADE
45 Risk: Extreme

Born: Aug. 2, 2002. **B-T:** R-R. **HT:** 6-2. **WT:** 223. **Signed:** Dominican Republic, 2018. **Signed by:** Victor Santana.

TRACK RECORD: Mojica signed with the Pirates for $390,000 on his 16th birthday in 2018. He hit .351/.468/.580 in his pro debut in the Dominican Summer League the following year to emerge as a young hitter to watch in Pittsburgh's system, but he got out of shape during the 2020 coronavirus shutdown and underwhelmed during instructional league in the fall.

SCOUTING REPORT: Mojica shows promising offensive tools with a smooth swing, a patient approach and plus raw power. The concern is he has a huge frame already and little mobility, raising concerns if he'll maintain the twitch and athleticism needed to catch up to better velocity once he starts facing it. Mojica signed as a third baseman but does not move well enough for the position and projects to move across the diamond to first base. He does have a plus arm.

THE FUTURE: Mojica's conditioning is going to be a key to his development. He is going to have to slim down in order to get the most from his natural abilities and become an everyday first baseman.

Year	Age	Club (League)	Class	AVG	G	AB	R	H	2B	3B	HR	RBI	BB	SO	SB	OBP	SLG
2019	16	Pirates2 (DSL)	R	.351	55	174	37	61	14	1	8	46	37	34	2	.468	.580
Minor League Totals				.351	55	174	37	61	14	1	8	46	37	34	2	.468	.580

25 SAMMY SIANI, OF

BA GRADE
45 Risk: Extreme

Born: Dec. 14, 2000. **B-T:** L-L. **HT:** 6-0. **WT:** 195. **Drafted:** HS—Philadelphia, 2019 (2nd round). **Signed by:** Dan Radcliff.

TRACK RECORD: The Pirates signed Siani for $2.15 million in 2019 after taking him with the 37th overall pick, pulling him away from a commitment to Duke. That came one year after his brother Mike was a fourth-round pick of the Reds. Siani shows good on-base skills but failed to impact the ball in his pro debut with Rookie-level Bristol after signing. The Pirates brought him to instructional league in 2020.

SCOUTING REPORT: Siani has a solid all-around foundation but doesn't wow evaluators with any one specific tool. The Pirates like his hitting ability, smooth swing and good pitch recognition, suggesting an ability to hit .270 or better down the road. However, Siani doesn't impact the ball in any way and will have to add significant strength to reach that potential. He has below-average power potential with a small, slight frame. Siani is an above-average runner and is an advanced defender in center field for his age. His average arm strength is enough for him to bounce around to all three outfield spots.

THE FUTURE: Siani needs to find a way to add strength and extract more power to project as a major leaguer. He's set to begin 2021 at low Class A.

Year	Age	Club (League)	Class	AVG	G	AB	R	H	2B	3B	HR	RBI	BB	SO	SB	OBP	SLG
2019	18	Pirates (GCL)	R	.241	39	133	21	32	3	3	0	9	26	41	5	.372	.308
Minor League Totals				.241	39	133	21	32	3	3	0	9	26	41	5	.372	.308

26 PO-YU CHEN, RHP

BA GRADE
45 Risk: Extreme

Born: Oct. 2, 2001. **B-T:** L-R. **HT:** 6-2. **WT:** 187. **Signed:** Taiwan, 2020. **Signed by:** Fu Chun Chiang.

TRACK RECORD: The Pirates scouted Chen for three years and finally landed him in October 2020 for $1.25 million shortly after clearing out international bonus pool space. Chen played for Taiwan's 18U national team and earned the save in the gold medal game of the 2019 World Baseball Softball Confederation 18U World Cup by pitching two innings against the U.S. Chen comes from a notably athletic family. His father played in the Taiwanese major league and his mother was a basketball player.

SCOUTING REPORT: Chen is a young pitcher with a four-pitch mix and above-average command. His fastball currently sits 89-91 mph and could add more velocity as he fills out his projectable frame. Chen's slider sits in the upper 70s, his curveball works in the lower 70s and his changeup is a low-80s offering. All three of them show average potential and he mixes them well. Chen throws everything for strikes with above-average control and shows impressive poise in high-pressure situations.

THE FUTURE: Chen is raw and far away from the majors, but his mix of pitches and projectability suggests the potential to be a back-end starter in time.

Year	Age	Club (League)	Class	W	L	ERA	G	GS	IP	H	HR	BB	SO	BB/9	SO/9	WHIP	AVG
2020	18	Did not play—Signed 2021 contract															

27 NICK MEARS, RHP

BA GRADE 40 **Risk:** High

Born: Oct. 7, 1996. **B-T:** R-R. **HT:** 6-2. **WT:** 215. **Signed:** Sacramento JC, 2018 (NDFA). **Signed by:** Mike Sansoe.

TRACK RECORD: The Pirates signed Mears after he went undrafted to fill out their roster after a wave of injuries hit their high Class A team in 2018. He saw a velocity increase in 2019, reaching 100 mph and sitting consistently in the mid-to-upper 90s. The Pirates called Mears up briefly in 2020, but he was overmatched in four relief appearances and logged a 5.40 ERA with as many walks as strikeouts.

SCOUTING REPORT: Mears' fastball has plenty of velocity. It comfortably sits 95-97 mph and has reached triple digits at its best. Mears' upper-70s curveball has above-average drop and pairs well with his fastball, getting swings and misses over the top. His issue in the majors is he often left his fastball up over the plate and struggled to land his curveball in the strike zone. Batters sat on his heater and crushed it. Mears' control is fringy at its best and was poor in every facet the majors, which he'll have to fix.

THE FUTURE: Mears has swing-and-miss stuff, but it won't matter if he doesn't improve his control. He should return to the Pirates' bullpen at some point in 2021 and will try to show the needed improvements.

Year	Age	Club (League)	Class	W	L	ERA	G	GS	IP	H	HR	BB	SO	BB/9	SO/9	WHIP	AVG
2020	23	Pittsburgh (NL)	MAJ	0	0	5.40	4	0	5	4	1	7	7	12.6	12.6	2.20	.222
Major League Totals				0	0	5.40	4	0	5	4	1	7	7	12.6	12.6	2.20	.222
Minor League Totals				5	3	3.02	37	0	50	32	5	19	77	3.4	13.7	1.01	.178

28 TRAVIS MacGREGOR, RHP

BA GRADE 45 **Risk:** Extreme

Born: Oct. 15, 1997. **B-T:** R-R. **HT:** 6-3. **WT:** 180. **Drafted:** HS—Tarpon Springs, Fla., 2016 (2nd round). **Signed by:** Nick Presto.

TRACK RECORD: The 68th overall pick in 2016, MacGregor started slowly as a pro but appeared to break out at low Class A in 2018. That progress was cut short by an elbow injury and he missed all of 2019 after having Tommy John surgery. MacGregor was set to return in 2020, but the canceled minor league season due to the coronavirus pandemic pushed his return back to 2021—three years after he last pitched in an official game.

TRACK RECORD: MacGregor showed improvements with his fastball prior to surgery, getting the pitch up to around 97 mph while generating lots of swings and misses and weak contact. He has an average changeup but is still looking for a third pitch. MacGregor worked on a slider during his Tommy John rehab and got tips from fellow rehabbers Chad Kuhl and Edgar Santana on the pitch. The slider is aimed at replacing his below-average 12-to-6 curveball. MacGregor previously showed fringe-average control and his durability is uncertain pending his return from surgery.

THE FUTURE: MacGregor is set to return to game action in 2021. Whether his stuff comes back and he can find a third pitch will determine if he's still a prospect.

Year	Age	Club (League)	Class	W	L	ERA	G	GS	IP	H	HR	BB	SO	BB/9	SO/9	WHIP	AVG
2018	20	Pirates (GCL)	R	0	0	2.57	2	2	7	6	1	1	6	1.3	7.7	1.00	.207
	20	West Virginia (SAL)	LoA	1	4	3.25	15	15	64	58	7	21	74	3.0	10.5	1.24	.212
Minor League Totals				3	9	4.51	38	38	143	154	12	52	131	3.3	8.2	1.43	.272

29 SANTIAGO FLOREZ, RHP

BA GRADE
45 Risk: Extreme

Born: May 9, 2000. **B-T:** R-R. **HT:** 6-4. **WT:** 239. **Signed:** Dominican Republic, 2016. **Signed by:** Rene Gayo, Orlando Covo and Jose Mosquera.

TRACK RECORD: Florez signed out of Colombia for $150,000 in 2016 and quickly impressed with his imposing frame and big velocity. He spent each of his first three pro seasons at the Rookie levels, capped by 3.46 ERA in 10 starts for Bristol in 2019. The Pirates brought him to instructional league in 2020.

SCOUTING REPORT: Florez has steadily gotten stronger and increased his velocity. His plus fastball lives in the 93-97 mph range and sits 95-97 on his best days. He has developed a changeup with average or better potential and switched from a loopy curveball to a hard slider, although none have developed into an out pitch to pair with his fastball. His slider shows the most promise with above-average spin rates. Florez has improved his control, but it's still below-average and has a long way to go.

THE FUTURE: Florez will continue starting for now in the minors. His future is likely a hard-throwing reliever barring significant jumps in his control and secondary pitches.

Year	Age	Club (League)	Class	W	L	ERA	G	GS	IP	H	HR	BB	SO	BB/9	SO/9	WHIP	AVG
2019	19	Bristol (APP)	R	2	2	3.46	10	10	42	35	4	21	36	4.5	7.8	1.34	.193
Minor League Totals				9	9	4.10	34	34	138	115	6	82	101	5.3	6.6	1.42	.225

30 RODOLFO NOLASCO, OF

Born: Sept. 23, 2001. **B-T:** R-R. **HT:** 6-1. **WT:** 175. **Signed:** Dominican Republic, 2018. **Signed by:** Victor Santana.

TRACK RECORD: Nolasco signed for $235,000 during the 2018 international signing period. He quickly emerged as one of the Pirates' most promising international prospects with a star turn in the Dominican Summer League the following year, batting .302/.373/.472 with some of the best exit velocities in the system. The Pirates brought him to instructional league at the end of 2020, where he continued this trend and opened more eyes.

SCOUTING REPORT: Nolasco's bat is his primary asset and has a lot of potential. He impacts the ball with authority and shows plus raw power from the right side. He has plus bat speed, a polished approach for his age and doesn't chase much out of the strike zone. Nolasco can hit a fastball and now must show he can handle higher-quality breaking stuff, but the tools are there for at least an average hitter with plus power. Nolasco makes the plays he should in right field, with average speed and an average arm that flashes plus on his best throws.

THE FUTURE: Nolasco has plenty of potential but is very far away. He'll make his U.S. debut in the Rookie-level Gulf Coast League in 2020.

Year	Age	Club (League)	Class	AVG	G	AB	R	H	2B	3B	HR	RBI	BB	SO	SB	OBP	SLG
2019	18	Pirates1 (DSL)	R	.328	37	131	26	43	5	1	0	11	11	28	12	.385	.382
Minor League Totals				.265	82	268	45	71	9	1	0	21	30	59	26	.343	.306

MORE PROSPECTS TO KNOW

31 JASE BOWEN, 2B

Bowen is very athletic and capable of playing all over the field. He's a fast runner with a strong arm, but needs to get his bat to average to project as a utility player.

32 MATT GORSKI, OF

SLEEPER

Gorski has plus power, plus speed and can stick in center field, but also has serious swing-and-miss issues. The Pirates are optimistic about the strides he made in 2020.

33 SOLOMAN MAGUIRE, OF

Signed out of Australia for $594,000 as a 17-year-old in February 2020, Maguire is a raw talent with plus speed, an above-average arm and strong defensive acumen in center field. The 5-foot-11 lefthanded hitter has above-average bat speed and shows surprising power for his lean frame.

34 OSVALDO BIDO, RHP

Bido works in the mid 90s and reaches 97 mph. He is already 25 but has the upside of a hard-throwing reliever or a potential depth starting option.

35 JACK HERMAN, OF

Herman shows impressive power at a young age, working the gaps and adding some over-the-fence power. That power came with an increase in strikeouts and he'll need to work to become an average hitter.

36 JC FLOWERS, RHP

Flowers played football in high school and was a two-way player at Florida State. The Pirates felt his best upside was on the mound, where he shows a mid-90s fastball and an above-average slider.

37 ANTHONY ALFORD, OF

The Pirates claimed Alford on waivers from the Blue Jays, then saw him go down quickly with a fractured right elbow. He'll try to show his power-speed combination can finally translate to results in the majors in 2021.

38 PHILLIP EVANS, 3B

Evans got into 11 games for the Pirates last season and posted a .932 OPS in 45 plate appearances. He could be a valuable super-utility player if his bat can come close to the small sample results of 2020.

39 NOE TORIBIO, RHP

Toribio has a fastball that sits in the low 90s as a starter and has gotten up to 97 mph. He also throws a curveball and a changeup that have a chance to be average pitches.

40 CODY PONCE, RHP

Ponce got the surprise call to the majors in 2020 and handled it well with a 3.18 ERA in 17 innings. He has a fastball that sits 93-94 mph and tops out at 96 to along with a swing-and-miss curveball as his primary pitches.

TOP PROSPECTS OF THE DECADE

Year	Player, Pos	2020 Org
2011	Jameson Taillon, RHP	Pirates
2012	Gerrit Cole, RHP	Yankees
2013	Gerrit Cole, RHP	Yankees
2014	Gregory Polanco, OF	Pirates
2015	Tyler Glasnow, RHP	Rays
2016	Tyler Glasnow, RHP	Rays
2017	Austin Meadows, OF	Rays
2018	Mitch Keller, RHP	Pirates
2019	Mitch Keller, RHP	Pirates
2020	Mitch Keller, RHP	Pirates

TOP DRAFT PICKS OF THE DECADE

Year	Player, Pos	2020 Org
2011	Gerrit Cole, RHP	Yankees
2012	*Mark Appel, RHP	Did not play
2013	Austin Meadows, OF	Rays
2014	Cole Tucker, SS	Pirates
2015	Kevin Newman, SS	Pirates
2016	Will Craig, 3B	Pirates
2017	Shane Baz, RHP	Rays
2018	Travis Swaggerty, OF	Pirates
2019	Quinn Priester, RHP	Pirates
2020	Nick Gonzales, SS	Pirates

*Did not sign

DEPTH CHART

PITTSBURGH PIRATES

TOP 2021 ROOKIES	RANK
Ke'Bryan Hayes, 3B	1
BREAKOUT PROSPECTS	**RANK**
Mason Martin, 1B	16
Braxton Ashcraft, RHP	17
Sammy Siani, OF	25

SOURCE OF TOP 30 TALENT

Homegrown	25	Acquired	5
College	8	Trade	4
Junior college	0	Rule 5 draft	0
High school	11	Independent league	1
Nondrafted free agent	0	Free agent/waivers	0
International	6		

LF
Cal Mitchell (19)

CF
Travis Swaggerty (11)
Jared Oliva (20)
Sammy Siani (25)
Solomon Maguire
Matt Gorski
Anthony Alford
Lolo Sanchez

RF
Oneil Cruz (2)
Rodolfo Nolasco (30)
Jack Herman

3B
Ke'Bryan Hayes (1)
Phillip Evans

SS
Liover Peguero (5)
Ji-Hwan Bae (9)

2B
Nick Gonzales (3)
Rodolfo Castro (22)
Jase Bowen

1B
Mason Martin (16)
Alexander Mojica (24)

C
Christian Kelley
Eli Wilson

LHP

LHSP	LHRP
Cam Vieaux	Braeden Ogle
	Blake Weiman

RHP

RHSP	RHRP
Quinn Priester (4)	Blake Cederlind (21)
Cody Bolton (6)	Nick Mears (27)
Tahnaj Thomas (7)	Santiago Florez (29)
Brennan Malone (8)	J.C. Flowers
Carmen Mlodzinski (10)	Cody Ponce
Jared Jones (12)	Yerry De Los Santos
JT Brubaker (13)	
Nick Garcia (14)	
Jose Soriano (15)	
Braxton Ashcraft (17)	
Michael Burrows (18)	
Max Kranick (23)	
Po-Yu Chen (26)	
Travis MacGregor (28)	
J.C. Flowers	
Noe Toribio	
Aaron Shortridge	
Osvaldo Bido	

St. Louis Cardinals

BY J.J. COOPER

It took winning eight of their final 12 games to ensure it, but once again the Cardinals finished above .500 and earned a playoff spot, albeit with a quick first-round exit.

When it comes to winning, the Cardinals' consistency is remarkable. Other teams rise and fall. St. Louis is exceptional every now and then—it has won 100 games twice since 2000 and took home World Series trophies in 2006 and 2011—but the team is rarely bad.

The Cardinals have one sub-.500 finish this century. For all of their consistency, the Dodgers have two, the Yankees have three and the Red Sox have five. St. Louis' biggest rival, the Cubs, have eight.

The Cardinals managed to overcome a coronavirus outbreak in 2020 that forced the team to postpone games for 16 straight days. They handled a compressed schedule that included 10 doubleheaders and were helped by 13 players who made their major league debuts.

But the pandemic did take away the Cardinals' not-so-secret weapon. Based on population, the St. Louis metropolitan area should make the Cardinals a small-market team. Instead, it ranks 20th in the U.S., just behind Denver and Tampa-St. Petersburg and just ahead of Baltimore and Charlotte (which doesn't have an MLB team).

But the Cardinals bring 3.4 to 3.5 million fans through the gates at Busch Stadium in a typical year and rank in the top three in attendance year after year. The Cardinals consistently draw as if Busch Stadium was in the middle of New York, Los Angeles or Chicago.

Whether it's an artifact of the sprawling Cardinals radio network and KMOX radio's massive reach for decades, excellent marketing or just an incredibly loyal fan base, the Cardinals are able to consistently spend like a team in a larger market because of their ability to draw fans at a rate far beyond their market.

In 2020, that superpower was eliminated, because every team played in ballparks without fans. The after-effects were seen after the season when, like almost every other team in their division, the Cardinals made moves to reduce payroll. Most notably, they did not exercise second baseman Kolten Wong's $12.5 million option.

If fans return to ballparks at some point in 2021, the Cardinals' ability to draw the masses should once again allow them to punch above their weight financially. And in a division where seemingly everyone is retrenching, the Cardinals' position is still strong.

St. Louis continues to have one of the top farm systems in the division. It still has a strong major league rotation and it has bullpen depth.

Now, the Cardinals need to figure out what has been ailing their offense. St. Louis finished 10th in the National League in runs scored in 2019. That was bad, but 2020 was much worse.

St. Louis hit .234/.323/.371 as a team and finished 14th in the NL in runs scored. While St. Louis struggled to hit, ex-Cardinals Randy Arozarena and Luke Voit starred with their new clubs, the Rays and Yankees.

The Cardinals still have a young outfield, but in 2021 they will need those youngsters to take big steps if their amazing run of winning is to continue. ■

The Cardinals declined Kolten Wong's $12.5 million option despite his steady production.

PROJECTED 2024 LINEUP

Position	Player	Age
Catcher	Ivan Herrera	24
First Base	Jordan Walker	22
Second Base	Tommy Edman	29
Third Base	Nolan Gorman	24
Shortstop	Paul DeJong	30
Left Field	Tyler O'Neill	29
Center Field	Harrison Bader	30
Right Field	Dylan Carlson	25
Designated Hitter	Paul Goldschmidt	36
No. 1 Starter	Jack Flaherty	28
No. 2 Starter	Dakota Hudson	29
No. 3 Starter	Matthew Liberatore	24
No. 4 Starter	Kwang Hyun Kim	36
No. 5 Starter	Zack Thompson	26
Closer	Alex Reyes	29

1 DYLAN CARLSON, OF

Born: Oct. 23, 1998. **B-T:** B-L. **HT:** 6-3. **WT:** 205.
Drafted: HS—Elk Grove, Calif., 2016. (1st round).
Signed by: Zach Mortimer.

TRACK RECORD: Before he retired at the end of the 2018 season, Elk Grove (Calif.) High coach Jeff Carlson was known for producing future big leaguers. Eight Elk Grove alums have reached the majors from Carlson's 16 seasons at the school, including his son Dylan. Dylan Carlson was one of the youngest players in the 2016 draft class and a late riser up draft boards. As one of the youngest players at every level of the minors he played, Carlson's first couple of years in pro ball were solid but unspectacular. He broke out with an excellent 2019 season at Double-A Springfield and won the Texas League MVP award while hitting .281/.364/.518 with 21 home runs and 18 stolen bases in 108 games. He was called up from the alternate training site in mid August for his big league debut, but he struggled and was demoted in early September. Carlson homered on his first day back 10 days later and hit .278/.325/.611 after he returned. He started all three of the Cardinals' playoff games and batted cleanup and was one of the team's most productive hitters in its Wild Card Series loss to San Diego.

SCOUTING REPORT: Carlson is more of a well-rounded player with few glaring weaknesses rather than a tools-laden star. A switch-hitter, Carlson is an all-fields hitter who likes to spread the ball around from both sides of the plate. He is just as comfortable taking a pitch on the outer third the other way as he is yanking a ball down and inside. Carlson has the approach and demeanor of a savvy veteran and draws rave reviews for his poise at the plate. He controls the strike zone, recognizes spin well and makes adjustments, ultimately projecting as an above-average hitter. Changeups gave him some trouble in his pro debut and he was also somewhat vulnerable against fastballs up in the zone, but he's a smart player who doesn't let a weakness hamper him for long. Carlson is one of the youngest players in the majors and should continue to get stronger and add power as he matures. His line-drive swing is more geared for singles and doubles than home runs, but more balls should travel over the fence as he fills out. Carlson is an above-average runner capable of stealing a base and playing all three outfield positions. He's best in a corner but can play center field. His fringe-average arm is his weakest tool, but its accuracy makes up for some of its strength shortcomings.

THE FUTURE: Carlson's strong finish and excellent playoff performance wiped away memories of a rough first month. He should begin 2021 in the Cardinals outfield and has a chance to grow into a well-rounded, first-division player. ■

BEST TOOLS

Best Hitter for Average	Dylan Carlson
Best Power Hitter	Nolan Gorman
Best Strike-Zone Discipline	John Nogowski
Fastest Baserunner	Lane Thomas
Best Athlete	Masyn Winn
Best Fastball	Edwin Nunez
Best Curveball	Zack Thompson
Best Slider	Johan Oviedo
Best Changeup	Kwang Hyun Kim
Best Control	Kodi Whitley
Best Defensive Catcher	Julio Rodriguez
Best Defensive Infielder	Delvin Perez
Best Infield Arm	Masyn Winn
Best Defensive Outfielder	Lane Thomas
Best Outfield Arm	Jhon Torres

Year	Age	Club (League)	Class	AVG	G	AB	R	H	2B	3B	HR	RBI	BB	SO	SB	OBP	SLG
2017	18	Peoria (MWL)	LoA	.240	115	383	63	92	18	1	7	42	52	116	6	.342	.347
2018	19	Palm Beach (FSL)	HiA	.247	99	376	63	93	19	3	9	53	52	78	6	.345	.386
	19	Peoria (MWL)	LoA	.234	13	47	5	11	3	0	2	9	10	10	2	.368	.426
2019	20	Memphis (PCL)	AAA	.361	18	72	14	26	4	2	5	9	6	18	2	.418	.681
	20	Springfield (TL)	AA	.281	108	417	81	117	24	6	21	59	52	98	18	.364	.518
2020	21	St. Louis (NL)	MAJ	.200	35	110	11	22	7	1	3	16	8	35	1	.252	.364
Major League Totals				.200	35	110	11	22	7	1	3	16	8	35	1	.252	.364
Minor League Totals				.260	403	1478	256	385	81	15	47	194	188	372	38	.350	.431

2 MATTHEW LIBERATORE, LHP

Born: Nov. 6, 1999. **B-T:** L-L. **HT:** 6-5. **WT:** 200. **Drafted:** HS—Glendale, Ariz., 2018 (1st round). **Signed by:** David Hamlett (Rays).

TRACK RECORD: Liberatore was the ace of USA Baseball's 18U World Cup-winning team in 2017 and was drafted 16th overall by the Rays the following year. The Rays traded him to the Cardinals before the 2020 season in a deal that quickly became known as the Randy Arozarena trade after Arozarena became the star of the 2020 postseason.

SCOUTING REPORT: Liberatore is one of the most promising young lefties in the game. His four-pitch mix is topped by a 92-96 mph fastball that may settle into the upper end of his velocity range as he matures, and he backs it up with an assortment of quality secondaries. His upper-70s, downer curveball gives him a second plus pitch and his average slider has flashes of intrigue as well with late tilt in the low 80s. His changeup is his fourth pitch but it still projects to be a potentially above-average offering. Liberatore ties his arsenal together with advanced command and control for a tall, young lefty. He repeats the delivery well with a clean arm action and should be at least an above-average strike-thrower without issue.

THE FUTURE: Liberatore has front-of-the-rotation potential but is many years from that ceiling. He will make his Cardinals organizational debut in 2021.

MARY DECICCO/MLB PHOTOS VIA GETTY IMAGES

BA GRADE
60 Risk: High

SCOUTING GRADES: Fastball: 60 Curveball: 60 Changeup: 55 Slider: 50 Control: 55

Year	Age	Club (League)	Class	W	L	ERA	G	GS	IP	H	HR	BB	SO	BB/9	SO/9	WHIP	AVG
2018	18	Princeton (APP)	R	1	0	3.60	1	1	5	5	0	2	5	3.6	9.0	1.40	.263
	18	Rays (GCL)	R	1	2	0.98	8	8	28	16	0	11	32	3.6	10.4	0.98	.148
2019	19	Bowling Green (MWL)	LoA	6	2	3.10	16	15	78	70	2	31	76	3.6	8.7	1.29	.205
Minor League Totals				8	4	2.59	25	24	111	91	2	44	113	3.6	9.2	1.22	.224

3 NOLAN GORMAN, 3B

Born: May 10, 2000. **B-T:** L-R. **HT:** 6-1. **WT:** 210. **Drafted:** HS—Phoenix, 2018 (1st round). **Signed by:** Mauricio Rubio.

TRACK RECORD: Gorman was considered the best high school power hitter in the 2018 draft class and was selected 19th overall by the Cardinals. He showcased his power immediately in his pro debut but scuffled as he advanced to the offense-suffocating Florida State League in 2019. Gorman stood out at 2020 spring training before camp shut down and spent the summer at the Cardinals' alternate training site, where he was one of the top offensive performers.

SCOUTING REPORT: Gorman is the epitome of a modern power hitter. He strikes out and has holes in his swing, but he makes pitchers pay when they make a mistake. Gorman feasts on pitches down and makes balls disappear with his plus-plus power. He can be beat by fastballs up and needs to become more selective, but he hits lefties well for a young hitter and shows enough feel for contact to hit .240-.250 to go with his power production. Gorman has solid hands, a quick exchange and plus arm strength at third base, but his lateral range needs to improve for him to be average defensively. He's a below-average runner.

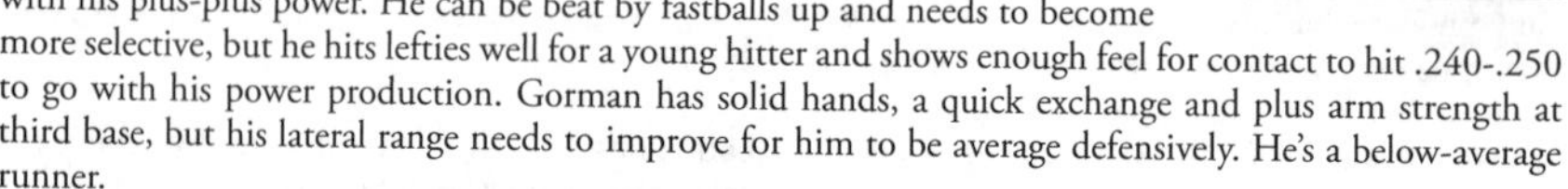

THE FUTURE: Gorman has the chance to hit 30-plus home runs in the majors if he puts it all together. He'll try to carry his gains from the alternate site forward to Double-A in 2021.

MARY DECICCO/MLB PHOTOS VIA GETTY IMAGES

BA GRADE
60 Risk: High

SCOUTING GRADES: Hitting: 45 Power: 70 Running: 40 Fielding: 45 Arm: 60

Year	Age	Club (League)	Class	AVG	G	AB	R	H	2B	3B	HR	RBI	BB	SO	SB	OBP	SLG
2018	18	Johnson City (APP)	R	.350	38	143	41	50	10	1	11	28	24	37	1	.443	.664
	18	Peoria (MWL)	LoA	.202	25	94	8	19	3	0	6	16	10	39	0	.280	.426
2019	19	Peoria (MWL)	LoA	.241	67	241	41	58	14	3	10	41	32	79	2	.344	.448
	19	Palm Beach (FSL)	HiA	.256	58	215	24	55	16	3	5	21	13	73	0	.304	.428
Minor League Totals				.263	188	693	114	182	43	7	32	106	79	228	3	.345	.483

4 IVAN HERRERA, C

MARY DECICCO/MLB PHOTOS VIA GETTY IMAGES

BA GRADE
55 Risk: High

Born: June 1, 2000. **B-T:** R-R. **HT:** 6-0. **WT:** 180. **Signed:** Panama, 2016. **Signed by:** Damaso Espino.

TRACK RECORD: Herrera earned an invitation to big league spring training in 2020 and took advantage of the opportunity to work with his boyhood hero Yadier Molina. Herrera stayed attached to the hip of the Cardinals great, whether it was early work in the batting cage at spring training or picking Molina's brain at summer camp. Herrera spent the summer putting his lessons to use at the Cardinals' alternate training site.

SCOUTING REPORT: While Herrera worked with Molina on how to run a pitching staff, his bat is his calling card. He is one of the best hitters in the Cardinals' system with a compact swing that is geared for contact and hard line drives. His exit velocities have steadily improved as he's gotten stronger and he'll flash above-average to plus raw power. Defensively, Herrera is a student of the game and has a tick above-average hands, which should allow him to present pitches well. His blocking and receiving still show signs of his youth, but he moves well and should eventually be at least an above-average defender. He's steadily improved his throwing mechanics, although his pop times are fringe-average.

THE FUTURE: Herrera's well-rounded skill set, excellent makeup and grinder mentality make him the team's likely catcher of the future.

SCOUTING GRADES: **Hitting:** 55 **Power:** 45 **Running:** 30 **Fielding:** 55 **Arm:** 50

Year	Age	Club (League)	Class	AVG	G	AB	R	H	2B	3B	HR	RBI	BB	SO	SB	OBP	SLG
2017	17	Cardinals (DSL)	R	.335	49	170	21	57	15	0	1	27	18	36	2	.425	.441
2018	18	Cardinals (GCL)	R	.348	28	112	23	39	6	4	1	25	11	20	1	.423	.500
	18	Springfield (TL)	AA	.000	2	4	0	0	0	0	0	0	0	2	0	.200	.000
2019	19	Peoria (MWL)	LoA	.286	69	248	41	71	10	0	8	42	35	56	1	.381	.423
	19	Palm Beach (FSL)	HiA	.276	18	58	7	16	0	0	1	5	5	16	0	.338	.328
Minor League Totals				.309	166	592	92	183	31	4	11	99	69	130	4	.397	.431

5 ZACK THOMPSON, LHP

MARY DECICCO/MLB PHOTOS VIA GETTY IMAGES

BA GRADE
55 Risk: High

Born: Oct. 28, 1997. **B-T:** L-L. **HT:** 6-2. **WT:** 225. **Drafted:** Kentucky, 2019 (1st round). **Signed by:** Jason Bryans.

TRACK RECORD: Thompson broke James Paxton's school record at Kentucky for strikeouts by a lefty with 130 punchouts in 90 innings as a junior. The Cardinals drafted him 19th overall and pushed him to high Class A Palm Beach in his pro debut. Thompson impressed at spring training and was tabbed as a potential breakout, but he instead spent the year at the alternate training site after the coronavirus pandemic canceled the 2020 minor league season.

SCOUTING REPORT: Thompson has loud stuff that brings to mind a front-of-the-rotation lefthander. His fastball sits 92-94 mph and touches 97, and his plus curveball has elite spin rates above 3,000 revolutions per minute. His mid-80s slider and mid-80s changeup give him two more average or better pitches and he is increasingly showing confidence in both of them. Thompson's consistency and control, however, have not come together. His control was an issue in college and wavered at the alternate training site. He had an elbow injury in college that also scared some teams, and his fastball velocity wavered at times in Springfield, as well.

THE FUTURE: Thompson's stuff gives him a chance to pitch in the middle or front of a rotation, but he could also end up in the bullpen if his control and consistency don't improve.

SCOUTING GRADES: **Fastball:** 55 **Curveball:** 60 **Slider:** 55 **Changeup:** 50 **Control:** 45

Year	Age	Club (League)	Class	W	L	ERA	G	GS	IP	H	HR	BB	SO	BB/9	K/9	WHIP	AVG
2019	21	Cardinals (GCL)	R	0	0	0.00	2	2	2	3	0	0	4	0.0	18.0	1.50	.300
	21	Palm Beach (FSL)	HiA	0	0	4.05	11	0	13	16	0	4	19	2.7	12.8	1.50	.302
Minor League Totals				0	0	3.52	13	2	15	19	0	4	23	2.3	13.5	1.50	.302

6 JORDAN WALKER, 3B

BILL MITCHELL

Born: May 22, 2002. **B-T:** R-R. **HT:** 6-5. **WT:** 220. **Drafted:** HS—Decatur, Ga., 2020 (1st round). **Signed by:** Charles Peterson.

TRACK RECORD: Walker was one of the few high school prospects who got to play meaningful games in the spring before the coronavirus pandemic shut everything down. He took advantage with a red-hot start to solidify himself as one of the top hitters and sluggers in the 2020 draft class. The Cardinals drafted him No. 21 overall and signed him for $2.9 million to forgo a Duke commitment. Walker was the last player signed by Cardinals area scout Charles Peterson, who died from Covid-19 three months later.

SCOUTING REPORT: Walker has the long arms and big frame befitting a power hitter. While he has some unavoidable length to his swing, he has shown a feel for hitting and can catch up to top velocity. He has a shot to be a fringe-average or even average hitter to go with his plus raw power, which will likely tick up to plus-plus as he continues to grow. Walker moves remarkably well for a big man and has an above-average arm at third base. His excellent work ethic gives him a shot to stick there, but he may have to move to first base depending on how much bigger he gets.

THE FUTURE: Walker has a chance to develop into a middle-of-the-order masher. He's still a teenager yet to make his pro debut and is many years away.

SCOUTING GRADES: **Hitting:** 45 **Power:** 60 **Running:** 45 **Fielding:** 45 **Arm:** 55

Year	Age	Club (League)	Class	AVG	G	AB	R	H	2B	3B	HR	RBI	BB	SO	SB	OBP	SLG
2020	17	Did not play—No minor league season															

7 KWANG HYUN KIM, LHP

MARY DECICCO/MLB PHOTOS VIA GETTY IMAGES

BA GRADE
45 Risk: Low

Born: July 22, 1988. **B-T:** L-L. **HT:** 6-2. **WT:** 195. **Signed:** South Korea, 2019. **Signed by:** Matt Slater.

TRACK RECORD: Kim was one of the stars of South Korea's gold medal-winning 2008 Olympic team and was the ace of the SK Wyverns in Korea's major league. The Cardinals signed him to a two-year, $8 million deal before the 2020 season. Kim began the year as the Cardinals' closer but moved to the rotation after the team's coronavirus outbreak and allowed one run or fewer in six of his seven starts.

SCOUTING REPORT: Kim locates on the edges of the strike zone and has a unique movement profile that helps his pitches play up. His 87-93 mph fastball has less vertical movement than most heaters, but he locates it to both sides of the plate and keeps hitters off of it with his assortment of secondary pitches. His low-80s changeup plays as a plus pitch because of his well above-average command, and his 85-87 mph slider has a short break that catches hitters off guard. Kim's fringe-average curveball is a big, slow breaker that locks up hitters while meandering to the plate at 67-72 mph. Kim mostly relies on soft contact for success and induces a high volume of ground balls, helping him to work quickly and avoid damage.

THE FUTURE: Kim can't blow away hitters, but he can keep them from squaring him up. He has earned a spot in the Cardinals' 2021 rotation.

SCOUTING GRADES: **Fastball:** 45 **Changeup:** 60 **Slider:** 55 **Curveball:** 45 **Control:** 60

Year	Age	Club (League)	Class	W	L	ERA	G	GS	IP	H	HR	BB	SO	BB/9	SO/9	WHIP	AVG
2017	28	Did not play															
2018	29	SK (KBO)	KOR	11	8	2.98	25	25	136	125	16	30	130	2.0	8.6	1.14	.226
2019	30	SK (KBO)	KOR	17	6	2.51	31	30	190	198	13	38	180	1.8	8.5	1.24	.252
2020	31	St. Louis (NL)	MAJ	3	0	1.62	8	7	39	28	3	12	24	2.8	5.5	1.03	.197
Major League Totals				3	0	1.62	8	7	39	28	3	12	24	2.8	5.5	1.03	.197

8 ANDREW KNIZNER, C

MARY DECICCO/MLB PHOTOS VIA GETTY IMAGES

BA GRADE

45 **Risk: Medium**

Born: Feb. 3, 1995. **B-T:** R-R. **HT:** 6-1. **WT:** 200. **Drafted:** North Carolina State, 2016, (7th round). **Signed by:** Charles Peterson.

TRACK RECORD: Knizner was a productive third baseman at North Carolina State but agreed to move behind the plate as a sophomore. The Cardinals drafted him in the seventh round in 2016 and he quickly made his way up the minors. Knizner has proven to be a better hitter than most catchers, but with Yadier Molina and Matt Wieters ahead of him, he's had just two brief big league callups so far.

SCOUTING REPORT: Knizner is an above-average hitter and hits the ball as hard as any Cardinals player—his 110 mph maximum exit velocity was fourth best on the team in 2020 even though he had only 17 plate appearances. Knizner hits more line drives than fly balls, but he has the strength for double-digit home run power if he can lift the ball in the air more. The big question is whether Knizner will be good enough defensively behind the plate. His hands are below-average, which limits his ability to frame pitches, and his blocking is also fringy. He has shown better understanding of pitch-calling, but—like everyone else—pales in comparison with Molina.

THE FUTURE: With Molina hitting free agency, Knizner entered the offseason as the team's internal option to start at catcher in 2021. He will have to improve defensively to nail down the everyday job.

SCOUTING GRADES: **Hitting:** 55 **Power:** 45 **Running:** 30 **Fielding:** 45 **Arm:** 45

Year	Age	Club (League)	Class	AVG	G	AB	R	H	2B	3B	HR	RBI	BB	SO	SB	OBP	SLG
2017	22	Springfield (TL)	AA	.324	51	182	27	59	13	0	4	22	14	27	0	.371	.462
	22	Peoria (MWL)	LoA	.279	44	179	18	50	10	1	8	29	9	22	1	.325	.480
2018	23	Memphis (PCL)	AAA	.315	17	54	3	17	5	0	0	4	4	8	0	.383	.407
	23	Springfield, MO (TL)	AA	.313	77	281	39	88	13	0	7	41	23	40	0	.365	.434
2019	24	St. Louis (NL)	MAJ	.226	18	53	7	12	2	0	2	7	4	14	2	.293	.377
	24	Memphis (PCL)	AAA	.276	66	246	41	68	10	0	12	34	24	37	2	.357	.463
2020	25	St. Louis (NL)	MAJ	.250	8	16	1	4	1	0	0	4	0	5	0	.235	.313
Major League Totals				.232	26	69	8	16	3	0	2	11	4	19	2	.280	.362
Minor League Totals				.303	308	1127	163	341	63	2	37	172	95	155	3	.369	.461

9 LANE THOMAS, OF

MARY DECICCO/MLB PHOTOS VIA GETTY IMAGES

BA GRADE

45 **Risk: Medium**

Born: Aug. 23, 1995. **B-T:** R-R. **HT:** 6-0. **WT:** 185. **Drafted:** HS—Knoxville, Tenn., 2014 (5th round). **Signed by:** Nate Murrie (Blue Jays).

TRACK RECORD: Acquired from the Blue Jays for international bonus pool space in 2017, Thomas has been productive when healthy but has had trouble staying on the field. He led the Cardinals system with 27 home runs in 2018 and had a loud big league debut in 2019, but it was cut short by a right wrist fracture. His 2020 season was derailed when he tested positive for Covid-19 amidst the teamwide outbreak. He missed almost all of August and looked overmatched when he returned in September.

SCOUTING REPORT: Thomas has some of the best tools in the system. He's a plus defender in center field, a plus-plus runner, has an average arm and average power. His only below-average tool is his fringy hitting ability. He expands his zone too much and is prone to over-aggressiveness, but when he focuses on line drives his power ensures that some of those drives clear the fence. Thomas' tools don't always add up to be the sum of his parts. His speed hasn't led to many stolen bases and he has concentration lapses in the outfield. He has the range to play center field and the arm for right.

THE FUTURE: Thomas has all the attributes teams look for in a fourth outfielder. He needs to stay healthy in order to gain a regular role.

SCOUTING GRADES: **Hitting:** 45 **Power:** 50 **Running:** 70 **Fielding:** 60 **Arm:** 50

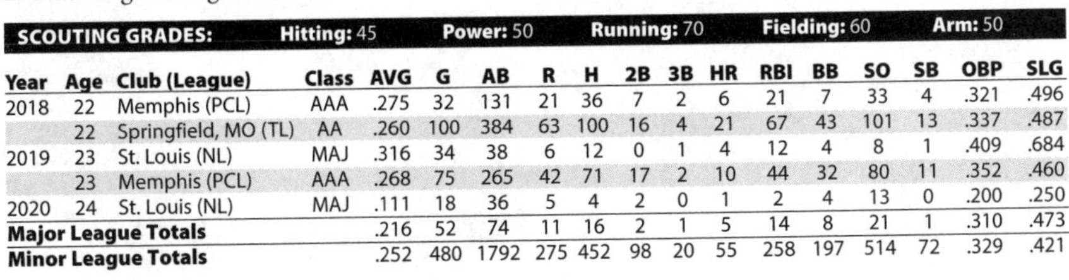

Year	Age	Club (League)	Class	AVG	G	AB	R	H	2B	3B	HR	RBI	BB	SO	SB	OBP	SLG
2018	22	Memphis (PCL)	AAA	.275	32	131	21	36	7	2	6	21	7	33	4	.321	.496
	22	Springfield, MO (TL)	AA	.260	100	384	63	100	16	4	21	67	43	101	13	.337	.487
2019	23	St. Louis (NL)	MAJ	.316	34	38	6	12	0	1	4	12	4	8	1	.409	.684
	23	Memphis (PCL)	AAA	.268	75	265	42	71	17	2	10	44	32	80	11	.352	.460
2020	24	St. Louis (NL)	MAJ	.111	18	36	5	4	2	0	1	2	4	13	0	.200	.250
Major League Totals				.216	52	74	11	16	2	1	5	14	8	21	1	.310	.473
Minor League Totals				.252	480	1792	275	452	98	20	55	258	197	514	72	.329	.421

10 JOHAN OVIEDO, RHP

Born: March 2, 1998. **B-T:** R-R. **HT:** 6-6. **WT:** 210. **Signed:** Cuba, 2016. **Signed by:** Angel Ovalles.

MARY DECICCO/MLB PHOTOS VIA GETTY IMAGES

BA GRADE
50 Risk: High

TRACK RECORD: Oviedo had an excellent spring training and was ticketed for the alternate training site, but he was forced into emergency duty in the Cardinals' rotation after the teamwide coronavirus outbreak decimated their pitching staff. Oviedo wasn't quite ready and got hit hard. He also had a stint on the injured list after being exposed to someone who tested positive for Covid-19.

SCOUTING REPORT: The 6-foot-6 Oviedo has long arms, excellent extension and two above-average to plus pitches. His fastball sits at 94-95 mph and has touched 98, and his slider sits in the mid 80s with bite to draw swings and misses. Oviedo is a long-limbed pitcher still learning to harness his body and has below-average command and control. The result was his fastball got too much of the plate and he often fell behind hitters, rendering him unable to bury his slider as a chase pitch in strikeout situations. Oviedo's average curveball with 11-to-5 shape proved better than expected in the majors. His changeup shows deception and drop but is inconsistent.

THE FUTURE: Oviedo is still developing and has a chance to be a back-of-the-rotation starter. He'll return to the minors in 2021 and could re-emerge in the majors at some point during the year.

SCOUTING GRADES: **Fastball:** 60 **Slider:** 55 **Curveball:** 50 **Changeup:** 45 **Control:** 40

Year	Age	Club (League)	Class	W	L	ERA	G	GS	IP	H	HR	BB	SO	BB/9	SO/9	WHIP	AVG
2017	19	Johnson City (APP)	R	2	1	4.88	6	6	28	22	0	18	31	5.9	10.1	1.45	.176
	19	State College (NYP)	SS	2	2	4.56	8	8	47	53	3	18	39	3.4	7.4	1.50	.255
2018	20	Peoria (MWL)	LoA	10	10	4.22	25	23	122	108	6	79	118	5.8	8.7	1.54	.199
2019	21	Palm Beach (FSL)	HiA	5	0	1.60	6	5	34	29	1	12	35	3.2	9.4	1.22	.206
	21	Springfield, MO (TL)	AA	7	8	5.65	23	23	113	120	9	64	128	5.1	10.2	1.63	.233
2020	22	St. Louis (NL)	MAJ	0	3	5.47	5	5	25	24	3	10	16	3.6	5.8	1.38	.253
Major League Totals				0	3	5.47	5	5	24	24	3	10	16	3.7	5.8	1.38	.253
Minor League Totals				26	22	4.36	75	72	365	351	19	197	380	4.9	9.4	1.50	.253

11 MASYN WINN, RHP/SS

BA GRADE
55 Risk: Extreme

Born: March 21, 2002. **B-T:** R-R. **HT:** 5-11. **WT:** 180. **Drafted:** HS—Kingwood, Texas, 2020 (2nd round). **Signed by:** Jabari Barnett.

TRACK RECORD: Generally, prospects who attempt to be two-way players in pro ball are pitchers who also play first base or DH. Winn is the rare player who could succeed as a shortstop and a righthander. No prominent draft pick has tried to do both since 2008 first-round pick Casey Kelly played shortstop and pitched in the lower levels of the minors for the Red Sox. He eventually moved to the mound full-time.

SCOUTING REPORT: Winn is going to make the Cardinals' decision on what is his best long-term home very difficult. He's an athletic, rangy shortstop with a plus-plus arm and plus speed. He plays a little too fast at times, but his arm gives him an extra step of range most shortstops don't have. Winn's performance at the World Wood Bat Championship in 2019 cemented his status as a two-way star. Winn sat at 95 mph and touched 98 for three innings while mixing in a potentially plus slider and changeup. He also went 3-for-4 with a home run and triple, with all three hits having 95 mph or better exit velocities. Winn has above-average raw power, in addition to being athletic and an intense competitor.

THE FUTURE: The Cardinals are expected to send Winn out first as a shortstop. It's hard to have him work on both because of the demands on his arm, but St. Louis is serious about letting him try to develop both as a position player and a pitcher.

Year	Age	Club (League)	Class	AVG	G	AB	R	H	2B	3B	HR	RBI	BB	SO	SB	OBP	SLG
2020	18	Did not play—No minor league season															

12 EDWIN NUNEZ, RHP

BREAKOUT
BA GRADE
55 Risk: Extreme

Born: Nov. 5, 2001. **B-T:** R-R. **HT:** 6-3. **WT:** 185. **Signed:** Dominican Republic, 2020. **Signed by:** Alix Martinez.

TRACK RECORD: MLB initially suspended Nunez from signing for a year because of an issue regarding his age. While he was ineligible, his stuff just kept getting better and better. On the first day after MLB ended the scouting/signing shutdown that had been put in place during the coronavirus pandemic, the Cardinals signed Nunez for $525,000.

SCOUTING REPORT: Nunez already can touch 100 mph with above-average spin. He also has an athletic build and a strong if lean frame. In addition to his potentially plus-plus fastball, Nunez also has a less consistent slider that flashes plus potential but sometimes gets slurvy. He's yet to throw in an official game, but Nunez's delivery has starter traits because he repeats it well. It's hard to project his control and command when he's so far away, but his delivery is clean.

THE FUTURE: Considering his age—he'll turn 19 before Opening Day—Nunez should jump straight to the U.S. and Class A in 2021. The Cardinals have plenty of successful experience at helping older Latin America signees make a speedy adjustment to pro ball. Throwing 100 mph has been found to help that transition.

Year	Age	Club (League)	Class	W	L	ERA	G	GS	IP	H	HR	BB	SO	BB/9	SO/9	WHIP	AVG
2020	18	Did not play—Signed 2021 contract															

13 TINK HENCE, RHP

Born: Aug. 6, 2002. **B-T:** R-R. **HT:** 6-1. **WT:** 175. **Drafted:** HS—Pine Bluff, Ark., 2020 (2nd round supplemental). **Signed by:** Dirk Kinney.

TRACK RECORD: As a child, Hence (whose given name is Markevian) was nicknamed Stinker, but his dad quickly changed it to Tink. He was a travel teammate of Cardinals' second-round pick Masyn Winn on a team coached by Cardinals area scout Dirk Kinney. Like Winn, Hence was committed to play at Arkansas.

SCOUTING REPORT: Hence has been a fixture on the baseball diamond since he ditched diapers. His stuff isn't consistent yet, but at his best it's already extremely impressive. His fastball sits between 90-93 mph but he can crank it up to 95-96 mph and get swings and misses at the top of the zone. His slider and curveball are two distinct pitches. Both flash plus and he has solid feel for locating them. He's even shown the potential for an average changeup. Hence is athletic and has plenty of room to fill out. He needs to continue to improve the consistency of his delivery as he gets stronger, but he has more upside than most supplemental second-round picks.

THE FUTURE: The sky's the limit with Hence, who shows feel for spinning breaking balls to go with a promising fastball. Like most pitchers drafted out of high school, patience will be required.

Year	Age	Club (League)	Class	W	L	ERA	G	GS	IP	H	HR	BB	SO	BB/9	SO/9	WHIP	AVG
2020	17	Did not play—No minor league season															

14 ELEHURIS MONTERO, 3B

BA GRADE
55 Risk: Extreme

Born: Aug. 17, 1998. **B-T:** R-R. **HT:** 6-3. **WT:** 215. **Signed:** Dominican Republic, 2014. **Signed by:** Angel Ovalles.

TRACK RECORD: The MVP of the Midwest League in 2018, Montero's speedy ascent through the system hit a detour in 2019 when injuries to his wrist and hand caused him to miss significant time. When he did play, he struggled. The Cardinals added him to their 40-man roster after the 2019 season. Montero spent 2020 at the Cardinals' alternate training site.

SCOUTING REPORT: Montero has a wide stance and starts his swing with a very modest load. His bat stays in the strike zone a long time, giving him a chance to remain on plane with the ball, which should lead to line drives but does limit his power. He's strong enough to still get to average power despite his hit-over-power approach. His pitch recognition needs to improve, but his swing, hand-eye coordination and bat speed give him the potential to be an above-average hitter. At third base, Montero has a plus arm that has earned some plus-plus grades, but his range is limited and his thick body could lead to an eventual move to first.

THE FUTURE: Montero's bounceback year had to be pushed to 2021 because of the pandemic. He struggled at times at the alternate site, but a return to Double-A Springfield could get him back on track.

Year	Age	Club (League)	Class	AVG	G	AB	R	H	2B	3B	HR	RBI	BB	SO	SB	OBP	SLG
2019	20	Springfield, MO (TL)	AA	.188	59	224	23	42	8	0	7	18	14	74	0	.235	.317
	20	Cardinals (GCL)	R	.308	4	13	1	4	0	0	0	0	1	2	0	.400	.308
Minor League Totals				.269	360	1347	207	362	84	7	32	192	129	319	5	.339	.413

15 ANGEL RONDON, RHP

Born: Dec. 1, 1997. **B-T:** R-R. **HT:** 6-2. **WT:** 185. **Signed:** Dominican Republic, 2016. **Signed by:** Raymi Dicent/Angel Ovalles.

TRACK RECORD: Yet another in a long line of savvy international signings by the Cardinals, Rondon was 18 when St. Louis signed him in 2016. Five years later, the Cardinals added him to their 40-man roster, further validating an impressive rise through the minors.

SCOUTING REPORT: Instead of an encore in games that count, Rondon had to settle for solid work at the club's alternate training site. Facing older hitters, his blend of savvy and stuff baffled once again. Rondon topped out at 93-94 at the ATS but has touched 96-97. He varies speeds well and is comfortable locating his fastball, slider, curveball and changeup at any point in the count. Rondon's slider is arguably his only above-average pitch, but he can make his average curve as big, slow or hard as he needs. His changeup, once average, has backed up. He has average control and lives at the edges of the zone.

THE FUTURE: After pitching with Aguillas in the Dominican League, Rondon should head to Triple-A to begin 2021. He's not overpowering, but evaluators rave about his feel for pitching. He could eventually be a multi-inning reliever, a back-end starter or even a setup man.

Year	Age	Club (League)	Class	W	L	ERA	G	GS	IP	H	HR	BB	SO	BB/9	SO/9	WHIP	AVG
2019	21	Palm Beach (FSL)	HiA	5	1	2.20	8	8	45	26	3	17	47	3.4	9.4	0.96	.145
	21	Springfield, MO (TL)	AA	6	6	3.21	20	20	115	99	11	42	112	3.3	8.8	1.23	.206
Minor League Totals				19	19	3.01	71	61	347	298	28	119	341	3.1	8.8	1.20	.229

16 JUSTIN WILLIAMS, OF

BA GRADE
45 Risk: Medium

Born: Aug. 20, 1995. **B-T:** L-R. **HT:** 6-2. **WT:** 215. **Drafted:** HS—Houma, La., 2013 (2nd round). **Signed by:** Rusty Pendergass (D-Backs).

TRACK RECORD: Williams' path to the majors has been long and winding. A D-Backs draftee, Williams was traded the next year to the Rays in a swap that brought Jeremy Hellickson to Arizona. He made his MLB debut in 2018 with the Rays. He was then dealt to the Cardinals for Tommy Pham at the trade deadline. A broken hand suffered punching a TV and hamstring injuries slowed him in 2019, but he returned to the majors briefly in September 2020.

SCOUTING REPORT: Williams hits the ball very hard. He just struggles to hit the ball very hard in the air. With his level swing, he hits stinging singles and doubles rather than home runs. Williams has above-average raw power. He will take a walk and he does a solid job of recognizing spin. He puts in good at-bats against lefthanders. A fringe-average runner, Williams' plus arm is an asset in right field, but he has struggled with reads and when to lay out and when to pull up, which is why he's considered a fringe-average defender.

THE FUTURE: Williams' ties a record with this Prospect Handbook appearance—he's been in eight books since 2014. He's out of options and will head to spring training looking to add a much-needed lefty bat to the very righthanded Cardinals' lineup.

Year	Age	Club (League)	Class	AVG	G	AB	R	H	2B	3B	HR	RBI	BB	SO	SB	OBP	SLG
2020	24	St. Louis (NL)	MAJ	.200	3	5	0	1	0	0	0	0	1	2	0	.333	.200
Major League Totals				.167	4	6	0	1	0	0	0	0	1	2	0	.286	.167
Minor League Totals				.296	601	2261	302	670	126	12	55	348	147	471	18	.342	.436

17 KODI WHITLEY, RHP

BA GRADE
45 Risk: Medium

Born: Feb. 21, 1995. **B-T:** R-R. **HT:** 6-4. **WT:** 220. **Drafted:** Mount Olive (N.C.), 2017 (27th round). **Signed by:** T. C. Calhoun.

TRACK RECORD: The Cardinals spotted and signed Whitley despite him throwing only 4.1 innings as a redshirt junior at Division II Mount Olive as he returned from Tommy John surgery. Whitley has reworked his delivery to better use his legs and drive off the mound, transforming himself into a fast-moving power reliever. He made the Cardinals' Opening Day roster but was added to the 10-day injured list during the Cardinals' coronavirus shutdown. He missed further time with a sore elbow, but returned late in September and made the postseason roster.

SCOUTING REPORT: Whitley's delivery is extremely short in the back, as he simply rocks into loading his plant leg and then explodes to the plate. It's a simple delivery and he repeats it well, showing above-average control. He works up and down in the strike zone, elevating a 92-95 mph above-average fastball that has above-average carry at the top of the zone. He has touched 97-98 in the past, but didn't reach those heights in the majors in 2020. Whitley's fastball sets up a mid-80s above-average slider that dives below the zone much more than it tilts. The former starter has more comfort throwing his straight mid-80s fringe-average changeup than most relievers. Because he works up and down, he doesn't have a significant platoon disadvantage.

THE FUTURE: Whitley should fit nicely in the Cardinals' 2021 bullpen. His combination of stuff and control gives him a shot at a significant role as a setup man.

Year	Age	Club (League)	Class	W	L	ERA	G	GS	IP	H	HR	BB	SO	BB/9	SO/9	WHIP	AVG
2020	25	St. Louis (NL)	MAJ	0	0	1.93	4	0	5	2	1	1	5	1.9	9.6	0.64	.125
Major League Totals				0	0	1.93	4	0	4	2	1	1	5	1.9	9.6	0.64	.125
Minor League Totals				7	6	2.01	104	2	156	136	5	49	168	2.8	9.7	1.18	.232

18 MALCOM NUNEZ, 3B

BA GRADE 50 **Risk: Extreme**

Born: March 9, 2001. **B-T:** R-R. **HT:** 5-11. **WT:** 205. **Signed:** Cuba, 2018.
Signed by: Alix Martinez/Angel Ovalles.

TRACK RECORD: One of the best players at the 2016 15U World Cup, Nunez has long been a productive hitter. The Cardinals may have landed a steal because they signed him in a year when they were unable to spend more than $300,000 on the international market. Nunez won the Dominican Summer League triple crown in his debut, hitting .415 with 13 home runs and 59 RBIs.

SCOUTING REPORT: Nunez's follow-up was not nearly as impressive. He was demoted after struggling at low Class A Peoria, but didn't set the world on fire in the Appalachian League either. In 2020, Nunez was invited to the Cardinals' alternate training site, where he spent a lot of time working on his defense at third base. Nunez is already on the borderline of getting too big for the position, but he moves well for his size. He has an inconsistent arm that flashes plus. Nunez has plus power, above-average bat speed and solid plate coverage, but right now he has a grip-and-rip approach.

THE FUTURE: It's fair to give a mulligan to a Cuban teenager jumping straight from the Dominican Summer League to the Midwest League. Nunez should get another shot at Class A. This year will be an important one to prove his bat is as advanced as advertised.

Year	Age	Club (League)	Class	AVG	G	AB	R	H	2B	3B	HR	RBI	BB	SO	SB	OBP	SLG
2019	18	Johnson City (APP)	R	.254	37	130	14	33	11	0	2	13	13	32	3	.336	.385
	18	Peoria (MWL)	LoA	.183	21	71	5	13	1	0	0	5	5	15	0	.247	.197
Minor League Totals				.312	102	365	63	114	28	2	15	77	44	76	6	.396	.523

19 JHON TORRES, OF

BA GRADE 50 **Risk: Extreme**

Born: March 29, 2000. **B-T:** R-R. **HT:** 6-4. **WT:** 199. **Signed:** Colombia, 2016.
Signed by: Domingo Toribio/Felix Nivar/Koby Perez (Indians).

TRACK RECORD: The Indians signed Torres out of Colombia for $150,000 and watched him quickly fill out and blossom. St. Louis picked him up along with Conner Capel in a deal that sent Oscar Mercado to the Indians in 2018. Torres struggled in 2019 with an aggressive jump to low Class A Peoria, but he was one of the better prospects in the Appalachian League after a midseason demotion. With a 60-player roster limit, Torres was not part of the Cardinals' alternate training site.

SCOUTING REPORT: Torres could develop plus power one day if he can learn to get into better counts and pounce on juicy pitches. He will likely always have some swing and miss, even on hittable pitches, because he has timing issues. Torres is an average runner, and an above-average defender in the corner outfield spots with an above-average arm. He has solid athleticism to go with his developing strength.

THE FUTURE: Torres is Rule 5 eligible even before he's established himself in full-season ball. The tools are there to be a well-rounded player, but like many prospects he'll need to add plate discipline and pitch recognition to get to his potential.

Year	Age	Club (League)	Class	AVG	G	AB	R	H	2B	3B	HR	RBI	BB	SO	SB	OBP	SLG
2019	19	Johnson City (APP)	R	.286	33	112	24	32	9	0	6	17	19	36	0	.391	.527
	19	Peoria (MWL)	LoA	.167	21	66	4	11	3	0	0	8	7	29	0	.240	.212
Minor League Totals				.271	152	524	80	142	28	3	19	90	73	143	8	.368	.445

20 JULIO RODRIGUEZ, C

Born: June 11, 1997. **B-T:** R-R. **HT:** 6-0. **WT:** 197. **Signed:** Dominican Republic, 2016. **Signed by:** Braly Guzman/Angel Ovalles.

TRACK RECORD: Rodriguez is a testament to the value of digging a little deeper to scout. He signed for $25,000 as an 18-year-old and turned 19 before his second game in the Dominican Summer League, but the Cardinals quickly found his catch-and-throw skills made him a very useful backstop. He was a Florida State League all-star in 2019, made it to Double-A at the end of that year, and spent the summer of 2020 at the alternate training site.

SCOUTING REPORT: Rodriguez does not have a plus tool, but his game-calling, receiving and blocking skills make him an above-average defender and give him a path to a useful MLB career. He's athletic for a catcher and has solid balance and flexibility in his setup. His arm strength is average, but he has a quick transfer and throws accurately. Rodriguez has a contact-oriented approach with a short stroke. He has below-average power, but he can yank a line drive over the left field fence. Like many catchers, he's a baseclogger.

THE FUTURE: Rodriguez was left off the 40-man roster but went unpicked in the Rule 5 draft. He's ready to head to Double-A. With his reliable glove, he's not far away from being a backup option in the major leagues.

Year	Age	Club (League)	Class	AVG	G	AB	R	H	2B	3B	HR	RBI	BB	SO	SB	OBP	SLG
2019	22	Palm Beach (FSL)	HiA	.276	71	268	28	74	14	0	7	31	16	53	0	.321	.407
	22	Springfield, MO (TL)	AA	.222	14	45	2	10	1	0	1	7	2	15	0	.255	.311
Minor League Totals				.275	249	932	114	256	54	6	28	158	67	178	0	.324	.436

21 TREJYN FLETCHER, OF

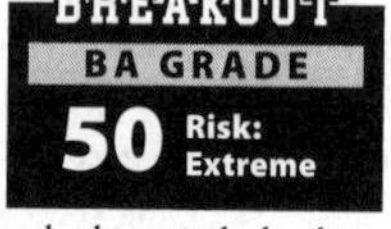

Born: April 30, 2001. **B-T:** R-R. **HT:** 6-2. **WT:** 200. **Drafted:** HS—Portland, Maine, 2019 (2nd round). **Signed by:** Jim Negrych.

TRACK RECORD: The Cardinals had to work hard to scout Fletcher, who reclassified to join the 2019 class six months before the draft. That meant teams had to circle back to scout him more heavily, but it's not easy to scout high school prospects in Maine during the spring. The Cardinals were confident in what they had seen from him in multiple showcase events. Fletcher became the third-highest Maine prep draftee ever.

SCOUTING REPORT: Fletcher is a plus-plus runner with some of the best athleticism in the organization. His twitchy athleticism also carries over to the plate, where he has a fast, handsy swing with above-average bat speed. There's not a lot Fletcher can't do—he was also 91-94 mph off the mound in high school, and that plus arm carries over to the outfield. Fletcher displays plus raw power in batting practice, but he has work to do at laying off breaking balls out of the zone.

THE FUTURE: Even with a lost year, Fletcher will play 2021 as a 19-year-old. His athleticism, speed and center field defense give him foundational tools that should ensure a lengthy pro career.

Year	Age	Club (League)	Class	AVG	G	AB	R	H	2B	3B	HR	RBI	BB	SO	SB	OBP	SLG
2019	18	Johnson City (APP)	R	.228	34	123	9	28	4	1	2	18	7	59	7	.271	.325
	18	Cardinals (GCL)	R	.297	9	37	6	11	3	0	2	8	4	17	0	.357	.541
Minor League Totals				.244	43	160	15	39	7	1	4	26	11	76	7	.291	.375

22 SETH ELLEDGE, RHP

BA GRADE
40 Risk: Medium

Born: May 20, 1996. **B-T:** R-R. **HT:** 6-3. **WT:** 230. **Drafted:** Dallas Baptist, 2017 (4th round). **Signed by:** Ty Bowman (Mariners).

TRACK RECORD: When the Cardinals traded Sam Tuiavaila to the Mariners at the trade deadline in 2018, they acquired an eventual replacement. Elledge had a dominating MLB debut on Aug. 16, when he struck out five in 2.2 hitless innings. He struggled with his control, but he was a regular option in the Cardinals' bullpen in September.

SCOUTING REPORT: There's little subtlety to Elledge's approach. He has two pitches, and likes to work up and away with his 92-95 mph, above-average fastball. The pitch has late life and run to get swings and misses at the top of the zone. The fastball sets up Elledge's plus, low-80s slider, which has above-average depth but generally is a chase pitch. Only one out of every four he threw in the majors finished in the strike zone, but he can start it out over the plate before it dives to the dirt down and away from righthanders. Lefties hit . 316/.458/.842 against Elledge because he doesn't throw anything that breaks away, so they can focus on the inner half of the plate. He can locate to his gloveside but not armside.

THE FUTURE: Elledge was entrusted with pitching the seventh and eighth innings when the Cardinals were behind. Now he needs to earn Mike Shildt's trust to work in higher-leverage situations.

Year	Age	Club (League)	Class	W	L	ERA	G	GS	IP	H	HR	BB	SO	BB/9	SO/9	WHIP	AVG
2020	24	St. Louis (NL)	MAJ	1	0	4.63	12	0	12	11	2	8	14	6.2	10.8	1.63	.262
Major League Totals				1	0	4.63	12	0	11	11	2	8	14	6.2	10.8	1.63	.262
Minor League Totals				17	6	3.29	110	3	147	109	11	61	191	3.7	11.6	1.15	.209

23 JUNIOR FERNANDEZ, RHP

BA GRADE
45 **Risk: High**

Born: March 2, 1997. **B-T:** R-R. **HT:** 6-1. **WT:** 180. **Signed:** Dominican Republic, 2014. **Signed by:** Rodney Jimenez/Angel Ovalles.

TRACK RECORD: Fernandez had a breakout season in 2019, when he leapt from high Class A to the majors. He made his MLB debut in August. He made the Cardinals' 2020 Opening Day rotation, but soon tested positive for Covid-19. He returned to action in September, then tried to make up for lost time by pitching in the Dominican League.

SCOUTING REPORT: Fernandez's stuff took a step back in 2020, which is troubling because his plus fastball has long paved his way to the majors. In 2019, Fernandez sat at 95-97 mph and bumped 99. In 2020, he sat at 93-95 mph and touched 97 once. Fernandez does not locate his fringe-average downer-breaking slider very well, and his above-average changeup is not as effective when paired with a less hairy fastball. His swing-and-miss rate in his admittedly short MLB stints dropped by half from 2019 to 2020. Fernandez's control is fringe-average, but his command wavers. He needs to get his fastball back or improve his slider to have success.

THE FUTURE: Fernandez did struggle in 2020, but his 2019 season was excellent, and his bout with the coronavirus explains some of his setback. He will compete for a spot in the Cardinals bullpen in 2021.

Year	Age	Club (League)	Class	W	L	ERA	G	GS	IP	H	HR	BB	SO	BB/9	SO/9	WHIP	AVG
2020	23	St. Louis (NL)	MAJ	0	0	18.00	3	0	3	6	1	2	2	6.0	6.0	2.67	.429
Major League Totals				0	1	7.98	16	0	14	15	3	8	18	4.9	11.1	1.57	.259
Minor League Totals				20	19	3.57	129	52	393	363	14	170	326	3.9	7.5	1.35	.247

24 IAN BEDELL, RHP

BA GRADE
45 **Risk: High**

Born: Sept. 5, 1999. **B-T:** R-R. **HT:** 6-2. **WT:** 198. **Drafted:** Missouri, 2020 (4th round). **Signed by:** Dirk Kinney.

TRACK RECORD: After an impressive sophomore season as a reliever, Bedell earned himself a lot of money by making six dominant starts in the Cape Cod League in the summer of 2019. He went 4-0, 0.59 in six starts with 36 strikeouts and three walks in 31 innings. Bedell's excellent summer became even more important when the 2020 college season was shut down in mid March. By then, he had made four solid starts in Missouri's weekend rotation.

SCOUTING REPORT: Nothing Bedell throws stands out, but his competitiveness and confidence are apparent. His 89-93 mph fastball is fringe-average, although some scouts see it as average because of his above-average command and plus control. His changeup is average as well. He also throws an average low-80s spike curveball and he's recently added a fringe-average slider.

THE FUTURE: Bedell is seen as a high-floor, quick mover with a solid track record of success. Bedell has had some success in the bullpen in college and will touch 94-95 more often as a reliever, but his command and control should give him a shot to prove he can be a starter.

Year	Age	Club (League)	Class	W	L	ERA	G	GS	IP	H	HR	BB	SO	BB/9	SO/9	WHIP	AVG
2020	20	Did not play—No minor league season															

25 JAKE WOODFORD, RHP

BA GRADE
40 **Risk: Medium**

Born: Oct. 28, 1996. **B-T:** R-R. **HT:** 6-4. **WT:** 220. **Drafted:** HS—Tampa, 2015 (1st round supplemental). **Signed by:** Mike Debiase.

TRACK RECORD: A high school teammate of Kyle Tucker at Tampa's Plant High, Woodford has taken a little longer than Tucker to develop but he's climbed the minor league ladder steadily, gotten stronger and thrown harder. Woodford has never dominated as a pro, but he's been dependable enough to work his way to the majors.

SCOUTING REPORT: Working out of the pen for multiple innings in his big league debut, Woodford pitched like a starter. He mixed fastballs, sliders, curveballs and even a couple of changeups, but his command strayed. Woodford's fringe-average 92-94 mph fastball is relatively straight. He gives up hard contact if he isn't around the edges of the zone. He showed little feel for his potentially above-average, mid-70s curveball. He bounces it or sails it, but it has exceptional depth if he can figure out better command. He commands his average slider the best, and it has solid depth but little tilt.

THE FUTURE: Woodford was hit hard in his MLB debut, but his curveball and slider give him a shot to develop into a multi-inning reliever or spot starter.

Year	Age	Club (League)	Class	W	L	ERA	G	GS	IP	H	HR	BB	SO	BB/9	SO/9	WHIP	AVG
2020	23	St. Louis (NL)	MAJ	1	0	5.57	12	1	21	20	7	5	16	2.1	6.9	1.19	.253
Major League Totals				1	0	5.57	12	1	21	20	7	5	16	2.1	6.9	1.19	.253
Minor League Totals				30	32	3.87	106	101	550	540	55	220	407	3.6	6.7	1.38	.258

26 TONY LOCEY, RHP

BA GRADE
45 Risk: High

Born: July 29, 1998. **B-T:** R-R. **HT:** 6-3. **WT:** 239. **Drafted:** Georgia, 2019 (3rd round). **Signed by:** Charles Peterson.

TRACK RECORD: A high school teammate of Orioles lefty D.L. Hall and Buffalo Bills quarterback Jake Fromm, Locey went from being a midweek starter and reliever as a sophomore to a fixture in Georgia's weekend rotation and eventually its Friday starter as a junior. When he was promoted to low Class A Peoria, he followed in his father's footsteps—Tony Sr. pitched for Peoria in 1994.

SCOUTING REPORT: Locey's plus fastball has long been his calling card. It sits 93-96 mph and will touch 98. He locates it well and has developed average control. His arm can be a little late catching up to his lower half in his delivery. His slider has the movement of a potentially plus pitch, but right now it's more of a chase pitch than one he can throw convincingly near the strike zone. He also has thrown a get-me-over curveball as a surprise early-count pitch.

THE FUTURE: Locey will need to develop a more reliable third pitch if he wants to stay a starter for the Cardinals, but even if he can't, his fastball/slider combo gives him a solid chance to be a power reliever.

Year	Age	Club (League)	Class	W	L	ERA	G	GS	IP	H	HR	BB	SO	BB/9	SO/9	WHIP	AVG
2019	20	Peoria (MWL)	LoA	1	2	6.00	10	0	15	15	1	10	28	6.0	16.8	1.67	.197
	20	Cardinals (GCL)	R	0	0	0.00	2	0	2	1	0	2	3	9.0	13.5	1.50	.111
Minor League Totals				1	2	5.29	12	0	17	16	1	12	31	6.4	16.4	1.65	.246

27 ALEC BURLESON, OF

BA GRADE
45 Risk: High

Born: Nov. 25, 1998. **B-T:** L-L. **HT:** 6-2. **WT:** 212. **Drafted:** East Carolina, 2020 (2nd round). **Signed by:** T.C. Calhoun.

TRACK RECORD: Burleson was a star from day one at East Carolina as a pitcher and in his sophomore season turned into one of the Pirates' best hitters as well. He was a member of USA Baseball's Collegiate National team as a two-way player. As the 70th overall pick, he became the fourth-highest draftee in school history.

SCOUTING REPORT: Burleson does not accept strikeouts as a price of power. He struck out just 37 times in his three years at ECU and just three times in 75 plate appearances as a junior. Despite his size and strength, Burleson is primarily a contact-oriented hitter who does not sell out to get to power. He hit .341/.387/.496 for his ECU career. There is hope that his focus on hitting will help him focus on getting even stronger, as his profile is somewhat dependent on him getting to more of his above-average raw power. The Cardinals are going to start Burleson in the outfield, a spot he played sporadically as an amateur. His below-average speed limits him to the corners, but he also has shown he's a nimble first baseman.

THE FUTURE: Pure hitters often get to their power eventually if they keep making solid contact, and Burleson generates loads of consistent contact.

Year	Age	Club (League)	Class	AVG	G	AB	R	H	2B	3B	HR	RBI	BB	SO	SB	OBP	SLG
2020	21	Did not play—No minor league season															

28 MATEO GIL, SS

BA GRADE
45 Risk: Very High

Born: July 24, 2000. **B-T:** R-R. **HT:** 6-1. **WT:** 180. **Drafted:** HS—Keller, Texas, 2018 (3rd round). **Signed by:** Tom Lipari.

TRACK RECORD: The son of former big league shortstop Benji Gil, Mateo is the type of player most negatively affected by the loss of a 2020 season. The Cardinals have been impressed by Gil's development so far, but the loss of the season means he will enter his fourth pro year looking to make a full-season roster for the first time.

SCOUTING REPORT: It's hard to find evaluators who see Gil as a big league regular, but it's easy to find those who see him as a future MLB utility infielder. Gil has some whip to his bat and solid barrel control, but he doesn't do a lot of damage when he makes contact. Gil's body is still filling out, so there is hope he'll add more power in his 20s. Gil has an above-average arm which should allow him to stick at shortstop. His hands and range are average and he has a solid understanding of positioning and getting a good first step. He's an above-average runner.

THE FUTURE: Gil is more than ready for full-season ball. His long-term role is likely bouncing around the infield and hitting at the bottom of the order, but further physical development could raise that ceiling.

Year	Age	Club (League)	Class	AVG	G	AB	R	H	2B	3B	HR	RBI	BB	SO	SB	OBP	SLG
2019	18	Palm Beach (FSL)	HiA	.000	2	6	0	0	0	0	0	0	0	2	0	.000	.000
	18	Johnson City (APP)	R	.270	51	204	42	55	8	2	7	30	17	56	1	.324	.431
Minor League Totals				.257	98	381	69	98	14	3	8	50	37	109	3	.327	.373

29 LEVI PRATER, LHP

BA GRADE
45 **Risk: Very High**

Born: June 20, 1999. **B-T:** B-L. **HT:** 6-2. **WT:** 175. **Drafted:** Oklahoma, 2020 (4th round). **Signed by:** Tom Lipari.

TRACK RECORD: Perseverance has never been a problem for Prater. He lost three fingers on his right hand in a lawnmower accident when he was 2. The injury never slowed him as a pitcher, and he's a switch-hitter too. He was an extremely reliable starter for Oklahoma as one-third of a weekend rotation that was all drafted in 2020's shortened five-round draft.

SCOUTING REPORT: Prater pitches with a lot of deception. He works from a lower arm slot and pitches from the first-base side of the rubber. Combined with his closed-off delivery, that means that lefties especially have a hard time picking up the ball. The deception has helped Prater's fringe-average 90-93 mph fastball be effective. His average slider works more because of location than power or bite—lefties don't see it well and he is comfortable back-footing it to righthanders. His average changeup keeps righthanders honest because it gives them something to worry about on the outer third of the plate. He has fringy control, but that's partly because he knows he has to nibble. His command is better than his control.

THE FUTURE: Prater is a back-end starter who may end up working in the bullpen to help his stuff play up. He has a knack for getting the most out of his stuff.

Year	Age	Club (League)	Class	W	L	ERA	G	GS	IP	H	HR	BB	SO	BB/9	SO/9	WHIP	AVG
2020	21	Did not play—No minor league season															

30 EDMUNDO SOSA, SS

BA GRADE
40 **Risk: Medium**

Born: March 6, 1996. **B-T:** R-R. **HT:** 5-11. **WT:** 170. **Signed:** Panama, 2012. **Signed by:** Arquimedes Nieto.

TRACK RECORD: Sosa was a high-profile international signing out of Panama in 2012, far enough back that he was a teammate of Jack Flaherty in the Gulf Coast League in 2014. Sosa's path to the majors has been frustrating. He made the Cardinals' Opening Day roster in 2020 but contracted Covid-19 before he played in a game. Once he recovered, he remained at the alternate training site.

SCOUTING REPORT: Sosa's value is as a reliable defender who can play second base, third base or shortstop without any issues. He's an above-average defender at all three. Offensively, Sosa has made steady improvements and found the more lively Triple-A ball to his liking, as he set a career high with 17 home runs in 2019. He projects as a below-average hitter with below-average power in the big leagues. His aggressiveness means he does not get on base very often.

THE FUTURE: This is an important season for Sosa, as he's already used four options. He either makes the Opening Day roster or will have to be placed on outright waivers. He's ready to be a utilityman but time is running out to claim that job.

Year	Age	Club (League)	Class	AVG	G	AB	R	H	2B	3B	HR	RBI	BB	SO	SB	OBP	SLG
2020	24	St. Louis (NL)	MAJ	--	0	0	0	0	0	0	0	0	0	0	0	--	--
Major League Totals				.200	11	10	3	2	0	0	0	0	2	3	1	.385	.200
Minor League Totals				.283	547	2090	312	592	96	22	44	237	129	389	37	.334	.413

MORE PROSPECTS TO KNOW

31 ALVARO SEIJAS, RHP

Seijas was outrighted off the Cardinals' 40-man roster in 2020, but he still has a shot to be a multi-inning reliever if he improves his command and pitch selection.

32 LUKEN BAKER, 1B

Baker's massive power hasn't turned into home runs in pro ball, but there's still reason to think they will. They'll need to if he's going to have a major league future because power is his carrying tool.

33 JOHN NOGOWSKI, 1B

Nogowski got a cameo in the majors in 2020. He's a first baseman who has never slugged .500 in a season in the minors, but his excellent strike-zone judgement makes him an on-base machine.

34 DELVIN PEREZ, SS

Perez will never reach the heights expected of him when he was the Cardinals' 2016 first-round pick, but he is still an impressive defender, which gives him a path to the majors.

35 JUSTIN TOERNER, OF

Toerner is a potential fourth outfielder who can play all three outfield spots but needs to bounce back from a rough finish to 2019 in his first taste of Double-A.

36 ANDRE PALLANTE, RHP

SLEEPER

A productive starter at UC Irvine, Pallante may end up as a reliever. He has a 92-95 mph fastball and a breaking ball with good shape and depth.

37 JUAN YEPEZ, 1B/3B

Yepez can play a solid first base and an adequate third. He's worked on adding corner outfield spots as options as well. He's a potential pinch-hitter and utilityman who is likely to have a long Triple-A career.

38 ROEL RAMIREZ, RHP

Ramirez is a fastball-slider reliever who doesn't have a plus pitch, but could fit as an up-and-down reliever who rides the Triple-A to St. Louis shuttle.

39 GRIFFIN ROBERTS, RHP

A 2018 supplemental first-round pick, Roberts was suspended for 50 games for testing positive for marijuana and has struggled to throw strikes. His slider remains an excellent pitch if he can gain consistency.

40 JEREMY RIVAS, SS

A teenage shortstop from Venezuela with a track record of performing, Rivas may end up moving to second or third but he has a solid glove and should hit for average.

TOP PROSPECTS OF THE DECADE

Year	Player, Pos	2020 Org
2011	Shelby Miller, RHP	Brewers
2012	Shelby Miller, RHP	Brewers
2013	Oscar Taveras, OF	Deceased
2014	Oscar Taveras, OF	Deceased
2015	Marco Gonzales, LHP	Mariners
2016	Alex Reyes, RHP	Cardinals
2017	Alex Reyes, RHP	Cardinals
2018	Alex Reyes, RHP	Cardinals
2019	Alex Reyes, RHP	Cardinals
2020	Dylan Carlson, OF	Cardinals

TOP DRAFT PICKS OF THE DECADE

Year	Player, Pos	2020 Org
2011	Kolten Wong, 2B	Cardinals
2012	Michael Wacha, RHP	Mets
2013	Marco Gonzales, LHP	Mariners
2014	Luke Weaver, RHP	D-backs
2015	Nick Plummer, OF	Cardinals
2016	Delvin Perez, SS	Cardinals
2017	Scott Hurst, OF (3rd round)	Cardinals
2018	Nolan Gorman, 3B	Cardinals
2019	Zack Thompson, LHP	Cardinals
2020	Jordan Walker, 3B	Cardinals

DEPTH CHART

ST. LOUIS CARDINALS

TOP 2021 ROOKIES	RANK
Dylan Carlson, OF	1
BREAKOUT PROSPECTS	**RANK**
Edwin Nunez, RHP	12
Trejyn Fletcher, OF	21

SOURCE OF TOP 30 TALENT

Homegrown	27	Acquired	3
College	8	Trade	3
Junior college	0	Rule 5 draft	0
High school	9	Independent league	0
Nondrafted free agent	0	Free agent/waivers	0
International	10		

LF
L.J. Jones
Diowill Burgos

CF
Dylan Carlson (1)
Lane Thomas (9)
Trejyn Fletcher (21)
Adanson Cruz
Conner Capel

RF
Justin Williams (16)
Jhon Torres (19)
Justin Toerner

3B
Nolan Gorman (3)
Jordan Walker (6)
Elehuris Montero (14)
Evan Mendoza

SS
Masyn Winn (11)
Mateo Gil (28)
Edmundo Sosa (30)
Delvin Perez
Jeremy Rivas

2B
Kramer Robertson

1B
Malcom Nunez (18)
Alec Burleson (27)
Luken Baker
John Nogowski
Juan Yepez

C
Ivan Herrera (4)
Andrew Knizner (8)
Julio Rodriguez (20)

LHP

LHSP	LHRP
Matthew Liberatore (2)	John Beller
Zack Thompson (5)	Connor Thomas
Kwang Hyun Kim (7)	
Levi Prater (29)	

RHP

RHSP	RHRP
Johan Oviedo (10)	Kodi Whitley (17)
Masyn Winn (11)	Seth Elledge (22)
Edwin Nunez (12)	Junior Fernandez (23)
Tink Hence (13)	Ian Bedell (24)
Angel Rondon (15)	Jake Woodford (25)
Alvaro Seijas	Tony Locey (26)
Gianluca Dalatri	Andre Pallante
Kyle Leahy	Roel Ramirez
	Griffin Roberts
	Connor Jones

San Diego Padres

BY KYLE GLASER

After years of unmet expectations and disappointing finishes, the Padres' long, painful rebuild finally came to fruition in 2020.

The Padres posted the second-best record in the National League during the pandemic-shortened season and ended a 14-year playoff drought. Manny Machado and Fernando Tatis Jr. finished third and fourth in National League MVP voting, Dinelson Lamet finished fourth in NL Cy Young Award voting, Jake Cronenworth finished tied for second in NL Rookie of the Year voting and first-year manager Jayce Tingler finished second in NL Manager of the Year voting.

The Padres got contributions from players old and young, acquired and homegrown, and became the talk of baseball when they hit a grand slam in a record four straight games in August, earning them the moniker "Slam Diego."

Everything changed for the Padres in 2020, from their uniforms—back to their traditional brown and yellow—to their status in the game. A bland franchise defined by a lack of stars for most of the previous decade, they became baseball's most exciting team led by their effervescent young superstar Tatis.

General manager A.J. Preller spent years building the farm system, and it paid dividends in the majors, mostly through trades. The Padres used homegrown players to acquire Cronenworth, Tommy Pham, Trent Grisham, Zach Davies and Jurickson Profar before the season. That accelerated at the trade deadline, when Preller made a whopping six trades involving 26 players, bringing Mike Clevinger, Trevor Rosenthal, Austin Nola, Austin Nola, Jason Castro and Mitch Moreland to San Diego.

Even after trading away so many homegrown products, the Padres still have a promising farm system. Lefthander MacKenzie Gore remains one of the top pitching prospects in baseball, while touted pitchers Luis Patiño, Adrian Morejon and Ryan Weathers all showed promising stuff in the majors in 2020. Catcher Luis Campusano's major league debut and the progress of shortstop CJ Abrams at the alternate training site give the Padres two potential standout position players to work with.

With a winning team in the major leagues and a farm system that features many promising players, the Padres' future outlook is the best it's been in decades.

Nothing, of course, is guaranteed. Clevinger will miss all of 2021 after having Tommy John surgery, Lamet missed the postseason with an arm injury and Chris Paddack took a step back in his second season. That puts the Padres' rotation in a precarious situation, especially if Gore, Patiño, Morejon and Weathers—all 22 or younger—aren't quite ready for the workload of a full major league season. The Padres also have payroll decisions to make with three players—Machado, Eric Hosmer and Wil Myers—due to make a combined $75.5 million in 2021 and '22, more than half the team's payroll.

But for a team that hadn't made the playoffs since 2006 and hadn't posted a winning record since 2010, the fact those are the concerns, rather than how to avoid last place, marks a step forward.

After "Slam Diego" stole the show in 2020, an encore awaits in 2021. ■

SEAN M. HAFFEY/GETTY IMAGES

Jake Cronenworth came from out of nowhere to finish second in Rookie of the Year balloting.

PROJECTED 2024 LINEUP

Position	Player	Age
Catcher	Luis Campusano	25
First Base	Eric Hosmer	34
Second Base	Jake Cronenworth	30
Third Base	Manny Machado	31
Shortstop	Fernando Tatis Jr.	25
Left Field	Robert Hassell	22
Center Field	CJ Abrams	23
Right Field	Trent Grisham	27
Designated Hitter	Francisco Mejia	28
No. 1 Starter	MacKenzie Gore	25
No. 2 Starter	Dinelson Lamet	31
No. 3 Starter	Luis Patiño	24
No. 4 Starter	Chris Paddack	28
No. 5 Starter	Adrian Morejon	25
Closer	Cole Wilcox	24

1 MacKENZIE GORE, LHP

Born: Feb. 24, 1999. **B-T:** L-L. **HT:** 6-4. **WT:** 197.
Drafted: HS—Whiteville, N.C., 2017 (1st round).
Signed by: Nick Brannon.

TRACK RECORD: Gore led tiny Whiteville (N.C.) High to three state championships in four years and won BA's High School Player of the Year award in 2017. The Padres drafted him third overall and signed him for a franchise-record $6.7 million to forgo an East Carolina commitment. Gore's first full season was interrupted by recurring blisters that sent him to the injured list three times, but he flourished with full health in 2019. Gore posted the lowest ERA (1.69) and WHIP (0.83) of any pitcher in the minors who threw at least 100 innings despite spending the year at hitter-friendly high Class A Lake Elsinore and Double-A Amarillo, and he entered 2020 considered arguably the top pitching prospect in baseball. Gore looked sharp in spring training, but after the coronavirus pandemic shut camps down, he arrived at summer camp in July with his delivery out of sync. He spent the season at the alternate training site smoothing that out and improved toward the end of the year.

SCOUTING REPORT: Gore is a tall, lanky lefthander whose elite athleticism is the foundation of his success. His delivery features a lot of moving parts, including a high leg kick where he brings his knee nearly to his collarbone, hands raised high above his head and a slight turn away from the batter, but he generally has the strength and body control to repeat his mechanics. Gore explodes out of his delivery with tremendous extension that helps his stuff play up. His fastball ranges from 91-96 mph and sits at 93-94. The pitch gets on hitters faster than they expect, resulting in a lot of late swings and misses in the strike zone. Gore's 83-87 mph slider with tight spin and late break is another plus pitch he can locate to both sides of the plate, but there are days his 76-79 mph curveball with late, 1-to-7 snap is his better breaking ball. He rarely has a feel for both of them in the same game and often has to pick one. Gore's 79-83 mph changeup features late sink at the bottom of the zone and is another plus pitch the few times he throws it. Gore throws everything for strikes with plus control when he's right, but his delivery fell out of rhythm over the summer. Different observers alternately saw problems with his direction to the plate, his upper and lower body being disconnected and inconsistent timing with his arm stroke and release point. The result was a velocity drop into the low 90s and sharply reduced command. Gore worked through the summer to get back in sync and began looking more like his best self by the end of the season. He still is working to get all four of his pitches working at the same time.

THE FUTURE: Gore's ability to throw four quality pitches for strikes gives him front-of-the-rotation potential, but he's going to have to maintain his high-maintenance delivery. The Padres plan to take it slow and start him back at Double-A in 2021. ■

TOP ROOKIE

SEAN M. HAFFEY/GETTY IMAGES

BA GRADE
70 Risk: High

SCOUTING GRADES
Fastball: 60. **SL:** 60. **CHG:** 60. **Curveball:** 55. **Control:** 60

Projected future grades on 20-80 scouting scale.

BEST TOOLS

Best Hitter for Average	CJ Abrams
Best Power Hitter	Luis Campusano
Best Strike-Zone Discipline	Robert Hassell
Fastest Baserunner	CJ Abrams
Best Athlete	CJ Abrams
Best Fastball	Luis Patiño
Best Curveball	Adrian Morejon
Best Slider	MacKenzie Gore
Best Changeup	Adrian Morejon
Best Control	Ryan Weathers
Best Defensive Catcher	Brandon Valenzuela
Best Defensive Infielder	CJ Abrams
Best Infield Arm	Eguy Rosario
Best Defensive Outfielder	Robert Hassell
Best Outfield Arm	Ismael Mena

Year	Age	Club (League)	Class	W	L	ERA	G	GS	IP	H	HR	BB	SO	BB/9	SO/9	WHIP	AVG
2017	18	Padres 1 (AZL)	R	0	1	1.27	7	7	21	14	0	7	34	3.0	14.3	0.98	.167
2018	19	Fort Wayne (MWL)	LoA	2	5	4.45	16	16	61	61	5	18	74	2.7	11.0	1.30	.234
2019	20	Lake Elsinore (CAL)	HiA	7	1	1.02	15	15	79	36	4	20	110	2.3	12.5	0.71	.125
	20	Amarillo (TL)	AA	2	1	4.15	5	5	22	20	3	8	25	3.3	10.4	1.29	.222
Minor League Totals				11	8	2.56	43	43	183	131	12	53	243	2.6	12.0	1.01	.201

2 CJ ABRAMS, SS

MATT THOMAS/SAN DIEGO PADRES

Born: Oct. 3, 2000. **B-T:** L-R. **HT:** 6-2. **WT:** 185. **Drafted:** HS—Roswell, Ga., 2019 (1st round). **Signed by:** Tyler Stubblefield.

TRACK RECORD: The Padres considered Abrams the top prep shortstop in the 2019 draft and were thrilled he fell to them at the sixth overall pick. After signing for $5.2 million, Abrams hit .401 in the Rookie-level Arizona League to win the league's MVP award and received a promotion to low Class A Fort Wayne. He spent 2020 at the alternate training site and excelled against older competition.

SCOUTING REPORT: Abrams is a rare blend of elite athleticism with a gifted feel for hitting. His flat, fluid swing consistently produces hard contact and allows him to drive the ball wherever it's pitched. Abrams has the direct stroke and bat speed to hit any fastball and the hand-eye coordination to barrel secondary pitches even when he's fooled or off-balance. He occasionally chases off the edges of the plate, but he rarely swings and misses in the strike zone. A potential .300 hitter, Abrams has the long, lean frame to add strength and reach 20-home run power at maturity. His elite speed makes him a premier stolen base threat. Abrams has rapidly improved defensively at shortstop. He makes highlight-reel plays with his wide range and reliable hands, though his average arm fits better at second base.

THE FUTURE: Abrams has the skills to be a dynamic talent atop the order. The Padres believe he'll move quickly in 2021.

SCOUTING GRADES: **Hitting:** 70 **Power:** 50 **Running:** 80 **Fielding:** 60 **Arm:** 50

Year	Age	Club (League)	Class	AVG	G	AB	R	H	2B	3B	HR	RBI	BB	SO	SB	OBP	SLG
2019	18	Padres 1 (AZL)	R	.401	32	142	40	57	12	8	3	22	10	14	14	.442	.662
	18	Fort Wayne (MWL)	LoA	.250	2	8	1	2	1	0	0	0	1	0	1	.333	.375
Minor League Totals				.393	34	150	41	59	13	8	3	22	11	14	15	.436	.647

3 LUIS PATIÑO, RHP

TOP ROOKIE

BA GRADE
60 Risk: High

ROBERT BINDER/MLB PHOTOS VIA GETTY IMAGES

Born: Oct. 26, 1999. **B-T:** R-R. **HT:** 6-1. **WT:** 192. **Signed:** Colombia, 2016. **Signed by:** Chris Kemp/Andres Cabadias.

TRACK RECORD: Patiño's fastball sat in the mid 80s when he signed with the Padres for $130,000 in 2016, but he rapidly gained weight and strength and was touching 99 mph by the 2019 Futures Game. Patiño spent the coronavirus shutdown in 2020 working out with fellow Colombian pitcher Jose Quintana in anticipation of his major league debut. That debut came on Aug. 5, and Patiño spent the bulk of the season pitching out of the Padres' bullpen as a 20-year-old.

SCOUTING REPORT: Patiño's strong lower half and electrifying arm speed allow him to generate explosive 94-99 mph fastballs. It's a plus-plus, swing-and-miss fastball with late life up in the zone, but he overthrows it when he gets too amped up and gets wild as a result. Patiño's tilting, biting mid-80s slider is another swing-and-miss pitch at its best, but he also struggles to locate it consistently. He commands his firm changeup better than his slider and gets swings and misses over the top when he dials it back to 85-87 mph. He also has an 82-84 mph curveball he can land for strikes early in the count to give batters a different look. Patiño pitches with a lot of emotion and adrenaline. He shows above-average control when he slows down and keeps a balanced tempo.

THE FUTURE: The Padres broke Patiño in as a reliever but still view him as a future starter. He has mid-to-front of the rotation potential if he can manage his energy level and control.

SCOUTING GRADES: **Fastball:** 70 **Slider:** 60 **Changeup:** 55 **Curveball:** 45 **Control:** 50

Year	Age	Club (League)	Class	W	L	ERA	G	GS	IP	H	HR	BB	SO	BB/9	SO/9	WHIP	AVG
2017	17	Padres 1 (AZL)	R	2	1	2.48	9	8	40	32	2	16	43	3.6	9.7	1.20	.190
	17	Padres (DSL)	R	2	1	1.69	4	4	16	11	0	2	15	1.1	8.4	0.81	.183
2018	18	Fort Wayne (MWL)	LoA	6	3	2.16	17	17	83	65	1	24	98	2.6	10.6	1.07	.197
2019	19	Lake Elsinore (CAL)	HiA	6	8	2.69	18	17	87	61	4	34	113	3.5	11.7	1.09	.171
	19	Amarillo (TL)	AA	0	0	1.17	2	2	8	8	0	4	10	4.7	11.7	1.57	.229
2020	20	San Diego (NL)	MAJ	1	0	5.19	11	1	17	18	3	14	21	7.3	10.9	1.85	.257
Major League Totals				1	0	5.19	11	1	17	18	3	14	21	7.3	10.9	1.85	.257
Minor League Totals				16	13	2.35	50	48	234	177	7	80	279	3.1	10.7	1.10	.208

4 LUIS CAMPUSANO, C

TOP ROOKIE

ROBERT BINDER/MLB PHOTOS VIA GETTY IMAGES

BA GRADE

60 Risk: High

Born: Sept. 29, 1998. **B-T:** R-R. **HT:** 5-11. **WT:** 232. **Drafted:** HS—Augusta, Ga., 2017 (2nd round). **Signed by:** Tyler Stubblefield.

TRACK RECORD: Campusano suffered a concussion shortly after the Padres drafted him in 2017 and had a season-ending concussion in 2018. He stayed healthy in 2019 and won the high Class A California League batting title (.325) and co-MVP award. He made his big league debut in 2020 and homered in his first game before missing the rest of the season with a left wrist sprain. In October, Campusano was arrested and charged with felony marijuana possession in Georgia.

SCOUTING REPORT: Campusano is one of the strongest players in the Padres' system. He occasionally swung a 40-ounce bat in the minors and still demonstrated some of the best bat speed among his peers. Campusano pummels baseballs on a line from foul pole to foul pole and is progressively learning to elevate for home runs. He's aggressive and swings hard, but he stays within the strike zone to limit his strikeouts and draw plenty of walks. Campusano has a strong, flexible lower half behind the plate and lost 10-15 pounds to improve his quickness. He's an excellent blocker and has improved his receiving to average to go with above-average arm strength.

THE FUTURE: Campusano's upcoming legal proceedings cloud his future. On talent, he could be an everyday catcher who hits in the middle of the order.

SCOUTING GRADES: **Hitting:** 55 **Power:** 55 **Running:** 30 **Fielding:** 50 **Arm:** 55

Year	Age	Club (League)	Class	AVG	G	AB	R	H	2B	3B	HR	RBI	BB	SO	SB	OBP	SLG
2018	19	Fort Wayne (MWL)	LoA	.288	70	260	26	75	11	0	3	40	19	43	0	.345	.365
2019	20	Lake Elsinore (CAL)	HiA	.325	110	422	63	137	31	1	15	81	52	57	0	.396	.509
2020	21	San Diego (NL)	MAJ	.333	1	3	2	1	0	0	1	1	0	2	0	.500	1.333
Major League Totals				.333	1	3	2	1	0	0	1	1	0	2	0	.500	1.333
Minor League Totals				.304	217	816	97	248	46	1	22	146	86	125	0	.372	.444

5 ADRIAN MOREJON, LHP

ROBERT BINDER/MLB PHOTOS VIA GETTY IMAGES

BA GRADE

55 Risk: High

Born: Feb. 27, 1999. **B-T:** L-L. **HT:** 5-11. **WT:** 224. **Signed:** Cuba, 2016. **Signed by:** Chris Kemp/Trevor Schumm/Felix Feliz.

TRACK RECORD: Morejon was the star pitcher on Cuba's junior national teams and signed with the Padres for a franchise-record $11 million in 2016. He battled a series of arm injuries after signing, including a season-ending shoulder injury after his major league debut in 2019, but he stayed healthy in 2020 and posted a 4.66 ERA as a long reliever and spot starter for the Padres.

SCOUTING REPORT: Morejon has long had premium stuff from the left side. His fastball sits 94-96 mph as a starter and touches 99 in short bursts with remarkably little effort. He's begun repeating his release point on his 79-82 mph curveball to make it a consistent plus offering that sweeps across the plate and finishes with sharp, late drop at the bottom of the strike zone. Morejon has a traditional changeup with sink and run, but his diving, swing-and-miss knuckle-change is the better offspeed pitch and has taken a more prominent role in his arsenal. He also introduced a vertical slider in 2020 that shows promise but is the clear final pitch in his arsenal. Morejon pitched with more confidence and improved his strike-throwing in his second stint in the majors, but he's still working on fastball command. He frequently leaves his fastball up over the plate and gets hit. He also has never pitched more than 65.1 innings in a season.

THE FUTURE: Morejon has potent stuff, but his durability and command are questions. He will try to win a rotation spot in 2021.

SCOUTING GRADES: **Fastball:** 60 **Slider:** 45 **Changeup:** 60 **Curveball:** 60 **Control:** 45

Year	Age	Club (League)	Class	W	L	ERA	G	GS	IP	H	HR	BB	SO	BB/9	SO/9	WHIP	AVG
2018	19	Lake Elsinore (CAL)	HiA	4	4	3.30	13	13	63	54	6	24	70	3.4	10.1	1.24	.205
	19	Padres 1 (AZL)	R	0	1	6.75	1	1	3	5	0	0	4	0.0	13.5	1.88	.385
2019	20	San Diego (NL)	MAJ	0	0	10.13	5	2	8	15	1	3	9	3.4	10.1	2.25	.357
	20	Amarillo (TL)	AA	0	4	4.25	16	16	36	29	3	15	44	3.8	11.0	1.22	.188
2020	21	San Diego (NL)	MAJ	2	2	4.66	9	4	19	20	7	4	25	1.9	11.6	1.24	.267
Major League Totals				2	2	6.26	14	6	27	35	8	7	34	2.3	11.2	1.54	.307
Minor League Totals				7	13	3.78	43	43	164	153	13	55	176	3.0	9.6	1.27	.245

6 RYAN WEATHERS, LHP

MATT THOMAS/SAN DIEGO PADRES

BA GRADE
55 **Risk: High**

Born: Dec. 17, 1999. **B-T:** R-L. **HT:** 6-1. **WT:** 230. **Drafted:** HS—Loretto, Tenn., 2018 (1st rd). **Signed by:** Tyler Stubblefield.

TRACK RECORD: The Padres went above industry consensus to draft Weathers seventh overall in 2018. He battled arm fatigue and conditioning issues in his first full season, but he rewarded the Padres in 2020. Weathers arrived at summer camp throwing 4-5 mph harder and impressed all summer at the alternate training site. The Padres put him on their Division Series roster despite the fact he had never pitched above low Class A. He became the second pitcher ever to make his big league debut in the postseason.

SCOUTING REPORT: Weathers is the son of former reliever David Weathers and shows the polish often seen in big league progeny. He shows an advanced feel for sequencing, is rarely fazed and locates to both sides of the plate. After previously sitting 88-92 mph, Weathers' fastball jumped to 92-95 as a starter and 95-97 in short bursts with carry through the strike zone. His slider also became a tighter, harder pitch in the mid 80s and his changeup with heavy fade remains potentially above-average, though he's sometimes too firm with it. Weathers has a portly, heavyset frame, but he's deceptively athletic and repeats his delivery for plus control.

THE FUTURE: Weathers draws comparisons to Hyun-Jin Ryu as a hefty lefthander who effectively locates his entire arsenal. He'll head back to the minors in 2021 to continue his development.

SCOUTING GRADES: **Fastball:** 60 **Slider:** 55 **Changeup:** 50 **Control:** 60

Year	Age	Club (League)	Class	W	L	ERA	G	GS	IP	H	HR	BB	SO	BB/9	SO/9	WHIP	AVG
2018	18	Fort Wayne (MWL)	LoA	0	1	3.00	3	3	9	11	0	1	9	1.0	9.0	1.33	.268
	18	Padres (AZL)	R	0	2	3.86	4	4	9	8	2	3	9	2.9	8.7	1.18	.190
2019	19	Fort Wayne (MWL)	LoA	3	7	3.84	22	22	96	101	6	18	90	1.7	8.4	1.24	.256
Minor League Totals				3	10	3.78	29	29	114	120	8	22	108	1.7	8.5	1.24	.270

7 ROBERT HASSELL, OF

MLB PHOTOS VIA GETTY IMAGES

BA GRADE
60 **Risk: Extreme**

Born: Aug. 15, 2001. **B-T:** L-L. **HT:** 6-2. **WT:** 195. **Drafted:** HS—Thompson's Sta., Tenn., 2020 (1). **Signed by:** Tyler Stubblefield.

TRACK RECORD: Hassell's precocious hitting ability first rose to national prominence when he played for Tennessee in the 2013 and 2014 Little League World Series. He later hit .514 to lead USA Baseball's 18U National Team to the silver medal at the 2019 World Cup, cementing his status as the top high school hitter in the 2020 class. The Padres made Hassell the first prep player drafted, No. 8 overall, and signed him for $4.3 million to forgo a Vanderbilt commitment. He reported to the alternate training site before finishing in instructional league.

SCOUTING REPORT: Hassell has a picturesque lefthanded swing geared for contact. It's an easy, loose, direct swing, and he has a preternatural ability to manipulate the barrel and cover all parts of the strike zone. Hassell has excellent strike-zone discipline and projects to be at least a plus hitter, but his lean, thin frame raises questions about his power potential. His long limbs and big hands provide hope he can add enough strength to reach 15-20 home runs. Hassell is an average runner down the line and ticks up to above-average in center field, where he glides naturally to the ball. He touched 92 mph as a pitcher and has the arm strength for right field if needed.

THE FUTURE: Hassell's pure hitting ability gives him an excellent foundation. His physical development will determine if he reaches his above-average, everyday potential.

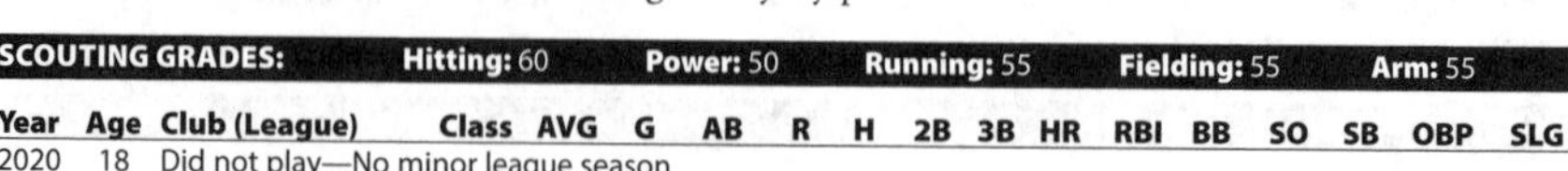

SCOUTING GRADES: **Hitting:** 60 **Power:** 50 **Running:** 55 **Fielding:** 55 **Arm:** 55

Year	Age	Club (League)	Class	AVG	G	AB	R	H	2B	3B	HR	RBI	BB	SO	SB	OBP	SLG
2020	18	Did not play—No minor league season															

8 HUDSON HEAD, OF

MATT THOMAS/SAN DIEGO PADRES

BA GRADE

55 Risk: Very High

Born: April 8, 2001. **B-T:** L-L. **HT:** 6-1. **WT:** 180. **Drafted:** HS—San Antonio, 2019 (3rd round). **Signed by:** Kevin Ham.

TRACK RECORD: Head played quarterback at his San Antonio high school and didn't draw baseball scouts' attention until he hit .645 with 13 home runs and 54 RBI his senior year. The Padres drafted him in the third round and signed him for $3 million, a then-record for a third-rounder. The Padres brought Head to their alternate training site in 2020, but he was limited by a recurring hamstring injury.

SCOUTING REPORT: Head is one of the best athletes in the Padres' system. He's a lean, twitchy athlete who is a plus runner, has explosive bat speed and is ambidextrous—he threw with his right hand when he rolled right and threw with his left hand when he rolled left as a quarterback. Head has a lot of extra movement in his swing, leading to questions whether he'll catch up to upper-end velocity. He drives balls with authority when he does connect and flashes surprising plus raw power out of his lean frame. Head is extremely aggressive on both sides of the ball. He needs to rein in his approach, and evaluators are concerned he'll hurt himself with how aggressively he plays center field. He's a potential above-average defender with an above-average arm when he plays under control.

THE FUTURE: Head has plenty of athleticism, but he still has to prove his swing works against advanced pitchers. He'll get the chance to show it does in 2021.

SCOUTING GRADES: **Hitting:** 50 **Power:** 55 **Running:** 60 **Fielding:** 50 **Arm:** 55

Year	Age	Club (League)	Class	AVG	G	AB	R	H	2B	3B	HR	RBI	BB	SO	SB	OBP	SLG
2019	18	Padres 1 (AZL)	R	.283	32	120	19	34	7	3	1	12	15	29	3	.383	.417
Minor League Totals				.283	32	120	19	34	7	3	1	12	15	29	3	.383	.417

9 COLE WILCOX, RHP

KRISTIN M. BRADSHAW

Born: July 14, 1999. **B-T:** R-R. **HT:** 6-5. **WT:** 232. **Drafted:** Georgia, 2020 (3rd round). **Signed by:** Tyler Stubblefield.

TRACK RECORD: Scouts viewed Wilcox as a potential first-round talent out of high school, but his strong commitment to Georgia deterred teams from picking him early. After struggling with his control as a Bulldogs freshman, Wilcox went 3-0, 1.57 with 32 strikeouts and two walks in four starts as a draft-eligible sophomore before the college season shut down in 2020. He dropped to the third round because teams were wary of his bonus demands, but the Padres stopped his slide and signed him for a third round-record $3.3 million.

SCOUTING REPORT: Wilcox is a big, physical righthander at 6-foot-5, 232 pounds with stuff to match his size. His fastball ranges from 93-97 mph with natural sink and run and touched 99 in short bursts at the alternate training site. His slider is a powerful offering at 86-89 mph with short, three-quarters break and projects to above-average when he stays on top of it. His hard changeup mirrors his fastball and dives with heavy sink at 85-87 mph. Wilcox has the physicality and durability to start, but he lacks a soft offering and his control can be inconsistent. As such, many observers predict a bullpen future.

THE FUTURE: The Padres will give Wilcox every chance to start. How his command and control progress will determine his ultimate role.

SCOUTING GRADES: **Fastball:** 60 **Slider:** 55 **Changeup:** 50 **Control:** 45

Year	Age	Club (League)	Class	W	L	ERA	G	GS	IP	H	HR	BB	SO	BB/9	SO/9	WHIP	AVG
2020	20	Did not play—No minor league season															

10 BLAKE HUNT, C

BRIAN WESTERHOLT/FOUR SEAM IMAGES

BA GRADE
45 Risk: High

Born: Nov. 21, 1998. **B-T:** R-R. **HT:** 6-4. **WT:** 180. **Drafted:** HS—Santa Ana, Calif., 2017 (2nd round supplemental). **Signed by:** Nick Long.

TRACK RECORD: Hunt failed to make the Area Code Games as a rising high school senior and used it as motivation to get stronger. The added strength and power made him one of the fastest risers in the 2017 draft, and the Padres selected him 69th overall and signed him for an above-slot $1.6 million. Hunt stood out as one of the top defensive catchers in the low Class A Midwest League in his full-season debut in 2019. The Padres made him a late addition to their alternate training site in 2020.

SCOUTING REPORT: Hunt's strength is his defense. Though tall for a catcher at nearly 6-foot-5, he moves well behind the plate, is a plus receiver and pitch framer and has the intelligence and work ethic to lead a pitching staff. He controls the run game with an above-average, accurate arm. Hunt has good timing at the plate and stays in the strike zone, but his upper-body, handsy swing limits his impact. He has the size to project 15-20 home runs once he adds more strength and learns to incorporate his lower half.

THE FUTURE: Hunt projects to be a defensively-minded catcher who starts in his peak years. He'll see high Class A in 2021.

SCOUTING GRADES: **Hitting:** 45 **Power:** 50 **Running:** 40 **Fielding:** 60 **Arm:** 55

Year	Age	Club (League)	Class	AVG	G	AB	R	H	2B	3B	HR	RBI	BB	SO	SB	OBP	SLG
2017	18	Padres 1 (AZL)	R	.214	8	28	7	6	2	0	1	4	3	13	0	.313	.393
	18	Padres (AZL)	R	.250	22	88	14	22	7	2	1	15	5	29	1	.316	.409
2018	19	Tri-City (NWL)	SS	.271	56	207	34	56	13	0	3	25	27	56	2	.371	.377
2019	20	Fort Wayne (MWL)	LoA	.255	89	333	40	85	21	3	5	39	35	67	4	.331	.381
Minor League Totals				.258	175	656	95	169	43	5	10	83	70	165	7	.341	.384

11 TUCUPITA MARCANO, 3B/2B

BA GRADE
45 Risk: High

Born: Sept. 16, 1999. **B-T:** L-R. **HT:** 6-0. **WT:** 165. **Signed:** Venezuela, 2016. **Signed by:** Antonio Alejos//Chris Kemp/Yfrain Linares.

TRACK RECORD: Marcano is the son of famed Venezuelan player Raul Marcano and signed with the Padres for $320,000 in 2016. After hitting .366 in his stateside debut, Marcano finished tied for fifth in the Midwest League in hits in his first full season in 2019 and hit .370 in the California League playoffs after being promoted. The Padres brought him to their alternate training site in 2020.

SCOUTING REPORT: Marcano is extraordinarily lean and lacks power, but he knows who he is and doesn't try to do too much. He's a smart hitter who controls the strike zone and makes consistent contact with a direct, compact stroke. He lines the ball to all fields and is a prolific bunter with a great feel for when to lay one down, including on squeeze plays. He beats bunts out for singles with his plus speed, but he makes poor decisions on the basepaths and frequently gets picked off or caught stealing. Marcano is an average defender whose best asset is his versatility—he is solid at third base and second base, can fill in at shortstop and began playing left field and first base at the alternate site.

THE FUTURE: Marcano is frequently described as a "winning player" who does the little things that make a difference. His contact skills and versatility have him ticketed for a utility role.

Year	Age	Club (League)	Class	AVG	G	AB	R	H	2B	3B	HR	RBI	BB	SO	SB	OBP	SLG
2019	19	Fort Wayne (MWL)	LoA	.270	111	460	55	124	19	3	2	45	35	45	15	.323	.337
Minor League Totals				.279	212	824	117	230	28	8	3	86	99	76	40	.357	.343

12 MICHEL BAEZ, RHP

BA GRADE
40 Risk: Medium

Born: Jan. 21, 1996. **B-T:** R-R. **HT:** 6-7. **WT:** 237. **Signed:** Cuba, 2016. **Signed by:** Trevor Schumm/Jake Koenig.

TRACK RECORD: Baez briefly pitched in Cuba's major league, Serie Nacional, as an 18-year-old before leaving the island. He signed with the Padres for $3 million in Dec. 2016. Baez worked as a starter in the low minors, but he broke into the majors as a reliever with the Padres in 2019. Expected to take on a bigger bullpen role in 2020, Baez instead regressed and spent most of the season at the alternate training site.

SCOUTING REPORT: Baez is physically enormous at nearly 6-foot-8, which is both a blessing and a curse. He generates easy 94-97 mph fastballs with his natural strength but struggles to keep his big body and long limbs in sync, resulting in inconsistent mechanics and wide fluctuations in his velocity and his control. Baez's breaking balls stalled in their development and remain well below-average pitches, leaving him to rely almost entirely on his fastball and above-average 86-88 mph changeup. He's also had minor back or shoulder injuries every year since he signed.

THE FUTURE: The Padres haven't given up on Baez as a starter, but his breaking balls and control need to come a long way for him to stick in the rotation. If they don't, his fastball-changeup combination gives him a chance to stick as a reliever.

Year	Age	Club (League)	Class	W	L	ERA	G	GS	IP	H	HR	BB	SO	BB/9	SO/9	WHIP	AVG
2020	24	San Diego (NL)	MAJ	0	0	7.71	3	1	5	7	0	2	7	3.9	13.5	1.93	.333
Major League Totals				1	1	3.67	27	2	34	32	3	16	35	4.2	9.2	1.40	.241
Minor League Totals				14	14	3.08	47	32	195	160	19	66	240	3.0	11.0	1.16	.221

13 JORGE OÑA, OF

BA GRADE
45 Risk: High

Born: Dec. 31, 1996. **B-T:** R-R. **HT:** 6-0. **WT:** 235. **Signed:** Cuba, 2016. **Signed by:** Felix Feliz/Trevor Schumm/Chris Kemp.

TRACK RECORD: Oña was arguably Cuba's best hitter for his age as an amateur and signed with the Padres for $7 million in 2016. He battled a host of injuries after signing and had season-ending right shoulder surgery in May 2019, but he returned healthy in 2020 and starred at the alternate training site. The Padres called him up in September and gave him four starts at designated hitter.

SCOUTING REPORT: Oña is a thick, bulky hitter with massive raw power. His brute strength and solid bat speed produce towering drives to all fields, especially the opposite way to right-center. Oña's swing was previously stiff and prevented him from making enough contact, but his swing looked much looser post-surgery. He showed the ability to wait back on breaking balls and handle varied stuff, although he's still extremely aggressive and has big holes in his swing, particularly against elevated fastballs or anything inside. Oña's bulk makes him a below-average defender with below-average speed in the outfield. He flashed above-average arm strength before surgery.

THE FUTURE: Oña has a better chance to reach his power with his looser swing. His outlook for playing time will improve if the National League permanently adopts the DH.

Year	Age	Club (League)	Class	AVG	G	AB	R	H	2B	3B	HR	RBI	BB	SO	SB	OBP	SLG
2020	23	San Diego (NL)	MAJ	.250	5	12	3	3	1	0	1	2	2	7	0	.400	.583
Major League Totals				.250	5	12	3	3	1	0	1	2	2	7	0	.400	.583
Minor League Totals				.268	232	872	109	234	44	3	24	126	84	251	10	.342	.408

14 REGGIE LAWSON, RHP

Born: Aug. 2, 1997. **B-T:** R-R. **HT:** 6-3. **WT:** 214. **Drafted:** HS—Victorville, Calif., 2016 (2nd round supplemental). **Signed by:** Jeff Stevens.

TRACK RECORD: A touted amateur drafted in the supplemental second round in 2016, Lawson interspersed flashes of brilliance with rough outings before missing most of 2019 with an elbow strain. He received a platelet-rich plasma injection and returned to make three dominant appearances in the Arizona Fall League, but the PRP didn't hold and he had Tommy John surgery in March 2020.

SCOUTING REPORT: Lawson looks like a pitcher straight out of central casting with a strong, well-proportioned frame and a loose, athletic delivery. He tops his three-pitch mix with a 93-96 mph fastball with late life he holds deep into games. His 76-80 mph curveball has steadily added power and bite to get swings and misses and his mid-80s changeup flashes above-average with sink at the bottom of the zone. Lawson's stuff is loud, but his secondaries and his control vary widely, leading to dominant outings mixed with disastrous ones. He's at his best in big games.

THE FUTURE: Lawson has the ingredients of a mid-rotation starter, but he has to get healthy and find consistency. He may return in mid-2021 depending on his rehab progress.

Year	Age	Club (League)	Class	W	L	ERA	G	GS	SV	IP	H	HR	BB	SO	K/9	WHIP	AVG
2019	21	Amarillo (TL)	AA	3	1	5.20	6	6	0	28	28	4	13	36	11.7	1.48	.262
Minor League Totals				15	12	5.09	52	48	0	226	235	23	102	249	9.9	1.49	.265

15 REGGIE PRECIADO, SS

Born: May 16, 2003. **B-T:** R-R. **HT:** 6-5. **WT:** 185. **Signed:** Panama, 2019. **Signed by:** Chris Kemp/Richard Montenegro.

TRACK RECORD: Preciado trained with his father Victor, a former Yankees minor leaguer, growing up and emerged as Panama's top prospect in the 2019 international class. The Padres signed him for $1.3 million. Preciado's professional debut was delayed by the coronavirus pandemic, but he participated in instructional league in the fall.

SCOUTING REPORT: Preciado grew since signing and now stands 6-foot-5 with a skinny, projectable frame. He isn't overly twitchy, but he has a knack for being on time at the plate. Preciado's lefthanded swing has an elliptical path and his righthanded swing is a more compact stroke. They're different swings, but he can drive the ball from both sides and has room to grow into power as he fills out. He is still learning to control the strike zone. Preciado is a fringe-average runner, but his advanced instincts and polished defensive skills allow him to handle shortstop. His above-average arm strength should improve.

THE FUTURE: Preciado's future hinges on how his body fills out. He'll be 17 years old on Opening Day and still has lots of growth ahead.

Year	Age	Club (League)	Class	AVG	G	AB	R	H	2B	3B	HR	RBI	BB	SO	SB	OBP	SLG
2019	16	Did not play—Signed 2020 contract															

16 EFRAIN CONTRERAS, RHP

Born: Jan. 2, 2000. **B-T:** R-R. **HT:** 5-10. **WT:** 185. **Signed:** Mexico, 2017. **Signed by:** Emmanuel Rangel/Bill McLaughlin.

TRACK RECORD: The Padres purchased Contreras' rights for $50,000 from the Mexican League's Veracruz franchise in 2017. He jumped on radars when he finished eighth in the low Class A Midwest League in strikeouts in his full-season debut in 2019 and took a leap in 2020, where he earned raves as the Padres' top pitcher in instructional league. He left one of his final instructs starts with an elbow injury, however, and had Tommy John surgery in November.

SCOUTING REPORT: Contreras long showed the ability to throw three pitches for strikes and has steadily improved his fastball velocity. Strong in his square, stocky build, Contreras' fastball now sits 92-93 mph and touches 95 with carry up in the zone. His combination of velocity, life and pinpoint command makes his fastball a swing-and-miss weapon, and he confidently challenges hitters with a hint of bravado. Contreras drops his sharp, downer curveball in the strike zone in any count and shows the makings of an above-average low-80s changeup with deception and fade. He fills up the strike zone with plus control and works quickly with a composed, business-like demeanor.

THE FUTURE: The Padres felt confident Contreras would pitch in the majors and be a potential back-of-the-rotation starter. He'll be out all of 2021 recovering and is set to return in 2022.

Year	Age	Club (League)	Class	W	L	ERA	G	GS	IP	H	HR	BB	SO	BB/9	SO/9	WHIP	AVG
2019	19	Fort Wayne (MWL)	LoA	6	6	3.61	25	23	110	97	12	32	121	2.6	9.9	1.18	.213
Minor League Totals				8	9	3.03	41	30	178	146	16	46	197	2.3	10.0	1.08	.223

17 ISMAEL MENA, OF

BREAKOUT
BA GRADE
50 Risk: Extreme

Born: Nov. 30, 2002. **B-T:** L-L. **HT:** 6-3. **WT:** 185. **Signed:** Dominican Republic, 2019. **Signed by:** Chris Kemp/Alvin Duran/Felix Feliz.

TRACK RECORD: Mena was one of the most athletic players in the 2019 international class and signed with the Padres for $2.2 million, the largest bonus the club awarded that year. His professional debut was delayed by the coronavirus pandemic, but he put on good weight and stood out in instructional league.

SCOUTING REPORT: Mena is a lean, sleek center fielder with plus-plus speed in the outfield and on the bases. He's a slashing hitter who sprays the ball around with a whippy swing from the left side, although he's added strength and leverage and has started to drive the ball in the air. Mena's swing can be too steep at times and he's prone to striking out, but that may improve with experience and maturity. Mena's routes and instincts in center field are a work in progress. He has the speed for the position but needs experience to refine his play. He has a plus arm that could become a plus-plus weapon as he gets stronger.

THE FUTURE: Mena shows hints of a potential top-of-the-order center fielder, but he's extremely raw and will need time. His professional debut awaits in 2021.

Year	Age	Club (League)	Class	AVG	G	AB	R	H	2B	3B	HR	RBI	BB	SO	SB	OBP	SLG
	16	Did not play—Signed 2020 contract															

18 YEISON SANTANA, SS

BA GRADE
50 Risk: Extreme

Born: Dec. 7, 2000. **B-T:** R-R. **HT:** 5-11. **WT:** 170. **Signed:** Dominican Republic, 2017. **Signed by:** Felix Felix/Chris Kemp.

TRACK RECORD: Santana trained with Rudy Santin in the Dominican Republic and signed with the Padres for $300,000 in 2017. He quickly added strength and emerged as one of the top players in the Rookie-level Arizona League in his stateside debut, finishing fourth in batting average (.346) and sixth in on-base percentage (.429). He continued to impress at instructional league in 2020.

SCOUTING REPORT: Santana has emerged as one of the more promising hitters in the Padres system. He's an aggressive hitter who swings hard but has the hand-eye coordination and barrel awareness to make consistent contact. He lines the ball to all fields, especially up the middle and the opposite way, and shows a keen eye for the strike zone. He is a lithe, twitchy athlete with explosive hands and may grow into power as he gets bigger. Santana plays with energy in the field and has a good awareness for the game. He occasionally plays too fast but has a chance to stay at shortstop with his solid range and improving arm strength.

THE FUTURE: Santana is frequently asked about in trade discussions. The Padres see a valuable middle infielder who can hit and want to hold onto him.

Year	Age	Club (League)	Class	AVG	G	AB	R	H	2B	3B	HR	RBI	BB	SO	SB	OBP	SLG
2019	18	Padres (AZL)	R	.346	41	162	38	56	5	5	3	30	23	38	4	.429	.494
Minor League Totals				.306	77	294	61	90	6	10	3	55	56	68	9	.418	.425

19 JUSTIN LANGE, RHP

BA GRADE
50 Risk: Extreme

Born: Sept. 11, 2001. **B-T:** R-R. **HT:** 6-4. **WT:** 220. **Drafted:** HS—Llano, Texas (1st round supplemental). **Signed by:** Kevin Ham.

TRACK RECORD: Lange topped out in the low 90s during the Area Code Games entering his senior year of high school, but came back sitting 95-98 mph in the spring and rocketed up draft boards. The Padres drafted him 34th overall and signed him for $2 million to forgo a Dallas Baptist commitment. Lange joined the alternate training site after signing but was limited by shoulder fatigue in instructional league.

SCOUTING REPORT: Lange has a projectable 6-foot-4 frame and is extraordinarily athletic. He originally committed to DBU as an infielder and is a plus-plus runner. Lange's fastball sits 94-95 mph, touches 98 with ease and has clipped 100 mph. He doesn't quite have command of it yet, but that should improve as he grows into his long limbs and gets stronger. Lange's secondaries are works in progress. He flashes an above-average slider at 86-89 mph but gets under the ball too often and has rarely used his mid-80s changeup. His control of his secondaries is behind his fastball control.

THE FUTURE: Lange is a bit of a lottery ticket. His athleticism and velocity are a good foundation, and the Padres will see if his secondaries and control come along.

Year	Age	Club (League)	Class	W	L	ERA	G	GS	IP	H	HR	BB	SO	BB/9	SO/9	WHIP	AVG
2020	18	Did not play—No minor league season															

20 OWEN CAISSIE, OF

BA GRADE
50 Risk: Extreme

Born: July 8, 2002. **B-T:** L-R. **HT:** 6-4. **WT:** 190. **Drafted:** HS—Burlington, Ont., 2020 (2nd round). **Signed by:** Chris Kemlo.

TRACK RECORD: Caissie starred as the top power hitter on Canada's junior national team and generated buzz in the spring when he hit a home run over the batter's eye at the Blue Jays' spring training stadium. The Padres drafted him 45th overall and signed him for just over $1.2 million to forgo a Michigan commitment. Caissie got hit by a pitch in his elbow at the alternate site camp and suffered a hairline fracture, but he recovered in time for instructional league.

SCOUTING REPORT: Caissie is a big lefthanded hitter with plus raw power and room to add even more strength. He posts some of the top exit velocities and longest home run distances in every environment he plays. Caissie's swing can get long and he is prone to striking out, but when he gets a fastball over the plate he crushes it. He is a hard worker who spends every free moment in the batting cage. Caissie is much more raw defensively. He has average speed and an average arm, but he's not comfortable with high fly balls and is still learning proper footwork.

THE FUTURE: Caissie has the power for 30-plus home runs if he can make enough contact. His pro debut awaits in 2021.

Year	Age	Club (League)	Class	AVG	G	AB	R	H	2B	3B	HR	RBI	BB	SO	SB	OBP	SLG
2020	17	Did not play—No minor league season															

21 JOSHUA MEARS, OF

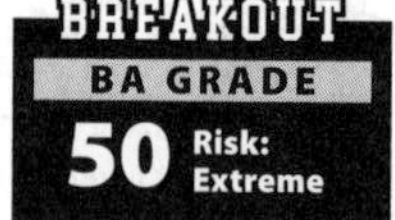

Born: Feb. 21, 2001. **B-T:** R-R. **HT:** 6-3. **WT:** 230. **Drafted:** HS—Federal Way, Wash., 2019 (2nd round). **Signed by:** Justin Baughman.

TRACK RECORD: Mears stood out for his physicality at the 2018 Area Code Games and showed prolific power throughout high school. The Padres drafted him 48th overall in 2019 and signed him for $1 million. Mears impressed in his pro debut in the Rookie-level Arizona League, but he suffered a broken hamate bone in 2020 that kept him off the field until the end of instructional league.

SCOUTING REPORT: Mears is built like a major league slugger at a chiseled 6-foot-3, 230 pounds. He destroys baseballs with plus-plus raw power and has already posted exit velocities as high as 117 mph—which would have been fourth-highest in the major leagues in 2020. Mears' power is monstrous, but it's a question how much he'll get to it. He has rarely faced good velocity and his swing length and pitch recognition need improvement for him to be an average hitter. Mears is athletic for his size but projects to slow down as he gets older. He fits in right field with his above-average arm strength.

THE FUTURE: Mears was committed to Purdue to study engineering and took college classes while still in high school. That intelligence and work ethic should help him get the most from his abilities.

Year	Age	Club (League)	Class	AVG	G	AB	R	H	2B	3B	HR	RBI	BB	SO	SB	OBP	SLG
2019	18	Padres 1 (AZL)	R	.253	43	166	30	42	4	3	7	24	23	59	9	.354	.440
Minor League Totals				.253	43	166	30	42	4	3	7	24	23	59	9	.354	.440

22 JORGE MATEO, OF/2B

BA GRADE
40 Risk: Medium

Born: June 23, 1995. **B-T:** R-R. **HT:** 6-0. **WT:** 182. **Signed:** Dominican Republic, 2012. **Signed by:** Juan Rosario (Yankees).

TRACK RECORD: Mateo was a top prospect when the Yankees traded him and two others to the A's for Sonny Gray at the 2017 trade deadline. Mateo's bat never came around, and the A's traded him to the Padres for a player to be named last June. He appeared in 22 big league games, mostly as a pinch-runner.

SCOUTING REPORT: Mateo is one of the fastest players in baseball. He's capable of stealing a base at any time and can score on shallow balls in play that others can't. Mateo's offensive value derives almost entirely from his speed. He has shown flashes of a quick, direct swing, but overall he's a bottom of the scale hitter who is tentative against velocity and doesn't recognize spin. He does have some gap power when he connects. Mateo came up as a shortstop but is better in the outfield, where he covers a lot of ground and his plus arm is less encumbered by iffy accuracy.

THE FUTURE: Mateo is purely a pinch-runner and defensive replacement, but he can create runs and add value at the bottom of a roster. He'll fill that role for the Padres in 2021.

Year	Age	Club (League)	Class	AVG	G	AB	R	H	2B	3B	HR	RBI	BB	SO	SB	OBP	SLG
2020	25	San Diego (NL)	MAJ	.154	22	26	4	4	3	0	0	2	1	11	1	.185	.269
Major League Totals				.154	22	26	4	4	3	0	0	2	1	11	1	.185	.269
Minor League Totals				.267	702	2818	445	751	131	76	52	302	227	714	283	.325	.422

23 OMAR CRUZ, LHP

BREAKOUT
BA GRADE
45 Risk: High

Born: Jan. 26, 1999. **B-T:** L-L. **HT:** 6-0. **WT:** 200. **Signed:** Mexico, 2017. **Signed by:** Bill McLaughlin/Chris Kemp.

TRACK RECORD: The Padres purchased Cruz's rights from the Mexican League's Mexico City franchise for $100,000 in 2017, the same club they purchased Luis Urias and Andres Muñoz from in previous years. Cruz dominated the short-season levels and jumped for high Class A Fort Wayne in 2019, where he posted a 2.76 ERA in 10 starts. He continued to shine during 2020 instructional league.

SCOUTING REPORT: Cruz's fastball has improved to 89-93 mph with room to keep growing. His fastball plays up with carry through the zone and gets swings and misses despite modest velocity. Cruz's primary weapon is a big, overhand curveball with a high arc. It can get loopy at times at 73-77 mph, but he shows an impressive feel to spin the ball and should add power to it as he gets stronger. His fading 78-82 mph changeup shows average potential and he attacks the strike zone with average control.

THE FUTURE: Cruz shows the makings of the back-of-the-rotation starter if he can continue adding velocity. He's a strong competitor who has a chance to move quickly in 2021.

Year	Age	Club (League)	Class	W	L	ERA	G	GS	IP	H	HR	BB	SO	BB/9	SO/9	WHIP	AVG
2019	20	Tri-City (NWL)	SS	0	1	2.57	2	2	7	4	0	6	14	7.7	18.0	1.43	.121
	20	Fort Wayne (MWL)	LoA	2	2	2.76	10	10	49	42	1	13	62	2.4	11.4	1.12	.211
Minor League Totals				3	4	2.38	23	22	98	80	1	41	135	3.8	12.4	1.23	.225

24 REISS KNEHR, RHP

BA GRADE
45 Risk: High

Born: Nov. 3, 1996. **B-T:** L-R. **HT:** 6-2. **WT:** 205. **Drafted:** Fordham, 2018 (20th round). **Signed by:** Jake Koenig.

TRACK RECORD: Knehr was a standout pitcher at Fordham and was the Rams' second baseman or designated hitter on days he didn't pitch. The Padres liked his athleticism and drafted him in the 20th round in 2018. Knehr struggled with an aggressive assignment to high Class A Lake Elsinore in his first full season, but he made adjustments and was the Padres' biggest breakout performer at instructional league in 2020.

SCOUTING REPORT: Knehr's stuff has improved now that he is focused on pitching only. His fastball sat in the low 90s in college and now comfortably sits 93-96 mph. His slider has ticked up from a low-80s pitch to an average 84-87 mph offering with shape and depth, and he is increasingly showing a feel for upper-80s changeup. Knehr has a history of walks and his control is inconsistent, but he's gradually challenging hitters and throwing more strikes. He is a good athlete with a big, durable frame and a quick arm.

THE FUTURE: Knehr's upward trend has the Padres excited. He may see Double-A in 2021.

Year	Age	Club (League)	Class	W	L	ERA	G	GS	IP	H	HR	BB	SO	BB/9	SO/9	WHIP	AVG
2019	22	Lake Elsinore (CAL)	HiA	3	5	5.43	17	12	66	71	11	28	83	3.8	11.3	1.49	.238
Minor League Totals				6	6	4.72	37	13	101	97	14	43	128	3.8	11.4	1.39	.245

25 MASON THOMPSON, RHP

Born: Feb, 20, 1998. **B-T:** R-R. **HT:** 6-7. **WT:** 223. **Drafted:** HS—Round Rock, Texas, 2016 (3rd round). **Signed by:** Matt Schaffner.

TRACK RECORD: Thompson had Tommy John surgery in high school and pitched only one inning his senior year. The Padres still drafted him in the third round in 2016 based on his pre-surgery success. Injuries continued to afflict Thompson in pro ball—he had biceps tendinitis and shoulder inflammation in 2017, a triceps strain in 2018 and elbow issues in 2019—and have contributed to a career 5.08 ERA. But Thompson used the 2020 shutdown to get healthy, and he turned heads at instructional league.

SCOUTING REPORT: Thompson has filled out his 6-foot-7 frame and now sits 94-98 mph on his fastball in short stints. His main secondary is a power slider at 88-90 mph that gets swings and misses. Thompson's 12-to-6 curveball and fading changeup each flashed above-average in the past, but they've taken a back seat to his fastball and slider. Thompson can only locate pitches to his glove side, but that's enough to dominate righthanded batters.

THE FUTURE: Thompson is a likely reliever moving forward. Staying healthy will be key in 2021.

Year	Age	Club (League)	Class	W	L	ERA	G	GS	IP	H	HR	BB	SO	BB/9	SO/9	WHIP	AVG
2019	21	Lake Elsinore (CAL)	HiA	0	5	7.66	7	6	22	22	3	19	22	7.7	8.9	1.84	.202
	21	Padres 1 (AZL)	R	0	0	0.00	1	0	1	0	0	0	0	0.0	0.0	0.00	.000
	21	Padres (AZL)	R	0	0	6.75	2	2	4	6	1	3	3	6.8	6.8	2.25	.300
Minor League Totals				8	17	5.08	44	40	159	154	14	76	162	4.3	9.2	1.44	.248

26 DAURIS VALDEZ, RHP

BA GRADE
45 Risk: High

Born: Oct. 22, 1995. **B-T:** R-R. **HT:** 6-8. **WT:** 254. **Signed:** Dominican Republic, 2016. **Signed by:** Chris Kemp/Alvin Duran.

TRACK RECORD: Valdez was lightly regarded as an amateur and signed with the Padres for just $10,000 late in the 2015-16 international signing period. He exploded physically into a 6-foot-8, 254-pound behemoth and quickly rose through the minors as a hard-throwing reliever. Valdez spent all of 2019 at Double-A and pitched at instructional league in 2020 before heading to the Dominican Winter League.

SCOUTING REPORT: Valdez is an enormous human being whose nickname is "Exxon" Valdez, after the oil tanker. He is an intimidating presence on the mound and blows hitters away with a fastball that averages 98-99 mph and touches 101-102 mph out of a short arm action. Valdez's slider has transformed from a loopy, 78-80 mph pitch into a hard, 87-88 mph power offering with late snap to give him a needed secondary offering. His 89-90 changeup with hard sink has also come along to be a solid pitch. Both of his secondaries flash plus at their best but need more consistency. Valdez's control is below-average, but he throws enough strikes to be an effective late-game reliever.

THE FUTURE: Valdez has a chance to be one of the hardest-throwing relievers in the majors. He is in position to make his major league debut in 2021.

Year	Age	Club (League)	Class	W	L	ERA	G	GS	IP	H	HR	BB	SO	BB/9	SO/9	WHIP	AVG
2019	23	Amarillo (TL)	AA	2	0	4.23	43	0	55	51	11	28	68	4.6	11.1	1.43	.219
Minor League Totals				8	9	3.97	122	12	199	174	19	83	245	3.8	11.1	1.29	.230

27 ANDERSON ESPINOZA, RHP

BA GRADE
50 Risk: Extreme

Born: March 9, 1998. **B-T:** R-R. **HT:** 6-0. **WT:** 190. **Signed:** Venezuela, 2014. **Signed by:** Eddie Romero/Manny Padron (Red Sox).

TRACK RECORD: Espinoza was one of baseball's top pitching prospects when the Red Sox traded him to the Padres for Drew Pomeranz at the 2016 all-star break. MLB later suspended Padres general manager A.J. Preller for 30 days after ruling he did not disclose Pomeranz's complete medical history to Boston. Espinoza, however, is the one whose injuries have been a bigger problem. He's had two Tommy John surgeries and has not pitched in a game since 2016.

SCOUTING REPORT: Despite having not pitched in four seasons, Espinoza will still be only 22 when spring training begins and has shown signs of his arm strength returning. He returned to the mound at the alternate training site and his fastball sat 94-96 mph and touched 98 mph with little effort during instructional league. He threw his fastball for strikes and, most importantly, had no setbacks. Espinoza's secondaries have further to go. He has not spun the ball well since returning and has yet to regain a feel for his once-dominant changeup after the long layoff.

THE FUTURE: Espinoza's youth and arm strength remain intriguing after all this time. Staying healthy will be his primary goal in 2021.

Year	Age	Club (League)	Class	W	L	ERA	G	GS	IP	H	HR	BB	SO	BB/9	SO/9	WHIP	AVG
2019	21	Did not play—Injured															
Minor League Totals				6	13	3.35	40	39	166	156	3	49	165	2.7	8.9	1.23	.248

28 TIRSO ORNELAS, OF

BA GRADE
45 Risk: Very High

Born: March 11, 2000. **B-T:** L-R. **HT:** 6-4. **WT:** 200. **Signed:** Mexico, 2016. **Signed by:** Chris Kemp/Bill McLaughlin.

TRACK RECORD: The Padres purchased Ornelas' rights from the Mexican League for $1.5 million and pushed him quickly up their system. He stumbled at high Class A Lake Elsinore in 2019, batting .220 with one home run and while being demoted at midseason. Ornelas showed signs of breaking out with a new swing at the end of the year and carried it forward in the Mexican Winter League in 2020.

SCOUTING REPORT: Ornelas is a physical lefthanded hitter with exceptional strike-zone recognition and above-average raw power. His swing got long, slow and steep during his 2019 struggles, so the Padres reset his hand position to get him quicker to the ball. Ornelas is not particularly twitchy so he needs to keep his swing short. He swings at the right pitches and has the strength to drive the ball. Ornelas moves well for his size and is playable in right field. His arm strength previously flashed above-average but has regressed.

THE FUTURE: Ornelas' swing improvements were a promising first step. They need to hold in 2021.

Year	Age	Club (League)	Class	AVG	G	AB	R	H	2B	3B	HR	RBI	BB	SO	SB	OBP	SLG
2019	19	Lake Elsinore (CAL)	HiA	.220	89	332	41	73	11	5	1	30	44	91	3	.309	.292
	19	Padres 1 (AZL)	R	.205	21	88	6	18	2	0	0	11	9	22	4	.278	.227
Minor League Totals				.241	249	925	138	223	37	11	12	107	133	242	12	.337	.344

29 JAGGER HAYNES, LHP

BA GRADE
45 Risk: Extreme

Born: Sept. 20, 2002. **B-T:** L-L. **HT:** 6-3. **WT:** 170. **Drafted:** HS—Cerro Gordo, N.C. (5th round). **Signed by:** Jake Koenig.

TRACK RECORD: Haynes went under the radar in tiny Cerro Gordo, N.C. and pitched only one game before the coronavirus pandemic canceled his high school senior season. Padres righthander Seth Frankoff, who also lives in Cerro Gordo, worked out with Haynes during the shutdown and recommended him to the Padres' scouting staff, who knew Haynes from previous showcases. The Padres drafted Haynes in the fifth round and signed him for an above-slot $300,000 to forgo a North Carolina commitment.

SCOUTING REPORT: Haynes is a tall, projectable lefthander who was the youngest pitcher selected in the 2020 draft. His fastball ranges from 87-93 mph with running life out of a clean, athletic delivery, and his wide shoulders portend future strength and velocity gains. Haynes' breaking ball is slurvy and he'll need to tighten it, but it shows average or better potential. He decently sells his fringy changeup with light fade. Haynes has the delivery and athleticism for average or better control, though he'll need time and experience to get there. He is an edgy competitor who isn't fazed by falling behind in the count.

THE FUTURE: Haynes is all projection but has lots of promising ingredients. The Padres think he could be a draft steal.

Year	Age	Club (League)	Class	W	L	ERA	G	GS	IP	H	HR	BB	SO	BB/9	SO/9	WHIP	AVG
2020	17	Did not play—No minor league season															

30 BRANDON VALENZUELA, C

BA GRADE 45 **Risk:** Extreme

Born: Oct. 2, 2000. **B-T:** B-R. **HT:** 6-3. **WT:** 230. **Signed:** Mexico, 2017.
Signed by: Bill McLaughlin/Trevor Schumm/Chris Kemp.

TRACK RECORD: The Padres scouted Mexico heavily during the 2017-18 international signing period and purchased Valenzuela's rights for $100,000 from the Mexico City Red Devils. The switch-hitting catcher grew three inches after signing and impressed with more walks (34) than strikeouts (32) in the Rookie-level Arizona League. He earned plaudits during 2020 instructional league for his ability to catch older, more advanced pitchers.

SCOUTING REPORT: Valenzuela is a physical backstop with premium defensive ability for his age. He's an excellent framer who takes low pitches and turns them into strikes, records pop times in the 1.9s with his above-average arm and is often the smartest player on the field. He remembers hitters' tendencies and expertly guides his pitchers through difficult situations. Valenzuela has a simple swing from both sides of the plate. His bat speed is limited, but he doesn't chase outside the strike zone and draws enough walks to be an offensive contributor. His strength gives him a chance to reach double-digit home runs at maturity.

THE FUTURE: Valenzuela has the look and defensive attributes of a future major league catcher. He'll move to full-season ball in 2021.

Year	Age	Club (League)	Class	AVG	G	AB	R	H	2B	3B	HR	RBI	BB	SO	SB	OBP	SLG
2019	18	Padres 1 (AZL)	R	.248	42	145	21	36	4	1	0	20	34	32	0	.399	.290
Minor League Totals				.251	96	343	55	86	11	3	1	47	73	91	2	.387	.309

MORE PROSPECTS TO KNOW

31 BRAYAN MEDINA, RHP

The Venezuelan righthander is a plus athlete who sits 92-94 mph and has the makings of a high-spin, swing-and-miss slider at 18 years old.

32 MASON FEOLE, LHP

SLEEPER

The all-time strikeout leader at UConn returned from Tommy John surgery throwing 94-98 mph with an excellent curveball.

33 IVAN CASTILLO, SS/2B

The switch-hitting middle infielder is a late bloomer who won the Texas League batting title in 2019 and has super-utility potential.

34 PEDRO AVILA, RHP

The polished righthaznder is back from Tommy John surgery and provides valuable starting depth.

35 LAKE BACHAR, RHP

A former college football kicker/punter, Bachar has a 92-95 mph fastball and a pair of high-spin breaking balls, but elbow issues cloud his immediate future.

36 EGUY ROSARIO, 3B/2B

The egg-shaped infielder has surprising thump, a big arm and a potential utility future.

37 JAVY GUERRA, RHP

The converted shortstop is still learning to pitch but has explosive stuff with a 98-101 mph fastball and 88-91 mph slider.

38 ESTEURY RUIZ, OF/2B

Ruiz is a toolsy athlete with plenty of power and speed, but his contact ability and defense have a long way to go.

39 JONNY HOMZA, C

The converted infielder from Alaska has gotten comfortable behind the plate and shows promising catch-and-throw skills.

40 DAVID BEDNAR, RHP

A late-round draft find, Bednar continues to show promising stuff in relief but needs to improve his command against major league hitters.

TOP PROSPECTS OF THE DECADE

Year	Player, Pos	2020 Org
2011	Casey Kelly, RHP	LG (Korea)
2012	Anthony Rizzo, 1B	Cubs
2013	Casey Kelly, RHP	LG (Korea)
2014	Austin Hedges, C	Indians
2015	Matt Wisler, RHP	Twins
2016	Javier Guerra, SS	Padres
2017	Anderson Espinoza, RHP	Padres
2018	Fernando Tatis Jr., SS	Padres
2019	Fernando Tatis Jr., SS	Padres
2020	MacKenzie Gore, LHP	Padres

TOP DRAFT PICKS OF THE DECADE

Year	Player, Pos	2020 Org
2011	Cory Spangenberg, 2B	Seibu (Japan)
2012	Max Fried, LHP	Braves
2013	Hunter Renfroe, OF	Rays
2014	Trea Turner, SS	Nationals
2015	Austin Smith, RHP (2nd round)	Padres
2016	Cal Quantrill, RHP	Indians
2017	MacKenzie Gore, LHP	Padres
2018	Ryan Weathers, LHP	Padres
2019	CJ Abrams, SS	Padres
2020	Robert Hassell, OF	Padres

DEPTH CHART

SAN DIEGO PADRES

TOP 2021 ROOKIES	RANK
MacKenzie Gore, LHP	1
Luis Patiño, RHP	3
Luis Campusano, C	4
BREAKOUT PROSPECTS	**RANK**
Ismael Mena, OF	17
Joshua Mears, OF	21
Omar Cruz, LHP	23

SOURCE OF TOP 30 TALENT

Homegrown	28	Acquired	2
College	2	Trade	2
Junior college	0	Rule 5 draft	0
High school	13	Independent league	0
Nondrafted free agent	0	Free agent/waivers	0
International	13		

LF
Jorge Mateo (22)
Esteury Ruiz

CF
Robert Hassell (7)
Hudson Head (8)
Ismael Mena (17)

RF
Jorge Oña (13)
Owen Caissie (20)
Joshua Mears (21)
Tirso Ornelas (28)
Cristian Heredia

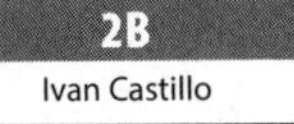

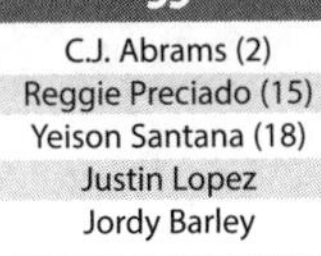

3B
Tucupita Marcano (11)
Eguy Rosario

SS
C.J. Abrams (2)
Reggie Preciado (15)
Yeison Santana (18)
Justin Lopez
Jordy Barley

2B
Ivan Castillo

1B
Brad Zunica

C
Luis Campusano (4)
Blake Hunt (10)
Logan Driscoll (27)
Brandon Valenzuela (30)
Jonny Homza

LHP

LHSP	LHRP
MacKenzie Gore (1)	Mason Feole
Adrian Morejon (5)	Jerry Keel
Ryan Weathers (6)	Cody Tyler
Omar Cruz (23)	
Jagger Haynes (29)	
Aaron Leasher	

RHP

RHSP	RHRP
Luis Patiño (3)	Cole Wilcox (9)
Reggie Lawson (14)	Michel Baez (12)
Efrain Contreras (16)	Reiss Knehr (24)
Justin Lange (19)	Mason Thompson (25)
Anderson Espinoza (27)	Dauris Valdez (26)
Brayan Medina	Lake Bachar
Pedro Avila	Javy Guerra
Jacob Nix	David Bednar
Luarbert Arias	Steven Wilson
Jesse Scholtens	Evan Miller
Carlos Guarate	Adrian Martinez

San Francisco Giants

BY JOSH NORRIS

Even with the agonizing end to the season, hope is on the way in San Francisco. The Giants missed a spot in the expanded playoffs by losing to the Padres in the final three games of the coronavirus-shortened season.

During the course of the season, however, they got glimpses of their future. Mike Yastrzemski put together an excellent encore to his 2019 breakout. Rookies Mauricio Dubon and Logan Webb each carved out spots on the roster.

The Giants got an encore from veteran infielder Donovan Solano, who earned the nickname "Donnie Barrels" by hitting .326/.365/.463 a year after producing an .815 OPS over a half-season. Veterans Alex Dickerson and Darin Ruf added punch to the lineup, as well.

Top catching prospect Joey Bart made his big league debut, albeit earlier than planned because of a lack of a minor league season and the absence of Buster Posey, who opted out of the season.

Bart's presence led some in the industry to raise their eyebrows when the Giants took North Carolina State catcher Patrick Bailey with their first-round selection, but the organization believes both can be long-term assets.

The Giants also added high school lefty Kyle Harrison in the draft and were extremely encouraged by his early performance in instructional league. The additions of Harrison and Bailey help strengthen a system headed by one of the game's best prospects in Marco Luciano.

The Giants felt strongly enough about Luciano's future that they made him part of their 60-man player pool, giving him the opportunity to compete against upper-level players despite having never played full-season ball.

San Francisco brought plenty of its other top prospects to the alternate site as well, including Bailey, outfielders Alexander Canario and Heliot Ramos and infielders Luis Toribio and Will Wilson.

Canario, one of the team's top prospects, had shoulder surgery after the season to repair a dislocation.

Though he wasn't at the alternate training site, one of the system's most eye-opening performances came from outfielder Luis Matos. Coronavirus restrictions meant Matos couldn't travel back home to Venezuela while the sport was shut down, so he mostly spent his time at the team hotel in Scottsdale, Ariz.

Nonetheless, when instructional league opened, he emerged as one of the system's best prospects, perhaps just a tick below the big three of Luciano, Bart and Ramos. Righthander Camilo Doval, too, made an impression on Giants evaluators and spent time with the big league taxi squad.

Going forth, the team's long-term starting pitching will need to be addressed. The Giants' rotation lacks a true top-end talent, with Kevin Gausman the closest facsimile. The system's best arms are years away.

Nobody is quite sure what the 2021 season will look like, but the young talent coming through the Giants pipeline and the team's ability to turn forgotten veterans into productive big leaguers should hearten fans about what's to come in the years ahead. ■

BRIAN ROTHMULLER/ICON SPORTSWIRE VIA GETTY IMAGES

Mike Yastrzemski kept raking in his age-29 season for a vastly improved Giants' offense.

PROJECTED 2024 LINEUP

Position	Player	Age
Catcher	Patrick Bailey	25
First Base	Joey Bart	27
Second Base	Mauricio Dubon	29
Third Base	Marco Luciano	22
Shortstop	Will Wilson	25
Left Field	Hunter Bishop	26
Center Field	Luis Matos	22
Right Field	Mike Yastrzemski	33
Designated Hitter	Heliot Ramos	24
No. 1 Starter	Kevin Gausman	34
No. 2 Starter	Kyle Harrison	22
No. 3 Starter	Seth Corry	25
No. 4 Starter	Logan Webb	27
No. 5 Starter	Tristan Beck	28
Closer	Tyler Rogers	33

1 MARCO LUCIANO, SS

Born: Sept. 10, 2001. **B-T:** R-R. **HT:** 6-1. **WT:** 198.
Signed: Dominican Republic, 2018.
Signed by: Jonathan Bautista.

TRACK RECORD: After two years under international signing restrictions, the Giants opened their wallet in 2018 to sign a star-studded class that included Luciano and outfielders Luis Matos and Jairo Pomares. Luciano was the undisputed gem and quickly showed why in his 2019 pro debut when he demolished the Rookie-level Arizona League, made a cameo at short-season Salem-Keizer and asserted himself as the most promising prospect in a Giants' system full of high-end offensive talent. Luciano got his first look at Oracle Park in January, when he was part of a group the Giants brought in for a preseason minicamp. He got there again when he was added to the 60-man player pool following baseball's resumption from the coronavirus pandemic shutdown. Luciano immediately announced his presence by hitting a home run in his first intrasquad at-bat as part of the ramp-up to the major league season. Because the minor league season was canceled, Luciano spent the summer at the team's alternate training site getting at-bats against a wide variety of pitchers before heading to instructional league in the fall.

SCOUTING REPORT: Luciano is one of the game's most electrifying prospects. He uses huge bat speed and strength to produce tons of loud contact—he was one of just five players 17 or younger who hit double-digit home runs in 2019—and reached a peak exit velocity of 118 mph at the alternate site. While Luciano has immense strength and feel for the barrel, there is still work to be done. He understandably struggled facing pitchers with much more experience at the alternate site. Initially, he struggled to get balls in the air, but as he learned how to make a plan at the plate and better understand how pitchers would attack him, he started taking better at-bats. Defensively, he has a chance to stay at shortstop, but his bat might push him too quickly to get the necessary development at the position. He shows fine actions and has plenty of arm strength, but hasn't quite mastered making throws on the run. If Luciano has to move, his plus arm will make third base an option. He is a fringe-average runner right now, which might also hasten a move off shortstop. His strong pre-pitch positioning—which has been a point of emphasis in Luciano's development—could mitigate a lack of range.

THE FUTURE: Luciano's bat is that of a potential everyday, middle-of-the-order standout. Although his glove will likely need more time, his bat might not allow that to happen in much the same way Nationals outfielder Juan Soto had his timetable accelerated because his bat was consistently better than the competition at every level of the minor leagues. Luciano has all-star potential even if he has to move to third base. If he can make the defensive improvements necessary, he could one day join the Padres' Fernando Tatis Jr. as a second Dominican superstar shortstop in the National League West. He is likely to open the 2021 season at low Class A. ■

CODY GLENN/ICON SPORTSWIRE VIA GETTY IMAGES

BA GRADE
70 **Risk:** **V. High**

SCOUTING GRADES
Hit: 60. **Power:** 70. **Run:** 40.
Field: 50. **Arm:** 60.

Projected future grades on 20-80 scouting scale.

BEST TOOLS

Best Hitter for Average	Marco Luciano
Best Power Hitter	Marco Luciano
Best Strike-Zone Discipline	Logan Wyatt
Fastest Baserunner	Simon Whiteman
Best Athlete	Hunter Bishop
Best Fastball	Camilo Doval
Best Curveball	Tristen Beck
Best Slider	Blake Rivera
Best Changeup	Nick Swiney
Best Control	Kyle Harrison
Best Defensive Catcher	Patrick Bailey
Best Defensive Infielder	Casey Schmitt
Best Infield Arm	Casey Schmitt
Best Defensive Outfielder	Hunter Bishop
Best Outfield Arm	Diego Rincones

Year	Age	Club (League)	Class	AVG	G	AB	R	H	2B	3B	HR	RBI	BB	SO	SB	OBP	SLG
2019	17	Giants Orange (AZL)	R	.322	38	146	46	47	9	2	10	38	27	39	8	.438	.616
	17	Salem-Keizer (NWL)	SS	.212	9	33	6	7	4	0	0	4	5	6	1	.316	.333
Minor League Totals				.302	47	179	52	54	13	2	10	42	32	45	9	.417	.564

2 JOEY BART, C

TOP ROOKIE

ROBERT BINDER/MLB PHOTOS VIA GETTY IMAGES

BA GRADE
60 Risk: High

Born: Dec. 5, 1996. **B-T:** R-R. **HT:** 6-2. **WT:** 238. **Drafted:** Georgia Tech, 2018 (1st round). **Signed by:** Luke Murton.

TRACK RECORD: Bart parlayed an excellent career at Georgia Tech into becoming the second overall pick in the 2018 draft. He made a splash in his pro debut, but suffered two hand injuries in 2019. He broke his left hand during the regular season and his right thumb in the Arizona Fall League, both the result of errant pitches. The Giants made Bart part of their 60-man player pool in 2020 and installed him as the regular catcher after calling him up on Aug. 20.

SCOUTING REPORT: Bart is a big, strong hitter who can impact the ball with tremendous force, but he still needs refinement. He struck out nearly 37% of the time in the majors as pitchers quickly learned to attack him with hard stuff inside before finishing him with breaking balls out of the zone. Bart has trouble catching up to velocity inside because of the way he moves his body while loading his swing. Bart has a strong arm and quick release but threw out just 18% of basestealers in the majors, which can be somewhat attributed to learning a new pitching staff on the fly. He's a strong blocker and receiver and a surprisingly swift runner.

THE FUTURE: Bart's major league debut came before he was ready. He will start 2021 in the upper levels of the minors to continue polishing his game.

SCOUTING GRADES: **Hitting:** 45 **Power:** 60 **Running:** 40 **Fielding:** 50 **Arm:** 60

Year	Age	Club (League)	Class	AVG	G	AB	R	H	2B	3B	HR	RBI	BB	SO	SB	OBP	SLG
2018	21	Salem-Keizer (NWL)	SS	.298	45	181	35	54	14	2	13	39	12	40	2	.369	.613
	21	Giants Orange (AZL)	R	.261	6	23	3	6	1	1	0	1	1	7	0	.320	.391
2019	22	San Jose (CAL)	HiA	.265	57	234	37	62	10	2	12	37	14	50	5	.315	.479
	22	Richmond (EL)	AA	.316	22	79	9	25	4	1	4	11	7	21	0	.368	.544
2020	23	San Francisco (NL)	MAJ	.233	33	103	15	24	5	2	0	7	3	41	0	.288	.320
Major League Totals				.233	33	103	15	24	5	2	0	7	3	41	0	.288	.320
Minor League Totals				.284	130	517	84	147	29	6	29	88	34	118	7	.343	.532

3 HELIOT RAMOS, OF

Born: Sept. 7, 1999. **B-T:** R-R. **HT:** 5-9. **WT:** 233. **Drafted:** HS—Guaynabo, P.R., 2017 (1st round). **Signed by:** Junior Roman.

TRACK RECORD: Ramos has moved quickly after the Giants drafted him 19th overall in 2017, reaching Double-A at 19 years old in 2019 even though he missed time with a knee injury. He spent 2020 at the alternate training site and instructional league before an oblique strain ended his season.

SCOUTING REPORT: Ramos is a thick, stocky outfielder who is built like a fullback and has a mixture of skills that are average or slightly above-average. Giants officials were pleased with his at-bats at the alternate site, especially with how he adjusted to the way pitchers attacked him. He was previously vulnerable to sliders down and away, but after last summer he no longer shows a weakness against any single pitch. As long as Ramos maintains that, his quick hands, balance and excellent barrel control should make him at least an average hitter with above-average power. Defensively, Ramos' average speed and good route-running make him playable in center field despite his body type. He's still better suited for a corner spot, with his above-average arm fitting in right field.

THE FUTURE: Ramos will head to an upper-level affiliate to start 2021. He has the potential to be an above-average, everyday outfielder and should be in San Francisco by 2022.

SCOUTING GRADES: **Hitting:** 50 **Power:** 55 **Running:** 50 **Fielding:** 55 **Arm:** 55

Year	Age	Club (League)	Class	AVG	G	AB	R	H	2B	3B	HR	RBI	BB	SO	SB	OBP	SLG
2017	17	Giants Black (AZL)	R	.348	35	138	33	48	11	6	6	27	10	48	10	.404	.645
2018	18	Augusta (SAL)	LoA	.245	124	485	61	119	24	8	11	52	35	136	8	.313	.396
2019	19	San Jose (CAL)	HiA	.306	77	294	51	90	18	0	13	40	32	85	6	.385	.500
	19	Richmond (EL)	AA	.242	25	95	13	23	6	1	3	15	10	33	2	.321	.421
Minor League Totals				.277	261	1012	158	280	59	15	33	134	87	302	26	.347	.462

4 LUIS MATOS, OF

BILL MITCHELL

BA GRADE

60 Risk: Extreme

Born: Jan. 28, 2002. **B-T:** R-R. **HT:** 6-0. **WT:** 186. **Signed:** Venezuela, 2018. **Signed by:** Edgar Fernandez.

TRACK RECORD: Matos was one of three big prizes the Giants landed in the 2018 international class along with Marco Luciano and Jairo Pomares. He starred in the Dominican Summer League in his 2019 pro debut and earned a brief look in the Rookie-level Arizona League. Like many Venezuelans, Matos was marooned by the coronavirus pandemic and spent the shutdown at the team hotel in Scottsdale, Ariz., until being unleashed for instructional league.

SCOUTING REPORT: Matos stands out for his above-average bat speed, electric hand speed and ability to maneuver the barrel up and down the strike zone. He produced exit velocities up to 111 mph during instructs. Matos is more than just a fastball hitter. He shows an impressive ability for his age to wait back on offspeed pitches, and hit a pair of same-side changeups for home runs during instructional league. Defensively, Matos is the organization's most surefire center field prospect. He shows the above-average speed, instincts and jumps to man the position. The Giants were especially pleased with the way Matos maintained his body during the shutdown.

THE FUTURE: No Giants prospect raised his stock more than Matos during the challenging conditions of the 2020 season. He is set to make his full-season debut in 2021.

SCOUTING GRADES: **Hitting:** 55 **Power:** 55 **Running:** 55 **Fielding:** 55 **Arm:** 55

Year	Age	Club (League)	Class	AVG	G	AB	R	H	2B	3B	HR	RBI	BB	SO	SB	OBP	SLG
2019	17	Giants (DSL)	R	.362	55	235	60	85	24	2	7	47	19	30	20	.430	.570
	17	Giants Orange (AZL)	R	.438	5	16	5	7	1	0	0	1	1	1	1	.550	.500
Minor League Totals				.367	60	251	65	92	25	2	7	48	20	31	21	.438	.566

5 KYLE HARRISON, LHP

BILL MITCHELL

BA GRADE

55 Risk: Extreme

Born: Aug. 12, 2001. **B-T:** L-L. **HT:** 6-2. **WT:** 200. **Drafted:** HS—Concord, Calif., 2020 (3rd round). **Signed by:** Keith Snider.

TRACK RECORD: Harrison was the top pitcher on USA Baseball's 18U National Team in 2019, a loaded squad that featured five future first-round picks. He continued with a dominant showing at the Area Code Games and during the abbreviated 2020 high school season. The Giants drafted him in the third round, No. 85 overall, and signed him for $2,497,500 to pry him from a UCLA commitment. He received the equivalent of first-round money.

SCOUTING REPORT: Harrison hit the weight room during the coronavirus shutdown and arrived at instructional league throwing harder than he did in the spring. After ranging from 90-94 mph as an amateur, he reached 96 at instructs and showed advanced command. The Giants worked with Harrison to reshape his curveball from a sweepier pitch into something with a sharper angle he could land on the back foot of righthanders. It requires some projection but should be at least an average pitch. His changeup projects as a solid third offering. Harrison impressed the Giants with how much he studies the game. He's a good athlete with a clean delivery and has above-average control out of his low three-quarters arm slot.

THE FUTURE: The Giants believe Harrison is the organization's best pitching prospect. He should see low Class A in 2021.

SCOUTING GRADES: **Fastball:** 60 **Curveball:** 50 **Changeup:** 50 **Control:** 55

Year	Age	Club (League)	Class	W	L	ERA	G	GS	IP	H	HR	BB	SO	BB/9	SO/9	WHIP	AVG
2020	18	Did not play—No minor league season															

6 HUNTER BISHOP, OF

BILL MITCHELL

BA GRADE
55 **Risk: Extreme**

Born: June 25, 1998. **B-T:** L-R. **HT:** 6-3. **WT:** 212. **Drafted:** Arizona State, 2019 (1st round). **Signed by:** Chuck Hensley.

TRACK RECORD: Bishop hit 22 home runs during a breakout junior year at Arizona State and the Giants drafted him 10th overall in 2019. He advanced quickly out of the Rookie-level Arizona League but struggled to make contact after a promotion to short-season Salem-Keizer. Bishop was delayed in 2020 after testing positive for Covid-19. He recovered in time to join the alternate training site in August and finished the year in instructional league.

SCOUTING REPORT: Bishop has plenty of physical tools with plus raw power, above-average speed and above-average arm strength. The question has always been how much contact will he make. Bishop has excellent bat speed and hand speed, but both his bat path and approach are targeted for adjustment. He's a patient hitter with a sharp eye, but the Giants want him to refine his approach to be more aggressive on pitches he can drive, noting part of the reason he struck out so often was because he was in many deep counts. Bishop's physicality makes him less than a slam dunk to stick in center field. He fits in best in a corner, with left field a possibility.

THE FUTURE: Bishop will likely begin 2021 at high Class A. He will continue to refine his hit tool in the hopes of reaching his ceiling as an everyday outfielder with plenty of power.

SCOUTING GRADES: **Hitting:** 40 **Power:** 60 **Running:** 55 **Fielding:** 50 **Arm:** 55

Year	Age	Club (League)	Class	AVG	G	AB	R	H	2B	3B	HR	RBI	BB	SO	SB	OBP	SLG
2019	21	Salem-Keizer (NWL)	SS	.224	25	85	21	19	1	1	4	9	29	28	6	.427	.400
	21	Giants Orange (AZL)	R	.250	7	20	4	5	3	0	1	3	9	11	2	.483	.550
Minor League Totals				.229	32	105	25	24	4	1	5	12	38	39	8	.438	.429

7 PATRICK BAILEY, C

BA GRADE
50 **Risk: High**

Born: May 29, 1999. **B-T:** B-R. **HT:** 6-1. **WT:** 210. **Drafted:** North Carolina State, 2020 (1st round). **Signed by:** Mark O'Sullivan.

TRACK RECORD: Bailey started all three years behind the plate at North Carolina State and was twice chosen for USA Baseball's Collegiate National Team. Known for his defense, he slammed six home runs in 17 games for the Wolfpack before the pandemic shut the 2020 season down. The Giants drafted Bailey 13th overall and signed him for $3,757,500. Bailey reported to the alternate training site after signing and finished the year in instructional league.

SCOUTING REPORT: Bailey's makeup and work ethic jump out as much as his physical abilities. He immediately impressed the Giants with his willingness to learn new pitchers and drew particular praise from Jeff Samardzija for his professionalism. Bailey is a skilled receiver, especially when it comes to presenting and handling balls low in the strike zone or in the dirt. He makes strong, accurate throws to the bases, even when letting it fly from his knees. The switch-hitting Bailey has different setups in each swing. He takes a loftier swing path from the left side, where he is more of a power threat, and a flatter, contact-oriented swing from the right side.

THE FUTURE: The Giants thought Bailey presented the best combination of skills at a premium position and were happy to draft him, even with the presence of Joey Bart.

SCOUTING GRADES: **Hitting:** 45 **Power:** 55 **Running:** 40 **Fielding:** 70 **Arm:** 60

Year	Age	Club (League)	Class	AVG	G	AB	R	H	2B	3B	HR	RBI	BB	SO	SB	OBP	SLG
2020	21	Did not play—No minor league season															

8 ALEXANDER CANARIO, OF

ZACHARY LUCY/FOUR SEAM IMAGES

Born: May 7, 2000. **B-T:** R-R. **HT:** 6-0. **WT:** 203. **Signed:** Dominican Republic, 2016. **Signed by:** Ruddy Moreta.

TRACK RECORD: Canario signed for $60,000 in 2016 and slowly worked his way through the system before breaking out in 2019. He hit .301/.365/.539 at short-season Salem-Keizer despite playing through a sprained left shoulder. Canario spent 2020 at the alternate training site and went to instructional league in the fall, where he dislocated the same shoulder while playing the outfield. He had surgery to repair a torn labrum.

SCOUTING REPORT: When Canario connects, he tends to do damage. He has plus raw power and ranked among the Giants' leaders in home runs and OPS during his breakout 2019 season. The biggest question is his plate discipline. Canario can be far too eager to swing, especially with two strikes. With that in mind, his work at the alternate site involved developing a more concrete plan and staying calm when behind in the count. Canario has plenty of work to do on defense. He has plenty of arm strength to stick in right field and the above-average speed to cover ground, but he does not get good jumps or reads and needs a lot more polish.

THE FUTURE: Canario is not expected to be ready for spring training. Once he recovers from his surgery, he will head to one of the organization's Class A affiliates.

SCOUTING GRADES: **Hitting:** 40 **Power:** 60 **Running:** 55 **Fielding:** 50 **Arm:** 60

Year	Age	Club (League)	Class	AVG	G	AB	R	H	2B	3B	HR	RBI	BB	SO	SB	OBP	SLG
2017	17	Giants (DSL)	R	.294	66	235	42	69	17	4	5	45	33	40	18	.391	.464
2018	18	Giants Black (AZL)	R	.250	45	176	36	44	5	2	6	19	27	51	8	.357	.403
2019	19	Salem-Keizer (NWL)	SS	.301	49	193	38	58	17	1	9	40	18	71	3	.365	.539
	19	Giants Orange (AZL)	R	.395	10	43	13	17	3	1	7	14	2	9	1	.435	1.000
Minor League Totals				.291	170	647	129	188	42	8	27	118	80	171	30	.377	.505

9 SETH CORRY, LHP

BA GRADE
50 Risk: High

Born: Nov. 3, 1998. **B-T:** L-L. **HT:** 6-2. **WT:** 210. **Drafted:** HS—Highland, Utah, 2017 (3rd round). **Signed by:** Chuck Hensley.

TRACK RECORD: Corry had electric stuff but spotty control coming out of high school. That remained true over his first two seasons, and he struggled again to open 2019, but he made gradual improvements and took off once June hit. Corry went 9-1, 1.28 over his final 17 starts at low Class A Augusta and finished tied for fourth in the minors with 172 strikeouts. He spent the 2020 season working out at home in Utah before reporting for instructional league.

SCOUTING REPORT: The Giants didn't bring Corry to the alternate training site because they believed young pitchers had a better chance to develop remotely than hitters. Corry showed no ill effects from being left home, looking much like the pitcher he was in 2019. Corry's fastball sits in the low-to-mid 90s and peaks at 96 mph. He complements it with a downer curveball and changeup that each have a chance to be average. His control and command remain below-average, but the quality of his arsenal—especially the way he can tunnel his curveball off his fastball—helps him overwhelm hitters and get swings and misses even when he misses his spot.

THE FUTURE: Corry will likely head to high Class A in 2021. He'll look to continue improving his command and control in the hopes of settling in as a starter.

SCOUTING GRADES: **Fastball:** 60 **Curveball:** 50 **Changeup:** 50 **Control:** 40

Year	Age	Club (League)	Class	W	L	ERA	G	GS	IP	H	HR	BB	SO	BB/9	SO/9	WHIP	AVG
2017	18	Giants Black (AZL)	R	0	2	5.55	13	10	24	14	1	22	21	8.1	7.8	1.48	.127
2018	19	Salem-Keizer (NWL)	SS	1	2	5.49	5	5	20	14	1	15	17	6.9	7.8	1.47	.161
	19	Giants Orange (AZL)	R	3	1	2.61	9	9	38	38	1	17	42	4.0	9.9	1.45	.225
2019	20	Augusta (SAL)	LoA	9	3	1.76	27	26	123	73	4	58	172	4.3	12.6	1.07	.139
Minor League Totals				13	8	2.73	54	50	204	139	7	112	252	4.9	11.1	1.23	.191

10 WILL WILSON, SS/2B

Born: July 21, 1998. **B-T:** R-R. **HT:** 5-8. **WT:** 202. **Drafted:** North Carolina State, 2019 (1st round). **Signed by:** Chris McAlpin (Angels).

COURTESY OF N.C. STATE

BA GRADE
50 Risk: High

TRACK RECORD: Wilson was teammates with fellow Giants prospects Patrick Bailey and Nick Swiney at North Carolina State. The Angels drafted him 14th overall in 2019 and dealt him to San Francisco with Zack Cozart that offseason in what amounted to a salary dump. Wilson spent 2020 at the Giants' alternate training site and finished the year at instructional league.

SCOUTING REPORT: After Wilson's vanilla pro debut in the Angels' system, the Giants made adjustments to his swing. They stood him more upright, tweaked his attack angle and focused on establishing a more consistent, closed stride direction to help stay on the ball better. Wilson is a line-drive hitter who can do the little things—such as hit with two strikes or hit behind runners—and occasionally does damage to pitches in his wheelhouse. He has a chance to hit for average, but his power figures to be modest. Wilson is a solid if unspectacular defender at shortstop who can make all the plays and has an above-average arm. The Giants are likely to get him time at second base and third base.

THE FUTURE: Wilson is more polished than some of the higher-upside prospects in the Giants' system. If he reaches his peak, he should be a solid contributor on both sides of the ball.

SCOUTING GRADES: Hitting: 55 Power: 45 Running: 45 Fielding: 50 Arm: 55

Year	Age	Club (League)	Class	AVG	G	AB	R	H	2B	3B	HR	RBI	BB	SO	SB	OBP	SLG
2019	20	Orem (PIO)	R	.275	46	189	23	52	10	3	5	18	14	47	0	.328	.439
Minor League Totals				.275	46	189	23	52	10	3	5	18	14	47	0	.328	.439

11 LUIS TORIBIO, 3B

Born: Sept. 28, 2000. **B-T:** L-R. **HT:** 6-1. **WT:** 213. **Signed:** Dominican Republic, 2017. **Signed by:** Ruddy Moreta.

BA GRADE
55 Risk: Extreme

TRACK RECORD: Toribio signed with the Giants for $300,000 and immediately impressed in each of his first two seasons at the Rookie levels. The Giants promoted him to short-season Salem-Keizer as an 18-year-old in 2019 when he helped the Volcanoes push toward the playoffs. The Giants brought him to the alternate training site in 2020.

SCOUTING REPORT: As a third baseman, there is going to be pressure for Toribio to show big power, but right now his profile leans toward hitting instead of mashing. The Giants believe he has raw juice—generated by above-average bat speed and average hand speed—but his passive approach and a flat bat path leaves it muted. They've suggested hunting fastballs might help him unlock his power, even if it comes at the expense of some batting average and on-base percentage. Toribio is a below-average defender at third base who gets into trouble when he tries to do too much. The Giants have toyed with the idea of moving him to second base, where his strong arm could be an asset in certain defensive shifts. Though the sample size was small, Toribio was eaten up by lefties in the Rookie-level Arizona League, and there are concerns about him hitting southpaws in the long term.

THE FUTURE: Understandably, Toribio struggled a bit at the alternate training site against older, more wily pitchers. He'll move to low Class A in 2021 and will try to steer his future toward staying at third base and showing more power.

Year	Age	Club (League)	Class	AVG	G	AB	R	H	2B	3B	HR	RBI	BB	SO	SB	OBP	SLG
2019	18	Salem-Keizer (NWL)	SS	.273	3	11	2	3	1	0	0	0	2	5	0	.385	.364
	18	Giants Orange (AZL)	R	.297	51	185	45	55	15	3	3	33	45	54	4	.436	.459
Minor League Totals				.282	118	411	91	116	29	4	13	72	98	121	8	.428	.467

12 TRISTAN BECK, RHP

Born: June 24, 1996. **B-T:** R-R. **HT:** 6-4. **WT:** 199. **Drafted:** Stanford, 2018 (4th round). **Signed by:** Jim Blueburg (Braves).

BA GRADE
50 Risk: High

TRACK RECORD: A back injury kept Beck out for his sophomore season at Stanford, but he rebounded well enough to return as a junior. Injury concerns remained, however, and he fell to the Braves in the fourth round. The Giants acquired Beck at the 2019 trade deadline in the deal that sent Mark Melancon to Atlanta, and the righthander's stuff immediately ticked up in his new organization. He spent 2020 working out on his own until reporting to instructional league in the fall.

SCOUTING REPORT: Beck has exactly the kind of pitch mix the Giants covet. He uses his 90-94 mph four-seam fastball at the top of the zone and tunnels it with a downer, mid-70s curveball that has a chance to be a plus pitch. Beck also throws a mid-80s changeup and a slider, but those are his third and fourth pitches and are well behind his fastball and curve. Unsurprisingly for a Stanford product, Beck earns high marks for how he approaches pitching from a mental standpoint. He repeats his delivery and throws strikes with average control.

THE FUTURE: After a 2019 season at high Class A, followed by a stint in the Arizona Fall League and more polish at instructional league, Beck should make his upper-level debut in 2020. He has the ceiling of a back-end starter.

Year	Age	Club (League)	Class	W	L	ERA	G	GS	IP	H	HR	BB	SO	BB/9	SO/9	WHIP	AVG
2019	23	Braves (GCL)	R	0	0	4.00	2	2	9	9	0	4	14	4.0	14.0	1.44	.231
	23	San Jose (CAL)	HiA	3	2	2.27	6	6	36	33	1	13	37	3.3	9.3	1.29	.224
	23	Florida (FSL)	HiA	2	2	5.65	8	8	37	45	2	14	39	3.4	9.6	1.61	.246
Minor League Totals				5	4	3.77	19	17	86	91	3	33	97	3.5	10.2	1.44	.277

13 SEAN HJELLE, RHP

BA GRADE
50 Risk: High

Born: May 7, 1997. **B-T:** R-R. **HT:** 6-11. **WT:** 230. **Drafted:** Kentucky, 2018 (2nd round). **Signed by:** Kevin Christman.

TRACK RECORD: Hjelle moved from closer to starter between his freshman and sophomore seasons at Kentucky, and ended his draft year with a better than 4-to-1 strikeout-to-walk ratio. The Giants drafted him 45th overall and he raced to Double-A in his first full season, but was not invited to the team's alternate training site in 2020 nor instructional league. Hjelle used the shutdown to complete his college degree.

SCOUTING REPORT: Hjelle's exceptional coordination and athleticism help him repeat his delivery despite his massive, 6-foot-11 frame. Away from coaches all year, Hjelle instead worked out at home in Richmond with fellow Giants farmhand Matt Winn. The angle created by Hjelle's height and overhand delivery means he doesn't necessarily have to elevate his low-90s fastball to be effective. Even so, the Giants wanted him to work on that this season in order to change hitters' eye levels and then create a tunnel for his 12-to-6 curveball to follow. Hjelle has a potentially average changeup as well.

THE FUTURE: The Giants estimate Hjelle threw as many as 110 simulated innings in 2020. He should start 2021 at one of the upper levels and has a ceiling as a back-end starter.

Year	Age	Club (League)	Class	W	L	ERA	G	GS	IP	H	HR	BB	SO	BB/9	SO/9	WHIP	AVG
2019	22	San Jose (CAL)	HiA	5	5	2.78	14	14	78	73	2	19	74	2.2	8.6	1.18	.225
	22	Augusta (SAL)	LoA	1	2	2.66	9	9	41	41	3	9	44	2.0	9.7	1.23	.265
	22	Richmond (EL)	AA	1	2	6.04	5	5	25	38	1	9	21	3.2	7.5	1.86	.319
Minor League Totals				7	9	3.55	40	40	165	176	10	41	161	2.2	8.8	1.32	.272

14 CASEY SCHMITT, 3B

BREAKOUT
BA GRADE
50 Risk: High

Born: March 1, 1999. **B-T:** R-R. **HT:** 6-1. **WT:** 216. **Drafted:** San Diego State, 2020 (2nd round). **Signed by:** Brad Cameron.

TRACK RECORD: Schmitt was a decorated two-way player at San Diego State and closed the final game of the Cape Cod League's championship series in 2019 while also hitting two home runs. He started his junior season nicely before things were shut down by the coronavirus pandemic, but the Giants were convinced enough to draft him 49th overall and sign him for $1,147,000.

SCOUTING REPORT: Though he proved himself in college as a pure hitter, Schmitt didn't show the kind of power that usually comes with a corner-infield position and hit just six home runs in 382 at-bats with the Aztecs. He has plenty of strength to impact the ball, but now must learn to add loft to his swing. To achieve that goal, Giants coaches worked with him to incentivize flyballs while at instructional league. Schmitt is a slam dunk to stick at the hot corner. He shows range in and out and side to side—though his footwork could stand to be improved—and a double-plus throwing arm.

THE FUTURE: Given his advanced nature, Schmitt has a chance to start 2021 at high Class A. With improved power, he could turn into an everyday third baseman who provides value on both sides of the ball.

Year	Age	Club (League)	Class	AVG	G	AB	R	H	2B	3B	HR	RBI	BB	SO	SB	OBP	SLG
2020	21	Did not play—No minor league season															

15 LOGAN WYATT, 1B

BA GRADE
50 **Risk: High**

Born: Nov. 15, 1997. **B-T:** L-R. **HT:** 6-4. **WT:** 230. **Drafted:** Louisville, 2019 (2nd round). **Signed by:** Todd Coryell.

TRACK RECORD: Wyatt was coveted at Louisville for his exceptional command of the strike zone and a frame that should easily produce the power required for first base. The Giants drafted him 51st overall and watched as he quickly advanced to low Class A after signing. Wyatt had to wait until instructional league to get back on the field in 2020 after the coronavirus pandemic canceled the minor league season.

SCOUTING REPORT: It's no secret that the Giants want to unlock Wyatt's power. To do so, in addition to extensive work with Giants coach Pat Burrell, they had Wyatt take part in daily faux home run derbies pitted against teammate Connor Cannon while facing the high-velocity pitching machine. The drill was designed to unleash Wyatt's selective aggression on pitches he can drive while still utilizing an all-fields approach. Defensively, Wyatt has soft hands and presents a big target but still needs to improve his footwork around the bag.

THE FUTURE: If Wyatt can sufficiently alter his approach, he could evolve into the prototypical masher at first base. He'll likely restart his path at high Class A.

Year	Age	Club (League)	Class	AVG	G	AB	R	H	2B	3B	HR	RBI	BB	SO	SB	OBP	SLG
2019	21	Giants Black (AZL)	R	.375	7	24	7	9	1	0	0	9	4	6	0	.448	.417
	21	Augusta (SAL)	LoA	.233	19	60	9	14	3	0	1	9	12	14	0	.368	.333
	21	Salem-Keizer (NWL)	SS	.284	18	67	10	19	2	0	2	12	10	9	0	.385	.403
Minor League Totals				.278	44	151	26	42	6	0	3	30	26	29	0	.388	.377

16 NICK SWINEY, LHP

BA GRADE
50 **Risk: High**

Born: Feb. 12, 1999. **B-T:** R-L. **HT:** 6-3. **WT:** 183. **Drafted:** North Carolina State, 2020 (2nd round supplemental). **Signed by:** Mark O'Sullivan.

TRACK RECORD: Swiney was a reliever for two seasons at North Carolina State before a planned move to the rotation in his junior season. He was limited to just four starts before the season shut down, but the Giants saw enough to draft him 67th overall and sign him for $1,197,500. Swiney's crowning moment in 2020 was a 15-strikeout game that marked the highest total for a Wolfpack pitcher since Carlos Rodon in 2014.

SCOUTING REPORT: Although Swiney's fastball has touched 94 mph, he was more in the 89-91 range at instructional league. He'll need to get stronger to tap into his top-end velocity more frequently and hold it throughout starts. Swiney backs up his fastball with a curveball and changeup. Evaluators are split on which pitch has the better future, but they believe that he accentuates his mix by tunnelling all three pitches off of one another. The Giants also worked with Swiney at instructional league to work from the bottom up in his delivery and extract more power from his lower half. He's had control issues in the past but was a plus strike-thrower as a junior.

THE FUTURE: Swiney should begin his first official pro season at one of the Class A levels. He has a ceiling of a back-end starter.

Year	Age	Club (League)	Class	W	L	ERA	G	GS	IP	H	HR	BB	SO	BB/9	SO/9	WHIP	AVG
2020	21	Did not play—No minor league season															

17 AEVERSON ARTEAGA, SS

Born: March 16, 2003. **B-T:** R-R. **HT:** 6-0. **WT:** 174. **Signed:** Venezuela, 2019. **Signed by:** Edgar Fernandez.

TRACK RECORD: The Giants signed Arteaga for $1 million out of Venezuela, the largest bonus they awarded in their 2019 international signing class. His father played professional basketball and clearly handed down some of his athleticism to his son. Arteaga's expected pro debut was delayed by the coronavirus pandemic in 2020, but he got on the field in instructional league in the fall.

SCOUTING REPORT: Arteaga is one of the Giants' better bets to stick at shortstop, where he has smooth, quick hands and an arm strong enough to make all the throws. He also possesses excellent body control and defensive instincts. Arteaga's future is a little more clouded at the plate. The Giants like the whippy action his swing shows in batting practice. They believe he can blossom into a hitter who can produce a little bit of average and a little bit of power, but even they don't think he'll be an impact hitter.

THE FUTURE: Arteaga will make his pro debut in 2021, likely in the Rookie-level Arizona League.

Year	Age	Club (League)	Class	AVG	G	AB	R	H	2B	3B	HR	RBI	BB	SO	SB	OBP	SLG
2019	16	Did not play—Signed 2020 contract															

18 ANTHONY RODRIGUEZ, SS

BA GRADE 50 Risk: Extreme

Born: Sept. 20, 2002. **B-T:** B-R. **HT:** 6-2. **WT:** 165. **Signed:** Venezuela, 2019. **Signed by:** Jonathan Arraiz.

TRACK RECORD: Rodriguez signed for $800,000 as part of the Giants' highly regarded 2019 international signing class, which also included fellow shortstop Aeverson Arteaga, lefthander Esmerlin Vinicio and catcher Adrian Sugastey. Rodriguez's expected pro debut was wiped out by the coronavirus pandemic in 2020 and he did not participate in instructional league.

SCOUTING REPORT: Rodriguez's balanced skill set probably leans toward his offensive tools over his defense. At the plate, he shows an easy swing geared for line drives. Rodriguez has a projectable body, so those line drives could turn into home runs as he gets older and adds strength to his frame. While his bat is the most prominent part of his game, Rodriguez has a solid chance to stick at shortstop with his strong footwork and plus arm strength.

THE FUTURE: Rodriguez will get another chance at a professional debut in 2021. He's likely to start in the Rookie-level Arizona League.

Year	Age	Club (League)	Class	AVG	G	AB	R	H	2B	3B	HR	RBI	BB	SO	SB	OBP	SLG
2019	16	Did not play—Signed 2020 contract															

19 JAIRO POMARES, OF

BA GRADE 45 Risk: Very High

Born: Aug. 4, 2000. **B-T:** L-R. **HT:** 6-1. **WT:** 185. **Signed:** Cuba, 2018. **Signed by:** Jonathan Bautista/Gabriel Elias.

TRACK RECORD: Pomares was one of the Giants' highest profile signings from 2018 along with top prospect Marco Luciano and rising star Luis Matos. He proved advanced enough in his first season as a pro to make it to the college-heavy short-season Northwest League. Pomares could not get his visa renewed for 2020, so the only in-person development he got was at instructional league in the Dominican Republic.

SCOUTING REPORT: Pomares earns strong marks for his calm, quiet approach, advanced knowledge of the strike zone and the way he drives the ball to all fields. He makes plenty of contact, but there are questions about how much power he'll produce. Right now, Pomares' power is only to the pull side, and even then it's only fringy. Pomares is unlikely to play center field, so he'll need to produce more juice if he is to carve out an everyday role as a corner outfielder.

THE FUTURE: Even with a year of lost development, Pomares still has youth on his side. He'll be just 20 years old for most of the 2021 season and should start at low Class A.

Year	Age	Club (League)	Class	AVG	G	AB	R	H	2B	3B	HR	RBI	BB	SO	SB	OBP	SLG
2019	18	Giants Black (AZL)	R	.368	37	155	17	57	10	4	3	33	10	26	5	.401	.542
	18	Salem-Keizer (NWL)	SS	.207	14	58	7	12	3	0	0	4	1	17	0	.258	.259
Minor League Totals				.324	51	213	24	69	13	4	3	37	11	43	5	.362	.465

20 CAMILO DOVAL, RHP

BA GRADE 40 Risk: High

Born: July 4, 1997. **B-T:** R-R. **HT:** 6-2. **WT:** 198. **Signed:** Dominican Republic, 2015. **Signed by:** Gabriel Elias.

TRACK RECORD: Doval has moved a level a year since signing in 2015, when the Giants gave him $100,000 on the strength of a loose arm, a promising slider and a fastball just beginning to scrape 90 mph. The Giants brought Doval to the team's alternate training site because they believed he had a chance to make his big league debut. He didn't quite get there, and he got more polish at instructional league in the fall.

SCOUTING REPORT: Doval's fastball has taken several jumps as he's matured, and now the pitch peaks at 102 mph. His slider, a sweepy pitch delivered from a lower, winding arm slot, also flashes plus. Given that his future is in the bullpen, the Giants have encouraged him to divide his pitches at something closer to a 50-50 ratio. More consistent finger placement on the fastball has led to improved velocity and movement patterns. He's toyed with a changeup before, but he should be a two-pitch guy going forth.

THE FUTURE: Doval was placed on the 40-man roster after the season and will get his first taste of the upper levels in 2021. He could move quickly enough to make his big league debut toward season's end.

Year	Age	Club (League)	Class	W	L	ERA	G	GS	IP	H	HR	BB	SO	BB/9	SO/9	WHIP	AVG
2019	21	San Jose (CAL)	HiA	3	5	3.83	45	0	56	41	2	34	80	5.4	12.8	1.33	.163
Minor League Totals				6	10	3.31	118	0	163	117	4	85	233	4.7	12.8	1.24	.199

21 GREGORY SANTOS, RHP

BA GRADE
40 Risk: High

Born: Aug. 28, 1999. **B-T:** R-R. **HT:** 6-4. **WT:** 240. **Signed:** Dominican Republic, 2015. **Signed by:** Eddie Romero/Manny Nanita (Red Sox).

TRACK RECORD: Santos came to the Giants with righthander Shaun Anderson in 2017 as part of the deal that sent Eduardo Nunez to the Red Sox. He struggled with command and control over his first two seasons with his new organization, then missed most of 2019 with injuries to his shoulder and hamstring. Santos was one of the Giants' most impressive pitchers at instructional league.

SCOUTING REPORT: Santos has a power fastball that averages 97 mph and touches 100. While his fastball's pure velocity is excellent, Santos' next goal will be to optimize the pitch by making it spin more efficiently. Outside evaluators noticed a bit of a downtick in his stuff when he pitched out of the stretch, which is something to monitor. His slider gives him a second potential plus pitch and he also throws a changeup, but he won't need the pitch much in the bullpen.

THE FUTURE: Despite no experience above low Class A, Santos was added to the 40-man roster based on the strength of his instructional league showing. He should start 2021 at high Class A and could move quickly as a one-inning power reliever.

Year	Age	Club (League)	Class	W	L	ERA	G	GS	IP	H	HR	BB	SO	BB/9	SO/9	WHIP	AVG
2019	19	Augusta (SAL)	LoA	1	5	2.86	8	8	35	34	4	9	26	2.3	6.8	1.24	.238
Minor League Totals				9	13	3.20	48	42	174	181	10	70	138	3.6	7.1	1.44	.267

22 KERVIN CASTRO, RHP

BA GRADE
40 Risk: High

Born: Feb. 7, 1999. **B-T:** R-R. **HT:** 5-11. **WT:** 234. **Signed:** Venezuela, 2015. **Signed by:** Edgar Fernandez.

TRACK RECORD: The Giants signed Castro in 2015 just three months after he'd converted from catching to pitching. He started his career in the Dominican Summer League in 2016 and missed most of the next two seasons after having Tommy John surgery. He returned in 2019 with short-season Salem-Keizer, where he showed excellent command while helping the Volcanoes reach the playoffs. Castro spent the 2020 coronavirus shutdown working out in Orlando with fellow Venezuelan players who were unable to return home due to travel restrictions. He got back on the mound during instructional league.

SCOUTING REPORT: Castro throws a fastball that sits 93-94 mph and has begun touching 96-97 mph, a significant spike from what he showed in his first year back from surgery. He pairs his fastball with a downer curveball that took significant steps forward and now flashes plus, especially when tunneled off of his four-seamer. He has a changeup, which he throws with excellent conviction and arm speed, but it is a clear third pitch. Castro commands his arsenal well with a short, compact arm stroke.

THE FUTURE: The Giants placed Castro on the 40-man roster after he starred in instructional league. He will likely begin 2021 at high Class A and could move quickly as a reliever.

Year	Age	Club (League)	Class	W	L	ERA	G	GS	IP	H	HR	BB	SO	BB/9	SO/9	WHIP	AVG
2019	20	Salem-Keizer (NWL)	SS	5	3	2.66	14	14	68	52	2	13	61	1.7	8.1	0.96	.194
Minor League Totals				8	4	3.11	28	14	89	69	2	26	88	2.6	8.8	1.06	.214

23 RICARDO GENOVES, C

BA GRADE
40 Risk: High

Born: May 14, 1999. **B-T:** R-R. **HT:** 6-2. **WT:** 254. **Signed:** Venezuela, 2015. **Signed by:** Jonathan Arraiz.

TRACK RECORD: Genoves signed with the Giants for $550,000 in 2015, the second highest bonus the club awarded that year behind the $6 million they gave since-traded shortstop Lucius Fox. Genoves made it to low Class A as a 19-year-old and earned a non-roster invitation to spring training in 2020. He returned to Arizona for instructional league in the fall.

SCOUTING REPORT: As an amateur, Genoves built his reputation on a strong defensive foundation that gave him a chance to be an above-average catcher. He has lived up to that billing throughout his career, and in 2019 allowed just eight passed balls while throwing out 41% of attempted basestealers. He's shown well with the bat throughout his career, too, and has average power out of a strong, righthanded frame. Genoves also earns high marks for his baseball IQ and ability to handle velocity.

THE FUTURE: Genoves has a future as a potential backup catcher who can handle a staff, control the running game and occasionally send a ball out of the park. He'll move to high Class A in 2021.

Year	Age	Club (League)	Class	AVG	G	AB	R	H	2B	3B	HR	RBI	BB	SO	SB	OBP	SLG
2019	20	Augusta (SAL)	LoA	.292	19	65	9	19	4	0	2	14	6	17	0	.361	.446
	20	Salem-Keizer (NWL)	SS	.252	32	131	19	33	7	1	7	31	11	24	1	.322	.481
Minor League Totals				.255	199	715	94	182	39	2	13	95	65	142	1	.334	.369

24 R.J. DABOVICH, RHP

BA GRADE 40 Risk: High

Born: Jan. 11, 1999. **B-T:** R-R. **HT:** 6-3. **WT:** 215. **Drafted:** Arizona State, 2020 (4th round). **Signed by:** Chuck Hensley.

TRACK RECORD: An 18th-round selection by the Royals in 2018 after a year at Central Arizona JC, Dabovich instead transferred to Arizona State. He spent his first season in Tempe shuttling between the rotation and the bullpen but took over closer duties in the shortened 2020 season. The Giants drafted him in the fourth round and included him on their instructional league roster in the fall.

SCOUTING REPORT: Dabovich's money pitch is a 93-96 mph fastball that has touched 98. He had a full four-pitch arsenal from his starting days, but the Giants prefer he focus on his upper-70s curveball because of the way it forms a tunnel with his four-seamer. Dabovich also shifted his arm slot from a high three-quarters to true overhand, which should make it easier for him to drive his curveball down through the zone.

THE FUTURE: Dabovich could move quickly through the system. He has the repertoire to be a middle reliever.

Year	Age	Club (League)	Class	W	L	ERA	G	GS	IP	H	HR	BB	SO	BB/9	SO/9	WHIP	AVG
2020	21	Did not play—No minor league season															

25 ADRIAN SUGASTEY, C

BA GRADE 45 Risk: Extreme

Born: Oct. 23, 2002. **B-T:** R-R. **HT:** 6-1. **WT:** 170. **Signed:** Panama, 2019. **Signed by:** Rogelio Castillo.

TRACK RECORD: Sugastey signed for $525,000 as part of the Giants' lauded 2019 international signing class. He represented Panama at tournaments across the world as an amateur, including Japan, Colombia and Nicaragua, and made his organizational debut in instructional league in the fall.

SCOUTING REPORT: Sugastey's raw package of tools teases a player who could impact the game on both sides of the ball. He's a strong player who already produces exit velocities up to 112 mph, although the Giants want to take some of the choppiness out of his swing in order to unlock more consistent contact. He's made big strides behind the plate and shows a potentially plus arm and solid receiving skills. Sugastey also shows the intangibles for the position, including an ability to work with pitchers and the leadership required behind the plate. Though promising, he is still very young and has a lot of rawness to his game that needs to be smoothed over.

THE FUTURE: Sugastey should begin his pro career in the Rookie-level Arizona League in 2021. He has a chance to add to the Giants' wealth of strong catching prospects.

Year	Age	Club (League)	Class	AVG	G	AB	R	H	2B	3B	HR	RBI	BB	SO	SB	OBP	SLG
2019	16	Did not play—Signed 2020 contract															

26 RAYNER SANTANA, C

BA GRADE 45 Risk: Extreme

Born: Aug. 15, 2002. **B-T:** R-R. **HT:** 6-3. **WT:** 232. **Signed:** Venezuela, 2018. **Signed by:** Daniel Mavarez.

TRACK RECORD: Santana was part of the Giants' heralded 2018 international class that also included Marco Luciano, Luis Matos and Jairo Pomares. He made his pro debut with a strong showing in the Dominican Summer League in 2019 and got back on the field in 2020 during instructional league.

SCOUTING REPORT: Santana's performance is going to be strongly driven by his bat, and he looks like he's going to have a power-over-hit profile. There are some swing-and-miss issues to his game, which the Giants have worked to correct. He's going to have to work to stay behind the plate as well. He's already a big-bodied player, and if he gets much bigger he'll likely have to move to first base. The move could be a bit of a blessing, though, if a less demanding defensive position allows him to focus more on his offense and unlocking his power. Santana is a catcher for now and has the hands and arm strength to stay there, but he's going to need to focus on remaining as mobile as possible.

THE FUTURE: Santana will be 18 years old for most of the 2021 season. He'll begin in the Rookie-level Arizona League.

Year	Age	Club (League)	Class	AVG	G	AB	R	H	2B	3B	HR	RBI	BB	SO	SB	OBP	SLG
2019	16	Giants (DSL)	R	.294	48	170	31	50	14	0	10	36	37	58	2	.439	.553
Minor League Totals				.294	48	170	31	50	14	0	10	36	37	58	2	.439	.553

27 BLAKE RIVERA, RHP

BA GRADE **40** Risk: High

Born: Jan. 9, 1998. **B-T:** R-R. **HT:** 6-4. **WT:** 221. **Drafted:** Wallace State (Ala.) JC, 2018 (4th round). **Signed by:** Jeff Wood.

TRACK RECORD: Rivera is a two-time Giants draftee. They took him in 2017 after his freshman season at Wallace State (Ala.) JC and again a year later in the fourth round. So far, he's proved to be worth the wait. Rivera skipped the short-season Northwest League in 2019, instead jumping from the Arizona League straight to low Class A. His only action in 2020 came during instructional league due to the coronavirus pandemic.

SCOUTING REPORT: Rivera showcases some of the best pure stuff in the Giants' system. He fronts his pitch mix with a mid-90s fastball that has reached 98 with heavy cut life. If he commands the pitch better, it could move from potentially plus to double-plus. Rivera pairs his fastball with a nasty slider with above-average potential. He also has a changeup, but it's a clear third pitch at this point. Rivera's stuff is explosive, but his velocity tends to drop off quickly and his control is firmly below-average. As such, evaluators overwhelmingly view him as a future reliever.

THE FUTURE: Rivera is likely to start 2021 at high Class A. He has a chance to move quickly if the Giants put him in the bullpen.

Year	Age	Club (League)	Class	W	L	ERA	G	GS	IP	H	HR	BB	SO	BB/9	SO/9	WHIP	AVG
2019	21	Augusta (SAL)	LoA	4	6	3.95	16	15	73	59	3	39	87	4.8	10.7	1.34	.186
	21	Giants Orange (AZL)	R	0	1	18.00	2	2	2	4	0	2	0	9.0	0.0	3.00	.364
Minor League Totals				4	7	4.69	27	25	94	83	5	52	101	5.0	9.7	1.44	.232

28 JOSE MARTE, RHP

BA GRADE **40** Risk: High

Born: June 14, 1996. **B-T:** R-R. **HT:** 6-5. **WT:** 236. **Signed:** Dominican Republic, 2015. **Signed by:** Ruddy Moreta.

TRACK RECORD: Marte has moved slowly through the system, advancing only as far as high Class A after six seasons as a pro—though most of the 2020 season was a wash because of the coronavirus pandemic. He got back into the swing of things at instructional league in the fall but was left unprotected on the 40-man roster in advance of the Rule 5 draft.

SCOUTING REPORT: Much like Blake Rivera, Marte has some of the best stuff in the organization and is likely a reliever barring significant improvements in his well below-average command and control. His fastball sits in the mid 90s and can touch 98. He complements his fastball with a low-90s slider and a third-pitch changeup. The goal is to get him to the point where he can finish hitters more consistently once he gets them in two-strike counts. He struggled to do that in instructional league, which Giants officials believe is more of a mental problem than an indicator of problems with his stuff.

THE FUTURE: Marte should be ready for Double-A in 2021. He has a chance to be a middle reliever if his control improves.

Year	Age	Club (League)	Class	W	L	ERA	G	GS	IP	H	HR	BB	SO	BB/9	SO/9	WHIP	AVG
2019	23	San Jose (CAL)	HiA	3	9	5.59	18	17	74	70	7	44	80	5.4	9.7	1.54	.215
Minor League Totals				13	22	4.86	63	61	266	270	19	138	254	4.7	8.6	1.53	.264

29 KAI-WEI TENG, RHP

BA GRADE **40** Risk: High

Born: Dec. 1, 1998. **B-T:** R-R. **HT:** 6-4. **WT:** 260. **Signed:** Taiwan, 2017. **Signed by:** Cary Broder (Twins).

TRACK RECORD: The Twins signed Teng in 2017 because of an intriguing combination of stuff and command. They dealt him to the Giants along with righthander Prelander Berroa in exchange for reliever Sam Dyson at the 2019 trade deadline. Teng stayed in his native Taiwan throughout the coronavirus pandemic and did not attend instructional league in the fall.

SCOUTING REPORT: Teng boasts a three-pitch mix with a low-90s fastball that topped out at 93 mph the last time he pitched. He pairs his fastball with a slider and changeup that each project as above-average with further refinement. Teng mixes his pitches a little bit differently than most in that he throws his fastball less than 50% of the time. The Giants previously worked with Teng to improve the spin efficiency on his fastball, which plays better than its velocity because of how often he can throw his offspeeds for strikes. He commands his arsenal expertly with above-average control.

THE FUTURE: Teng's varied mix and excellent pitchability give him a chance to move quickly. He has a chance to see the upper levels in 2021.

Year	Age	Club (League)	Class	W	L	ERA	G	GS	IP	H	HR	BB	SO	BB/9	SO/9	WHIP	AVG
2019	20	Augusta (SAL)	LoA	3	0	1.55	5	5	29	16	0	7	39	2.2	12.1	0.79	.145
	20	Cedar Rapids (MWL)	LoA	4	0	1.60	9	8	51	40	1	14	49	2.5	8.7	1.07	.190
Minor League Totals				10	3	2.28	24	22	122	92	1	36	135	2.7	9.9	1.05	.205

30 ALEXANDER SUAREZ, OF

BA GRADE
45 **Risk: Extreme**

Born: Dec. 20, 2001. **B-T:** R-R. **HT:** 6-2. **WT:** 160. **Signed:** Venezuela, 2018. **Signed by:** Cira Villalobos Jr.

TRACK RECORD: Suarez, who is a cousin of fellow Giants prospect Luis Matos, signed out of Venezuela in 2018 and hit well in a brief stint in the Dominican Summer League in his professional debut. He reported to instructional league in 2020 and opened eyes among evaluators.

SCOUTING REPORT: Suarez has the potential for average or above-average tools across the board, but it's going to take a little while for him to get there. His main goal right now is to improve his bat path to give him a better angle to the ball. His current path allows him to get to pitches up in the zone but otherwise produces less than ideal contact. Suarez is a good athlete who should have above-average speed and an above-average arm as he matures physically. He should fit in either center or right field. Giants officials are heartened by his makeup and believe his willingness to learn will help him reach his ceiling.

THE FUTURE: Suarez put himself on the map during instructional league. He will have a chance to reinforce the belief in him in the Rookie-level Arizona League in 2021.

Year	Age	Club (League)	Class	AVG	G	AB	R	H	2B	3B	HR	RBI	BB	SO	SB	OBP	SLG
2019	17	Giants (DSL)	R	.308	12	39	15	12	4	0	1	6	10	12	2	.472	.487
Minor League Totals				.308	12	39	15	12	4	0	1	6	10	12	2	.472	.487

MORE PROSPECTS TO KNOW

31 TYLER FITZGERALD, SS/2B

Fitzgerald is a polished college infielder from Louisville. He could settle in as a utility player who provides a little bit of everything but not a lot of anything.

32 JIMMY GLOWENKE, SS

The 2020 supplemental second-round pick showed well with the bat at Dallas Baptist but had elbow surgery that limited him to DH duties in the spring.

33 CALEB KILIAN, RHP

Kilian got into better shape during the shutdown and saw his stuff tick up in instructional league. If he can keep it up, he has a better chance of developing as a starter.

34 GRANT MCCRAY, OF

SLEEPER

McCray is a tooled-up outfielder who will show you flashes of brilliance but needs more consistency.

35 TREVOR MCDONALD, RHP

The 2019 11th-rounder has potential but a lot of rough edges to smooth out. A funky arm stroke limits his potential as a starter.

36 ESMERLIN VINICIO, LHP

Vinicio is an intriguing lefthander from the 2019 international class who needs to gain strength before he can move up the depth chart.

37 CONNER MENEZ, LHP

The veteran lefthander has pitched parts of two seasons in the majors and could work his way into a swingman's role with better control and command.

38 JAYLIN DAVIS, OF

The Appalachian State product has gotten a few cups of coffee and likely has a future as an up-and-down player.

39 DEDNIEL NUÑEZ, RHP

A Rule 5 pick from the Mets, Nuñez's velocity ticked up to 95 mph at instructional league and he commands his fastball well. A lack of a consistent breaking ball could limit his upside, but he has survival skills in his velocity and command.

40 CONNOR CANNON, 1B

Cannon has the best raw power in the organization and produces some of the top exit velocities in all of baseball, but he's got a long way to go to tap into it consistently.

TOP PROSPECTS OF THE DECADE

Year	Player, Pos	2020 Org
2011	Brandon Belt, 1B	Giants
2012	Gary Brown, OF	Did not play
2013	Kyle Crick, RHP	Pirates
2014	Kyle Crick, RHP	Pirates
2015	Andrew Susac, C	Pirates
2016	Christian Arroyo, SS	Red Sox
2017	Tyler Beede, RHP	Giants
2018	Heliot Ramos, OF	Giants
2019	Joey Bart, C	Giants
2020	Marco Luciano, SS	Giants

TOP DRAFT PICKS OF THE DECADE

Year	Player, Pos	2020 Org
2011	Joe Panik, SS	Blue Jays
2012	Chris Stratton, RHP	Pirates
2013	Christian Arroyo, SS	Red Sox
2014	Tyler Beede, RHP	Giants
2015	Phil Bickford, RHP	Brewers
2016	Bryan Reynolds, OF (2nd round)	Pirates
2017	Heliot Ramos, OF	Giants
2018	Joey Bart, C	Giants
2019	Hunter Bishop, OF	Giants
2020	Patrick Bailey, C	Giants

DEPTH CHART

SAN FRANCISCO GIANTS

TOP 2021 ROOKIES	RANK
Joey Bart, C	2
BREAKOUT PROSPECTS	**RANK**
Casey Schmitt, 3B	14

SOURCE OF TOP 30 TALENT

Homegrown	**26**	**Acquired**	**4**
College	8	Trade	4
Junior college	1	Rule 5 draft	0
High school	3	Independent league	0
Nondrafted free agent	0	Free agent/waivers	0
International	14		

LF
Hunter Bishop (6)
Vince Fernandez
Armani Smith
Kwan Adkins

CF
Luis Matos (4)
Alexander Suarez (30)
Grant McCray

RF
Heliot Ramos (3)
Alexander Canario (8)
Jairo Pomares (19)
Diego Rincones
Jaylin Davis

3B
Luis Toribio (11)
Casey Schmitt (14)

SS
Marco Luciano (1)
Will Wilson (10)
Aeverson Arteaga (17)
Anthony Rodriguez (18)
Jimmy Glowenke
Simon Whiteman

2B
Tyler Fitzgerald
Sean Roby

1B
Logan Wyatt (15)
Garrett Frechette
Victor Bericoto
Connor Cannon

C
Joey Bart (2)
Patrick Bailey (7)
Ricardo Genoves (23)
Adrian Sugastey (25)
Rayner Santana (26)
Ronaldo Flores
Onil Perez
Victor Coronil

LHP

LHSP
Kyle Harrison (5)
Seth Corry (9)
Nick Swiney (16)
Esmerlin Vinicio
Conner Menez

LHRP
Caleb Baragar
Mac Marshall

RHP

RHSP
Tristan Beck (12)
Sean Hjelle (13)
Caleb Kilian
Trevor McDonald
Jake Wong
Manuel Mercedes

RHRP
Camilo Doval (20)
Gregory Santos (21)
Kervin Castro (22)
R.J. Dabovich (24)
Blake Rivera (27)
Jose Marte (28)
Kai-Wei Teng (29)
Ronnie Williams
Dedniel Nunez
Prelander Berroa
Melvin Adon

Seattle Mariners

BY BILL MITCHELL

Though the Mariners missed the postseason for the 19th straight season—the longest dry spell in the North American sports—there were reasons to be hopeful for a brighter tomorrow.

Chief among the bright spots was outfielder Kyle Lewis' outstanding season, which earned him the American League Rookie of the Year award. Lewis, the team's first-round pick in 2016 out of Mercer who battled through a series of injuries before reaching the majors, hit .262/.364/.437 with 11 home runs and made numerous highlight-reel catches.

Seattle also got contributions from other prospects. First baseman Evan White, the club's 2017 first-rounder, played every day and lived up to his reputation as a stellar defender by winning the American League's Gold Glove award at first base. Justus Sheffield and righthander Justin Dunn each made 10 starts. The two pitchers were trade acquisitions, with Sheffield coming over from the Yankees in the James Paxton deal and Dunn as part of the package for Edwin Diaz and Robinson Cano. Before that, the Mariners bought low on J.P. Crawford and received him as part of the deal that sent Jean Segura to Philadelphia.

After years of languishing toward the bottom of the organizational talent rankings—including ranking dead last at No. 30 overall in 2018—the Mariners have spent the last two seasons bulking up their farm system through high draft picks, excellent international signings and shrewd trades. The top two prospects in the system—outfielders Julio Rodriguez and Jarred Kelenic—rank among the very best prospects in the sport.

Seattle's system was further replenished in 2020 through a couple of trades, specifically the deal with the Padres that centered around catcher Austin Nola and netted outfielder Taylor Trammell and reliever Andres Muñoz. Outfielder Alberto Rodriguez was acquired from the Blue Jays in a deal for veteran righthander Taijuan Walker.

Although the Mariners' prospect depth is fronted by Rodriguez and Kelenic, more than a third of Seattle's top prospects are starting pitchers, which was an emphasis in recent drafts.

The Mariners invested first-round picks in college righthanders in each of the last three drafts, taking Stetson's Logan Gilbert in 2018, Elon's George Kirby in 2019 and Georgia's Emerson Hancock in 2020.

Seattle's rejuvenated system was apparent at the alternate training site in Tacoma, where young prospects such as Kelenic and shortstop Noelvi Marte starred in addition to top draft picks from the last two years. Rodriguez would have participated if not for a broken left wrist suffered during the preseason summer camp.

The Mariners held instructional league after the end of the regular season, sending additional prospects to make up for the canceled 2020 minor league season. Among the surprises from this camp were pitchers Levi Stoudt and Adam Macko, both 2019 draft picks, who further added to the Mariners' wealth of pitchers.

After years with no success in the big leagues and a fallow farm system, hope is on the horizon in Seattle. ■

ABBIE PARR/MLB PHOTOS VIA GETTY IMAGES

Powerful center fielder Kyle Lewis captured the American League Rookie of the Year award

PROJECTED 2024 LINEUP

Position	Player	Age
Catcher	Cal Raleigh	27
First Base	Evan White	28
Second Base	Dylan Moore	31
Third Base	Noelvi Marte	22
Shortstop	JP Crawford	29
Left Field	Jarred Kelenic	24
Center Field	Kyle Lewis	28
Right Field	Julio Rodriguez	23
Designated Hitter	Ty France	29
No. 1 Starter	Marco Gonzales	32
No. 2 Starter	Logan Gilbert	27
No. 3 Starter	Emerson Hancock	25
No. 4 Starter	Justus Sheffield	28
No. 5 Starter	George Kirby	26
Closer	Andres Muñoz	25

1 JULIO RODRIGUEZ, OF

Born: Dec. 29, 2000. **B-T:** R-R. **HT:** 6-3. **WT:** 205.
Signed: Dominican Republic, 2017.
Signed by: Eddy Toledo/Tim Kissner.

JAMIE SCHWABEROW/GETTY IMAGES

TRACK RECORD: Rodriguez signed with the Mariners during the 2017 international period for $1.75 million. After starting his pro career in the Dominican Summer League in 2018, Rodriguez jumped to full-season ball for his first U.S. experience and put up strong numbers at both low Class A West Virginia and high Class A Modesto despite missing nearly two months with a broken left hand. Rodriguez was anything but intimidated by more advanced California League pitchers, batting .462/.514/.738 in 17 games with the Nuts and earning hyperbolic praise from league observers. He also spent time in the Arizona Fall League after the 2019 season to make up for the time he'd lost during the regular season. Rodriguez suffered a hairline fracture in his left wrist diving for a ball during summer camp in 2020 and sat out most of the summer recovering. He made up for lost time with a strong instructional league stint in the fall before reporting to Escogido of the Dominican League.

SCOUTING REPORT: Rodriguez is a precocious physical specimen often referred to as a "man-child." His elite bat speed and quick hands allow balls off his bat to register big exit velocities—he peaked at 111 mph during instructional league—and his swing takes a solid path through the zone. He has an excellent feel to hit and an advanced ability to make adjustments at the plate. With his natural hitting ability and comically easy plus-plus raw power, he projects to be a plus hitter capable of hitting 30-35 home runs per year with power to all fields. As Rodriguez continues to mature in his already-strong body, he projects to be a fringe-average runner who is faster underway than he is getting out of the box. Rodriguez gets good reads and jumps in the outfield and projects to be at least an average defender with solid instincts. He'll settle into right field as a polished defender with an accurate, plus-plus arm. Rodriguez still has some room for development, with scouts seeing him give away at-bats at times, and he'll need to continue to work on his conditioning to keep his solid, muscular body in shape. He is a bright, effervescent individual with outstanding makeup. He rapidly learned English after signing with the Mariners and shows the confidence and personality to be a leader both on and off the field. He started a YouTube show at instructional league in which he interviewed his teammates on a variety of topics.

THE FUTURE: Rodriguez will be just 20 years old in 2021 and is likely to begin the year in Double-A for his first true taste of the upper levels. While the Mariners have no reason to rush Rodriguez to Seattle, it wouldn't be surprising to see him there before the end of the year if he continues to perform as he can. His talent and personality give him a chance to join Jarred Kelenic as a perennial all-star and one of the Mariners' faces of the franchise through the 2020s, when the team hopes it will have ended the longest current postseason drought in all of North American sports. ■

BEST TOOLS

Best Hitter for Average	Jarred Kelenic
Best Power Hitter	Julio Rodriguez
Best Strike-Zone Discipline	Zach DeLoach
Fastest Baserunner	Jonatan Clase
Best Athlete	Jarred Kelenic
Best Fastball	Logan Gilbert
Best Curveball	Brandon Williamson
Best Slider	Emerson Hancock
Best Changeup	Levi Stoudt
Best Control	George Kirby
Best Defensive Catcher	Cal Raleigh
Best Defensive Infielder	Donovan Walton
Best Infield Arm	Milkar Perez
Best Defensive Outfielder	Luis Liberato
Best Outfield Arm	Julio Rodriguez

Year	Age	Club (League)	Class	AVG	G	AB	R	H	2B	3B	HR	RBI	BB	SO	SB	OBP	SLG
2018	17	Mariners (DSL)	R	.315	59	219	50	69	13	9	5	36	30	40	10	.404	.525
2019	18	West Virginia (SAL)	LoA	.293	67	263	50	77	20	1	10	50	20	66	1	.359	.490
	18	Modesto (CAL)	HiA	.462	17	65	13	30	6	3	2	19	5	10	0	.514	.738
Minor League Totals				.322	143	547	113	176	39	13	17	105	55	116	11	.395	.534

2 JARRED KELENIC, OF

TOP ROOKIE

ALEX TRAUTWIG/MLB PHOTOS VIA GETTY IMAGES

BA GRADE

65 Risk: High

Born: July 16, 1999. **B-T:** L-L. **HT:** 6-1. **WT:** 196. **Drafted:** HS—Waukesha, Wis., 2018 (1st round). **Signed by:** Chris Hervey (Mets).

TRACK RECORD: Kelenic was one of the top high school players in the 2018 draft and was selected sixth overall by the Mets. His time with the Mets lasted only one summer before he was traded to the Mariners in the deal that sent Robinson Cano and Edwin Diaz to New York. Kelenic jumped three levels up to Double-A in his first year with the Mariners. He spent the 2020 season at the alternate training site.

SCOUTING REPORT: Kelenic is an elite young hitter who projects to be an offensive force. He attacks pitches he can hit with authority and lays off pitches that might result in weak contact or swings and misses. Most impressive is his ability to learn and adapt to pitchers' plans of attack from at-bat to at-bat. Kelenic uses a swing so short and powerful it allows him to wait a beat longer before pulling the trigger. He has good strike-zone awareness, though at times he can get locked up on balls inside. Kelenic is a plus runner who may slow down as he matures but should still steal plenty of bases with his advanced instincts and athleticism. Kelenic's main focus at the alternate site was his defense. He is an average defender in center field but needs to improve his focus and decisiveness.

THE FUTURE: Kelenic has an all-star potential and his major league debut is on the horizon in 2021.

SCOUTING GRADES: **Hitting:** 70 **Power:** 60 **Running:** 55 **Fielding:** 50 **Arm:** 60

Year	Age	Club (League)	Class	AVG	G	AB	R	H	2B	3B	HR	RBI	BB	SO	SB	OBP	SLG
2018	18	Mets (GCL)	R	.413	12	46	9	19	2	2	1	9	4	11	4	.451	.609
	18	Kingsport (APP)	R	.253	44	174	33	44	8	4	5	33	22	39	11	.350	.431
2019	19	West Virginia (SAL)	LoA	.309	50	191	33	59	14	3	11	29	25	45	7	.394	.586
	19	Modesto (CAL)	HiA	.290	46	169	36	49	13	1	6	22	17	49	10	.353	.485
	19	Arkansas (TL)	AA	.253	21	83	11	21	4	1	6	17	8	17	3	.315	.542
Minor League Totals				.290	173	663	122	192	41	11	29	110	76	161	35	.366	.516

3 LOGAN GILBERT, RHP

TOP ROOKIE

ALEX TRAUTWIG/MLB PHOTOS VIA GETTY IMAGES

BA GRADE

60 Risk: High

Born: May 5, 1997. **B-T:** R-R. **HT:** 6-6. **WT:** 225. **Drafted:** Stetson, 2018 (1st round). **Signed by:** Rob Mummau.

TRACK RECORD: The Mariners drafted Gilbert 14th overall in 2018 after an impressive college career at Stetson that included winning Atlantic Sun Conference pitcher of the year honors as a sophomore. Gilbert battled mononucleosis and had toe surgery after signing, but he showed no ill effects in his pro debut. He was named the Mariners' minor league pitcher of the year in 2019 after jumping three levels to Double-A. He spent 2020 at the alternate training site and showed an uptick in stuff.

SCOUTING REPORT: Gilbert is a tall, long-limbed righthander who dominates with his fastball. His heater generally sits 93-95 mph and plays up with riding life. He generates tremendous extension from his 6-foot-6 frame. Gilbert's 11-to-5, downer curveball flashes plus, and his changeup made huge strides at the alternate site to give him a third potential plus offering. He also has a horizontal slider he boosted into the low 80s with increased sharpness. The pitch flashes above-average. Everything Gilbert throws plays up with his advanced pitchability and above-average control despite a long arm action.

THE FUTURE: Gilbert still has to show he can maintain his improved stuff over a full season. If he can, he has front-of-the-rotation upside.

SCOUTING GRADES: **Fastball:** 60 **Slider:** 55 **Curveball:** 60 **Changeup:** 60 **Control:** 55

Year	Age	Club (League)	Class	W	L	ERA	G	GS	IP	H	HR	BB	SO	BB/9	SO/9	WHIP	AVG
2018	21	Did not play—Injured															
2019	22	Modesto (CAL)	HiA	5	3	1.73	12	12	62	52	3	12	73	1.7	10.5	1.03	.240
	22	West Virginia (SAL)	LoA	1	0	1.59	5	5	23	9	2	6	36	2.4	14.3	0.66	.108
	22	Arkansas (TL)	AA	4	2	2.88	9	9	50	34	2	15	56	2.7	10.1	0.98	.174
Minor League Totals				10	5	2.13	26	26	135	95	7	33	165	2.2	11.0	0.95	.198

4 EMERSON HANCOCK, RHP

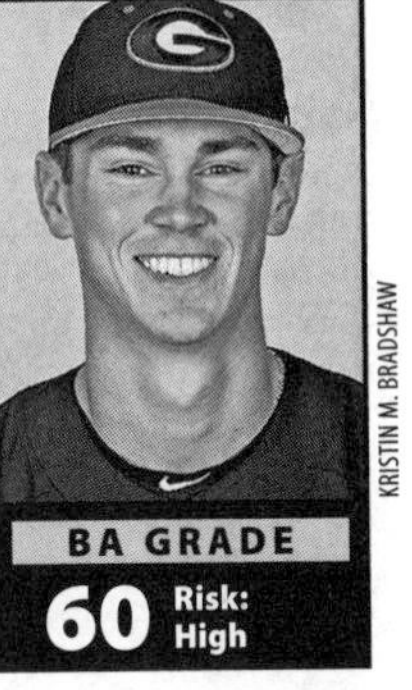

Born: May 31, 1999. **B-T:** R-R. **HT:** 6-4. **WT:** 213. **Drafted:** Georgia, 2020 (1st round). **Signed by:** John Wiedenbauer.

TRACK RECORD: Hancock zoomed up draft boards after an outstanding sophomore season at Georgia in 2019 that included a 1.99 ERA. His four college starts in 2020 before the season shut down weren't as gaudy, but his assortment of plus pitches and outstanding control were enough for the Mariners to draft him sixth overall and sign him for $5.7 million. Hancock participated at the Mariners' alternate training site and instructional league, but he did not pitch because of the long layoff after the college season.

SCOUTING REPORT: Hancock stands out for his command, frame, delivery and pitch mix. He starts with a plus fastball that sits 93-97 mph with heavy sinking action. The Mariners will try to optimize the life on Hancock's fastball to get it to play better up in the zone. Hancock's low-80s slider is above-average with the potential to be plus. His tumbling changeup consistently misses bats against both righthanded and lefthanded batters. Hancock rounds out his arsenal with a seldom-used curveball. He's a natural athlete with a clean delivery that allows him to show plus control.

THE FUTURE: Hancock profiles as at least a No. 3 starter and perhaps better if he refines his breaking pitches. High Class A is his likely assignment coming out of spring training.

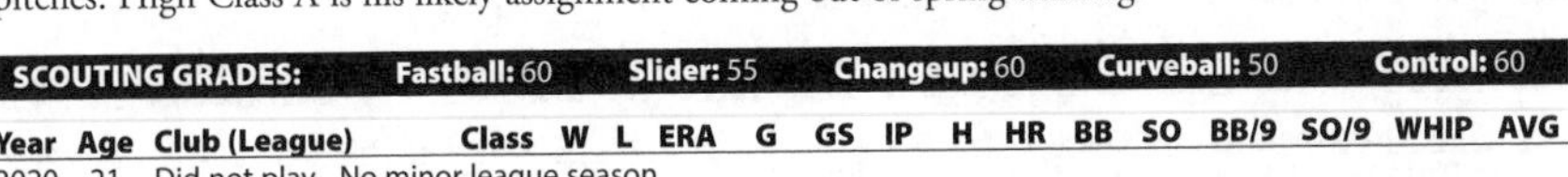
SCOUTING GRADES: **Fastball:** 60 **Slider:** 55 **Changeup:** 60 **Curveball:** 50 **Control:** 60

Year	Age	Club (League)	Class	W	L	ERA	G	GS	IP	H	HR	BB	SO	BB/9	SO/9	WHIP	AVG
2020	21	Did not play	No minor league season														

5 NOELVI MARTE, SS

BILL MITCHELL

BA GRADE
60 Risk: Very High

Born: Oct. 16, 2001. **B-T:** R-R. **HT:** 6-1. **WT:** 187. **Signed:** Dominican Republic, 2018. **Signed by:** Eddy Toledo/Tim Kissner.

TRACK RECORD: Marte signed with the Mariners for $1.55 million in 2018 and ranked as the Dominican Summer League's top prospect the following year after making his pro debut. He led the DSL with 134 total bases. Marte was poised to jump to the U.S. in 2020, but instead he spent the summer as one of the youngest players at the Mariners' alternate training site. He finished the year at instructional league in Arizona.

SCOUTING REPORT: Marte is extremely young but has a chance to be a special player at a premium position. His hands, bat speed and feel for the barrel allow him to make contact against all types of pitches and hit with power to all fields. He projects as a plus hitter with above-average power in the middle of the order. Marte has added muscle to his frame and is just an average runner, and he may slow down more if he keeps growing. Scouts are split on whether Marte can stay at shortstop. His range is a little short, but he has the actions and IQ to handle the position as long as he doesn't grow too much bigger. His plus arm is accurate and he can make throws on the move.

THE FUTURE: If Marte does eventually move to third base, he has more than enough bat to profile as a potential all-star. He should open the 2021 season in full-season ball.

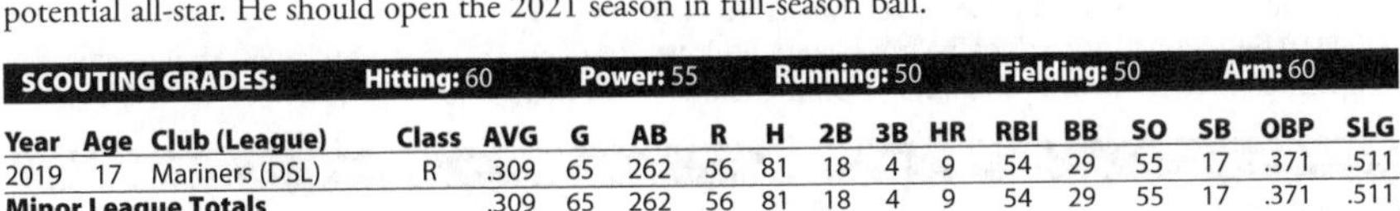
SCOUTING GRADES: **Hitting:** 60 **Power:** 55 **Running:** 50 **Fielding:** 50 **Arm:** 60

Year	Age	Club (League)	Class	AVG	G	AB	R	H	2B	3B	HR	RBI	BB	SO	SB	OBP	SLG
2019	17	Mariners (DSL)	R	.309	65	262	56	81	18	4	9	54	29	55	17	.371	.511
Minor League Totals				.309	65	262	56	81	18	4	9	54	29	55	17	.371	.511

6 TAYLOR TRAMMELL, OF

TOP ROOKIE

ROBERT BINDER/MLB PHOTOS VIA GETTY IMAGES

BA GRADE
55 Risk: High

Born: Sept. 13, 1997. **B-T:** L-L. **HT:** 6-2. **WT:** 215. **Drafted:** HS—Kennesaw, Ga., 2016 (1st round supplemental). **Signed by:** John Poloni (Reds).

TRACK RECORD: Trammell has been on the move frequently the last two seasons. The 2018 Futures Game MVP with the Reds, he was traded to the Padres at the 2019 trade deadline and sent to the Mariners at the 2020 deadline as part of the package for Austin Nola. He joined the Mariners at the alternate training site in Tacoma and finished the year at instructional league.

SCOUTING REPORT: Trammell has the ingredients to be an offensive asset, but he hasn't put them all together. He has size, strength and bat speed and showed improved plate discipline at instructional league. His swing is a bit long, and there are timing issues that lead to holes pitchers can exploit. Trammell stands out for elite athleticism stemming from his background as an all-state running back in high school. He's since filled out his lower half and is more of an above-average than plus runner. Trammell's improved instincts and routes in the outfield stood out this summer and give him a chance to stay in center field. His arm is below-average but accurate.

THE FUTURE: Trammell needs a full season at Triple-A, but his solid makeup and work ethic are positive signs that he will make the necessary adjustments.

SCOUTING GRADES: **Hitting:** 55 **Power:** 45 **Running:** 55 **Fielding:** 50 **Arm:** 40

Year	Age	Club (League)	Class	AVG	G	AB	R	H	2B	3B	HR	RBI	BB	SO	SB	OBP	SLG
2017	19	Dayton (MWL)	LoA	.281	129	491	80	138	24	10	13	77	71	123	41	.368	.450
2018	20	Daytona (FSL)	HiA	.277	110	397	71	110	19	4	8	41	58	105	25	.375	.406
2019	21	Chattanooga (SL)	AA	.236	94	318	47	75	8	3	6	33	54	86	17	.349	.336
	21	Amarillo (TL)	AA	.229	32	118	14	27	4	1	4	10	13	36	3	.316	.381
Minor League Totals				.270	426	1552	251	419	64	24	33	195	219	407	110	.363	.406

7 GEORGE KIRBY, RHP

ALEX TRAUTWIG/MLB PHOTOS VIA GETTY IMAGES

Born: Feb. 4, 1998. **B-T:** R-R. **HT:** 6-4. **WT:** 201. **Drafted:** Elon, 2019 (1st round). **Signed by:** Ty Holub.

TRACK RECORD: Kirby was known for impeccable control at Elon and was drafted 20th overall by the Mariners in 2019. That trait showed up in his professional debut at short-season Everett, when he went 23 innings without walking a batter. He spent 2020 at the Mariners' alternate training site remaking his body to add velocity and power to his arsenal.

SCOUTING REPORT: Kirby's fastball sat in the low 90s in college and touched 95 mph, but he showed an uptick in his pro debut and took another jump in 2020. Kirby's fastball averaged 96 mph and peaked at 99 at the alternate site, and that extra velocity did not come at the expense of his plus-plus control. He also added movement to his fastball, making it a bona fide plus pitch. Kirby's mid-80s slider with deep, crisp break is another plus pitch, while his low-80s, downer curveball projects as average. Kirby doesn't throw his 85-87 mph changeup often, but it has good action and has the potential to be an above-average pitch.

THE FUTURE: Kirby has to show he can maintain his velocity uptick over the course of a full season in a competitive environment. If he can, he'll be a potential mid-rotation starter or better.

SCOUTING GRADES: **Fastball:** 60 **Slider:** 60 **Curveball:** 50 **Changeup:** 55 **Control:** 70

Year	Age	Club (League)	Class	W	L	ERA	G	GS	IP	H	HR	BB	SO	BB/9	SO/9	WHIP	AVG
2019	21	Everett (NWL)	SS	0	0	2.35	9	8	23	24	1	0	25	0.0	9.8	1.04	.270
Minor League Totals				0	0	2.35	9	8	23	24	1	0	25	0.0	9.8	1.04	.270

8 CAL RALEIGH, C

Born: Nov. 26, 1996. **B-T:** B-R. **HT:** 6-3. **WT:** 215. **Drafted:** Florida State, 2018 (3rd round). **Signed by:** Rob Mummau.

ALEX TRAUTWIG/MLB PHOTOS VIA GETTY IMAGES

BA GRADE
50 Risk: High

TRACK RECORD: Raleigh's big power at Florida State led the Mariners to draft him in the third round in 2019, and he quickly showed it transferred to pro ball. Raleigh hit 29 home runs in his first full season as he jumped to Double-A. He spent 2020 at the alternate training site and stood out in instructional league, where his eight home runs led all Mariners prospects.

SCOUTING REPORT: The burly, switch-hitting Raleigh has plus raw power he gets to in games. He has slightly below-average bat speed, but he worked to shorten his swing at instructs and still barrels balls hard in the air. His home run power is almost exclusively from the left side, but he has enough strength to drive balls from the right side, too. Some scouts are concerned he'll struggle with better velocity, but his power should compensate for low batting averages. Whether Raleigh stays at catcher will depend on how he maintains his body and mobility. He has a thick lower half and keeps getting bigger. Because of his size, he catches on one knee but has a quick transfer and makes accurate throws. He is a solid receiver and communicates well with pitchers.

THE FUTURE: Raleigh could be the rare catcher who hits enough to DH on occasion. He'll see Triple-A in 2021.

SCOUTING GRADES: **Hitting:** 40 **Power:** 60 **Running:** 30 **Fielding:** 45 **Arm:** 55

Year	Age	Club (League)	Class	AVG	G	AB	R	H	2B	3B	HR	RBI	BB	SO	SB	OBP	SLG
2018	21	Everett (NWL)	SS	.288	38	146	25	42	10	1	8	29	18	29	1	.367	.534
2019	22	Modesto (CAL)	HiA	.261	82	310	48	81	19	0	22	66	33	69	4	.336	.535
	22	Arkansas (TL)	AA	.228	39	145	16	33	6	0	7	16	14	47	0	.296	.414
Minor League Totals				.260	159	601	89	156	35	1	37	111	65	145	5	.334	.506

9 JUAN THEN, RHP

Born: Feb. 7, 2000. **B-T:** R-R. **HT:** 6-0. **WT:** 178. **Signed:** Dominican Republic, 2016. **Signed by:** Eddy Toledo.

BA GRADE
50 Risk: High

TRACK RECORD: Then first signed with the Mariners in 2016 and was traded to the Yankees one year later. The Mariners reacquired the lanky righthander in 2019 in a trade for Edwin Encarnacion, and Then reached low Class A by the end of that season. Then spent 2020 at the Mariners' alternate training site before reporting to Arizona for instructional league.

SCOUTING REPORT: Then added 10 pounds of good weight prior to spring training and dropped his arm slot to a more natural position. Those changes resulted in a big uptick in his velocity. Then's plus fastball sat 96-97 mph in the fall and began touching triple-digits, up from his previous 92-96. It's a four-seamer with tail and sink, but he can also manipulate it to generate average movement to his glove side. His hard, sharp slider also added power to flash plus at 87-91 mph, and he has a good feel for an above-average changeup at 88-91 mph with deception and a good bottom. Then uses a low three-quarters slot with a smooth arm action and a clean, repeatable delivery that yields above-average control.

THE FUTURE: Then has the attributes to be a mid-rotation starter, but he could also thrive in a late-inning bullpen role. He will likely start 2021 in high Class A.

SCOUTING GRADES: **Fastball:** 60 **Slider:** 60 **Changeup:** 55 **Control:** 55

Year	Age	Club (League)	Class	W	L	ERA	G	GS	IP	H	HR	BB	SO	BB/9	SO/9	WHIP	AVG
2017	17	Mariners (DSL)	R	2	2	2.64	13	13	61	50	3	15	56	2.2	8.2	1.06	.204
2018	18	Yankees1 (GCL)	R	0	3	2.70	11	11	50	38	2	11	42	2.0	7.6	0.98	.195
2019	19	Everett (NWL)	SS	0	3	3.56	7	6	30	24	1	9	32	2.7	9.5	1.09	.202
	19	Mariners (AZL)	R	0	0	0.00	1	0	2	2	0	0	2	0.0	9.0	1.00	.286
	19	West Virginia (SAL)	LoA	1	2	2.25	3	3	16	7	1	4	14	2.3	7.9	0.69	.115
Minor League Totals				3	10	2.76	35	33	159	121	7	39	146	2.2	8.2	1.00	.209

10 ANDRES MUÑOZ, RHP

ROBERT BINDER/MLB PHOTOS VIA GETTY IMAGES

BA GRADE
55 **Risk: Extreme**

Born: Jan. 16, 1999. **B-T:** R-R. **HT:** 6-2. **WT:** 243. **Signed:** Mexico, 2015. **Signed by:** Trevor Schumm (Padres).

TRACK RECORD: The Padres purchased Muñoz's rights from the Mexican League for $700,000 in 2015. He quickly grew into one of the hardest throwers in baseball. He made his big league debut as a 20-year-old and struck out 30 of the 97 batters he faced in relief, but his 2020 season was wiped out by Tommy John surgery. The Mariners acquired him with Taylor Trammell, Ty France and Luis Torrens in the deadline trade that sent Austin Nola to San Diego.

SCOUTING REPORT: Muñoz's top-of-the-scale fastball and an above-average slider allow him to project as a late-innings weapon if he refines his control. Prior to the injury, his four-seamer sat 99-100 mph and touched 103 with explosive life that allowed the pitch to play up even further. He can elevate it to miss bats or spot it on either corner. His mid-80s slider needs consistency, but at its best the pitch generates swings and misses with short, late glove-side cut. Muñoz's control is below-average, but most concerning is his injury history. He battled elbow issues for years before surgery and has thrown more than 26 innings only once in five seasons.

THE FUTURE: Muñoz is set to complete his rehab in mid 2021 and could join Seattle's bullpen late in the season. He has the potential to become the Mariners' closer.

SCOUTING GRADES: **Fastball:** 80 **Slider:** 55 **Control:** 40

Year	Age	Club (League)	Class	W	L	ERA	G	GS	IP	H	HR	BB	SO	BB/9	K/9	WHIP	AVG
2017	18	Tri-City (NWL)	SS	3	0	3.80	21	0	24	15	2	16	35	6.1	13.3	1.31	.177
	18	Fort Wayne (MWL)	LoA	0	0	3.86	3	0	2	2	0	2	3	7.7	11.6	1.71	.222
2018	19	Tri-City (NWL)	SS	0	0	0.00	5	0	6	0	0	2	9	3.2	14.3	0.35	.000
	19	San Antonio (TL)	AA	2	1	0.95	20	0	19	11	0	11	19	5.2	9.0	1.16	.175
2019	20	El Paso (PCL)	AAA	3	2	3.79	19	0	19	16	3	7	24	3.3	11.4	1.21	.235
	20	Amarillo (TL)	AA	0	2	2.16	16	0	17	9	1	11	34	5.9	18.4	1.20	.153
	20	San Diego (NL)	MAJ	1	1	3.91	22	0	23	16	2	11	30	4.3	11.7	1.17	.188
Major League Totals				1	1	3.91	22	0	23	16	2	11	30	4.3	11.7	1.17	.188
Minor League Totals				9	6	3.14	100	1	106	69	7	65	150	5.5	12.7	1.26	.184

11 BRANDON WILLIAMSON, LHP

BA GRADE
50 **Risk: High**

Born: April 2, 1998. **B-T:** L-L. **HT:** 6-6. **WT:** 210. **Drafted:** Texas Christian, 2019 (2nd round). **Signed by:** Jordan Bley.

TRACK RECORD: Williamson spent one season at Texas Christian after transferring from North Iowa Area JC. Despite corrective surgery on both hips, he performed well enough to be drafted by the Mariners in the second round. He pitched minimally in his first pro season and spent 2020 at the Mariners' alternate training site.

SCOUTING REPORT: Williamson works with a powerful fastball-curveball combination that misses bats. His heater sits at 95-97 mph and generates plenty of swings and misses because of its electric life. Williamson's plus curveball has good 11-to-5 shape and a high spin rate that makes it another swing-and-miss pitch. He tried to be too much of a finesse pitcher during the summer, using his above-average changeup and average slider instead of pitching to his strengths with his fastball and curveball. He delivers his pitches from a deceptive three-quarters delivery that features a high front side. He has average control.

THE FUTURE: Williamson will get his first crack at full-season ball in 2021. He has a chance to become a mid-to-back-of-the-rotation-starter.

Year	Age	Club (League)	Class	W	L	ERA	G	GS	IP	H	HR	BB	SO	BB/9	SO/9	WHIP	AVG
2019	21	Everett (NWL)	SS	0	0	2.35	10	9	15	9	0	5	25	2.9	14.7	0.91	.148
Minor League Totals				0	0	2.35	10	9	15	9	0	5	25	2.9	14.7	0.91	.167

12 LEVI STOUDT, RHP

BREAKOUT
BA GRADE
50 **Risk: High**

Born: Dec. 4, 1997. **B-T:** R-R. **HT:** 6-1. **WT:** 195. **Drafted:** Lehigh, 2019 (3rd round). **Signed by:** Patrick O'Grady.

TRACK RECORD: Stoudt was selected by the Mariners in the third round in 2019 and had Tommy John surgery shortly after he was drafted. His first game action came at 2020 instructional league, where he struck out 10 batters and walked three over nine innings.

SCOUTING REPORT: Stoudt thrives with above-average control and command of four pitches. His fastball sat 93-94 mph and touched as high as 97 during instructs. He moves his fastball around the zone effectively with a good downhill plane. Stoudt's best secondary pitch is a split-changeup that has earned future plus-plus grades from observers. Thrown with a vulcan grip, it's a pitch he uses to get swings-and-misses from both righthanded and lefthanded batters. Stoudt has scrapped his curveball in favor of a sweepier slider with roughly 15 inches of horizontal break. His delivery has some effort but his arm action is fluid.
THE FUTURE: Stoudt will make his pro debut in 2021. He likely projects toward the back of a rotation, but his performance in the fall added a bit more ceiling.

Year	Age	Club (League)	Class	W	L	ERA	G	GS	IP	H	HR	BB	SO	BB/9	SO/9	WHIP	AVG
2019	21	Did not play—Injured															

13 ADAM MACKO, LHP

BREAKOUT
BA GRADE
50 Risk: High

Born: Dec. 30, 2000. **B-T:** L-L. **HT:** 6-0. **WT:** 170. **Drafted:** HS—Vauxhall, Alberta, 2019 (7th round). **Signed by:** Les McTavish/Alex Ross.
TRACK RECORD: If Levi Stoudt was the biggest surprise of instructional league, Macko at least deserves the consolation prize. After making his pro debut in the Rookie-level Arizona League in 2019, Macko, who was raised in Canada but born in Slovakia, reported to instructs after working out at home during the summer.
SCOUTING REPORT: Macko stands out for his pitchability, athleticism and above-average command of four pitches. He took a big step forward in 2020, and while he doesn't have any bat-missing pitches, he has the finesse to get batters out. Macko's fastball ranges from 88-94 mph, sitting 90 mph, with late armside tail. The Mariners see his curveball as a potentially plus pitch and his slider has progressed to average after he changed his grip. Macko rounds out his arsenal with a fringy changeup with fade and good separation from his fastball. He's a studious worker who keeps a journal about what he's learned.
THE FUTURE: Macko should begin at low Class A in 2021. His feel and pitchability from the left side give him the potential to be a back-of-the-rotation starter.

Year	Age	Club (League)	Class	W	L	ERA	G	GS	IP	H	HR	BB	SO	BB/9	SO/9	WHIP	AVG
2019	18	Everett (NWL)	SS	0	0	0.00	1	0	2	0	0	1	1	4.5	4.5	0.50	.000
	18	Mariners (AZL)	R	0	3	3.38	8	2	21	19	1	11	31	4.6	13.1	1.41	.202
Minor League Totals				0	3	3.09	9	2	23	19	1	12	32	4.6	12.3	1.33	.224

14 ISAIAH CAMPBELL, RHP

BA GRADE
50 Risk: High

Born: Aug. 15, 1997. **B-T:** R-R. **HT:** 6-4. **WT:** 225. **Drafted:** Arkansas, 2019 (2nd round supplemental). **Signed by:** Ben Collman.
TRACK RECORD: Campbell boosted his draft stock in 2019 after he went 12-1, 2.26 as Arkansas' Friday night starter. Taken in the supplemental second round by the Mariners, he sat after signing because of a heavy college workload and a history of elbow issues. Campbell began taking regular turns on the mound at the Mariners' alternate training site in 2020.
SCOUTING REPORT: A big-bodied righthander with arm strength, Campbell has an above-average fastball that sits 92-95 mph. He commands his heater well and complements it with a trio of competitive, if unspectacular, secondaries. Campbell slowed his slider a few ticks to average 81 mph, adding horizontal break and making it more sweepy. His 82 mph split-changeup can be an above-average pitch with deception and tumble, and his 71-75 mph curveball has lots of depth. He locates his pitches well with average control, keeping them in the bottom of the zone and elevating the fastball when needed. He is the son of an Air Force veteran and is lauded for his makeup.
THE FUTURE: Campbell profiles as a back-end starter. A full-season debut awaits in 2021.

Year	Age	Club (League)	Class	W	L	ERA	G	GS	IP	H	HR	BB	SO	BB/9	SO/9	WHIP	AVG
2019	21	Did not play															

15 WYATT MILLS, RHP

Born: Jan. 25, 1995. **B-T:** R-R. **HT:** 6-4. **WT:** 190. **Drafted:** Gonzaga, 2017 (3rd round). **Signed by:** Alex Ross/Jeff Sakamoto.
TRACK RECORD: A Spokane, Wash. native who went to Gonzaga, Mills was expected to move quickly after the Mariners drafted him in the third round in 2017. While that hasn't happened quite as planned, Mills' fastball showed a 3 mph increase at the alternate training site and instructional league in 2020. The Mariners added him to the 40-man roster after the season.

SCOUTING REPORT: Mills' strength is a mid-90s fastball that touches 97 mph and seems to come out of his hip with a deceptive, sidearm delivery. His heater has good run and sink and is especially tough for righthanded batters. Mills' above-average slider is a sweeping pitch with deception and tilt. He's dropped the use of his changeup to focus on his two best pitches. Mills is more of a control-over-command type of pitcher, and while his stuff has fluctuated over his career he's been consistently effective.
THE FUTURE: Often compared to Steve Cishek and Darren O'Day, Mills should have a similar major league career as a reliable reliever who gives hitters a different look. He is in position to make his MLB debut in 2021.

Year	Age	Club (League)	Class	W	L	ERA	G	GS	IP	H	HR	BB	SO	BB/9	SO/9	WHIP	AVG
2019	24	Arkansas (TL)	AA	4	2	4.27	41	0	53	43	2	17	66	2.9	11.3	1.14	.192
Minor League Totals				10	6	3.57	103	0	126	98	3	39	154	2.8	11.0	1.09	.212

16 ZACH DELOACH, OF

BA GRADE
50 Risk: High

Born: Aug. 8, 1998. **B-T:** L-R. **HT:** 6-1. **WT:** 205. **Drafted:** Texas A&M, 2020 (2nd round). **Signed by:** Derek Miller.

TRACK RECORD: DeLoach boosted his draft stock with a strong Cape Cod League in 2019 and was off to a good start at Texas A&M before the early end to the 2020 season. That performance led the Mariners to draft him 43rd overall and sign him for $1,729,800. DeLoach reported to the alternate training site in the summer and instructional league in the fall, when he was part of a starting outfield with Julio Rodriguez and Taylor Trammell.
SCOUTING REPORT: DeLoach stands out for his pure hitting ability. He has a sound swing, good strike-zone awareness and swings at the right pitches. He rarely strikes out and draws lots of walks. With no other carrying tools, DeLoach's upside will be determined by how much he hits. He has fringe-average raw power and will need to get to it with what is now a line-drive swing. He's an average runner and defender, with a tick below-average arm, and needs to improve his routes in the outfield. He may not have enough range to be a regular in center field, which puts more pressure on his power to emerge.
THE FUTURE: DeLoach could begin 2021 at high Class A. His power production will determine if he has a chance to be regular.

Year	Age	Club (League)	Class	AVG	G	AB	R	H	2B	3B	HR	RBI	BB	SO	SB	OBP	SLG
2020	21	Did not play—No minor league season															

17 CONNOR PHILLIPS, RHP

Born: May 4, 2001. **B-T:** R-R. **HT:** 6-2. **WT:** 190. **Drafted:** McLennan (Texas) JC, 2020 (2nd round supplemental). **Signed by:** Derek Miller.

TRACK RECORD: Phillips spent one year at McLennan (Texas) JC instead of following through on his commitment to Louisiana State. He made just four starts before the season was shut down but showed enough to be drafted by the Mariners in the supplemental second round. He signed for $1,050,300 and spent the summer working out remotely before reporting to instructional league.
SCOUTING REPORT: Phillips is best described as a projection pitcher, with his rawness showing in his instructional league outings. He's physical and athletic with a strong frame, but has below-average command and control due to a delivery that lacks direction and isn't repeatable. The stuff is there, though, including a fastball that sits 93-94 mph and touches 97 and a potentially plus slider with powerful two-plane break. After watching Logan Gilbert at the alternate site, Phillips started throwing a similar knuckle-curveball held deep in his palm. He rounds out his arsenal with an average circle changeup in the mid 80s.
THE FUTURE: A mound of clay for the Mariners to mold, Phillips won't be ready for full-season ball at the start of 2021. There's a lot to like if he can smooth out his delivery and improve his control.

Year	Age	Club (League)	Class	W	L	ERA	G	GS	IP	H	HR	BB	SO	BB/9	SO/9	WHIP	AVG
2020	19	Did not play—No minor league season															

18 AUSTIN SHENTON, 3B

BA GRADE
50 Risk: High

Born: Jan. 22, 1998. **B-T:** L-R. **HT:** 6-0. **WT:** 195. **Drafted:** Florida International, 2019 (5th round). **Signed by:** Dan Rovetto.

TRACK RECORD: After hitting .337 in his career at Florida International, Shenton made it to low Class A shortly after being drafted and asserted himself as one of the more advanced hitters in the Seattle organization. He got plenty of at-bats at the alternate training site in 2020.
SCOUTING REPORT: Shenton is an advanced hitter with emerging power. His advanced pitch recognition

allows him to control the strike zone and consistently barrel balls to all fields. He showed more pull-side power at the alternate site and should have average pop with more experience. While there are few questions about his bat, where Shenton plays defensively is still to be determined. He's not particularly athletic and is a below-average defender at third base with an average arm. Shenton is a hard worker and has outstanding makeup, so it's not out of the question that he can continue to improve his defense enough to be adequate. His most likely role will have him moving around the infield and outfield corners.
THE FUTURE: Shenton will get plenty of chances to prove his bat can make up for his defensive shortcomings. He has a chance to see the upper levels of the minors in 2021.

Year	Age	Club (League)	Class	AVG	G	AB	R	H	2B	3B	HR	RBI	BB	SO	SB	OBP	SLG
2019	21	Everett (NWL)	SS	.367	21	79	16	29	10	1	2	16	8	15	0	.446	.595
	21	West Virginia (SAL)	LoA	.252	32	119	13	30	7	1	5	20	11	29	0	.328	.454
Minor League Totals				.298	53	198	29	59	17	2	7	36	19	44	0	.376	.510

19 MILKAR PEREZ, 3B

BREAKOUT
BA GRADE
50 Risk: Extreme

Born: Oct. 16, 2001. **B-T:** B-R. **HT:** 5-11. **WT:** 175. **Signed:** Nicaragua, 2018. **Signed by:** Tom Shafer.

TRACK RECORD: After signing for $175,000, the top bonus for a player from Nicaragua in 2018, Perez had a strong pro debut in the Dominican Summer League in 2019. He was slated to make his stateside debit in 2020 before the coronavirus pandemic hit. He spent the year on his own until instructional league, where he started at third base in most games.
SCOUTING REPORT: The switch-hitting Perez is primarily a contact hitter with above-average bat speed, a strong feel for the strike zone and solid rhythm and timing from both sides of the plate. He's gotten stronger but will need to lengthen his stroke to get more separation and unlock his 12-15 home run potential. As his body has stiffened, Perez has lost some lateral movement at third base. He has below-average range, but his hands work well and his plus-plus arm is the best among infielders in the organization. He was already a below-average runner before adding the extra bulk.
THE FUTURE: Perez will likely spend most of 2021 in the Rookie-level Arizona League. His offensive potential gives him an everyday ceiling, but he has a long way to go.

Year	Age	Club (League)	Class	AVG	G	AB	R	H	2B	3B	HR	RBI	BB	SO	SB	OBP	SLG
2019	17	Mariners (DSL)	R	.274	64	237	38	65	11	2	4	44	37	55	8	.381	.388
Minor League Totals				.274	64	237	38	65	11	2	4	44	37	55	8	.381	.388

20 JOEY GERBER, RHP

BA GRADE
40 Risk: Medium

Born: May 3, 1997. **B-T:** R-R. **HT:** 6-4. **WT:** 215. **Drafted:** Illinois, 2018 (8th round). **Signed by:** Ben Collman.

TRACK RECORD: Gerber made it to the majors his third professional season, with the quick arrival primarily due to the need for extra pitching during the pandemic-afflicted 2020 season. The hard-throwing reliever made 17 appearances and posted a 4.02 ERA with six strikeouts in 15.2 innings. The low strikeout rate came after he averaged 13.6 strikeouts per nine innings in the minors.
SCOUTING REPORT: Gerber pitches with a funky, crossfire delivery that adds deception to an electric fastball. His stuff generally was down in the majors, with his fastball averaging 94 mph after sitting 96-98 mph in the minors. His heater has natural sink with armside run from a low three-quarters delivery that makes hitters uncomfortable, but also makes it difficult to command. Gerber's mid-80s slider has flashed plus, and he's shown the ability to command it better than his fastball. Overall his control is below-average.
THE FUTURE: Gerber had only pitched a partial season above high Class A, so more minor league seasoning is in order. If he gets his velocity back up, he has potential to be a high-leverage reliever.

Year	Age	Club (League)	Class	W	L	ERA	G	GS	IP	H	HR	BB	SO	BB/9	SO/9	WHIP	AVG
2020	23	Seattle (AL)	MAJ	1	1	4.02	17	0	16	13	1	5	6	2.9	3.4	1.15	.241
Major League Totals				1	1	4.02	17	0	15	13	1	5	6	2.9	3.5	1.15	.241
Minor League Totals				2	4	2.42	66	0	74	56	2	30	112	3.6	13.6	1.16	.211

21 ANTHONY MISIEWICZ, LHP

BA GRADE
40 **Risk: Medium**

Born: Nov. 1, 1994. **B-T:** R-L. **HT:** 6-1. **WT:** 200. **Drafted:** Michigan State, 2015 (18th round). **Signed by:** Jay Catalano.

TRACK RECORD: The question of what role would best suit Misiewicz was answered in 2020, when the Mariners made him a reliever. He made the Opening Day roster in 2020 and stayed in the majors throughout the abbreviated season, logging a 4.05 ERA in 21 appearances.

SCOUTING REPORT: With Misiewicz's role more clearly defined, his stuff took a step forward. His fastball sat 94 mph and played up with the nearly 6 feet of extension he generates out of his delivery. Misiewicz's primary pitch is a 90 mph cutter. He controls his cutter better than his four-seamer and it shows plus potential at times, although it got hit hard at times in the majors. His hard, low-80s curveball has sweeping movement but is a below-average pitch. Misiewicz has solid pitchability and above-average control. He was limited to one-inning stints in his debut but has the ability to go multiple innings as a former starter.

THE FUTURE: Misiewicz excelled against lefthanded batters but got hit hard by righties in his debut. With the three-batter minimum rule here to stay, he's going to have to fix that to nail down a permanent spot in the Mariners bullpen.

Year	Age	Club (League)	Class	W	L	ERA	G	GS	IP	H	HR	BB	SO	BB/9	SO/9	WHIP	AVG
2020	25	Seattle (AL)	MAJ	0	2	4.05	21	0	20	20	2	6	25	2.7	11.3	1.30	.263
Major League Totals				0	2	4.05	21	0	20	20	2	6	25	2.7	11.3	1.30	.263
Minor League Totals				33	38	4.55	120	111	586	610	66	164	516	2.5	7.9	1.32	.268

22 YOHAN RAMIREZ, RHP

BA GRADE
40 **Risk: Medium**

Born: May 6, 1995. **B-T:** R-R. **HT:** 6-4. **WT:** 190. **Signed:** Dominican Republic, 2016. **Signed by:** Oz Ocampo/Roman Ocumarez/David Brito (Astros).

TRACK RECORD: The Mariners selected Ramirez from the Astros in the 2019 Rule 5 draft, taking advantage of Houston's 40-man roster crunch. Despite well below-average control, Ramirez's lightning-fast arm was worth the risk. He walked nearly a batter an inning in his 20.2 major league innings in 2020, but still posted a 2.61 ERA and limited opponents to a .130 batting average over 26 appearances.

SCOUTING REPORT: Ramirez sits 95-96 mph with his fastball and it would be a plus-plus pitch if he had just a bit more command. His heater has natural sink and he gets plenty of swings and misses when he throws it in the strike zone. Ramirez also flashes a plus 82 mph slider with sweeping action. He has occasionally used a curveball and changeup, but moving forward he's going to focus strictly on his fastball and slider mix. Ramirez has some deception in his max-effort, high three-quarters delivery. His well below-average control works to his advantage somewhat because batters can't dig in and get comfortable in the box.

THE FUTURE: Considering his relative inexperience, there's a chance Ramirez can harness his control and take on a high-leverage bullpen role. Regardless, he should be back in the Seattle bullpen in 2021.

Year	Age	Club (League)	Class	W	L	ERA	G	GS	IP	H	HR	BB	SO	BB/9	SO/9	WHIP	AVG
2020	25	Seattle (AL)	MAJ	0	0	2.61	16	0	21	9	3	20	26	8.7	11.3	1.40	.130
Major League Totals				0	0	2.61	16	0	20	9	3	20	26	8.7	11.3	1.40	.130
Minor League Totals				16	21	3.73	88	40	289	212	16	176	323	5.5	10.0	1.34	.203

23 JAKE FRALEY, OF

BA GRADE
40 **Risk: Medium**

Born: May 25, 1995. **B-T:** L-L. **HT:** 6-0. **WT:** 195. **Drafted:** Louisiana State, 2016 (2nd round supplemental). **Signed by:** Rickey Drexler (Rays).

TRACK RECORD: Acquired from the Rays in the trade that sent Mike Zunino to Tampa Bay after the 2018 season, Fraley had a strong first year with the Mariners that culminated in his major league debut. He was expected to compete for a spot on the Opening Day roster in 2020, but instead stagnated at the plate and spent most of the season at the alternate training site. He got into seven major league games late in the season.

SCOUTING REPORT: Fraley has a solid approach at the plate with strong hands and gap power. He hasn't hit the ball particularly hard in the majors, registering an average exit of 83.1 mph, but he showed some over-the-fence pop in the minors. Fraley's best path toward sticking in the majors would be if he could stay in center field, which is complicated by his waning footspeed. A plus runner at his peak, Fraley has become just a tick above-average as he's aged. His fringe-average arm makes him a poor fit in right field.

THE FUTURE: Fraley is either going to have to hit better or find a way to stay in center field to have a steady role in the majors. He's still on the 40-man roster and will have a chance to win a bench role in 2021.

Year	Age	Club (League)	Class	AVG	G	AB	R	H	2B	3B	HR	RBI	BB	SO	SB	OBP	SLG
2020	25	Seattle (AL)	MAJ	.154	7	26	3	4	1	1	0	0	2	11	2	.241	.269
Major League Totals				.152	19	66	6	10	3	1	0	1	2	25	2	.200	.227
Minor League Totals				.286	250	922	153	264	61	20	26	153	95	194	70	.362	.480

24 ALBERTO RODRIGUEZ, OF

BA GRADE 45 Risk: Very High

Born: Oct. 6, 2000. **B-T:** L-L. **HT:** 5-11. **WT:** 180. **Signed:** Dominican Republic, 2017. **Signed by:** Sandy Rosario/Lorenzo Perez/Luciano del Rosario (Blue Jays).

TRACK RECORD: Signed by the Blue Jays for $500,000 in 2017, Rodriguez followed his debut in the Dominican Summer League with a strong showing in the Rookie-level Gulf Coast League. The Mariners acquired him to complete the deadline trade that sent righthander Taijuan Walker to Toronto, and he finished the summer at the Mariners' alternate training site.

SCOUTING REPORT: Rodriguez has whippy bat speed and good hitting instincts, coupled with a natural swing path geared to hit live drives. He uses his hands well and puts plenty of balls in play to project as an above-average hitter with 12-15-home run potential. Rodriguez is an average defender with an above-average arm that should help him in right field. He's added significant weight and strength to his upper half, and his once above-average speed is now below-average. He reported to instructional league and spent his time on conditioning instead of playing in games, and he reportedly lost about 10 pounds of excess weight.

THE FUTURE: Rodriguez should be ready for low Class A in 2021. He will need to continue his conditioning work and closely monitor his fitness.

Year	Age	Club (League)	Class	AVG	G	AB	R	H	2B	3B	HR	RBI	BB	SO	SB	OBP	SLG
2019	18	Blue Jays (GCL)	R	.301	47	173	19	52	13	1	2	29	19	32	13	.364	.422
Minor League Totals				.274	108	401	63	110	22	2	7	63	51	87	34	.356	.392

25 KADEN POLCOVICH, 2B/OF

BA GRADE 45 Risk: Very High

Born: Feb. 21, 1999. **B-T:** B-R. **HT:** 5-10. **WT:** 185. **Drafted:** Oklahoma State, 2020 (3rd round). **Signed by:** Jordan Bley.

TRACK RECORD: The son of former Pirates infielder Kevin Polcovich, Kaden played two years at Northwest Florida State JC before heading to Oklahoma State for his junior year. He hit .344 in 18 games for the Cowboys before the season shut down and was drafted by the Mariners in the third round. Polcovich signed for $575,000 and spent the summer at the Mariners' alternate training site.

SCOUTING REPORT: Like fellow OSU alum Donovan Walton, drafted four years earlier by the Mariners, Polcovich stands out for his versatility and grinder mentality. He split time at second and third base in college and saw significant time in the outfield in the Cape Cod League. A switch-hitter with a solid swing and excellent barrel control from both sides of the plate, Polcovich has a knack for getting on base and sneaky fringe-average power. He's not likely to be more than a fringe-average defender with an average arm because he struggles with his footwork on ground balls,

THE FUTURE: Polcovich should be adequate in a utility role provided his bat develops. He should be ready for a full-season assignment in 2021.

Year	Age	Club (League)	Class	AVG	G	AB	R	H	2B	3B	HR	RBI	BB	SO	SB	OBP	SLG
2020	21	Did not play—No minor league season															

26 JOSE CORNIELL, RHP

BA GRADE 45 Risk: Extreme

Born: June 22, 2003. **B-T:** R-R. **HT:** 6-3. **WT:** 185. **Signed:** Dominican Republic, 2019. **Signed by:** Francisco Rosario.

TRACK RECORD: After signing with the Mariners for $620,000 in 2019, Corniell was slated to make his pro debut in the Dominican Summer League in 2020 before the minor league season was canceled by the coronavirus pandemic. After a visa-related delay, he made it to Arizona in time to pitch in two games during instructional league before heading back to the Dominican Republic.

SCOUTING REPORT: Corniell has a tall, sturdy body that looks capable of eating innings as he matures. He pounds the bottom of the strike zone with a 90-93 mph fastball with natural sink. It projects as an above-average pitch and gets plenty of ground balls and soft contact. Corniell's curveball and changeup both play up to average because of how well he commands them to both sides of the plate. He's been toying with a slider in order to give himself a more complete repertoire. Corniell shows on excellent poise, especially for a pitcher who won't turn 18 until midway through 2021. He has a lot of projection remaining but shows the ingredients for plus control.

THE FUTURE: Corniell's pitchability and command make him advanced for his age. He should make his pro debut in the Rookie-level Arizona League in 2021.

Year	Age	Club (League)	Class	W	L	ERA	G	GS	IP	H	HR	BB	SO	BB/9	SO/9	WHIP	AVG
2019	16	Did not play—Signed 2020 contract															

27 SAM CARLSON, RHP

BA GRADE
45 Risk: Extreme

Born: Dec. 3, 1998. **B-T:** R-R. **HT:** 6-3. **WT:** 200. **Drafted:** HS—Burnsville, Minn., 2017 (2nd round). **Signed by:** Ben Collman.

TRACK RECORD: The most significant accomplishment for Carlson in 2020 was finally getting back on the mound after a litany of injuries, most notably Tommy John surgery in 2018. Carlson took regular turns on the mound during instructional league with mixed results, but most importantly he stayed healthy and built confidence.

SCOUTING REPORT: Carlson has not pitched in an official game since 2017 and is still shaking off the rust. He worked on developing cleaner mechanics during his injury rehab time, resulting in a more efficient and free delivery. Carlson's fastball reached 96 mph with late life and sink prior to surgery but sat 91-93 mph with sneaky darting action during instructs. His secondary pitches are all right around average, with his slider the most promising. His slider shows a good amount of sweep and depth, but he needs to throw it harder to make it an above-average pitch. Carlson commands his 11-to-5 curveball for strikes early in counts and also throws a potentially average changeup with soft fade. He throws them all for strikes with average control.

THE FUTURE: Carlson's future depends on how his stuff comes back. The hope is it will and that he can become a back-end starter.

Year	Age	Club (League)	Class	W	L	ERA	G	GS	IP	H	HR	BB	SO	BB/9	SO/9	WHIP	AVG
2017	18	Mariners (AZL)	R	0	0	3.00	2	2	3	4	0	0	3	0.0	9.0	1.33	.308
Minor League Totals				0	0	3.00	2	2	3	4	0	0	3	0.0	9.0	1.33	.364

28 CARTER BINS, C

BA GRADE
40 Risk: High

Born: Oct. 7, 1998. **B-T:** R-R. **HT:** 6-0. **WT:** 200. **Drafted:** Fresno State, 2019 (11th round). **Signed by:** Chris Hom.

TRACK RECORD: Bins got plenty of scout looks at Fresno State when he was the catcher for Cubs 2019 first-rounder Ryan Jensen. The Mariners drafted him in the 11th round and signed him for an over-slot $350,000. Bins made his pro debut after signing at short-season Everett and, after 2020 spring training was cut short by the coronavirus pandemic, got back on the field during instructional league.

SCOUTING REPORT: Bins has above-average raw power and makes plenty of loud contact. He shows feel for the barrel, but his below-average bat speed limits his offensive ceiling. He has a hitchy, shoulder-heavy rotational swing that leads to a lot of strikeouts. Bins controls the strike zone and draws his fair share of walks, leading to projections he'll be a three true outcomes—walk, strikeout or home run—hitter. Bins has made positive strides defensively. He's athletic and has good hands behind the plate but needs to be more consistent in blocking and receiving. His above-average arm strength plays down a bit because of a slow transfer.

THE FUTURE: Bins profiles best as a backup catcher. His solid makeup and the ability to learn gives him a chance to surpass that projection.

Year	Age	Club (League)	Class	AVG	G	AB	R	H	2B	3B	HR	RBI	BB	SO	SB	OBP	SLG
2019	20	Everett (NWL)	SS	.208	49	154	31	32	2	0	7	26	33	56	5	.391	.357
Minor League Totals				.208	49	154	31	32	2	0	7	26	33	56	5	.391	.357

29 JONATAN CLASE, OF

BA GRADE
45 Risk: Extreme

Born: May 23, 2002. **B-T:** L-R. **HT:** 5-9. **WT:** 180. **Signed:** Dominican Republic, 2018. **Signed by:** Audo Vicente.

TRACK RECORD: Clase signed with the Mariners for $35,000 in 2018 and delivered an intriguing pro debut in the Dominican Summer League the following year. He was set to make his stateside debut in 2020 before the coronavirus pandemic canceled the minor league season. He got back on the field for instructional league in the fall.

SCOUTING REPORT: Clase has packed on 30 pounds of muscle since signing, giving him a brick-like build. Impressively, he's maintained his plus-plus speed as he's added the weight. Clase has a slasher's approach in games with excellent bat speed and controls the strike zone. His approach and swing aren't conducive to hitting for power, so he'll need to make adjustments to get the most from his newfound strength. Namely, he needs to get better at learning which pitches he can impact. Clase relies on his natural speed and athleticism in the outfield but needs to improve his routes. He may project better as a corner outfielder even with his speed.

THE FUTURE: Clase has strength and athleticism to dream on, but he's still very raw. He'll be 18 on Opening Day 2021 and will begin in the Rookie-level Arizona League.

Year	Age	Club (League)	Class	AVG	G	AB	R	H	2B	3B	HR	RBI	BB	SO	SB	OBP	SLG
2019	17	Mariners (DSL)	R	.300	63	223	64	67	12	7	2	22	51	56	31	.434	.444
Minor League Totals				.300	63	223	64	67	12	7	2	22	51	56	31	.434	.444

30 SAM HAGGERTY, OF/2B

BA GRADE
40 **Risk: High**

Born: May 26, 1994. **B-T:** B-R. **HT:** 5-11. **WT:** 175. **Drafted:** New Mexico, 2015 (24th round). **Signed by:** Jon Heuerman (Indians).

TRACK RECORD: Originally drafted by the Indians in 2015, Haggerty made it to the big leagues for 11 games with the Mets in 2019. After the Mariners acquired the switch-hitting utilityman on waivers in the offseason, Haggerty started the summer at the alternate training site before getting into 13 games in the second half of August.

SCOUTING REPORT: Haggerty's plus-plus speed, good instincts on the bases and ability to play multiple positions are his primary assets. He's a spray hitter with below-average power, but his history of drawing walks allows him to get on base enough to make his speed play. He has enough raw power to occasionally run into a few balls. Haggerty's average defense at second base and in the outfield will suffice as a bench player.

THE FUTURE: Haggerty's speed and versatility may win him a spot on the 26-man roster. At the very least, he'll be a callup when his skill set is needed in Seattle.

Year	Age	Club (League)	Class	AVG	G	AB	R	H	2B	3B	HR	RBI	BB	SO	SB	OBP	SLG
2020	26	Seattle (AL)	MAJ	.260	13	50	7	13	4	0	1	6	4	16	4	.315	.400
Major League Totals				.241	24	54	9	13	4	0	1	6	4	19	4	.293	.370
Minor League Totals				.249	408	1431	236	357	82	27	15	143	226	401	113	.355	.376

MORE PROSPECTS TO KNOW

31 LOGAN RINEHART, RHP

SLEEPER

The 2019 draft pick from California Baptist has gotten stronger and added velocity to his fastball to make it a pitch with solid sink in the mid-90s. He also consistently lands his curveball for strikes.

32 TAYLOR DOLLARD, RHP

A 2020 fifth-round pick from Cal Poly, Dollard is a good athlete with plus strike-throwing ability and a slider that gets swings and misses.

33 AARON FLETCHER, LHP

Fletcher's stuff was down at the alternate training site, but he's a lefthander with a fastball up to 96 mph and a funky, deceptive delivery.

34 SAM DELAPLANE, RHP

Delaplane has a fastball up to 98 mph and has logged extremely high strikeout totals through his minor league career. His stuff was down significantly at the alternate training site in 2020, but there's still time to turn it around.

35 DONOVAN WALTON, 2B/SS

A perpetual grinder who can play all over the infield and do the little things that make coaches happy, Walton has had several callups to the majors over the last two seasons.

36 DEVIN SWEET, RHP

A nondrafted free agent signing, Sweet reached high Class A in 2019 and possesses the best changeup in the organization. He's been used both as a starter and a reliever and profiles best as a bullpen arm.

37 TYLER KEENAN, 3B

A fourth-round pick in 2020, Keenan checks in at 250 pounds and has plus raw power. He was out of shape when he reported to the alternate training site and then got hurt.

38 LJAY NEWSOME, RHP

An under-the-radar prospect who throws strikes and flashes a plus changeup, Newsome followed a strong finish to 2019 at Double-A by getting a callup to Seattle for five games in 2020.

39 MATT BRASH, RHP

Acquired from the Padres late in the summer, Brash has a small, wiry frame with a mid-90s fastball and unique movement on his pitches.

40 BRENDAN MCGUIGAN, RHP

Undrafted in 2019, McGuigan went to the Northwoods League after college and saw his velocity tick up to 98 mph, earning a free agent deal with the Mariners. He complements the fastball with a wipeout slider.

TOP PROSPECTS OF THE DECADE

Year	Player, Pos	2020 Org
2011	Dustin Ackley, 2B	Did not play
2012	Taijuan Walker, RHP	Blue Jays
2013	Mike Zunino, C	Rays
2014	Taijuan Walker, RHP	Blue Jays
2015	Alex Jackson, OF	Braves
2016	Alex Jackson, OF	Braves
2017	Kyle Lewis, OF	Mariners
2018	Kyle Lewis, OF	Mariners
2019	Justus Sheffield, LHP	Mariners
2020	Julio Rodriguez, OF	Mariners

TOP DRAFT PICKS OF THE DECADE

Year	Player, Pos	2020 Org
2011	Danny Hultzen, LHP	Cubs
2012	Mike Zunino, C	Rays
2013	D.J. Peterson, 3B	Independent League
2014	Alex Jackson, OF	Braves
2015	Nick Neidert, RHP (2nd round)	Marlins
2016	Kyle Lewis, OF	Mariners
2017	Evan White, 1B	Mariners
2018	Logan Gilbert, RHP	Mariners
2019	George Kirby, RHP	Mariners
2020	Emerson Hancock, RHP	Mariners

DEPTH CHART

SEATTLE MARINERS

TOP 2020 ROOKIES	RANK
Jarred Kelenic, OF	2
Logan Gilbert, RHP	3
Taylor Trammell, OF	6
BREAKOUT PROSPECTS	**RANK**
Levi Stoudt, RHP	12
Adam Macko, LHP	13
Milkar Perez, 3B	19

SOURCE OF TOP 30 TALENT

Homegrown	**22**	**Acquired**	**8**
College	14	Trade	6
Junior college	1	Rule 5 draft	1
High school	2	Independent league	0
Nondrafted free agent	0	Free agent/waivers	1
International	5		

LF
Keegan McGovern
Cade Marlowe

CF
Jarred Kelenic (2)
Taylor Trammell (6)
Jake Fraley (23)
Jonatan Clase (29)
Sam Haggerty (30)
Braden Bishop

RF
Julio Rodriguez (1)
Zach DeLoach (16)
Alberto Rodriguez (24)

3B
Austin Shenton (18)
Milkar Perez (19)
Tyler Keenan
Joe Rizzo

SS
Noelvi Marte (5)
Juan Querecuto
Connor Kopach
Cesar Izturis Jr.

2B
Kaden Polcovich (25)
Donovan Walton
Jose Caballero

1B
Jose Marmolejos
Robert Perez

C
Cal Raleigh (8)
Carter Bins (28)
Jake Anchia

LHP

LHSP	LHRP
Brandon Williamson (11)	Anthony Misiewicz (21)
Adam Macko (13)	Aaron Fletcher
Brayan Perez	Raymond Kerr
Holden Laws	Jorge Benitez

RHP

RHSP	RHRP
Logan Gilbert (3)	Andres Munoz (10)
Emerson Hancock (4)	Wyatt Mills (15)
George Kirby (7)	Joey Gerber (20)
Juan Then (9)	Yohan Ramirez (22)
Levi Stoudt (12)	Sam Delaplane
Isaiah Campbell (14)	Devin Sweet
Connor Phillips (17)	Matt Brash
Jose Corniell (26)	Brendan McGuigan
Sam Carlson (27)	Gerson Bautista
Logan Rinehart	
Taylor Dollard	
Ljay Newsome	
Tim Elliott	
Penn Murfee	
Yeury Tatiz	

Tampa Bay Rays

BY J.J. COOPER

Here they are again. Baseball's little-team-that-could was the class of the American League in 2020. The Rays finished the season with the best record in the league and then rolled through the longest-ever postseason before losing to the Dodgers in the World Series.

The last time the Rays went to the World Series was in 2008. They managed to remain a postseason contender for another five years after that. Their young core of Evan Longoria, David Price, James Shields and others kept the Rays relevant in a brutally tough AL East division year after year.

It's tougher now, because other teams in larger revenue markets keep hiring Rays' executives. The Rays' way has been exported to the World Series-champion Dodgers (Andrew Friedman), the Astros (James Click) and the Red Sox (Chaim Bloom).

But even as other teams have adopted many of the Rays' approaches, the Rays aren't changing what they have long done, partly because they don't have a choice. The team's payroll will never compete with other playoff contenders.

So they keep churning the roster. They keep trading players at their peak value to try to land a player whose peak is still a few years in the future. And they keep developing replacements for the stars who are departing.

Fresh off the most successful season in Rays history, Tampa Bay entered the offseason by deciding not to exercise its $15 million option for Charlie Morton. Weeks before, it had been Morton's excellent work in Game 7 of the AL Championship Series that had earned the Rays their second-ever AL pennant.

Soon after that, the Rays began to listen to offers for lefthander Blake Snell, the 2018 AL Cy Young Award winner.

Welcome to the high-wire act that is the Rays' long-term approach. The Rays have figured out a way to be a consistent playoff contender despite a payroll that almost always resides near the bottom of Major League Baseball.

The constant roster turnover is a feature of the Rays' way. The Rays exited the 2020 season with only one player, Kevin Kiermaier, who had more than six years of service time. The Rays continually shuffle more veteran players off their roster, replacing them with younger, less expensive talent.

To make that work requires managing to continually land underappreciated talent in trades, hitting on draft picks and international signings and doing an excellent job of player development. Somehow, Tampa Bay keeps managing to pull off that tricky trio.

ALEX TRAUTWIG/MLB PHOTOS VIA GETTY IMAGES

The Rays declined an option on Charlie Morton as they continue their annual search for value.

PROJECTED 2024 LINEUP

Position	Player	Age
Catcher	Ronaldo Hernandez	26
First Base	Ji-Man Choi	33
Second Base	Vidal Brujan	26
Third Base	Willy Adames	28
Shortstop	Wander Franco	23
Left Field	Randy Arozarena	29
Center Field	Manuel Margot	29
Right Field	Austin Meadows	29
Designated Hitter	Brandon Lowe	29
No. 1 Starter	Blake Snell	31
No. 2 Starter	Tyler Glasnow	30
No. 3 Starter	Shane McClanahan	27
No. 4 Starter	Brendan McKay	28
No. 5 Starter	Ryan Yarbrough	32
Closer	Diego Castillo	30

And the farm system gives them an opportunity to continue to do so in 2021 and beyond. The Rays have a nice mix of close-to-the-majors middle infielders and arms. And even after trading away 2018 first-rounder Matthew Liberatore in the Randy Arozarena deal, they continue to have a deep assortment of high-ceiling pitchers who are farther away.

With Willy Adames and Brandon Lowe established as the major league middle infield, and many other middle infielders not far behind, such as Wander Franco, Vidal Brujan, Xavier Edwards, Greg Jones and Taylor Walls, Tampa Bay will likely have to make further moves to ensure that solid major league talent doesn't stagnate in the upper levels of the minors.

That's just the kind of challenge and opportunity the Rays like to embrace. ■

1 WANDER FRANCO, SS

Born: March 1, 2001. **B-T:** B-R. **HT:** 5-10. **WT:** 170.
Signed: Dominican Republic, 2017.
Signed by: Danny Santana.

MICHAEL REAVES/GETTY IMAGES

TRACK RECORD: The No. 1 prospect in the 2017 international signing class, Franco has managed to exceed lofty expectations throughout his teenage years. He hit .339 in the offense-stifling Florida State League in his first full season as an 18-year-old—the third straight level he hit over .300—and began the year as the No. 1 prospect in baseball before spending the 2020 season at the Rays' alternate training site. Franco's time at the alternate site pushed him. He has long played against older players, but against pitchers with major league experience, he was pressed even further. He showed well enough that the Rays added him to their postseason taxi squad before he ever appeared in a major league game. He traveled with the team throughout the postseason and participated in pregame workouts, including during the World Series. Franco has a chance to be the first player to rank No. 1 on back-to-back Top 100 Prospects lists since Bryce Harper (2011-12). The only other two-time No. 1 prospects are Joe Mauer (2004-05) and Andruw Jones (1996-97).

SCOUTING REPORT: Franco is an exceptionally advanced hitter for his age. The switch-hitter's compact, level stroke and above-average bat speed from both sides of the plate grant him a controlled aggression most young hitters can't match. His bat control allows him to make consistent hard contact while rarely striking out. He also has an innate ability to adjust his swing, leaving few holes for pitchers to attack. Franco stings the ball and has plus power potential, but his level swing leads to more line drives and ground balls than fly balls. It will likely limit his power production if he does not make tweaks. He has shown in team competitions that he can put on a show in a home run derby. Franco's body has already filled out. He is an average runner who will have to work to keep his speed with a thick, muscular lower half. Defensively, Franco's soft hands, above-average arm and solid understanding of the game give him a shot to stay at shortstop, where he's a potentially average defender. The Rays played him at second base and third base at the alternate site to help prepare him for the possibility he could break into the majors at another spot. He has the tools to be an above-average or even plus defender at second or third.

THE FUTURE: There are prospects in the minors with louder tools than Franco, but few prospects can come close to Franco's likelihood of being a productive regular or all-star thanks to his exceptional hitting ability. He's more likely to win a batting title than a home run crown but has the chance to produce plenty of power as well. The Rays have a crowded infield, and Franco is unlikely to push Willy Adames off shortstop, but his bat and glove are ready to produce for the Rays in 2021 at any infield position. His bat should clear his path to St. Petersburg, even if he is likely to begin the season in Triple-A. ■

BEST TOOLS

Best Hitter for Average	Wander Franco
Best Power Hitter	Moises Gomez
Best Strike-Zone Discipline	Wander Franco
Fastest Baserunner	Vidal Brujan
Best Athlete	Greg Jones
Best Fastball	Shane Baz
Best Curveball	Shane McClanahan
Best Slider	Shane Baz
Best Changeup	Josh Fleming
Best Control	Brendan McKay
Best Defensive Catcher	Chris Betts
Best Defensive Infielder	Taylor Walls
Best Infield Arm	Taylor Walls
Best Defensive Outfielder	Josh Lowe
Best Outfield Arm	Josh Lowe

Year	Age	Club (League)	Class	AVG	G	AB	R	H	2B	3B	HR	RBI	BB	SO	SB	OBP	SLG
2018	17	Princeton (APP)	R	.351	61	242	46	85	10	7	11	57	27	19	4	.418	.587
2019	18	Bowling Green (MWL)	LoA	.318	62	233	42	74	16	5	6	29	30	20	14	.390	.506
	18	Charlotte (FSL)	HiA	.339	52	192	40	65	11	2	3	24	26	15	4	.408	.464
Minor League Totals				.336	175	667	128	224	37	14	20	110	83	54	22	.405	.523

2 RANDY AROZARENA, OF

TOP ROOKIE

MARY DECICCO/MLB PHOTOS VIA GETTY IMAGES

BA GRADE

60 Risk: Medium

Born: Feb. 28, 1995. **B-T:** R-R. **HT:** 5-11. **WT:** 185. **Signed:** Cuba 2016. **Signed by:** Ramon Garcia (Cardinals).

TRACK RECORD: When the Rays acquired Arozarena in a trade that sent touted lefthander Matthew Liberatore to the Cardinals, it seemed like a high price to pay. Those concerns quickly faded. A positive coronavirus test delayed Arozarena's 2020 debut until Aug. 30, but he was one of baseball's best hitters in September and in the playoffs. He hit seven home runs through the ALCS, breaking the rookie record for homers in a single postseason.

SCOUTING REPORT: Arozarena's electric hands and bat speed allow him to catch up to fastballs up in the zone, and he's gotten strong enough to do damage. He has solid pitch recognition skills, and his bat-to-ball ability has stood out for years through a long track record of hitting for average and getting on base. Arozarena takes some massive swings, but there's a method to it—his swing gets bigger in advantageous counts. Defensively, Arozarena is a fast-twitch athlete with plus-plus speed and an excellent burst, but his poor routes need to improve to make him more than an average defender.

THE FUTURE: Arozarena's postseason was one for the ages, but he'll have to make adjustments as the league finds his weaknesses. Most evaluators see him settling in as a .270 hitter with 20-25 home runs and 10-15 steals.

SCOUTING GRADES: **Hitting:** 55 **Power:** 60 **Running:** 70 **Fielding:** 50 **Arm:** 55

Year	Age	Club (League)	Class	AVG	G	AB	R	H	2B	3B	HR	RBI	BB	SO	SB	OBP	SLG
2018	23	Memphis (PCL)	AAA	.232	89	267	42	62	16	0	5	28	28	59	17	.328	.348
	23	Springfield, MO (TL)	AA	.396	24	91	22	36	5	0	7	21	6	25	9	.455	.681
2019	24	St. Louis (NL)	MAJ	.300	19	20	4	6	1	0	1	2	2	4	2	.391	.500
	24	Memphis (PCL)	AAA	.358	64	246	51	88	18	2	12	38	24	48	9	.435	.593
	24	Springfield, MO (TL)	AA	.309	28	97	14	30	7	2	3	15	13	23	8	.422	.515
2020	25	Tampa Bay (AL)	MAJ	.281	23	64	15	18	2	0	7	11	6	22	4	.382	.641
Major League Totals				.286	42	84	19	24	3	0	8	13	8	26	6	.384	.607
Minor League Totals				.289	331	1149	204	332	79	8	38	151	113	245	61	.373	.471

3 VIDAL BRUJAN, 2B/SS

Born: Feb. 9, 1998. **B-T:** B-R. **HT:** 5-9. **WT:** 180. **Signed:** Dominican Republic, 2014. **Signed by:** Danny Santana.

TRACK RECORD: The Rays spent big on the 2014 international class, including signing No. 1 prospect Adrian Rondon for $2.95 million. But Brujan, a $15,000 signing, looks like the best of the group. He quickly outpaced Rondon and finished the 2019 season at Double-A Montgomery. The Rays brought him to their alternate training site in 2020.

SCOUTING REPORT: The speedy Brujan is a throwback to when leadoff hitters got on base and immediately stole second. He's stolen 151 bases in five minor league seasons, including 48 in 2019. A switch-hitter, Brujan is hard to strike out with his excellent bat control and has sneaky power from the left side. His righthanded swing doesn't have much power. Brujan is a versatile defender who moved from shortstop to second base when he signed but looked capable when the Rays played him at short again in 2019. He has just enough arm for the position, but his accuracy has to improve and he tends to rush his throws. He got some work in center field at the alternate site and could be a rangy center fielder.

THE FUTURE: The Rays have a crowded infield situation, but Brujan's hitting ability, speed and athleticism should get him to the majors in due time.

SCOUTING GRADES: **Hitting:** 60 **Power:** 40 **Running:** 80 **Fielding:** 55 **Arm:** 50

Year	Age	Club (League)	Class	AVG	G	AB	R	H	2B	3B	HR	RBI	BB	SO	SB	OBP	SLG
2017	19	Hudson Valley (NYP)	SS	.285	67	260	51	74	15	5	3	20	34	36	16	.378	.415
2018	20	Bowling Green (MWL)	LoA	.313	95	377	86	118	18	5	5	41	48	53	43	.395	.427
	20	Charlotte (FSL)	HiA	.347	27	98	26	34	7	2	4	12	15	15	12	.434	.582
2019	21	Charlotte (FSL)	HiA	.290	44	176	28	51	8	3	1	15	17	26	24	.357	.386
	21	Montgomery (SL)	AA	.266	55	207	28	55	9	4	3	25	20	35	24	.336	.391
Minor League Totals				.294	399	1554	309	457	78	28	19	141	187	197	151	.377	.417

4 SHANE MCCLANAHAN, LHP

MARY DECICCO/MLB PHOTOS VIA GETTY IMAGES

BA GRADE
55 Risk: High

Born: April 28, 1997. **B-T:** L-L. **HT:** 6-1. **WT:** 190. **Drafted:** South Florida, 2018 (1st round). **Signed by:** Brett Foley.

TRACK RECORD: McClanahan had Tommy John surgery at South Florida but recovered to become one of the top pitchers in the 2018 draft class. The Rays drafted him 31st overall and signed him for just over $2.2 million. He spent most of 2020 working five-inning stints every fifth day at the alternate training site but moved to the bullpen as the major league playoffs neared. The Rays added him to their postseason roster, and he became the first pitcher in history to make his debut in the postseason.

SCOUTING REPORT: Few lefthanders can match McClanahan's fastball velocity, which sits 95-98 mph as a starter and touched 101 in the playoffs. What's even better is his 86-88 mph breaking ball. McClanahan can throw it tighter with more of a curveball shape or turn it into a wipeout slider that starts in the middle of the plate and ends up at a righthanded hitter's feet. In either form, it's a pitch that finishes hitters. McClanahan's fringe-average changeup plays up when he throws it with conviction. His control has improved as he's gotten better at maintaining a regular pace to his delivery, but it's still fringe-average.

THE FUTURE: McClanahan's improvements to his changeup and control give him a chance to start. His big fastball and wipeout breaking ball would also fit in high-leverage relief.

SCOUTING GRADES: **Fastball:** 70 **Slider:** 60 **Curveball:** 60 **Changeup:** 50 **Control:** 45

Year	Age	Club (League)	Class	W	L	ERA	G	GS	IP	H	HR	BB	SO	BB/9	SO/9	WHIP	AVG
2018	21	Princeton (APP)	R	0	0	0.00	2	2	4	2	0	1	7	2.3	15.8	0.75	.143
	21	Rays (GCL)	R	0	0	0.00	2	2	3	1	0	0	6	0.0	18.0	0.33	.100
2019	22	Montgomery (SL)	AA	1	1	8.35	4	4	18	30	3	6	21	2.9	10.3	1.96	.333
	22	Bowling Green (MWL)	LoA	4	4	3.40	11	10	53	38	3	31	74	5.3	12.6	1.30	.170
	22	Charlotte, FL (FSL)	HiA	6	1	1.46	9	8	49	33	1	8	59	1.5	10.8	0.83	.156
Minor League Totals				11	6	3.17	28	26	127	104	7	46	167	3.2	11.8	1.17	.218

5 SHANE BAZ, RHP

BA GRADE
60 Risk: Extreme

Born: June 17, 1999. **B-T:** R-R. **HT:** 6-3. **WT:** 190. **Drafted:** HS—Tomball, Texas, 2017 (1st round). **Signed by:** Wayne Mathis (Pirates).

TRACK RECORD: The Rays getting Austin Meadows and Tyler Glasnow from the Pirates for Chris Archer is a heist of a trade, but the fact that they also acquired Baz as the player to be named later seems like piling on. Baz, the 12th overall pick in the 2017 draft, had a solid Rays organizational debut in 2019 before struggling in the Arizona Fall League. He spent 2020 at the Rays' alternate training site.

SCOUTING REPORT: Much like Glasnow, Baz has responded well to the Rays' tweaks to his approach. He's now pumping upper-90s, high-spin, four-seam fastballs up in the strike zone and pairing them with a dastardly plus-plus 84-87 mph slider with tight, two-plane break. Everything else is still a work in progress. Baz's tempo in his delivery is too energetic and his lower half isn't always in sync with his arm, leading to below-average command and control. His fringe-average changeup improved at the alternate training site, but still has further to go. His curveball has become less of a factor every year.

THE FUTURE: Many scouts are confident Baz will wind up in the bullpen as a potentially dominant reliever. The Rays still see a path for him to be a starter, noting he's still quite young and has continued to improve his control.

SCOUTING GRADES: **Fastball:** 70 **Slider:** 70 **Changeup:** 45 **Curveball:** 40 **Control:** 40

Year	Age	Club (League)	Class	W	L	ERA	G	GS	IP	H	HR	BB	SO	BB/9	SO/9	WHIP	AVG
2017	18	Pirates (GCL)	R	0	3	3.80	10	10	24	26	2	14	19	5.3	7.2	1.69	.248
2018	19	Princeton (APP)	R	0	2	7.71	2	2	7	11	1	6	5	7.7	6.4	2.43	.297
	19	Bristol (APP)	R	4	3	3.97	10	10	45	45	2	23	54	4.6	10.7	1.50	.217
2019	20	Bowling Green (MWL)	LoA	3	2	2.99	17	17	81	63	5	37	87	4.1	9.6	1.23	.181
Minor League Totals				7	10	3.60	39	39	157	145	10	80	165	4.6	9.4	1.43	.243

6 BRENDAN MCKAY, LHP

Born: Dec. 18, 1995. **B-T:** L-L. **HT:** 6-2. **WT:** 212. **Drafted:** Louisville, 2017 (1st round). **Signed by:** James Bonnici.

MARY DECICCO/MLB PHOTOS VIA GETTY IMAGES

BA GRADE
60 **Risk: Extreme**

TRACK RECORD: McKay was a two-way star at Louisville and won the Golden Spikes Award in 2017. The Rays drafted him fourth overall that year and signed him for just over $7 million. McKay raced to the major leagues, debuting in 2019 and pitching 49 innings. He was expected to be a part of the Rays' plans in 2020, but he was delayed by a positive coronavirus test and then had season-ending shoulder surgery to repair a torn labrum in August.

SCOUTING REPORT: While McKay's power in the batter's box is intriguing, the Rays have shifted his focus to pitching exclusively. McKay's control and command have always been his biggest calling cards. He locates all four of his pitches for strikes, helping them play up beyond their raw qualities. McKay's 92-95 mph fastball was his best pitch in the minors, though it was less effective in the majors with its modest movement. His above-average 87-89 mph cutter avoids barrels as his main secondary. His curveball is an average offering and he busts out his average mid-80s changeup against righties. McKay struggled to put away hitters in his first big league stint and now must see what his stuff looks like post-surgery.

THE FUTURE: McKay's future outlook is muddied by his shoulder surgery. The Rays hope he'll be ready in the spring.

SCOUTING GRADES: **Fastball:** 60 **Cutter:** 55 **Curveball:** 50 **Changeup:** 50 **Control:** 60

Year	Age	Club (League)	Class	W	L	ERA	G	GS	IP	H	HR	BB	SO	BB/9	K/9	WHIP	AVG
2018	22	Bowling Green (MWL)	LoA	2	0	1.09	6	6	25	8	1	2	40	0.7	14.6	0.41	.096
	22	Rays (GCL)	R	0	0	1.50	2	2	6	2	0	1	9	1.5	13.5	0.50	.095
	22	Charlotte (FSL)	HiA	3	2	3.21	11	9	48	45	2	11	54	2.1	10.2	1.17	.256
2019	23	Montgomery (SL)	AA	3	0	1.30	8	7	42	25	2	9	62	1.9	13.4	0.82	.172
	23	Durham (IL)	AAA	3	0	0.84	7	6	32	17	1	9	40	2.5	11.3	0.81	.156
	23	Tampa Bay (AL)	MAJ	2	4	5.14	13	11	49	53	8	16	56	2.9	10.3	1.41	.268
2020	24	Did not play—Injured															
Major League Totals				2	4	5.14	13	11	49	53	8	16	56	2.9	10.3	1.41	.268
Minor League Totals				12	2	1.78	40	36	172	107	9	37	226	1.9	11.8	0.84	.178

7 XAVIER EDWARDS, 2B/SS

Born: Aug. 9, 1999. **B-T:** B-R. **HT:** 5-10. **WT:** 175. **Drafted:** HS—Coconut Creek, Fla., 2018 (1st round supplemental). **Signed by:** Brian Cruz (Padres).

BA GRADE
55 **Risk: High**

TRACK RECORD: Drafted 38th overall by the Padres in 2018, Edwards hit .322 and finished tied for third in the minors in hits in his first full season. The Rays acquired him with Hunter Renfroe in the trade that sent Tommy Pham and Jake Cronenworth to San Diego. The Rays sent Edwards to their alternate training site in mid August, where he joined the organization's collection of middle infielders with excellent bat-to-ball skills.

SCOUTING REPORT: Edwards is a smallish second baseman who rarely strikes out, consistently puts the barrel on the ball and can run with plus speed. But also like Nick Madrigal, the switch-hitting Edwards' plus hitting ability is tempered by concerns about his lack of power. Edwards has gotten a little stronger and will post 100 mph exit velocities on his hardest hits, but he still hits more balls in front of outfielders than in the gaps. He's a patient hitter with nearly as many walks (75) as strikeouts in his career (79), so he may get on base enough to make up for his lack of slugging. He's an efficient basestealer and reliable defender, though his fringy arm is stretched at shortstop.

THE FUTURE: Edwards fits the Rays' desire for athletic, multi-positional players. He projects as a table-setter who's contact and speed-based game is a throwback to earlier eras.

SCOUTING GRADES: **Hitting:** 60 **Power:** 30 **Running:** 60 **Fielding:** 55 **Arm:** 45

Year	Age	Club (League)	Class	AVG	G	AB	R	H	2B	3B	HR	RBI	BB	SO	SB	OBP	SLG
2018	18	Padres 1 (AZL)	R	.384	21	73	19	28	4	1	0	11	13	10	12	.471	.466
	18	Tri-City (NWL)	SS	.314	24	86	21	27	4	0	0	5	18	15	10	.438	.360
2019	19	Fort Wayne (MWL)	LoA	.336	77	307	44	103	13	4	1	30	30	35	20	.392	.414
	19	Lake Elsinore (CAL)	HiA	.301	46	196	32	59	5	4	0	13	14	19	14	.349	.367
Minor League Totals				.328	168	662	116	217	26	9	1	59	75	79	56	.395	.399

8 NICK BITSKO, RHP

MIKE JANES/FOUR SEAM IMAGES

Born: June 16, 2002. **B-T:** R-R. **HT:** 6-4. **WT:** 225. **Drafted:** HS—Doylestown, Pa., 2020 (1st round). **Signed by:** Zach Clark.

TRACK RECORD: Bitsko reclassified from the 2021 draft to 2020, but the coronavirus pandemic canceled his high school season before he got to throw a pitch. Teams scouted him exclusively off his bullpen sessions, and the Rays saw enough to draft him No. 24 overall and sign him for an above-slot $3 million to forgo a Virginia commitment. With the canceled season, Bitsko threw just 33 innings in his high school career.

SCOUTING REPORT: Bitsko has the traits of a major league starter with a physical 6-foot-4, 225-pound frame and a clean delivery. His fastball sits 92-96 mph and touches 98, and he pairs it with a hard, high-spin downer curveball that's been up to 2,500 revolutions per minute. Both project to be plus or better pitches. Bitsko has shown a feel for a changeup, but it's sometimes a little firm and lacks deception. He throws everything out of a high three-quarters release point which allows him to work up and down the strike zone.

THE FUTURE: Bitsko is very young and will require patience, but he has the building blocks to be a mid-rotation starter. If he makes it to low Class A in 2021, he would be the first Rays high school pitcher in the last decade to see full-season ball in his first full season.

SCOUTING GRADES: **Fastball:** 70 **Curveball:** 60 **Changeup:** 40 **Control:** 45

Year	Age	Club(League)	Class	W	L	ERA	G	GS	IP	H	HR	BB	SO	BB/9	K/9	WHIP	AVG
2020	18	Did not play—No minor league season															

9 JJ GOSS, RHP

BA GRADE
55 Risk: Extreme

MIKE JANES/FOUR SEAM IMAGES

Born: Dec. 25, 2000. **B-T:** R-R. **HT:** 6-3. **WT:** 185. **Drafted:** HS—Houston, 2019 (1st round supplemental). **Signed by:** Pat Murphy.

TRACK RECORD: Goss entered 2019 as the No. 2 starter on Houston's Cypress Ranch High team, behind Matthew Thompson. He graduated to co-ace after a strong senior season as his stuff ticked up. At pick No. 36, Goss was drafted nine spots earlier than Thompson, but Thompson's $2.1 million bonus edged out Goss' $2,042,900.

SCOUTING REPORT: Goss showed at instructional league that his stuff is only continuing to get better. His above-average 90-96 mph fastball in high school was sitting 92-95 and touching higher in instructs. He has solid feel and a steady maturity on the mound. His hard high-80s slider is average now and with his feel for spin it should eventually at least be above-average. His changeup isn't as consistent and needs to add either a little more action or a little more separation but he has feel and comfort with it and it should continue to improve. Goss' body has room to fill out further, which gives hope for further projection.

THE FUTURE: Goss' stuff is already major league-caliber, and it should just continue to get better. His delivery, knack for pitching and composure make him a safer bet to remain a starter than most young arms. He has potential to be a mid-rotation starter. He should be ready for full-season ball in 2021.

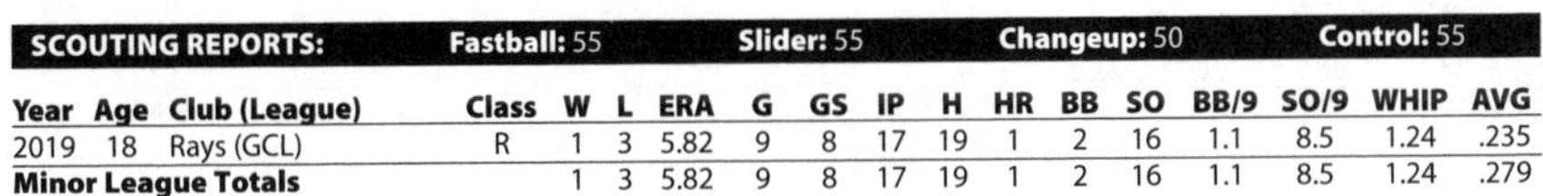
SCOUTING REPORTS: **Fastball:** 55 **Slider:** 55 **Changeup:** 50 **Control:** 55

Year	Age	Club (League)	Class	W	L	ERA	G	GS	IP	H	HR	BB	SO	BB/9	SO/9	WHIP	AVG
2019	18	Rays (GCL)	R	1	3	5.82	9	8	17	19	1	2	16	1.1	8.5	1.24	.235
Minor League Totals				1	3	5.82	9	8	17	19	1	2	16	1.1	8.5	1.24	.279

10 JOE RYAN, RHP

MARY DECICCO/MLB PHOTOS VIA GETTY IMAGES

BA GRADE
50 Risk: High

Born: June 5, 1996. **B-T:** R-R. **HT:** 6-1. **WT:** 185. **Drafted:** Cal State-Stanislaus, 2018 (7th round). **Signed by:** Alan Hull.

TRACK RECORD: A poorly timed lat injury crushed Ryan's draft stock in 2017, but a solid season after transferring to Division II Cal State Stanislaus made him a seventh-round steal for the Rays in 2018. He broke through in 2019 and finished second in the minors with 183 strikeouts as he climbed three levels to Double-A. The Rays added him to their 60-man player pool and brought him to their alternate training site in 2020.

SCOUTING REPORT: Ryan's fastball plays better than its 92-96 mph velocity and average spin rate indicate. He backspins the ball well and hides it in his delivery, leading to lots of swings and misses up in the zone. Ryan dominated the low minors almost exclusively with his fastball, so facing more advanced hitters at the alternate site helped him realize he needed to develop his secondaries. His fringy slider has surpassed his below-average curveball, but neither is consistent. Ryan's 83-85 mph changeup is his best secondary offering. It comes out of his hand looking like his fastball and has at least average potential, but he still uses it only sparingly.

THE FUTURE: Ryan was a fast mover in 2019, but he still has a ways to go before he is ready for the majors. The development of his secondaries will be critical in 2021.

SCOUTING GRADES: **Fastball:** 60 **Slider:** 40 **Curveball:** 30 **Changeup:** 50 **Control:** 55

Year	Age	Club (League)	Class	W	L	ERA	G	GS	IP	H	HR	BB	SO	BB/9	SO/9	WHIP	AVG
2018	22	Hudson Valley (NYP)	SS	2	1	3.72	12	7	36	26	3	14	51	3.5	12.6	1.10	.177
2019	23	Montgomery (SL)	AA	0	0	3.38	3	3	13	11	2	4	24	2.7	16.2	1.13	.204
	23	Bowling Green (MWL)	LoA	2	2	2.93	6	6	28	19	2	11	47	3.6	15.3	1.08	.202
	23	Charlotte, FL (FSL)	HiA	7	2	1.42	15	13	83	47	3	12	112	1.3	12.2	0.71	.141
Minor League Totals				11	5	2.36	36	29	160	103	10	41	234	2.3	13.2	0.90	.179

11 RONALDO HERNANDEZ, C

BA GRADE
50 Risk: High

Born: Nov. 11, 1997. **B-T:** R-R. **HT:** 6-1. **WT:** 230. **Signed:** Colombia, 2014. **Signed by:** Angel Contreras

TRACK RECORD: Signed for $225,000 in the same 2014 international class that produced righthander Diego Castillo, Hernandez was an infielder the Rays immediately converted to catcher. His bat has always outpaced his glove, but he mainly focused on his defense in 2020. He spent much of the year traveling with the Rays as a taxi squad member, catching bullpens and side sessions.

SCOUTING REPORT: Hernandez's stints on the taxi squad gave him experience catching premium stuff, but fewer opportunities to work on his hitting. Hernandez has the plus power to hit 20-25 home runs, but he has to do a better job selecting which pitches to hit. He makes frequent contact with his solid hand-eye coordination but often swings at pitches that are tough to drive. Hernandez's approach is very pull-heavy. Every home run of his pro career has been hit to left or left-center field. Hernandez has a plus arm behind the plate and moves well for a big catcher, but his receiving is fringe-average and needs to continue to improve.

THE FUTURE: The Rays added Hernandez to the 40-man roster after the 2019 season knowing he still needed time to develop. He is likely to open the 2021 season in Double-A.

Year	Age	Club (League)	Class	AVG	G	AB	R	H	2B	3B	HR	RBI	BB	SO	SB	OBP	SLG
2019	21	Charlotte, FL (FSL)	HiA	.265	103	393	43	104	19	3	9	60	17	65	7	.299	.397
Minor League Totals				.293	333	1271	190	373	73	6	41	218	87	191	22	.345	.457

12 GREG JONES, SS

BREAKOUT
BA GRADE
50 Risk: High

Born: March 7, 1998. **B-T:** B-R. **HT:** 6-2. **WT:** 175. **Drafted:** UNC Wilmington, 2019 (1st round). **Signed by:** Joe Hastings.

TRACK RECORD: Jones was considered one of the more intriguing prospects of the2017 high school class thanks to his speed, switch-hitting ability and his glove at shortstop. He made it to UNC Wilmington and followed up a mediocre freshman year and strikeout-filled Cape Cod League appearance with an excellent sophomore season (.341/.491/.543) that carried over into his pro debut.

SCOUTING REPORT: Jones had an inconsistent summer as a late addition to the Rays' alternate training site and sat out much of instructional league with a minor knee injury. He has a discerning eye at the plate with a level swing and adequate hand-eye coordination. He coils into his back leg before exploding

out of a compact stance with above-average bat speed. Jones could develop into a high on-base percentage table-setter with gap power that gives him a chance to hit 12-15 home runs a year. Once he gets on base, his plus-plus speed makes him a weapon on the basepaths. Defensively, his range, body control and plus arm are a fit at shortstop, but his hands need to get softer. Jones was limited at shortstop in 2019 because he had a sore shoulder early in his final college season. His arm bounced back in 2020. He showed plus arm strength and better accuracy. Center field is a viable backup plan.
THE FUTURE: The pandemic means Jones will get his first full-season at-bat as a 23-year-old. He's seven months older than Juan Soto. Jones' athleticism is exciting, but he needs to make up for lost time.

Year	Age	Club (League)	Class	AVG	G	AB	R	H	2B	3B	HR	RBI	BB	SO	SB	OBP	SLG
2019	21	Hudson Valley (NYP)	SS	.335	48	191	39	64	13	4	1	24	22	56	19	.413	.461
Minor League Totals				.335	48	191	39	64	13	4	1	24	22	56	19	.413	.461

13 TAYLOR WALLS, SS

BREAKOUT
BA GRADE
45 Risk: Medium

Born: July 10, 1996. **B-T:** B-R. **HT:** 5-10. **WT:** 180. **Drafted:** Florida State, 2017 (3rd round). **Signed by:** Brett Foley.

TRACK RECORD: A three-year starter at Florida State, Walls has managed to carve a path for himself despite the overflow of middle infielders in the Rays' system. Even in a system with so many options, Walls has managed to establish himself as the club's best defensive shortstop, with enough bat to be a potential major league regular.
SCOUTING REPORT: Walls is a plus defender at shortstop whose steady reliability and sticky hands are matched by above-average range and an above-average, accurate arm. Walls manages to slow the game down with an excellent internal clock. Walls can play other infield spots, but the Rays haven't had him work much at second or third because he's so reliable at short. Offensively, Walls is more likely a bottom-of-the-order hitter than someone who tops a lineup. He's a switch-hitter who is comfortable against lefthanders and righthanders. Walls is an average hitter with below-average power. He's best as a pest whose bat control makes it hard for pitchers to strike him out. His above-average speed is a useful bonus.
THE FUTURE: Where Walls fits on the Rays' roster is hard to decipher, but the more scouts from other teams have seen him, the more convinced they are that he'll be a starting shortstop. The question is whether it will be with the Rays or with another club after a trade.

Year	Age	Club (League)	Class	AVG	G	AB	R	H	2B	3B	HR	RBI	BB	SO	SB	OBP	SLG
2019	22	Montgomery (SL)	AA	.270	55	211	42	57	16	5	6	20	26	51	15	.346	.479
	22	Charlotte, FL (FSL)	HiA	.269	41	156	22	42	7	2	4	26	19	28	13	.339	.417
Minor League Totals				.277	262	998	173	276	60	13	17	124	140	212	64	.364	.414

14 JOSH LOWE, OF

BA GRADE
50 Risk: High

Born: Feb. 2, 1998. **B-T:** L-R. **HT:** 6-4. **WT:** 205. **Drafted:** HS—Marietta, Ga., 2016 (1st round). **Signed by:** Milt Hill.

TRACK RECORD: The younger brother of first baseman Nate Lowe, whom Tampa Bay traded to the Rangers in December, Josh was a first-round pick out of high school as a two-way third baseman/righthander. The Rays moved him to the outfield after his first pro season, reasoning that his speed was a better fit in center. Lowe was supposed to miss time in 2020 as he recovered from shoulder surgery, but the delayed start meant he was ready for the alternate training site. The Rays added him to their 40-man roster after the season.
SCOUTING REPORT: Lowe is a big league-ready center fielder. He is a plus defender with plus speed, and his plus arm fits in right field as well. Lowe's athleticism and defense should get him to the majors, but his bat is what could hold him back from a significant role. He's a fringe-average hitter with swing-and-miss and timing issues. His swing is a little grooved. He has struggled to handle pitchers who can locate up-and-in, as he prefers to get his long arms extended. Pitchers who do stay away can find that his average power gives him the ability to line balls the other way, and he yanks balls down-and-in over the fence.
THE FUTURE: Lowe should be at least a fourth outfielder, but unlike most potential fourth outfielders, he has impact potential. With three plus tools on his scouting report, Lowe could be a star if he takes a big step forward at the plate, but that's a big ask for any hitter.

Year	Age	Club (League)	Class	AVG	G	AB	R	H	2B	3B	HR	RBI	BB	SO	SB	OBP	SLG
2019	21	Montgomery (SL)	AA	.252	121	448	70	113	23	4	18	62	59	132	30	.341	.442
Minor League Totals				.253	398	1476	217	373	80	12	37	190	185	452	72	.336	.398

15 BRENT HONEYWELL, RHP

Born: March 31, 1995. **B-T:** R-R. **HT:** 6-2. **WT:** 180. **Drafted:** Walters State (Tenn.) JC, 2014 (2nd round supplemental). **Signed by:** Brian Hickman.

TRACK RECORD: If Honeywell's career had gone as planned, he would be arbitration eligible by now. Instead he ranks as a Rays Top 30 Prospect for the seventh time. Right before he was expected to join the Rays' rotation in 2018 he blew out his elbow. He fractured his repaired elbow in 2019. Then he had a further surgery in May 2020 to remove scar tissue that was compressing his ulnar nerve in that elbow. But he returned to the mound at the alternate training site, was added to the Rays' taxi squad for the playoffs and came close to making his big league debut.

SCOUTING REPORT: As hard as it may be to believe, Honeywell's stuff has returned to close to where it was before he missed three consecutive seasons. His average fastball is now more 91-93 mph rather than the 94-96 he flashed before his string of injuries, but his plus screwball and plus changeup are very close to what they were before. So too is his above-average mid-80s cutter. His command and control were not back yet to average in 2020.

THE FUTURE: Honeywell was able to get back to 90% of where he was pre-injury in an abbreviated 2020. If that's where he ends up, he will be a useful big league starter and could help the Rays in 2021. If he finds a little more as he puts distance between his last surgery, he could somehow still be a mid-rotation starter, though his durability is a significant question.

Year	Age	Club (League)	Class	W	L	ERA	G	GS	IP	H	HR	BB	SO	BB/9	SO/9	WHIP	AVG
2017	22	Durham (IL)	AAA	12	8	3.64	24	24	124	130	11	31	152	2.3	11.1	1.30	.249
2017	22	Montgomery (SL)	AA	1	1	2.08	2	2	13	4	1	4	20	2.8	13.8	0.62	.087
Minor League Totals				31	19	2.88	79	78	416	357	27	93	458	2.0	9.9	1.08	.230

16 SETH JOHNSON, RHP

BA GRADE
50 Risk: High

Born: Sept. 19, 1998. **B-T:** R-R. **HT:** 6-1. **WT:** 200. **Drafted:** Campbell, 2019 (1st round supplemental). **Signed by:** Joe Hastings.

TRACK RECORD: Losing the 2020 season may be a little more costly for Johnson than most prospects because he's still just getting started on his pitching career. Primarily a shortstop at Louisburg (N.C.) JC, he turned himself into a top 50 draft prospect when he moved to the mound for his junior year at Campbell. Johnson has just 89 innings of experience between college and pro ball.

SCOUTING REPORT: While he didn't play in an official game in 2020, Johnson didn't let the layoff go to waste. He attacked his throwing program with intensity and added some good weight. He showed up at instructional league with a plus mid-90s fastball that can now touch 99 mph with late run and a sharp, above-average slider with high spin at 2,700 to 2,800 revolutions per minute. Johnson also has worked on a fringe-average curveball, and his average changeup has modest fading action. Johnson is athletic and has impressed with his ability to quickly improve as a pitcher. His arm works well as part of a clean delivery, and his control and command are quickly getting to average with a chance to eventually be better than that.

THE FUTURE: Johnson just needs to wrack up the innings he hasn't been able to log yet. His present fastball/slider combo gives him a backup plan as a reliever, but his four-pitch assortment gives him a shot to be a mid-rotation starter.

Year	Age	Club (League)	Class	W	L	ERA	G	GS	IP	H	HR	BB	SO	BB/9	SO/9	WHIP	AVG
2019	20	Princeton (APP)	R	0	1	5.14	4	4	7	10	0	1	9	1.3	11.6	1.57	.333
	20	Rays (GCL)	R	0	0	0.00	5	5	10	7	0	2	7	1.8	6.3	0.90	.179
Minor League Totals				0	1	2.12	9	9	17	17	0	3	16	1.6	8.5	1.18	.258

17 ALIKA WILLIAMS, SS

BA GRADE
50 Risk: High

Born: March 12, 1999. **B-T:** R-R. **HT:** 6-2. **WT:** 180. **Drafted:** Arizona State, 2020 (1st round supplemental). **Signed by:** David Hamlett.

TRACK RECORD: Williams is the highest drafted Arizona State shortstop since Deven Marrero was a first-rounder in 2012. Marrero is an interesting analogue for Williams. Like Marrero, Williams is considered an excellent defensive shortstop who faced questions about his bat. He hit .300/.383/.400 for his Sun Devils career.

SCOUTING REPORT: Williams makes the shortstop position look easy because he is a fluid athlete who has such smooth actions. He's rangy with an excellent first step. His ability to be at least an above-average glove at shortstop and possibly plus is why he was a top-40 pick despite persistent questions about his bat. Williams puts the bat on the ball, but he just doesn't frighten pitchers. His contact ability makes him a bottom-of-the-order hitter who isn't a complete nothing offensively, but he projects as a below-average hitter with well below-average power.

THE FUTURE: The Rays love to collect athletic up-the-middle defenders with contact ability. If they can unlock a little more in Williams' bat, he's a future big league regular. If not, his glove still could pave a way to a role.

Year	Age	Club (League)	Class	AVG	G	AB	R	H	2B	3B	HR	RBI	BB	SO	SB	OBP	SLG
2020	21	Did not play—No minor league season															

18 KEVIN PADLO, 3B

BA GRADE 45 Risk: Medium

Born: July 15, 1996. **B-T:** R-R. **HT:** 6-2. **WT:** 200. **Drafted:** HS—Murietta, Calif., 2014 (5th round). **Signed by:** Jon Lukens (Rockies).

TRACK RECORD: Half of the 28 high school position players drafted ahead of Padlo in 2014 have either been released or have reached minor league free agency. In other words, Padlo has been a slow mover. Drafted by the Rockies, Padlo was dealt to the Rays in 2016, along with Corey Dickerson, in the deal that surrendered German Marquez to Colorado. Padlo came close to making his big league debut in 2020, when he was part of the Rays' taxi squad.

SCOUTING REPORT: Until 2019, the oft-injured Padlo was a slugger who didn't slug. More consistent at-bats and a better understanding of when to let loose in advantageous counts helped him start to tap into his plus-plus raw power. He's still likely a .220-.240 hitter if he plays every day in the majors thanks to a pull-heavy approach, but the Rays' clever platooning would likely keep him from facing many of the pitchers who would hamstring him. Padlo has made himself into an average defender at third base with an above-average arm, and he can also play first base. He's athletic with a decent first step, but he's a below-average runner.

THE FUTURE: Padlo's power is real. As a righthanded slugger, he could fill a need as a platoon option, but his next stop is a return to Triple-A. He has two minor league options remaining.

Year	Age	Club (League)	Class	AVG	G	AB	R	H	2B	3B	HR	RBI	BB	SO	SB	OBP	SLG
2019	22	Durham (IL)	AAA	.290	40	131	25	38	11	1	9	27	21	46	1	.400	.595
	22	Montgomery (SL)	AA	.250	70	220	39	55	20	0	12	35	47	70	11	.383	.505
Minor League Totals				.244	554	1885	307	460	134	14	70	314	322	556	77	.359	.441

19 TAJ BRADLEY, RHP

BA GRADE 50 Risk: Very High

Born: March 20, 2001. **B-T:** R-R. **HT:** 6-2. **WT:** 190. **Drafted:** HS—Stone Mountain, Ga., 2018 (5th round). **Signed by:** Milt Hill.

TRACK RECORD: The Rays take a patient approach with high school pitchers. They had even more reason to do so with Bradley, since he was young for his draft class. Instead of getting his first shot at full-season ball in 2020, his third pro season, Bradley instead had to wait for instructional league.

SCOUTING REPORT: Bradley was primarily an outfielder for most of his time in high school, and now that he's focused on pitching, his velocity has steadily climbed. He sat in the low 90s in his draft year and ticked that up to 92-94 mph in 2019. In shorter stints at instructs in 2020 he sat 94-97 mph on his best days. His plus fastball has some life, giving it swing-and-miss potential. His breaking ball keeps getting tighter. His breaking ball and his changeup are average at best, but he knows how to spot them, and he reads swings well. Bradley's intelligence and feel give him a solid chance to continue to get better.

THE FUTURE: Bradley's lack of a plus secondary pitch makes it hard to project him as more than a No. 4 starter. For someone who has come far in a short time, he may continue to exceed projection.

Year	Age	Club (League)	Class	W	L	ERA	G	GS	IP	H	HR	BB	SO	BB/9	SO/9	WHIP	AVG
2019	18	Princeton (APP)	R	2	5	3.18	12	11	51	42	4	19	57	3.4	10.1	1.20	.195
Minor League Totals				3	9	3.77	22	20	74	68	5	31	81	3.8	9.9	1.34	.238

20 MOISES GOMEZ, OF

BA GRADE 50 Risk: Very High

Born: Aug. 27, 1988. **B-T:** R-R. **HT:** 5-11. **WT:** 200. **Signed:** Venezuela, 2015. **Signed by:** Juan Castillo/Ronnie Blanco.

TRACK RECORD: Gomez turned in an outstanding debut in the Venezuelan Summer League in 2016 and an equally impressive full-season debut in the Midwest League in 2018. He hit for power but struggled to hit for average at high Class A Charlotte in 2019. The Rays left him unprotected for both the 2019 and 2020 Rule 5 drafts. He went unpicked both times.

SCOUTING REPORT: Gomez hits the ball as hard as anyone in the Rays' system when he makes contact.

He regularly stings balls with 105-plus mph exit velocities. Now he just has to figure out how to make contact more regularly. Gomez has above-average bat speed and plus power potential. His swing is quite simple, with a significant timing step as he loads with an aggressive weight transfer. But his swing has some stiffness to it. He swings through hittable pitches and his takes seem to at times be guesses, making it hard to project him as even a below-average hitter. Gomez has gotten bigger and stronger. He's still an average runner, but he is now a fringe-average defender in the corners with an average arm.

THE FUTURE: Gomez can be a 30-home run slugger in the majors, but only if he adds more adjustability to his swing. He needs a bounce-back season in his move to Double-A.

Year	Age	Club (League)	Class	AVG	G	AB	R	H	2B	3B	HR	RBI	BB	SO	SB	OBP	SLG
2019	20	Charlotte, FL (FSL)	HiA	.220	119	428	55	94	26	2	16	66	48	164	3	.297	.402
Minor League Totals				.259	388	1458	217	378	90	14	47	220	130	418	30	.320	.437

21 NICK SCHNELL, OF

Born: March 27, 2000. **B-T:** L-R. **HT:** 6-3. **WT:** 180. **Drafted:** HS—Indianapolis, 2018 (1st round). **Signed by:** James Bonnici.

TRACK RECORD: After battling wrist and knee injuries in the past, Schnell was healthy for the first time in three pro seasons in 2020. Unfortunately, Schnell's healthy season was spent at home thanks to the pandemic.

SCOUTING REPORT: Schnell leapt into the first round with an excellent senior year of high school where he showed plenty of home run power. That has yet to translate to pro ball, even though he shows plus raw power in batting practice. Schnell needs plenty of at-bats against lefthanders, because he doesn't seem to pick the ball up all that well against them. He also is vulnerable to pitches off the plate. Schnell's defense has steadily gotten better and he actually runs a little better now, turning in plus times at his best. He's a plausible long-term center fielder who can be an above-average defender.

THE FUTURE: Schnell is moving slower than his peers from the 2018 first round. He has a chance to be a center fielder with plus productive power, but there's a lot of projection involved in that. A solid 2021 at Class A would help kick-start Schnell's development.

Year	Age	Club (League)	Class	AVG	G	AB	R	H	2B	3B	HR	RBI	BB	SO	SB	OBP	SLG
2019	19	Bowling Green (MWL)	LoA	.236	14	55	7	13	3	1	0	3	2	24	0	.271	.327
	19	Princeton (APP)	R	.286	37	147	28	42	11	3	5	27	18	51	5	.361	.503
	19	Rays (GCL)	R	.190	4	21	4	4	0	2	0	1	0	9	0	.190	.381
Minor League Totals				.259	74	290	47	75	18	7	6	35	34	107	7	.338	.431

22 JOSH FLEMING, LHP

Born: May 18, 1996. **B-T:** L-L. **HT:** 6-2. **WT:** 190. **Drafted:** Webster (Mo.) 2017 (5th round). **Signed by:** Matt Allison.

TRACK RECORD: Fleming led all Division III pitchers with a 0.67 ERA in 2017, which helped him become the first Webster University player ever drafted. He embellished his credentials in 2020, when he not only became the school's first major leaguer, but he pitched in the World Series.

SCOUTING REPORT: Fleming is a modern version of the crafty lefty who used to fill the back end of many rotations. He likes to pepper the outside bottom corner against righthanded hitters, working on and off the edge of the zone with plus command. His 88-93 mph fringe-average sinker and his above-average low-80s changeup are thrown to that same spot, with the changeup's deception and fade baffling hitters looking to feast on a low-90s fastball. His below-average mid-80s slider lacks power, depth or tilt, but it pairs well as he sneaks it up-and-in on righthanded hitters looking to dive over the plate. Fleming's changeup and slider don't baffle same-side batters, so he's better against righthanded hitters. He has a quality pickoff move.

THE FUTURE: The Rays trusted Fleming enough to insert him into their rotation and use him in their playoff bullpen. He fits best as a bulk or long reliever, and the Rays have shown they can get the most out of pitchers like Fleming.

Year	Age	Club (League)	Class	W	L	ERA	G	GS	IP	H	HR	BB	SO	BB/9	SO/9	WHIP	AVG
2020	24	Tampa Bay (AL)	MAJ	5	0	2.78	7	5	32	28	5	7	25	1.9	7.0	1.08	.230
Major League Totals				5	0	2.78	7	5	32	28	5	7	25	2.0	7.0	1.08	.230
Minor League Totals				22	13	3.40	56	46	294	285	25	53	214	1.6	6.6	1.15	.254

23 RYAN THOMPSON, RHP

Born: June 26, 1992. **B-T:** R-R. **HT:** 6-6. **WT:** 221. **Drafted:** Campbell, 2014 (23rd round). **Signed by:** Tim Bittner (Astros).

TRACK RECORD: Thompson went from minor league afterthought to World Series reliever in the span of two seasons. He was a dominating sidearm reliever at Campbell, going 16-3, 1.12 over 70 appearances and 161 innings in two seasons. He missed all of 2018 because of Tommy John surgery. The Rays nabbed him for $24,000 in the minor league phase of the 2018 Rule 5 draft that December. A year and a half later he finished second among Rays pitchers with 25 appearances.

SCOUTING REPORT: As a pro, Thompson has gotten more athletic in his weight transfer into his rear leg, but he remains the epitome of a sidearm sinker/slider righthander. His plus low-90s sinker has one of the lowest spin rates in the majors, which gives it dramatically more sink than the average two-seamer to go with average run. He gave up only one extra-base hit and three flyball outs off his sinker in 2020. He'll occasionally sneak a low-90s four-seamer up in the zone to try to surprise a hitter. His plus mid-70s slider destroys normal notions of what a slider should be. It has no depth, but it runs away from righties and in on the hands of lefties. Its lack of depth makes it much tougher for lefties to hit.

THE FUTURE: Thompson's assortment is unusual, and he marries that with above-average command. He has the tools to be a productive, durable reliever.

Year	Age	Club (League)	Class	W	L	ERA	G	GS	IP	H	HR	BB	SO	BB/9	SO/9	WHIP	AVG
2020	28	Tampa Bay (AL)	MAJ	1	2	4.44	25	1	26	29	4	8	23	2.7	7.9	1.41	.274
Major League Totals				1	2	4.44	25	1	26	29	4	8	23	2.7	7.9	1.41	.274
Minor League Totals				15	10	3.35	162	5	252	249	15	64	230	2.3	8.2	1.24	.255

24 PEDRO MARTINEZ, SS

BA GRADE
50 Risk: Extreme

Born: Jan. 28, 2001. **B-T:** B-R. **HT:** 5-11. **WT:** 165. **Signed:** Venezuela, 2018. **Signed by:** Hector Ortega/Louis Eljaua/Julio Figueroa (Cubs).

TRACK RECORD: The Rays acquired Martinez for the unrelated Jose Martinez in a late-August deal with the Cubs. Pedro Martinez impressed in his two years with the Cubs—he was considered one of the more advanced teenage hitters in the Arizona and Northwest leagues in 2019. The Rays brought him to instructional league in the fall.

SCOUTING REPORT: Martinez has an advanced feel for hitting for his age. The switch-hitter has an understanding of the strike zone and has already demonstrated his bat-to-ball skills and good timing at the plate to go with average bat speed. His modest gap power should eventually turn into 10-12 home runs a year. He's an above-average runner. He has an above-average arm and could be an average shortstop and above-average second baseman. He'll probably bounce around multiple positions as a Rays prospect.

THE FUTURE: Martinez spent the winter as one of the younger players in the Venezuelan League, a further reminder of how he's advanced for his age. He's ready for full-season ball in 2021.

Year	Age	Club (League)	Class	AVG	G	AB	R	H	2B	3B	HR	RBI	BB	SO	SB	OBP	SLG
2019	18	Cubs 1 (AZL)	R	.352	27	108	12	38	6	3	2	17	12	27	8	.417	.519
	18	Eugene (NWL)	SS	.265	27	98	15	26	2	3	0	7	12	36	11	.357	.347
Minor League Totals				.310	108	403	64	125	11	11	4	49	50	89	50	.393	.422

25 HERIBERTO HERNANDEZ, OF/1B

BA GRADE
50 Risk: Extreme

Born: Dec. 16, 1999. **B-T:** R-R. **HT:** 6-1. **WT:** 180. **Signed:** Dominican Republic, 2017. **Signed by:** Willy Espinal (Rangers).

TRACK RECORD: Hernandez signed for $10,000 during the 2017 international signing period and quickly emerged as a potential bargain. He finished second in the Dominican Summer League in home runs (12) and OPS (1.099) in his pro debut in 2018 and kept it up by ranking tied for second in home runs (11) and third in OPS in the Rookie-level Arizona League (1.079) the following year. He was set to make his full-season debut in 2020, but instead he took a step back without the structure professional baseball provided. The Rays acquired him from the Rangers in December in the deal that sent Nate Lowe to Texas.

SCOUTING REPORT: The Rangers brought Hernandez to their alternate training site during the summer and found a player who had lost strength and weight. He didn't have access to quality facilities in the Dominican Republic, where he spent the shutdown, and wasn't back to where he should have been until the end of instructs. When he's right, Hernandez has plus power on par with anyone in the Rays' system. He has trouble recognizing pitches and needs work on his hit tool, but the power comes naturally. Hernandez generates force through proper sequencing, quick hands, good extension and good bat speed. Hernandez signed as a catcher, but he's exclusively a first baseman and left fielder now.

THE FUTURE: Hernandez will begin at low Class A in 2021. As long as he's hitting homers, he will keep rising.

Year	Age	Club (League)	Class	AVG	G	AB	R	H	2B	3B	HR	RBI	BB	SO	SB	OBP	SLG
2019	19	Rangers (AZL)	R	.344	50	192	42	66	17	4	11	48	27	57	3	.433	.646
	19	Spokane (NWL)	SS	.375	3	8	4	3	0	0	0	1	2	3	3	.500	.375
Minor League Totals				.320	113	378	102	121	32	9	23	98	82	101	11	.450	.635

26 JOHN DOXAKIS, LHP

BA GRADE **45** Risk: High

Born: Aug. 20, 1998. **B-T:** B-L. **HT:** 6-4. **WT:** 215. **Drafted:** Texas A&M, 2019 (2nd round). **Signed by:** Pat Murphy.

TRACK RECORD: Doxakis picked the perfect time for a breakout. A consistent performer at Texas A&M, he had been viewed as a soft-tosser. But he started throwing 91-93 mph more often as a junior, which turned him into a second-round pick in a pitching-poor 2019 draft class.

SCOUTING REPORT: Even with improved velocity, Doxakis pitches with a below-average fastball, though his funky delivery makes it hard to square up. He sits around 90 mph, though his fastball has quality life and he can run it and cut it. His ability to dot corners with above-average command and plus control lets his fastball work, and it sets up his above-average mid-80s slider. It has two-plane break and he's shown he can use it against lefties and righties. His fringy changeup will need to get better as he climbs the ladder.

THE FUTURE: Doxakis is yet another crafty Rays lefty whose fastball plays better than the radar gun readings would indicate. If he can continue to add further velocity, he has back-end starter potential.

Year	Age	Club (League)	Class	W	L	ERA	G	GS	IP	H	HR	BB	SO	BB/9	SO/9	WHIP	AVG
2019	20	Hudson Valley (NYP)	SS	0	0	1.93	12	10	33	20	0	11	31	3.0	8.5	0.95	.154
Minor League Totals				0	0	1.93	12	10	32	20	0	11	31	3.0	8.5	0.95	.174

27 IAN SEYMOUR, LHP

BA GRADE **45** Risk: High

Born: Dec. 13, 1998. **B-T:** L-L. **HT:** 6-0. **WT:** 190. **Drafted:** Virginia Tech, 2020 (2nd round). **Signed by:** Landon Lassiter.

TRACK RECORD: Seymour earned a spot in Virginia Tech's weekend rotation just a couple of weeks into his college career. He left as one of the best starters in program history. The coronavirus shutdown cost him his shot at topping Joe Saunders' school strikeout record. Saunders is the only Hokie to be drafted higher than Seymour in the 21st century.

SCOUTING REPORT: Seymour was one of the most competitive pitchers in college baseball in 2020. He wouldn't rank among the top 60 players in the class based on pure stuff, but his makeup and toughness help him get the most out of his ability. Setting up from the extreme third base side of the rubber, Seymour's closed-off delivery means that righthanded hitters are staring at his back because he hides the ball well. Seymour's delivery has plenty of effort and a hard finish, but his arm is consistently on time. He throws strikes and has been durable. Seymour generally has sat 91-93 mph and sometimes struggles to maintain that velocity, but he touched 95 more often in 2020. His changeup is an above-average pitch already. His cutterish short slider gives him a fringe-average breaking ball.

THE FUTURE: Despite Seymour's durability, scouts largely see him moving to the bullpen because of his delivery. His run-through-a-wall competitiveness should serve him well in any role.

Year	Age	Club (League)	Class	W	L	ERA	G	GS	IP	H	HR	BB	SO	BB/9	SO/9	WHIP	AVG
2020	21	Did not play—No minor league season															

28 OSLEIVIS BASABE, 2B

Born: Sept. 13, 2001. **B-T:** R-R. **HT:** 6-1. **WT:** 188. **Signed:** Venezuela, 2017. **Signed by:** Carlos Plaza/Rafic Saab (Rangers).

TRACK RECORD: The Rangers signed Basabe out of Venezuela for $550,000 in 2017. He was known as a toolsy athlete with a questionable bat at the time, but he's since hit .334 over his first two professional seasons. He carried on with a strong offensive performance during instructional league in 2020, reinforcing the belief in his bat. The Rays acquired him in the trade that sent Nate Lowe to the Rangers in December.

SCOUTING REPORT: Few players at Rangers instructs consistently hit the ball harder than Basabe, who produced exit velocities up to 110 mph. Unable to return to Venezuela during the pandemic, he used the time stuck in Arizona to add muscle to his frame. He's a gap-to-gap, line-drive hitter who lacks lift in his swing, but his excellent bat-to-ball skills and his ability to keep the bat in the zone give the Rays hope that home run power will eventually come. The team loves his makeup and lauds his advanced approach at the plate. Basabe has improved his movements and footwork enough defensively that scouts believe he could be a plausible big league shortstop. He's athletic enough to also play second base or center field. He has an above-average arm.

THE FUTURE: Basabe will open 2021 at Class A. His continued offensive growth and potential defensive versatility make him an intriguing prospect to watch.

Year	Age	Club (League)	Class	AVG	G	AB	R	H	2B	3B	HR	RBI	BB	SO	SB	OBP	SLG
2019	18	Rangers (AZL)	R	.325	35	151	29	49	2	5	0	31	8	20	7	.355	.404
	18	Spokane (NWL)	SS	.300	2	10	0	3	0	0	0	1	0	1	0	.300	.300
Minor League Totals				.334	89	353	66	118	18	8	1	66	31	46	19	.386	.439

29 CALEB SAMPEN, RHP

BA GRADE
45 Risk: High

Born: July 23, 1996. **B-T:** R-R. **HT:** 6-2. **WT:** 185. **Drafted:** Wright State, 2018 (20th round). **Signed by:** Marty Lamb (Dodgers).

TRACK RECORD: Sampen was an eye-opening discovery for Wright State as a freshman. After being sidelined for a year with ulnar nerve transposition surgery, he was once again Wright State's ace by the end of his redshirt sophomore season. The Rays acquired him from the Dodgers for Jamie Schultz in 2019.

SCOUTING REPORT: The Rays like college performers who seem to get the most out of their ability, and Sampen fits that description. As a pro, he's added a little velocity to his fringe-average 91-94 mph fastball, and he's continued to refine his hard 88-89 mph plus cutter. It has more tilt than most sliders and is effective against lefties. He didn't throw that pitch until late in his college career. Now it's his calling card. Hitters can't sit on his fastball or cutter because he also throws an average curve and a fringe-average changeup. Sampen's above-average control is key to his success as he has to stay away from the heart of the plate.

THE FUTURE: Sampen's stuff isn't flashy, but the Rays' pitching development staff keeps figuring out ways to maximize the ability of plus-makeup pitchers with average stuff. Sampen is another one who fits that bill.

Year	Age	Club (League)	Class	W	L	ERA	G	GS	IP	H	HR	BB	SO	BB/9	SO/9	WHIP	AVG
2019	22	Bowling Green (MWL)	LoA	9	4	2.68	22	21	121	91	3	32	104	2.4	7.7	1.02	.188
Minor League Totals				9	6	3.15	35	32	151	122	5	41	147	2.4	8.7	1.08	.216

30 DREW STROTMAN, RHP

BA GRADE
45 Risk: High

Born: Sept. 3, 1996. **B-T:** R-R. **HT:** 6-3. **WT:** 195. **Drafted:** St. Mary's, 2017 (4th round). **Signed by:** Alan Hull.

TRACK RECORD: Strotman's solid start to his pro career hit a detour when he tore his ulnar collateral ligament in his elbow in 2018. Tommy John surgery meant he didn't return to the mound until late 2019. Fully healthy for 2020, the coronavirus shutdown meant he was limited to work at the alternate training site. His work there was enough to convince the Rays to add him to the 40-man roster in November.

SCOUTING REPORT: Strotman's fastball and slider looked a little better at instructional league than they did in the Arizona Fall League in 2019. Strotman sat 93-95 mph pretty regularly at the Rays' fall camp. His average slider showed a little more power, and he's added an 88-92 mph cutter that ties in nicely with the other two pitches. Stroman has a high-tempo delivery. He showed average control pre-injury, but he has yet to demonstrate that consistently in his return to the mound.

THE FUTURE: After being added to the Rays' 40-man roster, Strotman enters 2021 ready for Double-A. The Rays have started him so far, but his best role likely is in the bullpen, where his fastball, slider and cutter would all play up.

Year	Age	Club (League)	Class	W	L	ERA	G	GS	IP	H	HR	BB	SO	BB/9	SO/9	WHIP	AVG
2019	22	Charlotte, FL (FSL)	HiA	0	2	5.06	5	5	16	20	3	9	13	5.1	7.3	1.81	.274
	22	Rays (GCL)	R	0	1	3.38	4	4	8	9	0	3	11	3.4	12.4	1.50	.237
Minor League Totals				5	6	2.98	29	25	120	98	3	39	109	2.9	8.1	1.14	.225

MORE PROSPECTS TO KNOW

31 TOMMY ROMERO, RHP

Romero was Rule 5 eligible and went unpicked, but he's not all that far away from being yet another multi-inning reliever who can work up in the zone with a deceptive fastball and down with his curveball.

32 FORD PROCTOR, C/INF

Procter may fly up this list next year. He's always hit, but his range at shortstop was limited. He's taken to a move to catcher and could take off as a smart conversion candidate.

33 HUNTER BARNHART, RHP

A star quarterback in high school, Barnhart's improving low-90s fastball and sharp curveball give him projection as a starting pitching prospect.

34 JHON DIAZ, OF

One of the best hitters in the 2019 international class, Diaz combines an advanced hitting tool with solid power potential.

35 RYAN SHERRIFF, LHP

A sinker-slider lefty, he should help the Rays bullpen as an up-and-down reliever who rides the St. Petersburg-Durham shuttle.

36 MICHAEL MERCADO, RHP

The Rays 2017 second-round pick missed the 2019 season recovering from Tommy John surgery. He was back on the mound for instructional league in 2020 and was once again bumping 95 mph with his fastball.

37 NIKO HULSIZER, OF

Hulsizer is a left fielder who can tattoo fastballs and has some of the best power in the organization, but it's a pretty all-or-nothing approach.

38 MICHAEL PLASSMEYER, LHP

Welcome to the next Josh Fleming. Plassmeyer has even better command to make his low-90s fastball, changeup and slider toy with hitters who think they should be able to square him up.

39 CURTIS MEAD, 3B

Picked up from the Phillies for lefthander Cristopher Sanchez, Mead has yet to make his Rays' pro debut, but he's shown his power in two seasons of Rays instructional leagues.

40 TRISTAN GRAY, 2B/3B

Gray has above-average power for a middle infielder. He's a solid second baseman and can play shortstop or third base, although he's much less reliable on that side of the diamond.

41 SHANE SASAKI, OF

SLEEPER

Sasaki is a rangy outfielder whose glove is far, far ahead of his bat. He has to get stronger to make any kind of impact at the plate.

TOP PROSPECTS OF THE DECADE

Year	Player, Pos	2020 Org
2011	Jeremy Hellickson, RHP	Did not play
2012	Matt Moore, LHP	Softbank (Japan)
2013	Wil Myers, OF	Padres
2014	Jake Odorizzi, RHP	Twins
2015	Willy Adames, SS	Rays
2016	Blake Snell, LHP	Rays
2017	Willy Adames, SS	Rays
2018	Brent Honeywell, RHP	Rays
2019	Wander Franco, SS	Rays
2020	Wander Franco, SS	Rays

TOP DRAFT PICKS OF THE DECADE

Year	Player, Pos	2020 Org
2011	Taylor Guerrieri, RHP	Rangers
2012	Richie Shaffer, 3B	Did not play
2013	Nick Ciuffo, C	Rangers
2014	Casey Gillaspie, 1B	Independent Lge
2015	Garrett Whitley, OF	Rays
2016	Josh Lowe, 3B	Rays
2017	Brendan McKay, LHP/1B	Rays
2018	Matthew Liberatore, LHP	Cardinals
2019	Greg Jones, SS	Rays
2020	Nick Bitsko, RHP	Rays

DEPTH CHART

TAMPA BAY RAYS

TOP 2021 ROOKIES	RANK
Wander Franco, SS	1
Randy Arozarena, OF	2
BREAKOUT PROSPECTS	**RANK**
Greg Jones, SS	12
Taylor Walls, SS	13

SOURCE OF TOP 30 TALENT

Homegrown	21	Acquired	9
College	11	Trade	8
High School	5	Rule 5 draft	1
Junior College	1	Independent leagues	0
Nondrafted free agent	0	Free agents/waivers	0
International	4		

LF
Randy Arozarena (2)
Moises Gomez (20)
Michael Gigliotti

CF
Josh Lowe (14)
Nick Schnell (21)
Jhon Diaz
Shane Sasaki

RF
Niko Hulsizer
Ruben Cardenas
Diego Infante

3B
Kevin Padlo (18)
Curtis Mead

SS
Wander Franco (1)
Greg Jones (12)
Taylor Walls (13)
Alika Williams (17)
Osleivis Basabe (28)
Tanner Murray

2B
Vidal Brujan (3)
Xavier Edwards (7)
Pedro Martinez (24)
Tristan Gray

1B
Heriberto Hernandez (25)
Dalton Kelly

C
Ronaldo Hernandez (11)
Ford Proctor
Chris Betts

LHP

LHSP	LHRP
Shane McClanahan (4)	Ian Seymour (27)
Brendan McKay (6)	Ryan Sherriff
Josh Fleming (22)	Ben Brecht
John Doxakis (26)	Graeme Stinson
Michael Plassmeyer	
Anthony Banda	

RHP

RHSP	RHRP
Shane Baz (5)	Seth Johnson (16)
Nick Bitsko (8)	Ryan Thompson (23)
JJ Goss (9)	Caleb Sampen (29)
Joe Ryan (10)	Neraldo Catalina
Brent Honeywell (15)	Jeff Hakanson
Taj Bradley (19)	Sandy Gaston
Drew Strotman (30)	Tanner Dodson
Tommy Romero	Tobias Myers
Hunter Barnhart	
Michael Mercado	

Texas Rangers

BY JEFF WILSON

The Rangers are rebuilding, again.

The organization shifted after quickly falling out of contention in the first half of the pandemic-shortened 2020 season. They finished 22-38, the worst record in the American League. In typical 2020 form, the rebuild launched during a season in which there were no minor league games.

One positive development was the opening of Globe Life Field, which has a retractable roof and played as one of the more pitcher-friendly parks in the majors in 2020.

Before the coronavirus pandemic canceled the minor league season, Rangers officials were looking forward to seeing the system at work. They were convinced the talent at the lower levels would mature, and the rest of baseball would see their system in a more favorable light.

Alas, the Rangers were stuck with only the instructional league to evaluate where they are as a system. Nothing the Rangers saw changed their minds on the promise they believe the system has.

For now, though, it's a depth-based system. That's what the Rangers heard from other organizations during instructs and what they also realize. The Rangers have few Top 100 Prospects, but many others project as solid players.

If the rebuild is going to take the Rangers where they want to be, they need to see those players develop into impact players. The sooner the better.

After a season in which the brakes were applied, the Rangers need to hit the gas.

The bulk of the Rangers top prospects haven't played above Class A, even as the Rangers have been aggressive with their assignments. Many players will have to take significant jumps in 2021.

The good news is the Rangers saw many prospects develop in 2020 at the alternate training site—and in Arlington. None impressed more than Leody Taveras, who planted his flag in center field in Texas after two years of questions about his future. He played terrific defense and was a menace on the bases. That he was able to get on base and hit for power is what gives the Rangers hope.

Catcher Sam Huff, shortstop Anderson Tejeda and righthander Kyle Cody all made their debuts, held their own and are in the picture for 2021. Third baseman Josh Jung spent the summer in Arlington getting at-bats at the alternate site and said he benefited more from the experience than he would have over a full minor league season.

One other bright spot? The addition of Mississippi State second baseman Justin Foscue with the 14th overall pick in the draft. He's an advanced college hitter, just as Jung was when selected eighth overall in 2019, and has immediately emerged as one of the system's top prospects.

Even the selection that might have been the most questioned in the draft has boosted the Rangers' opinion of the system. Tennessee high school outfielder Evan Carter, a shocking selection in the second round, shined at instructs and has the Rangers expecting him to be a top prospect by this time next year.

Add in the No. 2 overall pick in the 2021 draft, and the Rangers like the direction they are headed.

They just need their players to get going. ■

RONALD MARTINEZ/GETTY IMAGES

Rookie center fielder Leody Taveras surprisingly made the Opening Day roster and thrived.

PROJECTED 2024 LINEUP

Position	Player	Age
Catcher	Sam Huff	26
First Base	Nate Lowe	28
Second Base	Justin Foscue	25
Third Base	Josh Jung	26
Shortstop	Isiah Kiner-Falefa	29
Left Field	Nick Solak	29
Center Field	Leody Taveras	25
Right Field	Joey Gallo	30
Designated Hitter	Willie Calhoun	29
No. 1 Starter	Dane Dunning	29
No. 2 Starter	Cole Winn	24
No. 3 Starter	Hans Crouse	25
No. 4 Starter	Kolby Allard	26
No. 5 Starter	Ronny Henriquez	24
Closer	Jonathan Hernandez	27

1 JOSH JUNG, 3B

Born: Feb. 12, 1998. **B-T:** R-R. **HT:** 6-2. **WT:** 215.
Drafted: Texas Tech, 2019 (1st round).
Signed by: Josh Simpson.

TRACK RECORD: The Rangers made Jung the eighth overall pick in 2019 after a star-studded career at Texas Tech, where he was named co-player of the year for the Big 12 in 2019 after hitting .343/.474/.636 with 15 home runs and 58 RBIs. He signed for $4.4 million and got his feet wet with a productive but not flashy 44-game run in the Rookie-level Arizona League and low Class A Hickory. With the minor league season canceled in 2020, the Rangers added Jung to their 60-man player pool and made the most of his time facing older, more experienced players at the alternate training site. He finished the year at instructional league, where he starred as one of the top hitters in Arizona.

SCOUTING REPORT: The Rangers believe Jung is going to hit in the middle of their lineup for years to come. His bat-to-ball skills are the best in the organization, and he works over pitchers during an at-bat. It's not just his strike-zone judgment that stands out, but his ability to adjust within an at-bat. His ability to make contact, which might be his best tool, allows him to be aggressive early in counts and still line a ball into the gap if he falls behind. His hand speed fuels his ability to hit, and he has a sharp eye and an understanding of how to manipulate the barrel. Jung is going to be difficult to strike out, something that will stand out in the whiff-heavy Rangers lineup. The goal in 2020 was to transition Jung from simply a contact hitter, which he was in college, into a hitter who can do more damage. His power was mostly to right-center field at Texas Tech. He was that hitter again at low Class A, where he hit only one home run in 157 at-bats. Jung worked on pulling fastballs in 2020 and developed to the point where 30-homer power is possible. He should be around 20 homers on the low end, with even more doubles, but when a game is on the line, Jung is the hitter the Rangers will want at the plate. Though he played shortstop his final season in Lubbock and flirted with second base during instructs, Jung is a third baseman. He's not flashy, but he makes every play and has enough arm to handle the hot corner. His bat is going to force him into the lineup, and that helped influence the Rangers' decision to move Gold Glove third baseman Isiah Kiner-Falefa to shortstop, where Elvis Andrus is on the decline and not performing well enough to warrant everyday playing time.

TOP ROOKIE

BILL MITCHELL

BA GRADE
60 **Risk: High**

SCOUTING GRADES
Hit: 60. **Power:** 60. **Run:** 40.
Field: 50. **Arm:** 55.

Projected future grades on 20-80 scouting scale.

BEST TOOLS

Best Hitter for Average	Josh Jung
Best Power Hitter	Sam Huff
Best Strike-Zone Discipline	Justin Foscue
Fastest Baserunner	Bubba Thompson
Best Athlete	Bubba Thompson
Best Fastball	A.J. Alexy
Best Curveball	Cole Winn
Best Slider	Cole Winn
Best Changeup	John King
Best Control	Tyler Phillips
Best Defensive Catcher	David Garcia
Best Defensive Infielder	Anderson Tejeda
Best Infield Arm	Anderson Tejeda
Best Defensive Outfielder	Leody Taveras
Best Outfield Arm	Leody Taveras

THE FUTURE: The Rangers need some prospects to become stars for their rebuild to be a success, and Jung has a strong chance. He has what it takes to be a solid regular and possibly an impact player. He will begin 2021 at Double-A, with a chance he makes his big league debut by the all-star break. ■

Year	Age	Club (League)	Class	AVG	G	AB	R	H	2B	3B	HR	RBI	BB	SO	SB	OBP	SLG
2019	21	Rangers (AZL)	R	.588	4	17	5	10	1	1	1	5	2	3	0	.632	.941
	21	Hickory (SAL)	LoA	.287	40	157	18	45	13	0	1	23	16	29	4	.363	.389
Minor League Totals				.316	44	174	23	55	14	1	2	28	18	32	4	.389	.443

2 SAM HUFF, C

DAVID DUROCHIK/MLB PHOTOS VIA GETTY IMAGES

Born: Jan. 14, 1998. **B-T:** R-R. **HT:** 6-5. **WT:** 240. **Drafted:** HS—Phoenix, 2016 (7th round). **Signed by:** Josh Simpson.

TRACK RECORD: An unheralded seventh-round pick in 2016, Huff hit 28 home runs during a breakout 2019 season and won MVP at the Futures Game. The Rangers brought Huff to the alternate training site in 2020 and called him up to the majors for the final three weeks. He didn't disappoint.

SCOUTING REPORT: Huff struggled with game-calling and too often chased spin at the plate when he first came up, but he adjusted and was one of the Rangers' best hitters the final 10 games of the season. Huff's plus-plus power stands out, and his improved approach gives him a chance to get to it. He will likely never hit for a high average, but improved pitch recognition could help produce high-end offensive production at the catcher position. Huff's arm is the strongest among Rangers catchers, and his catching has improved after working with ex-big league backstop Bobby Wilson, a Rangers coach. Though massive for a catcher, Huff's athletic ability should allow him to stick there.

THE FUTURE: Huff would benefit from more time in the minor leagues, but the Rangers are open to the idea of him starting the season in the majors. If Huff's hit tool develops, he could be a star. At minimum, he and Jose Trevino could be the Rangers' catching tandem for years to come.

SCOUTING GRADES: **Hitting:** 40 **Power:** 70 **Running:** 40 **Fielding:** 45 **Arm:** 60

Year	Age	Club (League)	Class	AVG	G	AB	R	H	2B	3B	HR	RBI	BB	SO	SB	OBP	SLG
2017	19	Rangers (AZL)	R	.249	49	197	34	49	9	2	9	31	24	66	3	.329	.452
2018	20	Hickory (SAL)	LoA	.241	118	415	53	100	22	3	18	55	23	140	9	.292	.439
2019	21	Hickory (SAL)	LoA	.333	30	108	22	36	5	0	15	29	6	37	4	.368	.796
	21	Down East (CAR)	HiA	.262	97	367	49	96	17	2	13	43	27	117	2	.326	.425
2020	22	Texas (AL)	MAJ	.355	10	31	5	11	3	0	3	4	2	11	0	.394	.742
Major League Totals				.355	10	31	5	11	3	0	3	4	2	11	0	.394	.742
Minor League Totals				.264	322	1184	177	313	63	8	56	175	96	389	18	.328	.473

3 LEODY TAVERAS, OF

DAVID DUROCHIK/MLB PHOTOS VIA GETTY IMAGES

Born: Sept. 8, 1998. **B-T:** S-R. **HT:** 6-2. **WT:** 195. **Signed:** Dominican Republic, 2015. **Signed by:** Willy Espinal/Gil Kim/Thad Levine.

TRACK RECORD: After zooming to short-season Spokane in his pro debut, Taveras began moving more methodically through the minors and spent a year and a half at high Class A before finishing 2019 at Double-A Frisco. Taveras' offense had stagnated, so it was somewhat surprising to see him crack the Rangers' Opening Day roster in 2020. He performed admirably for a 21-year-old with modest upper-level experience and spent the year as the Rangers' primary center fielder.

SCOUTING REPORT: Rangers officials credit Taveras for showing more exit velocity and lift in his swing in 2020, as well as the first double-digit walk rate of his career. He's normally a disciplined hitter and struck out more than expected in the majors, but that was associated with him being more aggressive on pitches he believed he could drive. The goal is to find a happy medium and help him be an average hitter with double-digit home run power. Taveras is a plus-plus runner and finished in the 94th percentile for MLB Statcast's sprint speed. Taveras uses that speed to be a plus defender in center field and boasts a plus arm.

THE FUTURE: If Taveras' bat continues to trend upward, he could be an impact player on both sides of the ball.

SCOUTING GRADES: **Hitting:** 50 **Power:** 40 **Running:** 70 **Fielding:** 60 **Arm:** 60

Year	Age	Club (League)	Class	AVG	G	AB	R	H	2B	3B	HR	RBI	BB	SO	SB	OBP	SLG
2017	18	Hickory (SAL)	LoA	.249	134	522	73	130	20	7	8	50	47	92	20	.312	.360
2018	19	Down East (CAR)	HiA	.246	132	521	65	128	16	7	5	48	51	96	19	.312	.332
2019	20	Frisco (TL)	AA	.265	65	264	32	70	12	4	3	31	23	60	11	.320	.375
	20	Down East (CAR)	HiA	.294	66	255	44	75	7	4	2	25	31	62	21	.368	.376
2020	21	Texas (AL)	MAJ	.227	33	119	20	27	6	1	4	6	14	43	8	.308	.395
Major League Totals				.227	33	119	20	27	6	1	4	6	14	43	8	.308	.395
Minor League Totals				.260	470	1868	256	486	69	28	19	187	177	365	89	.323	.358

4 DANE DUNNING, RHP

Born: Dec. 20, 1994. **B-T:** R-R. **HT:** 6-4. **WT:** 225. **Drafted:** Florida, 2016 (1st rd). **Signed by:** Buddy Hernandez (Nationals).

DAVID DUROCHIIK/MLB PHOTOS VIA GETTY IMAGES

BA GRADE
50 Risk: Medium

TRACK RECORD: The Nationals selected Dunning in the first round in 2016 and sent him to the White Sox with Lucas Giolito and Reynaldo Lopez for outfielder Adam Eaton that winter. Dunning missed all of 2019 recovering from Tommy John surgery, but he returned in 2020 and went 2-0, 3.97 in seven starts for the White Sox to solidify the back of their rotation. The Rangers acquired him with righthander Avery Weems for Lance Lynn after the season.

SCOUTING REPORT: Dunning was primarily a sinker/slider pitcher in college but has expanded his repertoire as a pro. He added a four-seam fastball and tweaked his curveball grip with help from former White Sox righthander James Shields. Along with his changeup, the enhancements gave Dunning a varied, five-pitch mix. Nothing is overpowering, but Dunning mixes and matches to keep hitters off balance. His 91-93 mph sinker and low-80s slider remain his primary weapons, and he throws his four-seam fastball, curveball and changeup enough to keep lefthanded batters guessing. His walk rate was a tick high in his major league debut, but he throws everything for strikes and has demonstrated above-average control throughout his career.

THE FUTURE: Dunning will begin 2021 in the Rangers' rotation. His arsenal, control and pitchability will keep him there.

SCOUTING GRADES: **Fastball:** 55 **Slider:** 60 **Changeup:** 55 **Curveball:** 50 **Control:** 55

Year	Age	Club (League)	Class	W	L	ERA	G	GS	IP	H	HR	BB	SO	BB/9	SO/9	WHIP	AVG
2017	22	Kannapolis (SAL)	LoA	2	0	0.35	4	4	26	13	0	2	33	0.7	11.4	0.58	.138
	22	Winston-Salem (CAR)	HiA	6	8	3.51	22	22	118	114	15	36	135	2.7	10.3	1.27	.223
2018	23	Birmingham (SL)	AA	5	2	2.76	11	11	62	57	0	23	69	3.3	10.0	1.29	.218
	23	Winston-Salem (CAR)	HiA	1	1	2.59	4	4	24	20	2	3	31	1.1	11.5	0.95	.204
2019	24	Did not play—Injured															
2020	25	Chicago (AL)	MAJ	2	0	3.97	7	7	34	25	4	13	35	3.4	9.3	1.12	.197
Major League Totals				2	0	3.97	7	7	34	25	4	13	35	3.4	9.3	1.12	.197
Minor League Totals				17	13	2.74	49	49	266	230	18	71	300	2.4	10.2	1.13	.229

5 COLE WINN, RHP

Born: Nov. 25, 1999. **B-T:** R-R. **HT:** 6-2. **WT:** 203. **Drafted:** HS—Orange, Calif., 2018 (1st round). **Signed by:** Steve Flores.

BA GRADE
55 Risk: Extreme

TRACK RECORD: The 2018 High School Player of the Year and a product of prep powerhouse Orange (Calif.) Lutheran, Winn was drafted 15th overall by the Rangers and experienced the ups and downs of many young pitchers during his first full season of pro ball. He posted a 4.46 ERA at low Class A Hickory in 2019, but rebounded in 2020 with a strong showing at the alternate training site before dominating hitters in instructional league.

SCOUTING REPORT: Everything the Rangers thought they were getting when they drafted Winn came to fruition in 2020. He pitched confidently at the alternate training site against much older hitters and showed improved stuff in instructional league. Winn's fastball now sits 93-97 mph with good vertical break. His plus curveball, which has always been his best secondary pitch, has been joined by an above-average slider and a developing changeup. Winn throws strikes, remains composed and is a diligent worker. He succeeded at processing lessons quickly and translating them into games.

THE FUTURE: A quality four-pitch mix could allow Winn to become a mid-rotation starter, but there's a long way to go to reach that ceiling. The Rangers plan to start him at high Class A and hope he quickly earns a bump to Double-A.

SCOUTING GRADES: **Fastball:** 60 **Slider:** 55 **Curveball:** 60 **Changeup:** 50 **Control:** 50

Year	Age	Club (League)	Class	W	L	ERA	G	GS	IP	H	HR	BB	SO	BB/9	SO/9	WHIP	AVG
2018	18	Did not play—Injured															
2019	19	Hickory (SAL)	LoA	4	4	4.46	18	18	69	59	5	39	65	5.1	8.5	1.43	.198
Minor League Totals				4	4	4.46	18	18	68	59	5	39	65	5.1	8.5	1.43	.233

6 JUSTIN FOSCUE, 2B

AARON CORNIA/MISSISSIPPI STATE ATHLETICS

BA GRADE

50 **Risk: High**

Born: March 2, 1999. **B-T:** R-R. **HT:** 6-0. **WT:** 205. **Drafted:** Mississippi State, 2020 (1st round). **Signed by:** Brian Morrison.

TRACK RECORD: Foscue had a stellar sophomore season at Mississippi State in 2019 and was the starting second baseman for USA Baseball's Collegiate National Team that summer. He was off to a blazing start in 2020 before the coronavirus pandemic cut the college season short. The Rangers drafted him 14th overall and signed him for $3.25 million, more than $725,000 under slot. Foscue spent the summer at the Rangers' alternate training site and finished in instructional league.

SCOUTING REPORT: Foscue was the second straight college hitter the Rangers selected in the first round, after drafting Josh Jung in 2019. Foscue is an offensive-oriented second baseman who has the potential to hit .280 with 25 homers. He doesn't have a prototypical swing and has struggled swinging a wood bat in the past, but he took to a few tweaks the Rangers suggested and earned high praise from team officials. He understands how pitchers will attack him, works counts and covers the entire strike zone. Foscue's offense is well ahead of his defense. He is a below-average runner and fringe-average defender who needs a lot of refinement.

THE FUTURE: Foscue has a chance to launch his pro career at Double-A with a strong showing in spring training.

SCOUTING GRADES: **Hitting:** 55 **Power:** 55 **Running:** 40 **Fielding:** 45 **Arm:** 45

Year	Age	Club (League)	Class	AVG	G	AB	R	H	2B	3B	HR	RBI	BB	SO	SB	OBP	SLG
2020	21	Did not play—No minor league season															

7 MAXIMO ACOSTA, SS

BILL MITCHELL

BA GRADE

50 **Risk: Extreme**

Born: Oct. 29, 2002. **B-T:** R-R. **HT:** 6-1. **WT:** 187. **Signed:** Venezuela, 2019. **Signed by:** Carlos Gonzalez/Jhonny Gomez/Rafic Saab.

TRACK RECORD: The Rangers signed Acosta for $1.65 million out of Venezuela as part of their touted 2019 international signing class. His pro debut was delayed by the pandemic, but he spent the fall as one of the youngest players in instructional league and earned raves from Rangers player development.

SCOUTING REPORT: Acosta has drawn comparisons with the Yankees' Gleyber Torres as a potential offensive star who plays up the middle. Acosta's bat produces plenty of line drives and consistently finds the barrel, and the belief is he will have 20-25-homer power once he matures. He recognizes pitches, controls the strike zone and has an all-fields approach that portends an above-average hitter. Somewhat surprisingly, the Rangers clocked Acosta as a below-average runner but expect that to improve once he's in full game shape. He does have a thicker lower half that will have to be maintained. Acosta overcomes his lack of speed defensively with excellent anticipation at shortstop and plus arm strength.

THE FUTURE: It's easy to get excited about Acosta, even though he hasn't made his official pro debut and still has a lot of developing to do. He will likely begin 2021 in the Rookie-level Arizona League.

SCOUTING GRADES: **Hitting:** 55 **Power:** 50 **Running:** 50 **Fielding:** 50 **Arm:** 60

Year	Age	Club (League)	Class	AVG	G	AB	R	H	2B	3B	HR	RBI	BB	SO	SB	OBP	SLG
2020	17	Did not play—No minor league season															

8 LUISANGEL ACUÑA, SS

BILL MITCHELL

BA GRADE

50 Risk: Extreme

Born: March 12, 2002. **B-T:** R-R. **HT:** 5-8. **WT:** 181. **Signed:** Venezuela, 2018. **Signed by:** Rafic Saab.

TRACK RECORD: The younger brother of Braves superstar Ronald Acuña Jr., Luisangel Acuña packs a big punch into a smaller package. He lit up the Dominican Summer League in 2019, hitting .342 with more walks than strikeouts as a 17-year-old, and his bat was among the loudest during 2020 instructional league.

SCOUTING REPORT: Ask Acuña Jr., and little brother is already hitting balls at 18 farther and harder than he did at the same age. Still, the Rangers aren't sure what will become of the 5-foot-8 Luisangel. Ronald underwent a late growth spurt that the Rangers hope filters down the family tree. If not, they know Luisangel can find the barrel and has a good idea of the strike zone. He's fearless in the box, can hit velocity and projects to reach 15-20 homers at his current size. He does need work on hitting spin. Acuña needs reps defensively, and the Rangers worked him at third base and second base in addition to shortstop, which is a crowded position in the system. He has the range and arm to play around the infield.

THE FUTURE: Aggressive as always, the Rangers are planning for Acuña to open 2021 at low Class A. He might not be as good as his older brother, but his bat and potential defensive versatility give him a chance to join him in the majors.

SCOUTING GRADES: **Hitting:** 55 **Power:** 45 **Running:** 55 **Fielding:** 50 **Arm:** 60

Year	Age	Club (League)	Class	AVG	G	AB	R	H	2B	3B	HR	RBI	BB	SO	SB	OBP	SLG
2019	17	Rangers1 (DSL)	R	.342	51	202	61	69	11	3	2	29	34	26	17	.438	.455
Minor League Totals				.342	51	202	61	69	11	3	2	29	34	26	17	.438	.455

9 HANS CROUSE, RHP

BA GRADE

50 Risk: Extreme

Born: Sept. 15, 1998. **B-T:** R-R. **HT:** 6-5. **WT:** 208. **Drafted:** HS—Dana Point, Calif., 2017 (2nd round). **Signed by:** Steve Flores.

TRACK RECORD: Crouse has been one of the Rangers' most electric pitchers since they selected him 66th overall in 2017, but injuries have slowed him. He pitched with bone spurs in his elbow in 2019, which cost him a month of the season, and did not participate at the Rangers' alternate training site or in instructional league in 2020 because of undisclosed personal issues. The Rangers kept tabs on Crouse as he worked out on his own.

SCOUTING REPORT: Crouse didn't wow anyone in 2019 as he pitched through his injured elbow, but he showed drive as he kept pitching and putting innings on his shoulder. Crouse's fastball is his calling card. It's a four-seamer that sits 92-97 mph, but he also shows the ability to sink it. His slider is a plus pitch that generates plenty of swings and misses. With his elbow limiting his ability to throw breaking balls in 2019, he developed a changeup that is potentially above-average. Crouse remains a max-effort pitcher with a high motor, but he has toned down his delivery since making his pro debut and shows average control.

THE FUTURE: Crouse's combination of power and feel makes him a potential mid-rotation starter, but he has to show he's healthy. He has a chance to see Double-A in 2021.

SCOUTING GRADES: **Fastball:** 60 **Slider:** 60 **Changeup:** 55 **Control:** 50

Year	Age	Club (League)	Class	W	L	ERA	G	GS	IP	H	HR	BB	SO	BB/9	SO/9	WHIP	AVG
2017	18	Rangers (AZL)	R	0	0	0.45	10	6	20	7	1	7	30	3.2	13.5	0.70	.095
2018	19	Hickory (SAL)	LoA	0	2	2.70	5	5	17	18	1	8	15	4.3	8.1	1.56	.237
	19	Spokane (NWL)	SS	5	1	2.37	8	8	38	25	2	11	47	2.6	11.1	0.95	.166
2019	20	Hickory (SAL)	LoA	6	1	4.41	19	19	88	86	12	19	76	2.0	7.8	1.20	.234
Minor League Totals				11	4	3.27	42	38	162	136	16	45	168	2.5	9.3	1.11	.224

10 ANDERSON TEJEDA, SS

DAVID DUROCHIIK/MLB PHOTOS VIA GETTY IMAGES

BA GRADE
45 **Risk: High**

Born: May 1, 1998. **B-T:** S-R. **HT:** 6-0. **WT:** 200. **Signed:** Dominican Republic, 2014. **Signed by:** Roberto Aquino/Rodolfo Rosario.

TRACK RECORD: After missing almost all of 2019 with a separated shoulder, Tejeda reclaimed his status as a top prospect in 2020. He began the year at the alternate training site and impressed enough to earn his first major league callup despite not having played above high Class A. Tejeda made his debut in August and took over as the Rangers' primary shortstop in September.

SCOUTING REPORT: The Rangers have few concerns about Tejeda's defense. He can make all the plays at shortstop, particularly in the hole, and his plus-plus arm allows him to make throws most others cannot. Tejeda is a natural lefthanded hitter who recently began switch-hitting. He has natural loft in his swing, which will translate into big power for a middle infielder, if he can make enough contact. Tejeda is a free swinger and was too aggressive for major league pitchers, who didn't have to throw pitches in the strike zone to get him out. Pitchers will make life tough on him as long as he continues to chase.

THE FUTURE: Tejeda did plenty of good things in his major league debut but remains raw at the plate. With Isiah Kiner-Falefa moving from third base to shortstop, Tejeda will likely start 2021 back in the minors.

SCOUTING GRADES: **Hitting:** 40 **Power:** 55 **Running:** 50 **Fielding:** 70 **Arm:** 60

Year	Age	Club (League)	Class	AVG	G	AB	R	H	2B	3B	HR	RBI	BB	SO	SB	OBP	SLG
2017	19	Hickory (SAL)	LoA	.247	115	401	68	99	24	9	8	53	36	132	10	.309	.411
2018	20	Down East (CAR)	HiA	.259	121	467	76	121	17	5	19	74	49	142	11	.331	.439
2019	21	Down East (CAR)	HiA	.234	43	158	22	37	10	1	4	24	17	58	9	.315	.386
2020	22	Texas (AL)	MAJ	.253	23	75	7	19	4	1	3	8	2	30	4	.273	.453
Major League Totals				.253	23	75	7	19	4	1	3	8	2	30	4	.273	.453
Minor League Totals				.265	400	1500	248	397	84	31	45	238	145	454	46	.332	.452

11 BAYRON LORA, OF

BA GRADE
50 **Risk: Extreme**

Born: Sept. 29, 2002. **B-T:** R-R. **HT:** 6-5. **WT:** 240. **Signed:** Dominican Republic, 2019. **Signed by:** Willy Espinal.

TRACK RECORD: Lora was the top power hitter in the 2019 international signing class when he signed with the Rangers for $3.9 million. His pro debut was delayed when the coronavirus pandemic canceled the 2020 minor league season. Lora got on the field for instructional league after the season but was limited by a wrist injury.

SCOUTING REPORT: Those who worship exit velocity will go crazy for Lora, who produces readings of 115 mph. His batting practice sessions are comparable to those of the best power hitters in the game. His power is rooted in a good foundation, natural sequencing and plenty of leverage and torque. His massive size doesn't hurt, either, and the Rangers were encouraged by how well Lora took care of himself during the shutdown. While there was some concern Lora might grow too big and be limited to a designated hitter, the Rangers believe he can play right field. He's a below-average defender with below-average speed and will have to watch his weight. His arm strength is average, but accuracy needs work.

THE FUTURE: As long as his wrist is healthy, Lora should make his pro debut in 2021. He is likely to skip the Dominican Summer League and open in the Rookie-level Arizona League.

Year	Age	Club (League)	Class	AVG	G	AB	R	H	2B	3B	HR	RBI	BB	SO	SB	OBP	SLG
2020	17	Did not play—No minor league season															

12 SHERTEN APOSTEL, 1B

BA GRADE
45 **Risk: High**

Born: March 11, 1999. **B-T:** R-R. **HT:** 6-4. **WT:** 235. **Signed:** Curacao, 2015. **Signed by:** Rene Gayo/Juan Mercado/Mark VanZanten (Pirates).

TRACK RECORD: Acquired as the player to be named later in the Keone Kela trade with the Pirates in 2018, Apostel joined catcher Sam Huff, shortstop Anderson Tejeda and lefthander John King as players who jumped from high Class A straight to the majors in 2020. He went 2-for-20 with nine strikeouts in his debut and was understandably not quite ready.

SCOUTING REPORT: Apostel is a large man with power in his bat, and the Rangers see some quality hitting tools, too. Apostel understands the strike zone and looks to do damage when the ball is in the zone, though he is much more productive against lefthanders than righties. His power is to all fields. The main question is where Apostel ends up on defense. He moves well at third base with quick reactions and good range and has a plus arm. A switch to first base could be in the works because of the presence of Josh Jung and lack of depth at first base in the organization. Apostel logged time at first against lefthanders in his debut.

THE FUTURE: Apostel will begin 2021 back in the minors. He may get regular at-bats in the majors depending on how incumbent first baseman Ronald Guzman produces.

Year	Age	Club (League)	Class	AVG	G	AB	R	H	2B	3B	HR	RBI	BB	SO	SB	OBP	SLG
2020	21	Texas (AL)	MAJ	.100	7	20	1	2	1	0	0	0	1	9	0	.143	.150
Major League Totals				.100	7	20	1	2	1	0	0	0	1	9	0	.143	.150
Minor League Totals				.249	283	963	158	240	45	7	37	152	172	280	10	.368	.426

13 RONNY HENRIQUEZ, RHP

BA GRADE
45 **Risk: High**

Born: June 20, 2000. **B-T:** R-R. **HT:** 5-10. **WT:** 165. **Signed:** Dominican Republic, 2017. **Signed by:** Willy Espinal.

TRACK RECORD: A converted outfielder who signed for just $10,000, Henriquez had a sterling debut in the Dominican Summer League before hitting a few bumps in an aggressive assignment to low Class A Hickory in 2019. His only 2020 action came during instructional league.

SCOUTING REPORT: Henriquez might not look the part at 5-foot-10, but the Little Engine That Could stands out as a premium strike-thrower with the best delivery in the system. His fastball sits in the mid-90s, but it tends to be flat and plays down from its raw velocity, so he has worked to try to get more vertical movement to his heater. Henriquez's real weapons are his plus slider and a changeup that has flashed plus. He has a knack for controlling his emotions and staying calm when trouble arises.

THE FUTURE: Henriquez will likely never be a 200-inning starting pitcher but he may be able to cover 150-180 innings. The biggest test will be to see if his stuff, namely his fastball, is good enough once he gets to Double-A.

Year	Age	Club (League)	Class	W	L	ERA	G	GS	IP	H	HR	BB	SO	BB/9	K/9	WHIP	AVG
2019	19	Hickory (SAL)	LoA	6	6	4.50	21	19	82	91	6	27	99	3.0	10.9	1.44	.284
Minor League Totals				11	6	3.28	32	30	140	128	8	35	178	2.3	11.4	1.16	.242

14 DAVIS WENDZEL, 3B/2B

BA GRADE
45 **Risk: High**

Born: May 23, 1997. **B-T:** R-R. **HT:** 6-0. **WT:** 205. **Signed:** Baylor, 2019 (1st round supplemental). **Signed by:** Josh Simpson.

TRACK RECORD: Wendzel won the Big-12 Conference co-player of the year award with Josh Jung in 2019. The Rangers drafted both when they selected Jung eighth overall and Wendzel 41st overall after the season. Wendzel got into only seven games after signing, but he spent time at the alternate training site in 2020 and finished in instructional league.

SCOUTING REPORT: Wendzel's instincts at the plate and defensive versatility stand out the most about him. He controls the strike zone and makes quality swing decisions, which results in hard contact. The Rangers are confident he will rap plenty of doubles and believe there are more homers in his bat than they did a year ago. His defense isn't an issue, other than finding him a spot. He can play second base, third base and shortstop at an average clip as well as across the outfield. He played some center at the alternate site. He has the plus arm to fit in multiple spots.

THE FUTURE: Wendzel's status as a polished college hitter should serve him well. He has a chance to move quickly alongside fellow top picks Jung and Justin Foscue.

Year	Age	Club (League)	Class	AVG	G	AB	R	H	2B	3B	HR	RBI	BB	SO	SB	OBP	SLG
2019	22	Rangers (AZL)	R	.444	4	9	4	4	1	0	1	2	2	3	0	.545	.889
	22	Spokane (NWL)	SS	.200	3	10	4	2	0	0	0	0	3	3	2	.385	.200
Minor League Totals				.316	7	19	8	6	1	0	1	2	5	6	2	.458	.526

15 STEELE WALKER, OF

BA GRADE
45 Risk: High

Born: July 30, 1996. **B-T:** L-L. **HT:** 5-11. **WT:** 190. **Drafted:** Oklahoma, 2018 (2nd round). **Signed by:** Rob Cummings (White Sox).

TRACK RECORD: A native of Prosper, Texas, Walker was one of college baseball's top hitters at Oklahoma when the White Sox drafted him 41st overall in 2018. The Rangers acquired him for Nomar Mazara at the 2019 Winter Meetings. Walker joined the alternate training site in September and showed off an experienced, polished offensive game.

SCOUTING REPORT: Walker has a solid track record of hitting. He has an advanced approach and good plate discipline. He has excellent hand-eye coordination and hits the ball hard back up the middle and to right field. He has average power with enough natural lift in his swing to find gaps and clear fences. The power he has now is to his pull side. Though athletic enough to play center field, Walker projects as a solid right fielder. He's very confident, which has led some to see aloofness from time to time and questions about if he will bring his best every day.

THE FUTURE: Walker does a lot of things well, which makes the Rangers confident he will be a major league contributor sooner rather than later. He will likely open 2021 at Double A Frisco, only miles from his hometown.

Year	Age	Club (League)	Class	AVG	G	AB	R	H	2B	3B	HR	RBI	BB	SO	SB	OBP	SLG
2019	22	Kannapolis (SAL)	LoA	.365	20	74	6	27	10	3	0	11	8	15	4	.437	.581
	22	Winston-Salem (CAR)	HiA	.269	100	383	59	103	26	2	10	51	42	63	9	.346	.426
Minor League Totals				.265	164	615	82	163	42	5	15	83	60	115	19	.338	.423

16 EVAN CARTER, OF

BREAKOUT
BA GRADE
50 Risk: Extreme

Born: Aug. 29, 2002. **B-T:** L-R. **HT:** 6-4. **WT:** 190. **Drafted:** HS—Elizabethton, Tenn., 2020 (2nd round). **Signed by:** Derrick Tucker/Ryan Coe.

TRACK RECORD: The Rangers shocked the industry when they drafted Carter with the 50th overall pick in 2020. He signed for a below-slot $1.25 million to forgo a Duke commitment. The Rangers believed the prep outfielder would have been a big riser had the high school season not been canceled. Carter made that belief look prescient with an impressive showing at instructional league.

SCOUTING REPORT: The Rangers see five-tool potential in Carter, who was only 17 when drafted. He already hits for power, something assisted by how well he commands the strike zone, and should only get stronger as he physically matures. Carter posted a .304/.467/.446 slash line at instructs with as many walks as strikeouts. The Rangers believe Carter can add another 25 pounds to a long-levered frame that already passes the eye test. Carter has above-average speed and the athletic ability to play center field, where he already projects as above-average.

THE FUTURE: The Rangers plan to send Carter to low Class A Hickory to start 2021. He could be a draft steal if he lives up to the expectations created at instructs.

Year	Age	Club (League)	Class	AVG	G	AB	R	H	2B	3B	HR	RBI	BB	SO	SB	OBP	SLG
2020	17	Did not play—No minor league season															

17 DAVID GARCIA, C

BA GRADE
50 Risk: Extreme

Born: Feb. 6, 2000. **B-T:** S-R. **HT:** 5-11. **WT:** 2000. **Signed:** Venezuela, 2016. **Signed by:** Rafic Saab/Jhonny Gomez.

TRACK RECORD: Several clubs considered Garcia the top catcher in the 2016 international class when the Rangers signed him for $800,000. Garcia has moved slowly and is yet to play above short-season ball, but the Rangers opted to add him to their 40-man roster after the 2020 season.

SCOUTING REPORT: The switch-hitting Garcia has a good idea of the strike zone for his age. That allows him to be a line-drive, gap-to-gap hitter and fairly equal from both sides of the plate. Garcia isn't much of a power threat, and what power he does have is to the pull side. His bat is behind his defense, which is the best among catchers in the system and will be his ticket to the big leagues. He is an above-average receiver who moves well with quick footwork. He has an above-average, accurate arm that has allowed him to throw out 35 percent of attempted basestealers in his career.

THE FUTURE: Garcia will jump to full-season ball in 2021. He will try to distance himself from a pack of catchers system-wide and take the lead in the race to be Sam Huff's future backup.

Year	Age	Club (League)	Class	AVG	G	AB	R	H	2B	3B	HR	RBI	BB	SO	SB	OBP	SLG
2019	19	Spokane (NWL)	SS	.277	48	184	33	51	14	0	5	29	21	42	1	.351	.435
Minor League Totals				.252	140	489	70	123	29	1	7	75	55	117	2	.332	.358

18 RICKY VANASCO, RHP

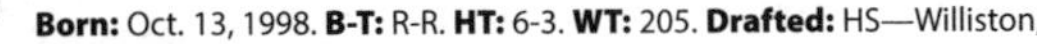

Born: Oct. 13, 1998. **B-T:** R-R. **HT:** 6-3. **WT:** 205. **Drafted:** HS—Williston, Fla., 2017 (15th round). **Signed by:** Brett Campbell.

TRACK RECORD: The Rangers signed Vanasco for an above-slot $200,000 as a 15th-round pick in 2017 after he created some buzz during Florida prep showcases. He quickly impressed with a 2.38 ERA through his first three professional seasons and pitched well at the Rangers alternate training site in 2020, but he suffered a torn elbow ligament and had Tommy John surgery in September.

SCOUTING REPORT: Vanasco's fastball velocity jumped to 94-98 mph in 2019 and he maintained it into 2020 after an offseason focus on adding quality weight. Once he arrived at the alternate site, he showed an 82-86 mph power curveball that remains his best offspeed pitch and a potentially average slider at 89-91 mph. He started to show the feel for an average changeup, which clocked 88-90 mph. Vanasco has the potential for four quality pitches, but he has below-average control and still needs to learn how to pitch as opposed to just throw. That comes only through reps, which he won't get until he returns from surgery.

THE FUTURE: Vanasco will miss all of 2021 recovering from surgery. He was trending toward a mid-rotation starter, but now must wait to see how his stuff comes back when he returns.

Year	Age	Club (League)	Class	W	L	ERA	G	GS	IP	H	HR	BB	SO	BB/9	K/9	WHIP	AVG
2019	20	Spokane (NWL)	SS	3	1	1.85	9	9	39	23	2	22	59	5.1	13.6	1.15	.173
	20	Hickory (SAL)	LoA	0	0	1.69	2	2	11	5	0	3	16	2.5	13.5	0.75	.143
Minor League Totals				6	5	2.38	28	14	83	61	3	43	116	4.6	12.5	1.25	.210

19 OWEN WHITE, RHP

BA GRADE
50 Risk: Extreme

Born: Aug. 9, 1999. **B-T:** R-R. **HT:** 6-3. **WT:** 200. **Drafted:** HS—China Grove, N.C., 2018 (2nd round). **Signed by:** Jay Heafner.

TRACK RECORD: The Rangers drafted White in the second round in 2018 and gave him an above-slot $1.5 million to pass up a South Carolina commitment. To date, that is the most noteworthy part of his professional career. White has not pitched in an official game in three seasons since signing. The Rangers rested him after the draft and he blew out his elbow in 2019, requiring season-ending Tommy John surgery. He did return to pitch in 2020 instructional league.

SCOUTING REPORT: Despite the missed time, White has starter written all over him. He features a four-pitch mix topped by a fastball that sat 93-97 mph during instructs. His best offspeed pitch is a 78-80 mph curveball with plus potential, and he throws an 83-87 mph slider and 84-87 mph changeup that flash average. Best of all, he throws a lot of strikes. He was a terrific prep athlete who is learning to repeat his delivery. He also fields his position well and keeps runners close.

THE FUTURE: The Rangers plan to send White to low Class A Hickory to open 2021. As he continues to develop his body and gain reps, his ceiling could be a mid-rotation starter.

Year	Age	Club (League)	Class	W	L	ERA	G	GS	IP	H	HR	BB	SO	BB/9	SO/9	WHIP	AVG
2019	19	Did not play—Injured															

20 KYLE CODY, RHP

BA GRADE
45 Risk: High

Born: Aug. 9, 1994. **B-T:** R-R. **HT:** 6-7. **WT:** 225. **Drafted:** Kentucky, 2016 (6th round). **Signed by:** Mike Medici.

TRACK RECORD: Cody was a fast riser in the Rangers' system before an elbow injury that eventually required Tommy John surgery in 2018. He returned in 2020, pitched well at the alternate training site and earned his first major league callup in late August. After beginning in the bullpen, Cody moved into the Rangers rotation and posted a 1.96 ERA in five starts, albeit with too many walks.

SCOUTING REPORT: Cody mostly relies on his 94-97 mph fastball and a plus slider that is the best in the Rangers system. His 83-86 mph slider is his primary pitch and has elite vertical movement, which major league hitters never adjusted to were nearly helpless against. Cody also has a changeup that should be an average pitch and possibly more. Like many tall pitchers, the 6-foot-7 Cody has trouble controlling his long limbs and has firmly below-average control. Though he checked all the health boxes in 2020, the Rangers are concerned about how many innings he can handle in 2021.

THE FUTURE: Cody is going to pitch in the major leagues in 2021. How much he pitches, and in what role, will be determined by his health and how much he improves his control.

Year	Age	Club (League)	Class	W	L	ERA	G	GS	IP	H	HR	BB	SO	BB/9	SO/9	WHIP	AVG
2020	25	Texas (AL)	MAJ	1	1	1.59	8	5	23	15	1	13	18	5.2	7.1	1.24	.190
Major League Totals				1	1	1.59	8	5	22	15	1	13	18	5.2	7.2	1.24	.190
Minor League Totals				11	11	3.23	37	34	178	160	8	57	198	2.9	10.0	1.22	.238

21 DEMARCUS EVANS, RHP

Born: Oct. 22, 1996. **B-T:** R-R. **HT:** 6-5. **WT:** 265. **Drafted:** HS—Petal, Miss., 2015 (25th round). **Signed by:** Brian Morrison.

TRACK RECORD: An unheralded 25th-round high school pick in 2015, Evans broke out as one of the most dominant relievers in the minors in back-to-back seasons in 2018 and 2019, capped by an ERA of 0.96 in 30 appearances at Double-A. He seemed like an easy choice to be in the Rangers' bullpen early in 2020, but instead spent most of the season at the alternate training site and made four brief appearances in September.

SCOUTING REPORT: Evans was never far away from the major leagues in 2020 but needed to refine some things. He works with a 92-96 mph fastball with an elite spin rate and 22 inches of vertical movement, making it a plus-plus pitch that plays beyond its pure velocity. It's a nasty pitch at the top of the strike zone and one he can dominate with. The Rangers asked him to focus on improving his below-average control, adding depth to his 82-86 mph curveball and bettering his mental approach while at the alternate site. Those things had been remedied by the time he debuted and helped him retire 11 of the 14 batters he faced.

THE FUTURE: With the Rangers in rebuild mode, Evans is a strong candidate to make the team out of spring training. If his command remains dialed in, he could work in high-leverage situations for years to come.

Year	Age	Club (League)	Class	W	L	ERA	G	GS	IP	H	HR	BB	SO	BB/9	SO/9	WHIP	AVG
2020	23	Texas (AL)	MAJ	0	0	2.25	4	0	4	3	1	0	4	0.0	9.0	0.75	.231
Major League Totals				0	0	2.25	4	0	4	3	1	0	4	0.0	9.0	0.75	.231
Minor League Totals				13	11	2.53	125	26	242	147	7	149	369	5.5	13.7	1.22	.173

22 JOE PALUMBO, LHP

BA GRADE
45 Risk: Very High

Born: Oct. 26, 1994. **B-T:** L-L. **HT:** 6-1. **WT:** 190. **Drafted:** HS—West Islip, N.Y., 2013 (30th round). **Signed by:** Takeshi Sakurayama.

TRACK RECORD: After making his major league debut in 2019, Palumbo made the Opening Day roster for the first time in his career in 2020, though as a reliever. As has been the case in his past chances in the majors, it didn't last long because of a health issue.

SCOUTING REPORT: For every step forward Palumbo takes, he seems to take two back with health issues. He arrived for spring training in 2020 having gained weight and strength and was healthy for summer camp. However, a significant bout with ulcerative colitis ended his season after only two appearances. Palumbo has a 92-94 mph fastball and a 77-80 mph curveball that makes life hard on lefthanded hitters. His third pitch is an average changeup. But he hasn't put it all together in the majors, in part because of below-average control and largely due to injury and a lack of reps since having Tommy John surgery in 2017. Durability is a major concern as he enters his age-26 season.

THE FUTURE: If Palumbo can manage his ulcerative colitis and find a way to maintain his weight and strength, he will contribute in 2021. The stuff is there to be a quality pitcher, but health remains an issue.

Year	Age	Club (League)	Class	W	L	ERA	G	GS	IP	H	HR	BB	SO	BB/9	SO/9	WHIP	AVG
2020	25	Texas (AL)	MAJ	0	1	11.57	2	0	2	3	1	3	5	11.6	19.3	2.57	.273
Major League Totals				0	4	9.47	9	4	19	24	8	11	26	5.2	12.3	1.84	.296
Minor League Totals				21	17	2.72	104	53	357	271	21	139	425	3.5	10.7	1.15	.207

23 CHRIS SEISE, SS

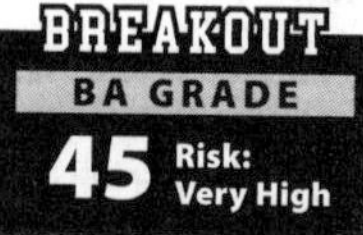

Born: Jan. 6, 1999. **B-T:** R-R. **HT:** 6-2. **WT:** 200. **Drafted:** HS—Winter Garden, Fla., 2017 (1st round). **Signed by:** Brett Campbell.

TRACK RECORD: The 29th overall pick in the 2017 draft, Seise has played just 72 career games in three seasons due to an assortment shoulder injuries. He missed all of 2018 after having rotator cuff surgery on his right shoulder and suffered a season-ending torn labrum in his left shoulder just 21 games into 2019. Seise returned healthy in 2020, and was one of the Rangers' best players in instructional league.

SCOUTING REPORT: Seise is a physical specimen with a major league body. It's that way because he has worked relentlessly to make sure his injury woes are a thing of the past. Physically, Seise can do everything on the field. He stings the ball hard and posted a top exit velocity of 111.1 mph at instructs, along with a .944 OPS. After three seasons with limited game action he does have holes pitchers can exploit, but he has the athleticism and intelligence to close them as he gets more reps. The Rangers see Seise as a shortstop with his plus speed, above-average hands and average arm. He ranges well to both sides and gets good reads off the bat.

THE FUTURE: The Rangers system is loaded with shortstops. If Seise can stay healthy, he could be the best of the bunch.

Year	Age	Club (League)	Class	AVG	G	AB	R	H	2B	3B	HR	RBI	BB	SO	SB	OBP	SLG
2019	20	Hickory (SAL)	LoA	.241	21	87	12	21	4	3	0	6	3	33	6	.272	.356
Minor League Totals				.272	72	302	45	82	12	7	3	42	16	93	12	.314	.387

24 A.J. ALEXY, RHP

BA GRADE
40 Risk: High

Born: April 21, 1998. **B-T:** R-R. **HT:** 6-4. **WT:** 235. **Drafted:** HS--Honey Brook, Pa., 2016 (11th round). **Signed by:** Rich Delucia (Dodgers).

TRACK RECORD: One of three players acquired from the Dodgers in the Yu Darvish trade, Alexy made only five starts for low Class A Hickory in 2019 before he suffered a season-ending strained lat and received a platelet-rich plasma injection. He was not invited to the alternate training site in 2020, but showed enough during instructional league that the Rangers added him to the 40-man roster in order to protect him from the Rule 5 draft.

SCOUTING REPORT: Alexy's bread and butter is his 94-98 mph fastball with big vertical movement. When his curveball is right, it's a nasty pitch with big 12-to-6 break. The pitch doesn't always hold its shape, but it's his best secondary offering. Alexy also has a feel for a fringy but usable changeup. Whether he can improve his below-average control will make or break Alexy's bid to be a starter. He impressed the Rangers with the dedication he showed during the shutdown, staying in Arizona to work on the mechanical side of things and also gain a better understanding of how to pitch.

THE FUTURE: Alexy will continue starting for now. His future is likely as a reliever, where his power fastball-curveball combination could be devastating in short bursts.

Year	Age	Club (League)	Class	W	L	ERA	G	GS	IP	H	HR	BB	SO	BB/9	SO/9	WHIP	AVG
2019	21	Down East (CAR)	HiA	0	3	5.12	5	5	19	14	1	13	23	6.1	10.7	1.40	.165
Minor League Totals				10	18	3.75	58	52	235	179	14	120	286	4.6	10.9	1.27	.214

25 AVERY WEEMS, RHP

BA GRADE
40 Risk: High

Born: June 6, 1997. **B-T:** R-L. **HT:** 6-2. **WT:** 205. **Drafted:** Arizona, 2019 (6th round). **Signed by:** John Kazanas (White Sox).

TRACK RECORD: After starting his career at Yavapai (Ariz.) JC, Weems transferred to Arizona and spent two seasons shuffling between the rotation and bullpen. The White Sox signed him for $10,000 as a senior sign and watched dominate out of the rotation at the Rookie levels. The Rangers acquired Weems with Dane Dunning for Lance Lynn after the 2020 season.

SCOUTING REPORT: Weems has taken a jump in pro ball and impressed evaluators with his performance at instructional league prior to the trade. His four-seam fastball sits 90-94 mph and has touched as high as 96. He pairs his heater with a potentially plus, low-80s curveball with 1-to-7 break as well as a mid-80s slider with slurvy shape. He also has a changeup and two-seamer. Weems' holds his velocity late into his outings and has improved his command after struggling with it in college.

THE FUTURE: Weems could be a quick mover through the lower levels of the system. He'll start for now, but questions about his command and consistency have most projecting him as a reliever long-term.

Year	Age	Club (League)	Class	W	L	ERA	G	GS	IP	H	HR	BB	SO	BB/9	SO/9	WHIP	AVG
2019	22	Great Falls (PIO)	R	4	3	2.47	10	10	47	43	1	7	60	1.3	11.4	1.06	.228
	22	White Sox (AZL)	R	1	1	0.69	4	4	13	10	0	3	14	2.1	9.7	1.00	.196
Minor League Totals				5	4	2.09	14	14	60	53	1	10	74	1.5	11.0	1.04	.235

26 BUBBA THOMPSON, OF

BA GRADE **40** Risk: High

Born: June 9, 1998. **B-T:** R-R. **HT:** 6-2. **WT:** 200. **Drafted:** HS—Mobile, Ala., 2017 (1st round). **Signed by:** Brian Morrison.

TRACK RECORD: The 26th overall pick in 2017, Thompson endured a 2019 to forget at high Class A Down East. A broken hamate bone knocked him out for two months, then he missed another month after running into an outfield wall and hit .178 in 57 games. He bounced back somewhat in the Arizona Fall League after the season and spent the final month of 2020 at the Rangers alternate training site.

SCOUTING REPORT: A football standout in high school, Thompson is the best pure athlete in the Rangers system. He has big power, plus-plus speed and is a plus defender in center field. The question is if Thompson can hit. He is a well below-average hitter with way too many swings and misses and little consistency from at-bat to at-bat. He needs to clean up his swing path and is trying to do that by staying connected. The Rangers want Thompson's swing on a better plane and for it to stay in the zone longer to create more margin for error. The good news is that he wants to be great and is willing to work for it.

THE FUTURE: Thompson has ability, but he needs to make significant improvements as a hitter to project as even a major league reserve. He'll try to do that in 2021.

Year	Age	Club (League)	Class	AVG	G	AB	R	H	2B	3B	HR	RBI	BB	SO	SB	OBP	SLG
2019	21	Down East (CAR)	HiA	.178	57	202	24	36	8	2	5	21	21	72	12	.261	.312
Minor League Totals				.249	171	647	99	161	33	9	16	75	50	204	49	.313	.402

27 KEITHRON MOSS, 2B

BREAKOUT

BA GRADE **45** Risk: Extreme

Born: Aug. 20, 2001. **B-T:** B-R. **HT:** 5-10. **WT:** 185. **Signed:** Bahamas, 2017. **Signed by:** Cliff Terracuso/Ross Fenstermaker.

TRACK RECORD: Moss signed with the Rangers for $800,000 out of the burgeoning baseball hotbed of The Bahamas. After struggling in his pro debut in the Dominican Summer League, Moss found his form in year two and hit .308/.425/.442 while earning plaudits as one of the best prospects in the Rookie-level Arizona League. He returned in 2020 during instructional league.

SCOUTING REPORT: Consider Moss a sleeper in the system, with speed and power to dream on offensively. He's freakishly strong for his size and hits balls out without finding the barrel. That power was on display during instructional league and earned him comparisons to Ray Durham. A switch-hitter, Moss has become more comfortable from the left-side, where he sees the ball better, but is a natural righthanded hitter. While Moss can play third base, the thought is he ends up as a second baseman due to his fringe-average arm.

THE FUTURE: Moss' offensive potential is exciting, but he still has to prove it outside of the complex leagues. He'll get the chance at low Class A in 2021.

Year	Age	Club (League)	Class	AVG	G	AB	R	H	2B	3B	HR	RBI	BB	SO	SB	OBP	SLG
2019	17	Rangers (AZL)	R	.308	34	120	27	37	4	3	2	14	21	40	8	.425	.442
Minor League Totals				.244	85	283	56	69	15	4	2	37	56	102	16	.381	.346

28 YERRY RODRIGUEZ, RHP

BA GRADE **40** Risk: High

Born: Oct. 15, 1997. **B-T:** R-R. **HT:** 6-2. **WT:** 215. **Signed:** Dominican Republic, 2015. **Signed by:** Willy Espinal.

TRACK RECORD: Signed for $60,000 out of the Dominican Republic, Rodriguez spent three years in short-season ball before breaking out with low Class A Hickory in 2019. He went 7-3, 2.08 in 13 starts and earned South Atlantic League all-star honors, but an elbow injury ended his season in July. Though the Rangers didn't bring Rodriguez to their alternate training site in 2020, they added him to the 40-man roster after the season.

SCOUTING REPORT: Rodriguez's fastball sits at 92-96 mph, which is a tick above-average, but its high spin rate makes it a plus pitch, to the point where he often dominated lower level hitters in 2019 with just that pitch. Rodriguez's secondary pitches are the concern. His fringe-average curveball is slurvy and his changeup is average, at best. Rodriguez has a unique ability to manipulate the ball and throws all of his pitches for strikes with above-average control.

THE FUTURE: Rodriguez's secondary pitches must improve for him to stay in the mix as a starting pitcher. He more likely ends up as a multi-inning reliever in the majors.

Year	Age	Club (League)	Class	W	L	ERA	G	GS	IP	H	HR	BB	SO	BB/9	SO/9	WHIP	AVG
2019	21	Hickory (SAL)	LoA	7	3	2.08	13	13	74	45	5	21	85	2.6	10.4	0.90	.159
Minor League Totals				17	8	2.42	43	30	193	164	8	40	208	1.9	9.7	1.06	.228

29 ALEX SPEAS, RHP

BA GRADE
45 **Risk: Extreme**

Born: March 4, 1998. **B-T:** R-R. **HT:** 6-3. **WT:** 225. **Drafted:** HS—Powder Springs, Ga., 2016 (2nd round). **Signed by:** Derrick Tucker.

TRACK RECORD: Speas had Tommy John surgery in 2018 and came back throwing 102 mph when he returned. The Rangers brought him to the alternate training site in 2020 but left him unprotected for the Rule 5 draft, reasoning a team could take a flier on Speas but would ultimately return him after witnessing some of his flaws, and he went undrafted.

SCOUTING REPORT: Speas can throw as hard as any pitcher in the Rangers system. He routinely touches 100 mph, the result of lightning-quick arm speed and an explosive lower half. His slider is above-average and he has the feel for a changeup. Speas' issue is finding the strike zone, which he hasn't done adequately pre- or post-surgery. His strike percentage was only 45% between the alternate training site and instructional league, well below-average control that won't play even in relief.

THE FUTURE: The Rangers will continue working with Speas on his control. If he finds it—and that's a big if—he could become a bullpen force.

Year	Age	Club (League)	Class	W	L	ERA	G	GS	IP	H	HR	BB	SO	BB/9	SO/9	WHIP	AVG
2019	21	Rangers (AZL)	R	0	0	0.00	2	2	1	1	0	2	2	18.0	18.0	3.00	.167
Minor League Totals				3	6	3.77	42	12	71	50	6	55	107	6.9	13.4	1.47	.188

30 TYLER PHILLIPS, RHP

Born: Oct. 27, 1997. **B-T:** R-R. **HT:** 6-5. **WT:** 225. **Drafted:** HS—Pennsauken, N.J., 2015 (16th round). **Signed by:** Takeshi Sakurayama.

TRACK RECORD: Phillips reached Double-A Frisco in 2019 and the Rangers added him to the 40-man roster after the season, but he was one of the few 40-man players who did play in the majors for the Rangers in 2020. Instead, he and the Rangers used his time at the alternate training site to overhaul the characteristics of his pitches.

SCOUTING REPORT: Phillips profiles as a classic workhorse with a strong, physical frame and a four-pitch mix. The Rangers wanted more vertical movement to his 92-95 mph four-seam fastball and he successfully added more depth to his average curveball. His changeup remains a plus pitch and he has added a slider. Phillips remains a premium strike-thrower with borderline plus-plus control.

THE FUTURE: Phillips still needs to sharpen his new pitches and show they play in live games. He has a chance to be a back-of-the-rotation starter if he can.

Year	Age	Club (League)	Class	W	L	ERA	G	GS	IP	H	HR	BB	SO	BB/9	SO/9	WHIP	AVG
2019	21	Frisco (TL)	AA	7	9	4.73	18	16	93	95	15	20	74	1.9	7.1	1.23	.245
	21	Down East (CAR)	HiA	2	2	1.19	6	6	38	28	1	6	28	1.4	6.7	0.90	.200
Minor League Totals				30	28	3.86	93	75	436	439	32	83	389	1.7	8.0	1.20	.257

MORE PROSPECTS TO KNOW

31 CURTIS TERRY, 1B

Terry is a bat-only masher, but the Rangers believe he is a future major leaguer despite his defensive deficiencies.

32 TEKOAH ROBY, RHP

The Rangers' third-round pick in 2020, Roby has already shown an uptick in velocity to 91-96 mph along with a curveball, a changeup and lots of strikes.

33 MARCUS SMITH, OF

Acquired from Oakland in the Mike Minor trade, Smith adds power and speed to an athletic crop of Rangers center fielders.

34 MASON ENGLERT, RHP

Englert returned from Tommy John surgery and impressed with his three-pitch mix during instructional league.

35 RANDY FLORENTINO, C

Florentino has a chance to develop 20-homer power and should stick at catcher, but he's behind David Garcia in the pecking order.

36 BROCK BURKE, LHP

Burke missed all of 2020 after having shoulder surgery, but his four-pitch mix makes him a back-of-the-rotation candidate if he can stay healthy.

37 TAYLOR HEARN, LHP

SLEEPER

Hearn's stock would be higher if he was a rotation lock, but a lack of command likely means his mid-90s fastball and sharp slider end up in the bullpen.

38 DYLAN MACLEAN, LHP

A projectable lefty drafted in the fourth round in 2020, the Rangers are waiting for MacLean's velocity to jump to better compliment his plus changeup and breaking ball.

39 JONATHAN ORNELAS, SS

Ornelas can play all over the diamond but needs to learn how to drive the ball at the plate rather than simply collide with it.

40 JOHN KING, LHP

King features the best changeup in the organization and attacks hitters, but he doesn't miss a ton of bats.

TOP PROSPECTS OF THE DECADE

Year	Player, Pos	2020 Org
2011	Martin Perez, LHP	Red Sox
2012	Jurickson Profar, SS	Padres
2013	Jurickson Profar, SS/2B	Padres
2014	Rougned Odor, 2B	Rangers
2015	Joey Gallo, 3B	Rangers
2016	Joey Gallo, 3B	Rangers
2017	Leody Taveras ,OF	Rangers
2018	Willie Calhoun, OF	Rangers
2019	Hans Crouse, RHP	Rangers
2020	Josh Jung, 3B	Rangers

TOP DRAFT PICKS OF THE DECADE

Year	Player, Pos	2020 Org
2011	Kevin Matthews, LHP	Did not play
2012	Lewis Brinson, OF	Marlins
2013	Chi Chi Gonzalez, RHP	Rockies
2014	Luis Ortiz, RHP	Orioles
2015	Dillon Tate, RHP	Orioles
2016	Cole Ragans, LHP	Rangers
2017	Bubba Thompson, OF	Rangers
2018	Cole Winn, RHP	Rangers
2019	Josh Jung, 3B	Rangers
2020	Justin Foscue, 2B	Rangers

DEPTH CHART

TEXAS RANGERS

TOP 2021 ROOKIES	RANK
Josh Jung, 3B	1
Sam Huff, C	2
BREAKOUT PROSPECTS	
Evan Carter, CF	16
Chris Seise, SS	23
Keithron Moss, 2B	27

SOURCE OF TOP 30 TALENT

Homegrown	27	Acquired	3
College	4	Trade	3
Junior college	0	Rule 5 draft	0
High school	14	Independent league	0
Nondrafted free agent	0	Free agent/waivers	0
International	9		

LF
Evan Carter (16)

CF
Leody Taveras (4)
Bubba Thompson (28)
Marcus Smith
Zion Bannister
Julio Pablo Martinez

RF
Bayron Lora (11)
Steele Walker (15)
Pedro Gonzalez

3B
Josh Jung (1)
Davis Wendzel (14)

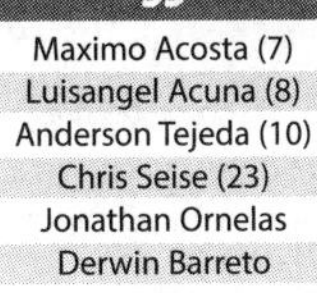

SS
Maximo Acosta (7)
Luisangel Acuna (8)
Anderson Tejeda (10)
Chris Seise (23)
Jonathan Ornelas
Derwin Barreto

2B
Justin Foscue (6)
Keithron Moss (27)

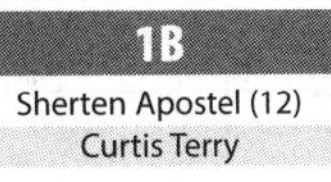

1B
Sherten Apostel (12)
Curtis Terry

C
Sam Huff (3)
David Garcia (17)
Randy Florentino
Matt Whatley
Cody Freeman

LHP

LHSP	LHRP
Joe Palumbo (22)	Taylor Hearn
Dylan MacLean	
Brock Burke	
John King	
Cole Ragans	
Cody Bradford	

RHP

RHSP	RHRP
Dane Dunning (2)	Demarcus Evans (21)
Cole Winn (5)	A.J. Alexy (24)
Hans Crouse (9)	Yerry Rodriguez (28)
Ronny Henriquez (13)	Alex Speas (29)
Ricky Vanasco (18)	Brett de Geus
Owen White (19)	
Kyle Cody (20)	
Avery Weems (25)	
Tyler Phillips (30)	
Tekoah Roby	
Mason Englert	
Justin Slaten	
Sean Chandler	
Ryan Garcia	

Toronto Blue Jays

BY BEN BADLER

The Blue Jays are in position to be a perennial playoff contender for the first half of the 2020s.

Aided by an expanded postseason in 2020, the Blue Jays started the decade with their first playoff appearance since 2016, building around a young, largely homegrown lineup of players in their 20s to rank seventh in the majors in runs scored.

Bo Bichette, Vladimir Guerrero Jr., Cavan Biggio and Lourdes Gurriel Jr. are all in their early-to-mid 20s, while outfielder Teoscar Hernandez is still in his prime as he enters his age-28 season coming off a .289/.340/.549 campaign.

Just as the Blue Jays have a team ready to compete in the American League East, they have one of the game's best farm systems, with a balance of talent from players at the upper levels down to the lowest rungs.

The Blue Jays badly need starting pitchers to support Hyun-Jin Ryu, and they have one in righthander Nate Pearson, who got brief exposure to Toronto in 2020. If Pearson stays healthy, he has the talent to develop into a frontline starter. Righthander Simeon Woods Richardson is another Top 100 Prospect and a polished pitcher who could reach Toronto later in the 2021 season.

The strength of the system still remains its hitters, a group that got stronger in 2020 when Toronto drafted Austin Martin out of Vanderbilt. Martin, who played third base, shortstop and center field in college, was a candidate to go No. 1 overall, so the Blue Jays were thrilled to get him with the fifth overall pick.

Martin and shortstop Jordan Groshans give the Blue Jays two of the game's best hitting prospects. Shortstop Orelvis Martinez, who was the No. 1 prospect in the Rookie-level Gulf Coast League in 2019 as a 17-year-old, has the talent to eventually jump into that tier, and catcher Gabriel Moreno is another with Top 100 Prospect potential, especially after a strong showing during his time at Toronto's alternate training site in Rochester.

Moreno adds to the Blue Jays' catching prospect depth behind Alejandro Kirk, who arrived in Toronto in 2020 having never played above high Class A, but showed the exceptional bat control and strike-zone discipline he has been known for throughout his career.

There's more talent beyond them, including righthanders Alek Manoah (the 11th overall pick in the 2019 draft), Adam Kloffenstein, whose velocity ticked up in 2020, C.J. Van Eyk (the 42nd overall pick in the 2020 draft) and Eric Pardinho, who is coming back from Tommy John surgery. There's also an array of hitters with breakout potential at the lower levels, with infielders Miguel Hiraldo and Leonardo Jimenez ready for their first full-season assignments in 2021. Recent international signings like shortstops Estiven Machado and Rikelbin de Castro and catcher Victor Mesia all show promise despite not having made their pro debuts.

To take the next step, the Blue Jays need smart moves to supplement their major league roster, but they are well positioned to do so, whether it's spending on free agents, promoting from within their farm system or using that wealth of prospects in trades. Those decisions could lead to a string of playoff appearances over the next five years. ■

JIN-TIMOTHY T LUDWIG/GETTY IMAGES

The Blue Jays have a position core in place, but need more pitchers to support Hyun-Jin Ryu.

PROJECTED 2024 LINEUP

Position	Player	Age
Catcher	Danny Jansen	29
First Base	Vladimir Guerrero Jr.	25
Second Base	Cavan Biggio	29
Third Base	Jordan Groshans	24
Shortstop	Bo Bichette	26
Left Field	Lourdes Gurriel Jr.	30
Center Field	Austin Martin	25
Right Field	Teoscar Hernandez	32
Designated Hitter	Alejandro Kirk	25
No. 1 Starter	Nate Pearson	27
No. 2 Starter	Hyun-Jin Ryu	37
No. 3 Starter	Simeon Woods Richardson	23
No. 4 Starter	Alek Manoah	26
No. 5 Starter	Adam Kloffenstein	23
Closer	Jordan Romano	31

TOP ROOKIE

DAVID J. GRIFFIN/ICON SPORTSWIRE VIA GETTY IMAGES

BA GRADE	SCOUTING GRADES
70 Risk: High	**FB:** 80. **SL:** 70. **CHG:** 55. **CB:** 50. **CTL:** 55.

Projected future grades on 20-80 scouting scale.

BEST TOOLS

Best Hitter for Average	Austin Martin
Best Power Hitter	Riley Adams
Best Strike-Zone Discipline	Alejandro Kirk
Fastest Baserunner	Dasan Brown
Best Athlete	Dasan Brown
Best Fastball	Nate Pearson
Best Curveball	Patrick Murphy
Best Slider	Nate Pearson
Best Changeup	Simeon Woods Richardson
Best Control	Simeon Woods Richardson
Best Defensive Catcher	Gabriel Moreno
Best Defensive Infielder	Rikelbin de Castro
Best Infield Arm	Jordan Groshans
Best Defensive Outfielder	Dasan Brown
Best Outfield Arm	Chavez Young

1 NATE PEARSON, RHP

Born: Aug. 20, 1996. **B-T:** R-R. **HT:** 6-6. **WT:** 250.
Drafted: JC of Central Florida, 2017 (1st round).
Signed by: Matt Bishoff.

TRACK RECORD: Pearson mostly pitched as a reliever when he was a freshman at Florida International. He transferred to the JC of Central Florida for 2017 and his stock soared as a starter. He was drafted 28th overall, signed for $2,452,900 and quickly looked like a steal. His 2018 season ended early—he didn't pitch until May 7, then threw 1.2 innings before a line drive fractured his right forearm—but he returned with an outstanding 2019 that put him in the conversation for the top pitching prospect in baseball. Pearson made his major league debut in 2020 and made four starts before going on the injured list with a flexor strain in his right elbow. He returned in time to make one relief appearance at the end of the season and made the Blue Jays' postseason roster. In his lone playoff appearance, he struck out five of six batters he faced over two perfect innings of relief.

SCOUTING REPORT: Pearson has a huge frame with a power fastball to match. He sits 94-98 mph, touched 101 in the majors and has previously been as high as 104, showing the ability to get empty swings when he elevates. Pearson significantly improved his mid-80s slider during his time in the minors and saw it carry over to the majors. It's a plus pitch that flashes as a 70 on the 20-80 scouting scale, with late bite and two-plane depth to dive underneath barrels. Pearson shows the feel to add and subtract from his slider, landing it in the strike zone or burying it for a chase pitch when necessary. Pearson leaned heavily on his fastball/slider combination in 2020. When he keeps his changeup down, it shows flashes of being a solid-average pitch at 86-89 mph. He didn't throw it much and lacked a consistent feel for it in the big leagues, where it played below-average. He sprinkles in an occasional 75-79 mph curveball, usually early in the count, showing better control of his curveball than he does with his changeup. Pearson showed electric stuff but got into trouble in the majors because of his control. That hasn't been an issue for Pearson in the past, and his athletic, efficient delivery suggests he should be able to throw more strikes. Pearson has plenty of starter traits, but durability is still a question. His 101.2 innings in 2019 were a career high, so his 2020 elbow injury and the fact that he throws so hard gives some scouts pause about his ability to handle a starter's workload.

THE FUTURE: If Pearson shows he can hold up as a starter and throw strikes, he has the stuff to develop into a true No. 1 starter. He should be an integral part of Toronto's rotation in 2021. ■

Year	Age	Club (League)	Class	W	L	ERA	G	GS	IP	H	HR	BB	SO	BB/9	SO/9	WHIP	AVG
2017	20	Vancouver (NWL)	SS	0	0	0.95	7	7	19	6	0	5	24	2.4	11.4	0.58	.090
	20	Blue Jays (GCL)	R	0	0	0.00	1	1	1	1	0	0	2	0.0	18.0	1.00	.250
2018	21	Dunedin (FSL)	HiA	0	1	10.80	1	1	2	5	1	0	1	0.0	5.4	3.00	.500
2019	22	Buffalo (IL)	AAA	1	0	3.00	3	3	18	12	2	3	15	1.5	7.5	0.83	.174
	22	Dunedin (FSL)	HiA	3	0	0.86	6	6	21	10	2	3	35	1.3	15.0	0.62	.133
	22	New Hampshire (EL)	AA	1	4	2.59	16	16	63	41	4	21	69	3.0	9.9	0.99	.164
2020	23	Toronto (AL)	MAJ	1	0	6.00	5	4	18	14	5	13	16	6.5	8.0	1.50	.209
Major League Totals				1	0	6.00	5	4	18	14	5	13	16	6.5	8.0	1.50	.209
Minor League Totals				5	5	2.19	34	34	123	75	9	32	146	2.3	10.7	0.87	.173

2 AUSTIN MARTIN, SS

VANDERBILT UNIVERSITY/JOE HOWELL

BA GRADE
65 Risk: High

Born: March 23, 1999. **B-T:** R-R. **HT:** 6-0. **WT:** 185. **Drafted:** Vanderbilt, 2020 (1st round). **Signed by:** Nate Murrie.

TRACK RECORD: Martin was an All-American at Vanderbilt who led the Southeastern Conference in on-base percentage in 2019, putting himself in the conversation to be the No. 1 overall pick in the 2020 draft. The Blue Jays were elated to get him with the fifth pick and signed him for $7,000,825. He spent the summer at the alternate training site and put together the most disciplined at-bats of any hitter in Rochester.

SCOUTING REPORT: Martin is a well-rounded player with quick hands and a short, direct swing geared for line drives. He has excellent hand-eye coordination which leads to a high contact rate and good plate coverage, with no problems barreling high-end velocity. Martin's bat speed and swing efficiency enable him to let the ball travel deeper before deciding whether to swing, which, along with his keen eye for the strike zone, helps him get on base at a high clip. Martin has solid-average raw power that was showing up more in games before the 2020 college season shut down. A tick above-average runner, Martin is athletic and spent a lot of time at shortstop at the alternate site but moved around to third base, second base and center field. He played mostly third base in 2020, with hands and feet that work well in the dirt, but throwing accuracy issues prompted Vanderbilt to move him to center field in 2020 and remain a point of emphasis in his development.

THE FUTURE: Martin's future position remains unsettled, but he has the hitting ability and versatility to develop into a standout at many different spots. He's advanced enough to start in high Class A in 2021.

SCOUTING GRADES: **Hitting:** 70 **Power:** 55 **Running:** 55 **Fielding:** 50 **Arm:** 50

Year	Age	Club (League)	Class	AVG	G	AB	R	H	2B	3B	HR	RBI	BB	SO	SB	OBP	SLG
2020	21	Did not play—No minor league season															

3 JORDAN GROSHANS, SS

Born: July 20, 1998. **B-T:** R-R. **HT:** 6-3. **WT:** 205. **Drafted:** HS—Magnolia, Texas, 2018 (1st round). **Signed by:** Brian Johnston.

TRACK RECORD: Groshans was the 12th overall pick in the 2018 draft and was crushing the low Class A Midwest League in 2019, but a left foot injury sidelined him after 23 games. He spent 2020 at the alternate site in Rochester, N.Y., where he led the team in home runs.

SCOUTING REPORT: Groshans has a long frame with an athletic, well-sequenced swing and an advanced offensive approach for his age. He has good bat speed, barrels quality fastballs and drives the ball with above-average raw power. With the moving parts in his swing, there are times Groshans opens early and works around the ball, leaving him vulnerable against breaking balls away. When he stays back and gets into a good hitting position, he stays through the ball and is able to manipulate the barrel and drive the ball from right-center over to his pull side. Groshans reads the ball well off the bat and has a plus arm at shortstop, but a lot of scouts think his range and quickness will play better at third base, where he would be a potentially above-average defender.

THE FUTURE: Groshans' foot injury followed by the pandemic have limited his development the last two years, but he has the potential to be a force in the middle of a lineup.

SCOUTING GRADES: **Hitting:** 60 **Power:** 60 **Running:** 50 **Fielding:** 50 **Arm:** 60

Year	Age	Club (League)	Class	AVG	G	AB	R	H	2B	3B	HR	RBI	BB	SO	SB	OBP	SLG
2018	18	Blue Jays (GCL)	R	.331	37	142	17	47	12	0	4	39	13	29	0	.390	.500
	18	Bluefield (APP)	R	.182	11	44	4	8	1	0	1	4	2	8	0	.229	.273
2019	19	Lansing (MWL)	LoA	.337	23	83	12	28	6	0	2	13	13	21	1	.427	.482
Minor League Totals				.309	71	269	33	83	19	0	7	56	28	58	1	.376	.457

4 SIMEON WOODS RICHARDSON, RHP

BA GRADE

60 Risk: High

Born: Sept. 27, 2000. **B-T:** R-R. **HT:** 6-3. **WT:** 215. **Drafted:** HS—Sugar Land, Texas, 2018 (2nd round). **Signed by:** Ray Corbett (Mets).

TRACK RECORD: Woods Richardson was one of the youngest players in the 2018 draft and played his first season at 17 years old after signing for $1.85 million as the 48th overall pick. One year later, the Mets traded him and lefthander Anthony Kay to the Blue Jays for Marcus Stroman. He spent 2020 at the alternate training site in Rochester, N.Y.

SCOUTING REPORT: Woods Richardson has a strong, powerful build and exceptional polish for his age, reaching high Class A Dunedin in 2019 as a 19-year-old. His athleticism helps him repeat his delivery consistently and locate his fastball to all quadrants of the strike zone, with a chance for plus or better control. He gets good extension on his 91-95 mph fastball, which has late, riding life up in the zone. He mixes and matches three secondary pitches to miss bats, including a tick above-average slider and a deceptive changeup that improved in 2020 to become a plus pitch. Woods Richardson also throws an average curveball, though he goes to his slider more with two strikes.

THE FUTURE: Woods Richardson is advanced enough to start 2021 in Double-A, with a chance to get to Toronto by the end of the year. He has the mix of stuff and control to develop into a No. 2 or 3 starter.

SCOUTING GRADES: **Fastball:** 60 **Slider:** 55 **Curveball:** 50 **Changeup:** 60 **Control:** 60

Year	Age	Club (League)	Class	W	L	ERA	G	GS	IP	H	HR	BB	SO	BB/9	SO/9	WHIP	AVG
2018	17	Mets (GCL)	R	1	0	0.00	5	2	11	9	0	4	15	3.2	11.9	1.15	.191
	17	Kingsport (APP)	R	0	0	4.50	2	2	6	6	1	0	11	0.0	16.5	1.00	.250
2019	18	Dunedin (FSL)	HiA	3	2	2.54	6	6	28	18	1	7	29	2.2	9.2	0.88	.168
	18	Columbia (SAL)	LoA	3	8	4.25	20	20	78	78	5	17	97	2.0	11.1	1.21	.240
Minor League Totals				7	10	3.48	33	30	124	111	7	28	152	2.0	11.0	1.12	.236

5 ALEJANDRO KIRK, C

TOP ROOKIE

MIKE CARLSON/MLB PHOTOS VIA GETTY IMAGES

BA GRADE

55 Risk: Medium

Born: Nov. 6, 1998. **B-T:** R-R. **HT:** 5-8. **WT:** 265. **Signed:** Mexico, 2016. **Signed by:** Dean Decillis/Sandy Rosario.

TRACK RECORD: It's easy to overlook Kirk because of his squatty body, but his track record of hitting continues to sparkle. Signed out of Mexico in 2016, Kirk reached high Class A in 2019 and spent most of 2020 at the alternate training site. He made the jump to Toronto in September and earned regular playing time down the stretch in the Blue Jays' playoff push.

SCOUTING REPORT: Built like a shorter Pablo Sandoval, Kirk matches Sandoval's innate ability to barrel the baseball. He has short arms, a short swing and makes frequent contact, striking out just 10% of the time in 2019 and showing the bat control that translated in his brief big league callup. He has a small strike zone and stays disciplined within it, tracking pitches well enough to drive fastballs and breaking pitches to all fields, especially fastballs at the top of the zone. It's an on-base over power profile, but he accesses his average raw power in games because of his ability to consistently find the sweet spot. Kirk's detractors worry about his body and question his defensive skills behind the plate, while others think he receives well, does a solid job blocking and works well with his pitchers. He has an average arm.

THE FUTURE: Kirk made a big jump to the majors at the end of the season, so more minor league time would be reasonable. Still, his performance catapulted him into the 2021 big league picture.

SCOUTING REPORTS: **Hitting:** 70 **Power:** 50 **Running:** 20 **Fielding:** 45 **Arm:** 50

Year	Age	Club (League)	Class	AVG	G	AB	R	H	2B	3B	HR	RBI	BB	SO	SB	OBP	SLG
2017	18	Blue Jays (GCL)	R	.000	1	2	0	0	0	0	0	0	0	0	0	.333	.000
2018	19	Bluefield (APP)	R	.354	58	206	31	73	10	1	10	57	33	21	2	.443	.558
2019	20	Dunedin (FSL)	HiA	.288	71	233	26	67	25	0	4	36	38	31	2	.395	.446
	20	Lansing (MWL)	LoA	.299	21	77	15	23	6	1	3	8	18	8	1	.427	.519
2020	21	Toronto (AL)	MAJ	.375	9	24	4	9	2	0	1	3	1	4	0	.400	.583
Major League Totals				.375	9	24	4	9	2	0	1	3	1	4	0	.400	.583
Minor League Totals				.315	151	518	72	163	41	2	17	101	89	60	5	.418	.500

6 ORELVIS MARTINEZ, SS/3B

Born: Nov. 19, 2001. **B-T:** R-R. **HT:** 6-1. **WT:** 190. **Signed:** Dominican Republic, 2018. **Signed by:** Alexis de la Cruz/Sandy Rosario.

MIKE JANES/FOUR SEAM IMAGES

BA GRADE
60 **Risk: Very High**

TRACK RECORD: Martinez signed for $3.51 million, the largest bonus for any 16-year-old in the 2018-19 international class. He immediately impressed in his pro debut as the No. 1 prospect in the Rookie-level Gulf Coast League in 2019. After training at home in the Dominican Republic in the summer of 2020, he joined the alternate training site for a week, homered there, and then hit four homers in his first two weeks of instructional league.

SCOUTING REPORT: Like several other young Blue Jays hitters, Martinez does a good job incorporating his whole body into his swing. He has to keep those moving parts in sync, but generally does so to generate fast bat speed and easy plus power. He uses his hands well at the plate, driving the ball with impressive carry to all fields. Martinez makes frequent contact and has an advanced approach for his age, shrinking his lower-half movement when he gets to two strikes, though he gets himself in trouble when he's too aggressive early in the count. Martinez has a plus arm and good hands at shortstop, but he needs to improve his footwork. The Blue Jays think he has a chance to play shortstop, but his range is already iffy. With how much bigger he projects to get, his best fit is likely third base.

THE FUTURE: Martinez has the upside to develop into an all-star, but he is still a teenager yet to make his full-season debut. He is likely to begin in low Class A in 2021.

SCOUTING GRADES: **Hitting:** 60 **Power:** 60 **Running:** 45 **Fielding:** 40 **Arm:** 60

Year	Age	Club (League)	Class	AVG	G	AB	R	H	2B	3B	HR	RBI	BB	SO	SB	OBP	SLG
2019	17	Blue Jays (GCL)	R	.275	40	142	20	39	8	5	7	32	14	29	2	.352	.549
Minor League Totals				.275	40	142	20	39	8	5	7	32	14	29	2	.352	.549

7 ALEK MANOAH, RHP

Born: Jan. 9, 1998. **B-T:** R-R. **HT:** 6-6. **WT:** 270. **Drafted:** West Virginia, 2019 (1st round). **Signed by:** Coulson Barbiche.

BA GRADE
55 **Risk: High**

TRACK RECORD: Manoah split time between starting and relieving his first two years at West Virginia. He had an outstanding summer in the Cape Cod League in 2018 and carried that success into 2019 as a junior, propelling him to become the 11th overall pick and land a $4,547,500 bonus.

SCOUTING REPORT: Manoah is a power pitcher with a gigantic frame. Built like Aaron Harang, Manoah will need to stay on top of his conditioning, but he leverages his size into a high-octane fastball. He sits at 93-96 mph with tailing life and can dial it up to 98. His slider flashes plus and is his putaway pitch. Manoah primarily relied on those two pitches at West Virginia and in the short-season Northwest League, where he continued to rack up strikeouts. His changeup lagged behind and was a developmental priority in 2020 at the alternate training site. It flashes enough movement that it could develop into an average pitch. Manoah is more athletic than his body suggests, which helps him throw strikes, though he does need to tighten his fastball command.

THE FUTURE: Manoah has the stuff to develop into a mid-rotation starter with a chance for more. Even with the shutdown, he could be in position to pitch in Toronto by the end of the 2021 season.

SCOUTING GRADES: **Fastball:** 60 **Slider:** 55 **Changeup:** 50 **Control:** 50

Year	Age	Club (League)	Class	W	L	ERA	G	GS	IP	H	HR	BB	SO	BB/9	K/9	WHIP	AVG
2019	21	Vancouver (NWL)	SS	0	1	2.65	6	6	17	13	1	5	27	2.6	14.3	1.06	.213
Minor League Totals				0	1	2.65	6	6	17	13	1	5	27	2.6	14.3	1.06	.213

8 GABRIEL MORENO, C

Born: Feb. 14, 2000. **B-T:** R-R. **HT:** 5-11. **WT:** 170. **Signed:** Venezuela, 2016. **Signed by:** Francisco Plasencia.

BA GRADE
55 Risk: High

TRACK RECORD: Signed out of Venezuela for $25,000 in 2016, Moreno has become one of the top catching prospects in the lower levels of the minors. He arrived at the alternate site in Rochester, N.Y. in mid-August and quickly impressed the veteran players there. He posted one of the top offensive performances in his brief stint, then played winter ball in Venezuela. The Blue Jays added him to the 40-man roster after the season.

SCOUTING REPORT: Moreno jumps out for his athleticism and elite hand-eye coordination. He has excellent control of the barrel and his body, striking out just 11% of the time in 2019. He has incorporated bigger, more athletic movements into his swing since signing to help him drive the ball with more impact, something that started to pop in 2019 and gives him a chance for 15-20 home runs. Moreno is adept at squaring up good velocity, though he has chase tendencies. He's working to tighten that while becoming more selective on borderline pitches. Moreno has a slightly above-average arm, a quick release and his athleticism is an asset behind the plate, but his blocking and receiving still need improvement.

THE FUTURE: Moreno continues to show positive trends with his bat. As long as they continue, he has a chance to develop into an average or better regular behind the plate.

SCOUTING GRADES: **Hitting:** 55 **Power:** 45 **Running:** 30 **Fielding:** 50 **Arm:** 55

Year	Age	Club (League)	Class	AVG	G	AB	R	H	2B	3B	HR	RBI	BB	SO	SB	OBP	SLG
2017	17	Blue Jays (DSL)	R	.248	32	125	9	31	4	1	0	17	6	5	5	.274	.296
2018	18	Bluefield (APP)	R	.279	17	61	10	17	5	0	2	14	3	13	1	.303	.459
	18	Blue Jays (GCL)	R	.413	23	92	14	38	12	2	2	22	4	7	1	.455	.652
2019	19	Lansing (MWL)	LoA	.280	82	307	47	86	17	5	12	52	22	38	7	.337	.485
Minor League Totals				.294	154	585	80	172	38	8	16	105	35	63	14	.339	.468

9 ADAM KLOFFENSTEIN, RHP

Born: Aug. 25, 2000. **B-T:** R-R. **HT:** 6-5. **WT:** 245. **Drafted:** HS—Magnolia, Texas, 2018 (3rd round). **Signed by:** Brian Johnston.

TRACK RECORD: A third-round pick in 2018, Kloffenstein was one of the top pitchers in the short-season Northwest League as a teenager in 2019. Instead of going to the alternate training site or instructional league in 2020, Kloffenstein stayed home in Texas to pitch in the independent Constellation Energy League. He had a 4.64 ERA with 20 strikeouts and 12 walks in 21.1 innings, throwing no more than three innings per appearance.

SCOUTING REPORT: Kloffenstein has the extra-large frame similar to other pitchers the Blue Jays have drafted in recent years. His touch and feel sticks out more than overpowering stuff, but he also saw a slight velocity bump in 2020. He's a strike-thrower whose fastball sits in the low-to-mid 90s with sink and now reaches 97 mph. He pairs his fastball with two breaking pitches he has natural feel to spin. Both his slider and curveball are average pitches with a chance to be plus, with his slider typically the more reliable of the two. His changeup, a focus in 2020, has good fade and gives him a chance to develop another average pitch.

THE FUTURE: Kloffenstein has mid-rotation potential with his control and arsenal. Low Class A is likely next.

SCOUTING GRADES: **Fastball:** 55 **Slider:** 55 **Curveball:** 50 **Changeup:** 50 **Control:** 50

Year	Age	Club (League)	Class	W	L	ERA	G	GS	IP	H	HR	BB	SO	BB/9	K/9	WHIP	AVG
2018	17	Blue Jays (GCL)	R	0	0	0.00	2	2	2	1	0	2	4	9.0	18.0	1.50	.143
2019	18	Vancouver (NWL)	SS	4	4	2.24	13	13	64	47	4	23	64	3.2	9.0	1.09	.205
Minor League Totals				4	4	2.17	15	15	66	48	4	25	68	3.4	9.2	1.10	.203

10 MIGUEL HIRALDO, SS/2B

Born: Sept. 4, 2000. **B-T:** R-R. **HT:** 5-11. **WT:** 175. **Signed:** Dominican Republic, 2017. **Signed by:** Luciano del Rosario.

BA GRADE 55 Risk: Very High

TRACK RECORD: Several clubs considered Hiraldo one of the best hitters in the 2017 international class when he signed with the Blue Jays for $750,000. He came as advertised in his first two seasons, including a strong showing in the Rookie-level Appalachian League in 2019. The Blue Jays did not bring him to their alternate training site in 2020, so Hiraldo instead trained at home in the Dominican Republic before coming over for instructional league.

SCOUTING REPORT: Hiraldo has an innate feel for barreling the baseball with a short, direct swing and a knack for being on time. His hands are so quick he's able to generate impressive bat speed, even though he doesn't get much separation with his load to start his swing. He gets his lower half into his swing well and generates solid-average raw power that could increase. Hiraldo is a good fastball hitter, but his approach can get pull-heavy and leaves him vulnerable on the outer third of the plate and against breaking pitches. His hands and solid-average arm fit at shortstop, but his range points to a future position change, with a skill set that could work well at third base. At instructional league he played shortstop, third base and second base, with most of his time spent at second.

THE FUTURE: The Blue Jays have a wealth of shortstops to find playing time for in 2021. Hiraldo is ready for one of the Class A levels and may move around the infield to get into the lineup regularly.

SCOUTING GRADES: Hitting: 55 | Power: 55 | Running: 45 | Fielding: 45 | Arm: 55

Year	Age	Club (League)	Class	AVG	G	AB	R	H	2B	3B	HR	RBI	BB	SO	SB	OBP	SLG
2018	17	Blue Jays (DSL)	R	.313	54	214	41	67	18	3	2	33	23	30	15	.381	.453
	17	Blue Jays (GCL)	R	.231	10	39	3	9	4	0	0	3	1	12	3	.250	.333
2019	18	Lansing (MWL)	LoA	.250	1	4	0	1	0	1	0	0	0	0	0	.250	.750
	18	Bluefield (APP)	R	.300	56	237	43	71	20	1	7	37	14	36	11	.348	.481
Minor League Totals				.300	121	494	87	148	42	5	9	73	38	78	29	.354	.460

11 C.J. VAN EYK, RHP

BA GRADE 50 Risk: High

Born: Sept. 15, 1998. **B-T:** R-R. **HT:** 6-1. **WT:** 205. **Drafted:** Florida State, 2020 (2nd round). **Signed by:** Brandon Bishoff.

TRACK RECORD: Van Eyk won a gold medal with USA Baseball's 18U national team in high school and entered his senior year as one of the top prospects in the 2017 draft. A forearm injury hurt his draft stock, and he instead went to Florida State. The move worked out, as Van Eyk became the 42nd overall pick in the 2020 draft and signed for $1,797,500. He went to the team's rookie camp at instructional league in the fall and pitched in one game.

SCOUTING REPORT: Van Eyk pitches off a fastball that sits in the low 90s and touches 95 mph. He throws an above-average curveball with good depth that can miss bats, along with an average changeup that has good sink and separation off his fastball. Van Eyk has a feel to spin a slider, but it doesn't generate the same swing-and-miss rate as his curveball. He throws strikes with easy, fluid arm action and simple, low-maintenance mechanics.

THE FUTURE: Van Eyk is a relatively safe bet to stick as a starter between his repertoire, delivery and pitchability. He should make his pro debut at one of the Class A levels in 2021.

Year	Age	Club (League)	Class	W	L	ERA	G	GS	IP	H	HR	BB	SO	BB/9	SO/9	WHIP	AVG
2020	21	Did not play—No minor league season															

12 OTTO LOPEZ, SS/2B

BA GRADE 50 Risk: High

Born: Oct. 1, 1998. **B-T:** R-R. **HT:** 5-10. **WT:** 170. **Signed:** Dominican Republic, 2016. **Signed by:** Sandy Rosario/Lorenzo Perez/Alexis de la Cruz.

TRACK RECORD: Signed for $60,000 out of the Dominican Republic in 2016, Lopez broke out in 2019 with a batting title in the low Class A Midwest League. In 2020, Lopez spent a few weeks in instructional league before going home to play winter ball for Escogido in the Dominican Republic. The Blue Jays added him to the 40-man roster after the season.

SCOUTING REPORT: Lopez won't jump out for his pure tools, but he has an innate feel for contact and a particular knack for barreling fastballs up in the zone. Lopez doesn't walk much and would benefit from a more selective hitting approach, as his bat control leads to light contact on pitches he should lay off. Lopez has average raw power, though it hasn't manifested itself in games yet with a swing geared for

low line drives and grounders. There's unlocked power for Lopez to tap into if he shifts his intent from a contact-oriented approach to one where he tries to drive certain pitches for extra-base damage. Lopez has primarily played shortstop with his slightly above-average speed and average arm strength, but he will be stretched to play there every day at higher levels. He has played second base and the outfield, as well.
THE FUTURE: Lopez's future may involve playing multiple positions. He has a chance to be an everyday player if he's able to hit for more power in games.

Year	Age	Club (League)	Class	AVG	G	AB	R	H	2B	3B	HR	RBI	BB	SO	SB	OBP	SLG
2019	20	Lansing (MWL)	LoA	.324	108	447	61	145	20	5	5	50	34	63	20	.371	.425
Minor League Totals				.310	217	833	130	258	38	14	9	93	79	112	41	.374	.421

13 ESTIVEN MACHADO, SS

BREAKOUT
BA GRADE
50 Risk: Extreme

Born: Oct. 4, 2002. **B-T:** B-R. **HT:** 5-10. **WT:** 165. **Signed:** Venezuela, 2019.
Signed by: Sandy Rosario/Francisco Plasencia.

TRACK RECORD: Machado was one of the top prospects in the 2019 international class and signed with the Blue Jays for $775,000. When the coronavirus pandemic shut down the 2020 season, Machado and a group of Venezuelan players stayed near the Blue Jays' complex in Dunedin, Fla., and worked out together at their hotel. Dominican Summer League manager Dane Fujinaka guided them through video workouts and drills in the parking lot before they got back on the field later in the summer.
SCOUTING REPORT: Machado combines an exciting mix of quick-twitch athleticism, tools and skills that translate in games. The switch-hitter's swings are fast, short and direct from both sides of the plate. His plate discipline is advanced for his age, leading to a high contact rate and consistent quality at-bats. Machado has mostly doubles power now, but he has the bat speed and projectable strength to potentially develop average power. Machado has average speed, but he has explosive movements with an easy running gait, so there's a chance he could get faster. His defense at shortstop isn't at the same level as fellow 2019 signing Rikelbin de Castro, but he has the athleticism, quick first step, footwork, range and hands to stay at shortstop. His above-average arm could become plus when he gets stronger.
THE FUTURE: Machado could develop into one of the most exciting players in the system, but needs to prove it in real games first. He should get that chance in the Rookie-level Gulf Coast League in 2021.

Year	Age	Club (League)	Class	AVG	G	AB	R	H	2B	3B	HR	RBI	BB	SO	SB	OBP	SLG
2020	17	Did not play—No minor league season															

14 ERIC PARDINHO, RHP

BA GRADE
50 Risk: Extreme

Born: Jan. 5, 2001. **B-T:** R-R. **HT:** 5-9. **WT:** 200. **Signed:** Brazil, 2017.
Signed by: Andrew Tinnish/Sandy Rosario.

TRACK RECORD: The top international pitching prospect in 2017, Pardinho signed with the Blue Jays out of Brazil for $1.4 million. He got off to a terrific start in his pro debut, skipping two levels and showing his polish in the Rookie-level Appalachian League as a 17-year-old. Pardinho battled a sore right elbow the following year and didn't have the same stuff or success when he returned. He eventually had Tommy John surgery in Feb. 2020 and spent the year rehabbing in Florida.
SCOUTING REPORT: When Pardinho was at his best in 2018, he sat in the low 90s and touched 96 mph. He complemented his heater with a curveball that flashed plus to get swings and misses and a slider that could develop into another above-average pitch. But when Pardinho returned to the mound after his elbow soreness in 2019, his stuff was not as crisp, with his velocity in the 88-92 mph range and his breaking stuff lacking its usual bite. He has shown feel for a changeup, though he hasn't been able to use it much. With Pardinho having surgery, there's reason to believe he wasn't 100% when he came back to pitch in 2019, and there's a chance his stuff will rebound once he's fully rehabbed. He has solid control from a smooth, easy delivery and a good arm action.
THE FUTURE: Pardinho is set to return in the middle of the 2021 season. His outlook depends on what his stuff looks like when he returns.

Year	Age	Club (League)	Class	W	L	ERA	G	GS	IP	H	HR	BB	SO	BB/9	K/9	WHIP	AVG
2019	18	Blue Jays (GCL)	R	1	0	0.00	1	0	4	1	0	3	5	6.8	11.3	1.00	.091
	18	Lansing (MWL)	LoA	1	1	2.41	7	7	34	29	1	13	30	3.5	8.0	1.25	.240
Minor League Totals				6	4	2.57	19	18	87	67	6	32	99	3.3	10.2	1.13	.211

15 THOMAS HATCH, RHP

BA GRADE **40** Risk: Medium

Born: Sept. 29, 1994. **B-T:** R-R. **HT:** 6-1. **WT:** 200. **Drafted:** Oklahoma State, 2016 (3rd round). **Signed by:** Ty Nichols (Cubs).

TRACK RECORD: Hatch won Big 12 Conference pitcher of the year in 2016 at Oklahoma State and was drafted by the Cubs in the third round. He made his way up to Double-A in the Cubs' system and was acquired by the Blue Jays at the 2019 trade deadline for David Phelps. Hatch's results improved when the Blue Jays encouraged him to throw his changeup more. He made his major league debut in 2020 as a reliever, with his stuff looking sharper out of the bullpen.

SCOUTING REPORT: Hatch's fastball sat in the low 90s as a starter but ticked up to 94-98 mph as a reliever. He generates above-average spin that helps his fastball play up, though he needs to improve his command. Hatch mainly threw his fastball and slider in college and with the Cubs, but his plus changeup is his best offspeed pitch, a weapon for whiffs against both lefties and righties. It looks like a fastball out of his hand before hitting the brakes at 84-88 mph, resulting in off-balance and empty swings. Hatch throws his solid-average slider with more power out of the bullpen than he did as a starter. It comes in at 86-91 mph with short, hard action and is capable of getting swings and misses as well.

THE FUTURE: Hatch has a smooth, controlled delivery and a three-pitch starter's mix, so a return to the rotation is possible. Given how much better his stuff played in relief, he might stay there going forward.

Year	Age	Club (League)	Class	W	L	ERA	G	GS	IP	H	HR	BB	SO	BB/9	SO/9	WHIP	AVG
2020	25	Toronto (AL)	MAJ	3	1	2.73	17	1	26	18	2	13	23	4.4	7.9	1.18	.191
Major League Totals				3	1	2.73	17	1	26	18	2	13	23	4.4	7.9	1.18	.191
Minor League Totals				19	30	3.99	79	79	403	382	36	150	370	3.3	8.3	1.32	.255

16 LEONARDO JIMENEZ, SS

BREAKOUT BA GRADE **50** Risk: Extreme

Born: May 17, 2001. **B-T:** R-R. **HT:** 6-0. **WT:** 195. **Signed:** Panama, 2017. **Signed by:** Alex Zapata/Sandy Rosario.

TRACK RECORD: Jimenez was Panama's top prospect in the 2017 international class and signed with the Blue Jays for $825,000. He performed well in his first two years of Rookie ball and showed up to instructional league in 2020 with added strength that made a notable impact.

SCOUTING REPORT: Jimenez is an instinctive player who isn't as flashy or explosive as other shortstops, but he's a fundamentally sound player with a good internal clock. He's a fluid defender at shortstop with soft hands, good body control and an average arm, with a throwing program a focal point for Jimenez to try to improve his arm strength. His first-step quickness and range lead some to believe he'll move off the position, but others believe his reads and instincts will keep him at short. After not hitting a home run in his first two seasons, Jimenez went deep in an early instructional league game and was driving the ball with more authority. Like many young hitters who start to grow into a little bit of power, Jimenez got caught up trying to sell out for power and began swinging and missing more than usual. That should settle in as he finds the right balance. The strength of Jimenez's offensive game has been his ability to manage his at-bats and put the ball in play from a simple swing

THE FUTURE: Jimenez's newfound strength should help his jump to a full-season league in 2021. He might end up a utilityman, but there's enough upside for him to develop into an everyday middle infielder.

Year	Age	Club (League)	Class	AVG	G	AB	R	H	2B	3B	HR	RBI	BB	SO	SB	OBP	SLG
2019	18	Lansing (MWL)	LoA	.167	2	6	0	1	0	0	0	0	0	2	0	.167	.167
	18	Bluefield (APP)	R	.298	56	215	34	64	13	2	0	22	21	42	2	.377	.377
Minor League Totals				.278	95	353	47	98	21	4	0	41	37	61	2	.358	.360

17 VICTOR MESIA, C

BREAKOUT BA GRADE **50** Risk: Extreme

Born: Jan. 18, 2003. **B-T:** R-R. **HT:** 5-10. **WT:** 205. **Signed:** Venezuela, 2019. **Signed by:** Sandy Rosario/Jose Contreras/Miguel Leal.

TRACK RECORD: Mesia signed for $300,000 as part of the deep Blue Jays international class in 2019. He made a strong impression after signing during Tricky League (an unofficial league for July 2 signings) and Dominican instructional league. The coronavirus pandemic prevented him from making his official pro debut in 2020, but he was a standout at instructional league in the fall.

SCOUTING REPORT: Mesia has a knack for making contact and driving the ball with impact. He has surprising explosiveness to his actions for his stocky build, producing fast bat speed and a compact, efficient stroke. He needs to become a more selective hitter, but he still makes a lot of contact, squares up high-end velocity and uses the whole field. Mesia's raw power is at least average with a chance for more to come. He has a strong, heavy lower half and moves athletically behind the plate, where he projects to stick with

a slightly above-average arm that could tick up as he gets stronger.
THE FUTURE: Mesia is far away, but he has the building blocks to develop into an everyday catcher. He's advanced enough to start 2021 in the Rookie-level Gulf Coast League.

Year	Age	Club (League)	Class	AVG	G	AB	R	H	2B	3B	HR	RBI	BB	SO	SB	OBP	SLG
2020	17	Did not play—No minor league season															

18 RIKELBIN DE CASTRO, SS

BA GRADE
50 Risk: Extreme

Born: Jan. 23, 2003. **B-T:** R-R. **HT:** 6-0. **WT:** 155. **Signed:** Dominican Republic, 2019. **Signed by:** Sand Rosario/Lorenzo Perez/Luis Natera.
TRACK RECORD: De Castro received the largest bonus in Toronto's deep 2019 international signing class, signing for $1.2 million. His expected pro debut was delayed by the coronavirus pandemic, but the Blue Jays brought him over in the fall for instructional league.
SCOUTING REPORT: De Castro is a wiry, thin-boned shortstop with quick-twitch athleticism and slick defensive actions. He's a high-energy player with a quick first step, nimble footwork, smooth hands and good range. His speed and arm strength are average but have a chance to tick up once he puts on strength, especially his throwing given his fast arm speed. The attributes are there for a future plus defender at shortstop, but de Castro is still a skinny teenager who needs to add weight. That holds back the damage he's able to do at the plate right now, but he has quick wrists and a loose, simple swing with a good path. He's not always consistent with his swing mechanics, but he has shown solid bat-to-ball skills so far, with a line-drive approach and gap power.
THE FUTURE: De Castro likely would have debuted in the Dominican Summer League if there was a 2020 season. He may be advanced enough to go to the Rookie-level Gulf Coast League for his debut in 2021.

Year	Age	Club (League)	Class	AVG	G	AB	R	H	2B	3B	HR	RBI	BB	SO	SB	OBP	SLG
2020	17	Did not play—No minor league season															

19 PATRICK MURPHY, RHP

BA GRADE
45 Risk: High

Born: June 10, 1995. **B-T:** R-R. **HT:** 6-5. **WT:** 235. **Drafted:** HS—Chandler, Ariz., 2013 (3rd round). **Signed by:** Blake Crosby.
TRACK RECORD: Murphy was pitching well for Double-A New Hampshire in 2019 before umpires informed him in the middle of the season that his toe tap with his left foot was illegal. He took time off to change his mechanics and struggled the rest of the way as he tried to adapt to his new delivery. He spent 2020 continuing to make adjustments at the alternate training site and earned his first major league callup in September, when he made four solid relief appearances.
SCOUTING REPORT: Murphy's fastball sat in the low-to-mid 90s as a starter and ticked up to 95-98 mph in relief in his debut. He likes to pitch up in the zone and to his arm side, though he tends to fly open in his delivery and has less success locating to his glove side. Murphy pairs his fastball with a power curveball that has slider-like velocity at 82-85 mph. It has a hard, sharp break and is a plus pitch at its best. Murphy has a below-average changeup and didn't throw it in the majors. His medical record includes Tommy John surgery, an operation for thoracic outlet syndrome and a surgery to reposition nerves in his pitching elbow early in his career.
THE FUTURE: Between his delivery, medical history and the way his powerful two-pitch mix has played up as a reliever, the bullpen may be the best place for Murphy. He could be a middle reliever with the upside to pitch in higher leverage situations.

Year	Age	Club (League)	Class	W	L	ERA	G	GS	IP	H	HR	BB	SO	BB/9	SO/9	WHIP	AVG
2020	25	Toronto (AL)	MAJ	0	0	1.50	4	0	6	6	0	2	5	3.0	7.5	1.33	.261
Major League Totals				0	0	1.50	4	0	6	6	0	2	5	3.0	7.5	1.33	.261
Minor League Totals				23	23	3.33	89	81	438	416	20	156	376	3.2	7.7	1.31	.250

20 ANTHONY KAY, LHP

BA GRADE
40 Risk: Medium

Born: March 21, 1995. **B-T:** L-L. **HT:** 6-0. **WT:** 218. **Drafted:** Connecticut, 2016 (1st round). **Signed by:** Michael Pesce (Mets).
TRACK RECORD: Kay was drafted by the Mets with the 31st overall pick in 2016 but missed the following year after having Tommy John surgery. He returned to pitch well in 2018 and the Blue Jays acquired him with Simeon Woods Richardson at the 2019 trade deadline in exchange for Marcus Stroman. Kay made his major league debut shortly after the trade and returned to the majors for 13 appearances in 2020.
SCOUTING REPORT: Kay's 91-96 mph fastball has above-average velocity from the left side, but it comes

in fairly straight and got hit hard in the majors, especially when he was behind in the count and hitters were looking for it. Kay throws an average curveball at 76-80 mph that can get swings and misses when he keeps it down. His 85-88 mph changeup is a tick below-average but flashes average. Kay threw strikes up through Double-A, but his command has been below-average in Triple-A and the majors.

THE FUTURE: Kay came up through the minors as a starter and some think he could still handle that role in the back of a rotation. But he will be 26 in 2021 and it's yet to click for him in the major leagues, so he could end up returning to relief.

Year	Age	Club (League)	Class	W	L	ERA	G	GS	IP	H	HR	BB	SO	BB/9	SO/9	WHIP	AVG
2020	25	Toronto (AL)	MAJ	2	0	5.14	13	0	21	22	3	14	22	6.0	9.4	1.71	.268
Major League Totals				3	0	5.40	16	2	35	37	3	19	35	4.9	9.0	1.60	.266
Minor League Totals				17	19	3.58	49	49	256	235	19	105	258	3.7	9.1	1.33	.248

21 SANTIAGO ESPINAL, SS/2B/3B

BA GRADE
40 **Risk: Medium**

Born: Nov. 13, 1994. **B-T:** R-R. **HT:** 5-10. **WT:** 181. **Drafted:** Miami-Dade JC, 2016 (10th round). **Signed by:** Willie Romay (Red Sox).

TRACK RECORD: Espinal was born in the Dominican Republic, grew up in Florida and spent one season at Miami-Dade JC, where he won the Southern Conference player of the year in 2016. The Red Sox signed him for $50,000 as a 10th-round pick and traded him to the Blue Jays at the 2018 trade deadline for Steve Pearce. Espinal steadily climbed the minors and made the Blue Jays' Opening Day roster in 2020, settling in as a reserve infielder.

SCOUTING REPORT: At 26, there isn't much projection left for Espinal, who has the skill set to fit as a utilityman between his bat control and ability to play multiple positions. He has been a high-contact hitter all the way up the minor league ladder, with a low swing-and-miss rate and a good two-strike approach. He manages his at-bats well with solid plate discipline. Espinal has well below-average power, so there's little impact when he connects. Espinal is an average runner with soft hands and a solid-average arm. He's a reliable defender at shortstop and has seen time at second base, third base and center field in his pro career.

THE FUTURE: Espinal lacks the power to be an everyday player. His ability to put the ball in play and move around the diamond are suited to a bench role.

Year	Age	Club (League)	Class	AVG	G	AB	R	H	2B	3B	HR	RBI	BB	SO	SB	OBP	SLG
2020	25	Toronto (AL)	MAJ	.267	26	60	10	16	4	0	0	6	4	16	1	.308	.333
Major League Totals				.267	26	60	10	16	4	0	0	6	4	16	1	.308	.333
Minor League Totals				.285	395	1517	208	433	74	11	21	187	129	218	44	.345	.390

22 WILL ROBERTSON, OF

BA GRADE
45 **Risk: Very High**

Born: Dec. 26, 1997. **B-T:** L-L. **HT:** 6-2. **WT:** 215. **Drafted:** Creighton, 2019 (4th round). **Signed by:** Wes Penick.

TRACK RECORD: Robertson had two loud offensive seasons at Creighton with a strong Cape Cod League summer in-between. He signed with the Blue Jays as a fourth-round pick in 2019 and debuted that summer in the short-season Northwest League. Robertson went to instructional league in 2020 and was one of the Blue Jays' top offensive performers, though at 22 he was one of the oldest hitters in camp.

SCOUTING REPORT: Robertson generates easy above-average raw power with his strength, bat speed and short lefthanded stroke. Pitchers were able to beat him with fastballs inside in his pro debut, so he backed off the plate in 2020 with better results at instructs. There's some stiffness in his swing that contributes to swing-and-miss concerns against more advanced pitchers, but he is working to create a better bat path to stay through the hitting zone longer. That showed early results at instructs, where Robertson was able to show more power through the middle of the field and to right-center. Robertson's value is tied to his bat. He's a below-average runner and defender in a corner with average arm strength.

THE FUTURE: Robertson showed encouraging signs in 2020. The real test will come once he faces Double-A pitching, possibly at some point in 2021.

Year	Age	Club (League)	Class	AVG	G	AB	R	H	2B	3B	HR	RBI	BB	SO	SB	OBP	SLG
2019	21	Vancouver (NWL)	SS	.268	61	228	33	61	11	1	6	33	31	49	1	.365	.404
Minor League Totals				.268	61	228	33	61	11	1	6	33	31	49	1	.365	.404

23 NICK FRASSO, RHP

BA GRADE 45 Risk: Very High

Born: Oct. 18, 1998. **B-T:** R-R. **HT:** 6-5. **WT:** 200. **Drafted:** Loyola Marymount, 2020 (4th round). **Signed by:** Bud Smith.

TRACK RECORD: Frasso was mostly a reliever his first two seasons at Loyola Marymount and led the Lions in saves as a sophomore. He moved to the rotation in 2020 but failed to get through five innings in either of his first two starts before he was sidelined with forearm and elbow tightness and the college season shut down. The Blue Jays still drafted him in the fourth round and signed him for $459,000.

SCOUTING REPORT: Frasso hits plenty of checkpoints scouts have for a young pitcher. He's a college arm who still has physical projection remaining in his 6-foot-5 frame and was a standout high school basketball player whose athleticism is evident on the mound. He throws strikes with a 92-95 mph fastball that plays up because of its high spin rate and his ability to generate extension out front. His slider is still inconsistent, but it has tight spin and flashes plus potential. Frasso has shown some feel for a changeup, but it's a third pitch that lags behind.

THE FUTURE: Frasso has the qualities to develop into a solid major league starter but needs to prove he can handle that workload. Otherwise, his stuff could play well in a multi-inning relief role.

Year	Age	Club (League)	Class	W	L	ERA	G	GS	IP	H	HR	BB	SO	BB/9	SO/9	WHIP	AVG
2020	21	Did not play—No minor league season															

24 TRENT PALMER, RHP

BA GRADE 45 Risk: Very High

Born: April 2, 1999. **B-T:** R-R. **HT:** 6-1. **WT:** 230. **Drafted:** Jacksonville, 2020 (3rd round). **Signed by:** Matt O'Brien.

TRACK RECORD: Palmer was a reliever as a freshman at Jacksonville, split time between starting and relieving his sophomore year and took off as a full-time starter as a junior before the coronavirus pandemic shut down the season. The Blue Jays drafted him in the third round and signed him for $847,500. Palmer made his organizational debut at instructional league in the fall.

SCOUTING REPORT: Palmer has a sturdy, heavy build that helps him generate a lot of power but he will have to maintain. His fastball comes in at 92-97 mph and he can both sink it or throw a four-seamer up in the zone. It will play better if he can improve its spin efficiency. Palmer's mid-80s slider flashes above-average potential and he has worked to mix in more of his splitter. Palmer has a repeatable delivery and showed better control as a starter than he did as a reliever at Jacksonville.

THE FUTURE: The Blue Jays will develop Palmer as a starter. He'll make his pro debut in 2021 at one of the Class A levels.

Year	Age	Club (League)	Class	W	L	ERA	G	GS	IP	H	HR	BB	SO	BB/9	SO/9	WHIP	AVG
2020	21	Did not play—No minor league season															

25 DASAN BROWN, OF

BA GRADE 45 Risk: Extreme

Born: Sept. 5, 2001. **B-T:** R-R. **HT:** 6-0. **WT:** 185. **Drafted:** HS—Oakville, Ont., 2019 (3rd round). **Signed by:** Kory Lafreniere.

TRACK RECORD: The Blue Jays drafted Brown with the 88th overall pick in 2019, making him the first Canadian player selected that year. Brown was raw coming out of high school and young for the class at 17 on draft day. The lack of development time with the canceled 2020 minor league season was evident to scouts when Brown arrived at instructional league in the fall.

SCOUTING REPORT: Brown is the best athlete in the Blue Jays' system and one of the fastest players in professional baseball. He's an explosive runner with a light, gliding gait and 80-grade speed on the 20-to-80 scouting scale. That speed, along with his solid instincts, gives him the attributes to develop into a plus or better defender in center field. Brown has an average arm, but he's working to improve his arm action and exchange to be more efficient. Brown is still crude as a hitter. He has plenty of bat speed to handle good velocity, and that bat speed gives him a chance to drive the ball with impact in the future despite his wiry build, but his pitch recognition, swing path, timing and contact skills all lag behind. Once he learns to read pitchers and get better jumps, he should pile up stolen bases.

THE FUTURE: The lost season hurt Brown's development more than most, but he's still an electric athlete and only 19. He probably starts 2021 in the Rookie-level Gulf Coast League.

Year	Age	Club (League)	Class	AVG	G	AB	R	H	2B	3B	HR	RBI	BB	SO	SB	OBP	SLG
2019	17	Blue Jays (GCL)	R	.222	14	45	8	10	2	2	0	5	9	17	6	.444	.356
Minor League Totals				.222	14	45	8	10	2	2	0	5	9	17	6	.444	.356

26 JOEY MURRAY, RHP

BA GRADE
40 Risk: High

Born: Sept. 23, 1996. **B-T:** R-R. **HT:** 6-2. **WT:** 195. **Drafted:** Kent State, 2018 (8th round). **Signed by:** Coulson Barbiche.

TRACK RECORD: Murray racked up strikeouts despite modest velocity at Kent State and was drafted in the eighth round by Toronto in 2018. He soared up to Double-A in his first full season in 2019 and led all Blue Jays minor leaguers in strikeouts. The Blue Jays brought him to their alternate training site in 2020.

SCOUTING REPORT: Murray piles up whiffs with a fastball that gets on hitters faster than they anticipate. It parks at 88-92 mph, with a slight uptick at the alternate site to 94 mph, and plays up with above-average spin and late riding life. On top of its movement, Murray has exceptional deception that makes it difficult for hitters to track the ball of his hand, leading to an abundance of empty swings when he elevates his fastball. Murray's slow curveball gets mixed reviews. Some scouts consider it a fringe-average pitch that better hitters might lay off. Others see good rotation and bite to keep hitters off-balance. He throws a fringy slider and hasn't used much of his below-average changeup, with his changeup a developmental focus. Murray is a solid strike-thrower and a student of the game who prepares for the strengths and weaknesses of opposing lineups.

THE FUTURE: Some scouts think Murray's act may be more smoke-and-mirrors that won't translate against major league hitters, but he could develop into a back-end starter similar to Josh Collmenter, with a chance to get starts with Toronto at some point in 2021.

Year	Age	Club (League)	Class	W	L	ERA	G	GS	IP	H	HR	BB	SO	BB/9	SO/9	WHIP	AVG
2019	22	Dunedin (FSL)	HiA	5	2	1.71	12	11	63	40	3	19	77	2.7	11.0	0.94	.152
	22	New Hampshire (EL)	AA	2	4	3.50	9	8	44	37	4	18	52	3.7	10.7	1.26	.218
	22	Lansing (MWL)	LoA	3	1	3.82	6	6	31	28	3	12	40	3.5	11.7	1.30	.214
Minor League Totals				11	8	2.60	40	31	163	124	11	59	208	3.3	11.5	1.12	.209

27 TANNER MORRIS, SS

BA GRADE
40 Risk: High

Born: Sept. 13, 1998. **B-T:** L-R. **HT:** 6-2. **WT:** 180. **Drafted:** Virginia, 2019 (5th round). **Signed by:** Coulson Barbiche.

TRACK RECORD: Morris had a strong summer in the Cape Cod League and followed it up by hitting .345/.452/.507 with more walks than strikeouts as a draft-eligible sophomore at Virginia in 2019. The Blue Jays drafted him in the fifth round and signed him for $397,500. Morris showed the same on-base skills in his pro debut in the short-season Northwest League after signing, but he arrived at instructional league in 2020 having lost weight, which took a toll on his performance.

SCOUTING REPORT: Morris is a disciplined hitter who doesn't expand the strike zone and puts himself in advantageous counts to manage his at-bats. He has a simple lefty stroke and good bat control with a swing geared for line drives and sending the ball to the opposite field. If he learns to turn on certain pitches, there could be more power coming, but he doesn't project as a power threat for now. Morris has a strong arm and generally makes the routine play on balls he can get to, but his first-step quickness and range is thin for shortstop, which should lead him to second or third base, with a focus on improving his body positioning on defense.

THE FUTURE: Morris has the components to be a high on-base threat if he can drive the ball with more impact. He is set to open 2021 at one of the Class A levels.

Year	Age	Club (League)	Class	AVG	G	AB	R	H	2B	3B	HR	RBI	BB	SO	SB	OBP	SLG
2019	20	Vancouver (NWL)	SS	.246	64	240	37	59	16	1	2	28	49	56	4	.384	.346
Minor League Totals				.246	64	240	37	59	16	1	2	28	49	56	4	.384	.346

28 YOSVER ZULUETA, RHP

BA GRADE
45 Risk: Extreme

Born: Jan. 23, 1998. **B-T:** R-R. **HT:** 6-1. **WT:** 190. **Signed:** Cuba, 2019. **Signed by:** Sandy Rosario/Luis Natera.

TRACK RECORD: The Blue Jays signed Zulueta at 21 for $1 million near the end of the 2018-19 international signing period, but he needed Tommy John surgery shortly afterward. He spent the 2020 season rehabbing in Florida and began showing his previous big velocity during live batting practice sessions in December.

SCOUTING REPORT: Zulueta's fastball ranges from 93-97 mph and tops out at 98. He's an athletic pitcher with a loose, quick arm and has late life on his four-seam fastball. Zulueta throws a hard, power curveball in the low 80s with good bite and three-quarters action. It's more advanced than his changeup, which has some depth. Zulueta's command remains scattered as he goes through the early stages of returning from surgery.

THE FUTURE: Zulueta is a wild card as an electric arm with a lot of uncertainty and a wide range of outcomes. He will develop as a starter and pitch his first official games in 2021.

Year	Age	Club (League)	Class	W	L	ERA	G	GS	IP	H	HR	BB	SO	BB/9	SO/9	WHIP	AVG
2020	22	Did not play—No minor league season															

29 SEM ROBBERSE, RHP

BA GRADE 45 Risk: Extreme

Born: Oct. 12, 2001. **B-T:** R-R. **HT:** 6-1. **WT:** 180. **Signed:** Netherlands, 2019. **Signed by:** Andrew Tinnish.

TRACK RECORD: In the summer of 2018, Robberse was a skinny 16-year-old throwing in the mid 80s. The following spring, he reached 88 mph before signing with the Blue Jays for $125,000. After signing, Robberse went to the United States and hit 90 mph. Once the Rookie-level Gulf Coast League started, he was up to 93 mph. Robberse has a host of projection indicators pointing in the right direction, but the 2020 season hampered his development. He stayed in Florida with a group of Venezuelan players the Blue Jays had in a hotel during the shutdown, training there over the summer before heading home prior to instructional league.

SCOUTING REPORT: Robberse pitches with incredible ease of operation, throwing with fluid, easy mechanics. Adding weight and getting stronger helped Robberse's velocity tick up in 2019, and between his remaining physical projection, arm speed and relatively clean delivery, there's probably more velocity coming. He mixes four- and two-seam fastballs with the athleticism to repeat his delivery and shows command of both. He shows a feel for a breaking ball that flashes solid-average and is in the early stages of learning to throw a changeup.

THE FUTURE: There is a wide range of possible outcomes for Robberse. He's a breakout candidate if his stuff continues its upward trend in 2021.

Year	Age	Club (League)	Class	W	L	ERA	G	GS	IP	H	HR	BB	SO	BB/9	SO/9	WHIP	AVG
2019	17	Blue Jays (GCL)	R	2	0	0.87	5	3	10	11	0	0	9	0.0	7.8	1.06	.268
Minor League Totals				2	0	0.87	5	3	10	11	0	0	9	0.0	7.8	1.06	.275

30 PHIL CLARKE, C

BA GRADE 40 Risk: High

Born: March 24, 1998. **B-T:** L-R. **HT:** 5-11. **WT:** 205. **Drafted:** Vanderbilt, 2019 (9th round). **Signed by:** Nate Murrie.

TRACK RECORD: An offensive-minded catcher at Vanderbilt, Clarke hit .308/.388/.480 as a draft-eligible sophomore in 2019 and signed with the Blue Jays for $497,5000 as a ninth-round pick. He made his pro debut in the short-season Northwest League and got his only game action in 2020 at instructional league, where he was one of the top hitters before he pulled a hamstring toward the end of camp.

SCOUTING REPORT: Clarke moves well in the batter's box, with explosive movements in a quick lefthanded swing and a knack for finding the barrel. An intelligent hitter with a good eye for the strike zone, Clarke showed up to instructional league bigger and stronger and began posting higher exit velocities than in previous years. He has never been a big power threat, but the added strength and barrel awareness give him a chance for 15-20 home runs. Clarke needs work defensively. He's not a great receiver, although his hands and blocking ability could be good enough. There are more questions about his throwing on account of his below-average arm strength and long release.

THE FUTURE: Clarke has to stick behind the plate to have a major league role, which would likely be an offensive-oriented backup. Low Class A is probably his next step.

Year	Age	Club (League)	Class	AVG	G	AB	R	H	2B	3B	HR	RBI	BB	SO	SB	OBP	SLG
2019	21	Vancouver (NWL)	SS	.257	37	144	24	37	5	0	2	16	21	22	1	.359	.333
Minor League Totals				.257	37	144	24	37	5	0	2	16	21	22	1	.359	.333

MORE PROSPECTS TO KNOW

31 RILEY ADAMS, C

Adams' strikeout rate is a red flag, but the 6-foot-4 catcher has plus raw power and a plus arm. With experience at Double-A in 2019 and time at the alternate training site in 2020, he could make his major league debut in 2021.

32 YENNSY DIAZ, RHP

A starter up through Double-A, Diaz made his major league debut as a reliever and a bullpen role might ultimately suit him best. He has a lively fastball that can touch 98 mph but lacks a reliable secondary pitch.

33 JOSH PALACIOS, OF

Palacios helped his stock at the Blue Jays' alternate training site over the summer, showing better plate discipline and contact frequency on pitches in the zone. He is in position to break in as a reserve outfielder at some point in 2021.

34 JULIAN MERRYWEATHER, RHP

Merryweather made his major league debut as a 28-year-old in 2020 out of Toronto's bullpen. His fastball, which is up to 99 mph, could keep him there if he improves his below-average control.

35 DAHIAN SANTOS, RHP

SLEEPER

A 2019 international signing out of Venezuela, Santos has a fastball that has ticked up to 94 mph with good movement. He is not very big at 5-foot-11, but he has an athletic delivery and throws strikes with a three-pitch mix that includes a curveball and changeup.

36 SAMAD TAYLOR, 2B

Taylor struggled at high Class A Dunedin in 2019 but had a much higher contact rate in 2020 at instructional league—albeit as a 22-year-old who was one of the older players in camp. He is an athletic player with plus speed who can put a surprising charge into the ball for his size.

37 KEVIN SMITH, SS

After a strong 2018, Smith never got a chance to rebound from a disastrous 2019 season. The Blue Jays left him unprotected for the Rule 5 draft in December, but he did not get picked.

38 T.J. ZEUCH, RHP

A 2016 first-round pick, Zeuch's upside now looks more muted at 25. He is a 6-foot-7 pitcher who sinks the ball and doesn't miss many bats, but he has MLB experience and could be a fifth starter or swingman.

39 JOSH WINCKOWSKI, RHP

A 15th-round pick in 2016, Winckowski reached high Class A Dunedin in 2019 with a fastball that has been up to 96 mph and good feel for a breaking ball.

40 ZACH BRITTON, OF

A fifth-round pick in 2020 out of Louisville, Britton hit well at instructional league on account of a nice lefthanded stroke with good bat speed and hard contact. He's likely a left fielder.

TOP PROSPECTS OF THE DECADE

Year	Player, Pos	2020 Org
2011	Kyle Drabek, RHP	Did not play
2012	Travis d'Arnaud, C	Braves
2013	Travis d'Arnaud, C	Braves
2014	Aaron Sanchez, RHP	Did not play
2015	Daniel Norris, LHP	Tigers
2016	Anthony Alford, OF	Pirates
2017	Vladimir Guerrero Jr., 3B	Blue Jays
2018	Vladimir Guerrero Jr., 3B	Blue Jays
2019	Vladimir Guerrero Jr., 3B	Blue Jays
2020	Nate Pearson, RHP	Blue Jays

TOP DRAFT PICKS OF THE DECADE

Year	Player, Pos	2020 Org
2011	*Tyler Beede, RHP	Giants
2012	D.J. Davis, OF	Did not play
2013	*Phil Bickford, RHP	Brewers
2014	Jeff Hoffman, RHP	Rockies
2015	Jon Harris, RHP	Blue Jays
2016	T.J. Zeuch, RHP	Blue Jays
2017	Logan Warmoth, SS	Blue Jays
2018	Jordan Groshans, SS	Blue Jays
2019	Alek Manoah, RHP	Blue Jays
2020	Austin Martin, SS	Blue Jays

* Did not sign

DEPTH CHART

TORONTO BLUE JAYS

TOP 2021 ROOKIES	RANK
Nate Pearson, RHP	1
Alejandro Kirk, C	5
BREAKOUT PROSPECTS	**RANK**
Estiven Machado, SS	13
Leonardo Jimenez, SS	16
Victor Mesia, C	17

SOURCE OF TOP 30 TALENT

Homegrown	25	Acquired	5
College	9	Trade	5
Junior college	1	Rule 5 draft	0
High school	4	Independent league	0
Nondrafted free agent	0	Free agent/waivers	0
International	11		

LF
Zach Britton
Cristian Feliz

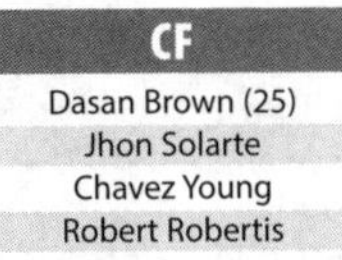

CF
Dasan Brown (25)
Jhon Solarte
Chavez Young
Robert Robertis

RF
Will Robertson (22)
Josh Palacios

3B
Peniel Brito

SS
Austin Martin (2)
Jordan Groshans (3)
Orelvis Martinez (6)
Estiven Machado (13)
Leonardo Jimenez (16)
Rikelbin de Castro (18)
Santiago Espinal (21)
Kevin Smith

2B
Miguel Hiraldo (10)
Otto Lopez (12)
Tanner Morris (27)
Samad Taylor

1B
Ryan Noda

C
Alejandro Kirk (5)
Gabriel Moreno (8)
Victor Mesia (17)
Phil Clarke (30)
Riley Adams

LHP

LHSP	LHRP
Rafael Monsion	Anthony Kay (20)

RHP

RHSP	RHRP
Nate Pearson (1)	Thomas Hatch (15)
S. Woods Richardson (4)	Patrick Murphy (19)
Alek Manoah (7)	Yennsy Diaz
Adam Kloffenstein (9)	Julian Merryweather
C.J. Van Eyk (11)	Anthony Castro
Eric Pardinho (14)	
Nick Frasso (23)	
Trent Palmer (24)	
Joey Murray (26)	
Yosver Zulueta (28)	
Sem Robberse (29)	
Dahian Santos	
T.J. Zeuch	
Josh Winckowski	

Washington Nationals

BY LACY LUSK

The Nationals started 19-31 in 2020—just as they did in 2019 before turning everything around and winning the World Series.

But in the Covid-19-shortened 60-game season, there was no time to make up for such a subpar start.

Washington missed out on its opportunity to celebrate at Nationals Park with its fans, and so much else felt absent in a 26-34 season.

Left fielder Juan Soto led the National League in batting average (.351), on-base percentage (.490), slugging (.695) and adjusted-OPS+ (212), in the process becoming the youngest National League batting champion at age 21. Shortstop Trea Turner had a terrific season, but World Series MVP Stephen Strasburg pitched just five innings and needed surgery to alleviate carpal tunnel neuritis.

Anthony Rendon, who left to sign with the Angels in free agency, proved irreplaceable at third base, where preseason top prospect Carter Kieboom hit .202/.344/.212 with only one extra-base hit in 99 at-bats.

Fellow top prospect Luis Garcia fared somewhat better, taking the injured Starlin Castro's spot at second base and hitting .276/.302/.366 in 134 at-bats while becoming the first player born in the 2000s to homer in the major leagues. The 20-year-old Garcia also hit a game-winning home run in extra innings at Tampa Bay.

The Nationals are hoping to see some breakthroughs down on the farm in 2021. They are excited about their 2020 draft picks, especially the four from the first three rounds: college righthanders Cade Cavalli and Cole Henry, high school shortstop Sammy Infante and college closer Holden Powell.

Even without a minor league season, several Nationals prospects made jumps forward at the team's alternate training site in Fredericksburg, Va. Righthander Jackson Rutledge, a 2019 first-round pick who finished his draft year in low Class A, could be ready to move quickly.

One prospect who leaped to the majors in 2020 was lefthander Seth Romero, a 2017 first-round pick who was coming off Tommy John surgery. He had never pitched above low Class A until he appeared in three games out of Washington's bullpen, but even that feel-good story took a bad turn when he fell down stairs and caught himself with his non-pitching hand. He needed surgery and was out for the season.

Fellow lefthander Ben Braymer also made his debut. In Braymer's one start, he held the Marlins to one hit over five scoreless innings. Righthander Wil Crowe also had a taste of the majors in 2020 and will be a potential option for the future.

NICOLE FRIDLING/ICON SPORTSWIRE VIA GETTY IMAGES

The Nationals don't have much on the farm but have Juan Soto for at least four more seasons.

PROJECTED 2024 LINEUP

Position	Player	Age
Catcher	Tres Barrera	29
First Base	Yasel Antuna	24
Second Base	Luis Garcia	24
Third Base	Carter Kieboom	26
Shortstop	Trea Turner	31
Left Field	Juan Soto	25
Center Field	Victor Robles	27
Right Field	Andrew Stevenson	30
Designated Hitter	Drew Mendoza	26
No. 1 Starter	Stephen Strasburg	36
No. 2 Starter	Patrick Corbin	34
No. 3 Starter	Cade Cavalli	25
No. 4 Starter	Jackson Rutledge	25
No. 5 Starter	Cole Henry	24
Closer	Tanner Rainey	31

The Nationals tied the Mets for fourth in the NL East after winning three of four from the Phillies and three of four from New York to close the season. Yadiel Hernandez, a 32-year-old outfielder who was Washington's 2019 minor league player of the year, made history in one of the wins over Philadelphia when he became the oldest player to hit a walk-off as his first major league homer.

Those magical moments were hard to come by in 2020, but the franchise looks forward to celebrating 2019 and starting fresh in 2021. ■

1 CADE CAVALLI, RHP

Born: Aug. 14, 1998. **B-T:** R-R. **HT:** 6-4. **WT:** 226.
Drafted: Oklahoma, 2020 (1st round).
Signed by: Jerad Head.

TOM DIPACE

BA GRADE
55 **Risk: High**

SCOUTING GRADES
FB: 70. **SL:** 60. **CB:** 55.
CHG: 55. **CTL:** 50.

Projected future grades on 20-80 scouting scale.

TRACK RECORD: After two seasons in a two-way role for Oklahoma where he pitched and served as a designated hitter, Cavalli focused on pitching as a junior in 2020. The move paid off as he showed significantly improved control in his four starts before the season was shut down because of coronavirus. The former USA Baseball Collegiate National Team member already was a known commodity to Nationals general manager Mike Rizzo and the entire scouting community–he was a 29th round pick of the Braves coming out of high school. Washington took him 22nd overall and signed him for $3.027 million in 2020. Cavalli fit right into a spot in the club's 60-man player pool and impressed the big leaguers with his performance in a simulated game at Nationals Park before the start of the delayed major league season. Cavalli had back issues in high school and a stress reaction in his arm in college, but he was healthy all summer while adjusting to pitching every sixth day instead of once a week. One of his off-the-field interests has helped him get to know teammates better. He estimates he has given more than 500 haircuts.

SCOUTING REPORT: Cavalli accurately described himself on draft night as a blend of power and pitchability. His fastball sits in the mid 90s with ease and touches 98 mph. More than just a thrower, he complements his heater with an array of impressive secondaries. His slider is a devastating offering at 87-90 mph with impressive tilt and gets swings and misses against both lefthanded and righthanded hitters . His curveball is a hard downer that hitters don't see well, and he can manipulate his changeup to throw it with diving action and either sink or run. He has an efficient delivery and elite makeup. Cavalli i s a former Big 12 Conference first baseman who hit six home runs as a freshman and four as a sophomore (as part of a .319/.393/.611 season as the team's DH). He has plenty of athleticism and good body control. Cavalli's father Brian was a catcher at Oklahoma and in the Angels' system, so Cade has also seen the game from the other side of the battery. The reason he was still available at No. 22 overall is he got hit more in college than his raw stuff would suggest, in part because he lacks deception and his control can be erratic. Scouts love Cavalli's smooth delivery, but that ease of effort means he lacks deception. The Nationals like the work Cavalli did with coach Skip Johnson and the rest of the Sooners staff, so any tweaks they've made have been minor. Cavalli has a strong work ethic and a desire to not just make the majors but to become a regular all-star.

THE FUTURE: Cavalli and Jackson Rutledge give the Nationals a pair of hard-throwing righthanders with a chance to develop into future anchors in the rotation. Cavalli logged more than 50 innings combined between the alternate training site and instructional league in Florida, so he should be ready to go in 2021. Health and control will dictate how fast he moves through the system. ■

BEST TOOLS

Best Hitter for Average	Yasel Antuna
Best Power Hitter	Yasel Antuna
Best Strike-Zone Discipline	Drew Mendoza
Fastest Baserunner	Cody Wilson
Best Athlete	Cody Wilson
Best Fastball	Jackson Rutledge
Best Curveball	Tim Cate
Best Slider	Jackson Rutledge
Best Changeup	Steven Fuentes
Best Control	Tim Cate
Best Defensive Catcher	Tres Barrera
Best Defensive Infielder	Jackson Cluff
Best Infield Arm	Jackson Cluff
Best Defensive Outfielder	Cody Wilson
Best Outfield Arm	Daniel Marte

Year	Age	Club (League)	Class	W	L	ERA	G	GS	IP	H	HR	BB	SO	BB/9	SO/9	WHIP	AVG
2020	21	Did not play—No minor league season															

2 JACKSON RUTLEDGE, RHP

MIKE JANES/FOUR SEAM IMAGES

Born: April 1, 1999. **B-T:** R-R. **HT:** 6-8. **WT:** 250. **Drafted:** San Jacinto (Texas) JC, 2019 (1st round). **Signed by:** Brandon Larson.

TRACK RECORD: The imposing, 6-foot-8 Rutledge hit 101 mph at San Jacinto (Texas) JC, where he became the fourth junior college player ever nominated as a Golden Spikes Award semifinalist. The Nationals drafted him 17th overall and signed him for $3.45 million. Rutledge then dominated hitters at three stops, culminating in the low Class A South Atlantic League in his pro debut. The Nationals brought him to their alternate training site in 2020.

SCOUTING REPORT: Rutledge is an intimidating, aggressive pitcher with a high-90s fastball and a wipeout slider. Both are plus pitches that draw swings and misses, and he complements them with a curveball and changeup that are average, usable offerings. Rutledge stays tall on the mound and uses a compact arm action. The ball appears to come out of his shoulder and gets on hitters quickly with explosive life. He's a decent athlete who improved in 2020 at slowing things down and pitching under control, helping him throw more strikes. Rutledge does a good job of holding baserunners. He prides himself on his craft and eagerly studies analytics.

THE FUTURE: Rutledge benefited from facing more experienced hitters at the alternate site. He is part of the Nationals' future rotation plans and may see the upper minors in 2021.

SCOUTING GRADES: **Fastball:** 70 **Slider:** 60 **Curveball:** 50 **Changeup:** 50 **Control:** 50

Year	Age	Club (League)	Class	W	L	ERA	G	GS	IP	H	HR	BB	SO	BB/9	SO/9	WHIP	AVG
2019	20	Auburn (NYP)	SS	0	0	3.00	3	3	9	4	2	3	6	3.0	6.0	0.78	.118
	20	Nationals (GCL)	R	0	0	27.00	1	1	1	4	0	1	2	9.0	18.0	5.00	.444
	20	Hagerstown (SAL)	LoA	2	0	2.30	6	6	27	14	0	11	31	3.6	10.2	0.91	.132
Minor League Totals				2	0	3.13	10	10	37	22	2	15	39	3.6	9.4	0.99	.169

3 COLE HENRY, RHP

WHITNEY WILLISTON/LSU ATHLETICS

Born: July 15, 1999. **B-T:** R-R. **HT:** 6-4. **WT:** 214. **Drafted:** Louisiana State, 2020 (2nd round). **Signed by:** Brandon Larson.

TRACK RECORD: Henry touched 97 mph in high school but fell to the 38th round due to his strong commitment to Louisiana State. He became the Tigers' Friday night starter immediately as a freshman and was off to another excellent start in 2020 before the season shut down. The Nationals drafted the eligible sophomore in the second round, No. 55 overall, and signed him for $2 million.

SCOUTING REPORT: Henry is a big, physical righthander with power stuff. His plus four-seam fastball sits at 94 mph and touches 97. He also has a two-seamer with solid sink in the mid 90s. Henry's curveball flashes the depth and power to be an above-average pitch as a top-to-bottom, 12-to-6 offering. His fading changeup has flashed plus as well. Henry flashes premium stuff, but it's not consistent and he has outings where he can't put hitters away. He struggles to land his secondaries in the strike zone, allowing batters to sit on his fastball and drive it. Henry is a fiery competitor who goes right after hitters. The Nationals are excited about the tall pitcher's frame and how his arm works.

THE FUTURE: Henry took part in instructional league and should open next year in full-season ball. How quickly he harnesses his command will determine how fast he rises.

SCOUTING GRADES: **Fastball:** 60 **Changeup:** 55 **Curveball:** 50 **Control:** 50

Year	Age	Club (League)	Class	W	L	ERA	G	GS	IP	H	HR	BB	SO	BB/9	SO/9	WHIP	AVG
2020	20	Did not play—No minor league season															

4 YASEL ANTUNA, SS

Born: Oct. 26, 1999. **B-T:** B-R. **HT:** 6-0. **WT:** 170. **Signed:** Dominican Republic, 2016. **Signed by:** Pablo Arias.

TRACK RECORD: The highly-touted Antuna struggled with injuries after signing for $3.85 million in 2016, but he accrued hundreds of reps at the alternate training site against upper-level pitchers in 2020 and thrived. He hit 11 home runs during one two-week period and showed arguably the best hitting ability and power potential in the Nationals' system.

SCOUTING REPORT: Finally clear from the Tommy John surgery and leg injuries that kept him off the field for nearly two years, Antuna showed what he can do when healthy. The switch-hitter has plus bat speed, a relaxed approach and a repeatable swing from both sides of the plate. He hits home runs to all fields from both sides and has no problem catching up to upper-90s velocity. He has among the best strike-zone judgment in the system and an advanced two-strike approach. He also showed improved ability to recognize and hit offspeed pitches. Antuna's future positional home is up for question. He has improved his footwork and exchanges around second base to give him a better chance to stay in the middle infield. He'll remain a shortstop for now but may move to a corner as he gets bigger.

THE FUTURE: Antuna's bat gives him a chance to move up the system quickly as long as he stays healthy. His fantastic summer gives him a chance to see the upper minors in 2021.

SCOUTING GRADES: **Hitting:** 50 **Power:** 60 **Running:** 50 **Fielding:** 45 **Arm:** 50

Year	Age	Club (League)	Class	AVG	G	AB	R	H	2B	3B	HR	RBI	BB	SO	SB	OBP	SLG
2017	17	Nationals (GCL)	R	.301	48	173	25	52	8	3	1	17	23	29	5	.382	.399
2018	18	Hagerstown (SAL)	LoA	.220	87	323	44	71	14	2	6	27	32	79	8	.293	.331
2019	19	Nationals (GCL)	R	.167	3	6	1	1	0	0	0	0	2	1	0	.375	.167
Minor League Totals				.247	138	502	70	124	22	5	7	44	57	109	13	.325	.353

5 ANDRY LARA, RHP

Born: Jan. 6, 2003. **B-T:** R-R. **HT:** 6-5. **WT:** 235. **Signed:** Venezuela, 2019. **Signed by:** Ronald Morillo.

TRACK RECORD: Lara was the Nationals' top signing in the 2019 international class and received a $1.25 million bonus. He was set to make his debut in 2020, but was delayed after the coronavirus pandemic canceled the minor league season. Lara spent the summer working out at the Nationals' facility in West Palm Beach, Fla., and impressed the strength and conditioning staff with his dedication in the weight room. He showed the same dedication in the classroom and completed the club's Rosetta Stone language program.

SCOUTING REPORT: Lara is a 6-foot-5 righthander who throws his 92-96 mph fastball downhill with little effort. He has a quick arm and still has room to get stronger and add more velocity to his fastball. His slider is developing and shows the potential to be a swing-and-miss pitch. He also shows a feel for a nascent sinking changeup. Lara has a big frame he will have to maintain, but he has generally been a solid strike-thrower to this point in his career.

THE FUTURE: After experience in instructional leagues in both the U.S. and the Dominican Republic, Lara may jump straight to low Class A as an 18-year-old. He has the potential to be a solid starter and shows the aptitude to move quickly for his age.

SCOUTING GRADES: **Fastball:** 60 **Slider:** 60 **Changeup:** 50 **Control:** 50

Year	Age	Club (League)	Class	W	L	ERA	G	GS	IP	H	HR	BB	SO	BB/9	SO/9	WHIP	AVG
2020	17	Did not play—No minor league season															

6 JEREMY DE LA ROSA, OF

TOM DIPACE

BA GRADE
50 Risk: Extreme

Born: Jan. 16, 2002. **B-T:** L-L. **HT:** 5-11. **WT:** 160. **Signed:** Dominican Republic, 2018. **Signed by:** Modesto Ulloa.

TRACK RECORD: The Nationals signed De La Rosa for $300,000 in 2018 and challenged him by skipping him over the Dominican Summer League to the Rookie-level Gulf Coast League. He showed enough promise to get tested again in 2020 when he made Washington's 60-man player pool and competed well against upper-level minor leaguers at the alternate training site. He hit a couple of the longest home runs to center field of anyone in camp at the new ballpark in Fredericksburg, Va.

SCOUTING REPORT: De La Rosa has already learned how to get into a good hitting position. He gets on plane early and looks to drive the ball on a line. Like several young hitters in the system, he has taken to imitating National League batting champion Juan Soto's two-strike approach. De La Rosa has juice in his bat and can hit high-velocity fastballs to all fields. He has made progress at laying off breaking balls out of the strike zone. He's a plus athlete who looks like an NFL wide receiver when he runs down fly balls. He's capable of playing all three outfield positions.

THE FUTURE: Though De La Rosa has yet to play in a full-season league, he showed in 2020 that he's not afraid of facing older competition. With his bat speed and his power, he has a chance to be an impact hitter.

SCOUTING GRADES: **Hitting:** 50 **Power:** 55 **Running:** 55 **Fielding:** 50 **Arm:** 50

Year	Age	Club (League)	Class	AVG	G	AB	R	H	2B	3B	HR	RBI	BB	SO	SB	OBP	SLG
2019	17	Nationals (GCL)	R	.232	26	82	14	19	1	2	2	10	12	29	3	.343	.366
Minor League Totals				.232	26	82	14	19	1	2	2	10	12	29	3	.343	.366

7 TIM CATE, LHP

BA GRADE
45 Risk: High

Born: Sept. 30, 1997. **B-T:** L-L. **HT:** 6-0. **WT:** 185. **Drafted:** Connecticut, 2018 (2nd round). **Signed by:** John Malone.

TRACK RECORD: The lefthanded Cate had Tommy John surgery in high school but was so eager to continue playing that he pitched with his right arm. He went on to set the University of Connecticut's career strikeout record and was drafted in the second round, No. 65 overall, by the Nationals in 2018. Cate won the organization's minor league pitcher of the year award in 2019, then spent 2020 at the alternate training site in Fredericksburg, Va.

SCOUTING REPORT: Cate is undersized but has shown moxie at each level he's pitched. He maintains a consistent effort level and has a smooth delivery. By moving the ball to all quadrants of the strike zone, he's able to stay away from hitters' barrels. That's important because his fastball is a fringy offering that lives in the 89-90 mph range. It plays up some with his ability to cut and sink it. Cate's curveball is his signature pitch as a hammer in the low 80s that he has an exceptional feel to command. His changeup made great strides at the alternate site and began flashing above-average. Cate is an excellent strike-thrower who can locate his pitches to both sides of the plate.

THE FUTURE: Cate is set to see the upper minors in 2021. He has a shot to make it as a back-of-the-rotation lefthander.

SCOUTING GRADES: **Fastball:** 45 **Curveball:** 60 **Changeup:** 55 **Control:** 55

Year	Age	Club (League)	Class	W	L	ERA	G	GS	IP	H	HR	BB	SO	BB/9	SO/9	WHIP	AVG
2018	20	Auburn (NYP)	SS	2	3	4.65	9	8	31	34	1	10	26	2.9	7.5	1.42	.246
	20	Hagerstown (SAL)	LoA	0	3	5.57	4	4	21	23	4	6	19	2.6	8.1	1.38	.247
2019	21	Fredericksburg (CAR)	HiA	7	4	3.31	13	13	73	71	4	19	66	2.3	8.1	1.23	.235
	21	Hagerstown (SAL)	LoA	4	5	2.82	13	13	70	61	2	13	73	1.7	9.3	1.05	.219
Minor League Totals				13	15	3.59	39	38	195	189	11	48	184	2.2	8.5	1.21	.252

8 EDDY YEAN, RHP

BA GRADE
50 Risk: Extreme

Born: June 25, 2001. **B-T:** R-R. **HT:** 6-1. **WT:** 230. **Signed:** Dominican Republic, 2017. **Signed by:** Modesto Ulloa.

TRACK RECORD: Yean was a projectable 180-pound righthander when he signed with the Nationals for $100,000 in 2017. He's grown quite a bit since then, bulking up to 230 pounds with a muscular, linebacker-like build. He made his U.S. debut in 2019 and reached short-season Auburn, but he did not get to pitch in 2020 with the cancellation of the minor league season. He picked up where he left off with an impressive turn at instructional league.

SCOUTING REPORT: Yean is a big, powerful pitcher who is aggressive and still growing. He has an explosive fastball that sits in the mid 90s and touches 97 mph with late life. He throws both a four-seam fastball and a two-seamer to keep batters guessing which one they'll see. Yean's slider is a little slurvy at this point but gets swings and misses and shows above-average potential, especially if he is able to firm it up. His changeup is improving as well and could be an average pitch in time. Yean has a clean, three-quarters arm slot and a feel for making adjustments.

THE FUTURE: Yean is still learning the details of pitching rather than throwing, but the Nationals are high on his upside. He should be ready for a full-season assignment at age 19 in 2021.

SCOUTING GRADES: **Fastball:** 60 **Slider:** 55 **Changeup:** 50 **Control:** 50

Year	Age	Club (League)	Class	W	L	ERA	G	GS	IP	H	HR	BB	SO	BB/9	SO/9	WHIP	AVG
2018	17	Nationals (DSL)	R	1	2	5.98	11	10	44	57	1	23	32	4.7	6.6	1.83	.275
2019	18	Auburn (NYP)	SS	1	1	2.45	2	2	11	7	0	5	7	4.1	5.7	1.09	.159
	18	Nationals (GCL)	R	1	2	3.82	8	8	35	30	3	12	36	3.1	9.2	1.19	.205
Minor League Totals				3	5	4.70	21	20	90	94	4	40	75	4.0	7.5	1.49	.272

9 MASON DENABURG, RHP

MIKE JANES/FOUR SEAM IMAGES

BA GRADE
50 Risk: Extreme

Born: Aug. 8, 1999. **B-T:** R-R. **HT:** 6-4. **WT:** 195. **Drafted:** HS—Merritt Island, Fla., 2018 (1st round). **Signed by:** Alan Marr.

TRACK RECORD: Denaburg was one of the top high school pitchers in the 2018 draft class but was limited to eight starts his senior year by biceps tendinitis. The Nationals still took him 27th overall and signed him for $3 million. Injuries have continued to limit Denaburg in pro ball. He had shoulder surgery after a disappointing 2019 season and dealt with tenderness in 2020 before the coronavirus pandemic shutdown. He began throwing with fewer restrictions at the start of instructional league.

SCOUTING REPORT: When healthy, Denaburg has a 91-94 mph fastball that touches 97. He didn't show that velocity in his pro debut, but he impressed team officials with his progression during his recovery. Rehab pitching coordinator Mark Grater sent video to colleagues who say Denaburg has built up his body and is in great shape. Denaburg also has a high-spin, upper-70s curveball that shows above-average potential. His developing changeup has potential to be average. Denaburg is a good athlete who caught as well as pitched in high school and fields his position well. He was wild in his pro debut and has to prove he can get to fringe-average control.

THE FUTURE: It all comes down to health for Denaburg. He's thrown just 20 professional innings and needs development time to catch up.

SCOUTING GRADES: **Fastball:** 60 **Curveball:** 55 **Changeup:** 50 **Control:** 45

Year	Age	Club (League)	Class	W	L	ERA	G	GS	IP	H	HR	BB	SO	BB/9	SO/9	WHIP	AVG
2019	19	Nationals (GCL)	R	1	1	7.52	7	4	20	23	1	14	19	6.2	8.4	1.82	.228
Minor League Totals				1	1	7.52	7	4	20	23	1	14	19	6.2	8.4	1.82	.288

10 WIL CROWE, RHP

MARY DECICCO/MLB PHOTOS VIA GETTY IMAGES

BA GRADE 45 Risk: High

Born: Sept. 9, 1994. **B-T:** R-R. **HT:** 6-2. **WT:** 240. **Drafted:** South Carolina, 2017 (2nd round). **Signed by:** Paul Faulk.

TRACK RECORD: Crowe had Tommy John surgery as a freshman at South Carolina but rebounded to become the Gamecocks' ace by his junior year. The Nationals drafted him in the second round in 2017 and signed him for $946,500. Crowe won the high Class A Carolina League pitcher of the year award in 2018, when he went 11-0, 2.69 in 87 innings, jumped to Triple-A in 2019 and made his major league debut in 2020. He tested positive for Covid-19 and missed summer camp but recovered in time to make his first three major league starts.

SCOUTING REPORT: Crowe didn't trust his stuff in his first major league outings, but the Nationals believe he has a future as a possible No. 5 starter or relief option. Crowe's fastball sits at 91-93 mph and touches 95. He can spin an average slider and curveball and shows the makings of a changeup with average potential, as well. Crowe's stuff is all average, but he's a tough competitor who has better command than he showed in his major league debut. He fell into too many deep counts and nibbled too much in his first taste of major league play.

THE FUTURE: Crowe will get another shot at the majors in 2021. The Nationals are intrigued to see what he learned from facing adversity at the highest level.

SCOUTING GRADES: **Fastball:** 50 **Curveball:** 50 **Slider:** 50 **Changeup:** 50 **Control:** 50

Year	Age	Club (League)	Class	W	L	ERA	G	GS	IP	H	HR	BB	SO	BB/9	SO/9	WHIP	AVG
2018	23	Fredericksburg (CAR)	HiA	11	0	2.69	16	15	87	71	6	30	78	3.1	8.1	1.16	.197
	23	Auburn (NYP)	SS	0	0	0.00	1	1	3	2	0	2	1	6.0	3.0	1.33	.182
	23	Harrisburg (EL)	AA	0	5	6.15	5	5	26	31	4	16	15	5.5	5.1	1.78	.261
2019	24	Fresno (PCL)	AAA	0	4	6.17	10	10	54	66	7	26	41	4.3	6.8	1.70	.264
	24	Harrisburg (EL)	AA	7	6	3.87	16	16	95	85	8	22	89	2.1	8.4	1.12	.222
2020	25	Washington (NL)	MAJ	0	2	11.88	3	3	8	14	5	8	8	8.6	8.6	2.64	.378
Major League Totals				0	2	11.88	3	3	8	14	5	8	8	8.6	8.6	2.64	.378
Minor League Totals				18	15	4.03	57	56	290	276	28	100	241	3.1	7.5	1.30	.253

11 MATT CRONIN, LHP

Born: Sept. 20, 1997. **B-T:** L-L. **HT:** 6-2. **WT:** 195. **Drafted:** Arkansas, 2019 (4th round). **Signed by:** Jerad Head.

TRACK RECORD: Cronin saved 14 games as a sophomore for Arkansas, helping lead the program to the College World Series finals. The next year, he had 12 saves as the Razorbacks returned to Omaha. He signed with the Nationals for $464,500 as a fourth-round pick in 2019 and struck out 16.8 batters per nine innings over 17 appearances at low Class A Hagerstown in his pro debut. The Nationals brought him to the alternate site in 2020 and he finished the year at instructional league.

SCOUTING REPORT: Cronin impresses with the spin on his 93-96 mph fastball and hammer 12-to-6 curveball, each of which grade as potential plus pitches. Cronin's fastball works at the top and bottom of the zone, and his curve has late break and good depth. Facing more experienced hitters at the alternate site taught him he needed to attack the strike zone earlier in counts. Cronin uses a split grip on his changeup, which has a chance to become a viable third—if below-average—pitch. His focus is on his big fastball, and he's not afraid to pitch inside to lefthanded and righthanded hitters.

THE FUTURE: Cronin's final dozen outings or so left team officials believing he could be on a fast track to Washington. With the Nats short on lefthanded options with Sean Doolittle set to depart in free agency, Cronin's major league debut could come in 2021.

Year	Age	Club (League)	Class	W	L	ERA	G	GS	IP	H	HR	BB	SO	BB/9	SO/9	WHIP	AVG
2019	21	Hagerstown (SAL)	LoA	0	0	0.82	17	0	22	11	1	11	41	4.5	16.8	1.00	.129
Minor League Totals				0	0	0.82	17	0	22	11	1	11	41	4.5	16.8	1.00	.153

12 DREW MENDOZA, 1B

Born: Oct. 10, 1997. **B-T:** L-R. **HT:** 6-5. **WT:** 230. **Drafted:** Florida State, 2019 (3rd round). **Signed by:** Alan Marr.

TRACK RECORD: Mendoza led the Atlantic Coast Conference in walks and on-base percentage in 2019 and helped lead Florida State to two College World Series trips in his three years in Tallahassee. He signed for $800,000 as a third-round pick in 2019 and immediately made the switch from third base to first base at low Class A Hagerstown. He reported to the alternate training site in August after what he called a "minimal" experience with Covid-19.

SCOUTING REPORT: The Nationals would like Mendoza to take more early-count swings, but he's begun to show more power to his pull side and use his legs better. His swing tends to get too long, but he has as much power potential as anybody in the system and shows enough feel for the barrel to project as an average hitter. He needs to make more consistent contact. Mendoza returned to third base at the alternate site and showed soft hands, above-average arm strength and improving footwork. His size still makes him a likely first baseman long term.

THE FUTURE: Mendoza will be tested by pitchers with better command at the upper levels. He'll take his first crack against them in 2021.

Year	Age	Club (League)	Class	AVG	G	AB	R	H	2B	3B	HR	RBI	BB	SO	SB	OBP	SLG
2019	21	Hagerstown (SAL)	LoA	.264	55	201	23	53	12	0	4	25	34	57	3	.377	.383
Minor League Totals				.264	55	201	23	53	12	0	4	25	34	57	3	.377	.383

13 JACKSON CLUFF, SS

BREAKOUT

BA GRADE

45 Risk: High

Born: Dec. 3, 1996. **B-T:** L-R. **HT:** 6-0. **WT:** 185. **Drafted:** Brigham Young, 2019 (6th round). **Signed by:** Mitch Sokol.

TRACK RECORD: The Nationals' player development staff was pleased to add Cluff to the system as a 2019 sixth-round pick for just $200,000. The quick, twitchy athlete served a two-year Mormon mission but didn't miss a beat upon his return to Brigham Young, where he hit .327/.458/.518 in his draft year. Cluff made his pro debut at low Class A Hagerstown and chased too many pitches en route to batting .229/.320/.367 in 62 games. The Nationals made him a late addition to their alternate training site in 2020.

SCOUTING REPORT: Cluff primarily worked on hitting to all fields at the alternate site, where he was challenged by more experienced pitchers. He has sneaky power in his bat and is improving at getting the barrel to the ball. He tends to get pull happy, which takes away his ability to line the ball to the gaps and rack up doubles and triples. Cluff is an advanced defender with a strong arm who is capable of sticking at shortstop. The Nationals rave about his makeup.

THE FUTURE: Cluff should start at high Class A once the 2021 minor league season begins. The Nationals see him as at least a potential super-utility option.

Year	Age	Club (League)	Class	AVG	G	AB	R	H	2B	3B	HR	RBI	BB	SO	SB	OBP	SLG
2019	22	Hagerstown (SAL)	LoA	.229	62	240	33	55	8	5	5	19	26	63	11	.320	.367
Minor League Totals				.229	62	240	33	55	8	5	5	19	26	63	11	.320	.367

14 SAMMY INFANTE, SS

BA GRADE

50 Risk: Extreme

Born: June 22, 2001. **B-T:** R-R. **HT:** 6-1. **WT:** 175. **Drafted:** HS—Miami, 2020 (2nd round supplemental). **Signed by:** Alex Morales.

TRACK RECORD: Infante emerged early as one of the most well-rounded prep shortstops in the 2020 draft class and got off to a hot start in the spring before the coronavirus pandemic shut down the high school season. The Nationals drafted him 71st overall and signed him for an above-slot $1 million to forgo a Miami commitment. Infante made his organizational debut at instructional league, where he impressed team officials with his maturity.

SCOUTING REPORT: Infante has average or above-average tools across the board as well as strong intangibles. He has soft hands, some pull-side power and a good head on his shoulders. Infante is advanced for a high school draftee, especially when it comes to defensive fundamentals. His plus arm is his strongest tool and he has dynamic infield actions to go with sound instincts. Infante tends to drift in his swing and he needs to show he can make more consistent contact, but he has the raw ingredients to be an average hitter in time. His passion for the game gives him a chance to be a quick learner.

THE FUTURE: Infante's defense and intangibles make him arguably the most promising shortstop in the Nationals' system. How his bat comes along will determine if he reaches his everyday potential.

Year	Age	Club (League)	Class	AVG	G	AB	R	H	2B	3B	HR	RBI	BB	SO	SB	OBP	SLG
2020	19	Did not play—No minor league season															

15 SETH ROMERO, LHP

BA GRADE 45 Risk: High

Born: April 19, 1996. **B-T:** L-L. **HT:** 6-3. **WT:** 240. **Drafted:** Houston, 2017 (1st round). **Signed by:** Tyler Wilt.

TRACK RECORD: Romero's impressive slider and changeup helped make him the 25th overall pick in 2017, but off-the-field troubles and Tommy John surgery delayed his progress. He never pitched above low Class A until 2020, when the Nationals brought him to their alternate training site and called him up for his major league debut in August. Romero made only three relief appearances before he injured his non-pitching hand when he caught himself during a fall, ending his season.

SCOUTING REPORT: Romero's fastball is a bit down from what he showed in college—he topped at 93 mph in his big league stint—but his low-80s, potentially plus slider has become even nastier. The development of his low-80s changeup, which he can throw well to both sides of the plate, is a separator. Romero is fearless and attacks the zone. He throws all of his pitches for strikes with average control.

THE FUTURE: Romero will continue developing as a starter in the minors. His durability and health will determine if he can stay in that role or has to transition to relief.

Year	Age	Club (League)	Class	W	L	ERA	G	GS	IP	H	HR	BB	SO	BB/9	SO/9	WHIP	AVG
2020	24	Washington (NL)	MAJ	0	0	13.50	3	0	3	5	1	3	5	10.1	16.9	3.00	.333
Major League Totals				0	0	13.50	3	0	2	5	1	3	5	10.1	16.9	3.00	.333
Minor League Totals				0	2	4.37	14	14	47	39	3	16	69	3.0	13.1	1.16	.215

16 ISRAEL PINEDA, C

BREAKOUT
BA GRADE 45 Risk: Very High

Born: April 3, 2000. **B-T:** R-R. **HT:** 5-11. **WT:** 190. **Signed:** Venezuela, 2016. **Signed by:** German Robles.

TRACK RECORD: Pineda signed with the Nationals for $450,000 out of Venezuela in 2016 and impressed his first two years in short-season ball. He made the jump to low Class A Hagerstown in 2019 and struggled with strike zone discipline, batting .217/.278/.305. The Nationals still brought him to their alternate training site in 2020 and he finished the year in instructional league.

SCOUTING REPORT: Pineda showed growth and maturity at the alternate site and at instructional league, providing hope his poor 2019 was a mirage. A bat-first catcher, Pineda has a quick swing, above-average raw power and crushes fastballs. He's been undone by breaking balls in the past, but he has learned to take more pitches and put himself in better counts. Pineda's size and strong arm give him a good foundation as a catcher. His mobility is limited and his defensive skills need polish, but he is making progress.

THE FUTURE: Barrera should see high Class A in 2021. He has a chance to emerge as a part-time catcher if he can sustain his offensive improvements.

Year	Age	Club (League)	Class	AVG	G	AB	R	H	2B	3B	HR	RBI	BB	SO	SB	OBP	SLG
2019	19	Hagerstown (SAL)	LoA	.217	101	374	48	81	12	0	7	35	30	102	1	.278	.305
Minor League Totals				.239	164	598	83	143	24	2	11	71	46	150	1	.300	.341

17 TRES BARRERA, C

Born: Sept. 15, 1994. **B-T:** R-R. **HT:** 6-0. **WT:** 215. **Drafted:** Texas, 2016 (6th round). **Signed by:** Tyler Wilt.

TRACK RECORD: Barrera earned all-star honors at high Class A and Double-A en route to making his major league debut in 2019. He was in line for more big league time in 2020 but was suspended for the season after testing positive for an anabolic–androgenic steroid on Major League Baseball's banned-substance list. Barrera said he was wrongfully suspended based on "junk science" and filed a class action lawsuit against MLB, the commissioner's office, two testing labs and a director of one of the labs.

SCOUTING REPORT: Barrera's strength is his defense. He's an excellent receiver, controls the running game with solid arm strength and a quick exchange and shows the requisite leadership skills for catching. He's a slow runner but makes up for it with good short-area quickness and athleticism behind the plate. Barrera is more of a contact hitter than a power bat offensively, but he has held his own at every stop. He keeps his hands inside the ball, has a repeatable swing and has decent strike-zone discipline.

THE FUTURE: Barrera was reinstated from the restricted list at the end of the season and played in the Dominican League in the winter. He has a chance to be a backup catcher and should be ready to assume that role in 2021.

Year	Age	Club (League)	Class	AVG	G	AB	R	H	2B	3B	HR	RBI	BB	SO	SB	OBP	SLG
2019	24	Washington (NL)	MAJ	.000	2	2	0	0	0	0	0	0	0	0	0	.000	.000
	24	Harrisburg (EL)	AA	.249	101	357	42	89	23	0	8	46	36	69	1	.323	.381
Major League Totals				.000	2	2	0	0	0	0	0	0	0	0	0	.000	.000
Minor League Totals				.259	284	1017	125	263	64	2	25	114	96	202	5	.336	.399

18 DANIEL MARTE, OF

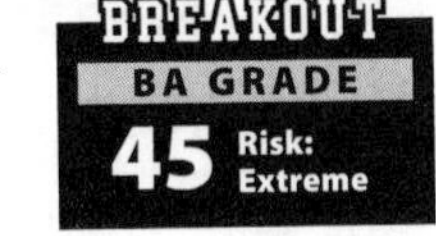

Born: Jan. 14. 2002. **B-T:** R-R. **HT:** 6-0. **WT:** 180. **Signed:** Dominican Republic, 2018. **Signed by:** Virgilio De Leon.

TRACK RECORD: Marte signed for $300,000 during the 2018 international signing period and had a loud debut in the Dominican Summer League in 2019. He tied for second in the league in triples, tied for his team lead in home runs and reeled off a 17-game hitting streak toward the end of the season. He reported to instructional league in 2020 and was one of the top standouts in camp.

SCOUTING REPORT: Still a teenager, Marte has made big improvements in a short time. He's a toolsy, powerfully built center fielder with a strong arm and plus speed. He has a short bat-to-the-ball approach and has improved his patience at the plate. He hits line drives to all fields and doesn't over-swing. Marte has gained 20 pounds since signing and has a good deal of untapped power potential. In instructional league games, he homered into the wind twice—once at home and once at cavernous Jupiter. The organization likes his confidence and his aggressiveness.

THE FUTURE: Marte is one of the most exciting, high-energy players in the system. He'll make his stateside debut in 2021 in the Rookie-level Gulf Coast League.

Year	Age	Club (League)	Class	AVG	G	AB	R	H	2B	3B	HR	RBI	BB	SO	SB	OBP	SLG
2019	17	Nationals (DSL)	R	.257	55	210	32	54	7	9	5	29	11	67	10	.310	.448
Minor League Totals				.257	55	210	32	54	7	9	5	29	11	67	10	.310	.448

19 BEN BRAYMER, LHP

BA GRADE
40 Risk: High

Born: April 28, 1994. **B-T:** L-L. **HT:** 6-2. **WT:** 215. **Drafted:** Auburn, 2016 (18th round). **Signed by:** Eric Robinson.

TRACK RECORD: Braymer has steadily risen up the minors since signing for $100,000 in 2016 after one season at Auburn. He won the Nationals' minor league co-pitcher of the year award in 2018, was added to the 40-man roster after the 2019 season and made his major league debut in 2020. He made three appearances for the Nationals, highlighted by five scoreless innings in a start against the Marlins on Sept. 20.

SCOUTING REPORT: The key for Braymer is locating his curveball. When it's on, it's an above-average sweeper that's particularly tough on lefthanded hitters. His fastball sits in the upper 80s but has decent carry through the zone. His upper-70s changeup has the potential to give him an armside option to keep righthanded hitters off-balance. Braymer succeeded both as a starter and in relief after his callup and has the ability to fill multiple roles on a pitching staff. He struggled with walks in his brief debut but showed average control throughout his minor league career.

THE FUTURE: Braymer is tentatively slated to open 2021 as a starter in Triple-A. He could feasibly settle in as a spot starter, long reliever or even middle reliever depending on the Nationals needs.

Year	Age	Club (League)	Class	W	L	ERA	G	GS	IP	H	HR	BB	SO	BB/9	SO/9	WHIP	AVG
2020	26	Washington (NL)	MAJ	1	0	1.23	3	1	7	7	0	5	8	6.1	9.8	1.64	.241
Major League Totals				1	0	1.23	3	1	7	7	0	5	8	6.1	9.8	1.64	.241
Minor League Totals				18	17	3.64	75	52	338	311	35	124	334	3.3	8.9	1.28	.243

20 HOLDEN POWELL, RHP

BA GRADE
40 Risk: High

Born: Sept. 9, 1999. **B-T:** R-R. **HT:** 6-0. **WT:** 185. **Drafted:** UCLA, 2020 (3rd round). **Signed by:** Steve Leavitt.

TRACK RECORD: Powell touched 93 mph with his fastball as a high school senior and immediately became UCLA's closer as a freshman. He won college baseball's Stopper of the Year award as the top closer in the nation as a sophomore and finished second all time in UCLA history with 26 career saves. After Powell looked particularly dominant during the abbreviated 2020 college season, the Nationals drafted him in the third round and signed him for $500,000.

SCOUTING REPORT: Powell has the mix of power and poise that portends a future closer. His fastball comfortably averages 94-95 mph and touches 97 with solid sinking action. He backs his fastball up with a wipeout 82-86 mph slider that is at least a plus pitch and potentially more. He has better command of his slider than his fastball. Powell is not overly physical, but he's strong and adds some deception with his arm action. He had some trouble with control as an underclassmen but was lights-out in 2020 and pounded the strike zone.

THE FUTURE: Powell has present stuff that should help him move quickly. As long as his control gains hold, he has a future in late relief.

Year	Age	Club (League)	Class	W	L	ERA	G	GS	IP	H	HR	BB	SO	BB/9	SO/9	WHIP	AVG
2020	20	Did not play—No minor league season															

21 STEVEN FUENTES, RHP

BA GRADE **40** Risk: High

Born: May 4, 1997. **B-T:** R-R. **HT:** 6-1. **WT:** 220. **Signed:** Panama, 2013. **Signed by:** Miguel Ruiz.

TRACK RECORD: It's been a long, slow climb for Fuentes, who signed with the Nationals out of Panama in 2013. He failed to stand out most of his career and his breakout 2019 at Double-A was cut short when was suspended 50 games after testing positive for a banned stimulant. Despite a delayed arrival at the alternate training site, Fuentes impressed team officials at camp, continued in instructional league and in a fall league in his native Panama. The Nationals added him to the 40-man roster after the season, just before he was set to hit minor league free agency.

SCOUTING REPORT: Fuentes keeps the ball on the ground with his low-to-mid-90s sinker. He has allowed just two home runs in his last 148 innings over his past two minor league seasons, while posting ground ball rates north of 50%. He has good command of his sinker and his plus changeup mirrors the pitch, allowing him to keep hitters off-balance. He also has a slider he can mix in. Fuentes has mostly worked in relief but was effective as a starter at Double-A Harrisburg. He's learning to repeat his east-west delivery and has flashed above-average control.

THE FUTURE: Fuentes lacks huge stuff but knows how to mix his offerings effectively. He's in position for his major league debut in 2021.

Year	Age	Club (League)	Class	W	L	ERA	G	GS	IP	H	HR	BB	SO	BB/9	SO/9	WHIP	AVG
2019	22	Fredericksburg (CAR)	HiA	1	1	0.53	8	0	17	8	0	7	26	3.7	13.8	0.88	.119
	22	Harrisburg (EL)	AA	5	4	2.69	15	11	64	63	1	15	63	2.1	8.9	1.23	.232
Minor League Totals				22	21	3.29	126	29	358	352	16	99	354	2.5	8.9	1.26	.252

22 ROISMAR QUINTANA, OF

BA GRADE **45** Risk: Extreme

Born: Feb. 6, 2003. **B-T:** R-R. **HT:** 6-1. **WT:** 190. **Signed:** Venezuela, 2019. **Signed by:** Ronald Morillo.

TRACK RECORD: Quintana signed with the Nationals for $820,000 out of Venezuela during the 2019 international signing period. His expected pro debut in 2020 was delayed by the coronavirus pandemic, but he impressed Nationals officials at instructional league, including hitting a home run off Seth Romero in live batting practice.

SCOUTING REPORT: Quintana has gained so much strength since signing that his build has been compared to a young Yasiel Puig. His bat will be his carrying tool. He already shows an aptitude for laying off breaking balls out of the strike zone and keeping his lower half stable. He has a feel to hit and legitimate plus power potential. Quintana stays through the ball and drives pitches to right-center field. A leg injury kept him out for part of instructional league, but he was healthy by the end of camp and consistently getting into a good hitting position. As he matures, Quintana will likely move from center field to right field.

THE FUTURE: The Nationals think Quintana is primed for a breakout in 2021. He'll make his pro debut in the Rookie-level Gulf Coast League.

Year	Age	Club (League)	Class	AVG	G	AB	R	H	2B	3B	HR	RBI	BB	SO	SB	OBP	SLG
2019	16	Did not play—Signed 2020 contract															

23 TYLER DYSON, RHP

BA GRADE **40** Risk: High

Born: Dec. 24, 1997. **B-T:** R-R. **HT:** 6-3. **WT:** 210. **Drafted:** Florida, 2019 (5th round). **Signed by:** Alan Marr.

TRACK RECORD: Dyson went 4-0, 3.23 in 39 innings as a dynamic freshman for the 2017 College World Series-champion Florida Gators. He wasn't quite as effective the following two seasons as a weekend starter, but the Nationals still drafted him in the fifth round and signed him for $500,000. Dyson posted a 1.07 ERA in starts after signing, enhancing the Nationals belief they got a good value.

SCOUTING REPORT: Dyson attacks the strike zone with his mid-90s fastball and potentially plus slider. He also has confidence in his curveball and changeup, which work well in combination. After metrics revealed the natural sink on his fastball, he added a two-seamer to what is now a five-pitch arsenal. An infielder for much of his high school career, Dyson is a good athlete who repeats his mechanics well. He's also well prepared, having pitched in big games in college.

THE FUTURE: Dyson has the pitch mix to remain a starter. He's ready for his first full minor league season in 2021.

Year	Age	Club (League)	Class	W	L	ERA	G	GS	IP	H	HR	BB	SO	BB/9	SO/9	WHIP	AVG
2019	21	Auburn (NYP)	SS	2	1	1.14	8	8	32	20	1	8	14	2.3	4.0	0.88	.169
	21	Nationals (GCL)	R	0	0	0.00	1	1	2	0	0	0	3	0.0	13.5	0.00	.000
Minor League Totals				2	1	1.07	9	9	33	20	1	8	17	2.1	4.5	0.83	.182

24 JAKE IRVIN, RHP

BA GRADE 45 Risk: Extreme

Born: Feb. 18, 1997. **B-T:** R-R. **HT:** 6-6. **WT:** 225. **Drafted:** Oklahoma, 2018 (4th round). **Signed by:** Ed Gustafson.

TRACK RECORD: A three-year starter and all-Big 12 Conference performer at Oklahoma, Irvin signed for $550,000 as a fourth-round pick in 2018 and has been a workhorse in the Nationals' system. He went at least five innings in 20 of his 25 starts in 2019 and finished the year strong, earning an invitation to the alternate training site in 2020. Irvin spent the summer pitching against more experienced players, but he suffered an elbow injury and had Tommy John surgery in October.

SCOUTING REPORT: Irvin has plenty of stuff and impressed Nationals manager Dave Martinez with his 94-97 mph fastball in a simulated game at Nationals Park. He also has a plus, power curveball that he throws in the 78-80 mph range and has at least an average changeup. Irvin has improved at attacking hitters and throwing inside, and he's capable of missing more bats. His mix and his durability give him a chance to remain a starter, but his arm action may be more suited toward relieving.

THE FUTURE: Irvin will miss the entire 2021 season recovering from surgery. His future outlook will depend on what his stuff looks like when he returns.

Year	Age	Club (League)	Class	W	L	ERA	G	GS	IP	H	HR	BB	SO	BB/9	SO/9	WHIP	AVG
2019	22	Hagerstown (SAL)	LoA	8	8	3.79	25	25	128	122	14	38	113	2.7	7.9	1.25	.228
Minor League Totals				9	8	3.50	36	32	149	138	14	45	128	2.7	7.7	1.23	.244

25 JOAN ADON, RHP

BA GRADE 45 Risk: Extreme

Born: Aug. 12, 1998. **B-T:** R-R. **HT:** 6-2. **WT:** 185. **Signed:** Dominican Republic, 2016. **Signed by:** Pablo Arias.

TRACK RECORD: With a $50,000 signing bonus, Adon was a seemingly small piece in the Nationals' international spending bonanza of 2016 that saw them spend more than $5 million. But he has already surpassed many of the players who signed for more. Adon went 11-3, 3.86 for low Class A Hagerstown in 2019 and impressed at the alternate training site in 2020. The Nationals added him to their 40-man roster after the season.

SCOUTING REPORT: Adon has a 95-96 mph fastball, a power slider and a changeup that has become effective against lefthanded and righthanded hitters. The workload of more than 100 innings with Hagerstown helped him improve at repeating his delivery and showing more consistent mechanics. He attacks the zone with all three of his pitches and brings good energy to the mound. Still, his control is below-average, leading many evaluators to project him to the bullpen.

THE FUTURE: Adon's control will determine if he stays in the rotation. His power stuff could play in relief.

Year	Age	Club (League)	Class	W	L	ERA	G	GS	IP	H	HR	BB	SO	BB/9	SO/9	WHIP	AVG
2019	20	Hagerstown (SAL)	LoA	11	3	3.86	22	21	105	93	8	44	90	3.8	7.7	1.30	.218
Minor League Totals				16	5	3.85	55	21	163	150	11	75	161	4.1	8.9	1.37	.244

26 JAKSON REETZ, C

BA GRADE 40 Risk: High

Born: Jan. 3, 1996. **B-T:** R-R. **HT:** 6-0. **WT:** 195. **Drafted:** HS—Firth, Neb., 2014 (3rd round). **Signed by:** Ed Gustafson.

TRACK RECORD: Reetz signed out of high school for $800,000 in 2014 instead of playing baseball at Nebraska, where his father was a linebacker on the football team. After scuffling at the plate throughout his pro career and spending a third straight season at high Class A, Reetz's bat finally broke out when he hit .282/.378/.563 with 12 home runs in 174 at-bats in the second half of 2019. The Nationals brought him to their alternate training site in 2020.

SCOUTING REPORT: Reetz has continued to make progress at the plate, namely by improving his bat path by allowing his hands to do more of the work. He has average to above-average power and has made progress in his strike-zone recognition skills and hitting to the right-center field gap. He still has a long way to go, but Reetz is at least moving in the right direction offensively. Defensively, Reetz has soft hands in receiving and is a good blocker behind the plate. He has a quick exchange and average arm strength. Reetz is a hard worker and good teammate, endearing him to scouts and coaches alike.

THE FUTURE: Reetz's offensive developments give him a shot to be a backup catcher. He'll make the move to Double-A in 2021.

Year	Age	Club (League)	Class	AVG	G	AB	R	H	2B	3B	HR	RBI	BB	SO	SB	OBP	SLG
2019	23	Fredericksburg (CAR)	HiA	.253	96	324	54	82	18	2	13	55	46	95	3	.370	.441
Minor League Totals				.238	395	1280	182	305	73	3	27	162	182	360	20	.357	.363

27 STERLING SHARP, RHP

BA GRADE 40 Risk: High

Born: May 30, 1995. **B-T:** R-R. **HT:** 6-3. **WT:** 170. **Drafted:** Drury (Mo.), 2016 (22nd round). **Signed by:** Brandon Larson.

TRACK RECORD: The Marlins took Sharp from the Nationals in the 2019 Rule 5 draft, even after he missed three months because of an oblique injury. Sharp's worst major league outing of 2020 was his last one, when he gave up five runs (four earned) in one-third of an inning against the Nationals. Less than a week later, he cleared waivers and was returned to Washington.

SCOUTING REPORT: Sharp's 89-93 mph sinker and extreme groundball rate in Double-A made for an intriguing possibility in the Marlins' bullpen, but they couldn't hold a roster spot for him once they became a playoff contender. Aside from his sinker, Sharp throws an above-average changeup in the upper 80s and a low-80s breaking ball. He hides the ball and repeats his delivery well, but he struggled with his control in the big leagues. He has a lean build but has gained strength without hurting the athleticism he shows in his slam dunks on the basketball court.

THE FUTURE: A starter throughout his minor league career, Sharp's best route for long-term success is likely as a groundball-inducing reliever. He'll continue on a more typical trajectory in 2021.

Year	Age	Club (League)	Class	W	L	ERA	G	GS	IP	H	HR	BB	SO	BB/9	SO/9	WHIP	AVG
2020	25	Miami (NL)	MAJ	0	0	10.13	4	0	5	7	1	5	3	8.4	5.1	2.25	.304
Major League Totals				0	0	10.13	4	0	5	7	1	5	3	8.4	5.1	2.25	.304
Minor League Totals				25	21	3.71	75	69	378	407	25	95	290	2.3	6.9	1.33	.274

28 ANDRY ARIAS, OF

BA GRADE 45 Risk: Extreme

Born: June 19, 2000. **B-T:** L-L. **HT:** 6-2. **WT:** 211. **Signed:** Dominican Republic, 2017. **Signed by:** Pablo Arias.

TRACK RECORD: Arias signed with the Nationals during the 2017 international signing period and immediately stood out for his big power potential from the left side. He had a strong pro debut in the Dominican Summer League before struggling in his stateside debut in 2019, especially facing lefthanded pitchers. The Nationals brought him to instructional league in 2020.

SCOUTING REPORT: Arias has a slender build but immense power. He has grown more explosive in his legs as he's matured and is working on getting into a stronger hitting position that will give him more leverage. Arias is willing to work counts, but he still swings and misses too much. It may be a prolonged process for the Nationals to try to get the most out of his powerful swing. Arias isn't known for his speed, but he moves well enough to be an average corner outfielder defensively. He also has the ability to play first base.

THE FUTURE: Arias' main focus is on getting physically stronger. That, combined with some swing development, could make him a breakout power threat.

Year	Age	Club (League)	Class	AVG	G	AB	R	H	2B	3B	HR	RBI	BB	SO	SB	OBP	SLG
2019	19	Nationals (GCL)	R	.195	32	113	19	22	4	0	3	10	19	39	7	.321	.310
Minor League Totals				.245	93	339	52	83	13	7	6	50	47	87	10	.347	.378

29 JACKSON TETREAULT, RHP

BA GRADE 40 Risk: Very High

Born: June 3, 1996. **B-T:** R-R. **HT:** 6-5. **WT:** 189. **Drafted:** State JC of Florida, 2017 (7th round). **Signed by:** Buddy Hernandez.

TRACK RECORD: Tetreault began his college career as a reliever at Division II Cameron (Okla.) before transferring to State JC of Florida, He struck out 105 batters in 80.1 innings as a sophomore and signed with the Nationals for $400,000 as a seventh-round pick in 2017. Tetrault cruised through the lower minors, but he hit a wall at Double-A Harrisburg in 2019. He logged a 4.73 ERA, had the highest walk rate and the lowest strikeout rate of his career.

SCOUTING REPORT: With a fast, whippy delivery, Tetreault is able to maintain the 93-95 mph velocity on his fastball, which still makes him a candidate for a starting role. His curveball is a work in progress, but it showed a later and sharper break in instructional league than it has in the past. His changeup is a fringe-average pitch. Tetreault is working on staying on the rubber longer and using more of the strength in his legs. His control is below-average.

THE FUTURE: Tetreault's velocity might tick up with a move to the bullpen. With a questionable third pitch and control, that is his best avenue to the majors.

Year	Age	Club (League)	Class	W	L	ERA	G	GS	IP	H	HR	BB	SO	BB/9	SO/9	WHIP	AVG
2019	23	Fredericksburg (CAR)	HiA	4	2	1.91	7	7	38	29	0	13	29	3.1	6.9	1.12	.191
	23	Harrisburg (EL)	AA	4	5	4.73	18	18	86	98	8	40	63	4.2	6.6	1.61	.257
Minor League Totals				14	18	3.80	61	55	296	289	22	111	268	3.4	8.1	1.35	.254

30 NICK BANKS, OF

BA GRADE
40 **Risk: Very High**

Born: Nov. 18, 1994. **B-T:** L-L. **HT:** 6-0. **WT:** 215. **Drafted:** Texas A&M, 2016 (4th round). **Signed by:** Tyler Wilt.

TRACK RECORD: Banks won MVP of the 2016 Southeastern Conference tournament after hitting two home runs in the championship-clinching victory over Florida. He signed with the Nationals for $500,000 as a fourth-round pick. After slowly moving through the lower minors, Banks won MVP of the high Class A Carolina League all-star game in 2019 and received a promotion to Double-A, where he hit. 288/.358/.410 in 45 games.

SCOUTING REPORT: Banks is a line-drive hitter who makes plenty of contact. His plate discipline is iffy at times and he has had to work to use his legs in his swing better, limiting his power production to fringe-average, although he does hit a lot of doubles. He has some pull power and shows glimpses of it in games. Banks is a capable defender at all three outfield spots. He primarily plays the corners and is a smart runner who uses his instincts to cover ground in the outfield and be an efficient basestealer.

THE FUTURE: Banks profiles as a potential fourth outfielder. He should begin 2021 in Triple-A and has a chance to make his major league debut during the season.

Year	Age	Club (League)	Class	AVG	G	AB	R	H	2B	3B	HR	RBI	BB	SO	SB	OBP	SLG
2019	24	Fredericksburg (CAR)	HiA	.271	69	280	41	76	21	0	9	35	19	54	2	.327	.443
	24	Harrisburg (EL)	AA	.288	45	156	19	45	12	2	1	21	15	41	6	.358	.410
Minor League Totals				.266	416	1539	182	409	85	9	27	190	103	319	40	.316	.385

MORE PROSPECTS TO KNOW

31 REID SCHALLER, RHP

A 2018 third-round pick from Vanderbilt, Schaller has an excellent fastball/changeup combination, but his future as a starter hinges on the development of his slider.

32 BRYAN SANCHEZ, RHP

The 18-year-old from the Dominican Republic has a 90-95 mph fastball, a high-spin curveball and a plus changeup. He adds and subtracts well and throws all three pitches for strikes.

33 VIANDEL PENA, 2B

The undersized switch-hitter batted .359 to win the Rookie-level Gulf Coast League batting title in 2019. He repeats his simple, effective swing from both sides of the plate and has good defensive actions.

34 CODY WILSON, OF

An instinctual defender, Wilson makes highlight-reel plays in center field and is one of the fastest runners in the system. He needs to focus on making contact, especially against high-velocity fastballs.

35 EVAN LEE, LHP

SLEEPER

After playing sparingly as a DH and pitcher at Arkansas, Lee's stuff has jumped now that he's focused solely on pitching. He has high spin rates on his fastball and curveball and is capable of missing bats.

36 TODD PETERSON, RHP

Peterson's fastball touches 98 mph and he pitches well inside with his 87-88 mph slider. He also has an average changeup and remains a starter at this point.

37 NIOMAR GOMEZ, RHP

The 22-year-old Venezuelan stayed with a group of fellow Nationals minor leaguers in a West Palm Beach hotel in 2020, using the gym for workouts and the parking lot for throwing sessions. He spots his fastball well and has good feel for pitching to all four quadrants.

38 MITCHELL PARKER, LHP

The 2020 fifth-round pick out of San Jacinto (Texas) JC has a quirky delivery, but he has above-average stuff and the full complement of a four-pitch mix.

39 ZACH BRZYKCY, RHP

A nondrafted free agent signee out of Virginia Tech, Brzykcy (pronounced Brick-see) has a mid-90s fastball and a developing breaking ball. He made a positive first impression in pitching sessions in his North Carolina hometown with Sam Narron, one of the Nationals' minor league pitching coaches.

40 GERALDI DIAZ, C

The 20-year-old lefthanded hitter has a high baseball IQ, plus receiving skills and a plus arm. He also has above-average power, which sometimes gets him in trouble when it becomes too much of his focus at the plate.

TOP PROSPECTS OF THE DECADE

Year	Player, Pos	2020 Org
2011	Bryce Harper, OF	Phillies
2012	Bryce Harper, OF	Phillies
2013	Anthony Rendon, 3B	Angels
2014	Lucas Giolito, RHP	White Sox
2015	Lucas Giolito, RHP	White Sox
2016	Lucas Giolito, RHP	White Sox
2017	Victor Robles, OF	Nationals
2018	Victor Robles, OF	Nationals
2019	Victor Robles, OF	Nationals
2020	Carter Kieboom, SS/2B	Nationals

TOP DRAFT PICKS OF THE DECADE

Year	Player, Pos	2020 Org
2011	Anthony Rendon, 3B	Angels
2012	Lucas Giolito, RHP	White Sox
2013	Jake Johansen, RHP (2nd round)	Did not play
2014	Erick Fedde, RHP	Nationals
2015	Andrew Stevenson, OF (2nd round)	Nationals
2016	Carter Kieboom, SS	Nationals
2017	Seth Romero, LHP	Nationals
2018	Mason Denaburg, RHP	Nationals
2019	Jackson Rutledge, RHP	Nationals
2020	Cade Cavalli, RHP	Nationals

DEPTH CHART

WASHINGTON NATIONALS

TOP 2021 ROOKIES	RANK
Matt Cronin, LHP	11
BREAKOUT PROSPECTS	
Jackson Cluff, SS	13
Israel Pineda, C	16
Daniel Marte, OF	18

SOURCE OF TOP 30 TALENT

Homegrown	30	Acquired	0
College	15	Trade	0
Junior college	2	Rule 5 draft	0
High school	3	Independent league	0
Nondrafted free agent	0	Free agent/waivers	0
International	10		

LF
Nick Banks (30)
Jacob Rhinesmith

CF
Daniel Marte (18)
Cody Wilson
Cole Freeman

RF
Jeremy De La Rosa (6)
Roismar Quintana (22)
Andry Arias (28)
Gage Canning

3B
Junior Martina
Jake Noll
Gilbert Lara

SS
Yasel Antuna (4)
Jackson Cluff (13)
Sammy Infante (14)
Juan Garcia
Jose Sanchez

2B
Viandel Pena
Quade Tomlin
J.T. Arruda

1B
Drew Mendoza (12)
Leandro Emiliani

C
Israel Pineda (16)
Tres Barrera (17)
Jakson Reetz (26)
Geraldi Diaz

LHP

LHSP	LHRP
Tim Cate (7)	Matt Cronin (11)
Seth Romero (15)	Ben Braymer (19)
Evan Lee	Nick Wells
Mitchell Parker	

RHP

RHSP	RHRP
Cade Cavalli (1)	Holden Powell (20)
Jackson Rutledge (2)	Sterling Sharp (27)
Cole Henry (3)	Jackson Tetreault (29)
Andry Lara (5)	Reid Schaller
Eddy Yean (8)	Zach Brzykcy
Mason Denaburg (9)	Mirton Blanco
Wil Crowe (10)	Jhonatan German
Steven Fuentes (21)	Jacob Condra-Bogan
Tyler Dyson (23)	Tyler Eppler
Jake Irvin (24)	Bryan Bonnell
Joan Adon (25)	
Bryan Sanchez	
Todd Peterson	
Niomar Gomez	

Kyle Glaser reports on international professionals who were eligible to sign with major league organizations as the Prospect Handbook went to press. The players highlighted are from Japan's Nippon Professional Baseball (NPB) or Korea Baseball Organization (KBO).

TOMOYUKI SUGANO, RHP

YUKI TAGUCHI/WBCI/MLB VIA GETTY IMAGES

BA GRADE

55 Risk: Medium

Age: 31. **Born:** Oct. 11, 1989. **B-T:** R-R. **HT:** 6-1. **WT:** 183.

TRACK RECORD: Sugano spent the last eight seasons as the Yomiuri Giants' ace and twice won the Sawamura Award, Japan's equivalent of the Cy Young Award. He showed his stuff played against major leaguers when he pitched six innings without allowing an earned run against Team USA in the semifinals of the 2017 World Baseball Classic, leading U.S. manager Jim Leyland to say "he's a big league pitcher." Sugano went 14-2, 1.97 with 131 strikeouts and 25 walks in 137.1 innings for the Giants in 2020 and was posted after the season.

SCOUTING REPORT: Sugano is a poised, unflappable righthander who carves through lineups with plus command of a varied arsenal. His fastball velocity has dropped from 96-97 mph at his peak to 92-93 as he's dealt with injuries and age, but he's able to move his fastball around the strike zone and put it where he wants. Sugano's out pitch is a plus slider he can manipulate. He can give it a longer arc or throw it tighter with late movement and depth and tilt. In either form, he will throw his slider in any count and can locate it wherever he wants to get called strikes or swings and misses. He also has an above-average splitter and a fringe-average curveball. Sugano is durable, but he's also 31 years old and has a lot of innings on his arm. He dealt with back discomfort in 2019 but stayed healthy in 2020.

THE FUTURE: Sugano projects as a No. 3 or 4 starter on a championship-level club. His workload and velocity need to be monitored, but he has the stuff, command and poise to be an impact starter.

Year	Age	Club (League)	Class	W	L	ERA	G	GS	SV	IP	H	HR	BB	SO	K/9	BB/9	WHIP
2020	30	Yomiuri (NPB)	JPN	14	2	1.97	20	—	0	137	97	8	25	131	8.6	1.6	0.89

HA-SEONG KIM, SS

SHUGO TAKEMI/WBCI/MLB VIA GETTY IMAGES

BA GRADE

55 Risk: High

Age: 25. **Born:** Oct. 17, 1995. **B-T:** R-R. **HT:** 5-9. **WT:** 167.

TRACK RECORD: Kim showed rare athleticism from an early age and became an everyday shortstop at 19 years old in KBO. He quickly drew scouts' attention and blossomed into one of Korea's biggest stars from 2015-20, averaging more than 20 home runs and 20 stolen bases per season. Kim saved his best for last and hit .330 with a career-high 30 home runs, 109 RBIs and 23 stolen bases for Kiwoom in 2020. The Heroes posted him after the season.

SCOUTING REPORT: Kim will likely face an adjustment period in the U.S., but his excellent athleticism and instincts give him a chance to be an impact player over time. He's a twitchy, athletic defender with good instincts at shortstop and has the versatility to play second or third base. He puts himself in good positions to make throws and has sneaky, above-average arm strength. Kim rarely faced fastballs above 90 mph in Korea and may struggle initially against MLB pitching, but he has the twitch and athleticism to adjust and the natural contact skills to eventually be an above-average hitter. He has the power to drive balls out to his pull side and projects for 12-15 home runs. Kim adds value on the bases, where his average speed plays up.

THE FUTURE: Kim's well-rounded skill set allows him to impact the game in a variety of ways. He has the ability to be anything from an everyday shortstop to a multi-positional regular.

Year	Age	Club (League)	Class	AVG	G	AB	R	H	2B	3B	HR	RBI	BB	SO	SB	OBP	SLG
2020	24	Kiwoom (KBO)	KOR	.306	138	533	111	163	24	1	30	109	75	68	23	.397	.523

KOHEI ARIHARA, RHP

Age: 28. **Born:** Aug. 11, 1992. **B-T:** R-R. **HT:** 6-2. **WT:** 211.

BA GRADE

45 Risk: High

STR/JIJI PRESS/AFP VIA GETTY IMAGES

TRACK RECORD: Arihara was one of Japan's top college pitchers at Waseda University and won the Pacific League rookie of the year award in 2016 pitching in the Nippon Ham rotation with Shohei Ohtani. Arihara was more solid than spectacular over the next four seasons, including going 8-9, 3.46 in 2020. The Fighters posted him after the 2020 season.

SCOUTING REPORT: Arihara's fastball velocity has dropped over the years from 96-98 mph to 92-94, but he has the command and varied pitch mix to succeed even at his lower velocity. He shows average command on his worst days and plus command on his best, and fills the strike zone with five pitches. Arihara's changeup and splitter are both above-average pitches and tunnel well off each other. His changeup moves late to his arm side and his splitter plunges with late downward movement. He mainly throws his changeup to lefties and his splitter to righties, but he can use either effectively in any situation. Arihara also has a curveball and slider that are both fringy. He is durable and efficient.

THE FUTURE: Arihara projects as a back-of-the-rotation starter. He will be 28 years old on Opening Day in 2021 and still has a few years left in his prime.

Year	Age	Club (League)	Class	W	L	ERA	G	GS	SV	IP	H	HR	BB	SO	K/9	BB/9	WHIP
2020	27	Nippon Ham (NPB)	JPN	8	9	3.46	20	—	0	133	125	11	30	106	7.2	2.0	1.17

HYEON-JONG YANG, LHP

Age: 33. **Born:** March 1, 1988. **B-T:** L-L. **HT:** 6-0. **WT:** 190.

SHUGO TAKEMI/WBCI/MLB VIA GETTY IMAGES

TRACK RECORD: Yang emerged as one of KBO's top pitchers in the late 2000s and was posted for MLB clubs in 2014, but his club felt the highest bid was too low and pulled him back. Yang went on to win the KBO's MVP award in 2017 and ERA title in 2019 and helped South Korea qualify for the 2020 Olympics with a dominant showing during qualifying. He went 11-10, 4.70 for the Kia Tigers in 2020 and became a free agent after the season.

SCOUTING REPORT: Yang is the prototypical soft-tossing lefty who succeeds with feel and command. His fastball ranges from 88-91 mph, his changeup is his best offering as an average pitch, his slider is fringy and his curveball is a below-average offering. What Yang does is pitch in, out, up and down to prevent hitters from keying in on one part of the plate. His fastball gets on hitters quicker than they expect out his clean delivery, and he has plus command of his breaking pitches, landing them in places hitters can't reach them. He keeps his walks to a minimum, is consistent from start to start and frustrates hitters who struggle to square him up despite his modest stuff.

THE FUTURE: Yang projects as a back-of-the-rotation starter or a swingman depending on the caliber of team he's on. He'll be 33 years old when the 2021 season begins.

Year	Age	Club (League)	Class	W	L	ERA	G	GS	SV	IP	H	HR	BB	SO	K/9	BB/9	WHIP
2020	32	Kia (KBO)	KOR	11	10	4.70	31	31	0	172	180	13	64	149	7.8	3.3	1.42

SUNG-BUM NA, OF

CHUNG SUNG-JUN/GETTY IMAGES

AGE: 31. **Born:** Oct. 3, 1989. **B-T:** L-L. **HT:** 6-0. **WT:** 220.

TRACK RECORD: Na averaged 24 home runs per season from 2013-18 and hired Scott Boras as his agent in preparation for a move to MLB, but he suffered a gruesome knee injury on a slide 23 games into the 2019 season and missed the rest of the year. He returned to KBO in 2020 to show he was healthy and hit .324 with a career-high 34 home runs and 112 RBIs for the NC Dinos. He was posted after the season.

SCOUTING REPORT: Na is a thick, physical lefthanded hitter with a strong lower half and above-average power to all fields. He stays inside the ball and uses his hands well, allowing him to drive the ball where it's pitched. Na can turn on fastballs but struggles with offspeed pitches and changing speeds in general, leading to a lot of swings and misses. He notably struggled against American pitchers in KBO, resulting in projections of a below-average hitter in the major leagues. Na moves well for his size and will flash average run times down the line, but his agility and lateral movement have suffered since his knee injury. He primarily served as a designated hitter in 2020 and was below-average in right field in limited action. His arm is at least average.

THE FUTURE: Na doesn't project to hit enough to play every day, but his lefthanded power gives him a chance to stick as a platoon or reserve outfielder. Whether his mobility returns will be key to watch.

Year	Age	Club (League)	Class	AVG	G	AB	R	H	2B	3B	HR	RBI	BB	SO	SB	OBP	SLG
2020	30	NC Dinos (KBO)	KOR	.324	130	525	115	170	37	2	34	112	49	148	3	.390	.596

HIROKAZU SAWAMURA, RHP

YUKI TAGUCHI/WBCI/MLB VIA GETTY IMAGES

Age: 33. **Born:** April 3, 1988. **B-T:** R-R. **HT:** 6-0. **WT:** 212.

TRACK RECORD: Sawamura began his career as a starter for the Yomiuri Giants, later transitioned to relief and became a dominant closer, highlighted by 73 combined saves in 2015-16. An accident during a team acupuncture treatment in 2017 left him with nerve damage and his career took a downward turn, capped by a 6.08 ERA and a demotion to the minor leagues in 2020. He was traded to Chiba Lotte at midseason and looked reinvigorated with his new club, touching 99 mph in the playoffs.

SCOUTING REPORT: Sawamura went from ordinary to dominant in a matter of months following the trade. His fastball sits 97-98 mph and touches 99 at its best. He's short at 6 feet tall and his fastball is fairly straight, but he can get the ball elevated enough for swings and misses at the top of the strike zone. Sawamura pairs his fastball with an above-average splitter that gets swings and misses over the top and keeps hitters from keying in on his heater. He also has a slider, but it's a poor pitch many scouts think he should shelve. Sawamura is a bit wild, but he is able to work out of trouble by blowing hitters away in big spots.

THE FUTURE: Sawamura's resurgence has clubs interested as a potential late-innings reliever. He is a free agent and does not require a posting fee. He will turn 33 shortly after Opening Day.

Year	Age	Club (League)	Class	W	L	ERA	G	GS	SV	IP	H	HR	BB	SO	K/9	BB/9	WHIP
2020	32	Yomiuri/Lotte (NPB)	JPN	1	3	3.41	35	0	1	34	24	3	18	40	10.5	4.7	1.22

HARUKI NISHIKAWA, OF

Age: 29. **Born:** April 16, 1992. **B-T:** L-R. **HT:** 5-10. **WT:** 160.

TRACK RECORD: Nishikawa began his career as a second baseman but transitioned to the outfield midway through his career and became one of the best defensive center fielders in Japan. He won three Gold Gloves for Nippon Ham and, after modest offensive performance for most of his career, set career highs with a .306 batting average and .430 on-base percentage in 2020. The Fighters posted him after the season.

SCOUTING REPORT: Nishikawa's game is built around his legs. He has plus-plus speed, is a prolific basestealing threat and has exceptional range in center field. He runs balls down in every direction in the outfield, with his speed helping him outrun any bad routes or reads. Nishikawa has excellent baserunning skills in addition to his speed and can steal a bag at any time. He went 42-for-49 on stolen bases in 2020 and has been successful on more than 86% of his career attempts. The question is how often Nishikawa will get on base. He's a well below-average hitter but draws plenty of walks. He often swings early in counts and tries to hit the ball on the ground and beat out hits with his speed. He lacks strength and has well below-average power.

THE FUTURE: Scouts see Nishikawa is a lesser version of Shogo Akiyama, who hit .245/.357/.297 in his MLB debut. He projects as a reserve who moves up and down from Triple-A based on when a team needs his speed and outfield defense.

Year	Age	Club (League)	Class	AVG	G	AB	R	H	2B	3B	HR	RBI	BB	SO	SB	OBP	SLG
2020	28	Nippon Ham (NPB)	JPN	.306	115	422	82	129	17	3	5	39	92	84	42	.430	.396

APPENDIX

2020-21 INTERNATIONAL SIGNING PERIOD: PROJECTED TOP BONUSES

BY BEN BADLER

July 2 is usually the biggest day of the year for international prospects, marking the first date of the annual signing period when players who are 16 can sign.

However, due to the coronavirus pandemic, Major League Baseball postponed the start date of the 2020-21 signing period to Jan. 15, 2021. The Prospect Handbook went to press before that date, so these players aren't included in any of our team Top 30 Prospects rankings.

Still, we know who the big names are and where they're almost certain to sign.

Our ranking presented here is NOT an assessment of talent. Instead, it's a board of 30 international prospects ranked in order of their expected signing bonus amounts. Teams often line up commitments from players multiple years in advance of their official signing date, at which point they generally are no longer seen by other clubs. There was also a long pause due to the pandemic in 2020 when MLB banned all in-person scouting.

While it is premature to provide a talent ranking, this should be a guide to many of the biggest names to know from this year's international signing class.

This list does not include Cuban players who don't have agreements lined up yet, such as Yoelquis Cespedes.

BILL MITCHELL

The Cubs are expected to sign shortstop Cristian Hernandez.

1. PEDRO LEON, OF, CUBA

Born: May 28, 1998. **B-T:** R-R. **Ht.:** 5-9. **Wt.:** 185. **Expected Signing Team:** Astros.

Soon after new general manager James Click took over in Houston, the Astros had most of their 2020-21 international bonus pool still uncommitted in February, when they reached a deal to sign Leon for around $4 million. Leon didn't play much in Serie Nacional in Cuba and wasn't scouted heavily by clubs when he left the country and began training in the Dominican Republic, so there's a lot of uncertainty about him at the moment. He has a smaller, muscled-up build and has shown the raw power to drive the ball out of the park from the middle of the field to his pull side.

2. ARMANDO CRUZ, SS, DOMINICAN REPUBLIC

Born: Jan. 16, 2004. **B-T:** R-R. **Ht.:** 5-11. **Wt.:** 165. **Expected Signing Team:** Nationals.

The Nationals are expected to sign Cruz, with a bonus likely to be around $4 million. He's a defensive wizard with phenomenal hands and a strong arm, combining the ability to make acrobatic, highlight plays along with the internal clock and game savvy well beyond his years. There's more of a split camp on his offensive potential, but Cruz has a chance to be an elite defensive shortstop.

3. CRISTIAN HERNANDEZ, SS, DOMINICAN REPUBLIC

Born: Dec. 13, 2003. **B-T:** R-R. **Ht.:** 6-2. **Wt.:** 165. **Expected Signing Team:** Cubs.

On pure talent, Hernandez has a case as the top overall player in the 2020-21 international class. He has an outstanding, high-level swing, with fast bat speed and a barrel that stays on plane through the hitting zone for a long time. He has performed well in games and drives the ball with impact, giving him a chance for plus or better raw power, especially once he fills out his projectable build. Hernandez's bat is what generates the most attention, but he's also a good athlete and a plus runner. The Cubs are expected to sign Hernandez.

4. YIDDI CAPPE, SS, CUBA

Born: Sept. 17, 2002. **B-T:** R-R. **Ht.:** 6-3. **Wt.:** 178. **Expected Signing Team:** Marlins.

Cappe has a tall, extremely thin body type. He immediately draws attention in the field for his quickness, smooth hands and slick actions. Cappe has long, lanky limbs, which can add some length to his swing, and a lot of his future will depend on his physical development.

5. CARLOS COLMENAREZ, SS, VENEZUELA

Born: Nov. 15, 2003. **B-T:** L-R. **Ht.:** 5-10. **Wt.:** 175. **Expected Signing Team:** Rays.

Colmenarez is arguably the best Venezuelan player in the class and is in the conversation among the top overall 2020 players. He makes everything look easy, starting with his pure, smooth swing from the left side. He stays calm with good rhythm and balance in the box, unleashing an explosive, efficient stroke with good bat path. That leads to a lot of contact in games, with the strength and bat speed to generate impressive power. He has easy, fluid actions at shortstop as well.

6. CRISTIAN SANTANA, SS, DOMINICAN REPUBLIC

Born: Nov. 25, 2003. **B-T:** R-R. **Ht.:** 6-0. **Wt.:** 175. **Expected Signing Team:** Tigers.

Santana is the top target in this class for the Tigers, who should know him well—he's a cousin of the organization's Wenceel Perez. Santana, one of the top shortstops in the class, stands out for his athleticism and ability to hit in games with a short swing and an advanced offensive approach.

7. WILMAN DIAZ, SS, VENEZUELA

Born: Nov. 15, 2003. **B-T.:** R-R. **Ht.:** 6-2. **Wt.:** 165. **Expected Signing Team:** Dodgers.

The Dodgers signed the top player in Venezuela in 2018 (Diego Cartaya) and 2019 (Luis Rodriguez). In 2020, they're again expected to sign a player in the mix as Venezuela's top prospect. The Dodgers have followed Diaz closely for years. Has has an athletic, projectable frame and high offensive upside, performing well in games with a loose, easy swing, good bat speed, a mature approach and big power.

8. SHALIN POLANCO, OF, DOMINICAN REPUBLIC

Born: Feb. 6, 2004. **B-T:** L-L. **Ht.:** 6-0. **Wt.:** 170. **Expected Signing Team:** Pirates.

The Pirates signed many players in 2019, with their highest bonus ($850,000) going to Dominican righty Cristopher Cruz. Their top signing in 2020 is expected to be Polanco for significantly more. Scouts like his short, fluid swing and power potential once he strengthens his projectable frame.

9. DANNY DE ANDRADE, SS, VENEZUELA

Born: April 10, 2004. **B-T:** R-R. **Ht.:** 6-0. **Wt.:** 165. **Expected Signing Team:** Twins.

De Andrade has been training in the Dominican Republic and has quick hands, a sound swing and has performed well in games, with an approach geared to hit the ball to all fields. He has grown into more over-the-fence power lately as he's added strength. He has shown good instincts in the field, getting quick reads off the bat with good body control at shortstop, though some scouts see him moving to third base.

10. MANUEL BELTRE, SS, DOMINICAN REPUBLIC

Born: June 9, 2004. **B-T:** R-R. **Ht.:** 5-11. **Wt.:** 165. **Expected Signing Team:** Blue Jays.

One of the best hitters in the class, Beltre is a baseball rat who has spent years documenting his development on social media. He has a short, simple swing, a good feel for the strike zone and gap power. Beltre isn't as tooled-up as some of the other top prospects in the class, but he has a ton of game experience relative to his peers, which is evident in his all-around instincts and fundamentally sound play.

2020-21 INTERNATIONAL SIGNING PERIOD: PROJECTED TOP BONUSES

11. PEDRO PINEDA, OF, DOMINICAN REPUBLIC

Born: Sept. 6, 2003. **B-T:** R-R. **Ht.:** 6-0. **Wt.:** 180. **Expected Signing Team:** Athletics.

Pineda is a strong, athletic, physical center fielder with a loud tool set. He has excellent speed, a fast bat and the power potential to hit 25-plus home runs.

12. DENZER GUZMAN, SS, DOMINICAN REPUBLIC

Born: Feb. 8, 2004. **B-T:** R-R. **Ht.:** 6-2. **Wt.:** 178. **Expected Signing Team:** Angels.

Guzman is a physical, offensive-oriented shortstop. He makes a lot of contact against live pitching with a loose, easy swing, and has the bat speed and physical projection to grow into considerable power as well. His strong arm should play on the left side of the infield, though his defense might fit better at third base.

13. YEMAL FLORES, OF, DOMINICAN REPUBLIC

Born: Nov. 22, 2003. **B-T:** R-R. **Ht.:** 6-1. **Wt.:** 170. **Expected Signing Team:** Phillies.

Flores has a strong, sturdy build and big power. It comes at the expense of some swing-and-miss tendencies, but he generates loft, backspin and drives the ball with impact when he connects. A former third baseman, Flores moved to the outfield and fits best in a corner, with a strong arm for right field.

14. JACKSON BRAYAN CHOURIO, SS/OF, VENEZUELA

Born: March 11, 2004. **B-T:** R-R. **Ht.:** 6-1 Wt.: **150.** **Expected Signing Team:** Brewers.

The Brewers' top signings are again likely to be Venezuelans, led by Chourio, who has split time between shortstop and center field. A quick-twitch athlete with plus speed, he has a skinny frame but drives the ball with surprising impact, generating lift and backspin with his swing.

15. MALVIN VALDEZ, OF, DOMINICAN REPUBLIC

Born: Oct. 14, 2003. **B-T:** R-R. **Ht.:** 6-2. **Wt.:** 174. **Expected Signing Team:** Reds.

Valdez is one of the most athletic, toolsy outfielders in the class. He's an explosive player with plus-plus speed and a plus arm, giving him the tools to be a high-level defender in the middle of the diamond. Valdez shines in a workout, though he's still raw in other facets of the game, with quick bat speed and a chance to hit for power, though his pitch recognition will need to improve.

16. YEISON MORROBEL, OF, DOMINICAN REPUBLIC

Born: Dec. 8, 2003. **B-T:** L-L. **Ht.:** 6-1. **Wt.:** 170. **Expected Signing Team:** Rangers.

The Rangers are in on multiple players who are expected to sign seven-figure deals, with the biggest bonus expected to go to Morrobel. He has plenty of room to add strength to a lean, athletic frame. He has good bat speed and feel for finding the sweet spot in games, with a line-drive approach and gap power that has started to increase with strength gains. He's an average runner who could stick in center field.

17. JHONNY PIRON, OF, DOMINICAN REPUBLIC

Born: June 2, 2004. **B-T:** R-R. **Ht.:** 6-1. **Wt.:** 178. **Expected Signing Team:** Rays.

Piron is a lean, fast-twitch athlete, standing out for his quickness and speed in the middle of the field. He's a plus or better runner underway who accelerates quickly to cover a lot of ground in center field. Piron's pure hitting ability isn't as advanced as his raw athleticism, but he has a quick bat and has started to drive the ball with more impact as he's added weight over the past year.

18. MIGUEL BLEIS, OF, DOMINICAN REPUBLIC

Born: March 1, 2004. **B-T:** R-R. **Ht.:** 6-2. **Wt.:** 170. **Expected Signing Team:** Red Sox.

Bleis is one of the top athletes in the international class. He has a sleek, athletic frame with high physical upside. He glides around center field with an easy gait and long strides, with average speed that might tick up as he gets stronger along with a strong arm. He has a quick bat with gap power.

19. ARIEL ALMONTE, OF, DOMINICAN REPUBLIC

Born: Dec. 1, 2003. **B-T:** L-L. **Ht.:** 6-4. **Wt.:** 190. **Expected Signing Team:** Reds.

Almonte is a tall, physical corner outfielder, with a short swing for his size from the left side. He recognizes pitches well for his age and has easy power that projects to be plus once he's physically mature. He's not much of a runner but has a plus arm that should fit in right field.

20. VICTOR ACOSTA, SS, DOMINICAN REPUBLIC

Born: June 10, 2004. **B-T:** B-R. **Ht.:** 5-11. **Wt.:** 165. **Expected Signing Team:** Padres.

Acosta has a chance to be a plus defender at the position. A plus runner with an above-average arm, he has quick reactions off the bat and nimble footwork, with good body control and instincts in the field. A switch-hitter, Acosta has a slashing offensive approach, with more bat speed and power from the left side.

21. DANIEL VASQUEZ, SS, DOMINICAN REPUBLIC

Born: Dec. 15, 2003. **Ht.:** 6-2. **Wt.:** 158. **Expected Signing Team:** Royals.

Vasquez has continued to grow taller while remaining lean over the past year, with a promising mix of athleticism, strength projection and good actions on both sides of the ball. He has a short, line-drive swing with good contact skills and gap power that should grow as he gets stronger, along with smooth actions and good body control in the field.

22. HANS MONTERO, SS, DOMINICAN REPUBLIC

Born: Dec. 25, 2003. **B-T:** R-R. **Ht.:** 5-10. **Wt.:** 160. **Expected Signing Team:** Yankees.

The Yankees landed the top international prospect in 2019, signing Dominican outfielder Jasson Dominguez for $5.1 million. This year they're going to spread their money around more, with Montero their top target. Montero projects to stay at shortstop, with soft hands, a strong arm and above-average speed. He has a short righthanded swing with a line-drive approach and gap power.

23. STARLIN AGUILAR, SS/3B, DOMINICAN REPUBLIC

Born: Jan. 26, 2004. **B-T:** L-R. **Ht.:** 5-10. **Wt.:** 177. **Expected Signing Team:** Mariners.

Aguilar has a sweet, compact swing with excellent bat speed and a good path through the hitting zone. He has good feel for manipulating the barrel and an all-fields approach, with the potential to grow into plus power. Aguilar has spent time at shortstop, but he's a bat-first player who should move to third base.

24. AMBIORIS TAVAREZ, SS, DOMINICAN REPUBLIC

Born: Nov. 12, 2003. **B-T:** R-R. **Ht.:** 6-2. **Wt.:** 175. **Expected Signing Team:** Braves.

As a penalty for their international signing violations, the Braves could not sign anyone for more than $10,000 during the 2019-20 signing period, and their 2020-21 bonus pool was reduced by half. They are expected to make Tavarez their top target. He has shown good strength projection, fast bat speed, big raw power and a strong arm at shortstop. Some scouts think he will fit better at third base or in the outfield.

25. NORGE VERA, RHP, CUBA

Born: June 1, 2000. **B-T:** R-R. **Ht.:** 6-4. **Wt.:** 185. **Expected Signing Team:** White Sox.

Vera looks like he will be the top paid pitcher in the 2020-21 signing period. He is the son of Norge Luis Vera, who was a standout pitcher in Cuba's Serie Nacional and pitched for the Cuban national team. The junior Vera garnered attention pitching in international tournaments prior to leaving Cuba. He has a lean, projectable frame, with a fastball that sat 90-94 mph and ran up to 96. Scouts who saw Vera later were more mixed on his command and secondary stuff, possibly stemming from mechanical adjustments he was making. His hard slider is his main offspeed pitch and is ahead of his changeup, which he has started throwing more after dropping his splitter.

26. RICARDO PEREZ, C, VENEZUELA

Born: Dec. 4, 2003. **B-T:** L-R. **Ht.:** 6-1. **Wt.:** 165. **Expected Signing Team:** Phillies.

Perez has a loose, fluid swing from the left side with good bat control and a knack for getting the ball airborne. He projects to hit for power once he fills out his lean frame. He has the defensive attributes to stay behind the plate with a tick above-average arm strength.

27. MANUEL PEÑA, SS, DOMINICAN REPUBLIC

Born: Dec. 5, 2003. **B-T:** L-R. **Ht.:** 6-2. **Wt.:** 175. **Expected Signing Team:** D-backs.

Peña has grown into a lean, well-proportioned frame with good strength projection. Scouts highest on him are drawn to his offensive upside. He has a compact lefthanded swing with emerging power that should continue to grow as he fills out and an approach conducive to hitting the ball in the air. Peña should begin his career at shortstop, though he might end up at third base or possibly second base.

28. SAMUEL BASALLO, C, DOMINICAN REPUBLIC

Born: Aug. 13, 2004. **B-T:** L-R. **Ht.:** 6-3. **Wt:** 198. **Expected Signing Team:** Orioles.

Basallo is one of the youngest players in the class and was once connected to the Yankees, but he's now expected to sign with the Orioles. He is a tall, physical catcher with a plus arm, above-average raw power and a sound swing from the left side. Already 6-foot-3 at 15, Basallo might outgrow catcher if he keeps getting bigger, but right now he's lean and agile with good flexibility behind the plate for his size.

29. GABRIEL GONZALEZ, OF, VENEZUELA

Born: April 1, 2004. **B-T:** R-R. **Ht.:** 6-0. **Wt.:** 195. **Expected Signing Team:** Mariners.

Gonzalez has trended up as one of the top players in Venezuela. With a strong, stocky build for a center fielder, he is physically advanced for his age and shows a mix of strength, bat speed and leverage in his swing to drive the ball out of the park. He has a good track record of hitting and hitting for power against live pitching, with an aggressive approach and swing that might ultimately lead to a power-over-hit profile. He's an average runner with good defensive instincts, so he should start his career as a center fielder with a chance to stick there, although he might end eventually up in a corner with his build.

30. MOISES BALLESTEROS, C, VENEZUELA

Born: Nov. 17, 2003. **B-T:** L-R. **Ht.:** 5-10. **Wt.:** 185. **Expected Signing Team:** Cubs

Ballesteros has experience representing his country at international tournaments going back to when he hit cleanup as the youngest player on the Venezuelan team in the 2015 U-12 World Cup in Taiwan. He is an offensive-oriented catcher with a stout, boxy frame and a strong upper body. He has performed well in games in Venezuela, with good bat control and ability to drive the ball with a sound approach for his age. Ballesteros has a strong arm, but he will need to stay on top of his mobility.

SIGNING BONUSES

2020 DRAFT — TOP 100 PICKS

FIRST ROUND

No.	Team: Player, Pos.	Bonus
1.	Tigers: Spencer Torkelson, 3B	$8,416,300
2.	Orioles: Heston Kjerstad, OF	$5,200,000
3.	Marlins: Max Meyer, RHP	$6,700,000
4.	Royals: Asa Lacy, LHP	$6,670,000
5.	Blue Jays: Austin Martin, SS	$7,000,825
6.	Mariners: Emerson Hancock, RHP	$5,700,000
7.	Pirates: Nick Gonzales, SS	$5,432,400
8.	Padres: Robert Hassell, OF	$4,300,000
9.	Rockies: Zac Veen, OF	$5,000,000
10.	Angels: Reid Detmers, LHP	$4,670,000
11.	White Sox: Garrett Crochet, LHP	$4,547,500
12.	Reds: Austin Hendrick, OF	$4,000,000
13.	Giants: Patrick Bailey, C	$3,797,500
14.	Rangers: Justin Foscue, 2B	$3,250,000
15.	Phillies: Mick Abel, RHP	$4,075,000
16.	Cubs: Ed Howard, SS	$3,745,500
17.	Red Sox: Nick Yorke, 2B	$2,700,000
18.	D-backs: Bryce Jarvis, RHP	$2,650,000
19.	Mets: Pete Crow-Armstrong, OF	$3,359,000
20.	Brewers: Garrett Mitchell, OF	$3,242,900
21.	Cardinals: Jordan Walker, 3B	$2,900,000
22.	Nationals: Cade Cavalli, RHP	$3,027,000
23.	Indians: Carson Tucker, SS	$2,000,000
24.	Rays: Nick Bitsko, RHP	$3,000,000
25.	Braves: Jared Shuster, LHP	$2,197,500
26.	Athletics: Tyler Soderstrom, C	$3,300,000
27.	Twins: Aaron Sabato, 1B	$2,750,000
28.	Yankees: Austin Wells, C	$2,500,000
29.	Dodgers: Bobby Miller, RHP	$2,197,500

SUPPLEMENTAL FIRST ROUND

No.	Team: Player, Pos.	Bonus
30.	Orioles: Jordan Westburg, SS	$2,365,500
31.	Pirates: Carmen Mlodzinski, RHP	$2,050,000
32.	Royals: Nick Loftin, SS	$3,000,000
33.	D-backs: Slade Cecconi, RHP	$2,384,900
34.	Padres: Justin Lange, RHP	$2,000,000
35.	Rockies: Drew Romo, C	$2,095,800
36.	Indians: Tanner Burns, RHP	$1,600,000
37.	Rays: Alika Williams, SS	$1,850,000

SECOND ROUND

No.	Team: Player, Pos.	Bonus
38.	Tigers: Dillon Dingler, C	$1,952,300
39.	Orioles: Hudson Haskin, OF	$1,906,800
40.	Marlins: Dax Fulton, LHP	$2,400,000
41.	Royals: Ben Hernandez, RHP	$1,450,000
42.	Blue Jays: C.J. Van Eyk, RHP	$1,797,500
43.	Mariners: Zach DeLoach, OF	$1,729,800
44.	Pirates: Jared Jones, RHP	$2,200,000
45.	Padres: Owen Caissie, OF	$1,200,004
46.	Rockies: Chris McMahon, RHP	$1,637,400
47.	White Sox: Jared Kelley, RHP	$3,000,000
48.	Reds: Christian Roa, RHP	$1,543,600
49.	Giants: Casey Schmitt, 3B	$1,147,500
50.	Rangers: Evan Carter, OF	$1,250,000
51.	Cubs: Burl Carraway, LHP	$1,050,000
52.	Mets: J.T. Ginn, RHP	$2,900,000
53.	Brewers: Freddy Zamora, SS	$1,150,000
54.	Cardinals: Masyn Winn, SS/RHP	$2,100,000
55.	Nationals: Cole Henry, RHP	$2,000,000
56.	Indians: Logan Allen, LHP	$1,125,000
57.	Rays: Ian Seymour, LHP	$1,243,600
58.	Athletics: Jeff Criswell, RHP	$1,000,000
59.	Twins: Alerick Soularie, OF	$900,000
60.	Dodgers: Landon Knack, RHP	$712,500

SUPPLEMENTAL SECOND ROUND

No.	Team: Player, Pos.	Bonus
61.	Marlins: Kyle Nicolas, RHP	$1,129,700
62.	Tigers: Daniel Cabrera, OF	$1,210,000
63.	Cardinals: Tink Hence, RHP	$1,115,000
64.	Mariners: Connor Phillips, RHP	$1,050,300
65.	Reds: Jackson Miller, C	$1,290,000
66.	Dodgers: Clayton Beeter, RHP	$1,196,500
67.	Giants: Nick Swiney, LHP	$1,197,500
68.	Giants: Jimmy Glowenke, SS	$597,500
69.	Mets: Isaiah Greene, OF	$850,000
70.	Cardinals: Alec Burleson, OF	$700,000
71.	Nationals: Sammy Infante, SS	$1,000,000
72.	Astros: Alex Santos, RHP	$1,250,000

THIRD ROUND

No.	Team: Player, Pos.	Bonus
73.	Tigers: Trei Cruz, SS	$900,000
74.	Orioles: Anthony Servideo, SS	$950,000
75.	Marlins: Zach McCambley, RHP	$775,000
76.	Royals: Tyler Gentry, OF	$750,000
77.	Blue Jays: Trent Palmer, RHP	$847,500
78.	Mariners: Kaden Polcovich, 2B	$575,000
79.	Pirates: Nick Garcia, RHP	$1,200,000
80.	Padres: Cole Wilcox, RHP	$3,300,000
81.	Rockies: Sam Weatherly, LHP	$755,300
82.	Angels: David Calabrese, OF	$744,200
83.	White Sox: Adisyn Coffey, RHP	$50,000
84.	Reds: Bryce Bonnin, RHP	$700,000
85.	Giants: Kyle Harrison, LHP	$2,497,500
86.	Rangers: Tekoah Roby, RHP	$775,000
87.	Phillies: Casey Martin, SS	$1,300,000
88.	Cubs: Jordan Nwogu, OF	$678,600
89.	Red Sox: Blaze Jordan, 3B	$1,750,000
90.	D-backs: Liam Norris, LHP	$800,000
91.	Mets: Anthony Walters, SS	$20,000
92.	Brewers: Zavier Warren, C	$575,000
93.	Cardinals: Levi Prater, LHP	$575,000
94.	Nationals: Holden Powell, RHP	$500,000
95.	Indians: Petey Halpin, OF	$1,525,000
96.	Rays: Hunter Barnhart, RHP	$585,000
97.	Braves: Jesse Franklin, OF	$497,500
98.	Athletics: Michael Guldberg, OF	$300,000
99.	Yankees: Trevor Hauver, 2B	$587,400
100.	Dodgers: Jake Vogel, OF	$1,622,500

INDEX

A

B

C

D

INDEX

INDEX